COMPREHENSIVE INDEX OF GROUP PSYCHOTHERAPY WRITINGS

BERNARD LUBIN, Ph.D.
and
ALICE W. LUBIN, B.A.

Monograph 2
AMERICAN GROUP PSYCHOTHERAPY ASSOCIATION
MONOGRAPH SERIES

Series Consulting Editor:
Fern J. Cramer Azima, Ph.D.

INTERNATIONAL UNIVERSITIES PRESS, INC.
Madison Connecticut

Library of Congress Cataloging-in-Publication Data

Lubin, Bernard, 1923-
Comprehensive index of group psychotherapy writings.

(Monograph series / American Group Psychotherapy Association; monograph 2)
Bibliography: p.
Includes index.
1. Group psychotherapy—Bibliography. 2. Group psychotherapy—Indexes. I. Lubin, Alice W. II. Title. III. Series: Monograph series (American Group Psychotherapy Association); monograph 2. [DNLM: 1. Psychotherapy, Group—indexes. W1 M0559PU monograph 2 / ZWM 430 L929c]
Z6665.7.G76L82 1982 016.61689'152 86-10683
[RC488]
ISBN 0-8236-1045-4

Manufactured in the United States of America

Contents

Foreword—Zanvel A. Liff, Ph.D. vii

Preface—Berard Lubin, Ph.D. and Alice W. Lubin, B.A. ix

Comprehensive Index 1
Subject Index 611
Cited Periodicals 653

Foreword

The publication of this comprehensive bibliography of the world's group psychotherapy literature represents a major historic event in the ever widening development of the field. As compilers of the annual reviews for the *International Journal of Group Psychotherapy* for many years, Alice and Bernard Lubin have earned the utmost gratitude of researchers, scholars and clinicians for undertaking this challenging and arduous task. They have collected all the relevant references since the pioneering efforts of Joseph Hersey Pratt who utilized groups in Boston to help tuberculosis patients. Thus, it may also be timely to note that this volume will appear on the 80th anniversary of Pratt's printed account of his work in 1906.

As a former Editor of the *International Journal of Group Psychotherapy*, I applaud the arrival of this exhaustive project by the Lubins. Their efforts should considerably ease the burden as well as upgrade the work of the literature searchers. The importance of authors relating their own work to parallel streams of investigation and thought cannot be sufficiently stressed. This literature relatedness enhances the scientific and creative processes and would be largely facilitated by the Lubins' bibliographical contribution. The cross indexing of this volume, by both author and subject, should help users enrich the quality of their work.

Furthermore, this world wide compilation of more than 13,000 items dispels any lingering doubts readers may have concerning the field of group psychotherapy as a highly important, vital and flourishing enterprise in areas of clinical practice, research and specialized training.

This volume is also testimony to how the growth of the literature was stimulated by the organization of the American Group Psychotherapy Association in 1942 and by the inauguration of the International Journal in 1951. It was actually the primary purpose of A.G.P.A. "to provide a forum for the exchange among qualified professional persons interested in group psychotherapy and to publish and to make publications available in all subjects relating to group psychotherapy" (A.G.P.A. By-laws, Article II).

Finally, this massive collation should thrust our field forward from its ever widening base of interest to higher levels of competence in research, scholarship and hopefully clinical practice. Alice and Bernard Lubin merit our extreme praise for their most worthy and historical contribution.

Zanvel A. Liff, Ph.D.
Editor,
International Journal of Group Psychotherapy

Preface

Publications in the area of group psychotherapy have appeared in a large variety of journals. While some of the publication outlets have "treatment," "psychotherapy," "group," or similar terms in their titles, a great many of them do not. Thus scholars, researchers, and practitioners have experienced considerable frustration for many years with the fact that it was quite difficult, if not impossible, to conduct a meaningful and reasonably thorough literature search in subareas of group therapy. It was out of this need experienced by the editors and frequently expressed by colleagues that we undertook the task of compiling the world's literature on group therapy.

This compilation of the writings on group therapy, 1906 through 1980, has required several years to complete. Our main search has concentrated upon *Psychological Abstracts, Cumulative Index Medicus, Sociological Abstracts*, and *Dissertation Abstracts International*. In addition, lists of references cited in books that were listed in *Books in Print* over the years were searched. Using this procedure, 13,304 items were identified between 1906 when Pratt published "The home sanatorium treatment of consumption"—the acknowledged beginning of the group therapy movement—and the end of the 1980 literature. Most of this productivity occurred since 1945 and was spurred by the formation of the American Group Psychotherapy Association.

Despite our attempt to be thorough and accurate, we realize that some errors and omissions are likely to have occurred. The current plan is to publish a supplement to the bibliography at suitable intervals. It is our intention to include in each supplement a section on Errata and Omissions so as to make the bibliography as accurate and complete as possible. Readers are urged to send such information to the editors.

Because many terms in the field of group psychotherapy lack precise definition and are used interchangeably, readers should check for items under synonyms or possibly related terms, e.g., encounter groups, sensitivity groups, and T groups. Indeed the terms "psychotherapy" and "therapy" are used interchangeably by some authors but not by others. The same is true in many cases for "therapy," "psychotherapy," and "counseling." Generally, we have classified items according to the authors' use of these terms in their titles.

In order to avoid redundancy and reduce probable increased costs, theses and dissertations have not been cross-referenced under "Research" even though most theses and dissertations represent empirical investigations. Therefore, readers with research interests are advised to review the items under "Theses and Dissertations."

Items on family therapy, couples therapy, and marital therapy are included in this compilation if the title also mentions "group therapy." Otherwise the items will appear in a forthcoming bibliography on Family Therapy.

Three things stand out to us as this work is brought to completion: a sense of satisfaction in having accomplished something that can be useful to others, a feeling of liberation from a confining task, and an increased appreciation for the important and exacting work of the librarian.

We wish to thank the many people who helped with this project in a number of ways. A few of them are David Tanquary, Gary Hamilton, Jill Montaleon, Sally Conrad, Catherine Stansberry, Audrey Taylor, and Sheila Zimmerman. We want to express our appreciation particularly to Mrs. Patricia Falk for her consistent, good humored and high quality assistance at various stages in the completion of this project. Also we wish to thank the publishers of *Science Citation Index* and *Social Science Citation Index* for permission to use and cite their system of journal title abbreviations.

It is obvious to us that the use of small groups to bring about change in individuals, groups and organizations is alive and vigorous. We feel privileged to be a part of the development of this field and we hope that this compilation will facilitate the work of scholars, researchers, and practitioners.

Bernard Lubin, Ph.D. and
Alice W. Lubin, B.A.

A

00001 **AACH, S.** (1976), Drama: a means of self-expression for the visually impaired child. *New Outlook for Blind*, 70:282-285.

00002 **AARDWEG, G. J. van den** (1962), (Auto-psychodrama: theory and therapy of neuroses by the J. L. Arndt method.) *Nederl. Tijdschr. Psychol.* (Amsterdam), 17:561-584.

00003 **AARDWEG, G. J. van den** (1964), Autopsychodrama: theory and therapy of neurosis according to J. L. Arndt. *Amer. J. Psychother.*, 18:259-271.

00004 **AARKROG, T.** (1971), (Group therapy in an adolescent psychiatric department.) *Ugeskr. for Laeger* (Copenhagen), 133:2079-2083.

00005 **ABARBANEL, A. R.** (1960), Psychosocial factors in fertility: management by means of "attitude" psychotherapy in limited groups. *Ginecol. & Obstet. Mexicana*, 15:513-523.

00006 **ABARBANEL, A. R.**, and **BACK, G.** (1959), Group psychotherapy for the infertile couple. *Internat. J. Fertility*, 4:151.

00007 **ABBATE, G. M.** (1942), Group procedures found effective in the prevention and handling of emotional disorders. *Ment. Health*, 26:394-409.

00008 **ABELL, R. G.** (1964), Group psychoanalysis. *Curr. Psychiat. Ther.*, 4:175-182.

00009 **ABELL, R. G.** (1959), Personality development during group psychotherapy: its relation to the etiology and treatment of the neuroses. *Amer. J. Psychoanal.*, 19:53-72.

00010 **ABELS, P.** (1969), Riding with Batman, Superman, and the Green Hornet: experiences in a very special group. *Ment. Retard.*, 7:37-39.

00011 **ABELS, P. A.** (1970), On the nature of supervision: the medium is the group. *Child Welfare*, 49:303-304.

00012 **ABELSON, H. H.** (1968), Group psychotherapeutic process and the educative process. *J. Group Psychoanal. Process*, (London) 1:76-82.

00013 **ABELY, P.**, and **MELMAN, C.** (1963), (Games, play and the parade in mental pathology: clinical study and psychoanalytic approach to play therapy.) *Annales Medico-Psychol.*, (Paris) 121:353-390.

00014 **ABIUSO, D., AHUMADA, J.**, and **FERSCHTUT, G.** (1973), (Notes about supervision in groups.) *Acta Psiquiat. Psicol. Amer. Latina*, (Buenos Aires) 19:349-354.

00015 **ABLESSER, H.** (1962), Role-reversal in a group psychotherapy session. *Group Psychother., Psychodrama & Sociometry*, 15:321-325.

00016 **ABRAHAM, A.** (1972), Death and psychodrama. *Group Psychother., Psychodrama & Sociometry*, 25:84-92.

00017 **ABRAHAM, A.** (1978), Group intervention for teachers in time of war. *Group*, 2:40-53.

00018 **ABRAHAM, A.** (1973), A model for exploring intra- and interindividual process in groups. *Internat. J. Group Psychother.*, 23:3-22.

00019 **ABRAHAM, K. A.** (1972), The effectiveness of structured sociodrama in altering the classroom behavior of fifth grade students. *Dissert. Abstr. Internat.*, 33:3677A.

00020 **ABRAHAMS, D.**, and **ENRIGHT, J. B.** (1965), Psychiatric intake in groups: a pilot study of procedures, problems and prospects. *Amer. J. Psychiat.*, 122:170-174.

00021 **ABRAHAMS, D. Y.** (1956), Observations on transference in a group of teen-age "delinquents." *Internat. J. Group Psychother.*, 6:286-290.

00022 **ABRAHAMS, J.** (1958), Correlations in combined treatment by group and individual psychoanalysis. *J. Amer. Psychoanal. Assn.*, 6:126-128.

00023 **ABRAHAMS, J.** (1949), Group psychotherapy: implications for direct and supervision of mentally ill patients. In: *Mental Health in Nursing*, ed., T. Muller. Washington, D.C.: Catholic University of America Press.

00024 **ABRAHAMS, J.** (1947), Group psychotherapy: remarks on its basis and application. *Med. Annals D.C.*, 16:612-617.

00025 **ABRAHAMS, J.** (1948), Preliminary report of an experience in the group psychotherapy of schizophrenics. *Amer. J. Psychiat.*, 104:613-617.

00026 **ABRAHAMS, J.** (1956), Some views of group psychotherapy in the mental hospital. *Neuropsychiatry*, 4:3-9.

00027 **ABRAHAMS, J.**, and **McCORKLE, L. W.** (1947), Group psychotherapy at an army rehabilitation center. *Diseases Nerv. System*, 8:50-62.

00028 **ABRAHAMS, J.**, and **McCORKLE, L. W.** (1946), Group psychotherapy of military offenders. *Amer. J. Sociol.*, 51:455-464.

00029 **ABRAHAMS, J.**, and **VARON, E.** (1953), *Maternal Dependence and Schizophrenia: Mothers and Daughters in a Therapeutic Group*. New York: International Universities Press.

00030 **ABRAHAMS, J. L.** (1979), Cognitive–behavioral versus non-directive group treatment program for opioid addicted persons: adjunct to methadone maintenance. *Inter. J. Addict.*, 14:503-512.

00031 **ABRAHMS, J. L.**, and **ALLEN, G. J.** (1974), Comparative effectiveness of situational programming: financial pay-offs and group pressure in weight reduction. *Behav. Ther.*, 5:391-400.

00032 **ABRAMCZUK, J.** (1966), Reports from Poland: an experiment in the development of a therapeutic community in psychiatric unit. *Inter. J. Soc. Psychiat.*, (London) 12:309-314.

00033 **ABRAMCZUK, J.** (1972), The type of leadership and the topics of discussion in a large open group: observations on community meetings. *Inter. J. Soc. Psychiat.*, (London) 18:53-60.

00034 **ABRAMCZUK, J., GAJEWSKA, G., GROCHOCKA, Z.**, and **SKRZYWAN, T.** (1968), Some difficulties encountered in the management of a psychiatric day unit. *Inter. J. Soc. Psychiat.*, (London) 14:141-144.

00035 **ABRAMOWITZ, C. V., ABRAMOWITZ, S. L., ROBACK, H. B.**, and **JACKSON, C.** (1974), Differential effectiveness of directive and non–directive group therapies as a function of client internal–external control. *J. Consult. & Clin. Psychol.*, 42:849.

00036 **ABRAMOWITZ, S. S.**, and **ABRAMOWITZ, C. V.** (1974), Psychological mindedness and benefit from insight oriented group therapy. *Arch. Gen. Psychiat.*, 30:610-615.

00037 **ABRAMS, L.** (1968), Action group training techniques. *Group Psychother., Psychodrama & Sociometry*, 21:151-154.

00038 **ABRAMSON, H. A.** (1979), Psychosomatic group therapy with parents of children with intractable asthma: ix. the Peters family. part 1. *J. Asthma Res.*, 16:103-117.

00039 **ABRAMSON, H. A.**, and **PESHKIN, M. M.** (1979), Psychosomatic group therapy with parents of children with intractable asthma: x. the Peters family. *J. Asthma Res.*, 16:149.

00040 **ABRAMSON, H. A.**, and **PESHKIN, M. M.** (1979), Psychosomatic group therapy with parents of children with intractable asthma. ix. the Peters family. *J. Asthma Res.*, 16:103.

00041 **ABRAMSON, H. A.**, and **PESHKIN, M. M.** (1978), Psychosomatic group therapy with parents with children with intractable asthma: viii. the Kohl family. *J. Asthma Res.*, 16:63-81.

00042 **ABRAMOWITZ, C. V.** (1977), Blaming the mother: an experimental investigation of sex-role bias in countertransference. *Psychol. Women Quart.*, 2:24-34.

00043 **ABRAMOWITZ, C. V.** (1976), Effectiveness of group psychotherapy with children. *Arch. Gen. Psychiat.*, 33:321-326.

00044 **ABRAMOWITZ, S. I.**, and **ABRAMOWITZ, C. V.** (1974), Psychological mindedness and benefit from insight-oriented group therapy. *Arch. Gen. Psychiat.*, 30:210-216.

00045 **ABRAMOWITZ, S. I.**, and **JACKSON, C.** (1974), Comparative effectiveness of there-and-then vs. here-and-now therapist interpretations in group psychotherapy. *J. Couns. Psychol.*, 21:288-293.

00046 **ABRAMOWITZ, S. I., ROBACK, H. B., SCHWARTZ, J. M., YASUNA, A., ABRAMOWITZ, C. V.**, and **GOMES, B.** (1976), Sex bias in psychotherapy: a failure to confirm. *Amer. J. Psychiat.*, 133:706-709.

00047 **ABRAMOWITZ, S. I., SCHWARTZ, J. M.**, and **ROBACK, H. B.** (1977), Effects of professional discipline and experience on group therapists' clinical reactions. *Internat. J. Group Psychother.*, 27:165-176.

00048 **ABRAMS, A.** (1953), Effects of group therapy upon certain personality characteristics of a selected group of institutionalized male sex offenders. *Dissert. Abstr. Internat.*, 13:114.

00049 **ABRAMS, A.** (1968), Nurses supervise family care. *Hosp. & Community Psychiat.*, 19:154-155.

00050 **ABRAMS, A., ROTH, D.**, and **BOSHES, B.** (1958), Group therapy with narcotic addicts, method and evaluation. *Group Psychother., Psychodrama & Sociometry*, 11:244-256.

00051 **ABRAMSON, H. A.**, and **PESHKIN, M. M.** (1980), Psychosomatic group therapy with parents of children with intractable asthma: xiii. the Goldey family. part 3. *J. Asthma Res.*, 17:123-147.

00052 **ABRAMSON, H. A.** (1980), Psychosomatic group therapy with parents of children with intractable asthma: xii. the Goldey family. part 2. *J. Asthma Res.*, 17:81-99.

00053 **ABRAMSON, H. A.** (1979), Psychosomatic group therapy with parents of children with intractable asthma: xi. the Goldey family. part 1. *J. Asthma Res.*, 17:31-47.

00054 **ABRAMSON, H. A.**, and **PESHKIN, M. M.** (1961), Group psychotherapy of the parents of intractably asthmatic children. *J. Child Asthma Res.*, 1:77-91.

00055 **ABRAMSON, H. A.**, and **PESHKIN, M. M.** (1965), Psychosomatic group therapy with parents of children with intractable asthma: iii. sibling rivalry and sibling support. *Psychosomatics*, 6:161-165.

00056 **ABRAMSON, H. A.**, and **PESHKIN, M. M.** (1960), Psychosomatic group therapy with parents of children with intractable asthma: ii. adaption mechanisms. *Annals of Allergy*, 18:87-91.

00057 **ABRAMSON, J.** (1972), An activity program for the disturbed retardate. *Hosp. & Community Psychiat.*, 23:14-15.

00058 **ABRAMSON, R. M., HOFFMAN, L.**, and **JOHNS, C. A.** (1979), Play group psychotherapy for early latency-age children on an inpatient psychiatric unit. *Internat. J. Group Psychother.*, 29:383-392.

00059 **ABROMS, G. M.** (1969), The new eclecticism. *Arch. Gen. Psychiat.*, 20:514-523.

00060 **ABRUZZ, W.** (1979), Failure of therapeutic communities drug treatment and rehabilitation programs. *Internat. J. Addict.*, 14:1023.

00061 **ABSE, D. W.** (1974), *Clinical Notes on Group–Analytic Psychotherapy*. Charlottesville, VA: University Press.

00062 **ABT, B. A.** (1976), Predicting casualties in experimental groups. *Dissert. Abstr. Internat.*, 36:5777B.

00063 **ABUDABBEH, N., PRANDONI, J. R.**, and **JENSEN, D. E.** (1972), Application of behavior principles to group therapy techniques with juvenile delinquents. *Psychol. Reports*, 3:375-380.

00064 **ACHILLE, P. A.** (1964), Schema evolutivo della terapia di gruppo con i giovani delinquenti. (Developmental phases of group therapy with young offenders.) *Arch. Psicol., Neurol. & Psichiat.*, (Milan) 25:269-285.

00065 **ACHTE, K. A.** (1963), (Milieu therapy in the hesperia hospital.) *Nordisk Psykiat. Tidsskr.*, (Kungsbacha) 17:367-375.

00066 **ACKERKNECT, L. K.** (1971), Marathon, Adlerian style. *J. Individ. Psychol.*, 27:176-180.

00067 **ACKERMAN, B. L.** (1980), Review of D. Gordon's *Therapeutic Metaphors. J. Marital & Fam. Ther.*, 6:95.

00068 **ACKERMAN, M.**, and **ACKERMAN, S.** (1962), Emergency psychodrama for an acute psychosomatic syndrome. *Group Psychother., Psychodrama, & Sociometry*, 15:84-88.

00069 **ACKERMAN, M.**, and **ACKERMAN, S.** (1962), Therapeutic psychodrama. *J. Amer. Coll. Neuropsychiat.*, 1:65-67.

00070 **ACKERMAN, M.**, and **ACKERMAN, S.** (1962), The use of psychodrama in a postpartum depression. *J. Amer. Coll. Neuropsychiat.*, 1:67-70.

00071 **ACKERMAN, N. W.** (1944), Dynamic patterns in group psychotherapy. *Psychiatry*, 7:341-348.

00072 **ACKERMAN, N. W.** (1957), Five issues in group psychotherapy. *Ziet. Diagnost. Psychol.*, 5:167-178.

00073 **ACKERMAN, N. W.** (1955), Group psychotherapy with a mixed group of adolescents. *Inter. J. Group Psychother.*, 5:249-260.

00074 **ACKERMAN, N. W.** (1946), Group psychotherapy with veterans. *Ment. Health*, 30:559-570.

00075 **ACKERMAN, N. W.** (1946), Group psychotherapy with veterans. *Psychosomatic Med.*, 8:118-119.

00076 **ACKERMAN, N. W.** (1943), Group therapy from the viewpoint of a psychiatrist. *Amer. J. Orthopsychiat.*, 13:678-687.

00077 **ACKERMAN, N. W.** (1955), Interaction processes in a group and the role of the leader. In: *Psychoanalysis and the social sciences. Vol. IV*. eds. W. Muensterberg and S. Axelrod. New York: International Universities Press, pp. 111-120.

00078 **ACKERMAN, N. W.** (1955), Moreno's transference, countertransference and tele: their relations to group research and group psychotherapy. *Group Psychother., Psychodrama & Sociometry*, 8:57-60.

00079 **ACKERMAN, N. W.** (1950), Psychoanalysis and group psychotherapy. *Group Psychother., Psychodrama & Sociometry*, 3:204-215.

00080 **ACKERMAN, N. W.** (1975), Psychoanalysis and group psychotherapy. In: *Group Psychotherapy and Group Function*, 2d ed., eds. M. Rosenbaum and M. M. Berger. New York: Basic Books.

00081 **ACKERMAN, N. W.** (1944), Psychotherapy and giving love. *Psychiatry*, 7:129-137.

00082 **ACKERMAN, N. W.** (1951), Round table conference, group psychotherapy and the treatment of minority problems. *Group Psychother., Psychodrama & Sociometry*, 4:74-76.

00083 **ACKERMAN, N. W.** (1946), Some general principles in the use of group psychotherapy. In: *Current Therapies of Behavior Disorders*, ed. B. Glueck. New York: Grune and Stratton, pp. 275-280.

00084 **ACKERMAN, N. W.** (1954), Some structural problems in the relations of psychoanalysis and group psychotherapy. *Internat. J. Group Psychother.*, 4:131-145.

00085 **ACKERMAN, N. W.** (1945), Some theoretical aspects of group psychotherapy. *Sociometry*, 8:355-362.

00086 **ACKERMAN, N. W.** (1961), Symptom, defense, and growth in group process. *Internat. J. Group Psychother.*, 11:131-142.

00087 **ACKERMAN, P. H.** (1972), A staff group in a women's prison. *Internat. J. Group Psychother.*, 22:364-373.

00088 **ACKLAND, V. L. B.** (1971), A comparison of two group counseling models in facilitating verbal interaction among delinquent girls. *Dissert. Abstr. Internat.*, 31:5752A.

00089 **ACPA** statement regarding the use of group experiences in higher education (1975). *J. Coll. Student Personnel*, 16:342-347.

00090 **ADAMS, B., BROWNSTEIN, C. A., RENNALLS, G. M.,** and **SCHMIDT, M. H.** (1976), The pregnant adolescent: a group approach. *Adolescence*, 11:467.

00091 **ADAMS, G.** (1961), The heartening response of patients to an experiment in dual purpose remotivation. *Ment. Hosp.*, 12:28.

00092 **ADAMS, G. K.** (1974), Perceptions of abortion: the circle of choice—a decision-making process observed in women considering abortions. *ANA. Clin. Sessions*, 47-59.

00093 **ADAMS, H. J.,** and **BARR, D. J.** (1971), A model for training group counselors. *Counselor Educat. & Supervision*, 11:36-40.

00094 **ADAMS, J.** (1971), Student evaluations of an interactional group experience. *J. Psychiat. Nursing*, 9:28-36.

00095 **ADAMS, J. D.,** and **HOPSON, B.** (1975), Sensitivity training and the school counselor. *Brit. J. Guid. & Couns.*, (Cambridge) 3:45-55.

00096 **ADAMS, O. T.** (1973), The effects of the response demand technique on self-directed groups of hospitalized psychiatric patients. *Dissert. Abstr. Internat.*, 34:2917.

00097 **ADAMS, P. L.** (1970), Experiential group counseling with intern teachers. *Dissert. Abstr. Internat.*, 31:605A.

00098 **ADAMSON, K.** (1978), Silence in psychotherapy groups. *Nursing Mirror*, (London) 146:25-27.

00099 **ADAMSON, J. D.** (1980), Tears of joy. *Can. J. Psychiat., (Ottawa)* 25:264-265.

00100 **ADAMSON, W. C.** (1947), Group psychotherapy: an aid to diagnosis and treatment. *Delaware State Med. J.*, 19:94-97.

00101 **ADAMSON, W. C.** (1972), Helping parents of children with learning disabilities. *J. Learn Disabil.*, 5:326-330.

00102 **ADDISON, R. E.** (1977), Racially different patients in individual and group psychotherapy. *J. Contemp. Psychother.*, 9:39-40.

00103 **ADDY, M. F.** (1974), Changes in self-regard and regard for others as a function of interaction group experiences. *Dissert. Abstr. Internat.*, 34:6376A.

00104 **ADELSON, E.** (1953), Die psychotherapeutische gruppe in der heilanstalt. (The psychotherapeutic group in mental hospitals.) *Psyche (Heidelburg)*, 7:464-480.

00105 **ADELSON, G.,** and **PERESS, E.** (1979), Single–couple and group sex therapy. *Soc. Casework*, 60:471-478.

00106 **ADELSON, J. P.** (1975), Feedback and group development. *Small Group Behav.*, 6:389-401.

00107 **ADELSON, J. P.** (1974), Feedback and group development. *Dissert. Abstr. Internat.*, 34:4648B.

00108 **ADILMAN, P. H.** (1973), Some concepts of adolescent residential treatment. *Adolescence*, 8:547-568.

00109 **ADINOLFI, A. A., McCOURT, W. F.,** and **GEOGHEGAN, S.** (1976), Group assertiveness training for alcoholics. *J. Studies on Alcohol*, 37:311-320.

00110 **ADLER, A.** (1963), Adlerian psychotherapy and recent trends. *J. Individ. Psychol.*, 19:55-60.

00111 **ADLER, A.** (1962), Group therapy and individual psychology. *Exper. Med. & Surgery*, 20:5-9.

00112 **ADLER, A.** (Chm.) (1958), Symposium on Adlerian concepts of schizophrenia. *J. Individ. Psychol.*, 14:73-78.

00113 **ADLER, E. M.** (1977), A review of M. S. Bergmann's and F. R. Hartman's *The Evolution of Psychoanalytic Technique. Group*, 1:140-141.

00114 **ADLER, E. M.** (1977), A review of O. Kernberg's *Object Relations, Theory and Clinical Psychoanalysis. Group*, 1:267-268.

00115 **ADLER, H. M.** (1977), Interpersonal psychotherapy: a communications perspective. *Amer. J. Psychother.*, 31:570-576.

00116 **ADLER, J.** (1979), The child care worker's leadership in group process. *Child Care Quart.*, 8:196-205.

00117 **ADLER, J.** (1969), The delinquent-oriented adolescent in residential placement. *Child Welfare*, 48:142-147.

00118 **ADLER, J.** (1953), Therapeutic group work with tuberculous displaced persons. *Internat. J. Group Psychother.*, 3:302-308.

00119 **ADLER, J., BERMAN, I. R.,** and **SLAVSON, S. R.** (1960), Multiple leadership in group treatment of delinquent adolescents. *Internat. J. Group Psychother.*, 10:213-226.

00120 **ADLER, K. A.** (1970), Adlerian view of the present-day scene. *J. Individ. Psychol.*, 26:113-121.

00121 **ADLER, M. S.** (1972), Non-winner script, type b: the plastic prince. *Transactional Anal. J.*, 2:19-20.

00122 **ADLER, N. E.,** and **GOLEMAN, D.** (1975), Goal setting, t-group participation, and self-rated change: an experimental study. *J. Appl. Behav. Science*, 11:197-209.

00123 **ADORJANI, C.,** and **GALFI, B.** (1961), Csoportos pszichoterapia idult elmebetegekkel. (Group therapy of chronically insane persons.) *Psychol. Studies Pszichol. Tanulmanyok*, 685-702.

00124 **ADSETT, C. A.,** and **BRUHN, J. G.** (1968), Short–term group psychotherapy for post-myocardial infarction patients and their wives. *Can. Med. Assn. J.*, (Ottawa) 99:577-584.

00125 **AGATI, G. J.,** and **IOVINO, J. W.** (1974), Implementation of a parent counseling program. *School Counselor*, 22:126-129.

00126 **AGITOVA, N. A.** (1965), (V. M. Bekhterev and his views on group therapy of alcoholics.) *Vop. Psikhiat. & Nevropatol.*, (Leningrad) 11:300-355.

00127 **AGLER, C. F.** (1966), Psychodrama with the criminally insane. *Group Psychother., Psychodrama & Sociometry*, 19:176-181.

00128 **AGOSTON, T., LANDMAN, L.,** and **PAPANEK, H.** (1961), The management of anxiety in group psychoanalysis: a round table discussion. *Amer. J. Psychoanal.*, 21:74-84.

00129 **AGRANOWITZ, A., BOONE, D. R., RUFF, M., SEACAT, G.,** and **TERR, A. L.** (1954), Group therapy as a method of retraining aphasics. *Quart. J. Speech*, 40:170-182.

00130 **AGRIN, A.** (1960), The Georgian Clinic: a therapeutic community for alcoholics. *Quart. J. Studies Alcohol*, 21:113-124.

00131 **AGUIRRE de CÁRCER, A.** (1969), (Group dynamics in pregnant women.) *Acta Obstet. Ginecolog. Hispano-Lusitania,* (Barcelona) 17:257-261.

00132 **AHEARN, T. R.** (1969), An interaction process analysis of extended group counseling with prospective counselors. *Dissert. Abstr. Internat.*, 29:4271A.

00133 **AHUMADA, J. L.** (1976), Limited time group psychotherapy: group process. *Brit. J. Med. Psychol.*, (London) 49:81-88.

00134 **AHUMADA, J. L., ABIUSO, D. B., AIGUERA, N.,** and **GALLO, A.** (1974), On limited-time group psychotherapy: i. setting, admission, and therapeutic ideology. *Psychiatry*, 37:254-260.

00135 **AIKEN, J.,** and **JOHNSTON, J. A.** (1973), Promoting career information seeking behaviors in college students. *J. Vocat. Behav.*, 3:81-87.

00136 **AITKEN, J. R.** (1970), A study of attitudes and attitudinal change of institutionalized delinquents through group guidance techniques. *Dissert. Abstr. Internat.*, 30:4762A.

00137 **AJA, J. H.** (1977), Brief group treatment of obesity through ancillary self-hypnosis. *Amer. J. Clin. Hypnosis*, 19:231-234.

00138 **AKIN, C.**, and **KUNYMAN, G. G.** (1974), A group desensitization approach to public speaking anxiety. *Can. Counselor*, (Ottawa) 8:106-112.

00139 **AKMAN, D. D.** (1968), The group treatment literature in correctional institutions: an international bibliography, 1945-1967. *J. Crim. Law & Criminol.*, 59:41-56.

00140 **AKSTEIN, D.** (1974), Psychosocial perspectives of the application of terpsichoretrance therapy. *Psychopathol. Africaine*, (Dakar-Fann) 10:121-129.

00141 **AKSTEIN, D.** (1977), Socio-cultural basis of terpsichoretrancetherapy. *Amer. J. Clin. Hypnosis*, 19:221-225.

00142 **AKSTEIN, D.** (1973), Terpsichoretrancetherapy: a new hypnopsychotherapeutic method. *Internat. J. Clin. & Exper. Hypnosis*, 21:131-143.

00143 **AKUTAGAWA, D., SISKO, F. J.**, and **KEITEL, N. B.** (1965), "Beartrapping": a study in interpersonal behavior. *Amer. J. Psychiat.*, 19:54-65.

00144 **ALANEN, Y. O.**, and **TAHKA, V.** (1961), (On somatic methods, group therapeutic procedures, and allied measures in the treatment of schizophrenia.) *Duodecim.*, (Helsinki) 77:254-268.

00145 **ALARCON, F. M.** (1974), The effects of human potential group counseling on the self-concept and anxiety level of drug addicts in a therapeutic rehabilitation program. *Dissert. Abstr. Internat.*, 35:813A.

00146 **ALBERT, S.**, and **MOLL, A. E.** (1948), Group psychotherapy: preliminary report. *Treatment Serv. Bull.*, 3:38-40.

00147 **ALBERTI, G.** (1965), (Ways of its appearance in group psychotherapy of the families of chronic schizophrenics.) *Ospedale Psichiat.*, (Naples) 33:597-610.

00148 **ALBRECHT, W.** (1952), (Viennese psychotherapeutic schools.) *Monatsschr. Psychiat. & Neurol.*, (Basel) 124:146-160.

00149 **ALBRETSEN, C. S.** (1966), (Family therapy in puerperal psychosis in a hospital unit: joint hospitalization of the patient, the baby and the husband.) *Sykepleien*, (Oslo) 53:508-511.

00150 **ALBRETSEN, C. S.** (1968), (Treatment of post–partum psychosis with hospitalization of the baby, the patient and her husband.) *Sykepleien*, (Oslo) 55:82-84.

00151 **ALBRETSEN, C. S.** (1963), (Group activities with therapeutic intention in military infractions.) *Nordisk Psykiat. Tidsskr.*, (Kungsbacha) 17:386-397.

00152 **ALBRETSEN, S.** (1968), Hospitalization of post partum psychotic patients, together with babies and husbands. *Acta Psychiat. Scand. Suppl.*, (Copenhagen) 203:179.

00153 **ALCOHOLICS ANONYMOUS** (1952), *Twelve steps and twelve traditions.* New York: Alcoholics Anonymous.

00154 **ALDEN, A. R., WEDDINGTON, W. W., JACOBSON, C.**, and **GIANTUCCO, D. T.** (1979), Group aftercare for chronic schizophrenia. *J. Clin. Psychiat.*, 40:249.

00155 **ALECKSANDROWICZ, D. R.**, and **GAYE, Z.** (1971), A therapeutic club for schizophrenic adolescents. *Bull. Menninger Clinic*, 35:199-202.

00156 **ALEDORT, S.**, and **GRUNEBAUM, H.** (1969), Group psychotherapy on alien turf. *Psychiat. Quart.*, 43:512-524.

00157 **ALEKSANDROWICZ, J. W.** (1972), (Effects of therapeutic roles upon the course of group therapy.) *Psychiat. Polska*, (Warsaw) 6:169-174.

00158 **ALEKSANDROWICZ, J. W.** (1972), (The influence of role conflict on the course of group psychotherapy.) *Psychiat. Polska*, (Warsaw) 6:169.
00159 **ALEKSANDROWICZ, J. W.** (1971), (Some features of open psychotherapy groups.) *Przeglad. Lekarski*, (Warsaw) 27:643-646.
00160 **ALEVY, D. I.**, and **BUNKER, B. B.** (1974), Rationale, research, and role relations in the Stirling Workshop. *J. Confl. Resolut.*, 18:276-284.
00161 **ALEXANDER, E. D.** (1969), From play-therapy to the encounter marathon. *Psychother.: Theory, Res. & Pract.*, 6:188-193.
00162 **ALEXANDER, F.** (1954), Comments on Moreno's "Transference, countertransference and tele." *Group Psychother., Psychodrama & Sociometry*, 7:317-318.
00163 **ALEXANDER, W. B.** (1970), The development of a therapeutic social club. *Hosp. & Community Psychiat.*, 21:230-233.
00164 **ALFARO, R. R.** (1970), A group therapy approach to suicide prevention. *Bull. Suicidol.*, 6:56-59.
00165 **ALGER, J.** (1970), The superego in time of social conflict. *J. Contemp. Psychother.*, 3:51-56.
00166 **ALI, B. B.** (1958), An experience with a frustrated group. *Group Psychother., Psychodrama & Sociometry*, 11:153-158.
00167 **ALI, S.** (1957), A note on social climates in group psychoanalysis. *Internat. J. Group Psychother.*, 7:261-263.
00168 **ALIAKOS, L. C.** (1965), Analytical group treatment of the post-hospital schizophrenic. *Internat. J. Group Psychother.*, 15:492-504.
00169 **ALIAKOS, L. C., STARER, E.**, and **WINICH, W.** (1956), Observations on the meaning of behavior in groups of chronic schizophrenics. *Internat. J. Group Psychother.*, 6:180-192.
00170 **ALISSI, A. S.** (1965), Social influences on group values. *Soc. Work*, 10:14-22.
00171 **ALLAHYARI, H.** (1975), Productive films in patient groups. *Confinia. Psychiat.*, (Basel) 18:136-138.
00172 **ALLAIS, C. M.** (1971), Social and psychological characteristics of students participating in encounter groups. *Dissert. Abstr. Internat.*, 32:1184-1185B.
00173 **ALLAN, T. K.**, and **ALLAN, K. H.** (1971), Sensitivity training for community leaders. *Proceed., 79th Annual Convention*, American Psychological Assn., 577-578.
00174 **ALLEN, D. T.** (1969), "The crib scene": a psychodramatic exercise. *Psychother.: Theory, Res. & Pract.*, 6:206-208.
00175 **ALLEN, D. T.** (1960), The essence of psychodrama. *Group Psychother., Psychodrama & Sociometry*, 13:188-194.
00176 **ALLEN, D. W.**, and **HOUSTON, M.** (1959), The management of hysterioid acting-out patients in a training clinic. *Psychiatry*, 22:41-49.
00177 **ALLEN, H. A.** (1971), The use of cognitive structuring and verbal reinforcement of positive self-reference statements within a short term group therapy session to enhance self-concept. *Dissert. Abstr. Internat.*, 32:730A.
00178 **ALLEN, J. E.** (1970), The silent observer: a new approach to group therapy for delinquents. *Crime & Delinquency*, 16:324-328.
00179 **ALLEN, J. G.** (1973), Implications of research in self-disclosure for group psychotherapy. *Internat. J. Group Psychother.*, 23:306-321.
00180 **ALLEN, K. S.** (1976), A group experience for elderly patients with organic brain syndrome: Soundview-Throgs Neck Community Mental Health Center. *Health & Soc. Work*, 1:61-69.
00181 **ALLEN, M. G.** (1979), Peer review of group therapy, Washington, D.C., 1972-77. *Amer. J. Psychiat.*, 136:444.
00182 **ALLEN, R. F.** (1969), Conflict resolution-team building for police and ghetto residents. *J. Crim. Law & Criminol.*, 60:251-255.

00183 **ALLERHAND, M. E.** (1953), A comparison of two approaches to group psychotherapy and psychodrama. *Group Psychother., Psychodrama & Sociometry*, 5:199-204.

00184 **ALLGEYER, J.** (1973), Using groups in a crisis-oriented outpatient setting. *Internat. J. Group Psychother.*, 23:217-222.

00185 **ALLGEYER, J. M.** (1970), The crisis group: its unique usefulness to the disadvantaged. *Internat. J. Group Psychother.*, 20:235-240.

00186 **ALLISON, R. B., JR., KORNER, I. N.,** and **ZWANZIGER, M. D.** (1966), Matching patients and therapists: a methodological approach. *J. Psychology*, 64:33-40.

00187 **ALLISON, S. G.** (1952), Nondirective group therapy of alcoholics in a state hospital. *Quart. J. Studies Alcohol*, 13:596-601.

00188 **ALLODI, F.** (1972), The community group program: evaluation of a multiagency therapeutic social club. *Can. Psychologist*, S-45-S-50.

00189 **ALLPORT, G. W.** (1954), Comments on J. L. Moreno's "Transference, countertransference and tele: their relation to group research and group psychotherapy." *Group Psychother., Psychodrama & Sociometry*, 7:307-308.

00190 **ALMOND, R.** (1969), Milieu therapeutic process. *Arch. Gen. Psychiat.*, 21:431-442.

00191 **ALMOND, R.** (1969), Patient value change in milieu therapy. *Arch. Gen. Psychiat.*, 20:339-351.

00192 **ALMOND, R.** (1971), The therapeutic community. *Scient. Amer.*, 224:34-42.

00193 **ALMOND, R.,** and **ASTRACHAN, B.** (1969), Social system training for psychiatric residents. *Psychiatry*, 32:277-291.

00194 **ALNAES, R.** (1963), (Clinical sociotherapy: experiences in a psychiatric hospital.) *Zeit. Psychother. Med. Psychol.*, (Stuttgart) 13:37-48.

00195 **ALNAES, R.** (1963), Sociometry and group analysis. *Acta Psychiat. Scand., Suppl.*, (Copenhagen) 169:402.

00196 **ALNOES, R.,** and **SIGRELL, B.** (1975), Evaluation of the outcome of training groups using an analytic group psychotherapy technique. *Psychother. & Psychosomatics*, (Basel) 25:168-175.

00197 **ALPERT, A.** (1936), Educational group therapy: an experiment. *Progr. Educat.*, 13:170-173.

00198 **ALPERT, A.** (1941), Education as therapy. *Psychoanal. Quart.*, 10:468-474.

00199 **ALPERT, H. S., WEINGARTEN, L. L.,** and **DOLINS, R. S.** (1966), Content and process in modified group psychotherapy: an experiment in observation. *Psychiat. Quart. Suppl.*, 40:256-272.

00200 **AL-SAADI, L. C.,** and **GOOS, D.** (1970), *Help Me: A Way to Guide Troubled Youth*. Kaukauna, WI: C. C. Thomas.

00201 **AL SALIH, H. A.** (1969), Phobics in group psychotherapy. *Internat. J. Group Psychother.*, 19:28-34.

00202 **ALSTON, P. P.** (1974), Multidiscipline group facilitation training: an aid to the team approach. *Rehab. Couns. Bull.*, 18:21-25.

00203 **ALSTRUP, K.** (1950), (Group therapy of alcoholism in Denmark.) *Ugeskrift for Laeger*, (Copenhagen) 112:807-812.

00204 **ALTENBERG, H. E.** (1970), Beginning the therapy. *Voices*, 6:33-34.

00205 **ALTHOUSE, R. H.** (1976), Enhancing self-disclosure in psychotherapy groups: an analogue study. *Dissert. Abstr. Internat.*, 36:3668B.

00206 **ALTSHULER, A.** (1977), Teen meetings: a way to help adolescents cope with hospitalization. *Amer. J. Maternal & Child Nursing*, 2:348-353.

00207 **ALTSHULER, I. M.** (1940), One year's experience with group psychotherapy. *Ment. Health*, 24:290-296.

00208 **ALTSHULER, I. M.** (1945), The organism–as–a–whole and music therapy. *Sociometry*, 8:465-470.

00209 **ALUMBAUGH, R. V.** (1971), The management of social behavior of chronic psychiatric patients: an empirical analysis of small group behaviors. *J. Clin. Psychol.*, 27:525-528.

00210 **ALVAREZ, G. A.** (1964), Un ensayo de grupoterapia en la Guayana Inglesa. (A group therapy experiment in British Guiana.) *Acta Psiquiat. Psicol. Amer. Latina*, (Buenos Aires) 10:280-283.

00211 **ALVERSON, L. G.** (1979), An evaluation of group play therapy techniques with acting out headstart children. *Dissert. Abstr. Internat.*, 39:4566B.

00212 **ALVIN, J.** (1959), The response of severely retarded children to music. *Amer. J. Ment. Deficiency*, 63:988-996.

00213 **AMADO, H.** (1967), (The psychiatric hospital.) *Rev. de Enfermagem*, (Lisbon) 6:246-262.

00214 **AMARANTO, E.** (1970), The group within the group: an experimental clinical approach in combining two psychotherapy groups. *Sandoz Psychiat. Spectator*, 6:4-6.

00215 **AMARO, J. W.** (1969), Contribution to the study of pathological grief in group psychotherapy. *Rev. Hosp. Clin. Fac. Med.*, (Sao Paulo) 24:185-192.

00216 **AMARO, J. W.** (1970), Group therapy: paranoid anxiety in the therapist-observer relationship. *Rev. Hosp. Clin. Fac. Med.*, (Sao Paulo) 25:77-81.

00217 **AMARO, J. W.**, and **SOEIRO, A. C.** (1969), Psychodrama at a psychiatric clinic. *Group Psychother., Psychodrama & Sociometry*, 22:157-163.

00218 **ABERCROMBIE, M. L. J.** (1980), Review of W. Bramley's *Group Tutoring: Concepts and Case Studies. Group Analysis*, (London) 13:219-221.

00219 **ABRAMOVITCH, R., KONSTANTAREAS, M.**, and **SLOMAN, I.** (1980), An observational assessment of change in two groups of behaviourally disturbed boys. *J. Child Psychol. & Psychiat.*, 21:133-141.

00220 **ABRAMOWITZ, C. V.** (1977), The effectiveness of group psychotherapy with children. *Annals Prog. Child Psychiat.*, 393-408.

00221 **ADORJANI, C., BOSZORMENYI, Z.**, and **HAJTMAN, P.** (1965), Csoportpszichoterapia es a szkizofren betegek konfrontativ stimulacioja. (Group psychotherapy and confrontative stimulation of schizophrenic patients.) *Psychol. Studies Psizochol. Tanulmanyok*, 8:439-448.

00222 **ADRIAN, S. A.** (1980), A systematic approach to selecting group participants. *J. Psychiatr. Nursing*, 18:37-41.

00223 **AKISTER, J.**, and **CANEVER, N.** (1980), A year in the life of an adolescent group. *J. Adolescence*, 3:155-163.

00224 **ALMOND, R., KENISTON, K.**, and **BOLTAX, S.** (1968), The value system of a milieu therapy unit. *Arch. Gen. Psychiat.*, 19:545-561.

00225 **ALPERT, H. S.** (1980), The dynamics of individual resistance and techniques for handling these manifestations in group psychotherapy. *Group*, 4:49-59.

00226 **ALTHOF, S. E.**, and **KELLER, A. C.** (1980), Group therapy with gender identity patients. *Internat. J. Group Psychother.*, 30:481-490.

00227 **AMADO, G.**, and **GUITTET, A.** (1975), *La Dynamique des Communications dans les Groupes. (The Dynamics of Communication in Group.)* Paris: A. Colin.

00228 **AMBRAMORWITZ, C. V.** (1976), The effectiveness of group psychotherapy with children. *Arch. Gen. Psychiat.*, 33:320-326.

00229 **AMENDOLARA, F. R.** (1974), Group therapy for mothers of drug addicts. *Brit. J. Addict.*, 69:181-182.

00230 **AMENTA, R. B.** (1974), The development of an observation instrument for the evaluation of small group discussion. *Dissert. Abstr. Internat.*, 35:162A.

00231 Current concepts and methodological issues in group psychotherapy research: ii. (1967), *Proceed., 23d Annual Conference*, American Group Psychotherapy Association, Philadelphia, Jan. 1966, *Internat. J. Group Psychother.*, 17:192-242.

00232 **AMERICAN SOCIETY OF GROUP PSYCHOTHERAPY AND PSYCHODRAMA** (1957), *Group Psychother., Psychodrama & Sociometry*, 10:73-74.

00233 **AMERICAN SOCIETY OF GROUP PSYCHOTHERAPY AND PSYCHODRAMA** (1951), *Report on Round Table Conference on 9th Annual Meeting on Group Psychotherapy and the Treatment of Minority Problems. Group Psychother., Psychodrama & Sociometry*, 4:74-76.

00234 **AMMON, G.** (1973), (Aggression and ego development in groups: a contribution to psychoanalytical aggression theory.) *Zeit. Psychother. Med. Psychol.*, (Stuttgart) 23:61-72.

00235 **AMMON, G.** (1975), Analytic group psychotherapy as an instrument for the treatment and research of psychosomatic disorders. In: *Group Therapy 1975: An Overview*, eds. L. R. Wolberg and M. L. Aronson. New York: Stratton Intercontinental Medical Books.

00236 **AMMON, G.** (1973), Der traum als ich- und gruppenfunktion. *Dynam. Psychiatry*, (Berlin) 6:145-164.

00237 **AMMON, G.** (1973), Ego-psychological and group dynamic aspects of psychoanalytic group psychotherapy. *Dynam. Psychiat.*, 6:207-230.

00238 **AMMON, G.** (1977), Ego-psychological and group dynamic aspects of psychoanalytic group psychotherapy. In: *Group Therapy 1977: An Overview*, ed. L. R. Wolberg. New York: Stratton Intercontinental Medical Books.

00239 **AMMON, G.** (1974), (Group psychotherapy: i.) *Hippokrates*, (Stuttgart) 45:126-129.

00240 **AMMON, G.** (1974), (Group psychotherapy. ii.) *Hippokrates*, (Stuttgart) 45:129-131.

00241 **AMMON, G.** (1970), Psychoanalyse und gruppentherapie: anpassung oder emanzipation? (Psychoanalysis and group therapy: adaptation or emancipation?) *Ziet. Psychother. Med. Psychol.*, (Stuttgart) 20:1-10.

00242 **AMMON, G.** (1973), Psychoanalytic milieu therapy. *Dynam. Psychiat.*, (Berlin) 6:112-130.

00243 **AMMON, G.** (1978), Psychoanalytische gruppendynamik. (Psychoanalytic group dynamics.) *Dynam. Psychiat.*, (Berlin) 48:1-22.

00244 **AMMON, G.**, and **AMENT, A.** (1967), The terminal phase of the dynamic process of group-dynamic teaching group. *Internat. J. Group Psychother.*, 17:35-43.

00245 **AMMON, G.**, and **HAMEISTER, H. J.** (1975), Ego-psychological and group-dynamic aspects of death and dying. *Dynam. Psychiat.*, (Berlin) 8:129-142.

00246 **AMMON, K.** (1977), Adaptation as a defense formation in borderline symptomatics. *Dynam. Psychiat.*, (Berlin) 10:183-197.

00247 **AMMONS, G.** (1971), (Structuring of leisure time in the framework of group dynamics work therapy.) *Praxis der Psychother.*, 16:310-314.

00248 **AMORE, G. S.** (1972), A role play approach to group counseling with educable mentally retarded children. *Dissert. Abstr. Internat.*, 33:4165A.

00240 **AMSTER, F.** (1954), Applications of group therapy principles to nonstructured groups. *Internat. J. Group Psychother.*, 4:285-292.

00250 **AMSTER, F.** (1944), Collective psychotherapy of mothers of emotionally disturbed children. *Amer. J. Orthopsychiat.*, 14:44-51.

00251 **AMUNDSON, C. L.** (1954), Increasing interpersonal relationships in the high school with the aid of sociometric procedures. *Group Psychother., Psychodrama & Sociometry*, 6:183-188.

00252 **AMUNDSON, N. E.** (1975), TA with elementary school children: a pilot study. *Transactional Anal. J.*, 5:247-250.

00253 **ANANT, S. S.** (1968), Alcoholics Anonymous and aversion therapy. *Can. Ment. Health*, (Ottawa) 16:23-27.

00254 **ANCELIN-SCHUTZENBERG, A.** (1965), Development of the helper-helped relationship. *Inform. Psychiat.*, 41:673-685.

00255 **ANCELIN-SCHUTZENBERG, A.** (1969/1970), An introduction to psychodrama. *Bull. de Psychol.*, (Paris) 23:713-714.

00256 **ANCELIN-SCHÜTZENBERGER, A.** (1977), *Le Corps et le Groupe: Les Nouvelles Thérapies de Groupe: de la Gestalt à la Bio-énergie, aux Groupes de Rencontre et à la Méditation.* (*The Body and the Group: The New Group Therapies: Gestalt and Bioenergetics in Meditation Groups.*) Toulouse: Privat.

00257 **ANCELIN-SCHUTZENBERG, A.** (1969/1970), (Presentation of psychodrama.) *Bull. de Psychol.*, (Paris) 23:969-993.

00258 **ANCELIN-SCHUTZENBERGER, A.** (1955), Psychodrame et milieu professionnel. (Psychodrama and the professional milieu.) *Travail et Methodes*, 94:39-43.

00259 **ANCHOR, K. N.** (1979), High and low-risk self-disclosure in group psychotherapy. *Small Group Behav.*, 10:279-283.

00260 **ANCHOR, K. N.** (1972), Social desirability as a predictor of self-disclosure in groups. *Psychother.: Theory, Res. & Pract.*, 9:262-264.

00261 **ANCHOR, K. N., VEJTISEK, J. E.,** and **PATTERSON, R. L.** (1973), Trait anxiety, initial structuring and self-disclosure in groups of schizophrenic patients. *Psychother.: Theory, Res. & Pract.*, 10:155-158.

00262 **ANCONA, L.** (1975), Group analysis of homosexuality. *Arch. Psicol., Neurol. & Psichiat.*, (Milan) 36:445.

00263 **ANCONA, L.** (1977), Shortened group analysis as an instrument of therapy. *Arch. Psicol., Neurol. & Psichiat.*, (Milan) 38:7-20.

00264 **ANDERE, M.** (1967), Breaking down the barrier. *Ment. Health*, 26:9-11.

00265 **ANDERSON, A. R.** (1970), An experimental assessment of videotape feedback and two pregroup orientation procedures in a human relations training laboratory. *Compar. Group Studies*, 1:156-176.

00266 **ANDERSON, A. V.** (1969), Predicting response to group psychotherapy. Ann Arbor: University Microfilms.

00267 **ANDERSON, A. V.** (1959), Predicting response to group psychotherapy. Unpublished doctoral dissertation, University of Oklahoma.

00268 **ANDERSON, B. N., PINE, L.,** and **MEE-LEE, D.** (1972), Resident training in cotherapy groups. *Internat. J. Group Psychother.*, 22:192-198.

00269 **ANDERSON, C.,** and **SLOCUM, J. W.** (1973), Personality traits and their impact on t-group training success. *Training & Develop. J.*, 27:18-25.

00270 **ANDERSON, C. M., HARROW, M., SCHWARTZ, A. H.,** and **KUPFER, D. J.** (1972), Impact of therapist on patient satisfaction in group psychotherapy. *Comprehens. Psychiatry*, 13:33-40.

00271 **ANDERSON, D.** (1977), The effects of group counseling on the incidence of fear of success motives, role orientation and personal orientation of college women. *Dissert. Abstr. Internat.*, 38:1881A.

00272 **ANDERSON, D. B.** (1969), Nursing therapy with families. *Perspect. Psychiat. Care*, 7:21-27.

00273 **ANDERSON, H. W.** (1978), Remotivation therapy. *Dimens. Health Serv.*, (Toronto) 55:18-19.

00274 **ANDERSON, H. W.,** and **KAUFMAN, S. J.** (1973), The group method in adoption of children with special needs. *Child Welfare*, 52:45-51.

00275 **ANDERSSON, I.** (1970), (Group therapy or individual therapy: a psychiatric dilemma.) *Tidskr. Sveriges Sjukskoeterskor*, (Stockholm) 37:956-8 passim.

00276 **ANDERSON, J.** (1977), Group theory integrated: a model for baccalaureate nursing programs. *J. Nursing Educat.*, 16:16-21.

00277 **ANDERSON, J. D.** (1978), Growth groups and alienation: a comparative study of Rogerian encounter, self-directed encounter and gestalt. *Group & Organizat. Studies*, 3:85-107.

00278 **ANDERSON, J. D.** (1975), Human relations training and group work. *Soc. Work*, 20:195-199.

00279 **ANDERSON, J. E.** (1968), Group therapy with brain-damaged children. *Hosp. & Community Psychiat.*, 19:175-176.

00280 **ANDERSON, K.** (1948), A Detroit case study in the group-talking technique. *Personnel J.*, 27:93-98.

00281 **ANDERSON, L. M.**, and **SHAFER, G.** (1979), The character disordered family: a community treatment model for family sexual abuse. *Amer. J. Orthopsychiat.*, 49:436.

00282 **ANDERSON, L. R.** (1965), Some effects of leadership training on intercultural discussion groups. *Dissert. Abstr. Internat.*, 25:6796.

00283 **ANDERSON, N.**, and **MARRONE, R. T.** (1977), Group therapy for emotionally disturbed children: key to affective education. *Amer. J. Orthopsychiat.*, 47:97-103.

00284 **ANDERSON, N.**, and **MARRONE, R. T.** (1979), Therapeutic discussion groups in public school classes for emotionally disturbed children. *Focus Except. Children*, 12:1-16.

00285 **ANDERSON, N. J.**, and **LOVE, B.** (1973), Psychological education for racial awareness. *Personnel & Guid. J.*, 51:666-670.

00286 **ANDERSON, R. E.** (1969), The exchange of tape recordings as a catalyst in group psychotherapy with sex offenders. *Internat. J. Group Psychiat.*, 19:214-220.

00287 **ANDERSON, R. L.** (1956), An experimental investigation of group counseling with freshmen in a women's college. Unpublished doctoral dissertation, New York University.

00288 **ANDERSON, S.** (1971), Group counseling in drug awareness. *School Counselor*, 19:123-125.

00289 **ANDERSON, W.** (1970), Services offered by college counseling centers. *J. Couns. Psychol.*, 17:380-382.

00290 **ANDRE, C. S. C.** (1974), An exploration of the sex variable as a determinant in the interaction and outcome of marathon group sessions. *Dissert. Abstr. Internat.*, 35:2669A.

00291 **ANDRE, R.**, **HEILIGMAN, A.**, **HIGGINS, R.**, **KARATZ, J.**, and **KOTTLER, A.** (1966), Short-term social group work in the hospital. *Ment. Health*, 50:266-269.

00292 **ANDREWS, D. A.**, **WORMITH, J. S.**, **DIAGLEZINN, W. J.**, **KENNEDY, D. J.**, and **NELSON, S.** (1980), Low and high functioning volunteers in group counseling with anxious and non-anxious prisoners: the effects of interpersonal skills on group process and attitude change. *Can. J. Criminol. and Correct.*, (Ottawa) 22:433-456.

00293 **ANDREWS, D. A.**, **YOUNG, J. G.**, and **WORMITH, J. S.** (1974), The attitudinal effects of group discussions between young criminal offenders and community volunteers. *J. Community Psychol.*, 1:417-422.

00294 **ANDREWS, E. E.** (1964), Identity maintenance operations and group therapy process. *Internat. J. Group Psychother.*, 14:491-498.

00295 **ANDREWS, E. E.** (1962), Some group dynamics in therapy groups of mothers. *Internat. J. Group Psychother.*, 12:476-491.

00296 **ANDREWS, E. E.** (1963), The struggle for identity in mothers undergoing group therapy. *Internat. J. Group Psychother.*, 13:346-353.

00297 **ANDREWS, G.** (1967), Theoretical and therapeutic considerations: ii. syllable timed speech group therapy and recovery from stuttering. *Austral. Psychologist*, (Brisbane) 2:162-164.

00298 **ANDREWS, J. D.** (1974/1975), Interpersonal challenge workshop. *Interpersonal Develop.*, 5:26-36.
00299 **ANDREWS, J. D. W.** (1973), Interpersonal challenge: a source of growth in laboratory training. *J. Appl. Behav.*, 9:514-533.
00300 **ANDREWS, J. M.** (1962), Community therapy: its effect on training psychiatric nurses. *Nursing Times*, (London) 58:206-208.
00301 **ANDREWS, K. W.** (1978), Family training in contingency management: preparation of the work furloughee for family reentry. *Dissert. Abstr. Internat.*, 38:4436B.
00302 **ANDRONICO, M. P., FIDLER, J., GUERNEY, B.**, and **GUERNEY, L. F.** (1967), The combination of didactic and dynamic elements in filial therapy. *Internat. J. Group Psychother.*, 17:10-17.
00303 **ANDRUS, R. S.** (1964), Instant therapy: a study of group process at the Utah State Hospital. *Provo Papers*, 8:1-14.
00304 **ANGEL, J.**, and **GAY, A.** (1952), Une psychotherapie de groupe: L'esthesiotherapie. (Esthetic therapy: a group psychotherapy.) *Annales Medico-Psychol.*, (Paris) 110:284-290.
00305 **ANGEL, S. L.** (1981), The emotion identification group. *Amer. J. Occupat. Ther.*, 35:256-262.
00306 **ANGLIKER, C. C.** (1971), (Therapeutic community: whom are we training?) *Laval Med.*, (Quebec) 42:12-14.
00307 **ANKER, J. M.**, and **DUFFEY, R. F.** (1958), Training group psychotherapists: a method and evaluation. *Group Psychother., Psychodrama & Sociometry,* 11:314-319.
00308 **ANKER, J. M.**, and **WALSH, R. P.** (1961), Group psychotherapy: a special activity program and structure in the treatment of chronic schizophrenics. *J. Consult. & Clin. Psychol.*, 25:476-481.
00309 **ANNESLEY, P. T.** (1959), Group psychotherapy and rehabilitation of long-stay patients. *Internat. J. Group Psychother.*, 9:167-175.
00310 **ANNESLEY, P. T.** (1963), Group psychotherapy in an adolescent psychiatric unit. *Internat. J. Soc. Psychiat.*, (London) 9:283-291.
00311 **ANNESLEY, P. T.** (1961), A rehabilitation unit on group therapy lines for long–stay patients. *Psychiat. Quart.*, 35:321-357.
00312 **ANNIS, L. V.**, and **PERRY, D. F.** (1978), Self-disclosure in unsupervised groups: effects of videotaped models. *Small Group Behav.*, 9:102-108.
00313 **ANON.** (1939), *Alcoholics anonymous.* New York: The Works Co.
00314 **ANON.** (1949), Group psychotherapy. *Brit. Med. J.*, (London) 1:227-228.
00315 **ANON.** (1938), Group psychotherapy at the Psychiatric Institute. *Lost & Found*, 1:32-39.
00316 **ANON.** (1939), Group psychotherapy: indifference breeds ill will in a group. *Lost & Found*, 2:13-16.
00317 **ANON.** (1948), Group psychotherapy in New Jersey correctional institutions. *Prison World*, 10 passim.
00318 **ANON.** (1949), Group therapy at St. Elizabeth's hospital. *Newsweek*, (Aug. 22), 34:44-46.
00319 **ANON.** (1957), Impressions of an inmate after reading Corsini. *J. Correct. Psychol.*, 2:17-23.
00320 **ANON.** (1973), Philadelphia Center House: inpatient treatment program for the pre-skid-row man. *Alcohol Health & Res. World*, 1:8.
00321 **ANSBACHER, H. L.** (1955), J. L. Moreno's "Transference, countertransference, and tele" in relation to certain formulations by Alfred Adler. *Group Psychother., Psychodrama & Sociometry*, 8:179-180.
00322 **ANSHIN, R. N.** (1970), The role of a psychiatric consultant to a public high school in racial transition: challenge and response. *Amer. J. Orthopsychiat.*, 40:304-305.

00323 **ANTELYES, J.** (1968), Group therapy in the veterinary office. *Veterinary Med.*, 36:975-976.
00324 **ANTENEV, W. W.** (1964), Change in topic and affect during group counseling: its relationship to outcome of group counseling. *Dissert. Abstr. Internat.*, 24:5185.
00325 **ANTHONY, E. J.** (1965), Age and syndrome in group psychotherapy. *Topical Probl. Psychol. & Psychother.*, 5:80-89.
00326 **ANTHONY, E. J.** (1957), Die psychotherapeutische gruppenbehandlung von kindern in verschiedenen stadien ihrer entwicklung. (Psycho-therapeutic group treatment of children in their various developmental stages.) *Praxis Kinderpsychol. & Kinderpsychiat.*, (Goettingen) 6:15-20.
00327 **ANTHONY, E. J.** (1968), Discussion of F. H. Stoller's accelerated interaction. *Internat. J. Group Psychother.*, 18:249-254.
00328 **ANTHONY, E. J.** (1967), The generic elements in dyadic and group psychotherapy. *Internat. J. Group Psychother.*, 17:57-70.
00329 **ANTHONY, E. J.** (1968), Reflections on twenty-five years of group psychotherapy. *Internat. J. Group Psychother.*, 18:277-301.
00330 **ANTHONY, E. J.** (1975), There and then and here and now. *Internat. J. Group Psychother.*, 25:163-167.
00331 **ANTHONY, E. J.**, and **FOULKES, S. H.** (1972), *Group Psychotherapy,* rev. ed. Baltimore: Penguin.
00333 **ANTHONY, W. A.** (1973), Human relations skills and training: implications for rehabilitation counseling. *Rehab. Couns. Bull.*, 16:180-186.
00334 **ANTHONY, W. A.** (1974), Human relations training and rehabilitation counseling: further implications. *Rehab. Couns. Bull.*, 17:171-175.
00335 **ANTON, W. D.** (1976), An evaluation of outcome variables in the systematic desensitization of test anxiety. *Behav. Res. & Ther.*, 14:217-224.
00336 **ANTONIJEVIC, M., VIDOJKOVIC, S., MARINKOV, M.**, and **JOJIC-MILENKOVIC, M.** (1979), (Psychotherapy in large groups of neurotic and borderline patients.) *Psihijat. Danas*, (Belgrade) 11:373-380.
00337 **ANTONS, K.** (1976), (Outpatient group therapy with alcoholics: possibilities and limits.) *Gruppenpsychother. und Gruppendynam.*, (Goettingen) 11:100-104.
00338 **ANZIEU, D.** (1960), Aspects of analytic psychodrama applied to children. *Internat. J. Sociometry & Sociatry*, 2:42-47.
00339 **ANZIEU, D.** (1962), Contribution du psychodrama analytique à la maturation chez l'enfant. *Internat. J. Sociometry & Sociatry*, 2:123-124.
00340 **ANZIEU, D.** (1969/1970), (Group analytic psychodrama in clinical training of psychology students.) *Bull. de Psychol.*, (Paris) 23:908-914.
00341 **ANZIEU, D.** (1975), *Le Groupe et l'Inconscient.* (*The Group and the Unconscious.*) Paris: Dunod.
00342 **ANZIEU, D.** (1956), *Le psychodrame analytique chez l'enfant.* (*Analytic Psychodrama in a Children's Home.*) Paris: Presses Universitaires de France.
00343 **ANZIEU, D.** (1962), (Some problems laid by depth analysis training.) *Psychol. Francaise*, (Paris) 7:85-93.
00344 **ANZIEU, D., BÉJARANO, A., KAËS, R.**, and **MISSENARD, A.** (1976), *Le Travail Psychanalytique dans les Groupes.* (*Psychoanalytic Work in Groups.*) Paris: Dunod.
00345 **APAKA, T. K., GIRSCH, G.**, and **KLEIDMAN, S.** (1967), Establishing group supervision in a hospital social work department. *Soc. Work*, 12:54-60.
00346 New professional association formed: focus certification and public education. (1971), *Amer. Psychol. Assn. Monitor*, 2:7-ff.
00347 **APER, N. E., DEBBANE, E. G., GARRANT, J.**, and **BIENUENO, J. P.** (1979), Pretraining for group psychotherapy. *Arch. Gen. Psychiat.*, 36:1250-1260.

00348 **APFEL, A.**, and **RAMIREZ, J.** (1973), The corridor group. *J. Bronx State Hosp.*, 1:62-66.

00349 **APFEL-SAVITZ, R., SILVERMAN, D.**, and **BENNETT, M. I.** (1977), Group psychotherapy of patients with somatic illnesses and alexithymia. *Psychother. & Psychosomatics*, (Basel) 28:323-329.

00350 **APONTE, J. F.** (1970), Group systematic desensitization: a test of the counterconditioning hypothesis with cognitive and emotional modes of test anxiety. *Dissert. Abstr. Internat.*, 31:6251B.

00351 **APONTE, J. F.**, and **APONTE, C. E.** (1971), Group preprogrammed systematic desensitization without the simultaneous presentation of aversive scenes with relaxation training. *Behav. Res. & Ther.*, 9:337-346.

00352 **APOSTAL, R. A.**, and **MURO, J. J.** (1970), Effects of group counseling on self-reports and on self-recognition abilities of counselors in training. *Counselor Educat. & Supervision*, 10:56-63.

00353 **APPEL, E.**, and **MARTIN, C. H.** (1957), Group counselling for social adjustment. *Amer. J. Ment. Deficiency*, 62:517-520.

00354 **APPELBAUM, S. A.** (1979), *Out in Inner Space*. Garden City, NY: Doubleday.

00355 **APPELBAUM, S. A.** (1963), The pleasure and reality principles in group process teaching. *Brit. J. Med. Psychol.*, (London) 36:49-56.

00356 **APPELL, M. J., WILLIAMS, C. M.**, and **FISHELL, K. N.** (1964), Changes in attitudes of parents of retarded children effected through group counseling. *Amer. J. Ment. Deficiency*, 68:807-812.

00357 **APPLEY, D. G.**, and **WINDER, A. E.** (1973), *T-Groups and Therapy Groups in a Changing Society*. San Francisco: Jossey-Bass.

00358 **APTER, A.**, and **TYANO, S.** (1976), Review of Rachman's "Identity group psychotherapy with adolescents." *Isr. Annals Psychiat.*, (Jerusalem) 14:206.

00359 **ARAGONA, J., CASSADY, J.**, and **ORABMAN, R. S.** (1975), Treating overweight children through parental training and contingency contracting. *J. Appl. Behav. Anal.*, 8:269-278.

00360 **ARANGO, C. R.** (1964), (Group psychotherapy.) *Folia Clin. Internac.*, (Barcelona) 14:380-387.

00361 **ARANN, L.**, and **HORNER, V. M.** (1972), Contingency management in an open psychiatric ward. *J. Behav. Ther. & Exper. Psychiat.*, 3:31-38.

00362 **ARAOZ, D. L.** (1978), Clinical hypnosis in couple therapy. *J. Amer. Soc. Psychosomat. Dent. & Med.*, 25:58.

00363 **ARBES, B. H.**, and **HUBBELL, R. N.** (1973), Packaged impact: a structured communication skills workshop. *J. Couns. Psychol.*, 20:332-337.

00364 **ARBISER, S.** (1973), (Schemes of group psychotherapy.) *Acta Psiquiat. Psicol. Amer. Latina*, (Buenos Aires) 19:372-377.

00365 **ARCAN, P.** (1976), Group autogenic therapy. *Rev. Med. Internal., Neurolog. Psihiatr.*, (Bucharest) 21:15-20.

00366 **ARCHER, D.** (1974), Power in groups: self-concept changes of powerful and powerless group members. *J. Appl. Behav. Science*, 10:208-220.

00367 **ARCHIBALD, H. C.** (1954), Therapy group as dream content. *Group Psychother., Psychodrama & Sociometry*, 7:146-147.

00368 **ARDOINO, J.** (1967), *Propos Actuels sur l'Éducation Contribution à l'Éducation des Adultes*, 3d ed. Paris: Gauthier-Villard.

00369 **ARDOINO, J.** (1969/1970), (Reflections on psychodrama as a crucial experience.) *Bull. de Psycholog.*, (Paris) 23:740-744.

00370 **ARENDSEN HEIN, G. W.** (1959), Group therapy with criminal psychopaths. *Acta Psychother., Psychosomat. Orthopaedagog. Suppl.*, (Basel) 7:6-16.

00371 **ARENDSEN HEIN, G. W.** (1963), Treatment of the neurotic patient, resistant to the usual techniques of psychotherapy, with special reference to LSD. *Topical Probl. Psychol. & Psychother.*, 4:50-57.

00372 **ARFSTEN, A. J.**, and **HOFFMANN, S. O.** (1978), (Psychoanalysis in hospital as an independent treatment: considerations and results based on a model of group therapy.) *Praxis der Psychother.*, 23:233-245.

00373 **ARFSTEN, J.** (1975), (Treatment of psychotherapeutic problem-patients in a ward or: another model of inpatient psychotherapy.) *Gruppenpsychother. & Gruppendynam.*, (Goettingen) 9:212-218.

00374 **ARGELAND, R.** (1976), (Results of group psychotherapy and problems of outcome studies.) *Gruppenpsychother. & Gruppendynam.*, (Goettingen) 10:293-312.

00375 **ARGELANDER, H.** (1963), (The analysis of group psychological processes.) *Psyche,* (Stuttgart) 17:450-479.

00376 **ARGELANDER, H.** (1963), (The analysis of psychic processes in groups ii.) *Psyche*, (Stuttgart) 17:481-515.

00377 **ARGELANDER, H.** (1968), (Group analysis using a structural model.) *Psyche*, (Stuttgart) 22:915-933.

00378 **ARGELANDER, H.** (1974), (Individual psychotherapy and group psychotherapy in combination.) *Gruppenpsychother. & Gruppendynam.*, (Goettingen) 8:141-151.

00379 **ARGELANDER, H.** (1974), (The psychoanalytic situation of a group in comparison with individual therapy.) *Psyche*, (Stuttgart) 28:310-327.

00380 **ARGUE, D. H.** (1969), A research study of the effects of behavioral group counseling upon college freshmen. *Dissert. Abstr. Internat.*, 30:1852A.

00381 **ARGYLE, M., LALLJEE, M.**, and **COOK, M.** (1968), The effects of visibility on interaction in a dyad. *Human Relat.*, 21:3-17.

00382 **ARGYRIS, C.** (1972), Do personal growth laboratories represent an alternative culture? *J. Appl. Behav. Science*, 8:7-28.

00383 **ARGYRIS, C.** (1969), The incompleteness of social-psychological theory: examples from small group, cognitive consistency, and attribution research. *Amer. Psychologist*, 24:893-908.

00384 **ARIAS DUQUE, H.** (1975), (Group psychoanalytic psychotherapy.) *Rev. Colombiana Psiquiat.*, (Bogota) 4:277-284.

00385 **ARIES, E.** (1976), Interaction patterns and themes of male, female and mixed groups. *Small Group Behav.*, 7:7-18.

00386 **ARIES, E. J.** (1974), Interaction patterns and themes of male, female and mixed groups. *Dissert. Abstr. Internat.*, 35:3084B.

00387 **ARMOR, T. H.** (1970), Peak-experiences and sensitivity training groups. *Dissert. Abstr. Internat.*, 30:5218B.

00388 **ARMSBY, R. E.** (1971), Adolescent crisis team: An experiment in community crisis intervention. *Proceed., 79th Annual Convention, American Psychological Association*, 735-736.

00389 **ARMSTRONG, J. D.**, and **TYNDEL, M.** (1965), A therapeutic waiting area experience for alcoholics and drug addicts. *Comprehen. Psychiat.*, 6:137-138.

00390 **ARMSTRONG, J. H.** (1978), The effects of group counseling on the self-concept, academic performance, and reading level of a selected group of high school students. *Dissert. Abstr. Internat.*, 39:1332A.

00391 **ARMSTRONG, J. J.**, and **GIBBONS, R. J.** (1956), A psychotherapeutic technique with large groups in the treatment of alcoholics: a preliminary report. *Quart. J. Studies Alcohol*, 17:461-478.

00392 **ARMSTRONG, R. G.** (1974), A comparison between group therapists and members of the desired degree of self-disclosure by therapists. *Newsl. Res. Ment. Health & Behav. Sciences*, 16:20.

00393 **ARMSTRONG, R. G.** (1964), Playback technique in group psychotherapy. *Psychiat. Quart.*, 38:247-252.

00394 **ARMSTRONG, S.**, and **ROBACK, H.** (1977), An empirical test of Schutz' three–dimensional theory of group process in adolescent dyads. *Small Group Behav.*, 8:443-456.

00395 **ARMSTRONG, S. W.**, and **ROUSLIN, S.** (1963), *Group Psychotherapy in Nursing Practice*. New York: Macmillan.

00396 **ARN, I.** (1974), (Group therapy in alcoholism.) *Svenska Lakartidningen*, (Stockholm) 71:3914-3916.

00397 **ARNETOLI, C., del LUNGO, A.**, and **PONTALTI, C.** (1979), (Relational paradoxes: systemic strategies for early intervention in paranoid symptomatology.) *Arch. Psicol., Neurol. & Psychiat.*, (Milan) 40:173-190.

00398 **ARNETTE, J. L.** (1967), The effect of short term group counseling on anxiety and hostility of newly incarcerated prison inmates. *Dissert. Abstr. Internat.*, 27:3299A.

00399 **ARNHART, E. A.** (1975), Establishing group work in a psychiatric unit of a general hospital. *J. Psychiat. Nursing*, 13:5-9.

00400 **ARNOLD, L. E., TOLBERT, H. A., MOLINARI, V. J.**, and **PASS, A.** (1980), Observation room therapy for aggressive adolescence. *Amer. J. Psychiat.*, 37:130-131.

00401 **ARNOLD, O. H.**, and **SCHINDLER, R.** (1952), Bifokale gruppentherapie bei schizophren. (Bifocal group therapy with schizophrenics.) *Weiner Zeit., Nervenheilk.*, (Vienna) 5:155-174.

00402 **ARNOLD, T. J.**, and **SIMPSON, R. L.** (1975), The effects of a t group on emotionally disturbed school-age boys. *Transactional Anal. J.*, 5:238-241.

00403 **ARNOLD, W. R.**, and **STILES, B.** (1972), A summary of increasing use of group methods in correctional institutions. *Internat. J. Group Psychother.*, 22:77-92.

00404 **ARNSON, A. N.**, and **COLLINS, R.** (1970), Treating low-income patients in a neighborhood center. *Hosp. & Community Psychiat.*, 21:111-113.

00405 **ARON, W. S.**, and **DAILY, D. W.** (1976), Graduates and splitters from therapeutic drug treatment programs: a comparison. *Internat. J. Addict.*, 11:1-18.

00406 **ARONIN, E.** (1974), Activity group therapy to strengthen self-concepts. *Elem. School Guid. & Coun.*, 9:233-235.

00407 **ARONOFF, R.** (1976), Parent group or student group counseling: a question of efficiency. *Dissert. Abstr. Internat.*, 36:4249A.

00408 **ARONOWITZ, E.** (1968), Ulterior motives in games: implications for group work with children. *Soc. Work*, 13:50-55.

00409 **ARONS, B. S.** (1978), First reported dreams in psychoanalytic group psychotherapy. *Amer. J. Psychother.*, 32:544-551.

00410 **ARONS, B. S.** (1978), Review of M. Seligman's "Group-counseling and group-psychotherapy with rehabilitation clients." *Amer. J. Psychother.*, 32:619-620.

00411 **ARONSON, M. L.** (1964), Acting out in individual and group psychotherapy. *J. Hillside Hosp.*, 13:43-48.

00412 **ARONSON, M. L.** (1976), Advanced training of analytic group therapists at the Postgraduate Center for Mental Health. *Trans. Ment. Health Res. Newsl.*, 18:15-16.

00413 **ARONSON, M. L.** (1974), A group program for overcoming the fear of flying. In: *Group Therapy 1974: An Overview*, eds. L. R. Wolberg and M. L. Aronson. New York: Stratton Intercontinental Medical Books.

00414 **ARONSON, M. L.** (1972), Intensifying the group process: i. techniques to raise intensity. *Psychiat. Annals*, 2:39-51.

00415 **ARONSON, M. L.** (1967), Resistance in individual and group psychotherapy. *Amer. J. Psychother.*, 21:86-94.

00416 **ARONSON, M. L.** (1964), A symposium on combined individual and group psychotherapy: technical problems in combined therapy. *Internat. J. Group Psychother.*, 14:425-432.

00418 **ARONSON, M. L., FURST, H. B., KRASNER, J. D.**, and **LIFF, Z. A.** (1962), The impact of the death of a leader on a group process. *Amer. J. Psychother.*, 16:460-468.

00419 **ARONSON, S. R.** (1971), A comparison of cognitive vs. focused activities techniques in sensitivity group training. *Dissert. Abstr. Internat.*, 32:548B.

00420 **ARRIAGA, K., ESPINOZA, E.,** and **GUTHRIE, M. B.** (1978), Group therapy evaluation for psychiatric inpatients. *Internat. J. Group Psychother.*, 28:359-364.

00421 **ARROYAVE, F.** (1978), Review of D. J. Drum's and J. E. Knott's "Structured groups for facilitating development: acquiring life skills, resolving life themes, and making life transitions." *Brit. J. Psychiatry*, (Ashford) 133:473.

00422 **ARSENAULT, R. E.** (1979), The role and impact of the leader in group psychotherapy. *Dissert. Abstr. Internat.*, 40:4992B. (University Microfilms No. 8007703.)

00423 **ARSENAULT, R. E.** (1979), The role and impact of the leader in group psychotherapy. *Dissert. Abstr. Internat.*, 40:4992B.

00424 **ARSENIAN, J.,** and **SEMRAD, E. V.** (1951), Application of analytic observations to teaching group dynamics. *J. Psychiat. Soc. Work*, 20:150-158.

00425 **ARSENIAN, J.,** and **SEMRAD, E. V.** (1967), Individual and group manifestations. *Internat. J. Group Psychother.*, 17:82-98.

00426 **ARSENIAN, J.,** and **SEMRAD, E. V.** (1966), Schizophrenia and language: some formulations based on experience in group therapy. *Psychiat. Quart.*, 40:449-458.

00427 **ARSENIAN, J., SEMRAD, E. V.,** and **SHAPIRO, D.** (1962), An analysis of integral functions in small groups. *Internat. J. Group Psychother.*, 12:421-434.

00428 **ARTHUR, G. L., SISSON, P. J.,** and **McCLUNG, C. E.** (1980), Use of group process in teaching communication and life skills for law enforcement personnel. *J. Special. Group Work*, 5:196-204.

00429 **ARTINIAN, B. M.** (1976), Identity change in a therapeutic community. *Dissert. Abstr. Internat.*, 36:7684A.

00430 **ARTISS, K. L.** (1962), *Milieu Therapy in Schizophrenia*. New York: Grune and Stratton.

00431 **ÅS, A.** (1951), Psykodrama. (Psychodrama.) *Norsk Pedagog. Tidsskr.*, (Troundheim) 35:177-185.

00432 **ASCH, M. J.,** and **CALHOUN, S. H.** (1966), Group therapy with patients in a respiratory center. *Internat. J. Group Psychother.*, 16:372-376.

00433 **ASCH, S. E.** (1975), Opinions and social pressure. In: *Group Psychotherapy and Group Function*, 2d ed. eds. M. Rosenbaum and M. M. Berger. New York: Basic Books.

00434 **ASHBY, W. A.** (1977), Long-term maintenance: a comparative investigation of the long–term efficacy of different maintenance strategies following a group behavioral treatment for obesity. *Dissert. Abstr. Internat.*, 38:884B.

00435 **ASHKENAS, R.,** and **TANDON, R.** (1979), An eclectic approach to small group facilitation. *Small Group Behav.*, 10:224-241.

00436 **ASIMOS, C. T.,** and **ROSEN, D. H.** (1978), Group treatment of suicidal and depressed persons: indications for an open-ended group-therapy program. *Bull. Menninger Clinic*, 42:515-519.

00437 **ASKENASY, G. H.** (1974), Humor: aggression, defense, and conservatism group characteristics and differential humor appreciation. *Dissert. Abstr. Internat.*, 34:4618B.

00438 **ASKEVOLD, F.** (1960), Group psychotherapy at the Oslo Psychiatric University Clinic. *Internat. J. Group Psychother.*, 10:298-300.

00439 **ASKEVOLD, F.** (1955), Preliminary clinical experiences. *Tidsskr. Norske Laegeforen*, 75:718-720.

00440 **ASKEVOLD, F.**, and **LEHMANN, H.** (1959), Special problems connected with group psychotherapy in a psychiatric clinic. *Acta Psychiat. Scand. Suppl.*, (Copenhagen) 34:179-186.

00441 **ASNES, D. P.** (1979), Review of S. Stevry's and M. L. Blank's *Readings in Psychotherapy with Older People. J. Geriat. Psychiat.*, 12:116.

00442 **ASPEREN, G. H.** (1963), (Pedagogical aspects of group psychotherapy with delinquents.) *Nederl. Tijdschr. Geneeskunde*, 107:1291-1293.

00443 **ASTIQUETO, F. D.** (1974), Bion, Tavistok the Argentine school and psychoanalytic group psychotherapy. *Internat. Ment. Health Res. Newsl.*, 16:6.

00444 **ASTIGUETA, F. D.** (1977), The use of nicknames in delineating character patterns in group psychotherapy. In: *Group Therapy 1977: An Overview*, ed. L. R. Wolberg. New York: Stratton Intercontinental Medical Books.

00445 **ASTON, P. J.** (1971), Predicting participation length in group therapy. *Brit. J. Psychiat.*, (Ashford) 119:57-58.

00446 **ASTON, P. J.** (1970), Predicting verbal participation in group therapy. *Brit. J. Psychiat.*, (Ashford) 116:45-50.

00447 **ASTRACHAN, B. M.** (1974), Learning theory and a social systems perspective. *J. Appl. Behav. Science*, 10:175-179.

00448 **ASTRACHAN, B. M.** (1970), Systems approach to day hospitalization. *Arch. Gen. Psychiat.*, 22:550-559.

00449 **ASTRACHAN, B. M.** (1970), Towards a social systems model of therapeutic groups. *Soc. Psychiat.*, 5:110-119.

00450 **ASTRACHAN, B. M.** (1968), Post-hospital treatment of the psychotic patient. *Comprehens. Psychiat.*, 9:71-80.

00451 **ASTRACHAN, B. M., HARROW, M., BECKER, R. E., SCHWARTZ, A. H.**, and **MILLER, J. C.** (1967), The unled patient group as a therapeutic tool. *Internat. J. Group Psychother.*, 17:178-191.

00452 **ASTRACHAN, B. M.**, and **REDLICH, F. C.** (1969), Leadership ambiguity and its effects on residents' study groups. *Internat. J. Group Psychother.*, 19:259-267.

00453 **ASTRACHAN, B. M.**, and **REDLICH, F. C.** (1968), The study group. *Sandoz Psychiat. Spectator*, 5:14-16.

00454 **ASTRACHAN, B. M., SCHWARTZ, A. H., BECKER, R.**, and **HARROW, M.** (1967), The psychiatrist's effect on the behavior and interaction of therapy groups. *Amer. J. Psychiat.*, 123:1379-1387.

00455 **ASTRACHAN, U.** (1955), Group psychotherapy with mentally retarded female adolescents and adults. *Amer. J. Ment. Deficiency*, 60:152-160.

00456 **ASTRUP, C.** (1958), Group therapy in a mental hospital with special regard to schizophrenics. *Acta Psychiat. Neurol.*, 33:1-20.

00457 **ASTRUP, C.** (1961), A note on clinical and experimental observations of the application of group therapy. *Internat. J. Group Psychother.*, 11:74-77.

00458 **ASTRUP C.**, and **HARZSTEIN, N. G.** (1960), The influence of psychotherapy on the higher nervous activity of schizophrenics. *Internat. J. Group Psychother.*, 10:394-407.

00459 **ASTRUP, C., HASETH, K.**, and **UGELSTAD, E.** (1966), Psychophysiological studies of schizophrenics treated with group therapy. *Activ. Nerv. Superior*, (Prague) 8:78-80.

00460 **ASTRUP, K. H.** (1961), Kliniko-eksperimental'noe izuchenie mekhanizmov psikhoterapii. (Experimental clinical study of the mechanisms of psychotherapy.) *Zh. Vysshei Nerv. Deyatel'nosti Povlova*, (Moscow) 11:216-224.

00461 **ASUNI, T.** (1967), Nigerian experiment in group psychotherapy. *Amer. J. Psychother.*, 21:95-104.

00462 **ATEIN, A.** (1970), The nature and significance of interaction in group psychotherapy. *Internat. J. Group Psychother.*, 20:153-162.

00463 **ATEROY, E. T.** (1979), Effects of member and leader expectations on group outcome. *J. Couns. Psychol.*, 26:534.

00464 **ATKESON, P.**, and **GUTTENTAG, M.** (1975), A parent discussion group in a nursery school. *Soc. Casework*, 56:515-520.

00465 **ATKINS, C. D.** (1977), The effects of group, group-individual, and individual counseling on changes in self-perceptions of high school sophomores of low-economic background. *Dissert. Abstr. Internat.*, 38:1219A.

00466 **ATKINS, S.** (1967), A moment in forever: the personal story of a trainer. *J. Appl. Behav. Science*, 3:556-569.

00467 **ATTERBURY, G. P.** (1945), Psychodrama as an instrument for diagnostic testing. *Sociometry*, 8:79-81.

00468 **ATTNEAVE, C. L.** (1979), Therapeutic effectiveness of social network interventions compared to groups of "intimate strangers." *Group Psychother., Psychodrama, & Sociometry*, 32:173-177.

00469 **ATWOOD, N.**, and **WILLIAMS, M. E. D.** (1978), Group support for the families of the mentally ill. *Schiz. Bull.*, 4:415-425.

00470 **AUERBACH, A. B.** (1968), *Parents Learn Through Discussion: Principles and Practices of Parent Group Education.* New York: J. Wiley and Sons.

00471 **AUG, R.** (1976), Review of I. D. Yalom's *Theory and Practice of Group Psychotherapy. J. Amer. Acad. Child Psychiatry*, 15:589-591.

00472 **AUGENBRAUN, B.**, and **TASEM, M.** (1966), Differential techniques in family interviewing with both parents and preschool child. *J. Amer. Acad. Child Psychiatry*, 5:721-730.

00473 **AUIROL, B.** (1972), Group yogatherapy: instructions and prohibitions of a new psychosomatic technique. *Psychother. & Psychosomatics*, (Basel) 20:162.

00474 **AUKEN, K.**, and **ARNTZEN, B.** (1963), On group therapy of medicine and alcohol abusing women. *Acta Psychiat. Scand. Suppl.*, (Copenhagen) 39:400-401.

00475 **AULICINO, J.** (1954), Critique of Moreno's spontaneity theory. *Group Psychother., Psychodrama & Sociometry*, 7:148-158.

00476 **AULT, A. L.** (1972), The effects of interpersonal communication: training on the educable mentally retarded. *Dissert. Abstr. Internat.*, 32:3679A.

00477 **AURIOL, B.** (1972), Group yogatherapy: instructions and prohibitions of a new psychosomatic technique. *Group Psychother., Psychodrama & Sociometry*, 20:162-168.

00478 **AUSTIN, B. M.** (1970), The effects of group supervisor roles on practicum students' interview behavior. *Dissert. Abstr. Internat.*, 30:4213A.

00479 **AUSTIN, N. K., LIBERMAN, R. P., KING, L. W.**, and **DeRISI, W. J. A.** (1973), A comparative evaluation of two day hospitals; goal attainment scaling of behavior therapy vs. milieu therapy. *J. Nerv. & Ment. Disease*, 163:253-262.

00480 **AUTHIER, J.**, and **FIX, A. J.** (1977), A step-group therapy program based on levels of interpersonal communication. *Small Group Behav.*, 8:101-107.

00481 **AUTHIER, J.**, and **GUSTAFSON, K.** (1976), Group intervention techniques: a practical guide for psychiatric team members. *J. Psychiat. Nursing*, 14:19-22.

00482 **AUVENSHINE, W. B.** (1973), The parent discussion group: an additional dimension to the role of the school counselor. *Dissert. Abstr. Internat.*, 34:3859A.

00483 **AVERILL, S.** (1976), A brighter future: Kansas Boys Industrial School. *Ment. Hygiene*, 60:14-16.

00484 **AVERILL, S. C., CADMAN, W. H., CRAIG, L. P.,** and **LINDEN, R. E.** (1973), Group psychotherapy with young delinquents: report from a residential treatment center. *Bull. Menninger Clinic*, 37:1-70.

00485 **AVERY, C.** (1968), Para-analytic group therapy with adolescent multi-handicapped blind. *New Outlook for Blind*, 62:65-72.

00486 **AVERY, J. B.** (1980), Effects of the interaction of patient characteristics and therapeutic method on outcome of therapy. *Dissert. Abstr. Internat.*, 41:1489B. (University Microfilms No. 8021733.)

00487 **AVIS, W. E.** (1973), *Shared Participation*. Garden City, NY: Doubleday.

00488 **AXELROD, P. L., CAMERON, M. S.,** and **SOLOMON, J. C.** (1944), An experiment in group therapy with shy adolescent girls. *Amer. J. Orthopsychiat.*, 14:616-627.

00489 **AXELROD, P. L.** (1950), Group treatment of social anxiety in college women. *J. Psychiat. Soc. Work*, 19:107-115.

00490 **AXLINE, V.** (1955), Group therapy as a means of self discovery for parents and children. *Group Psychother., Psychodrama & Sociometry*, 8:152-160.

00491 **AXLINE, V. M.** (1947), Nondirective therapy for poor readers. *J. Couns. Psychol.*, 11:61-69.

00492 **AXLINE, V. M.** (1947), *Play Therapy*. New York: Houghton-Mifflin.

00493 **AXMAKER, L. W.** (1970), The effect of group counseling on the self-concept, on the motivation to achieve and on the proportion of dropouts among unselected community college students at Southwestern Oregon Community College. *Dissert. Abstr. Internat.*, 30:4214A.

00494 **AYD, F. J.** (1972), Neuroleptic therapy for chronic schizophrenia. *Diseases Nerv. System*, 33:35-39.

00495 **AYER, W. A.,** and **FRANKEL, A. S.** (1972), Implosive therapy: a review. *Psychother.: Theory, Res. & Pract.*, 4:242.

00496 **AYERS, G. W.** (1977), A structured group as a potentiator of treatment. *Psychiat. Forum*, 6:31-36.

00497 **AYESTARÁN ETXEBERRIA, S.** (1980), *Manual de Psicoterapia de Grupo: nueva Sinteses de Psicoánalyisis Existencial.* (*Manual of Group Psychotherapy: New Syntheses of Existential Psychoanalysis.*) Salamanca: Universidad Pontificia.

00498 **AYLESWORTH, D. R.** (1954), A group approach to problems of polio patients. *Soc. Casework*, 35:161-166.

00499 **AZIMA, F. J.** (1977), Effective communication in adolescent group psychotherapy. In: *Psychotherapy: The Promised Land?* ed. M. Dinoff. Tuscaloosa: University of Alabama Press.

00500 **AZIMA, F. J.** (1976), Group psychotherapy for latency–age children. *Can. Psychiat. Assn. J.*, (Ottawa) 21:210-211.

00501 **AZIMA, F. J.** (1969), Interaction and insight in group psychotherapy: the case for insight. *Internat. J. Group Psychother.*, 19:259-267.

00502 **AZIMA, H.,** and **AZIMA, F. J.** (1959), Projective group therapy. *Internat. J. Group Psychother.*, 9:176-183.

00503 **AZIMA, H., CRAMER-AZIMA, F.,** and **WITTKOWER, E. D.** (1957), Analytic group art therapy. *Internat. J. Group Psychother.*, 7:243-260.

00504 **AZOUBEL NETO, D.** (1957), Localizacao em psicoterapia de grupo. (Position in group psychotherapy.) *Rev. Psicolog. Normal & Pateolog.*, (São Paulo) 3:547-555.

00505 **AZOUBEL NETO, D.** (1964), (Some aspects of seating arrangement as a form of non-verbal communication in the therapeutic group.) *J. Brasil. Psiquiat.*, (Rio de Janeiro) 13:331-338.

00506 **AZRIN, N. H.** (1975), Job finding club: a group assisted program for obtaining employment. *Behav. Res. & Ther.*, 13:17-22.

00507 **AZULAY, J. D.** (1966), Estudo sobre o Papel da "ovelha negra" no grupo terapeutico. (Study on the role of the "black sheep" in the therapeutic group.) *J. Brasil. Psiquiat.*, (Rio de Janeiro) 15:15-23.

00508 **AZULAY, J. D.** (1967), (Early defenses (and anxieties) in a group.) *J. Brasil. Psiquiat.*, (Rio de Janeiro) 16:319-326.

00509 **AZULAY, J. D.** (1967), (Progress of the group as seen in a patient.) *J. Brasil. Psiquiat.*, (Rio de Janeiro) 16:339-345.

B

00510 **BAADE, L. E.** (1974), Mother study groups in behavior modification and Adlerian child rearing practices: an empirical evaluation and comparison of behavior change. *Dissert. Abstr. Internat.*, 34:4650B.

00511 **BAAK, W. W., CLOWER, C. G., KALMAN, G. J., MITTEL, N. S.,** and **STERN, S.** (1966), Therapeutic leadership in milieu treatment. *Internat. J. Group Psychother.*, 16:163-173.

00512 **BAAS, B. M.,** and **NORTON, F. M.** (1951), Group size and leaderless discussions. *J. Appl. Psychol.*, 35:397-400.

00513 **BABAD, E. Y.,** and **AMIR, L.** (1978), Trainer's liking, Bion's emotional modalities, and t-group effect. *J. Appl. Behav. Science*, 14:511-522.

00514 **BABAD, E. Y.,** and **MELNICK, J.** (1976), Effects of a t-group as a function of trainer's liking and member's participation, involvement, quantity, and quality of received feedback. *J. Appl. Behav. Science*, 12:543-562.

00515 **BABAD, E. Y., OPPENHEIMEN, B. T.,** and **SHAITIEL, A.** (1977), An all-purpose model for group work. *Human Rel.*, 30:389-401.

00516 **BABB, H. E.** (1969), The verbal behavior of schizophrenic women in four types of group situations. *Dissert. Abstr. Internat.*, 39:2430B-2431B.

00517 **BABBITTS, R. M.** (1979), Cognitive and autonomic group procedures with speech-anxious children. *Dissert. Abstr. Internat.*, 40:5789B.

00518 **BABCOCK, C. I.** (1956), A study of the interrelationships between group guidance and subject matter as reported by selected secondary schools. Unpublished doctoral dissertation, Washington State University.

00519 **BABCOCK, P., GROSS, D.,** and **GOHL, A.** (1962), Occupational therapy for disturbed adolescents. *Amer. J. Occupat. Ther.*, 16:176-181.

00520 **BABER, M.** (1968), Group work with foster care parents. *Hosp. & Community Psychiat.*, 19:277-279.

00521 **BABINEAU, R.** (1979), Review of I. H. Paul's *Form and Techniques of Psychotherapy*. *Amer. J. Psychiat.*, 136:1488.

00522 **BACAL, H. A.** (1972), Balint groups: training or treatment? *Psychiat. Med.*, 3:373-377.

00523 **BACH, G. R.** (1957), Basic concept in group psychotherapy: a field-theoretical view. *Z. Diagnost. Psychol.*, 5:161-166.

00524 **BACH, G. R.** (1956), Current trends in group psychotherapy. In: *Progress in Clinical Psychology, II*, eds. D. Brower and L. E. Abt. New York: Grune and Stratton, pp. 114-145.

00525 **BACH, G. R.** (1968), Discussion of F. H. Stoller's "Accelerated interaction." *Internat. J. Group Psychother.*, 18:244-249.

00526 **BACH, G. R.** (1950), Dramatic play therapy with adult groups. *J. Psychology*, 29:225-246.

00527 **BACH, G. R.** (1974), Fight with me in group therapy. In: *Group Therapy 1974: An Overview*, eds. L. R. Wolberg and M. L. Aronson. New York: Stratton Intercontinental Medical Books.

00528 **BACH, G. R.** (1956), Freud's time bounded group concepts. *Group Psychother., Psychodrama & Sociometry*, 9:301-304.

00529 **BACH, G. R.** (1970), From the first to the hundredth marathon: a report to Fred Stoller. *Compar. Group Studies*, 1:341-347.

00530 **BACH, G. R.** (1967), Group and leader-phobias in marathon groups. *Voices*, 3:41-46.

00531 **BACH, G. R.** (1953), (Intelligence testing as an ego-mirroring technique in group psychotherapy.) *Rev. Psychol. Appl.*, (Paris) 3:298-300.

00532 **BACH, G. R.** (1954), *Intensive Group Psychotherapy*. New York: Ronald Press.

00533 **BACH, G. R.** (1966), The marathon group: intensive practice of intimate interaction. *Psychol. Reports*, 18:995-1002.
00534 **BACH, G. R.** (1967), Marathon group dynamics: i. some functions of the professional group facilitator. *Psychol. Reports*, 20:995-999.
00535 **BACH, G. R.** (1967), Marathon group dynamics: ii. dimensions of helpfulness: therapeutic aggression. *Psychol. Reports*, 20:1147-1158.
00536 **BACH, G. R.** (1967), Marathon group dynamics: iii. disjunctive contacts. *Psychol. Reports*, 20:1163-1172.
00537 **BACH, G. R.** (1977), (Narcissism and group therapy: considerations on three failures.) *Gruppenpsychother. & Gruppendynam.*, 12:100-107.
00538 **BACH, G. R.** (1957), Observations on transference and object relations in the light of group dynamics. *Internat. J. Group Psychother.*, 7:64-76.
00539 **BACH, G. R.** (1956), Pathological aspects of therapeutic groups. *Group Psychother., Psychodrama & Sociometry*, 9:133-148.
00540 **BACH, G. R.** (1957), Specific group cultures as release mechanisms for individual behavior patterns. *Group Psychother., Psychodrama & Sociometry*, 10:277-286.
00541 **BACH, G. R.** (1950), Toward a theoretical foundation for group psychotherapy. *Amer. Psychologist*, 5:470.
00542 **BACH, G. R., ARMON, V., BARKER, G., LINDT, H., SHAPIRO, S.,** and **YOUNG, N.** (1948), Theoretical and technical explorations in group methods of psychotherapy. *Amer. Psychologist*, 3:346.
00543 **BACH, G. R.,** and **ILLING, H. A.** (1955), Eine historische perspective zur gruppentherapie. (One historical perspective on group therapy.) *Zeit. Psychosomat. Med. & Psychoanal.*, (Goettingen) 1:131-147.
00544 **BACH, O., FELDES, D., KRIEGEL, A.,** and **SMOLIVSKY, B.** (1972), (Group therapy with married couples.) *Psychiat., Neurol. & Med. Psychol.*, (Leipzig) 24:90-97.
00545 **BACK, K. W.** (1973), *Beyond Words: The Story of Sensitivity Training and the Encounter Movement.* New York: Penguin Books.
00546 **BACK, K. W.** (1972), *Beyond Words: The Story of Sensitivity Training and the Encounter Movement.* New York: Russell Sage Foundation.
00547 **BACK, K. W.** (1973), The experiential group and society. *J. Appl. Behav. Science*, 9:7-20.
00548 **BACK, K. W.** (1978), *In Search for Community: Encounter Groups and Social Change.* Boulder: Westview Press.
00549 **BACK, K. W.** (1974), Intervention techniques: small groups. In: *Annual Review of Psychology*, eds. M. R. Rosenzweig and L. W. Porter. Palo Alto: Annual Reviews.
00550 **BACK, K. W.** (1971), Sensitivity training: questions and quest. *Personnel Administration*, 34:22-26.
00551 **BACK, K. W.** (1979), Small group tightrope between sociology and personality. *J. Appl. Behav. Science*, 15:283-295.
00552 **BACKLI, H. R.** (1955), *Moreno's Sociometric und Ihre Psychohygienische Bedeutung. (Moreno's Sociometry and Its Psychohygienic Importance.)* Wenththur: Keller.
00553 **BACKNER, B. L.** (1961), "Attraction-to-group," as a function of style of leadership, follower personality, and group composition. Unpublished doctoral dissertation, University of Buffalo.
00554 **BACKUS, O. L.,** and **DUNN, H. M.** (1947), Intensive group therapy in speech rehabilitation. *J. Speech & Hearing Disorders*, 12:39-60.
00555 **BACON, C. T.** (1945), Psychodrama. *Hosp. Corps Quart.*, 18:44-46.
00556 **BACON, S.** (1971), I became a bum to understand their problems: societal sensitivity program. *Science Digest*, 69:40-47.
00557 **BADARACCO, J. G., PROVERLIO, N.,** and **CANSUARO, A.** (1972), (Treatment of psychiatric patients.) *Acta Psiquiat. Psicol. Amer. Latina*, (Buenos Aires) 18:232-243.

00558 **BADER, B. R.** (1975), The effects of a group training program and cognitive style on mother-child interactions. *Dissert. Abstr. Internat.*, 36:3496A.

00559 **BADER, E.**, and **ZEIG, J. K.** (1976), Fifty-seven discounts. *Transactional Anal. J.*, 6:133-134.

00560 **BADER, L. J.** (1976), Review of S. de Schill's *The Challenge for Group Psychotherapy: Present and Future. Internat. J. Group Psychother.*, 26:251-253.

00561 **BADLER, D. S.** (1970), Group screening of adolescents in an outpatient psychiatric clinic. *Smith Coll. Studies Soc. Work*, 41:57-58.

00562 **BADOLATO, G.**, and **DiIULLO, M. G.** (1979), *Gruppi Terapeutici e Gruppi di Formazione. (Group Therapy and Group Formations.)* Rome: Bulzoni.

00563 **BADURA, H. O.**, and **STEINMEYER, E. M.** (1978), Objektivierung des behandlungserfolges einer analytischen gruppentherapie mit dem giessen-test. (Objective evaluation of treatment results from analytic group therapy using Giessen test.) *Psychother. & Psychosomat.*, (Basel) 29:118-124.

00564 **BADURA, H. O.**, and **STEINMEYER, E. M.** (1976), Therapeutic success of an analytic group-psychotherapy demonstrated objectively by Giessen-test.) *Psychother. & Med. Psychol.*, (Stuttgart) 26:205-208.

00565 **BADURA, W.** (1971), (Group psychotherapy for convalescents.) *Psychiat. Polska*, (Warsaw) 5:295-300.

00566 **BAEHR, G. O.** (1954), The comparative effectiveness of individual psychotherapy, group psychotherapy, and a combination of these methods. *J. Couns. Psychol.*, 18:179-183.

00567 **BAFF, W. A.** (1976), The effects of group counseling in a naval correction facility. *Dissert. Abstr. Internat.*, 37:797A.

00568 **BAGADIA, V. N.** (1975), Diabetes mellitus: a psychosomatic study of 147 cases. *J. Postgrad. Med.*, 21:17-29.

00569 **BAGDASSARROFF, B. J.**, and **CHAMBERS, N. E.** (1970), An evaluation of the encounter group process through assessment of value shifts and patterns of black and white educators. *Dissert. Abstr. Internat.*, 31:3685B.

00570 **BAGGOTT, E.** (1967), Role of the hospital nurse in the wider psychiatric service. *Nursing Times*, (London) 63:993-994.

00571 **BAHART, J. B. S.** (1977), The impact of death and dying counseling groups on death anxiety for college student volunteers. *Dissert. Abstr. Internat.*, 37:4853A.

00572 **BAHIA, A. B.** (1954), Experiências psicanalticas em terapia de grupo. (Psychoanalytic techniques in group psychotherapy.) *Med. Cir. Farm., Rio*, 220: 333-349.

00573 **BAHN, J. J.** (1972), Value of the action lab in police training. *Group Psychother., Psychodrama & Sociometry*, 25:27-29.

00574 **BAIDER, L.** (1973), Group work with addicts and therapists: observations in a drug addiction clinic. *Drug Forum*, 3:91-102.

00575 **BAILEY, J. P.** (1977), Consciousness raising groups for women: implications of Pavlo Freire's theory of critical consciousness for psychotherapy and education. *Dissert. Abstr. Internat.*, 38:164A.

00576 **BAILEY, J. S.** (1974), The effects of marathon group counseling on selected self-concept factors of future teachers. *Dissert. Abstr. Internat.*, 34:5614A.

00577 **BAILEY, K. G.** (1970), Audiotape self-confrontation in group psychotherapy. *Psychol. Reports*, 27:439-444.

00578 **BAILEY, K. G.**, and **SOWDER, W. T.** (1970), Audiotape and videotape self-confrontation in psychotherapy. *Psychol. Bull.*, 74:127-137.

00579 **BAILEY, M. B.** (1965), Al-Anon family groups as an aid to wives of alcoholics. *Soc. Work*, 10:68-74.

00580 **BAILEY, W. L.** (1972), A comparison of the effects of visual-sensory-commitment-action group therapy with commitment-action group therapy only and no-treatment control group of obese university females. *Dissert. Abstr. Internat.*, 3773A.

00581 **BAILINE, S. H., KATCH, M.,** and **GOLDEN, H. K.** (1977), Mini-groups: maximizing the therapeutic milieu on an acute psychiatric unit. *Hosp. & Community Psychiat.*, 28:445-447.

00582 **BAILIS, S. S., LAMBERT, S. R.,** and **BERNSTEIN, S. B.** (1978), The legacy of the group: a study of group therapy with a transient membership. *Soc. Work & Health Care*, 3:405-418.

00583 **BAIN, R.** (1955), Johnathan and role reversal. *Group Psychother., Psychodrama & Sociometry*, 8:329-337.

00584 **BAINBRIDGE, G., DUDDINGTON, A. E., COLLINGDON, M.,** and **GARDNER, C. E.** (1953), Dance-mime: a contribution to treatment in psychiatry. *J. Ment. Science*, (London) 99:308-314.

00585 **BAISDEN, M. J.,** and **BAISDEN, J. R.** (1979), A profile of women who seek counseling for sexual dysfunction. *Amer. J. Fam. Ther.*, 7:68-76.

00586 **BAITHER, R. C.,** and **GODSEY, R.** (1979), Rational emotive education and relaxation training in large group treatment of test anxiety. *Psychol. Reports*, 45:326.

00587 **BAKER, A. A., JONES, M., MERRY, J.,** and **POMRYN, B. A.** (1953), A community method of psychotherapy. *Brit. J. Med. Psychol.*, (London) 26:222-244.

00588 **BAKER, B. S.** (1980), The presentation of self in consciousness-raising groups. *Dissert. Abstr. Internat.*, 41:2300A. (University Microfilms No. 8025903.)

00589 **BAKER, J. M.,** and **NADA, J. E.** (1966), Anger in group therapy. *J. Psychiat. Nursing*, 4:50-55, 58-63.

00590 **BAKER, J. M.,** and **NADA, J. E.** (1965), Anger in group therapy. *Amer. J. Nursing*, 65:96-100.

00591 **BAKER, R. R.** (1971), Use of patient groups in evaluation and treatment planning. *Hosp. & Community Psychiat.*, 22:37-39.

00592 **BALAZS-PIRI, T.,** and **HEGEDUS, A.** (1968), (Play acting therapy as a specific class of group therapy in the cure of alcoholics.) *Magyar Pszichol. Szemle*, (Budapest) 25:123-132.

00593 **BALCH, P.,** and **ROSS, A. W.** (1974), A behaviorally oriented didactic group treatment of obesity: an exploratory study. *J. Behav. Ther. & Exper. Psychiat.*, 5:239-243.

00594 **BALDWIN, B. A.** (1972), Change in interpersonal cognitive complexity as a function of a training group experience. *Psychol. Reports*, 30:935-940.

00595 **BALDWIN, C. A.** (1975), Using media techniques in group therapy: why, how, when and which ones? *Michigan Nurse*, 48:10-11.

00596 **BALES, R. F.** (1950), *Interaction Process Analysis: A Method for the Study of Small Groups*. Cambridge, MA: Addison Wesley Press.

00597 **BALES, R. F.** (1945), Social therapy for a social disorder: compulsive drinking. *J. Soc. Issues*, 1:14-22.

00598 **BALES, R. F.** (1944), The therapeutic role of AA as seen by a sociologist. *Quart. J. Studies Alcohol*, 5:267-278.

00599 **BALES, R. F.** (1942), Types of social structure as factors in cures for alcohol addiction. *Appl. Anthropology*, 1:1-13.

00600 **BALES, R. F.,** and **GERBRANDS, H.** (1948), The "interaction recorder": an apparatus and check list for sequential content analysis of social interaction. *Human Relat.*, 1:456-463.

00601 **BALGOOYEN, T. J.** (1974), A comparison of the effect of Synanon game verbal attack therapy and standard group therapy practice on hospitalized chronic alcoholics. *J. Community Psychol.*, 2:54-58.

00602 **BALGOPAL, P. R.** (1974), Sensitivity training: A conceptual model for social work education. *J. Educat. Soc. Work,* 10:5-11.

00603 **BALGOPAL, P. R.,** and **HULL, R. F.** (1973), Keeping secrets: group resistance for patients and therapists. *Psychother.: Theory, Res. & Pract.,* 10:334-336.

00604 **BALGOPAL, P. R.,** and **VASSIL, T. V.** (1979), The group psychotherapist: a new breed. *Perspect. Psychiat. Care,* 17:132-142.

00605 **BALINT, E.** (1972), Fair shares and mutual concern. *Internat. J. Psycho-Analysis,* (London) 53:61-65.

00606 **BALINT, E.,** and **BALINT, M.** (1955), Dynamics of training in groups for psychotherapy. *Brit. J. Med. Psychol.,* (London) 28:135-143.

00607 **BALINT, M.** (1954), Training general practitioners in psychotherapy. *Brit. Med. J.,* (London) 1:115-120.

00608 **BALL, J. D.,** and **GRIEGER, R. M.** (1978), Leader's guide to time-limited rational-emotive group psychotherapy. *Cat. Selected Docum. Psychol.,* 8:41.

00609 **BALL, J. D.,** and **MECK, D. S.** (1979), Implications of developmental theories of counseling adolescents in groups. *Adolescence,* 14:529-534.

00610 **BALL, W. R.** (1971), Physical contact as a variable in encounter group programming of counselors training. *Dissert. Abstr. Internat.,* 32:1265A.

00611 **BALLARD, J.** (1977), *Stop a Moment: A Group Leader's Handbook of Energizing Experiences.* Amherst, MA: Mandala.

00612 **BALLERING, L. R.** (1980), The effects of a structured group approach on anxiety in junior high youth: a technique for paraprofessionals. *Dissert. Abstr. Internat.,* 40:5195B. (University Microfilms No. 8005093.)

00613 **BALLINE, S. H., KATCH, M.,** and **GOLDEN, H. K.** (1977), Mini-groups: maximizing the therapeutic milieu on an acute psychiatric unit—Long Island Jewish-Hillside Medical Center. *Hosp. & Community Psychiat.,* 28:445-447.

00614 **BALLIS, S. S., LAMBERT, S. R.,** and **BERNSTEIN, S. B.** (1978), The legacy of the group: a study of group therapy with a transient membership. *Soc. Work & Health Care,* 3:405-418.

00615 **BALLOU, M., REUTER, J.,** and **DINERO, T.** (1979), An audio-taped consciousness-raising group for women: evaluation of the process dimension. *Psychol. Women Quart.,* 4:185-193.

00616 **BALOGH, P.** (1975), New ways of getting more real: or does the encounter culture herald the end of psychoanalysis. *Internat. J. Soc. Psychiat.,* (London) 21:126-129.

00617 **BALTER, L.** (1976), Psychological consultation for preschool parent groups: an educational–psychological intervention to promote mental health. *Children Today,* 5:19-22.

00618 **BAMBRICK, A. F.** (1980), Defining the terms of go between process. *Internat. J. Fam. Ther.,* 2:99-105.

00619 **BAMMEN, J.** (1971), The human relations movement in Canada. *Can. Ment. Health,* (Ottawa) 19:18-23.

00620 **BANDER, K. W., STEINKE, G. V., ALLEN, G. J.,** and **MOSHER, D. L.** (1975), Evaluation of three dating-specified treatment approaches for heterosexual dating anxiety. *J. Consult. & Clin. Psychol.,* 43:259-265.

00621 **BANDOLI, L. R.** (1977), Leaderless support groups in child protective srvices. *Soc. Work,* 22:150-151.

00622 **BANIK, S. N.,** and **MENDELSON, M. A.** (1978), Group psychotherapy with a paraplegic group, with an emphasis on specific problems of sexuality. *Internat. J. Group Psychother.,* 28:123-128.

00623 **BANTA, G. W.** (1967), A comparison of the leaderless group discussion and the individual interview techniques for the selection of student orientation assistants. *Dissert. Abstr. Internat.,* 28:937.

00624 **BARABASZ, A. F.** (1975), Classroom teachers as paraprofessional therapists in group systematic desensitization of test anxiety. *Psychiatry*, 38:388-392.

00625 **BARABASZ, A. F.** (1974), Enlarging temporal orientation: a test of alternative counseling approaches. *J. Soc. Psychol.*, 93:67-74.

00626 **BARABASZ, A. F.** (1973), Group desensitization of test anxiety in elementary school. *J. Psychology*, 83:295-301.

00627 **BARAN, F. N.** (1972), Group therapy improves mental retardates' behavior. *Hosp. & Community Psychiat. Suppl.*, No. 23.

00628 **BARATA, A. M.** (1967), A countertransferential experience of uncontrolled laughter. *J. Brasil. Psiquiat.*, (Rio de Janeiro) 16:327-338.

00629 **BARBACH, L.**, and **FLAHERTY, M.** (1980), Group treatment of situationally orgasmic women. *J. Sex & Marital Ther.*, 6:19-29.

00630 **BARBACH, L. G.** (1974), Group treatment of preorgasmic women. *J. Sex & Marital Ther.*, 1:139-145.

00631 **BARBACH, L. G.**, and **AYRES, T.** (1976), Group process for women with orgasmic difficulties. *Personnel & Guid. J.*, 54:389-391.

00632 **BARBARA, D. A., GOLDART, N.**, and **ORAM, C.** (1961), Group psychoanalysis with adult stutterers. *Amer. J. Psychoanal.*, 21:40-57.

00633 **BARBATO, L.** (1945), Drama therapy. *Sociometry*, 8:396-398.

00634 **BARBER, V.** (1939), Studies in the psychology of stuttering: xv. chorus reading as a distraction in stuttering. *J. Speech & Hearing Disorders*, 4:371-383.

00635 **BARBER, W. H.** (1961), Social interaction and severity of emotional disturbance. Unpublished doctoral dissertation, St. Louis University.

00636 **BARBOUR, A.** (1972), The self disclosure aspect of the psychodrama sharing session. *Group Psychother., Psychodrama & Sociometry*, 25:132.

00637 **BARBOUR, A.** (1977), Variations on psychodramatic sharing. *Group Psychother., Psychodrama & Sociometry*, 30:122-126.

00638 **BARCAI, A.**, and **ROBINSON, E. H.** (1969), Conventional group therapy with preadolescent children. *Internat. J. Group Psychother.*, 19:334-345.

00639 **BARCAI, A., UMBARGER, C., PIERCE, T. W.**, and **CHAMBERLAIN, P.** (1973), A comparison of three group approaches to underachieving children. *Amer. J. Orthopsychiat.*, 43:133-141.

00640 **BARCLAY, L. E.** (1969), A group approach to young unwed mothers. *Soc. Casework*, 50:379-384.

00641 **BARD, J. A.**, and **CREELMAN, M. B.** (1954), Parent education in a group therapy setting. *Internat. J. Group Psychother.*, 4:429-436.

00642 **BARDACH, J. L.** (1969), Group sessions with wives of aphasic patients. *Internat. J. Group Psychother.*, 19:361-365.

00643 **BARDILL, D. R.** (1972), Behavior contracting and group therapy with preadolescent males in a residential setting. *Internat. J. Group Psychother.*, 23:333-342.

00644 **BARDILL, D. R.** (1977), A behavior-contributing program of group treatment for early adolescents in a residential treatment setting. *Internat. J. Group Psychother.*, 27:389-400.

00645 **BARDILL, D. R.** (1966), The group process in group therapy. *Ment. Hygiene*, 50:117-123.

00646 **BARDILL, D. R.** (1973), Group therapy techniques for preadolescent boys in a residential treatment center. *Child Welfare*, 52:533-541.

00647 **BARDON, E. J.** (1966), Transference reactions to the relationship between male and female co-therapists in group psychotherapy. *J. Amer. Coll. Health Assn.*, 14:287-289.

00648 **BARE, C. E.**, and **MITCHELL, R. R.** (1972), Experimental evaluation of sensitivity training. *J. Appl. Behav. Science*, 8:263-276.

00649 **BARENDREGT, J. T.** (1957), A psychological investigation of the effect of group psychotherapy in patients with bronchial asthma. *J. Psychosomatic Res.*, 2:115-119.

00650 **BARENDREGT, J. T.** (1957), Psychologisch onderzoek van effect van groepstherapie bij asthmapatienten. (Psychological investigation of the effect of group therapy in asthma patients.) *Nederl. Tijdschr. Psychol.*, (Amsterdam) 12:57-67.

00651 **BARENTSEN, A. C.** (1952), *Bijdrage tot de Kennis der Techniek der Groepspsychotherapie voor Volwassenen: een Clinisch-Psychiatrische Studie.* Leiden: Pompe.

00652 **BARKER, B. W.**, and **WEISMAN, M. N.** (1966), Residential camping: imaginative program helps chronic mental patients. *J. Rehab.*, 32:26-27.

00653 **BARKER, P.**, and **MUIR, A. M.** (1969), The role of occupational therapy in a children's inpatient psychiatric unit. *Amer. J. Occupat. Ther.*, 23:431-436.

00654 **BARKER, R. G.** (1947), Psychodrama in teaching scientific method in the social sciences. *Sociatry*, 1:179-182.

00655 **BAR-LEVAV, R.** (1970), A method for dealing with a forbidden oedipal wish. *Internat. J. Group Psychother.*, 20:224-229.

00656 **BAR-LEVAV, R.** (1976), Review of P. de Mare's and L. C. Kreeger's *Introduction to Group Treatments in Psychiatry. Internat. J. Group Psychother.*, 26:119-120.

00657 **BAR-LEVAV, R.**, and **RENNEN, M. D.** (1977), The treatment of preverbal hunger and rage in a group. *Internat. J. Group Psychother.*, 27:457-469.

00658 **BARLOW, I. D.** (1975), The use of media in counseling male homosexual groups. *J. Sex & Marital Ther.*, 1:267-270.

00659 **BARMETTLER, D.**, and **FIELDS, G. L.** (1975-76), Using the group method to study and treat parents of asthmatic children. *Soc. Work & Health Care*, 1:167-176.

00660 **BARNARD, J. E.** (1970), Peer group instruction for primigravid adolescents. *Nursing Outlook*, 18:42-43.

00661 **BARNES, G. G.** (1975), Deprived adolescents: a use for groupwork. *Brit. J. Soc. Work*, (Birmingham) 5:149-160.

00662 **BARNES, L. W.** (1978), The effects of group counseling on the self concept and achievement of primary grade Mexican-American pupils. *Dissert. Abstr. Internat.*, 38:5920A.

00663 **BARNES, M., SCHIFF, E.**, and **ALBEE, C.** (1957), The collaboration of child psychiatry, casework and group work in dealing with the mechanism of acting out. *Amer. J. Orthopsychiat.*, 27:377-386.

00664 **BARNES, R. E.** (1977), Communication anxiety: a psychotherapeutic perspective. Annual meeting of the international communication association convention. Berlin, 1977.

00665 **BARNES, R. H., BUSSE, E. W.**, and **DINKEN, H.** (1954), The alleviation of emotional problems in multiple sclerosis by group psychotherapy. *Group Psychol.*, 6:193-201.

00666 **BARNETT, G. J.** (1959), Group psychotherapy as an adjunct to insulin subcoma treatment. *Internat. J. Group Psychother.*, 9:62-70.

00667 **BARNWELL, J. E.** (1965), Group methods in public welfare. *Internat. J. Group Psychother.*, 15:446-463.

00668 **BAROLIN, G. S.** (1970), (Experience with various methods of group psychotherapy.) *Wiener Klin. Wochenschr.*, (Vienna) 82:265-272.

00669 **BAROLIN, G. S.** (1961), (Spontaneous regression of age in the symbolic drama and its clinical significance. Results with experimental catathymic picture reactions: viii.) *Zeit. Psychother. Med. Psychol.*, (Stuttgart) 11:77-91.

00670 **BARR, J. E.** (1978), A study of relationships between premature termination in group counseling and select client variables. *Dissert. Abstr. Internat.*, 39:5319A.
00671 **BARRERA, M., Jr.** (1979), An evaluation of a brief group therapy for depression. *J. Consult. Clin. Psychol.*, 47:413-415.
00672 **BARRERA, M.** (1977), An evaluation of a brief group therapy for depression. *Dissert. Abstr. Internat.*, 38:2842B.
00673 **BARRES, P.** (1964), (Apropos of psychodrama and its applications.) *Toulouse Med.*, 65:1284.
00674 **BARRETT, B. C.** (1974), Drugs, adolescence and group therapy: behavioral change relationships with drug prevention. *Disst. Abstr. Internat.*, 35:1398B.
00675 **BARRETT, C. J.** (1975), The development and evaluation of three therapeutic group interventions for widows. *Dissert. Abstr. Internat.*, 35:3569-3570.
00676 **BARRETT, C. J.** (1978), Effectiveness of widow's groups in facilitating change. *J. Consult. & Clin. Psychol.*, 46:20-31.
00677 **BARRETT, J. E.** (1955), Summarization of group psychotherapy of parents in a child guidance clinic. *Virginia Med. Monthly*, 82:326-328.
00678 **BARRETT-LENNARD, G. T.** (1974), Experiential learning groups. *Psychother.: Theory, Res. & Pract.*, 11:71-75.
00679 **BARRETT-LENNARD, G. T.** (1973), The intensive group experience: experiential learning groups in practice—general process description and guidelines. *Can. Ment. Health*, (Ottawa) 21:3-12.
00680 **BARRETT-LENNARD, G. T.** (1973), The intensive group experience: experiential learning groups in practice: General process description and guidelines. *Can. Ment. Health Suppl.*, 73:1-12.
00681 **BARRETT-LENNARD, G. T.** (1979), New model of communicational –relational systems in intensive groups. *Human Relat.*, 32:841-850.
00682 **BARRETT-LENNARD, G. T.** (1975), Outcomes of residential encounter group workshops. Descriptive analysis of follow-up structured questionnaire data. *Interpersonal Develop.*, 5:86-93.
00683 **BARRETT-LENNARD, G. T.** (1973/1974), Some effects of participation in encounter group workshops: an analysis of written follow-up reports. *Interpersonal Develop.*, 4:35-41.
00684 **BARRILLEAUX, S. P.**, and **BAUER, R. H.** (1976), The effects of gestalt awareness training on experiencing levels. *Internat. J. Group Psychother.*, 26:431-440.
00685 **BARRIOS, B. A.**, and **SHIGETOMI, C. C.** (1979), Coping-skills training for the management of anxiety. *Behav. Ther.*, 10:491-522.
00686 **BARRON, D. B.** (1965), New horizons in schizophrenia. *Illinois Med. J.*, 128:526-528.
00687 **BARRON, J.** (1970), Beginning the therapy. *Voices*, 6:32-33.
00688 **BARRON, J.** (1970), Group psychotherapy: evolution and process. *J. Contemp. Psychother.*, 3:27-30.
00689 **BARRON, M. E.** (1947), Role practice in interview training. *Sociatry*, 1:198-208.
00690 **BARRUCAND, D.** (1969/1970), (Catharsis and psychodrama.) *Bull. de Psychol.*, (Paris) 23:736-738.
00691 **BARRUCAND, D.** (1970), *La Catharsis dans le Théâtre, la Psychoanalyse, et la Psychothérapie de Groupe.* (*The Catharsis in the Theater, Psychoanalysis, and Group Psychotherapy.*) Paris: Epi.
00692 **BARSKY, M.**, and **MOZENTER, G.** (1976), The use of creative drama in a children's group. *Internat. J. Group Psychother.*, 26:105-114.
00693 **BARTHOLOMEW, A. A.** (1964), Some medical problems encountered in the setting up and running of a psychiatric unit within a prison. *New Zeal. Med. J.*, (Dunedin) 63:219-224.

00694 **BARTLETT, C. J.** (1959), Dimensions of leadership behavior in classroom discussion groups. *J. Educat. Psychol.*, 50:280-284.

00695 **BARTLETT, R. M.** (1970), A training model for group leadership. *Soc. Worker*, (Ottawa) 38:11-15.

00696 **BARTOLETTI, M.** (1973), A community counsellor training program for both volunteers and professionals. *Ontario Psychol.*, (Toronto) 5:32-37.

00697 **BARTON, G. M.**, and **SCHWENK, T.** (1976), Group care for psychiatric patients. *Amer. Fam. Physician*, 13:79-82.

00698 **BARTON, W. B.** (1946), Convalescent reconditioning program for neuropsychiatric casualties in the U.S. army. *Res. Pub. Assess. Nerv. & Ment. Diseases*, 25:271-284.

00699 **BARTON, W. E.** (1953), Group psychotherapy of the psychoses. *Digest Neurol. & Psychiat.*, 21:148.

00700 **BARTOS, O. J.** (1967), *Simple Models of Group Behavior*. New York: Columbia University Press.

00701 **BARTSCH, K.** (1970), The effectiveness of small group vs. individualized procedures for teaching occupational information-gathering and career decision-making skills to college students. *Dissert. Abstr. Internat.*, 30:4763A.

00702 **BARTZ, W. R.** (1970), A small-group approach on state hospital wards. *Hosp. & Community Psychiat.*, 21:390-393.

00703 **BARUCH, D. W.** (1959), Adaptations from the field of group psychotherapy to educational procedures in the classroom. *Acta Psychother., Psychosomat. Orthopaedagog. Suppl.*, (Basel) 7:16-24.

00705 **BARUCH, D. W.** (1945), Description of a project in group therapy. *Psychol. Bull.*, 42:538-539.

00704 **BARUCH, D. W.** (1945), Description of a project in group therapy. *J. Couns. Psychol.*, 9:271-280.

00706 **BARUCH, D. W.**, and **MILLER, H.** (1946), Group and individual psychotherapy as an adjunct in the treatment of allergy. *Amer. Psychologist*, 1:452-453.

00707 **BARUCH, D. W.**, and **MILLER, H.** (1959), The use of spontaneous drawings in group therapy. *Amer. J. Psychother.*, 5:45-58.

00708 **BARUCH, D. W.**, and **MILLER, H.** (1950), The use of spontaneous drawing in group therapy. *Amer. Psychologist*, 5:470.

00709 **BASCUE, L. O.** (1978), Conceptual model for training group therapists. *Internat. J. Group Psychother.*, 28:445-482.

00710 **BASECQZ, G.** (1972), Curative factors in group therapy. *Feuillets Psychiat. Liège*, 5:306-316.

00711 **BASHAM, J.** (1960), An investigation of the role of the group therapist as a determiner of the verbal behavior of schizophrenic patients. *Dissert. Abstr. Internat.*, 20:3825. (University Microfilms No. 60-00630.)

00712 **BASS, B. M.** (1963), Amount of participation, coalescence, and profitability of decision-making discussions. *J. Abnorm. & Soc. Psychol.*, 67:92-94.

00713 **BASS, B. M.**, and **DUNTEMAN, G.** (1963), Behavior in groups as a function of self-interaction, and task orientation. *J. Abnorm. & Soc. Psychol.*, 66:419-428.

00714 **BASS, G.** (1975), Working with the ego's healthy parts: the analytic milieu therapy. *Dynam. Psychiat.*, (Berlin) 8:8-16.

00715 **BASS, R. D.** (1969), Group counseling in vocational adjustment. *J. Rehab.*, 30:25-28.

00716 **BASS, R. D.** (1967), Potential of group therapy in vocational rehabilitation. *J. Rehab.*, 33:26-28.

00717 **BASS, T. A.** (1970), Analysis of functional and non-functional role behaviors of culturally different children participating in a group guidance program. *Dissert. Abstr. Internat.*, 31:5115-5116A.

00718 **BASSAGE, H. E.** (1967), *A Book, a Group, and You: Some Suggestions for Leaders about Using Books in Discussion Groups.* New York: Seabury Press.

00719 **BASSETT, R. L.** (1978), Group therapy and social impact theory: an exploratory study. *Dissert. Abstr. Internat.*, 38:3951B-3952B. (University Microfilms No. 7731822.)

00720 **BASSIN, A.,** and **SMITH, A. B.** (1959), Group therapy with adult offenders on probation and parole. *Group Psychother., Psychodrama & Sociometry*, 12:52-57.

00721 **BASSIN, A.,** and **SMITH, A. B.** (1962), Verbal participation and improvement in group therapy. *Internat. J. Group Psychother.*, 12:369-373.

00722 **BASTIAANS, J.** (1958), (Psychodynamic aspects of group therapy for asthmatics.) *Nederl. Tijdschr. Geneeskunde*, (Amsterdam) 120:257-260.

00723 **BATES, E.,** and **LEYTON, H.** (1968), Therapeutic communities and admission centres: what of the future? *Med. J. Austral.*, (Glebe) 1:663-664.

00724 **BATES, J. P.** (1973), An analysis of two variables in group process training as measured by Cattell's Sixteen Personality Factors. *Dissert. Abstr. Internat.*, 33:4704A.

00725 **BATES, M.** (1968), A test of group counseling. *Personnel & Guid. J.*, 46:749-753.

00726 **BATES, M. M.,** and **JOHNSON, C. D.** (1973), *Group Leadership.* Denver: Love Publishing.

00727 **BATMAN, R. H.,** and **BINZLEY, V. A.** (1968), Group meetings with charge aides. *Nursing Outlook*, 16:38-40.

00728 **BATTEGAY, R.** (1975), Activité de groupe avec les collaborateurs d'un hospital. (Group activities with hospital workers.) In: *Therapie de Group et Milieu Social*, (*Group Therapy and Social Environment,*) eds. R. Battegay, A. Uchtenhagen, and A. Friedmann. Berne: H. Huber, pp. 820-823.

00729 **BATTEGAY, R.** (1972), Analisi dei contenuti e decondizionamento nel gruppo therapeutico. *Aggiornam. Psicother. Psicol. Clin.*, 2:35-41.

00730 **BATTEGAY, R.** (1968), Analysieren von inhalten und dekonditionieren von haltungen in der therapeutischen gruppe: erfahrungen mit analyt. aerztegruppen. *Gruppenpsychother. & Gruppendynam.*, (Goettingen) 2:104.

00731 **BATTEGAY, R.** (1969), Anpassung und widerstand in her gruppe. *Basler Nationalzeitung No. 214*, (May 13).

00732 **BATTEGAY, R.** (1975), (Basic principles for the training of group psychotherapists.) In: *Therapie de Group et Milieu Social*, (*Group Therapy and Social Environment,*) eds. R. Battegay, A. Uchtenhagen, and A. Friedmann. Berne: H. Huber.

00733 **BATTEGAY, R.** (1969), Bericht ueber die gruppen-psychotherapie in der Schweiz. *Gruppenpsychother. & Gruppendynam.*, (Goettingen) 3:129-154.

00734 **BATTEGAY, R.** (1977), Characteristics and new trends in group psychotherapy. *Acta Psychiat. Scand.*, (Copenhagen) 56:21-31.

00735 **BATTEGAY, R.** (1967), Das therapeutische gruppengesprach. (Therapeutic groupwork.) *Praxis der Psychother.*, 12:32-41.

00736 **BATTEGAY, R.** (1976), The concept of narcissistic group-self. *Group Analysis*, (London) 9:217-220.

00737 **BATTEGAY, R.** (1975), (Defective developments of therapeutic groups.) In: *Therapie de Group et Milieu Social*, (*Group Therapy and Social Environment,*) eds. R. Battegay, A. Uchtenhagen, and A. Friedmann. Berne: H. Huber.

00738 **BATTEGAY, R.** (1971), Der beitrag der gruppenpsychotherapie zu einem umfassenden verstaendnis des psychiatrischen patienten. *Gruppenpsychother. & Gruppendynam.*, (Goettingen) 5:62-66.

00739 **BATTEGAY, R.** (1974), *Der Mensch in der Gruppe.* (*Man in the Group.*) Berne: H. Huber.

00740 **BATTEGAY, R.** (1976), *Der Mensch in der Gruppe.* (*Man in the Group, Vol.* 1,) 5th ed. Berne: H. Huber.

00741 **BATTEGAY, R.** (1973), *Der Mensch in der Gruppe,Vol. 1*, (*Man in the Group, Vol. 1,*) 4th ed. Berne: H. Huber.

00742 **BATTEGAY, R.** (1970), *Der Mensch in der Gruppe, Vol. 1*, (*Man in the Group, Vol. 1,*) 3rd ed. Berne: H. Huber.

00743 **BATTEGAY, R.** (1968), *Der Mensch in der Gruppe, Vol. 1.* (*Man in the Group, Vol. 1,*) 2d ed. Berne: H. Huber.

00744 **BATTEGAY, R.** (1967), *Der Mensch in der Gruppe, Vol. 1: Sozialpsychol. und Dynamische Aspekte*, (*Man in the Group, Vol. 1: Social Psychology and Dynamic Aspects,*) Berne: H. Huber.

00745 **BATTEGAY, R.** (1973), *Der Mensch in der Gruppe, Vol. 2*, (*Man in the Group, Vol. 2*) 4th ed. Berne: H. Huber.

00746 **BATTEGAY, R.** (1971), *Der Mensch in der Gruppe, Vol. 2, (Man in the Group, Vol. 2,*) 3d ed. Berne: H. Huber.

00747 **BATTEGAY, R.** (1969), *Der Mensch in der Gruppe, Vol. 2*, (*Man in the Group, Vol. 2,*) 2d ed. Berne: H. Huber.

00748 **BATTEGAY, R.** (1967), *Der Mensch in der Gruppe, Vol. 2: Allegeine und Spezielle Gruppenpsychotherapeutische Aspekte.* (*Man in the Group, Vol. 2: General and Special Aspects of Group Psychotherapy.*) Berne: H. Huber.

00749 **BATTEGAY, R.** (1979), *Der Mensch in der Gruppe, Vol. 3*, (*Man in the Group, Vol. 3,*) 3d ed. Berne: H. Huber.

00750 **BATTEGAY, R.** (1972), *Der Mensch in der Gruppe, Vol. 3*, (*Man in the Group, Vol. 3,*) 2d ed. Berne: H. Huber.

00751 **BATTEGAY, R.** (1970), *Der Mensch in der Gruppe, Vol. 3*, (*Man in the Group, Vol. 3,*) Berne: H. Huber.

00752 **BATTEGAY, R.** (1969), *Der Mensch in der Gruppe, Vol. 3: Gruppendynamik und Gruppenpsychotherapie.* (*Man in the Group, Vol. 3: Group Dynamics and Group Psychotherapy.*) Berne: H. Huber.

00753 **BATTEGAY, R.** (1976), Die bedeutung des traumes in der gruppenpsychotherapie. (The significance of trauma in group psychotherapy.) In: *Der Traum.* (*Trauma.*) eds. R. Battegay and A. Trenkel. Berne: H. Huber.

00754 **BATTEGAY, R.** (1971), Die gruppe als konfliktaustragungsmilieu. (The group as conflict resolving setting.) *Wirklichkeit & Weischeit*, (Dusseldorf) 4:235.

00755 **BATTEGAY, R.** (1971), Die gruppe als konfliktaustragungsort. (The group in conflict resolution.) *Reformatio*, (Berne) 9:533-539.

00756 **BATTEGAY, R.** (1970), Die gruppe als medium der sozialen psychiatrie. (The group as a method of social psychiatry.) *Schweiz. Arch. Neurol., Neurochir. & Psychiat.*, (Zurich) 106:359-365.

00757 **BATTEGAY, R.** (1966), Die gruppe als medium zur behandlung suechtiger. In: *Analyt. Gruppenpsychotherapie*, ed. G. Preuss. Berlin: Schwarzenberg Munchin.

00758 **BATTEGAY, R.** (1972), Die gruppe als mittel zur psychiatrischen rehabilitation. (The group as a means of psychiatric rehabilitation.) *Praxis*, (Berne) 61:971-978.

00759 **BATTEGAY, R.** (1978), Die gruppe als ort des haltes in der behandlung suechtiger: drogenabhangigkeit, wissenschaftl. *Praxis der Psychother.*, 11:31-190.

00760 **BATTEGAY, R.** (1966), Die gruppe als therapeutisches milieu. (The group in the therapeutic environment.) In: *International Handbook of Group Psychotherapy*, eds. R. Battegay, J. L. Moreno, and A. Friedmann. New York: Philosophical Library.

00761 **BATTEGAY, R.** (1971), Die psychosomatische krankheit als phaenomen der gruppe. (Psychosomatic illness in group phenomena.) *Therapeut. Umschau*, (Berne) 28:359-363.
00762 **BATTEGAY, R.** (1977), Die psychotherapeutische gruppe als mittlerin zwischen individuum. (The psychotherapeutic group as a means to individual change.) *Psychosomat. Med.*, 7:142-151.
00763 **BATTEGAY, R.** (1967), Die psychotherapeutische gruppe als ort der begegnung. In: *Die Begegnung mit dem Kranken Menschen*, ed. A. Friedman. Berne: H. Huber.
00764 **BATTEGAY, R.** (1978), Die therapeutische beziehung in der gruppenpsychotherapie. In: *Die Therapeut. Beziehung unter dem Aspekt Versch. Psychotherap. Schulen*, eds. R. Battegay and A. Trenkel. Berne: H. Huber.
00765 **BATTEGAY, R.** (1961), Die verstarkerwirkung der therapeutischen gruppe. (Strengthening the therapeutic group.) *Praxis der Psychother.*, 6:9-13.
00766 **BATTEGAY, R.** (1974), Die zukunft der gruppenpsychotherapie. (The future of group psychotherapy.) *Arch. Neurol., Neurochir. & Psychiat.*, (Zurich) 115:67.
00767 **BATTEGAY, R.** (1977), Different kinds of group psychotherapy with patients with different diagnoses. *Acta Psychiat. Scand.*, (Copenhagen) 55:345-354.
00768 **BATTEGAY, R.** (1972), Dorrinos grupne terapije cjelovitom razumijevanju psihijatrijskog bolesnika. *Psihoter. Zagreb*, 2:3.
00769 **BATTEGAY, R.** (1978), *El Hombre en el Grupo: Biblioteca de Psicologia.* (*Man and the Group: Readings in Psychology.*) Barcelona: Herder.
00770 **BATTEGAY, R.** (1977), Erinnern, einsicht, soziales lernen in der therapeutischen gruppen: vom umang mit den informationen in der gruppe. (Memory, insight, and social learning in the therapeutic group: the sharing of information in the group.) *Praxis der Psychother.*, 22:165-178.
00771 **BATTEGAY, R.** (1968), Gegenseitiger einfluss von psychopharmaka und gruppenpsychotherapie in der klinischen und ambulanten behandlung. (The influence of countertransference on psychopharmacy and group psychotherapy in the clinic and an outpatient unit.) *4th Internat. Congress on Group Psychotherapy*. Vienna.
00772 **BATTEGAY, R.** (1966), Geschwisterrelationen als funktionsmuster der therapeutischen gruppen. (Good relations in running the therapeutic group.) *Psychother. & Psychosomat.*, (Basel) 14:251-263.
00773 **BATTEGAY, R.** (1971), The group as link between sick and healthy community. *Internat. J. Group Psychother.*, 21:3-10.
00774 **BATTEGAY, R.** (1964), (The group as a therapeutic environment.) *Zeit. Psychother. Med. Psychol.*, (Stuttgart) 14:29-35.
00775 **BATTEGAY, R.** (1977), The group dream. In: *Group Therapy 1977: An Overview*, ed. L. R. Wolberg. New York: Stratton Intercontinental Medical Books.
00776 **BATTEGAY, R.** (1971), Group dynamics. *Acta Psychiat. Scand. Suppl.* (Copenhagen) 224:21-30.
00777 **BATTEGAY, R.** (1977), Group models, group dynamics, sociological and psychological aspects of group formation and evaluation. *Acta Psychiat. Scand.*, (Copenhagen) 55:330-344.
00778 **BATTEGAY, R.** (1976), Group psychology and group dynamics. In: *Encyclopedic Handbook of Medical Psychology*, ed. Krauss St. London: Butterworths.
00779 **BATTEGAY, R.** (1978), Group psychotherapy according to S. R. Slavson. *Group Anal.*, (London) 11:29-33.
00780 **BATTEGAY, R.** (1965), (Group psychotherapy and a modern psychiatric hospital.) *Nervenarzt*, 36:250-253.

00781 **BATTEGAY, R.** (1963), (Group psychotherapy and clinical psychiatry.) *Bibl. Psychiat. & Neurol.*, (Basel) 119:1-116.

00782 **BATTEGAY, R.** (1966), Group psychotherapy and the modern psychiatric hospital. *Internat. J. Group Psychother.*, 16:270-278.

00783 **BATTEGAY, R.** (1974), Group psychotherapy as a method of treatment in a psychiatric hospital. In: *The Challenge for Group Psychotherapy: Present and Future*, ed. S. de Shill. New York: International Universities Press.

00784 **BATTEGAY, R.** (1959), Group psychotherapy as a treatment method for hospitalized patients. *Acta Psychother., Psychosomat. Orthopaedagog. Suppl.*, (Basel) 7:24-30.

00785 **BATTEGAY, R.** (1976), (Group psychotherapy in psychiatry.) *Schweiz. Med. Wochenschr.*, (Basel) 106:1877-1882.

00786 **BATTEGAY, R.** (1972), Group psychotherapy: its characteristics in comparison with individual treatment. *Schweiz. Arch. Neurol., Neurochir., & Psychiat.*, (Zurich) 108:113-124.

00787 **BATTEGAY, R.** (1958), Group therapy with alcoholics and analgesic addicts. *Internat. J. Group Psychother.*, 8:428-434.

00788 **BATTEGAY, R.** (1963), Group psychotherapy with neglected children. *Schweiz. Arch. Neurol., Neurochir. & Psichiat.*, (Zurich) 92:528-532.

00789 **BATTEGAY, R.** (1967), Gruppenaspekte der angst. (The apathetic group.) In: *Angst, Psych. und Som. Aspekte*, ed. P. Kielholz. Berne: H. Huber.

00790 **BATTEGAY, R.** (1975), Gruppendynamik und lernprozess. (Group dynamics and the learning process.) *Schweiz. Aerztezeit.*, (Berne) 51:1862-1865.

00791 **BATTEGAY, R.** (1966), Gruppendynamische prozesse, ii: katharsis-einsicht-wandlung. In: *Analyt. Gruppenpsychotherapie Urban u.*, ed. G. Preuss. Berlin: Schwarzenberg Munich.

00792 **BATTEGAY, R.** (1964), Gruppengespraeche und gruppentherapie mit dem pflegepersonal. (Group work and group therapy with nurses.) *Prakt. Psychiat. Nr.*, 2:3.

00793 **BATTEGAY, R.** (1971), Gruppenpsychotherapie als behandlungsmethode im psychiatrischen spital. In: *Psychoanalytische Therapie in Gruppen, (Psychoanalytic Therapy in Groups.)* ed. S. de Schill. Stuttgart: E. Klett, pp. 200-258.

00794 **BATTEGAY, R.** (1971), Gruppenpsychotherapie, ihre charakteristika, im vergleich zur individuellen behandlung. *Schweiz. Arch. Neurol., Neurochir., & Psychiat.*, (Zurich) 108:113-124.

00795 **BATTEGAY, R.** (1970), Gruppenpsychotherapie im klinischen rahmen. (Group psychotherapy in the clinical setting.) In: *Klinische Psychologie*, ed. W. J. Schraml. Berne: H. Huber.

00796 **BATTEGAY, R.** (1973), Gruppenpsychotherapie: indikationen und verwirklichung in klinik und praxis. *Tägl. Praxis*, (Munich) 14:315-319.

00797 **BATTEGAY, R.** (1972), Gruppenpsychotherapie: indikationen und verwirklichung in klinik und praxis. *Internist. Praxis*, (Munich) 12:641-645.

00798 **BATTEGAY, R.** (1968), Gruppenpsychotherapie mit depressiven. (Group psychotherapy with the depressed.) In: *Labhard F. Fortbildungskurse Schweiz: Ges. Psych.* Basel: S. Karger, 1:66-76.

00799 **BATTEGAY, R.** (1971), Gruppenpsychotherapie mit schizophrenen als defktprophylaxe. (Group psychotherapy in the treatment of schizophrenics.) In: *Schizophrenie und Umwelt, 6*, (Schizophrenia and Environment, 6,) Bad Kreuznacher Symposium, 1970, eds. H. Kranz and K. Heinrich. Stuttgart: H. Huber, pp. 142-148.

00800 **BATTEGAY, R.** (1975), Gruppenpsychotherapie: moeglichkeiten und formen zur einsicht in unbewusste motivationen und zur einleitung von sozialen lernprozessen. *Informat. Gruppendynam. & Gruppenpadagog.*, (Zurich) 4:41-56.

00801 **BATTEGAY, R.** (1971), Gruppenpsychotherapie und aerztliche praxis. *Therapiewoche*, (Karlsruhe) 26:1-5.

00802 **BATTEGAY, R.** (1975), Gruppenpsychotherapie und gruppenarbeit. (Group psychotherapy and group work.) In: *Psychiatrie der Gegenwart: Fortschung und Praxis, 2d ed.*, (*Current Psychiatry: Theory and Practice, 2d ed.*,) eds. K. P. Kisker, J. E. Meyer, C. Müller, and E. Strömgren. Berlin: Springer Verlag, pp. 620-668.

00803 **BATTEGAY, R.** (1973), Gruppenpsychotherapie und gruppendynamik: therapeutisches konzept. (Group psychotherapy and group dynamics: therapeutic concepts.) *Gruppenpsychother. & Gruppendynam.*, (Goettingen) 7:1-4.

00804 **BATTEGAY, R.** (1963), *Gruppenpsychotherapie und Klinische Psychiatrie.* (*Group Psychotherapy and Clinical Psychiatry.*) Basel: S. Karger.

00805 **BATTEGAY, R.** (1970), Gruppenpsychotherapie versus individuelle psychotherapy. (Group psychotherapy as opposed to individual psychotherapy.) *Nervenarzt*, 41:429-433.

00806 **BATTEGAY, R.** (1972), Gruppenpsychotherapie von drogenabhaengigen. (Group psychotherapy with the drug dependent.) In: *Fortbildungskurse Schweiz. Ges. Psych.*, ed. F. Labhard. Basel: S. Karger, 5:58-61.

00807 **BATTEGAY, R.** (1973), Gruppentherapie in der hand des arztes fuer allgemeinmedizin. *Praxis*, 62:935-939.

00808 **BATTEGAY, R.** (1972), Individual psychotherapy and group psychotherapy as single treatment methods and in combination. *Acta Psychiat. Scand.*, (Copenhagen) 48:43-48.

00809 **BATTEGAY, R.** (1971), Individuen brachen ein gruppenfuegl. *G.D.I. Topics*, (Zurich) 8:11-15.

00810 **BATTEGAY, R.** (1971), Individuum und gruppe. (Individual and group.) *Basler Nationalzeitung No. 222*, (May 18).

00811 **BATTEGAY, R.** (1971), Individuum und gruppe, quellen und auswirkungen der aggression. *Schweiz. Spital. Veska*, (Aarau) 4:187-189.

00812 **BATTEGAY, R.** (1978), The influence of group dynamic approaches in psychotherapy. *Group Anal.*, (London) 11:259-264.

00813 **BATTEGAY, R.** (1969), Klinische gruppenpsychotherapie in ihrer analytische und verhaltenstherapeutischen potenz. *Psychother. & Psychosomatics*, (Basel) 17:281-294.

00814 **BATTEGAY, R.** (1968), Konfliktinhalte und haltung in der therapeutischen gruppe unter dem aspekte analytischer selbsterfahrungsgruppen mit arzten. *Praxis der Psychother.*, 13:58-66.

00815 **BATTEGAY, R.** (1973), La formation des psychotherapeutes de groupe. (The formation of psychotherapeutic groups.) *Med. Hygiene*, (Paris) 31:1238.

00816 **BATTEGAY, R.** (1973), La position de l'individu dans le groupe therapeutique. (The position of the individual in group therapy.) *Schweiz. Arch. Neurol., Neurochir., & Psychiat.*, (Zurich) 113:394-398.

00817 **BATTEGAY, R.** (1965), La psychotherapie de groupe en clinique psychiatrique. (Group psychotherapy in clinical psychiatry.) In: *Practique de la Psychotherapie de Groupe*, (*The Practice of Group Psychotherapy*,) ed. P. B. Schneider. Paris: Presses Universités de France, pp. 121-132.

00818 **BATTEGAY, R.** (1975), The leader and group structure. In: *The Leader in the Group*, ed. Z. A. Liff. New York: Jason Aronson.

00819 **BATTEGAY, R.** (1974), L'influence a l'hopital de la relation médecimalade par le group Balint. *Rev. de Med. Psychosomat.*, (Toulouse) 16:431-435.

00820 **BATTEGAY, R.** (1973), Moeglichkeiten, grenzen und gefahren der gruppenpsychotherapie. *Gruppenpsychother. & Gruppendynam.*, (Goettingen) 7:115-131.

00821 **BATTEGAY, R.** (1976), Oedipuskomplex, rivalitaetsokonflikt, narzistisches gruppenselbst: drei kernprobleme. *Dynam. Psychiatry*, (Berlin) 9:300-313.

00822 **BATTEGAY, R.** (1964), Zur ausbilung von gruppenpsychotherapeuten. (On training of group psychotherapists: work with groups practicing psychoanalytic self-experience.) *Schweiz. Arch. Neurol., Neurochir., & Psichiat.*, (Zurich) 93:346-361.

00823 **BATTEGAY, R.** (1977), Perspectives in the development of group psychotherapy in Switzerland with special consideration of the years 1966-1976. *Group Anal.*, (London) 10:273-276.

00824 **BATTEGAY, R.** (1959), Pharmacotherapy, individual and group psychotherapy in one psychiatric clinic. *Schweiz. Arch. Neurol., Neurochir., & Psichiat.*, (Zurich) 84:337-340.

00825 **BATTEGAY, R.** (1977), Possibilities and risks of group psychotherapy. *Zeit. Klin. Psychol. & Psychother.*, (Freiburg) 25:52-63.

00826 **BATTEGAY, R.** (1971), Psychoactive drugs and the group. *Triangle*, (Basel) 10:105-108.

00827 **BATTEGAY, R.** (1960), (Psychodynamic relations in group psychotherapy.) *Psychiat. Neurol. Neurochir.*, (Amsterdam) 63:333-342.

00828 **BATTEGAY, R.** (1977), The psychotherapeutic group as mediator between individual family and society. In: *New Dimensions in Psychiatry: A World View*, eds. S. Arieti and G. Chrzanowski. New York: J. Wiley and Sons.

00829 **BATTEGAY, R.** (1977), Psychotherapie in der aerztlichen praxis. *Schweiz. Med. Wochenschr.*, (Basel) 107:1-3.

00830 **BATTEGAY, R.** (1965), Psychotherapy of schizophrenics in small groups. *Internat. J. Group Psychother.*, 15:316-320.

00831 **BATTEGAY, R.** (1978), Therapeutische gruppenarbeit in der stationaeren behandlung drogen-und alkoholabhaengiger. *Gruppenpsychother. & Gruppendynam.*, (Goettingen) 4:162-171.

00832 **BATTEGAY, R.** (1976), Three central factors of group psychotherapy: oedipal complex, rivalry conflict, narcissistic group-self. In: *Group Therapy*, ed. R. Wolberg and M. L. Aronson. New York: Stratton Intercontinental Medical Books Corp.

00833 **BATTEGAY, R.** (1972), Training in group psychotherapy. *Psychother. & Psychosomatics*, (Basel) 20:82-91.

00834 **BATTEGAY, R.** (1957), Unsere methoden und erfahrungen mit gruppenpsychotherapie. (Our technique and method of group psychotherapy.) *Schweiz. Arch. Neurol., Neurochir. & Psychiat.*, (Zurich) 80:1-3.

00835 **BATTEGAY, R.** (1966), The verbal exchange in the therapeutic group. *Group Psychother., Psychodrama & Sociometry*, 19:166-175.

00836 **BATTEGAY, R.** (1971), Vergleich des einflusses der Balint-gruppe und der analytischen gruppen auf den allgemeinpraktiker. *Gruppenpsychother. & Gruppendynam.*, (Goettingen) 4:296-299.

00837 **BATTEGAY, R.** (1977), Was will und kann die gruppenpsychotherapie? *Uni Nova*, (Basel) (Dec. 77).

00838 **BATTEGAY, R.** (1969), Wesen und ziele der gruppenpsychotherapie. In: *Sandorama II*, (Basel) pp. 22-23.

00839 **BATTEGAY, R.** (1975), What takes place during group psychotherapy? *Hexagon Roche*, (Basel) 3:18-24.

00840 **BATTEGAY, R.** (1964), Zur ausbilung von gruppenpsychotherapeuten. *Schweiz. Arch. Neurol., Neurochir., & Psichiat.*, (Zurich) 93:346-361.

00841 **BATTEGAY, R., ABT, K., BOGDAN-PATAKI, N., BURGER, H.**, and **SPIEGEL, R.** (1974), Vergleichende untersuchungen der verbalen interaktionen in einer gruppe von gesunden probanden unter der wirkung von psychopharmaka. *Schweiz. Arch. Neurol., Neurochir., & Psychiat.*, (Zurich) 114:339-350.

00842 **BATTEGAY, R.**, and **BENEDETTI, G.** (1971), Clinical group psychotherapy. *Acta Psychiat. Scand.*, (Copenhagen) 224:31-40.

00843 **BATTEGAY, R.**, and **BENEDETTI, G.** (1971), *Psychodynamic Approach to Group Therapy and to Psychotherapy of Psychotics. Acta Psychiat. Scand. Suppl.*, (Copenhagen) pp. 9-30.

00844 **BATTEGAY, R.** (1975), (Group psychotherapy as contribution to rehabilitation of prisoners.) *Gruppenpsychother. & Gruppendynam.*, (Goettingen) 9:106-117.

00845 **BATTEGAY, R., CAHN, T. H., LUTZ, K. S.**, and **OSPELT, M.** (1976), Gruppenpsychotherapie mit alterspatienten, gruppendynamische gesichtspunkte. *Akt. Gerontol.*, (Stuttgart) 6:507-517.

00846 **BATTEGAY, R.**, and **HOLE, G.** (1966), (Group therapy experiences with drug addicts.) *Schweiz. Arch. Neurol., Neurochir., & Psichiat.*, (Zurich) 97:318-328.

00847 **BATTEGAY, R.**, and **LADEWIG, D.** (1970), Gruppentherapie und gruppenarbeit mit suchtigen frauen. (Group psychotherapy and group work with affected wives.) In: *Alkoholismus mit Frauen, (The Wives of Alcoholics,) Schrift. Reihe zur Problem Suchtgefahren, 15.* Hamburg: Hoeneck-Verlag; and *Brit. J. Addict.*, (Edinburgh) 65:89-98.

00848 **BATTEGAY, R.**, and **LADEWIG, D.** (1970), Therapeutische gruppenarbeit in der stationaeren behandlung drogen-und alkoholabhaengiger. *Gruppenpsychother. & Gruppendynam.*, (Goettingen) 4:162-171.

00849 **BATTEGAY, R., RAUCHFLEISCH, U.**, and **BRUNNER, M.** (1973), Gruppendynamik im social club. (Group dynamics in a social club.) *Gruppenpsychother. & Gruppendynam.*, (Goettingen) 6:308-320.

00850 **BATTEGAY, R.**, and **ROHRBACH, P.** (1966), Gruppenpsychotherapie mit schizophrenen und deren angehorigen. (Group psychotherapy with schizophrenics and their relatives.) *Zeit. Psychother. Med. & Psychoanal.*, (Goettingen) 16:134-146.

00851 **BATTEGAY, R., UCHTENHAGEN, A.**, and **FRIEDMANN, A.** (1975), *Gruppentherapie und Soziale Umwelt. (Group Psychotherapy and Social Environment.)* Berne: H. Huber.

00852 **BATTEGAY, R.**, and **von MARSCHALL, R.** (1978), Dynamics and effects of long-term group psychotherapy with schizophrenics. In: *Group Therapy: 1978*, ed. L. R. Wolberg and M. L. Aronson. New York: Stratton Intercontinental Medical Books.

00853 **BATTEGAY, R.**, and **von MARSCHALL, R.** (1978), Results of long-term group psychotherapy with schizophrenics. *Compar. Psychiat.*, 19:349-353.

00854 **BATTENBERG, F.** (1978), Das Körper-Ich und seine nacholende entwicklung im rahmen der milieutherapie. (Working with the body-ego and the significance of psychosomatic illness in milieu therapy.) *Dynam. Psychiat.*, (Berlin) 52/53:510-527.

00855 **BATTLE, E.**, and **ZWIER, M.** (1973), Efficacy of small group process with intractable neuropsychiatric patients. *Newsl. Res. Ment. Health & Behav. Sciences*, 15:15-17.

00856 **BAUER, I.**, and **GUREVITZ, S.** (1952), Group therapy with parents of schizophrenic children. *Internat. J. Group Psychother.*, 2:344-357.

00857 **BAUER, J.**, and **FRIEDMAN, R.** (1969), Structured group psychoeducational therapy. *Amer. J. Orthopsychiat.*, 39:294-295.

00858 **BAUER, R. E.** (1970), The effects of cognitive structuring on the outcomes of group counseling. *Dissert. Abstr. Internat.*, 30:5227A.

00859 **BAUER, R. E.** (1972), Verbal and motor components of leader behavior in a leaderless group discussion. *Dissert. Abstr. Internat.*, 33:1835B.

00860 **BAUM, C.** (1974), Brief group therapy for single mothers: some observations by a paraprofessional. *Amer. J. Orthopsychiat.*, 44:214-215.

00861 **BAUM, R. E.** (1972), Self-disclosure in small groups as a function of groups composition. *Dissert. Abstr. Internat.*, 32:4200-4201B.

00862 **BAUMAN, M. K.**, and **WIEGLE, H. H.** (1951), Amateur theatre as a technique in adjustment training. *New Outlook for Blind*, 45:275-277.

00863 **BAUMAN, W. F.** (1972), The effect of time variations in videotape feedback on the verbal behavior of members in group counseling. *Dissert. Abstr. Internat.*, 32:7300-7301B.

00864 **BAUMAN, W. F.** (1972), Games counselor trainees play: dealing with trainee resistance. *Couns. Educat. & Supervision*, 11:251-256.

00865 **BAUMEL, L. N.** (1973), Psychiatrist as music therapist. *J. Music Ther.*, 10:83-85.

00866 **BAUMLER, F.** (1957), (Multidimensional treatment of stuttering of children and adolescents in speech therapy groups.) *Zeit. Psychother. Med. Psychol.*, (Stuttgart) 7:99-104.

00867 **BAUTE, P. B.** (1975), Termination and the autonomy chair: a new ritual for group intimacy. *Transactional Anal. J.*, 5:180-182.

00868 **BAVELAS, A.** (1973), The five-squares problem: an instructional aid in group cooperation. *Studies Personnel Psychol.*, (Ottawa) 5:29-38.

00869 **BAVELAS, A.** (1947), Role playing and management training. *Sociatry*, 1:183-191.

00870 **BAVER, H.** (1971), To diagnose or not to diagnose: a naive inquiry. *Internat. J. Group Psychother.*, 21:470-475.

00871 **BAXT, R.**, and **CHINLUND, S. J.** (1975), Some examples of the helpfulness of group sessions for individual probations. *Correct. & Soc. Psychiat.*, 21:11-16.

00872 **BAXTER, W. M.** (1960), Fragments of a psychodramatic experience within a religious setting. *Group Psychother., Psychodrama & Sociometry*, 13:40-46.

00873 **BAY, A. V.** (1971), Group procedures in counseling: influences affecting its credibility. *Psychother.: Theory, Res. & Pract.*, 8:333.

00874 **BAYNE, R.** (1972), Psychology and encounter groups. *Brit. Psychol. Soc. Bull.*, (London) 25:285-289.

00875 **BAYNE, R. D.** (1972), A process analysis of negative affect in a laboratory training group. *Dissert. Abstr. Internat.*, 32:6179A.

00876 **BAYRAKAL, S.** (1975), A group experience with chronically disabled adolescents. *Amer. J. Psychiat.*, 132:1291-1294.

00877 **BEACH, L.** (1976), A note on self-reported long-term effects of encounter groups. *Interpersonal Develop.*, 6:65-68.

00878 **BEACHER, A. I.** (1962), Psychoanalytic treatment of a sociopath in a group situation. *Amer. J. Psychiat.*, 16:278-288.

00879 **BEAHRS, J. O.**, and **HILL, M. M.** (1971), Treatment of alcoholism by group-interaction psychotherapy under hypnosis. *Amer. J. Clin. Hypnosis*, 14:60-62.

00880 **BEAL, D., DUCKRO, P., ELIAS, J.**, and **HECHT, E.** (1977), Graded group procedures for long-term regressed schizophrenics. *J. Nerv. & Ment. Diseases*, 164:102-106.

00881 **BEAL, D., DUCKRO, P., ELIAS, J.**, and **HECHT, E.** (1977), Increased verbal interaction via group techniques with regressed schizophrenics. *Psychol. Reports*, 40:319-325.

00882 **BEALE, A. V.** (1974), Working with parents: a guidance drama. *Elem. School Guid. & Couns.*, 8:182-188.

00883 **BEALL, L.** (1972), The corrupt contract: problems in conjoint therapy with parents and children. *Amer. J. Orthopsychiat.*, 42:77-81.

00884 **BEAN, H. B.** (1972), The effects of a role-model and instructions on group interpersonal openness and cohesiveness. *Dissert. Abstr. Internat.*, 4201B.

00885 **BEAN, S. L.** (1971), The parents' center project: a multiservice approach to the prevention of child abuse. *Child Welfare*, 50:277-282.

00886 **BEARD, J. H., GOERTZEL, V.,** and **PEARCE, A. J.** (1958), The effectiveness of activity group therapy with chronically regressed adult schizophrenics. *Internat. J. Group Psychother.*, 8:123-136.

00887 **BEARD, M. T.** (1976), (The efficacy of group therapy by nurses for hospitalized patients.) *Japanese J. Nursing Res.*, (Tokyo) 9:31-37.

00888 **BEARD, M. T.,** and **SCOTT, P. Y.** (1975), The efficacy of group therapy by nurses for hospitalized patients. *Nursing Res.*, 24:120-124.

00889 **BEARDON, A.** (1969), Group work training for child care officers. *Soc. Serv. Quart.*, (London) 42:136-140.

00890 **BEASLEY, J.** (1951), Group therapy in the field of speech correction. *J. Except. Children*, 17:102-107.

00891 **BEATTIE, D. G.,** and **ERSKINE, R. G.** (1976), Permissions: a cure for sexual problems. *Transactional Anal. J.*, 6:413-415.

00892 **BEAUBRUN, M. H.** (1967), Treatment of alcoholism in Trinidad and Tobago, 1956-65. *Brit. J. Psychiat.*, (Ashford) 113:643-658.

00893 **BEAUCHAMP, A., GRAVELINE, G.,** and **QUIVIGER, C.** (1976), *Comment Animer un Groupe.* (*How to Enliven a Group.*) Montreal: Éditions de l'Homme.

00894 **BEAUCHESNE, H.** (1976), (A therapeutic group for whom? a rehabilitation of the body?) *Perspect. Psychiat.*, (Paris) 57:235-241.

00895 **BEBCHUK, J.** (1973), (The therapeutic group as an atomist and gestaltic totality: the therapeutic group as a whole.) *Acta Psiquiat. Psicol. Amer. Latina*, (Buenos Aires) 19:386-395.

00896 **BEBCHUK, J.** (1973), (The therapeutic group as concrete totality: ii.) *Acta Psiquiat. Psicol. Amer. Latina*, (Buenos Aires) 19:451-461.

00897 **BEBJAKOVÁ, V.,** and **HEFTYOVA, F.** (1978), (The role of leader in a psychotherapeutic group of sadopsychiatric patients from the psychosocial point of view.) *Ceskoslov. Psychiat.*, (Prague) 74:139-144.

00898 **BEBOUT, J.** (1973), A study of group encounter in higher education. *Educat. Technol.*, 13:63-67.

00899 **BEBOUT, J.,** and **GORDON, B.** (1973), The use of encounter groups for interpersonal growth: initial results of the TIE project. *Interpersonal Develop.*, 2:91-104.

00900 **BECK, A. A.** (1974), The application of small group techniques to training in community participation: a field experiment. *Dissert. Abstr. Internat.*, 34:6189B.

00901 **BECK, D. F.** (1950), The dynamics of group psychotherapy as seen by a sociologist, part i: the basic process. *Sociometry*, 21:98-128.

00902 **BECK, D. F.** (1958), The dynamics of group psychotherapy as seen by a sociologist, part ii: some puzzling questions on leadership, contextual relation and outcomes. *Sociometry*, 21:180-197.

00903 **BECK, F. S.** (1972), Affective sensitivity of counselor supervisors as a dimension of growth in their trainee groups. *Dissert. Abstr. Internat.*, 33:3277A.

00904 **BECK, J. C., BUTTENWIESER, P.,** and **GRUNEBAUM, H.** (1968), Learning to treat the poor: a group experience. *Internat. J. Group Psychother.*, 18:325-336.

00905 **BECK, J. E.** (1980), Learning from experience in sensitivity training groups: a personal construct theory model and framework for research. *Small Group Behav.*, 11:279-298.

00906 **BECK, K. E.** (1979), Differential response of speech-anxious repressors and sensitizers to systematic desensitization and rational-emotive therapy. *Dissert. Abstr. Internat.*, 40:5800B.

00907 **BECK, L., LATTIMER, J. K.,** and **BRAUN, E.** (1979), Group psychotherapy on a children's urology service. *Soc. Work & Health Care*, 4:275.

00908 **BECKENSTEIN, N.** (1959), Group psychotherapy: the promise it holds. *Internat. J. Group Psychother.*, 9:147-149.

00909 **BECKER, B. J.** (1971), Adolescent group psychotherapy in a psychiatric training center. *Amer. J. Psychol.*, 31:95-101.

00910 **BECKER, B. J.** (1969), A concept of total psychiatric theory. *Penn. Psychiat. Quart.*, 9:5-14.

00911 **BECKER, B. J.** (1960), The obese patient in group psychoanalysis. *Amer. J. Psychother.*, 14:322-337.

00912 **BECKER, B. J.** (1957), Observations on the process of group psychoanalysis. *Amer. J. Psychother.*, 11:345-358.

00913 **BECKER, B. J.** (1972), The psychodynamics of analytic group psychotherapy. *Amer. J. Psychoan.*, 32:177-185.

00914 **BECKER, B. J.** (1958), Relatedness and alienation in group psychoanalysis. *Amer. J. Psychoanal.*, 18:150-157.

00915 **BECKER, B. J., GUSRAE, R.,** and **BERGER, E.** (1956), Adolescent group psychotherapy: a community mental health program. *Internat. J. Group Psychother.*, 6:300-316.

00916 **BECKER, B. J., GUSRAE, R.,** and **MacNICOL, E.** (1963), A clinical study of a group psychotherapy program for adolescents. *Psychiat. Quart.*, 37:685-703.

00917 **BECKER, G. S.,** and **ISRAEL, P.** (1961), Integrated drug and psychotherapy in the treatment of alcoholism. *Quart. J. Studies Alcohol*, 22:610-633.

00918 **BECKER, H.** (1956), Empathy, sympathy and Scheler. *Internat. J. Soc. Psychiat.*, (London) 1:15-22.

00919 **BECKER, J. L.** (1970), The effects of instructional audio-tape in self-directed encounter groups. *Dissert. Abstr. Internat.*, 31:4325-4326.

00920 **BECKER, M. C.** (1948), The effects of activity group therapy on sibling rivalry. *J. Soc. Casework*, 29:217-221.

00921 **BECKER, M. C.** (1945), The effects of group therapy upon sibling rivalry. *Smith Coll. Studies Soc. Work*, 16:131-132.

00922 **BECKER, P. W.** (1978), Beer and social therapy treatment with geriatric psychiatric patient groups. *Addict. Diseases*, 3:429-436.

00923 **BECKER, R.** (1971), Group preparation for discharge and group placement of chronically hospitalized schizophrenic patients. *Diseases Nerv. System*, 32:176-180.

00924 **BECKER, R. E., HARROW, M.,** and **ASTRACHAN, B.** (1970), Leadership and content in group psychotherapy. *J. Nerv. & Ment. Diseases*, 150:346-353.

00925 **BECKER, R. E., HARROW, M., ASTRACHAN, B. M., DETRE, T.,** and **MILLER, J. C.** (1968), Influence of the leader on the activity level of therapy groups. *J. Soc. Psychol.*, 74:39-51.

00926 **BECKER, R. E.,** and **PAGE, M. S.** (1973), Psychotherapeutically oriented rehabilitation in chronic mental illness. *Amer. J. Occupat. Ther.*, 27:34-38.

00927 **BECKMANN, J. W.** (1944), The "opportunity" class: a study of children with problems. *Amer. J. Orthopsychiat.*, 14:113-128.

00928 **BECKWITH, E. G.** (1979), Behavioral predispositions in group situations inventory: a construct validity study using naturally occurring small groups. *Dissert. Abstr. Internat.*, 40:2428B.

00929 **BEDAT, M.** (1968), (Psychotherapeutic techniques.) *Infirmiere Francaise*, (Paris) 31-34.

00930 **BEDEE, C.** (1968), (Activities as a therapeutic aid.) *Nederl. Tijdschr. Geneeskunde*, (Amsterdam) 112:725-727.

00931 **BEDFORD, A., MEIVER, D.,** and **PEARSON, P. R.** (1978), Further test of poulds personality and personal illness differentiae in a psychiatric group. *Psychol. Med.*, (London) 8:467-470.

00932 **BEDNAR, M. A.** (1965), Changes in social perception in adolescents during group psychotherapy. *Dissert. Abstr. Internat.*, 26:1166-1167.

00933 **BEDNAR, R. L.** (1970), Group psychotherapy research variables. *Internat. J. Group Psychother.*, 20:146-152.

00934 **BEDNAR, R. L.** (1980), Review of B. Levine's *Group Psychotherapy: Practice and Development. J. Contemp. Psychol.*, 25:167.

00935 **BEDNAR, R. L.** (1974), Risk, responsibility, and structure: a conceptual framework for initiating group counseling and psychotherapy. *J. Couns. Psychol.*, 21:31-37.

00936 **BEDNAR, R. L.,** and **BATTERSBY, C. B.** (1976), The effects of specific cognitive structure on early group development. *J. Appl. Behav. Science*, 12:513-522.

00937 **BEDNAR, R. L.,** and **KAUL, T. J.** (1979), Experiential group research: what never happened. *J. Appl. Behav. Science*, 15:311-319.

00938 **BEDNAR, R. L., WEET, C., EVENSEN, P., LANIER, D.,** and **MELNICK, J.** (1974), Empirical guidelines for group therapy: pre-training, cohesion and modeling. *J. Appl. Behav. Science*, 10:149-165.

00939 **BEDNAR, R. L.,** and **WEINBERG, S. L.** (1970), Ingredients of successful treatment programs for underachievers. *J. Couns. Psychol.*, 17:1-7.

00940 **BEHYMER, A. F., CANIDA, J., COOPER, S., FADEN, P. D.,** and **KAHNE, M. J.** (1957), Mental health films in group psychotherapy. *Psychiatry*, 20:27-38.

00941 **BEHZADI, B.** (1976), Review of Yalom's *Group Psychotherapy: Principles and Methods. Psychology*, 184:289-290.

00942 **BEIGEL, A.,** and **FEDER, S. L.** (1970), A night hospital program. *Hosp. & Community Psychiat.*, 21:146-149.

00943 **BEIGEL, A.,** and **FEDER, S. L.** (1970), Patterns of utilization in partial hospitalization. *Amer. J. Psychiat.*, 126:1267-1274.

00944 **BEKAOUCHE, A.** (1975), A study of the effectiveness of transactional analysis and transactional analysis modified on juvenile delinquents. *Dissert. Abstr. Internat.*, 35:7150-7151.

00945 **BELASCO, J. A.,** and **TRICE, H. M.** (1969), *The Assessment of Change in Training and Therapy*. Hightstown, NJ: McGraw-Hill Book Co.

00946 **BELETSIS, J., Jr.** (1956), Group psychotherapy with chronic male schizophrenics: an evaluation of the frequency of group psychotherapy sessions as a factor affecting the results of the therapy. Unpublished doctoral dissertation, New York University.

00947 **BELFORD, R. Q.** (1970), An evaluation of relative effectiveness of role-playing and group therapy on the subsequent socialization of parolees. *Dissert. Abstr. Internat.*, 551B.

00948 **BELINKOFF, J., BROSS, R.,** and **STEIN, A.** (1964), The effect of group psychotherapy on anaclitic transference. *Internat. J. Group Psychother.*, 14:474-481.

00949 **BELINKOFF, J., RESNICK, E. V., STEIN, A., ALPERT, H., BOOKHALTER, S., BROSS, R., GOLUB, M., WACHTEL, A.,** and **BRALOVE, R.** (1962), The effect of a change of therapist on the group psychotherapy in an outpatient clinic. *Internat. J. Group Psychother.*, 12:456-466.

00950 **BELL, G. E.** (1970), An application of differential counseling techniques to groups of male college students experiencing vocational and educational problems. *Dissert. Abstr. Internat.*, 32:551B.

00951 **BELL, J. L.,** and **BARNETT, C. J.** (1955), Intensive insulin sub-coma treatments combined with group therapy in a mental hygiene clinic. *Diseases Nerv. System*, 16:80-85.

00952 **BELL, R.** (1973), Facilitating progress in group therapy by means of the basic human relations laboratory. *Newsl. Res. Ment. Health & Behav. Sciences*, 15:11-12.

00953 **BELL, R.** (1972), The glass ark: a drug abuse treatment program. *Newsl. Res. Psychol.*, 14:41.

00954 **BELL, R. L.** (1973), Can addicts relate to "straights"? *Drug Forum*, 2:265-270.

00955 **BELL, R. L.** (1970), Practical applications of psychodrama: systematic role-playing teaches social skills. *Hosp. & Community Psychiat.*, 21:189-191.

00956 **BELL, R. L.** (1969), Small group dialogue and discussion: an approach to police-community relationships. *J. Crim. Law & Criminol.*, 60:242-246.

00957 **BELL, R. W.** (1970), Activity as a tool in group therapy. *Perspect. Psychiat. Care*, 8:84-91.

00958 **BELL, S.**, and **LEDFORD, T.** (1978), The effects of sociodrama on the behaviors and attitudes of elementary school boys. *Group Psychother., Psychodrama, & Sociometry*, 31:117.

00959 **BELLAK, L.** (1976), Nature and interaction of community psychiatric treatment and the schizophrenic syndrome. In: *Treatment of Schizophrenia: Progress and Prospects*, eds. L. J. West and D. E. Flinn. New York: Grune and Stratton.

00960 **BELLAK, L.** (1980), On some limitations of dyadic psychotherapy and the role of group modalities. *Internat. J. Group Psychother.*, 30:7-21.

00961 **BELLANTI, J.** (1972), The effects of an encounter group experience on empathy, respect, congruence, and self actualization. *Dissert. Abstr. Internat.*, 33:6668B.

00962 **BELLEMY, N. D.** (1966), A study of the effectiveness of group guidance on a behavior determinant. *Dissert. Abstr. Internat.*, 26:4322.

00963 **BELLIN, E. H.** (1977), A review of J. F. Masterson's *Psychotherapy of the Borderline Adult. Group*, 1:203-205.

00964 **BELLOMO, E.** (1974), Art therapy and its use in a psychiatric setting. *J. Bronx State Hosp.*, 2:203.

00965 **BELLSMITH, V.** (1964), The impact of two decades of group psychotherapy on social work. *Internat. J. Group Psychother.*, 14:32-40.

00967 **BELLUCCI, M. T.** (1972), Group treatment of mothers in child protection cases. *Child Welfare*, 51:110-116.

00968 **BELLUCCI, M. T.** (1975), Treatment of latency-age adopted children and parents. *Soc. Casework*, 56:297-301.

00969 **BEMPORAD, J. R.** (1977), Resistance encountered in the psychotherapy of depressed individuals. *Amer. J. Psychoanal.*, 39:207.

00970 **BENAIM, S.** (1957), Group psychotherapy within a geriatric unit: an experiment. *Internat. J. Soc. Psychiat.*, (London) 3:123-128.

00971 **BEN-AARON, M.**, and **JARUS, A.** (1978), Remarks on the communication of psychotic children as seen in group therapy. *Ment. Health*, 5:224.

00972 **BENASSI, P.** (1970), (Amateur acting and other group activities in psychiatric institutions.) *Riv. Sper. Freniatria*, (Emilia) 94:792-795.

00973 **BENDER, E. I.** (1971), The citizen as emotional activist: an appraisal of self-help groups in North America. *Can. Ment. Health*, 19:3-7.

00974 **BENDER, L.** (1952), *Child Psychiatric Techniques: Diagnostic and Therapeutic Approach to Normal and Abnormal Development through Patterned, Expressive, and Group Behavior.* Springfield, IL: Thomas.

00975 **BENDER, L.** (1937), Group activities in a children's ward as methods of psychotherapy. *Amer. J. Psychiat.*, 93:1151-1173.

00976 **BENDER, L.**, and **WOLTMAN, A. G.** (1937), Puppetry as a psychotherapeutic measure with problem children. *N.Y. State Assn. Occupat. Ther.*, 7:1-7.

00977 **BENDER, L.**, and **WOLTMAN, A. G.** (1936), The use of puppet shows as a psychotherapeutic measure for behavior problem children. *Amer. J. Orthopsychiat.*, 6:341-354.

00978 **BENDORF, G.** (1976), (Therapeutic play as clinical short-term group therapy in rehabilitative and preventive internal medicine.) *Psychother. & Med. Psychol.*, (Stuttgart) 26:158-163.

00979 **BEN-ELI, T.**, and **SELA, M.** (1980), (Terrorists in Nahariya: description of coping under stress.) *Isr. J. Psychol. Couns. Educat.*, 13:94-101.

00980 **BENFARI, R. C.** (1976), Type a-b behavior and outcome of group process. *Psychol. Reports*, 38:415-419.

00981 **BENGS, H. A.** (1951), Presentation of psychodrama at the third mental hospital institute. *Group Psychother., Psychodrama & Sociometry*, 4:213-214.

00982 **BENJAFIELD, J.**, **POMEROY, E.**, and **JORDAN, D.** (1976), Encounter groups: a return to the fundamental. *Psychother.: Theory, Res. & Pract.*, 13:387-389.

00983 **BENJAMIN, A.** (1978), *Behavior in Small Groups*. Boston: Houghton Mifflin.

00984 **BENJAMIN, A.**, and **WEATHERLY, H. E.** (1947), Hospital ward therapy of emotionally disturbed children. *Amer. J. Orthopsychiat.*, 17:665-674.

00985 **BENJAMIN, S. E., Jr.** (1972), Cotherapy: a growth experience for therapists. *Internat. J. Group Psychother.*, 22:199-209.

00986 **BENNE, K. D.**, **BRADFORD, L. P.**, **GIBB, J. R.**, and **LIPPITT, R. O.** (1975), *The Laboratory Method of Changing and Learning: Theory and Application*. Palo Alto: Science and Behavior Books.

00987 **BENNE, K. D.**, and **SHEATS, P.** (1948), Functional roles of group members. *J. Soc. Issues*, 4:41-49.

00988 **BENNET, E. A.** (1950), Psychotherapy. In: *Recent Progress in Psychiatry, Vol. 2*, 2d ed., ed. G. W. Fleming. London: Churchill.

00989 **BENNET, E. A.** (1944), Psychotherapy. In: *Recent Progress in Psychiatry*, ed. G. W. Fleming. London: Churchill, pp. 615-634.

00990 **BENNETT, F. D.** (1970), Encounter groups: growth or addiction? *J. Human Psychol.*, 16:59-70.

00991 **BENNIS, W. G.** (1960), A critique of group therapy research. *Internat. J. Group Psychother.*, 10:63-77.

00992 **BENNIS, W. G.** (1957), Decision-making in groups: some specific aboulias. *Group Psychother., Psychodrama & Sociometry*, 10:287-299.

00993 **BENNIS, W. G.**, **BURKE, R. C.**, **HENRY, H. H.**, and **HOFFMAN, J.** (1957), A note on some problems of measurement and prediction in a training group. *Group Psychother., Psychodrama & Sociometry*, 10:328-341.

00994 **BENOIT, J. C.**, and **BEAUJEAN, J.** (1975), (Exchanges in an expression group studied in videotape recordings: preliminary study centered on observer reactions.) *Annales Medico-Psychol.*, (Paris) 133:377-382.

00995 **BENOIT, J. C.**, **FORZY, CL.**, and **LaFORÊT, M.** (1973), (Study of the therapeutic process in group psychotherapy: program of research.) *Annales Medico-Psychol.*, (Paris) 1:406-411.

00996 **BENSMAN, J.**, and **LILIENFELD, R.** (1972), Psychological techniques and role relationships. *Psychoanal. Rev.*, 58:529-552.

00997 **BENSON, A. N.** (1973), A differential approach to orientation to group counseling. *Dissert. Abstr. Internat.*, 34:3560A.

00998 **BENSON, H. A., Jr.** (1967), A therapy group in a child guidance clinic. *Penn. Psychiat. Quart.*, 7:21-27.

00999 **BENTHAM, J. E.** (1974), The effects of Tavistock Conference, encountertape, and theme-centered group approaches on certain personality variables. *Dissert. Abstr. Internat.*, 34:4652B.

01000 **BENTLEY, J.** (1976), Group therapy for parents of mentally handicapped children. *Nursing Mirror*, (London) 142:53.

01001 **BENTON, D. W.** (1980), The significance of the absent member in milieu therapy. *Perspect. Psychiat. Care*, 18:21-25.

01002 **BEN-YAKAR, M., DASBERG, H.,** and **PLOTKIN, I.** (1978), The influence of various therapeutic milieus on the course of group treatments in two groups of soldiers with combat reaction. *Isr. Annals Psychiat.*, (Jerusalem) 16:183-198.

01003 **BENYEHUDA, N.** (1980), Group therapy with methadone-maintenance patients: structural problems and solutions. *Internat. J. Group Psychother.*, 30:331-346.

01004 **BEQUART, P.** (1965), (The therapeutic relationship in hospital and extra-hospital practice.) *Inform. Psychiat.*, (Paris) 41:99-117.

01005 **BERAN, M.** (1961), Combined individual and group therapy within a hospital team set-up. *Internat. J. Group Psychother.*, 11:313-318.

01006 **BERBERICH, R. R., GABEL, H.,** and **ANCHOR, K. N.** (1979), Self-disclosure in reflective, behavioral, and discussion parent-counseling groups. *J. Community Psychol.*, 7:259-263.

01007 **BERENSTEIN, F.** (1973), The homosexual retardate: theory and group work. *J. Spec. Educat. & Ment. Retard.*, 9:74-79.

01008 **BERG, C. D.** (1978), Helping children accept death and dying through group counseling. *Personnel & Guid. J.*, 57:169-171.

01009 **BERG, R. B.** (1960), Combining group and casework treatment in a camp setting. *Soc. Work*, 5:56-62.

01010 **BERG, R. C.** (1968), The effect of group counseling on students placed on academic probation at Rock Valley College, Rockford, Illinois. *Dissert. Abstr. Internat.*, 29:115A.

01011 **BERG, R. C.,** and **LANDRETH, G. L.** (1979), *Group Counseling: Fundamental Concepts and Procedures*. Muncie, IN: Accelerated Development.

01012 **BERGEEST, H.G., STEINBACH, I.,** and **TAUSCH, A. M.** (1980), (Speech contents in person-centered discussion groups and their relationship to process variables in non-clients.) *Zeit. Klin. Psychol. & Psychother.*, (Freiburg) 28:259-266.

01013 **BERGEN, R. H.** (1972), An investigation of Frederiek Peres' gestalt therapy method as a functioning religious involvement. *Dissert. Abstr. Internat.*, 33:2477A.

01014 **BERGER, G.** (1949), The group worker and psychiatry. *Amer. J. Orthopsychiat.*, 19:455-462.

01015 **BERGER, I. L.** (1967), Group psychotherapy training institutes: group process, therapy, or resistance to learning? *Internat. J. Group Psychother.*, 17:505-512.

01016 **BERGER, I. L.** (1960), Modifications of the transference as observed in combined individual and group psychotherapy. *Internat. J. Group Psychother.*, 10:456-470.

01017 **BERGER, I. L.** (1978), Presidential address: group psychotherapy today—ideologies and issues. *Internat. J. Group Psychother.*, 28:307-318.

01018 **BERGER, I. L.** (1969), Resistances to learning process in group dynamics programs. *Amer. J. Psychiat.*, 126:850-857.

01019 **BERGER, I. L.** (1956), Some reflections on group psychotherapy, a growing force in psychiatry. *Ohio State Med. J.*, 52:827-832.

01020 **BERGER, I. L.,** and **SHOSKIN, D. A.** (1973/1974), What is treatment and what is training in group psychotherapy. *Groups J. Group Dynam. Psychiat.*, 5:49-52.

01021 **BERGER, J.,** and **VRANJEŠEVIĆ, L.** (1978), (A demonstration of the work of transactional groups.) *Psihijat. Danas*, (Belgrade) 10:89-94.

01022 **BERGER, J.**, and **VRANJEŠEVIĆ, L.** (1978), (Transactional group psychotherapy.) *Psihijat. Danas*, (Belgrade) 10:37-42.

01023 **BERGER, L. F.** (1978), Activating a psychogeriatric group. *Psychiat. Quart.*, 50:63-66.

01024 **BERGER, L. F.**, and **BERGER, M. M.** (1973), A holistic group approach to psychogeriatric outpatients. *Internat. J. Group Psychother.*, 23:432-444.

01025 **BERGER, M. L.**, and **BERGER, P. J.** (1973), *Group Training Techniques: Cases, Applications and Research.* New York: J. Wiley & Sons.

01026 **BERGER, M. M.** (1962), An overview of group psychotherapy: its past, present and future development. *Internat. J. Group Psychother.*, 12:287-294.

01027 **BERGER, M. M.** (1969), Experiential and didactic aspects of training in therapeutic group approaches. *Amer. J. Psychiat.*, 126:845-850.

01028 **BERGER, M. M.** (1967), Extending our use of fantasies. *Voices*, 3:91-92.

01029 **BERGER, M. M.** (1965), Group approaches in the therapeutic community: opening remarks. *Internat. J. Group Psychother.*, 15:3-4.

01030 **BERGER, M. M.** (1970), Group therapy for diagnosis and treatment, 1905-1970. *Med. Insight*, 2:40-56.

01031 **BERGER, M. M.** (1974), The impact of the therapist's personality on group process. *Amer. J. Psychoanal.*, 34:213-219.

02032 **BERGER, M. M.** (1970), Integrating video into private psychiatric practice. *Voices*, 5:78-85.

01033 **BERGER, M. M.** (1975), Nonverbal communications in group psychotherapy. In: *Group Psychotherapy and Group Function*, 2d ed., eds. M. Rosenbaum and M. M. Berger. New York: Basic Books.

01034 **BERGER, M. M.** (1958), Nonverbal communications in group psychotherapy. *Internat. J. Group Psychother.*, 8:161-178.

01035 **BERGER, M. M.** (1969), Notes on the communication process in group psychotherapy. *J. Group Psychoanal. & Process*, (London) 2:29-36.

01036 **BERGER, M. M.** (1960), The place of psychoanalysis in contemporary group psychotherapy. *Topical Probl. Psychol. & Psychother.*, 2:155-163.

01037 **BERGER, M. M.** (1968), Similarities and differences between group psychotherapy and intensive short term group process experiences: clinical impressions. *J. Group Psychoanal. & Process*, (London) 1:11-30.

01038 **BERGER, M. M.** (1958), Training in group psychotherapy, v: problems of anxiety in group psychotherapy trainees. *Amer. J. Psychother.*, 12:505-507.

01039 **BERGER, M. M.** (1975), The use of videotape with psychotherapy groups in a community mental health service program. In: *The Innovative Psychological Therapies: Critical and Creative Contributions*, eds. R. M. Suinn and R. G. Weigel. New York: Harper and Row.

01040 **BERGER, M. M.**, and **GALLANT, D. M.** (1965), The use of closed-circuit television in the teaching of group psychotherapy. *Psychosomatics*, 6:16-18.

01041 **BERGER, M. M.**, and **MENDELL, D.** (1967), A preliminary report on participation of patients in more than one psychotherapy group concurrently. *Internat. J. Soc. Psychiat.*, (London) 13:192-198.

01042 **BERGER, M. M.**, and **ROSENBAUM, M.** (1975), Notes on help-rejecting complainers. In: *Group Psychotherapy and Group Function*, 2d ed., eds. M. Rosenbaum and M. M. Berger. New York: Basic Books.

01043 **BERGER, M. M.**, and **ROSENBAUM, M.** (1967), Notes on help-rejecting complainers. *Internat. J. Group Psychother.*, 17:357-370.

01044 **BERGER, M. M.**, **SHERMAN, B.**, **SPALDING, J.**, and **WESTLAKE, R.** (1968), The use of videotape with psychotherapy groups in a community mental health service program. *Internat. J. Group Psychother.*, 18:504-515.

01045 **BERGER, R. M.** (1979), Training the institutionalized elderly in interpersonal skills. *Soc. Work*, 24:420.

01046 **BERGER, S. E.**, and **ANCHOR, K. N.** (1970), Disclosure process in group interaction. *Proceed., 78th annual convention.* American Psychological Association, 529-530.

01047 **BERGER, S. E.**, and **ANCHOR, K. N.** (1978), The disclosure process in group interaction. *Small Group Behav.*, 9:59-63.

01048 **BERGIER, J.** (1955), Influencing parents by means of groups of mothers. *Schweiz. Arch. Neurol., Neurochir., & Psychiat.*, (Zurich) 75:415-418.

01049 **BERGMAN, A. S.** (1980), Marital stress and medical training: an experience with a support group for medical house staff wives. *Pediatrics*, 65:944-947.

01050 **BERGMAN, P.** (1958), The role of faith in psychotherapy. *Bull. Menninger Clinic*, 22:92-103.

01051 **BERGONZI, P.** (1976), Relational models and psychopathology of epileptics in a group-psychotherapy perspective. *Riv. Patol. Nerv. & Ment.*, (Florence) 96:378-392.

01052 **BERK, T. J. C.** (1967), (Some experiences with mime-play with children.) *Tijdschr. Orthopedagog.*, 6:61-73.

01053 **BERKEN, G. H.**, and **EISENSTAT, M. B.** (1969), Chaplaincy sponsored group-therapy: a military treatment modality with jeopardy. *Military Med.*, 134:360-362.

01054 **BERKOVITZ, I. H.** (1972), *Adolescents Grow in Groups: Clinical Experiences in Adolescent Group Psychotherapy.* New York: Brunner/Mazel.

01055 **BERKOVITZ, I. H.** (1975), *When Schools Care: Creative Use of Groups in Secondary Schools.* New York: Brunner/Mazel.

01056 **BERKOVITZ, I. H., CHIKAHISA, P., LEE, M. L.**, and **MURASKI, E. M.** (1966), Psychosexual development of latency-age children and adolescents in group therapy in a residential setting. *Internat. J. Group Psychother.*, 16:344-356.

01057 **BERKOVITZ, I. H.**, and **SUGAR, M.** (1976), Experience in teaching adolescent group psychotherapy: observers become participants. *Internat. J. Group Psychother.*, 26:441-453.

01058 **BERKOVITZ, I. H.**, and **SUGAR, M.** (1975), Indications and contraindications for adolescent group psychotherapy. In: *The Adolescent in Group and Family Therapy*, ed. M. Sugar. New York: Brunner/Mazel.

01059 **BERKOWITZ, B.** (1965), Evaluating the effects of psychotherapy orientation in groups: an investigation of orientation for psychotherapy in small groups as a means of maintaining motivation and as preparation for psychotherapy. *Dissert. Abstr. Internat.*, 26:4070.

01060 **BERKOWITZ, L.** (1978), *Group Processes.* New York: Academic Press.

01061 **BERKOWITZ, P. H.**, and **ROTHMAN, E. P.** (1968), *The Disturbed Child: Recognition and Psychoeducational Therapy in the Classroom.* New York: New York University Press.

01062 **BERL, M. E.** (1951), The relationship of group psychotherapy to remedial reading. *Group Psychother., Psychodrama & Sociometry*, 4:60-62.

01063 **BERLAND, D. I.**, and **POGGI, R.** (1979), Expressive group psychotherapy with the aging. *Internat. J. Group Psychother.*, 29:87-108.

01064 **BERLEIN, I. C.** (1945), Rehabilitation center: psychiatry and group therapy. *J. Crim. Law & Criminol.*, 36:249-255.

01065 **BERLIN, I. N.** (1970), From confrontation to collaboration. *Amer. J. Orthopsychiat.*, 40:473-480.

01066 **BERLIN, I. N.** (1978), Psychotherapeutic work with parents of psychotic children. In: *Autism: A Reappraisal of Concepts and Treatment*, eds. M. Rutter and E. Shopler. New York: Plenum Press.

01067 **BERLIN, J. S.,** and **DIES, R. R.** (1974), Differential group structure: the effects on socially isolated college students. *Small Group Behav.*, 5:462-472.

01068 **BERMAN, A. L.** (1975), Group psychotherapy training: issues and models. *Small Group Behav.*, 6:325-344.

01069 **BERMAN, A. L., MESSERSMITH, C. E.,** and **MULLENS, B. M.** (1972), Profile of group therapy practice in university counseling centers. *J. Couns. Psychol.*, 19:353-354.

01070 **BERMAN, H. H.** (1946), Audio-visual psychotherapeutics. *Psychiat. Quart. Suppl.*, 20:197-203.

01071 **BERMAN, J. J.,** and **ZIMPFER, D. G.** (1980), Growth groups: do the outcomes really last? *Rev. Educat. Res.*, 50:505-524.

01072 **BERMAN, L.** (1953), Mental hygiene for educators. *Psychoanal. Rev.*, 40:319-332.

01073 **BERMAN, L.** (1953), Problems of supervision and training in clinical psychology. round table, 1952. 6: a group psychotherapeutic technique for training in clinical psychology. *Amer. J. Orthopsychiat.*, 23:322-327.

01074 **BERMAN, L.** (1950), Psychoanalysis and group psychotherapy. *Psychoanal. Rev.*, 37:156-163.

01075 **BERMUDEZ, J. C.** (1964), Primeras experiencias de psychodrama publico en Buenos Aires. (Primary experiences in public psychodrama in Buenos Aires.) *Internat. J. Sociometry & Sociatry*, 4:33-36.

01076 **BERMUDEZ, J. G.,** and **PAVLOVSKY, E. A.** (1966), Psychodramatic exploration of doctor-patient relations in the permanent theater of psychodrama. *Group Psychother., Psychodrama & Sociometry*, 19:37-42.

01077 **BERNARD, F.** (1943), Notes from a psychiatric social worker in North Africa: use of individual and group techniques. *Newsl. Amer. Assn. Psychiat. Soc. Work*, 13:75-76.

01078 **BERNARD, H. S.** (1977), The women's movement. a new challenge for the psychotherapist. *Fam. Ther.*, 4:1-10.

01079 **BERNARD, H. S.,** and **KLEIN, R. H.** (1977), Some perspectives on time-limited group psychotherapy. *Comprehens. Psychiat.*, 18:579-584.

01080 **BERNARD, H. S.,** and **KLEIN, R. H.** (1979), Time–limited group psychotherapy: a case report. *Group Psychother., Psychodrama & Sociometry*, 32:31-37.

01081 **BERNARD, J.** (1961), Nurses and psychotherapy. *Ment. Hosp.*, 12:32-34.

01082 **BERNARD, J. L., KINZIE, W. B., TOLLMAN, G. P.,** and **WEBB, R. A.** (1965), Some effects of a brief course in the psychology of adjustment on a psychiatric admissions ward. *J. Clin. Psychol.*, 21:322-326.

01083 **BERNARDEZ, T.** (1969), The role of the observer in group psychotherapy. *Internat. J. Group Psychother.*, 19:234-239.

01084 **BERNARDEZ, T.,** and **STEIN, T. S.** (1979), Separating the sexes in group therapy: an experiment with men's and women's groups. *Internat. J. Group Psychother.*, 29:493-502.

01085 **BERNE, E.** (1971), Away from a theory of the impact of interpersonal interaction on non-verbal participation. *Transactional Anal. J.*, 1:6-13.

01086 **BERNE, E.** (1975), Four books on group therapy: a review. In: *Group Psychotherapy and Group Function*, 2d ed., eds. M. Rosenbaum and M. M. Berger. New York: Basic Books.

01087 **BERNE, E.** (1955), Group attendance: clinical and theoretical considerations. *Internat. J. Group Psychother.*, 5:392-403.

01088 **BERNE, E.** (1958), Group therapy abroad. *Internat. J. Group Psychother.*, 8:466-469.

01089 **BERNE, E.** (1970), *Group Treatment*. New York: Grove Press.

01090 **BERNE, E.** (1954), The natural history of a spontaneous therapy group. *Internat. J. Group Psychother.*, 4:74-85.

01091 **BERNE, E.** (1968), *Principles of Group Treatment.* New York: Grove Press.
01092 **BERNE, E.** (1966), *Principles of Group Treatment.* New York: Oxford Univ. Press.
01093 **BERNE, E.** (1960), "Psychoanalytic" versus "dynamic" group therapy. *Internat. J. Group Psychother.*, 10:98-103.
01094 **BERNE, E.** (1968), Staff-patient conferences. *Amer. J. Psychother.*, 125:286-293.
01095 **BERNE, E.** (1966), *The Structure and Dynamics of Organizations and Groups.* New York: Grove Press.
01096 **BERNE, E.** (1963), *The Structure and Dynamics of Organizations and Groups.* Philadelphia: J. B. Lippincott.
01097 **BERNE, E.** (1958), Transactional analysis: a new and effective method of group therapy. *Amer. J. Psychother.*, 12:735-743.
01098 **BERNE, E., STARRELS, R. J.,** and **TRINCHERO, A.** (1960), Leadership hunger in a therapy group. *Arch. Gen. Psychiat.*, 2:75-80.
01099 **BERNE, E. L.** (1961), *Transactional Analysis in Psychotherapy: A Systematic Individual and Social Psychiatry.* New York: Grove Press.
01100 **BERNER, P.** (1971), (The videocorder as a therapeutic aid: a behavior therapy technique for criminals.) *Zeit. Psychother. Med. Psychol.*, (Stuttgart) 21:21-27.
01101 **BERNSTEIN, D. A.** (1970), The modification of smoking behavior: a search for effective variables. *Behav. Res. & Ther.*, 8:133-146.
01102 **BERNSTEIN, I.,** and **BELMONT, H. S.** (1946), Group psychotherapy in a convalescent hospital. *Diseases Nerv. System*, 7:133-138.
01103 **BERNSTEIN, N. R.,** and **TINKHAM, C. B.** (1971), Group therapy following abortion. *J. Nerv. & Ment. Diseases*, 152:303-314.
01104 **BERNSTEIN, S.** (1970), *Further Explorations in Group Work.* Boston: Boston University School of Social Work.
01105 **BERNSTEIN, S.,** and **HERZBERG, J.** (1970), Small group experience with psychiatric aides. *Ment. Hygiene*, 54:113-117.
01106 **BERNSTEIN, S., WACKS, J.,** and **CHRIST, J.** (1969), The effect of group therapy on the psychotherapist. *Amer. J. Psychother.*, 23:271-282.
01107 **BERRETT, R. D.,** and **KELLEY, R.** (1975), Discipline and the hearing impaired child. *Volta Rev.*, 77:117-124.
01108 **BERRY, K. K., TURONE, R. J.,** and **HARDT, P.** (1980), Comparison of group therapy and behavioral modification with children. *Psychol. Reports*, 46:975-978.
01109 **BERRYMAN, B. W.** (1970), The effects of group counseling upon visual perception and its relationship to other forms of perception. *Dissert. Abstr. Internat.*, 30:2793A-2794A.
01110 **BERSADSKY, L.** (1949), Concepts of psychodrama. *Persona*, 1:20-23.
01111 **BERSCHLING, C.,** and **HOMANN, J.** (1966), A proposal for the establishment of a group psychotherapy program for adolescents. *Psychiat. Communicat.*, 8:17-36.
01112 **BERTCHER, H.** (1974), Developing group leadership skills. *Manpower Informat. Jew.*, 6:10-13.
01113 **BERTCHER, H. J.** (1972), *Group Composition: An Instructional Program.* Ann Arbor, MI: Campus Publishers.
01114 **BERTRAND, R.** (1966), Rééducation psycho-cinétique d'asthmatiques en groupe. (Group psychokinetic rehabilitation of asthmatics.) *Bronches*, (Paris) 16:240-243.
01115 **BERTUCELLI, L.** (1967), (Structure and dynamics of a "group discussion" in a psychiatric hospital.) *Riv. Sper. Freniatria*, (Emilia) 91:842-847.
01116 **BERZOK, R. S.** (1978), Self-disclosure as a function of trust in an encounter group setting. *Dissert. Abstr. Internat.*, 39:3498B.

01117 **BERZON, B.** (1969), Peer: an audio tape program for self-directed small groups. *J. Human Psychol.*, 9:71-86.
01118 **BERZON, B.** (1962), Residual parental threat and selective interaction in group psychotherapy. *Internat. J. Group Psychother.*, 12:347-354.
01119 **BERZON, B.** (1968), Tape programs for self-directed groups. *Rehab. Record*, 9:35-37.
01120 **BERZON, B.** (1973), Encountertapes for black/white groups: a new approach to race relations. *Interpersonal Develop.*, 2:73-90.
01121 **BERZON, B., PIOUS, C.,** and **FARSON, R. E.** (1963), The therapeutic event in group psychotherapy: a study of subjective reports by group members. *J. Individ. Psychol.*, 19:204-212.
01122 **BERZON, B.,** and **SOLOMON, L. N.** (1966), Research frontiers: the self-directed therapeutic group—three studies. *J. Couns. Psychol.*, 13:491-497.
01123 **BERZON, B.,** and **SOLOMON, L. N.** (1964), The self-directed therapeutic group: an exploratory study. *Internat. J. Group Psychother.*, 14:366-369.
01124 **BETLHEIM, S.** (1963), Das problem der einzelbesprechung innerhalb de gruppenpsychotherapie. (The problem of individual interview in group psychotherapy.) *Zeit. Psychother. Med. Psychol.*, (Stuttgart) 13:21-27.
01125 **BETLHEIM, S.** (1963), (On the question of group psychotherapy of homosexuals.) *Topical Probl. Psychol. & Psychother.*, 4:154-162.
01126 **BETLHEIM, S.** (1963), (The relationship between group and individual psychotherapy.) *Neuropsihijatrija*, (Zagreb) 11:253-260.
01127 **BETLHEIM, S.** (1958), Über die bedeutung der träume in der gruppentherapie. (The meaning of dreams in group therapy.) *Acta Psychother. Psychosomat. Orthopaedagog.*, (Basel) 6:56-67.
01128 **BETLHEIM, S.** (1957), Über gruppentherapie von verheirhateten psychisch impotenten. (Concerning group therapy of psychologically impotent married men.) *Z. Diagnost. Psychol.*, 5:251-259.
01129 **BETTELHEIM, B.,** and **SYLVESTER, E.** (1947), Therapeutic influence of the group on the individual. *Amer. J. Orthopsychiat.*, 17:684-692.
01130 **BETTELHEIM, R.** (1946), Psychotherapy of the individual in the group. *Amer. Psychologist*, 1:296.
01131 **BETTIS, M. C.** (1947), A method of group therapy. *Diseases Nerv. System*, 8:235-246.
01132 **BETTIS, M. C., MALAMUD, D. I.,** and **MALAMUD, R. F.** (1949), Deepening a group's insight into human relations; a compilation of aids. *J. Clin. Psychol.*, 5:114-122.
01133 **BETTS, E. L.** (1976), Effects of behavioral group counseling on community college students. *Dissert. Abstr. Internat.*, 37:799A.
01134 **BETTSCHART, W.** (1977), Some reflections on therapeutic measures with parents at a child's day hospital. *Acta Paedopsychiat.*, (Basel) 43:23-31.
01135 **BETZ, K.** (1951), Gruppentraining und bilderleben. (Group therapy and imagining of scenes.) *Zeit. Psychother. Med. Psychol.*, (Stuttgart) 1:71-76.
01136 **BETZ, R. L.** (1969), Effects of group counseling as an adjunctive practicum experience. *J. Couns. Psychol.*, 16:528-533.
01137 **BEUKENKAMP, C., Jr.** (1959), Anxiety activated by the idea of marriage as observed in group psychotherapy. *Ment. Hygiene*, 43:532-538.
01138 **BEUKENKAMP, C., Jr.** (1956), Beyond transference behavior. *Amer. J. Psychother.*, 10:467-470.
01139 **BEUKENKAMP, C.** (1975), Beyond transference behavior. In: *Group Psychotherapy and Group Function*, 2d ed., eds. M. Rosenbaum and M. M. Berger. New York: Basic Books.
01140 **BEUKENKAMP, C.** (1956), Clinical observations on the effect of analytically oriented group therapy and group supervision on the therapist. *Psychoanal. Rev.*, 43:82-90.

01141 **BEUKENKAMP, C.** (1958), *Fortunate Strangers.* New York: Rinehart.

01142 **BEUKENKAMP, C.** (1956), Further developments of the transference life concept in therapeutic groups. *J. Hillside Hosp.*, 5:441-448.

01144 **BEUKENKAMP, C.** (1959), Identification in group psychotherapy. *Acta Psychother. Psychosomat. Orthopaedagog. Suppl.*, (Basel) 7:30-33.

01143 **BEUKENKAMP, C.** (1955), General remarks pertaining to the first two lectures (1954) by J. L. Moreno on transference and the unconscious. *Group Psychother., Psychodrama & Sociometry*, 8:78-89.

01145 **BEUKENKAMP, C.** (1963), (The importance of despair.) *Bibl. Psychiat. & Neurol.*, (Basel) 118:69-75.

01146 **BEUKENKAMP, C.** (1955), An indication for group psychotherapy. *J. Hillside Hosp.*, 4:93-98.

01147 **BEUKENKAMP, C.** (1955), The multidimensional orientation in analytic group therapy. *Amer. J. Psychother.*, 9:477-483.

01148 **BEUKENKAMP, C.** (1955), The nature of orality as revealed in group psychotherapy. *Internat. J. Group Psychother.*, 5:339-345.

01149 **BEUKENKAMP, C.** (1961), Parental suicide as a source of resistance to marriage. *Internat. J. Group Psychother.*, 11:204-208.

01150 **BEUKENKAMP, C.** (1952), Some observations made during group therapy. *Psychiat. Quart. Suppl.*, 26:22-26.

01151 **BEUKENKAMP, C.** (1958), Training in group psychotherapy: a symposium. *Amer. J. Psychother.*, 12:493-507.

01152 **BEUKENKAMP, C.** (1958), Graining in group psychotherapy: a symposium. (i) some of the values involved in training group psychotherapists. *Amer. J. Psychother.*, 12:493-495.

01153 **BEUTLER, L. E., JOBE, A. M.,** and **ELKINS, D.** (1974), Outcomes in group psychotherapy: using persuasion theory to increase treatment efficiency. *J. Consult. & Clin. Psychol.*, 42:547-553.

01154 **BEUTLER, L. E., ORO-BEUTLER, M. E.,** and **MITCHELL, R.** (1979), Systematic comparison of two parent training programs in child-management. *J. Couns. Psychol.*, 26:531-533.

01155 **BEVINS, S. M. C.** (1970), A comparison of the effectiveness of individual and group counseling in the improvement of social adjustment of fifth and sixth grade children. *Dissert. Abstr. Internat.*, 30:5277A.

01156 **BEY, D. R.** (1972), Group dynamics and the "F.N.G." in Vietnam: a potential focus of stress. *Internat. J. Group Psychother.*, 22:22-30.

01157 **BHATTACHARYYA, A., HICKS, S. E.,** and **STURGESS, P.** (1971), Some experiences in sociodrama in a county psychiatric hospital. *Internat. J. Soc. Psychiat.*, (London) 17:230-238.

01158 **BIASCI, G.** (1970), (Influence of psychotherapeutic activities on society.) *Riv. Sper. Freniatria*, (Emilia) 94:805-806.

01159 **BIASCO, F.,** and **REDFERING, D. L.** (1976), Effects of counselor supervision of group counseling: clients' perceived outcomes. *Counselor Educat. & Supervision*, 15:216-221.

01160 **BIASCO, F.,** and **REDFERING, D.** (1980), Group counseling with navy prisoners. *J. Special Group Work*, 5:15-19.

01161 **BIASE, D. V.,** and **De LEON, G.** (1969), The encounter group: measurement of some affect changes. *Proceed., 77th Annual Convention,* American Psychological Association, 4:497-498.

01162 **BIBERMAN, G.** (1978), Trainer behavior in a t-group setting: a survey of current practice. *Dissert. Abstr. Internat.*, 39:768A.

01163 **BIBERMAN, G.** (1979), Trainer behavior in a t-group setting. *Small Group Behav.*, 10:501-522.

01164 **BICE, H. V.,** and **HOLDEN, M. G. D.** (1949), Group counseling with mothers of children with cerebral palsy. *J. Soc. Casework*, 30:104-109.

01165 **BIEBER, T.** (1974), Group and individual psychotherapy with male homosexuals. *J. Amer. Acad. Psychoanal.*, 2:255-260.

01166 **BIEBER, T. B.** (1957), The emphasis on the individual in psychoanalytic group therapy. *Internat. J. Soc. Psychiat.*, (London) 2:275-280.

01167 **BIEBER, T. B.** (1965), Group psychotherapy today: case discussion. *Topical Probl. Psychol. & Psychother.*, 5:189-193.

01168 **BIEBER, T. B.** (1959), The individual and the group. *Amer. J. Psychother.*, 13:635-650.

01169 **BIEBER, T. B., CAPPON, D.,** and **DURKIN, H. E.** (1964), Discussion of papers presented at a symposium on combined individual and group psychotherapy. *Internat. J. Group Psychother.*, 14:433-454.

01170 **BIELE, H.** (1967), (Development of a plan for advancement of phase-retarded children during stationary therapy.) *Paediat. & Grenzgebiete*, (Berlin) 6:157-164.

01171 **BIELE, H.,** and **FARBER, H.** (1969), (Child guidance in pediatric psychiatry: group discussions with parents of behaviorally disturbed children in a special form of therapy.) *Psychiat., Neurol. & Med. Psychol.*, (Leipzig) 21:99-106.

01172 **BIER, E.** (1951), Experimental therapy with a group. *Focus*, 30:97-102.

01173 **BIERER, J.** (1954), Clubs de thérapie sociale. (Social therapy clubs.) *Hygiene Ment. Can.*, (Ottawa) 3:75-84.

01174 **BIERER, J.** (1959), Critical analysis of some concepts in present day group psychotherapy. *Acta Psychother., Psychosomat. & Orthopaedagog.*, (Basel) 7:110-118.

01175 **BIERER, J.** (1962), The day hospital: therapy in a guided democracy. *Ment. Hosp.*, 13:246-252.

01176 **BIERER, J.** (1955), Die therapeutischen social clubs. (Therapeutic social clubs.) *Zeit. Psychother. Med. Psychol.*, (Stuttgart) 5:58-64.

01177 **BIERER, J.** (1942), Group psychotherapy. *Br. Med. J.*, (London) 1:214-217.

01178 **BIERER, J.** (1948), Modern social and group therapy. In: *Modern Trends in Psychological Medicine*, ed. N. G. Harris. New York: Hoeber.

01179 **BIERER, J.** (1943), A new form of group psychotherapy. *Lancet*, 245:799-800.

01180 **BIERER, J.** (1944), A new form of group therapy. *Ment. Health*, (London) 5:23-26.

01181 **BIERER, J.** (1944), A new form of group psychotherapy. *Royal Soc. Med. Proceed.*, (London) 37:208-209.

01182 **BIERER, J.** (1940), Psychotherapy in mental hospital practice. *J. Ment. Science*, (London) 86:928-947.

01183 **BIERER, J.** (1948), *Therapeutic Social Clubs*. London: Lewis.

01184 **BIERER, J.** (1950), Thérapies collectives. (Group therapies.) *Psyché*, (Stuttgart) 5:633-639.

01185 **BIERER, J.,** and **BUCKMAN, J.** (1961), Marlborough night hospital, 2: treatment with LSD and group therapy. *Nursing Times*, (London) 57:637-639.

01186 **BIERMAN, R., CARKHUFF, R. R.,** and **SANTILLI, M.** (1972), Efficacy of empathic communication training groups for inner city preschool teachers and family workers. *J. Appl. Behav. Science*, 8:188-202.

01187 **BIERMANN, G.** (1967), Die rolle der mutter in der erziehungsberatung und psychotherapie des kindes: ii. (Mother's role in the child's educational counselling and psychotherapy: ii.) *Praxis Kinderpsychol. & Kinderpsychiat.*, (Goettingen) 16:295-298.

01188 **BIERMANN, G.** (1964), (Group therapy in children and adolescents with behavior disorders and their parents.) *Praxis Kinderpsychol. & Kinderpsychiat.*, (Goettingen) 13:40-47.

01189 **BIERSDORF, K. R.** (1958), The effectiveness of two group vocational guidance treatments. Unpublished doctoral dissertation, University of Maryland.

01190 **BIFERNO, K. G.** (1978), A comparison of the effects of cognitive developmental and Adlerian parent education groups on parental expectation, parental acceptance, and parental acceptance as perceived by children. *Dissert. Abstr. Internat.*, 38:4999B-5000B. (University Microfilms No. 7802818.)

01191 **BIGGS, B. E., FELTON, G. S.,** and **HIRSCH, B. T.** (1976), Contract groups and transition groups: a working formula for a weekend retreat. *Psychother.: Theory, Res., & Pract.*, 13:384-386.

01192 **BIKALES, V. W.** (1949), Drama therapy at Winter Veterans Administration Hospital: a preliminary report. *Bull. Menninger Clinic*, 13:127-133.

01193 **BIKALES, V. W., EBERT, G., WEIL, R.,** and **HOWE, L. P.** (1952), The effects of leadership upon morale in a group therapeutic setting. *Bull. Menninger Clinic*, 16:202-210.

01194 **BILL, A. Z.** (1958), The development of sociometry, psychodrama, and group psychotherapy in Turkey. *Group Psychother., Psychodrama & Sociometry*, 11:341-342.

01195 **BILLER, H. B.,** and **SMITH, A. E.** (1972), An AFDC mothers' group: an exploratory effort in community mental health. *Fam. Coordinator*, 21:287-290.

01196 **BILLINGS, A. G., McDOWELL, S. W., GOMBERG, C. A., KESSLER, M.,** and **WEINER, S.** (1978), Validity of time-sampling in group interactions. *J. Soc. Psychol.*, 104:223-230.

01197 **BILLINGS, J. H.** (1974), Observations on long-term group therapy with suicidal and depressed persons. *Life-Threatening Behav.*, 4:160-170.

01198 **BILLINGSLEY, P.** (1977), Sex bias in psychotherapy: an examination of the effects of client sex, client pathology, and therapist sex on treatment planning. *J. Consult. & Clin. Psychol.*, 45:250-256.

01199 **BILLS, L. E.** (1976), The development and validation of an instrument to measure the attitudes of women toward joining a consciousness-raising group. *Dissert. Abstr. Internat.*, 36:5338B.

01200 **BILLS, R. E.** (1950), Play therapy with well-adjusted retarded readers. *J. Consult. & Clin. Psychol.*, 14:246-249.

01201 **BILLUPS, F. H.** (1970), Comparative effects of orientation by group counseling and group guidance on the adjustment, attitudes, and achievement of foundation students in a community college. *Dissert. Abstr. Internat.*, 31:4449A.

01202 **BILODEAU, C. B.,** and **HACKETT, T. P.** (1971), Issues raised in a group setting by patients recovering from myocardial infarction. *Amer. J. Psychiat.*, 128:73-78.

01203 **BILODEAU, C. B.,** and **HACKETT, T. P.** (1975), Issues raised in a group setting by patients recovering from myocardial infarction. In: *Group Psychotherapy and Group Function*, 2d ed., eds. M. Rosenbaum and M. M. Berger. New York: Basic Books.

01204 **BILON, L. R.** (1967), Improving children's creative thinking through group discussion treatment of mothers: an experimental study of the impact of group discussion on maternal attitudes and on children's creative thinking. *Dissert. Abstr. Internat.*, 28:261B.

01205 **BINDELGLAS, P. M.,** and **GOSLINE, E.** (1957), Differential reactions of patients receiving group psychotherapy with concomitant somatic and drug therapies. *Internat. J. Group Psychother.*, 7:275-280.

01206 **BINDER, H.** (1969), (Group psychotherapy aspects in conducting autogenic training with patients suffering from seizures, especially patients

with brain injuries and epileptics.) *Zeit. Allgemeinmed,* (Stuttgart) 45:407-408.
01207 **BINDER, H.** (1966), *Seminar uber Gruppentherapie mit dem Autogenen Training.* (*Seminar on Group Therapy with Autogenic Training.*) Munich: J. F. Lehmann.
01208 **BINDER, H.** (1960), Le training autogène dans la pratique courante et chez les traumatises du crâne. (Autogenous training in current practice and in brain damaged patients.) *Evolut. Psychiat.,* (Toulouse) 25:617-622.
01209 **BINDER, J.** (1976), A method for small group training of psychiatric ward staff. *Psychiatry,* 39:364-375.
01210 **BINDER, S.** (1971), (New approaches to the treatment of alcoholics.) *Zeit. Psychother. Med. Psychol.,* (Stuttgart) 21:239.
01211 **BINDRAM, P.** (1980), Group therapy: protecting privacy. *Psychol. Today,* 14:24-33.
01212 **BINDRIM, P.** (1969), Nudity as a quick grab for intimacy in group therapy. *Psychol. Today,* 3:24-28.
01213 **BINDRIM, P.** (1968), A report on a nude marathon: the effect of physical nudity upon the practice of interaction in the marathon group. *Psychother.: Theory, Res. & Pract.,* 5:180-188.
01214 **BINES, J.,** and **MASTERSON, P.** (1978), The effect of pregnancy on patients receiving group therapy. *Nursing Times,* (London) 74:1220-1221.
01215 **BINGHAM, M. D.** (1978), The effects of Adlerian group counseling on goal-oriented behavior and adjustment of children in a parochial high school. *Dissert. Abstr. Internat.,* 36:5920A.
01216 **BINLEY, E. C.** (1977), Group psychotherapy with persons on probation who have had alcohol related offenses. *Dissert. Abstr. Internat.,* 39:5537B.
01217 **BINOT, E.** (1973), (Group therapy for hospitalized drug addicts: review of four years of experience.) *Toxicomanies,* (Quebec) 5:31-45.
01218 **BION, W. R.** (1948), Advances in group and individual therapy. In: *International Congress on Mental Health, Vol. 3,* Proceed., International Conference on Medical Psychotherapy. ed. J. C. Flugel. New York: Columbia University Press.
01219 **BION, W. R.** (1975), *Attention and Interpretation.* London: Tavistock Publications.
01220 **BION, W. R.** (1970), *Attention and Interpretation: A Scientific Approach to Insight in Psycho-Analysis and Groups.* London: Tavistock Publications.
01221 **BION, W. R.** (1948), Experiences in groups: i. *Human Relat.,* 1:314-320.
01222 **BION, W. R.** (1948), Experiences in groups: ii. *Human Relat.,* 1:487-496.
01223 **BION, W. R.** (1949), Experiences in groups: iii. *Human Relat.,* 2:13-22.
01224 **BION, W. R.** (1949), Experiences in groups: iv. *Human Relat.,* 2:295-303.
01225 **BION, W. R.** (1950), Experiences in groups: v. *Human Relat.,* 3:3-14.
01226 **BION, W. R.** (1950), Experiences in groups: vi. *Human Relat.,* 3:395-402.
01227 **BION, W. R.** (1951), Experiences in groups: vii. *Human Relat.,* 4:221-227.
01228 **BION, W. R.** (1961), *Experiences in Groups and Other Papers.* London: Tavistock Publications.
01229 **BION, W. R.** (1974), *Experiences in Groups and Other Papers.* New York: Ballantine.
01230 **BION, W. R.** (1961), *Experiences in Groups and Other Papers.* New York: Basic Books.
01231 **BION, W. R.** (1946), The leaderless group project. *Bull. Menninger Clinic,* 10:77-81.
01232 **BION, W. R.,** and **RICKMAN, J.** (1943), Intra-group tensions in therapy: their study as a task of the group. *Lancet,* 245:678-681.
01233 **BIRD, J. R.** (1980), Group approaches and army health. *Royal Army Med. Corps J.,* (Liverpool) 126:112-119.

01234 **BIRD, J. R.** (1980), A method of brief group psychotherapy. *Royal Army Med. Corps J.*, (Liverpool) 126:120-127.
01235 **BIRDWHISTELL, R. L.** (1963), Research in the structure of group psychotherapy. *Internat. J. Group Psychother.*, 13:485-493.
01236 **BIRK, L.** (1974), Group psychotherapy for men who are homosexual. *J. Sex & Marital Ther.*, 1:27-52.
01237 **BIRK, L.** (1974), Intensive group therapy: an effective behavioral-psychoanalytic method. *Amer. J. Psychiat.*, 131:11-16.
01238 **BIRK, L.** (1980), Intensive group therapy: effective behavioral-psychoanalytic method. In: *Interface between the Psychodynamic and Behavioral Therapies*, eds. J. Marmor and S. M. Woods. New York: Plenum.
01239 **BIRK, L.**, and **BRINKLEY-BIRK, A. W.** (1974), Psychoanalysis and behavior therapy. *Amer. J. Psychiat.*, 131:499-510.
01240 **BIRK, L., MILLER, E.**, and **COHLER, B.** (1970), Group psychotherapy for homosexual men by male-female cotherapists. *Acta Psychiat. Scand. Suppl.*, 218:1.
01241 **BIRKETT, O. P.**, and **BOLTVICH, B.** (1973), Remotivation therapy. *J. Amer. Geriat. Soc.*, 21:368-371.
01242 **BISCHOF, L. J.** (1966), Are we climbing Jacob's ladder? *Group Psychother., Psychodrama & Sociometry*, 19:10-16.
01243 **BISHOP, D. W.** (1968), Group member adjustment as related to interpersonal and task success and affiliation and achievement motives. *Dissert. Abstr. Internat.*, 28:3259-3260.
01244 **BISHOP, J. H.** (1978), Comparative effects of cognitive and affective group counseling on self-esteem of second grade students. *Dissert. Abstr. Internat.*, 38:3948A.
01245 **BISTER, W.**, and **LINNEMANN, F.** (1974), (Changing planes of interaction in group therapy for schizophrenics.) *Psychother. & Med. Psychol.*, (Stuttgart) 24:215-224.
01246 **BITNER, J. A.** (1972), Diabetes, self-concept, and the encounter group: a pilot study using phenomenological analysis and the Tennessee Self Concept Scale. *Dissert. Abstr. Internat.*, 33:1264B.
01247 **BIXBY, F. L.** (1965), The group psychotherapy movement since 1932: a look backwards and forward. *Group Psychother., Psychodrama & Sociometry*, 18:6-10.
01248 **BIXBY, F. L.**, and **McCORKLE, L. W.** (1950), Applying the principles of group therapy in correctional institutions. *Fed. Probat.*, 14:36-40.
01249 **BIXBY, F. L.**, and **McCORKLE, L. W.** (1951), Guided group interaction in correctional work. *Amer. Sociol. Rev.*, 16:455-461.
01250 **BIXBY, F. L.**, and **McCORKLE, L. W.** (1948), A recorded presentation of a program of guided group interaction in New Jersey correctional institutions. *Proceed. Amer. Prison Assn.*, 190-199.
01251 **BJERSTEDT, A.** (1959), Controlling value judgements in group therapy. an experimental approach to the intervening link between sociometric description and therapeutic action. *Acta Psychother., Psychosomat. Orthopaedagog. Suppl.*, (Basel) 7:34-47.
01252 **BJERSTEDT, A.** (1956), The dynamics of the moment: ontogenetic conserves in the warming-up to a new situation. *Internat. J. Soc. Psychiat.*, (London) 1:100-108.
01253 **BLACHLY, P. H., PEPPER, B., SCOTT, W.**, and **BAGANZ, P.** (1961), Group therapy and hospitalization of narcotic addicts. *Arch. Gen. Psychiat.*, 5:393-396.
01254 **BLACK, J.** (1967), Group therapy of parents who have children in residential or day care psychiatric treatment. *J. Asthma Res.*, 4:251-252.
01255 **BLACK, J. C.** (1976), Review of S. R. Slavson's and M. Schiffer's *Group Psychotherapies for Children. Psychiat. Annals*, 6:100.

01256 **BLACK, J. M.** (1972), The marathon as an adjunct to ongoing group process. *Dissert. Abstr. Internat.*, 32:4852B.
01257 **BLACK, S.** (1972), Group therapy for pregnant and nonpregnant adolescents. *Child Welfare*, 51:514-518.
01258 **BLACKER, K. H.** (1962), Group psychotherapy in the treatment of acute emotional disorders. *Internat. J. Group Psychother.*, 13:365-369.
01259 **BLACKHURST, A. E.** (1966), Sociodrama for the adolescent mentally retarded. *Training School Bull.*, 63:136-142.
01260 **BLACKMAN, N.** (1959), Changing community attitudes toward social maladjustment through group psychotherapeutic techniques. *Acta Psychother. Psychosomat. Orthopaedagog. Suppl.*, (Basel) 7:47-55.
01261 **BLACKMAN, N.** (1950), Group psychotherapy with aphasics. *J. Nerv. & Ment. Diseases*, 111:154-163.
01262 **BLACKMAN, N.** (1948), Sequelae of military service and their treatment in a Veterans Administration mental hygiene clinic. *J. Missouri Med. Assn.*, 45:579-582.
01263 **BLACKMAN, N. W.** (1940), Experiences with a library club in the group treatment of schizophrenia. *Occupat. Ther. & Rehab.*, 19:293-305.
01264 **BLACKMAN, N. W.** (1948), Psychotherapy in a Veterans Administration mental hygiene clinic. *Psychiat. Quart.*, 22:89-102.
01265 **BLACKMAN, N. W.** (1942), Ward treatment: a new method of group psychotherapy. *Psychiat. Quart.*, 16:660-667.
01266 **BLAIN, D.** (1948), Advances in group and individual therapy. In: *International Congress on Mental Health, Vol. 3*, Proceed., International Conference on Medical Psychotherapy. ed. J. C. Flugel. New York: Columbia University Press.
01267 **BLAIR, D.** (1943), Group psychotherapy of war neuroses. *Lancet*, 244:204-205.
01268 **BLAIR, D. A. S.** (1955), The therapeutic social club: an important measure of social rehabilitation in the treatment of psychiatric cases. *Ment. Hygiene*, 39:54-62.
01269 **BLAIR, D.**, and **BROOKING, M.** (1957), Music as a therapeutic agent. *Ment. Hygiene*, 41:228-237.
01270 **BLAKE, A.** (1976), Group approach to weight control: behavior modification, nutrition, and health education. *J. Amer. Dietetic Assn.*, 69:645-649.
01271 **BLAKE, R.** (1980), The group matrix. *Group Analysis*, (London) 13:177-183.
01272 **BLAKE, R. R.** (1958), Comments on "code of ethics of group psychotherapists." *Group Psychother., Psychodrama & Sociometry*, 11:356-360.
01273 **BLAKE, R. R.** (1955), Experimental psychodrama with children. *Group Psychother., Psychodrama & Sociometry*, 8:347-350.
01274 **BLAKE, R. R.** (1957), Group training vs. group therapy. *Group Psychother., Psychodrama & Sociometry*, 10:271-276.
01275 **BLAKE, R. R.** (1958), *Group Training vs. Group Therapy*. New York: Beacon House.
01276 **BLAKE, R. R.** (1953), The interaction feeling hypothesis applied to psychotherapy groups. *Sociometry*, 16:253-265.
01277 **BLAKE, R. R.** (1955), Transference and tele viewed from the standpoint of therapy and training. *Group Psychother., Psychodrama & Sociometry*, 8:178-179.
01278 **BLAKE, R. R.** (1955), The treatment of relational conflict by individual, group and interpersonal methods. *Group Psychother., Psychodrama & Sociometry*, 8:182-185.
01279 **BLAKE, R. R.**, and **MOUTON, J. H.** (1961), *Group Dynamics*. Houston: Gulf.

01280 **BLAKE, R. R.**, and **MOUTON, J. S.** (1956), Human relations problem areas in work. *Group Psychother., Psychodrama & Sociometry*, 9:253-264.

01281 **BLAKE, R. R.**, and **MOUTON, J. S.** (1956), Perspectives on housing architectures and social interaction. *Internat. J. Soc. Psychiat.*, (London) 1:95-98.

01282 **BLAKE, R. R., MOUTON, J. S.**, and **SLOMA, R. L.** (1965), The union-management inter-group laboratory. *J. Appl. Behav. Science*, 1:25-57.

01283 **BLAKEMAN, J. D.** (1967), The effects of activity group counseling on behavior problem boys. *Dissert. Abstr. Internat.*, 28:2066A.

01284 **BLAKENEY, P. M.**, and **CRESON, D. L.** (1970), Status and stability in an adolescent milieu patient group. *Diseases Nerv. System*, 31:756-762.

01285 **BLAKER, K. E.**, and **SAMO, J.** (1973), Communications games: a group counseling technique. *School Counselor*, 21:46-51.

01286 **BLANCHARD, E. R.**, and **MILLER, S. T.** (1977), Psychological treatment of cardiovascular disease. *Arch. Gen. Psychiat.*, 34:1402-1413.

01287 **BLANCHARD, F. A., WEIGEL, R. H.**, and **COOK, S. W.** (1975), The effect of relative competence of group members upon interpersonal attraction in cooperating interracial groups. *J. Personality & Soc. Psychol.*, 32:519-530.

01288 **BLANCHARD, W. H.** (1970), Ecstasy without agony is baloney. *Psychol. Today*, 3:8-10, 64.

01289 **BLANCHETTE, M.** (1973), (Function of a multidisciplinarian mini-team in the treatment of drug addiction.) *Infirmiere Can.*, (Ottawa) 15:12-16.

01290 **BLAND, J. R.** (1975), The effects of focused feedback on counseling groups. *Dissert. Abstr. Internat.*, 36:2015A.

01291 **BLANE, H.** (1972), Leadership training program in alcoholism: comment. *Amer. J. Orthopsychiat.*, 42:314-315.

01292 **BLANK, H.** (1975), Crisis consultation. *Internat. J. Soc. Psychiat.*, (London) 21:179-189.

01293 **BLANK, L.** (1971), *Confrontation*. New York: Macmillan.

01294 **BLANK, L.** (1971), The uses and abuses of encounter groups. *Group Process*, (London) 4:106-116.

01295 **BLANK, L., GOTTSEGEN, G. B.**, and **GOTTSEGEN, M. G.** (1971), *Confrontation: Encounters in Self and Interpersonal Awareness*. New York: Macmillan.

01296 **BLANK, L.** (1972), The value of intense encounters in interactional group process training. *Compar. Group Studies*, 3:51-76.

01297 **BLANKENBERG, W.** (1969), Dances in the therapy of schizophrenics. Relation between mannerism and schizophrenic mannerism. *Psychother. & Psychosomat.*, (Basel) 17:336-342.

01298 **BLASI, A.** (1971), A developmental approach to responsibility training. *Dissert. Abstr. Internat.*, 32:1233B.

01299 **BLATNER, H.** (1968), (Comments on some commonly held reservations about psychodrama.) *Bull. de Psychol.*, (Paris) 23:957-968.

01300 **BLATNER, H. A.** (1973), *Acting-in: Practical Applications of Psychodramatic Methods*. New York: Springer.

01301 **BLATT, A.** (1957), Group therapy with parents of severely retarded children: a preliminary report. *Group Psychother., Psychodrama & Sociometry*, 10:133-140.

01302 **BLAU, D.**, and **ZILBACH, J.** (1954), The use of group psychotherapy in posthospitalization treatment. *Amer. J. Psychiat.*, 111:244-247.

01303 **BLAU, H. J.** (1977), (Group talks with parents of leukemic children.) *Kinderaerztliche Praxis*, (Leipzig) 45:278-280.

01304 **BLAY NETO, B.** (1966), Aspectos de contratransferencia em grupo. (Some aspects of group counter-transference.) *Rev. Psicol. Normal & Patol.*, (Sao Paulo) 12:436-440.

01305 **BLAY NETO, B.** (1966), Conceito de interpretacao grupal. (Meaning of group interpretation.) *Rev. Psicol. Normal & Patol.*, (Sao Paulo) 12:25-31.

01306 **BLAY NETO, B.** (1966), Frequency of sessions in group psychotherapy. *Rev. Psicol. Normal & Patol.*, (Sao Paulo) 12:419-423.

01307 **BLAY NETO, B.** (1968), (Frequency of sessions in group psychotherapy.) *Rev. Paulista Med.*, (Sao Paulo) 72:18-22.

01308 **BLAY NETO, B.** (1969), (The masking of group fantasy performance.) *Zeit. Psychosomat. Med. & Psychoanal.*, 15:277-282.

01309 **BLAY NETO, B.** (1966), (Meaning of group interpretation.) *Rev. Psicol. Normal & Patol.*, (Sao Paulo) 12:25-31.

01310 **BLAY NETO, B.** (1965), (Some aspects of countertransference in the group.) *J. Brasil. Psiquiat.*, (Rio de Janeiro) 14:235-243.

01311 **BLAY NETO, B.** (1971), Some aspects of countertransference in group psychotherapy. *Internat. J. Group Psychother.*, 21:95-98.

01312 **BLAY NETO, B.** (1959), (Technical aspects of group psychotherapy.) *Arq. Neuro-Psiquiat.*, (Sao Paulo) 17:285-296.

01313 **BLAYA, M.** (1966), (The treatment of psychotic patients through group psychoanalysis.) *J. Brasil. Psiquiat.*, (Rio de Janeiro) 15:33-52.

01314 **BLAYA, P. M.** (1968), (Hospital group practice.) *Arch. Neurobiol.*, (Madrid) 31:249-260.

01315 **BLAYLOCK, M. E. W.** (1979), Variables predictive of success in treatment of obesity by group hypnotherapy. *Dissert. Abstr. Internat.*, 40:5801B.

01316 **BLAYLOCK, M. E. W.** (1980), Variables predictive of success in treatment of obesity by group hypnotherapy. *Dissert. Abstr. Internat.*, 40:5801B. (University Microfilms No. 8012152.)

01317 **BLAŽEVIC, D.** (1966), Psihodinamika rada u grupamaz. (Psychodynamics of group therapy.) *Lijecnicki Vjesnik*, (Zagreb) 88:837-838.

01318 **BLAZEVIC, D.** (1966), Psychodynamics of group work. *J. Med.*, 88:75-77.

01319 **BLAZEVIC, D.**, and **JOVIC, N.** (1972), The position of the psychotherapist in group psychotherapy as seen by the therapist himself. *Psychother. & Psychosomat.*, (Basel) 20:169-171.

01320 **BLEANDONU, G.** (1970), *Les Communautés Thérapeutiques. (The Therapeutic Communities.)* Paris: Éditions de Scarabée.

01321 **BLECK, R. T.** (1978), Developmental group counseling using a structured play with elementary school disruptive children. *Dissert. Abstr. Internat.*, 38:3949A.

01322 **BLEDSOE, J. C.**, and **LAYSER, G. R.** (1977), Effects of human relations training with houseparents on attainment of group facilitation skills. *Psychol. Reports*, 40:787-791.

01323 **BLOCH, C.** (1962), Psychothérapie par groupes de discussion chez des malades mentaux hospitalisés. (Psychotherapy through group discussion with hospitalized mental patients.) *Acta Neurol. & Psychiat. Belgica*, (Brussels) 62:264-278.

01324 **BLOCH, D. A.** (1976), Family therapy: group therapy. *Internat. J. Group Psychother.*, 26:289-299.

01325 **BLOCH, G.** (1959), Remarks on psychotherapeutic activities in Israel. *Internat. J. Group Psychother.*, 9:303-307.

01326 **BLOCH, H. S.** (1968), An open-ended crisis-oriented group for the poor who are sick. *Arch. Gen. Psychiat.*, 18:178-185.

01327 **BLOCH, J.** (1970), A preschool workshop for emotionally disturbed children. *Children*, 17:10-14.

01328 **BLOCH, S.** (1979), A method for the study of therapeutic factors in group psychotherapy. *Brit. J. Psychiat.*, (Ashford) 134:257-263.

01329 **BLOCH, S.** (1979), Review of H. Mullan's and M. Rosenbaum's *Group Psychotherapy: Theory and Practice. Brit. J. Psychiat.*, (Ashford) 135:184.

01330 **BLOCH, S.** (1980), Review of S. R. Slavson's and M. Schiffer's *Dynamics of Group Psychotherapy. Brit. J. Psychiat.*, (Ashford) 136:605.
01331 **BLOCH, S.** (1979), Review of J. S. Whiteley's and J. Gordon's *Group Approaches. Brit. J. Psychiat.*, (Ashford) 135:184.
01332 **BLOCH, S., BOND, G., QUALLS, B., YALOM, I.,** and **ZIMMERMAN, E.** (1976), Patients' expectations of therapeutic improvement and their outcomes. *Amer. J. Psychiat.*, 133:1457-1460.
01333 **BLOCH, S., BROWN, S., DAVIS, K.,** and **DISHOTSKY, N.** (1975), The use of a written summary in group psychotherapy supervision. *Amer. J. Psychiat.*, 132:1055-1057.
01334 **BLOCH, S.,** and **REIBSTEIN, J.** (1980), Perceptions by patients and therapists of therapeutic factors in group psychotherapy. *Brit. J. Psychiat.*, (Ashford) 137:274-278.
01335 **BLOCK, A. M.** (1979), (The person-centered method and its application in the resolution of social problems: A contribution from humanistic psychology.) *Ensenanza & Investig. Psicol.*, (Mexico City) 5:405-409.
01336 **BLOCK, J. D.** (1970), A comparison of the verbal interaction in counseling groups differing in member interpersonal compatibility. *Dissert. Abstr. Internat.*, 32:780A.
01337 **BLOCK, S. L.** (1961), Multi-leadership as a teaching and therapeutic tool in group psychotherapy. *Comprehens. Psychiat.*, 2:211-218.
01338 **BLOCK, S. L.** (1969), Notes on regression in groups. *Comprehens. Psychiat.*, 10:128-135.
01339 **BLOCK, S. L.** (1966), Some notes on transference in group psychotherapy. *Comprehens. Psychiat.*, 7:31-38.
01340 **BLOHM, A. L.** (1978), Group counseling with moderately mentally retarded and learning disabled elementary school children. *Dissert. Abstr. Internat.*, 39:3367A.
01341 **BLOLAND, P. A.** (1967), *Student Group Advising in Higher Education.* Washington, D.C.: American Personnel and Guidance Association.
01342 **BLOMFIELD, O. A.** (1972), Group: the more primitive psychology? a review of some paradigms in group dynamics. *Austral. & New Zeal. J. Psychiat.*, (Carlton) 6:238-246.
01343 **BLOOM, J.,** and **WINOKUR, M.** (1972), Stability and variability of seat preference in a therapy group: their relationship to patient behavior. *Psychiatry*, 35:78-87.
01344 **BLOOM, L. M.** (1962), A rationale for group treatment of aphasic patients. *J. Speech & Hearing Disorders*, 27:11-16.
01345 **BLOOM, N. D.** (1979), Group work in a hospital waiting room. *Health & Soc. Work*, 4:48.
01346 **BLOOM, V.** (1977), Bioenergetics in group psychotherapy. *Group*, 1:172-183.
01347 **BLOOM, V.,** and **DOBIE, S. I.** (1969), The effect of observers on the process of group therapy. *Internat. J. Group Psychother.*, 19:79-87.
01348 **BLOOMBERG, P.,** and **BLOOMBERG, L. I.** (1969), Using intensive groups for developing community. *Voices*, 5:60-67.
01349 **BLOOMBURG, L. I.** (1969), The intensive group as a founding experience. *J. Human Psychol.*, 9:93-99.
01350 **BLOTCKY, M. J., SHEINBEIN, M., WIGGINS, K. M.,** and **FORGOTSON, J. H.** (1980), A verbal group technique for ego-disturbed children: action to words. *Internat. J. Psychoanal. Psychother.*, 8:203-232.
01351 **BLOUIN, G. A.** (1973), (Beyond pharmacotherapy.) *Union Med. Can.*, (Montreal) 102:2308-2313.
01352 **BLOYER, R. O.** (1966), The effects of group counseling with a college disciplinary problem. *Dissert. Abstr. Internat.*, 27:944A.

01353 **BLUM, M.** (1954), Group dynamics in industry. *Internat. J. Group Psychother.*, 4:172-176.

01354 **BLUMBERG, A.** (1971), *Sensitivity Training: Processes, Problems and Applications*. Syracuse: Syracuse University Continuing Education.

01355 **BLUMBERG, A.** (1972), Teachers and managers: some differential effects of sensitivity training. *Interpersonal Develop.*, 2:246-254.

01356 **BLUMBERG, A.**, and **GOLEMBIEWSKI, R. T.** (1976), *Learning and Change in Groups*. New York: Penguin.

01357 **BLUMBERG, M. L.** (1979), Collateral therapy for the abused child and the problem parent. *Amer. J. Psychother.*, 3:339.

01358 **BLUMBERG, R. W.**, and **LOCKHART-MUMMERY, L.** (1972), Training groups and professional training for mental health workers. *Psychol. Reports*, 30:379-382.

01359 **BLUME, S. B.** (1978), Group psychotherapy in the treatment of alcoholism. In: *Practical Approaches to Alcoholism Psychotherapy*, eds. S. Zimberg, J. Wallace and S. B. Blime. New York: Plenum Press.

01360 **BLUME, S. B.** (1971), Group role reversal as a teaching technique in an alcoholism rehabilitation unit. *Group Psychother., Psychodrama & Sociometry*, 24:135-137.

01361 **BLUMENFELD, H.** (1973), Group treatment with parents of outpatients: an experiment. *J. Bronx State Hosp.*, pp. 173-176.

01362 **BLUMENTHAL, R.** (1966), Sociometric choice patterns in outpatient schizophrenics. *Internat. J. Soc. Psychiat.*, (London) 12:279-282.

01363 **BLURTON, R. R.** (1969), Effects of group behavior therapy imagery on basketball performance. *Dissert. Abstr. Internat.*, 29:3476B.

01364 **BLYTH, Z.** (1969), Group treatment for handicapped children. *J. Psychiat. Nursing*, 7:172-173.

01365 **BLYTHE, P. W.** (1971), Considerations for design of college student t-group. *Can. Counselor*, (Ottawa) 5:153-160.

01366 **BLYTHE, P. W.** (1975), Silence is golden. *Can. Counselor*, (Ottawa) 9:69-70.

01367 **BOARD, C., KING, J., TIERNEY, A. M.**, and **LICHTENBERG, P.** (1959), Time perspective and intimacy: their effect on patient behavior in occupational therapy. *Arch. Gen. Psychiat.*, 1:425-433.

01368 **BOBBIS, B. R., HARRISON, R. M.**, and **TRAUB, L.** (1955), Activity group therapy. *Amer. J. Occupat. Ther.*, 9:19-21, 50.

01369 **BOBROFF, A. J.** (1962), Biblical psychodrama. *Group Psychother., Psychodrama & Sociometry*, 15:129-131.

01370 **BOBROFF, A. J.** (1963), Religious psychodrama. *Group Psychother., Psychodrama & Sociometry*, 16:36-38.

01371 **BOCHNER, A. O.**, and **YERBY, J.** (1977), Factors affecting instruction in interpersonal competence. *Comment on Educat.*, (Toronto) 26:91-104.

01372 **BOCHNER, A. P., DISALVO, V.**, and **JONAS, T.** (1975), A computer-assisted analysis of small group process: an investigation of two machiavellian groups. *Small Group Behav.*, 6:187-203.

01373 **BOCK, J. C.** (1975), Psychology and medicine: rehabilitation of the industrially injured. *Ontario Psychologist*, (Toronto) 7:24-25.

01374 **BOCK, J. C.** (1961), Self-orientation and orientation to others during non-directive group psychotherapy. *Med. Serv. J.*, 17:111-117.

01375 **BOCK, J. C., LEWIS, D. J.**, and **TUCK, J.** (1954), Role-divided, three-cornered therapy. *Psychiatry*, 17:277-282.

01376 **BODENHEIMER, J. T.** (1978), (Experiences in group-therapy with discharged soldiers.) *Gruppenpsychother. & Gruppendynam.*, (Goettingen) 13:364-373.

01377 **BODERMAN, A., FREED, D. W.**, and **KINNUCAN, M. T.** (1972), "Touch me like me": testing an encounter group assumption. *J. Appl. Behav. Science*, 8:527-533.

01378 **BÖDIKER, M.-L.**, and **LANGE, W. H.** (1975), *Gruppendynamische Trainingsformen: Techniken, Fallbeisp., Auswirkungen im Krit. Überblick.* Reinbek bei Hamburg, Germany: Rowohlt.

01379 **BODIN, A. M.** (1969), Videotape applications in training family therapists. *J. Nerv. & Ment. Diseases*, 148:251-261.

01380 **BODWIN, R. F.** (1954), The use of psychodrama in the psychiatric clinic. *Group Psychother., Psychodrama & Sociometry,* 6:222-226.

01381 **BOE, E. E., GOCKA, E. F.**, and **KOGAN, W. S.** (1966), The effect of group psychotherapy on interpersonal perceptions of psychiatric patients. *Multivar. Behav. Res.*, 1:177-187.

01382 **BOEHRINGER, G. H., ZERUOLIS, V., BAYLEY, J.**, and **BOEHRINGER, K.** (1974), Stirling: the destructive application of group techniques to a conflict. *J. Confl. Resolut.*, 18:257-275.

01383 **BOENHEIM, C.** (1959), The closing of a group. *Acta Psychother. Psychosomat. Orthopaedagog. Suppl.*, (Basel) 7:56-61.

01384 **BOENHEIM, C.** (1963), Dynamic doctor groups as a training method for group psychotherapy. *Ment. Hygiene*, 47:84-88.

01385 **BOENHEIM, C.** (1959), A follow-up study of group psychotherapy patients. *Internat. J. Group Psychother.*, 9:463-474.

01386 **BOENHEIM, C.** (1959), Group psychotherapy with adolescents. *Internat. J. Group Psychother.*, 7:398-405.

01387 **BOENHEIM, C.** (1957), Gruppen-psychotherapie bei jugendlichen. (Group psychotherapy with adolescents.) *Praxis Kinderpsychol. & Kinderpsychiat.*, (Goettingen) 6:21-24; *Internat. J. Group Psychother.*, 7:398.

01388 **BOENHEIM, C.** (1965), Group therapy for personnel. *Ment. Hosp.*, 16:242-244.

01389 **BOENHEIM, C.** (1966), Music and group therapy. *J. Music Ther.*, 3:49-52.

01390 **BOENHEIM, C.** (1967), New developments in hospital group psychotherapy. *Psychother. & Psychosomat.*, (Basel) 15:10.

01391 **BOENHEIM, C.** (1971), Some reflections about contemporary dynamic psychotherapy. *Internat. J. Group Psychother.*, 21:239-243.

01392 **BOENHEIM, C.**, and **DILLON, L. O.** (1962), Group psychotherapy in the mental hospital. *Ment. Hosp.*, 13:380-381.

01393 **BOER, A. K.**, and **LANTZ, J. E.** (1974), Adolescent group therapy membership selection. *Clin. Soc. Work J.*, 2:172.

01394 **BOETTCHER, H.** (1961), (Variants in the use of autogenic training.) *Deutsche Gesundh.*, (Berlin) 16:708-715.

01395 **BOFSKY, R. B.** (1970), Learning from group experience: an analysis of the experiential structure of therapeutic dialogue. *Dissert. Abstr. Internat.*, 31:389.

01396 **BOGARDUS, E. S.** (1936), The use of sociodrama in teaching sociology. *Sociometry*, 18:542-547.

01397 **BOGDANOFF, M.**, and **ELBAUM, P. L.** (1978), Role lock: dealing with monopolizers, mistrusters, isolates, helpful hannahs, and other assorted characters in group-psychotherapy. *Internat. J. Group Psychother.*, 28:247-262.

01398 **BOGLIOLO, C.**, and **BACHERINI, A. M.** (1977), *Terapia Familiare e Psichiatria di Territorio.* Firenze: Uncini Pierucci.

01399 **BOGUSLAW, R.**, and **BACH, G. R.** (1959), Work culture management in industry: a role for the social science consultant. *Group Psychother., Psychodrama & Sociometry*, 12:134-142.

01400 **BOHM, K. H.** (1970), Group behavior and freedom of movement as measured by locus of reinforcement control and time orientation. *Dissert. Abstr. Internat.*, 30:3381B.

01401 **BOISEN, A. T.** (1954), Group therapy: the Elgin plan. *Pastoral Psychol.*, 5:33-38.
01402 **BOISEN, A. T.** (1948), The service of worship in a mental hospital: its therapeutic significance. *J. Clin. & Pastoral Soc. Work*, 1:19-25.
01403 **BOISSET, J.** (1955), Le psychodrama. (Psychodrama.) *Science & Vie*, (Paris) 88:26-118.
01404 **BOJANIN, S.** (1973), (A mental-hygiene approach to adolescence.) *Anali Zavoda Ment. Zdrovlge*, 5:105-116.
01405 **BOJANIN, S.**, and **MIHALJEVIĆ, K.** (1975), (Group therapy with teachers: group education.) *Anali Zavoda Ment. Zdravlge*, 7:49-56.
01406 **BOJANOVSKY, J.**, and **CHOLOUPKOVA, K.** (1964), Activating training in the treatment of depressions. *Activ. Nerv. Superior*, (Prague) 6:101-102.
01407 **BOJANOVSKY, J.** (1968), Single administration of diazepam in group psychotherapy. *Activ. Nerv. Superior*, (Prague) 10:260-261, 263.
01408 **BOLAN, S. L.** (1973), A study exploring two different approaches to encounter groups: the combination of verbal encounter and designed nonverbal activity only. *Dissert. Abstr. Internat.*, 33:6070B.
01409 **BOLEN, D. W.** (1968), Treatment of compulsive gambling. *Lancet*, 1:1253-1258.
01410 **BOLES, G.** (1959), Simultaneous group therapy with cerebral palsied children and their parents. *Internat. J. Group Psychother.*, 9:488-495.
01411 **BOIES, K. G.** (1972), Role playing as a behavior change technique: review of the empirical literature. *Psychother.: Theory, Res. & Pract.*, 9:185-192.
01412 **BOLK-WEISCHEDEL, D.** (1977), (Group therapy and group work.) *Zeit. Psychosomat. Med. & Psychoanal.*, (Goettingen) 23:289-293.
01413 **BOLL, T. J.** (1971), Systematic observation of behavior change with older children in group therapy. *Psychol. Reports*, 28:26-28.
01414 **BOLLER, J. D.**, and **BOLLER, J. D.** (1973), Sensitivity training and the school teacher: an experiment in favorable publicity. *J. Educat. Res.*, 66:309-312.
01415 **BOLMAN, L.** (1973), Some effects of trainers on their groups: a partial replication. *J. Appl. Behav. Science*, 9:534-539.
01416 **BOMHARD, K. V.** (1977), (Review of A. Uchtenhagen's *Group Therapy and Social Environment.*) *Praxis des Psychother.*, 22:93.
01417 **BONABESSE, M.** (1969/1970), (The utilization of psychodrama in the treatment of alcoholics.) *Bull. de Psychol.*, (Brussels) 23:834-838.
01418 **BOND, G. M., BLOCH, S.**, and **YALOM, I. D.** (1979), The evaluation of a "target problem" approach to outcome measurement. *Psychother.: Theory, Res., & Pract.*, 16:48.
01419 **BOND, G. R.** (1976), Norm formation in therapy groups. *Dissert. Abstr. Internat.*, 36:3590.
01420 **BONIER, R. J.**, and **KOPLOUSKI, A.** (1971), The borderline adolescent in crisis intervention. *Proceed., Annual Convention*, American Psychological Association, 6:437-438.
01421 **BONNEY, W. C.** (1974), The maturation of groups. *Small Group Behav.*, 5:445-461.
01422 **BONNEY, W. C.**, and **FOLEY, W. J.** (1963), The transition stage in group counseling in terms of congruence theory. *J. Couns. Psychol.*, 10:136-138.
01423 **BOON, E. M.** (1969), A therapeutic community in an open state hospital: administrative-therapeutic links. *Hosp. & Community Psychiat.*, 20:269-278.
01424 **BOORER, D.** (1964), Psychiatric prison. *Nursing Times*, (London) 60:1293-1296.
01425 **BOORSTEIN, S.** (1979), Troubled relationships: transpersonal and psychoanalytic approaches. *J. Transpersonal Psychol.*, 11:129-139.

01426 **BORAK, W.** (1963), (Our experience with the application of group psychotherapy in a pediatric psychiatry department. Preliminary communication.) *Neurol. & Neurochir. Polska*, (Warsaw) 13:527-533.

01427 **BORDEN, R.** (1940), The use of the psychodrama in an institution for delinquent girls. *Sociometry*, 3:81-90.

01428 **BORENS, R.** (1974), (Combination of individual and group therapy in schizophrenics.) *Psyche*, (Stuttgart) 28:706-718.

01429 **BORENZWEIG, H.** (1970), Social group work in the field of mental retardation: a review of the literature. *Soc. Serv. Rev.*, 44:177-183.

01430 **BORENZWEIG, H.,** and **DOMBEY, D.** (1969), The use of social group work in a vocational training program. *J. Rehab.*, 30:30-32.

01431 **BORG, V.** (1964), (Clinical treatment of alcoholism.) *Tidskr. Norsk. Laegeforen*, 84:1117-1120.

01432 **BORGATTA, E. F.** (1967), Methodological notes on a model new research of small groups. *Sociol. Quart.*, 8:133-138.

01433 **BORGATTA, E. F.** (1955), Research: pure and applied. *Group Psychother., Psychodrama & Sociometry*, 8:263-277.

01434 **BORGATTA, E. F.** (1953), Some research findings on the validity of group psychotherapy as a diagnostic and therapeutic approach. *Amer. J. Psychiat.*, 110:362-365.

01435 **BORGATTA, E. F.,** and **COTTRELL, L. S.** (1959), Control-group experimentation in psychotherapy. *Psychiatry*, 22:97-100.

01436 **BORGATTA, E. F.,** and **PHILIP, H.** (1953), The definition of some problem areas for research: a theoretical formulation of some problems of relevance to diagnostics. *Group Psychother., Psychodrama & Sociometry*, 6:90-101.

01437 **BORGEAT, F.** (1971), "Acting out" et psychothérapie de groupe pour adolescents en milieu institutionnel. ("Acting out" and group psychotherapy for adolescents in an institutional environment.) *Laval Med.*, (Quebec) 42:237-241.

01438 **BORGERS, S. B.** (1980), An examination of the use of contracts in groups. *J. Special. Group Work*, 5:68-72.

01439 **BORGHESI, R.** (1965), (Apropos of a form of group psychotherapy in chronic alcoholism: critical considerations on Alcoholics Anonymous.) *Rass. Studi Psichiat.*, (Siena) 54:79-92.

01440 **BORING, R. O.,** and **DEABLER, H. L.** (1951), A simplified psychodramatic approach in group therapy. *J. Clin. Psychol.*, 7:371-375.

01441 **BORIS, H. N.** (1970), The medium, the message, and the good group dream. *Internat. J. Group Psychother.*, 20:91-98.

01442 **BORIS, H. N.** (1970), The medium, the message, and the good group dream. *Sandoz Psychiat. Spectator*, 6:16-17.

01443 **BORIS, H. N.** (1971), The seelsorger in rural Vermont. *Internat. J. Group Psychother.*, 21:159-173.

01444 **BORIS, H. N., ZINBERG, N. E.,** and **BORIS, M.** (1975), Fantasies in group situations. *Contemp. Psychoanal.*, 11:15-45.

01445 **BORNSTEIN, P. H.** (1975), (Innovation in technique: a group-based induced anxiety.) *Rev. Mexicana Anal. Conducta*, (Mexico City) 1:299-301.

01446 **BORNSTEIN, P. H.,** and **SIPPRELLE, C. N.** (1973), Group treatment of obesity by induced anxiety. *Behav. Res. & Ther.*, 11:339-341.

01447 **BOROFSKY, R. B.** (1970), Learning from group experience: an analysis of the experiential structure of therapeutic dialogue. *Dissert. Abstr. Internat.*, 31:389B.

01448 **BOROWSKI, T.,** and **TOLWINSKI, T.** (1969), Treatment of paranoid schizophrenics with chlorpromazine and group therapy. *Diseases Nerv. System*, 30:201-202.

01449 **BORRIELLO, J. F.** (1979), Group psychotherapy with acting-out patients: specific problems and technique. *Amer. J. Psychother.*, 33:521.

01450 **BORRIELLO, J. F.** (1976), Leadership in the therapist–centered group-as-a-whole psychotherapy approach. *Internat. J. Group Psychother.*, 26:149-162.

01451 **BORRIELLO, J. F.** (1973), Patients with acting-out character disorders. *Amer. J. Psychother.*, 27:4-14.

01452 **BORRIELLO, J. F.** (1980), Review of F. L. Shapiro's *Methods of Group Psychotherapy and Encounter: Tradition of Innovation. Contemp. Psychol.*, 25:163.

01453 **BORRIELLO, J. F.** (1974), The role of the leader in the Bion-Ezriel model of group psychotherapy. *Amer. J. Orthopsychiat.*, 44:215-216.

01454 **BORRIELLO, J. F.** (1980), Trainee selection in group psychotherapy. In: *Psychotherapy Research and Training*, eds. W. Demoor and H. R. Wijngaarden. Amsterdam: Elsevier.

01455 **BÖRSIG, A.**, and **FREY, D.** (1979), Satisfaction with group process and group decision as a function of group structure. *Psychol. Reports*, 44:699-705.

01456 **BOSS, M.** (1956), Moreno's "Existentialism, daseinsanalyse and psychodrama"; a discussion. *Internat. J. Group Psychother.*, 1:111-113.

01457 **BOSSMAN, L. J., Jr.** (1968), An analysis of interagent residual effects upon members of small, decision-making groups. *Behav. Science*, 13:220-233.

01458 **BOTTCHER, H. F.** (1973), (Experience with psychoprophylactic groups in industrial factories.) *Zeit. Aerztl. Fortbildung*, (Jena) 67:393-396.

01459 **BÖTTCHER, H. R.** (1976), Methods of research on group therapy. *Psychiatr., Neurol. & Med. Psychol.*, (Leipzig) 28:259-266.

01460 **BOTUINIK, G.** (1973), (Consolation, symptoms, listening.) *Rev. Neuropsychiat. Infantile*, (Paris) 21:517-528.

01461 **de BOUCAUD, M.** (1972), (Conjugal Psychotherapy). *Annales Medico-Psychol.*, (Paris) 2:33-48.

01462 **de BOUCAUD, M.** (1978), Psychothérapie conjugale et phases processuelles. (Conjugal psychotherapy and phase processing.) *Psychother. & Psychosomat.*, (Basel) 29:192-197.

01463 **BOUCHAL, M.** (1976), (Group talks: a form of self-regulating group in the psychotherapeutic system.) *Ceskoslov. Psychiat.*, (Prague) 72:32-50.

01464 **BOUCHARD, V. C.** (1972), Hemiplegic exercise and discussion group. *Amer. J. Occupat. Ther.*, 26:330-331.

01465 **BOUDRY, C.**, and **PFAEHLER, P.** (1976), (Double-focus treatment of a psychotic young girl and her parents.) *Rev. Neuropsychiat. Infantile*, (Paris) 24:25-33.

01466 **BOUILLION, K. R.** (1974), The comparative efficacy of nondirective group play therapy with preschool, speech or language delayed children. *Dissert. Abstr. Internat.*, 35:495B.

01467 **BOULANGER, J. B.** (1965), Group analytic psychodrama in child psychiatry. *Can. Psychiat. Assn. J.*, (Ottawa) 10:427-432.

01468 **BOULANGER, J. B.** (1961), Group psychoanalytic therapy in child psychiatry. *Can. Psychiat. Assn. J.*, (Ottawa) 6:272-275.

01469 **BOULANGER, J. B.** (1968), Les psychothérapies collectives chez l'enfant et l'adolescent. (Collective psychotherapy in the child and adolescent.) *Can. Psychiat. Assn. J.*, (Ottawa) 13:323-326.

01470 **BOULETTE, T. R.** (1976), Group therapy with low-income Mexican Americans. *Soc. Work*, 20:403-404.

01471 **BOUR, P.** (1964), (Catalytic elements in group psychotherapy of schizophrenics.) *Annales Medico-Psychol.*, (Paris) 122:491-514.

01472 **BOUR, P.** (1967), (Discovery and management of unconscious aggression in group psychotherapy.) *Evolut. Psychiat.*, (Toulouse) 32:961-983.

01473 **BOUR, P.** (1961), (Group psychotherapy and psychodrama in the psychiatric hospital.) *Annales Medico-Psychol.*, (Paris) 119:849-876.

01474 **BOUR, P.** (1970), Objet intermédiaire et psychodrame. (Intermediate object and psychodrama.) *Annales Medico-Psychol.*, (Paris) 2:742-750.

01475 **BOUR, P.** (1960), (Overlapping therapy with a neurotic couple.) *Evolut. Psychiat.*, (Toulouse) 25:255-267.

01476 **BOUR, P.** (1962), Psychodrama in a psychiatric hospital in France. *Group Psychother., Psychodrama & Sociometry*, 15:304-311.

01477 **BOUR, P.**, and **SAISSE, S.** (1959), (Experience with psychodrama in a psychiatric hospital centered on unconscious aggression.) *Annales Medico-Psychol.*, (Paris) 117:711-721.

01478 **BOURESTOM, N. C.** (1961), Self-government for patients on a geriatric service. *Group Psychother., Psychodrama & Sociometry*, 14:73-77.

01479 **BOURESTOM, N. C.**, and **SMITH, W. L.** (1954), A comparison between fantasy productions and social behavior in experimental group psychotherapy. *Group Psychother., Psychodrama & Sociometry*, 7:205-213.

01480 **BOUSINGEN, R. D.** (1963), (Relaxation and group psychotherapy, collective therapeutic use of autogenic training.) *Strasbourg Med.*, 14:983-988.

01481 **BOUTTE, M. A.** (1971), Play therapy practices in approved counseling agencies. *J. Clin. Psychol.*, 27:150-152.

01482 **BOVARD, E. W.** (1952), Clinical insight as a function of group process. *J. Abnorm. & Soc. Psychol.*, 47:534-539.

01483 **BOVILL, D.** (1977), An outcome study of group psychotherapy. *Brit. J. Psychiat.*, (Ashford) 131:95-98.

01484 **BOVILL, D.** (1972), A trial of group psychotherapy for neurotics. *Brit. J. Psychiat.*, (Ashford) 120:285-292.

01485 **BOVILSKY, D. M.**, and **SINGER, D. L.** (1977), Confrontational group treatment of smoking: a report of three comparative studies. *Internat. J. Group Psychother.*, 27:481-498.

01486 **BOWERS, D. G.**, and **SEASHORE, S. E.** (1967), Peer leadership within work groups. *Personnel Administrator*, 30:45-50.

01487 **BOWERS, M.**, **BERKOWITZ, B.**, and **BRECHER, S.** (1958), Therapeutic implications of analytic group psychotherapy of religious personnel. *Internat. J. Group Psychother.*, 8:243-256.

01488 **BOWERS, M. K.** (1963), *Conflicts of the Clergy*. New York: T. Nelson and Sons.

01489 **BOWERS, M. K.**, **MULLAN, H.**, and **BERKOWITZ, B.** (1959), Observations on suicide occurring during group psychotherapy. *Amer. J. Psychother.*, 13:93-106.

01490 **BOWERS, M. K.** (1971), Therapy of multiple personality. *Internat. J. Clin. & Exper. Hypnosis*, 19:57-65.

01491 **BOWERS, P. F.**, **BANQUER, M.**, and **BLOOMFIELD, H. H.** (1974), Utilization of nonverbal exercises in the group therapy of outpatient chronic schizophrenics. *Internat. J. Group Psychother.*, 24:13-24.

01492 **BOWLBY, J.** (1947), The study of human relations in the child guidance clinic. *J. Soc. Issues*, 3:35-41.

01493 **BOWMAN, C. C.** (1948), The psychodramatic method in collegiate instruction: a case study. *Sociometry*, 1:421-430.

01494 **BOWMAN, R. L.** (1976), A study of the marathon group tension function via telemetered radioelectrocardiography and self report. *Dissert. Abstr. Internat.*, 36:4679.

01495 **BOYD, N. J.** (1977), Clinician's perceptions of black families in therapy. *Dissert. Abstr. Internat.*, 38:346B.

01496 **BOYD, R. D.**, and **WILSON, J. P.** (1974), Three channel theory of communication in small groups. *Adult Educat.*, 24:167-183.
01497 **BOYD, W. H.**, and **BOLEN, D. W.** (1970), The compulsive gambler and spouse in group psychotherapy. *Internat. J. Group Psychother.*, 20:77-90.
01498 **BOYLE, D. E.** (1980), The effects of two different small group short term treatments on sixth grade social isolates. *Dissert. Abstr. Internat.*, 40:5370A. (University Microfilms No. 8009626.)
01499 **BOYLE, H. C.** (1972), The comparative effects of a dyadic program on group interpersonal relationships. *Dissert. Abstr. Internat.*, 33:1429A.
01500 **BOYLE, T. J.** (1977), Effects of group counseling on the self-concept of students identified as deviant. *Dissert. Abstr. Internat.*, 38:1884A.
01501 **BOYLIN, E. R.** (1975), Gestalt encounter in the treatment of hospitalized alcoholic patients. *Amer. J. Psychother.*, 29:524-534.
01502 **BOYLIN, E. R.** (1971), Using psychodrama to introduce a new drug addict to members of a concept house: a case study. *Group Psychother., Psychodrama & Sociometry*, 24:31-33.
01503 **BOYSEN, K.**, and **SPIEL, W.** (1949), Vorlaiifiger bericht über gruppen behandlung vegetativer. (Group psychotherapy of neurovegetative exhaustion: preliminary report.) *Weiner Zeit. Nervenheilk.*, (Vienna) 2:270-279.
01504 **BOYSON, M. A.** (1975), Helping the alcoholic cope with sobriety: Bedford, Mass., V.A. Hospital. *RN*, 38:37.
01505 **BOZZETTI, L. P.** (1972), Group psychotherapy with addicted smokers. *Psychother. & Psychosomat.*, (Basel) 20:172-175.
01506 **BRAATEN, L. J.** (1975), Developmental phases of encounter groups and related intensive groups. *Interpersonal Develop.*, 5:112-129.
01507 **BRAATEN, L. J.** (1971), (Insight-oriented therapy in student groups: some client-centered viewpoints.) *Nordisk Psykiat. Tidsskr.*, (Kungshacha) 25:413-423.
01508 **BRACELAND, F. J.** (1945), Group psychotherapy. *Sociometry*, 8:283-287.
01509 **BRACK, E.** (1962), Bifckale gruppentherapie von schizophrenen: einige erfahrungen nach zweijaehrigem versuch. (Bifocal group therapy of schizophrenics: some experiences after two years of trial.) *Zeit. Psychosomat. Med. & Psychoanal.*, (Goettingen) 8:133-141.
10510 **BRACONNIER, A.** (1971), (Therapeutic methods in psychiatry.) *Rev. de l'Infirmiere,* (Paris) 21:557-563.
01511 **BRADFER, J.** (1965), The Antonin Artaud Club. *Inform. Psychiat.*, 41:119-135.
01512 **BRADFORD, L.**, and **SHEATS, P.** (1948), Complacency shock as a prerequisite to training. *Sociatry*, 2:37-46.
01513 **BRADFORD, L. P.** (1963), *Group Development.* Washington, DC: National Education Association.
01514 **BRADFORD, L. P.** (1947), The use of psychodrama for group consultants. *Sociatry*, 1:192-197.
01515 **BRADFORD, L. P., GIBB, J. R.,** and **BENNE, K. D.** (1964), *T-Group Theory and Laboratory Method: Innovation in Re-education.* New York: J. Wiley and Sons.
01516 **BRADLEY, H. B.** (1969), Community-based treatment for young adult offenders. *Crime & Delinquency*, 15:359-370.
01517 **BRADSHAW, W. H., Jr.** (1972), The coffee-pot affair: an episode in the life of a therapeutic community. *Hosp. & Community Psychiat.*, 23:33-38.
01518 **BRAEN, B. B.** (1969), Evolution of a group therapeutic approach to school age pregnant girls. *Proceed., 77th Annual Convention,* American Psychological Association, 4:547-548.

01519 **BRAEN, B. B.** (1970), The evolution of a therapeutic group approach to school-age pregnant girls. *Adolescence*, 5:171-186.

01520 **BRAEN, B. B., DiFLORIO, R., HAGEN, J. H., LONG, R., OSOFSKY, H. J.**, and **WOOD, P. W.** (1968), A multidisciplinary program for the pregnant adolescents: a progress report. *Amer. J. Orthopsychiat.*, 38:367-368.

01521 **BRAGUINSKY, J.**, and **MUNDET, M. J.** (1978), Group psychotherapy in extreme obesity: diet vs. therapeutic insight. *Internat. J. Obesity*, 2:471.

01522 **BRAINAN, S. G.** (1977), The establishment of a therapeutic alliance with parents of psychiatrically hospitalized children. *Soc. Work & Health Care*, 3:19-27.

01523 **BRAM, J.** (1954), L'application du psychodrame aux recherches d'anthropologie sociale. (The application of psychodrama to research in social anthropology.) *Rev. Psychol. Peuples*, (Le Havre) 9:415-422.

01524 **BRAMLETTE, C. A.**, and **TUCKER, J. H.** (1981), Encounter groups: positive change or deterioration? more data and a partial replication. *Human Relat.*, 34:303-314.

01525 **BRAMLEY, W.** (1980), Influencing the culture of an academic department: impressions of a group analytical consultant. *Group Anal.*, (London) 13:110-118.

01526 **BRANAN, J. M.** (1967), Client reaction to counselor's use of self-experience. *Personnel & Guid. J.*, 45:568-572.

01527 **BRANCALE, R., VUOCOLO, A.**, and **PRENDERGAST, W.** (1972), The New Jersey program for sex offenders. In: *Sexual Behaviors: Social, Clinical, and Legal Aspects*, eds. H. L. Resnik and M. E. Wolfgang. Boston: Little, Brown.

01528 **BRAND, R. R.** (1974), The frequency and consequences of therapist-to-member confrontation in ongoing psychotherapy groups. *Dissert. Abstr. Internat.*, 35:4161B.

01529 **BRANDEL, I. W.** (1975), The relationship between the quantity of verbal performance and selected variables in the group counseling process. *Dissert. Abstr. Internat.*, 36:2623A.

01530 **BRANDES, N. C.** (1967), Group therapy and the psychiatrist. *Psychiat. Quart. Suppl.*, 41:69-76.

01531 **BRANDES, N. S.** (1977), Adolescent therapy through the eyes of a group therapist. *Groups*, 8:2-7.

01532 **BRANDES, N. S.** (1964), Challenges in the management of troubled adolescents. *Clin. Pediat.*, 3:647-650.

01533 **BRANDES, N. S.** (1968), The disturbed adolescent: discussion of an outpatient psychotherapeutic approach. *Ohio Med. J.*, 64:1272-1274.

01534 **BRANDES, N. S.** (1971), Group psychotherapy for the adolescent. *Curr. Psychiat. Ther.*, 11:18-26.

01535 **BRANDES, N. S.** (1969), Group psychotherapy in the treatment of emotional disturbance. *Ment. Hygiene*, 53:105-109.

01536 **BRANDES, N. S.** (1965), Understanding the adolescent in group psychotherapy. *Clin. Pediat.*, 4:203-209.

01538 **BRANDES, N. S.** (1977), Group therapy is not for every adolescent: two case illustrations. *Internat. J. Group Psychother.*, 27:507-510.

01539 **BRANDES, N. S.** (1976), Multidimensional treatment of adolescents and young adults. *Groups*, 7:1-6.

01540 **BRANDES, N. S.**, and **GARDNER, M. L.** (1973), *Group Therapy for the Adolescent*. New York: J. Aronson.

01541 **BRANDES, N. S.**, and **TODD, W. E.** (1972), Dissolution of a peer supervision group of individual psychotherapists. *Internat. J. Group Psychother.*, 22:54-59.

01542 **BRANDL, G.** (1975), *Das Gruppengespräch als Lernweg: fine Tiefenpsychologische und Religionspädagogische Grundlegung*. Vienna: Herder Verlag.

01543 **BRANDNER, P.** (1974), Women in groups. *Amer. J. Nursing*, 74:1661-1664.

01544 **BRANDT, D. E.** (1973), A descriptive analysis of selected aspects of group therapy with severely delinquent boys. *J. Amer. Acad. Child Psychiat.*, 12:473-481.

01545 **BRANDZEL, R.** (1963), Role playing as a training device in preparing multiple handicapped youth for employment. *Group Psychother., Psychodrama & Sociometry*, 16:16-21.

01546 **BRANHAM, V. C.** (1950), Comment on relation of social psychiatry to group psychotherapy. *Group Psychother., Psychodrama & Sociometry*, 3:196.

01547 **BRANT, H.** (1957), Group therapy with large groups of psychotic patients. *Group Psychother., Psychodrama & Sociometry*, 10:129-132.

01548 **BRANT, H.** (1959), Values of self-government on a psychiatric ward. *Internat. J. Group Psychother.*, 9:322-325.

01549 **BRASFIELD, C. R.**, and **CUBITT, A.** (1974), Changes in self-disclosure behavior following an intensive "encounter" group experience. *Can. Counselor*, (Ottawa) 8:12-21.

01550 **BRASHEAR, E. L.**, **KENNY, E. T.**, **BUCHMUELLER, A. D.**, and **GILDEA, M. C. L.** (1954), Community (St. Louis) program of mental health education using group discussion methods. *Amer. J. Orthopsychiat.*, 24:554-562.

01551 **BRATFOS, O.**, and **SAGEDAL, E.** (1961), (Simple group therapy in a mental hospital.) *Nordisk Med.*, (Copenhagen) 66:1535-1537.

01552 **BRATTER, T. E.** (1978), Classroom meetings: the teacher and group process. *Together: Special. Group Work*, 3:78-85.

01553 **BRATTER, T. E.** (1974), Confrontation: a group psychotherapeutic treatment model for alienated, acting-out, unmotivated, adolescent drug abusers and addicts. *Dissert. Abstr. Internat.*, 35:1902B.

01554 **BRATTER, T. E.** (1977), Confrontation groups: the therapeutic community's gift to psychotherapy. In: *Proceed., First World Conference on Therapeutic Communities*, eds. P. Vamos and J. J. Dovlin. Montreal: Portage Press.

01555 **BRATTER, T. E.** (1967), Dynamics of role reversal. *J. Group Psychother.*, 20:88-95.

01556 **BRATTER, T. E.** (1976), Group psychotherapy: restructuring of probation process. *Correct. & Soc. Psychol.*, 22:1-5.

01557 **BRATTER, T. E.** (1978), Group therapy with affluent, alienated, adolescent drug abusers: a reality therapy and confrontation approach. *Psychother.: Theory, Res. & Pract.*, 9:308-313.

01558 **BRATTER, T. E.** (1977), Guest editor's comments. *Together: J. Special. Group Work*, 2:50.

01559 **BRATTER, T. E.** (1977), Motivating the unmotivated: the self help therapeutic communities biggest challenge. In: *Proceed., Second World Congress of Therapeutic Communities*, eds. P. Vamos and J. E. Brown. Montreal: Portage Press, pp. 84-93.

01560 **BRATTER, T. E.** (1974), Reality therapy: a group psychotherapeutic approach with adolescent alcoholics. *Annals N.Y. Acad. Science*, 233:104-114.

01561 **BRATTER, T. E.** (1971), Treating adolescent drug abusers in a community-based interaction group program: some philosophical considerations. *J. Drug Issues*, 1:237-252.

01562 **BRAUN, M. C.** (1974), Heroin: phenomenological aspects of its use and group treatment. *Dissert. Abstr. Internat.*, 34:3487B.

01563 **BRAUNTHAL, H.** (1952), A casework training course as a group therapeutic experience. *Internat. J. Group Psychother.*, 2:239-244.

01564 **BRÄUTIGAM, W.** (1959), Gemeinschaftsfaktoren in der behandlung von alkoholsüchtigen. (Group factors in treatment of alcoholics.) *Zeit. Psychother. Med. Psychol.*, (Stuttgart) 9:146-147.

01565 **BRAVERMAN, M., GILL, P. L.,** and **STANDISH, C.** (1958), Beginning group therapy in a prison. *Group Psychother., Psychodrama & Sociometry*, 11:203-210.

01566 **BRAY, R. E.** (1962), Psychiatric group assignment. *Nursing Times*, (London) 58:468-470.

01567 **BRAYBOY, T.** (1971), The Black patient in group therapy. *Internat. J. Group Psychother.*, 21:288-293.

01568 **BRAYBOY, T. L.,** and **MARKS, M. J.** (1968), Transference variations evoked by racial differences in cotherapists. *Amer. J. Psychother.*, 22:474-480.

01569 **BREAKWELL, G. M.** (1979), Illegitimate group membership and intergroup differentiation. *Brit. J. Soc. & Clin. Psychol.*, (London) 18:141-150.

01570 **BRECKHILL, J. A.** (1972), The effectiveness of group counseling with alienated ninth grade boys in a residential school. *Dissert. Abstr. Internat.*, 32:4935-4936A.

01571 **BRECKIR, N. J.** (1951), Group psychotherapy with psychotic patients. *Internat. J. Group Psychother.*, 1:129-132.

01572 **BRECKIR, N. J.** (1950), Hospital orientation and training program for group psychotherapy of schizophrenic patients. *Psychiat. Quart.*, 24:131-143.

01573 **BREDSEN, K. N.** (1969), Small group work: the need for some guidelines. *Amer. J. Psychiat.*, 126:876-877.

01574 **BREEN, D.** (1977), Brief communications: some differences between group and individual therapy in connection with the therapist's pregnancy. *Internat. J. Group Psychother.*, 27:499-506.

01575 **BREESKIN, J.** (1970), The airmen's readjustment group therapy program. *Correct. Psychiat. & J. Soc. Ther.*, 16:103-113.

01576 **BREGANT, L.** (1978), (The countertransference experience in didactic group analysis.) *Psihijat. Danas*, (Belgrade) 10:109-110.

01577 **BREGANT, L.** (1978), (An example of group dydactic analysis.) *Psihijat. Danas*, (Belgrade) 10:83-88.

01578 **BRENDEL, M.** (1974), Changes in positive personality traits as a function of teaching encouraging transactions. *Dissert. Abstr. Internat.*, 34:5669.

01579 **BRENNAN, M. E.,** and **STEINITZ, M.** (1949), Interpretation of group therapy to parents. *Amer. J. Orthopsychiat.*, 19:61-68.

01580 **BRENNAN, M. M.** (1977), Self-concept change among pregnant adolescent girls as a result of small group counseling. *Dissert. Abstr. Internat.*, 39:5538B.

01581 **BRENNER, A. M.** (1971), Self-directed t-groups for elementary teachers: impetus for innovation. *J. Appl. Behav. Science*, 7:327-341.

01582 **BRENNER, H.** (1977), Effects of group psychotherapy on patients after heart infarction. *Cardiology*, (Basel) 62:159-160.

01583 **BRENNER, R. S.** (1973), The effects of systematic feedback to leaders on outcomes in human relations training groups. *Dissert. Abstr. Internat.*, 34:129A.

01584 **BRETT, S. R.,** and **VILLENEUVE, A.** (1963), Evolution of group therapy policies with hospitalized drug addicts in the narcotic unit at Central Islip State Hospital. *Psychiat. Quart.*, 37:666-670.

01585 **BREWER, M. B.** (1979), In-group bias in the minimal intergroup situation: a cognitive motivational analysis. *Psychol. Bull.*, 86:307-324.

01586 **BREWSTER, R. J.** (1978), Group counseling as an alternative to school suspension for high school smoking violators: help or hindrance? *Dissert. Abstr. Internat.*, 39:370B. (University Microfilms No. 7800181.)

01587 **BRICKMAN, P.** (1969), Predicting behavior from first impressions of a t-group member. *Internat. J. Group Psychother.*, 19:53-62.
01588 **BRIDGES, W. W., Jr.** (1972), The use of peers as facilitators in small group procedures with underachieving college freshman. *Dissert. Abstr. Internat.*, 32:4936A.
01589 **BRIGANTE, T. R.**, and **KINNE, M. J.** (1958), The use of mental health films in group psychotherapy with psychotic patients. *Group Psychother., Psychodrama & Sociometry*, 11:219-226.
01590 **BRIGL, H.** (1963), On hither to gained experiences with group psychotherapy combined with occupational therapy in a psychiatric treatment home. *Wiener Zeit. Nervenheilk*, (Vienna) 21:169-176.
01591 **BRILL, L.** (1971), Some comments on the paper "Social control in therapeutic communities." *Internat. J. Addict*, 6:45-50.
01592 **BRILL, N. Q.** (1947), Group psychotherapy. *Proceed. Nat. Conference Soc. Work*, pp. 237-243.
01593 **BRIND, A. B.**, and **BRIND, N. B.** (1963), The "drama" in psychodrama. *Internat. J. Soc. Psychiat.*, (London) 3:3-5.
01594 **BRIND, A. B.**, and **BRIND, N. B.** (1958), Group psychotherapy and psychodrama, a footnote to their history. *Group Psychother., Psychodrama & Sociometry*, 11:275-277.
01595 **BRIND, A. B.**, and **BRIND, N. B.** (1964), The therapeutic hour of psychodrama and the rest of the week. *Group Psychother., Psychodrama & Sociometry*, 17:139-142.
01596 **BRIND, A. B.**, and **BRIND, N. B.** (1966), The tragic origins and counteragic evolution of psychodrama. *Group Psychother., Psychodrama & Sociometry*, 19:94-100.
01597 **BRINEGAR, J. R.** (1978), A behavioral study of group counseling process: member self-disclosure and leader social reinforcement. *Dissert. Abstr. Internat.*, 39:5320A.
01598 **BRINLING, T.** (1971), Tearing down a wall. *Amer. J. Nursing*, 71:1406-1409.
01599 **BRISCOE, R. V., HOFFMAN, D. B.**, and **BAILEY, J. S.** (1975), Behavioral community psychology: training a community board to problem solve. *J. Appl. Behav. Analysis*, 8:157-168.
01600 **BRISKIN, G. J.** (1955), An exploratory study of identification in group therapy. *Dissert. Abstr. Internat.*, 16:626-627.
01601 **BRISKIN, G. J.** (1955), *An Exploratory Study of Identification in Group Therapy*. Ann Arbor: University Microfilms.
01602 **BRISKIN, G. J.** (1958), Identification in group psychotherapy. *J. Abnorm. & Soc. Psychol.*, 56:195-198.
01603 **BRISTOW, W. H.** (1948), Sociometry, sociodrama and the curriculum. *Sociatry*, 2:73-74.
01604 **BRITO, M. E.** (1967), (Sociotherapy in psychiatric hospitals, 2.) *Rev. de Enfermagen*, (Lisbon) 6:74-75.
01605 **BROCHER, T.** (1975), Group methods in parent education. *Internat. J. Group Psychother.*, 25:315-322.
01606 **BROCHER, T.** (1970), Orientation on group dynamics. *Psychiat. Communicat.*, 13:3-12.
01607 **BROCHU, L.** (1977), (Psychiatric intervention in a school setting.) *Rev. Neuropsychiat. Infantite*, (Paris) 25:339-346.
01608 **BROCKBANK, R.** (1966), Analytic group psychotherapy. *Curr. Psychiat. Ther.*, 6:145-156.
01609 **BROCKBANK, R.** (1971), Theory of therapeutic rationale in analytic group psychotherapy. *Group Process*, (London) 4:73-86.
01610 **BROCKMELE, M. J.** (1968), Nursing in two community health settings. *Nursing Outlook*, 16:55-58.

01611 **BRODEY, J. F.**, and **DETRE, T.** (1972), Criteria used by clinicians in referring patients to individual or group therapy. *Amer. J. Psychother.*, 26:176-184.

01612 **BRODSKY, A. M.** (1973), The consciousness-raising group as a model for therapy with women. *Psychother.: Theory, Res. & Pract.*, 10:24-29.

01613 **BRODY, M. W.**, and **HARRISON, S. I.** (1953), Group psychotherapy with male stutterers. *Arch. Neurol. Psychiat.*, 69:401-402.

01614 **BRODY, M. W.**, and **HARRISON, S. I.** (1954), Group psychotherapy with male stutterers. *Internat. J. Group Psychother.*, 4:154-162.

01615 **BRODY, M. W.**, and **HARRISON, S. I.** (1956), Stutterers. In: *The Fields of Group Psychotherapy*, ed. S. R. Slavson. New York: International Universities Press.

01616 **BRODY, S.** (1959), Value of group psychotherapy in patients with "polysurgery addiction." *Psychiat. Quart.*, 33:260-283.

01617 **BRODY, V. A.** (1969), An approach to the treatment of disadvantaged, preschool preverbal psychotic children and their parents in an outpatient clinic. *Amer. J. Orthopsychiat.*, 39:259-260.

01618 **BROEDEL, J. W.** (1959), A study of the effects of group counseling on the academic performance and mental health of underachieving gifted adolescents. *Dissert. Abstr. Internat.*, 19:3019.

01619 **BROK, A. J.**, (1980), Review of J. Cappon's *El Movimiento de Encuentro en Psicoterapia de Grupo. Group*, 4:63.

01620 **BROMBACH, C. J.** (1980), The effects of systematic group desensitization and marathon group desensitization on mathematics anxiety and confidence in learning mathematics in freshmen college females. *Dissert. Abstr. Internat.*, 41:2445A. (University Microfilms No. 8028399.)

01621 **BROMBERG, W.** (1961), Advances in group therapy. *Curr. Psychiat. Ther.*, 1:152-158.

01622 **BROMBERG, W.** (1956), An aspect of therapeutic theory. *Group Psychother., Psychodrama & Sociometry*, 9:265-267.

01623 **BROMBERG, W.** (1955), Comments on "Interpersonal therapy, group psychotherapy and the function of the unconscious." *Group Psychother., Psychodrama & Sociometry*, 8:61-62.

01624 **BROMBERG, W.** (1954), Comments on Moreno's "Transference, countertransference and tele." *Group Psychother., Psychodrama & Sociometry*, 7:319-320.

01625 **BROMBERG, W.** (1956), A critical appraisal of "The practice of dynamic psychiatry" by Jules H. Masserman. *Group Psychother., Psychodrama & Sociometry*, 9:69-71.

01626 **BROMBERG, W.** (1960), Developments in group and action methods. *Progr. Psychother.*, 5:59-66.

01627 **BROMBERG, W.** (1957), Evolution of group psychotherapy. *Group Psychother., Psychodrama & Sociometry*, 10:111-113.

01628 **BROMBERG, W.** (1955), "The significance of the therapeutic format and the place of acting out in psychotherapy," a comment. *Group Psychother., Psychodrama & Sociometry*, 8:169-170.

01629 **BROMBERG, W.**, and **FRANKLIN, G.** (1952), The treatment of sexual deviates with group psychodrama. *Group Psychother., Psychodrama & Sociometry*, 4:274-289.

01630 **BROMS, D. S.** (1971), Group processes and the preschool retarded child. *Group Process*, (London) 4:39-51.

01631 **BRONFENBRENNER, U.**, and **NEWCOMB, T. M.** (1948), Improvisations: an application of psychodrama in personality diagnosis. *Sociatry*, 1:367-382.

01632 **BRONNER, A.** (1954), Observations on group therapy in private practice. *Amer. J. Psychother.*, 8:54-62.

01633 **BROOK, D.** (1978), Review of I. A. Greenberg's *Group Hypnotherapy and Hypnodrama. Internat. J. Group Psychother.*, 28:568-570.

01634 **BROOK, R. C.**, and **WHITEHEAD, P. C.** (1973), "414": a therapeutic community for the treatment of adolescent amphetamine abusers. *Correct. Soc. Psychol.*, 19:10-19.

01635 **BROOK, R. M.** (1975), A note on two types of anxiety in the human potential group and marathon experience. *Interpersonal Develop.*, 6:38-41.

01636 **BROOKS, D. D.** (1976), "Teletherapy": or how to use videotape feedback to enhance group process. *Perspect. Psychiat. Care*, 14:83-87.

01637 **BROSS, R. B.** (1956), The "deserter" in group psychotherapy. *Internat. J. Group Psychother.*, 6:392-404.

01638 **BROSS, R. B.** (1952), Mother and child in group psychotherapy: a preliminary report. *Internat. J. Group Psychother.*, 2:358-368.

01639 **BROSS, R. B.** (1959), The silent schizophrenic patient among severe neurotics in group psychotherapy. *Acta Psychother., Psychosomat. Orthopaedagog. Suppl.*, (Basel) 7:61-69.

01640 **BROSS, R. B.** (1959), Termination of analytically oriented psychotherapy in groups. *Internat. J. Group Psychother.*, 9:326-337.

01641 **BROTMAN, R., MEYER, A. S.**, and **FREEDMAN, A. M.** (1965), An approach to treating narcotic addicts based on a community mental health diagnosis. *Comprehens. Psychiat.*, 6:104-118.

01642 **BROWER, J. L.** (1962), Patient-personnel interpersonal choice on a state mental hospital ward. Unpublished doctoral dissertation, University of Buffalo.

01643 **BROWN, A.** (1978), A case study in family systems consultation for community health nurses working with Sudden Infant Death Syndrome (SIDS) families. *Fam. Therapy*, 5:233.

01644 **BROWN, A.** (1978), Review of N. Mccaughan's *Groupwork: Learning and Practice. Brit. J. Soc. Work*, (Birmingham) 8:367.

01645 **BROWN, A.**, and **DAVIES, M.** (1980), *Groupwork*. Exeter, NH: Heinemann Educational Books.

01646 **BROWN, B. M.** (1976), The effects of consciousness-raising group participation on stereotypic interests, behavior, self perception and self actualization. *Dissert. Abstr. Internat.*, 37:518B.

01647 **BROWN, B. S., JACKSON, C. S.**, and **BASS, U. F.** (1973), Methadone and abstinent clients in group counseling sessions. *Internat. J. Addict.*, 8:309-316.

01648 **BROWN, C. C.** (1980), The effect of videotape feedback on self concept in elementary school counseling groups. *Dissert. Abstr. Internat.*, 40:5721A. (University Microfilms No. 8008561).

01649 **BROWN, D. I.** (1962), Nurses participate in group therapy. *Amer. J. Nursing*, 62:68-69.

01650 **BROWN, D. T.** (1966), Staff development through ward-group consultation. *Internat. J. Group Psychother.*, 16:405-412.

01651 **BROWN, G. D.** (1970), A comparison of the effects of "intrusive" and "permissive" group treatments of hospitalized chronic schizophrenic patients. *Dissert. Abstr. Internat.*, 30:5233B.

01652 **BROWN, J.** (1972), The influence of a contract approach and/or encounter group on attitudes toward self and others. *Dissert. Abstr. Internat.*, 32:909B.

01653 **BROWN, J. B.** (1969), Some factors in response to criticism in group therapy. *Dissert. Abstr. Internat.*, 30:376B.

01654 **BROWN, J. E.** (1972), The effects of instant visual feedback of congruence in group counseling. *Dissert. Abstr. Internat.*, 33:436-437B.

01655 **BROWN, J. M.**, and **CHAVES, J. F.** (1980), Hypnosis in the treatment of sexual dysfunction. *J. Sex & Marital Ther.*, 6:63-74.
01656 **BROWN, J. W.**, and **SAPORTA, J.** (1971), Community training for mental health professionals. *Soc. Change*, 3:3-4.
01657 **BROWN, L. B.**, and **CAWTE, J. E.** (1958), A method of establishing a social audit in a mental hospital. *Austral. J. Psychol.*, (Parkville) 10:278-286.
01658 **BROWN, M. S.** (1977), The Gordons need all the help they could get. *Nursing*, (Horsham) 7:40-43.
01659 **BROWN, P. M.** (1957), A comparative study of three therapy techniques used to effect behavioral and social status changes in a group of institutionalized delinquent Negro boys. Unpublished doctoral dissertation, New York University.
01660 **BROWN, R. D.** (1969), Effects of structured and unstructured group counseling with high-and-low-anxious college underachievers. *J. Couns. Psychol.*, 16:209-214.
01661 **BROWN, R. M.** (1977), Bibliotherapy as a technique for increasing individuality among elderly patients. *Hosp. & Community Psychiat.*, 28:347.
01662 **BROWN, R. S.** (1973-1974), A note on body readiness in encounter groups. *Interpersonal Develop.*, 4:58-61.
01663 **BROWN, S.**, and **YALOM, I. D.** (1977), Interactional group therapy with alcoholics. *J. Studies Alcohol*, 38:426-456.
01664 **BROWN, S. R.**, and **ROTHENBERG, A.** (1976), The analysis of group episodes. *Small Group Behav.*, 7:287-306.
01665 **BROWN, T. H.** (1974), Change of self-concept with an intact group by a transactional analysis approach. *Dissert. Abstr. Internat.*, 34:5705A.
01666 **BROWN, W.**, and **KINGSLEY, R. F.** (1975), The effect of individual contracting and guided group interaction upon behavior-disordered youth's self-concept. *J. School Health*, 45:399-401.
01667 **BROWNE, L. J.**, **GOLDSBERRY, J. H.**, and **BULL, J. K.** (1968), Rehabilitating blind psychiatric patients. *Hosp. & Community Psychiat.*, 19:116-117.
01668 **BROWNELL, A. J.** (1970), "Warm-up techniques" as a function of small group involvement. *Dissert. Abstr. Internat.*, 30:4766A.
01669 **BROWNELL, K. D.**, **HECKERMAN, C. L.**, and **WESTLAKE, R. J.** (1978), Therapist and group contact as variables in the behavioral treatment of obesity. *J. Consult. Clin. Psychol.*, 46:593
01670 **BROWNE-MAYERS, A. N.**, (1977), Participation in group therapy: outcome in treatment. *Alcohol Clin. Exch.*, 1:168.
01671 **BROWNSTEIN, S. M.** (1966), Is group treatment feasible for the small and intermediate Jewish family and children's service? *J. Jewish Communal Serv.*, 42:250-254.
01672 **BROWNSTONE, J.**, **PENICK, E. C.**, **LARCEN, S. W.**, **POWELL, B. J.**, and **NORD, A. F.** (1977), Disaster-relief training and mental health. *Hosp. & Community Psychiat.*, 28:30-32.
01673 **BRUCE, J. H.** (1972), The effects of group counseling on selected rehabilitation clients. *Dissert. Abstr. Internat.*, 32:4936A.
01674 **BRUCE, T.** (1978), Group work with adolescents. *J. Adolescence*, 1:47-54.
01675 **BRUCK, M.** (1954), An example of the use of psychodrama in the relieving of an acute symptom in a psychiatric children's clinic. *Group Psychother., Psychodrama & Sociometry*, 6:216-221.
01676 **BRUDNO, J. J.**, and **SELTZER, H.** (1968), Re-socialization therapy through group process with senile patients in a geriatric hospital. *Gerontologist*, 8:211-214.

01677 **BRUHN, M., SCHWAB, R.,** and **TAUSCH, R.** (1980), (The effects of intensive person-centered encounter groups on clients with psychic complaints.) *Zeit. Klin. Psychol.-Forschung & Praxis*, (Goettingen) 9:266-280.

01678 **BRULLEMAN, L. H.** (1972), Group-therapy with epileptic patients at the "institut voor epilepsiebestrijding." *Epilepsia*, 13:225-231.

01679 **BRUNELLE, P.** (1948), Action projects from children's literature: an indirect approach to intercultural relations in the elementary school. *Sociatry*, 2:235-242.

01680 **BRUNI, F.** (1960), (Group psychotherapy and psychodrama.) *Policlinico*, (Rome) 67:1376-1377.

01681 **BRUNNER-ORNE, M.** (1958), The role of a general hospital in the treatment and rehabilitation of alcoholics. *Quart. J. Studies Alcohol*, 19:108-117.

01682 **BRUNNER-ORNE, M.** (1956), The utilization of group psychotherapy in enforced treatment programs for alcoholics and addicts. *Internat. J. Group Psychother.*, 6:272-279.

01683 **BRUNNER-ORNE, M.** (1959), Ward group sessions in the framework of daily hospital rounds. a new therapeutic tool. *Acta Psychother., Psychosomat. Orthopaedagog. Suppl.*, (Basel) 7:70-78.

01684 **BRUNNER-ORNE, M.** (1959), Ward group sessions with hospitalized alcoholics as motivation for psychotherapy. *Internat. J. Group Psychother.*, 9:219-224.

01685 **BRUNNER-ORNE, M.,** and **ORNE, M. T.** (1956), Alcoholics. In: *The Fields of Group Psychotherapy*, ed. S. R. Slavson. New York: International Universities Press, pp. 76-95.

01686 **BRUNNER-ORNE, M.,** and **ORNE, M. T.** (1954), Directive group therapy in the treatment of alcoholics: technique and rationale. *Internat. J. Group Psychother.*, 4:293-302.

01687 **BRUNNERWERNER, R., BRUNNER, E. J.,** and **BINTIG, H.** (1978), (Attitude change as criterion for success of a therapeutic counseling group.) *Gruppenpsychother. & Gruppendynam.*, (Goettingen) 13:152-163.

01688 **BRUNO, N.,** and **DUQUE, R. T.** (1967), Can group therapy replace individual therapy? *Jahrb. Psychol., Psychother. & Med. Anthropol.*, (Freiburg) 15:256-262.

01689 **BRUNO, N.,** and **TANCO DUQUE, R.** (1967), Puede substituierla terapia analitica de grupo al psicoanalisis individual? (Can analytic group therapy be substituted for individual psychoanalysis?) *Arch. Estudios Psicoanal. Psicolog. Med.*, 4:115-124.

01690 **BRUNSE, A.** (1958), West coast foundation for psychodrama and group psychotherapy. *Group Psychother., Psychodrama & Sociometry*, 11:165-166.

01691 **BRUSNAHAN, J.** (1970), A study of the effects of small-group counseling on ninth-grade underachievers. *Dissert. Abstr. Internat.*, 30:3273A-3274A.

01692 **BRUSSEL, B. B.** (1967), The educational and therapeutic effects of the group process experience. *Ment. Hygiene*, 51:495-500.

01693 **BRUWER, M.** (1966), Psychiatric case study. *So. Africa Nursing J.*, (Pretoria) 33:13-14.

01694 **BRUYERE, P. H.** (1975), The effects of client-centered and behavioral group counseling on classroom behavior and self concept of junior high school students who exhibited disruptive classroom behavior. *Dissert. Abstr. Internat.*, 36:1299A.

01695 **BRY, T.** (1953), Acting out in group psychotherapy. *Internat. J. Group Psychother.*, 3:42-48.

01696 **BRY, T.** (1951), Varieties of resistance in group psychotherapy. *Internat. J. Group Psychother.*, 1:106-114.

01697 **BRYAN, W. V.** (1973), The effects of short-term individual and group counseling on the self concept of physically handicapped workers in a sheltered workshop setting. *Dissert. Abstr. Internat.*, 34:4729A.

01698 **BRYER, S. J.**, and **WAGNER, R.** (1963), The didactic value of role-playing for institutionalized retardates. *Group Psychother., Psychodrama & Sociometry*, 16:177-181.

01699 **BRYNGELSON, B.** (1966), *Clinical Group Therapy for Problem People: A Practical Treatise for Stutterers and Normal Speakers.* Minneapolis: T. S. Denison.

01700 **BUCHANAN, D. C.** (1978), Group therapy for chronic physically ill patients. *Psychosomatics*, 19:425-431.

01701 **BUCHANAN, D. C.** (1975), Group therapy for kidney transplant patients. *Internat. J. Psychiat. Med.*, 6:523-531.

01702 **BUCHANAN, D. M.**, and **ROGERS, A. S.** (1980), A comprehensive adolescent treatment program: an inpatient interdisciplinary approach. *J. Psychiat. Nursing*, 18:42-45.

01703 **BUCHANAN, D. R.** (1980), The central concern model: a framework for structuring psychodramatic production. *Group Psychother., Psychodrama & Sociometry*, 33:47-62.

01704 **BUCHANAN, J. R.**, and **RUBIN, T. J.** (1973), Five year analytic study of obesity. *Amer. J. Psychoanal.*, 33:30-41.

01705 **BUCHER, J.** (1967), Group therapy as a disposition following individual therapy. *Psychiat. Communicat.*, 5:25-30.

01706 **BUCHMUELLER, A. D.**, and **GILDEA, M. C. L.** (1949), A group therapy project with parents of behavior problem children in public schools. *Amer. J. Psychiat.*, 106:46-52.

01707 **BUCHMUELLER, A. D.**, and **GILDEN, M. C. L.** (1955), Group therapy for parents of behavior problem children in public schools. *Internat. J. Soc. Psychiat.*, (London) 1:51-56.

01708 **BUCK, A. E.**, and **GRYGIER, T.** (1952), A new attempt in psychotherapy with juvenile delinquents. *Amer. J. Psychother.*, 6:711-724.

01709 **BUCK, B.** (1952), Psychodrama of drug addiction. *Group Psychother., Psychodrama & Sociometry*, 4:301-321.

01710 **BUCK, L. A.**, and **KRAMER, A.** (1974), Poetry as a means of group facilitation. *J. Human. Psychol.*, 14:57-71.

01711 **BUCK, R. E.** (1972), A large milieu therapy group. *Amer. J. Psychother.*, 25:384-393.

01712 **BUCK, R. W.** (1937), The class method in the treatment of essential hypertension. *Annals Internal Med.*, 11:514-518.

01713 **BUCZYNSKI, R. M.** (1980), The effect of method of instruction, amount of previous group experience, amount of previous training, and satisfaction with the instruction, upon counselor trainees' behavior when leading groups. *Dissert. Abstr. Internat.*, 40:4482A. (University Microfilms No. 8003741.)

01714 **BUDA, B.** (1974), Strategy and tactics in group psychotherapy. *Dynam. Psychiat.*, (Berlin) 7:301.

01715 **BUDMAN, S. H.**, **BENNET, M. J.**, and **WISNESKI, M. J.** (1980), Short-term group psychotherapy: an adult developmental model. *Internat. J. Group Psychother.*, 30:63-76.

01716 **BUDMAN, S. H.**, and **CLIFFORD, M.** (1979), Short-term group therapy for couples in a health maintenance organization. *Prof. Psychol.*, 10:419-429.

01717 **BUDMAN, S. H.**, **DEMBY, A.**, and **RANDALL, M.** (1980), Short-term group psychotherapy: who succeeds, who fails? *Group*, 4:3-16.

01718 **BUEKER, K.** (1957), Group therapy in a new setting. *Amer. J. Nursing*, 57:1581-1595.

01719 **BUEKER, K.** (1966), The treatment role of the psychiatric nurse: one point of view. *Perspect. Psychiat. Care*, 4:15-19.

01720 **BUEKER, K.**, and **WARRICK, A.** (1964), Can nurses be group therapists? *Amer. J. Nursing*, 64:114-116.

01721 **BUFFARD, S.** (1963), (Group psychotherapy of criminals: initial results of a clinical experiment.) *Annals Med. Legale*, (Paris) 43:362-365.

01722 **BUGEN, L. A.** (1977), Composition and orientation effects on group cohesion. *Psychol. Reports*, 40:175-181.

01723 **BUGENTAL, J. F. T.** (1973/1974), Confronting the existential meaning of "my death" through group exercises. *Interpersonal Develop.*, 4:148-163.

01724 **BUGENTAL, J. F. T.** (1962), Five paradigms for group psychotherapy. *Psychol. Reports*, 10:607-610.

01725 **BUGH, V. G.** (1972), Group psychotherapy in the mental hospital. *Compar. Group Studies*, 3:99-103.

01726 **BUHLER, C.** (1953), Group therapy with adolescents. *First Annual Report, Group Psychotherapy Association of Southern California*, pp. 17-19.

01727 **BÜHLING, W.** (1978), (Acting-out of addicts in t- or patient-psychotherapy.) *Dynam. Psychiat.*, (Berlin) 52/53: 554-562.

01728 **BUIRSKI, P.** (1975), Some contributions of ethology to group therapy: dominance and hierarchies. *Internat. J. Group Psychother.*, 25:227-235.

01729 **BUIRSKI, P.** (1980), Toward a theory of adaptation of analytic group psychotherapy. *Internat. J. Group Psychother.*, 30:447-460.

01730 **BUIRSKI, P.**, and **WRIGHT, F.** (1977), Dominance and personality in short-term process groups. *Group*, 1:48-55.

01731 **BUIS, C.** (1966), (Pictorial therapy as group therapy.) *Psychiat., Neurol., Neurochir.*, (Amsterdam) 69:181-196.

01732 **BUKELIE, J.** (1976), The group psychiatric work pattern in a diagnostically homogeneous group of adolescent drug addicts. *Soc. Psihijat.*, (Belgrade) 4:47-59.

01733 **BUKI, R.** (1964), A treatment program for homosexuals. *Diseases Nerv. System*, 25:304-307.

01734 **BULACH, C. R.** (1974), An investigation of the relationship of group openness and group trust to group decisions involving risk. *Dissert. Abstr. Internat.*, 35:2760A.

01735 **BULBULYAN, A. A.** (1969), The psychiatric nurse as family therapist. *Perspect. Psychiat. Care*, 7:58-68.

01736 **BULL, P.** (1978), The interpretation of posture through an alternative methodology to role play. *Brit. J. Sociol. & Clin. Psychol.*, (London) 171:1-6.

01737 **BULLIVANT, B. M.** (1978), Towards a neo-ethnographic method for small-group research. *Austral. & New Zeal. J. Sociol.*, (Christchurch) 14:239-250.

01738 **BULLOCK, D.**, and **KOBAYASKI, K.** (1978), The use of live consultation in family therapy. *Fam. Ther.*, 5:245.

01739 **BUMBALO, J. A.**, and **YOUNG, D. E.** (1973), The self-help phenomenon. *Amer. J. Nursing*, 73:1588-1591.

01740 **BUNKER, B. B.**, and **SINGER, D. L.** (1978), Independent nonprofessionals in the community: a case history analysis of a human relations program. *Psychiatry*, 41:377-390.

01741 **BUNZEL, G.** (1948), Psychokinetics and dance therapy. *J. Health, Physical Educat. & Recreation*, (Tokyo) 19:180-181, 227-229.

01742 **BURCHARD, E. M. L., MICHAELS, J. J.**, and **KOTKOV, B.** (1948) Criteria for the evaluation of group therapy. *Psychosomat. Med.*, 10:257-274.

01743 **BURCK, J. L.** (1969), A corrective use of reality group therapy within the institutional ministry. *J. Pastoral Care*, 23:15-25.

01744 **BURDMAN, M.** (1974), Ethnic self-help groups in prison and on parole. *Crime & Delinquency*, 20:107-118.

01745 **BURDON, A. P.** (1967), Levels and goals in group psychotherapy: presented at joint session of AGPA and AOA. *Amer. J. Orthopsychiat.*, 37:271-273.

01746 **BURDON, A. P., NEELY, J. A.**, and **THORPE, A. L.** (1964), Emotionally disturbed boys failing in school: treatment in an outpatient clinic school. *Southern Med. J.*, 57:829-835.

01747 **BURDON, A. P.**, and **NEELY, J. H.** (1966), Chronic school failure in boys: a short-term group therapy and educational approach. *Amer. J. Psychiat.*, 122:1211-1219.

01748 **BURDON, A. P.**, and **RYAN, W.** (1963), The broadest practical effective application of group psychotherapy in a community outpatient psychiatric clinic. *Psychiat. Quart. Suppl.*, 37:270-281.

01749 **BURDON, A. P.**, and **RYAN, W.** (1963), Group psychotherapy as a primary treatment in an outpatient clinic. *Diseases Nerv. System*, 24:534-537.

01750 **BURDON, A. P.**, and **RYAN, W.** (1963), Group therapy as primary treatment in an outpatient setting. *Curr. Psychiat. Ther.*, 3:229-233.

01751 **BURESH, M. C.** (1980), Sensitivity training as a method of increasing the therapeutic effectiveness of group members. *Dissert. Abstr. Internat.*, 40:3383B.

01752 **BURGIN, V. D.** (1978), Group treatment of test anxiety on college students by undergraduate group leaders. *Dissert. Abstr. Internat.*, 39:1468B.

01753 **BURKE, J. L.**, and **LAFAVE, H. G.** (1964), A structured group programme for patient-staff communication. *Internat. J. Soc. Psychiat.*, (London) 10:142-148.

01754 **BURKE, J. L.**, and **LEE, H.** (1964), An acting-out patient in a psychotic group. *Internat. J. Group Psychother.*, 14:194-201.

01755 **BURKE, P. J.** (1974), Participation and leadership in small groups. *Amer. Sociol. Rev.*, 39:832-843.

01756 **BURKS, H. J., Jr.** (1973), Training to counsel in a system: a systems approach for training employment counselors. *J. Employment Couns.*, 10:145-148.

01757 **BURLINGHAM, S.** (1938), Therapeutic effects of a play group for preschool children. *Amer. J. Orthopsychiat.*, 8:627-638.

01758 **BURMAN, O.** (1964), (Treatment of the intoxicated.) *Svenska Lakartidningen*, (Stockholm) 61:4175-4183.

01759 **BURNELL, G. M., DWORSKY, W. A.**, and **HARRINGTON, R. L.** (1972), Post-abortion group therapy. *Amer. J. Psychiat.*, 129:220-223.

01760 **BURNER, M.** (1971), Prevention and therapeutic possibilities in ambulatory care of drug addicts. *Schweiz. Akad. Med. Wissenschaften Bull.*, (Basel) 27:109-120.

01761 **BURNER, M.**, and **VILLA, J. L.** (1961), (Structure and functions of the Policlinique Psychiatrique Universitaire of Lausanne: importance of the use of individual and group psychotherapy methods.) *Cahiers Psychiat.*, 15:7-18.

01762 **BURNS, G. W.** (1972), Religious influences on behavior of the group therapist. *Psychol. Reports*, 31:638.

01763 **BURNS, W. J.** (1974), The effects of a group process staff development program upon psychiatric attendants' attitudes toward psychopathology and treatment. *Dissert. Abstr. Internat.*, 34:7038A.

01764 **BURNSIDE, I. M.** (1969), Group work among the aged. *Nursing Outlook*, 17:68-71.

01765 **BURNSIDE, I. M.** (1970), Group work with the aged: selected literature. *Gerontologist*, 10:241-246.

01766 **BURNSIDE, I. M.** (1971), Long-term group work with hospitalized aged. *Gerontologist*, 11:213-218.

01767 **BURNSIDE, I. M.** (1970), Loss: a constant theme in group work with the aged. *Hosp. & Community Psychiat.*, 21:173-177.

01768 **BURNSIDE, I. M.** (1976), Overview of group work with the aged. *J. Gerontol. Nursing*, 2:14-17.

01769 **BURNSIDE, I. M.** (1969), Sensory stimulation: an adjunct to group work with the disabled aged. *Ment. Hygiene*, 53:381-388.

01770 **BURNSIDE, R. W.** (1974), Group counseling technique for adults returning to college. *J. Coll. Student Personnel*, 15:62.

01771 **BURRELL, N. E.** (1960), A report of an experiment to facilitate learning in a sophomore course in educational psychology through cooperative group procedures of teaching and learning. Ph.D. thesis, Columbia University.

01772 **BURROW, B.** (1979), The dilemma of the alcoholic female in treatment. *Curr. Alcoholism*, 6:223.

01773 **BURROW, T.** (1928), The basis of group analysis, or the analysis of the reactions of normal and neurotic individuals. *Brit. J. Med. Psychol.*, (London) 8:198-206.

01774 **BURROW, T.** (1975), The group method of analysis. In: *Group Psychotherapy and Group Function*, 2d ed., eds. M. Rosenbaum and M. M. Berger. New York: Basic Books.

01775 **BURROW, T.** (1927), The group method of analysis. *Psychoanal. Rev.*, 10:268-280.

01777 **BURTON, A.** (1969), *Encounter: Theory and Practice of Encounter Groups*. San Francisco: Jossey-Bass.

01778 **BURTON, A.** (1969), To seek and encounter critical people. *Voices*, 5:26-28.

01779 **BURTON, G.** (1962), Group counseling with alcoholic husbands and their non-alcoholic wives. *Marriage & Fam. Living*, 24:56-61.

01780 **BURWELL, D.** (1977), Psychodrama and the depressed elderly. *Can. Nurse*, (Ottawa) 73:54-55.

01781 **BURWELL, D. M.** (1969), Psychodrama. *Can. Nurse*, 65:44-46.

01782 **BUSCH, R. A.** (1978), Facilitator's presence and locus of control in the short-term group desensitization of public speaking anxiety. *Dissert. Abstr. Internat.*, 39:4725A.

01783 **BUSER, M.** (1970), Group structures and group therapy in the hospital for internal medicine. *Helvetica Med. Acta,* (Basel) 50:91-92.

01784 **BUSFIELD, B. L., Jr., HAUGHEY, D. W.,** and **DiBIASE, V.** (1969), *Out of Wedlock Pregnancy: What Happens Next? An Indepth Survey of Post-Natal Unwed Mothers Treated by Long Term Group Therapy*. Boston: Hastings House.

01785 **BUSH, H.** (1972), Adolescents: personality correlates of self and group-ratings of empathy. *Dissert. Abstr. Internat.*, 33:1282B.

01786 **BUSH, J. F.** (1972), The effect of sexed and random principal actor interaction on individual goal attainment in group counseling. *Dissert. Abstr. Internat.*, 32:6118A.

01787 **BUSH, M.** (1975), Sex offenders are people! *J. Psychiat. Nursing*, 13:38-40.

01788 **BUSTAMANTE, J. A.** (1959), Group psychotherapy and psychodrama in Cuba. *Acta Psychother. Psychosomat. Orthopaedagog. Suppl.*, (Basel) 7:78-83.

01789 **BUSTAMANTE, J. A.** (1961), Importance of cultural patterns in group psychotherapy and psychodrama. *Acta Psychother. Psychosomat. Orthopaedagog.*, (Basel) 9:262-276.

01790 **BUSTAMANTE, J. A.** (1960), Psychodrama and cultural constellation in Cuba. *Internat. J. Sociometry & Sociatry*, 2:28-34.
01791 **BUSTAMANTE, J. A.** (1957), (Psychodrama, its technique and psychotherapeutic importance.) *Arch. Hosp. Univers.*, (Havana) 9, No. 3.
01792 **BUSTOS, D. M.** (1969), Moreno Academy, World Center of psychodrama at Beacon, New York as seen by an Argentinian. *Group Psychother., Psychodrama & Sociometry*, 22:155-156.
01793 **BUTCHER, T., NEWTON, W. B.,** and **MELLETTE, R. R.** (1965), Scholastic suicide: an emerging problem area for community mental health. *Amer. J. Orthopsychiat.*, 35:346-347.
01794 **BUTKOVICH, P., CARLISLE, J., DUNCAN, R.,** and **MOSS, M.** (1975), Social system and psychoanalytic approaches to group dynamics: complementary or contradictory? *Internat. J. Group Psychother.*, 25:3-31.
01795 **BUTLER, B.** (1966), Music group psychotherapy. *J. Music Ther.*, 3:53-56.
01796 **BUTLER, J. M.** (1955), Comments on Dr. Moreno's "Transference, countertransference and tele." *Group Psychother., Psychodrama & Sociometry*, 8:181-182.
01797 **BUTLER, P. E.** (1976), Techniques of assertive training in groups. *Internat. J. Group Psychother.*, 26:361-372.
01798 **BUTLER, R.** (1980), Actualizing counselors in training: three small group approaches. *Small Group Behav.*, 11:13-22.
01799 **BUTLER, R.** (1980), Growth groups vs. traditional classroom experience: which contributes more to counselor growth? *J. Special. Group Work*, 5:20-23.
01800 **BUTLER, R. R.** (1977), Self-actualization: myth or reality? *Group & Organizat. Studies*, 2:228-233.
01801 **BUTLER, T.,** and **FUHRIMAN, A.** (1980), Patient perspective on the curative process: a comparison of day treatment and outpatient psychotherapy groups. *Small Group Behav.*, 11:371-388.
01802 **BUTTERBAUGH, R. L.** (1979), The analysis of the Graphic Awareness Projective Therapeutic Technique. *Dissert. Abstr. Internat.*, 40:5802B.
01803 **BUTTON, L.** (1974), *Developmental Group Work with Adolescents.* London: University of London Press.
01804 **BUTTON, L.** (1974), *Development Group Work with Adolescents.* New York: Halsted Press.
01805 **BUTTS, W. M.** (1962), Psychodrama with students and their wives. *Group Psychother., Psychodrama & Sociometry*, 15:55-57.
01806 **BUXBAUM, E.** (1945), Transference and group formation in children and adolescents. *Psychoanalytic Study of the Child*, 1:351-365.
01807 **BUXBAUM, H.,** and **HREBICEK, S.** (1963), The effectiveness of group psychotherapy in the treatment of female psychotic patients at a rehabilitation center. *Internat. J. Sociometry & Sociatry*, 3:25-28.
01808 **BUXBAUM, H.,** and **SIROKY, H.** (1960), Psychodrama in Czechoslovakia. *Internat. J. Sociometry & Sociatry*, 2:39-41.
01809 **BUXBAUM, H.,** and **SIROKY, H.** (1960), (Psychodrama: methodological and theoretical considerations.) *Ceskoslov. Psychiat.*, (Prague) 56:343-349.
01810 **BYRNE, M.** (1968), Resocialization of the chronic alcoholic. *Amer. J. Nursing*, 68:99-100.
01811 **BYRNE, W. A.** (1954), Current concepts of group psychotherapy. *Delaware State Med. J.*, 26:197-199.
01812 **BYRNE, W. C.** (1953), Group psychotherapy. *Delaware State Med. J.*, 25:214-216.
01813 **BYRON, E. M.** (1978), Reversing senile behavior patterns through RO-Sensory Stimulation Group Therapy. *J. Nat. Assn. Priv. Psychiat. Hosp.*, 10:68-72.

01814 **BZDEK, V. M.** (1980), Effects of a self esteem skill building program on a group of women. *Dissert. Abstr. Internat.*, 41:1962A.

C

01815 **CABANISS, A. K.** (1966), Family conferences for rehabilitation of long-term psychiatric patients. *J. Psychiat. Nursing*, 4:451-457.

01816 **CABEEN, C. W.**, and **COLEMAN, J. C.** (1961), Group therapy with sex offenders: description and evaluation of a group therapy program in an institutional setting. *J. Clin. Psychol.*, 17:122-129.

01817 **CABEEN, C. W.**, and **COLEMAN, J. C.** (1962), The selection of sex-offender patients for group psychotherapy. *Internat. J. Group Psychother.*, 12:326-334.

01818 **CABERNITE, L.** (1974), *O Grupo Terapêutico e a Psicanálise. (On the Therapeutic Group and Psychoanalysis.)* Rio de Janiero : Imago Editora.

01819 **CABIBI, J. V.** (1975), Body talk: a group therapy approach to facilitate dyadic interaction. *Dissert. Abstr. Internat.*, 35:5101.

01820 **CABRAL, D. A.** (1977), (Psychodramatic experiences with psychotic patients.) *Acta Psiquiat. Psicol. Amer. Latina*, (Buenos Aires) 23:44-49.

01821 **CABRAL, R., BEST, J.**, and **PATON, A.** (1975), Patients' and observers' assessments of process and outcome in group therapy: a follow-up study. *Amer. J. Psychiat.*, 132:1052-1054.

01822 **CABRAL, R.**, and **PATON, A.** (1975), Evaluation of group therapy: correlations between clients' and observers' assessments. *Brit. J. Psychiat.*, 126:475-477.

01823 **CABRERA, F. J.** (1961), Group psychotherapy and psychodrama for alcoholic patients in a state hospital rehabilitation program. *Group Psychother., Psychodrama & Sociometry*, 14:154-159.

01824 **CADDEN, J. J., FLACH, F. F., BLAKESLEE, S.**, and **CHARLTON, R.** (1969), Growth in medical students through group process. *Amer. J. Psychiat.*, 126:862-868.

01825 **CADDY, G. R.**, and **KRETCHMER, R. S.** (1980), Evaluation of the alternate leaderless group in a military psychiatric hospital. *Group Psychother., Psychodrama & Sociometry*, 33:33-46.

01826 **CADE, B.** (1979), Family therapy: an interactional approach to problems. *Health Visitor*, (London) 52:33-34.

01827 **CADE, B. W.** (1980), Resolving therapeutic deadlocks using a contrived team conflict. *Internat. J. Fam. Ther.*, 2:253-262.

01828 **CADMAN, W. H., MISBACH, L.**, and **BROWN, D. V.** (1954), An assessment of round-table psychotherapy. *Psychol. Monogr.*, *68*, No. 384.

01829 **CADMAN, W. H., MISBACH, L.**, and **BROWN, D. V.** (1954), *An Assessment of Round-Table Psychotherapy.* Washington, DC: American Psychological Association.

01830 **CAHILL, R. F.** (1969), Group counseling: a syllabus. *Dissert. Abstr. Internat.*, 30:2324A.

01831 **CAHILL, T. J.** (1976), The effectiveness of familial involvement on the psychodynamics of adolescent drug user therapy. *Dissert. Abstr. Internat.*, 36:4128-4129.

01832 **CAHN, C. H.** (1950), The use of drugs in group therapy. *Amer. J. Psychiat.*, 107:135-136.

01833 **CAHN, M. M.** (1973/1974), Desacralization as a response to group change. *Interpersonal Develop.*, 4:62-64.

01834 **CAHN, R., WEILL, D.**, and **DION, Y.** (1974), Understanding the parents of psychotic children by means of the countertransference process. *Psychiat. de l'Enfant*, 17:413-478.

01835 **CAHNERS, S. S.** (1978), Group meetings for families of burned children. *Health & Soc. Work*, 3:165-172.

01836 **CAILLÉ, P.** (1978), Psychothérapie du psychotique et de sa famille: les processus thérapeutique dans le cadre de la théorie des systèmes. (Psychotherapy with the psychotic and his family: therapeutic processes in the group and systems theory.) *Psychother. & Psychosomat.*, (Stuttgart) 29:217-220.

01837 **CAIN, A.** (1978), Pratique du psychodrame Freudien. (Practice of Freudian psychodrama.) *Psychother. & Psychosomat.*, (Stuttgart) 29:267-270.

01838 **CAIN, A. O.** (1972), The relationship between growth in self actualization and the numbers of perceived and mutually perceived relationships in sensitivity drawing groups. *Dissert. Abstr. Internat.*, 33:2232A.

01839 **CAIN, J., CHARPIN, J.,** and **PLANSON, C.** (1959), Psychosomatic considerations on 50 cases of allergic asthma: attempted group psychotherapy. *Acta Allergologica*, (Copenhagen) 14:134-145.

01840 **CAINE, T. M.,** and **WIJESINGHE, B.** (1976), Personality, expectancies and group psychotherapy. *Brit. J. Psychiat.*, (Ashford) 129:384-387.

01841 **CAJIAO, R. G.** (1960), Die forschungsarbeit in der gruppentherapie: ihre probleme, methoden und aufgaben. (Research in group therapy: its problems, methods, and goals.) *Psyche*, (Stuttgart) 14:524-537.

01842 **CALDWELL, H. S., LEVEQUE, K. L.,** and **LANE, D. M.** (1974), Group psychotherapy in the management of hemophilia. *Psychol. Reports*, 35:339-342.

01843 **CALEF, R. A., CALEF, R. S., SUNDSTROM, P., JARRETT, J.,** and **DAVIS, B.** (1974), Facilitation of group desensitization of test anxiety. *Psychol. Reports*, 35:1285-1286.

01844 **CÁLEK, O.** (1975), (Group psychotherapy in rationalization courses for the later blind.) *Ceskoslov. Psychol.*, (Prague) 19:529-535.

01845 **CALHOUN, K. S.** (1971), Change in group psychotherapy as function of interaction between patient and therapist styles. *Dissert. Abstr. Internat.*, 32:1204B.

01846 **CALHOUN, L. D.** (1969), The effect of group counseling on academic achievement. *Dissert. Abstr. Internat.*, 30:981A.

01847 **CALIFORNIA DEPT. OF MENTAL HYGIENE.** (1952), *Group Psychotherapy for the Psychoneurotic: Report of Activities During May, 1952*. Sacramento: Department Mental Hygiene.

01848 **CALIGOR, J.** (1980), The analytic therapist in the group 1980: continuities and discontinuities with Sigmund Freud. *Group*, 4:32-39.

01849 **CALIGOR, J. A.** (1976), Perceptions of the group therapist and the dropout from group. *Dissert. Abstr. Internat.*, 36:3594B.

01850 **CALLAN, J. E. B.** (1970), A measure of self-disclosure in intensive small groups. *Dissert. Abstr. Internat.*, 31:4306B.

01851 **CALLAO, M. J.** (1972), Sociometric change among elementary school children involved in a shared goals model of group counseling. *Dissert. Abstr. Internat.*, 32:4937A.

01852 **CALLIOTTE, J. A.** (1971), The effects of basic encounter groups on student teachers' personality traits and subsequent teaching behaviors. *Dissert. Abstr. Internat.*, 32:4462A.

01853 **CALVIN, A. D., HOFFMAN, F. K.,** and **HARDEN, E. L.** (1957), The effect of intelligence and social atmosphere of group problem solving behavior. *J. Soc. Psychol.*, 45:61-74.

01854 **CAMBELL, R. S.,** and **STEWART, C. H.** (1976), Dimensions of narcotic addiction treatment. *Drug Forum*, 5:149-161.

01855 **CAMERON, D. E.** (1950), *General Psychotherapy: Dynamics and Procedures*. New York: Grune and Stratton.

01856 **CAMERON, J.,** and **STEWART, R.** (1955), Observations on group psychotherapy with chronic psychoneurotic patients in a mental hospital. *Internat. J. Group Psychother.*, 5:346-360.

01857 **CAMERON, J. L.** (1957), Some implications of ego psychology for group psychotherapy of chronic schizophrenia. *Internat. J. Group Psychother.*, 7:355-362.

01858 **CAMERON, J. L.**, and **FREEMAN, T.** (1956), Group psychotherapy in affective disorders. *Internat. J. Group Psychother.*, 6:235-257.

01859 **CAMERON, K.** (1953), Group approach to inpatient adolescents. *Amer. J. Psychiat.*, 109:657-661.

01860 **CAMPBELL, D. R.**, and **SINHA, B. K.** (1980), Brief group psychotherapy with chronic hemodialysis patients. *Amer. J. Psychiatry*, 137:1234-1237.

01861 **CAMPBELL, D. T.**, and **MEHRA, K.** (1960), Individual differences in evaluations of group discussions as a projective measure of attitudes toward leadership. *J. Soc. Psychol.*, 47:101-106.

01862 **CAMPBELL, J.**, and **CLAUNON, T. L.** (1969), From the medical facility of the California Department of Correction: questionnaire-study of the aspects considered relevant by its group therapists. *Internat. J. Offender Ther.*, (London) 13:158-164.

01863 **CAMPBELL, J. P.**, and **DUNNETTE, M. D.** (1968), Effectiveness of t-group experiences in managerial training and development. *Psychol. Bull.*, 70:73-104.

01864 **CAMPO, A.**, and **CARPELAN, H.** (1962), (The manifestation of manic defense in a psychoanalytic psychodrama group.) *Acta Psychother. Psychosomat. Orthopaedagog.*, (Basel) 10:439-453.

01865 **CAMPOS, L. P.** (1971), Transactional analysis: group leadership operations. *Transactional Anal. J.*, 1:219-222.

01866 **CAMPOY GUERRERO, A.**, and **GALLEGO MERE, A.** (1970), Intensive gruppenpsychotherapie. (Intensive group therapy.) *Fortsch. Psychoanal.*, 4:135-144.

01867 **CAMPUZANO MONTOYA, M.** (1977), A model of group psychotherapy for adolescent drug addicts. *Neurol.-Neurocir.-Psiquiat.*, (Mexico City) 18:222-232.

01868 **CANADA, A. T.** (1972), Methadone in a 30 day detoxification program for narcotics addicts: a critical review. *Internat. J. Addict.*, 7:613.

01869 **CANDEIAS, N. M. F.**, and **MARCONDES, R. S.** (1977), Group dynamics at a school for public health: pioneer experiment. *Internat. J. Health Educat.*, (Geneva) 20:271-278.

01870 **CANFIELD, S. F., ELEY, J., ROLLMAN, L. P.**, and **SCHUR, E. L.** (1975), A laboratory training model for the development of effective interpersonal communications in social work. *J. Educat. Sociol.*, 11:45-50.

01871 **CANINO-STOLBERG, G.** (1976), The effects of physical contact exercises in marathon encounter leaderless groups, on dimensions of self-concept, self-disclosure and touching behavior. *Dissert. Abstr. Internat.*, 36:3592B.

01872 **CANTANZARO, R. J.** (1967), Tape-a-drama in treating alcoholics. *Quart. J. Studies Alcohol*, 28:138-140.

01873 **CANTER, A. H.** (1955), Observations on group psychotherapy with hospitalized patients. *Amer. J. Psychother.*, 10:66-73.

01874 **CANTER, A. H.** (1955), Observations on group psychotherapy with hospitalized patients. *Amer. J. Psychiat.*, 112:297-298.

01875 **CANTER, F. M.** (1971), Authoritarian attitudes, degree of pathology and preference for structured versus unstructured psychotherapy in hospitalized mental patients. *Psychol. Reports*, 28:231-234.

01876 **CANTER, F. M.** (1969), Motivation for self-confrontation in alcoholic patients. *Psychother.: Theory, Res. & Pract.*, 6:21-23.

01877 **CANTER, F. M.** (1966), Personality factors related to participation in treatment of hospitalized male alcoholics. *J. Clin. Psychol.*, 22:114-116.

01878 **CANTER, F. M.** (1969), A self-help project with hospitalized alcoholics. *Internat. J. Group Psychother.*, 19:16-27.

01879 **CANTER, I.** (1957), A study of the relationship of education to social group work through an analysis of theory and practice. Unpublished doctoral dissertation, Maryland University.

01880 **CANTRELL, W. A.** (1978), Review of G. L. Paul's and R. J. Lentz's *Psychosocial Treatment of Chronic Mental Patients: Milieu Versus Social-Learning Programs. Amer. J. Psychiat.*, 135:1133.

01881 **CAPALDO, T.** (1971), (Some general aspects of group psychotherapy in psychiatric institutions.) *Riv. Sper. Freniatria*, (Emilia) 95:808-817.

01882 **CAPANI, R.** (1970), (Positive and negative aspects of amateur dramatic festivals.) *Riv. Sper. Freniatria*, (Emilia) 94:777-780.

01883 **CAPELLE, R. G.** (1979), *Changing Human Systems.* Toronto: International Human Systems Institute.

01884 **CAPITAIN, J. P.** (1978), A propos d'un groupe de biolnergie à l'*h*ôpital genéral. sa peace, éléments pour une discuscion. (Group use of bioenergy in general hospital: report of an experience and discussion.) *Dissert. Abstr. Internat.*, 38:5345C.

01885 **CAPLAN, G.** (1951), Mental–hygiene work with expectant mothers—a group psychotherapeutic approach. *Ment. Hygiene*, 35:41-50.

01886 **CAPLAN, H. L., ROHDE, P. D., SHAPIRO, D. A.,** and **WATSON, D. P.** (1975), Some correlates of repertory grid measures used to study a psychotherapeutic group. *Brit. J. Med. Psychol.*, (London) 48:217-226.

01887 **CAPLOWLIDNER, E., HARPAZ, L.,** and **SAMBERG, S.** (1979), Therapeutic dance–movement: expressive activities for older adults. *Rehab. Lit.*, 40:318.

01888 **CAPP, L. A.** (1971), A projective cartoon investigation of nurse-patient psychodramatic role perception and expectation. *Nursing Res.*, 20:100-112.

01889 **CAPPON, D.** (1963), Group therapy in private practice. *Amer. J. Psychother.*, 17:213-229.

01890 **CAPUZZI, D.,** and **MUFFETT, L.** (1980), An overview of ethical standards for group facilitators. *J. Special. Group Work*, 5:98-106.

01891 **CAREK, D. J.** (1964), Group therapy as a study in behavioral expression. *Internat. Psychiat. Clinics*, 1:123-135.

01892 **CAREY, R. W.** (1960), Group counseling with scholastic underachievers in high school. Ph.D. thesis, University of California, Berkeley.

01893 **CARINI, E. M., COSKEY, S. A., MICHLEWSKI, J.,** and **RAMSDEN, W. A.** (1971), Remotivation groups: too structured for current needs? *Hosp. & Community Psychiat.*, 22:313-314.

01894 **CARKHUFF, R.** (1973), A human technology for group helping processes. *Educat. Technol.*, 13:31-38.

01895 **CARKHUFF, R. R.** (1971), The sensitivity fraud. *J. Clin. Psychol.*, 27:158-159.

01896 **CARKHUFF, R. R.,** and **BIERMAN, R.** (1970), Training as a preferred mode of treatment of parents of emotionally disturbed children. *J. Consult. & Clin. Psychol.*, 17:157-161.

01897 **CARKHUFF, R. R.** (1965), Lay mental health counseling: the effects of lay group counseling. *J. Consult. & Clin. Psychol.*, 29:26-31.

01898 **CARLIN, A. S.,** and **ARMSTRONG, H. E.** (1968), Rewarding social responsibility in disturbed children: a group play technique. *Psychother.: Theory, Res. & Pract.*, 5:169-174.

01899 **CARLISLE, L. A.** (1978), A nonfunctioning group. *Issues Ment. Health Nursing*, 1:85-90.

01900 **CARLSON, C. R.** (1976), The relationship of anxiety openness and group psychotherapy experience with perceptions of therapist self-disclosure among psychiatric patients. *Dissert. Abstr. Internat.*, 37:453B.

01901 **CARLSON, N. D.**, and **WEINBERGER, G.** (1964), Experimental group therapy in a senior high school. *J. Soc. Psychol.*, 64:241-247.

01902 **CARLSON, P. M.** (1970), An analysis of the motor, cognitive, and physiological components of psychotherapeutically induced changes in phobic behavior. *Dissert. Abstr. Internat.*, 30:5233-5234.

01903 **CARLSON, W. A.** (1962), The relationship between success in group counseling and discrepancy in levels of personality. *Dissert. Abstr. Internat.*, 22:3516.

01904 **CARMAN, M. B.** (1977), Effects of emotional innoculation and supportive therapy on stress incurred from nursing home placement. *Dissert. Abstr. Internat.*, 37:4132B.

01905 **CARMENT, D. W., SCHWARTZ, F. S.**, and **MILES, C. G.** (1964), Participation and opinion changes as related to cohesiveness and sex of ss in two-person groups. *Psychol. Reports*, 14:695-702.

01906 **CARMICHAEL, D. M.** (1953), Potential of group practices in mental hospitals. *Internat. J. Group Psychother.*, 3:309-314.

01907 **CARNER, C.** (1968), Now: clubs for mutual mental help. *Today's Health*, 46:40-41, 72-73.

01908 **CARNES, G. D., CLELAND, R. S.**, and **BEHA, W.** (1964), Group counseling with student nurses during their psychiatric affiliation. *J. Psychiat. Nursing*, 2:304-312.

01909 **CARNEY, F. L.** (1977), Outpatient treatment of the aggressive offender. *Amer. J. Psychother.*, 31:265-274.

01910 **CARNEY, F. L.** (1972), Some recurring therapeutic issues in group psychotherapy with criminal patients. *Amer. J. Psychother.*, 26:34-41.

01911 **CARNEY, F. L.** (1973), Three important factors in psychotherapy with criminal patients. *Amer. J. Psychother.*, 27:220-231.

01912 **CARNEY, P.** (1967), Nurse–conducted group therapy. *UNA Nursing J.*, (Melbourne) 65:41-43.

01913 **CARNEY, T. F.** (1976), *Mind-Expanding Techniques*. Winnipeg: Harbeck.

01914 **CAROFF, P., LEIBERMAN, F.**, and **GOTTESFELD, M.** (1970), The drug problem: treating preaddictive adolescents. *Soc. Casework*, 51:527-532.

01915 **CARP, E. A. D. E.** (1960), Group-selection. *Acta Psychother. Psychosomat. Orthopaedagog.*, (Basel) 8:449-456.

01916 **CARP, E. A. D. E.** (1953), *Problemen der Groepsychotherapie.* (*The Problem of Group Psychotherapy.*) Lochem: De Tijdstroom.

01917 **CARP, E. A. D. E.** (1949), *Psychodrama: Dramatisering als Vorm van Psychotherapie.* (*Psychodrama: Dramatizing as a Form of Psychotherapy.*) Amsterdam: Scheltema and Holkema.

01918 **CARP E. A. D. E.** (1953), Remarques sur la sociotherapie francais. (Remarks on French psychotherapy.) *Acta Psychother. Psychosomat. Orthopaedagog.*, (Basel) 1:281-286.

01919 **CARP, E. A. D. E.** (1955), *Sociotherapie Actieve Aanpassingstherapie.* Lochem: De Tijdstroom.

01920 **CARPELAN, H.** (1977), (On insight in psychoanalytic group psychotherapy.) *Psychiat. Fennica*, 167-170.

01921 **CARPENTER, J. R.** (1968), Role reversal in the classroom. *Group Psychother., Psychodrama & Sociometry*, 21:155-167.

01922 **CARPENTER, J. T.** (1977), Further considerations on "A theoretical framework for group psychotherapy": a summary and culture. *J. Contemp. Psychother.*, 9:83-88.

01923 **CARPENTER, P.**, and **SANDBERG, S.** (1973), "The things inside:" psychodrama with delinquent adolescents. *Psychother.: Theory, Res. & Pract.*, 10:245-247.

01924 **CARPILOVSKY, J. C.** (1966), Concepcão oral da cena primária em un grupo terapeutico. (Oral phase of the primary scene in group therapy).*J. Brasil. Psiquiat.*, (Rio de Janeiro) 15:211-218.

01925 **CARPILOVSKY, J. C.** (1964), Frustracão, Inveja e Ódio em un Grupo Terapêutico. (Frustration, envy and hate in a therapeutic group). *J. Brasil. Psiquiat.*, (Rio de Janeiro) 13:365-371.

01926 **CARPILOVSKY, J. C.** (1965), (Fantasies of a therapeutic group concerning the admission of the "observer.") *J. Brasil. Psiquiat.*, (Rio de Janeiro) 14:277-284.

01927 **CARPILOVSKY, J. C.** (1967), (Readjustment of honoraria in group psychotherapy.) *J. Brasil. Psiquiat.*, (Rio de Janeiro) 16:187-192.

01928 **CARPILOVSKY, J. C.** (1967), (The function of projective identification in group therapy.) *J. Brasil. Psiquiat.*, (Rio de Janeiro) 16:355-362.

01929 **CARR, J. E.**, and **WHITTENBAUGH, J.** (1965), Perception of "improvement" and interjudge reliability in therapy-outcome studies. *Proceed., 73d Annual Convention,* American Psychological Association, pp. 197-198.

01930 **CARRASCO, J. S.**, and **GARCIA, J. M.** (1965), Psicoterapia de grupo en alcoholicos. (Group psychotherapy with alcoholics.) *Rev. Psiquiat. & Psicol. Med.*, 7:132-143.

01931 **CARRERA, R. N.**, and **LOTT, D. L.** (1978), The effect of group implosive therapy on snake phobias. *J. Clin. Psychol.*, 34:177-181.

01932 **CARRÈRE, J.**, and **SEGUIER, R.** (1965), (Value of dynamic group psychotherapy of drinkers by participation in anonymous alcoholics and their wives.) *Annales Medico-Psychol.*, (Paris) 123:87-92.

01933 **CARRIER, J. A. J.** (1972), The comparison of a team/group dynamics training model with a team/traditional training model within leadership training workshops. *Dissert. Abstr. Internat.*, 32:6754A.

01934 **CARRILLO CARILLO, J. A.** (1975), (Psychoanalytic psychodrama in group therapy.) *Neurol.-Neurocir-Psiquiat.*, (Mexico City) 16:101-108.

01935 **CARROLL, L. J.** (1979), Success prediction in behavioral vs. self-help weight control groups. *Dissert. Abstr. Internat.*, 40:4993B.

01936 **CARROLL, L. J.** (1980), Success prediction in behavioral versus self-help weight control groups. *Dissert. Abstr. Internat.*, 40:4993B. (University Microfilms No. 8008559.)

01937 **CARROLL, W. T.** (1960), The use of group counseling in the modification of parental attitudes concerning the guidance of children. Ph.D. thesis, Florida State University.

01938 **CARRUTH, B. F.** (1976), Modifying behavior through social learning. *Amer. J. Nursing*, 76:1804-1806.

01939 **CARSKY, M.** (1978), An elaboration of Bion's group theory. *Dissert. Abstr. Internat.*, 39:3501B.

01940 **CARSON, W. M.** (1974), A study of the effects of training teachers through group consultation to decrease pupils' attention-getting behaviors. *Dissert. Abstr. Internat.*, 34:5618A.

01941 **CARSTENSON, B.** (1955), The auxiliary chair technique. *Group Psychother., Psychodrama & Sociometry*, 8:50-56.

01942 **CARSWELL, R. W.** (1976), A study of the effects of an experiential learning model in group counseling with juvenile delinquents. *Dissert. Abstr. Internat.*, 36:7201A.

01943 **CARTER, A. L.** (1975), An analysis of the use of contemporary Black literature and music and its effects upon self-concept in group counseling procedures. *Dissert. Abstr. Internat.*, 35:7052-7053.

01944 **CARTER, F. M.** (1959), The critical incident technique in identification of the patients' perception of therapeutic patient-patient interaction on a psychiatric ward. *Nursing Res.*, 8:207-211.

01945 **CARTER, H. L.** (1970), An investigation of two methods of short-term group counseling with white preadolescents rated low on social status by their peers. *Dissert. Abstr. Internat.*, 31:5757A.

01946 **CARTER, J. H.,** and **DUNSTON, J. C.** (1973), Treating the black college drug abuser. a preliminary report. *Nat. Med. Assn. J.*, 65:127-131.
01947 **CARTER, J. H.,** and **JORDAN, B. M.** (1972), Inpatient therapy for black paranoid men. *Hosp. & Community Psychiat.*, 23:180-182.
01948 **CARTER, L. M.** (1961), Psychodrama and the new role of the school principal. *Group Psychother., Psychodrama & Sociometry*, 14:169-171.
01949 **CARTER, W.** (1978), A student group art therapy experience. *Amer. J. Art Ther.*, 17:131-139.
01950 **CARTER, W. W.** (1968), Group counseling for adolescent foster children. *Children*, 15:22-27.
01951 **CARTWRIGHT, D.** (1975), Risk taking by individuals and groups: an assessment of research employing choice dilemmas. In: *Group Psychotherapy and Group Function*, 2d ed., eds. M. Rosenbaum and M. M. Berger. New York: Basic Books.
01952 **CARTWRIGHT, D.,** and **LIPPITT, R.** (1957), Group dynamics and the individual. *Internat. J. Group Psychother.*, 7:86-102.
01953 **CARTWRIGHT, D.,** and **ZANDER, A. R.** (1965), *Group Dynamics*. London: Tavistock.
01954 **CARTWRIGHT, M. H.** (1976), Preparatory method for group counseling. *J. Couns. Psychol.*, 23:75-76.
01955 **CARTWRIGHT, M. H.** (1972), A preparatory process for group counseling and/or group therapy. *Dissert. Abstr. Internat.*, 33:2315B.
01956 **CARTWRIGHT, R. D.** (1968), Psychotherapeutic processes. In: *Annual Review of Psychology*, ed. P. R. Farnsworth. Palo Alto: Annual Reviews.
01957 **CARTWRIGHT, R. D., SEEMAN, J.,** and **GRUMMON, D. I.** (1956), Patterns of perceived interpersonal relations. *Sociometry*, 19:166-177.
01958 **CARUSO, I. A., FRANK-RIESER, E., RUBNER, A.,** and **RUBNER, E.** (1976), (The relationship of psychoanalysis and group dynamics as a method of socialization.) *Zeit. Klin. Psychol. & Psychother.*, (Freiburg) 24:49-55.
01959 **CARUTHERS, J. D.** (1975), The effects of small group counseling on the self concept of disadvantaged students. *Dissert. Abstr. Internat.*, 36:2017A.
01960 **CASE, M. E.** (1951), The forgotten ones: an exploratory project in the use of group activities for the treatment of deteriorated psychotic patients. *Smith Coll. Studies Soc. Work.*, 21:199-231.
01961 **CASELLA, B. M.** (1972), Group process in training catholic seminarians. *Internat. J. Group Psychother.*, 22:384-389.
01962 **CASEY, N. A.,** and **SOLOMON, L.** (1971/1972), The effect of seating arrangements on t-group interaction and sociometric choices. *Interpersonal Develop.*, 2:9-20.
01963 **CASHDAN, S.** (1970), Sensitivity groups: problems and promise. *Prof. Psychol.*, 1:217-224.
01964 **CASRIEL, D.** (1972), *A Scream Away from Happiness*. New York: Grosset and Dunlap.
01965 **CASRIEL, D. H.,** and **DEITCH, D.** (1968), The marathon: time extended. In: *Current Psychiatric Therapies*, ed. J. H. Masserman. New York: Grune and Stratton.
01966 **CASSEL, R. N.,** and **MARTIN, G.** (1964), Comparing peer status ratings of elementary pupils with their guidance data and learning efficiency indices. *J. Genetic Psychol.*, 105:39-42.
01967 **CASTETS, B.,** and **LEFORT, R.** (1962), (Remarks on the indications for psychodrama.) *Annales Medico-Psychol.*, (Paris) 120:574-578.
01968 **CASTLE, N.** (1980), A group experience with physically handicapped children. *Child Welfare*, 59:235.
01969 **CASTRILLON de la ROSA, C.** (1976), (Psychological approach in pediatric oncology.) *Annales Espan. Pediat.*, (Madrid) 9:59-63.

01970 **CASTRO GUEYARA, N. P.** (1967), La entrevista con el niño y sus padres en una clinica de la conducta. (Interview with child and parents in a behavior clinic.) *Rev. Clin. Conducta*, 1:17-25.
01971 **CATANZARO, R. J.** (1970), Group therapies in the problem habit, alcoholism. *Texas Med.*, 66:60-62.
01973 **CATHCART, R. S.**, and **SAMOVAR, L. A.** (1974), *Small Group Communication: A Reader*, 2d ed., Dubuque, IA: Brown.
01974 **CATRON, D. W.** (1966), Educational-vocational group counseling: the effects on perception of self and others. *J. Couns. Psychol.*, 13:202-207.
01975 **CATRON, D. W.** (1965), The effects of educational–vocational group counseling on perception of self and others. *Dissert. Abstr. Internat.*, 25:6756.
01976 **CAUFFMAN, J.** (1971), Outcomes of a reality therapy workshop. *School Health Rev.*, 2:2-4.
01977 **CAULFIELD, T. F.** (1969), The effects of using video-taped social models in elementary school group counseling with low sociometric status students. *Dissert. Abstr. Internat.*, 30:1813A.
01978 **CAVANAGH, J. K.**, and **GERSTEIN, S.** (1949), Group psychotherapy in a naval disciplinary barracks: preliminary report. *U.S. Navy Med. Bull.*, 49:645-654.
01979 **CECERE, G. J.**, (1969), Change in certain personality variables of counselor education candidates as a function of t-group. *Dissert. Abstr. Internat.*, 30:1427A-1428A.
01980 **CECIL, E. A., CHERTKOFF, J. M.**, and **CUMMINGS, L. L.** (1970), Risk taking in groups as a function of group pressure. *J. Soc. Psychol.*, 81:273-274.
01981 **CELIA, S. A. H.** (1970), The club as an integrative factor in a therapeutic community for children. *Amer. J. Orthopsychiat.*, 40:130-134.
01982 **CERANSKI, J.** (1976), (Ambulatory group psychotherapy in the treatment of psychoses.) *Psychiat. Polska*, (Warsaw) 10:661-665.
01983 **CERBONE, A. R.** (1974), An analysis of the Bennis model of small group development as related to leadership style. *Dissert. Abstr. Internat.*, 34:3982A.
01984 **CERIO, J. E.** (1979), Structured experiences with the educational growth group. *Personnel & Guid. J.*, 57:398-401.
01985 **CERMAK, S. A., STEIN, F.**, and **ABELSON, C.** (1973), Hyperactive children and an activity group therapy model. *Amer. J. Occupat. Ther.*, 27:311-315.
01986 **CERNÝ, J.** (1964), (On "bifocal" group psychotherapy of schizophrenia.) *Ceskoslov. Psychiat.*, (Prague) 60:262-268.
01987 **CERNÝ, J.** (1968), (On some newer psychopathological aspects of the Japanese concept of Morita's psychotherapy and on the studies of Zazem.) *Ceskoslov. Psychiat.*, (Warsaw) 64:194-204.
01988 **CERNÝ, J.**, and **SVOBODOVA, D.** (1966), Nase zkusenosti s diskusni skupinovou psychoterapii u deti. (Our experiences with discussion group psychotherapy with children.) *Ceskoslov. Psychiat.*, (Warsaw) 62:153-159.
01989 **CERRA, V.** (1974), A comparison of structured and unstructured time limited sensitivity groups. *Dissert. Abstr. Internat.*, 34:6970A.
01990 **CHABOT, F.**, and **DOYON, Y.** (1973), (Group psychotherapy of preadolescents presenting behavior problems of neurotic origin.) *Vie Med. Can. Francaise*, (Quebec) 2:115-117.
01991 **CHACE, M.** (1953), Dance as an adjunctive therapy with hospitalized mental patients. *Bull. Menninger Clinic*, 17:219-225.
01992 **CHACE, M.** (1945), Rhythm in movement as used in St. Elizabeth's Hospital. *Sociometry*, 8:481-483.
01993 **CHADBOURNE, J.** (1980), Training groups: a basic life cycle model. *Personnel & Guid. J.*, 59:55-58.

01994 **CHAFETZ, M. E.** (1954), An active treatment program for chronically ill mental patients. *J. Nerv. & Ment. Diseases*, 119:428-436.

01995 **CHAFETZ, M. E.** (1958), The role of psychiatry in the treatment of Parkinson's disease. *Geriatrics*, 13:435-440.

01996 **CHAFETZ, M. E., BERNSTEIN, N., SHARPE, W.,** and **SCHWAB, R. S.** (1955), Short-term therapy of patients with Parkinson's disease. *New Engl. J. Med.*, 253:961-964.

01997 **CHALFEN, L.** (1964), The use of dreams in psychoanalytic group psychotherapy. *Psychoanal. Rev.*, 51:125-132.

01998 **CHALPIN, G.** (1966), The fathers' group: an effective therapy medium for involving fathers in a child psychiatric clinic treatment program. *J. Amer. Acad. Child Psychiat.*, 5:125-133.

01999 **CHAMBERS, J. L.,** and **LIEBERMANN, L. R.** (1965), Differences between normal and clinical groups in judging, evaluating and associating needs. *J. Clin. Psychol.*, 21:145-149.

02000 **CHAMBERS, N. S.** (1970), An investigation into group and individual assessment of creativity. *Dissert. Abstr. Internat.*, 31:1614A.

02001 **CHAMBERS, W. M.,** and **FICEK, D. E.** (1970), An evaluation of marathon counseling. *Internat. J. Group Psychother.*, 20:372-379.

02002 **CHAMPAGNE, D. W.** (1971), A training design for decision making. *Soc. Change*, 3:4-5.

02003 **CHAMPERNOWNE, H. I.,** and **LEWIS, E.** (1966), Psychodynamics of therapy in a residential group. *J. Anal. Psychol.*, (London) 11:163-180.

02004 **CHAN, D. C.** (1973), Using patients as group leaders in a VA hospital. *Hosp. & Community Psychiat.*, 24:531.

02005 **CHANCE, E.** (1968), Group psychotherapy in community mental health programs. *Amer. J. Orthopsychiat.*, 37:921-925.

02006 **CHANCE, E.** (1948), Group psychotherapy and the psychiatric social worker. *Ment. Health*, (London) 8:8-12.

02007 **CHANCE, E.** (1971), Recurrent problems in the management of treatment groups. *Internat. J. Soc. Psychiat.*, (London) 17:210-216.

02008 **CHANCE, E.** (1975), Recurrent problems in the management of treatment groups. In: *Group Psychotherapy and Group Function*, 2d ed., eds. M. Rosenbaum and M. M. Berger. New York: Basic Books.

02009 **CHANCE, E.** (1974), Some implications of variations in techniques of group therapy. *Amer. J. Orthopsychiat.*, 44:216-217.

02010 **CHANCE, E.** (1976), Some implications of variations in techniques of group therapy for social controls. *Internat. J. Soc. Psychiat.*, (London) 22:147-152.

02011 **CHANCE, E.** (1952), A study of transference in group psychotherapy. *Internat. J. Group Psychother.*, 2:40-53.

02012 **CHANCE, E.** (1965), Training in analytic group psychotherapy: observations on some learning problems in the dimension of power. *Internat. J. Group Psychother.*, 15:291-302.

02013 **CHANDLER, C. S.,** and **SHAFTER, A. J.** (1953), A critique of the group placement concept. *Amer. J. Ment. Deficiency*, 59:517-521.

02014 **CHANDLER, E. S.** (1978), Videotape feedback in group counseling: improving self concepts of children. *Dissert. Abstr. Internat.*, 38:5921A.

02015 **CHANG, T. M.** (1962), Estimate of behavioral characteristics in group psychotherapy. *Internat. J. Sociometry & Sociatry*, 2:125-135.

02016 **CHANG, T. M. C.** (1957), Predicting selected behavioral characteristics on the basis of observation of a group psychotherapy session with mental patients. *Dissert. Abstr. Internat.*, 17:2312-2313.

02017 **CHAPMAN, A. L.** (1953), An experiment with group conferences for weight reduction. *Pub. Health Reports*, 68:439-440.

02018 **CHAPMAN, M.** (1971), Movement therapy in the treatment of suicidal patients. *Perspect. Psychiat. Care*, 9:119-122.
02019 **CHAPMAN, M.** (1959), *Self-Inventory: Group Therapy for Those Who Stutter*, 3rd ed. Minneapolis: Burgess.
02020 **CHAPMAN, M. E.** (1959), *Self-Inventory: Group Therapy for Those who Stutter*, 3d ed. Minneapolis: Burgess Publishing.
02021 **CHAPPELL, C. L.** (1969), Participation Training: an instrument for milieu change. *Hosp. & Community Psychiat.*, 20:355-357.
02022 **CHAPPELL, M. H., STEFANO, J. J., ROGERSON, J. S.,** and **PIKE, P. H.** (1937), Value of group psychological procedures in the treatment of peptic ulcers. *Amer. J. Digestive Diseases*, 3:813-817.
02023 **CHARLIN, V., SEPULVEDA, M.,** and **VINET, E.** (1980), (Two strategies in Gestalt therapy: a group with periodic sessions and a group with marathon sessions: comparison of the efficacy and role of the time factor.) *Rev. Chilean Psicol.*, (Santiago) 3:55-61.
02024 **CHARNEY, M.** (1975), Psychodrama and self-identity. *Group Psychother., Psychodrama & Sociometry*, 28:118-127.
02025 **CHARNY, I. W.** (1974), The new psychotherapies and encounters of the seventies: progress or fads. *Humanist*, 34:
02026 **CHARNY, I. W.** (1972), Parental intervention with one another on behalf of their child: a breaking-through tool for preventing emotional disturbances. *J. Contemp. Psychother.*, 5:19-29.
02027 **CHASE, B. S.** (1973), A study of the effects of the duration of group counseling on study habits. *Dissert. Abstr. Internat.*, 32:152A.
02028 **CHASE, C.** (1978), No joking matter: a study of laughter in sensitivity training groups. *Dissert. Abstr. Internat.*, 39:4023B.
02029 **CHASE, M.** (1960), A note on dance therapy. *Group Psychother., Psychodrama, & Sociometry*, 13:205.
02030 **CHASE, P.,** and **FARNHAM, B.** (1966), Psychodrama in a mental hospital. *Ment. Hygiene*, 50:262-265.
02031 **CHASE, P.,** and **FARNHAM, B.** (1965), A report on religious psychodrama. *Group Psychother., Psychodrama & Sociometry*, 18:177-190.
02032 **CHASE, P. H.,** and **FARNHAM, B. T.** (1980), Group rhythms: action . . . assessment . . . assimilation. *J. Special. Group Work*, 5:77-80.
02033 **CHASONOFF, E.,** and **SCHRADER, C.** (1979), Behaviorally oriented activities therapy program for adolescents. *Adolescence*, 14:567-578.
02034 **CHATEAU, J. F.** (1968), (Outline of a methodology for an approach to group neuroses: choice of the analyst's place.) *Rev. Neuropsychiat. Infantile*, (Paris) 16:499-503.
02035 **CHATEL, M. M.** (1969/1970), Encounter groups. *Bull. de Psychol.*, (Paris) 23:994-997.
02036 **CHATMAN, V. A. S.** (1976), Career planning in decision making: a group counseling approach. *Dissert. Abstr. Internat.*, 37:1982A.
02037 **CHATWIN, M. W.** (1972), Interpersonal truth and leadership style in group counseling. *Dissert. Abstr. Internat.*, 32:6120A.
02038 **CHEATHAM, R. B.** (1968), A study of the effects of group counseling on the self-concept and on the reading efficiency of low-achieving readers in a public-intermediate school. *Dissert. Abstr. Internat.*, 29:2200B.
02039 **CHEN, C.** (1962), Therapeutic effects of spontaneous patient subgroups formed on a state hospital ward. *Internat. J. Group Psychother.*, 12:301-311.
02040 **CHEN, C. C.** (1972), Experiences with group psychotherapy in Taiwan. *Internat. J. Group Psychother.*, 22:210-227.
02041 **CHEN, C. C.,** and **CHU, H. M.** (1962), Evaluation of patient's attendance in open group psychotherapeutic sessions on a psychiatric ward. *Formosa Med. Assn. J.*, (Taipei) 61:345-351.

02042 **CHEN, M. E.** (1978), Applying Yalom's principles to crisis work: some intriguing results—at the Community Mental Health Center at Strong Memorial Hospital. *J. Psychiat. Nursing*, 16:15-22.

02043 **CHENEY, W. D.** (1971), Eric Berne: biographical sketch. *Transactional Anal. J.*, 1:14-22.

02044 **CHENVEN, H.** (1953), Effects of group therapy upon language recovery in predominantly expressive aphasic patients. Unpublished doctoral dissertation, New York University.

02045 **CHERCHIA, P. J.** (1974), Effects of communication skill training on high school students' ability to function as peer group facilitators. *Dissert. Abstr. Internat.*, 34:6970A.

02046 **CHERTOFF, H. R.**, and **BERGER, M. M.** (1971), A technique for overcoming resistance to group therapy in psychotic patients on a community mental health service. *Internat. J. Group Psychother.*, 21:53-61.

02047 **CHERTOFF, H. R.**, and **BERGER, M. M.** (1970), A technique for overcoming resistance to group therapy in psychotic patients on a community mental health service. *Sandoz Psychiat. Spectator*, 6:17-18, 20.

02048 **CHERTOK, L. G.** (1972), The Balint group and preventive industrial medicine. *Psychiat. in Med.*, 3:395-402.

02049 **CHESARO, F. J.** (1978), Pillow talk: a comfort for new mothers. *MCN: Amer. J. Maternal Child Nursing*, 3:183-184.

02050 **CHESEBORO, J. W., GRAGAN, J. F.**, and **McCULLOUGH, P.** (1973), The small group technique of the radical revolutionary: a synthetic study of consciousness raising. *Speech Monogr.*, 40:136-146.

02051 **CHESTEEN, H. E., Jr.** (1961), Breaking through the resistance in a group of psychotic patients. *Internat. J. Group Psychother.*, 11:462-467.

02052 **CHESTNUT, W.**, and **GILBREATH, S.** (1969), Differential group counseling with male college underachievers: a three-year follow-up. *J. Couns. Psychol.*, 16:365-367.

02053 **CHEVROLET, D.**, and **PHILIPPOT, M.** (1967), La substitution des stereotypes normatifs a l'objectivite au cours de la formation de groupes a forte cohesion socio-professionnelle, par la methode des cas. (The replacement of normative stereotypes by objectivity in the course of forming groups with strong social and professional cohesion.) *Informat. Psychol.*, 27-28:91-104.

02054 **CHIGLER, E.** (1963), Group therapy in a school by the school physician in Israel. *J. School Health*, 33:471-473.

02055 **CHIGLER, E.** (1977), Use of group techniques in rehabilitation of retarded in Israel. In: *Research to Practice in Mental Retardation, Vol. 2*, ed. P. Mittler. Baltimore: University Park Press.

02056 **CHILD, I. L.** (1943), The use of interview data in quantifying the individual's role in the group. *J. Abnorm. & Soc. Psychol.*, 38:305-318.

02057 **CHILDERS, B.** (1967), A ward program based on graduated activities and group effort. *Hosp. & Community Psychiat.*, 18:289-295.

02058 **CHILDREN'S BUREAU.** (1969), The closed, short-term group: a treatment adjunct for parents of mentally retarded children. Washington, D.C. Superintendent of Documents, U.S. Government Printing Office, 1965. *Ment. Retard. Abstr.*, 6:141.

02059 **CHILDS, A. W.** (1976), A tale of two groups: an observational study of targeted humor. *Dissert. Abstr. Internat.*, 36:5960.

02060 **CHILDS-GOWELL, E.** (1977), A study of schizophrenics in transactional analysis treatment: report of ethnographic research. *Internat. J. Nursing Studies*, 14:215-221.

02061 **CHILES, J. A., MARSHALL, J.**, and **GRIEGT, T. H.** (1972), Group intake, brief therapy, and the use of expertise: evolving changes in intake procedure. *Comprehens. Psychiat.*, 13:489-492.

02062 **CHILES, J. A.,** and **SANGER, E.** (1977), The use of groups in brief inpatient treatment of adolescents. *Hosp. & Community Psychiat.*, 28:443-444.

02063 **CHING, W.,** and **PROSEN, S. S.** (1980), Asian-Americans in group counseling: a case of cultural dissonance. *J. Special. Group Work*, 5:228-232.

02064 **CHISHOLM, M.** (1970), A study to determine the influence of actual self-observation on selected aspects of the self awareness of participants in t-groups. *Dissert. Abstr. Internat.*, 31:2171A.

02065 **CHOLDEN, L.** (1953), Group therapy with the blind. *Group Psychother., Psychodrama & Sociometry*, 6:21-29.

02066 **CHOLDEN, L. S.** (1955), Discussion of Dr. Moreno's article, "Transference, countertransference and tele." *Group Psychother., Psychodrama & Sociometry*, 8:64-67.

02067 **CHRIST, J.** (1967), Volunteer training as an education. *Ment. Hygiene*, 51:433-439.

02068 **CHRIST, J.,** and **GOLDSTEIN, S.** (1970), Four techniques in dealing with psychotic disorders in the outpatient clinic. *Ment. Hygiene*, 54:105-108.

02069 **CHRISTEN, C. A.** (1973), An analysis of the changes in career exploration, school satisfaction and vocational maturity effected by individual, small and large group counseling. *Dissert. Abstr. Internat.*, 34:130A.

02070 **CHRISTENSEN, E. W.** (1963), Group counseling with selected scholarship students. *Dissert. Abstr. Internat.*, 24:619.

02071 **CHRISTIE, G. L.** (1970), Group psychotherapy in private practice. *Austral. & New Zeal. J. Psychiat.*, (Carlton) 4:42-48.

02072 **CHRISTIE, G. L.** (1964), Therapeutic community and psychotherapy: the Austen Riggs Centre. *Med. J. Austral.*, (Glebe) 1:458-460.

02073 **CHRISTIE, H.** (1976), Reality therapy. *Nursing Times*, (London) 72:1896-1899.

02074 **CHRISTIE, U. A.** (1977), Behavior rehearsal, verbal conditioning and reinforcement counseling in group therapy. *Dissert. Abstr. Internat.*, 37:3601B.

02075 **CHRISTMAS, J. J.** (1965), Group methods in training and practice: nonprofessional mental health personnel in a deprived community. *Amer. J. Orthopsychiat.*, 35:380-381.

02076 **CHRISTMAS, J. J.** (1966), Group therapy with the disadvantaged. *Curr. Psychiat. Ther.*, 6:163-171.

02077 **CHRISTMAS, J. J.,** and **DAVIS, E. B.** (1965), Group therapy programs with the socially deprived in community psychiatry. *Internat. J. Group Psychother.*, 15:464-476.

02078 **CHU, V.** (1975), (Aspects of different identifications in group therapy observers.) *Gruppenpsychother. & Gruppendynam.*, (Goettingen) 9:165-184.

02079 **CHURCH, G.,** and **CARNES, C. D.** (1972), *The Pit.* New York: Outerbridge and Lazard.

02080 **CHURCH, J. S.** (1972), Effect of individual and group cue-reinforcement counseling as interventional techniques for modifying elementary classroom behaviors. *Dissert. Abstr. Internat.*, 33:4083A.

02081 **CHURCHILL, S. R.** (1959), Prestructuring group content. *Soc. Work*, 4:52-59.

02082 **CHURCHILL, S. R.** (1974), Preventive, short-term groups for siblings of child mental hospital patients. In: *Individual Change through Small Groups*, eds. P. Glasser, R. Sarri, and R. Vinter. New York: Free Press.

02083 **CHURCHILL, S. R.** (1965), Social group work: a diagnostic tool in child guidance. *Amer. J. Orthopsychiat.*, 35:581-588.

02084 **CHURVEN, P.** (1977), A group approach to the emotional needs of parents of leukemic children. *Aust. Paedia.*, 13:290-294.

02085 **CHURVEN, P. G.** (1978), Families: parental attitude to family assessment in a child psychiatric setting. *J. Child Psychol. & Psychiat.*, 19:33.
02086 **CHWAST, J., HARARI, C.,** and **DELANY, L.** (1961), Experimental techniques in group psychotherapy with delinquents. *J. Crim. Law & Criminol.*, 52:156-165.
02087 **CHYATTE, C.** (1960), Changes in adjustment during a course in mental hygiene. *Group Psychother., Psychodrama & Sociometry*, 13:200-204.
02088 **CIARAMELLA, V. A.** (1973), A comparative study of ethnic versus dominant culture group counseling: an interaction process analysis. *Dissert. Abstr. Internat.*, 34:2289A.
02089 **CICCATI, S. M.** (1970), Comparison of three methods of facilitating encounter groups in a college environment. *Dissert. Abstr. Internat.*, 31:2954B-2955B.
02090 **CIERPKA, M., OHLMEIER, D.,** and **SCHAUMBURG, C.** (1980), (Personal pronouns as indicators of interpersonal relations in psychoanalytic group therapy.) *Psychother. & Med. Psychol.*, (Stuttgart) 30:212-217.
02091 **CIMBOLIC, P.** (1973), T-group effects on Black clients' perceptions of counselors. *J. Coll. Student Personnel*, 14:296-302.
02092 **CIMPERMAN, A.,** and **DUNN, M.** (1974), Group therapy with spinal cord injured patients: a case study. *Rehab. Psychol.*, 21:44.
02093 **CINNAMON, K. M.,** and **FARSON, D.** (1979), *Cults and Cons: The Exploration of the Emotional Growth Consumer.* Chicago: Nelson-Hall.
02094 **CIRIGLIANO, R. J.** (1972), Group encounter effects upon the self-concepts of high school students. *Dissert. Abstr. Internat.*, 33:2760A.
02095 **CITRIN, R. S.,** and **DIXON, D. N.** (1977), Reality orientation: a milieu therapy in an institution for the aged. *Gerontologist*, 17:39-43.
02096 **CIVIDINI, E.** (1966), (Countertransference and interactions in group psychotherapy.) *Neuropsihijatrija*, (Zagreb) 14:109-117.
02097 **CIVIDINI, E.** (1975), (Group analysis.) *Anali Zavoda Ment. Zdravlge*, 7:73-80.
02098 **CIVIDINI, E.** (1967), (Transference and countertransference in group psychotherapy.) *Neuropsihijatrija*, (Zagreb) 15:191-199.
02099 **CIVIDINI, E.,** and **KLAIN, E.** (1967), The influence of socio-cultural factors on the dynamics of group psychotherapy. *Psychother. & Psychosomat.*, (Basel) 15:12.
02100 **CIVIDINI, E.,** and **KLAIN, E.** (1973), (Psychotherapy in a cotherapeutic group.) *Soc. Psihijat.*, (Belgrade) 1:65-74.
02101 **CIVIDINI-STRANIĆ, E.** (1973), (The influence of socio-cultural factors on the dynamics of group psychotherapy.) *Psyhoterapija*, (Zagreb) 1:31-44.
02102 **CIVIDINI-STRANIĆ, E.** (1978), (Our experience in group analytical psychotherapy.) *Psihijat. Danas*, (Belgrade) 10:15-21.
02103 **CLACK, J.,** and **WACKERMAN, A.** (1962), Five patients in group therapy. *Amer. J. Nursing*, 62:70.
02104 **CLACK, R. J., CONYNE, R. K.,** and **STRAND, K. H.** (1975), Interpersonal skills workshop: a laboratory-based microcounseling experience. *J. Coll. Student Personnel*, 16:149-153.
02105 **CLAGHORN, J. L., JOHNSTONE, E. E., COOK, T. H.,** and **ITSCHNER, L.** (1974), Group therapy and maintenance treatment of schizophrenics. *Arch. Gen. Psychiat.*, 31:361-365.
02106 **CLAMPITT, R. R.** (1955), *An Experimentally Controlled Investigation of the Effect of Group Therapy.* Ann Arbor: University Microfilms.
02107 **CLAMPITT, R. R.** (1955), An experimentally controlled investigation of the effect of group therapy. Unpublished doctoral dissertation, University of Iowa.
02108 **CLANCY, J.** (1962), The use of intellectual processes in group psychotherapy with alcoholics. *Quart. J. Studies Alcohol*, 23:432-441.

02109 **CLANON, T. L.** (1966), Group psychotherapy with prisoners. *Curr. Psychiat. Ther.*, 6:197-201.

02110 **CLANTON, E. M.** (1976), Changes in the level of depression & self-concept of suicidal clients following nursing intervention in a small group setting. *Dissert. Abstr. Internat.*, 36:4942-4943.

02111 **CLAPHAM, H. I.**, and **SCLARE, A. B.** (1958), Group psychotherapy with asthmatic patients. *Internat. J. Group Psychother.*, 8:44-54.

02112 **CLARK, A. J.**, and **DOBSON, J. E.** (1980), Moral development: a factor in the group counseling process. *J. Special. Group Work*, 5:81-86.

02113 **CLARK, A. W.**, and **YEOMANS, N. T.** (1969), *Fraser House: Theory, Practice, and Evaluation of a Therapeutic Community.* New York: Springer.

02114 **CLARK, C. C.** (1972), A social systems approach to short-term psychiatric care. *Perspect. Psychiat. Care*, 10:178-182.

02115 **CLARK, D. B.** (1975), Group work with early school leavers. *J. Curriculum Studies*, (London) 7:42-54.

02116 **CLARK, J. B.**, and **CULBERT, S. A.** (1965), Mutually therapeutic perception and self-awareness in a t-group. *J. Appl. Behav. Science*, 1:180-194.

02117 **CLARK, J. V.** (1970), Task group therapy: i. goals and the client system. *Human Relat.*, 23:263-277.

02118 **CLARK, J. V.** (1970), Task group therapy: ii. intervention and problems of practice. *Human Relat.*, 23:383.

02119 **CLARK, M.**, and **SNYDER, M.** (1955), Group therapy for parents of preadolescent stutterers. *Group Psychother., Psychodrama & Sociometry*, 8:226-232.

02120 **CLARK, W. H.** (1972), A study of the relationships between the client personality traits of dogmatism, empathy, self-disclosure and the behavioral changes resulting from a therapeutic group experience. *Dissert. Abstr. Internat.*, 33:5488A.

02121 **CLARKE, E. K.** (1952), Group therapy in rehabilitation. *Fed. Probat.*, 16:28-32.

02122 **CLARKE, D. L.** (1978), Rogerian conditions in group therapy with mastectomy patients. *Dissert. Abstr. Internat.*, 41:343B.

02123 **CLARKE, M.** (1974), Treating frigidity means treating the couple. *Med. J. Austral.*, (Glebe) 2:405-409.

02124 **CLARKSON, G. P.** (1968), Decision making in small groups: a simulation study. *Behav. Science Res.*, 13:288-305.

02125 **CLARKSON, G. P.**, and **TUGGLE, F. D.** (1966), Toward a theory of group-decision behavior. *Behav. Science Res.*, 11:33-42.

02126 **CLARKSON, P. J.** (1978), Effects of parent training and group counseling on children's functioning in elementary school. *Dissert. Abstr. Internat.*, 39:4726A.

02127 **CLARY, T. C.** (1972), Transactional analysis. *Training & Develop. J.*, 26:14-19.

02128 **CLAUSEN, R. D.** (1971), The effects of group counseling on selected attitudes of economically disadvantaged high school age youth in a residential setting. *Dissert. Abstr. Internat.*, 32:1847A.

02129 **CLAXTON, G.** (1978), Reviewing A. Blumberg's and R. T. Golembiewski's *Learning and Change in Groups. Brit. Psychol. Soc. Bull.*, (London) 31:16.

02130 **CLAYTON, G. M.** (1971), Sociodrama in a church group. *Group Psychother., Psychodrama & Sociometry*, 24:97-100.

02131 **CLAYTON, L.** (1977), A rating scale of warm-up in psychodrama. *Group Psychother., Psychodrama & Sociometry*, 30:18-36.

02132 **CLEGG, H. C.** (1974), Group analytic practice in the therapeutic community. *Deveveaux Forum*, 9:1.

02133 **CLELAND, J. F.** (1973), Changes in sensitivity training groups associated with changes in trainer characteristics. *Dissert. Abstr. Internat.*, 34:1271B.
02134 **CLEMENT, J. A.** (1977), Family therapy: the transferability of theory to practice. *J. Psychiat. Nursing*, 15:33-37.
02135 **CLEMENT, P. W.** (1968), Operant conditioning in group psychotherapy with children. *J. School Health*, 38:271-278.
02136 **CLEMENT, P. W.** (1971), Please mother, I'd rather you did it yourself: training parents to treat their own children. *J. School Health*, 41:65-69.
02137 **CLEMENT, P. W.**, and **MILNE, D. C.** (1967), Group play therapy and tangible reinforcers used to modify the behavior of eight-year-old boys. *Behav. Res. & Ther.*, 5:301-312.
02138 **CLEMENT, P. W., FAZZONE, R. A.**, and **GOLDSTEIN, B.** (1970), Tangible reinforcers and child group therapy. *J. Amer. Acad. Child Psychiat.*, 9:409-427.
02139 **CLEMENT, P. W., ROBERTS, P. W.**, and **LANTZ, C. E.** (1976), Mothers and peers as child behavior therapists. *Internat. J. Group Psychother.*, 26:335-359.
02140 **CLEMENTS, B. E.** (1965), The effects of group counseling with college bound high-school seniors on their anxiety and parent child empathy. *Dissert. Abstr. Internat.*, 25:3966.
02141 **CLEMENTS, B. E.** (1966), Transitional adolescents, anxiety, and group counseling. *Personnel & Guid. J.*, 45:67-71.
02142 **CLIFFORD, M.**, and **CROSS, T.** (1980), Group therapy for seriously disturbed boys in residential treatment. *Child Welfare*, 59:560-565.
02143 **CLINARD, M. B.** (1949), The group approach to social reintegration. *Amer. Sociol. Rev.*, 14:257-262.
02144 **CLINEBELL, H. J.** (1977), *Growth Groups*. Nashville: Abingdon Press.
02145 **CLINEBELL, H. J., Jr.** (1972), *The People Dynamic: Changing Self and Society through Growth Groups*, 1st ed. New York: Harper and Row.
02146 **COCHÉ, E.** (1977), (Problem-solving training as a special form of group psychotherapy.) *Gruppenpsychother. & Gruppendynam.*, (Goettingen) 12:49-67.
02147 **COCHE, E.** (1980), (Self-disclosure and group-therapy.) *Gruppenpsychother. & Gruppendynam.*, (Goettingen) 16:229-239.
02148 **COCHÉ, E.**, and **DOUGLAS, A. A.** (1977), Therapeutic effects of problem-solving training and play-reading groups. *J. Clin. Psychol.*, 33:820-827.
02149 **COCHÉ, E.**, and **FLICK, A.** (1975), Problem-solving training groups for hospitalized psychiatric patients. *J. Psychology*, 91:19-29.
02150 **COCHÉ, E.**, and **SPECTOR, J.** (1978), TAT derived affiliation scores and social behavior in therapy groups. *Psychol. Reports*, 42:739.
02151 **COCHÉ, E., POLIKOFF, B.**, and **COOPER J.** (1980), Participant self-disclosure in group therapy. *Group*, 4:28-35.
02152 **COCHÉ, J.**, and **GOLDMAN, J.** (1979), Brief group psychotherapy for women after divorce: planning a focused experience. *J. Divorce*, 3:153-160.
02153 **COCHE, J. A.**, and **FREEDMAN, P.** (1975), (The treatment of a child with psychogenic megacolon through fantasy therapy in a group of children.) *Praxis Kinderpsychol. & Kinderpsychiat.*, (Goettingen) 24:26-32.
02154 **COCHRAN, M. L.**, and **YEAWORTH, R. C.** (1967), Ward meetings for teen-age mothers. *Amer. J. Nursing*, 67:1044-1047.
02155 **CODOL, J. P.** (1974), On the system of representations in a group situation. *European J. Soc. Psychol.*, (The Hague) 4:343-365.
02156 **COE, W. C., CURRY, A. E.**, and **HUELS, M. A.** (1967), A method of group therapy training for nurses in psychiatric hospitals. *Perspect. Psychiat. Care*, 5:231-234.

02157 **COELHO, J. M.** (1970), (Adaptation of imagery to a group of children.) *Riv. Sper. Freniat.*, (Emilia) 94:1248-1255.
02158 **COFER, D. H.**, and **NIR, Y.** (1975), Theme-focused group therapy on a pediatric ward. *Internat. J. Psychiat. Med.*, 6:541-550.
02159 **COFFEY, H. S.** (1954), Group psychotherapy. In: *An Introduction to Clinical Psychology*, ed. L. A. Pennington, and I. A. Berge. New York: Ronald Press, pp. 586-607.
02160 **COFFEY, H. S.** (1952), Socio and psyche group processes: integrative concepts. *J. Soc. Issues*, 8:65-74.
02161 **COFFEY, H. S.**, and **WEINER, L. L.** (1967), *Group Treatment of Autistic Children*. Englewood Cliffs, NJ: Prentice-Hall.
02162 **COFFEY, H. S., FREEDMAN, M., LEARY, T.**, and **OSSORIO, A.** (1950), Results and implications of the group therapy program. *J. Soc. Issues*, 6:37-43.
02163 **COFFEY, H. S., FREEDMAN, M., LEARY, T.**, and **OSSORIO, A.** (1950), A technique of group therapy. *J. Soc. Issues*, 6:25-36.
02164 **COFFMAN, R.**, and **BACKUS, O.** (1953), Group therapy with preschool children having cerebral palsy. *J. Speech & Hearing Disorders*, 18:350-354.
02165 **COGAN, F., MONSON, L.**, and **BRUGGEMAN, W.** (1966), Concurrent group and individual treatment of the mentally retarded. *Correct. Psychiat. & J. Soc. Ther.*, 12:404-409.
02166 **COGHILL, M. A.** (1967), *Sensitivity Training: A Review of the Controversy*. Ithaca, NY: New York State School of Industrial and Labor Relations, Cornell University.
02167 **COHEN, A. A.** (1956), Use of group process in an institution. *Soc. Work*, 1:57-61.
02168 **COHEN, A. I.** (1976), The impact of the death of a group member on a therapy group. *Internat. J. Group Psychother.*, 26:203-212.
02169 **COHEN, A. M.** (1976), *Critical Incident in Growth Groups: Theory and Technique*. La Jolla: University Associates.
02170 **COHEN, A. M.** (1964), Predicting organization in changed communication networks: iii. *J. Psychology*, 58:115-129.
02171 **COHEN, A. M.**, and **FOERST, J. R., Jr.** (1968), Organizational behaviors and adaptations to organizational change of sensitizer and represser problem-solving groups. *J. Personality & Soc. Psychol.*, 8:209-216.
02172 **COHEN, C. A.**, and **CORWIN, J.** (1978), A further application of balance theory to multiple family therapy. *Internat. J. Group Psychother.*, 28:195.
02173 **COHEN, C. P.**, and **JOHNSON, D. L.** (1971), Interpersonal changes among psychiatric patients in human relations training. *J. Personality Assessment*, 35:472-479.
02174 **COHEN, H.** (1962), Psychodrama with an adolescent group. *Internat. J. Sociometry & Sociatry*, 2:136-140.
02175 **COHEN, H. J.** (1975), The effectiveness of training in interpersonal skills as treatment in a chronic psychiatric setting. *Dissert. Abstr. Internat.*, 36:1912-1913.
02176 **COHEN, I.** (1973), Group therapy: an effective method of self-supervision. *Small Group Behav.*, 4:69-80.
02177 **COHEN, L.** (1964), How to reverse chronic behavior. *Ment. Hosp.*, 15:39-41.
02178 **COHEN, L. B.** (1959), The use of extramural activities in group psychotherapy with hospitalized female chronic schizophrenics. *Group Psychother., Psychodrama & Sociometry*, 12:315-321.
02179 **COHEN, M.** (1949), A study of casework–group-work cooperation. *J. Psychiat. Soc. Work*, 19:69-76.

02180 **COHEN, M. F.** (1974), Group methods and the new careerists. *Internat. J. Group Psychother.*, 24:393-399.

02181 **COHEN, R.** (1969), Cognitive orientation for patients in group psychotherapy. *Perspect. Psychiat. Care*, 7:76-79.

02182 **COHEN, R.** (1971), EST + group therapy = improved care. *Amer. J. Nursing*, 71:1195-1198.

02183 **COHEN, R.** (1969), The effects of group interaction and progressive hierarchy presentation on desensitization of test anxiety. *Behav. Res. & Ther.*, 7:15-26.

02184 **COHEN, R.** (1968), Group desensitization of test anxiety. *Dissert. Abstr. Internat.*, 29:1504B-1505B.

02185 **COHEN, R. A.** (1947), Military group psychotherapy. *Ment. Hygiene*, 31:94-102.

02186 **COHEN, R. G.**, and **LIPKIN, G. B.** (1979), *Therapeutic Group Work for Health Professionals.* New York: Springer Publishing.

02187 **COHEN, R. R.** (1944), Factors in adjustment to army life: plan for preventive psychiatry by mass psychotherapy. *War Med.*, (Chicago) 5:83-91.

02188 **COHEN, R. R.** (1945), Visual aids in group psychotherapy: puppetry. *Sociometry*, 8:311-314.

02189 **COHEN, R. R.** (1944), Visual aids in preventive psychiatry. *War Med.*, (Chicago) 6:18-23.

02190 **COHEN, R. Y.** (1978), The development of a group education and management program for low income diabetic and hypertensive patients. *Dissert. Abstr. Internat.*, 38:3869B-3870B. (University Microfilms No. 7731026.)

02191 **COHLER, J.** (1977), Review of L. Wolberg's, M. Aronson's, and A. Wolberg's *Group Therapy 1976: An Overview. Group*, 1:141-142.

02192 **COHLER, J., EPSTEIN, L.**, and **ISSACHAROFF, A.** (1977), A psychoanalytic evaluation of the leader-absent or coordinated group therapy format. *Group*, 1:75-89.

02193 **COHN, A. I.** (1971), Process in t-groups: some observations. *J. Contemp. Psychother.*, 3:127-130.

02194 **COHN, B.** (1973), Absentee-Cueing: a technical innovation in the training of group counselors. *Educat. Technol.*, 13:61-62.

02195 **COHN, I. H.** (1965), Intra-psychic changes in an adolescent girl during group psychotherapy. *Topical Probl. Psychol. & Psychother.*, 5:176-188.

02196 **COHN, I. H.**, and **HULSE, W. C.** (1961), The use of a group psychotherapy program for adolescents as a training unit in child psychiatry. *Amer. J. Orthopsychiat.*, 31:521-535.

02197 **COHN, L. M.** (1973), Effects of group counseling on freshmen nursing students. *Dissert. Abstr. Internat.*, 33:5489A.

02198 **COHN, R. C.** (1969), Psychoanalytic or experiential group psychotherapy: a false dichotomy. *Psychoanal. Rev.*, 56:333-345.

02199 **COHN, R. C.** (1972), (Big groups—little groups: little steps—big steps.) *Praxis der Psychother.*, 17:1-13.

02200 **COHN, R. C.** (1965), Group therapeutic techniques as educational means in the training of psychoanalysts. *Topical Probl. Psychol. & Psychother.*, 5:48-58.

02201 **COHN, R. C.** (1961), A group-therapeutic workshop on countertransference. *Internat. J. Group Psychother.*, 11:284-296.

02202 **COHN, R. C.** (1970), The theme-centered interactional method: group therapists as group educators. *J. Group Psychoanal. & Process*, (London) 2:19-36.

02203 **COHN, R. C.** (1974), (Therapy in groups: psychoanalytic, experiential and gestalt.) *Gruppenpsychother. & Gruppendynam.*, (Goettingen) 8:1-14.

02204 **COIRO, C.** (1971), Sensitivity: new awareness of yourself. *Harvest Years*, 11:6-10.

02205 **COLBERT, E. G.** (1959), Group psychotherapy for mothers of schizophrenic children in a state hospital. *Internat. J. Group Psychother.*, 9:93-98.

02206 **COLBY, K. M.** (1964), Psychotherapeutic processes. In: *Annual Review of Psychology, Volume 15*, eds. P. R. Farnsworth, O. McNemar, and Q. McNemar. Palo Alto: Annual Reviews, pp. 347-370.

02207 **COLE, B. L.** (1973), The effect of group size on organizational climate in elementary schools. *Small Group Behav.*, 4:503-507.

02208 **COLE, C.**, and **MORROW, W. R.** (1976), Refractory parent behaviors in behavior modification training groups. *Psychother.: Theory, Res. & Pract.*, 13:162.

02209 **COLE, C. M., CHAN, F. A., BLAKENEY, P. E.,** and **CHESNEY, A. P.** (1980), Participants' reactions to components of a rapid-treatment workshop for sexual dysfunction. *J. Sex & Marital Ther.*, 6:30-39.

02210 **COLE, N. R.** (1948), Exploring psychodrama at the fifth grade level. *Sociatry*, 2:243-245.

02211 **COLEMAN, J. C.** (1952), Group therapy with parents of mentally deficient children. *Amer. J. Ment. Deficiency*, 57:700-708.

02212 **COLEMAN, J. V.** (1946), The group factor in military psychiatry. *Amer. J. Orthopsychiat.*, 16:222-226.

02213 **COLEMAN, M.**, and **GLOFKA, P. T.** (1969), Effect of group therapy on self-concept of senior nursing students. *Nursing Res.*, 18:274-275.

02214 **COLEMAN, S. B.** (1978), Sib group therapy: a prevention program for siblings from drug-addicted families. *Internat. J. Addict.*, 13:115-127.

02215 **COLEMAN, S. B.**, and **STANTON, M. D.** (1978), An index for measuring agency involvement in family therapy. *Fam. Process*, 17:479.

02216 **COLES, R. B.** (1967), Group treatment in the skin department. *Trans., St. John Hosp. Dermatol. Soc.*, 53:82-85.

02217 **COLIN, L.**, and **LEMAITRE, J. M.** (1975), *Le Potentiel Humain.* (*Human Potential.*) Paris: J. P. Delarge.

02218 **COLLER, C. F.** (1978), The effective personal integration model and its impact upon locus of control with clients in group counseling. *Dissert. Abstr. Internat.*, 38:3386B.

02219 **COLLINGWOOD, T. R.** (1970), Toward identification of plus and minus training groups. *Rehab. Res. & Pract. Rev.*, 1:27-31.

02220 **COLLINS, B. E.**, and **RAVEN, B. H.** (1969), Group structure: attraction, coalitions, communication and power. In: *The Handbook of Social Psychology*, 2d ed., eds. G. Lindzey and E. Aronson. Reading, MA: Addison-Wesley.

02221 **COLLINS, J. E.** (1964), Group counseling method with underachieving ninth grade students. *Dissert. Abstr. Internat.*, 25:3389.

02222 **COLLINS, M. C.** (Ed.) (1978), *Child Abuses: A Study of Child Abusers in Self-Help Group Therapy.* Littleton, MA: P&G Publishing.

02223 **COLLOMB, H.**, and **de PRENEUF, C.** (1969/1970), N'doep and psychodrama. *Bull. de Psycholog.*, (Paris) 23:745-749.

02224 **COLLUM, H. L.** (1972), An investigation of a group approach to weight reduction involving modified group involvement feedback training. *Dissert. Abstr. Internat.*, 4937A.

02225 **COLMAN, A.** (1971), Psychology of a first-baby group. *Internat. J. Group Psychother.*, 21:74-83.

02226 **COLMAN, A. D.** (1965), The effect of group and family emphasis on the role of the psychiatric resident of an acute treatment ward. *Internat. J. Group Psychother.*, 15:516-525.

02227 **COLMAN, A. D.,** and **BEXTON, W. H.** (1975), *Group Relations Reader.* Sausalito, CA: GREX.

02228 **COLMAN, M. D., DOUGHER, C. A.,** and **TANNER, M. R.** (1976), Group therapy for physically–handicapped toddlers with delayed speech and language development. *J. Amer. Acad. Child Psychiat.*, 15:395-413.

02229 **COLSON, D.** (1976), What psychoanalytic group therapy situation evokes. *Bull. Menninger Clin.*, 40:508-512.

02230 **COLTHORP, R. W.** (1947), Group psychotherapy in patients recovering from psychoses. *Amer. J. Psychiat.*, 104:414-417.

02231 **COMEAUX, C. R.** (1970), Intensity of group interactions as a factor in change in self-concept and dogmatism. *Dissert. Abstr. Internat.*, 30:4218A.

02232 **COMER, N. L., MORRIS, H. H.,** and **ORLAND, F.** (1961), Experiences with milieu therapy in a general hospital. *Nat. Med. Assn. J.*, 53:36-38.

02233 **COMMISSION ON GROUP PSYCHOTHERAPY.** (1952), Report to the World Federation for Mental Health: i. group treatment of preschool children and their mothers. *Internat. J. Group Psychother.*, 2:72-75.

02234 **COMMISSION ON GROUP PSYCHOTHERAPY.** (1952), Report to the World Federation for Mental Health: ii. group therapy for children in latency. *Internat. J. Group Psychother.*, 2:77-82.

02235 **COMMISSION ON GROUP PSYCHOTHERAPY.** (1952), Report to the World Federation for Mental Health: iii. group psychotherapy with adolescents. *Internat. J. Group Psychother.*, 2:173-176.

02236 **COMMISSION ON GROUP PSYCHOTHERAPY.** (1952), Report to the World Federation for Mental Health: iv. group psychotherapy with adults, a review of recent trends and practices. *Internat. J. Group Psychother.*, 2:177-184.

02237 **COMMISSION ON GROUP PSYCHOTHERAPY.** (1952), Report to the World Federation for Mental Health: v. group psychotherapy in institutions. *Internat. J. Group Psychother.*, 2:274-279.

02238 **COMMISSION ON GROUP PSYCHOTHERAPY.** (1952), Report to the World Federation for Mental Health: vi. summary, conclusions and recommendations. *Internat. J. Group Psychother.*, 2:280-283.

02239 **COMMITTEE ON HISTORY.** (1971), A brief history of the American Group Psychotherapy Association, 1943-1968. *Internat. J. Group Psychother.*, 21:406-435.

02240 **COMMUNITY APPROACH KEEPS ADDICTS IN CONTACT WITH SOCIETY.** (1969). *Roche Report: Front Hosp. Psychiat.*, 20:44-49.

02241 **COMSTOCK, B. S.,** and **JONES, M. A.** (1975), Group therapy as a treatment technique for severely disturbed outpatients. *Hosp. & Comm. Psychiat.*, 26:677-679.

02242 **COMSTOCK, B. S.,** and **McDERMOTT, M.** (1975), Group therapy for patients who attempt suicide. *Internat. J. Group Psychother.*, 25:44-49.

02243 **CONFORTO, C.** (1979), (Transference in analytic group therapy: clinical experiences and theoretical considerations.) *Minerva Psichiat.* (Turin) 20:191.

02244 **CONIGLIARO, V.,** and **PELZMAN, O.** (1954), Il servizi psicoterapeutici di gruppo in un ospedale psichiatrico americano. (Group psychotherapy in an American hospital.) *Cervello*, 30:459-484.

02245 **CONIGLIARO, V.,** and **PELZMAN, O.** (1954), La psicoterapia di gruppo. (Group psychotherapy.) *Cervello*, 30:361-390.

02246 **CONNELL, R. H.,** and **RYBACK, D.** (1978), The relative effects of three pretraining procedures on encounter group participants' behaviors. *Psychiat. J.*, 3:121-125.

02247 **CONRAD, G. J.,** and **ELKINS, H. K.** (1959), The first 18 months of group counseling in a family service agency. *Soc. Casework*, 40:123-129.

02248 **CONRAD, W. K.** (1974), A group therapy program with older adults in a high-risk neighborhood setting. *Internat. J. Group Psychother.*, 24:358-360.

02249 **CONTE, A., BRANDZEL, M.,** and **WHITEHEAD, S.** (1974), Group work with hypertensive patients. *Amer. J. Nursing*, 74:910-912.

02250 **CONTE, P.** (1971), The effects of group centered and nongroup-centered instruction on group cohesion of psychiatric patients. *Amer. Corrective Ther. J.*, 25:129-131.

02251 **CONTE, W. R.,** and **SHIMOTA, H. E.** (1962), The relationship between psychiatry and occupational therapy. *Amer. J. Occupat. Ther.*, 16:119-123.

02252 **CONTE, W. R.,** and **WAGGONER, E. R.** (1970), The group dynamic approach to professional maturation. *Amer. J. Occupat. Ther.*, 24:343-346.

02253 **CONVERY, E.,** and **SMOCHEK, M. R.** (1969), Student-patient discussion groups. *Amer. J. Nursing*, 69:1942-1944.

02254 **CONWAY, F.,** and **SIEGELMAN, J.** (1978), *Snapping: America's Epidemic of Sudden Personality Change*. Philadelphia: Lippincott.

02255 **CONYNE, R. K.** (1974), Effects of facilitator-directed and self-directed group experiences. *Counselor Educat. & Supervision*, 13:184-189.

02256 **CONYNE, R. K.** (1973), Guidelines for group experiences in the college and university counseling center: a statement of opinion. *J. Coll. Student Personnel*, 14:63-67.

02257 **CONYNE, R. K.** (1978), Review of J. P. Trotzer's The *Counselor and the Group: Integrating Theory, Training, and Practice. Contemp. Psychol.*, 23:581.

02258 **CONYNE, R. K.** (1975), Group experiences in counseling centers: a national survey. *J. Coll. Student Personnel*, 16:196-200.

02259 **CONYNE, R. K.,** and **RAPIN, L. S.** (1977), Facilitator- and self-directed groups: a statement-by-statement interaction study. *Small Group Behav.*, 8:341-350.

02260 **CONYNE, R. K.,** and **RAPIN, L. S.** (1977), A Hill Interaction Process analysis study of facilitator- and self-directed groups. *Small Group Behav.*, 8:333-340.

02261 **CONYNE, R. K.,** and **RAPIN, L. S.** (1977), Programmed groups: a process analysis of facilitator and self-directed treatments. *Small Group Behav.*, 8:403-414.

02262 **CONYNE, R. K.,** and **SILVER, R. J.** (1980), Direct, vicarious, and vicarious-process experiences: effects on increasing group therapeutic attraction. *Small Group Behav.*, 11:419-430.

02263 **COOK, D. W., KUNCE, J. T.,** and **SLEATER, S. M.** (1974), Vicarious behavior induction and training psychiatric aides. *J. Community Psychol.*, 2:293-297.

02264 **COOK, E. L.** (1964), Group therapy in a military community. *Internat. J. Group Psychother.*, 14:374-377.

02265 **COOK, E. L.** (1966), Short term group psychotherapy. *Med. Soc. N.J. J.*, 63:83-85.

02266 **COOK, F. J.** (1970), The use of three types of group procedures with ninth grade underachieving students and their parents. *Dissert. Abstr. Internat.*, 31:3869A.

02267 **COOK, J. H.** (1973), The effects of small group counseling on the classroom behavior of sociometrically underchosen adolescents. *Dissert. Abstr. Internat.*, 33:4827A.

02268 **COOK, V. J.** (1967), Group decision, social comparison, and persuasion in changing attitudes. *J. Advert. Res.*, 7:31-37.

02269 **COOKE, C. C.** (1980), Some effects of a teacher-directed group guidance program on middle school students' attitudes toward school. *Dissert. Abstr. Internat.*, 40:5319A. (University Microfilms No. 8009644.)

02270 **COOKER, P. G.**, and **CHERCHIA, P. J.** (1976), Effects of communication skill training on high school students' ability to function as peer group facilitators. *J. Couns. Psychol.*, 23:464-467.

02271 **COOLEY, M. L.** (1974), The effects of interaction and information on group systematic desensitization of test anxiety. *Dissert. Abstr. Internat.*, 35:3010B.

02272 **COOLIDGE, J. C.**, and **GRUNEBAUM, M. G.** (1964), Individual and group therapy of a latency age child. *Internat. J. Group Psychother.*, 14:84-96.

02273 **COOMBES, D. B.**, and **ROGERS, W. H.** (1962), The way back: a resettlement unit in a mental hospital. *Nursing Times*, (London) 58:334-337.

02274 **COONS, W. H.** (1957), Interaction and insight in group psychotherapy. *Can. J. Psychol.*, (Toronto) 11:1-8.

02275 **COONS, W. H.**, and **PEACOCK, E. P.** (1970), Interpersonal interaction and personality change in group psychotherapy. *Can. Psychiat. Assn. J.*, (Ottawa) 15:347-355.

02276 **COOPER, C. L.** (1972), An attempt to assess the psychologically disturbing effects of t-group training. *Brit. J. Soc. & Clin. Psychol.*, (London) 11:342-345.

02277 **COOPER, C. L.** (1973/1974), A bibliography of current encounter and t-group research: 1971-1973. *Interpersonal Develop.*, 4:65-75.

02278 **COOPER, C. L.** (1971/1972), A bibliography of current sensitivity or t-group training research: 1969-1971. *Interpersonal Develop.*, 2:61-64.

02279 **COOPER, C. L.** (1972), Coping with life stress after sensitivity training. *Psychol. Reports*, 31:602-603.

02280 **COOPER, C. L.** (1976), *Developing Social Skills in Managers: Advances in Group Training*. New York: J. Wiley and Sons.

02281 **COOPER, C. L.** (1975), Experiential learning groups: a substitute for therapy? *Brit. Psychol. Soc. Bull.*, (London) 28:337-341.

02282 **COOPER, C. L.** (1972), *Group Training for Individual and Organizational Development*. Basel: S. Karger.

02283 **COOPER, C. L.** (1975), How psychologically dangerous are t-groups and encounter groups? *Human Relat.*, 28:249-260.

02284 **COOPER, C. L.** (1975), The impact of marathon encounters on teacher-student relationships. *Interpersonal Develop.*, 5:71-77.

02285 **COOPER, C. L.** (1979), *Learning from Others in Groups*. Chicago: Associated Business Press.

02286 **COOPER, C. L.** (1974), Psychological disturbance following t-groups: relationship between the Eysenck Personality Inventory and family/friends perceptions. *Brit. J. Soc. Work*, (Birmingham) 4:39-49.

02287 **COOPER, C. L.** (1980), Risk factors in experiential learning groups. *Small Group Behav.*, 11:251-278.

02288 **COOPER, C. L.** (1971), T-group training and self-actualization. *Psychol. Reports*, 28:391-394

02289 **COOPER, C. L.** (1975), *Theories of Group Processes*. New York: J. Wiley and Sons.

02290 **COOPER, C. L.** (1977), *Theories of Group Processes*. New York: J. Wiley and Sons.

02291 **COOPER, C. L.**, and **KOYBAYASHI, K.** (1976), Changes in self-actualization as a result of sensitivity training in England and Japan. *Small Group Behav.*, 7:387-396.

02292 **COOPER, C. L.**, and **MANGHAM, I. L.** (1971), *T-Groups: A Survey of Research*. London: Wiley-Interscience.

02293 **COOPER, E. J.** (1977), Groups and the hispanic prenatal patient. *Amer. J. Orthopsychiat.*, 47:689-700.

02294 **COOPER, J. F.**, and **KITTRELL, E.** (1958), One group for both parents: an experiment. *Soc. Work*, 3:24-29.

02295 **COOPER, L.** (1974), Application group: broadening the patient experience in a psychiatric organization. *Brit. J. Psychiat.*, (Ashford) 124:247-251.

02296 **COOPER, L.** (1976), Co-therapy relationship in groups. *Small Group Behav.*, 7:473-498.

02297 **COOPER, L.** (1971), Systematic use of groups in an acute psychiatric unit. *Group Anal.*, (London) 4:152-156.

02298 **COOPER, L.**, and **GOLDBART, S.** (1976), Safety in groups: an existential analysis. *Small Group Behav.*, 7:237-256.

02299 **COOPER, L.**, and **GUSTAFSON, J. P.** (1978), Collaboration in small groups: theory and technique for the study of small group processes. *Human Relat.*, 31:155-171.

02300 **COOPER, L.**, and **GUSTAFSON, J. P.** (1979), Planning and mastery in group therapy: a contribution to theory and technique. *Human Relat.*, 32:689-703.

02301 **COOPER, L.**, and **GUSTAFSON, J. P.** (1979), Toward a general theory of group therapy. *Human Relat.*, 32:967-973.

02302 **COOPER, L.**, and **GUSTAFSON, J. P.** (1978), Towards an open institution for the study of the working problems of society in microcosm: critical problems of group relations conferences. *Human Relat.*, 31:843-862.

02303 **COOPER, M.**, and **KATZ, J.** (1956), The treatment of migraine and tension headache with group psychotherapy. *Internat. J. Group Psychother.*, 6:266-271.

02304 **COOPER, S.**, and **KAHNE, M. J.** (1957), Mental health and group psychotherapy. *Arch. Neurol. Psychiat.*, 77:274-276.

02305 **COOPER, S.**, and **KAHNE, M. J.** (1956), Mental health film and group psychotherapy. *J. Nerv. & Ment. Diseases*, 123:191-192.

02306 **COOPER, W. L.** (1975), A test of group semantic desensitization with moderate to highly fearful mixed/folic females. *Dissert. Abstr. Internat.*, 36:2463B.

02307 **COPELAND, H.** (1980), The beginning groups. *Internat. J. Group Psychother.*, 30:201-212.

02308 **COPELAND, H.**, and **RESNICK, E. V.** (1975), The Tuesday Evening Club: using community resources to treat chronically ill patients. *Hosp. & Community Psychiat.*, 26:227-230.

02309 **COPEMANN, C. D.** (1976), Drug addiction: ii. an aversive counter-conditioning technique for treatment. *Psychol. Reports*, 38:1271-1281.

02310 **COPP, L. A.** (1966), The use of pictures as a projective technique in group therapy. *Perspect. Psychiat. Care*, 4:24-31.

02311 **CORAZZINI, J. G.**, and **ANDERSON, S. M.** (1980), An apprentice model for training group leaders: revitalizing group treatment. *J. Special. Group Work*, 5:29-35.

02312 **CORBIN, M. L.**, (1951), Group speech therapy for mother aphasia and dysarthria. *J. Speech & Hearing Disorders*, 16:21-34.

02313 **CORDELL, L. G.** (1973), The effect of structured group counseling on the self-concept, attendance, and achievement of absentee–prone high school students. *Dissert. Abstr. Internat.*, 34:4733A.

02314 **CORDER, B. F.** (1977), Therapeutic game for structuring and facilitating group psychotherapy with adolescents. *Adolescence*, 12:261-268.

02315 **CORDER, B. F.**, **CORDER, R. F.**, and **HENDRICKS, A.** (1971), An experimental study of the effect of paired-patient meetings on the group therapy process. *Internat. J. Group Psychother.*, 21:310-318.

02316 **CORDER, B. F.**, **CORDER, R. F.**, and **LAIDLAW, N. D.** (1972), An intensive treatment program for alcoholics and their wives. *Quart. J. Studies Alcohol*, 33:1144-1146.

02317 **CORDER, B. F., HAIZLIP, T. M.,** and **WALKER, P. A.** (1980), Critical areas of therapists' functioning in adolescent group psychotherapy: a comparison with self-perception of functioning in adult groups by experienced and inexperienced therapists. *Adolescence*, 15:435-442.

02318 **CORDER, B. F., HAIZLIP, T., WHITESIDE, R.** and **VOGEL, M.** (1980), Pretherapy training for adolescents in group psychotherapy: contracts, guidelines, and pre-therapy preparation. *Adolescence*, 15:699-706.

02319 **CORDER, M. P.,** and **ANDERS, R. L.** (1974), Death and dying: oncology discussion group. *J. Psychiat. Nursing*, 12:10-14.

02320 **CORDISCO, W. S., Jr.** (1980), The effect of a self-awareness group on the self-acceptance of counselors in training. *Dissert. Abstr. Internat.*, 40:4407A. (University Microfilms No. 8004796).

02321 **COREN BLUM, B.,** and **FISCHER, D. G.** (1975), Some correlates of Al-Anon group membership. *J. Studies Alcohol*, 36:675-677.

02322 **COREY, G. F.** (1981), *Manual for Theory and Practice of Group Counseling*. Monterey, CA: Brooks/Cole Publishing.

02323 **COREY, G.** (1980), *Theory and Practice of Group Counseling. Monterey, CA: Brooks/Cole Publishing.*

02324 **COREY, G.,** and **COREY, M. S.** (1977), *Groups: Process and Practice*. Monterey,CA: Brooks/Cole Publishing.

02325 **COREY, G., COREY, M. A., CALLANAN, P.,** and **RUSSELL, J. M.** (1980), A residential workshop for personal growth. *J. Special. Group Work*, 5:205-211.

02326 **COREY, S. M.,** and **COREY, E. K.** (1971), Sensitivity education. *Educat. Digest*, 36:23-25.

02327 **CORK, R. M.** (1956), Case work in a group setting with wives of alcoholics. *Soc. Worker*, (Ottawa) 24:1-6.

02328 **CORMAN, L.** (1973), (On the possibility of game psychotherapy without interpretation in children.) *Rev. Neuropsychiat. Infantile*, (Paris) 21:543-550.

02329 **CORMIER, A.** (1972), Group versus individual dietary instruction in the treatment of obesity. *Can. J. Pub. Health*, (Ottawa) 63:327-332.

02330 **CORMIER, L. S., HACKNEY, H.,** and **SEGRIST, A.** (1974), Three counselor training models: a comparative study. *Counselor Educat. & Supervision*, 14:95-104.

02331 **CORNACCHIA, A.** (1967), A layman's view of group therapy in weight control. *Can. J. Pub. Health*, (Ottawa) 58:505-507.

02332 **CORNETTE, R. A.** (1976), The aptitude for social learning as shown by therapy vs. non-therapy subjects. *Dissert. Abstr. Internat.*, 40:5805B.

02333 **CORNFELD, C.,** and **GOLDSTEIN, A.** (1970), Group counseling with college students: a cooperative project. *J. Jewish Communal Serv.*, 47:64-69.

02334 **CORNYETZ, P.** (1945), The warming up process of an audience. *Sociometry*, 8:456-463.

02335 **CORROTHERS, M. L.** (1963), Sexual themes in an adolescent girls' group. *Internat. J. Group Psychother.*, 13:43-51.

02336 **CORSINI, R. J.** (1953), The "behind your back" technique in group psychotherapy and psychodrama. *Group Psychother., Psychodrama & Sociometry*, 6:102-109.

02337 **CORSINI, R. J.** (1954), Group psychotherapy with a hostile group. *Group Psychother., Psychodrama & Socimetry*, 6:168-173.

02338 **CORSINI, R. J.** (1955), Historic background of group psychotherapy: a critique. *Group Psychother., Psychodrama & Sociometry*, 8:219-225.

02339 **CORSINI, R. J.** (1952), Immediate therapy: with special emphasis on psychoanalysis and psychodrama. *Group Psychother., Psychodrama & Sociometry*, 4:322-330.

02340 **CORSINI, R. J.** (1978), Impossible cases. *Individ. Psychologist*, 15:5.

02341 **CORSINI, R. J.** (1957), *Methods of Group Psychotherapy*. New York: Blakiston Division.

02342 **CORSINI, R. J.** (1957), *Methods of Group Psychotherapy*. New York: McGraw-Hill.

02343 **CORSINI, R. J.** (1951), The method of psychodrama in prison. *Group Psychother., Psychodrama & Sociometry*, 3:321-326.

02344 **CORSINI, R. J.** (1955), Moreno's theory of interpersonal therapy. *Group Psychother., Psychodrama & Sociometry*, 8:73-76.

02345 **CORSINI, R. J.** (1951), On the theory of change resulting from group therapy. *Group Psychother., Psychodrama & Sociometry*, 4:179-180.

02346 **CORSINI, R. J.** (1958), Psychodrama with a psychopath. *Group Psychother., Psychodrama & Sociometry*, 11:33-39.

02347 **CORSINI, R. J.** (1951), Psychodramatic treatment of a pedophile. *Group Psychother., Psychodrama & Sociometry*, 4:166-171.

02348 **CORSINI, R. J.** (1957), *The Role-Playing Technique in Business and Industry*. Chicago: Industrial Relations Center, University of Chicago.

02349 **CORSINI, R. J.** (1955), Towards a definition of group psychotherapy. *Ment. Hygiene*, 39:647-656.

02350 **CORSINI, R. J.** (1956), Two therapeutic groups that failed. *J. Correct. Psychol.*, 1:16-22.

02351 **CORSINI, R. J.**, and **LUNDIN, W. H.** (1955), Group psychotherapy in the mid-west. *Group Psychother., Psychodrama & Sociometry*, 8:316-320.

02352 **CORSINI, R. J.**, and **PUTZEY, L. J.** (1956), Bibliography of group psychotherapy. Group Psychother., Psychodrama & Sociometry, 9:178-249.

02353 **CORSINI, R. J.**, and **PUTZEY, L. J.** (1957), *Bibliography of Group Psychotherapy, 1906-1956*. New York: Beacon House.

02354 **CORSINI, R. J.**, and **ROSENBERG, B.** (1955), Mechanisms of group psychotherapy. *J. Abnorm. & Soc. Psychol.*, 51:406-411.

02355 **CORSINI, R. J.**, and **ROSENBERG, B.** (1975), Mechanisms of group psychotherapy: processes and dynamics. In: *Group Psychotherapy and Group Function*, 2d ed., eds. M. Rosenbaum and M. M. Berger. New York: Basic Books.

02356 **CORT, C. C.** (1973), Effects of a group approach emphasizing student development on the academic performance and social/psychological adjustment of high risk college freshmen. *Dissert. Abstr. Internat.*, 34:4776A.

02357 **CORTAZZI, D.**, and **ROOTE, S.** (1975), *Illuminative Incident Analysis*. New York: McGraw-Hill.

02358 **CORTESÃO, E. L.** (1960), (Psychodynamics of depressive neuroses and syndromes in group analytical psychotherapy.) *J. Medico*, (Porto) 42:730-734.

02359 **CORTESÃO, E. L.** (1963), (Psychotherapy and psychotherapeutists.) *J. Medico*, (Porto) 51:791-799.

02360 **CORTNER, R. H.** (1961), The relation between morale and informal group structure in hospitals. Ph.D. thesis, St. Louis University.

02361 **CORY, T. L.**, and **PAGE, D.** (1978), Group techniques for effecting change in the more disturbed patient. *Group*, 2:149-155.

02362 **CORY, T. L.**, and **PAGE, D.** (1978), Playing games in group therapy. *Transactional Anal. J.*, 8:229.

02363 **COSNIER, J.** (1971), (Experience with group dramatic psychoanalysis and children.) *Rev. Neuropsychiat. Infantile*, (Paris) 19:497-517.

02364 **COSTELL, R.**, and **YALOM, I.** (1971), Treatment of the sex offender: institutional group therapy. *Internat. Psychiat. Clinics*, 8:119-144.

02365 **COSTELL, R. M.**, and **KORAN, L. M.** (1972), Compatibility and cohesiveness in group psychotherapy: a re-evaluation and extension. *J. Nerv. & Ment. Disease*, 155:99-104.

02366 **COSTINEW, A. E.** (1971), The basic encounter group as an innovation in counselor education. *Dissert. Abstr. Internat.*, 32:170A.

02367 **COTSONAS, N. J., Jr., KAISER, R. J.,** and **DOWLING, H. F.** (1958), Adapting the group discussion technique for use with large classes. *J. Med. Educat.*, 33:152-163.

02368 **COTTLE, T. J.** (1967), Encounter in color. *Psychol. Today*, 1:22-27, 40-41.

02369 **COTTLE, T. J.** (1968), Facing the patients: notes on group therapy observation. *Psychother.: Theory, Res. & Pract.*, 5:254-261.

02370 **COTTLE, T. J.** (1973), Notes on leader disclosure in self-analytic groups. *Sociol. Inquiry*, 43:51-66.

02371 **COTTON, J. M.** (1948), Group psychotherapy: an appraisal. In: *Failures in Psychiatric Treatment*, ed. P. H. Hoch. New York: Grune & Stratton.

02372 **COTTON, J. M.** (1950), Group structure and group psychotherapy. *Group Psychother., Psychodrama & Sociometry*, 3:216-217.

02373 **COTTON, J. M.** (1945), *Manual of Group Psychotherapy. Daytona Beach, FL. Neuropsychiatric Treatment Branch, Welsch Convalescent Hospital*, mimeographed.

02374 **COTZIN, M.** (1948), Group psychotherapy with mentally defective problem boys. *Amer. J. Ment. Deficiency*, 53:268-283.

02375 **COUGHLIN, F.,** and **WIMBERGER, H. C.** (1968), Group Family Therapy. *Fam. Process*, 7:37-50.

02376 **COULSON, W. R.** (1972), *Groups, Gimmicks, and Instant Gurus: An Examination of Encounter Groups and Their Distortions*, 1st ed. New York: Harper and Row.

02377 **COULTER, W. R.** (1973), Communications content and style as operants in group therapy. *Dissert. Abstr. Internat.*, 33:3932B.

02378 **COUNSELING CENTER STAFF.** (1972), Effects of three types of sensitivity groups on changes in measures of self-actualization. *J. Couns. Psychol.*, 1:253-254.

02379 **COURCHET, J.,** and **MAUCORPS, P. H.** (1966), *Le Vide Social: Ses Conséquences et Leur Traitement par la Revendication—Recherches Biologiques et Sociologiques. (The Social Life: Its Consequences and Their Treatment by Reclaimation—Sociological and Biological Research.)* Paris: Mouton.

02380 **COURTNEY, P.** (1969), *Beware Sensitivity Training*. New Orleans: Free Men Speak.

02381 **COVEN, A. B.** (1977), Using gestalt psychodrama experiments in rehabilitation counseling. *Personnel & Guid. J.*, 56:143-148.

02382 **COVI, L.** (1972), A group psychotherapy approach to the treatment of neurotic symptoms in male and female patients of homosexual preference. *Psychother. & Psychosomat.*, (Basel) 20:176-180.

02383 **COVI, L.** (1974), Drugs and group psychotherapy in neurotic depression. *Amer. J. Psychiat.*, 131:210-220.

02384 **COWDEN, R. C.** (1961), Group psychotherapy with chronic schizophrenics. *Group Psychother., Psychodrama & Sociometry*, 14:209-214.

02385 **COWDEN, R. C., ZAX, M.,** and **SPROLES, J. A.** (1956), Group psychotherapy in conjunction with a physical treatment. *J. Clin. Psychol.*, 12:53-56.

02386 **COWDEN, R. C., ZAX, M., HAGUE, J. R.,** and **FINNEY, R. C.** (1956), Chlorpromazine: alone and as an adjunct to group psychotherapy in the treatment of psychiatric patients. *Amer. J. Psychiat.*, 113:898-902.

02387 **COWEN, E. L.,** and **CRUICKSHANK, W. M.** (1948), Group therapy with physically handicapped children: ii. evaluation. *J. Educat. Psychol.*, 39:281-297.

02388 **COWEN, L.**, and **SMITH, C.** (1973), The ultimate group. *Psychother.: Theory, Res. & Pract.*, 10:339-340.

02389 **COWEN, L., McNEIL, M.**, and **ROBINSON, M. R.** (1973), Group physical activity as therapy. *Soc. Work*, 18:96-97.

02390 **COX, F. N.** (1953), Sociometric status and individual adjustment before and after play therapy. *J. Abnorm. & Soc. Psychol.*, 48:354-356.

02391 **COX, M.** (1973), Group psychotherapy as a redefining process. *Internat. J. Group Psychother.*, 23:465-473.

02392 **COX, M.** (1976), *Group Psychotherapy in a Secure Setting. Royal Soc. Med. Proceed.*, (London) 69:215-220.

02393 **COX, M.** (1973), The group therapy interaction chronogram. *Brit. J. Soc. Work*, (Birmingham) 3:243-256.

02394 **COX, M.** (1978), *Structuring the Therapeutic Process: Compromise with Chaos—A Therapist's Response to the Individual and the Group.* Elmsford, NY: Pergamon Press.

02395 **COYLE, G. L.** (1959), Group work in psychiatric settings: its roots and branches. *Soc. Work*, 4:74-81.

02396 **CRABTREE, L. H., Jr.**, and **COX, J. L. D.** (1972), The overthrow of a therapeutic community. *Internat. J. Group Psychother.*, 22:31-41.

02397 **CRABTREE, L. H.**, and **GRALLER, J. L.** (1971), The group psychotherapy of natural relationships. *Psychother.: Theory, Res. & Pract.*, 8:55-58.

02398 **CRABTREE, L. H.**, and **HOROWITZ, H.** (1974), Impromptu group: beyond crisis intervention. *Psychother.: Theory, Res. & Pract.*, 11:356-359.

02399 **CRADDICK, R. A.** (1962), Group therapy with inmates in a Canadian prison. *Group Psychother., Psychodrama & Sociometry*, 15:312-320.

02400 **CRAFOORD, C.** (1973), (Elementary confidence and confrontation: experiences from the Fruängen day hospital 1968-1972.) *Svenska Lakartidningen*, (Stockholm) 70:1640-1647.

02401 **CRAFT, M., STEPHENSON, G.**, and **GRANGER, C.** (1964), A controlled trial of authoritarian and self-governing regimes with adolescent psychopaths. *Amer. J. Orthopsychiat.*, 34:543-554.

02402 **CRAFTS, G.** (1975), The effect of group counseling on self-concept and reading improvement of selected community college students. *Dissert. Abstr. Internat.*, 35:4181A.

02403 **CRAIG, R. J.** (1971), Alumni group therapy for chronic schizophrenic outpatients. *Hosp. & Community Psychiat.*, 22:204-205.

02404 **CRAIG, Y.** (1978), Counseling and the schizophrenias. *Brit. J. Guid. & Couns.*, (Cambridge) 16:35-44.

02405 **CRAMPTON, M.** (1972), Toward a psychosynthetic approach to the group. *Psychosynth. Res. Found.*, 28:18.

02406 **CRANDALL, R.** (1978), The assimilation of newcomers into groups. *Small Group Behav.*, 9:331-336.

02407 **CRARY, W. G.** (1968), Goals and techniques of transitory group therapy. *Hosp. & Community Psychiat.*, 19:389-391.

02408 **CRAVENS, R. W.**, and **WORCHEL, P.** (1977), The differential effects of rewarding and coercive leaders on group members differing in locus of control. *J. Personality & Soc. Psychol.*, 45:150-169.

02409 **CRAWSHAW, R.** (1969), How sensitive is sensitivity training? *Amer. J. Psychiat.*, 126:868-873.

02410 **CREMERIUS, J.** (1964), (Experiences with group work not conducted by a physician aiming at the social rehabilitation of chronic hospital patients.) *Schweiz. Arch. Neurol., Neurochir. & Psychiat.*, (Zurich) 93:425-427.

02411 **CRESCI, M. B.** (1974), The interaction of trainer's leadership style and member's level of dominance: submissiveness in sensitivity groups. *Dissert. Abstr. Internat.*, 135:1043B.

02412 **CRESON, D. L., and BLAKEREY, P. M.** (1970), Social structure in an adolescent milieu program: implications for treatment. *Adolescence*, 5:407-426.

02413 **CRESSEY, M. R.** (1954), Contradictory theories in correctional group therapy programs. *Fed. Probation*, 18:20-26.

02414 **CRETEKOS, C., HALPERIN, D., and FIDLER, J.** (1966), Group communication with chronic "rehabilitated" psychiatric patients. *Internat. J. Group Psychother.*, 16:51-57.

02415 **CREWS, C. Y.** (1978), The effects of participant sex role orientation and some parameters of structure on group development in analogue CR groups. *Dissert. Abstr. Internat.*, 39:2977B. (University Microfilms No. 7824385.)

02416 **CREWS, G. Y., and MELNICK, J.** (1976), Use of initial and delayed structure in facilitating group development. *J. Couns. Psychol.*, 23:92-98.

02417 **CRICHTON, A.** (1966), Developing understanding of group behavior in social studies students. *Soc. Worker*, (London) 23:19-24.

02418 **CRICHTON, A.** (1967), Training for management in the social services. *Soc. Worker*, (London) 24:20-26.

02419 **CRIDER, M. M.** (1966), A study of the effectiveness of group counseling upon personality conflict and reading retardation. *Dissert. Abstr. Internat.*, 26:4438.

02420 **CRIGHTON, J., and JEHU, D.** (1969), Treatment of examination anxiety by systematic desensitization or psychotherapy in groups. *Behav. Res. & Ther.*, 7:245-248.

02421 **CRISHAM, M. J., and DANIELSEN, S. L.** (1965), An experience with group orientation sessions. *Perspect. Psychiat. Care*, 3:34-41.

02422 **CRISLER, J. R.** (1970), The effects and utility of training and using subprofessional rehabilitation personnel as group facilitators. *Dissert. Abstr. Internat.*, 30:3274A.

02423 **CRISLER, J. R., and LONG, E. G.** (1978), The effects of human relations training upon the self concept of severely disabled persons. *J. Appl. Rehab. Couns.*, 9:50-52.

02424 **CRISS, F. L., and GOODWIN, R. C.** (1970), Short-term group counseling for parents of children in residential treatment. *Child Welfare*, 49:45-48.

02425 **CRISTANTIELLO, P. D.** (1968), Group process for developing a faculty adviser program. *Nursing Outlook*, 16:27-29.

02426 **CRITTENDEN, R. L.** (1973), Comment on group reactive inhibition and reciprocal inhibition therapies with anxious college students. *J. Couns. Psychol.*, 20:353-354.

02427 **CROAKE, J. W.** (1970), Group counseling: a first attempt. *Psychol. in Schools*, 7:57-60.

02428 **CROCE, V. M.** (1979), Natural high therapy: innovative approach to drug dependency. *J. Psychiat. Nurs.*, 17:20-22.

02429 **CROCKET, R.** (1966), Acting-out as a mode of communication in the psychotherapeutic community. *Brit. J. Psychiat.*, (Ashford) 112:383-388.

02430 **CROCKET, R., and ST. BLAIZE-MOLONY, R.** (1964), Social ramifications of the therapeutic community approach in psychotherapy. *Brit. J. Med. Psychol.*, (London) 37:153-156.

02431 **CROCKET, R. W.** (1962), Initiation of the therapeutic community approach to treatment in a neurosis center. *Internat. J. Group Psychother.*, 12:180-193.

02432 **CROGHAN, L. M.** (1974), Encounter groups and the necessity for ethical guidelines. *J. Clin. Psychol.*, 30:438-446.

02433 **CROLEY, H. T.** (1951), A method of analyzing the process of group psychotherapy. Unpublished doctoral dissertation, University of Denver.

02434 **CROMES, G. F.** (1971), The effect of a group therapy experience on juvenile offenders relative to their classification as neurotic or sociopathic. *Dissert. Abstr. Internat.*, 32:5435B.

02435 **CROMWELL, R. E.**, and **KENNEY, B. P.** (1979), Diagnosing marital and family systems: a training model. *Fam. Coordinator*, 28:101.

02436 **CROSA, G.** (1964), (Autogenic training and group psychotherapy.) *Sistemo Nerv.*, (Milan) 16:53-63.

02437 **CROSA, G.** (1966), Grappi terapeutici e distensione. (Therapeutic groups and relaxation.) *Minerva Med.*, (Turin) 57:1063-1065.

02438 **CROSBIE, P. V., PETRONI, F. A.**, and **STITT, B. G.** (1972), The dynamics of "corrective" groups. *J. Health & Soc. Behav.*, 13:294-302.

02439 **CROSS, F. M.** (1967), An analysis of verbal interaction in a therapy group of elderly psychiatric patients. *Dissert. Abstr. Internat.*, 28:961B.

02440 **CROT, M.**, and **BETTSCHART, W.** (1969), Psychotherapeutic treatment by means of analytic psychodrama. *Acta Paedopsychiat.*, (Basel) 36:130-141.

02441 **CROUCH, K. D.** (1970), The application of group counseling and behavior modification procedures to number anxiety in a college population. *Dissert. Abstr. Internat.*, 31:5758A.

02442 **CROW, M. L.** (1971), A comparison of three group counseling techniques with sixth graders. *Elem. School Guid. & Couns.*, 6:37-42.

02443 **CROW, M. S.** (1967), Preventive intervention through parent group education. *Soc. Casework*, 48:161-165.

02444 **CROWDES, N. E.** (1975), Group therapy for pre-adolescent boys. *Amer. J. Nursing*, 75:92-95.

02445 **CROWE, M. J.** (1976), The effectiveness of paraprofessionally-run social skills training groups for psychiatric inpatients. *Dissert. Abstr. Internat.*, 36:6375B.

02446 **CROWLEY, J. J.** (1974), Reality versus client–centered group therapy with adolescent males. *Dissert. Abstr. Internat.*, 34:4657B.

02447 **CROWLEY, P. M.** (1977), Review of A. W. Rachman's *Identity Group Psychotherapy with Adolescents. Internat. J. Group Psychother.*, 27:121-122.

02448 **CROWN, S.** (1976), Review of I. D. Yalom's *Theory and Practice of Group Psychotherapy. Brit. J. Psychiat.*, (Ashford) 130:91-92.

02449 **CROWTHER, B.**, and **PANTLEO, P. M.** (1971), Marathon therapy and changes in attitude toward treatment and behavior ratings. *Ment. Hygiene*, 55:165-170.

02450 **CROWTHER, B.**, and **PANTLEO, P.** (1970), Measurement of group interaction rate. *Psychol. Reports*, 27:707-712.

02451 **CRUICKSHANK, W. M.**, and **COWEN, E. L.** (1948), Group therapy with physically handicapped children: i. report of study. *J. Educat. Psychol.*, 39:193-215.

02452 **CRUMBAUGH, J. C.**, and **CARR, G. L.** (1979), Treatment of alcoholics with logotherapy. *Internat. J. Addict.*, 14:847-853.

02453 **CRUTCHER, R.** (1961), The usefulness of group therapy with character disorders. *Internat. J. Group Psychother.*, 11:431-439.

02454 **CRUVANT, B. A.** (1953), The function of the "administrative group" in a mental hospital group therapy program. *Amer. J. Psychiat.*, 110:342-436.

02455 **CRYER, L.**, and **BEUTLER, L.** (1980), Group therapy: an alternative treatment approach for rape victims. *J. Sex & Marital Ther.*, 6:40.

02456 **CUILHOT, M. A.** (1978), Les Groupes d'entr'aide thérapeutique en sexologie. *Psychother. & Psychosomat.*, (Basel) 29:214-216.

02457 **CULBERT, S. A.** (1972), Tone and intent: consciousness-raising. *J. Appl. Behav. Science*, 8:53-55.

02458 **CULBERTSON, E. L.** (1972), Changes in perceived attitudes of mentally gifted minors following individual and group counseling. *Dissert. Abstr. Internat.*, 33:419B.

02459 **CULEMANN, T.**, and **MEILICKE, A.** (1976), (Group dynamics as a delineation of group therapy.) *Hippokrates*, (Stuttgart) 47:284-286.

02460 **CULLEN, J. S.** (1968), The effectiveness of parent discussion groups: a follow-up study. *Ment. Hygiene*, 52:590-599.

02461 **CULP, W. H.** (1970), Changes in behavior and attitude as a result of receiving direct feedback and participating in group counseling. *Dissert. Abstr. Internat.*, 31:1007A.

02462 **CULPAN, F. M.** (1979), Studying action sociometry: an element in the personal growth of the therapist. *Group Psychother., Psychodrama & Sociometry*, 32:122-127.

02463 **CUMISKEY, P. A.**, and **MUDD, P.** (1972), Postpartum group therapy with unwell mothers. *Child Welfare*, 51:241-246.

02464 **CUMMING, J. H.**, and **CUMMING, E.** (1962), *Ego and Milieu: Theory and Practice of Environmental Therapy*. New York: Atherton Press.

02465 **CUMMINGS, S. T.**, and **STOCK, D.** (1962), Brief group therapy of mothers of retarded children outside of the specialty clinic setting. *Amer. J. Ment. Deficiency*, 66:739-748.

02466 **CUNNICK, D. G.**, and **FINBERG, L.** (1954), Group work with foster children in a pediatric clinic. *Pediatrics*, 13:103-106.

02467 **CUNNINGHAM, C., HELMERING, D.**, and **KORNBLUM, E.** (1975), A corner for the "kick me" player. *Transactional Anal. J.*, 5:404-410.

02468 **CUNNINGHAM, J., STRASSBERG, D.**, and **ROBACK, H.** (1978), Group psychotherapy for medical patients. *Comprehens. Psychiat.*, 19:133-140.

02469 **CURLEE, J.** (1971), Combined use of alcoholics anonymous and outpatient psychotherapy. *Bull. Menninger Clinic*, 35:368-371.

02470 **CURRAN, C. A.** (1969), *Religious Values in Counseling and Psychotherapy*. New York: Sheed and Ward.

02471 **CURRAN, F. J.** (1952), Group therapy: introductory remarks. *Neuropsychiatry*, 2:43-47.

02472 **CURRAN, F. J.** (1947), Group treatment in rehabilitation of offenders. In: *Handbook of correctional psychology*, eds. R. M. Lindner and R. V. Seliger. New York: Philosophical Library, pp. 571-588.

02473 **CURRAN, F. J., STRAUSS, B. V.**, and **VOGEL, B. F.** (1943), Group sex conference as a diagnostic, therapeutic and pedagogic method. *J. Crim. Psychopathol.*, 5:289-301.

02474 **CURRAN, J. J.** (1939), The drama as a therapeutic measure in adolescents. *Amer. J. Orthopsychiat.*, 9:215-231.

02475 **CURRAN, J. P.** (1975), Social skills training and systematic desensitization in reducing dating anxiety. *Behav. Res. & Ther.*, 13:65-68.

02476 **CURRAN, J. P.**, and **GILBERT, F. S.** (1975), A test of the relative effectiveness of a systematic desensitization program and an interpersonal skills training program with date anxious subjects. *Behav. Ther.*, 6:510-521.

02477 **CURRAN, J. P., GILBERT, S. S.**, and **LITTLE, L. M.** (1976), A comparison between behavioral replication training and sensitivity approaches to heterosexual dating anxiety. *J. Couns. Psychol.*, 23:190-196.

02478 **CURRAN, T. F.** (1978), Increasing motivation to change in group treatment. *Small Group Behav.*, 9:337-348.

02479 **CURRY, A. E.** (1966), Group psychotherapy: phenomenological considerations. *Rev. Exist. Psychol. & Psychiat.*, 6:63-70.

02480 **CURRY, A. E.** (1967), Large therapeutic groups: a critique and appraisal of selected literature. *Internat. J. Group Psychother.*, 17:536-547.

02481 **CURRY, A. E.** (1964), Meditations on group psychotherapy: and the role of the psychiatric nurse. *Perspect. Psychiat. Care*, 2:12-16.

02482 **CURRY, A. E.** (1963), Some comments on transference when group therapist is negro. *Internat. J. Group Psychother.*, 13:363-365.

02483 **CURTIS, J. H.** (1980), Review of M. C. Collins's *Child Abuser: A Study of Child Abusers in Self-Help Group Therapy. Fam. Relat.*, 29:256.

02484 **CURTIS, T. E., CLARKE, M. G.,** and **ABSE, D. W.** (1960), Etiological factors in peptic ulcer as revealed in group analytic psychotherapy. *Internat. Rec. Med.*, 173:92-96.

02485 **CUTFORTH, N. B.** (1980), The effect of group bibliotherapy in reducing the anxieties of children in grades one, two, and three. *Dissert. Abstr. Internat.*, 41:932A. (University Microfilms No. 8020654.)

02486 **CUTLER, M. O.** (1978), Symbolism and imagery in a group of chronic schizophrenics. *Internat. J. Group Psychother.*, 28:73-80.

02487 **CUTTER, F.** (1960), Patient-led discussion groups in a state hospital. *Ment. Hygiene*, 44:545-550.

02488 **CUTTER, H. S., SAMARAWEERA, A. B., FISH, R. A.,** and **MORRIS, L.** (1974), Emotional openness and mood change in marathon group psychotherapy. *Internat. J. Addict.*, 9:741-748.

02489 **CUTTS, N. B.** (1973), Group therapy leadership style and patient-perceived therapist ideal qualities. *Dissert. Abstr. Internat.*, 34:2300B.

02490 **CUVELIER, F.,** and **MATTHEEUWS, A.** (1969/1970), Psychodrama for the alcoholic. *Bull. de Psychol.*, (Brussels) 23:829-833.

02491 **CVETKOVICH, G.,** and **BAUMGARDNER, S. R.** (1973), Attitude polarization: the relative influence of discussion group structure and reference group norms. *J. Personality & Soc. Psychol.*, 26:15-165.

02492 **CYPREANSEN, L.** (1948), Group therapy for adult stutterers. *J. Speech & Hearing Disorders*, 13:313-319.

02493 **CYRUS, A. S.** (1967), Group treatment of ten disadvantaged mothers. *Soc. Casework*, 48:80-84.

02494 **CZABALA, J. C.,** and **KOSEWSKA, A.** (1976), (Personality and popularity in a psychotherapeutic group.) *Prezeglad, Psychol.*, (Warsaw) 19:311-322.

02495 **CZAJKOSKI, E. H.** (1968), The use of videotape recordings to facilitate the group therapy process. *Internat. J. Group Psychother.*, 18:516-524.

02496 **CZAPOW, G.,** and **CZAPOW, C.** (1968), Psychodrama w psychoterapii i w wychowaniu. (Psychodrama in psychotherapy and upbringing.) *Psychol. Wychowawcza*, (Warsaw) 11:51-68.

02497 **CZAPOW, G.,** and **CZAPOW, C.** (1968), Psychodrama w psychoterapii i w wychowaniw. (Psychodrama in psychotherapy and education.) *Psychol. Wychowawcza*, (Warsaw) 11:201-214.

02498 **CZECHOWICZ, A. S.** (1977), Retirement and beyond: therapeutic groups—a clue to management. part 6. *Australasian Nurses J.*, (Port Adelaide) 7:13-14.

02499 **CZERNIK, A.,** and **STEINMEYER, E. M.** (1978), Empirische untersuchungen zu einer quantitativen soziometrie in verlauf einer gruppentherapie. (Empirical study on quantitative sociometry during group psychotherapy.) *Psychother. & Med. Psychol.*, (Stuttgart) 28:152-157.

D

02500 **DABROWSKI, S.**, and **SEK, H.** (1976), Cognitive aspects of physicians' and psychologists' attitudes to the traditional psychiatric medical service and to the therapeutic community. *Polish Psychol. Bull.*, (Warsaw) 7:257-261.

02501 **DAEHLIN, D.**, and **HYNES, J.** (1974), A mother's discussion group in a women's prison. *Child Welfare*, 53:464-470.

02502 **D'AFFLITTI, J. G.**, and **SWANSON, D.** (1975), Group sessions for the wives of home–hemodialysis patients. *Amer. J. Nursing*, 75:633-635.

02503 **DAGUE, P. B.** (1974), The effects of an encounter-group intervention on levels of dogmatism. *Dissert. Abstr. Internat.*, 35:2423B.

02504 **DAILEY, A. L.** (1972), Group counseling parameters for pregnant non-residential high school students. *Dissert. Abstr. Internat.*, 32:6122A.

02505 **DALE,J. H.** (1972), The significance of sibling position and the frequency of participation by adults in group counseling activities. *Dissert. Abstr. Internat.*, 33:4041A.

02506 **DALL, A. G.** (1967), Group-learning for foster parents: in a public agency. *Children*, 14:185-187.

02507 **DALL'OGLIO, G. N.** (1956), Sputi critici in un esame storico di alcune esperienze di psicoterapia di gruppo. (Critical notes in a historic analysis of certain experiments in group psychotherapy.) *Neurone*, 4:13-20.

02508 **DALY, D. C.** (1962), Psychodrama as a care technique in milieu therapy. *Dissert. Abstr. Internat.*, 12:3266.

02509 **DALY, N. A.**, and **HEINE, H. C.** (1970), Honesty is the secret in sensitivity training. *Nursing Outlook*, 18:36-39.

02510 **DALY, V. J.** (1950), *Understanding Mental Illness: A Patient's Manual for Group Therapy*. Whitfield, MS: Mississippi State Hospital.

02512 **DALZELL-WARD, A. J.** (1960), Group discussion with male V.D. patients. *Brit. J. Venereal Diseases*, (London) 36:106-112.

02513 **DAMGAARD, J. A.** (1974), Structured versus unstructured procedures for training groups in the expression of feeling-cause relations. *Dissert. Abstr. Internat.*, 35:499B.

02514 **DANA, R. H.**, and **DANA, J. M.** (1969), Systematic observation of children's behavior in group therapy. *Psychol. Reports*, 24:134.

02515 **D'ANDREA, F. F.** (1963), (Psychodrama.) *Rev. Paulista Med.*, (Sao Paulo) 62:397-407.

02516 **DANE, P. G.** (1949), Observations upon group therapy. *Med. J. Austral.*, (Glebe) 36:127-129.

02517 **DANESH, H. B.** (1977), The angry group. *Internat. J. Group Psychother.*, 27:59-66.

02518 **DANESH, H. B.** (1980), The angry group for couples: a model for short-term group psychotherapy. *Univ. Ottawa Psychiat. J.*, 5:118-124.

02519 **DANET, B. N.** (1969), Impact of audio-visual feedback on group psychotherapy. *J. Consult. & Clin. Psychol.*, 33:632.

02520 **DANET, B. N.**, (1968), Self-confrontation by videotape in group psychotherapy. *Dissert. Abstr. Internat.*, 28:3058.

02521 **DANET, B. N.** (1969), Videotape playback as a therapeutic device in group psychotherapy. *Internat. J. Group Psychother.*, 19:433-440.

02522 **DANET, B. N.** (1968), Witnessed group therapy on television: therapeutic or not? *Amer. Psychol.*, 23:759.

02523 **D'ANGELO, R. J.** (1970), Relationships among agreement with therapist and self-concept changes. *Dissert. Abstr. Internat.*, 31:1532.

02524 **D'ANGELO, R. Y.** (1962), An evaluation of group psychotherapy with institutionalized delinquent girls. *Dissert. Abstr. Internat.*, 23:306-307.

02525 **DANIEL, S. J.** (1970), The influence of leader empathy (affective sensitivity) participant motivation to change and leader-participant relationship on changes in affective sensitivity of t-group participants. *Dissert. Abstr. Internat.*, 30:5229A-5230A

02526 **DANIELE, S. M.,** and **WOLIN, H.** (1973), Treatment of regressed schizophrenics: the nurse's role. *J. Bronx State Hosp.*, 1:57-61.

02527 **DANIELS, A. C.** (1966), Verbal behavior in group psychotherapy. *Dissert. Abstr. Internat.*, 27:962.

02528 **DANIELS, A. M.** (1969), Reaching unwed mothers. *Amer. J. Nursing*, 69:332-335.

02529 **DANIELS, A. M.** (1966), Training school nurses to work with groups of adolescents. *Children*, 13:210-216.

02530 **DANIELS, A. M.,** and **KRIM, A.** (1969), Helping adolescents explore emotional issues. *Amer. J. Nursing*, 69:1482-1485.

02531 **DANIELS, C. R.,** (1964), Play group therapy with children. *Acta Psychother. Psychosomat. Orthopaedagog.*, (Basel) 12:45-52.

02532 **DANIELS, D. N.** (1969), Task groups in the therapy of mental patients. In: *Current Psychiatric Therapies*, ed. J. H. Masserman. New York: Grune and Stratton.

02533 **DANIELS, D. N.,** and **RUBIN, R. S.** (1968), The community meeting. an analytical study and a theoretical statement. *Arch. Gen. Psychiat.*, 18:60-75.

02534 **DANIELS, E. M., SNYDER, B. R., WOOL, M.,** and **BERMAN, L.** (1960), A group approach to predelinquent boys, their teachers and parents, in a junior high school. *Internat. J. Group Psychother.*, 10:346-352.

02535 **DANIELS, M.** (1958), The influence of the sex of the therapist and of the co-therapist technique in group psychotherapy with boys: an investigation of the effectiveness of group psychotherapy with eighth grade, behavior problem boys, comparing results achieved by a male therapist, by a female therapist, and by the two therapists in combination. *Dissert. Abstr. Internat.*, 18:1489.

02536 **DANIELS, N.** (1967), Participation of relatives in a group centered program. *Internat. J. Group Psychother.*, 17:336-341.

02537 **DANIELS, R. S.** (1965), *Group psychotherapy. Progr. Neurol. Psychiat.*, 20:717-722.

02538 **DANIELS, R. S.,** and **PROSEN, H.** (1962), The contribution of visual observation to the understanding of an interview. *Internat. J. Group Psychother.*, 12:230-239.

02539 **DANISH, S. J.** (1971), Factors influencing changes in empathy following a group experience. *J. Couns. Psychol.*, 8:262-267.

02540 **DANISH, S. J.,** and **KAGAN, N.** (1969), Emotional stimulation in counseling and psychotherapy. *Psychother.: Theory, Res. & Pract.*, 6:261-263.

02541 **DANISH, S. J.,** and **KAGAN, N.** (1971), Measurement of affective sensitivity: toward a valid measure of interpersonal perception. *J. Couns. Psychol.*, 18:51-54.

02542 **DANISH, S. J.,** and **ZELENSKI, J. F., Jr.** (1972), Structured group interaction. *J. Coll. Student Personnel*, 13:53-56.

02543 **DANNEFER, E., BROWN, R.,** and **EPSTEIN, N.** (1975), Experience in developing a combined activity and verbal group therapy program with latency-age boys. *Internat. J. Group Psychother.*, 25:331-337.

02544 **DANZIG, M. E.** (1970), Education of the community mental health assistant: dovetailing theory with practice. *Ment. Hygiene*, 54:357.

02545 **DARRAGH, E.,** and **GENTLES, R.** (1980), Role playing in leadership training. *Dimens. Health Serv.*, 57:21-22.

02546 **DARS, E.**, and **BENOIT, J. C.** (1967), La pratique de l'expression scénique en groupe. (The use of scenic expression in a group.) *Encéphale Suppl.*, (Paris) 56:5-17.

02547 **DARSONO, A.** (1970), Van Gestalt-theorie tot groep-theorie: de evolutie van een psychologisch kernbegrip. (From Gestalt-therapy to group therapy: the development of a basic idea in psychology.) *Nederl. Tijdschr. Psychol.*, (Amsterdam) 25:144-177.

02548 **DASHEF, S. S., ESPEY, W. M.**, and **LAZARUS, J. A.** (1974), Time-limited sensitivity groups for medical students. *Amer. J. Psychiat.*, 131:287-292.

02549 **DASHEW, L.** (1977), Art-therapy group for latency age children. *Soc. Work*, 22:57-59.

02550 **da SILVA, G.** (1963), The role of the father with chronic schizophrenic patients: a study in group therapy. *Can. Psychiat. Assn. J.*, (Ottawa) 8:190-203.

02551 **DASTE, B. M.** (1973), Institutionalized aggressives in Louisiana. *Internat. J. Offender Ther.*, (London) 17:285-289.

02552 **D'AUGELLI, A. R.** (1974), Changes in self-reported anxiety during a small group experience. *J. Couns. Psychol.*, 21:202-205.

02553 **D'AUGELLI, A. R.** (1977), The effects of a leaderless encounter group experience on helping skills training. *Counselor Educat. & Supervision*, 17:92-97.

02554 **D'AUGELLI, A. R.** (1973), Group composition using interpersonal skills: an analogue study on the effects of members' interpersonal skills on peer ratings and group cohesiveness. *J. Couns. Psychol.*, 20:531-534.

02555 **D'AUGELLI, A. R.**, and **CHINSKY, J. M.** (1974), Interpersonal skills and pretraining: implications for the use of group procedures for interpersonal learning and for the selection of nonprofessional mental health workers. *J. Consult. & Clin. Psychol.*, 42:65-72.

02556 **D'AUGELLI, A. R., CHINSKY, J. M.**, and **GETTER, H.** (1974), The effect of group composition and duration on sensitivity training. *Small Group Behav.*, 5:56-64.

02557 **DAUMEZON, G.** (1964), Essai de sémiologie de l'observation en groupe. (Attempt at a semiology of group observation.) *Evolut. Psychiat.*, (Toulouse) 29:533-558.

02558 **DAVID, A. C.**, and **DONOVAN, E. H.** (1975/1976), Initiating group process with parents of multihandicapped children. *Soc. Work & Health Care*, 1:177-183.

02559 **DAVID, H. P.** (1966), International trends. *J. Psychiat. Nursing*, 4:183-185.

02560 **DAVIDOFF, E.**, and **BUCKLAND, G.** (1939), Reaction of a juvenile delinquent group to story and drama technique. *Psychiat. Quart.*, 13:245-258.

02561 **DAVIDOFF, I. F., LAUGA, A. C.**, and **WALZER, R. S.** (1969), The mental health rehabilitation worker: a new member of the psychiatric team. *Community Ment. H.*, 5:46-54.

02562 **DAVIDSON, G. C., GOLDFRIED, M. R.**, and **KRASNER, L.** (1970), A postdoctoral program in behavior modification: theory and practice. *Amer. Psychologist*, 25:767-772.

02563 **DAVIDSON, P. W.** (1965), Comment on the small activity group (SAG) project of the Montebello Unified School District. *J. School Health J.*, 35:423-429.

02564 **DAVIDSON, S.** (1946), Notes on a group of ex-prisoners of war. *Bull. Menninger Clinic*, 10:90-100.

02565 **DAVIDSON, S.**, and **BEHR, H.** (1980), Group analysis: an Israeli experience. *Group Anal.*, (London) 13:121-124.

02566 **DAVIES, E.** (1973), The use of t-groups in training social workers. *Brit. J. Soc. Work*, (Birmingham) 3:65-77.

02567 **DAVIES, M. H.** (1976), The origins and practice of psychodrama. *Brit. J. Psychiat.*, (Ashford) 129:201-206.

02568 **DAVIS, C. A.** (1970), The effect of group approaches in hospital management. *Sandoz Psychiat. Spectator*, 6:8-9.

02569 **DAVIS, C. P.** (1970), An assessment of the effectiveness of small group counseling. *Dissert. Abstr. Internat.*, 30:3275A.

02570 **DAVIS, C. S.** (1970), An assessment of the effectiveness of small group counseling on selected groups of seventh and ninth grade underachieving boys. *Dissert. Abstr. Internat.*, 30:3275A.

02571 **DAVIS, D.** (1979), Review of T. J. Paolino's and B. S. McCrady's *Alcoholic Marriage: Alternative Perspective. Amer. J. Fam. Ther.*, 7:86.

02572 **DAVIS, D. M.** (1977), An implementation of therapeutic community in a private mental health center. *Diseases Nerv. System*, 38:189-191.

02573 **DAVIS, F. B.**, and **LOHR, N. E.** (1971), Special problems with the use of cotherapists in group psychotherapy. *Internat. J. Group Psychother.*, 21:143-158.

02574 **DAVIS, F. M.**, and **DITMAN, K. S.** (1963), The effect of court referral and disulfiram on motivation of alcoholics: a preliminary report. *Quart. J. Studies Alcohol*, 24:276-279.

02575 **DAVIS, H. K.**, and **DORMAN, K. R.** (1974), Group therapy versus ward rounds. *Diseases Nerv. System*, 35:316-319.

02576 **DAVIS, J. A.** (1971), Outpatient group therapy with schizophrenic patients. *Soc. Casework*, 52:172-178.

02577 **DAVIS, J. H.** (1969), *Group Performance*. Reading, MA: Addison-Wesley.

02578 **DAVIS, J. H.** (1969), Individual-group problem solving, subject preference, and problem type. *J. Personality & Soc. Psychol.*, 13:362-374.

02579 **DAVIS, J. H., HOPPE, R. A.**, and **HORNSETH, J. P.** (1968), Risk-taking: task, response pattern, and grouping. *Organiz. Behav. & Human Perf.*, 2:124-142.

02580 **DAVIS, J. L.** (1969), The effect of group counseling on teacher affectiveness. *Dissert. Abstr. Internat.*, 30:2328A.

02581 **DAVIS, K. L.** (1980), Is confidentiality in group counseling realistic? *Personnel & Guid. J.*, 59:197-201.

02582 **DAVIS, K. L.** (1968), The sensitivity of selected instruments to personality changes produced by group counseling. *Dissert. Abstr. Internat.*, 28:3968A.

02583 **DAVIS, L. H.** (1970), The effects of group counseling for vocational choice upon adolescents expressed occupational preference. *Dissert. Abstr. Internat.*, 31:1007A.

02584 **DAVIS, M.** (1972), A self-confrontation technique in alcoholism treatment. *Quart. J. Studies Alcohol*, 22:191-192.

02585 **DAVIS, M. C.** (1967), Evaluation of therapy and discontinuation of treatment as perceived by patients. *Smith College Studies Soc. Work*, 38:60-61.

02586 **DAVIS, M. D.**, and **FEINSTEIN, S. C.** (1968), A therapeutic day program for emotionally disturbed students in a public school. *Amer. J. Orthopsychiat.*, 38:275-276.

02587 **DAVIS, M. I., SHARFSTEIN, S.**, and **OWEN, M.** (1974), Separate and together: all Black therapy group in the white hospital. *Amer. J. Orthopsychiat.*, 44:19-25.

02588 **DAVIS, M. M.** (1978), The effects of group counseling on the self-concept and achievement of black college freshmen. *Dissert. Abstr. Internat.*, 38:1335A.

02589 **DAVIS, M. S.** (1978), Poetry group therapy vs. interpersonal group therapy: comparison of treatment effectiveness with depressed women. *Dissert. Abstr. Internat.*, 39:5543B.

02590 **DAVIS, R.** (1980), Review of S. R. Slavson's and M. Schiffer's *Dynamics of Group Psychotherapy, Group Anal.*, (London) 13:148-149.

02591 **DAVIS, R. E.** (1976), Review of A. W. Rachman's *Identity Group Psychotherapy with Adolescents. Amer. J. Psychiat.*, 133:982-983.

02592 **DAVIS, R. G.** (1948), Group therapy and social acceptance in a first-second grade. *Elem. School J.*, 49:219-223.

02593 **DAVIS, S.**, and **MARCUS, L. M.** (1980), Involving parents in the treatment of severely communication disordered children. *J. Pediat. Psychol.*, 5:189.

02594 **DAVIS, S. H.** (1969), The effects of participation in group psychotherapy on the imitative behavior of chronic schizophrenics. *Dissert. Abstr. Internat.*, 29:4376B.

02595 **DAVIS, S. L.** (1980), The training of entry level group counselors: a descriptive survey. *Dissert. Abstr. Internat.*, 40:4891A-4892A. (University Microfilms No. 8005857.)

02596 **DAVIS, T. M.** (1974), Differential gain in grade point average in response to structured group counseling as a function of personality traits. *Dissert. Abstr. Internat.*, 34:6380A.

02597 **DAVIS, W. S.** (1965), Group psychotherapy today. case discussion. *Topics & Probl. Psychother.*, 5:194-196.

02598 **DAWLEY, H. H.** (1972), Group implosive therapy in the treatment of test anxiety. *Dissert. Abstr. Internat.*, 33:1018A.

02599 **DAWLEY, H. H.**, and **WENRICH, W. W.** (1973), Group implosive therapy in the treatment of test anxiety: a brief report. *Behav. Ther.*, 4:261-263.

02600 **DAWLEY, H. H.**, and **WENRICH, W. W.** (1973), Massed group desensitization in reduction of test anxiety. *Psychol. Reports*, 33:359-363.

02601 **DAWLEY, H. H.**, and **WENRICH, W. W.** (1973), Treatment of test anxiety by group implosive therapy. *Psychol. Reports*, 33:383-388.

02602 **DAWLING, E.**, and **JONES, H. V.** (1978), Small children seen and heard in family therapy. *J. Child Psychother.*, 4:87.

02603 **DAWS, P. P.** (1973), Mental health and education: counseling as prophylaxis. *Brit. J. Guid. & Couns.*, (Cambridge) 1:2-10.

02604 **DAY, G. A.** (1965), A program for teenage unwed mothers. *Amer. J. Pub. Health*, 55:978-981.

02605 **DAY, M.** (1952), Expectations as a source of pitfalls in group psychotherapy. *J. Nerv. & Ment. Diseases*, 115:273-274.

02606 **DAY, M.** (1967), The natural history of training groups. *Internat. J. Group Psychother.*, 17:436-446.

02607 **DAY, M.**, and **SEMRAD, E. V.** (1968), Group interactions. *Sandoz Psychiat. Spectator*, 5:17-18.

02608 **DAY, M.**, and **SEMRAD, E. V.** (1975), Group therapy with psychotics: twenty years later. In: *Group Psychotherapy and Group Function*, 2d ed., eds. M. Rosenbaum and M. M. Berger. New York: Basic Books.

02609 **DAY, M., DAY, E.**, and **HERMANN, R.** (1953), Group therapy of patients with multiple sclerosis, a preliminary report. *Arch. Neurol. Psychiat.*, 69:193-196.

02610 **DAY, S. K.** (1968), The effects of activity group counseling on selected behavior characteristics of culturally disoriented Negro boys. *Dissert. Abstr. Internat.*, 28:3969A.

02611 **DAY, S. R.** (1970), Discussant: marathon papers. *Compar. Group Studies*, 1:419-423.

02612 **DAYMAS, S.** (1978), (Psychotherapeutic approach to the young child: mother-child psychotherapy.) *Rev. Neuropsychiat. Infantile*, (Paris) 26:321-327.

02613 **DEAN, S. R.** (1971), Role of self-conducted group therapy in psychorehabilitation: a look at recovery, inc. *Amer. J. Psychiat.*, 127:934-937.

02614 **DEAN, S. R.** (1973), (On the self-directed group: Its role in psychiatric care.) *Actas Luso Espanoles Neurol. Psiquiat.*, (Madrid) 1:467-470.

02615 **DEAN, S. R.** (1971), Self-help group psychotherapy: mental patients rediscover will power. *Internat. J. Soc. Psychiat.*, (London) 17:72-78.

02616 **DeANDEADE, L. F. G.** (1962), A maturacao emocional no grupo terapeutico. (Emotional maturation in group therapy.) *J. Brasil. Psiquiat.*, (Rio de Janeiro) 1:23-43.

02617 **DEANE, W. N.** (1964), Preliminary report of psychodrama. *Group Psychother., Psychodrama & Sociometry*, 17:134-138.

02618 **DEANE, W. N.** (1973), Three criteria for evaluating sensitivity training. *Hosp. & Community Psychiat.*, 23:169-170.

02619 **DEANE, W. N.**, and **DODD, M. L.** (1960), Educational techniques for the rehabilitation of chronic schizophrenic patients. *Amer. J. Occupat. Ther.*, 14:7-12.

02620 **DEANE, W. N.**, and **MARSHALL, E. B.** (1965), A validation study of a psychodrama group experience: a preliminary survey. *Group Psychother., Psychodrama & Sociometry*, 18:217-240.

02621 **DEARDOROFF, C. M.** (1973), Interpersonal values and behaviors associated with positive change in one form of encounter groups. *Dissert. Abstr. Internat.*, 34:1742B.

02622 **DEBOUTTE, D., van WANING, A.,** and **van ENGELAND, H.** (1979), ("May I join in?" behavioral group therapy for children with social anxiety.) *Tijdschr. Psychother.*, 5:295-304.

02623 **DEBOW, S. L.** (1975), Identical twins concordant for anorexia nervosa: a preliminary case report. *Can. Psychiat. Assn. J.*, (Ottawa) 20:215-217.

02624 **de CÉSAR, H. M.**, and **ABUISO, D.** (1971), El tiempo limitado como distorsión de la problemática y la técnica in terapia de grupos. (Limited time as a distortion of the problematic and the technique in group therapy.) *Acta Psichiat. Psicol. Amer. Latina.*, (Buenos Aires) 17:106-109.

02625 **DECHERF, G.** (1976), (Specific aspects of a recent technique: the development group for children.) *Perspect. Psychiat.*, (Paris) 57:205-214.

02626 **DeCHESARO, C.** (1970), Treatment of outpatient adolescents and their parents in separate–simultaneous group psychotherapy. *Psychiat. Communicat.*, 13:29-33.

02627 **DECK, E. S., HURLEY, J. E.,** and **CRUMTON, E.** (1963), Effects of group psychotherapy on attitudes of nursing students. *Group Psychother., Psychodrama & Sociometry*, 16:46-54.

02628 **DECKER, R. E.** (1976), The effects of visual observation, videotape and recording on verbal and non-verbal behavior in group psychotherapy. *Dissert. Abstr. Internat.*, 37:1428.

02629 **DEE, G. H.** (1970), The effects of parent group counseling on children with school adjustment problems. *Dissert. Abstr. Internat.*, 31:1008A.

02630 **DEE, V. D.** (1972), Contingency management in a crisis class. *Except. Children*, 38:631-634.

02631 **DEETHS, A.** (1970), Psychodrama crisis intervention with delinquent male drug users. *Group Psychother., Psychodrama & Sociometry*, 23:41-44.

02632 **DEFFENBACHER, J. L.** (1976), Group desensitization of dissimilar anxieties. *Community Ment. Health J.*, 12:263-265.

02633 **DEFFENBACHER, J. L.** (1974), Group desensitization for heterogeneous phobias. *J. Behav. Ther. & Exper. Psychiat.*, 5:305.

02634 **DEFFENBACHER, J. L.** (1974), Hierarchies for desensitization of test and speech anxieties. *J. Coll. Student Personnel*, 15:452-454.

02635 **DEFFENBACHER, J. L.**, and **KEMPER, C. C.** (1974), Counseling test-anxious sixth graders. *Elem. School Guid. & Couns.*, 9:22-29.

02636 **DEFFENBACHER, J. L.**, and **KEMPER, C. C.** (1974), Systematic desensitization of test anxiety in junior high students. *School Counselor*, 21:216-222.

02637 Defining role of psychotherapy in treating schizophrenia (1970), *Roche Report: Front. Hosp. Psychiat.*, 7:5-6.

02638 **deFRIES, Z.**, and **BROWDER, S.** (1952), Group psychotherapy with epileptic children and their mothers. *Arch. Neurol. Psychiat.*, 67:826-827.

02639 **deFRIES, Z.**, and **BROWDER, S.** (1952), Group therapy with epileptic children and their parents. *Proceed., N.Y. Acad. Science*, 28:235.

02640 **DeGIOVANNI, P.** (1959), A comparison between orthodox group psychotherapy and activity-group therapy in the treatment of chronic hospitalized schizophrenics. Ann Arbor: University Microfilms.

02641 **DEIBEL, A. W.** (1969), Geriatrics. *J. Psychiat. Nursing*, 7:238.

02642 **deJULIO, S. S.** (1974), The effects of pregroup norm setting in encounter groups. *Dissert. Abstr. Internat.*, 34:3491B.

02643 **deJULIO, S. S., BENTLEY, J.**, and **COCKAYNE, T.** (1979), Pregroup norm setting: effects on encounter group interactions. *Small Group Behav.*, 10:368-388.

02644 **deJULIO, S. S., LAMBERT, M. J.**, and **BENTLEY, J.** (1977), Personal satisfaction as a criterion for evaluating group success. *Psychol. Reports*, 40:409-410.

02645 **DELACROIX, J. M.** (1978), Les psychothérapies de groupe corporelles avec des psychotiques. (Group psychotherapies with psychotics.) *L'inform. Psychiat.*, 54:379-396.

02646 **DELACROIX, J. M.** (1977), Psychothérapie de groupe en hôspital psychiatrique pour malades difficiles. (Group psychotherapy in a psychiatric hospital for the seriously ill.) *L'inform. Psychiat.*, 53:929-935.

02647 **DELACROIX, J. M.** (1978), Psychothérapie de groupe en hôpital psychiatrique à sécurité maximale. (Group psychotherapy in a maximum security psychiatric hospital.) *Psychother. & Psychosomat.*, (Basel) 29:130-136.

02648 **DELACROIX, J. M.** (1978), Psychothérapie de groupe—verbale—chez les délinquants et parole "perverse." (Group psychotherapy: working with delinquents and sexual offenders.) *L'inform. Psychiat.*, 54:149-152.

02649 **DELANEY, D. J.**, and **HEIMANN, R. A.** (1966), Effectiveness of sensitivity training on the perception of non-verbal communications. *J. Couns. Psychol.*, 13:436-440.

02650 **DELANEY, E. T.** (1971), The effects of a group experience on the self-awareness of supervisor trainees and teacher trainees in supervision. *Dissert. Abstr. Internat.*, 31:6397A.

02651 **DeLARA, L. E.** (1969), Listening is a challenge: group counseling in the school. *Ment. Hygiene*, 53:600-605.

02652 **DeLATIL, P.** (1963), Sociometry: the science of human groups. *Internat. J. Sociometry & Sociatry*, 3:39-41.

02653 **DELBECQ, A. L.**, and **VAN de VEN, A. H.** (1971), A group process model for problem identification and program planning. *J. Appl. Behav. Science*, 7:466-492.

02654 **deLEON, G.**, and **BIASE, D. V.** (1975), Encounter group: measurement of systolic blood pressure. *Psychol. Reports*, 37:439-445.

02655 **deLEON, G., ROSENTHAL, M.**, and **BRODNEY, K.** (1971), Therapeutic community for drug addicts, long-term measurement of emotional changes. *Psychol. Reports*, 29:595-600.

02656 **deLIMA, O. R.** (1963), (Genetico-historical interpretations in group psychotherapy.) *Rev. Paulista Med.* (Sao Paulo), 63:339-341.

02657 **deLIMA, O. R.** (1966), (The schizoid stage preceding the schizo-paranoid phase, as seen through group psychotherapy.) *Rev. Paulista Med., (Sao Paulo) 69:129-133.*

02658 **DELK, J. L.**, and **RYAN, T. T.** (1977), A-B status and sex stereotyping among psychotherapists and patients. *J. Nerv. & Ment. Diseases*, 164:253-262.

02659 **DELL, D. F.** (1980), Review of F. Farrelly's and J. Brandsma's *Provocative Therapy. J. Marital & Fam. Ther.*, 6:93.

02660 **DELLA PIETRA, V.** (1969), (Specular action in group psychotherapy studied by the comical imitation sketch.) *Ospedale Psichiat.*, (Naples) 37:67-88.

02661 **DELLAROSSA, A.** (1971), Grupoterapia institucional. (Institutional group therapy.) *Acta Psichiat. Psicol. Amer. Latina*, (Buenos Aires) 17:97-101.

02662 **DELLAROSSA, A.** (1971), Grupoterapia institucional: introduccion. (Institutional group therapy: introduction.) *Acta Psichiat. Psicol. Amer. Latina*, (Buenos Aires) 17:90-97.

02663 **DELLAROSSA, A.** (1968), La spicoterapia en grupos y las instituciones asistenciales. (Group psychotherapy and treatment centers.) *Acta Psichiat. Psicol. Amer. Latina*, (Buenos Aires) 14:144-148.

02664 **DELLIS, N. P.**, and **STONE, H. K.** (1960), *The Training of Psychotherapists*, Baton Rouge: Louisiana State University Press.

02665 **DELL ORTO, A. E.** (1975), Goal group therapy: a structured group experience applied to drug treatment and rehabilitation. *J. Psychedelic Drugs*, 7:363-371.

02666 **Del NUOVO, F. A., SPIELBERG, G.**, and **GILLIS, H.** (1978), A preliminary investigation of the psychodramatic experience of spontaneity. *Group Psychother., Psychodrama & Sociometry*, 31:86.

02667 **Del TORTO, J.**, and **CORNYETZ, P.** (1944), How to organize a psychodramatic unit. *Sociometry*, 7:250-256.

02668 **Del TORTO, J.**, and **CORNYETZ, P.** (1944), Psychodrama as expressive and projective technique. *Sociometry*, 7:356-375.

02669 **DELUCA, F.** (1976), The effects of group counseling as influenced by group size on junior high school students in academic difficulty. *Dissert. Abstr. Internat.*, 36:5837A.

02670 **DELWORTH, U.** (1973), Raising consciousness about sexism. *Personnel & Guid. J.*, 51:672-674.

02671 **DELWORTH, U. M.** (1972), Interpersonal skill development for occupational therapists. *Amer. J. Occupat. Ther.*, 26:27-29.

02672 **de LYRA CHEBABI, W.** (1963), Esquema Da Situacão Terapêutica De Grupo. (A method of group therapy.) *J. Brasil. Psiquiat.*, (Rio de Janeiro) 12:277-300.

02673 **de LYRA CHEBABI, W.**, and **de ANDRADE LIMA, H.** (1963), Fantasías de "Acasalamento" no grupo terapêútico. (The pairing fantasy in a therapeutic group.) *J. Brasil. Psiquiat.*, (Rio de Janeiro) 12:327-342.

02674 **de MACEDO, G.** (1954), Group psychotherapy. *Neurobiologia*, (Pernambuco) 17:58-65.

02675 **de MACEDO, G.** (1955), Group psychotherapy in juvenile criminology. *Internat. J. Group Psychother.*, 5:54-59.

02676 **DEMANGEAT, M.** (1963), (Rehabilitation and sociotherapy.) *J. Med. Bordeaux*, 140:709-719.

02677 **de MARÉ, P.** (1972), *Perspectives in Group Psychotherapy: A Theoretical Background*. New York: Science House.

02678 **DEMAREST, E. W.**, and **TEICHER, A.** (1954), Transference in group therapy: its use by co-therapists of opposite sexes. *Psychiatry*, 17:187-202.

02679 **DEMBROSKI, B. G.** (1970), Role specialization in small leaderless psychiatric groups. *Dissert. Abstr. Internat.*, 30:3384B.

02680 **DEMCSAK-KELEN, I.**, and **SZAKACS, F.** (1972/1973), Attempt to employ simultaneously autogenic training and group therapy at puberty. *Psychother. & Psychosomat.*, (Basel) 21:67-70.

02681 **de MELLO FILHO, J.** (1977), (Group analytic technique: past and present.) *J. Brasil. Psiquiat.*, (Rio de Janeiro) 26:29-39.
02682 **DeMINICIS, C.**, and **RAUZATO, F. P.** (1969), (The borderline as the disrupting element in group psychotherapy.) *Riv. Psychiat.*, (Rome) 4:366-368.
02683 **de MONTMOLLIN, G.** (1959), Effet de l'âge sur le comportement en groupes. (Effect of age on group behavior.) *Annee Psychol.*, (Paris) 59:93-106.
02684 **de MONTMOLLIN, G.** (1966), Processus d'influence sociale et modalites d'interaction. (Process of social influence and modalities of interaction.) *Psychol. Francaise*, (Paris) 11:169-178.
02685 **DEMOS, G. D.** (1967), Marathon therapy: a new therapeutic modality. *Psychother. & Psychosomat.*, (Basel) 15:14-15.
02686 **DENBER, H. C. B.** (1963), Group process in a state hospital. *Amer. J. Orthopsychiat.*, 33:900-911.
02687 **DENBER, H. C.**, and **RAJOTTE, P.** (1961), (The therapeutic community: a systematized form of sociotherapy and its application to a group of schizophrenics.) *Annales Medico-Psychol.*, (Paris) 119:115-128.
02688 **DENCKER, S. J.** (1965), (Environmental therapy of severe chronic mental disorders: attempt at group therapy outside the hospital.) *Svenska Lakartidningen*, (Stockholm) 62:2471-2476.
02689 **DENES, M.** (1975), The ethos of sensitivity training. *Psychother.: Theory, Res. & Pract.*, 12:52-55.
02690 **DENES-RADOMISLI, M.** (1974), Gestalt group therapy: sense in sensitivity. In: *Group Process Today: Evaluation and Perspective*, eds. D. S. Milmas and G. D. Goldman. Springfield, IL: C. C. Thomas.
02691 **de NEUTER, P.** (1974), Some processes of change in psychotherapeutic groups and in psychodrama. *Feuillet Psychiat. Liege*, 7:352.
02692 **de NEUTER, P.**, and **de NEUTER-STRYCKMAN, N.** (1973), Individual interviews associated with psychodrama sessions. *Rev. Psychol. & Sci. Educat.*, (Liege) 8:23-38.
02693 **DENHOLTZ, M. S.**, and **MANN, E. T.** (1974), An audiovisual program for group desensitization. *J. Behav. Ther. & Exper. Psychiat.*, 5:27-29.
02694 **DENICOLA, J.**, and **SANDLER, J.** (1980), Training abusive parents in child management and self-control skills. *Behav. Ther.*, 11:263-270.
02695 **DENMAN, L.** (1963), Mental patients as "line workers," "machines," and "outputs." *J. Health & Human Behav.*, 4:211-214.
02696 **DENMAN, S. B.**, and **RUFFIN, W. C.** (1968), The sociologist's contribution to milieu therapy. *Hosp. & Community Psychiat.*, 19:79-80.
02697 **DENNIS, H.** (1976), Remotivation therapy for the elderly: a surprising outcome. *J. Gerontol. Nursing*, 2:28-30.
02698 **DENNY, J. M.** (1972), Techniques for individual and group art therapy. *Amer. J. Art. Ther.*, 11:117-134.
02699 **DENNY, J. M.**, and **FAGEN, A. C.** (1970), Group art therapy with university students: a comparative case analysis. *Psychother.: Theory, Res. & Pract.*, 7:164-168.
02700 **DENTON, G.** (1972), The effects of group counselling on selected aspects of the self concepts of undergraduate students when group composition had been controlled. *Dissert. Abstr. Internat.*, 32:4343-4344A.
02701 **de OLIVEIRA, W. I.** (1963), The psychoanalytic approach to group psychotherapy. *J. Hillside Hosp.*, 12:156-166.
02702 **de OLIVEIRA, W. I.**, and **deANDRADE, L. F. H.** (1961), Integracio do novo paciente no grupo terapeutico. (New patient admissions in group therapy.) *J. Brasil. Psiquiat*, (Rio de Janeiro) 10:235-252.
02703 **de OLIVEIRA, W. I.**, **LEME PEREIRA, W.**, and **CANDIDO BASTOS, J.** (1974), (Brief group psychotherapy.) *Jornal Brasil. Psiquiat.*, (Rio de Janeiro) 23:377-392.

02704 **DePALMA, D.** (1970), A work group model for social work intervention. *Soc. Casework*, 51:91-94.

02705 **DePALMA, N.** (1956), Group psychotherapy with high grade imbeciles and low grade morons. *Delaware State Med. J.*, 28:200-203.

02706 **de PAZ, L. R.** (1969), (The ruled games in group dynamics.) *Acta Psiquiat. Psicol. Amer. Latina*, (Buenos Aires) 15:251-256.

02707 **de PERROT, E.**, and **LAI, G.** (1967), Incidences de la co-therapie sur la psychotherapie d'un groupe de psychotiques. (Incidences of co-therapy in the psychotherapy of a group of psychotics.) *Soc. Psychiat.*, 1:182-187.

02708 **DERBOLOWSKY, G.** (1968), Dealing and working with materials in group-analysis and with "LSD-25." *Brit. J. Sociol. & Clin. Psychol.*, (London) 2:67-72.

02709 **DERBOLOWSKY, U.** (1959), Analytic group psychotherapy in private practice. *Acta Psychother. Psychosomat. Orthopaedagog. Suppl.*, (Basel) 7:83-90.

02710 **DERBOLOWSKY, U.** (1969), (Group dynamic position change as a technique in group analysis.) *Zeit. Psychother. Med. Psychol.*, (Stuttgart) 19:204-207.

02711 **DERBOLOWSKY, U.** (1964), (Multilateral resistance in patient groups.) *Zeit. Psychother. Med. Psychol.*, (Stuttgart) 14:74-79.

02712 **DERBOLOWSKY, U.** (1969), Mutual immunity in analysis groups and Freud's conception of abstinence. *Psychother. & Psychosomat.*, (Basel) 17:325-335.

02713 **DERBOLOWSKY, U.** (1968), (On the concept of abstinence by Sigmund Freud with its consequences for group psychotherapy.) *Zeit. Psychother. Med. Psychol.*, (Stuttgart) 18:177-184.

02714 **DERBOLOWSKY, U.** (1972), (Role change in group dynamics as a psychoanalytic technique in individual and group psychotherapy.) *Rev. Psicoanal.*, (Buenos Aires) 21:53-59.

02715 **DERBOLOWSKY, U.** (1969), (The three-sentence technique in role play in group-oriented psychotherapy.) *Zeit. Psychother. Med. Psychol.*, (Stuttgart) 19:202-204.

02716 **DERBOLOWSKY, U.** (1959), Voraussetzungen ambulanter analytischer gruppenpsychotherapie. (Principles of analytical oupatient group psychotherapy.) *Zeit. Psychother. Med. Psychol.*, 9:201-204.

02717 **DERBOLOWSKY, U.** (1970), Zum problem de gegenseitigen immunitat in analysegruppen. (Notes on the problem of mutual immunity in analytic groups.) *Fortschr. Psychoanal.*, 4:145-156.

02718 **DeROSIS, H. A.** (1969), A primary preventive program with parent groups in public schools. *J. School Health*, 39:102-109.

02719 **DeROSIS, H. A.**, and **DeROSIS, L. E.** (1971), Concurrent psychoanalysis. *Internat. J. Group Psychother.*, 21:294-300.

02720 **DeROSIS, L.** (1975), Karen Horney's theory applied to psychoanalysis in groups. In: *Group Psychotherapy and Group Function*, 2d ed., eds. M. Rosenbaum an M. M. Berger. New York: Basic Books.

02721 **DeROSIS, L. E.** (1961), Alienation and group analysis. *Amer. J. Psychoanal.*, 21:263-272.

02722 **DeROSIS, L. E.** (1952), Some techniques of group therapy. *Amer. J. Psychoanal.*, 12:79.

02723 **DeROSIS, L. E., BECKER, B. J., WASSELL, B. B., KRAFT, I. A.**, and **ABELL, R. G.** (1960), Sexuality in group psychoanalysis: a round table discussion. *Amer. J. Psychoanal.*, 20:197-200.

02724 **DERR, J.**, and **SILVER, A. W.** (1962), Predicting participation and behavior in group therapy from test protocols. *J. Clin. Psychol.*, 18:322-325.

02725 **deSCHAZER, S.** (1978), Brief therapy with couples. *Internat. J. Fam. Couns.*, 6:17.
02726 **deSCHILL, S.** (1974), *The Challenge for Group Psychotherapy: Present and Future*. New York: International Universities Press.
02727 **deSCHILL, S.** (1974), Introduction to psychoanalytic group psychotherapy. In: *The Challenge for Group Psychotherapy: Present and Future*, ed. S. deSchill. New York: International Universities Press.
02728 **deSCHILL, S.** (1958), *Introduction to Psychoanalytic Group Therapy: Remarks for the Psychotherapist*. New York: American Mental Health Foundation.
02729 **deSCHILL, S.** (1959), Mental health groups: an effective form of low-cost psychoanalytic therapy. *Acta Pychother. Psychosomat. Orthopaedagog. Suppl.*, (Basel) 7:328-337.
02730 **deSCHILL, S.**, and **LaHULLIER, D.** (1974), Mental health groups: an intensive, low-cost treatment method. In: *The Challenge for Group Psychotherapy: Present and Future*, ed. S. deSchill. New York: International Universities Press.
02731 **De SHONG, H. G.** (1972), A factor analytic investigation of a measure of self disclosure in intensive small groups. *Dissert. Abstr. Internat.*, 33:612A.
02732 **DeSIMONE, G.**, and **ALBERTI, G.** (1966), (Problems of the treatment of chronic mental disease patients: bifocal group psychotherapy.) *Minerva Med.*, (Turin) 57:4013-4015.
02733 **DeSIMONE, G.**, and **de PERROT, E.** (1963), Premieres observations sur une experience de psychotherapie en groupe bifocal. (Preliminary observations on experience with bifocal group psychotherapy.) *Annales Medico-Psychol.*, (Paris) 121:205-213.
02734 **DeSIMONE GABURRI, G.** (1967), (Problems of group psychotherapy in the psychiatric hospital. the dynamic aspect of the regressive experience in groups of psychotics.) *G. Psichiat. & Neuropat.*, (Ferrara) 95:41-58.
02735 **DESKIN, G.** (1968), Effects of different treatment procedures on reading ability and anxiety level in children with learning difficulties. *Dissert. Abstr. Internat.*, 28:3469B-3470B.
02736 **DESMEDT, D.** (1967), (Analytical psychodrama in a teaching medico-pedagogic clinic for retarded children.) *Rev. Neuropsychiat. Infantile*, (Paris) 15:869-882.
02737 **DESMOND, R. E.**, and **SELIGMAN, M.** (1977), A review of research on leaderless groups. *Small Group Behav.*, 8:3-24.
02738 **DESPOTOVIĆ, M.** (1978), (A demonstration of work with a group of paranoid patients.) *Psihijat. Danas*, (Belgrade) 10:77-82.
02739 **DESPOTOVIĆ, M.** (1975), (Some characteristics of group work with paranoid patients.) *Anali Zavoda Ment. Zdravlje*, 7:119-121.
02740 **DETERD OUDE, WEME, J. L.**, and **DOHMEN, G. B.** (1979), (Group therapy with myocardial infarction patients and their spouses.) *Gedrag*, (Tilburg) 7:115-128.
02741 **DEUTCH, M.** (1949), Effects of cooperation and competition upon group process. Unpublished doctoral dissertation, Massachusetts Institute of Technology.
02742 **DEUTSCH, A. L.**, and **LIPPMAN, A.** (1964), Group psychotherapy for patients with psychosomatic illness. *Psychosomatics*, 5:14-20.
02743 **DEUTSCH, A. L.**, and **ZIMMERMAN, J.** (1948), Group psychotherapy as adjunct treatment of epileptic patients. *Amer. J. Psychiat.*, 104:783-785.
02744 **DEUTSCH, D.** (1958), Didactic group discussions with mothers in a child guidance setting: a theoretical statement. *Group Psychother., Psychodrama & Sociometry*, 11:52-56.

02745 **DEUTSCH, H.** (1968), *Selected Problems of Adolescence: With Special Emphasis on Group Formation. The Psychoanalytic Study of the Child,* Monogr. 3. New York: International Universities Press.

02746 **DEVOGE, S.** (1975), A behavioral analysis of a group hypnosis treatment method. *Amer. J. Clin. Hypnosis,* 18:127-131.

02747 **DEVOTO, A.** (1964), (Milieu therapy and therapeutic community.) *Rass. Studi Psichiat.,* (Siena) 53:301-306.

02748 **deVRIES, D. L.,** and **EDWARDS, K. J.** (1973), Learning games and student teams: their effects on classroom process. *Amer. Educat. Res. J.,* 10:307-318.

02749 **DEW, F. E.** (1970), The effect of varying racial composition during group counseling undertaken to improve intergroup attitude among elementary school children. *Dissert. Abstr. Internat.,* 31:3870A.

02750 **DEWAR, M. C.** (1946), The technique of group therapy. *Bull. Menninger Clinic,* 10:82-84.

02751 **deWASONGARZ, A. J.** (1975), (The evolution of group psychotherapy.) *Fortschr. Neurol., Neurocir. Psiquiat. & Grenzgebiete,* (Stuttgart) 16:75-83.

02752 **DeWIT, F.** (1957), Therapist behavior in group therapy. *Provo Papers,* 1:1-11.

02753 **DeWOLFE, A. S., BARRELL, R. P., CONTE, P.,** and **KLEIN, J.** (1972), Group-oriented activity and the change in teamwork of chronic psychotic patients. *J. Nerv. & Ment. Diseases,* 154:363-367.

02754 **DIAL, K. B.** (1968), A report of group work to increase social skills of females in a vocational rehabilitation program. *Mental Retard.,* 6:11-14.

02755 **DIAMENT, C.** (1977), A training program in behavior modification for parents: an evaluation of a group approach. *Dissert. Abstr. Internat.,* 38:892B.

02756 **DIAMENT, C.,** and **COLLETTI, G.** (1978), Evaluation of behavioral group counseling for parents of learning-disabled children. *J. Abnorm. Child Psychol.,* 6:385-400.

02757 **DIAMOND, M. J.** (1974), From Skinner to Satori? toward a social learning analysis of encounter group behavior change. *J. Appl. Behav. Science,* 10:133-148.

02758 **DIAMOND, M. J.,** and **SHAPIRO, J. L.** (1973), Changes in locus of control as a function of encounter group experiences: a study and replication. *J. Abnorm. & Soc. Psychol.,* 82:514-518.

02759 **DIAMOND, M. J.,** and **SHAPIRO, J. L.** (1975), An expedient model of encounter group learning. *Psychother.: Theory, Res. & Pract.,* 12:56-59.

02760 **DIAMOND, M. J.,** and **SHAPIRO, J. L.** (1975), Method and paradigm in encounter group research. *J. Human. Psychol.,* 15:59-70.

02761 **DIAS, M. C. N.** (1972), The effect of counseling on adjustment of foreign students. *Dissert. Abstr. Internat.,* 32:6123A.

02762 **DIATKINE, R.** (1958), Activité de psychotherapie de groupe et de psychodrame. (Group psychotherapy activities and psychodrama.) *Group Psychother., Psychodrama & Sociometry,* 11:187-188.

02763 **DIATKINE, R., SOCARRAS, F.,** and **KESTEMBERG, E.** (1950), Le transfert en psychotherapie collective. (Transference in collective psychotherapy.) *Encephale,* (Paris) 39:248-274.

02764 **DIBNER, A. S., GOFTSTEIN, A. G.,** and **COHEN, N. B.** (1964), Open-ended group psychotherapy as a clinic intake procedure. *Curr. Psychiat. Ther.,* 4:183-190.

02765 **DIBNER, A. S., PALMER, R. D.,** and **COHEN, B.** (1962), Screening for psychotherapy by an open-ended group. *Internat. J. Group Psychother.,* 12:373-374.

02766 **DIBNER, A. S., PALMER, R. D., COHEN, B.,** and **GOFSTEIN, A. G.** (1963), The use of an open-ended group in the intake procedure of a mental hygiene unit. *J. Consult. & Clin. Psychol.*, 27:83-88.

02767 **DICHTER, E.** (1944), Psychodramatic research project on commodities as intersocial media. *Sociometry*, 7:432.

02768 **DICHTER, M., DRISCOLL, G. Z., OTTENBERG, D. J.,** and **ROSEN, A.** (1971), Marathon therapy with alcoholics. *Quart. J. Studies Alcohol*, 32:66-77.

02769 **DICK, B., LESSLER, K.,** and **WHITESIDE, J.** (1980), A developmental framework for cotherapy. *Internat. J. Group Psychother.*, 30:273-285.

02770 **DICK, B. M.** (1975), A ten-year study of outpatient analytic group therapy. *Brit. J. Psychiat.*, (Ashford) 127:365-375.

02771 **DICKEN, C., BRYSON, R.,** and **KASS, N.** (1977), Companionship therapy: a replication in experimental community psychology. *J. Consult. & Clin. Psychol.*, 45:637-646.

02772 **DICKENS, D. L.** (1979), Mental health program for the deaf of Saint Elizabeth's Hospital. In: *Hearing and Hearing Impairment*, eds. L. J. Bradford and W. G. Hardy. New York: Grune and Stratton.

02773 **DICKENS, G.,** and **SHARPE, M.** (1970), Music therapy in the setting of a psychotherapeutic centre. *Brit. J. Med. Psychol.*, (London) 43:83-94.

02774 **DICKENS, H. O., MUDD, E. H.,** and **HUGGINS, G. R.** (1975), Teenagers, contraception and pregnancy. *J. Marriage & Fam. Couns.*, 1:175-181.

02775 **DICKENSON, W. A.,** and **TRUAX, C. B.** (1966), Group counseling with college underachievers. *Personnel & Guid. J.*, 45:243-247.

02776 **DICKER, J.** (1970), Group treatment of emotionally disturbed children. *Nursing Mirror*, (London) 130:19-21.

02777 **DICKERSON, J. A.** (1976), Group vocational counseling: its effectiveness on changing Black attitudes and work performance for emotionally disturbed and educable retarded adolescents. *Dissert. Abstr. Internat.*, 36:6468A.

02778 **DICKOFF, H.,** and **LAKIN, M.** (1963), Patients' views of group therapy: retrospections and interpretations. *Internat. J. Group Psychother.*, 13:61-73.

02779 **DICKSON, M.** (1974), Involvement of the spouse in the treatment of the alcoholic. *Nursing Mirror*, (London) 139:77-79.

02780 **DIDATO, S. U.** (1970), Delinquents in group therapy: some new techniques. *Adolescence*, 5:207-222.

02781 **DIDIER, M. C.** (1967), An investigation of non-verbal communication in clinicians' observation process. *Smith Coll. Studies Soc. Work*, 38:17-18.

02782 **DIEDRICH, R. C.,** and **DEP, H. A.** (1972), *Group Procedures: Purposes, Processes, and Outcomes*. San Jose, CA: Houghton-Mifflin.

02783 **DIEPOLD, P.** (1975), (Group dynamics in pre-service teacher training.) *Paedagog. Rundschau*, (Kastellaun) 29:672-689.

02784 **DIERGARTEN, F.,** and **HAMM, A.** (1978), (Report on 21st Conference on Group-Dynamics of German Society for Group-Psychotherapy.) *Dynam. Psychiat.*, (Berlin) 11:97-98.

02785 **DIERS, D.,** and **JOHNSON, J. E.** (1969), How workshops prepare nurses for the therapeutic role. *Nursing Outlook*, 17:30-34.

02786 **DIES, R. R.** (1974), Attitudes toward the training of group psychotherapists: some interprofessional and experience-associated differences. *Small Group Behav.*, 5:65-79.

02787 **DIES, R. R.** (1980), Current practice in the training of group psychotherapists. *Internat. J. Group Psychother.*, 30:169-185.

02788 **DIES, R. R.** (1978), Encounter group volunteering: implications for research and practice. *Small Group Behav.*, 9:23-42.

02789 **DIES, R. R.** (1973), Group therapist self-disclosure: development and validation of a scale. *J. Consult. & Clin. Psychol.*, 41:97-103.
02790 **DIES, R. R.** (1973), Group therapist self-disclosure: an evaluation by clients. *J. Couns. Psychol.*, 20:344-348.
02791 **DIES, R. R.** (1977), Group therapist transparency: a critique of theory and research. *Internat. J. Group Psychother.*, 27:177-200.
02792 **DIES, R. R.** (1979), Group psychotherapy: reflections on three decades of research. *J. Appl. Behav. Science*, 15:361-374.
02793 **DIES, R. R.** (1977), Pragmatics of leadership in psychotherapy and encounter group research. *Small Group Behav.*, 8:229-248.
02794 **DIES, R. R.** (1980), Review of R. G. Cohen's and G. B. Lipkin's *Therapeutic Group Work for Health Professionals. Contemp. Psychol.*, 25:543.
02795 **DIES, R. R.,** and **COHEN, L.** (1976), Content considerations in group therapist self-disclosure. *Internat. J. Group Psychother.*, 26:71-88.
02796 **DIES, R. R.,** and **HESS, A. K.** (1971), An experimental investigation of cohesiveness in marathon and conventional group psychotherapy. *J. Abnorm. & Soc. Psychol.*, 77:258-262.
02797 **DIES, R. R.,** and **HESS, A. K.** (1970), Self-disclosure, time perspective and semantic-differential changes: marathon and short-term group psychotherapy. *Compar. Group Studies*, 1:387-395.
02798 **DIES, R. R.,** and **HESS, A. K.** (1970), Time perspective, intimacy and semantic-differential changes in marathon and conventional group psychotherapy. *Proceed., 78th Annual Convention*, American Psychological Association, pp. 531-532.
02799 **DIES, R. R., MALLET, J.,** and **JOHNSON, F.** (1979), Openness in the coleader relationship. *Small Group Behav.*, 10:523-546.
02800 **DIES, R. R.,** and **SADOWSKY, R.** (1974), A brief encounter group experience and social relationships in a dormitory. *J. Couns. Psychol.*, 21:112-115.
02801 **DIES, R. R.** (1973), Content considerations in group therapist self-disclosure. *Proceed., 81st Annual Convention*, American Psychological Association, 8:483-484.
02802 **DIETHELM, D. R.** (1974), Changes in levels of self disclosure and perceived self disclosure between partners following participation in a weekend encounter group for couples. *Dissert. Abstr. Internat.*, 34:5622A.
02803 **DIETRICH, G.** (1976), Nurses in the therapeutic community. *J. Advanced Nursing*, 1:139-154.
02804 **DIETZAL, C. S.** (1972), Client-therapist complementarity and therapeutic outcome. *Dissert. Abstr. Internat.*, 32:7305-7306.
02805 **DiFABIO, S.,** and **ACKERHALT, E. J.** (1978), Teaching the use of restraint through role play. *Perspect. Psychiat. Care*, 16:218-222.
02806 **DiGIOVANNI, P.** (1958), A comparison between orthodox group psychotherapy and activity group therapy in the treatment of chronic hospitalized schizophrenics. Unpublished doctoral dissertation, University of Illinois.
02807 **DILL, J. S.** (1971), An experimental comparison of single therapist and multiple therapist group counseling with incarcerated female delinquents. *Dissert. Abstr. Internat.*, 31:5120A.
02808 **DILLER, J. V.** (1971), The encounter group as a means of reducing prejudice. *Dissert. Abstr. Internat.*, 32:2191A.
02809 **DILLEY, J. S.** (1972), Anti-shrinkthink. *Personnel & Guid. J.*, 50:567-573.
02810 **DILLOW, L. B.** (1968), The group process in adoptive homefinding. *Children*, 15:153-157.
02811 **DiLORETO, A. O.** (1970), A comparison of the relative effectiveness of systematic desensitization. *Dissert. Abstr. Internat.*, 30:5230A.

02812 **DiLORETO, A. O.** (1970), A comparison of the relative effectiveness of systematic desensitization, rational-emotive and client-centered group psychotherapy in the reduction of interpersonal anxiety in introverts and extroverts. *Dissert. Abstr. Internat.*, 30:5230A-5231A.

02813 **DILTHEY, E.** (1971), Konzentrative bewegungstherapie im rahmen intensivierter analytischer gruppentherapie. (Concentrative movement therapy in the context of intensified analytic group therapy.) *Praxis der Psychother.*, 16:124-129.

02814 **DiMARCO, N.** (1973), T-group and workgroup climates and participants' thoughts about transfer. *J. Appl. Behav. Science*, 9:757-764.

02815 **Di MATTIA, D. J.**, and **ARNDT, G. M.** (1974), A comparison of microcounseling and reflective listening techniques. *Counselor Educat. & Supervision*, 14:61-64.

02816 **DIMOCK, H. G.** (1971), Sensitivity training in Canada: perspective and comments. *Can. Ment. Health*, (Ottawa) 69:1-17.

02817 **DINGES, N. G.**, and **WEIGEL, R. G.** (1975), Evaluation of marathon groups and the group movement. In: *The Innovative Psychological Therapies: Critical and Creative Contributions*, eds. R. M. Suinn and R. G. Weigel. New York: Harper and Row.

02818 **DINGES, N. G.**, and **WEIGEL, R. G.** (1971), The marathon group: a review of practice and research. *Compar. Group Studies*, 2:339-458.

02819 **DINGMAN, P. R.** (1965), Day hospital service in a community child guidance setting. *Amer. J. Orthopsychiat.*, 35:408-409.

02820 **DINKMEYER, D.** (1975), Adlerian group psychotherapy. *Internat. J. Group Psychother.*, 25:219-226.

02821 **DINKMEYER, D.** (1970), Developmental group counseling. *Elem. School Guid. & Couns.*, 4:267-272.

02822 **DINKMEYER, D.** (1971), Group approaches to understanding and changing behavior. *Nat. Cath. Guid. Conf. J.*, 15:163-166.

02823 **DINKMEYER, D.** (1973), The parent "c" group. *Personnel & Guid. J.*, 52:252-256.

02824 **DINKMEYER, D.**, and **McKAY, G. D.** (1974), Leading effective parent study groups. *Elem. School Guid. Couns.*, 9:108-115.

02825 **DINKMEYER, D. C.**, and **CARLSON, J.** (1973), *Consulting: Facilitating Human Potential and Change Processes*. Columbus, OH: Merrill.

02826 **DINKMEYER, D. C.**, and **MURO, J. J.** (1971), *Group Counseling: Theory and Practice*. Ithaca, IL: F. T. Peacock.

02827 **DINNEN, A.** (1971), Change of therapists as a cause of absences from group psychotherapy. *Brit. J. Psychiat.*, (Ashford) 119:625-628.

02828 **DINNEN, A.** (1977), No speak much English: or how I stopped worrying about the theory and began treating the indigent Greek. *Mental Health*, 4:26-35.

02829 **DINNEN, A.**, and **BELL, D. S.** (1972), Transference in a group with different therapists. *Austral. & New Zeal. J. Psychiat.*, (Carlton) 6:176-179.

02830 **DINOFF, M., HORNER, R. F., KURPIEWSKI, B. S.**, and **TIMMONS, E. O.** (1960), Conditioning verbal behavior of schizophrenics in a group therapy-like situation. *J. Clin. Psychol.*, 16:367-370.

02831 **DINOFF, M., HORNER, R. F., KURPIEWSKI, B. S., RICKARD, H. C.**, and **TIMMONS, E. O.** (1960), Conditioning verbal behavior of a psychiatric population in a group therapy-like situation. *J. Clin. Psychol.*, 16:371-372.

02832 **DINOFF, M.** (1977), Psychotherapy: The Promised Land? *POCA Perspective No. 6*. Proceed., 13th and 14th Annual Meetings of Psychiatric Outpatient Centers of America. Tuscaloosa, AL: University of Alabama Press.

02833 **DINOZZO, T. M.** (1978), Effects of a group career counseling model on vocational maturity and personal growth of female undergraduates over age 25. *Dissert. Abstr. Internat.*, 38:6529A.
02834 **DION, K. L.** (1979), Status equity, sex composition of group and intergroup bias. *J. Personnel & Soc. Psychiat.*, 5:240-244.
02835 **DION, K. L.** (1970), Cohesiveness and social responsibility as determinants of group risk taking. *Proceed., 78th Annual Convention*, American Psychological Association, pp. 335-336.
02836 **DITMAN, K. S., ENELOW, A. J.,** and **MacANDREW, C.** (1959), Psychotherapy of alcoholics: the concept of psychotherapeutic motivation. *California Med.*, 90:138.
02837 **DITZ, G. W.** (1965), Role theory applied to life insurance selling. *Group Psychother., Psychodrama & Sociometry*, 18:17-26.
02838 **DITZLER, J.** (1976), Rehabilitation for alcoholics. *Amer. J. Nursing*, 76:1772-1775.
02839 **DIVITA, E. C.,** and **OLSSON, P. A.** (1975), The use of sex therapy in a patient with penile prosthesis. *J. Sex & Marital Ther.*, 1:305-311.
02840 **DIX, D. M.** (1962), Role playing in nursing education in the psychiatric field. *Group Psychother., Psychodrama & Sociometry*, 15:231-235.
02841 **DIXON, D. R.,** and **ROWLEY, M.** (1968), Public information panels as therapy for disturbed young patients. *Children*, 15:111.
02842 **DLABACOVA, E.** (1977), (Uses of group psychotherapy in marital consultation service.) *Ceskoslov. Psychiatr.*, (Prague) 73:85-89.
02843 **DOCTOR, R. M., SPONTE, J., BURRY, A.,** and **WELCH, R.** (1970), Group counseling versus behavior therapy in treatment of college underachievement. *Behav. Res. & Ther.*, 8:87-89.
02844 **DODD, B. B.,** and **PETROVICH, D. V.** (1967), Out of the back ward. *Amer. J. Nursing*, 67:2124-2128.
02845 **DODSON, J. P.** (1971), Participation in a biracial encounter group: its relation to acceptance of self and others, racial attitudes, and interpersonal orientations. *Dissert. Abstr. Internat.*, 31:5120-5121A.
02846 **DOERING, R.** (1964), A study of the process and the effects of therapy with groups of adolescent boys in a public school setting. *Dissert. Abstr. Internat.*, 25:289.
02847 **DOHERTY, E. G.** (1976), Length of hospitalization on a short-term therapeutic community: a multivariate study by sex across time. *Arch. Gen. Psychiat.*, 33:87-92.
02848 **DOHERTY, E. G.** (1974), Therapeutic community meetings: a study of communication patterns, sex, status and staff attendance. *Small Group Behav.*, 5:244-256.
02849 **DOHERTY, E. G.,** and **HARRY, J.** (1976), Structural dissensus in the therapeutic community. *J. Health & Soc. Behav.*, 17:272-279.
02850 **DOISE, W.** (1969), Intergroup relations and polarization of individual and collective judgments. *J. Personal. & Soc. Psychol.*, 12:136-143.
02851 **DOISE, W., DESCHAMPS, J-C.,** and **DESCHAMPS, J.** (1979), *Expériences entre Groupes. (Experiences with Groups.)* Paris: École des Hautes Études en Sciences Sociales.
02852 **DOLAN, L. P.** (1975), Intake group in the alcoholism outpatient clinic. *J. Studies Alcohol.*, 36:996-999.
02853 **DOLAN, M.** (1976), A return to laughter . . . and tears. *Nursing '76*, 6:43.
02854 **DOLEŽAL, V.,** and **HAUSNER, M.** (1962), Our experiences with individual and group psychotherapy with the aid of LSD. *Activ. Nerv. Superior*, (Prague) 4:241-242.
02855 **DOLLINS, C. N.** (1967), The effect of group discussion as a learning procedure on the adaptive social behavior of educable adult mental retardates. *Dissert. Abstr. Internat.*, 28:2056-2057.

02856 **DONADIO, G.** (1975), (An external experiment by psychotherapeutic groups.) *Lavoro Neuropsichiat.*, (Rome) 56:271-274.
02857 **DONAHOE, P. M.** (1978), A comparison of the effects of group assertiveness training and unstructured group counseling on changes in focus of control. *Dissert. Abstr. Internat.*, 38:5922A.
02858 **DONALDSON, H.** (1972), Intensive therapy for adult stutterers. *Can. Ment. Health*, (Ottawa) 20:14-18.
02859 **DONALDSON, L.**, and **SCANNELL, E. E.** (1978), *Human Resource Development.* Reading, MA: Addison-Wesley.
02860 **DONÁTH, B. G.** (1980), *Személyiségformáló Kiscsoportmunka az Iskolában.* Budapest: Akademiai Kiado.
02861 **DONAVAN, L. P.** (1976), Family environment: significance for continuance in a day treatment program. *Clin. Psychologist*, 29:10-12.
02862 **DONKER, F. J. S.**, and **LANGE, M. M.** (1977), (Training for self-assertion: development toward group therapy on behavior-therapeutic basis.) *Gedrag*, (Tilburg) 5:352-377.
02863 **DONLON, P. J.**, **RADA, R. T.**, and **KNIGHT, S. W.** (1973), A therapeutic aftercare setting for "refractory" chronic schizophrenic patients. *Amer. J. Psychiat.*, 130:682-684.
02864 **DONNAN, H. H.**, and **MITCHELL, H. O., Jr.** (1979), Preferences for older versus younger counselors among a group of elderly persons. *J. Couns. Psychol.*, 26:514-518.
02865 **DONNELLY, G.** (1978), Group survival. *Nursing Times*, (London) 74:252-253.
02866 **DONNER, J.**, and **GAMSOM, A.** (1968), Experience with multifamily, time limited, outpatient groups at a community psychiatric clinic. *Psychiatry*, 31:126-137.
02867 **DONNER, L.** (1970), Automated group desensitization: a follow-up report. *Behav. Res. & Ther.*, 8:241-247.
02868 **DONNER, L.** (1968), Effectiveness of a pre-programmed group desensitization treatment for test anxiety with and without a therapist present. *Dissert. Abstr. Internat.*, 28:5201B.
02869 **DONNER, L.**, and **GUERNEY, B. G., Jr.** (1969), Automated group desensitization for test anxiety. *Behav. Res. & Ther.*, 7:1-13.
02870 **DONOFRIO, A. F.** (1976), Parent education vs. child psychotherapy. *Psychol. in Schools*, 13:176-180.
02871 **DONOGHUE, P. J.** (1970), A study of the relationship of basic encounter group experience to change in teacher attitudes towards students and towards self and to student perceptions of these teachers. *Dissert. Abstr. Internat.*, 31:4001A.
02872 **DONOHUE, S. T.** (1970), The effects of three video tape critique methods in practicum upon prospective counselors' nonverbal behavior. *Dissert. Abstr. Internat.*, 30:3721A-3722A.
02873 **DONOVAN, J. N.** (1979), Crisis group: outcome study. *Amer. J. Psychiat.*, 136:906.
02874 **DONOVAN, W. B.**, and **MARVIT, R. C.** (1970), Alienation-reduction of brief group therapy. *Amer. J. Psychiat.*, 127:825-827.
02875 **DOOB, L. W.** (1976), Cyprus Workshop: intervention methodology during a continuing crisis. *J. Soc. Psychol.*, 98:143-144.
02876 **DOOB, L. W.**, and **FOLTZ, W. J.** (1973), The Belfast Workshop: an application of group techniques to a destructive conflict. *J. Confl. Resolut.*, 17:489-512.
02877 **DOOB, L. W.**, and **FOLTZ, W. J.** (1974), The impact of a workshop upon grass-roots leaders in Belfast. *J. Confl. Resolut.*, 18:237-256.
02878 **DOOLEY, C. D.** (1974), Effects of response interaction training on the group assessment of interpersonal traits. *Dissert. Abstr. Internat.*, 34:3492B.

02879 **DORDEVIĆ-BANKOVIĆ, V.,** and **SEDMAK, T.** (1979), (A practical demonstration of group psychotherapy for adolescents.) *Psihijat. Danas,* (Belgrade) 11:81-86.

02880 **DORE, MARY, D.** (1974), Change as a function of sensitivity group experiences and selected personality characteristics in graduate students. *Dissert. Abstr. Internat.,* 35:5015A.

02881 **DOREY, M. R.** (1964), (On psychosociologic formation by group methods.) *Bull. Soc. Med. Milit. Francaise,* 58:399-408.

02882 **DORFMAN LERNER, B.** (1975), (Combined individual and group psychotherapy.) *Acta Psichiat. Psicol. Amer. Latina,* (Buenos Aires) 21:118-128.

02883 **DORMAN, W., SLATER, S.,** and **GOTTLIEB, N.** (1959), Drug and placebo in group treatment of obesity. *Internat. J. Group Psychother.,* 9:345-351.

02884 **DORKEN, H.,** and **WEBB, J. T.** (1979), The hospital practice of psychology: an interstate comparison. *Prof. Psychol.,* 10:619-630.

02885 **DORN, R. S.** (1975), The effects of sex role awareness groups on fear of success, verbal task performance, and sex role attitudes of undergraduate women. *Dissert. Abstr. Internat.,* 36:1386A.

02886 **DORNA, M. A.** (1972), Description of several techniques for work with groups. *Cuadernas de Psicol.,* 2:25.

02887 **DORON, M.** (1968), Psychodrama and basic group: development therapy. *Annales Medico-Psychol.,* (Paris) 2:759.

02888 **DOSAMANTES-ALPERSON, E.,** and **MERRILL, N.** (1980), Growth effects of experiential movement psychotherapy. *Psychother.: Theory, Res. & Pract.,* 17:63-68.

02889 **DOSUŽKOV, T.** (1969), (Psychodrama from the viewpoint of psychoanalysis.) *Zeit. Psychother. Med. Psychol.,* (Stuttgart) 19:163-164.

02890 **DOUGHERTY, C. A.** (1974), Group art therapy: a Jungian approach. *Amer. J. Art Ther.,* 13:229.

02891 **DOUGLAS, T.** (1979), *Group Processes in Social Work.* New York: J. Wiley and Sons.

02892 **DOUGLAS, T.** (1979), Review of K. Heap's *Group Theory for Social Workers. Brit. J. Soc. Work,* (Birmingham) 9:403.

02893 **DOVERSPIKE, J. E.** (1973), Group and individual goals: their development and utilization. *Educat. Technol.,* 13:24-26.

02894 **DOVERSPIKE, J. E., WEIS, D. M.,** and **WANGERIN, M. B.** (1971), Themes of individual and group counseling sessions. *Nat. Cath. Guid. Conf. J.,* 15:180-182.

02895 **DOW, R. A.** (1971), *Learning Through Encounter.* Valley Forge, PA: Judson Press.

02896 **DOWNS, C. W.** (1974), The impact of laboratory training on leadership orientation, values, and self-image. *Speech Teacher,* 23:197-205.

02897 **DOYLE, I.** (1955), (Teaching and regulation of psychotherapy.) *J. Brasil. Psiquiat.,* (Rio de Janeiro) 4:37-48.

02898 **DOYLE, M. C.** (1975), Rabbitt: therapeutic prescription. *Perspect. Psychiat. Care,* 13:79-82.

02899 **DOYLE, R. E.** (1978), Group counseling and counselor-teacher consultation with poorly achieving ninth grade students. *Dissert. Abstr. Internat.,* 38:6531A.

02900 **DOYLE, R. P.** (1957), A group study approach to improved guidance services. Unpublished doctoral dissertation, Columbia University.

02901 **DOYNE, S. E.** (1972), The relationship between self-disclosure and self-esteem in encounter groups. *Dissert. Abstr. Internat.,* 33:1786B.

02902 **DOYON, D.** (1967), (The use of psychodrama for hospitalized patients in a general hospital.) *Laval Med.,* (Quebec) 38:67-70.

02903 **DRABKOVA, H.** (1966), Experiences resulting from clinical use of psychodrama with children. *Group Psychother., Psychodrama & Sociometry*, 19:32-36.

02904 **DRACOULIDES, N. N.** (1966), Aristophanes: "The Clouds" and "The Wasps:" foreshadowing of psychoanalysis and psychodrama. *Amer. Imago*, 23:48-62.

02905 **DRACOULIDÈS, N. N.** (1963), (The psychopedagogical education of future parents and teachers and the preschool education of children: should they be made obligatory?) *Hygiene Ment., Can.*, (Ottawa) 52:203-220.

02906 **DRAGE, E.**, and **LANGE, B.** (1969), Ethical considerations in the use of patients for demonstration. *Amer. J. Nursing*, 69:2161-2165.

02907 **DRAGIČEVIĆ, D.** (1979), (How to direct the group to itself.) *Psihijat. Danas*, (Belgrade) 11:87-91.

02908 **DRAKEFORD, J. W.** (1967), *Integrity Therapy*. Nashville: Broadman.

02909 **DRAPELA, V. J.** (1974), In-service training for pastoral counselors. *J. Religion & Health*, 13:142-146.

02910 **DRAPER, P. A.** (1948), Psychiatric group therapy. *Rocky Mtn. Med. J.*, 45:212-214.

02911 **DREES, A.** (1977), (Conflict oriented problem-solving: consultation and psychotherapy in dialysis units.) *Gruppenpsychother. & Gruppendynam.*, (Goettingen) 11:150-158.

02912 **DREES, L.** (1969), (Group therapy of chronic psychiatric patients with theater playing.) *Nervenarzt.*, 40:517-521.

02913 **DREESE, M.** (1957), Group guidance and group therapy. *Rev. Educat. Res.*, 27:219-228.

02914 **DREIKURS, R.** (1955), Adlerian analysis of interaction. *Group Psychother., Psychodrama & Sociometry*, 8:298-307.

02915 **DREIKURS, R.** (1956), The contribution of group psychotherapy to psychiatry. *Group Psychother., Psychodrama & Sociometry*, 9:115-125.

02916 **DREIKURS, R.** (1957), The cultural implications of group psychotherapy. *Zeit. Diagnost. Psychol.*, 5:186-197.

02917 **DREIKURS, R.** (1938), Die entwicklung der psychischen hygiene in Wien. (The retreat of mental hygiene in Vienna.) *Allgemaine Zeit. Psychiat.*, 88:2-27.

02918 **DREIKURS, R.** (1959), Early experiments with group psychotherapy: a historical review. *Amer. J. Psychother.*, 13:882-891.

02919 **DREIKURS, R.** (1932), Einige wirksame faktoren in der psychotherapie. (The effective leader in psychotherapy.) *Internat. Zeit. Individ.-Psychol.*, (Munich) 10:161-176.

02920 **DREIKURS, R.** (1960), *Group Approaches: Collected Papers of Rudolf Dreikurs*. Chicago: Alfred Adler Institute.

02921 **DREIKURS, R.** (1975), Group psychotherapy from the point of view of Alderian psychology. In: *Group Psychotherapy and Group Function*, 2d ed., eds. M. Rosenbaum and M. M. Berger. New York: Basic Books.

02922 **DREIKURS, R.** (1957), Group psychotherapy from the points of view of various schools of psychology: i. group psychotherapy from the point of view of Adlerian psychology. *Internat. J. Group Psychother.*, 7:363-375.

02923 **DREIKURS, R.** (1955), Group psychotherapy and the third revolution in psychiatry. *Internat. J. Soc. Psychiat.*, (London) 1:23-32.

02924 **DREIKURS, R.** (1943), Our child guidance clinics in Chicago. *Individ. Psychol. Bull.*, 2:11-18.

02925 **DREIKURS, R.** (1954), The psychodynamics of disability: a group therapy approach. *Amer. Arch. Rehab. Ther.*, 2:5.

02926 **DREIKURS, R.** (1950), Techniques and dynamics of multiple psychotherapy. *Psychiat. Quart.*, 24:788-799.

02027 **DREIKURS, R.** (1955), Tele and interpersonal therapy: an appraisal of Moreno's concept from the Adlerian point of view. *Group Psychother., Psychodrama & Sociometry*, 8:185-191.
02928 **DREIKURS, R.** (1951), The unique social climate experienced in group psychotherapy. *Group Psychother., Psychodrama & Sociometry*, 3:292-299.
02929 **DREIKURS, R.** (1928), Von der geistenkrankenfursorge uber die sociale psychiatric zur psychischen hygiene. *Allgemaine Zeit. Psychiat.*, 88:67-73.
02930 **DREIKURS, R.**, and **CORSINI, R. J.** (1954), Twenty years of group psychotherapy: purposes, methods, and mechanisms. *Amer. J. Psychiat.*, 110:567-575.
02931 **DREIKURS, R., CORSINI, R., LOWE, R.,** and **SONSTEGARD, M.** (1959), *Adlerian Family Counseling: A Manual for Counseling Center*. Eugene, OR: University Press.
02932 **DREIKURS, R., SHULMAN, B. H.,** and **MOSAK** (1952), Patient-therapist relationship in multiple psychotherapy: i. its advantages to the therapist. *Psychiat. Quart.*, 26:219-227.
02933 **DREIKURS, S. E.** (1976), Art therapy: an Alderian group approach. *J. Individ. Psychol.*, 32:69-80.
02934 **DREIKURS, S. G.** (1945), Psychological techniques applied in a group situation. *Individ. Psychol. Bull.*, 4:110-125.
02935 **DRENNEN, W. T.,** and **WIGGINS, S. L.** (1964), Manipulation of verbal behavior of chronic hospitalized schizophrenics in group therapy situation. *Internat. J. Group Psychother.*, 14:189-193.
02936 **DRESSLER, D. M., ACCETTELLO, D.,** and **PONCINI, S.** (1976), A group treatment program for emotionally disturbed rest home patients. *Hosp. & Community Psychiat.*, 27:770-771.
02937 **DREWS, R. S.** (1959), Psychodrama in private practice. *Acta Psychother. Psychosomat. Orthopaedagog. Suppl.*, (Basel) 7:90-95.
02938 **DREWS, R. S.** (1952), Psychodrama in private practice. *Group Psychother., Psychodrama & Sociometry*, 5:70-72.
02939 **DREYER, A. H.** (1963), The citizen as a decision maker. *Group Psychother., Psychodrama & Sociometry*, 16:59-64.
02940 **DREYER, A. H., Jr.** (1958), Group training vs. group psychotherapy: a challenge in truth. *Group Psychother., Psychodrama & Sociometry*, 11:46-49.
02941 **DREYER, A. H., Jr.** (1957), Some comments on "role playing and sociometric peer status." *Group Psychother., Psychodrama & Sociometry*, 10:141-142.
02942 **DREYER, M. M.** (1965), Psychodrama with a changing group in a U.S. Navy Hospital. *Group Psychother., Psychodrama & Sociometry*, 18:267-270.
02943 **DREYFUS, A.,** and **KLINE, N. S.** (1948), Group psychotherapy in veterans administration hospitals. *Amer. J. Psychiat.*, 104:618.
02944 **DREYFUS, C.,** and **PIGEAT, J-P.** (1975), *Les Groupes de Rencontre. (Self-Discovery Groups.)* Paris: Retz-C.E.P.L.
02945 **DREYFUS, E. A.** (1974), From group therapy to a therapeutic collective. *Nursing Digest*, 2:87-91.
02946 **DREYFUS, E. A.** (1973), Private practice: a therapeutic collective. *Psychother.: Theory, Res. & Pract.*, 10:236-241.
02947 **DREYFUS-MOREAU, J.** (1955), Bilan d'une experience de psychanalyse collective. (Balance sheet of an experiment in collective psychoanalysis.) *Rev. Francaise Psychanal.*, (Paris) 19:333-356.
02948 **DREYFUS-MOREAU, J.** (1950), A propos du transfert en psychothérapie collective. (Transfer in group therapy.) *Rev. Française Psychanal.*, (Paris) 14:244-257.

02949 **DRIVER, H.** (1952), Learning self and social adjustment through small group discussion. *Ment. Hygiene*, 36:600-606.

02950 **DRIVER, H. I.** (1958), *Counseling and Learning through Small-Group Discussion.* Madison, WI: Monona Publications.

02951 **DRIVER, H. I.** (1954), *Multiple Counseling: A Small-Group Discussion Method for Personal Growth.* Madison, WI: Monona Publications.

02952 **DROBITS, R.**, and **EWING, G. B.** (1967), Multiple problems beset trial unit for alcoholics. *Hosp. & Community Psychiat.*, 18:152-155.

02953 **DROWNE, J.** (1972), A study of three group counselling approaches and their effectiveness in modifying selected aspects of self-concept and selected personality characteristics of third grade children. *Dissert. Abstr. Internat.*, 32:4344A.

02954 **DRUCK, A. B.** (1978), The role of didactic group psychotherapy in short-term psychiatric settings. *Group*, 98:109.

02955 **DRUM, D. J.**, and **KNOTT, J. E.** (1977), *Structured Groups for Facilitating Development: Acquiring Life Skills, Resolving Life Themes, and Making Life Transitions.* New York: Human Science Press.

02956 **DRYE, R. C.** (1974), Leadership styles in transactional analysis and gestalt groups. *Amer. J. Orthopsychiat.*, 44:219-225.

02957 **DUA, P. S.** (1972), Group desensitization of a phobia with three massing procedures. *J. Couns. Psychol*, 19:125-129.

02958 **DUBE, B. D.** (1980), Uses of the self run group in a child guidance setting. *Internat. J. Group Psychother.*, 30:461.

02959 **DUBISSON, M.** (1979), *Les Groupements d'Entreprises pour les Marchés Internationaux. (The International Movement for Group Work.)* Paris: F.E.D.U.C.I: Éditions du Moniteur.

02960 **DUBLIN, J. E.** (1971), A further motive for psychotherapists: community intimacy. *Psychiatry*, 34:401-409.

02961 **DUBLIN, J. E.** (1973), Gestalting psychotic persons. *Psychother.: Theory, Res. & Pract.*, 10:149-152.

02962 **DUBLIN, J. E.** (1972), Whose image of what?: open letters of Sigmund Koch. *J. Human. Psychol.*, 12:79-85.

02963 **DUBNO, P.** (1968), Group congruency patterns and leadership characteristics. *Personnel Psychol.*, 21:335-344.

02964 **DUBO, S.** (1951), Opportunities for group therapy in a pediatric service. *Internat. J. Group Psychother.*, 1:235-242.

02965 **du BOIS, R. D.**, and **LI, M. S.** (1971), *Reducing Social Tension and Conflict Through the Group Conversation Method.* New York: Associated Press.

02966 **du BOIS, E.** (1970), (Attempt to assess changes in neurotic patients after group psychotherapy.) *Psychiat. Polska*, (Warsaw) 4:49-56.

02967 **DUCKERT, K.** (1959), Trial of group therapy of alcoholics in general practice. *Tidskr. Norske Laegeforen.*, 79:1050-1054.

02968 **DUCKWORTH, G. L.** (1967), A project in crisis intervention. *Soc. Casework*, 48:227-231.

02969 **DUDEK, S. Z.** (1969), Interaction testing as a measure of therapeutic change in groups. *J. Project. Tech. & Personal. Assessment*, 33:127-137.

02970 **DUDLEY, D. L.**, and **PATTISON, E. M.** (1969), Group psychotherapy in patients with severe diffuse obstructive pulmonary syndrome. *Amer. Rev. Respirat. Disease*, 100:575-576.

02971 **DUDLEY, H. K.**, **WILLIAMS, J. D.**, and **GUINN, T. J.** (1970), Treating inpatients as day patients. *Hosp. & Community Psychiat.*, 21:160-161.

02972 **DUEHN, W. D.**, and **MAYADAS, N. S.** (1975/1976), Behavioral rehearsals in group counseling with parents. *Groups*, 7:13-23.

02973 **DUEHN, W. D.** (1978), Covert sensitization in group treatment of adolescent drug abusers. *Internat. J. Addict.*, 13:485–491.

02974 **DUEHN, W. D.**, and **MAYADAS, N. S.** (1976), A study of client content expectancies as related to interactional processes during short-term group sexual counseling. *Small Group Behav.*, 7:457-472.

02975 **DUETSCH, C. B.**, and **KRAMER, N.** (1977), Outpatient group psychotherapy for elderly: alternative to institutionalization. *Hosp. & Community Psychiat.*, 28:440-442.

02976 **DUFFY, J.** (1965), An experience in group psychotherapy. *J. Psychiat. Nursing*, 3:104-118.

02977 **DUFFY, J. H.**, AND **KRAFT, I. A.** (1965), Group therapy of early adolescents: an evaluation of one year of group therapy with a mixed group of early adolescents. *Amer. J. Orthopsychiat.*, 35:372.

02978 **DUFOUR, R.**, and **NADAL, J.** (1975), (Directed reverie and group imagery.) *Etudes Psychother.*, 20:69-79.

02979 **DÜHRSSEN, A.** (1964), (Catamnestic studies on group therapy: results in 270 treated patients 5 years after the termination of therapy.) *Zeit. Psychosomat. Med. Psychol.*, (Stuttgart) 10:120-126.

02980 **DÜHRSSEN, A.** (1966), Investigaciones catamnesicas de la terapia de grupo. (Catamnestic investigations in group therapy.) *Rev. Psicoanal. Psiquiat. Psicol.*, (Buenos Aires) 3:36-42.

02981 **DÜHSLER, K.** (1976), (Family therapy by means of symbol interpretation.) *Praxis. Kinderpsychol. & Kinderpsychiat.*, (Goettingen) 25:96-99.

02982 **DUKIĆ, T.** (1975), (Group work after the home care of chronic psychoses.) *Anali Zavoda Ment. Zdravlje*, 7:67-72.

02983 **DUKIĆ, T.**, and **VIDOJKOVIC, S.** (1979), (Countertransference in group psychotherapy.) *Psihijat. Danas*, (Belgrade) 11:15-20.

02984 **DULIT, E.** (1977), Adolescent therapy through the eyes of an individual therapist. *Groups*, 8:8-16.

02985 **DUMONT, M. P.** (1966), Death of the leader in a therapy group of schizophrenics. *Internat. J. Group Psychother.*, 16:209-216.

02986 **DUNCAN, J. A.** (1966), The effects of short term group counseling on selected characteristics of culturally deprived ninth grade students. *Dissert. Abstr. Internat.*, 27:387A.

02987 **DUNCAN, M.** (1953), Environmental therapy in a hostel for maladjusted children. *Brit. J. Delinquency*, 3:248-268.

02988 **DUNKAS, N.**, and **NIKELLY, A. G.** (1975), Group psychotherapy with Greek immigrants. *Internat. J. Group Psychother.*, 25:402-409.

02989 **DUNKLEBERGER, C. P.** (1967), Group or individual counseling: an analysis of the effective and efficient use of counselors in personal counseling. *Dissert. Abstr. Internat.*, 28:1677A.

02990 **DUNN, W. H.**, and **SELINSKI, H.** (1947), An army neurosis center. *U.S. Army Med. Serv. Bull.*, 7:868-876.

02991 **DUPELJ, M.**, and **GORETA, M.** (1979), (Reeducation by conventional communication group psychotherapy of biologically treated schizophrenics.) *Soc. Psihijat.*, (Belgrade) 7:83-86.

02992 **DUPONT, M. A.** (1975), The observer in the analytic psychotherapy group. In: *Group Therapy 1975: An Overview*, eds. L. R. Wolberg and M. L. Aronson. New York: Stratton Intercontinental Medical Books.

02993 **DURALD, M. M.**, and **HANKS, D.** (1980), The evaluation of coleading a Gestalt group. *J. Psychiat. Nursing*, 18:19-23.

02994 **DURAND-DASSIER, J.** (1969), *Structure et psychologie de la Relation. (The Structure and Psychology of Communications.)* Paris: Editions de l'Ep.

02995 **DURBIN, H. J.** (1977), An evaluation of media therapy with groups of hospitalized schizophrenics. *Dissert. Abstr. Internat.*, 38:2360B.

02996 **DURELL, J.**, **ARNSON, A.**, and **KELLAM, S. G.** (1965), A community–oriented therapeutic milieu. *Med. Annals D.C.*, 34:468-474.

02997 **DURELL, V. G.** (1969), Adolescents in multiple family group therapy in a school setting. *Internat. J. Group Psychother.*, 19:44-52.
02998 **DURET-COSYNS, S.** (1969), Therapy in psychosomatic medicine. *Acta Neurol. & Psychiat. Belgica*, (Brussels) 69:101-122.
02999 **DURHAM, M. S.** (1971), Re-entry in psychotherapy. *Voices*, 7:46-50.
03000 **DURKIN, H.** (1975), The development of systems theory and its implications for the theory and practice of group therapy. In: *Group Therapy 1975: An Overview*, eds. L. R. Wolberg and M. L. Aronson. New York: Stratton Intercontinental Medical Books.
03001 **DURKIN, H. E.** (1955), Acting out in group psychotherapy. *Amer. J. Orthopsychiat.*, 25:664-652.
03002 **DURKIN, H. E.** (1951), The analysis of character traits in group therapy. *Internat. J. Group Psychother.*, 1:133-143.
03003 **DURKIN, H. E.** (1969), Concluding remarks (as part of panel on interaction and insight in group psychotherapy, AGPA Conf., 1968). *Internat. J. Group Psychother.*, 19:288-291.
03004 **DURKIN, H. E.** (1974), Current problems of group therapy in historical context. In: *Group Therapy 1974: An Overview*, eds. L. R. Wolberg and M. L. Aronson. New York: Stratton Intercontinental Medical Books.
03005 **DURKIN, H. E.** (1939), Dr. John Levy's relationship therapy as applied to a play group. *Amer. J. Orthopsychiat.*, 9:583-598.
03006 **DURKIN, H. E.** (1972), General systems theory and group therapy: an introduction. *Internat. J. Group Psychother.*, 22:159-166.
03007 **DURKIN, H. E.** (1954), Group dynamics and group psychotherapy. *Internat. J. Group Psychother.*, 4:56-64.
03008 **DURKIN, H. E.** (1965), *The Group in Depth*. New York: International Universities Press.
03009 **DURKIN, H. E.** (1969), *Group Psychotherapy for Mothers*. Springfield, IL: C. C. Thomas.
03010 **DURKIN, H. E.** (1955), *Group Psychotherapy for the Mothers of Disturbed Children*. Springfield, IL: C. C. Thomas.
03011 **DURKIN, H. E.** (1954), *Group Therapy for Mothers of Disturbed Children*. Springfield, IL: C. C. Thomas.
03012 **DURKIN, H. E.** (1972), The group therapy movement. *Psychiat. Annals*, 2:14-23.
03013 **DURKIN, H. E.** (1967), Levels of group therapy in large hospitals. *Amer. J. Orthopsychiat.*, 37:272.
03014 **DURKIN, H. E.** (1956), Mothers. In: *The Fields of Group Psychotherapy*, ed. S. R. Slavson. New York: International Universities Press.
03015 **DURKIN, H. E.** (1972), Summary and Conclusions. *Internat. J. Group Psychother.*, 22:469-470.
03016 **DURKIN, H. E.** (1974), Theoretical foundations of group psychotherapy: i. In: *The Challenge for Group Psychotherapy: Present and Future*, ed. S. deSchill. New York: International Universities Press.
03017 **DURKIN, H. E.** (1948), The theory and practice of group psychotherapy. *Annals N.Y. Acad. Science*, 49:889-901.
03018 **DURKIN, H. E.** (1965), A therapist's experience as a patient in group therapy. *Topical Probl. Psychol. & Psychother.*, 5:24-28.
03019 **DURKIN, H. E.** (1972), To touch or not to touch: chairman's introduction. *Internat. J. Group Psychother.*, 22:444-445.
03020 **DURKIN, H. E.** (1957), Toward a common basis for group dynamics: group and therapeutic processes in group psychotherapy. *Internat. J. Group Psychother.*, 7:115-130.
03021 **DURKIN, H. E.** (1971), Transference in group psychotherapy revisited. *Internat. J. Group Psychother.*, 21:11-22.

03022 **DURKIN, H. E.**, and **GLATZER, H. T.** (1960), Combined individual and group psychoanalysis: symposium, 1959. 3. discussion. *Amer. J. Orthopsychiat.*, 30:242-246.

03023 **DURKIN, H. E., GLATZER, H. T.**, and **HIRSCH, J. S.** (1944), Therapy of mothers in groups. *Amer. J. Orthopsychiat.*, 14:68-76.

03024 **DURKIN, H. E., GLATZER, H. T., KADIS, A. L., WOLF, A.**, and **HULSE, W. C.** (1958), Acting out in group psychotherapy: a panel discussion. *Amer. J. Psychother.*, 12:87-105.

03025 **DURKIN, R.** (1967), Social functions of psychological interpretations. *Amer. J. Orthopsychiat.*, 37:956-962.

03026 **DURLAK, J. A.** (1980), Comparative effectiveness of behavioral and relationship group treatment in the secondary prevention of school maladjustment. *Amer. J. Community Psychol.*, 8:327.

03027 **DUSAY, J. M.** (1972), Editorial. *Transactional Anal. J.*, 2:57-58.

03028 **DUSAY, J. M.** (1972), Egograms and the "constancy hypothesis." *Transactional Anal. J.*, 2:133-137.

03029 **DUSAY, J. M.** (1971), Eric Berne's studies of intuition. *Transactional Anal J.*, 1:34-44.

03030 **DUSAY, J. M.** (1970), Script rehearsal. *Transactional Anal. Bull.*, 9:117-121.

03031 **DUVALL, W. B.** (1972), The effects of group counseling upon the classroom behavior of second grade boys. *Dissert. Abstr. Internat.*, 32:5544A.

03032 **DWAN, C.** (1978), Group approach to hypochondriasis. *Amer. Fam. Physician*, 18:23.

03033 **DWIGHT, R. B.** (1972), A group counseling methodology to help suburban adults develop an increased courage to live with anxiety. *Dissert. Abstr. Internat.*, 32:4943-4944A.

03034 **DWORIN, J.** (1970), The alternate session in group psychotherapy. *Voices*, 5:105-107.

03035 **DYCK, G.** (1969), "Talking the dozens:" a game of insults played in a group of adolescent boys. *Bull. Menninger Clinic*, 33:108-116.

03036 **DYE, C. A.** (1972), An analysis of the effects of human relations training upon student nurses measured anxiety, self-concept and group participation. *Dissert. Abstr. Internat.*, 33:795B.

03037 **DYE, C. A.** (1974), Self-concept, anxiety, and group participation as affected by human relations training. *Nursing Res.*, 23:301-306.

03038 **DYE, G. R.** (1976), Group vocational counseling with college students: analysis of program effectiveness. *Dissert. Abstr. Internat.*, 36:7865A.

03039 **DYER, W.**, and **VRIEND, J.** (1973), Effective group counseling process interventions. *Educat. Technol.*, 13:61-67.

03040 **DYER, W.**, and **VRIEND, J.** (1973), Role-working in group counseling. *Educat. Technol.*, 13:32-36.

03041 **DYER, W. G.** (1972), *Modern Theory and Method in Group Training*. New York: Van Nostrand Reinhold.

03042 **DEYER, W. G.** (1972), *The Sensitive Manipulator: The Change Agent Who Builds With Others*. Provo: Brigham Young University Press.

03043 **DYER, W. W.** (1970), Group counseling leadership training in counselor education. *Dissert. Abstr. Internat.*, 31:3263A.

03044 **DYER, W. W.**, and **VRIEND, J.** (1980), *Group Counseling for Personal Mastery: Everything You Need to Know to Lead Any Group in Any Setting*. New York: Sovereign Books.

03045 **DYNES, J. B.**, and **HAMILTON, F. J.** (1945), Group psychotherapy of psychiatric war casualties. *U.S. Navy Med. Bull.*, 44:549-597.

03046 **DYRUD, J. E.**, and **RIOCH, M.** (1953), Multiple therapy in the treatment program of a mental hospital. *Psychiatry*, 16:21-26.

03047 **DYSON, J. W., FLEITAS, D. W.**, and **SCIOLI, F. P.** (1972), The interaction of leadership, personality, and decisional environments. *J. Soc. Psychol.*, 86:29-33.

03048 **DYSON, J. W., GODWIN, D. H. B.**, and **HAZELWOOD, L. A.** (1976), Group composition, leadership orientation, and decisional outcomes. *Small Group Behav.*, 7:114-128.

03049 **D'ZURILLA, T. J.** (1966), Persuasion and Praise as techniques for modifying verbal behavior in a "real-life" group setting. *J. Abnorm. Psychol.*, 7:369-376.

E

03050 **EAGER, M.**, and **EXOO, R.** (1980), Parents visiting parents for unequaled support. *Amer. J. Maternal Child Nursing*, 5:35-36.

03051 **EAGLIN, R. G.** (1970), An experimental study of the effect of positive, negative, and no verbal reinforcers on assigned leaders in 8-member decision making groups. *Dissert. Abstr. Internat.*, 31:3688B-3689B.

03052 **EAGLY, A. H.** (1970), Leadership style and role differentiation as determinants of group effectiveness. *J. Personality*, 38:509-524.

03053 **EARLE, A., LYNN, F., MANASER, J.**, and **SELBY, N.** (1970), The role of the psychiatric nurse in the rehabilitation of the schizophrenic patient. *J. Psychiat. Nursing*, 8:16.

03054 **EASTERWOOD, H. B.** (1973), An investigation of the effectiveness of group versus group-individual counseling with potential high school dropouts. *Dissert. Abstr. Internat.*, 34:3865A.

03055 **EASLMAN, J. N.**, and **SAUR, W. G.** (1979), Group model for building strengths in families with handicapped children. In: *Building Family Strengths*, eds. N. Stinnett, B. Chesser and J. Defrain. Lincoln: University of Nebraska Press.

03056 **EASTMAN, P. C.** (1973), Consciousness-raising as a resocialization process for women. *Smith Coll. Studies Soc. Work*, 43:153-183.

03057 **EASTON, C. W.** (1972), The effect of the structure and emphasis of group training methods on communication skills, attitude change and problem-solving ability. *Dissert. Abstr. Internat.*, 32:6190A.

03058 **EATON, A.** (1962), Some implications and effects of intragroup acting out of pregenital conflicts. *Internat. J. Group Psychother.*, 12:435-447.

03059 **EATON, J. W.** (1957), On the validity of treatment evaluation by client associates. *Group Psychother., Psychodrama & Sociometry*, 10:198-211.

03060 **EBAUGH, F.** (1951), Group therapy. *Neuropsychiatry*, 1:19-32.

03061 **EBENSTEIN, N.** (1976), The effect of a group counseling program on the self concept and the sense of independence in women. *Dissert. Abstr. Internat.*, 37:2633A.

03062 **EBERSOLE, G. O.** (1969), Training the nonprofessional group therapist: a controlled study. *J. Nerv. & Ment. Diseases*, 149:294-302.

03063 **EBERSOLE, G. O., LELDERMAN, P. H.**, and **YALOM, I. D.** (1969), Training the non-professional group therapist: a controlled study. *J. Nerv. & Ment. Diseases*, 149:294-302.

03064 **EBERSOLE, P.** (1974), Management of mental health problems in the aging: from despair to integrity through group reminiscing with the aged. part i. *ANA Clin. Sessions*, 135-142.

03065 **EBERSOLE, P.** (1976), Problems of group reminiscing with the institutionalized aged. *J. Gerontol. Nursing*, 2:23-27.

03066 **EBERSOLE, P. D.** (1969), Investigation of Fiedler's leadership model in a quasi-therapeutic situation with hospitalized patients. *Dissert. Abstr. Internat.*, 30:1894-1985.

03068 **ECHANIZ, J. S.** (1972), (Psychodramatic study of the family structure. *Acta Psiquiat. Psychol. Amer. Latina*, (Buenos Aires) 18:160-167.

03069 **ECHANIZ, J. S.**, and **ZURETTI, M.** (1973), (Psychodrama with couples.) *Acta Psiquiat. Psicol. Amer. Latina*, (Buenos Aires) 19:140-147.

03070 **ECKMAN, B. K.** (1980), Seating pattern and working in a Gestalt therapy group. *Gestalt J.*, 3:99-106.

03071 **ECKSTEIN, D. G.** (1980), The use of early recollections in group counseling. *J. Special. Group Work*, 5:87-92.

03072 **EDDING, C.** (1978), (Invitations to group training: problem of professional standards.) *Gruppenpsychother. & Gruppendynam.*, (Goettingen) 13:274.

03073 **EDDY, F. L., O'NEILL, E.**, and **ASTRACHAN, B. M.** (1968), Group work on a long term psychiatric service as conducted by nurses and aides. *Perspect. Psychiat. Care*, 6:9-15.

03074 **EDDY, W. B.**, and **LUBIN, B.** (1971), Laboratory training and encounter groups. *Personnel & Guid. J.*, 49:625-636.

03075 **EDELSON, J. S.** (1972), Group work in the institution. *Can. Ment. Health*, (Ottawa) 20:42-43.

03076 **EDELSON, M.** (1964), *Ego Psychology, Group Dynamics, and the Therapeutic Community.* New York: Grune and Stratton.

03077 **EDELSON, M.** (1970), *The Practice of Sociotherapy: A Case Study.* New Haven: Yale University Press.

03078 **EDELSTEIN, E. L.**, and **KNELLER, D.** (1976), A combined art therapy group. *Isr. Annals Psychiat.*, (Jerusalem) 14:322-332.

03079 **EDELSTEIN, E. L.**, and **NOY, P.** (1972), Open groups within a changing psychiatric ward in Israel. *Internat. J. Group Psychother.*, 22:379-383.

03080 **EDENFIELD, W. H.**, and **MYRICK, R. D.** (1973), The effect of group sensitivity experience on learning facilitative verbal responses. *Small Group Behav.*, 4:249-256.

03081 **EDINGER, H. B.** (1970), Reuniting children and parents through casework and group work. *Children*, 17:183-187.

03082 **EDINGER, J. D.** (1979), Exploration of a live together, group together paradigm with incarcerated drug offenders. *Internat. J. Addict*, 14:715.

03083 **Editorial:** psychotherapy and the danger of suicide (1961), *Amer. J. Psychother.*, 15:181-183.

03084 **EDLESON, J. L.** (1980), Group social skills training for children: an evaluative study. *Dissert. Abstr. Internat.*, 40:4747A. (University Microfilms No. 7928639.)

03085 **EDLS, S. C.** (1971), The effect of group counseling upon classroom behavior and anxiety of school teachers. *Dissert. Abstr. Internat.*, 32:2524.

03086 **EDNEY, J. J.**, and **UHLIG, S. R.** (1977), Individual and small group territories. *Small Group Behav.*, 8:457-468.

03087 **EDWARDS, D. D.** (1972), Effects of an extended group experience upon counselor facilitation of client self-exploration. *Dissert. Abstr. Internat.*, 3683A.

03088 **EDWARDS, G., HENSMAN, C., HAWKER, A.**, and **WILLIAMSON, V.** (1967), Alcoholics anonymous: the anatomy of a self-help group. *Soc. Psychiat.*, 1:195-204.

03089 **EDWARDS, J. D., Jr.**, and **DILL, J. E.** (1974), Alcoholism clinic in a military setting: a combined disulfiram and group therapy outpatient program. *Military Med.*, 139:206-209.

03090 **EDWARDS, N.** (1980), A contribution to the understanding of the role of the superego in dreams: further development of an approach to dreams in analytic group psychotherapy. *Group*, 4:3-20.

03091 **EDWARDS, N.** (1977), Dreams, ego psychology, and group interaction in analytic group psychotherapy. *Group*, 1:32-47.

03092 **EDWARDS, S. L.** (1967), Group work with brain damaged patients. *Hosp. & Community Psychiat.*, 18:267-270.

03093 **EDWARDS, W. P.** (1969), Interpersonal relations orientation compatibility as related to outcome variables in group psychotherapy. *Dissert. Abstr. Internat.*, 29:3909B-3910B.

03094 **EDWARDS, W. R.** (1970), The use of focused audio feedback in group counseling with adolescent boys. *Dissert. Abstr. Internat.*, 30:5232A.

03095 **ANON.** (1966), Effective therapy for "back ward" patients. *Roche Report: Front. Hosp. Psychiat.*, 5:5-6.

03096 **EFRAN, J. S.**, and **BOYLIN, E. R.** (1967), Social desirability and willingness to participate in a group discussion. *Psychol. Reports*, 20:402.
03097 **EFRON, H. Y., MARKS, H. K.**, and **HALL, R.** (1959), A comparison of group-centered and individual-centered activity programs. *Arch. Gen. Psychiat.*, 1:552-555.
03098 **EFTIHIADES, T. D.** (1969), Community meetings in a prison setting. *Ment. Hygiene*, 53:289-294.
03099 **EGAN, G.** (1970), *Encounter: Group Processes for Interpersonal Growth.* Belmont, CA: Brooks/Cole Publishing.
03100 **EGAN, G.** (1971), *Encounter Groups: Basic Readings.* Belmont, CA: Brooks/Cole Publishing.
03101 **EGAN, G.** (1973), *Face to Face.* Monterey, CA: Brooks/Cole Publishing.
03102 **EGAN, G.** (1973), *Face to Face: The Small-Group Experience and Interpersonal Growth.* Monterey, CA: Wadsworth.
03103 **EGAN, G.** (1976), *Interpersonal Living: A Skill Contract Approach to Human Relations Training in Groups.* Monterey, CA: Brooks/Cole Publishing.
03104 **EGAN, G.** (1977), *You and Me: The Skills of Communicating and Relating to Others.* Monterey, CA: Brooks/Cole Publishing.
03105 **EGAN, M. H.** (1975), Dynamisms in activity discussion group therapy (ADGT). *Internat. J. Group Psychother.*, 25:199-218.
03106 **EGELHOFF, E. A.** (1970), Encounter group feedback and self-perception change. *Dissert. Abstr. Internat.*, 31:3334A.
03107 **EGENDORF, A.** (1975), Vietnam veteran rap groups and themes of postwar life. *J. Soc. Issues*, 31:111-124.
03108 **EGGER, J.** (1980), Group psychotherapy in the treatment of cardiovascular diseases: health and disease education in inpatient rehabilitation. *Psychiat. Praxis*, (Stuttgart) 7:34.
03109 **EGGER, J.** (1980), Psychologische gruppenarbeit mit herzinfarktpatientsen. (Group work psychology with depressed patients.) *Oesterreich. Aerztezeit.*, (Vienna) 35:419-426.
03110 **EHRENWALD, J.** (1960), Psychoanalyst vs. psychodramatist: a dialogue. *Group Psychother., Psychodrama & Sociometry*, 13:69-73.
03111 **EHRLICH, F.** (1967), The use of group techniques in physical rehabilitation. *Med. J. Austral.*, (Glebe) 1:843-846.
03112 **EHRLICH, I. F.** (1968), Supervision: process not position. *Amer. J. Nursing*, 68:115-119.
03113 **EIBEN, R.**, and **CLACK, R. J.** (1973), Impact of a participatory group experience on counselors in training. *Small Group Behav.*, 4:486-495.
03114 **EICHEL, E.** (1978), Assessment with a family focus. *J. Psychiat. Nursing*, 16:11-14.
03115 **EICKE, D.** (1978), Analytische gruppentherapie als selbsterfahrung im rahmen der weiterbildung in psychotherapie. (Analytical group therapy as self-encounter in continuing psychotherapeutic education.) *Praxis der Psychother.*, 23:73-79.
03116 **EICKE, D.** (1966), (Problems encountered with clinical indications of psychotherapy of schizophrenic patients with reference to modern socio-psychiatric aspects.) *Zeit. Psychother. Med. Psychol.*, (Stuttgart) 16:70-78.
03117 **EICKE, D.** (1967), Therapeutische gruppen-arbeit mit schizophrenen. (Therapeutic group work with schizophrenics.) *Zeit. Psychother. Med. Psychol.*, (Stuttgart) 17:100-111.
03118 **EINSTEIN, G.**, and **MOSS, M. S.** (1967), Some thoughts on sibling relationships. *Soc. Casework*, 48:549-555.
03119 **EISEMAN, R.** (1965), Operant conditioning of the sequence of speakers in conversation and group psychotherapy. *J. Psychology*, 61:267-270.

03120 **EISEN, A., LURIE, A.,** and **ROBBINS, L. L.** (1963), Group processes in a voluntary psychiatric hospital. *Amer. J. Orthopsychiat.*, 33:750-754.
03121 **EISENBEISS, M. J.** (1972), The effects of a sensitivity group experience on counselors-in-training and their understanding of counselee communication. *Dissert. Abstr. Internat.*, 33:154A.
03122 **EISENBERG, J.,** and **ABBOTT, R. D.** (1968), The monopolizing patient in group therapy. *Perspect. Psychiat. Care*, 6:66-69, 92-93.
03123 **EISENBERG, T., GLICKMAN, A.,** and **FOSEN, R. H.** (1969), Action for change in police–community behaviors. *Crime and Delinquency*, 15:393-406.
03124 **EISENMAN, R.** (1967), Birth order, anxiety, and verbal interaction in group psychotherapy. *Dissert. Abstr. Internat.*, 27:3670.
03125 **EISENMAN, R.** (1966), Birth order, anxiety, and verbalizations in group psychotherapy. *J. Consult. & Clin. Psychol.*, 30:521-526.
03126 **EISENMAN, R.** (1965), Operant conditioning of the sequence of speakers in conversation and group psychotherapy. *J. Psychology*, 61:305-309.
03127 **EISENMAN, R.** (1965), Usefulness of the concepts of inferiority feeling and life style with schizophrenics. *J. Individ. Psychol.*, 21:171-177.
03128 **EISLER, R. M.** (1972), Crisis intervention in the family of a firesetter. *Psychother.: Theory, Res. & Pract.*, 9:76-79.
03129 **EISMAN, E. J.** (1975), The effects of leader sex and self-disclosure on member self-disclosure in marathon encounter groups. *Dissert. Abstr. Internat.*, 36:1429B.
03130 **EISNER, B. G.** (1964), Notes on the use of drugs to facilitate group psychotherapy. *Psychiat. Quart.*, 38:310-328.
03131 **EITINGTON, J. E.** (1971), Assessing laboratory training using psychology of learning concepts. *Training & Develop. J.*, 25:8-15.
03132 **EKSTEIN, R.** (1978), The search and yearning for and the rebellion against the father: a group dilemma. *Internat. J. Group Psychother.*, 28:435-444.
03133 **ELASESSER, E.** (1963), On the revival of the single child situation in psychoanalytic group therapy following individual psychotherapy. *Praxis. Kinderpsychol. & Kinderpsychiat.*, (Goettingen) 12:208-210.
03134 **ELBERT, B.** (1978), Homeostasis. *Fam. Therapy*, 5:171.
03135 **ELBERT, W. E.** (1970), Changes in self-concept, self-actualization, and interpersonal relations as a result of video feedback in sensitivity training. *Dissert. Abstr. Internat.*, 30:5233A.
03136 **ELDER-JUCKER, P. L.** (1979), Effects of group therapy on self esteem, social interaction and depression of female residents in a home for the aged. *Dissert. Abstr. Internat.*, 39:5514B.
03137 **ELEFTHERY, D. G.,** and **ELEFTHERY, D. M.** (1966), Our psychodrama demonstration in the permanent theater of psychodrama. *Group Psychother., Psychodrama & Sociometry*, 19:17-21.
03138 **ELENEWSKI, I. J.** (1972), The effects of a racial confrontation group on self-reported interpersonal attitudes and on the intrapersonal behavior. *Dissert. Abstr. Internat.*, 33:968A.
03139 **ELGEN, M.** (1975), Psychopathy and individuation. *Psychother.: Theory, Res. & Pract.*, 12:286.
03140 **ELIAS, A.** (1980), Group treatment of delinquents: a review of guided group interaction. *Annals N.Y. Acad. Science*, 347:167-175.
03141 **ELIAS, A.** (1968), Group treatment program for juvenile delinquents. *Child Welfare*, 47:281-290.
03142 **ELIASBERG, W. G.** (1954), Group treatment of homosexuals on probation. *Group Psychother., Psychodrama & Sociometry*, 7:218-226.
03143 **ELIASBERG, W.** (1945), Newer viewpoints in the application and research of group psychotherapy. *Sociometry*, 8:350-354.

03144 **ELIASBERG, W. G.** (1954), Transference, countertransference and tele: remarks to J. L. Moreno's article. *Group Psychother., Psychodrama & Sociometry*, 7:320-321.

03145 **ELIASOPH, E.** (1962), Comment on creativity and destruction. *Group Psychother., Psychodrama & Sociometry*, 15:336-338.

03146 **ELIASOPH, E.** (1955), Concepts and techniques of role playing and role training utilizing psychodramatic methods in group psychotherapy with adolescent drug addicts. *Group Psychother., Psychodrama & Sociometry*, 8:308-315.

03147 **ELIASOPH, E.** (1960), Existence, spontaneity and anxiety, as related to the process of "merging." *Progr. Psychother.*, 5:195-200.

03148 **ELIASOPH, E.** (1955), A group therapy and psychodrama approach with adolescent drug addicts. *Group Psychother., Psychodrama & Sociometry*, 8:161-167.

03149 **ELIASOPH, E.** (1958), A group therapy-psychodrama program at Berkshire Industrial Farm. *Group Psychother., Psychodrama & Sociometry*, 11:57-62.

03150 **ELIASOPH, E.** (1960), Some different dimensions of group and individual therapy. *Group Psychother., Psychodrama & Sociometry*, 13:153-160.

03151 **ELISEO, T. S.** (1964), Effectiveness of remotivation technique with chronic psychiatric patients. *Psychol. Reports*, 14:171-178.

03152 **ELKES, R.** (1947), Group casework experiment with mothers of children with cerebral palsy. *J. Soc. Casework*, 28:95-101.

03153 **ELKINS, D.** (1951), How the classroom teacher can help the emotionally disturbed child. *Understanding the Child*, 20:63-73.

03154 **ELKINS, G. R.**, and **KEE, A. F.** (1978), Review of S. D. Rose's *Group-Therapy: A Behavioral Approach. Psychology*, 15:51.

03155 **ELLENBERG, J.** (1980), A lithium clinic in a community mental health center. *Hosp. & Community Psychiat.*, 31:834.

03156 **ELLIOT, A. E.** (1966), A group treatment for mentally ill offenders. *Crime & Delinquency*, 12:29-37.

03157 **ELLIOTT, D. S.**, **VOSS, H. L.**, and **WENDLING, A.** (1966), Dropout and the social milieu of the high school: a preliminary analysis. *Amer. J. Orthopsychiat.*, 36:808-817.

03158 **ELLIOT, G. R.** (1972), The effects of the T-group method upon the communication and discrimination skills of counselor trainees. *Dissert. Abstr. Internat.*, 4944A.

03159 **ELLIOTT, G. R.** (1978), Effects of T-group training on the communication skills of counselor trainees. *Small Group Behav.*, 9:49-58.

03160 **ELLIOTT, J.** (1977), *The Theory and Practice of Encounter Group Leadership*. Berkeley, CA: Exploration Institute.

03161 **ELLIOTT, M. A.** (1963), Group therapy in dealing with juvenile and adult offenders. *Fed. Probat.*, 27:48-54.

03162 **ELLIS, A.** (1969), Rational-emotive therapy. *J. Contemp. Psychother.*, 1:82-90.

03163 **ELLIS, A.** (1962), *Reason and Emotion in Psychotherapy*. New York: Lyle Stuart.

03164 **ELLIS, A.** (1974), Rational-emotive therapy in groups. *Rational Living*, 9:15.

03165 **ELLIS, A.** (1974), Rationality and irrationality in the group therapy process. In: *Group Process Today: Evaluation and Perspective*, eds. D. S. Milmon and G. D. Goldman. Springfield, IL: C. C. Thomas.

03166 **ELLIS, A.** (1970), A weekend of rational encounter. *Rational Living*, 4:1-8.

03167 **ELLIS, A. S.**, and **KRUPINSKI, J.** (1964), The evaluation of a treatment programme for alcoholics: a follow-up study. *Med. J. Austral.*, (Glebe) 1:8-13.

03168 **ELLIS, E. M.** (1977), A comparative study of feminist vs. traditional group assertiveness training with unassertive women. *Dissert. Abstr. Internat.*, 38:1397B.

03169 **ELLIS, E. M.,** and **NICHOLS, M. P.** (1979), A comparative study of feminist and traditional group assertiveness training with women. *Psychother.: Theory, Res. & Pract.*, 16:467.

03170 **ELLIS, H. E., SPENCER, C. P.,** and **OXFIELD-BOX, H.** (1969), Matched groups and the risky shift phenomenon: a defense of the extreme member hypothesis. *Brit. J. Soc. & Clin. Psychol.*, (London) 8:333-339.

03171 **ELLSWEIG, P. L.** (1972), The effects of group experiences on college resident advisors and their advisees. *Dissert. Abstr. Internat.*, 33:6085A.

03172 **ELLSWORTH, P. D.,** and **COLMAN, A. D.** (1969), A model program: the application of operant conditioning principles to work group experience. *Amer. J. Occupat. Ther.*, 23:495-501.

03173 **ELLSWORTH, R., MERONETT, R., KLETT, W., GORDON, H.,** and **GUNN, R.** (1971), Milieu characteristic of successful psychiatric treatment programs. *Amer. J. Orthopsychiat.*, 41:427-441.

03174 **ELLSWORTH, R. B.** (1973), Feedback: asset or liability in improving treatment effectiveness? *J. Consult. & Clin. Psychol.*, 40:383-393.

03175 **ELMAN, D.,** and **RUPPLE, D.** (1978), Group discussion members' reactions to a structured opening exercise. *Small Group Behav.*, 9:363-372.

03176 **ELMORE, J. L.,** and **FOWLER, D. R.** (1970), Brief group psychotherapy with unwed mothers. *J. Med. Soc. N.J.*, 67:19-23.

03177 **ELMORE, J. L.,** and **SAUNDERS, R.** (1972), Group encounter techniques in the short-term psychiatric hospital. *Amer. J. Psychother.*, 26:490-500.

03178 **ELPERS, J. R.** (1971), A support group for maintaining chronic patients outside the hospital. *Hosp. & Communty Psychiat.*, 22:31-34.

03179 **ELRICK, M. F.** (1977), Leader, she: dynamics of a female-led self-analytic group. *Human Relat.*, 30:869-878.

03180 **ELSAESSER, E.** (1964), (Contribution to the role of the co-therapist in analytic group therapy of adolescents with special reference to fundamental differences between psychoanalytic individual and group therapy.) *Praxis Kinderpsychol. & Kinderpsychiat.*, (Goettingen) 13:47-51.

03181 **ELSAESSER, E.** (1963), (On the revival of the single child situation in psychoanalytic group therapy following individual psychotherapy.) *Praxis Kinderpsychol. & Kinderpsychiat.*, (Goettingen) 12:208-210.

03182 **ELWELL, R.** (1970), Community mental health centers. *Amer. J. Nursing*, 70:1014-1018.

03183 **ELY, A. L., GVERNEY, B. G.,** and **STOVER, L.** (1973), Efficacy of the training phase of conjugal therapy. *Psychother.: Theory, Res. & Pract.*, 10:201-207.

03184 **ELY, J. W.** (1958), Parents help furnish supportive role in classroom problem solving. *Group Psychother., Psychodrama & Sociometry*, 11:128-136.

03185 **EMDE, R. N.** (1967), Limiting regression in the therapeutic community. *Amer. J. Nursing*, 67:1010-1015.

03186 **van EMDE BOAS, C.** (1966), (Determination of the indications for analytical group psychotherapy.) *Nederl. Tijdschr. Geneeskunde*, (Amsterdam) 110:2186-2190.

03187 **EMENER, W. G., Jr.** (1972), A comparison of programed machine training and leader-led group training on interpersonal behavior. *Dissert. Abstr. Internat.*, 32:3684A.

03188 **EMENER, W. G.** (1973), A prepracticum laboratory training experience. *Counselor Educat. & Supervision*, 12:213-220.

03189 **EMERSON, R. M.** (1955), Submission to social influence in face-to-face groups. *Dissert. Abstr. Internat.*, 15:1130.

03190 **EMERSON, R. W.** (1980), Changes in depression and self-esteem of spouses of stroke patients with aphasia as a result of group counseling. *Dissert. Abstr. Internat.*, 49:4893A. (University Microfilms No. 8005612.)

03191 **EMERY, P., LEVITAN, J.**, and **GADLIN, W.** (1980), Modified group therapy for psychotic and depressed patients. *Group*, 4:21-32.

03192 **EMMELKAMP, P. M.** (1975), Effects of historically portrayed modeling and group treatment on self-observation: a comparison with agoraphobics. *Behav. Res. & Ther.*, 13:135-139.

03193 **EMPEY, L. J.** (1977), Clinical group work with multihandicapped adolescents. *Soc. Casework*, 58:593-599.

03194 **EMPEY, L. T.** (1968), Sociological perspectives and small-group work with socially deprived youth. *Soc. Serv. Rev.*, 42:448-463.

03195 "Encounter" techniques held useful in marathon group therapy (1970), *Roche Report: Front. Hosp. Psychiat.*, 7:3.

03196 **ENDLEMAN, S.** (1963), Comparison of the sociometric structure of two college classes. *Internat. J. Sociometry & Sociatry*, 3:72-76.

03197 **ENDS, E. J.** (1958), Therapeutic understanding and patient change in group therapy. Unpublished doctoral dissertation, Denver University.

03198 **ENDS, E. J.**, and **PAGE, C. W.** (1959), Group psychotherapy and concomitant psychological change. *Psychol. Monogr.*, 73 (Whole No. 480).

03199 **ENDS, E. J.**, and **PAGE, C. W.** (1959), *Group Psychotherapy and Concomitant Psychological Change.* Washington, D.C.: American Psychological Association.

03200 **ENDS, E. J.**, and **PAGE, C. W.** (1957), A study of three types of group psychotherapy with hospitalized male inebriates. *Quart. J. Studies Alcohol*, 18:263-277.

03201 **ENFIELD, C. C.** (1967), A review on a novel psychotherapeutic approach. *Psychother. & Psychosomat.*, (Basel) 15:18.

03202 **ENFIELD, S. C. E.** (1971), The feasibility of freshman student development groups in a state university setting. *Dissert. Abstr. Internat.*, 31:7594B.

03203 **ENGELHARD, H. M.** (1969/1970), (A conceptual bond between psychoanalysis and psychodrama.) *Bull. de Psychol.*, (Paris) 23:889-894.

03204 **ENGELMAYER, O.** (1958), *Das Soziogramm in der Modernen Schule.* (*The Sociogram in the Modern School.*) Munich: Chr. Kaiser Verlag.

03205 **ENGELMAYER, O. A.** (1956), Die entwicklung des sozioalbewussteins im volkschulalter im lichte der soziometrischen motivationsanalyse. (The development of social consciousness in primary school children in light of sociometric motivation analysis.) *Internat. J. Sociometry & Sociatry*, 1:37-45.

03206 **ENGLE, M.** (1960), Shifting levels of communication in treatment of adolescent character disorders. *Arch. Gen. Psychiat.*, 2:104-109.

03207 **ENGLISH, F.** (1972), Rackets and real feelings: ii. *Transactional Anal. J.*, 2:23-25.

03208 **ENGLISH, F.** (1971), The substitution factor: rackets and real feelings. *Transactional Anal. J.*, 1:225-230.

03209 **ENGLISH, J. T.** (1969), Sensitivity training: promise and performance. *Amer. J. Psychiat.*, 126:874-876.

03210 **ENGLISH, R. W.**, and **HIGGINS, T. E.** (1971), Client-centered group counseling with pre-adolescents. *J. School Health*, 41:507-510.

03211 **ENKE, H.** (1965), Bipolare gruppenpsychotherapie als moeglichkeit psychoanalytischer arbeit in der stationaeren psychotherapie. (Bipolar group psychotherapy as possibility for psychoanalytic work in stationary psychotherapy.) *Zeit. Psychother. Med. Psychol.*, (Stuttgart) 15:116-122.

03212 **ENKE, H.** (1967), Patientengespräche. (Conversations of patients.) *Praxis der Psychother.*, 12:79-88.

03213 **ENKE, H.** (1968), Somatisierung und gruppenpsychotherapie. (Somatization and group psychotherapy.) *Psychiat. Neurol. & Med. Psychol.*, (Leipzig) 20:41-45.

03214 **ENNEIS, J. M.** (1951), The dynamics of group and action processes in therapy. *Group Psychother., Psychodrama & Sociometry*, 4:17-22.

03215 **ENNEIS, J. M.** (1952), Establishing a psychodrama program. *Group Psychother., Psychodrama & Sociometry*, 5:111-119.

03216 **ENNEIS, J. M.** (1950), The hypnodramatic technique. *Group Psychother., Psychodrama & Sociometry*, 3:11-54.

03217 **ENNEIS, J. M.** (1950), A note on the organization of the St. Elizabeths Hospital psychodrama program. *Group Psychother., Psychodrama & Sociometry*, 3:253-255.

03218 **ENNIS, D. L.** (1973), The effects of videotape feedback versus verbal feedback on the behavior of schizophrenics in group psychotherapy. *Dissert. Abstr. Internat.*, 34:2926B.

03219 **ENNS, H.** (1975), Activating a group of passive boys. In: *Adolescents Grow in Groups*, ed. I. Berkovitz. New York: Brunner/Mazel.

03220 **ENOMOTO, J. J.** (1972), Participation in correctional management by offender self-help groups. *Fed. Probat.*, 36:36-38.

03221 **ENRIGHT, J. B.** (1972), Thou art that: projection and play in therapy and growth. *Psychother.: Theory, Res. & Pract.*, 9:153-156.

03222 **ENRIGHT, M. F.** (1978), The effects of leadership style on development and productivity in encounter groups. *Dissert. Abstr. Internat.*, 39:2567B.

03223 **EPHROSS, P. H.**, and **BALGOPAL, P. R.** (1978), Educating students for the practice of creative groupwork. *J. Educ. Soc. Work*, 14:42-48.

03224 **EPPERSON, D. L.** (1980), Investigation of positive and negative, observational, reactive, and inferential feedback in experiential groups. *Dissert. Abstr. Internat.*, 40:3922B. (University Microfilms No. 8001725.)

03225 **EPPS, J. D.**, and **SIKES, W. W.** (1977), Personal-growth groups: who joins and who benefits? *Group & Organizat. Studies*, 2:88-100.

03226 **EPSTEIN, H. L.**, and **SLAVIN, S.** (1952), Common elements in group influence attempts. *J. Soc. Issues*, 8:45-53.

03227 **EPSTEIN, N.** (1970), Brief group therapy in a child guidance clinic. *Soc. Work*, 15:33-38.

03228 **EPSTEIN, N.** (1977), Group therapy with autistic-schizophrenic adolescents. *Soc. Casework*, 58:350-358.

03229 **EPSTEIN, N.** (1960), Recent observations on group psychotherapy with adolescent delinquent boys in residential treatment: activity group therapy. *Internat. J. Group Psychother.*, 10:180-194.

03230 **EPSTEIN, N.** (1976), Techniques of brief therapy with children and parents. *Soc. Casework*, 57:317-323.

03231 **EPSTEIN, N.**, and **ALTMAN, S.** (1972), Experiences in converting an activity group into verbal group therapy with latency-age boys. *Internat. J. Group Psychother.*, 22:93-100.

03232 **EPSTEIN, N.**, and **SLAVSON, S. R.** (1962), "Breakthrough" in group treatment of hardened delinquent adolescent boys. *Internat. J. Group Psychother.*, 12:199-210.

03233 **ERDMAN, D.** (1977), Neonatal intensive care. parent-to-parent support: the best for those with sick newborns—Children's Health Center Neonatal Intensive Care Unit, Minneapolis, MN. part 2. *MCN: Amer. J. Maternal Child Nursing*, 2:291-292.

03234 **ERDMANN, M.** (1964), (Speech therapy as a way to the formation of personality.) *Praxis Kinderpsychol. & Kinderpsychiat.*, (Goettingen) 13:76-79.

03235 Eric Berne as group therapist (1970). *Transactional Anal. Bull.*, 9:75-83.

03236 **ERICKSON, K. V.** (1974), The process of group communication; small group decision making; communication and the group process; discussion: the process of group decision making; problem solving group interaction. *Speech Teacher*, 23:277-282.

03237 **ERIKSON, C. R.**, and **LEJEUNE, R.** (1972), Poetry as a subtle therapy. *Hosp. & Community Psychiat.*, 23:56-57.

03238 **ERINOSHO, O. A.** (1977), Cultural factors in mental illness among the Yoruba. *Internat. J. Group Psychother.*, 27:511-515.

03239 **ERMALINSKI, R.** (1971), The training and importance of relevance in self-directed groups of psychiatric patients. *Dissert. Abstr. Internat.*, 32:3652B.

03240 **ERMANN, G.**, and **ENKE, H.** (1978), (Interventions and heart-rate in group-psychotherapy: ii.) *Gruppenpsychother. & Gruppendynam.*, Goettingen), 13:56-63.

03241 **ERMANN, G.** (1976), (Interventions and heart rate in group psychotherapy: group leader and group attendance.) *Gruppenpsychother. & Gruppendynam.*, (Goettingen) 11:23-32.

03242 **ERMANN, M.** (1973), (The group as theme: theme-centered interactional group performance with adolescents as a possibility for social experience.) *Praxis Kinderpsychol. & Kinderpsychiat.*, (Goettingen) 22:267-271.

03243 **ERMANN, M.** (1977), (Merging and individualization: the courage to be an individual in a group.) *Praxis der Psychother.*, 22:153-158.

03244 **ERMANN, M.** (1976), Object representations in group psychotherapy after loss and change of psychotherapist: empirical-causalistic study using impression differential. *Gruppenpsychol. & Gruppenpsychiat.*, (Goettingen) 11:33-46.

03245 **ERMANN, M.** (1977), (Theme centered interaction (TCI) in group work and group psychotherapy.) *Gruppenpsychother. & Gruppendynam.*, (Goettingen) 12:266.

03246 **ERMANN, M.**, and **ERMANN, G.** (1976), (Differential indications in the clinical field: empirical study of management of indications for analytic individual and group psychotherapy respectively in a psychotherapy clinic.) *Zeit. Psychosomat. Med. & Psychoanal.*, (Goettingen) 22:342-355.

03247 **ERNEY, T. A.** (1980), The effects of a peer facilitator-led group on the moral development, school attitudes, and self-esteem of middle school students. *Dissert. Abstr. Internat.*, 40:4408A. (University Microfilms No. 8002855.)

03248 **ERNSPERGER, B.** (1973), *Gruppendynamik und Didaktrik der Erwachsenenbildung.* (*Group Dynamics and the Teaching of Adolescents.*) Stuttgart: Klett.

03249 **ERNST, F. H.** (1971), The diagrammed parent: Eric Berne's most significant contribution. *Transactional Anal. J.*, 1:49-58.

03250 **ERNST, F. H.** (1971), The fourth millenium of the alphabet fetes the t.a. diagram. *Transactional Anal. J.*, 1:204-208.

03251 **ERNST, F. H.** (1962), Use of transactional analysis in prison therapy groups. *Correct. Psychiat. & J. Soc. Ther.*, 8:120-132.

03252 **ERNST, F. H.**, and **KEATING, W. C., Jr.** (1964), Psychiatric treatment of the California felon. *Amer. J. Psychiat.*, 120:974-979.

03253 **ERNST, P., BERAN, B., BADASH, B., KOSOVSKY, R.**, and **KLEINHAUZ, M.** (1977), Treatment of the aged mentally ill: further unmasking of the effects of a diagnosis of chronic brain syndrome. *J. Amer. Geriat. Soc.*, 25:466-469.

03254 **ERSKINE, R. G.**, and **MAISENBACHER, J.** (1975), The effects of a t.a. class on socially maladjusted high school students. *Transactional Anal. J.*, 5:252-255.

03255 **ERSKINE, R. G., CLINTON, L.**, and **OLMSTEAD, A. E.** (1975), Graphs as measures of care. *Transactional Anal. J.*, 5:255-256.

03256 **ERSNER-HERSHFIELD, R. R.,** (1978), Evaluation of two components of group treatment for pre-orgasmic women: couples versus women format and massed versus distributed spacing. *Dissert. Abstr. Internat.*, 39:3507B.

03257 **ERSNER-HERSHFIELD, R. R.,** and **KOPEL, S.** (1979), Group treatment of pre-orgasmic women: evaluation of partner involvement and spacing of sessions. *J. Consult. & Clin. Psychol.*, 47:750-759.

03258 **ESAU, T. G.** (1970), Group psychotherapy. *Sandoz Psychiat. Spectator*, 6:18.

03259 **ESKILSON, A.,** and **WILEY, M. G.** (1976), Sex composition and leadership in small groups. *Sociometry*, 39:183-193.

03260 **ESPIRO, N.** (1973), (The place of psychoanalytical theory in psychotherapy with small groups: a model of the group as a productive unit.) *Acta Psichiat. Psicol. Amer. Latina* (Buenos Aires), 19:362-371.

03261 **ESQUIBEL, E. V.,** and **BOWER, W. H.** (1965), Changeover of a mental hospital unit into a therapeutic community. *Internat. J. Group Psychother.*, 15:11-16.

03262 **ESQUIBEL, E. V.,** and **KORT, G.** (1973), Some practical and empirical aspects of group approaches in psychiatric facilities: epilogue on a therapeutic community. *Internat. J. Group Psychother.*, 23:93-103.

03263 **ESQUIBEL, E. V.,** and **KORT, G.** (1969), Structured separation of a key physician from a therapeutic community. *Internat. J. Group Psychother.*, 19:448-453.

03264 **ESSER, P. H.** (1961), (Group psychotherapy with alcoholics.) *Psychiat., Neurol., Neurochir.*, (Amsterdam) 64:365-367.

03265 **ESSER, P. H.** (1961), Group psychotherapy with alcoholics. *Quart. J. Studies Alcohol*, 22:646-651.

03266 **ESSER, P. H.** (1965), (Group therapy for alcoholics.) *Nederl. Tijdschr. Geneeskunde*, (Amsterdam) 109:873-875.

03267 **ESSER, P. H.** (1963), (Psychotherapy for alcoholics. Prognostic aspects.) *Psychiat., Neurol., Neurochir.*, (Amsterdam) 66:138-144.

03268 **ESSER, P. H.** (1963), (Psychotherapy for alcoholics. Prognostic aspects.) *Wiener Med. Wochenschr.*, (Vienna) 113:629-631.

03269 **ESTER, N. J.,** and **HANSON, K. J.** (1976), Sobriety: problems challenges and solutions. *Amer. J. Psychother.*, 30:256.

03270 **ESTERSON, H.** (1973), Time-limited group counseling with parents of preadolescent underachievers: a pilot program. *Proceed., 81st Annual Convention*, American Psychological Association, 8:703-704.

03271 **ESTERSON, H., FELDMAN, C., KRUGSMAN, N. L.,** and **WARSHAW, S.** (1975), Time-limited group counseling with parents of pre-adolescent underachievers: a pilot program. *Psychol. in Schools*, 12:79-84.

03272 **ESTRADE ESPINOSA, M.** (1977), Group psychotherapy aspects of mental health in a program of community psychiatry. *Psquiat., Neurol., Neurocir.*, (Amsterdam) 18:129-133.

03273 **ETHAN, S.** (1978), The question of the dilution of transference in group psychotherapy. *Psychol. Rev.*, 65:569-578.

03274 **ETTERS, L. E.** (1975), Adolescent retardates in a therapy group. *Amer. J. Nursing*, 75:1174-1175.

03275 **ETTKIN, L.,** and **SNIDER, L.** (1972), A model for peer group counseling based on role-playing. *School Counselor*, 19:215-218.

03276 **EUSTER, G. L.** (1980), Review of B. Levine's *Group Psychotherapy: Practice and Development. Soc. Work*, 25:421.

03277 **EUSTER, G. L.** (1971), A system of groups in institutions for the aged. *Soc. Casework*, 52:523-529.

03278 **EVANGELAKIS, M. G.** (1961), De-institutionalization of patients. *Diseases Nerv. System*, 22:26-32.

03279 **EVANS, C.** (1967), An attempt at group therapy as a cure for the smoking habit. *Med. J. Austral.*, (Glebe) 2:702-705.
03280 **EVANS, D. F.** (1971), Clinical papers: Cindy. *Utah Nurse*, 22:8-10.
03281 **EVANS, J.** (1966), Analytic group therapy with delinquents. *Adolescence*, 1:180-196.
03282 **EVANS, J.** (1965), In-patient analytic group therapy of neurotic and delinquent adolescents: some specific problems associated with these groups. *Psychother. & Psychosomat.*, (Basel) 13:265-270.
03283 **EVANS, J. T.** (1950), Objective measurement of the therapeutic group process. Unpublished doctoral dissertation, Harvard University.
03284 **EVANS, N. J.**, and **JARVIS, P. A.** (1980), Group cohesion: a review and evaluation. *Small Group Behav.*, 11:359-370.
03285 **EVANS, R. A.** (1971), *Belief and the Counter Culture*. Philadelphia: Westminster Press.
03286 **EVENSON, E. P.** (1976), The effects of specific cognitive and behavioral structure on early group interaction. *Dissert. Abstr. Internat.*, 37:1430.
03287 **EVERETT, C. A.** (1980), An analysis of AAMFT supervisors: their identity, roles and resources. *J. Marriage & Fam. Ther.*, 6:215.
03288 **EVERETT, H. C.** (1963), Psychiatric seminars for patients. *Ment. Hosp.*, 14:540-544.
03289 **EVERSON, S.** (1977), Sibling counseling. *Amer. J. Nursing*, 77:644-646.
03290 **EVERLY, G. S.** (1975), Leaderless therapy groups: a word of caution. *Group Psychother., Psychodrama & Sociometry*, 28:180-183.
03291 **EVSEEFF, G. S.** (1948), Group psychotherapy in the state hospital. *Diseases Nerv. System*, 9:214-218.
03292 **EWALT, J. R.** (1963), Group psychotherapy and mental health. *Internat. J. Group Psychother.*, 13:263-268.
03293 **EWING, J. A., LONG, V.**, and **WENZEL, G. G.** (1961), Concurrent group psychotherapy of alcoholic patients and their wives. *Internat. J. Group Psychother.*, 11:329-338.
03294 **EXLINE, R. V.** (1963), Explorations in the process of person perception: visual interaction in relation to competition, sex, and need for affiliation. *J. Personality*, 31:1-20.
03295 Experiential training group modified emotional problems. *Roche Report: Front. Hosp. Psychiat.*, 6:2.
03296 **EYSENCK, H. J.** (1952), The effects of psychotherapy: an evaluation. *J. Consult. & Clin. Psychol.*, 16:319-324.
03297 **EZBIEL, H.** (1967), The first session in psychoanalytic group treatment. *Nederl. Tijdschr. Geneeskunde*, (Amsterdam) 111:711-716.
03298 **EZRIEL, H.** (1952), Notes on psychoanalytic group therapy: ii. interpretation and research. *Psychiatry*, 15:119-126.
03299 **EZRIEL, H.** (1950), A psycho-analytic approach to group treatment. *Brit. J. Med. Psychol.*, (London) 23:59-74.
03300 **EZRIEL, H.** (1950), A psychoanalytic approach to the treatment of patients in groups. *J. Ment. Science*, (London) 96:774-779.
03301 **EZRIEL, H.** (1959), The role of transference in psychoanalytic and other approaches to group treatment. *Acta Psychother. Psychosomat. Orthopaedagog. Suppl.*, (Basel) 7:101-116.
03302 **EZRIEL, H.** (1950), Some principles of a psychoanalytic method of group treatment. *Comptes Rendus*, Premier Congres Mondial de Psychiatrie, 5.
03303 **EZRIEL, H.** (1960), Übertragung und psychoanalytische deutung in der einzel-und gruppenpsychotherapie. (Transference and psychoanalytic interpretation in individual and group psychotherapy.) *Psyche*, (Stuttgart) 14:496-523.

F

03304 **FABERHAUGH, S. Y.** (1974), Pain expression and control on a burn care unit: part 2. *Nursing Outlook*, 22:645-650.
03305 **FABIAN, A. A.** (1954), Group treatment of chronic patients in a child guidance clinic. *Internat. J. Group Psychother.*, 4:243-252.
03306 **FABIAN, A. A., CRAMPTON, J. E., and HOLDEN, M. A.** (1951), Parallel group treatment of preschool children and their mothers. *Internat. J. Group Psychother.*, 1:37-50.
03307 **FABRY, J. B.** (1974), Application of logotherapy in small sharing groups. *J. Religion & Health*, 13:128-136.
03308 **FACOS, J.** (1963), Group psychotherapy and psychodrama in a college classroom. *Group Psychother., Psychodrama & Sociometry*, 16:173-176.
03309 **FACOS, J.** (1965), Group psychotherapy and psychodrama in the college classroom: the application of Möreno techniques to the nursery-school trainee. *Group Psychother., Psychodrama & Sociometry*, 18:162-165.
03310 **FADALE, V. E.** (1970), An experimental study of the effects of videotape feedback in a basic encounter group. *Dissert. Abstr. Internat.*, 30:5234A-5235A.
03311 **FAGAN, J., SMITH, R. D., and TIMMS, R. J.** (1968), Three views of an incident at a marathon. *Voices*, 4:54-66.
03312 **FAGIN, C. M.** (1970), *Family-Centered Nursing in Community Psychiatry: Treatment in the Home*. Philadelphia: F. A. Davis.
03313 **FAGIN, C. M.** (1967), Psychotherapeutic nursing, *Amer. J. Nursing*, 67:298-304.
03314 **FAGIN, D. R., DANIELS, R. S., and MARGOLIS, P. M.** (1962), The effect of staff leadership roles on patient participation in activity therapy. *Internat. J. Soc. Psychiat.*, (London) 8:122-128.
03315 **FAGIOLI, M.** (1963), (Group insulin shock therapy and psychotherapy: psychotherapeutic value of the "feeling of schizophrenia.") *Arch. Psicol. Neurol. & Psichiat.*, (Milan) 24:545-557.
03316 **FAHLBERG, E.** (1965), (Group activity and group therapy with alcoholic wives: a few theoretical and methodologic reflections and practical experiences.) *Nordisk Psykiat. Tidsskr.*, (Kungsbacha) 19:11-22.
03317 **FAHNERT, J.** (1970), Group therapy. *Agnes Karll Schwest*, 24:52-53.
03318 **FAIRES, T. M.** (1976-77), A group experience to foster mothering skills in drug-using mothers. *Drug Forum*, 5:229-235.
03319 **FAIRWEATHER, G. W.** (1964), *Social Psychology in Treating Mental Illness: An Experimental Approach*. New York: J. Wiley and Sons.
03320 **FAISON, R. A.** (1972), A study of specified behavioral changes in four groups of sixth grade boys using: (1) group counseling, 2) group counseling and multi-media presentation, 3) multi-media presentation, and 4) no treatment. *Dissert. Abstr. Internat.*, 33:969A.
03321 **FALEK, A.** (1973), Issues and ethics in genetic counseling with Huntington's Disease families. *Psychiat. Forum*, 4:51-60.
03322 **FALGUIERE, J., and OUZILOU, C.** (1978), Practique du psychodrame en groupe. (Practice of group psychodrama.) *Psychother. & Psychosomat.*, (Basel) 29:271-275.
03323 **FALICK, M. D., RUBENSTEIN, B., and LEVITT, M.** (1955), A critical evaluation of the therapeutic use of a club in a school-based mental-hygiene program. *Ment. Hygiene*, 39:63-78.
03324 **FALK-KESSLER, J., and FROSCHAUER, K. H.** (1978), The soap opera: a dynamic group approach for psychiatric patients. *Amer. J. Occupat. Ther.*, 32:317-319.

03325 **FALLOON, I. R., LINDLEY, P., McDONALD, R.,** and **MARKS, I. M.** (1977), Social skills training of out-patient groups: a controlled study of rehearsal and homework. *Brit. J. Psychiat.*, (Ashford) 131:599-609.
03326 **FALTICO, G. J.** (1975), An after-school school without failure: a new therapy model for juvenile probationers. *Correct. & Soc. Psychiat.*, 21:17-20.
03327 **FAMILY SERVICE ASSOCIATION OF AMERICA** (1959), The use of group techniques in the family agency. *New York*: Family Service Association of America.
03328 **FANGER, M.** (1978), A study of autonomy and client-subjects' expectations in a transactional analysis group therapy marathon. *Dissert. Abstr. Internat.*, 38:6146B. (University Microfilms No. 7808059.)
03329 **FANNING, L.** (1972), Massed vs. spaced experiences in personal growth groups. *Dissert. Abstr. Internat.*, 32:4344A.
03330 **FANTEL, E.** (1951), The civilian and army social atom before and after. *Group Psychother., Psychodrama & Sociometry*, 4:66-69.
03331 **FANTEL, E.** (1952), Psychodrama in an army general hospital. *Group Psychother., Psychodrama & Sociometry*, 4:290-300.
03332 **FANTEL, E.** (1945), Psychodrama in an evacuation hospital. *Psychodr. Monogr., No. 18.*
03333 **FANTEL, E.** (1969), Psychodrama in Army and Veterans Administration hospitals: summary. *Group Psychother., Psychodrama & Sociometry*, 22:189-190.
03334 **FANTEL, E.** (1948), Psychodrama in a veteran's hospital. *Sociatry*, 2:47-64.
03335 **FANTEL, E.** (1948), Psychodrama in the counseling of industrial personnel. *Sociatry*, 2:384-398.
03336 **FANTEL, E.** (1947), Repetition and psychodrama. *Sociatry*, 1:236-238.
03337 **FANTEL, E.** (1950), Report on psychodramatic therapy. *Group Psychother., Psychodrama & Sociometry*, 3:55-58.
03338 **FANTEL, E.,** and **SCHNEIDMAN, E. S.** (1947), Psychodrama and the make-a-picture story. *Rorschach Res. Exch.*, 11:42-67.
03339 **FANTUS, R. A., PALMER, H. F.,** and **COLE, E. Y.** (1956), A flexible approach to group therapy. *J. Nerv. & Ment. Diseases*, 124:594-603.
03340 **FANZINO, M. A., GEREN, J. J.,** and **MEIMAN, G. L.** (1976), Group discussion among the terminally ill. *Internat. J. Group Psychother.*, 26:43-48.
03341 **FARBER, L. H.** (1958), The therapeutic despair. *Psychiatry*, 21:7-20.
03342 **FARBEROW, N. L.** (1968), Group psychotherapy with suicidal persons. In: *Suicidal Behaviors: Diagnosis and Management*, ed. H. L. Resnik. Boston: Little, Brown.
03343 **FARBEROW, N. L.** (1972), Vital process in suicide prevention: group psychotherapy as a community of concern. *Life-Threatening Behav.*, 2:239-251.
03344 **FARHOOD, L.** (1975), Choosing a partner for co-therapy. *Perspect. Psychiat. Care*, 13:177-179.
03345 **FARKAS, A.,** and **SHWACHMAN, H.** (1973), Psychological adaptation to chronic illness: a group discussion with cystic fibrosis patients. *Amer. J. Orthopsychiat.*, 43:259-260.
03346 **FARLEY, J. E.** (1979), Family separation-individuation tolerance: a developmental conceptualization of the nuclear family. *J. Marital & Fam. Ther.*, 5:61.
03347 **FARLEY, J. M.** (1980), Leadership variables and self-actualization of participants in short-term counseling groups. *Dissert. Abstr. Internat.*, 40:5390B. (University Microfilms No. 8010885.)

03348 **FARNHAM, R. C.** (1971), The effect of group therapy and grief on mothers' attitudes toward retarded children. *Dissert. Abstr. Internat.*, 3:6713B.

03349 **FARR, G.**, and **LEIK, R. K.** (1971), Computer simulation of interpersonal choice. *Compar. Group Studies*, 2:125-148.

03350 **FARRELL, M. P.** (1976), Patterns in the development of self-analytic groups. *J. Appl. Behav. Science*, 12:523-542.

03351 **FARRELL, M. P., Jr.** (1962), Transference dynamics of group psychotherapy. *Arch. Gen. Psychiat.*, 6:66-76.

03352 **FARRINGTON, J.** (1972), Utilization of psychological constructs by group therapy participants. *Psychol. Record*, 22:387-394.

03353 **FARWELL, G. F., GAMSKY, N. R.**, and **MATHEIU-COUGHLAN, P.** (1974), *The Counselor's Handbook*. New York: Intext.

03354 **FATKA, N. J.** (1963), Dynamic supervision. *Amer. J. Nursing*, 63:104-106.

03355 **FATZER, G.** (1980), *Die Gruppe als Methode: Gruppendynamische und Gruppentherapeutische Verfahren und ihre Wirksamkeit.* (*Group Methods: Group Dynamic and Group Therapy Techniques and Their Efficacy.*) Basel: Beltz.

03356 **FAURE, H.** (1958), *Cure de Sommeil Collective et Psychothérapie de Groupe.* (*Collective Sleep Therapy and Group Psychotherapy.*) Paris: Masson and Cie.

03357 **FAURE, H.** (1957), La cure de sommeil collective avec psychotherapie de groupe: ses rythmes évolutifs. (Collective sleep therapy with group psychotherapy: its evolutional rhythms.) *Evolut. Psychiat.*, (Toulouse) 2:273-302.

03358 **FAURE, H.** (1961), (Drawings of dreams of children during and at the termination of group sleep therapy: their projective richness and psychotherapeutic use.) *Annales Medico-Psychol.*, (Paris) 119:687-712.

03359 **FAURE, H.** (1960), Sleep-induced group psychotherapy: a new utilization of prolonged sleep, with pharmacological sleep induction, monotonous environment and psychosocial interactions. *Internat. J. Group Psychother.*, 10:22-38.

03360 **FAURE, H.**, and **FAURE, M. L.** (1960), (Collective sleep therapy with group psychotherapy in child neuropsychiatry.) *Annales Medico-Psychol.*, (Paris) 118:47-82.

03361 **FAUSTMAN, W. O.** (1978), Comments on use of group-therapy and written instruction in treatment of sexual dysfunction. *Psychol. Reports*, 43:539-542.

03362 **FAVAZZA, A. R.** (1970), Group therapy with schizophrenic patients. *Michigan Med.*, 69:123-126.

03363 **FAVELL, J. E., FAVELL, J. E.**, and **McGIMSEY, J. F.** (1978), Relative effectiveness and efficacy of group vs. individual training of severely retarded persons. *Amer. J. Ment. Deficiency*, 83:104-109.

03364 **FAWCETT, M. S.** (1961), Motivating group therapy in narcotic addicts in a women's prison. *Internat. J. Group Psychother.*, 11:339-346.

03365 **FAWCUS, M.** (1970), Intensive treatment and group therapy programme for the child and adult stammerer. *Brit. J. Disorders Communicat.*, (London) 5:59-65.

03366 **FAY, F. A.** (1974), Effects of a film, a discussion group, and a role-playing experience on architecture students' attitudes, behavioral intentions and actual behavior toward barrier-free design. *Dissert. Abstr. Internat.*, 34:6445A.

03367 **FAY, F. A.** (1968), Ego-stage development and interaction. *Dissert. Abstr. Internat.*, 28:4437-4438.

03368 **FAZEKAS, H.**, and **VARGA, E.** (1969), (Therapeutic possibilities and distortions in a specific form of group therapy in the activity of the psychopath.) *Maggar. Pszichol. Szemle*, (Budapest) 26:242-251.

03369 **FEARING, J. M.**, and **McGREGOR, R.** (1951), Analysis of the group process in the therapeutic session. *Internat. J. Group Psychother.*, 1:126-129.

03370 **FEARING, V. G.** (1978), An authors group for extended care patients. *Amer. J. Occupat. Ther.*, 32:526.

03371 **FEATHERSTONAIGH, H. G.** (1978), A test of a rational-emotive therapy homework hypothesis in self-management counseling groups. *Dissert. Abstr. Internat.*, 39:3390A.

03372 **FEDDER, R.** (1962), *The High School Principal and Staff Develop Group Guidance.* New York: Bureau of Publications, Teachers College, Columbia University.

03373 **FEDER, B.** (1962), Limited goals in short-term group psychotherapy with institutionalized delinquent adolescent boys. *Internat. J. Group Psychother.*, 12:503-507.

03374 **FEDER, B.**, and **RONALL, R. E.** (1980), *Beyond the Hot Seat: Gestalt Approaches to Group.* New York: Brunner/Mazel.

03375 **FEDER, S.** (1973), Motivational factors in self-deferral to experiential groups. *J. Amer. Psychoanal. Assn.*, 21:851-866.

03376 **FEDER, S. M.** (1961), Limited goals in short-term group psychotherapy with institutionalized adolescent delinquent boys. *Dissert. Abstr. Internat.*, 22:1250.

03377 **FEENEY, D. J.**, and **DRANGER, P.** (1976), Alcoholics view group therapy: process and goals. *J. Studies Alcohol*, 37:611-618.

03378 **FEIBEL, C.** (1960), The archaic personality structure of alcoholics and its implications for group therapy. *Internat. J. Group Psychother.*, 10:39-45.

03379 **FEIFEL, H.**, and **SCHWARTZ, A. D.** (1953), Group psychotherapy with acutely disturbed psychotic patients. *J. Consult. & Clin. Psychol.*, 12:113-121.

03380 **FEIL, N. W.** (1967), Group therapy in a home for the aged. *Gerontologist*, 7:192-195.

03381 **FEIN, E.** (1972), Motivating attendance in parent education groups. *Soc. Work*, 17:105-107.

03382 **FEIN, L. G.** (1962), Psychodrama in the treatment of disciplinary problems. *Group Psychother., Psychodrama & Sociometry*, 15:147-153.

03383 **FEIN, L. G.** (1963), The use of psychodrama to strengthen self concepts of student nurses. *Group Psychother., Psychodrama & Sociometry*, 16:161-163.

03384 **FEINBERG, H.** (1959), The ego building technique. *Group Psychother., Psychodrama & Sociometry*, 12:230-235.

03385 **FEINSTEIN, B. B.**, and **CAVANAUGH, C. C.** (1974), Treatment of long-term hospitalized mental patients through the use of volunteers as group leaders. *Internat. J. Group Psychother.*, 24:439-451.

03386 **FEINSTEIN, H. M.**, and **WAXLER, N. E.** (1963), Group dynamics and external life cycles. *Internat. J. Group Psychother.*, 13:141-155.

03387 **FEINSTEIN, H. M., PAUL, N.**, and **ESMIOL, P.** (1964), Group therapy for mothers with infanticidal impulses. *Amer. J. Psychiat.*, 120:882-886.

03388 **FEIT, M.**, and **KOESTERICH, E.** (1969), The need for a shift in emphasis in research relevant to social group workers. *J. Jewish Communal Serv.*, 45:349-360.

03389 **FELDBERG, T. M.** (1969), Group therapy: process and practice. *Mod. Treatm.*, 6:821-841.

03390 **FELDBERG, T. M.** (1958), Treatment of "borderline" psychotics in groups of neurotic patients. *Internat. J. Group Psychother.*, 8:76-84.

03391 **FELDE, R.** (1973), Alcoholics before and after treatment: a study of self-concept changes. *Newsl. Res. Ment. Health & Behav. Sciences*, 15:32-34.

03392 **FELDES, D.** (1978), (Empirical investigations on the position of the therapist in group psychotherapy.) *Psychiat. Neurol. & Med. Psychol.*, (Leipzig) 30:648-656.

03393 **FELDHUSEN, J.**, and **WANG, H.** (1966), Discussion groups in educational psychology. *J. Teacher Educat.*, 17:83-88.

03394 **FELDMAN, D. J.** (1956), The treatment of chronic alcoholism: a survey of current methods. *Annals Internal Med.*, 44:78-87.

03395 **FELDMAN, F.** (1946), Group techniques in a general hospital. *Psychiat. Quart. Suppl.*, 20:276-288.

03396 **FELDMAN, J. G.** (1973), Evaluating the effect of group therapy in the prognosis of coronary patients. *Dissert. Abstr. Internat.*, 34:94B.

03397 **FELDMAN, R. A.** (1974), An experimental study of conformity behavior as a small group phenomenon. *Small Group Behav.*, 5:404-426.

03398 **FELDMAN, R. A.** (1969), Group integration, intense interpersonal dislike, and social group work intervention. *Soc. Work*, 14:30-39.

03399 **FELDMAN, R. A.** (1968), Interrelationships among three bases of group integration. *Sociometry*, 31:30-46.

03400 **FELDMAN, R. A.**, and **WODARSKI, J. S.** (1975), *Contemporary Approaches to Group Treatment.* San Francisco: Jossey-Bass.

03401 **FELDMAN, W.** (1959), Forsg med forskellige former for gruppebehandling of alkoholister pa overforstergarden. (Trials of various forms of group therapy of alcoholics in Overforstergarden.) *Ugeskr. for Laeger*, (Copenhagen) 121:1728-1734.

03402 **FELSTEIN, I.** (1979), Finding safety in numbers. *Health & Soc. Serv. J.*, (London) 89:253.

03403 **FELTON, G. S.** (1973), Changes in i.q. scores of Black low achievers in a process-oriented learning program. *Coll. Student J.*, 7:83-86.

03404 **FELTON, G. S.** (1973), Teaching internalization to middle-level mental health workers in training. *Psychol. Reports*, 32:1279-1282.

03405 **FELTON, G. S.**, and **BIGGS, B. E.** (1973), Psychotherapy and responsibility: teaching internalization behavior to black low achievers through group therapy. *Small Group Behav.*, 4:147-155.

03406 **FELTON, G. S.**, and **BIGGS, B. E.** (1972), Teaching internalization behavior to collegiate low achievers in group psychotherapy. *Psychother.: Theory, Res. & Pract.*, 9:281-283.

03407 **FELTON, G. S.**, and **DAVIDSON, H. R.** (1973), Group counseling can work in the classroom. *Acad. Ther.*, 8:461-468.

03408 **FELTON, R.** (1978), Gestalt therapy and social work. *Internat. J. Soc. Psychiat.*, (London) 24:139.

03409 **FENGLER, J.** (1977), (Group therapy: therapy without therapists—self-help approach.) *Gruppendynamik*, (Stuttgart) 8:307-310.

03410 **FENGLER, J.** (1975), *Verhaltensänderung in Gruppenprozessen.* (*Change in Group Process.*) Heidelberg: Quelle and Meyer.

03411 **FENGLER, J.** (1978), (What is group therapy: an attempt at a more narrow definition.) *Praxis der Psychother.*, 23:41-47.

03412 **FENNELL, N. W.**, and **KENTON, R. W.** (1970), Some effects on personality of a basic encounter group in a community college class. *Dissert. Abstr. Internat.*, 31:2493A.

03413 **FENTON, N.** (1962), *Explorations in the Use of Group Counseling in the County Correctional Program.* Mountain View, CA: Pacific Press.

03414 **FENTON, N.** (1974), *Group Counseling: A Preface to Its Use in Correctional and Welfare Agencies.* Westport, CT: Greenwood Publishers.

03415 **FERCHLAND, E.**, and **WITTICH, G. H.** (1967), Gruppen dynamik und gruppenpsychotherapie einer psychosomatischen kurklinik. (Group dynamics and group psychotherapy at a psychosomatic clinic.) *Psychother. & Psychosomat.*, (Basel) 15:19.

03416 **FERGUSON, B. B.** (1979), A parents' group. *J. Psychiat. Nursing*, 17:24-27.
03417 **FERGUSON, R. E.** (1956), An investigation of behavior of chronic schizophrenics in experimental group psychotherapy. Unpublished doctoral dissertation, Denver University.
03418 **FERNANDES, M. A.**, and **NEVES, F. S. P.** (1951), Psicoterapia de grupo na esquizofrenia: Fundamentos psicopatológicos de uma hipótese de trabalho. (Group psychotherapy of schizophrenia: psychopathologic fundamentals of working hypothesis.) *Portugal Méd.*, 35:483-508.
03419 **FERRACCIOLI, E.** (1968), (Community experiences in juvenile maladjustment syndromes.) *G. Psichiat. & Neuropat.*, (Ferrara) 96:503-517.
03420 **FERRANT, J. P.** (1976), (Group therapy for alcoholics.) *Rev. de Alcoolisme*, (Paris) 22:221-227.
03421 **FERRARA, J. W.** (1973), A verbal interaction technique for studying individuals in small groups. *J. Soc. Psychol.*, 90:207-212.
03422 **FERRARA, L. S.** (1970), Aconselhamento de grupo. (Group counseling.) *Arq. Brasil. Psicol. Apl.*, (Rio de Janeiro) 22:103-121.
03423 **FERREIRA, A. G.** (1980), Transference and transference neurosis in group analysis. *Group Anal.*, (London) 13:93-99.
03424 **FERREIRA, A. J.** (1967), Psychosis and family myth. *Amer. J. Psychiat.*, 21:186-197.
03425 **FERRERO, P.** (1969), New psychological and sociological orientations in Italian psychiatric assistance. *Rev. Psicol. Soc. & Arch. Ital. Psicol. Gen.*, 36:143-166.
03426 **FERRIOLO, M. F.** (1974), The effect of homogeneity and heterogeneity, in terms of group experience, on success in group among counseling students. *Dissert. Abstr. Internat.*, 35:185A.
03427 **FERSCHTUT, G.** (1969), (On group mentality and acting out their transferential interpretation.) *Acta Psichiat. Psicol. Amer. Latina,* (Buenos Aires) 15:324-333.
03428 **FERSCHTUT, G.** (1973), (Group therapist formation.) *Acta Psichiat. Psicol. Amer. Latina*, (Buenos Aires) 19:336-348.
03429 **FERSH, I. J.** (1954), Group therapy as a technique to release tension and anxiety existing prior to regents examinations: an experiment in mental hygiene. *Dissert. Abstr. Internat.*, 14:2393.
03430 **FESHBACH, N. D.** (1967), Nonconformity to experimentally induced group norms of high-status versus low-status members. *J. Personality & Soc. Psychol.*, 6:55-63.
03431 **FEUERLEIN, W.** (1972), Treatment of alcoholics in medical practice. *Soc. Psychiat.*, 7:36-46.
03432 **FICEK, D. E.** (1970), The effects of marathon group counseling on two indices of phenomenological assessment. *Dissert. Abstr. Internat.*, 31:1010A.
03433 **FICHT, J. C.** (1973), Social perception and verbal interactions in tape-directed and counselor-directed encounter groups. *Dissert. Abstr. Internat.*, 34:1611A.
03434 **FIDLER, G. S.** (1969), The task-oriented group as a context for treatment. *Amer. J. Occupat. Ther.*, 23:43-48.
03435 **FIDLER, J. W., Jr.** (1951), The concept of levels in group therapy with psychotics. *Internat. J. Group Psychother.*, 1:51-54.
03436 **FIDLER, J. W., Jr.** (1975), The day hospital: a multimodal group therapy. In: *Group Therapy 1975: An Overiew*, eds. L. R. Wolberg and M. L. Aronson. New York: Stratton Intercontinental Medical Books.
03437 **FIDLER, J. W., Jr.** (1967), Discussion: bridge building in group therapy research. *Internat. J. Group Psychother.*, 17:99-104.
03438 **FIDLER, J. W., Jr.** (1972), Group therapy: future prospects. *Psychiat. Annals*, 2:51-62.

03439 **FIDLER, J. W., Jr.** (1965), Group psychotherapy of psychotics. *Amer. J. Orthopsychiat.*, 35:688-694.

03440 **FIDLER, J. W., Jr.** (1972), A niche for group psychotherapy. *Internat. J. Group Psychother.*, 22:287-305.

03441 **FIDLER, J. W., Jr.** (1951), Possibilities of group therapy with female offenders. *Internat. J. Group Psychother.*, 1:330-336.

03442 **FIDLER, J. W., Jr.** (1970), The relationship of group psychotherapy to "therapeutic" group approaches. *Internat. J. Group Psychother.*, 20:473-494.

03443 **FIDLER, J. W., Jr.** (1980), Review of H. Kellerman's *Group Psychotherapy and Personality: Intersecting Structures.* Amer. J. Psychiat., 137:641.

03444 **FIDLER, J. W., Jr.** (1976), Review of I. D. Yalom's *Theory and Practice of Group Psychotherapy. Internat. J. Group Psychother.*, 26:550-552.

03445 **FIDLER, J. W., Jr.** (1978), Review of J. L. Shapiro's *Methods of Group Psychotherapy and Encounter: A Tradition of Innovation. Amer. J. Psychiat.*, 136:244.

03446 **FIDLER, J. W., Jr.** (1978), Review of M. Grotjahn's and J. Aronson's *The Art and Technique of Analytic Group Therapy.* Amer. J. Psychiat., 135:637.

03447 **FIDLER, J. W., Jr.** (1969), Group psychotherapy with latency age children. *Newsl. Amer. Orthopsychiat. Assn.*, 13:8-9.

03448 **FIDLER, J. W., Jr.**, and **STANDISH, C.** (1948), Observations noted during course of group treatment of psychoses. *Diseases Nerv. System*, 9:24-28.

03449 **FIDLER, J. W., Jr.**, and **WAXENBERG, S. E.** (1971), A profile of group psychotherapy practice among A.G.P.A. members. *Internat. J. Group Psychother.*, 21:34-43.

03450 **FIEBERT, M. S.** (1968), Sensitivity training: an analysis of trainer intervention and group process. *Psychol. Reports*, 22:829-838.

03451 **FIEDLER, F. E.** (1950), A comparison of therapeutic relationships in psychoanalysis, nondirective and Adlerian therapy. *J. Consult. & Clin. Psychol.*, 14:436-445.

03452 **FIEDLER, F. E.** (1949), An experimental approach to preventive psychotherapy. *J. Abnorm. & Soc. Psychol.*, 44:386-393.

03453 **FIEDLER, K.** (1972), (Group therapy in adiposity.) *Zeit. Gesamte Hygiene*, (Berlin) 8:249-254.

03454 **FIEDLER, K.** (1974), (Group therapy in obesity: useful way for reduction of body weight.) *Zeit. Gesamte Hygiene*, (Berlin) 25:33-35.

03455 **FIEDLER, P. E., ORENSTEIN, H., CHILES, J., FRITZ, G.**, and **BREITTS, S.** (1979), Effects of assertive training on hospitalized adolescents and young adults. *Adolescence*, 14:523-528.

03456 **FIELD, G. D.**, and **TECH, M. A.** (1975), Group assertive training for severely disturbed patients. *J. Behav. Ther. & Exper. Psychiat.*, 6:129-134.

03457 **FIELD, L. W.** (1966), An ego-programmed group treatment approach with emotionally disturbed boys. *Psychol. Reports*, 18:47-50.

03458 **FIELDING, B.** (1967), Dreams in group psychotherapy. *Psychother.: Theory, Res. & Pract.*, 4:74-77.

03459 **FIELDING, B.** (1966), The dream and the session. *Psychother. & Psychosomat.*, (Basel) 14:298-312.

03460 **FIELDING, B. B.** (1966), Intense transference reactions and the group therapist. *Psychother. & Psychosomat.*, (Basel) 14:161-170.

03461 **FIELDING, J., GUY, L., HARRY, M.**, and **HOOK, R. H.** (1971), A therapy group observed by medical students. *Internat. J. Group Psychother.*, 21:476-488.

03462 **FIELDING, J. M.** (1974), Problems of evaluative research into group psychotherapy outcome. *Austral. & New Zeal. J. Psychiat.*, (Carlton) 8:97-102.

03463 **FIELDING, J. M.** (1975), A technique for measuring outcome in group psychotherapy. *Brit. J. Med. Psychol.*, (London) 48:189-198.

03464 **FIELDS, B. L.** (1979), Adolescent alcoholism: treatment and rehabilitation. *Fam. & Community Health*, 2:61-90.

03465 **FIELDS, S. J.** (1967), The natural history of a therapy group program. *J. Arkansas Med. Soc.*, 63:275-278.

03466 **FIELDS, S. J.** (1976), *Person Circle: A First Book on Group Psychotherapy and the Small Group Field.* Hicksville, N.Y.: Exposition Press.

03467 **FIELDSTEEL, N. D.** (1980), Therapist or leader: group and family therapy experiences. *Group*, 4:40-42.

03468 **FIENBERG, S. E.**, and **LARNTZ, F. K., Jr.** (1971), Some models for individual-group comparisons and group behavior. *Psychometrika*, 36:349-368.

03469 **FIERZ, H.** (1948), Das problem der masse in der psychotherapie. (The problem of the group in psychotherapy.) *Schweiz. Arch. Neurol., Neurochir. & Psichiat.*, (Zurich) 61:410.

03470 **FIERZ, H. K.** (1947), Das Problem der masse in der psychotherapie. (The problem of the group in psychotherapy.) *Schweiz. Zeit. Psychol. Anwendungen*, (Berne) 6:215-220.

03471 **FIESTER, T. L.** (1972), An investigation of the process and outcomes of the elimination of self-defeating behavior workshops: a group treatment for specific college student problems. *Dissert. Abstr. Internat.*, 33:4830A.

03472 **FIGGE, H. H.** (1972), (Trance mediumism as group therapy: an aspect of the Brazilian Umbanda.) *Zeit. Psychother. Med. Psychol.*, (Stuttgart) 22:149-156.

03473 **FIGLER, H. E.**, and **MANDELL, R. B.** (1976), A network of helpers: part ii. *J. Coll. Placement*, 36:53-57.

03474 **FIKKENS, W. L.** (1972), A participant observation study which examines the development and implementation of a peer group counseling project. *Dissert. Abstr. Internat.*, 33:6086A.

03475 **FIKSO, A.** (1970), Vicarious vs. participant group psychotherapy of underachievers. *Dissert. Abstr. Internat.*, 31:912B.

03476 **FILMER-BENNET, G.**, and **HILLSON, J. S.** (1959), Some child therapy practices. *J. Clin. Psychol.*, 15:105-106.

03477 **FILTER, T. A.** (1978), Individual differences, group process, and change in group psychotherapy. *Dissert. Abstr. Internat.*, 39:2982B. (University Microfilms No. 7822894.)

03478 **FINANDO, S. J., CROTEAU, J. M., SANZ, D.**, and **WOODSON, R.** (1977), The effects of group type on changes concept. *Small Group Behav.*, 8:123-134.

03479 **FINDLEY, J. R.** (1974), The relative effectiveness of rational encounter and basic encounter groups in facilitating changes in self-actualization, self-perception, and interpersonal sensitivity. *Dissert. Abstr. Internat.*, 35:502B.

03480 **FINE, H. J.** (1953), Interaction process: the analysis of a group therapeutic experience in a human relations seminar. Unpublished doctoral dissertation, University of Syracuse.

03481 **FINE, H. J.**, and **ZIMET, C. N.** (1961), Clinical evaluation in psychotherapy. *J. Genetic Psychol.*, 65:353-356.

03482 **FINE, H. J.**, and **ZIMET, C. N.** (1956), A quantitative method of scaling communication and interaction process. *J. Clin. Psychol.*, 12:268-271.

03483 **FINE, L. J.** (1967), Therapist position: report in psychodrama as a function of frame of reference and behavioral stance. *Dissert. Abstr. Internat.*, 28:1189-1190.

03484 **FINE, M. J.** (1969), Counseling with the educable mentally retarded. *Training School Bull.*, 66:105-110.

03485 **FINE, R., DALY, D., and FINE, L.** (1962), Psychodance: an experiment in psychotherapy and training. *Group Psychother., Psychodrama & Sociometry*, 15:203-223.
03486 **FINE, R. H., and DAWSON, J. C.** (1964), A therapy program for the mildly retarded adolescent. *Amer. J. Ment. Deficiency*, 69:23-30
03487 **FINE, S., KNIGHT-WEBB, G., and BREAU, K.** (1976), Volunteer adolescents in adolescent group therapy: effects on patients and volunteers. *Brit. J. Psychiat.*, (Ashford) 129:407-413.
03488 **FINE, S., KNIGHT-WEBB, G., and VERNON, J.** (1977), Selected volunteer adolescents in adolescent group therapy. *Adolescence*, 12:189-197.
03489 **FINEBERG, H. H., and JOHNSON, M.** (1957), Preliminary report of a preschool therapy group in a children's hospital. *Amer. J. Orthopsychiat.*, 27:808-814.
03490 **FINEBERG, H.H., JOHNSON, M., LEIDEN, I., and LYNCH, H.** (1956), Group therapy in a children's hospital: preliminary report. *Pediatrics*, 17:544-548.
03491 **FINEGAN, R., and FINEGAN, K.** (1951), Mixed groups in recreation therapy. *Psychiat. Quart. Suppl.*, 25:206-213.
03492 **FINGER, S.** (1965), Concurrent group therapy with adolescent unmarried mothers and their parents. *Confinia Psychiat.*, (Basel) 8:21-26.
03493 **FINGER, U. D.** (1977), *Narzissmus und Grüppe. (Narcissism and the Group.)* Frankfurt: Fachbuchhandlung Psychologie Verlag.
03494 **FINK, A. B.** (1960), The case for the "open" psychodramatic session: a dialogue. *Group Psychother., Psychodrama & Sociometry*, 13:94-100.
03495 **FINK, A. K.** (1963), The democratic essence of psychodrama. *Group Psychother., Psychodrama & Sociometry*, 16:156-160.
03496 **FINK, A. K.** (1962), Some implications of Moreno's concept of warm-up for education. *Group Psychother., Psychodrama & Sociometry*, 15:69-73.
03497 **FINK, A. K.** (1968), When is a director not a director? when he is a protagonist! (reactions to a session on therapist resistance, annual meeting. ASGPP, 1967). *Group Psychother., Psychodrama & Sociometry*, 21:38-39.
03498 **FINK, B., and HAVILAND, D.** (1976), The rap session. *Amer. Health Care Assn. J.*, 2:10-12.
03499 **FINK, H. K.** (1956), Some therapeutic departures in group therapy. *Psychol Newsl.*, 8:1-11.
03500 **FINKE, J., and WANIEK, W.** (1979), (Different psychiatric inpatients in common group therapy?). *Psychother. & Med. Psychol.*, (Stuttgart) 29:62-65.
03501 **FINKEL, S., and FILLMORE, W.** (1971), Experiences with an older adult group at a private psychiatric hospital. *J. Geriat. Psychiat.*, 4:188-199.
03502 **FINKELSTEIN, L., and BERENT, I.** (1960), Group therapy in a receiving hospital. *Ment. Hosp.*, 11:43-44.
03503 **FINLAY, D. G.** (1974), Acoholism: illness or problem in interaction. *Soc. Work*, 19:398.
03504 **FINN, A.** (1977), (Approach to problems in adolescents through development groups with therapeutic option.) *Rev. Neuropsychiat. Infantile*, (Paris) 25:139-150.
03505 **FINNEY, B. C.** (1954), A scale to measure inter-personal relationships in group psychotherapy. *Group Psychother., Psychodrama & Sociometry*, 7:52-66.
03506 **FINNEY, B. C.** (1968), Some techniques and procedures for teaching psychotherapy. *Psychother.: Theory, Res. & Pract.*, 5:115-119.
03507 **FINNEY, B. C., and van DALSEM, E.** (1969), Group counseling for gifted underachieving high school students. *J. Couns. Psychol.*, 16:87-94.

03508 **FINNEY, J. C.** (1968), Double reversal group psychotherapy: a method of teaching and treatment. *Internat. J. Group Psychother.*, 18:100-103.
03509 **FINNEY, J. C.** (1960), Homosexuality treated by combined psychotherapy. *J. Soc. Ther.*, 6:27-34.
03510 **FINNEY, J. C.** (1955), Interrelationships among three psychotic patients treated simultaneously in individual and group psychotherapy by the same therapist. *Acta Psychother. Psychosomat. Orthopaedagog.*, (Basel) 3:89-99.
03511 **FINOL, G. J.** (1973), The influence of three methods of interpersonal process recall upon parental verbal interaction with a mentally retarded child using short term family psychotherapy. *Dissert. Abstr. Internat.*, 34:1274.
03512 **FINSLEY, F.** (1953), Who gets parole? *Fed. Probation*, 17:26-29.
03513 **FISCHER, D. J.** (1972), Group psychotherapy with manic–depressives. *Med. Annals D.C.*, 41:512-515.
03514 **FISCHER, H. K.** (1973), Some aspects of psychotherapy in patients with addictive personality traits. *Psychosomatics*, 14:27-32.
03515 **FISCHER, I. K.** (1954), Gruppenterapi of tunghore. *Ugeskr. for Laeger*, (Copenhagen) 116:1231-1236.
03516 **FISCHER, J. J.** (1971), Effects of a simulated society experience on interpersonal behavior of a junior college faculty. *Dissert. Abstr. Internat.*, 31:4485-4486.
03517 **FISCHER, K.** (1974), Chemically dependent—but only for one week. *School Health Rev.*, 5:29-31.
03518 **FISCHER, J.**, and **COYLE, B.** (1977), A specialized treatment service for young problem drinkers (16-30 years): treatment results obtained during the first months of the treatment program. *Brit. J. Addict.*, 72:317-319.
03519 **FISCHER, N.**, and **CRABTREE, L. H.** (1969), Sadomasochistic struggle in group psychotherapy. *Amer. J. Psychother.*, 23:495-504.
03528 **FISCHER, W. G.**, and **SAMELSON, C. F.** (1971), Group psychotherapy for selected patients with lower extremity amputations. *Arch. Physical, Med. & Rehab.*, 52:79.
03521 **FISCHHOFF, J.** (1976), After the child dies. *J. Pediat. Psychol.*, 88:140-146.
03522 **FISH, J. M.** (1973), Dissolution of a fused identity in one therapeutic session: a case study. *J. Consult. & Clin. Psychol.*, 41:462-465.
03523 **FISH, L.** (1971), Using social-systems techniques on a crisis unit. *Hosp. & Community Psychiat.*, 22:252-255.
03524 **FISH, N.**, and **CHANDLER, B. E., Jr.** (1969), Group psychotherapy is effective. *J. Maine Med. Assn.*, 60:94-101.
03525 **FISHER, B.** (1953), Group therapy with retarded readers. *J. Educat. Psychol.*, 44:354-360.
03526 **FISHER, B.** (1953), An investigation of the effectiveness of group therapy for the remediation of reading disabilities. Unpublished doctoral dissertation, New York University.
03527 **FISHER, B. A.** (1970), The process of decision modification in small discussion groups. *J. Communicat., 20:51-64.*
03528 **FISHER, B. A.**, and **WERBEL, W. S.** (1979), T-group and therapy group communication. *Small Group Behav.*, 10:475-500.
03529 **FISHER, E. O.** (1975), Divorce counseling and values. *J. Religion & Health*, 14:265-270.
03530 **FISHER, H. S.** (1977), Adolescent group psychotherapy: collaborative opportunity for patients, parents, and therapist. *Internat. J. Group Psychother.*, 27:233-239.
03531 **FISHER, H. S.** (1976), Credo for responsible group therapy with hospitalized adolescents: a menopausal traditionalist copes with fads, feelies,

freaks, and phuck-ups or therapy without ploys, games, or gambits or getting it all together by talking—forgotten therapy. *Clin. Soc. Work J.*, 4:121-126.

03532 **FISHER, I. S.** (1970), The relationship between selected personality characteristics and the effects of training to develop small group productivity skills and interpersonal competence. *Dissert. Abstr. Internat.*, 31:1617A-1618A.

03533 **FISHER, L.** (1977), On the classification of families: a progress report. *Arch. Gen. Psychiat.*, 34:424-433.

03534 **FISHER, L.**, and **WOLFSON, I.** (1953), Group therapy of mental defectives. *Amer. J. Ment. Disease*, 57:463-476.

03535 **FISHER, L. P.** (1974), Small group facilitation of participant goals: the participants' views. *Dissert. Abstr. Internat.*, 35:4169B.

03536 **FISHER, R.** (1948), Therapeutic implications in the use of the group in recreation with psychotics. *Ment. Hygiene*, 32:465-473.

03537 **FISHER, R. J.**, and **WHITE, J. H.** (1976), (A prescriptive model: intergroup conflicts resolved by outside consultants.) *Community Develop. Soc.*, 7:88-98.

03538 **FISHER, S. H.** (1960), The individual psychotherapist looks at group psychotherapy. *Topical Probl. Psychol. & Psychother.*, 2:57-63.

03539 **FISHMAN, C. A.**, and **FISHMAN, D. B.** (1975), A group training program on behavior modification for mothers of children with birth defects: an exploratory study. *Child Psychiat., & Human Develop.*, 6:344.

03540 **FISHMAN, D. B.** (1966), Need and expectancy as determinants of affiliative behavior in small groups. *J. Personality & Soc. Psychol.*, 4:155-164.

03541 **FISHMAN, J. R.**, and **McCORMACK, J.** (1970), "Mental health without walls": community mental health in the ghetto. *Amer. J. Psychiat.*, 126:1461-1467.

03542 **FISHMAN, R.** (1964), The use of a group in dealing with excessive guilt. *J. Hillside Hosp.*, 13:170-176.

03543 **FISHMAN, S. T.**, and **NAWAS, M. M.** (1971), Standardized desensitization method in group treatments. *J. Couns. Psychol.*, 18:520-523.

03544 **FISKO, A.** (1970), Vicarious vs. participant group psychotherapy of underachievers. *Dissert. Abstr. Internat.*, 31:912B.

03545 **FITZIG, C.** (1966), Nursing in an alcohol program. *Amer. J. Nursing*, 66:2218-2221.

03546 **FITZSIMMONS, B. L.** (1971), A comparative study of the effectiveness of three types of hierarchies in the group systematic desensitization of test anxiety. *Dissert. Abstr. Internat.*, 32:1210B.

03547 **FITZSIMMONS, C. J.** (1966), Change in self-concept of adolescents in residential treatment. *Smith Coll. Studies Soc. Work*, 37:35-36.

03548 **FIUMARA, R.** (1976), Therapeutic group analysis and analytical psychology. *J. Anal. Psychol.*, (London) 21:1-24.

03549 **FIX, J. A.**, and **HAFFKE, E. A.** (1976), *Basic Psychological Therapies: Comparative Effectiveness*. New York: Human Science Press.

03550 **FLACK, R.**, and **GRAYER, E.** (1975), A consciousness-raising group for obese women. *Soc. Work*, 20:484-487.

03551 **FLAHERTY, R. W., Jr.** (1974), The effect of muscular relaxation training upon the self-actualization of encounter group participants. *Dissert. Abstr. Internat.*, 35:1443A.

03552 **FLAKE, J. K.** (1961), Milieu therapy for the mentally ill. *J. Rehab.*, 27:12-14.

03553 **FLANAGAN, B. D.** (1977), The effects of group orientation therapy on the adjustment of mobile seventh and eighth grade transfer students. *Dissert. Abstr. Internat.*, 38:1879B.

03554 **FLANDERS, J. P.**, and **THISTLETHWAITE, D. L.** (1967), Effects of familiarization and group discussion upon risk taking. *J. Personality & Soc. Psychol.*, 5:91-97.

03555 **FLANZER, J. P.**, and **APRILL, F. A.** (1977), A diagnostic-treatment model for effective group treatment of drug abusers. *J. Psychedelic Drugs*, 9:143-150.

03556 **FLANZER, J. P.**, and **O'BRIEN, G. M. S. L.** (1977), Family focused treatment and management: multi-discipline training approach. In: *Alcoholism and Drug Dependence: A Multidisciplinary Approach*, eds. J. S. Madden, R. Walker, and W. H. Kenyon. New York: Plenum Press.

03557 **FLECK, R.** (1979), Group dynamic work in balint groups for educators. *Dynam. Psychiat.*, (Berlin) 12:321.

03558 **FLECK, S.** (1976), A general systems approach to severe family pathology. *Amer. J. Psychiat.*, 133:669-673.

03559 **FLEGEL, H.** (1968), (From the custodial room to therapeutic community: the psychiatric hospital on the way to psychotherapeutic institute.) *Zeit. Psychother. Med. Psychol.*, (Stuttgart) 18:41-49.

03560 **FLEGEL, H.** (1963), (Group changes in a psychiatric ward as sociotherapy. Contribution to the sociology of hospital psychiatry.) *Nervenarzt.*, 34:384-391.

03561 **FLEGEL, H.** (1968), Problems and institution of a department of group psychiatry and behavioral research. *Psychiat. Clin.*, (Basel) 1:329-339.

03562 **FLEGEL, H.** (1968), (The role and concept of a department for group psychiatry and clinical behavioral research.) *Psychiat. Clin.*, (Basel) 1:329-339.

03563 **FLEGEL, H.** (1963), (Selective regrouping in a closed psychiatric ward with a view toward favoring social behavior.) *Annales Medico-Psychol.*, (Paris) 121:41-48.

03564 **FLEIGER, D. L.**, and **ZINGLE, H. W.** (1973), Covert sensitization treatment with alcoholics. *Can. Counselor*, (Ottawa) 7:269-277.

03565 **FLEISCHL, M. F.** (1962), The understanding and utilization of social and adjunctive therapies. *Amer. J. Psychother.*, 16:255-265.

03566 **FLEISHER, A. N.** (1977), Diagnostic and selection consideration in group therapy with latency children. *Smith Coll. Studies Soc. Work*, 48:48-49.

03567 **FLEISHER, D. S.** (1968), Composition of small learning groups in medical education. *J. Med. Educat.*, 43:349-355.

03568 **FLEISHER, D. S.**, and **LEVIN, J. L.** (1970), A second study in composition of small learning groups in medical education. *J. Med. Educat.*, 45:929-938.

03569 **FLEMING, C. M.** (1959), Therapies in the school situation. *Acta Psychother. Psychosomat. Orthopaedagog. Suppl.*, (Basel) 7:117-123.

03570 **FLEMING, L.**, and **SNYDER, W. U.** (1947), Social and personal changes following nondirective group play therapy. *Amer. J. Orthopsychiat.*, 17:101-116.

03571 **FLESCHER, J.** (1957), The economy of aggression and anxiety in group formations. *Internat. J. Group Psychother.*, 7:31-39.

03572 **FLESCHER, J.** (1951), Observations on S. R. Slavson's film "Activity group therapy." *Internat. J. Group Psychother.*, 1:278-280.

03573 **FLESCHER, J.** (1953), On different types of countertransference. *Internat. J. Group Psychother.*, 3:357-372.

03574 **FLETCHER, R.** (1971), Correlations of personality traits and intramural participation. *Percept. & Motor Skills*, 32:242.

03575 **FLEXO, P. A.** (1976), Self-concept change in encounter groups: the effects of verbalization and feedback. *Dissert. Abstr. Internat.*, 36:5789.

03576 **FLINT, W.**, and **DELOACH, C.** (1975), A parent involvement program model for handicapped children and their parents. *Except. Children*, 41:556-557.

03577 **FLOCH, M.** (1946), Group therapy in a women's prison. *Fed. Probat.*, 10:34-36.

03578 **FLOOD, B. J.** (1972), Development of group "language." *Dissert. Abstr. Internat.*, 33:1835A.

03579 **FLORAK, E. L.** (1970), Changes in selected variables resulting from group counseling in a developmental reading course. *Dissert. Abstr. Internat.*, 31:5123A.

03580 **FLÓREZ, B. H.** (1979), (Group psychotherapy in cancer patients.) *Rev. Latinoamer. Psicol.*, (Bogota) 11:47-63.

03581 **FLOWERMAN, S. H.** (1948), The sociodramatic denotation of the status of a secondary school principal. *Sociatry*, 2:220-225.

03582 **FLOWERMAN, S. H.** (1960), Status affirmation and status denial in group psychotherapy. *Topical Probl. Psychol. & Psychother.*, 2:97-118.

03583 **FLOWERS, C. R.** (1979), Review of R. E. Hartbauer's *Counseling in Communicative Disorders*. *Quart. J. Speech*, 65:344.

03584 **FLOWERS, J. V.** (1979), Differential outcome effects of simple advice, alternatives, and instruction in group psychotherapy. *Internat. J. Group Psychother.*, 29:305-316.

03585 **FLOWERS, J. V.** (1978), The effect of therapist support and encounter on the percentage of client-client interactions in group therapy. *J. Community Psychol.*, 6:69-73.

03586 **FLOWERS, J. V.**, and **BOORAEM, C. D.** (1976), Use of tokens to facilitate outcome and monitor process in group psychotherapy. *Internat. J. Group Psychother.*, 26:191-201.

03587 **FLOWERS, J. V., BOORAEM, C. D.**, and **SEACAT, G. F.** (1974), The effect of positive and negative feedback on members' sensitivity to other members in group therapy. *Psychother.: Theory, Res. & Pract.*, 11:346-350.

03588 **FLOWERS, J. V., BOORAEM, C. D., BROWN, T. R.**, and **HARRIS, D. E.** (1974), An investigation of a technique for facilitating patient to patient therapeutic interactions in group therapy. *J. Community Psychol.*, 2:39-42.

03589 **FLOWERS, J. V.**, and **GUERRA, J.** (1974), The use of client coaching in assertion training with large groups. *Community Ment. Health J.*, 10:414-417.

03590 **FLOWERS, L. K.** (1976), The development of a program for treating obesity. *Hosp. & Community Psychiat.*, 27:342-345.

03591 **FLUET, N. R., HOLMES, G. R.**, and **GORDOL, L. C.** (1980), Adolescent group psychotherapy: a modified fishbowl format. *Adolescence*, 15:75-82.

03592 **FOGEL, A. J.** (1974), Development of a replicable group vocational counseling procedure for use with community college students. *Dissert. Abstr. Internat.*, 34:6972A.

03593 **FOGELMAN, E.**, and **SAVRAN, B.** (1980), Brief group therapy with offspring of holocaust survivors: leaders' reactions. *Amer. J. Orthopsychiat.*, 50:96.

03594 **FOLEY, T. J.** (1970), The efficiency of group psychotherapy with first-term airmen at an air force technical training center. *Correct. Psychiat. & J. Soc. Ther.*, 16:46-50.

03595 **FOLLINGSTAD, D. R., KILMANN, P. R.**, and **ROBINSON, E. A.** (1976), Prediction of self-actualization in male participants in a group conducted by female leaders. *J. Clin. Psychol.*, 32:706-712.

03596 Follow-up of discharged patients called major "treatment" modality. (1968), *Roche Report: Front. Hosp. Psychiat.*, 5:3, 11.

03597 **FONG, J. Y., SCHNEIDER, M.**, and **WALLS-COOKE, P.** (1978), Multiple family group therapy with a tri-therapist team. *Nurs. Clinics North Amer.*, 13:685-699.

03598 **FONSECA FILHO, J. de S.** (1970), Abandonment in group therapy. The problem of the initial session. *Hospital*, (Rio de Janeiro) 77:2101-2102.
03599 **FONTAINE, P. J.** (1969/1970), (Psychodrama with institutionalized handicapped adolescents.) *Bull. de Psychol.*, (Paris) 23:923-926.
03600 **FONTAN, M.**, and **LANGE, G.** (1966), Les activités de groupe dans le service de desintoxication ethylique de l'Hôpital de la Charité de Lille. (Group activities on the dealcoholization service of l'Hôpital de la Charité de Lille.) *Annales Medico-Psychol.*, (Paris) 2:137-154.
03601 **FONTANA, A. E.** (1968), Investigacion y aplicacion de diferentes tecnicas psicoterapeuticas durante un lapso de diez años. (The study and application of different psychotherapeutic techniques over a ten year period.) *Acta Psiquiat. Psicol. Amer. Latina*, (Buenos Aires) 14:124-133.
03602 **FONTANA, A. E.** (1967), Techniques of psychotherapy applied in a therapeutic community: particularly on intensive group psychotherapy. *Psychother. & Psychosomat.*, (Basel) 15:22.
03603 **FONTANA, A. E.** (1977), *El Tiempo y los Grupos. (Time and Groups.)* Buenos Aires: Editorial Vancu.
03604 **FONTANA, A. F.**, and **DOWDS, B. N.** (1976), AA and group therapy for alcoholics: application of world hypothesis scale. *J. Studies Alcohol*, 37:675-682.
03605 **FORD, B. G.**, and **WEST, L. W.** (1979), Human relations training for families: a comparative strategy. *Can. Counselor*, (Ottawa) 13:102.
03606 **FORD, C. V.**, and **LONG, K. D.** (1977), Group psychotherapy of somatizing patients. *Psychother. & Psychosomat.*, (Basel) 28:294-304.
03607 **FORD, D. H.** (1962), Group and individual counseling in modifying behavior. *Personnel & Guid. J.*, 40:770-773.
03608 **FORD, L. A.** (1972), A process analysis of changes in positive affect in a weekend laboratory training group. *Dissert. Abstr. Internat.*, 33:4831A.
03609 **FOREMAN, M. E.** (1966), Some empirical correlates of psychological health. *J. Coun. Psychother.*, 13:3-11.
03610 **FORER, B. R.** (1961), Group psychotherapy with outpatient schizophrenics. *Internat. J. Group Psychother.*, 11:188-195.
03611 **FOREST, J.** (1969/1970), (Psychodrama, sociometry and the teaching of architecture.) *Bull. de Psychol.*, (Paris) 23:799-815.
03612 **FOREST, J. L. P.** (1950), *Psychotherapy in a small mental hospital. Edgewood Med. Monogr.*, 1:169-176.
03613 **FORESTER, B. M.**, and **SWILLER, H.** (1972), Transsexualism: review of syndrome and presentation of possible successful therapeutic approach. *Internat. J. Group Psychother.*, 22:343-351.
03614 **FOREYT, J. P.**, and **FELTON, G. S.** (1970), Change in behavior of hospitalized psychiatric patients in a milieu therapy setting. *Psychother.: Theory, Res. & Pract.*, 7:139-141.
03615 **FORISHA, B. L., HOFFMAN, M.**, and **HOLTZMAN, R.** (1979), The gestalt growth experience. *Small Group Behav.*, 10:332-342.
03616 **FORIZS, L.** (1955), Brief intensive group psychotherapy for treatment of alcoholics. *Psychiat. Quart. Suppl.*, 29:43-70.
03617 **FORIZS, L.** (1974), A schizophrenic patient in a large group treatment setting. *J. Nat. Assn. Priv. Psychiat. Hosp.*, 6:27-34.
03618 **FORIZS, L.** (1966), Some common denominators in psychotherapeutic modalities. *Diseases Nerv. System*, 27:783-788.
03619 **FORMAN, L. H.** (1972), Results of transactional analysis weekend group therapy. *Transactional Anal. J.*, 2:163-164.
03620 **FORMAN, M.** (1971), The alienated resident and the alienating institution: a case for peer group intervention. *Soc. Work*, 16:47-55.
03621 **FORMAN, M.** (1967), Conflict, controversy, and confrontations in group work with older adults. *Soc. Work*, 12:80-85.

03622 **FORSTER, V.**, and **STROTZKA, H.** (1958), Sociometric investigation with Hungarian refugees as a basis for a mental health program. *Group Psychother., Psychodrama & Sociometry*, 11:345-348.

03623 **FORT, J. P.** (1955), The psychodynamics of drug addiction and group psychotherapy. *Internat. J. Group Psychother.*, 5:150-156.

03624 **FORTH, M. W.**, and **JACKSON, M.** (1976), Group psychotherapy in management of bronchial asthma. *Brit. J. Med. Psychol.*, 49:257-260.

03625 **FORTIN, J. N.**, and **ABSE, D. W.** (1956), Group psychotherapy with peptic ulcer: a preliminary report. *Internat. J. Group Psychother.*, 6:383-391.

03626 **FORTUNE, H. O.** (1970), The pros and cons of sensitivity training. *Nursing Outlook*, 18:24-29.

03627 **FORWARD, J. R.** (1969), Group achievement motivation and individual motives to achieve success and to avoid failure. *J. Personality*, 37:297-309.

03628 **FOSDICK, C. J. H.** (1972), The effect of time organization on the process and outcome of encounter groups. *Dissert. Abstr. Internat.*, 33:5491A.

03629 **FOSTER, A. L.** (1972), The use of encounter groups in the church. *J. Pastoral Care*, 26:148-155.

03630 **FOSTER, B. W.** (1972), An investigation of changes in levels of dogmatism, self-concept, needs for inclusion, affection and control as a result of encounter group experiences with selected graduate students. *Dissert. Abstr. Internat.*, 33:2708A.

03631 **FOSTER, J.** (1978), Loneliness: the group solution to isolation. part 2. *Nursing Mirror*, (London) 147:28-29.

03632 **FOSTER, L. M.** (1975), Group psychotherapy: a pool of legal witnesses? *Internat. J. Group Psychother.*, 25:50-53.

03633 **FOSTER, R. M.** (1977), Parenting the child with a behavior disorder: a family approach. *Pediat. Annual*, 6:637-645.

03634 **FOSTER, T.** (1978), Inpatient group therapy with observer feedback: a pilot study. *Psychiat. Forum*, 7:23-27.

03635 **FOULDS, M. L.** (1971), Changes in locus of internal-external control: a growth group experience. *Compar. Group Studies*, 2:293-300.

03636 **FOULDS, M. L.** (1970), Effects of a personal growth group on a measure of self-actualization. *J. Human. Psychol.*, 10:33-38.

03637 **FOULDS, M. L.** (1973), Effects of a personal growth on ratings of self and others. *Small Group Behav.*, 4:508-512.

03638 **FOULDS, M. L.** (1972), The experiential-gestalt growth group experience. *J. Coll. Student Personnel*, 13:48-52.

03639 **FOULDS, M. L.** (1975), The experiential-gestalt growth group experience. In: *The Innovative Therapies: Critical and Creative Contributions*, eds. R. M. Suinn and R. G. Weigel. New York: Harper and Row.

03640 **FOULDS, M. L.** (1972), The growth center model: proactive programs of a university counseling service. *Compar. Group Studies*, 3:77-88.

03641 **FOULDS, M. L.** (1974), Marathon groups: changes in perceived locus of control. *J. Coll. Student Personnel*, 15:8-11.

03642 **FOULDS, M. L.**, and **GUINAN, J. F.** (1973), Marathon groups: changes in ratings of self and others. *Psychother.: Theory, Res. & Pract.*, 10:30-32.

03643 **FOULDS, M. L.**, **GUINAN, J. F.**, and **HANNIGAN, P.** (1974), Marathon groups: changes in scores on the California Psychological Inventory. *J. Coll. Student Personnel*, 15:474-479.

03644 **FOULDS, M. L.**, **GUINAN, J. F.**, and **WAREHIME, R. G.** (1974), Marathon group: changes in a measure of dogmatism. *Small Group Behav.*, 5:387-392.

03645 **FOULDS, M. L.**, and **HANNIGAN, P. S.** (1976), Effects of gestalt marathon workshops on measured self-actualization: a replication and follow-up. *J. Couns. Psychol.*, 23:60-65.

03646 **FOULDS, M. L., and HANNIGAN, P. S.** (1976), Effects of psychomotor group therapy on locus of control and social desirability. *J. Human. Psychol.*, 16:81-88.

03647 **FOULDS, M. L., and HANNIGAN, P. S.** (1976), Gestalt marathon group: does it increase reported self-actualization? *Psychother.: Theory, Res. & Pract.*, 13:378-383.

03648 **FOULDS, M. L., and HANNIGAN, P. S.** (1976), A gestalt marathon workshop: effects on extroversion and neuroticism. *J. Coll. Student Personnel*, 17:50-54.

03649 **FOULDS, M. L., WRIGHT, J. C., and GUINAN, J. F.** (1970), Marathon group: a six month follow-up. *J. Coll. Student Personnel*, 11:426-431.

03650 **FOULDS, M. L.** (1970), Changes in ratings of self and others as a result of a marathon group. *Compar. Group Studies*, 1:349-355.

03651 **FOULKES, S. H.** (1960), The application of group concepts to the treatment of the individual in the group. *Topical Probl. Psychol. & Psychother.*, 2:1-56.

03652 **FOULKES, S. H.** (1960), The application of group concepts to the treatment of the individual in the group. In: *Sources of Conflict in Contemporary Group Psychotherapy*, ed. H. C. Hulse. Basel: S. Karger.

03653 **FOULKES, S. H.** (1951), Concerning leadership in group-analytic psychotherapy. *Internat. J. Group Psychother.*, 1:319-329.

03654 **FOULKES, S. H.** (1952), Contributions to a symposium on group therapy. *Brit. J. Med. Psychol.*, (London) 25:229-234.

03655 **FOULKES, S. H.** (1965), Einige grundbegriffe der gruppen-psychotherapie. (Some basic notions of group psychotherapy.) *Zeit. Psychother. Med. Psychol.*, (Stuttgart) 15:125-19.

03656 **FOULKES, S. H.** (1946), Group analysis in a military neurosis center. *Lancet*, 250:303-306.

03657 **FOULKES, S. H.** (1976), Group-analytic approach and problems of large groups. *Arch. Psicol., Neurol. & Psichiat.*, (Milan) 35:423-445.

03658 **FOULKES, S. H.** (1957), Group-analytic dynamics with specific reference to psychoanalytic concepts. *Internat. J. Group Psychother.*, 7:40-52.

03659 **FOULKES, S. H.** (1954), Group analytic observation as indicator for psycho-analytic treatment. *Internat. J. Psycho-Anal.*, (London) 35:263-266.

03660 **FOULKES, S. H.** (1975), *Group Analytic Psychotherapy: Method and Principles*. London: Gordon and Breach.

03661 **FOULKES, S. H.** (1955), Group analytic psychotherapy: a short account. *Acta Psychother. Psychosom. Orthopaedagog.*, (Basel) 3:313-319.

03662 **FOULKES, S. H.** (1965), Group psychotherapy: the group-analytic view—a contribution to the discussion. *Psychother. & Psychosomat.*, (Basel) 13:150-154.

03663 **FOULKES, S. H.** (1968), Group dynamics and group analysis: a transatlantic view. *J. Group Psychoanal. & Process*, (London) 1:47-75.

03664 **FOULKES, S. H.** (1961), Group processes and the individual in the therapeutic group. *Brit. J. Med. Psychol.*, (London) 34:23-31.

03665 **FOULKES, S. H.** (1950), Group therapy: a short survey and orientation with particular reference to group analysis. *Brit. J. Med. Psychol.*, (London) 23:199-205.

03666 **FOULKES, S. H.** (1966), Illness as a social process. *Psychother. & Psychosomat.*, (Basel) 14:217-225.

03667 **FOULKES, S. H.** (1948), *Introduction to Group-Analytic psychotherapy*. London: W. Heinemann.

03668 **FOULKES, S. H.** (1972), Oedipus conflict and regression. *Internat. J. Group Psychother.*, 22:3-15.

03669 **FOULKES, S. H.** (1946), On group analysis. *Internat. J. Psycho-Anal.*, (London) 27:46-51.

03670 **FOULKES, S. H.** (1975), On group-analytic psychotherapy. In: *Group Psychotherapy and Group Function*, 2d ed., eds. M. Rosenbaum and M. M. Berger. New York: Basic Books.

03671 **FOULKES, S. H.** (1968), On interpretation in group analysis. *Internat. J. Group Psychother.*, 18:432-434.

03672 **FOULKES, S. H.** (1946), Principles and practice of group therapy. *Bull. Menninger Clinic*, 10:85-89.

03673 **FOULKES, S. H.** (1975), Problems of the large group from a group analytic point of view. In: *The Large Group: Dynamics and Therapy*, ed. L. Kreeger. London: Constable.

03674 **FOULKES, S. H.** (1956), Progress in psychotherapy, 1956: comments. *Group Psychother., Psychodrama & Sociometry*, 9:305-310.

03675 **FOULKES, S. H.** (1959), Psychoanalysis, group psychotherapy, group analysis: a bird's eye view of present trends. *Acta. Psychother. Psychosomat. Orthopaedagog.*, (Basel) 7:119-131.

03676 **FOULKES, S. H.** (1951), Remarks on group analytic psychotherapy. *Group Psychother., Psychodrama & Sociometry*, 4:56-59.

03677 **FOULKES, S. H.** (1975), Some personal observations. *Internat. J. Group Psychother.*, 25:169-172.

03678 **FOULKES, S. H.** (1953), Some similarities and differences between psychoanalytic principles and group analytic principles. *Brit. J. Med. Psychol.*, (London) 26:30-35.

03679 **FOULKES, S. H.** (1965), *Therapeutic Group Analysis*. New York: International Universities Press.

03680 **FOULKES, S. H.**, and **ANTHONY, E. J.** (1957), *Group Psychotherapy: The Psychoanalytic Approach*. Baltimore: Penguin Books.

03681 **FOULKES, S. H.**, and **ANTHONY, E. J.** (1965), *Group Psychotherapy: The Psychoanalytic Approach*, 2d ed. Baltimore: Penguin Books.

03682 **FOULKES, S. H.**, and **ANTHONY, E. J.** (1965), *Group Psychotherapy: The Psychoanalytic Approach*. Middlesex, England: Penguin.

03683 **FOULKES, S. H.**, and **ANTHONY, E. J.** (1957), *Group Psychotherapy: The Psychoanalytic Approach*. Harmondsworth, Middlesex: Penguin Books.

03684 **FOULKES, S. H.**, and **LEWIS, E.** (1944), Group analysis. *Brit. J. Med. Psychol.*, (London) 20:175-184.

03685 **FOX, D. J.** (1955), The effect of increasing the available time for problem solving on the relative quality of decisions: written by individuals and by groups. *Dissert. Abstr. Internat.*, 15:1250-1251.

03686 **FOX, J.** (1960), The systematic use of hypnosis in individual and group psychotherapy. *Internat. J. Clin. & Exper. Hypnosis*, 8:109-114.

03687 **FOX, P. B.** (1973), The effects of a modeling procedure on the verbal behavior of delinquent boys in a counseling group. *Dissert. Abstr. Internat.*, 33:5491.

03688 **FOX, R.** (1962), Group psychotherapy with alcoholics. *Internat. J. Group Psychother.*, 12:56-63.

03689 **FOX, R.** (1975), Group psychotherapy with alcoholics. In: *Group Psychotherapy and Group Function*, 2d ed., eds. M. Rosenbaum and M. M. Berger. New York: Basic Books.

03690 **FOX, R.** (1965), Modifications of group psychotherapy for alcoholics. *Amer. J. Orthopsychiat.*, 35:258-259.

03691 **FOX, R.** (1966), Modified group psychotherapy for alcoholics. *Postgrad. Med.*, 39:134 passim.

03692 **FOX, R.** (1968), A multidisciplinary approach to the treatment of alcoholism. *Internat. J. Psychiat.*, 5:34-44.

03693 **FOX, R. E.** (1968), The effect of psychotherapy on the spouse. *Fam. Process*, 7:7-16.

03694 **FOX, R. P., GRAHAM, M. B.,** and **GILL, M. J.** (1972), A therapeutic revolving door. *Arch. Gen. Psychiat.*, 26:179-182.

03695 **FOX, V.** (1962), Group methods in criminology. *Group Psychother., Psychodrama & Sociometry*, 15:40-45.

03696 **FOX, V.,** and **LOWE, G. D.** (1968), Day-hospital treatment of the alcoholic patient. *Quart. J. Studies Alcohol*, 29:634-641.

03697 **FRAAS, L. A.** (1972), Differential effects of reward and punishment on group performance by normal and psychiatric males. *Psychol. Reports*, 30:399-403.

03698 **FRAAS, L. A.** (1972), Leadership selection and group performance: an expanded replication. *J. Soc. Psychol.*, 87:317-318

03699 **FRAGES, S.** (1978), Family therapy: a literature review. *Fam. Ther.*, 5:105.

03700 **FRAILBERG, S.** (1978), Psychoanalysis and social work: a reexamination of the issues. *Smith Coll. Studies Soc. Work*, 48:87.

03701 **FRAIBERG, S. H.** (1947), Studies in group symptom formations. *Amer. J. Orthopsychiat.*, 17:278-289.

03702 **FRAMO, J. L.** (1979), Family theory and therapy. *Amer. Psychologist*, 34:998.

03703 **FRAMO, J. L.** (1973), Marriage therapy in a couples group. *Sem. Psychiat.*, 5:207-217.

03704 **FRAN, K.** (1968), Indications for psychoanalytic group therapy. *Psyche*, (Stuttgart) 22:778-785.

03705 **FRANCE, A. W.** (1977), Redefining and paraphrasing. *Transactional Anal. J.*, 7:318-322.

03706 **FRANCES, A., CLARKIN, J. F.,** and **MARACHI, J. P.** (1980), Selection criteria for outpatient group psychotherapy. *Hosp. & Community Psychiat.*, 31:245.

03707 **FRANCES, A.,** and **SCHIFF, M.** (1976), Popular music as a catalyst in the induction of therapy groups for teenagers. *Internat. J. Group Psychother.*, 26:393-398.

03708 **FRANCES, D.** (1980), Review of T. Douglas's *Basic Groupwork. Group*, 4:59-60.

03709 **FRANCH i BATTLE, J.** (1974), *El Grup-Classe.* (*The Group Class.*) Barcelona: Editorial Nova Terra.

03710 **FRANCK, B. M.** (1972), Phases of development of a multinational training group. *Compar. Group Studies*, 3:3-50.

03711 **FRANCK, P.** (1969), Psychodrama offers new vista to parolees. *J. Rehab.*, 35:28-29.

03712 **FRANK, B.** (1953), Areas of cooperation between psychiatry, psychology and education. *Proceed., Amer. Prison Assn.*, 83:4-6.

03713 **FRANK, G. H.** (1953), The literature on countertransference: a survey. *Internat. J. Group Psychother.*, 3:441-452.

03714 **FRANK, J.** (1959), Treatment approach to acting-out character disorders. *J. Hillside Hosp.*, 8:42-53.

03715 **FRANK, J.,** and **ASCHER, E.** (1956), Therapeutic emotional interactions in group treatment. *Postgrad. Med.*, 19:36-40.

03716 **FRANK, J. D.** (1953), Areas of research in group psychotherapy. *Proceed. Assn. Res. Nerv. Diseases*, 31:119-130.

03717 **FRANK, J. D.** (1952), The effects of interpatient and group influences in a general hospital. *Internat. J. Group Psychother.*, 2:127-138.

03718 **FRANK, J. D.** (1952), Group methods in psychotherapy. *J. Soc. Issues*, 8:35-44.

03719 **FRANK, J. D.** (1959), *Group Methods in Therapy*, 1st ed. New York: Public Affairs Committee.

03720 **FRANK, J. D.** (1964), Group psychology and the elimination of war. *Internat. J. Group Psychother.*, 14:41-48.

03721 **FRANK, J. D.** (1963), Group psychotherapy with psychiatric out-patients. *Group Psychother., Psychodrama & Sociometry*, 16:132-140.

03722 **FRANK, J. D.** (1950), Group psychotherapy in relation to research. *Group Psychother., Psychodrama & Sociometry*, 3:197-203.

03723 **FRANK, J. D.** (1975), Group psychotherapy research 25 years later. *Internat. J. Group Psychother.*, 25:159-162.

03724 **FRANK, J. D.** (1953), Group psychotherapy. *U.S. Vet. Admin. Tech. Bull.*, (June 30) pp. 10-91.

03725 **FRANK, J. D.** (1975), Group therapy in the mental hospital. In: *Group Psychotherapy and Group Function*, 2d ed., eds. M. Rosenbaum and M. M. Berger. New York: Basic Books.

03726 **FRANK, J. D.** (1961), *Persuasion and Healing: A Comparative Study of Psychotherapy*. Baltimore: Johns Hopkins University Press.

03727 **FRANK, J. D.** (1957), Some aspects of cohesiveness and conflict in psychiatric outpatient groups. *Bull. Johns Hopkins Hosp.*, 101:224-231.

03728 **FRANK, J. D.** (1957), Some determinants, manifestations, and effects of cohesiveness in therapy groups. *Internat. J. Group Psychother.*, 7:53-63.

03729 **FRANK, J. D.** (1951), Some problems of research in group psychotherapy. *Internat. J. Group Psychother.*, 1:78-81.

03730 **FRANK, J. D.** (1975), Some problems of research in group psychotherapy. *Internat. J. Group Psychother.*, 25:141-145.

03731 **FRANK, J. D.** (1955), Some values of conflict in therapeutic groups. *Group Psychother., Psychodrama & Sociometry*, 8:142-151.

03732 **FRANK, J. D.** (1961), Therapy in a group setting. In: *Contemporary Psychotherapies*, ed. M. I. Stein. New York: Free Press.

03733 **FRANK, J. D.**, and **ASCHER, E.** (1951), Corrective emotional experiences in group therapy. *Amer. J. Psychiat.*, 108:126-131.

03734 **FRANK, J. D., ASCHER, E., MARGOLIN, J. B., NASH, H., STONE, A. R.**, and **VARON, E. J.** (1952), Behavioral patterns in early meetings of therapeutic groups. *Amer. J. Psychiat.*, 108:771-778.

03735 **FRANK, J. D., GLIEDMAN, L. H., IMBER, S. D., NASH, E. H., Jr.**, and **STONE, A. R.** (1957), Why patients leave psychotherapy. *Arch. Neurol. Psychiat.*, 77:283-299.

03736 **FRANK, J. D., GLIEDMAN, L. H., IMBER, S. D., STONE, A. R.**, and **NASH, E. H., Jr.** (1959), Patients' expectancies and relearning as factors determining improvement in psychotherapy. *Amer. J. Psychiat.*, 115:961-968.

03737 **FRANK, J. D., MARGOLIN, J., NASH, H. T., STONE, A. R., VARON, E.**, and **ASCHER, E.** (1952), Two behavior patterns in therapeutic groups and their apparent motivation. *Human Relat.*, 5:289-317.

03738 **FRANK, J. D., MASTRANGELO, G., SLAVSON, S. R., JORGENSEN, C., RICKMAN, J., ALONSO, A. M.**, and **KEMPER W.** (1948), Advances in group and individual therapy: discussion. In: *International Congress on Mental Health, Vol. 3*, ed. J. C. Flugel. Proceed., Internat. Conf. Med. Psychother. New York: Columbia University Press.

03739 **FRANK, J. L.** (1978), A weekly group meeting for children on a pediatric ward: therapeutic and practical functions. *Internat. J. Psychiat. Med.*, 8:267-284.

03740 **FRANK, K.** (1968), (Indications for psychoanalytic group therapy.) *Psyche*, (Stuttgart) 22:778-785.

03741 **FRANK, L. K.** (1956), The place of the mental hygiene clinic in a group work agency. *Ment. Hygiene*, 40:237-250.

03742 **FRANK, M., FERDINAND, B.**, and **BAILEY, W.** (1975), Peer group counseling: a challenge to grow. *School Counselor*, 22:267-272.

03743 **FRANK, M. G.** (1976), Modifications of activity group therapy: responses of ego-impoverished children. *Clin. Soc. Work J.*, 4:102-109.
03744 **FRANK, M. G.**, and **ZILBACH, J.** (1968), Current trends in group therapy with children. *Internat. J. Group Psychother.*, 18:447-460.
03745 **FRANK, R.** (1973), Rotating leadership in a group therapy setting. *Psychother.: Theory, Res. & Pract.*, 10:337-338.
03746 **FRANKE, A.** (1978), *Die Klienten-Zentrierte Gruppenpsychotherapie. (Client-Centered Group Psychotherapy.)* Stuttgart: Kohlhammer.
03747 **FRANKE, A.** (1977), (Verification of process of client-centered group psychotherapy.) *Zeit. Klin. Psychol.-Forschung & Praxis*, (Goettingen) 6:244-258.
03748 **FRANKEL, A.**, and **SLOAT, W. E.** (1971), The odyssey of a self-help group. *Psychol. Aspects Disease*, 18:46-51.
03749 **FRANKEL, A. J.**, and **GLASSER, P. H.** (1974), Behavioral approaches to group work. *Soc. Work*, 19:163-175.
03750 **FRANKEL, B.** (1965), The resistance of a group therapist to being a patient in a therapy group. *Topical Probl. Psychol. & Psychother.*, 5:17-23.
03751 **FRANKEL, F. H.** (1967), Psychiatric consultation for nursing homes. *Hosp. & Community Psychiat.*, 18:331-334.
03752 **FRANKEL, S.** (1977), An indication for conjoint treatment: an application based on an assessment of individual psychopathology. *Psychiat. Quart.*, 49:97-109.
03753 **FRANKIEL, H. H.** (1971), Mutually perceived therapeutic relationships in t-groups: the co-trainer puzzle. *J. Appl. Behav. Science*, 7:449-465.
03754 **FRANKL, V. E.** (1973), Encounter: the concept and its vulgarization. *J. Amer. Acad. Psychoanal.*, 1:73-83.
03755 **FRANKL, V. E.** (1954), Group therapeutic experiences in a concentration camp. *Group Psychother., Psychodrama & Sociometry*, 7:81-90.
03756 **FRANKL, V. E.** (1975), Paradoxical intention and dereflection. *Psychother.: Theory, Res. & Pract.*, 12:226.
03757 **FRANKLIN, G.**, and **NOTTAGE, W.** (1969), Psychoanalytic treatment of severely disturbed juvenile delinquents in a therapy group. *Internat. J. Group Psychother.*, 19:165-175.
03758 **FRANKLIN, G. H.** (1957), The effect of group therapy on the attitudes toward self and others of institutionalized delinquent boys. Unpublished doctoral dissertation, New York University.
03759 **FRANKLIN, G. H.** (1959), Group psychotherapy with delinquent boys in a training school setting. *Internat. J. Group Psychother.*, 9:213-218.
03760 **FRANKLIN-PANEK, C. E.** (1978), Effects of personal growth groups on the self-concept and decision-making ability of normal adults. *Psychology*, 15:25-29.
03761 **FRANKNOI, J.** (1972), Psychodrama with respect to unraveling the multileveled meanings of social and racial prejudices. *Internat. J. Group Psychother.*, 22:374-378.
03762 **FRANKS, T. W.** (1952), A note on role playing in an industrial setting. *Group Psychother., Psychodrama & Sociometry*, 5:59-63.
03763 **FRANKS, T. W.** (1959), Project-centered group treatment. *Group Psychother., Psychodrama & Sociometry*, 12:161-165.
03764 **FRANSELLA, F.**, and **JOYSTON-BECHAL, M.** (1971), An investigation of conceptual process and pattern change in a psychotherapy group. *Brit. J. Psychiat.*, (Ashford) 119:199-206.
03765 **FRANZ, J. G.** (1940), The place of the psychodrama in research. *Sociometry*, 3:49-61.
03766 **FRANZ, J. G.** (1942), The psychodrama and interviewing. *Amer. Sociol. Rev.*, 7:27-33.

03767 **FRANZ, J. G.** (1946), Psychodrama at St. Elizabeth's. *Sociometry*, 9:169-170.

03768 **FRANZKE, E.** (1971), Psychodynamic approach to group therapy and to psychotherapy of psychotics. *Acta Psychiat. Scand. Suppl.*, (Copenhagen) 224:7.

03769 **FRASER, W. H.** (1955), Group psychotherapy. *Med. J. Austral.*, (Glebe) 42:521-524.

03770 **FRAZIER, F. K.** (1975), Parent education: a comparison of the impact of the Adlerian and the behavioral approaches. *Dissert. Abstr. Internat.*, 35:4155-4156.

03771 **FRAZIER, T. L.** (1971), The application of transactional analysis principles in the classroom of a correctional school. *Transactional Anal. J.*, 1:214-218.

03772 **FRAZIER, T. L.** (1972), Transactional analysis training and treatment of staff in a correctional school. *Fed. Probat.*, 36:41.

03773 **FREDERICK, C. J.** (1978), Review of I. A. Greenberg's *Group Hypnotherapy and Hypnodrama. Contemp. Psychol.*, 23:463.

03774 **FREDERICK, C. J.**, and **FARBEROW, N. L.** (1970), Group psychotherapy with suicidal persons: a comparison with standard group methods. *Internat. J. Soc. Psychiat.*, (London) 16:103-111.

03775 **FREDERICK, C. J.**, and **RESNICK, H. L.** (1970), Interventions with suicidal patients. *J. Contemp. Psychother.*, 2:103-109.

03776 **FREDERIK, L. W.**, and **MILLER, P. M.** (1976), Peer-determined and self-determined reinforcement in group therapy with alcoholics. *Behav. Res. & Ther.*, 14:385-388.

03777 **FREE, J. E.** (1964), An experiment to show the possible contribution of social group work to counseling in improving the adjustment of deviant high school students. *Dissert. Abstr. Internat.*, 25:2849.

03778 **FREED, A. M.** (1972), I'll do it when I get damn good and ready. *Transactional Anal. J.*, 2:26-27.

03779 **FREED, A. M.** (1972), TA and relaxation therapy. *Transactional Anal. J.*, 2:113-115.

03780 **FREED, L. F.** (1979), Review of G. R. Patterson's, I. M. Marks's, J. D. Matarrazo's, R. A. Myers', G. E. Schwartz's, and H. H. Strupp's *Behavior Change: Aldine Annual Conference, Symposium on Psychotherapy, Counseling and Behavior Modification. Internat. J. Soc. Psychiat.*, (London) 25:74.

03781 **FREEDLAND, R. C.** (1973), Some effects of verbal feedback on perceptions of members in two marathon groups. *Dissert. Abstr. Internat.*, 34:2303B.

03782 **FREEDMAN, D. X.** (1969), The psycho-pharmacology of hallucinogenic agents. *Annual Rev. Med.*, 20:409-418.

03783 **FREEDMAN, H. L.** (1945), The mental hygiene unit approach to reconditioning neuropsychiatric casualties. *Ment. Hygiene*, 29:269-302.

03784 **FREEDMAN, M.** (1966), T-group training for psychology trainees. *Newsl. Res. Psychol.*, 8:21-23.

03785 **FREEDMAN, M.**, and **SWEET, B.** (1954), Some specific features of group psychotherapy and their implications for selection of patients. *Internat. J. Group Psychother.*, 4:355-368.

03786 **FREEDMAN, N., ENGELHARDT, D. M., SCHWARTZ, S., ZOBEL, H.**, and **HANKOFF, L. D.** (1961), Patterns of verbal group participation in the drug treatment of chronic schizophrenic patients. *Internat. J. Group Psychother.*, 11:60-73.

03787 **FREEDMAN, R. J.** (1976), The effects of extra-group socializing and alternate sessions on group psychotherapy outcome. *Dissert. Abstr. Internat.*, 37:1896B.

03788 **FREEDMAN, S. M.,** and **HORLEY, J. R.** (1979), Maslow's needs: individual perceptions of helpful factors in growth groups. *Small Group Behav.*, 10:355-367.

03789 **FREEDMAN, S. M.,** and **HURLEY, J. R.** (1980), Perceptions of helpfulness and behavior in groups. *Group*, 4:51-58.

03790 **FREEMAN, A. M.,** and **APPLEGATE, W. R.** (1976), Psychiatric consultation to a rehabilitation program for amputees. *Hosp. & Community Psychiat.*, 27:40-42.

03791 **FREEMAN, C. W.** (1975), Adlerian mother study groups: effects on attitudes and behavior. *J. Individ. Psychol.*, 31:37-50.

03792 **FREEMAN, H.,** and **KING, C.** (1957), The role of visitors in activity group therapy. *Internat. J. Group Psychother.*, 7:289-301.

03793 **FREEMAN, P.** (1962), Treatment of chronic schizophrenia in a day center. *Arch. Gen. Psychiat.*, 7:259-265.

03794 **FREEMAN, R. V.,** and **SCHWARTZ, A.** (1953), A motivation center: a new concept in total neuropsychiatric hospital care. *Amer. J. Psychiat.*, 110:139-142.

03795 **FREEMAN, T.** (1967), The ambulant patient and community care. *New Zeal. Med. J.*, (Dunedin) 66:730-733.

03796 **FREEMAN, T.** (1967), Group psychotherapy in a mental hospital. *New Zeal. Med. J.*, (Dunedin) 66:726-730.

03797 **FREEMAN, T.** (1967), Psychoanalytical psychotherapy in the National Health Service. *Brit. J. Psychiat.*, (Ashford) 113:321-327.

03798 **FREEMAN, W. J.** (1969), Focused group discussion as an aid to bright high school underachievers. *Amer. J. Orthopsychiat.*, 39:302-303.

03799 **FREESE, A. L.** (1972), Group therapy with exhibitionists and voyeurs. *Soc. Work*, 17:44-52.

03800 **FREETLY, D. R.** (1965), Developing positive mental health concepts through group counseling. *Dissert. Abstr. Internat.*, 25:6389.

03801 **FREITAS, L.,** and **JOHNSON, L.** (1975), Behavior modification approach in a partial day treatment center. *J. Psychiat. Nurs.*, 13:14-18.

03802 **FREL, S.** (1978), Effects of counselor gender on changes in masculinity, femininity, and androgyny in short-term group counseling. *Dissert. Abstr. Internat.*, 38:5923A.

03803 **FRENCH, A. P.** (1977), *Disturbed Children and Their Families: Innovations in Evaluation and Treatment.* New York: Human Sciences Press.

03804 **FRENCH, J. R. P.** (1945), Role playing as a method of training foremen. *Sociometry*, 8:410-425.

03805 **FRENKL, S.** (1974), (Frustration reactions in small groups.) *Magyar Pszichol. Szemle*, (Budapest) 31:422.

03806 **FREUD, S.** (1922), *Group Psychology and Analysis of the Ego.* London: International Psychoanalytic Press.

03807 **FREUDENBERG, D.** (1956), (Group therapy with children.) *Praxis Kinderpsychol. & Kinderpsychiat.*, (Goettingen) 5:81-87.

03808 **FREUDENBERGER, H. J.** (1974), Crisis intervention, individual and group counseling, and the psychology of the counseling staff in a free clinic. *J. Soc. Issues*, 30:77-86.

03809 **FREUDENBERGER, H. J.** (1969), The drug "scene" in Haight-Ashbury, U.S.A. *Internat. J. Offender Ther.*, (London) 13:13-17.

03810 **FREUDENBERGER, H. J.** (1976), The gay addict in a drug and alcohol abuse therapeutic community. *Homosexual Couns. J.*, 3:34-45.

03811 **FREUDENBERGER, H. J.,** and **MARRERO, F.** (1972), A therapeutic marathon with Vietnam veteran addicts at S.E.R.A. *Voices*, 4:34-41.

03812 **FREUDENREICH, D.,** and **WAGNER, A.** (1974), (Experiences with a model in group dynamics at a pedagogic university.) *Gruppendynamik*, (Stuttgart) 5:39-50.

03813 **FREUND, J. C.**, and **CARDWELL, G. F.** (1977), A multi-faceted response to an adolescent's school failure. *J. Marriage & Fam. Couns.*, 3:49-57.

03814 **FREUND, R. B.** (1959), A patient's autonomous society as a method of group psychotherapy. *Psychiat. Quart. Suppl.*, 33:317-332.

03815 **FREUNDLICH, D.** (1973), The impact of nudity on therapy and encounter groups. *Voices*, 9:48-55.

03816 **FREUNDLICH, D.** (1976), Primal experience groups: a flexible structure. *Internat. J. Group Psychother.*, 26:29-41.

03817 **FREUNDLICH, D.** (1972), A psychoanalytic hypothesis of change mechanisms in encounter groups. *Internat. J. Group Psychother.*, 22:42-53.

03818 **FREY, D. H.**, and **RAMING, H. E.** (1979), Taxonomy of counseling goals and methods. *Personnel & Guid. J.*, 58:26-34.

03819 **FREY, L. A.** (1962), Support and the group: generic treatment form. *Soc. Work*, 7:35-42.

03820 **FREY, L. A.**, and **KOLODNY, R. L.** (1966), Group treatment for the alienated child in the school. *Internat. J. Group Psychother.*, 16:321-337.

03821 **FREY, L. A.**, and **KOLODNY, R. L.** (1964), Illusions and realities in current social work with groups. *Soc. Work*, 9:80-89.

03822 **FREY, N. C.**, and **PIZZITOLA, D.** (1973), Group therapy with schizophrenics. *Soc. Work*, 18:94-95.

03823 **FREYBERGER, H.** (1979), Psychosomatic aspects of self-help groups made up of medical patients: presented on the example of the ostomy group. *Psychother. & Psychosomat.*, (Basel) 31:114-120.

03824 **FREYBERGER, H.** (1958), Zurfrage der gruppen psychotherapie bei primar organischen inneren erkrankungen. (Group therapy in primary organic internal disease.) *Acta Psychother. Psychosomat. Orthopaedagog.*, (Basel) 6:327-336.

03825 **FREYHAN, F. A.** (1970), Clinical aspects of the revolution in mental health services. *Comprehens. Psychiat.*, 11:17.

03826 **FRICK, B.** (1954), Psychotherapie di gruppo in clinica. (Group psychotherapy in the clinic.) *Riv. Sper. Freniatria*, (Emilia) 78:285-296.

03827 **FRIED, E.** (1954), Benefits of "combined therapy" for the hostile withdrawn and the hostile dependent personality. *Amer. J. Orthopsychiat.*, 24:529-537.

03828 **FRIED, E.** (1955), Combined group and individual therapy with passive-narcissistic patients. *Internat. J. Group Psychother.*, 5:194-203.

03829 **FRIED, E.** (1974), Does woman's new self-concept call for new approaches in group psychotherapy? *Internat. J. Group Psychother.*, 24:265-272.

03830 **FRIED, E.** (1954), The effect of combined therapy on the productivity of patients. *Internat. J. Group Psychother.*, 4:42-55.

03831 **FRIED, E.** (1956), Ego emancipation of adolescents through group psychotherapy. *Internat. J. Group Psychother.*, 6:358-373.

03832 **FRIED, E.** (1970), Group dynamics and individuation. *Sandoz Psychiat. Spectator*, 6:3-4.

03833 **FRIED, E.** (1970), Individuation through group psychotherapy. *Internat. J. Group Psychother.*, 20:450-459.

03834 **FRIED, E.** (1971), The narcissistic cocoon: how it curbs and can be curbed. *Group Process*, (London) 4:87-95.

03835 **FRIED, E.** (1965), Some aspects of group dynamics and the analysis of transference and defenses. *Internat. J. Group Psychother.*, 15:44-56.

03836 **FRIED, E.** (1961), Techniques of psychotherapy going beyond insight. *Internat. J. Group Psychother.*, 11:297-304.

03837 **FRIED, E.** (1972), The use of action and confrontation. *Psychiat. Annals*, 2:40-47.

03838 **FRIED, E.** (1977), When "splitting" occurs in the group. *Group*, 1:26-31.

03839 **FRIED, F. E.** (1972), Six months on a commune: a comparison of a therapeutic community with a kibbutz. *Isr. Annals Psychiat.*, (Jerusalem) 10:101-105.

03840 **FRIED, K. W.** (1977), Some effects of the leader's abstinent role on group experience. *Group*, 1:118-131.

03841 **FRIEDEMANN, A.** (1964), Die tietenpsychologisch wirksame dynamik in der gruppe. *Internat. J. Sociometry & Sociatry*, 4:3-9.

03842 **FRIEDEMANN, A.** (1957), Group therapy and group diagnosis in children. *Zeit. Diagnost. Psychol.*, 5:295-304.

03843 **FRIEDEMANN, A.** (1963), In memoriam Berthold Stokvis. *Group Psychother., Psychodrama & Sociometry*, 16:193-196.

03844 **FRIEDEMANN, A.** (1975), Psychodrama and its role in psychoanalysis. *Gruppendynamik*, (Stuttgart) 2:92-96.

03845 **FRIEDEMANN, A.** (1961), Soziogramm, aktogramm und die dynamik der gruppe, insbesondere der schulgruppe. (Sociogram, actogram and group dynamics, particularly of the school group.) *Schweiz. Zeit. Psychol. Anwendungen*, (Berne) 20:56-60.

03846 **FRIEDEMANN, A.** (1974), Theoretical foundations of group psychotherapy: 2. In: *The Challenge for Group Psychotherapy: Present and Future*, ed. S. deSchill. New York: International Universities Press.

03847 **FRIEDLAND, B. U.** (1972), Changes in problems of ninth grade students as an outcome of Adlerian group counseling. *Dissert. Abstr. Internat.*, 53:1511A.

03848 **FRIEDLAND, D. M.** (1960), Group counseling as a factor in reducing runaway behavior from an open treatment institution for delinquent and pre-delinquent boys. The evaluation of changes in frustration tolerance, self-concept, attitude toward maternal figures, attitude toward paternal figures, attitude toward other authority and in reality testing of runaway delinquent boys. *Dissert. Abstr. Internat.*, 21:273.

03849 **FRIEDLAND, J.**, and **MURPHY, M.** (1965), A group approach in psychiatric occupational therapy. *Can. J. Occupat. Ther.*, (Toronto) 32:109-118.

03850 **FRIEDLANDER, K.** (1953), Varieties of group therapy patterns in a child guidance service. *Internat. J. Group Psychother.*, 3:59-66.

03851 **FRIEDMAN, A.** (1960), Some notes on psychotherapy with a group of adolescents. *Acta Psychother. Psychosomat. Orthopaedagog.*, (Basel) 8:147-151.

03852 **FRIEDMAN, A. R.** (1962), Education as part of a group therapy program. *Ment. Hosp.*, 13:274.

03853 **FRIEDMAN, A. R.** (1961), Group psychotherapy as a way of life. *Group Psychother., Psychodrama & Sociometry*, 14:78-81.

03854 **FRIEDMAN, A. R.** (1960), Group psychotherapy in the treatment of the Medea complex. *Acta Psychother. Psychosomat. Orthopaedagog.*, (Basel) 8:457-461.

03855 **FRIEDMAN, A. R.** (1963), Rorschach responses and treatment results under drug and group psychotherapy. *Acta Psychother. Psychosomat. Orthopaedagog.*, (Basel) 11:28-32.

03856 **FRIEDMAN, B.** (1973), Cotherapy: a behavioral and attitudinal survey of third-year psychiatric residents. *Internat. J. Group Psychother.*, 23:228-234.

03857 **FRIEDMAN, I.** (1968), A youth activity group. *Hosp. & Community Psychiat.*, 19:247-250.

03858 **FRIEDMAN, J.**, and **PASTRAK, R.** (1973), Accelerated acquisition of classification skills by blind children. *Develop. Psychol.*, 9:333-337.

03859 **FRIEDMAN, J. H.**, and **GERHART, L. W.** (1947), The "question-box" method of group therapy. *Ment. Hygiene*, 31:246-256.

03860 **FRIEDMAN, J. H.**, and **SPADA, A. R.** (1970), A psychiatric training program for high school students assigned to a geriatric service. *Ment. Hygiene*, 54:427-429.

03861 **FRIEDMAN, L. J.**, and **ZINBERG, N. E.** (1964), Application of group methods in college teaching. *Internat. J. Group Psychother.*, 14:344-359.

03862 **FRIEDMAN, M.** (1976), Aiming at the self: the paradox of encounter and the human potential movement. *J. Human. Psychol.*, 16:5-34.

03863 **FRIEDMAN, M.** (1960), Dialogue and the "essential we": the bases of values in the philosophy of Martin Buber. *Amer. J. Psychoanal.*, 20:26-34.

03864 **FRIEDMAN, M.** (1975), Dialogue and the "essential we": the bases of values in the philosophy of Martin Buber. In: *Group Psychotherapy and Group Function*, 2d ed., eds. M. Rosenbaum and M. M. Berger. New York: Basic Books.

03865 **FRIEDMAN, R.**, **SCHLISE, S.**, and **SELIGMAN, S.** (1975), Issues involved in the treatment of an adolescent group. *Adolescence*, 10:357-368.

03866 **FRIEDMAN, R.** (1978), Parent power: holding technique in the treatment of imnipotent children. *Internat. J. Fam. Couns.*, 6:66.

03867 **FRIEDMAN, R. R.**, and **COHEN, K.** (1980), The peer support group: a model for dealing with the emotional aspects of miscarriage. *Group*, 4:42-48.

03868 **FRIEDMAN, S.** (1970), Role-playing in a youth employment office. *Group Psychother., Psychodrama & Sociometry*, 23:21-26.

03869 **FRIEDMAN, S.** (1972), Role-playing with rehabilitation clients. *Group Psychother., Psychodrama & Sociometry*, 25:53-55.

03870 **FRIEDMAN, S. B.**, **ELLENHORN, L. J.**, and **SNORTUM, J. R.** (1976), A comparison of four warm-up techniques for initiating encounter groups. *J. Couns. Psychol.*, 23:514-519.

03871 **FRIEDMAN, W. H.** (1979), *How to Do Groups*. New York: J. Aronson and Sons.

03872 **FRIEDMAN, W. H.** (1976), Referring patients for group psychotherapy: some guidelines (letter). *Hosp. & Community Psychiat.*, 27:121-123.

03873 **FRIEDMAN, W. H.**, **JELLY, E.**, and **JELLY, P.** (1979), Group therapy for psychosomatic patients at a family practice center. *Psychosomatics*, 20:671-677.

03874 **FRIEDMAN, W. H.**, **JELLY, E.**, and **JELLY, P.** (1978), Group therapy in family medicine: part 1. *J. Fam. Practice*, 6:1015-1018.

03875 **FRIEDMAN, W. H.**, **JELLY, E.**, and **JELLY, P.** (1978), Group therapy in family medicine: part 2. establishing the group. *J. Fam. Practice*, 6:1243-1247.

03876 **FRIEDMAN, W. H.**, **JELLY, E.**, and **JELLY, P.** (1978), Group therapy in family medicine: part 3. starting the group. *J. Fam. Practice*, 7:317-320.

03877 **FRIEDMAN, W. H.**, **JELLY, E.**, and **JELLY, P.** (1978), Group therapy in family medicine: part 4. a case report. *J. Fam. Practice*, 7:501-503.

03878 **FRIEDMANN, C. T.**, **SCHIEBEL, D.**, and **McGUIRE, M. T.** (1980), Behavioral study of two patient groups during psychotherapy. *Psychol. Reports*, 47:575-579.

03879 **FRIEDMANN, C. T.**, and **SILVERS, F. M.** (1977), A multimodality approach to inpatient treatment of obsessive-compulsive disorders. *Amer. J. Psychother.*, 31:456-465.

03880 **FRIEDRICH, H.** (1979), Coordination problems of professional and nonprofessional counseling institutions. *Gruppenpsychother. & Gruppendynam.*, (Goettingen) 14:146-154.

03881 **FRIEND, K. E.** (1974), An information processing approach to small group interaction in a coalition formation game. *Dissert. Abstr. Internat.*, 34:5309A.

03882 **FRIEND, M. R.**, and **OLINICK, S. L.** (1945), Indirect group therapy of psychoneurotic soldiers. *Psychiatry*, 8:147-153.

03883 **FRIEND, M. R.**, and **OLINICK, S. L.** (1945), Therapy through a group of neurotic soldiers in an experimental military setting. *Amer. J. Orthopsychiat.*, 15:483-488.

03884 **FRIEND, M. R.**, and **SULLIVAN, W. F.** (1947), Group psychotherapy in an army general hospital relating to civilian readjustment. *Amer. J. Orthopsychiat.*, 17:254-265.

03885 **FRIEND-NASH, W.**, and **PHILLIPS, L.** (1978), A venture in community care. *Health Visitor*, (London) 51:248-251.

03886 **FRIESEN, A.** (1953), Training psychiatrists for group psychotherapy. *First Annual Report*, Group Psychotherapy Association of Southern California, pp. 12-16.

03887 **FRIESS, G.**, and **NEUBER, U.** (1976), (The care for drug addicts in a release condominium.) *Med. Klinik*, (Munich) 71:554-556.

03888 **FRIGHI, L.** (1967), Organizzazione di esperimenti pilota di psicoterapia di gruppo nell'ambito del servizio d' Igiene Mentale dell' Universita di Roma. (Organization of pilot experiments in group psychotherapy at the University of Rome Mental Hygiene Service.) *Riv. Psichiat.*, (Rome) 2:557-560.

03889 **FRIGNITO, N. G.**, and **ORCHINIK, C. W.** (1963), The therapy of adolescent offenders. *Curr. Psychiat. Ther.*, 3:188-196.

03890 **FRINGS-BAUMANN, E.** (1951), Praktische erfahrungen über die gruppen-psychotherapie (autogenes training) im sanatorium bzw in der allgemeinpraxis. (Practical studies of group psychotherapy [autogenous training] in sanatorium and general practice.) *München. Med. Wochenschr.*, (Munich) 93:1311-1313.

03891 **FRITZSCH, M.**, and **GOLLNER, R.** (1976), Patients as reference persons: investigation of results of an ambulatory group therapy. *Gruppenpsychother. & Gruppendynam.*, (Goettingen) 11:47-59.

03892 **FRIZZELL, M. K.** (1968), Group therapy for diabetic mental patients. *Hosp. & Commun. Psychiat.*, 19:297-298.

03893 **FROEHLICH, C. P.** (1954), Group guidance approaches in educational institutions. *Rev. Educat. Res.*, 24:147-155.

03894 **FROMAN, F.** (1972), Effects of peer tutoring, brief individual and group counselling, and reinforcement on the academic achievement of risk college students. *Dissert. Abstr. Internat.*, 32:4346A.

03895 **FROMKIN, H. L.**, and **SHERWOOD, J. J.** (1976), *Intergroup and Minority Relations: An Experiential Handbook.* La Jolla, CA: University Associates.

03896 **FROMKIN, H. L.** (1975), An evaluation of human relations training for police. *Cat. Selected Docum. Psychol.*, 5:206-207.

03897 **FROMME, D. K.**, and **CLOSE, S. R.** (1976), Group compatibility and the modification of affective verbalization. *Brit. J. Soc. & Clin. Psychol.*, (London) 15:189-198.

03898 **FROMME, D. K., JONES, W. H.**, and **DAVIS, J. O.** (1974), Experiential group training with conservative populations: a potential for negative effects. *J. Clin. Psychol.*, 30:290-296.

03899 **FROMME, D. K., STOMMEL, J. A.**, and **DUVAL, R. D.** (1976), Group modification of affective verbalizations: resistance to extinction and generalization effects. *Br. J. Soc. & Clin. Psychol.*, (London) 15:395-402.

03900 **FROMME, D. K., WHISENANT, W. F.**, and **SUSKY, H. H.** (1974), Group modification of affective verbalizations. *J. Consult. & Clin. Psychol.*, 42:866-871.

03901 **FROMMER, E. A.** (1969), (A day hospital for mentally disturbed children.) *Tijdschr. Ziekenverpleging*, (Lochem) 22:635-636.

03902 **FROMM-REICHMANN, F.** (1954), Transference, countertransference and tele. *Group Psychother., Psychodrama & Sociometry*, 7:309-310.

03903 **FROMM-REICHMANN, F.**, and **MORENO, J. L.** (1956), *Progress in Psychotherapy*. New York: Grune & Stratton.

03904 **FROST, B. E.** (1970), The "active leader" in group therapy for chronic schizophrenic patients. *Perspect. Psychiat. Care*, 8:268-272.

03905 **FROST, J. M.** (1972), Counseling outcomes with fourth, fifth and sixth grade pupils. *Dissert. Abstr. Internat.*, 33:6663A.

03906 **FROST, M.** (1975), Schizophrenia 7: group treatment of the acute and chronic patient. *Nursing Times*, (London) 71:587-589.

03907 **FRÜHMANN, E.** (1974), (The trend towards groups as a symptom of the crisis in psychoanalysis.) *Zeit. Klin. Psychol. & Psychother.*, (Freiburg) 22:261-266.

03908 **FRY, C. L.** (1966), Training children to communicate to listeners. *Child Develop.*, 37:675-685.

03909 **FRYE, R. L.**, and **ADAMS, H. E.** (1959), Effect of the volunteer variable on leaderless group discussion experiments. *Psychol. Reports*, 5:184.

03910 **FRYE, R. L.**, and **STRITCH, T. M.** (1964), Effect of timed vs. nontimed discussion upon measures of influence and change in small groups. *J. Soc. Psychol.*, 63:139-143.

03911 **FRYE, R. L., VIDULICH, R. N., MEIERHOEFER, B.**, and **JOURE, S. A.** (1972), Differential t-group behaviors of high and low dogmatic participants. *J. Psychology*, 81:301-310.

03912 **FUCHS, C. Z.**, and **REHM, L. P.** (1977), A self-control behavior therapy program for depression. *Consult. & Clin. Psychol.*, 45:206-215.

03913 **FUCHS-KAMP, D.** (1959), Aims and possibilities of polyclinical group therapy. *Acta Psychother. Psychosomat. Orthopaedagog. Suppl.*, (Basel) 7:126-134.

03914 **FUERSTEIN, C. W.** (1959), The effects of intra-group and inter-group competitive conditions on the performance and level of aspiration of male paranoid schizophrenics. Unpublished doctoral dissertation, New York University.

03915 **FUJISOWA, K.**, and **OBONAI, T.** (1960), Psychophysiological studies of hypnotic sleep. *Japanese J. Psychol.*, (Tokyo) 31:94.

03916 **FULLER, G. M.**, and **PERV, W. L.** (1978), Family and marriage education "recording." *Individ. Psychologist*, 15:46.

03917 **FULLER, J. B.** (1971), An investigation of self-disclosing behavior and the affective response within a t-group setting. *Dissert. Abstr. Internat.*, 32:1852A.

03918 **FULLER, J. K.** (1952), Extension of group therapy to parolees. *Prison World*, (Jul-Aug), 8-11.

03919 **FULLER, J. S.** (1977), Duo therapy case studies: process and techniques. *Soc. Casework*, 58:84-91.

03920 **FULLER, J. S.** (1977), Duo therapy: a potential treatment of choice for latency children. *J. Amer. Acad. Child Psychiat.*, 16:469-477.

03921 **FULLMER, D. W.** (1971), *Counseling: Group Theory and System*. Scranton: Educational Publishers.

03922 **FULLMER, D. W.**, and **BERNARD, H. W.** (1964), *Counseling: Content and Process*. Chicago: Science Research Association.

03923 **FUNK, I. C., SHATIN, L., FREED, E. X.**, and **ROCKMORE, L.** (1955), Somatopsychotherapeutic approach to long-term schizophrenic patients: demonstration program. *J. Nerv. & Ment. Diseases*, 121:423-437.

03924 **FÜREDI, J.** (1969), (Group psychotherapy under double direction.) *Orvosi Hetilap*, (Budapest) 110:2695-2701.

03925 **FÜREDI, J.** (1969), (Of the methodological questions of groups.) *Magyar Pszichol. Szemle*, (Budapest) 26:252-260.

03926 **FÜREDI, J., MÓROTZ, K., and SZOMBATHELYI, E.** (1969), (Of the methodological questions of groups.) *Magyar Pszichol. Szemle*, 26:252-260.

03927 **FÜREDI, J., SZEDEGI, M., and KUN, M.** (1974), Methodological problems of the therapeutic community's large groups. *Internat. J. Group Psychother.*, 24:190-198.

03928 **FUREDY, R., CROWDER, M., and SILVERS, F.** (1977), Transitional care: a new approach to aftercare. *Hosp. & Community Psychiat.*, 28:122-124.

03929 **FURGERI, L. B.** (1978), The celebration of death in group process. *Clin. Soc. Work J.*, 6:90.

03930 **FURLONG, F. W.** (1977), Review of L. Wolberg's and M. L. Aronson's *Group Therapy 1975: An Overview. Can. Psychiat.*, (Ottawa) 22:192-194.

03931 **FURMAN, S., and FEIGHNER, A.** (1973), Video feedback in treating hyperkinetic children: a preliminary report. *Amer. J. Psychiat.*, 130:792-796.

03932 **FURST, W.** (1951), Homogeneous versus heterogeneous groups. *Internat. J. Group Psychother.*, 1:120-123.

03933 **FURST, W.** (1960), Homogeneous versus heterogeneous groups. *Topical Probl. Psychol. & Psychother.*, 2:170-173.

03934 **FURST, W.** (1975), Homogeneous versus heterogeneous groups. In: *Group Psychotherapy and Group Function*, 2d ed., eds. M. Rosenbaum and M. M. Berger. New York: Basic Books.

03935 **FURSTENAU, P., et al.** (1970), (Experiences with a group therapy neurotic station.) *Zeit. Psychother. Med. Psychol.*, (Stuttgart) 20:95-104.

03936 **FURTAK, C. H.** (1973), A descriptive analysis of excitatory assertive exercises in multiple therapy and individual counseling in the active emotive approach to counseling. *Dissert. Abstr. Internat.*, 33:4087A.

03937 **FYBISH, I.** (1964), A study of the difficulties encountered in negative criteria for sociometric testing. *Internat. J. Sociometry & Sociatry*, 4:37-42.

03938 **FYFFE, D.** (1971), Encounter groups in industry. *Hydrocarb. Processing*, 50:151-153.

G

03939 **GABBY, J. I.**, and **LEAVITT, A.** (1970), Providing low-cost psychotherapy to middle-income patients. *Community Ment. Health J.*, 6:210-214.

03940 **GABEL, H.** (1975), Effects of parent group discussion of adolescents' perceptions of maternal behavior. *J. Community Psychol.*, 3:32-35.

03941 **GABEL, H. D.** (1973), Effects of parent group education and group play psychotherapy on maternal child-rearing attitudes. *Dissert. Abstr. Internat.*, 33:6077B.

03942 **GABRIEL, B.** (1951), Analytic group psychotherapy with a borderline psychotic woman. *Internat. J. Group Psychother.*, 1:243-253.

03943 **GABRIEL, B.** (1939), An experiment in group treatment. *Amer. J. Orthopsychiat.*, 9:146-169.

03944 **GABRIEL, B.** (1943), Group therapy of six adolescent girls. *Newsl. Amer. Assn. Psychiat. Soc. Workers*, 13:65-72.

03945 **GABRIEL, B.** (1944), Interview group therapy for adolescent girls. *Amer. J. Orthopsychiat.*, 14:593-602.

03946 **GABRIEL, B.** (1947), Interview group therapy with a neurotic adolescent girl suffering from chorea. In: *The Practice of Group Therapy*, ed. S. R. Slavson. London: Pushkin Press; New York: International Universities Press.

03947 **GABRIEL, B.**, and **HALPERT, A.** (1952), The effect of group therapy for mothers on their children. *Internat. J. Group Psychother.*, 2:159-171.

03948 **GABURRI, E.**, and **DeSIMONE GABURRI, G.** (1969), (Borderline in institutional psychotherapy.) *Riv. Psichiat.*, (Rome) 4:357-362.

03949 **GADLIN, W.** (1978), Review of L. Wolberg's, M. Aronson's, and A. Wolberg's *Group Therapy 1977: An Overview*. *Group*, 2:126-127.

03950 **GADPAILLE, W. J.** (1959), Observations on the sequence of resistances in groups of adolescent delinquents. *Internat. J. Group Psychother.*, 9:275-286.

03951 **GAGLIANO, T. E.**, and **FORIZS, L.** (1967), Intensive hospital treatment of severe psychiatric disorders. *Hosp. & Community Psychiat.*, 18:74-82.

03952 **GAGNON, J.** (1969), (Analytical group psychotherapy of preadolescents.) *Laval Med.*, (Quebec) 40:1028-1036.

03953 **GAGNON, J.** (1970), Experience de therapie analytique de groupe chez des preadolescentes. (An experience of analytic therapy in a group home for preadolescents.) *Can. Psychiat. Assn. J.*, (Ottawa) 15:361-363.

03954 **GAINES, T.** (1978), A technique for reducing parental obsessions in family therapy. *Fam. Ther.*, 5:91.

03955 **GALANTER, M.** (1978), The "relief effect": a sociobiological model for neurotic distress and large-group therapy. *Amer. J. Psychiat.*, 135:588-591.

03956 **GALASSI, J. P.**, and **GALASSI, M. D.** (1978), Promise of things to come: review of S. D. Rose's *Group Therapy: A Behavioral Approach*. *Contemp. Psychol.*, 23:512-513.

03957 **GALASSI, J. P., GALASSI, M. D.**, and **LIFZ, C.** (1974), Assertive training in groups using video feedback. *J. Couns. Psychol.*, 21:390-395.

03958 **GALASSI, J. P., KOSTKA, M. P.**, and **GALASSI, M. D.** (1975), Assertive training: a one year follow-up. *J. Couns. Psychol.*, 22:451-452.

03959 **GALBRAITH, K. J.** (1972), Evaluation of a token economy in the treatment of a chronic psychiatric population. *Can. J. Behav. Science*, (Montreal) 4:91-100.

03960 **GÁLDI, Z.**, and **FÜREDI, J.** (1965), Kisérlet indült elmebetegek rehabilitációjára. (Experiment aimed at the rehabilitation of chronic psychotic patients.) *Pszichol. Tanulmányok*, 8:455-463.

03961 **GALDSTON, R.** (1979), Review of M. C. Collins' *Child Abusers in Self-Help Group Therapy. Amer. J. Psychiat.*, 136:263.

03962 **GÁLFI, B.** (1969), Csopartterapias lehetosegek az elmegyogyaszatban. (Group therapy in psychiatry.) *Dissert. Abstr. Internat.*, 43:5489.

03963 **GÁLFI, B.** (1965), Cosoportterápiás lehetöségek az elmegyógyászatban. (Group therapy in psychiatry.) *Pszichol. Tanulmányok*, 8:465-475.

03964 **GÁLFI, B.** (1961), (Labor therapy in the Institute for Labor Therapy at Pomaz.) *Magyar Pszichol. Szemle*, (Budapest) 18:173-183.

03965 **GÁLFI, B., KISS-VAMOSI, J., SOOKY, A.,** and **SZOLLAR, E.** (1966), Idult elmebetegek csoport-pszichoterapiaja tomegjellegu csoportokban. (Group psychotherapy with chronic mental patients in mass groups.) *Magyar Pszichol. Szemle*, (Budapest) 23:409-414.

03966 **GÁLFI, B., KOCZKÁS, I.,** and **KURUEZ, L.** (1965), A kórusénekl és mint csoportmunka. (Community singing as a group activity.) *Pszichol. Tanulmányok*, 8:573-579.

03967 **GALIGARCÍA, J.** (1948), Psicoterapia de grupo. (Group psychotherapy.) *Bolivian Col. Méd. Camagũey*, 11:35-41.

03968 **GALINSKA, E.** (1975), (Receptive group musicotherapy in the comprehensive therapy of neuroses.) *Psychiatria Polska*, (Warsaw) 9:435-442.

03969 **GALINSKA, E.** (1976), Receptive group music therapy at the Neurological Clinic of the Psychoneurological Institute, Warsaw. *Psychiat. Neurol. Med. Psychol.*, (Leipzig) 26:714-721.

03970 **GALINSKY, M. J.,** and **SCHEPLER, J. H.** (1977), Warning: groups may be dangerous. *Soc. Work*, 22:89-94.

03971 **GALIONI, E., ALMADA, A. A., NEWHALL, C. M.,** and **PETERSON, A.** (1954), Group techniques in rehabilitating "backward" patients. *Amer. J. Nursing*, 54:977-979.

03972 **GALLAGHER, C. C.,** and **KNIGHT, W. A.** (1973), *Group Technology*. London: Butterworth.

03973 **GALLAGHER, D. E.** (1979), Comparative effectiveness of group psychotherapies for reduction of depression in elderly outpatients. *Dissert. Abstr. Internat.*, 39:5550B.

03974 **GALLAGHER, J.,** and **BURKE, P. J.** (1974), Scapegoating and leader behavior. *Soc. Forces*, 52:481-488.

03975 **GALLANT, D. M.** (1964), Group staffing on an alcoholism treatment service. *Internat. J. Group Psychother.*, 4:218-220.

03976 **GALLANT, D. M., BISHOP, P., STOY, B., FAULKNER, M. A.,** and **PATERNOSTRO, L.** (1966), The value of a "first contact" group intake session in an alcoholism outpatient clinic: statistical confirmation. *Psychosomatics*, 7:349-352.

03977 **GALLANT, D. M., BISHOP, M. A., FAULKNER, M. A., SIMPSON, L., COOPER, A., LATHROP, D., BRISOLARA, A. M.,** and **BOSSETTA, J. R.** (1968), A comparative evaluation of compulsory (group therapy and-or antiabuse) and voluntary treatment of the chronic alcoholic municipal court offender. *Psychosomatics*, 9:306-310.

03978 **GALLO, A. I.** (1971), Revisión de historiales clinicos de pucientes que abandonaron grupos de psicoterapia. (Review of the clinical histories of patients who abandoned group psychotherapy.) *Acta Psichiat., Psicol. Amer. Latina*, (Buenos Aires) 17:109-113.

03979 **GALM, D.** (1963), (The psychotherapeutic treatment of a nine-year-old boy subject to encopresis.) *Praxis Kinderpsychol. & Kinderpsychiat.*, (Goettingen) 12:284-288.

03980 **GALPER, J.** (1970), Nonverbal communication exercises in groups. *Soc. Work*, 15:71-78.

03981 **GALT, W.** (1940), The principle of cooperation in behavior. *Quart. Rev. Biol.*, 15:401-410.

03982 **GAMEZ, G. L.** (1970), T-groups as a tool for developing trust and cooperation between Mexican-American and Anglo-American college students. *Dissert. Abstr. Internat.*, 31:2305.

03983 **GAMEZ, K. B.** (1970), Transfer of learning from t-groups to other groups. *Dissert. Abstr. Internat.*, 31:2305-2306.

03984 **GAMMEL, J. B.** (1974), A study of the effects of self-actualization on communication in small structured experiential groups. *Dissert. Abstr. Internat.*, 34:4740A.

03985 **GANNON, R. A.** (1979), Psychotherapy: teaching group therapy to learner psychiatric nurses. *Nursing Times*, (London) 75:2128-2129.

03986 **GANNON, W. J.** (1972), The effects of the gestalt oriented group approach on the interpersonal contact attitudes of selected high school students. *Dissert. Abstr. Internat.*, 33:1434A.

03987 **GANS, J. S.** (1978), Review of M. Seligman's *Group-Counseling and Group-Psychotherapy with Rehabilitation Clients. J. Geriat. Psychiat.*, 11:102-105.

03988 **GANS, R. W.** (1962), Group cotherapists and the therapeutic situation: a critical evaluation. *Internat. J. Group Psychother.*, 12:82-88.

03989 **GANS, R. W.** (1957), The use of group co-therapists in the teaching of psychotherapy. *Amer. J. Psychother.*, 11:618-625.

03990 **GANTEN, G., YEAKEL, M.,** and **POLANSKY, N. A.** (1967), *Retrieval from Limbo: The Intermediary Group Treatment of Inaccessible Children.* New York: Child Welfare League of America.

03991 **GANTER, G.,** and **POLANSKY, N. A.** (1964), Predicting a child's accessibility to individual treatment from diagnostic groups. *Soc. Work*, 9:56-63.

03992 **GANTER, G., YEAKEL, M.,** and **POLANSKY, N. A.** (1965), Intermediary group treatment of inaccessible children. *Amer. J. Orthopsychiat.*, 35:739-746.

03993 **GANTZ, J. R.** (1973), Group therapy in education: toward a new humanism. *Dissert. Abstr. Internat.*, 34:2913A.

03994 **GANZARAIN, R.** (1977), General systems and object-relations theories: their usefulness in group psychotherapy. *Internat. J. Group Psychother.*, 27:441-456.

03995 **GANZARAIN, R.** (1951), Primeras impresiones sobre la psicoterapia de grupo despues de un año de experiencia. (First impressions after one year's experience of group psychotherapy.) *Rev. Psiquiat.*, (Santiago) 16:56-65.

03996 **GANZARAIN, R.** (1974/1975), A psychoanalytic study of sensitivity training. *Interpersonal Develop.*, 5:60-70.

03997 **GANZARAIN, R., DAVANZO, H.,** and **CIZALETTI, J.** (1958), Group psychotherapy in the psychiatric training of medical students. *Internat. J. Group Psychother.*, 8:137-153.

03998 **GANZARAIN, R., DAVANZO, H., FLORES, O.,** and **DROBNY, E.** (1959), Study of effectiveness of group psychotherapy in the training of medical students. *Internat. J. Group Psychother.*, 9:475-487.

03999 **GANZARAIN, CAJIAO R.** (1960), (Research work in group therapy: its problems, methods and tasks.) *Psyche*, (Stuttgart) 14:524-537.

04000 **GANZEVOORT, J.** (1973), (New roles for psychiatric nurses.) *Tijdschr. Ziekenverpleging*, (Lochem) 26:872-876.

04001 **GANZEVOORT, J.** (1975), New tasks for psychiatric nurses: "zuideroord vogelenzang" mental health hospital. *Internat. Nursing Rev.*, (Geneva) 22:109-112.

04002 **GARBER, B.**, and **POLSKY, R.** (1970), Follow-up study of hospitalized adolescents. *Arch. Gen. Psychiat.*, 22:179-187.

04003 **GARBER, J.** (1976), A psychoeducational therapy program for delinquent boys: an evaluation report. *J. Drug Educat.*, 6:331.

04004 **GARCIA, J.** (1978), (Review of G. W. Speierer's *Dimensions of Experience in Group-Therapy.*) *Psychother. & Med. Psychol.*, (Stuttgart) 28:35.

04005 **GARCIA-SHELTON, L. M.** (1979), An evaluation of two treatment programs for families with acting-out adolescents. *Dissert. Abstr. Internat.*, 40:5810B.

04006 **GARD, J. G.** (1962), Fundamental interpersonal relations orientations in clinical groups. *Dissert. Abstr. Internat.*, 22:4080.

04007 **GARD, J. G.** (1964), Interpersonal orientations in clinical groups. *J. Abnorm. & Soc. Psychol.*, 69:516-521.

04008 **GARDINER, C. F.** (1980), *A First Course in Group Therapy.* New York: Springer Verlag.

04009 **GARDNER, G. E.** (1951), Evaluation of therapeutic results in child guidance programs. *Res. Pub. Assess. Nerv. & Ment. Diseases*, 31:131-137.

04010 **GARDNER, J.**, and **LIEBERMAN, M. A.** (1973), Alternative helping systems: a summary comparison between participants in growth center activities and patients in psychiatric clinics. *Proceed., 81st Annual Convention*, American Psychological Association, 8:499-500.

04011 **GARDNER, K.** (1971), Patient groups in a therapeutic community. *Amer. J. Nursing*, 71:528-531.

04012 **GARDNER, W. J.** (1966), A handful of people: a group-oriented, comprehensive psychiatric care center in a general hospital. *J. Kansas Med. Soc.*, 67:22-25.

04013 **GARETZ, C.**, and **FIX, A. J.** (1972), Difficult problems in therapy: group leadership. *Hosp. & Community Psychiat.*, 23:248-250.

04014 **GARFIELD, S. J.** (1968), Creativity, mental health, and psychotherapy. *Dissert. Abstr. Internat.*, 28:4295B.

04015 **GARFIELD, S. J., COHEN, H. A.**, and **ROTH, R. M.** (1969), Creativity and mental health. *J. Educat. Res.*, 63:147-149.

04016 **GARFIELD, S. J., COHEN, H. A., ROTH, R. M.**, and **BERENBAUM, H. L.** (1971), Effects of group counseling on creativity. *J. Educat. Res.*, 64:235-237.

04017 **GARFUNKEL, J.** (1976), Effect of feedback-reinforcement for patients on frequency and duration of therapeutic verbalization in group therapy. *Dissert. Abstr. Internat.*, 37:2503.

04018 **GARIBAY, P. M.** (1970), Análisis de una psicoterapia de grupo con alcoholicos. (Analysis of group psychotherapy with alcoholics.) *Rev. Mex. Psicother.*, 4:117-124.

04019 **GARLAND, C.** (1980), Face to face. *Group Anal.*, (London) 13:42-43.

04020 **GARLAND, J. A.**, and **KOLODNY, R.** (1980), *The Treatment of Children through Social Group Work: A Developmental Approach.* Boston: Charles River.

04021 **GARLAND, J. A., KOLODNY, R. L.**, and **WALDFOGEL, S.** (1962), Social group work as adjunctive treatment for the emotionally disturbed adolescent: the experience of a specialized group work department. *Amer. J. Orthopsychiat.*, 32:691-706.

04022 **GARLOFF, L.** (1974), (Psychotherapeutic treatment of an outpatient group of schizophrenic women.) *Gruppenpsychother. & Gruppendynam.*, (Goettingen) 8:68-79.

04023 **GARMA, A.** (1973), Gruppenpsychoanalyse bei patienten mit ulcus pepticum. (Psychoanalysis of a special group of peptic ulcer patients.) *Dynam. Psychiat.*, (Berlin) 6:2-10.

04024 **GARNER, H. G.** (1974), Mental health benefits of small group experiences in the affective domain. *J. School Health*, 44:314-318.

04025 **GARNER, J.** (1980), Some thoughts on group analysis. *Group Anal.*, (London) 13:43-46.

04026 **GARNI, K. F.** (1972), The effects of Adlerian group counseling on the academic performance of marginal commuter college students. *Dissert. Abstr. Internat.*, 33:1434A.

04027 **GARRIDO MARTÍN, E.** (1978), *Jacob Leví Moreno: Psicología del Encuentro.* (*Jacob Levi Moreno: The Psychology of Encounter.*) Madrid: Sociedad de Educatión Atenas.

04028 **GARRIGAN, J. J.,** and **BAMBRICK, A. F.** (1979), New findings in research on go-between process. *Internat. J. Fam. Ther.*, 1:76.

04029 **GARRISON, C. B.** (1971), A comparative investigation of behavioral counseling group techniques used to modify study skills, attitudes, and achievement of selected high school pupils. *Dissert. Abstr. Internat.*, 32:1271A.

04030 **GARRISON, J.,** and **SCOTT, P. A.** (1979), A group self care approach to stress management. *J. Psychiat. Nursing*, 17:9-14.

04031 **GARRISON, J., KULP, C.,** and **ROSEN, S.** (1977), Community mental health nursing: a social network approach. *J. Psychiat. Nursing*, 15:32-36.

04032 **GARRISON, J. E.** (1972), Effects of systematic preparation of patients for group psychotherapy. *Dissert. Abstr. Internat.*, 33:2808B.

04033 **GARRISON, J. E.** (1978), Written vs. verbal preparation of patients for group psychotherapy. *Psychother.: Theory, Res. & Pract.*, 15:130-134.

04034 **GARRITY, L. I.,** and **LEFF, R. M.** (1977), Training emotionally disturbed children in role-taking: a structured technique. *Psychol. Reports*, 40:599-565.

04035 **GARTNER, D.** (1979), Group sessions for adolescents and for parents awaiting therapy in a child guidance clinic. *Hosp. & Community Psychiat.*, 30:161-162.

04036 **GARVIN, C.** (1978), Review of S. D. Rose's *Group Therapy: A Behavioral Approach. Soc. Serv. Rev.*, 52:145-147.

04037 **GARVIN, C.** (1974), Task-centered group work. *Soc. Serv. Rev.*, 48:494-507.

04038 **GARWOOD, D. S.** (1967), The significance and dynamics of sensitivity training programs. *Internat. J. Group Psychother.*, 17:457-472.

04039 **GARWOOD, D. S.,** and **AUGENBRAUN, B.** (1968), Coordinated psychotherapeutic approaches to a familial dysautonomic preschool boy and his parents. *Psychoanal. Rev.*, 55:62-78.

04040 **GARY, A. L., DAVIS, L.,** and **HOWELL, T.** (1977), Melanin distribution and sensitivity to group therapy. *J. Psychology*, 96:315-320.

04041 **GASKILL, E. R.,** and **MUDD, E. H.** (1950), A decade of group counseling. *Soc. Casework*, 31:194-201.

04042 **GASTAGER, H.** (1964), (Experience with the principle of the therapeutic community in a psychiatric ward.) *Wiener Med. Wochenschr.*, (Vienna) 114:301-308.

04043 **GASTAGER, H.** (1959), Group psychotherapy in connection with a general treatment plan of schizophrenic psychoses. *Acta Psychother. Psychosomat. Orthopaedagog. Suppl.*, (Basel) 7:134-141.

04044 **GASTAGER, H.** (1963), (Group psychotherapy in a psychotherapeutic outpatient service.) *Zeit. Psychosomat. Med. Psychol.*, (Stuttgart) 9:115-118.

04045 **GASTAGER, H.** (1962), (The therapeutic club and its group dynamics.) *Zeit. Psychosomat. Med. Psychol.*, (Stuttgart) 12:238-245.

04046 **GASTAGER, H.** (1963), (The therapeutic club and the aftercare of psychoses.) *Wiener. Zeit. Nervenheilk.*, (Vienna) 21:159-165.
04047 **GASTAGER, H.** (1976), (What is sociotherapy?) *Zeit. Klin. Psychol. & Psychother.*, (Freiburg) 24:156-159.
04048 **GASTON, E. T.** (1957), *Music Therapy 1957: Seventh Book of Proceedings of the National Association for Music Therapy*. Lawrence, KS: National Association Music Therapy.
04049 **GASTON, M. M.** (1972), Group counseling as a means of changing the self-concept of the economically disadvantaged. *Dissert. Abstr. Internat.*, 33:2709A.
04050 **GATES, J. C.** (1980), Comparison of behavior modification and self-help groups with conventional therapy of diabetes. *Dissert. Abstr. Internat.*, 40:3084B. (University Microfilms No. 8000255.)
04051 **GATHERS, M. A.** (1977), The comparative effectiveness of two methods of group counseling of potential drop-outs in an urban high school. *Dissert. Abstr. Internat.*, 37:4130A.
04052 **GATZ, M., TYLER, F. B.,** and **PARGAMENT, K. I.** (1978), Goal attainment, locus of control, and coping style in adolescent group counseling. ,*J. Couns. Psychol.*, 25:310.
04053 **GAULDEN, G. L.** (1975), Developmental play group counseling with early primary grade students exhibiting behavioral problems. *Dissert. Abstr. Internat.*, 36:2628A.
04054 **GAURON, E. F.,** and **RAWLINGS, E. I.** (1975), A procedure for orienting new members to group psychotherapy. *Small Group Behav.*, 6:293-307.
04055 **GAURON, E. F.,** and **RAWLINGS, E. I.** (1974), Using video-tapes to treat chronic patients in vicarious therapy groups. *Hosp. & Community Psychiat.*, 25:277-282.
04056 **GAURON, E. F., PROCTOR, S. A.,** and **SCHRODER, P. J.** (1970), Group therapy training: a multidisciplinary approach. *Perspect. Psychiat. Care*, 8:262-267.
04057 **GAURON, E. F., STEINMARK, S. W.,** and **GERSH, S. F.** (1977), The orientation group in pre-therapy training. *Perspect. Psychiat. Care*, 15:32-37.
04058 **GAUTHIER, R.** (1972), Comparative therapeutic factors in schizophrenia. *Can. Psychiat. Assn. J. Suppl.*, (Ottawa) 17:SS145.
04059 **GAVALAS, N.** (1977), Group systematic desensitization with test-anxious ninth grade students of differing locus of control orientations. *Dissert. Abstr. Internat.*, 38:171A.
04060 **GAVALES, D.** (1966), Effects of combined counseling and vocational training on personal adjustment. *J. Appl. Psychol.*, 50:18-21.
04061 **GAZDA, G. M.** (1979), *Basic Approaches to Group Psychotherapy and Group Counseling*, 2d ed. Springfield, IL: C C Thomas.
04062 **GAZDA, G. M.** (1968), *Basic Approaches to Group Psychotherapy and Group Counseling*. Springfield, IL: C C Thomas.
04063 **GAZDA, G. M.** (1975), *Basic Approaches to Group Psychotherapy and Group Counseling*. Springfield, IL: C C Thomas.
04064 **GAZDA, G. M.** (1959), The effect of short-term group counseling on prospective counselors. Unpublished doctoral dissertation, Illinois University.
04065 **GAZDA, G. M.** (1971), *Group Counseling: A Developmental Approach*. Rockleigh, NJ: Allyn and Bacon.
04066 **GAZDA, G, M,** (1968), *Innovations to Group Psychotherapy*. Springfield, IL: C C Thomas.
04067 **GAZDA, G. M.** (1971), Professional issues in group work. *Personnel & Guid. J.*, 49:637-644.
04068 **GAZDA, G. M.** (1972), Symposium on the use of group procedures in the

prevention and treatment of drug and alcohol addiction. Athens, GA: Athens Center for Continuing Education, University of Georgia.

04069 **GAZDA, G. M.** (1969), *Theories and Methods of Group Counseling in the Schools*. Springfield, IL: C. C. Thomas.

04070 **GAZDA, G. M.**, and **LARSEN, M. J.** (1968), A comprehensive appraisal of group and multiple counseling research. *J. Res. Develop. Educat.*, 1:57-132.

04071 **GAZDA, G.**, and **OHLSEN, M.** (1961), The effects of short-term group counseling on prospective counselors. *Personnel & Guid. J.*, 39:634-638.

04072 **GAZDA, G. M.**, and **PETERS, R. W.** (1973), Analysis of research in group procedures. *Educat. Technol.*, 13:68-75.

04073 **GAZDA, G. M.**, and **PETERS, R.** (1975), An analysis of research in group psychotherapy, group counseling, and human relations training. In: *Basic Approaches to Group Psychotherapy and Group Counseling*, ed. G. Gazda. Springfield, IL: C. C. Thomas.

04074 **GAZDA, G. M.**, and **PITTMAN, W.** (1977), Evaluative report of a participant approach to teaching group therapy to psychiatry residents. *Group Psychother., Psychodrama & Sociometry*, 30:13-17.

04075 **GAZDA, G. M., DUNCAN, J. A.**, and **SISSON, P. J.** (1971), Professional issues in group work. *Personnel & Guid. J.*, 49:637-644.

04076 **GAZDA, G. M., PARKS, J.**, and **SISSON, J.** (1971), The use of a modified marathon in conjunction with group counseling in short-term treatment of alcoholics. *Rehab. Couns. Bull.*, 15:97-105.

04077 **GEDDES, D.** (1955), A preliminary report on the mass psychotherapeutic treatment of sex offenders in California. *Acta Psychother., Psychosomat. Orthopaedagog.*, (Basel) 3:116.

04078 **GEE, H.**, and **KEMP, P.** (1969), Starting an adolescent group: some anxieties and solutions. *Brit. J. Psychiat. Soc. Work*, 10:12-16.

04079 **GEER, J. K.** (1972), The effect of group counseling model on the attitudes of high and low dogmatic non-Black college students toward Black people. *Dissert. Abstr. Internat.*, 32:4346A.

04080 **GEERT-JORGENSEN, E.** (1963), Group treatment of patients suffering from paranoid psychosis. *Acta Psychiat. Scand. Suppl.*, (Copenhagen) 39:152.

04081 **GEEVER, G.** (1954), Transference elements in a fathers' group in a child guidance clinic. *J. Psychiat. Social Work*, 23:227-230.

04082 **GEHL, R. H., WELKIND, A.**, and **UCKO, F. A.** (1966), Providing a therapeutic climate by pairing patients: a preliminary report. *Ment. Hygiene*, 50:36-46.

04083 **GEIDT, F. H.** (1956), Factor analysis of roles patients take in therapy groups. *J. Soc. Psychol.*, 44:165-171.

04084 **GEIS, H. J.** (1973), Effectively leading a group in the present moment: a highly artistic probabilistic and professional task if one would by-pass traditional myths about group work—1. *Educat. Technol.*, 13:76-88.

04085 **GEISLER, J.**, and **GILLINGHAM, W.** (1971), The effects of a personal growth group experience. *Nat. Cath. Guid. Conf. J.*, 15:183-186.

04086 **GEISSLER, K. A.** (1975), Significance of group dynamics for training of economics teachers. *Gruppenpsychother. & Gruppendynam.*, (Goettingen) 9:142-155.

04087 **GEITGEY, D. A.** (1968), *A Study of Some Effects of Sensitivity Training on the Performance of Students in Associate Degree Programs of Nursing Education*. New York: National League for Nursing, Department of Associate Degree Programs.

04088 **GELBER, H.** (1967), The use of psychological learning theory in the development of assertion. *Can. Psychiat. Assn. J.*, (Ottawa) 12:207-208.

04089 **GELDER, J. G.** (1963), Psychodrama in industry: pitfalls, cautions and requirements. *Group Psychother., Psychodrama & Sociometry*, 16:22-24.

04090 **GELDER, M. G.,** and **MARKS, I. M.** (1968), Desensitization and phobias: a cross-over study. *Brit. J. Psychiat.*, (Ashford) 114:323-328.

04091 **GELDER, M. G., MARKS, I. M.,** and **WOLFF, H. H.** (1967), Desensitization and psychotherapy in the treatment of phobic states: a controlled inquiry. *Brit. J. Psychiat.*, (Ashford) 113:53-73.

04092 **GELLER, J. J.** (1969), (Application of group psychotherapy for long-term analytical treatment.) *Zeit. Psychosomat. Med. Psychoanal.*, (Goettingen) 15:44-51.

04093 **GELLER, J. J.** (1975), Concerning the size of therapy groups. In: *Group Psychotherapy and Group Function*, 2d ed., eds. M. Rosenbaum and M. M. Berger. New York: Basic Books.

04094 **GELLER, J. J.** (1951), Concerning the size of therapy groups. *Internat. J. Group Psychother.*, 1:118-120.

04095 **GELLER, J. J.** (1974), Contribution of the interpersonal school of psychoanalysis to analytic group psychotherapy. In: *Group Therapy 1974: An Overview*, eds. L. R. Wolberg and M. L. Aronson. New York: Stratton Intercontinental Medical Books.

04096 **GELLER, J. J.** (1950), Current status of group psychotherapy practices in the state hospitals for mental disease. *Group Psychother., Psychodrama & Sociometry*, 3:231-240.

04097 **GELLER, J. J.** (1954), An experience in group psychotherapy as a teaching device. *Group Psychother., Psychodrama & Sociometry*, 7:130-138.

04098 **GELLER, J. J.** (1963), Group psychotherapy in child guidance clinics. *Curr. Psychiat. Ther.*, 3:219-228.

04099 **GELLER, J. J.** (1954), Group psychotherapy in a community psychiatric clinic. *Internat. J. Group Psychother.*, 4:103-108.

04100 **GELLER, J. J.** (1963), Group psychotherapy in the treatment of the schizophrenic syndromes. *Psychiat. Quart.*, 37:710-722.

04101 **GELLER, J. J.** (1962), Parataxic distortions in the initial stages of group relationships. *Internat. J. Group Psychother.*, 12:27-34.

04102 **GELLER, J. J.** (1949), A program of group psychotherapy in the treatment of chronic mental illness. *Psychiat. Quart.*, 23:425-438.

04103 **GELLER, J. J.** (1950), Proposed plan for institutional group psychotherapy. *Psychiatric Quart. Suppl.*, 24:270-277.

04104 **GELLER, J. J.** (1978), Review of M. Rosenbaum's and M. M. Berger's *Group Psychotherapy and Group Function. Comprehens. Psychiat.*, 19:478.

04105 **GELLER, J. J.** (1958), Supervision in a hospital psychotherapy program. *Internat. J. Group Psychother.*, 8:313-322.

04106 **GELLER, M.** (1953), Group psychotherapy with girls institutionalized for mental deficiency: a study of psychotherapeutic process and effects. Unpublished doctoral dissertation, New York University.

04107 **GELLER, R. E.** (1970), Reaching the deaf: report of an in-hospital group. *Ment. Hygiene*, 54:388-392.

04108 **GELMAN, S. R.** (1969), Admission groups for mentally retarded girls. *Hosp. & Community Psychiat.*, 20:31-33.

04109 **GENDLIN, E. T.** (1968), Psychotherapy and community psychology. *Psychother.: Theory, Res. & Pract.*, 5:67-72.

04110 **GENDLIN, E. T.,** and **BEEBE, J.** (1968), An experiential approach to group therapy. *J. Res. Develop. Educat.*, 1:19-29.

04111 **GENDREAU, P.,** and **ROSS, B.** (1979), Effective correctional treatment: bibliotherapy for cynics. *Crime & Delinquency*, 25:463-489.

04112 **GENDZEL, I. B.** (1970), Marathon group therapy and nonverbal methods. *Amer. J. Psychiat.*, 127:286-290.

04113 **GENDZEL, I. B.** (1972), Marathon group therapy: rationale and techniques. *Curr. Psychiat. Ther.*, 12:151-160.

04114 **GENDZEL, I. B.** (1978), Review of A. Starr's *Psychodrama: Rehearsal for Living. Internat. J. Group Psychother.*, 28:574.

04115 **GENEVARD, G.** (1969), Group analytic psychotherapy. *Annales Medico-Psychol.*, (Paris) 2:469-478.

04116 **GENEVARD, G., SCHNEIDER, P. B., JORDI, P., DELALOYE, R., GENTON, M., GLOOR, C.,** and **VILLA, J. L.** (1961), (Contribution of group psychotherapy to the comprehension of neurosis.) *Evolut. Psychiat.*, (Toulouse) 26:399-416.

04117 **GENIS, A.** (1966), El concepto de grupo en psicoterapia. (The group concept in psychotherapy.) *Rev. Psiquiat. Psicolog. Med.*, 7:394-398.

04118 **GENTHNER, R. W.,** and **FALKENBERG, V.** (1977), Changes in personal responsibility as a function of interpersonal skills training. *Small Group Behav.*, 8:533-539.

04119 **GENTRY, J. E.,** and **WATKINS, J. F.** (1974), Organizational training for improving race relations in schools. *Educat. & Urban Society*, 6:269-283.

04120 **GENTRY, M. E.** (1974), Initial group meetings: member expectations and information distribution process. *Dissert. Abstr. Internat.*, 35:2397A.

04121 **GEOGHAGAN, J. L.** (1970), An action approach to group counseling: an experimental study. *Dissert. Abstr. Internat.*, 31:4458A.

04122 **GEOGHEGAN, J. T.** (1960), Art therapy. *Diseases Nerv. System*, 21:638-639.

04123 **GEORGE, M.** (1967), In–patient care in a comprehensive community mental health center. *J. Psychiat. Nursing*, 5:22-29.

04124 **GEORGII, R.** (1970), Gruppenhilfe untereinander: beispiele der verschiedenen situationen eines gruppenverlaufes von 30 studen. (Mutual group aid: samples of various situations in a course of group therapy of 30 hours.) *Praxis Kinderpsychol. & Kinderpsychiat.*, (Goettingen) 19:130-134.

04125 **GEORGII, R.** (1971), Mechanisms of individual discussions and group care with child and mother. *Praxis Kinderpsychol. & Kinderpsychiat.*, (Goettingen) 20:46-51.

04126 **GERACE, L.,** and **ROSENBERG, L.** (1979), The use of art prints in group therapy with aftercare patients. *Perspect. Psychiat. Care*, 17:83-86.

04127 **GERARD, H. B.** (1964), Conformity and commitment to the group. *J. Abnorm. & Soc. Psychol.*, 68:209-211.

04128 **GERARD, H. B.,** and **MILLER, N.** (1967), Group dynamics. In: *Annual Review of Psychology, Vol. 18*, ed. P. S. Farnsworth. Palo Alto: Annual Reviews.

04129 **GERARD, H. B., WILHELMY, R. A.,** and **CONOLLEY, E. S.** (1968), Conformity and group size. *J. Personality & Soc. Psychol.*, 8:79-82.

04130 **GERBER, S. A.,** and **SINGER, D.** (1969), Dynamic group counseling with mothers of students in special classes. *Corrective Psychiat. & J. Soc. Ther.*, 15:25-33.

04131 **GERBRANDT, G. L.** (1974), *An Idea Book for Acting Out and Writing Language, K-8.* Urbana, IL: National Council of Teachers of English.

04132 **GERE, F.** (1975), Developing the ok miniscript. *Transactional Anal. J.*, 5:285-289.

04133 **GERINDEN, W. E.,** and **SEABER, J. A.** (1971), Adlerian psychology as a basis for group counseling of socially maladjusted students. *Nat. Cath. Guid. Conf. J.*, 15:106-112.

04134 **GERLER, E. R.** (1980), Physical exercise and multimodal counseling groups. *J. Special. Group Work*, 5:157-162.

04135 **GERMAN, M. L.** (1975), The effects of group reality therapy on institu-

tionalized adolescents and group leaders. *Dissert. Abstr. Internat.*, 36:1916B.
04136 **GERMAN, S. A.** (1964), A group approach to rehabilitation occupational therapy in a psychiatric setting. *Amer. J. Occupat. Ther.*, 18:209-214.
04137 **GERRISH, M. J.** (1968), The family therapist is a nurse. *Amer. J. Nursing*, 68:320-323.
04138 **GERSHAM, L.**, and **CLAUSER, R. A.** (1974), Treating insomnia with relaxation and desensitization in a group setting by an automated approach. *J. Behav. Ther. & Exper. Psychiat.*, 5:31.
04139 **GERSHMAN, H.** (1976), The effect of group therapy on compulsive homosexuality in men and women. *Amer. J. Psychoanal.*, 35:303-312.
04140 **GERSON, B.** (1974), Consciousness-raising groups with elementary school girls: a case study. *Psychother.: Theory, Res. & Pract.*, 11:30-35.
04141 **GERSTEIN, A. I.** (1974), Variations in treatment technique in group activity therapy. *Psychother.: Theory, Res. & Pract.*, 11:343-345.
04142 **GERSTEIN, A. I.** (1969), Variation in treatment techniques in group activity therapy for children. *Amer. J. Orthopsychiat.*, 39:261-262.
04143 **GERSTEN, C.** (1951), An experimental evaluation of group therapy with juvenile delinquents. *Internat. J. Group Psychother.*, 1:311-318.
04144 **GERSTEN, C.** (1952), Group therapy with institutionalized juvenile delinquents. *J. Genetic Psychol.*, 80:35-64.
04145 **GERSTENBERG, W.** (1979), (Psychodramatic therapy with out-patient children and their parents.) *Praxis Kinderpsychol. & Kinderpsychiat.*, (Goettingen) 28:293-302.
04146 **GERSTENBERG, W.**, and **SIEVERS, E. F.** (1978), (Experiences as a leader and co-leader of an analytic group.) *Gruppenpsychother. & Gruppendynam.*, (Goettingen) 13:25-30.
04147 **GERSTENLAUER, C.** (1950), A comparative evaluation of the effects of group therapy on some aspects of behavior and emotional and social adjustment of a selected group of institutionalized male juvenile delinquents. *Microfilm Abstr.*, 10:101-103.
04148 **GERSTENLAUER, C.** (1950), Group therapy with institutionalized male juvenile delinquents. *Amer. Psychol.*, 5:325.
04149 **GERSTL, T. L.** (1970), Sensitivity training with underachieving junior high school students. *Dissert. Abstr. Internat.*, 30:3724A-3725A.
04150 **GERTZ, B.**, and **VAN HORN, L.** (1971), Sensitivity training for college professors. *Training & Develop. J.*, 25:12-16.
04151 **GERVAIS, L.** (1968), La dynamique de groupe chez les residents en psychiatrie. (Group dynamics in psychiatric residents.) *Can. Psychiat. Assn. J.*, (Ottawa) 13:159-162.
04152 **GERVAIS, L.** (1969), Group dynamics as therapy. *Amer. J. Psychiat.*, 126:579-580.
04153 **GESENWAY, D. B.** (1973), Emotional involvement in psychotherapy. *Amer. J. Psychiat.*, 130:937-939.
04154 **GESUE, A.** (1980), (The treatment group and the 'acute' alcoholic in psychiatric hospital undergoing reform.) *Minerva Psichiat.*, (Turin) 21:139-153.
04155 **GETTY, C.**, and **SHANNON, A. M.** (1969), Cotherapy as an egalitarian relationship. *Amer. J. Nursing*, 69:767-771.
04156 **GETTY, C.** (1967), Nurses as co-therapists in a family-therapy setting. *Perspect. Psychiat. Care*, 5:38-46.
04157 **GETZEL, G. S., GOLDBERG, J. R.**, and **SALMON, R.** (1971), Supervising in groups as a model for today. *Soc. Casework*, 52:154-163.
04158 **GEYER, P.** (1970), Oregon's group homes for juveniles. *Rehab. Record*, 11:28-31.

04159 **GIALLOMBARDO, R.** (1966), Social roles in a prison for women. *Soc. Problems*, 13:268-288.

04160 **GIANNEL, A. S.** (1973), (Criminosynthesis and therapy of an LSD dependent criminal arsonist.) *Quad. Criminol. Clin.*, (Rome) 15:345-358.

04161 **GIARDINA, R. C.** (1972), Teaching international organization: the use of role-playing techniques. *New Dir. Teaching*, 3:22-28.

04162 **GIBB, C. A.** (1969), Leadership. In: *The Handbook of Social Psychology*, 2d ed., eds. G. Lindzey and E. Aronson. Reading, MA: Addison-Wesley.

04163 **GIBB, J. R.** (1974), The message from research. In: *The 1974 Annual Handbook for Group Facilitators*, eds. J. W. Pfeiffer and J. E. Jones. La Jolla: University Associates.

04164 **GIBB, J. R.** (1972), TORI theory: nonverbal behavior and the experience of community. *Compar. Group Studies*, 3:461-472.

04165 **GIBBARD, G. S.**, and **HARTMAN, J. J.** (1973), The oedipal paradigm in group development: a clinical and empirical study. *Small Group Behav.*, 4:305-354.

04166 **GIBBARD, G. S.**, and **HARTMAN, J. J.** (1973), Relationship patterns in self-analytic groups: a clinical and empirical study. *Behav. Sci. Res.*, 18:335-353.

04167 **GIBBARD, G. S.**, and **HARTMAN, J. J.** (1973), The significance of utopian fantasies in small groups. *Internat. J. Group Psychother.*, 23:125-147.

04168 **GIBBARD, G. S.**, **HARTMAN, J. J.**, and **MANN, R. D.** (1974), *Analysis of Groups*. San Francisco: Jossey-Bass.

04169 **GIBBARD, G. S.** (1973), *Analysis of Groups: Contributions to Theory, Research, and Practice*. San Francisco: Jossey-Bass.

04170 **GIBBONS, T. J.**, and **LEE, M. K.** (1972), Group counseling: impetus to learning. *Elem. School Guid. & Couns.*, 7:32-36.

04171 **GIBBS, G. I.** (1974), *Handbook of Games and Simulation Exercises*. Los Angeles: Sage Publications.

04172 **GIBBS, J. M.** (1945), Group play therapy. *Brit. J. Med. Psychol.*, (London) 20:244-251.

04173 **GIBERTI, E.** (1971), Grupos de orientacion de parejas. (Orientation groups for couples.) *Rev. Latinoamer. Psicol.*, (Bogota) 3:145-162.

04174 **GIBLIN, T. R.** (1972), The effect of group systematic desensitization treatment on the reported anxiety and self-concepts of secondary teacher education students. *Dissert. Abstr. Internat.*, 32:6265A.

04175 **GIBSON, A.** (1967), *The Remotivators' Guide Book*. Philadelphia: Davis.

04176 **GIBSON, D. L.** (1971), Prediction of verbal behavior of individuals in small counseling groups. *Dissert. Abstr. Internat.*, 32:559B.

04177 **GIBSON, J.** (1975), Human awareness in the medical school curriculum: a small group communication approach to improve human dimensions of medical education. *Bioscience Communicat.*, 1:69-84.

04178 **GIEDT, H. F.** (1961), Predicting suitability for group psychotherapy. *Amer. J. Psychother.*, 15:582-591.

04179 **GIFFIN, K.**, and **BRADLEY, K.** (1969), An exploratory study of group counseling for speech anxiety. *J. Clin. Psychol.*, 25:99-101.

04180 **GIFFIN, K.**, and **BRADLEY, K.** (1969), Group counseling for speech anxiety: an approach and a rationale. *J. Communicat.*, 19:22-29.

04181 **GIFFIN, K.**, and **EHRLICH, L.** (1963), The attitudinal effects of a group discussion on a proposed change in company policy. *Speech Monogr.*, 30:377-379.

04182 **GIFFORD, C. G.** (1968), Sensitivity training and social work. *Soc. Work*, 13:78-86.

04183 **GIFFORD, C. G.**, **LANDIS, E. E.**, and **ACKERLY, S. S.** (1953), The use of social group work as a therapeutic factor in the hospital setting. *Amer. J. Orthopsychiat.*, 23:142-155.

04184 **GIFFORD, S.**, and **MACKENZIE, J.** (1948), Review of literature on group treatment of psychoses. *Diseases Nerv. System*, 9:19-24.
04185 **GILBERT, J. G.** (1969), Dynamics of group formation and behavior. *Nat. Cath. Guid. Conf. J.*, 13:96-106.
04186 **GILBERT, J. G.** (1970), Group guidance, counseling, and psychotherapy. *Nat. Cath. Guid. Conf. J.*, 14:162-165.
04187 **GILBERT, L. A.** (1979), Review of L. S. Hansen's and R. S. Rapoza's *Career Development and Counseling of Women. J. Higher Educat.*, 50:782.
04188 **GILBREATH, S.** (1968), Appropriate and inappropriate group counseling with academic underachievers. *J. Couns. Psychol.*, 15:506-511.
04189 **GILBREATH, S. H.** (1967), Group counseling, dependence, and college male underachievement. *J. Couns. Psychol.*, 14:449-453.
04190 **GILBREATH, S. H.** (1967), Group counseling with male underachieving college volunteers. *Personnel & Guid. J.*, 45:469-476.
04191 **GILDEA, M. C. L.** (1948), Social function and group therapy. *Mental Hygiene*, 32:203-216.
04192 **GILDER, R., BUSCHMAN, P. R., SITARZ, A. L.**, and **WOLFF, J. A.** (1978), Group therapy with parents of children with leukemia. *Amer. J. Psychother.*, 32:276-287.
04193 **GILES, H. H.**, and **KRONEMEYER, R.** (1965), Self-evaluation of a group therapy experience by graduate students and its implication. *Internat. J. Soc. Psychiat.*, (London) 11:180-187.
04194 **GILI, E.**, and **O'DONNELL, P.** (1978), *El Juego: Técnica Lúdicas en Psicoterapia Grupal de Adultos*, 1st ed. Barcelona: Granica.
04195 **GILL, H. S.** (1972), Treatment of the marital dyad in a foursome: an illustrative case study. *Postgrad. Med. J.*, (Oxford) 48:555-562.
04196 **GILLAN, P.** (1980), Psychological methods in sex therapy for the disabled. *Sex. Disabil.*, 3:199-202.
04197 **GILLAN, P.** (1979), Sex therapy. *Midwife, Health Visitor & Community Nurse*, (London) 15:182.
04198 **GILLIARD, W.** (1973), The analysis of personality types and their relationship to perceived group behavior in a training group session. *Dissert. Abstr. Internat.*, 34:3868A.
04199 **GILLICK, J. J.** (1978), Al-Anon: a self-help group for co-alcoholics. *Dissert. Abstr. Internat.*, 39:1478B. (University Microfilms No. 7810621.)
04200 **GILLIES, E. P.** (1948), Therapy dramatics for the public schoolroom. *Nerv. Child*, 7:328-336.
04201 **GILLIGAN, J. F.** (1973), Personality characteristics of selectors and non-selectors on sensitivity training. *J. Couns. Psychol.*, 20:265-268.
04202 **GILLIGAN, J. F.** (1972), Personality characteristics of selectors and non-selectors on sensitivity training and the relationship between selector characteristics and training outcomes. *Dissert. Abstr. Internat.*, 33:2101A.
04203 **GILLIGAN, J. F.** (1974), Sensitivity training and self-actualization. *Psychol. Reports*, 34:319-325.
04204 **GILLILAND, B. E.** (1967), An evaluation of the effects of small group counseling with Negro adolescents. *Dissert. Abstr. Internat.*, 27:2878A.
04205 **GILLILAND, B. E.** (1968), Small group counseling with Negro adolescents in a public high school. *J. Couns. Psychol.*, 15:147-152.
04206 **GILLILAND, E. G.** (1961), Uses of music therapy. *Group Psychother., Psychodrama & Sociometry*, 14:68-72.
04207 **GILLIS, J. S.**, and **JESSOR, R.** (1970), Effects of brief psychotherapy on belief in internal control: an exploratory study. *Psychother.: Theory, Res. & Pract.*, 7:135-137.
04208 **GILLIS, L. S.** (1956), Group psychotherapy: an outline of some modern procedures. *Med. Proceed.*, 2:405-411.
04209 **GILMAN, M. C.**, and **GORLICH, E.** (1968), *Group Counseling with Delin-*

quent Youth. Washington, D.C.: U.S. Department of Health, Education, and Welfare.

04210 **GILPIN, C. R.**, and **NEUFELD, E.** (1970), Community consultation and a shoestring budget: Rx for an activity therapy program. *Ment. Hygiene*, 54:397-400.

04211 **GIMMESTAD, M. J.**, and **GREENWOOD, J. D.** (1974), A new twist on ipr: concurrent recall by supervisory group. *Counselor Educat. & Supervision*, 14:71-73.

04212 **GIMPEL, H. S.** (1968), Group work with adolescent girls. *Nursing Outlook*, 16:46-48.

04213 **GINOTT, H. G.** (1961), *Group Psychotherapy with Children*. New York: McGraw-Hill.

04214 **GINOTT, H. G.** (1961), *Group Psychotherapy with Children: The Theory and Practice of Play-Therapy*. New York: McGraw-Hill.

04215 **GINOTT, H. G.** (1956), Group screening of parents in a child guidance setting. *Internat. J. Group Psychother.*, 6:405-409.

04216 **GINOTT, H. G.** (1965), Interaction in child group therapy. *Topical Probl. Psychol. & Psychother.*, 5:205-210.

04217 **GINOTT, H. G.** (1957), Parent education groups in a child guidance clinic. *Ment. Hygiene*, 41:82-86.

04218 **GINOTT, H. G.** (1958), Play group therapy: a theoretical framework. *Internat. J. Group Psychother.*, 8:410-418.

04219 **GINOTT, H. G.**, **BLECK, L.**, and **BARNES, R. I.** (1959), A study in nonattendance of initial interviews in a community clinic. *Internat. J. Group Psychother.*, 9:314-321.

04220 **GINOTT, H. G.**, and **LEBO, D.** (1963), Most and least used play therapy limits. *J. Genetic Psychol.*, 103:153-159.

04221 **GINOTT, H. G.**, and **LEBO, D.** (1961), Play therapy limits and theoretical orientation. *J. Couns. Psychol.*, 25:337-340.

04222 **GINSBERG, B. G.**, **STUTMAN, S. S.**, and **HUMMEL, J.** (1978), Group filial therapy. *Soc. Work*, 23:154-156.

04223 **GINZBERG, R.** (1953), Geriatric ward psychiatry: techniques in the psychological management of elderly psychotics. *Amer. J. Psychiat.*, 110:296-300.

04224 **GIORANO, J. L.**, **LURIE, A.**, and **RON, H.** (1968), Socialization of the younger psychiatric patients: the community and the hospital—a dual responsibility. *Amer. J. Orthopsychiat.*, 38:243-244.

04225 **GIORDANO, J. L.** (1966), Group work in a home for the aged: the role of the worker. *J. Jewish Communal Serv.*, 42:364-370.

04226 **GIOVANNONI, J. M.**, and **BILINGSLEY, A.** (1971), Child neglect among the poor: a study of parental adequacy in families of three ethnic groups. *Child Welfare*, 49:187-195.

04227 **GIRSHICK, E.** (1978), The effects of psychodrama on verbal skills in high school students. *Dissert. Abstr. Internat.*, 38:6616A.

04228 **GITCHOFF, G. T.**, and **SHOPE, R. D.** (1971), Kids vs. cops: the police-youth discussion group. *Police*, (Surrey) 16:9-13.

04229 **GITELSON, M.** (1941), Group psychotherapy. *Illinois Psychiat. J.*, 1:5-6.

04230 **GLAD, D. D.** (1959), *Operational Values in Psychotherapy: A Conceptual Framework of Interpersonality*. New York: Oxford University Press.

04231 **GLAD, D. D.**, and **BARNES, R. H.** (1965), The network of psychiatric services. *Internat. J. Group Psychother.*, 15:477-482.

04232 **GLAD, D. D.**, and **DURKIN, H. E.** (1969), Summary (as part of panel on interaction and insight in group psychotherapy, AGPA Conf., 1968). *Internat. J. Group Psychother.*, 19:279-280.

04233 **GLAD, D. D.**, and **GLAD, V. B.** (1963), *Interpersonality Synopsis*. New York: Libra Publishers.

04234 **GLAD, D. D., HAYNES, M. L., GLAD, V. B.,** and **FERGUSON, R. D.** (1963), Schizophrenic factor reactions to four group psychotherapy methods. *Internat. J. Group Psychother.*, 13:196-210.

04235 **GLAD, D. D.,** and **RAINEY, R. V.** (1950), Group therapy with paranoid schizophrenics: a method of investigation. *J. Colorado-Wyoming Acad. Sci.*, 4:66.

04236 **GLAD, D. D., SMITH, W. L.,** and **GLAD, V. B.** (1957), Behavior factor reactions to leader emphasis upon feelings or social expressions. *Internat. J. Soc. Psychiat.*, (London) 3:129-132.

04237 **GLADFELTER, J.** (1977), Review of M. Rosenbaum's and M. M. Berger's *Group Psychotherapy and Group Function. Internat. J. Group Psychother.*, 27:117-119.

04238 **GLADFELTER, J.** (1970), The use of video-tape recording for supervision of group psychotherapists. *J. Contemp. Psychother.*, 2:119-123.

04239 **GLADFELTER, J. H.** (1970), Videotape supervision of co-therapists. *J. Group Psychoanal. & Process*, (London) 2:45-56.

04240 **GLADSTONE, H. P.** (1962), Educative psychotherapy with student nurse classes: an investigation of socially shared conflicts and value distortions. *Ment. Hygiene*, 46:408-419.

04241 **GLANZ, E. C.,** and **HAYES, R. W.** (1962), *Groups in Guidance: The Dynamics of Groups and the Application of Groups in Guidance*. Rockleigh, NJ: Allyn and Bacon.

04242 **GLANZ, E. C.,** and **HAYES, R. W.** (1967), *Groups in Guidance*, 2d ed. Rockleigh, NJ: Allyn and Bacon.

04243 **GLASER, J. S.** (1972), The stairwell society of public housing: from small groups to social organizations. *Compar. Group Studies*, 3:159-173.

04244 **GLASER, K.** (1976), Women's self-help groups as an alternative to therapy. *Psychother.: Theory, Res. & Pract.*, 13:77-81.

04245 **GLASGOW, D.,** and **LURIE, A.** (1966), Milieu therapy program in a psychiatric hospital. *Hospitals*, 40:79-90.

04246 **GLASS, J. F.** (1973), The presentation of self and the encounter culture: notes on the sociology of t-groups. *Small Group Behav.*, 4:449-458.

04247 **GLASS, M.** (1965), A group leader program for regressed patients. *Psychother.: Theory, Res. & Pract.*, 2:73-77.

04248 **GLASS, R.** (1968), The current dilemma in social group work methodology. *J. Jewish Communal Serv.*, 44:310-315.

04249 **GLASS, S. D.** (1969), *The Practical Handbook of Group Counseling*. Baltimore: Behavioral Consultation Services.

04250 **GLASSER, M. A.** (1952), Group therapy in the community. *Neuropsychiatry*, 2:74-77.

04251 **GLASSER, P., SARRI, R.,** and **VINTER, R.** (1974), *Individual Change through Small Groups*. New York: Free Press.

04253 **GLASSER, P. H.** (1974), Group work intervention in the social environment. In: *Individual Change through Small Groups*, eds. P. Glasser, R. Sarri, and R. Vinter. New York: Free Press.

04254 **GLASSFORD, P. V.** (1972), Staff experimental relaxation group. *Austral. Occupat. Ther. J.*, 19:51-54.

04255 **GLASSMANN, R., LIPTON, H.,** and **DUNSTAN, P. L.** (1959), Group discussions with a hospitalized schizophrenic and his family. *Internat. J. Group Psychother.*, 9:204-212.

04256 **GLATT, M. M.** (1958), Group therapy in alcoholism. *Brit. J. Addict.*, (Edinburgh) 54:133-147.

04257 **GLATT, M. M.** (1963), (Group therapy of alcoholics in "open" British hospitals: a retrospect on 10 years of personal experiences.) *Psychiat., Neurol. & Med. Psychol.*, (Leipzig) 146:1-15.

04258 **GLATT, M. M.** (1967), Group therapy with young drug addicts: the addicts' point of view. *Nursing Times*, (London) 63:519-521.

04259 **GLATT, M. M.** (1965), (Psychological bases of the treatment of alcoholics: a report of experiences of "alcoholics units.") *Munchen Med. Wochenschr.*, (Munich) 107:2477-2481.

04260 **GLATZER, H. T.** (1959), Analysis of masochism in group therapy. *Internat. J. Group Psychother.*, 9:158-166.

04261 **GLATZER, H. T.** (1971), Analytic supervision in group psychotherapy. *Internat. J. Group Psychother.*, 21:436-443.

04262 **GLATZER, H. T.** (1965), Aspects of transference in group psychotherapy. *Internat. J. Group Psychother.*, 15:167-176.

04263 **GLATZER, H. T.** (1965), Clinical aspects on interaction between the group and its leader in adult group psychotherapy. *Topical Probl. Psychol. & Psychother.*, 5:197-204.

04264 **GLATZER, H. T.** (1972), Discussion. *Internat. J. Group Psychother.*, 22:467-468.

04265 **GLATZER, H. T.** (1962), Handling narcissistic problems in group psychotherapy. *Internat. J. Group Psychother.*, 12:448-455.

04266 **GLATZER, H. T.** (1953), Handling transference resistance in group therapy. *Psychoanal. Rev.*, 40:36-43.

04267 **GLATZER, H. T.** (1967), Neurotic factors of voyeurism and exhibitionism in group psychotherapy. *Internat. J. Group Psychother.*, 17:3-9.

04268 **GLATZER, H. T.** (1964), Practice of group psychotherapy on classical psychoanalytic concepts. *Amer. J. Orthopsychiat.*, 34:395-396.

04269 **GLATZER, H T.** (1976), Presidential address: service to patients—the ultimate priority. *Internat. J. Group Psychother.*, 26:267-280.

04270 **GLATZER, H. T.** (1956), The relative effectiveness of clinically homogeneous and heterogeneous psychotherapy groups. *Internat. J. Group Psychother.*, 6:258-265.

04271 **GLATZER, H. T.** (1947), Selection of mothers for group therapy. *Amer. J. Orthopsychiat.*, 17:477-483.

04272 **GLATZER, H. T.** (1952), Transference in group therapy. *Amer. J. Orthopsychiat.*, 22:499-509.

04273 **GLATZER, H. T.** (1978), The working alliance in analytic group psychotherapy. *Internat. J. Group Psychother.*, 28:147-161.

04274 **GLATZER, H. T.** (1969), Working through in analytic group psychotherapy. *Internat. J. Group Psychother.*, 19:292-306.

04275 **GLATZER, H. T.**, and **DURKIN, H. E.** (1945), The role of the therapist in group relationships. *Nerv. Child*, 4:243-251.

04276 **GLATZER, H. T.**, and **PEDERSON-KRAG, G.** (1947), Relationship group therapy with a mother of a problem child. In: *The Practice of Group Therapy*, ed. S. R. Slavson. London: Pushkin Press; New York: International Universities Press.

04277 **GLAUBER, H.** (1943), Group therapy from the view-point of a psychiatric case worker. *Amer. J. Orthopsychiat.*, 13:671-677.

04278 **GLENN, J.** (1951), Values of group discussion with psychiatric aids in a mental hospital. *Internat. J. Group Psychother.*, 1:254-263.

04279 **GLENN, K. C.** (1969), "Gang work" in a psychiatric hospital. *Bull. Menninger Clinic*, 33:233-243.

04280 **GLENN, R. N.** (1978), Application of structured experience. *Health & Soc. Work*, 3:175-180.

04281 **GLICKMAN, E.** (1968), Professional social work with Headstart mothers. *Children*, 15:59-65.

04282 **GLIEDMAN, L. H.** (1957), Concurrent and combined group treatment of chronic alcoholics and their wives. *Internat. J. Group Psychother.*, 7:414-424.

04283 **GLIEDMAN, L. H.** (1958), Some contributions of group therapy in the treatment of chronic alcoholism. In: *Problems of Addiction and Habituation*, eds. P. H. Hock and J. Zubin. New York: Grune and Stratton.

04284 **GLIEDMAN, L. H., NASH, H. T.,** and **WEBB, W. L.** (1956), Group psychotherapy of male alcoholics and their wives. *Diseases Nerv. System*, 17:90-93.

04285 **GLIEDMAN, L. H., ROSENTHAL, D., FRANK, J. D.,** and **NASH, H. T.** (1956), Group therapy of alcoholics with concurrent group meetings of their wives. *Quart. J. Studies Alcohol*, 17:655-670.

04286 **GLIEDMAN, L. H.** (1975), Group therapy of alcoholics with concurrent group meetings of their wives. In: *Group Psychotherapy and Group Function*, 2d ed., eds. M. Rosenbaum and M. M. Berger. New York: Basic Books.

04287 **GLOCER, F.** (1973), (Laboratory group experiences.) *Acta Psiquiat. Psicol. Amer. Latina*, (Buenos Aires) 19:396-401.

04288 **GLOTZER, S.** (1973), Dynamics of a counseling group: the counselor as leader. *Internat. Assn. Pupil Personnel Workers J.*, 17:184-187.

04289 **GLOVER, B. H.** (1967), A new nurse therapist. *Amer. J. Nursing*, 67:1003-1005.

04290 **GLOVER, W. C.** (1973), Selected effects of individual and group counseling on disadvantaged elementary pupils. *Dissert. Abstr. Internat.*, 34:3869A.

04291 **GLÜCK, A.** (1974), Group therapy after remission of endogenous depression. In: *Zur Systematik, Provokation und Therapie Depressiver Psychosen*, ed. W. Walcher. Vienna: Hollinek.

04292 **GLUCK, M. M.** (1980), Group therapy in a pain management program. *J. Psychiat. Nursing*, 18:21-25.

04293 **GLUSKIN, S. W.** (1956), Changes in two groups of institutionalized mentally retarded delinquent boys following a series of individual and group blame avoidance interview sessions: the evaluation of changes in self-concept, in attitude toward others, and in certain aspects of institutional behavior and adjustment. Unpublished doctoral dissertation, New York University.

04294 **GODENNE, G. D.** (1964), Outpatient adolescent group psychotherapy: i. review of the literature on use of co-therapists, psychodrama and parent group therapy. *Amer. J. Psychother.*, 18:584-593.

04295 **GODENNE, G. D.** (1965), Outpatient adolescent group psychotherapy: ii. use of co-therapists, psychodrama and parent group therapy. *Amer. J. Psychother.*, 19:40-53.

04296 **GOEBEL, S. R.** (1978), Infantile play and infantile fantasies as indicators of group dynamical processes in a group of children at a klausurtagung. *Dynam. Psychiat.*, (Berlin) 11:52-63.

04297 **GOEBL, D. R.** (1978), A study of the effects of cotherapist mutuality on therapist team functioning in an analogue therapy session. *Dissert. Abstr. Internat.*, 39:2496B.

04298 **GOEHRING, D. J.** (1974), The effects of group size and task competitiveness upon cooperation. *Dissert. Abstr. Internat.*, 34:3529B.

04299 **GOFF, L. V.** (1972), The effect of film-medicated models on the verbal behavior and selected attitudinal variables of participants in group counseling. *Dissert. Abstr. Internat.*, 32:6758A.

04300 **GOFORTH, E. G., MOWATT, M. H.,** and **CLARKE, O. N. J.** (1966), Effect of the presence of an observer and a hidden observer on the defensive patterns of an on-going group. *Internat. J. Group Psychother.*, 16:338-343.

04301 **GÖHLER, I.** (1973), (First experiences in group conversation with mothers of cleft carriers.) *Paediat. & Grenzgebiete*, (Berlin) 12:313-319.

04302 **GÖKNAR, M. K.** (1966), Therapeutic considerations for long-term services. *Can. Psychiat. Assn. J.*, (Ottawa) 11:395-400.

04303 **GOLANN, S. E.** (1969), Emerging areas of ethical concern. *Amer. Psychologist*, 24:454-459.

04304 **GOLANT, M. C.** (1980), The effects of group counseling on locus of control with pregnant teenagers. *Dissert. Abstr. Internat.*, 40:5321A.

04305 **GOLD, H. A.** (1961), Ideology and sociometric position. *Group Psychother., Psychodrama & Sociometry*, 14:39-43.

04306 **GOLD, H. A.** (1962), The importance of ideology in sociometric evaluation of leadership. *Group Psychother., Psychodrama & Sociometry*, 15:224-230.

04307 **GOLD, H. A.** (1963), Sociometry and the teacher. *Internat. J. Sociometry & Sociatry*, 3:65-71.

04308 **GOLD, H. R.** (1959), Variety of cultural contacts as an aid in group psychotherapy: an introduction to ethnotherapy. *Acta Psychother., Psychosomat. Orthopaedagog. Suppl.*, (Basel) 7:142-146.

04309 **GOLD, J. S.** (1968), An evaluation of a laboratory human relations training program for college undergraduates. *Dissert. Abstr. Internat.*, 28:3262-3263.

04310 **GOLD, R. D.** (1971), Alteration of the self concept and attitudes toward others using group behavior modification techniques. *Dissert. Abstr. Internat.*, 31:5125A.

04311 **GOLD, V. J.** (1973), Dreams in group therapy: a review of the literature. *Internat. J. Group Psychother.*, 23:394-407.

04312 **GOLDBART, S.**, and **COOPER, L.** (1976), Safety in groups: an existential analysis. *Small Group Behav.*, 7:237-256.

04313 **GOLDBERG, A. A.**, and **LARSON, C. E.** (1975), *Group Communication.* New York: Prentice-Hall.

04314 **GOLDBERG, C.** (1970), *Encounter: Group Sensitivity Training Experience.* New York: Science House.

04315 **GOLDBERG, C.** (1971), An encounter with the sensitivity training movement. *Can. Ment. Health*, (Ottawa) 19:10-17.

04316 **GOLDBERG, C.** (1970), Group sensitivity training. *Internat. J. Psychiat.*, 9:165-192. Reply to the discussants. *Internat. J. Psychiat.*, 9:226-232.

04317 **GOLDBERG, C.** (1971), *Group Sensitivity Training Experience: "Encounter."* New York: J. Aronson and Sons.

04318 **GOLDBERG, C.** (1975), Peer influence in contemporary group psychotherapy. In: *Group Therapy 1975: An Overview*, eds. L. R. Wolberg and M. L. Aronson. New York: Stratton Intercontinental Medical Books.

04319 **GOLDBERG, C.** (1980), The utilization and limitations of paradoxical intervention in group psychotherapy. *Internat. J. Group Psychother.*, 30:287-298.

04320 **GOLDBERG, C.**, and **GOLDBERG, M. C.** (1973), *The Human Circle: An Existential Approach to the New Group Therapies.* Chicago: Nelson-Hall.

04321 **GOLDBERG, C.**, and **STANITIS, M.** (1977), The enhancement of self-esteem through the communication process in group therapy. *J. Psychiat. Nursing*, 15:5-8.

04322 **GOLDBERG, D. A.**, and **GOODMAN, B.** (1973), The small-group system and training on an acute psychiatric ward. *Psychiat. in Med.*, 4:173-181.

04323 **GOLDBERG, H. L.** (1973), Home treatment. *Psychiat. Annals*, 3:59-61.

04324 **GOLDBERG, M.** (1974), Confrontation groups in a girls' approved school. *Brit. J. Criminol.*, (London) 14:132-138.

04325 **GOLDBERG, M., DUMAS, P. A., DINENBERG, S.**, and **WINICK, W.** (1955), Comparative effectiveness of analytic and psychodramatic group therapy with psychotics. *Internat. J. Group Psychother.*, 5:367-379.

04326 **GOLDBERG, P. B.** (1970), A study to determine the effects of stimulated recall on the process and outcome of group counseling with underachieving junior high school students. *Dissert. Abstr. Internat.*, 30:2797A.

04327 **GOLDEN, J. S.**, and **ROSEN, A. C.** (1975), A group dynamics course for medical students. *Internat. J. Group Psychother.*, 25:305-314.

04328 **GOLDEN, M. M.** (1953), Some mechanisms of analytic group psychotherapy. *Internat. J. Group Psychother.*, 3:280-284.

04329 **GOLDEN, N., CHIRLIN, P.**, and **SHORE, B.** (1970), Tuesday children. *Soc. Casework*, 5:599-605.

04330 **GOLDENBERG de ANTIN, L. R.** (1961), La psicoterapía colectiva racional como forma de tratamiento en los adolescentes. (Rational group psychotherapy as a form of treatment for adolescents.) *Acta Neuropsiquiat. Argent.*, 7:204-206.

04332 **GOLDENBERG, E.**, and **COWDEN, J. E.** (1977), Evaluation of intensive group psychotherapy with male offenders in isolation units. *Correct. & Soc. Psychiat. J. Soc. Ther.*, 23:69-72.

04333 **GOLDFARB, R. L.**, and **SINGER, L. R.** (1970), Maryland's defective delinquency law and the patuxent institution. *Bull. Menninger Clinic*, 34:223-235.

04334 **GOLDFARB, W.** (1980), Effect of group counseling on self-reported problem as influenced by group composition and time arrangement. *Dissert. Abstr. Internat.*, 40:4488A. (University Microfilms No. 8002362.)

04335 **GOLDFARB, W.** (1953), Principles of group psychotherapy. *Amer. J. Psychother.*, 7:418-432.

04336 **GOLDFARB, W.**, and **PARK, P. D.** (1951), Dynamic role of group therapy in the total treatment program of psychotic patients. *Amer. J. Psychother.*, 5:514-520.

04337 **GOLDFARB, W.**, and **RADIN, S. S.** (1964), Group behavior of schizophrenic children. *Internat. J. Soc. Psychiat.*, (London) 10:199-208.

04338 **GOLDFARB-MAOR, S.**, and **MAOR, D.** (1973), Group therapy. *Acta Neurol. & Psychiat. Belgica*, (Brussels) 73:142-154.

04339 **GOLDFIELD, M. D.**, and **LEVY, R.** (1968), The use of television videotape to enhance the therapeutic value of psychodrama. *Amer. J. Psychiat.*, 125:690-692.

04340 **GOLDIN, P.** (1970), Preparing mental health professionals as race relations consultants. *Prof. Psychol.*, 1:343-350.

04341 **GOLDMAN, A. P.** (1973), Empathy, self-disclosure confrontation and cohesiveness in marathon and conventional encounter groups. *Dissert. Abstr. Internat.*, 34:1275B.

04342 **GOLDMAN, A. S., MURPHY, R. J.**, and **BABIKIAN, H.** (1973), Group therapy in obstetric management of pregnant teenagers. *N.Y. State J. Med.*, 73:407-411.

04343 **GOLDMAN, G.** (1955), Group psychotherapy and the lonely person in our changing times. *Group Psychother., Psychodrama & Sociometry*, 8:247-254.

04344 **GOLDMAN, G. D.** (1957), Group psychotherapy from the points of view of various schools of psychology: iii. some applications of Harry Stack Sullivan's theories to group psychotherapy. *Internat. J. Group Psychother.*, 7:385-391.

04345 **GOLDMAN, G. D.** (1975), Some applications of Harry Stack Sullivan's theories to group psychotherapy. In: *Group Psychotherapy and Group Function*, eds. M. Rosenbaum and M. M. Berger. New York: Basic Books.

04346 **GOLDMAN, G. D.**, and **BRODY, H. M.** (1970), An analytic and a behavioristic view of an encounter weekend. *Group Process*, (London) 3:101-121.

04347 **GOLDMAN, H.** (1971), Rehabilitation meets the encounter group. *J. Rehab.*, 37:42.

04348 **GOLDMAN, M.** (1966), A comparison of group and individual performance where subjects have varying tendencies to solve problems. *J. Personnel & Soc. Psychol.*, 3:604-607.

04349 **GOLDMAN, M., WESTERGARD, N.,** and **KRETCHMANN, J. G.** (1972), A comparison of mechanically and group induced reinforcement of verbal behavior. *J. Psychology*, 80:223-236.

04350 **GOLDMAN, M. S.** (1974), To drink or not to drink: an experimental analysis of group drinking decisions by four alcoholics. *Amer. J. Psychiat.*, 131:1123-1130.

04351 **GOLDMAN, M. S., TAYLOR, H. A., CARRUTH, M. L.,** and **NATHAN, P. E.** (1973), Effects of group decision-making on group drinking by alcoholics. *Quart. J. Studies Alcohol*, 34:807-822.

04352 **GOLDSTEIN, A. P.** (1967), The use of planted patients in group psychotherapy. *Amer. J. Psychother.*, 21:767-773.

04353 **GOLDSTEIN, A. P., GERSHAW, N. J.,** and **SPRAFKIN, R. P.** (1979), Structured learning therapy: development and evaluation. *Amer. J. Occupat. Ther.*, 33:635.

04354 **GOLDSTEIN, A. P., HELLER, K.,** and **SECHREST, L. B.** (1966), *Psychotherapy and the Psychology of Behavior Change*. New York: J. Wiley and Sons.

04355 **GOLDSTEIN, H.** (1967), Group learning for foster parents: in a voluntary agency. *Children*, 14:180-184.

04356 **GOLDSTEIN, H. K., COHEN, A., THAMES, M.,** and **GALLOWAY, J. P.** (1974), The influence of group therapy with relatives on rehabilitation clients and their families. *Small Group Behav.*, 5:372-384.

04357 **GOLDSTEIN, J. A.** (1971), Investigation of doubling as a technique for involving severely withdrawn patients in group psychotherapy. *J. Consult. & Clin. Psychol.*, 37:155-162.

04358 **GOLDSTEIN, J. A.** (1969), An investigation of the efficacy of a psychodrama technique in teaching withdrawn and silent psychiatric patients to participate verbally in a therapy group. *Dissert. Abstr. Internat.*, 29:3085B-3086B.

04359 **GOLDSTEIN, M. J., BEDNAR, R. L.,** and **YANDELL, B.** (1978), Personal risk associated with self-disclosure, interpersonal feedback, and group confrontation in group-psychotherapy. *Small Group Behav.*, 9:579-587.

04360 **GOLDSTEIN, N.** (1974), Editorial: group psychotherapy. *N. Y. State J. Med.*, 74:1082.

04361 **GOLDSTEIN, N.,** and **SEMON, R. G.** (1954), The group therapy process and its effectiveness with chronic schizophrenic patients as a function of the role of the leader. Unpublished doctoral dissertation, Boston University.

04362 **GOLDSTEIN, S. E.,** and **BIRNBOM, F.** (1976), Hypochondriasis and the elderly. *J. Amer. Geriat. Soc.*, 24:150-154.

04363 **GOLDSTEIN, S. G.** (1967), The effects of doubling in involvement in group psychotherapy as measured by number and duration of patient utterances. *Psychother.: Theory, Res. & Pract.*, 4:57-60.

04364 **GOLDSTEIN, S. R.** (1971), Differential effects of physical and non-physical encounter group techniques on dimensions of self-esteem, interpersonal relations and defense. *Dissert. Abstr. Internat.*, 31:6257B.

04365 **GOLDSTONE, M. W.** (1974), Verbal participation in small groups as a function of group composition. *Dissert. Abstr. Internat.*, 35:1910B.

04366 **GOLEMBIEWSKI, R. T.** (1979), *Approaches to Planned Change*. New York: Marcel Dekker.

04367 **GOLEMBIEWSKI, R. T.,** and **BLUMBERG, A.** (1970), *Sensitivity Training and the Laboratory Approach: Readings about Concepts and Applications*. Itasca, IL: F. E. Peacock Publishers.

04368 **GOLEMBIEWSKI, R. T.**, and **BLUMBERG, A.** (1973), *Sensitivity Training and the Laboratory Approach: Readings about Concepts and Applications*, 2d ed. Itasca, IL: F. E. Peacock Publishers.

04369 **GOLF, D. B., SHAMES, G. H.**, and **SELTZER, H. N.** (1971), The effects of time-out on the fluency of stutters in group therapy. *J. Communicat. Disorders*, 4:111-118.

04370 **GOLLAND, J. H.** (1972), A "hello" and "goodbye" group. *Internat. J. Group Psychother.*, 22:258-261.

04371 **GOLLER, G.** (1942), Criteria for referral to group therapy in a child guidance clinic. *Smith Coll. Studies Soc. Work*, 13:148-149.

04372 **GOLNER, J. H., GEDDES, H. M.**, and **ARSENIAN, J.** (1959), Notes on the use of recorded minutes in group therapy with chronic psychotic patients. *Psychiat. Quart.*, 33:312-325.

04373 **GOLOB, R. S.** (1978), Assertion training for children: a cognitive-behavioral group program for improving social problem solving in peer relationships. *Dissert. Abstr. Internat.*, 39:358B.

04374 **GOLOMBEK, H.** (1966), Group admission of adolescents to a day program. *Hosp. & Community Psychiat.*, 17:108-109.

04375 **GOLONKA, L. M.** (1977), The use of group counseling with breast cancer patients receiving chemotherapy. *Dissert. Abstr. Internat.*, 37:6362A.

04376 **GONDOR, L. H.**, and **GONGOR, E. I.** (1969), Changing times. *Amer. J. Psychother.*, 23:67-76.

04377 **GONEN, J. Y.** (1971), The use of psychodrama combined with videotape playback on an inpatient floor. *Psychiatry*, 34:198-213.

04378 **GONIN, D.** (1967), *Psychothérapie de Groupe du Délinquant Adulte en Milieu Pénitentiaire. (Group Psychotherapy with Adult Delinquents in the Prison Environment.)* Paris: C. Masson et Cie.

04379 **GONZALEZ, H. S.** (1980), The use and effect of training groups as pretherapy. *Dissert. Abstr. Internat.*, 41:165A. (University Microfilms No. 8009968.)

04380 **GONZALES, J. L., DORING, R.**, and **DEMATHMANN, C. D.** (1979), Cotherapy in a group of lower class psychosomatic patients. *Dynam. Psychiat.*, (Berlin) 12:73.

04381 **GONZÁLEZ, M.** (1975), (Psychodynamics of ideological democracy.) *Acta Psiquiat. Psicol. Amer. Latina*, (Buenos Aires) 21:137-142.

04382 **GONZÁLEZ CMGOYÁN, J. L.** (1975), (Psychoanalytic group therapy: theory of the technique.) *Neurol.-Neurocir.-Psiquiat.*, (Mexico City) 16:83-89.

04383 **GONZALEZ MURILLO, G.** (1963), (The importance of incorporating group techniques in our hospitals.) *Rev. Med. Costa Rica*, (San Jose) 20:105-107.

04384 **GOODACRE, D.** (1973), Experiences of group work in a rehabilitation unit. *Gerontology*, (Basel) 15:352-356.

04385 **GOODENOUGH, D. S.** (1965), Self-study groups: hope for the troubled normal. *Community Ment. Health J.*, 1:184-187.

04386 **GOODMAN, D. W., RANDOLPH, D. L.**, and **BROWN, H. J. D.** (1978), Attitudinal group-centered counseling: effects on openmindedness. *Small Group Behav.*, 9:403-408.

04387 **GOODMAN, J. C.** (1976), Group counseling with seventh graders. *Personnel & Guid. J.*, 54:519-520.

04388 **GOODMAN, J. I., SCHWARTZ, E. D.**, and **FRANKEL, L.** (1953), Group therapy of obese diabetic patients. *Diabetes*, 3:280-284.

04389 **GOODMAN, J. M.** (1962), Nondirective psychodrama play therapy. *Amer. J. Orthopsychiat.*, 32:532-534.

04390 **GOODMAN, L.**, and **ROTHMAN, R.** (1961), The development of a group counseling program in a clinic for retarded children. *Amer. J. Ment. Deficiency*, 65:789-795.

04391 **GOODMAN, M.**, and **MARKS, M.** (1963), Oral regression as manifested and treated analytically in group psychotherapy. *Internat. J. Group Psychother.*, 13:3-9.

04392 **GOODMAN, M., MARKS, M.**, and **ROCKBERGER, H.** (1964), Resistance in group psychotherapy enhanced by the countertransference reactions of the therapist: a peer group experience. *Internat. J. Group Psychother.*, 14:332-343.

04393 **GOODNICK, B.** (1957), Interpersonal relationships within a special class group. *Amer. J. Ment. Deficiency*, 62:310-321.

04394 **GOODRICH, D. W., MAZER, J.**, and **CLINE, B.** (1958), Fostering the involvement of the psychiatric patient in group activities. *Psychiatry*, 21:259-268.

04395 **GOODRIDGE, C.** (1975), Special techniques in the group adoptive study for children with special needs. *Child Welfare*, 54:35-39.

04396 **GOODSON, M. D.** (1964), Group therapy with regressed patients. *Perspect. Psychiat. Care*, 2:23-31.

04397 **GOODSPEED, E. J.** (1948), The use of psychodrama in the vocational guidance of eighth grade boys. *Sociatry*, 2:268-280.

04398 **GOODSTEIN, L. D., D'ORTA, C. V.**, and **GOODMAN, M. A.** (1976), Measurement of self-disclosure in encounter groups: a methodological study. *J. Couns. Psychol.*, 23:142-146.

04399 **GOODSTEIN, L. D.**, and **DOVICO, M.** (1979), Decline and fall of the small group. *J. Appl. Behav. Science*, 15:320-329.

04400 **GOODSTEIN, M.** (1972), A comparison of gestalt and transactional analysis therapies in marathons. *Dissert. Abstr. Internat.*, 33:1286B.

04401 **GOODSTEIN, M. A.** (1969), The relationship of personality change to therapeutic system and diagnosis. *Dissert. Abstr. Internat.*, 30:2419.

04402 **GOOTNICK, I.** (1975), Transference in psychotherapy with schizophrenic patients. *Internat. J. Group Psychother.*, 25:379-388.

04403 **GOOTZEIT, J. M., LOMBARDO, A. J.**, and **MILNER, S.** (1960), Situational diagnosis and therapy. *Amer. J. Ment. Deficiency*, 64:921-25.

04404 **GORAJ, J. T.** (1974), Stuttering therapy as crisis intervention. *Brit. J. Disorders Communication*, 9:51-57.

04405 **GORBAN, J. S.** (1978), Construct change of the thought disordered schizophrenic as a function of group psychotherapy. *Dissert. Abstr. Internat.*, 39:2984B-2985B. (University Microfilms No. 7823912.)

04406 **GORDON, A. S.** (1970), A comparison of homogeneous versus heterogeneous grouping using client-centered therapy with neurotics and schizophrenics. *Dissert. Abstr. Internat.*, 31:3705.

04407 **GORDON, D. W.** (1966), Topics, norms and social validators in psychotherapy sessions. *Dissert. Abstr. Internat.*, 26:7474. (University Microfilms No. 66-02790.)

04408 **GORDON, F. E.** (1974), The effects of disclosing different types and amounts of evaluative information on interpersonal relations and group performance. *Dissert. Abstr. Internat.*, 34:7328A.

04409 **GORDON, G.**, and **BOWMAN, K. M.** (1953), The auxiliary treatment of psychotic women: group psychotherapy for their husbands. *California Med.*, 78:303-308.

04410 **GORDON, J. E.**, and **FRESTON, MARJORIE.** (1964), Role-playing and age regression in hypnotized and nonhypnotized subjects. *J. Personality*, 32:411-419.

04411 **GORDON, L. V.** (1973), The therapeutic personality in the therapeutic community. *J. Appl. Psychol.*, 58:108-112.

04412 **GORDON, M.** (1971), Group psychotherapy: being and becoming. *Personnel & Guid. J.*, 49:611-618.
04413 **GORDON, M.** (1959), Role playing in industry. *Group Psychother., Psychodrama & Sociometry*, 12:187-191.
04414 **GORDON, M.**, and **LIBERMAN, N. J.** (1972), *Theme-Centered Interaction: An Original Focus on Counseling and Education.* Baltimore: National Educational Press.
04415 **GORDON, M. H.**, and **LIBERMAN, N. J.** (1973), *Theme-Centered Interaction.* Hyattsville, MD: Education Press.
04416 **GORDON, R. D.** (1972), A quantitative investigation of selected dynamics and outcomes of the basic encounter group. *Dissert. Abstr. Internat.*, 6046B.
04417 **GORDON, R. H.** (1978), Efficacy of a group crisis-counseling program for men who accompany women seeking abortions. *Amer. J. Community Psychol.*, 6:239-246.
04418 **GORDON, R. V.**, and **KILPATRICK, C. A.** (1977), A program of group counseling for men who accompany women seeking legal abortions. *Community Ment. Health J.*, 13:291-295.
04419 **GORDON, S.** (1967), Group psychotherapy as the treatment of choice. *Can. Ment. Health*, (Ottawa) 15:8-14.
04420 **GORDON, T.** (1951), Some theoretical notions regarding changes during group psychotherapy. *Group Psychother., Psychodrama & Sociometry*, 4:172-178.
04421 **GORDON, W. P.** (1972), A method to study the effect of a marathon experience on counselor effectiveness with practicum students: a pilot study. *Dissert. Abstr. Internat.*, 33:2709A.
04422 **GORFEIN, D. S.** (1964),The effects of a nonunanimous majority on attitude change. *J. Soc. Psychol.*, 63:333-338.
04423 **GORHAM, D. R.**, **HUBBARD, R. M.**, and **RAY, T. B.** (1953), Group therapy sessions. *Case Rep. Clin. Psychol.*, 3:39-53.
04424 **GORHAM, D. R.**, and **POKORNY, A. D.** (1964), Effects of a phenothiazine and/or group psychotherapy with schizophrenics. *Diseases Nerv. System*, 25:77-86.
04425 **GORE, R.** (1972), The object of speech in therapeutic groups. *Bull. de Psychol.*, (Paris) 20:634-648.
04426 **GORLICK, H. S.** (1967), Group psychotherapy: what it is and does. *RN*, 30:41-46.
04427 **GORLICK, H. S.** (1967), Psychodrama: the "action method" in group psychotherapy. *RN*, 30:67-77.
04428 **GORLOW, L.** (1951), Nondirective group psychotherapy: an analysis of the behavior of members as therapists. *Microfilm Abstr.*, 11:167-169.
04429 **GORLOW, L.**, **BUTLER, A.**, **EINIG, K. G.**, and **SMITH, J. A.** (1963), An appraisal of self-attitudes and behavior following group psychotherapy with retarded young adults. *Amer. J. Ment. Deficiency*, 67:893-898.
04430 **GORLOW, L.**, **HOCH, E. L.**, and **TELSCHOW, E. F.** (1952), *The Nature of Nondirective Group Psychotherapy: An Experimental Investigation.* New York: Bureau of Publications, Teachers College, Columbia University.
04431 **GORMALLY, J.** (1975), A behavioral analysis of structured skills training. *J. Couns. Psychol.*, 22:458-460.
04432 **GOROFF, N. N.** (1967), Confrontation with reality: a social group work approach. *Mental Hygiene*, 51:426-432.
04433 **GOSLINE, E.** (1951), A report on the application of group psychotherapy at Utica State Hospital. *Psychiat. Quart. Suppl.*, 25:65-75.
04434 **GOSLING, R.** (1967), *The Use of Small Groups in Training.* New York: Grune and Stratton.

04435 **GOSNELL, D.** (1964), Some similarities and dissimilarities between the psychodramaturgical approaches of J. L. Moreno and Erving Goffman. *Internat. J. Sociometry & Sociatry*, 4:94-106.

04436 **GOTCHEL, R. J.** (1980), Effectiveness of two procedures for reducing dental fear: group administered desensitization and group education and discussion. *J. Amer. Dental Assn.*, 101:634.

04437 **GOTO, T.** (1967), Improving everyday living in group psychiatric rehabilitation therapy. *Comprehens. Nursing Monthly*, 2:735-749.

04438 **GÖTTE, J.** (1976), (Method and form of therapeutic groups in stationary psychiatry.) *Psychiat. Praxis*, (Stuttgart) 3:130-135.

04439 **GÖTTE, J.** (1977), (Process of a special stationary group therapy demonstrated as part of work in a therapeutic community.) *Med. Welt*, (Stuttgart) 28:1753-1754.

04440 **GOTTSEGEN, G. B.** (1979), *Group Behavior*. Detroit: Gale Research.

04441 **GOTTESEGEN, M. G.** (1963), The role of assessment group in a hospital setting. *Amer. J. Psychother.*, 17:94-104.

04442 **GOTTESFELD, H.** (1963), A social interest scale for patients in group psychotherapy. *J. Individ. Psychol.*, 19:77-79.

04443 **GOTTESMAN, L. E.** (1967), The response of long-hospitalized aged psychiatric patients to milieu treatment. *Gerontologist*, 7:47-48.

04444 **GOTTLIEB, A.**, and **KRAMER, M.** (1965), Alternate-therapist group meetings: an approach to the severely ambivalent patient. *Internat. J. Group Psychother.*, 15:187-197.

04445 **GOTTSCHALK, L. A.** (1966), Psychoanalytic notes on t-groups at the Human Relations Laboratory, Bethel, Maine. *Comprehens. Psychiat.*, 7:472-487.

04446 **GOTTSCHALK, L. A., BROWN, S. B., BRUNEX, E. H., SHUMATE, L. W.,** and **ULIANA, R. L.** (1973), An evaluation of a parents' group in a child-centered clinic. *Psychiatry*, 36:157-171.

04447 **GOTTSCHALK, L. A.**, and **PATTISON, E. M.** (1969), Psychiatric perspectives on t-groups and the laboratory movement: an overview. *Amer. J. Psychiat.*, 126:823-839.

04448 **GOTTSEGEN, G. B.** (1967), The relationship between group psychotherapist professed activity level and awareness of group psychotherpy interaction: group psychotherapists' awareness of group interaction as a function of orientation to therapeutic technique with particular reference to the relationship between group psychotherapists' professed activity levels and their recall of group members' interactions. *Dissert. Abstr. Internat.*, 28:1194.

04449 **GOTTSEGEN, M. G.**, and **GRASSO, M.** (1973), Group treatment of the mother-daughter relationship. *Internat. J. Group Psychother.*, 23:69-81.

04450 **GOUDSMIT, W.** (1964), (Psychotherapy of delinquents.) *Psyche*, (Stuttgart) 17:664-684.

04451 **GOUGH, J. J.** (1969), How a group reacts. *Amer. J. Nursing*, 69:2400-2402.

04452 **GOULD, E. G., GARRIGUES, C. S.,**and **SCHEIKOWITZ, K.** (1975), Interaction in hospitalized patient-led and staff-led psychotherapy groups. *Amer. J. Psychother.*, 29:383-391.

04453 **GOULD, V. A.** (1975), Self-disclosure in small interaction groups in relation to the self-disclosure of the group leader. *Dissert. Abstr. Internat.*, 36:1304A.

04454 **GOUNAD, S., MIRIEL, M.-A.,** and **PROCHASSON, J.** (1976), (Is the body unrecognized in groups?) *Perspect. Psychiat.*, (Paris) 57:195-204.

04455 **GOURAN, D. S.** (1973), Correlates of member satisfaction in group decision-making discussion. *Cent. Studies Speech*, 24:91-96.

04456 **GOWELL, E. C.** (1966), An experience with the use of group work methods and process with student nurse groups over a period of 5 years. *J. Psychiat. Nursing*, 4:351-367.

04457 **GOWELL, E. C.** (1972), The health unit: a therapeutic community — psychodrama, play therapy and transactional analysis. *Internat. J. Nursing Studies*, 9:159-166.

04458 **GRABER, G. H.** (1976), (Review of J. Rattner's *Living and Learning with Each Other. Psychologie*, (Paris) 35:74.

04459 **GRAEBER, M. P., BROWN, G. C., PILLSBURY, R. M.,** and **ENTERLINE, J. D.** (1954), Group therapy on an acute service. *Amer. J. Psychiat.*, 110:677-680.

04460 **GRAF, A. K.** (1959), Modified children's groups and Moreno's impromptu therapy. *Group Psychother., Psychodrama & Sociometry*, 12:322-326.

04461 **GRAF, A. K.** (1958), Modified group therapy for children. *Internat. J. Soc. Psychiat.*, (London) 4:211-213.

04462 **GRAFF, B. D.** (1970), Group therapy and individual therapy: a comparison. *Dissert. Abstr. Internat.*, 31:1536B.

04463 **GRAFF, H.** (1972), Vicissitudes in the development of a psychoanalytic research group. *J. Amer. Psychoanal. Assn.*, 20:820-830.

04464 **GRAFF, R. W., DANISU, S.,** and **AUSTIN, B.** (1972), Reactions and three kinds of vocational-educational counseling. *J. Couns. Psychol.*, 19:224-228.

04465 **GRAFF, R. W., MacLEAN, D.,** and **LOVING, A.** (1971), Group reactive inhibition and reciprocal inhibition therapies with anxious college students. *J. Couns. Psychol.*, 18:431-436.

04466 **GRAHAM, F. W.** (1964), A case treated by psychoanalysis and analytic group psychotherapy. *Internat. J. Group Psychother.*, 14:267-290.

04467 **GRAHAM, F. W.** (1960), Group psychotherapy in the rehabilitation of the physically disabled. *Med. J. Austral.*, (Glebe) 47:537-538.

04468 **GRAHAM, F. W.** (1959), Observations on analytic group psychotherapy. *Internat. J. Group Psychother.*, 9:150-157.

04469 **GRAINGER, A. J.** (1967), *Bullring Assn. Psychother. Bull.*, 7:48-60.

04470 **GRALEWICZ, A., HILL, B.,** and **MACKINSON, M.** (1968), Restoration therapy: an approach to group therapy for the chronically ill. *Amer. J. Occupat. Ther.*, 22:294-299.

04471 **GRALNICK, A.,** and **D'ELIA, F.** (1973), "Administration" as therapy of the inpatient's family. *J. Nat. Assn. Priv. Psychiat. Hosp.*, 5:22-27.

04472 **GRALNICK, A.,** and **D'ELIA, F.** (1969), A psychoanalytic hospital becomes a therapeutic community. *Hosp. & Community Psychiat.*, 20:144-146.

04473 **GRAMBS, J. D.** (1948), Dynamics of psychodrama in the teaching situation. *Sociatry*, 1:383-399.

04474 **GRAND, S., FREEDMAN, N.,** and **JORTNER, S.** (1969), Variations in rem dreaming and the effectiveness of behavior in group therapy. *Amer. J. Psychother.*, 23:667-680.

04475 **GRANDOLPH, P. C.,** and **SIEGEL, B.** (1967), Adolescent day treatment project. *Amer. J. Orthopsychiat.*, 37:273-274.

04476 **GRANT, F. F.** (1950), The "Kasperl" theatre as play therapy. *Amer. J. Psychother.*, 4:279-285.

04477 **GRANT, J. D.,** and **GRANT, M.** (1959), A group dynamic approach to the treatment of nonconformists in the Navy. *Amer. Acad. Political & Soc. Sciences*, 322:126-135.

04478 **GRANT, M.** (1951), The group approach for weight control: report of a pilot study in Boston area, 1949-1950. *Group Psychother., Psychodrama & Sociometry*, 4:156-165.

04479 **GRANT, M.,** and **ROSENTHAL, J.** (1950), Group psychotherapy for weight control. *Massachusetts Health J.*, 31:89.

04480 **GRANT, S. J.** (1970), The effects of a basic encounter group experience on supervision by supervisor trainees. *Dissert. Abstr. Internat.*, 31:6343A.
04481 **GRANT, W. B.** (1972), The "human relations" movement and psychiatry. *Austral. & New Zeal. J. Psychiat.*, (Carlton) 6:184-190.
04482 **GRANVOLD, D. K.**, and **WELCH, G. J.** (1979), Structured, short-term group treatment of post-divorce adjustment. *Internat. J. Group Psychother.*, 29:347-358.
04483 **GRATKE, B. E.**, and **LUX, P. A.** (1960), Psychiatric occupational therapy in a milieu setting. *Amer. J. Occupat. Ther.*, 14:13-16.
04484 **GRATTON, L.** (1962), Essai d'une thérapie psychoanalytique de groupe pour les enfants d'âge préscolaire. (Psychoanalytical group therapy for preschool children.) *Can. Psychiat. Assn. J.*, (Ottawa) 7:90-96.
04485 **GRATTON, L., LAFONTAINE, C.**, and **GUIBEAUTT, J.** (1966), Group psychoanalytic work with children. *Can. Psychiat. Assn. J.*, (Ottawa) 11:430-442.
04486 **GRATTON, L.**, and **RIZZO, A. E.** (1969), Group therapy with young psychotic children. *Internat. J. Group Psychother.*, 19:63-71.
04487 **GRATTON, L.** (1972), Group diagnosis and therapy for young school children. *Hosp. & Community Psychiat.*, 23:188-190.
04488 **GRAU, J. J. R.** (1963), Permissive treatment of disabled persons: a sociological study. *Dissert. Abstr. Internat.*, 24:2168-2169.
04489 **GRAUBARD, P. S.**, and **UNOBSKEY, S.** (1969), Behavior modification, group process and attitude of group members. *Amer. J. Orthopsychiat.*, 39:295-296.
04490 **GRAVES, M. H.** (1970), *Help for Troubled Parents*. New York: Vantage Press.
04491 **GRAVES, W. H.**, and **GRAVES, L. H.** (1973), Analysis of feedback among group practicum members. *Counselor & Educat. Supervision*, 13:111-116.
04492 **GRAY, H.** (1962), Psychotherapeutic hours and outcomes. *Med. Times*, 90:388-392.
04493 **GRAY, H. D.**, and **TINDALL, J.** (1974), Communication training study: a model for training junior high school peer counselors. *School Counselor*, 22:107-112.
04494 **GRAY, P.**, and **STEVENSON, J. S.** (1980), Changes in verbal interaction among members of resocialization groups. *J. Gerontol. Nursing*, 6:86-90.
04495 **GRAY, P. D.** (1968), The influence of preparation on patients' use of group psychotherapy. *Smith Coll. Studies Soc. Work*, 39:59-60.
04496 **GRAY, W.** (1948), Group psychotherapy in a state hospital. *J. Nerv. & Ment. Diseases*, 108:485-495.
04497 **GRAY, W.** (1973), Multiple therapist therapy: a preliminary report. *Gen. Systems*, 18:175-176.
04498 **GRAYSON, H.** (1972), The psychoanalytic use of encounter techniques. *Psychiat. Annals*, 2:16-31.
04499 **GRAYSON, H.** (1977), Toward a theory of integration in group psychotherapy. In: *Group Therapy 1977: An Overview*, ed. L. R. Wolberg. New York: Stratton Intercontinental Medical Books.
04500 **GRAZIANO, A. M.** (1974), *Child Without Tomorrow*. Elmsford, NY: Pergamon Press.
04501 **GRAZIANO, A. M.** (1972), *Group Behavior Modification for Children*. New York: Pergamon.
04502 **GRAZIANO, A. M.** (1970), A group treatment approach to multiple problem behaviors of autistic children. *Except. Children*, 36:765-770.
04503 **GREEN, F. N.** (1970), The effects of a task-encounter workshop on the administrative staff of a public school system. *Dissert. Abstr. Internat.*, 31:2180A.
04504 **GREEN, J.** (1953), A treatment plan combining group and individual

psychotherapeutic procedures in a state mental hospital. *Psychiat. Quart.*, 27:245-253.

04505 **GREEN, J. R.** (1961), Sociodrama in a church setting. *Group Psychother., Psychodrama & Sociometry*, 14:62-65.

04506 **GREEN, P. S.** (1970), Group work with welfare recipients. *Soc. Work*, 15:3-4, 121.

04507 **GREEN, R.**, and **FULLER, M.** (1973), Group therapy with feminine boys and their parents. *Internat. J. Group Psychother.*, 23:54-68.

04508 **GREEN, R. B.** (1978), Counseling techniques for working with the family of the hearing impaired child. *Hearing Rehab. Quart.*, 3:17.

04509 **GREEN, T. L.** (1956), Note on sociometry in Ceylon. *Internat. J. Sociometry & Sociatry*, 1:45-48.

04510 **GREENBANK, R. K.** (1966), Special techniques in psychotherapy. *Curr. Psychiat. Ther.*, 6:64-69.

04511 **GREENBANK, R. K.**, and **GILBERT, A.** (1969), Mental health education for parents. In: *Current Psychiatric Therapies*, ed. J. M. Masserman. New York: Grune and Stratton.

04512 **GREENBANK, R. K.**, and **GREENBANK, S. J.** (1965), New ideas in psychotherapy. *Amer. J. Orthopsychiat.*, 35:256.

04513 **GREENBAUM, C. W.** (1979), Small group under the sun: uses of small group in battle conditions. *J. Appl. Behav. Science*, 15:392-406.

04514 **GREENBAUM, C. W.**, and **ZEMACH, M.** (1972), Role-playing and change of attitude toward the police after a campus riot: effects of situational demand and justification. *Human Relat.*, 25:87-99.

04515 **GREENBAUM, H.** (1954), Group therapy with alcoholics in conjunction with antabuse treatment. *Internat. J. Group Psychother.*, 4:30-41.

04516 **GREENBAUM, H.** (1979), The learning process in combined psychotherapy. *Amer. J. Psychoanal.*, 39:303.

04517 **GREENBAUM, H.** (1959), Three stages of group psychotherapy. *Acta Psychother. Psychosomat. Orthopaedagog. Suppl.*, (Basel) 7:146-149.

04518 **GREENBERG, D. J.**, and **O'DONNELL, W. J.** (1972), A note on the effects of group and individual contingencies upon deviant classroom behavior. *J. Child Psychol. & Psychiat.*, 13:55-58.

04519 **GREENBERG, H. C.** (1972), Self-concept changes in therapy marathon. *Dissert. Abstr. Internat.*, 33:1790-1791B.

04520 **GREENBERG, L.** (1964), Audience in action through psychodrama. *Group Psychother., Psychodrama & Sociometry*, 17:104-122.

04521 **GREENBERG, I. A.** (1977), *Group Hypnotherapy and Hypnodrama*. Chicago: Nelson-Hall.

04522 **GREENBERG, I. A.** (1968), Psychodrama and audience change. *Dissert. Abstr. Internat.*, 29:673.

04523 **GREENBERG, J.** (1976), The role of seating position in group interaction: a review, with applications for group trainers. *Group & Organizat. Studies*, 1:310-327.

04524 **GREENBERGER, P. A.** (1963), A reaction to an experience, the psychodrama. *Group Psychother., Psychodrama & Sociometry*, 16:250-254.

04525 **GREENBERG, P. V.** (1972), Group home care as an adjunct to residential treatment. *Child Welfare*, 51:423-435.

04526 **GREENBERG, R. P.** (1969), The effects of pre-session information on perception of the therapist and receptivity to influence in a psychotherapy analogue. *Dissert. Abstr. Internat.*, 29:4377B.

04527 **GREENBLATT, M.** (1950), Altruism in the psychotherapeutic relationship. In: *Explorations in Altruistic Love and Behavior*, ed. P. A. Sorokin. Boston: Beacon Press.

04528 **GREENBLATT, M.** (1963), Beyond the therapeutic community. *J. Hillside Hosp.*, 12:167-194.

04529 **GREENBLATT, M.** (1961), Formal and informal groups in a therapeutic community. *Internat. J. Group Psychother.*, 11:398-409.

04530 **GREENE, F. B.** (1979), A comparison of self-disclosure patterns of the schizophrenic and non-schizophrenic sibling within the family system. *Dissert. Abstr. Internat.*, 40:4482B.

04531 **GREENE, J. S.** (1939), Speech and voice disorders. *Med. World*, (London) 57:719-722.

04532 **GREENE, J. S.** (1935), Treatment of the stutter-type personality in a medical social clinic. *J. Amer. Med. Assn.*, 104:2239-2242.

04533 **GREENE, L. R., ABRAMOWITZ, S. I., DAVIDSON, C. V.,** and **EDWARDS, D. W.** (1980), Gender, race, and referral to group psychotherapy: further empirical evidence of countertransference. *Internat. J. Group Psychother.*, 30:357-364.

04534 **GREENE, L. R., MORRISON, T. L.,** and **TISCHLER, N. G.** (1980), Aspects of identification in the large group. *J. Soc. Psychol.*, 111:91-97.

04535 **GREENE, R. J.,** and **CROWDER, D. L.** (1972), Group psychotherapy with adolescents: an integrative approach. *J. Contemp. Psychother.*, 5:55-61.

04536 **GREENFIELD, R. C.** (1974), Trial by fire: rites of passage into psychotherapy groups. *Perspect. Psychiat. Care*, 12:152-156.

04537 **GREENGROSS, W.** (1980), Some problems that professionals experience in counseling the disabled. *Sex. & Disabil.*, 3:187-192.

04538 **GREENHILL, M.** (1945), Psycho-dramatic play therapy in disorders of childhood. *Proceed. Inst. Child Res. Clin. Woods Schools*, 12:107-122.

04539 **GREENING, T. C.** (1973), When a group rejects its leader. *Small Group Behav.*, 4:245-248.

04540 **GREENING, T. C.,** and **COFFEY, H. S.** (1966), Working with an "impersonal" t group. *J. Appl. Behav. Science*, 2:401-411.

04541 **GREENING, T. C.,** and **HAIGH, G. V.** (1968), The psychomat. *Voices*, 4:46-51.

04542 **GREENING, T. C.,** and **ZIELONKA, W.** (1973), Special applications of humanistic learning: a workshop on attorney-client relationships. *Interpersonal Develop.*, 2:194-199.

04543 **GREENLEAF, E.** (1973), "Senol" dream groups. *Psychother.: Theory, Res. & Pract.*, 10:218-222.

04544 **GREENLEAF, E.** (1971), The Red House: hypnotherapy of hysterical blindness. *Amer. J. Clin. Hypnosis*, 13:155-161.

04545 **GREENSPAN, S. I., SILVER, D.,** and **ALLEN, M. G.** (1977), Psychodynamically oriented group training program for early childhood care givers. *Amer. J. Psychiat.*, 134:1104-1108.

04546 **GREENWALD, H.** (1965), Failures in group psychotherapy. *Topical Probl. Psychol. & Psychother.*, 5:157-163.

04547 **GREENWALD, H.** (1967), Special problems of the psychotherapist as patient in group psychotherapy. *J. Long Island Consult. Ctr.*, 5:51-54.

04548 **GREENWOOD, C. R., HOPS, H., DELQUARDI, J.,** and **GUILD, J.** (1974), Group contingencies for group consequences in classroom management: a further analysis. *J. Appl. Behav. Anal.*, 7:413-425.

04549 **GREENWOOD, C. R., SLOANE, H. N.,** and **BASKIN, A.** (1974), Training elementary aged peer-behavior managers to control small group programmed mathematics. *J. Appl. Behav. Anal.*, 7:103-114.

04550 **GREENWOOD, D.** (1956), *Essays in Human Relations*, Washington, D.C.: Public Affairs Press.

04551 **GREGG, G. S.** (1968), Comprehensive professional help for the retarded child and his family. *Hosp. & Community Psychiat.*, 19:122-124.

04552 **GREGORY, H.** (1968), Parent guidance and early training for the hearing impaired pre-schooler. *Can. J. Pub. Health*, (Ottawa) 59:349-352.

04553 **GREGORY, L.** (1966), A voice in the people's choice. *J. Psychiat. Nursing*, 4:46-49.

04554 **GRENCIK, J. A.** (1972), The effects of a model on verbal behavior in group counseling. *Dissert. Abstr. Internat.*, 32:6807A.

04555 **GREVE, W.** (1977), Group therapy with schizophrenic patients. *Gruppenpsychother. & Gruppendynam.*, (Goettingen) 11:130-149.

04556 **GREVING, A., BLACK, H.,** and **SCHUPPER, F. X.** (1968), Group intake in an outpatient psychiatric clinic in a general hospital. *Amer. J. Orthopsychiat.*, 38:293-294.

04557 **GREVING, F. T.** (1947), Group treatment potentialities in an authoritative setting. *Ment. Hygiene*, 31:397-408.

04558 **GREW, R. S.** (1979), Personal construct theory and self-analytic groups: an examination of group constructs. *Dissert. Abstr. Internat.*, 41:352B.

04559 **GREW, R. S.** (1980), Personal construct theory and self-analytic groups: an examination of group constructs. *Dissert. Abstr. Internat.*, 41:352B. (University Microfilms No.8013948.)

04560 **GRIENEEKS, J. R.** (1978), Self-image and an encounter group experience: a study of focused feedback. *Dissert. Abstr. Internat.*, 39:2753A.

04561 **GRIEPENSTROH, G. D.** (1976), The effect of t-groups on the pupil control ideology of student teachers in secondary schools. *Dissert. Abstr. Internat.*, 36:4156A.

04562 **GRIESINGER, W. S.** (1978), Short-term group counseling of parents of handicapped children. *Dissert. Abstr. Internat.*, 39:675A.

04563 **GRIFFIN, K.,** and **BRADLEY, K.** (1969), An exploratory study of group counseling for speech anxiety. *J. Clin. Psychol.*, 25:98-101.

04564 **GRIFFIN, K.,** and **BRADLEY, K.** (1969), Group counseling for speech anxiety: an approach and a rationale. *J. Communicat.*, 19:22-29.

04565 **GRIFFIN, K.,** and **PATTON, B. R.** (1974), *Personal Communication in Human Relations*. Columbus, OH: C. E. Merrill Publishing.

04566 **GRIFFIN, N.** (1980), Effectiveness of group behavioral treatment with paraplegics and quadriplegics. *Dissert. Abstr. Internat.*, 40:5406B. (University Microfilms No. 8011334.)

04567 **GRIFFIN, R. S.** (1968), The role of the aide in transition. *Hosp. & Community Psychiat.*, 19:138-139.

04568 **GRIMM, J. E.** (1972), The effect of traditional and creative group counseling upon the degree of openness and creativity of male college students. *Dissert. Abstr. Internat.*, 33:1436A.

04569 **GRINBERG, L., LANGER, M.,** and **RODRIGUÉ, E.** (1959), Bildung einer gruppe. (Formation of a group.) *Psyche*, (Stuttgart) 13:195-214.

04570 **GRINBERG, L., LANGER, M.,** and **RODRIGUÉ, E.** (1960), *Psychoanalytische Gruppentherapie.* (*Psychoanalytic Group Therapy.*) Stuttgart: Ernst Klett.

04571 **GRINDER, J.,** and **BANDLER, R.** (1976), *The Structure of Magic: II*. Palo Alto: Science & Behavior.

04572 **GRINKER, R. R., Jr.** (1966), Complementary psychotherapy: treatment of "associated" pairs. *Amer. J. Psychiat.*, 123:633-638.

04573 **GRINSTEIN, A.** (1958), *The Index of Psychoanalytic Writings*. New York: International Universities Press.

04574 **GRISHAM, J. H.** (1972), A study of the effect of encounter type group experiences on the level of communication-discrimination skills and self-actualization of graduate counseling practicum students. *Dissert. Abstr. Internat.*, 33:6174A.

04575 **GROB, H. E., Jr.,** and **van DOREN, E. E.** (1969), Aggressive group work with teenage delinquent boys *Children*, 16:103-108.

04576 **GROB, H. E., Jr.,** and **van DOREN, E. E.** (1970), Helping houseparents find and use their creativity. *Children*, 17:97-102.

04577 **GROB, S.** (1951), A clinical investigation of the role of the therapist in group psychotherapy. Unpublished doctoral dissertation, Harvard University.

04578 **GROB, S.** (1970), Psychiatric social clubs come of age. *Ment. Hygiene*, 54:129-136.

04579 **GROBMAN, J.** (1978), Achieving cohesiveness in therapy groups of chronically disturbed patients. *Group*, 2:141-145.

04580 **GROBMAN, J.** (1980), The borderline patient in group psychotherapy: a case report. *Internat. J. Group Psychother.*, 30:299-318.

04581 **GROEN, J.** (1954), Behandeling van asthma bronchiale met die combintie van ACTH in groeps psychotherapie, nederlandsh. (The treatment of bronchial asthma through combined ACTH and group psychotherapy in the Netherlands.) *Nederl. Tijdschr. Geneeskunde*, (Amsterdam) 98:2212-2223.

04582 **GROEN, J. J.**, and **PELSER, H. E.** (1960), Experience with, and results of group psychotherapy in patients with bronchial asthma. *J. Psychosomat. Res.*, 4:191-205.

04583 **GROENEVELD, L. C.** (1970), The positive experience group encounter and its effect upon self-actualization. *Dissert. Abstr. Internat.*, 30:3726A.

04584 **GROFFMAN, L.**, and **DODSON, A. G.** (1971), Group guidance: sibling sessions as a means of establishing rapport in an inner city elementary school. *Elem. School Guid. Counselor*, 6:104-107.

04585 **GROFMAN, B.** (1974), Helping behavior and group size: some exploratory stochastic models. *Behav. Science Res.*, 4:219-224.

04586 **GROH, T. R.** (1976), A preliminary study of patient characteristics in a correctional setting. *Correct. & Soc. Psychol.*, 22:21-23.

04587 **GROLD, J.** (1975), The value of a youth group to hospitalized adolescents. In: *Adolescents Grow in Groups*, ed. I. Berkovitz. New York: Brunner/Mazel.

04588 **GROLD, L. J.** (1967), The continuous process of controlling milieu. *Hosp. & Community Psychiat.*, 18:182-183.

04589 **GROLL, M.** (1978), (Review of H. M. Ruitenbeck's *New Forms of Group-Therapy.*) *Praxis der Psychother.*, 23:92-93.

04590 **GROMUS, B.** (1977), Experiences with interdisciplinary treatment of obesity: model for group therapy. *Ernahr. Umschau*, 24:367-368.

04591 **GRONLUND, N. E.** (1959), *Sociometry in the Classroom*. New York: Harper and Row.

04592 **GROSS, D.** (1974), (Autogenic training in an open group.) *Zeit. Allgemeinmed.*, (Stuttgart) 50:131-134.

04593 **GROSS, G.** (1979), The family angel: the scapegoats counterpart. *Fam. Therapy*, 6:133.

04594 **GROSS, I.**, **WHEELER, M.**, and **HESS, K.** (1976), The treatment of obesity in adolescents using behavioral self-control. *Clin. Pediat.*, 15:920-924.

04595 **GROSS, P. K.**, and **BUSSARD, F.** (1970), A group method for finding and developing foster homes. *Child Welfare*, 49:521-524.

04596 **GROSS, R. L.** (1960), Therapy group composition: personal–interpersonal variable. *Dissert. Abstr. Internat.*, 20:3377-3378. (University Microfilms No. 59-06975.)

04597 **GROSS, R. S.** (1970), The effects of structuring and therapist presence or absence on behavior in a group psychotherapy setting. *Dissert. Abstr. Internat.*, 31:2986-2987.

04598 **GROSS, W. F.**, **CURTIN, M. E.**, and **MOORE, K. B.** (1970), Appraisal of a milieu therapy environment by treatment team and patients. *J. Clin. Psychol.*, 26:541-545.

04599 **GROSSMAN, D.** (1952), An experimental investigation of a psychotherapeutic technique. *J. Couns. Psychol.*, 16:325-331.

04600 **GROSSMAN, F.**, and **RETISH, P. M.** (1976), Classroom counseling: an approach to improve student self concept. *Couns. & Values*, 21:64-66.
04601 **GROSSMAN, J. S.** (1952), *How to Use Hand Puppets in Group Discussions*. New York: Play Schools Assn.
04602 **GROSSMAN, M.** (1944), A group therapy program in a neuropsychiatric hospital. *U.S. Vet. Admin. Med. Bull.*, 21:149-170.
04603 **GROSSMAN, W. K.**, and **KARMIOL, E.** (1973), Group psychotherapy supervision and its effect on resident training. *Amer. J. Psychiat.*, 130:920-921.
04604 **GROSSNER, L. A.** (1969), Developing a therapy group in a residential treatment center. *J. Jewish Communal Serv.*, 45:254-256.
04605 **GROSZ, H. J.** (1971), Self-help through Recovery, Inc. *Curr. Psychiat. Ther.*, 11:156-160.
04606 **GROSZ, H. J.**, **CLARK, J. R.**, and **WRIGHT, C. S.** (1965), A group participation-demonstration method of introducing patients to group psychotherapy. *Internat. J. Group Psychother.*, 15:246-250.
04607 **GROSZ, H. J.**, **STERN, H.**, and **WRIGHT, C. S.** (1965), Interactions in therapy groups as a function of differences among therapists and group size. *Psychol. Reports*, 17:827-834.
04608 **GROSZ, H. J.**, and **WAGONER, R.** (1971), MMPI and EPPS profiles of high and low verbal interactors in therapy groups. *Psychol. Reports*, 28:951-955.
04609 **GROSZ, H. J.**, and **WRIGHT, C. S.** (1967), The tempo of verbal interaction in an open therapy group conducted in rotation by three different therapists. *Internat. J. Group Psychother.*, 17:513-523.
04610 **GROTJAHN, M.** (1970), The analytic group experience in the training of therapists. *Voices*, 5:108-109.
04611 **GROTJAHN, M.** (1969), The analytic group therapy with psychotherapists. *Internat. J. Group Psychother.*, 19:326-333.
04613 **GROTJAHN, M.** (1977), *The Art and Technique of Analytic Group Therapy*. New York: J. Aronson and Sons.
04614 **GROTJAHN, M.** (1977), An attempt to analyze the therapeutic process in groups. *Group*, 1:5-9.
04615 **GROTJAHN, M.** (1973), The changing pattern of sexual pathology. *Contemp. Psychoanal.*, 10:
04616 **GROTJAHN, M.** (1971), Collectors items from the correspondence between Sigmund Freud and Otto Rank; and from the first *Rundbriefe of the ring-holders. Otto Rank Assn. J.*, 6:7-31.
04617 **GROTJAHN, M.** (1969), Das psycho-analytische gruppenerlebnis im rahmen der psychotherapeuthischen ausbildung. (The psychoanalytic group experience in psychotherapeutic training.) *Dynam. Psychiat.*, (Berlin) 2:1-12.
04619 **GROTJAHN, M.** (1973), Discussion remark in the Jonas Salk's talks: part 1. *The Center Report*. Santa Barbara: Center for the Study of Democratic Institutions.
04620 **GROTJAHN, M.** (1973), Do I read you correctly, Dr. Foukles and Dr. DeMare: an informal inquiry—with response by Drs. P. DeMare and S. H. Foulkes. *Group Anal.*, (London) 6:172-176.
04621 **GROTJAHN, M.** (1947), Experience with group psychotherapy as a method of treatment for veterans. *Amer. J. Psychiat.*, 103:637-643.
04622 **GROTJAHN, M.** (1949), Footnote: on group psychotherapy. In: *Modern Trends in Abnormal Psychology*. New York: Philosophical Library.
04623 **GROTJAHN, M.** (1971), Foreward to: *Group Sex Tapes*, by P. Rubinstein and H. Margolis. New York: David McKay.
04624 **GROTJAHN, M.** (1978), Group communication and group therapy with

the aged: a promising project. In: *Aging into the 21st Century: Middle Agers Today*, ed. L. Jarvik. New York: Gardner Press.
04625 **GROTJAHN, M.** (1977), The inroads of reality into the therapeutic group process. In: *Group Therapy 1977: An Overview*, ed. L. R. Wolberg. New York: Stratton Intercontinental Medical Books.
04626 **GROTJAHN, M.** (1971), Laughter in group psychotherapy. *Internat. J. Group Psychother.*, 21:234-238.
04627 **GROTJAHN, M.** (1972), Learning from dropout patients: a clinical view of patients who discontinued group psychotherapy. *Inernat. J. Group Psychother.*, 22:296-310.
04628 **GROTJAHN, M.** (1973), Letter of response to the July issue of Group Analysis from your observor in outer space. *Group Anal.*, (London) 6:133-134.
04629 **GROTJAHN, M.** (1979), Mistakes in analytic group psychotherapy. *Internat. J. Group Psychother.*, 29:317-324.
04630 **GROTJAHN, M.** (1973), Open letter to S. H. Foulkes, M.D., Group Anal., (London) 6:67-68.
04631 **GROTJAHN, M.** (1950), The process of maturation in group psychotherapy and in the group therapist. *Psychiatry*, 13:63-67.
04632 **GROTJAHN, M.** (1970), Psychiatric consultations for psychiatrists. *Amer. J. Psychiat.*, 126:932-937.
04633 **GROTJAHN, M.** (1970), Psychiatric consultations for psychiatrists. *Mental Health Digest*, 2:49-52.
04634 **GROTJAHN, M.** (1956), Psychoanalysis and group therapy. In: *Progress in Psychotherapy*, eds. I. Ziferstein, and M. Grotjahn. New York: Grune and Stratton, pp. 248-255.
04635 **GROTJAHN, M.** (1962), Psychoanalysis and the family neurosis. *J. Med. Assn. Georgia*, 51:459.
04636 **GROTJAHN, M. (Ed.)** (1960), *Psychoanalysis and the Family Neurosis*. New York: W. W. Norton and Co.
04637 **GROTJAHN, M.** (1970), Psychoanalytic group psychotherapy for psychiatrists and their wives: a report on David Morgan's work. *So. California Psychoanal. Inst. Bull.*
04638 **GROTJAHN, M.** (1970), Psychoanalytic group psychotherapy for therapists and their wives: a report on David Morgan's work. *Group Anal.*, (London) 3:62-63.
04639 **GROTJAHN, M.** (1971), The qualities of the group therapist. In: *Comprehensive Group Psychotherapy*, eds. H. L. Kaplan and B. J. Sadock. Baltimore: Williams and Wilkins, pp. 757-773.
04640 **GROTJAHN, M.** (1964), Review of group psychotherapy and group function. In: *Group Psychotherapy and Group Function*, eds. M. Rosenbaum and M. M. Berger. New York: Basic Books.
04641 **GROTJAHN, M.** (1976), Review of L. R. Wolberg's and M. Aronson's *Group Therapy 1975: An Overview*. *Internat. J. Group Psychother.*, 26:250-251.
04642 **GROTJAHN, M.** (1973), Selected clinical observations from psychoanalytic group psychotherapy. In: *Group Psychotherapy, 1973*. International Medical Books.
04643 **GROTJAHN, M.** (1953), Special aspects of countertransference in analytic group psychotherapy. *Internat. J. Group Psychother.*, 3:407-415.
04644 **GROTJAHN, M.** (1951), Special problems in the supervision of group psychotherapy. *Group Psychother. Sociopsychiat. Soc.*, 3:308-315.
04645 **GROTJAHN, M.** (1960), Supervision of analytic group psychotherapy. *Group Psychother., Psychodrama & Sociometry*, 13:161-169.
04646 **GROTJAHN, M.** (1955), (Teaching, problems and technics of supervision in psychiatric situations.) *Psychiatry*, 18:9-15.

04647 **GROTJAHN, M.** (1957), Theorie und praxis der gruppenpsychotherapie. (Theory and practice of group psychotherapy.) *Zeit. Diagnost. Psychol.*, 5:178-186.

04648 **GROTJAHN, M.** (1970), Thoughts on the obvious difference between psychoanalysis and group therapy. *Group Anal.*, (London) 3:42-45.

04649 **GROTJAHN, M.** (1972), The transference dynamics of the therapeutic group experience. In: *Adolescents Grow in Groups: Experiences in Adolescent Group Psychotherapy*, ed. H. Berkowitz. New York: Brunner/Mazel, pp. 173-178.

04650 **GROTJAHN, M.** (1975), The treatment of the famous and the "beautiful people" in groups. In: *Group Therapy 1975: An Overview*, eds. L. R. Wolberg and M. L. Aronson. New York: Stratton Intercontinental Medical Books.

04651 **GROTJAHN, M.** (1960), Trends in contemporary psychotherapy and the future of mental health. *Brit. J. Med. Psychol.*, (London) 33:263-267.

04652 **GROTJAHN, M.** (1978), A walk with Michael F. Foulkes. *Group Ther.*, 11:6-8.

04653 Group counselling in Wakefield Prison. (1959), *Lancet*, 2:1022-1023.

04654 The group: joy on Thursday. (1969), *Newsweek*, (May 12) 104-106.

04655 Group psychotherapy. (1968), *Drug Ther. Bull.*, 6:74-76.

04656 Group psychotherapy training program: first convocation. (1967), *Psychiatry*, 30:302.

04657 Group therapists can extend reach of mental health center. (1969), *Roche Report: Front. Clin. Psychiat.*, 6:1.

04658 Group therapy for alcoholism. (1965), *Lancet*, 2:538-539.

04659 Group therapy of deaf adolescents discussed. (1968), *Roche Report: Front. Hosp. Psychiat.*, 5:3.

04660 **GRUBER, L. N.** (1978), Group techniques for acutely psychotic inpatients. *Group*, 2:31-39.

04661 **GRUEN, B. J.** (1978), Self concept changes in women through the self-disclosing process in group counseling. *Dissert. Abstr. Internat.*, 38:7152A.

04662 **GRUEN, W.** (1977), Effects of executive and cognitive control of therapist on work climate in group therapy. *Internat. J. Group Psychother.*, 27:139-152.

04663 **GRUEN, W.** (1966), Emotional encapsulation as a predictor of outcome in therapeutic discussion groups. *Internat. J. Group Psychother.*, 16:93-97.

04664 **GRUEN, W.** (1968), Positive reaction to group therapy can be a reflection of behavior during group meetings. *Internat. J. Group Psychother.*, 18:361-365.

04665 **GRUEN, W.** (1978), Review of E. E. Sampson's and M. S. Marthas' *Group Process for the Health Professions. Contemp. Psychol.*, 23:919-

04666 **GRUEN, W.** (1978), Review of G. Corey's and M. S. Corey's *Groups: Process and Practice. Contemp. Psychol.*, 23:919.

04667 **GRUEN, W.** (1973), Some current issues in group psychotherapy research: discussion. *Internat. J. Group Psychother.*, 23:279-291.

04668 **GRUEN, W.** (1977), The stages in the development of a therapy group: tell-tale symptoms and their origin in the dynamic group forces. *Group*, 1:10-25.

04669 **GRUEN, W.** (1978), Use of the leader and of the group process in gestalt therapy groups. *Group*, 2:195-209.

04670 **GRUNEBAUM, H.** (1962), Group psychotherapy of fathers: problems of technique. *Brit. J. Med. Psychol.*, (London) 35:147-154.

04671 **GRUNEBAUM, H.** (1979), Selection of couples for group therapy. *Amer. J. Fam. Ther.*, 7:6-8.

04672 **GRUNEBAUM, H.** (1975), A soft-hearted review of hard-nosed research on groups. *Internat. J. Group Psychother.*, 25:185-197.
04673 **GRUNEBAUM, H.**, and **CHASIN, R.** (1978), Relabeling and reframing reconsidered: the beneficial effects of a pathological label. *Fam. Process*, 17:449.
04674 **GRUNEBAUM, H.**, and **KATES, W.** (1977), Whom to refer for group psychotherapy. *Amer. J. Psychiat.*, 134:130-133.
04675 **GRUNEBAUM, H.**, and **ROEMELE, V.** (1966), Problems of the indigenous worker. *Psychiat. Spectator*, 3:6-7.
04676 **GRUNEBAUM, H.** and **SOLOMON, L.** (1980), Toward a peer theory of group psychotherapy: i. developmental significance of peers and play. *Internat. J. Group Psychother.*, 30:23-50.
04677 **GRUNWALD, B.** (1951), The application of adlerian principles in a classroom. *Amer. J. Individ. Psychol.*, 10:131-141.
04678 **GRUNWALD, H.** (1954), Group counseling in a casework agency. *Internat. J. Group Psychother.*, 4:183-192.
04679 **GRUNWALD, H., HEADLEY, D., STEVENS, R. B.**, and **SLAVSON, S. R.** (1951), The case of Jean Case. *Internat. J. Group Psychother.*, 1:64-77.
04680 **GRUNWALD, H., HEADLEY, D., STEVENS, R. B.**, and **SLAVSON, S. R.** (1951), The case of Jean Case. *Internat. J. Group Psychother.*, 1:154-169.
04681 **GRUVER, G. G.** (1971), The use of a process measure in student development groups. *Dissert. Abstr. Internat.*, 31:6901B.
04682 **GRZESIAK, R. C.** (1979), Psychological services in rehabilitation medicine: clinical aspects of rehabilitation psychology. *Prof. Psychol.*, 10:511-520.
04683 **GUBI, M.**, and **DOBO, M.** (1976), (Group therapy with the parents of children treated in the department for neurotics.) *Magyar Pszichol. Szemle*, (Budapest) 33:24-31.
04684 **GUENZEL, Q. G.** (1970), The effect of need for social approval upon group discussion and the perception of persons in fiction. *Dissert. Abstr. Internat.*, 30:4791B-4792B.
04685 **GUERIN, Q. W.** (1969), Confrontation is the media of change. *Training & Develop. J.*, 23:5-7.
04686 **GUERNEY, B., Jr.** (1978), Evaluation of consultation-supervision in training conjugal therapists. *Prof. Psychol.*, 9:203-209.
04687 **GUERNEY, B., Jr.** (1964), Filial therapy: description and rationale. *J. Consult. & Clin. Psychol.*, 28:304-310.
04688 **GUGEL, R. N.** (1979), The effects of group therapy on orientation, memory, reasoning ability, social involvement and depression of brain damaged and non-brain damaged aged patients exhibiting senile behavior. *Dissert. Abstr. Internat.*, 40:2365B.
04689 **GUIDROZ, F. T.** (1971), Evaluation of four treatment approaches for drug addiction. *Dissert. Abstr. Internat.*, 31:5623.
04690 **GUIDRY, L. S.**, and **RANDOLPH, D. L.** (1974), Covert reinforcement in the treatment of test anxiety. *J. Couns. Psychol.*, 21:260-264.
04691 **GUILE, L. A.** (1977), Psychodrama as part of an integrated therapeutic programme. *Austral. & New Zeal. J. Psychiat.*, (Carlton) 11:185-188.
04692 **GUILFORD, J. S.** (1972), Group treatment versus individual initiative in the cessation of smoking. *J. Appl. Psychol.*, 56:162-167.
04693 **GUILHOT, J.**, and **GUILHOT, M. A.** (1975), A technique centered on group imagination: group-elicited revue. *Etudes Psychother.*, 20:94-99.
04694 **GUILHOT, M. A.** (1978), Mutual therapy groups in sexology. *Psychother. & Psychosomat.*, (Basel) 29:214-216.
04695 **GUINAN, A.** (1966), Human relations in the classroom. *Cath. School J.*, 66:53-56.

04696 **GUINAN, J. F.**, and **FOULDS, M. L.** (1970), Marathon group: facilitator of personal growth? *J. Couns. Psychol.*, 17:145-149.
04697 **GUINAN, J. F.** (1973), Do the changes last? a six-month follow-up of a marathon group. *Small Group Behav.*, 4:177-180.
04698 **GULA, M.** (1944), Boys' house: the use of a group for observation and treatment. *Ment. Hygiene*, 28:430-437.
04699 **GUMAER, J.** (1973), Peer-facilitated groups. *Elem. School Guid. Counselor*, 8:4-11.
04700 **GUMAER, J., BLECK, R.**, and **LOESCH, L. C.** (1975), Affective education through role playing: the feelings class. *Personnel & Guid. J.*, 53:604-608.
04701 **GUMAER, J.**, and **MYRICK, R. D.** (1974), Behavioral group counseling with disruptive children. *School Counselor*, 21:313-316.
04702 **GUMAER, J.**, and **SIMON, R. S.** (1979), Behavioral group counseling and schoolwide reinforcement program with obese trainable mentally retarded students. *Educat. & Training*, (London) 14:106-111.
04703 **GUMINA, J. M.** (1980), Sentence-completion as an aid to sex therapy. *J. Marital & Fam. Ther.*, 6:201-206.
04704 **GUMRUKCU, M. A.**, and **MIKELS, E.** (1965), Combating post-hospital bends: patterns of success in a psychiatric half way house. *Ment. Hygiene*, 49:244-249.
04705 **GUNDERSON, R. G.** (1951), Dangers in group dynamics. *Religious Educat.*, 46:342-344.
04706 **GUNDLACH, R. H.** (1967), Overview of outcome studies in group psychotherapy. *Internat. J. Group Psychother.*, 17:196-210.
04707 **GUNDLACH, R. H.** (1961), Problem: to convert a clinical judgment into a research design. *Internat. J. Group Psychother.*, 11:265-271.
04708 **GUNN, J. C.** (1967), Group psychotherapy on a geriatric ward. *Psychother. & Psychosomat.*, (Basel) 15:26.
04709 **GUNN, J. C.** (1968), An objective evaluation of geriatric ward meetings. *J. Neurol., Neurosurg. & Psychiat.*, (London) 31:403-407.
04710 **GUNN, R. C.** (1978), A use of videotape with inpatient therapy groups. *Internat. J. Group Psychother.*, 28:365-370.
04711 **GUNN, R. L., NAVRAN, L., SULLIVAN, D.**, and **JERDEN, L.** (1963), The live presentation of dramatic scenes as a stimulus to patient interaction in group psychotherapy. *Group Psychother., Psychodrama & Sociometry*, 16:164-172.
04712 **GUNTHER, B.** (1971), *How the West Is One*. New York: Macmillan.
04713 **GUNTHER, B.** (1971), *What to Do Till the Messiah Comes*. New York: Collier Books.
04714 **GURMAN, A. S.** (1980), Behavioral marriage therapy in the 1980's: the challenge of integration. *Amer. J. Fam. Ther.*, 8:86.
04715 **GURMAN, A. S.** (1969), Group counseling with underachievers: a review and evaluation of methodology. *Internat. J. Group Psychother.*, 19:463-474.
04716 **GURMAN, A. S.** (1978), Review of A. P. French's *Disturbed Children and Their Families: Innovations in Evaluation and Treatment. Contemp. Psychol.*, 23:247.
04717 **GURMAN, A. S.**, and **GUSTAFSON, J. P.** (1976), Patients' perceptions of therapeutic relationship and group therapy outcome. *Amer. J. Psychiat.*, 133:1290-1294.
04718 **GURMAN, E. B.** (1968), Creativity as a function of orientation and group participation. *Psychol. Reports*, 22:471-478.
04719 **GURMAN, E B.**, and **BASS, B. M.** (1961), Objective compared with subjective measures of the same behavior in groups. *J. Abnorm. Soc. Psychol.*, 63:368-374.

04720 **GUROWITZ, E. M.** (1975), Group boundaries and leadership potency. *Transactional Anal. J.*, 5:183-185.

04721 **GURRI, J.**, and **CHASEN, M.** (1948), Preliminary survey of the results of group treatment of psychoses. *Diseases Nerv. System*, 9:52-54.

04722 **GURSTELLE, E.** (1974), Reducing anxiety in interracial situations through systematic desensitization: a group approach. *Dissert. Abstr. Internat.*, 35:2431B.

04723 **GUSSOW, Z.** (1964), The observer-observed relationship as information about structure in small group research. *Psychiatry*, 27:230-247.

04724 **GUST, T.** (1970), Group counseling with rehabilitation clients. *Rehab. Record*, 11:18-25.

04725 **GUST, T.** (1978), Review of Seligman's *Group Counseling and Group Psychotherapy with Rehabilitation Clients. Contemp. Psychol.*, 23:299.

04726 **GUSTAFSON, D. P.**, and **GAUMNITZ, J. E.** (1972), Consensus rankings in small groups: self-rankings included and excluded. *Sociometry*, 35:610-618.

04727 **GUSTAFSON, J. P.** (1976), The group matrix of individual psychotherapy with Plains Indian people. *Contemp. Psychoanal.*, 12:227-239.

04728 **GUSTAFSON, J. P.** (1977), Injury to the self-concept in the working small group, in perspective. *J. Personality Soc. Syst.*, 1:39-52.

04729 **GUSTAFSON, J. P.** (1976), The mirror transference in the psychoanalytic psychotherapy of alcoholism: a case report. *Internat. J. Psychoanal. & Psychother.*, 5:65-85.

04730 **GUSTAFSON, J. P.** (1976), The passive small group: working concepts. *Human Relat.*, 29:793-803.

04731 **GUSTAFSON, J. P.** (1976), The pseudo–mutual small group or organization. *Human Relat.*, 29:989-997.

04732 **GUSTAFSON, J. P.** (1978), Schismatic groups. *Human Relat.*, 31:139-154.

04733 **GUSTAFSON, J. P.** (1978), The work of the student doctor. *Brit. J. Med. Educat.*, (Oxford) 12:300-305.

04734 **GUSTAFSON, J. P., COLEMAN, F., KIPPERMAN, A., WHITMAN, H.**, and **HANKINS, R.** (1978), A cancer patients group: the problem of containment. *J. Personality Soc. Syst.*, 1:6-18.

04735 **GUSTAFSON, J. P.**, and **COOPER, L.** (1978), Collaboration in small groups. *Human Relat.*, 31:155-171.

04736 **GUSTAFSON, J. P.**, and **COOPER, L.** (1978), Toward the study of society in microcosm. *Human. Relat.*, 31:843-862.

04737 **GUSTAFSON, J. P.**, and **HARTMAN, J. J.** (1978), Self-esteem in group-therapy. *Contemp. Psychoanal.*, 14:311-329.

04738 **GUSTAFSON, J. P.**, and **HAUSMAN, W.** (1975), The phenomenon of splitting in a small psychiatric organization. *Soc. Psychiat.*, 10:199-203.

04739 **GUSTAFSON, J. P.**, and **KIPPERMAN, A. L.** (1978), Introductory and preparatory therapeutic groups: the problems of joining in transient small groups—theory and technique. In: *Group Therapy 1978: An Overview*, eds. L. R. Wolberg and M. L. Aronson. New York: Stratton Intercontinental Medical Books.

04740 **GUSTAFSON, J. P.**, and **WHITMAN, H.** (1978), Towards a balanced social environment: an oncology service–cancer patients group. *Soc. Psychiat.*, 13:147-152.

04741 **GUSTAFSSON, R.** (1976), (Milieu therapy on a ward for patients with senile dementia.) *Scand. J. Behav. Ther.*, 5:27-37.

04742 **GUSTAITIS, R.** (1968), *Turning On*. New York: Macmillan.

04743 **GUTSCH, K. U.**, and **HOLMES, W. R.** (1974), Training counselors using an attitudinal group-centered approach. *Small Group Behav.*, 5:93-104.

04744 **GUTTMACHER, J. A.** (1972), Cohesion and hostility. *Amer. J. Psychiat.*, 129:361-363.

04745 **GUTTMACHER, J. A.** (1973), The concept of character, character problems, and group therapy. *Comprehens. Psychiat.*, 14:513-522.

04746 **GUTTMACHER, J. A.**, and **BIRK, L.** (1971), Group therapy: what specific therapeutic advantages? *Comprehens. Psychiat.*, 12:546-556.

04747 **GUY, W. B., SHOEMAKER, R. J.**, and **McLAUGHLIN, J. T.** (1954), Group psychotherapy in adult atopic eczema. *Arch. Dermatol. & Syph.*, 70:767-781.

04748 **GUYER, C. G.** (1978), The effects of nonverbal warm-up exercises upon group counseling effectiveness with adolescent groups. *Dissert. Abstr. Internat.*, 39:2754A.

04749 **GUYER, E. G., Jr.** (1956), *The Effect of Varying a Therapeutic Technique in Group Psychotherapy with Hospitalized Psychoneurotic Patients.* Ann Arbor: University Microfilms.

04750 **GUYER, E. G., Jr.** (1956), The effect of varying a therapeutic technique in group psychotherapy with hospitalized psychoneurotic patients. Unpublished doctoral dissertation, Pennsylvania State University.

H

04751 **HAAGEN, E. K., ROSENBERG, J.,** and **RICHMAND, A.** (1976), A group therapy experience with unwed adolescent mothers: repairing the mother-child bond. *Transnat. Ment. Health Res. Newsl.*, 18:11-15.

04752 **HAAKEN, J. K.,** and **DAVIS, F. B.** (1975), Group therapy with latency-age psychotic children. *Child Welfare*, 54:703-711.

04753 **HAAR, R.** (1980), (Group psychotherapy with children and adolescents in hospital treatment.) *Praxis Kinderpsychol. & Kinderpsychiat.*, (Goettingen) 29:182-193.

04754 **HAAS, A. B.** (1950), The therapeutic value of hymns. *Pastoral Psychol.*, 1:39-42.

04755 **HAAS, K.** (1975), *Growth Encounter: A Guide for Groups.* Chicago: Nelson-Hall.

04756 **HAAS, K.,** and **CABIN, S. H.** (1966), Role playing ability and clinical progress in a psychiatric state hospital. *J. Gen. Psychol.*, 75:161-165.

04757 **HAAS, R. B.** (1948), Action counseling and process analysis: a psychodramatic approach. *Psychodrama Monographs*, No. 25.

04758 **HAAS, R. B.** (1947), Action counseling and process analysis: a psychodramatic approach. *Sociatry*, 1:256-332.

04759 **HAAS, R. B.** (1948), The consultant in sociometry and the sociodrama speaks. *Sociatry*, 2:257-259.

04760 **HAAS, R. B.** (1958), Contagion for psychodramatic ideas in a large metropolitan community. *Group Psychother., Psychodrama & Sociometry*, 11:159-164.

04761 **HAAS, R. B.** (1948), Leaves from an educator's notebook illustrating action applications in several forms of production. *Sociatry*, 2:283-321.

04762 **HAAS, R. B.** (1946), Projects in psychodrama and sociometry. *Sociometry*, 9:173-174.

04763 **HAAS, R. B.** (1949), *Psychodrama and Sociodrama in American Education.* New York: Beacon House.

04764 **HAAS, R. B.** (1946), Psychodrama as a guidance technique in an experimental school. *Sociometry*, 9:254-262.

04765 **HAAS, R. B.** (1947), Psychodramatic retraining of stutterers. *Sociatry*, 1:293-295.

04766 **HAAS, R. B.** (1948), Sociodrama in education. *Sociatry*, 2:420-429.

04767 **HAAS, R. B.** (1949), Sociodrama in education: an exploratory study. *Stanford Univ. Bull.*, 24:362-366.

04768 **HAASZ, I.,** and **HAASZ, A.** (1976), (Positive motivating procedures in the acute therapy of alcoholics.) *Soc. Psihijat.*, (Belgrade) 4:61-66.

04769 **HABER, L. C.** (1977), The effect of short term group psychotherapy on the elderly. *Can. J. Psychiat. Nursing*, (Winnipeg) 18:8-11.

04770 **HABER, R.,** and **SMALL, J.** (1980), Structured exercises: a review and study. *J. Special. Group Work*, 5:63-67.

04771 **HABER, S., PALEY, A.,** and **BLOCK, A. S.** (1949), Treatment of problem drinkers at Winter Veteran's Administration Hospital. *Bull. Menninger Clinic*, 13:24-30.

04772 **HABERMAN, P. W.** (1966), Factors related to increased sobriety in group psychotherapy with alcoholics. *J. Clin. Psychol.*, 22:229-235.

04773 **HÄCHEZ, E.** (1954), Gruppentherapie des praktikers. (Group therapy practitioners.) *Hippokrates* (Stuttgart) 25:213-215.

04774 **HACKEL, J.,** and **ASIMOS, C. T.** (1980), Resistances encountered in starting a group therapy program for suicide attempters in varied administrative settings. *Life Threatening Behav.*, 10:100-105.

04775 **HACKETT, T. P.** (1977), Group therapy in cardiac rehabilitation. *Cardiology*, (Basel) 62:75.

04776 **HACKETT, T. P.** (1976), Psychological assistance for the dying patient and his family. *Annual Rev. Med.*, 27:371-378.

04777 **HACKETT, W. R.** (1945), Child care as a means of group therapy. *Amer. J. Orthopsychiat.*, 15:675-680.

04778 **HACKFIELD, A. W.** (1937), Can a reorientation through mass therapy correct the fallacious concept of the incurability of mental disease? *J. Nerv. & Ment. Disease*, 86:39-51.

04779 **HACKMAN, J. R.,** and **VIDMAR, N.** (1970), Effects of size and task type on group performance and member reactions. *Sociometry*, 33:37-54.

04780 **HACKSTEIN, F. G.** (1966), Rehabilitation schizophrener: die gruppentherapie und ihre voraussetzungen. (Rehabilitation of schizophrenics: group psychotherapy and its conditions.) *Nervenarzt*, 37:164-168.

04781 **HADDEN, S. B.** (1953), Countertransference in the group psychotherapist. *Internat. J. Group Psychother.*, 3:417-423.

04782 **HADDEN, S. B.** (1951), Dynamics and clinical application of group psychotherapy. *Res. Pub. Assess. Nerv. & Ment. Diseases*, 31:127-130.

04783 **HADDEN, S. B.** (1951), Dynamics of group psychotherapy. *Arch. Neurol. Pychiat.*, 65:125.

04784 **HADDEN, S. B.** (1959), Dynamics of group psychotherapy. *Diseases Nerv. System*, 20:258-262.

04785 **HADDEN, S. B.** (1975), A glimpse of pioneers in group psychotherapy. *Internat. J. Group Psychother.*, 25:371-378.

04786 **HADDEN, S. B.** (1943), Group psychotherapy. *Arch. Neurol. Psychiat.*, 50:625-628.

04787 **HADDEN, S. B.** (1945), Group psychotherapy. *Sociometry*, 8:306-310.

04788 **HADDEN, S. B.** (1943), Group psychotherapy. *Trans. Amer. Neurol. Assn.*, 69:132-135.

04789 **HADDEN, S. B.** (1944), Group psychotherapy: a superior method of treating larger numbers of neurotic patients. *Amer. J. Psychiat.*, 101:68-72.

04790 **HADDEN, S. B.** (1968), Group psychotherapy for sexual maladjustments. *Amer. J. Psychiat.*, 125:327-332.

04791 **HADDEN, S. B.** (1957), Group psychotherapy in a general hospital. *Diseases Nerv. System*, 18:379-382.

04792 **HADDEN, S. B.** (1951), Group psychotherapy in general hospitals. *Internat. J. Group Psychother.*, 1:31-36.

04793 **HADDEN, S. B.** (1961), Group psychotherapy in medicine. *Pennsylvania Med. J.*, 64:617-620.

04794 **HADDEN, S. B.** (1966), Group psychotherapy of male homosexuals. *Curr. Psychiat. Ther.*, 6:177-186.

04795 **HADDEN, S. B.** (1971), Group psychotherapy with homosexual men. *Internat. Psychiat. Clinics*, 8:81-94.

04796 **HADDEN, S. B.** (1972), Group psychotherapy with homosexual men. In: *Sexual Behaviors: Social, Clinical, and Legal Aspects*, eds. H. L. Resnik and M. E. Wolfgang. Boston: Little Brown.

04797 **HADDEN, S. B.** (1948), Group therapy in prisons. *Proceed. Amer. Prison Assn.*, pp. 178-183.

04798 **HADDEN, S. B.** (1955), Historic background of group psychotherapy. *Internat. J. Group Psychother.*, 5:162-168.

04799 **HADDEN, S. B.** (1959), A note on the impact of group psychotherapy on psychiatry. *Acta Psychother., Psychosomat. Orthopaedagog.*, 7:131-137.

04800 **HADDEN, S. B.** (1947), Post-military group therapy with psychoneurotics. *Ment. Hygiene*, 31:89-93.

04801 **HADDEN, S. B.** (1969), Rehabilitation of the sexual delinquent with special reference to the homosexually oriented. *Pennsylvania Med. J.*, 72:49-51.

04802 **HADDEN, S. B.** (1956), Training. In: *The Fields of Group Psychotherapy*, ed. S. R. Slavson. New York: International Universities Press.

04803 **HADDEN, S. B.** (1958), Treatment of homosexuality by individual and group psychotherapy. *Amer. J. Psychiat.*, 114:810-815.

04804 **HADDEN, S. B.** (1966), Treatment of male homosexuals in groups. *Internat. J. Group Psychother.*, 16:13-22.

04805 **HADDEN, S. B.** (1942), Treatment of the neuroses by class technic. *Annals Internal Med.*, 16:33-37.

04806 **HADDEN, S. B.** (1947), The utilization of a therapy group in teaching psychotherapy. *Amer. J. Psychiat.*, 103:644-648.

04807 **HADDEN, S. B.** (1975), The utilization of a therapy group in teaching psychotherapy. In: *Group Psychotherapy and Group Function*, 2d ed., eds. M. Rosenbaum and M. M. Berger. New York: Basic Books.

04808 **HADDLE, H. W. R.** (1974), The efficacy of automated group systematic desensitization as a strategy to modify attitudes toward disabled persons. *Dissert. Abstr. Internat.*, 34:4742A.

04809 **HADER, M.** (1966), The psychiatrist as consultant to the social worker in a home for the aged. *J. Amer. Geriat. Soc.*, 14:407-413.

04810 **HADLEY, J. M., TRUE, J. E.,** and **KEPES, S. Y.** (1970), An experiment in the education of the preprofessional mental health worker: the Purdue Program. *Community Ment. Health J.*, 6:40-50.

04811 **HADLEY, R. G., LEVY, W. V.,** and **MANSON, M. P.** (1963), Group psychotherapy in a mental hospital. *Geriatrics*, 18:910-915.

04812 **HAER, J. L.** (1968), Anger in relation to aggression in psychotherapy groups. *J. Soc. Psychol.*, 76:123-127.

04813 **HAER, J. L.** (1967), Aspects of aggression in psychotherapy groups. *Dissert. Abstr. Internat.*, 28:2138B.

04814 **HAESLER, W. T.** (1967), Einzel-und gruppenpsychotherapie im strafvollzug. (Individual and group psychotherapy in a penal institution.) *Psychother. & Psychosomat.*, (Basel) 15:26.

04815 **HAESLER, W. T.** (1969), Individual and group psychotherapy during the serving of sentence. *Zeit. Psychother. Med. Psychol.*, (Stuttgart) 19:11-17.

04816 **HAESLER, W. T.** (1970), Psychotherapy in delinquents under penal law. *Zeit. Psychother. Med. Psychol.*, (Stuttgart) 20:104-114.

04817 **HÄFNER, H.** (1965), (Experiences with schizophrenics in a transitional clinical treatment and after-care system.) *Zeit. Psychother. Med. Psychol.*, (Stuttgart) 15:97-116.

04818 **HAFNER, J.,** and **MARKS, I.** (1976), Exposure in vivo of agoraphobics: contributions of diazepam, group exposure, and anxiety evocation. *Psychol. Med.*, (London) 6:71-88.

04819 **HAGAN, M.,** and **KENWORTHY, M.** (1951), The use of psychodrama as a training device for professional groups working in the field of human relations. *Group Psychother., Psychodrama & Sociometry*, 4:23-27.

04820 **HAGAN, M.,** and **WRIGHT, E.** (1945), Psychodramatic techniques as a teaching device in an accelerated course for workers with neuropsychiatric patients. *Sociometry*, 8:384-388.

04821 **HAGBERG, K. L.** (1969), Combining social casework and group work methods in a children's hospital. *Children*, 16:192-197.

04822 **HAGEMANN, T.** (1964), (Psychotherapeutic attitude.) *Tidsskr. Norske Laegeforen*, 84:250-254.

04823 **HAGEN, D. S.** (1970), Group counseling, individual counseling, and teacher consultation as means of modifying self-reports on personality inventory items by elementary school children. *Dissert. Abstr. Internat.*, 30:5236A.

04824 **HAGEN, R. L.** (1974), Group therapy versus bibliotherapy in weight reduction. *Behav. Ther.*, 5:222-234.

04825 **HAGEN, R. L.** (1970), Group therapy versus bibliotherapy in weight reduction. *Dissert. Abstr. Internat.*, 31:2985-2986.

04826 **HAGER, R.** (1978), Evaluation of group psychotherapy: a question of values. *J. Psychiat. Nursing*, 16:26-33.

04827 **HÄGGLUND, T. B.** (1964), (A female and a male therapist in activity group therapy with boys in the latency period.) *Nordisk Psykiat. Tidsskr.*, (Kungsbacha) 18:521-529.

04829 **HAHN, J.**, and **BURNS, K. R.** (1973), Mrs. Richards, a rabbit, and remotivation. *Amer. J. Nursing*, 73:302-305.

04829 **HAHN, P.** (1966), (Direct observations of psychotherapy in the U.S.S.R.) *Psyche*, (Stuttgart) 20:222-230.

04830 **HAHN, P.**, and **LEISNER, R.** (1970), The influence of biographical anamnesis and group psychotherapy on postmyocardial patients. *Psychother. & Psychosomat.*, (Basel) 18:299-306.

04831 **HAHN, P.**, and **HILLEMANN, K. D.** (1972), (Out-patient group therapy and rehabilitation following myocardial infarction.) *Praxis der Psychother.*, 17:96.

04832 **HAIGH, G.**, and **KELL, B. L.** (1950), Multiple therapy as a method for training and research in psychotherapy. *J. Abnorm. & Soc. Psychol.*, 45:659-666.

04833 **HAIGH, G. V.** (1971), Response to Koch's assumption about group process. *J. Human. Psychol.*, 11:129-132.

04834 **HAIMAN, F. S.** (1963), Effects of training in group processes on open-mindedness. *J. Communications*, 13:236-245.

04835 **HAIMOWITZ, M.**, and **HAIMOWITZ, N.** (1976), Free therapy: free atmosphere, free training. *Transactional Anal. J.*, 6:138-139.

04836 **HAIMOWITZ, M. L.** (1975), Training and therapy in large groups without charge. *Transactional Anal. J.*, 5:36-37.

04837 **HAINES, D. B.**, and **McKENCHIE, W. J.** (1967), Cooperative versus competitive discussion methods in teaching introductory psychology. *J. Educat. Psychol.*, 58:386-390.

04838 **HAISCH, E.** (1955), Entwicklung und stand der gruppenpsychotherapie. (Puberty and development in group psychotherapy.) *Fortschr. Neurol. Psychiat. & Grenzgebiete,* (Stuttgart) 23:474-489.

04839 **HAISCH, E. O.** (1965), (Reform of institutional psychiatry, a goal to be reached.) *Nervenarzt*, 36:346-349.

04840 **HAIZLIP, T., McREE, C.**, and **CORDER, B. F.** (1975), Issues in developing psychotherapy groups for preschool children in out-patient clinics. *Amer. J. Psychiat.*, 132:1061-1063.

04841 **HÁJEK, P.** (1977), (Art therapy in group psychotherapy of neuroses.) *Ceskoslov. Psychiat.*, (Prague) 73:30-34.

04842 **HÁJEK, P.** (1979), (Written dialog: the sample of pair interaction and its use in psychotherapy.) *Ceskoslov. Psychol.*, (Prague) 23:317-320.

04843 **HAJEK, P.**, and **KRATOCHVIL, S.** (1979), (Review of R. E. Merrit's and D. O. Walley's *Group Leaders Handbook.*) *Ceskoslov. Psychol.*, (Prague) 23:256.

04844 **HÁJEK, P.**, and **MIKULA, V.** (1977), (Non-verbal psychotherapeutic techniques and group psychotherapy in rehabilitation of psychoses.) *Ceskoslov. Psychiat.*, (Prague) 73:35-38.

04845 **HAJNAL, A.** (1967), Au sujet d'une expérience de psychothérapie pavillonnaire en hôpital psychiatrique. (An experience with ward psychotherapy in a psychiatric hospital.) *Psychother. & Psychosomat.*, (Basel) 15:313-325.

04846 **HAKALA, I.** (1966), Newspaper survey: a new method of group therapy. *Sairaanhoitaja Sjukskotersken*, (Helsinki) 42:502.

04847 **HALA, M. P.** (1975), Reminiscence group therapy project. *J. Gerontol. Nursing*, 1:34-41.

04848 **HALAS, C.** (1973), All-women's groups: a view from inside. *Personnel & Guid. J.*, 52:91-95.

04849 **HALDANE, F. P.** (1975), A technique of insight-directed psychotherapy for health service use. *Brit. J. Psychiat.*, (Ashford) 126:469-474.

04850 **HALE, A. E.** (1975), The role diagram expanded. *Group Psychother., Psychodrama & Sociometry*, 28:77-104.

04851 **HALEY, J.** (1971), *Changing Families: A Family Therapy Reader*. New York: Grune & Stratton.

04852 **HALEY, J.** (1980), *Leaving Home: The Therapy of Disturbed Young People*. New York: McGraw-Hill.

04853 **HALL, B. A.** (1976), The effect of sex of the leader on the development of assertiveness in women undergoing assertive training. *Dissert. Abstr. Internat.*, 3:7208.

04854 **HALL, B. A.** (1976), Mutual withdrawal: the nonparticipant in a therapeutic community. *Perspect. Psychiat. Care*, 14:75-77, 93.

04855 **HALL, B. L.**, and **LITTLE, D. E.** (1969), Group project and learning outcomes. *Nursing Outlook*, 17:82-83.

04856 **HALL, D. M.** (1960), *Dynamics of Group Action*. Danville, IL: Interstate.

04857 **HALL, H. L.** (1974), The effect of personal and impersonal participant models on interpersonal openness in same and mixed sex groups. *Dissert. Abstr. Internat.*, 34:5192B.

04858 **HALL, I.** (1978), The effects of an intensive weekend psychodrama vs. spaced psychodrama sessions on anxiety, distress, and attitude toward group interaction in nursing students. *Dissert. Abstr. Internat.*, 39:3514B.

04859 **HALL, J.**, and **WILLIAMS, M.** (1971), Personality and group encounter style (a). *J. Personality & Soc. Psychol.*, 18:163.

04860 **HALL, J. R.** (1973), Structural characteristics of a psychiatric patient community and the therapeutic milieu. *Human Relat.*, 26:787-809.

04861 **HALL, K. E.** (1972), The effects of a teacher-led guidance program on selected personal and interpersonal variables among fourth grade pupils. *Dissert. Abstr. Internat.*, 33:1436A.

04863 **HALL, N. M.** (1978), Symposium on directions in psychiatric nursing: group treatment for sexually abused children. *Nursing Clinics North Amer.*, 13:701-705.

04864 **HALL, P. L.** (1976), A group behavioral treatment for primary anogasmia. *Dissert. Abstr. Internat.*, 37:973B.

04865 **HALL, R. P.** (1973), An examination of the effect of video-tape playback on a counseling practicum which includes group counseling. *Dissert. Abstr. Internat.*, 34:3061A.

04866 **HALL, R. V.**, and **BRODEN, M.** (1967), Behavior changes in brain-injured children through social reinforcement. *J. Exper. Child Psychol.*, 5:463-479.

04867 **HALL, R. W.** (1945), Group psychotherapy: introductory remarks. *Sociometry*, 8:279-282.

04868 **HALLANGER, F. T.** (1977), Speeches, performances and resolutions. *Transactional Anal. J.*, 7:166-167.

04869 **HALLE, L.**, and **LANDY, A.** (1948), Integration of group activity and group therapy. *Occupat. Ther. & Rehab.*, 27:286-298.

04870 **HALLECK, S. L.** (1967), Psychiatric treatment of the alienated college student. *Sandoz Psychiat. Spectator*, 4:5-6.

04871 **HALLIBURTON, J. K.** (1944), A note on the resolution of aggressive impulses through creative-destructive activity. *Occupat. Ther. & Rehab.*, 23:284-295.

04872 **HALLOWITZ, E.** (1951), Activity group psychotherapy as preparation for individual treatment. *Internat. J. Group Psychother.*, 1:337-347.

04873 **HALLOWITZ, E.** (1970), The challenge to the group psychotherapist created by a society in flux. *Internat. J. Group Psychother.*, 20:423-434.

04874 **HALLOWITZ, E.** (1970), Presidential address: the challenge to the group psychotherapist created by a society in flux. *Sandoz Psychiat. Spectator*, 6:11-14.

04875 **HALLOWITZ, E., ROSENTHAL, L.,** and **HENIG, T.** (1955), The group psychotherapy literature: 1954. *Internat. J. Group Psychother.*, 5:299-321.

04876 **HALPERIN, D. A.** (1970), Group psychotherapy with youth problems and challenges. *J. Psychoanal. Groups*, 3:15.

04877 **HALPERN, A. S.** (1968), Why not psychotherapy? *Ment. Retard.*, 6:48-50.

04878 **HALS, H.** (1962), (Experiment with youth groups in a "somatic" hospital.) *Nordisk Psykiat. Tidsskr.*, (Kungsbacha) 16:366-375.

04879 **HALSTEAD, H.** (1968), Group psychotherapy for the middle-aged. *Brit. J. Med. Psychol.*, (London) 41:139-148.

04880 **HAMILTON, D. M.** (1953), Cultural treatment in a psychiatric hospital. *Internat. J. Group Psychother.*, 3:204-209.

04881 **HAMILTON, D. M.** (1946), The psychiatric hospital as a cultural pattern. In: *Current Therapy of Personality Disorders*, ed. B. Glueck. New York: Grune & Stratton.

04882 **HAMILTON, F. J.** (1944), Group psychotherapy in military medicine. *Northwestern Med.*, 43:247-252.

04883 **HAMILTON, F. J.,** and **DYNES, J. B.** (1945), Group therapy of psychiatric war casualties. *U.S. Navy Med. Bull.*, 44:549-557.

04884 **HAMILTON, G. K.** (1972), The changes in perception of self resulting from a small group laboratory experience as measured by a semantic differential. *Dissert. Abstr. Internat.*, 32:6759A.

04885 **HAMILTON, J. A.** (1970), Encouraging career decision-making with group modeling and structured group counseling. *Dissert. Abstr. Internat.*, 30:2799A.

04886 **HAMILTON, J. A.,** and **BERGLAND, B. W.** (1971), Interactive relationships among student characteristics and group counseling methods. *Psychol. in Schools*, 8:50-55.

04887 **HAMILTON, J. L.** (1943), Psychodrama and its implications in speech adjustment. *Quart. J. Speech*, 29:61-67.

04888 **HAMILTON, L. S.** (1970), An experimental study of the effectiveness of small group discussions in facilitating inter-ethnic group communication and understanding. *Dissert. Abstr. Internat.*, 30:2849A.

04889 **HAMILTON, R. H.** (1972), *Dynamic Thinking: A Method for Effective Group Action.* Salem, OR: Reach.

04890 **HAMM, A.** (1978), (Observations and reflections on body language in group dynamical groups.) *Dynam. Psychiat.*, (Berlin) 11:40-51.

04891 **HAMM, N. H.,** and **WEDEMEYER, A.** (1974), Measuring the effects of racial encounter groups: a proposed assessment technique. *Urban Educat.*, 9:279-283.

04892 **HAMMAR, S.** (1971), Treating adolescent obesity: long-range evaluation of previous therapy. *Clin. Pediat.*, 10:46-52.

04893 **HAMMEN, C. L.,** and **PETERS, S. D.** (1978), Interpersonal consequences of depression: responses to men and women enacting a depressed role. *J. Abnorm. Psychol.*, 87:322-332.

04894 **HAMMER, M. L.** (1972), *The Theory and Practice of Psychotherapy with Specific Disorders.* Springfield, IL: C C Thomas.

04895 **HAMMER, M. L.** (1976), Trust restored through group action. *J. Psychiat. Nursing*, 14:22-23.
04896 **HAMMER, O.** (1971), The bad Nauheim smoking withdrawal therapy. *Verh Deutsch Ges Kreislaufforsch*, 37:473-475.
04897 **HAMMER, O.** (1970), (Group therapy "free of smoking.") *München Med. Wochenschr.*, (Munich) 112:1329-1335.
04898 **HAMMERSCHLAG, C. A.** (1974), Using t-groups to train American Indians as physician assistants. *Hosp. & Community Psychiat.*, 25:210-211.
04899 **HAMMERSCHLAG, C. A.**, and **ASTROCHON, B. M.** (1971), The Kennedy Airport snow-in: an inquiry into intergroup phenomena. *Psychiatry*, 34:301-308.
04900 **HAMMOND, D. C.** (1974), Dimensions of helpfulness in saturation marathon couples group therapy with prison inmates and their partners. *Dissert. Abstr. Internat.*, 35:1912B.
04901 **HAMMOND, J. G.** (1972), Ward discussion groups. *Nursing Times*, (London) 68:1106.
04902 **HAMPDEN-TURNER, C. M.** (1966), An existential "learning theory" and the integration of t-group research. *J. Appl. Behav. Science*, 2:367-386.
04903 **HAMPSHIRE, A.** (1954), The use of groups as motivation for analytic group psychotherapy. *Internat. J. Group Psychother.*, 4:95-102.
04904 **HAMPSON, R. G.**, and **TAVORMINA, J. B.** (1980), Relative effectiveness of behavioral and reflective group training with foster mothers. *J. Consult. & Clin. Psychol.*, 48:294-295.
04905 **HAMPTON, K. R.** (1970), Comparison of the behavior of recidivists and nonrecidivists during group psychotherapy in prison as reflected by therapist ratings. *Dissert. Abstr. Internat.*, 32:560B.
04906 **HAMPTON, P. J.** (1962), Group psychotherapy with parents. *Amer. J. Orthopsychiat.*, 32:918-926.
04907 **HANCOCK, E.** (1976), Crisis intervention in a newborn nursery intensive care unit. *Soc. Work & Health Care*, 1:421-432.
04908 **HAND, A. H., RICHARDS, M. D.**, and **SLOCOM, J. W.** (1973), Organizational climate and the effectiveness of a human relations training program. *Acad. Manage. J.*, 16:185-195.
04909 **HAND, H. H.**, and **SLOCUM, J. R., Jr.** (1972), A longitudinal study of the effects of a human relations training program on managerial effectiveness. *J. Appl. Psychol.*, 56:412-417.
04910 **HAND, I.** (1973), (A new treatment of agoraphobia: in-vivo group immersion—flooding. *Encephale*, (Paris) 62:513-541.
04911 **HAND, I.** (1975), (Symptom-centered group therapy for phobias: a problem-oriented workshop in psychotherapy.) *Fortschr. Neurol. Psychiat. & Grenzgebiete*, (Stuttgart), 43:285-304.
04912 **HAND, I., LAMONTAGNE, Y.**, and **MARKS, I. M.** (1975), Group therapy for agoraphobics: real-live retraining by flooding in vivo. *Psychother. & Psychosomat.*, (Basel) 25:76-82.
04913 **HANDAL, P. J.** (1970), Individual and group problem solving and type or orientation as a function repression-sensitization of death anxiety. *Dissert. Abstr. Internat.*, 31:2986.
04914 **HANDELSMAN, R. D.** (1971), Group counseling: the effects of participation on the dimensions of cognitive flexibility and psychological openness. *Dissert. Abstr. Internat.*, 32:176A.
04915 **HANDLIN, V., BREED, G., NOLL, G.**, and **WATKINS, J.** (1974), Encounter group process as a function of group length: the race toward confrontation, support, and living in the here and now. *Small Group Behav.*, 5:259-273.
04916 **HANKINS-McNARY, L.** (1979), The use of humor in group therapy. *Perspect. Psychiat. Care*, 17:228-231.

04917 **HANLEY, B. L.** (1971), Outcome effects of short term group counseling on the stated concerns and anxiety of students. *Dissert. Abstr. Internat.*, 32:3028A.

04918 **HANNA, N. J.** (1970), The effects of differential styles of group counseling on academic underachievers. *Dissert. Abstr. Internat.*, 31:5763A.

04919 **HANNAFORD, M. J.** (1974), A ta approach to teacher group counseling. *Elem. School Guid. Counselor*, 9:6-13.

04920 **HANNAM, J. C.** (1972), Congruence of the psychometric assessment and counselor perceptions of outcome of group counseling with college men and women. *Dissert. Abstr. Internat.*, 33:2810-2811B.

04921 **HANNIGAR, P. S.** (1976), An investigation of the comparative effects of a 16 hour marathon gestalt workshop on a measure of self-actualization. *Dissert. Abstr. Internat.*, 36:6471-6472.

04922 **HANNING, P. J.** (1975), Hypnosis and group process in weight reduction. *J. Res. Music Educat.*, 23:22-27.

04923 **HANNON, J. E., BATTLE, C. C.,** and **ADAMS, J. V.** (1962), Manipulation of direction of speech in a neuropsychiatric group. *J. Clin. Psychol.*, 18:428-431.

04924 **HANSEN, B.** (1948), Sociodrama: methodology for democratic action. *Sociatry*, 2:347-363.

04925 **HANSEN, B.** (1947), Sociodrama in a small community therapy program. *Sociatry*, 1:92-95.

04926 **HANSEN, B.** (1947), Sociodrama in the class room. *Sociatry*, 1:334-350.

04927 **HANSEN, B.** (1947), A tale of the bitter root: pageantry as sociodrama. *Quart. J. Speech*, 33:162-166.

04928 **HANSEN, E.** (1945), The child guidance clinic of Abraham Lincoln Center. *Individ. Psychol. Bull.*, 4:49-58.

04929 **HANSEN, J., WERNER, R. W.,** and **SMITH, E. M.** (1976), *Group Counseling: Theory and Process*. Chicago: Rand/McNally.

04930 **HANSEN, J. C.,** and **CRAMER, S. H.** (1971), *Group Guidance and Counseling in the Schools: Selected Readings*. New York: Appleton Century Crofts.

04931 **HANSEN, J. C., NILARD, T. M.,** and **ZANI, L. P.** (1969), Model reinforcement in group counseling with elementary school children. *Personnel & Guid. J.*, 47:741-744.

04932 **HANSEN, J. C., WARNER, R. W.,** and **SMITH, E. J.** (1980), *Group Counseling: Theory and Process*, 2d ed. Chicago: Rand McNally.

04933 **HANSEN, W. D.** (1978), Impact of leader verbal communication style on t-groups. *Dissert. Abstr. Internat.*, 39:2961B-2962B. (University Microfilms No. 7822830.)

04934 **HANSON, P. G.,** and **PECK, C. P.** (1974), Training for individual and group effectiveness and resourcefulness. *Newsl. Res. Ment. Health & Behav. Sciences*, 16:1-2.

04935 **HANSON, P. G., SANDS, P. M.,** and **SHELDON, R. B.** (1968), Patterns of communication in alcoholic marital couples. *Psychiat. Quart.*, 42:538-547.

04936 **HANSON, P. G., ROTHAUS, P., O'CONNELL, W. E.,** and **WIGGINS, G.** (1969), Training patients for effective participation in back-home groups. *Amer. J. Psychiat.*, 126:857-862.

04937 **HANSSEN, H.** (1977), *Weglopen of Doorvechten: Groepstherapie met Jongeren*. Bloemendaal: H. Nelissen.

04938 **HARARI, H.** (1972), Cognitive manipulation with delinquent adolescents in group therapy. *Psychother.: Theory, Res. & Pract.*, 9:303.

04939 **HARBIN, H. T.** (1978), Families and hospitals: collusion or cooperation. *Amer. J. Psychiat.*, 135:1496-1499.

04940 **HARBIN, H. T.** (1979), A family-oriented psychiatric inpatient unit. *Fam. Process*, 18:281-291.

04941 **HARDAGE, A. C.** (1972), A comparison of the efficacy of treatments of classroom behavior management and group counseling for use with potential dropouts. *Dissert. Abstr. Internat.*, 33:1436A.

04942 **HARDING, G. T., ISRAEL, J.,** and **BERNSTEIN, L.** (1951), Group therapy in Sweden. *Internat. J. Group Psychother.*, 1:82-85.

04943 **HARDING, M. D.** (1970), A comparison of the effectiveness of three approaches to altering behavior of seventh grade boys. *Dissert. Abstr. Internat.*, 30:2799A-2800A.

04944 **HARDT, H. D.,** and **SCHULZ, H.** (1973), Hospital takes group therapy to released alcoholics in distant community. *Hosp. & Community Psychiat.*, 24:221.

04945 **HARDY, R. C.** (1971), Effect of leadership style on the performance of small classroom groups. *J. Personality & Soc. Psychol.*, 19:367-374.

04946 **HARDY, R. E.,** and **CULL, J. G.** (1973), *Group Counseling and Therapy Techniques in Special Settings.* Springfield, IL: C. C. Thomas.

04947 **HARE, A. P.** (1972), Bibliography of small group research. *Sociometry*, 35:1-150.

04948 **HARE, A. P.** (1976), *Handbook of Small Group Research.* New York: The Free Press.

04949 **HARE, A. P.** (1963), A review of small-group research for group therapists. *Internat. J. Group Psychother.*, 13:476-484.

04950 **HARE, A. P.** (1973), Theories of group development and categories for interaction analysis. *Small Group Behav.*, 4:259-304.

04951 **HARE, A. P.,** and **BALES, R. F.** (1963), Seating position and small group interaction. *Sociometry*, 26:480-486.

04952 **HARE, R. T.,** and **FRANKENA, S. T.** (1972), Peer group supervision. *Amer. J. Orthopsychiat.*, 42:527-529.

04953 **HARGRAVE, G. E.,** and **HARGRAVE, M. C.** (1979), Peer group socialization therapy program in the school: outcome investigation. *Psychol. in Schools*, 16:546-550.

04954 **HARGREAVES, A. C.** (1967), The nurse group therapist in a variety of settings: community hospital, school, and prison. *ANA in Action, Reg. Clin. Conf.*, 281-288.

04955 **HARGREAVES, A. G.** (1967), The group culture and nursing practice. *Amer. J. Nursing*, 67:1840-1846.

04956 **HARGREAVES, A. G.,** and **ROBINSON, A. M.** (1950), The nurse-leader in group psychotherapy. *Amer. J. Nursing*, 50:713-716.

04957 **HARGREAVES, W. A., SHOWSTACK, J., FLOHR, R., BRADY, C.,** and **HARRIS, S.** (1974), Treatment acceptance following intake assignment to individual therapy, group therapy, or contact group. *Arch. Gen. Psychiat.*, 31:343-349.

04958 **HARLANDER, U.** (1978), (On expansion of identity in groups: the concept of identity expansion according to Günter Ammon.) *Dynam. Psychiat.*, (Berlin) 11:23-29.

04959 **HARLEY, A. B., Jr.** (1963), Group psychotherapy for parents of disturbed children. *Ment. Hosp.*, 14:14-19.

04960 **HARLFINGER, H.** (1958), Gruppengesprache mit psychotisch kranken in der Heilanstalt. (Group discussions with psychotic patients in the mental hospital.) *Zeit. Psychother. Med. Psychol.*, (Stuttgart) 8:51-66.

04961 **HARMAN, R. L.** (1978), Gestalt marriage and family therapy. *Gestalt J.*, 1:92.

04962 **HARMAN, R. L.,** and **DUTT, L. G.** (1974), Career counseling workshop: a new approach for undecided college students. *Vocat. Guid. Quart.*, 23:68-70.

04963 **HARMAN, R. L.,** and **FRANKLIN, R. W.** (1975), Gestalt interactional groups. *Personnel & Guid. J.*, 34:49-50.
04964 **HARMATTA, J.** (1975), (Report on research into the methods of group psychotherapy.) *Psychiat. Neurol. & Med. Psychol.*, (Leipzig) 27:418-422.
04965 **HARMELING, P. C.** (1950), Therapeutic theater of Alaska Eskimos. *Group Psychother., Psychodrama & Sociometry*, 3:74-76.
04966 **HARMS, E.** (1945), Group therapy: farce, fashion or sociologically sound? *Nerv. Child.*, 4:186-195.
04967 **HARMS, E., JOERGENSEN, C.,** and **MORENO, J. L.** (1958), On the history of psychodrama. *Group Psychother., Psychodrama & Sociometry*, 11:257-260.
04968 **HARNETT, D. L.** (1967), A level of aspiration model for group decision making. *J. Personality & Soc. Psychol.*, 5:58-66.
04969 **HARPEL, R. L.** (1970), The effect of encounter group composition upon social and political attitudes. *Dissert. Abstr. Internat.*, 31:2683A.
04970 **HARPER, A. E., Jr.** (1961), Role playing in the training of counselors. *Group Psychother., Psychodrama & Sociometry*, 14:12-137.
04971 **HARPER, J.** (1973), Embracement and enticement: a therapeutic nursery group for autistic children. *Slow Learning Child*, (Brisbane) 20:173-182.
04972 **HARPER. R. A.** (1973), The effects of sex and levels of acquaintance on risk-taking in groups. *Midwest Educat. Rev.*, 5:13-28.
04973 **HARPER, R. A.** (1975), *The New Psychotherapies*. Englewood Cliffs, NJ: Prentice-Hall.
04974 **HARRELL, B. E.** (1972), Effects of short-term confrontational group counseling on the risk taking behavior of counselor education graduate students. *Dissert. Abstr. Internat.*, 32:6136-6137A.
04975 **HARRIGAN, J. E.** (1979), Brainwashing in small groups, China or America. *Personnel & Guid. J.*, 58:16-19.
04976 **HARRIMAN, B. L.** (1956), *Influence of Group-Centered Therapy and Mental Health Films on Attitudes of Prisoners*. Ann Arbor: University Microfilms.
04977 **HARRIMAN, B. L.** (1956), Influence of group-centered therapy and mental health films on attitudes of prisoners. *Dissert. Abstr. Internat.*, 16:1494-1495.
04978 **HARRINGTON, J. A.** (1978), Art and technique of analytic group-therapy. *Brit. J. Psychiat.*, (Ashford) 132:611-612.
04979 **HARRINGTON, M.** (1941), A new design for psychotherapy. *Med. Rec., N.Y.*, 153:163-167.
04980 **HARRINGTON, R. C., STINSON, S. R.,** and **MARKEY, O. B.** (1965), Poor academic performance in bright adolescent boys: a study in group psychotherapy. *Amer. J. Orthopsychiat.*, 35:345-346.
04981 **HARRIS, A.** (1972), Good guys and sweethearts. *Transactional Anal. J.*, 2:13-18.
04982 **HARRIS, B.** (1976), The effects of cohesiveness and sequences of positive and negative feedback on acceptance of feedback on personal growth groups. *Dissert. Abstr. Internat.*, 36:6381B.
04983 **HARRIS, C. E. M., BROWN, L. B.,** and **CAWTE, J. E.** (1960), Problems of developing of a group-centered mental hospital. *Internat. J. Group Psychother.*, 10:408-418.
04984 **HARRIS, E. F.** (1971), Early treatment for motivated alcoholics. *Hosp. & Community Psychiat.*, 22:176-178.
04985 **HARRIS, F. G.** (1979), The behavioral approach to group therapy. *Internat. J. Group Psychother.*, 29:453-469.
04986 **HARRIS, G. G.** (1977), *The Group Treatment of Human Problems: A Social Learning Approach*. New York: Grune and Stratton.

04987 **HARRIS, H. I.** (1939), Efficient psychotherapy for the large outpatient clinic. *New Engl. J. Med.*, 221:1-15.
04988 **HARRIS, J.** (1980), Psychiatric referrals by a juvenile court. *Brit. J. Guid. & Couns.*, (Cambridge) 8:99-103.
04989 **HARRIS, J.**, and **JOSEPH, C.** (1973), *Murals of the Mind: Image of a Psychiatric Community*. New York: International Universities Press.
04990 **HARRIS, J. E.**, and **BODDEN, J. L.** (1978), An activity group experience for disengaged elderly persons. *J. Couns. Psychol.*, 25:325.
04991 **HARRIS, J. L.** (1973), Counselor reputation and previous performance as an influence upon counselee interaction and attitude in group experience. *Dissert. Abstr. Internat.*, 34:1080A.
04992 **HARRIS, L. M.**, and **SIEVERS, D. J.** (1959), A study to measure changes in behavior of aggressive mentally retarded adolescent girls in a permissive classroom. *Amer. J. Ment. Deficiency*, 63:975-980.
04993 **HARRIS, M. B.**, and **TRUJILLO, A. E.** (1975), Improving study habits of junior high school students through self-management versus group discussion. *J. Couns. Psychol.*, 22:513-517.
04994 **HARRIS, N. C., Jr.** (1974), Effectiveness of group techniques with socially anxious children. *Dissert. Abstr. Internat.*, 35:5118A.
04995 **HARRIS, N. G.** (1948), *Modern Trends in Psychological Medicine*. New York: Hoeber.
04996 **HARRIS, P.**, and **TROTTA, F.** (1962), An experiment with underachievers. *Education*, 82:347-349.
04997 **HARRIS, T. L.** (1980), Relationship of self-disclosure to several aspects of trust in a group. *J. Special. Group Work*, 5:24-28.
04998 **HARRISON, C. H.** (1971), Teacher and the t-group: NTL's Center for the Development of Educational Leadership. *Scholastic Teacher*, 34:30.
04999 **HARRISON, K.**, and **COOPER, C. L.** (1976), The use of groups in education: identifying the issues. *Small Group Behav.*, 7:259-270.
05000 **HARRISON, M. R.** (1972), Group counseling with secondary school norm violations. *Dissert. Abstr. Internat.*, 32:6200A.
05001 **HARRISON, R.** (1968), *Problems in the Design and Interpretation of Research on Human Relations Training*. Washington, D.C.: National Institute for Applied Behavioral Science.
05002 **HARROD, M. J. E.** (1978), Genetic counseling for ushers syndrome patients and their families. *Amer. Annals Deaf*, 123:377-380.
05003 **HARROW, G. S.** (1951), The effects of psychodrama group therapy on role behavior of schizophrenic patients. *Group Psychother., Psychodrama & Sociometry*, 3:316-320.
05004 **HARROW, G. S.** (1952), Psychodrama group therapy: its effects upon the role behaviour of schizophrenic patients. *Group Psychother., Psychodrama & Sociometry*, 5:120-172.
05005 **HARROW, G. S.**, and **HAAS, R. B.** (1947), Psychodrama in the guidance clinic. *Sociatry*, 1:70-81.
05006 **HARROW, M., ASTRACHAN, B. M., BECKER, R. E., MILLER, J. C.**, and **SCHWARTZ, A. H.** (1967), Influence of the psychotherapist on the emotional climate in group therapy. *Human Relat.*, 20:49-64.
05007 **HARROW, M., ASTRACHAN, B. M., TUCKER, G. J., KLEIN, E. B.**, and **MILLER, J. C.** (1971), The t-group and study group laboratory experiences. *J. Soc. Psychol.*, 85:225-238.
05008 **HARRUP, T., HENSEN, B. A.**, and **SOGHIKIAN, K.** (1979), Clinical methods in smoking cessation: description and evaluation of a stop smoking clinic. *Amer. J. Pub. Health*, 69:1226.
05009 **HARSHFIELD, H. W.**, and **SCHMIDT, J. P.** (1948), Playing out our problems in sociodrama. *Sociatry*, 2:363-367.
05010 **HARSHMAN, G. A.** (1964), Group counseling in a neuropsychiatric hos-

pital in continued treatment and extended privilege setting. *Dissert. Abstr. Internat.*, 24:4796.

05011 **HART, E. W.** (1975), The problem diagram. *Transactional Anal. J.*, 5:274-279.

05012 **HART, G.** (1975), Preparing students for small group work in the classroom. *Education*, 95:351-353.

05013 **HART, I. H.** (1975), Multi-disciplinary group therapy for revolving door patients. *Small Group Behav.*, 6:204-209.

05014 **HART, J. W.** (1964), Rejection patterns and group maintenance: rejection between racial subgroups. *Internat. J. Sociometry & Sociatry*, 4:26-32.

05015 **HART, L.** (1976), Attitudes regarding drug abuse among a group of ex-addict staff members. *Internat. J. Addict.*, 11:35-39.

05016 **HARTFORD, M. E.** (1972), *Groups in Social Work: Application of Small Group Theory and Research to Social Work Practice*. New York: Columbia University Press.

05017 **HART, W. T.** (1971), Rapid intake and group psychotherapy in a mental health center. *Hosp. & Community Psychiat.*, 22:212-214.

05018 **HART, W. T.** (1970), The treatment of alcoholism in a comprehensive community mental health center. *Amer. J. Psychiat.*, 126:1275-1281.

05019 **HARTLEY, D., ROBACK, H. B.,** and **ABRAMOWITZ, S. I.** (1976), Deterioration effects in encounter groups. *Amer. Psychologist*, 31:247-255.

05020 **HARTLEY, E.,** and **ROSENBAUM, M.** (1963), Criteria used by group psychotherapists for judging improvement in patients. *Internat. J. Group Psychother.*, 13:80-83.

05021 **HARTLEY, E. L.** (1975), An exhortation: group process analysis—past is prologue. In: *Group Psychotherapy and Group Function*, 2d ed., eds. M. Rosenbaum and M. M. Berger. New York: Basic Books.

05022 **HARTLEY, R. B.,** and **GLAD, D. D.** (1952), Changes in schizophrenic behavior in group therapy as a function of the type of therapist activity. *J. Colorado-Wyoming Acad. Science*, 4:81-82.

05023 **HARTMAN, B. J.** (1969), Group hypnotherapy in a university counseling center. *Amer. J. Clin. Hypnosis*, 12:16-19.

05024 **HARTMAN, J. J.** (1970), The role of ego state distress in the development of self-analytic groups. *Dissert. Abstr. Internat.*, 31:2986-2987B.

05025 **HARTMAN, J. J.** (1979), Small group methods of personal change. *Ann. Rev. Psychol.*, 30:453-476.

05026 **HARTMAN, J. J.,** and **GIBBARD, G. S.** (1973), Bisexual fantasy and group process. *Contemp. Psychoanal.*, 9:303-326.

05027 **HARTMAN, L. M.** (1980), The interface between sexual dysfunction and marital conflict. *Amer. J. Psychiat.*, 137:576.

05028 **HARTMAN, V.** (1965), Notes on group psychotherapy with pedophiles. *Can. Psychiat. Assn. J.*, (Ottawa) 10:283-289.

05029 **HARTMANN, O.** (1963), (Rehabilitation in a treatment and nursing home.) *Weiner Zeit. Nervenheilk*, (Vienna) 21:166-168.

05030 **HARTNETT, R. C.** (1977), Six month follow-up study on the effects of group psychotherapy with persons who have been arrested for alcohol related offenses. *Dissert. Abstr. Internat.*, 39:5557B.

05031 **HARTOCOLLIS, P.,** and **SHEAFOR, D.** (1968), Group psychotherapy with alcoholics: a critical review. *Psychiat. Digest*, 29:15-22.

05032 **HARTOG, J.** (1966), Group therapy with psychotic and borderline military wives. *Amer. J. Psychiat.*, 122:1125-1131.

05033 **HARTOG, J.** (1967), Nonprofessionals as mental health consultants. *Hosp. & Community Psychiat.*, 18:223-225.

05034 **HARTSON, D. J.,** and **KUNCE, J. T.** (1973), Videotape replay and recall in group work. *J. Couns. Psychol.*, 20:437-441.

05035 **HARTSOOK, J. E., OLCH, D. R.,** and **deWOLF, V. A.** (1976), Personality characteristics of women's assertiveness training group participants. *J. Couns. Psychol.*, 23:322-326.

05036 **HARTWELL, L. J.** (1980), The effects of an assertiveness training group on the levels of assertiveness and anxiety in females. *Dissert. Abstr. Internat.*, 41:689B. (University Microfilms No. 8018480.)

05037 **HARTZELL, R. E., ANTHONY, W. A.,** and **WAIN, H. J.** (1973), Comparative effectiveness of human relations training for elementary school teachers. *J. Educat. Res.*, 66:457-461.

05038 **HARVE, B. J., HOWE, S. R.,** and **PECK, B. B.** (1978), Working from the outside: administrative considerations in the psychotherapy of a family with disrupted boundaries. *Fam. Ther.*, 5:193.

05039 **HARVEY, H. I.,** and **SIMMONS, W. D.** (1953), Weight reduction: a study of the group method, preliminary report. *Amer. J. Med. Science*, 225:623-625.

05040 **HARVEY, H. I.,** and **SIMMONS, W. D.** (1954), Weight reduction: a study of the group method: report of progress. *Amer. J. Med. Science*, 227:521-525.

05041 **HARVEY, V., DILUZIO, G.,** and **HUNTER, W. J.** (1975), A comparison of verbal and nonverbal groups. *Small Group Behav.*, 6:210-219.

05042 **HASCHEL, M. R.** (1967), Ensenanza de un papel psicodramatico para la prevencion de la delincuencia juvenil. (Psychodramatic character education for the prevention of juvenile delinquency.) *Rev. Psiquiat. Psicol. Med.*, 8:161-164.

05043 **HASHMI, H.** (1968), Determinants of the sociometric pattern in an educational group. *Group Psychother., Psychodrama & Sociometry*, 21:49-61.

05044 **HASKELL, M. R.** (1961), An alternative to more and larger prisons: a role training program for social reconnection. *Group Psychother., Psychodrama & Sociometry*, 14:30-38.

05045 **HASKELL, M. R.** (1958), The drug addict, role playing and group psychotherapy, the need for a new approach. *Group Psychother., Psychodrama & Sociometry*, 11:197-202.

05046 **HASKELL, M. R.** (1960), Group psychotherapy and psychodrama in prison. *Group Psychother., Psychodrama & Sociometry*, 13:22-23.

05047 **HASKELL, M. R.** (1957), Psychodramatic role training in preparation for release on parole. *Group Psychother., Psychodrama & Sociometry*, 10:51-59.

05048 **HASKELL, M. R.** (1959), Role training and job placement of adolescent delinquents: the Berkshire Farm after-care program. *Group Psychother., Psychodrama & Sociometry*, 12:250-257.

05049 **HASKELL, M. R.** (1962), Socioanalysis and psychoanalysis. *Group Psychother., Psychodrama & Sociometry*, 15:105-113.

05050 **HASKELL, M. R.** (1968), Techniques of group psychotherapy. *Group Psychother., Psychodrama & Sociometry*, 21:100-105.

05051 **HASKELL, R. E.** (1978), An analogic model of small group behavior. *Internat. J. Group Psychother.*, 28:27-54.

05052 **HASKELL, R. E.** (1975), Presumptions of group work: a value analysis. *Small Group Behav.*, 6:469-486.

05053 **HASSALL, E.,** and **MADAR, D.** (1980), Crisis group therapy with the separated and divorced. *Fam. Relat.*, 29:591-597.

05054 **HATCH, E. J.,** and **GUERNEY, B.** (1975), A pupil relationship enhancement program. *Personnel & Guid. J.*, 54:102-105.

05055 **HATCHER, N. C.** (1970), Two methods of group psychotherapy with hospitalized psychiatric patients. *Dissert. Abstr. Internat.*, 31:1536B.

05056 **HATFIELD, L. D.** (1965), *As the Twig Is Bent: Therapeutic Values in the Use of Drama and the Dramatic in the Church.* New York: Vantage.

05057 **HATHORNE, B. C.** (1966), Frontiers in religion and psychotherapy. *J. Religion & Health*, 5:296-306.

05058 **HATTINGBERG, I.** (1967), Erfahrungen mit gruppenbehandlungen und einzelaussprächen bei der rehabilitation von infarktkranken. (Experiences with group therapy and individual consultations in the rehabilitation of infarct patients.) *Psychother. & Psychosomat.*, (Basel) 15:27.

05059 **HATTON, K. B.** (1962), Sociometry of peer-groups. *Internat. J. Sociometry & Sociatry*, 2:107-115.

05060 **HAU, T. F.** (1971), (Critical views on the comparison of psychoanalytic single therapy and psychoanalytic group therapy.) *Zeit. Psychother. Med. Psychol.*, (Stuttgart) 21:138-141.

05061 **HAU, T. F.** (1970), (Introduction to group dynamics.) *Praxis Kinderpsychol. & Kinderpsychiat.*, (Goettingen) 19:41-44.

05062 **HAUMAN, R. T.** (1976), The relationship of group counseling models and group facilitator personality profile to group member characteristics. *Dissert. Abstr. Internat.*, 36:5822A.

05063 **HAUMONTE, M. T.** (1969), (Three and a half years of experience in the psychotherapy of a group of alcoholics in a psychiatric hospital.) *Annales Medico-Psychol.*, (Paris) 2:323-335.

05064 **HAUPT, R.** (1975), (Theme centered group therapy as a connecting link in the chain of therapy of psychiatric patients: report of an experience.) *Deutsch Krankenpflege-Zeit.*, (Stuttgart) 28:537-540.

05065 **HAUPTMAN, A.** (1943), Group therapy for psychoneuroses. *Diseases Nerv. System*, 4:22-25.

05066 **HAUSERMAN, N., ZWEBACK, S.,** and **PLOTKIN, A.** (1972), Use of concrete reinforcement to facilitate verbal initiations in adolescent group therapy. *J. Consult. Clin. Psychol.*, 38:90-96.

05067 **HAUSMAN, M.** (1974), Parents' groups: how group members perceive curative factors. *Smith Coll. Studies Soc. Work*, 44:179-198.

05068 **HAUSNER, M.** (1974), (The fractioned weekend psychotherapy of chronic psychogenic, characterogenic, and sociogenic disturbances.) *Ceskoslov. Psychiat.*, (Prague) 70:195-199.

05069 **HAUSNER, M.** (1969), Occupational psychiatry and group psychotherapy in Czechoslovakia. *Internat. Psychiat. Clinics*, 6:175-191.

05070 **HAUSNER, M.** (1975), The psychotogenic "double-blind" model in psychoanalysis: case study contribution to the sociogenic theory of schizophrenia. *Psychother. & Psychosomat.*, (Basel) 25:26-28.

05071 **HAUSNER, M.** (1968), (Therapeutic community at the psychiatric department of a faculty hospital.) *Ceskoslov. Psychiat.*, (Prague) 64:241-245.

05072 **HAUSNER, M.,** and **DOLEZAL, V.** (1963), Group and individual psychotherapy under LSD. *Acta Psychother. Psychosomat. Orthopaedagog.*, (Basel) 11:39-59.

05073 **HAUTS, P. S.,** and **SERLER, M.** (1972), *After the Turn On, What? Learning Perspectives on Humanistic Groups*. Champaign, IL: Research Press.

05074 **HAVEN, G. A., Jr.,** and **WOOD, B. S.** (1970), The effectiveness of eclectic group psychotherapy in reducing recidivism in hospitalized patients. *Psychother.: Theory, Res. & Pract.*, 7:153-154.

05075 **HAW, T. F.** (1970), Einführung in die grouppendynamik. (Introduction to group dynamics.) *Praxis Kinderpsychol. & Kinderpsychiat.*, (Goettingen) 19:41-44.

05076 **HAWKEY, L.** (1951), The use of puppets in child psychotherapy. *Brit. J. Med. Psychol.*, (London) 24:206-214.

05077 **HAWKINS, D. M., NORTON, C. B., EISDORFER, C.,** and **GIANTURCO, D.** (1973), Group process research: a factor analytical study. *Amer. J. Psychiat.*, 130:916-919.

05078 **HAWKINS, J. D.** (1980), Some suggestions for "self-help" approaches with street drug abusers. *J. Psychedelic Drugs*, 12:131-137.

05079 **HAWORTH, M. R.** (1956), An exploratory study to determine the effectiveness of a filmed puppet show as a group projective technique for use with children. Unpublished doctoral dissertation, Pennsylvania State University.

05080 **HAWXHURST, D.**, and **WALZER, H.** (1970), Patients helping patients. *Ment. Hygiene*, 54:370-373.

05081 **HAYALIAN, T.** (1976), The effect of trainers' level of self-disclosure and participants' inclusion orientation on participants' self-disclosures in an encounter group. *Dissert. Abstr. Internat.*, 36:3674B.

05082 **HAYDEN, L. K., HANNAH, H. D.**, and **COZART, N. R.** (1966), Attitudes in action. *Amer. J. Nursing*, 66:2693-2695.

05083 **HAYDON, D.** (1976), A therapeutic community in Birmingham (England). *Internat. J. Offender Ther.*, (London) 20:263-271.

05084 **HAYMAN, K. A.**, and **LEWIS, J. S.** (1968), Hospital treatment of alcoholics: a realistic approach. *Hospitals*, 42:59-62.

05085 **HAYNAL, A.** (1967), (An experience with ward psychotherapy in a psychiatric hospital.) *Psychother. & Psychosomat.*, (Basel) 15:313-325.

05086 **HAYNE, M. L.** (1958), An inverse factor analysis of behavior of paranoid schizophrenics. Unpublished doctoral dissertation, University of Denver.

05087 **HAYNES, L. A.**, and **AVERY, A. W.** (1979), Training adolescents in self-disclosure and empathy skills. *J. Couns. Psychol.*, 26:526-530.

05088 **HAYNES, M., Jr.** (1973), The effects of group counseling on undergraduate teacher corps interns. *Dissert. Abstr. Internat.*, 34:4743A.

05089 **HAYS, D. S.** (1960), Problems involved in organizing and operating a group therapy program in the New York state parole setting. *Psychiat. Quart.*, 34:623-633.

05090 **HAYS, D. S.** (1968), Similarities and differences in the group process and group therapy experience: the role of co-leaders (therapists). *J. Group Psychoanal. & Process*, (London) 1:35-36.

05091 **HAYTHORN, W. W.** (1968), The composition of groups: a review of the literature. *Acta Psychol.*, (Amsterdam) 28:97-128.

05092 **HAYWARD, M. L., PETERS, J. J.**, and **TAYLOR, J. E.** (1952), Some values of the use of multiple therapists in the treatment of psychoses. *Psychiat. Quart.*, 26:244-249.

05093 **HAZEL, E. R.** (1976), Group counseling for occupational choice. *Personnel & Guid. J.*, 54:437.

05094 **HAZELL, J. W.** (1975), Query: an action-insight exercise. *Small Group Behav.*, 6:494-500.

05095 **HEACOCK, D. R.** (1965), Modifications of standard techniques for outpatient group psychotherapy with delinquent boys. *Amer. J. Orthopsychiat.*, 35:371.

05096 **HEACOCK, D. R.** (1966), Modifications of the standard techniques for out-patient group psychotherapy with delinquent boys. *Nat. Med. Assn. J.*, 58:41-47.

05097 **HEACOCK, D. R.** (1961), Pharmacotherapy of the mothers of schizophrenics. *Nat. Med. Assn. J.*, 53:282-285.

05098 **HEAD, V. B.** (1975), Experiences with art therapy in short-term groups of day clinic addicted patients. *Ontario Psychol.*, (Toronto) 7:42-49.

05099 **HEAD, W. A.** (1966), Sociodrama and group discussion with institutionalized delinquent adolescents. *Insights*, 1:26-39.

05100 **HEAD, W. A.** (1962), Sociodrama and group discussion with institutionalized delinquent adolescents. *Ment. Hosp.*, 46:127-135.

05101 **HEALEY, J. C., SENAY, E. C., ALTSHUL, V.**, and **LEVINSON, D. J.** (1968),

Innovations in administering a day program. *Hosp. & Community Psychiat.*, 19:180-186.
05102 **HEALY, C. C.** (1974), Evaluation of a replicable group career counseling procedure. *Vocat. Guid. Quart.*, 23:34-40.
05103 **HEALY, J. M.** (1980), Predicting benefit from a gestalt therapy marathon workshop. *Dissert. Abstr. Internat.*, 40:3782A. (University Microfilms No. 8001101.)
05104 **HEALY, P. J.** (1973), Comparison of the effectiveness of parental involvement in group counseling with peer group counseling in the seventh and eighth grades. *Dissert. Abstr. Internat.*, 34:171A.
05105 **HEAPS, K. A., RICKABAUGH, K.,** and **FUHRIMAN, A.** (1972), Academic recovery and client perceptions of group counselors. *Psychol. Reports*, 30:691-694.
05106 **HEATH, E. S.,** and **BACAL, H. A.** (1968), A method of group psychotherapy at the Tavistock Clinic. *Internat. J. Group Psychother.*, 18:21-30.
05107 **HEATH, R. G.** (1946), Group psychotherapy. *Psychosomat. Med.*, 8:118.
05108 **HEATH, R. G.** (1945), Group psychotherapy of alcohol addiction. *Quart. J. Studies Alcohol*, 5:555-562.
05109 **HEATH, S.** (1971), Group psychodynamics and the psychiatric case conference. *Can. Psychiat. Assn. J.*, (Ottawa) 16:223-226.
05110 **HEATH, T.** (1980), The talking pictures: art therapy. *Nursing Mirror*, (London) 150:30-32.
05111 **HEATHER, N., EDWARDS, S.,** and **HORE, B. D.** (1975), Changes in construing and outcome of group therapy for alcoholism. *J. Studies Alcohol*, 36:1238-1253.
05112 **HEBEISEN, A.** (1973), *Peer Program for Youth*. Minneapolis: Augsburg Publishing House.
05113 **HECKEL, R. V.** (1965), Characteristics of early dropouts from group psychotherapy. *Ment. Hygiene*, 49:574-576.
05114 **HECKEL, R. V.** (1963), Comment on Oakes: "Reinforcement of Bales' categories in group discussion." *Psychol. Reports*, 13:301-302.
05115 **HECKEL, R. V.** (1966), Effects of northern and southern therapists on racially mixed psychotherapy groups. *Ment. Hygiene*, 50:304-307.
05116 **HECKEL, R. V.** (1964), The nurse as co-therapist in group psychotherapy. *Perspect. Psychiat. Care*, 2:18-22.
05117 **HECKEL, R. V.** (1971), Precausal thinking as a criterion of therapy choice. *Psychiat. Forum*, 2:22-26.
05118 **HECKEL, R. V.** (1972), Predicting role flexibility in group therapy by means of a screening scale. *J. Clin. Psychol.*, 28:570-573.
05119 **HECKEL, R. V.** (1975), Relationship problems: the White therapist treating Blacks in the South. *Internat. J. Group Psychother.*, 25:421-428.
05120 **HECKEL, R. V.** (1963), A resocialization and rehabilitation program for patients on a psychology service. ii. *J. Assn. Phys. Ment. Rehab.*, 17:168.
05121 **HECKEL, R. V.** (1975), The television camera as co-therapist in group psychotherapy. *Psychiat. Forum*, 5:20-23.
05122 **HECKEL, R. V.,** and **SALZBERG, H. C.** (1976), *Group Therapy: A Behavioral Approach*. Columbia, SC: University of South Carolina Press.
05123 **HECKEL, R. V.,** and **SALZBERG, H. C.** (1967), Predicting verbal behavioral change in group therapy using a screening scale. *Psychol. Reports*, 20:403-406.
05124 **HECKEL, R. V., FROELICH, R. E.,** and **SALZBERG, H. C.** (1962), Interaction and redirection in group therapy. *Psychol. Reports*, 10:14.
05125 **HECKEL, R. V., HOLMES, G. B.,** and **ROSECRANS, C. J.** (1971), Factor analytic study of process variables in group therapy. *J. Clin. Psychol.*, 27:146-150.
05126 **HECKEL, R. V., HOLMES, G. R.,** and **SALZBERG, H. C.** (1967), Emer-

gence of distinct verbal phrases in group therapy. *Psychol. Reports*, 21:630-632.
05127 **HECKEL, R. V., HURSH, L.,** and **HIERS, J. M.** (1977), Analysis of process data from token groups in a summer camp. *J. Clin. Psychol.*, 33:241-244.
05128 **HECKEL, R. V., KRAUS, R.,** and **BECK, E. W.** (1963), Measurement of attitude change in nursing aides. *Psychol. Reports*, 13:639-642.
05129 **HECKEL, R. V., WIGGINS, S. L.,** and **SALZBERG, H. C.** (1962), Conditioning against silences in group therapy. *J. Clin. Psychol.*, 18:216-217.
05130 **HECKEL, R. V., WIGGINS, S. L.,** and **SALZBERG, H. C.** (1963), The effect of musical tempo in varying operant speech levels in group therapy. *J. Clin. Psychol.*, 19:129.
05131 **HEDMAN, L.** (1966), More than custodial care: experiences in group therapy in five state mental institutions. *Perspect. Psychiat. Care*, 4:22-32.
05132 **HEDQUIST, F. J.,** and **WEINHOLD, B. K.** (1970), Behavioral group counseling with socially anxious and unassertive college students. *J. Couns. Psychol.*, 17:237-242.
05133 **HEDRICK, R. P.** (1972), The differential effect of two group experiences upon the adjustment of college freshmen. *Dissert. Abstr. Internat.*, 33:2711A.
05134 **HEFETS, A.** (1963), Nisayon betipul kevutsati im holim psikhotiyim khroniyim. (Attempts of group treatment with chronic psychotics.) *Harefuah*, (Tel Aviv) 64:331-334.
05135 **HEFFERMAN, A.** (1959), An experiment in group therapy with the mothers of diabetic children. *Acta Psychother. Psychosomat. Orthopaedagog. Suppl.*, (Basel) 7:155-162.
05136 **HEFFRON, W. A.** (1974), Group therapy in family practice. *Amer. Fam. Physician*, 10:176-180.
05137 **HEFFRON, W. A., BOMMEHAERE, K.,** and **MASTERS, R.** (1973), Group discussions with the parents of leukemia children. *Pediatrics*, 52:831-840.
05138 **HEFTNER, E.,** and **TIZEK, H.** (1978), (Therapeutic wander-group.) *Gruppenpsychother. & Gruppendynam.*, (Goettingen) 13:97.
05139 **HEIDER, J.** (1974), Catharsis in human potential encounter. *J. Human. Psychol.*, 14:27-48.
05140 **HEIGL, F.** (1965), (Analytic group psychotherapy in a children's home: indication and prognosis: iii.) *Praxis Kinderpsychol. & Kinderpsychiat.*, (Goettingen) 14:46-51.
05142 **HEIGL, F.** (1963), Die analytische gruppenpsychotherapie im heim: indikation und prognose. (Analytical group psychotherapy in the institution: indication and prognosis.) *Praxis Kinderpsychol. & Kinderpsychiat.*, (Goettingen) 12:115-122.
05143 **HEIGL, F.** (1964), (Analytic group psychotherapy in a home: indication and prognosis. ii.) *Praxis Kinderpsychol. & Kinderpsychiat.*, (Goettingen) 13:113-116.
05144 **HEIGL, F.** (1977), (Duration and change, structure and process in group psychotherapy.) *Praxis der Psychother.*, 22:241-248.
05145 **HEIGL, F.** (1975), (Group work in neurosis clinic.) *Gruppenpsychother. & Gruppendynam.*, (Goettingen) 9:96-105.
05146 **HEIGL, F.** (1962), Ein prognostisch entscheidender charakterzug bei verwahrlosten jugendlichen. (A prognostically decisive character trait in neglected youth.) *Praxis Kinderpsychol. & Kinderpsychiat.*, (Goettingen) 11:197-201.
05147 **HEIGL, F.** (1970), Einige gedanken zur gruppendynamik. (Some thoughts on group dynamics.) *Zeit. Psychosomat. Med. & Psychoanal.*, (Goettingen) 16:80-98.
05148 **HEIGLEVE, A.,** and **HEIGL, F.** (1976), (Concept of unconscious fantasy in

psychoanalytic group therapy of gottinger model.) *Gruppenpsychother. & Gruppendynam.*, (Goettingen) 11:6-22.

05149 **HEIGL-EVERS, A.** (1967), Gruppendynamik und die position des therapeuten. (Group dynamics and the position of the therapist.) *Zeit. Psychosomat. Med. & Psychoanal.*, (Goettingen) 13:31-38.

05150 **HEIGL-EVERS, A.** (1972), (Group psychotherapy: methods and technics.) *Nervenarzt*, 43:605-613.

05151 **HEIGL-EVERS, A.** (1978), *Konzepte der Analytischen Gruppenpsychotherapie.* (*The Concept of Analytic Group Psychotherapy.*) Goettingen: Verlag Vanderhoeck und Ruprecht.

05152 **HEIGL-EVERS, A.** (1967), Berufliche wiedereingliederung durch klinische analytische gruppenpsychotherapy: ergebnisse einer katamnestischen untersuchung. (Professional reclassification through clinical analytic group therapy: results of a catamnestic experiment.) *Psychother. & Psychosomat.*, (Basel) 15:28.

05153 **HEIGL-EVERS, A.** (1969), On the social effect of clinical analytic group psychotherapy. *Psychother. & Psychosomat.*, (Basel) 17:50-62.

05154 **HEIGL-EVERS, A.** (1967), Zur behandlungstechnik in der analytischen gruppentherapie. (On treatment techniques in analytical group therapy.) *Zeit. Psychosomat. Med. & Psychoanal.*, (Goettingen) 13:266-276.

05155 **HEIGL-EVERS, A.** (1978), (What is group-therapy? principles of psychotherapy in groups.) *Praxis der Psychother.*, 23:53-62.

05156 **HEIGL-EVERS, A.**, and **HEIGL, F.** (1974), (On combination of psychoanalytic individual and group therapy.) *Gruppenpsychother. & Gruppendynam.*, (Goettingen) 8:97-121.

05157 **HEIGL-EVERS, A.**, and **HEIGL, F.** (1979), Initial phase in group work. *Gruppenpsychother. & Gruppendynam.*, (Goettingen) 14:105-116.

05158 **HEIGL-EVERS, A.**, and **LAUX, G.** (1968), (Fear and aggression in the group.) *Zeit. Psychosomat. Med. Psychol.*, (Stuttgart) 14:137-147.

05159 **HEIKKINEN, C. A.** (1979), Counseling for personal loss. *Personnel & Guid. J.*, 58:46.

05160 **HEILFRON, M.** (1969), Co-therapy: the relationship between therapists. *Internat. J. Group Psychother.*, 19:366-381.

05161 **HEILFRON, M.** (1972), Leading here and now groups. *Personnel & Guid. J.*, 50:673-674.

05162 **HEILIGMAN, A. C.** (1971), Establishing a drug clinic in Minneapolis. *Drug Forum*, 1:83.

05163 **HEIM, R. B.** (1957), Changes in expressed attitudes in prison inmates following group counseling. Unpublished doctoral dissertation, Claremont University.

05164 **HEIMAN, M.** (1953), *Psychoanalysis and Social Work.* New York: International Universities Press.

05165 **HEIMBACH, S. R.** (1962), Note on Gronlund's "Sociometry in the classroom." *Internat. J. Sociometry & Sociatry*, 2:141-145.

05166 **HEIMBACH, S. R.** (1959), Role playing as an aid in improving reading ability and empathy. *Group Psychother., Psychodrama & Sociometry*, 12:42-51.

05167 **HEIMLER, A.**, and **CHABOT, A.** (1974), Sickle cell counseling in a children and youth project. *Amer. J. Pub. Health*, 64:995-997.

05168 **HEINLICH, E. P.** (1973), Using a patient as "assistant" therapist in paraverbal therapy. *Internat. J. Child Psychiat.*, 2:23-52.

05169 **HEIN, A.** (1960), Group psychotherapy and psychodrama in Holland. *Internat. J. Sociometry & Sociatry*, 2:104.

05170 **HEIN, G. W.** (1963), (Psychotherapeutic possibilities for overcoming treatment resistance with special reference to a psychoanalytic method.) *Zeit. Psychother. Med. Psychol.*, (Stuttgart) 13:81-87.

05171 **HEIN, V. L.** (1970), A study of group counseling with selected high school freshmen. *Dissert. Abstr. Internat.*, 30:2800A.

05172 **HEINE, D. B.** (1975), Daily living group: focus on transition from hospital to community. *Amer. J. Occupat. Ther.*, 29:628-630.

05173 **HEINICKE, C. M.** (1976), Aiding "at risk" children through psychoanalytic social work with parents. *Amer. J. Orthopsychiat.*, 46:89-103.

05174 **HEISING, G.** (1974), (Iatrogenic structuring of closed subgroups within an open patient group.) *Zeit. Psychother. Med. Psychol.*, (Stuttgart) 24:1-12.

05175 **HEISING, G.** (1972), (Role and transference availability of the group analyst.) *Zeit. Psychother. Med. Psychol.*, (Stuttgart) 22:199-210.

05176 **HEISING, G.** (1973), (Role problems in cotherapy.) *Zeit. Psychother. Med. Psychol.*, (Stuttgart) 23:186-191.

05177 **HEISING, G.**, and **WOLFF, E.** (1976), *Kotherapie in Gruppen: E. Einf. in d. Probleme de. Praxis.* Göttingen: Verlag Vandenhoeck and Reprecht.

05178 **HEISLER, J. C.** (1980), The one-interview client. *Brit. J. Guid. & Couns.*, (Cambridge) 8:35-43.

05179 **HEISLER, V.** (1967), The catalytic effect of asking a group to admit a new patient. *Psychother.: Theory, Res. & Pract.*, 4:71-73.

05180 **HEISLER, V.** (1974), Dynamic group psychotherapy with parents of cerebral palsied children. *Rehab. Lit.*, 35:329-330.

05181 **HEISS, J. S.** (1963), The dyad views the newcomer: a study of perception. *Human Relat.*, 16:241-248.

05182 **HEIST, P.** (1956), An experiment utilizing group psychotherapy in a self analytic procedure for counselors in training. Unpublished doctoral dissertation, University of Minnesota.

05183 **HEIST, P. A.** (1956), *An Experiment Utilizing Group Psychotherapy in a Self-Analytic Procedure for Counselors in Training.* Ann Arbor: University Microfilms.

05184 **HEITLER, J. B.** (1974), Clinical impressions of an experimental attempt to prepare lower-class patients for expressive group psychotherapy. *Internat. J. Group Psychother.*, 24:308-322.

05185 **HEITLER, J. B.** (1973), Preparation of lower-class patients for expressive group psychotherapy. *J. Consult. & Clin. Psychol.*, 41:251-260.

05186 **HEITLER, J. B.** (1972), Preparation of lower-class patients for group psychotherapy. *Dissert. Abstr. Internat.*, 32:4215B-4216B.

05187 **HEIZER, M.**, and **WEDLER, H. L.** (1976), (Group therapy in clinical practice.) *München. Med. Wochenschr.*, (Munich) 118:645-648.

05188 **HELBERG, D. H.** (1970), The effects of educational-vocational group guidance and client centered group counseling on personality factors, student problems, and vocational direction of junior college students in a developmental program. *Dissert. Abstr. Internat.*, 30:4222-4223.

05189 **HELFAND, I.** (1955), Role playing in schizophrenia: a study in empathy. *Dissert. Abstr. Internat.*, 15:1117-1118.

05190 **HELFAT, L.** (1967), Parents of adolescents need help too. *N.Y. State J. Med.*, 67:2764-2768.

05191 **HELFMANN, B.** (1978), Role differentiation in group development: the emergence of the scapegoat in self-analytic groups. *Dissert. Abstr. Internat.*, 39:381.

05192 **HELLEBRANDT, E. T.**, and **STINSON, J. E.** (1971), The effects of t-group training on business game results. *J. Psychology*, 77:271-272.

05193 **HELLER, K.** (1969), Effects of modeling procedures in helping relationships. *J. Consult. & Clin. Psychol.*, 33:522-526.

05194 **HELLINGA, G.** (1977), Review of J. Huinck's *Getting Acquainted with Group Therapy. TIJD Psych.*, 19:816.

05195 **HELLMAN, I.** (1963), (Simultaneous psychoanalysis of mother and child.) *Rev. Française Psychoanal.*, (Paris) 27:619-639.

05196 **HELLWIG, K.** (1978), Partners in therapy: using the co-therapists' relationship in a group. *J. Psychiat. Nursing*, 16:41-44.

05197 **HELMERING, D. W.** (1976), *Group Therapy: Who Needs It?* Millbrae, CA: Celestial Arts.

05198 **HELMREICH, R., BAKEMAN, R.,** and **SHERWITZ, L.** (1973), The study of small groups. In: *Annual Review Psychology*, eds. P. H. Mussen and M. R. Rosenzweig. Palo Alto: Annual Reviews.

05199 Helping alcoholic patients overcome denial mechanisms (1970). *Roche Report: Front. Hosp. Psychiat.*, 7:1-2, 11.

05200 **HELPS, R.** (1979), The effectiveness of an intensive group speech therapy program for adult stammerers. *Brit. J. Disorders Communicat.*, (London) 14:17.

05201 **HEMPLE, W. F.** (1978), Review of R. E. Merritt's and D. D. Walley's *Group Leaders Handbook: Resources, Techniques, and Survival Skills. Fed. Probat.*, 42:79.

05202 **HEMSTRUP HANSEN, R.** (1977), (Course in therapeutic communication: close cooperation with the patient needs improved communication.) *Sygeplejersken*, (Copenhagen) 77:16-19, 26.

05203 **HENDERSON, G.** (1974), *Human Relations: From Theory to Practice.* Norman, OK: University of Oklahoma Press.

05204 **HENDERSON, J.** (1973), Training groups for public health nurses. *Can. Ment. Health*, (Ottawa) 21:12-14.

05205 **HENDERSON, J. L.** (1964), Factors related to amount of early participation in a development group. *Dissert. Abstr. Internat.*, 25:2611.

05206 **HENDERSON, S., DUNCAN-JONES, P., McAULEY, H.,** and **RITCHIE, K.** (1978), The patient's primary group. *Brit. J. Psychiat.*, (Ashford) 132:74-86.

05207 **HENDRICK, C., GEISEN, M.,** and **COY, S.** (1974), The social ecology of free seating arrangements in a small group interaction context. *Sociometry*, 37:262-274.

05208 **HENDRICK, H. W.** (1979), Differences in group problem solving behavior and effectiveness as a function of abstractness. *J. Appl. Psychol.*, 64:518-525.

05209 **HENDRICKS, L. J.** (1972), A descriptive analysis of the process of client-centered play therapy. *Dissert. Abstr. Internat.*, 32:3689A.

05210 **HENDRIX, J.,** and **HENDRIX, L.** (1975), *Experiential Education: X-ED.* Nashville, TN: Abingdon Press.

05211 **HENDRY, C. E.** (1948), *A Decade of Group Work.* New York: Association Press.

05212 **HENNEMANN, U., MULLENDER, J.,** and **BRUCKMANN, J. U.** (1980), (Group therapy with the theme-centered interaction method within the framework of a stationary psychiatric treatment.) *Psychother. & Med. Psychol.*, (Stuttgart) 30:274-279.

05213 **HENRY, B.** (1966), Association between content and affect in group therapy with prisoners: abstract of thesis. *Smith Coll. Studies Soc. Work*, 37:76.

05214 **HENTHORN, J. W.** (1980), An experimental study of a group counseling approach to improve the perceived self-concept and cognitive skills of title 1 primary school children. *Dissert. Abstr. Internat.*, 41:1404A. (University Microfilms No. 8021169.)

05215 **HERBERT, W. L.,** and **JARVIS, F. V.** (1960), *The Art of Marriage Counseling: A Modern Approach.* New York: Emerson Books.

05216 **HEREFORD, C. F.** (1963), *Changing Parental Attitudes Through Group Discussion.* Austin, TX: University of Texas Press.

05217 **HERMALIN, J., MELENDEZ, L., KAMARCK, T., KLEVANS, F., BALLEN, E.,** and **GORDON, M.** (1979), Enhancing primary prevention: marriage of self-help groups and familial health care delivery systems. *J. Clin. Child Psychol.*, 8:125-129.

05218 **HERMAN, S.** (1966), Some observations on group therapy with the blind. *Internat. J. Group Psychother.*, 16:367-372.

05219 **HERMAN, S. H.,** and **TRAMONTANA, J.** (1971), Instructions and group versus individual reinforcement in modifying disruptive group behavior. *J. Appl. Behav. Annal.*, 4:113-120.

05220 **HERMAN, B.** (1972), An investigation to determine the relationship of anxiety and reading disability and to study the effects of group and individual counseling on reading improvement. *Dissert. Abstr. Internat.*, 33:2711A.

05221 **HERNANDEZ, H. R.** (1977), (Institutional group therapy with a specific goal.) *Neurol.-Neurocir.-Psiquiat.*, (Mexico City) 18:113-116.

05222 **HERRARA, A. E.,** and **SANCHEZ, V. C.** (1980), Prescriptive group psychotherapy: a successful application in the treatment of low-income Spanish-speaking clients. *Psychother.: Theor., Res., & Pract.*, 17:169-174.

05223 **HERRENKOHL, E. C.** (1978), Parallels in the process of achieving personal growth by abusing parents through participation in group therapy programs or in religious groups. *Fam. Coordinator*, 27:279-282.

05224 **HERRERA, J. J.,** and **ESPINOSA, N.** (1965), Encuentro y abandono: a propósito de una fenomenología de la actitud corporal en la relación médico-enfermo, en psiquiatría. (Encounter and abandonment: concerning a phenomenology of the corporal attitude in the doctor-patient relationship in psychiatry.) *Rev. Psiquiat. Psicol. Méd.*, 7:229-242.

05225 **HERRICK, R. H.,** and **BINGER, C. M.** (1974), Group psychotherapy for early adolescents: an adjunct to a comprehensive treatment program. *J. Amer. Acad. Child Psychiat.*, 13:110-125.

05226 **HERRING, B.** (1973), (Training in group dynamics in social service education.) *Tidskr. Sveriges Sjukskoeterskor*, (Stockholm) 40:38-43.

05227 **HERRIOTT, F.** (1940), Diagnostic examination of mental patients on the psychodramatic stage. *Sociometry*, 3:383-398.

05228 **HERRIOTT, F.** (1949), Psychodrama. In: *Mental Health in Nursing*, ed. T. Muller. Washington, DC: Catholic University of America Press.

05229 **HERRIOTT, F.** (1946), Psychodrama. *Quart. Rev. Psychiat.*, 1:458-462.

05230 **HERRIOTT, F.** (1945), Some uses of psychodrama at St. Elizabeth's Hospital. *Sociometry*, 8:292-295.

05231 **HERRIOTT, F.,** and **HAGAN, M.** (1941), The theatre for psychodrama at St. Elizabeth's Hospital. *Sociometry*, 4:168-176.

05232 **HERROLD, K. F.** (1954), Applications of group principles to education. *Internat. J. Group Psychother.*, 4:177-182.

05233 **HERSAM, R. A.** (1970), The human development institute's relationship improvement program used as an adjunct to the group counseling process. *Dissert. Abstr. Internat.*, 31:5127A.

05234 **HERSCHELMAN, P.,** and **FREUNDLICH, D.** (1970), Group therapy with multiple therapists in a large group. *Amer. J. Psychiat.*, 127:457-461.

05235 **HERSCHELMAN, P.,** and **FREUNDLICH, D.** (1972), Large-group therapy with multiple therapists. *Curr. Psychiat. Ther.*, 12:161-167.

05236 **HERSEN, M.,** and **LUBER, R. F.** (1977), Use of group psychotherapy in a partial hospitalization service: remediation of basic skill deficits. *Internat. J. Group Psychother.*, 27:361-376.

05237 **HERSKO, M.** (1962), Group psychotherapy with delinquent adolescent girls. *Amer. J. Orthopsychiat.*, 32:169-175.

05238 **HERSKO, M.,** and **WINDER, A. E.** (1958), Changes in patients' attitudes toward self and others during group psychotherapy. *Group Psychother., Psychodrama & Sociometry*, 11:309-313.

05239 **HERSKO, M.**, and **SIMON, N.** (1977), A group social for principal treatment. *Child Welfare*, 56:601-611.

05240 **HERTZMAN, J.** (1959), Dynamic group experiences for teachers and students in the classroom. *Internat. J. Group Psychother.*, 9:99-109.

05241 **HERZ, M. I., SPITZER, R. L., GIBBON, M., GREENSPAN, K.**, and **RELBEL, S.** (1974), Individual versus group aftercare treatment. *Amer. J. Psychiat.*, 131:808-812.

05242 **HERZOFF, N. E.** (1979), A therapeutic group for cancer patients and their families. *Cancer Nursing*, 2:469-474.

05243 **HES, J. P.**, and **HANDLER, S. L.** (1961), Multidimensional group psychotherapy. *Arch. Gen. Psychiat.*, 5:70-75.

05244 **HESS, H.** (1970), Zur metrischen erfassung soziodynamischer aspekte der gruppenpsychotherapie. (The metric registration of socio-dynamic aspects of group psychotherapy.) *Psychiat., Neurol. & Med. Psychol.*, 22:373-378.

05245 **HESS, T.** (1970), A comparison of group counseling with individual counseling in the modification of self-adjustment and social adjustment of fifteen year old males identified as potential dropouts. *Dissert. Abstr. Internat.*, 31:998A.

05246 **HEUER, A.** (1977), (Group therapy of obesity in children and youth.) *Aerztl. Jugendkunde*, (Leipzig) 68:93-100.

05247 **HEWITT, H.**, and **GILDEA, M. C. L.** (1945), An experiment in group psychotherapy. *Amer. J. Orthopsychiat.*, 15:112-127.

05248 **HEWITT, J.**, and **KRAFT, M.** (1973), Effects of an encounter group experience on self-perception and interpersonal relations. *J. Consult. & Clin. Psychol.*, 40:162.

05249 **HEY, R. B.** (1980), The relationship among theoretical orientation, leader style, and group process variables: a taxonomy of leader and process variables. *Dissert. Abstr. Internat.*, 40:3933B. (University Microfilms No. 8004046.)

05250 **HEYMAN, E.** (1968), Alternate use of individual and group counseling with husbands of psychiatric patients. *J. Group Psychoanal. & Process*, (London) 1:49-61.

05251 **HEYMAN, E.** (1964), Group work and the interdisciplinary approach. *J. Hillside Hosp.*, 13:184-195.

05252 **HICKS, C. F.** (1972), An experimental approach to determine the effect of a group leader's programmed nonverbal social behavior upon group members' perception of the leader. *Dissert. Abstr. Internat.*, 32:4778A.

05253 **HICKS, C. J.** (1972), The effects of short-term group counseling on the interpersonal behaviors of urban teacher education students. *Dissert. Abstr. Internat.*, 32:3840A.

05254 **HICKS, H. A.** (1968), Selected system properties of four observed psychotherapy groups: a quantitative study of interaction processes of children's groups in psychotherapy. *Dissert. Abstr. Internat.*, 28:4312-4314.

05255 **HICKS, J. S.**, and **WIEDER, D.** (1973), The effects of intergeneration group counseling on clients and parents in a vocational rehabilitation agency. *Rehab. Lit.*, 34:358-363.

05256 **HIDAS, G.** (1963), (Clinical group psychotherapy of neurotics.) *Ideggyogyaszati Szemle*, (Budapest) 16:198-206.

05257 **HIDAS, G.** (1975), Greetings and reflections. *Internat. J. Group Psychother.*, 25:175-176.

05258 **HIDAS, G.** (1977), (The group-psychotherapeutic process, examined by complex methods: ii. the application of Hill's interaction analysis.) *Magyar Pszichol. Szemle*, (Budapest) 34:113-125.

05259 **HIDAS, G.** (1967), The problem of relationship of individual and group psychotherapy. *Pszichol. Tanulmanyok*, 10:791-795.

05260 **HIDAS, G.** (1974), (Psychotherapy and group process.) *Magyar Pszichol. Szemle*, (Budapest) 31:189-193.

05261 **HIDAS, G.**, and **BUDA, B.** (1973), Communication and aggression in psychoanalytic groups: the group process from the standpoint of interpersonal communication theory. *Internat. J. Group Psychother.*, 23:148-154.

05262 **HIDAS, G.**, and **BUDA, B.** (1968), A csoportpszichoterapias folyamat vizsgalata az interperszonalis kommunikacioselmelet szempontjal szerint. (Examination of group psychotherapeutic processes from the point of view of interpersonal communication theory.) *Magyar Pszichol. Szemle*, (Budapest) 25:104-122.

05263 **HIETT, R. M.** (1978), Verbal tongenital response pattern in troubled families. *Dissert. Abstr. Internat.*, 38:6535.

05264 **HIFT, E.**, and **REINELT, T.** (1977), (Training program for group psychotherapy in children.) *Zeit. Kinder- & Jugendpsychiat.*, (Berne) 5:25-35.

05265 **HIGASHI, H.** (1972), Behavioral analysis of group play therapy: diagramatic and quantitative representation for therapeutic relationship. *Psychiat. & Neurol. Japonica*, (Tokyo) 74:326-338.

05266 **HIGASHIYAMA, H.** (1975), (Group play communication therapy with autistic children.) *Japanese J. Child Psychiat.*, (Tokyo) 16:224-236.

05267 **HIGGIN, G.**, and **BRIDGER, H.** (1965), *The Psychodynamics of an Inter-Group Experience*. London: Tavistock Publications.

05268 **HIGGINS, P. S.** (1968), Changes in laymen's expectations of the minister's roles. *Ministry Studies*, 2:5-23.

05269 **HIGGINS, R. T.** (1976), Group maintenance: a common theme in group psychotherapy and pastoral leadership. *J. Pastoral Care*, 30:46-49.

05270 **HIGGINS, W. H.**, and **IVEY, A. E.** (1970), Media therapy: a programmed approach to teaching behavioral skills. *J. Couns. Psychol.*, 17:20-26.

05271 **HIGH, B. H.** (1970), Group counseling with underachieving tenth graders. *Dissert. Abstr. Internat.*, 31:5127A.

05272 **HIGHAM, D. P.** (1971), The effects of a marathon SIMSOC group experience on the self concepts of junior college freshmen. *Dissert. Abstr. Internat.*, 32:1853-1854A.

05273 **HIGHAM, E.** (1976), Case management of the gender incongruity syndrome in childhood and adolescence. *J. Homosexuality*, 2:49-57.

05274 Highlights from American Group Psychotherapy Association meeting (1967), *Roche Report: Front. Hosp. Psychiat.*, 4:1-2, 8, 11.

05275 Highlights from American Group Psychotherapy Association meeting (1968), *Roche Report: Front. Hosp. Psychiat.*, 5:1-2, 8.

05276 **HILER, E. G.**, and **BERKOWITZ, A.** (1960), Expanding goals of short-term group psychotherapy. *Diseases Nerv. System*, 21:573-574.

05277 **HILGARD, J. R.**, **STRAIGHT, D. C.**, and **MOORE, U. S.** (1969), Better-adjusted peers as resources in group therapy with adolescents. *J. Psychology*, 73:75-100.

05278 **HILREY, J.** (1976), The effects of video-tape pretraining and guided performance on selected process and outcome variables of group counseling. *Dissert. Abstr. Internat.*, 36:4261A.

05279 **HILL, B.** (1953), An experiment in treating seriously disturbed juvenile delinquent boys. *Psychiat. Quart. Suppl.*, 27:105-119.

05280 **HILL, F. A.** (1972), *Conflict Utilization: The Role of the Black Professional*. Washington: Black Affairs Center/Nat. Institute for Applied Behavioral Science.

05281 **HILL, G.**, and **ARMITAGE, S.** (1954), An analysis of combined therapy—individual and group—in patients with schizoid, obsessive, compulsive or aggressive defenses. *J. Nerv. & Ment. Disease*, 119:113-134.

05282 **HILL, J. G.** (1977), Reducing aggressive behavior in the institutional setting through psychodrama. *Group Psychother., Psychodrama & Sociometry*, 30:86-96.

05283 **HILL, L. B.** (1958), On being rather than doing in psychotherapy. *Internat. J. Group Psychother.*, 8:115-122.

05284 **HILL, P. S.** (1971), Verbal interaction styles of three marathon encounter groups. *Dissert. Abstr. Internat.*, 32:1845B.

05285 **HILL, R. E.** (1975), Interpersonal compatibility and workgroup performance. *J. Appl. Behav. Science*, 11:210-219.

05286 **HILL, W.** (1968), Some aspects of group psychotherapy and psychodrama used in a modern religious cult. *Group Psychother., Psychodrama & Sociometry*, 21:214-218.

05287 **HILL, W. F.** (1957), Analysis of interviews of group therapists practicing in the Rocky Mountain area. *Provo. Papers*, 1:25-39.

05288 **HILL, W. F.** (1975), Further consideration of therapeutic mechanisms in group therapy. *Small Group Behav.*, 6:421-429.

05289 **HILL, W. F.** (1971), The Hill Interaction Matrix. *Personnel & Guid. J.*, 49:619.

05290 **HILL, W. F.** (1977), The Hill Interaction Matrix: the conceptual framework served rating scales, and an updated bibliography. *Small Group Behav.*, 8:251-268.

05291 **HILL, W. G.** (1966), The family as a treatment unit: differential techniques and procedures. *Soc. Work*, 11:62-68.

05292 **HILLMAN, B. W.** (1975), Activity group guidance: a developmental approach. *Personnel & Guid. J.*, 53:761-767.

05293 **HILLMAN, B. W.**, and **PERRY, T.** (1975), The parent-teacher education center: evaluation of a program for improving family relations. *J. Fam. Couns.*, 3:11-16.

05294 **HILLS, C.**, and **STONE, R. B.** (1970), *Conduct Your Own Awareness Sessions*. New York: New American Library.

05295 **HILTZ, S. R.** (1975), Helping widows: group discussions as a therapeutic technique. *Fam. Coordinator*, 24:331-336.

05296 **HIMBER, C.** (1975), Evaluating sensitivity training for teenagers. In: *Four Psychologies Applied to Education: Freudian, Behavioral, Humanistic, Transpersonal*, ed. T. B. Roberts. Cambridge, MA: Schenkman.

05297 **HINCKLE, T. W.** (1975), Group systematic desensitization of test anxiety: a comparison of methods and an investigation of the effects of social facilitation. *Dissert. Abstr. Internat.*, 36:2025A.

05298 **HINCKLEY, R. G.** (1953), College mental hygiene and group therapy. *Internat. J. Group Psychother.*, 3:88-96.

05299 **HINCKLEY, R. G.** and **HERMANN, L.** (1951), *Group Treatment in Psychotherapy: A Report of Experience*. Minneapolis: University of Minnesota Press.

05300 **HINCKLEY, W. W.** (1957), The Chestnut Lodge Kiosk: part one. *Internat. J. Group Psychother.*, 7:327-336.

05301 **HINCKLEY, W. W.** (1957), The Chestnut Lodge Kiosk: part two. *Internat. J. Group Psychother.*, 7:437-449.

05302 **HINDS, P. S.** (1980), Music: a milieu factor with implications for the nurse-therapist. *J. Psychiat. Nursing*, 18:28-33.

05303 **HINDS, W. C.** (1969), A learning theory approach to group counseling with elementary school children. *Dissert. Abstr. Internat.*, 29:2524-2525.

05304 **HINDS, W. C.**, and **ROEHLKE, H. J.** (1970), A learning theory approach to group counseling with elementary school children. *J. Couns. Psychol.*, 17:49-55.

05305 **HINES, L.** (1970), A nonprofessional discusses her role in mental health. *Amer. J. Psychiat.*, 126:1467-1472.
05306 **HINES, P. M.**, and **HARE-MUSTIN, R. T.** (1978), Ethical considerations in family therapy. *Prof. Psychol.*, 9:165.
05307 **HINKLE, D. E., ARNOLD, C. F., CROAKE, J. W.**, and **KELLER, J. F.** (1980), Adlerian parent education: changes in parents' attitudes and behaviors, and children's self-esteem. *Amer. J. Fam. Ther.*, 8:32-43.
05308 **HINSHELWOOD, R. D.** (1972), Patients who lapse from group psychotherapy. *Brit. J. Psychiat.*, (Ashford) 120:587-588.
05309 **HINTERKOPF, E.** (1979), Promoting interpersonal interaction among mental patients by teaching them therapeutic skills. *Psychosoc. Rehab. J.*, 3:20-26.
05311 **HIPPLE, J. L.** (1974), Comparison of applicants and nonapplicants to human relations training laboratories. *J. Youth Adolescence*, 3:161-169.
05312 **HIPPLE, J. L.** (1976), Effects of differential human relations laboratory designs on personal growth. *Small Group Behav.*, 7:407-422.
05313 **HIPPLE, J. L.** (1973), Personal growth outcomes due to human relations training experiences. *J. Coll. Student Personnel*, 14:156-164.
05314 **HIPPLE, J. L.** (1975), Sex differences in residence hall advisor training programs. *J. Coll. Student Personnel*, 16:34-39.
05315 **HIPPLE, J. L.**, and **MUTO, L.** (1974), The ta group for adolescents. *Personnel & Guid. J.*, 52:675-681.
05316 **HIRSCH, M.** (1978), Therapeutische gemeinschaft und analytische milieutherapie: beitröge zu einer reform der psychiatrie. (Therapeutic community and analytic milieu therapy-contributions to a reform of psychiatry.) *Dynam. Psychiat.*, (Berlin) 52/53:509.
05317 **HIRSCH, R.** (1961), Group therapy with parents of adolescent drug addicts. *Psychiat. Quart.*, 35:702-710.
05318 **HIRSCH, S.** (1969), Group program in a general hospital: a consideration of differential factors. *J. Jewish Communal Serv.*, 45:248-253.
05319 **HIRSCH, S. L.** (1979), Home climate in the Black single-parent, mother-led family: a social-ecological, interactional approach. *Dissert. Abstr. Internat.*, 40:4485B.
05320 **HIRSCHFELD, A. H.** (1945), Group psychotherapy for neurotics. *Proceed. Neuropsychiat. Conf. Sixth Serv. Command*, 98-102.
05321 **HIRSCHHORN, T.** (1971), Encounter in a therapeutic community. *J. Emot. Educat.*, 11:203-215.
05322 **HIRSCHMAN, B.** (1961), The closing of a ward: a group experience. *Internat. J. Group Psychother.*, 11:305-312.
05323 **HIRSCHMAN, L. N.** (1979), Incest and seduction: a comparison of two client groups. *Dissert. Abstr. Internat.*, 40:4485B.
05324 **HIRSCHOWITZ, R. G.**, and **RALPH, D. E.** (1973), Communication about communication problems in psychiatric organizations: an intervention model. *Adult Leadership*, 21:285-288.
05325 **HITCH, C. R.** (1975), The effects of an experimental career oriented group guidance program on selected ninth grade students. *Dissert. Abstr. Internat.*, 36:2127A.
05326 **HITCHENS, E. A.** (1977), Helping psychiatric outpatients accept drug therapy. *Amer. J. Nursing*, 77:464-466.
05327 **HITCHENS, E. W.** (1972), Denial: an identified theme in marital relationships of sex offenders. *Perspect. Psychiat. Care.* 10:152-159.
05328 **HIZER, D. D.** (1972), The use of milieu rehabilitation in the adjustment training of the socio-culturally disadvantaged. *Vocat. Eval. & Work Adjustment Bull.*, 5:11-15.
05329 **HO, M. K.** (1971), Problems and results of a shift to heterogeneous age groups in cottages at a boys home. *Child Welfare*, 50:524-527.

05330 **HO, M. K.** (1970), The effect of group counseling on the academic performance, study habits and attitudes, and the interpersonal adjustment of foreign students. *Dissert. Abstr. Internat.*, 30:5237A-5238A.

05331 **HOBBS, G. W.** (1978), A program evaluation of individual and group psychotherapy in a university counseling center. *Dissert. Abstr. Internat.*, 38:5572B. (University Microfilms No. 7804275.)

05332 **HOBBS, N.** (1955), Client-centered psychotherapy. In: *Six Approaches to Psychotherapy*, eds. J. L. McCary & D. E. Sheer. New York: Dryden Press.

05333 **HOBBS, N.** (1951), Group-centered psychotherapy. In: *Client-Centered Therapy: Its Current Practice, Implications, and Theory*, ed. C. R. Rogers. Boston: Houghton Mifflin.

05334 **HOBBS, N.** (1948), Group psychotherapy in preventive mental hygiene. *Teachers Coll. Record*, 50:170-178.

05335 **HOBBS, N.**, and **PASCAL, G. R.** (1946), A method for the quantitative analysis of group psychotherapy. *Amer. Psychologist*, 1:297.

05336 **HOBBS, T. R.**, and **RADKA, J. E.** (1975), A short-term therapeutic camping program for emotionally disturbed adolescent boys. *Adolescence*, 10:447-455.

05337 **HOCH, E. L.** (1950), The nature of the group process in nondirective group psychotherapy. *Dissert. Abstr. Internat.*, 10:221. (University Microfilms No. 00-01859.)

05338 **HOCH, E. L.**, and **DENIS, M. I.** (1955), The role of group therapy in a general medical and surgical hospital. *J. Maine Med. Assn.*, 46:192-193.

05339 **HOCH, E. L.**, and **KAUFER, G.** (1955), A process analysis of "transient" therapy groups. *Internat. J. Group Psychother.*, 5:415-421.

05340 **HOCH, P. H.** (1948), *Failures in Psychiatric Treatment*. New York: Grune and Stratton.

05341 **HOCH, P. H.**, and **LEWIS, N. D. C.** (1950), General clinical psychiatry, psychosomatic medicine, psychotherapy, and group therapy. *Amer. J. Psychiat.*, 106:512-515.

05342 **HOCH, P. H.**, and **LEWIS, N. D. C.** (1951), General clinical psychiatry, psychosomatic medicine, psychotherapy and group therapy. *Amer. J. Psychiat.*, 107:516-519.

05343 **HOCH, P. H.**, and **LEWIS, N. D. C.** (1952), Review of psychiatric progress, 1951: general clinical psychiatry, psychosomatic medicine, psychotherapy, and group therapy. *Amer. J. Psychiat.*, 108:515-517.

05344 **HOCH, P. H.**, and **LEWIS, N. D. C.** (1953), Review of psychiatric progress 1952: general clinical psychiatry, psychosomatic medicine, psychotherapy, and group therapy. *Amer. J. Psychiat.*, 109:503-505.

05345 **HOCH, P. H.**, and **ZUBIN, J.** (1960), *Problems of Addiction and Habituation*. New York: Grune and Stratton.

05346 **HÖCK, K.** (1967), *Group Therapy in the Clinic and in Practice*. Jena: Gustav Fisher.

05347 **HÖCK, K.** (1975), (Use of the MMPI for the study of the progress of clinical group psychotherapy.) *Psychiat., Neurol. & Med. Psychol.*, (Leipzig) 24:465-474.

05348 **HOCK, R. A.** (1977), Model for conjoint group therapy for asthmatic children and their parents. *Group Psychother., Psychodrama & Sociometry*, 30:108-113.

05349 **HODGER, K. K.** (1975), Teaching of problem solving skills and internal locus of control as factors in the effectiveness of group counseling. *Dissert. Abstr. Internat.*, 36:912B.

05350 **HODGES, W. E.** (1975), The effects of an intensive group counseling process on family Chicano mates. *Dissert. Abstr. Internat.*, 36:2630A.

05351 **HODGMAN, C. H.,** and **STEWART, W. H.** (1972), The adolescent screening group. *Internat. J. Group Psychother.*, 22:177-185.

05352 **HÓDOSI, R.** (1975), (The role of psychotherapy in treating pre-adolescents at neurosis departments.) *Magyar Pszichol. Szemle*, (Budapest) 32:591-597.

05353 **HOEK, A.** (1960), Tipul nafshi bemisgeret kevutsatit: hadgamat tahalikh. (Group mental treatment: an illustration of the process.) *Megamot*, (Jerusalem) 11:160-172.

05354 **HOERL, R. T.** (1974), Encounter groups: their effect on rigidity. *Hum. Relat.*, 27:431-438.

05355 **HOFF, E. C.** (1968), Group therapy with alcoholics. *Psychiat. Res. Report, Amer. Psychiat. Assn.*, 24:61-70.

05356 **HOFFMAN, I.** (1979), Psychological versus medical psychotherapy. *Prof. Psychol.*, 10:571-579.

05357 **HOFFMAN, J. J.** (1961), Psychodrama with in-patients. *Group Psychother., Psychodrama & Sociometry*, 14:186-189.

05358 **HOFFMAN, J. M.,** and **ARSENIAN, J.** (1965), An examination of some models applied to group structure and process. *Internat. J. Group Psychother.*, 15:131-153.

05359 **HOFFMAN, L. R.** (1979), Applying experimental research on group problem solving to organizations. *J. Appl. Behav. Science*, 15:375-391.

05360 **HOFFMAN, L. R.,** and **MAIER, N. R. F.** (1967), Valence in the adoption of solutions by problem-solving groups: ii. quality and acceptance as goals of leaders and members. *J. Personality & Soc. Psychol.*, 6:175-182.

05361 **HOFFMAN, R. W.** (1974), The relative effectiveness of three types of group assertive training. *Dissert. Abstr. Internat.*, 35:261A.

05362 **HOFFMAN, R. W.,** and **PLUTCHICK, R.** (1959), *Small-Group Discussion in Orientation and Teaching*. New York: Putnam.

05363 **HOFFMAN, S. D.** (1973), A comparison of two "future group" approaches to self-exploration/career development of college students. *Dissert. Abstr. Internat.*, 34:1615A.

05364 **HOFFMAN, S. R.** (1980), The effect of the developmental parent group approach upon parent attitudes and ability. *Dissert. Abstr. Internat.*, 40:4895A-4896A. (University Microfilms No. 9004585.)

05365 **HOFFNUNG, R. J.,** and **MILLS, R. B.** (1970), Situational group counseling with disadvantaged youth. *Personnel & Guid. J.*, 48:458-464.

05366 **HOFRICHTER, D. A.** (1976), Trying-out a different comportment through psychodrama: the process of the "possible" becoming viable. *Dissert. Abstr. Internat.*, 37:1902B.

05367 **HOFSTEDE, G.** (1975), Perceptions of others after a t-group. *J. Appl. Behav. Science*, 11:367-377.

05368 **HOGAN, D. B.** (1974), Encounter groups and human relations training: the case against applying traditional forms of statutory regulation. *Harvard J. Legislat.*, 11:659-701.

05369 **HOGAN, D. B.** (1976), The experiential group and the psychotherapeutic enterprise revisited: a response to Strupp. *Internat. J. Group Psychother.*, 26:321-334.

05370 **HOGAN, P.,** and **ALGER, I.** (1969), The impact of videotape recording on insight in group psychotherapy. *Internat. J. Group Psychother.*, 19:158-164.

05371 **HOGAN, P. D.,** and **ROYCE, J. R.** (1976), Four-way sessions: the cotherapy of couples in individual and conjoint treatment groups. *Group Dynam. Psychother.*, 7:7-11.

05372 **HOGAN, R.** (1980), *Group Psychotherapy: A Peer-Focused Approach*. New York: Holt, Rinehart and Winston.

05373 **HOGAN, W.** (1978), Development of a rural psychiatric aftercare group. *Psychosoc. Rehab. J.*, 2:9-15.

05374 **HOGENRAAD, R.** (1966), L'evolution de la constrainte du contexte sur le processus de signification dans deux cas d'analyse de groupe. (Contextual constraints and the signification process in group therapy.) *J. Psychol. Normal. Pathol.*, 63:437-462.

05375 **HOGG, W. F.**, and **NORTHMAN, J. E.** (1979), The resonating parental bind and delinquency. *Fam. Therapy*, 6:21-26.

05376 **HOIRISCH, A.** (1963), Substitúi-se o observador: as reacões iniciais de um grupo. (Observer substitution: the initial reactions of a group.) *J. Brasil. Psiquiat.*, (Rio de Janeiro) 12:351-362.

05377 **HOIRISCH, A.** (1964), (Some aspects of "coming alone.") *J. Brasil. Psiquiat.*, (Rio de Janeiro) 13:73-88.

05378 **HOIRISCH, A.**, and **da CONCEICÃO LEVY, M.** (1964), (The arrival of a new patient: his reactions and those of the group.) *J. Brasil. Psiquiat.*, (Rio de Janeiro) 13:339-353.

05379 **HOIRISCH, A.** (1967), (Observations with relatives of analysts in group psychotherapy.) *J. Brasil. Psiquiat.*, (Rio de Janeiro) 16:259-266.

05380 **HOLAHAN, C.** (1972), Seating patterns and patient behavior in an experimental dayroom. *J. Abnorm. Psychol.*, 80:115-124.

05381 **HOLBERT, W. M.** (1971), The semantic differential in sensitivity training: an exploratory study. *Compar. Group Studies*, 2:36-42.

05382 **HOLBROOK, B.** (1976), The quiet group. *Nursing Mirror*, (London) 142:69-70.

05383 **HOLLAND, J. McW.** (1970), The effects of counseling on the decision-making behavior of high school seniors. *Dissert. Abstr. Internat.*, 30:3278A.

05384 **HOLLAND, P. W.**, and **LEINHARDT, S.** (1971), Transitivity in structural models of small groups. *Compar. Group Studies*, 2:107-124.

05385 **HOLLANDER, C.** (1967), The social dynamics of therapeutic recreation. *Hosp. & Community Psychiat.*, 18:226-229.

05386 **HOLLANDER, C.**, and **MOORE, C.** (1972), Rationale and guidelines for the combined use of psychodrama and videotape self-confrontation. *Group Psychother., Psychodrama & Sociometry*, 25:75-83.

05387 **HOLLANDER, E. P., FALLON, B. J.**, and **EDWARDS, M. T.** (1977), Some aspects of influence and acceptability for appointed and elected group leaders. *J. Psychology*, 95:289-297.

05388 **HOLLANDSWORTH, J. G.**, and **WALL, K. E.** (1977), Sex differences in assertive behavior: an empirical investigation. *J. Couns. Psychol.*, 24:217-222.

05389 **HOLLENBECK, G. P.** (1965), Conditions and outcomes in the student-parent relationship. *J. Consult. & Clin. Psychol.*, 29:237-241.

05390 **HOLLERAN, B. P.**, and **HOLLERAN, P. R.** (1976), Creativity revisited: a new role for group dynamics. *J. Creative Behav.*, 10:130-137.

05391 **HOLLIMAN, C. I.** (1970), A differential analysis of the comparative effectiveness of group counseling and individual counseling processes in producing behavior changes of juvenile delinquents using direct behavioral referents as measures of change. *Dissert. Abstr. Internat.*, 31:1511A.

05392 **HOLLISTER, W. G.**, and **HUSBAND, G. W.** (1955), Two role-playing methods of using mental health films and plays. *Ment. Hygiene*, 39:277-283.

05393 **HOLLOMAN, C. R.**, and **HENDRICK, H. W.** (1972), Effect of sensitivity training on tolerance for dissonance. *J. Appl. Behav. Science*, 8:174-187.

05394 **HOLLOMAN, C. R.**, and **HENDRICK, H. W.** (1970), Individual versus group effectiveness in solving factual and nonfactual problems. *Proceed., 78th Annual Convention,* American Psychological Association, 1970, 673-674.

05395 **HOLLOMAN, C. R.**, and **HENDRICK, H. W.** (1971), Problem-solving in different sized groups. *Personnel Psychol.*, 24:489-500.

05396 **HOLLON, T. H.** (1972), Modified group therapy in the treatment of patients on chronic hemodialysis. *Amer. J. Psychother.*, 26:501-510.

05397 **HOLLON, T. H.**, and **ZOLIK, E. S.** (1962), Self-esteem and symptomatic complaints in the initial phase of psychoanalytically oriented psychotherapy. *Amer. J. Psychother.*, 16:83-93.

05398 **HOLLOWAY, W. H.** (1972), The crazy child in the parent. *Transactional Anal. J.*, 2:128-130.

05399 **HOLLWEG, A.** (1964), The dialogue between group dynamics and interpersonal theology. *J. Pastoral Care*, 18:13-22.

05400 **HOLMES, C.**, and **BAUER, W.** (1970), Establishing an occupational therapy department in a community hospital. *Amer. J. Occupat. Ther.*, 24:219-221.

05401 **HOLMES, C. B.** (1972), The effect of sensitivity training on counseling behavior. *Dissert. Abstr. Internat.*, 32:3690A.

05402 **HOLMES, J. S.** (1969), Comparison of group leader and non-participant observer judgments of certain objective interaction variables. *Psychol. Reports*, 24:655-659.

05403 **HOLMES, J. S.** (1965), The effects of selected therapist verbal behaviors on patient verbal activity in group therapy. *Dissert. Abstr. Internat.*, 26:2868.

05404 **HOLMES, J. S.** (1966), The effects of selected therapist verbal behaviors on patient verbal activity in group therapy. *Newsl. Res. Psychol.*, 8:8-9.

05405 **HOLMES, J. S.** (1967), Relation of depression and verbal interaction in group therapy. *Psychol. Reports*, 20:1039-1042.

05406 **HOLMES, J. S.**, and **CURETON, E. E.** (1970), Group therapy interaction with and without the leader. *J. Soc. Psychol.*, 81:127-128.

05407 **HOLMES, M.**, and **HOLMES, D.** (1959), An attempt to categorize cultural variables in the application of psychodramatic techniques. *Group Psychother., Psychodrama & Sociometry*, 12:308-314.

05408 **HOLMES, M. J., LEFLEY, D.**, and **WERNER, J. A.** (1962), Creative nursing in day and night care centers. *Amer. J. Nursing*, 62:86.

05409 **HOLMES, R. M.** (1970), Alcoholics anonymous as group logotherapy. *Pastoral Psychol.*, 21:30-36.

05410 **HOLROYD, K. A.** (1976), Cognition and desensitization in the group treatment of test anxiety. *J. Consult. & Clin. Psychol.*, 44:991-1001.

05411 **HOLROYD, K. A.** (1976), Cognition and sensitization in the group treatment of test anxiety. *Dissert. Abstr. Internat.*, 36:4689B.

05412 **HOLT, H.** (1976), *Free to Be Good or Bad.* New York: M. Evans.

05413 **HOLT, H.**, and **WINICK, C.** (1961), Group psychotherapy with obese women. *Arch. Gen. Psychiat.*, 5:156-168.

05414 **HOLT, W. L.** (1950), Modern psychiatric treatment. *Med. Clinics No. Amer.*, 34:1499-1506.

05415 **HOLTBY, M. E.** (1975), Transactional analysis and psychodrama. *Transactional Anal. J.*, 4:133-136.

05416 **HOLUB, N., EKLUND, P.**, and **KEENAN, P.** (1975), Teaching the patient and the family: family conferences as an adjunct to total coronary care at Mercy Hospital—part 2. *Heart & Lung*, 4:767-769.

05417 **HOLYOAK, W. H.** (1972), Playing out family conflicts in a female homosexual "family" group (chick-vot) among institutional juveniles: a case presentation. *Adolescence*, 7:153-168.

05418 **HOLZHAUER, R. A.** (1979), A new focus for self-help groups. *Humanist*, 39:51.

05419 **HOLZINGER, R.** (1965), Synanon through the eyes of a visiting psychologist. *Quart. J. Studies Alcohol*, 26:304-309.

05420 **HOLZMAN, I. L.,** and **CARPENTER, W. A.** (1972), The confrontation method in sales training. *Training & Develop. J.*, 26:6-7.
05421 **HOME, A. M.** (1978), Change in women's consciousness raising groups: a study of four types of change and of some factors associated with them. *Dissert. Abstr. Internat.*, 40:1075A.
05422 **HOMER, C. E.** (1973), Community-based resource for runaway girls. *Soc. Casework*, 54:473-479.
05423 **HOMMERS, W.** (1978), (Improvement of role games by juvenile delinquents in social interaction through model-assisted role training.) *Praxis Kinderpsychol. & Kinderpsychiat.*, (Goettingen) 27:164-167.
05424 **HONEY, P.,** and **LINDSAY, J. S. B.** (1960), Occupational therapy for long term psychotic patients. *Amer. J. Occupat. Ther.*, 14:134-136.
05425 **HONFFY, M.** (1976), (Group work as behavior modification for school children at the educational psychology advisory board in Innsbruck.) *Praxis Kinderpsychol. & Kinderpsychiat.*, (Goettingen) 25:259-264.
05426 **HONIG, P.** (1946), Psychodrama and the stutterer. *Sociometry*, 9:175-176.
05427 **HONIGFELD, G., ROSENBLUM, M. P., BLUMENTHAL, I. J., LAMBERT, H. L.,** and **ROBERTS, A. J.** (1965), Behavioral improvement in the older schizophrenic patient: drug and social therapies. *J. Amer. Geriat. Soc.*, 13:57-72.
05428 **HONKALA, K.** (1961), Social class and visiting patterns in two Finnish villages. *Group Psychother., Psychodrama & Sociometry*, 14:190-197.
05429 **HOOFDAKKER, R. H.** (1962), (Some aspects of group psychotherapy in the H.O.C.) *Psychiat., Neurol., Neurochir.*, (Amsterdam) 65:201-213.
05430 **HOOPES, M. H.** (1970), The effects of structuring goals in the process of group counseling for academic improvement. *Dissert. Abstr. Internat.*, 31:1012A.
05431 **HOOVER, J.** (1971), Training for political awareness and commitment. *Soc. Change*, 1:3-5.
05432 **HOOVER, K. K., RAULINAITIS, V. B.,** and **SPANER, F. E.** (1965), Therapeutic democracy: group process as a corrective emotional experience. *Internat. J. Soc. Psychiat.*, (London) 11:26-31.
05433 **HOPER, C.** (1976), *Awareness Games: Personal Growth Through Group Interaction.* New York: St. Martin's Press.
05434 **HÖPER, C. J.** (1975), *Die Spielende Gruppe: 115 Vorschläge für Soziales Lernen. (The Play Group: 115 Examples for Social Studies.)* Wuppertal: Jugenddienst-Verlag.
05435 **HOPPOCK, R.** (1963), *Occupational Information: Where to Get It and How to Use It in Counseling and in Teaching*, 2d ed. New York: McGraw-Hill.
05436 **HORA, T.** (1959), Existential group psychotherapy. *Amer. J. Psychother.*, 13:83-92.
05437 **HORA, T.** (1961), Existential psychiatry and group psycotherapy. *Amer. J. Psychoanal.*, 21:58-73.
05438 **HORA, R.** (1959), Group psychotherapy and the human condition. *Acta Psychother., Psychosomat. Orthopaedagog. Suppl.*, (Basel) 7:162-171.
05439 **HORA, T.** (1958), Group psychotherapy, human values and mental health. *Internat. J. Group Psychother.*, 8:154-160.
05440 **HORA, T.** (1957), Group psychotherapy in the rehabilitation process of the borderline patient. *Internat. J. Group Psychother.*, 7:406-413.
05441 **HORA, T.** (1958), The schizophrenic patient in the therapy group: a study in communication. *J. Hillside Hosp.*, 7:110-115.
05442 **HORAN, J. J., ROBB, N. S.,** and **HUDSON, G. R.** (1975), Behavior therapy for chubby behavior therapists. *J. Couns. Psychol.*, 22:456-457.
05443 **HORE, B. D.** (1979), Review of D. Robinson's *Talking Out of Alcoholism:*

Self-Help Processes of Alcoholics Anonymous. Brit. J. Psychiat., (Ashford) 135:373.

05444 **HORETZKY, O.** (1963), Das gezielte pantomimenspiel inder gruppenpsychotherapie. (Directive pantomime drama in group psychotherapy.) *Topical Probl. Psychol. & Psychother.*, 4:163-168.

05445 **HORETZKY, O.** (1967), Individuelle pantomimepsychotherapie in der gruppe. (Individual pantomime psychotherapy in the group.) *Psychother. & Psychosomat.*, (Basel) 15:30.

05446 **HORETZKY, O.** (1960), Pantomime in group psychotherapy. *Internat. J. Sociometry & Sociatry*, 2:99-102.

05447 **HORETZKY, O.** (1960), Pantomime in der gruppenpsychotherapie. (Pantomime in group psychotherapy.) *Praxis der Psychother.*, 5:122-127.

05448 **HORETZKY, O.** (1966), La pantomime sur des themes individuels: technique psychotherapique de groupe de malades hospitalisés. (Pantomime of individual themes: psychotherapeutic technique for a group of hospitalized ill.) *Rev. Med. Psychosomat.*, (Toulouse) 7:401-406.

05449 **HORETZKY, O.** (1965), (The pantomime as a method of group psychotherapy.) *Zeit. Psychother. Med. Psychol.*, (Stuttgart) 15:130-135.

05450 **HORMUTH, R.** (1955), The utilization of group approaches in aiding mentally retarded adults adjust to community living. *Group Psychother., Psychodrama & Sociometry*, 8:233-241.

05451 **HORN, G.** (1979), (Open-house form of parental counseling.) *Praxis Kinderpsychol. & Kinderpsychiat.*, (Goettingen) 28:100-110.

05452 **HORNE, A. M.** (1972), A comparative study of three group counseling techniques for reducing test anxiety. *Dissert. Abstr. Internat.*, 32:4952A.

05453 **HORNE, W. C.** (1970), Group influence on ethical risk taking: the inadequacy of two hypotheses. *J. Soc. Psychol.*, 80:237-238.

05454 **HORNE, W. C.**, and **LONG, G.** (1972), Effect of group discussion on universalistic-particularistic orientation. *J. Exper. Soc. Psychol.*, 8:236-246.

05455 **HORNER, A. J.** (1975), A characterological contraindication for group psychotherapy. *J. Amer. Acad. Psychoanal.*, 3:301-306.

05456 **HORNER, A. J.** (1970), Self-deception and the search for intimacy. *Voices*, 6:34-36.

05457 **HORNSBY, J. L.** (1974), The effects of group composition on systematic human relations training. *Dissert. Abstr. Internat.*, 34:4871A.

05458 **HORNYAK, R. A.** (1980), The effect of a pre-practicum disability awareness group on counselor state anxiety and attitudes toward the disabled. *Dissert. Abstr. Internat.*, 40:4410A. (University Microfilms No. 8004810.)

05459 **HOROWITZ, J. A.** (1978), Sexual difficulties as indicators of broader personal and interpersonal problems as reflected in psychotherapy group. *Perspect. Psychiat. Care*, 16:66-69.

05460 **HOROWITZ, M. J.** (1966), Group psychotherapy of psychosis. *Curr. Psychiat. Ther.*, 6:204-210.

05461 **HOROWITZ, M. J.**, and **WEISBERG, P. S.** (1966), Techniques for the group psychotherapy of acute psychosis. *Internat. J. Group Psychother.*, 16:42-50.

05462 **HOROWITZ, R. H.** (1973), The influence of various group counseling procedures on certain personality traits and weight control among obese women. *Dissert. Abstr. Internat.*, 34:2299A.

05463 **HORSKY, D.** (1977), The efficacy of a significant other upon generalization in assertion training groups. *Dissert. Abstr. Internat.*, 38:1883B.

05464 **HORSLEY, J. A.** (1973), Psychiatric and mental health nursing: patient contingency managers in a small group token economy. *ANA Clin. Sessions*, 197-207.

05465 **HORSTMAN, P.** (1974), Leaderless group discussions as an assessment tool for supervisory and command promotions. *J. Polit. Science Admin.*, 2:34-37.

05466 **HORTON, E. B.** (1973), An experimental study to compare the effectiveness of two methods of group counseling for black junior high school students. *Dissert. Abstr. Internat.*, 34:567A.

05467 **HORVATH, S.** (1971), (Thematic analysis of group psychotherapy sessions.) *Magyar Pszichol. Szemle*, (Budapest) 28:509.

05468 **HORVATH, W. J.** (1965), A mathematical model of participation in small group discussions. *Behav. Science Res.*, 10:164-166.

05469 **HORWITZ, L.** (1977), A group-centered approach to group psychotherapy. *Internat. J. Group Psychother.*, 27:423-439.

05470 **HORWITZ, L.** (1971), Group-centered interventions in therapy groups. *Compar. Group Studies*, 2:311-331.

05471 **HORWITZ, L.** (1978), Groups for suicidal persons: a reply. *Bull. Menninger Clinic*, 42:518-519.

05472 **HORWITZ, L.** (1980), Group psychotherapy for borderline and narcissistic patients. *Bull. Menninger Clinic*, 44:181-200.

05473 **HORWITZ, L.** (1977), Group psychotherapy of borderline patients. In: *Borderline Personality Disorders: The Concept of Syndrome, the Patient*, ed. P. Hartocollis. New York: International Universities Press.

05474 **HORWITZ, L.** (1968), Group psychotherapy training for psychiatric residents. In: *Current Psychiatric Therapies*, ed. J. H. Masserman. New York: Grune and Stratton.

05475 **HORWITZ, L.** (1976), Indications and contraindications for group psychotherapy. *Bull. Menninger Clinic*, 40:505-507.

05476 **HORWITZ, L.** (1967), Training groups for psychiatric residents. *Internat. J. Group Psychother.*, 17:421-435.

05477 **HORWITZ, L.** (1971), Training issues in group psychotherapy. *Bull. Menninger Clinic*, 35:249-261.

05478 **HORWITZ, L.** (1964), Transference in training groups and therapy groups. *Internat. J. Group Psychother.*, 14:202-213.

05479 **HORWITZ, S.** (1945), The spontaneous drama as a technique in group therapy. *Nerv. Child*, 4:252-273.

05480 **HOSKOVCOVÁ, L.** (1973), (Group psychotherapy in schizophrenic adolescents.) *Ceskoslov. Psychiat.*, (Prague) 69:377-380.

05481 **HOTARD, S. R.** (1971), Increase in cognitive complexity: a comparison of human relations training and group psychotherapy. *Dissert. Abstr. Internat.*, 31:5624-5625.

05482 **HOTFELDER, P.**, and **SACHS, A. D.** (1979), Intake group counseling. *Fed. Probat.*, 43:48-54.

05483 **HOTKINS, A. S., KRIEGSFELD, M.**, and **SANDS, R. M.** (1958), An interview group therapy program for the waiting list problem. *Soc. Work*, 3:29-34.

05484 **HOTT, J. R.** (1978), Principles in sex therapy. *Amer. J. Psychoanal.*, 38:41-48.

05485 **HOTT, L. R.** (1967), The changing role of psychoanalysis in the clinic. *Amer. J. Psychoanal.*, 27:50-60.

05486 **HOULIHAN, J. P.** (1977), Contribution of an intake group to psychiatric inpatient milieu therapy. *Internat. J. Group Psychother.*, 27:215-224.

05487 **HOUPT, J. L., LIPSTICH, L.**, and **ANDERSON, C.** (1972), Re-entry groups: bridging the hospital-community gap. *Soc. Psychiat.*, 7:144-149.

05488 **HOUSE, J. W.**, and **MARQUIT, S.** (1950), Reactions of mental patients to attendance at a businessmen's luncheon club meeting. *J. Abnorm. & Soc. Psychol.*, 45:738-742.

05489 **HOUSE, R. J.** (1968), T-group education and leadership effectiveness: a

review of the empiric literature and a critical evaluation. *Personnel Psychol.*, 20:1-32.
05490 **HOUSE, R. M.** (1970), The effects of non-directive group play therapy upon the sociometric status and self-concept of selected second grade children. *Dissert. Abstr. Internat.*, 31:2685.
05491 **HOUSTON, J.** (1980), *Lifeforce: The Psycho-Historical Recovery of the Self.* New York: Delacorte Press.
05492 **HOUTS, P. S.**, and **SERBER, M.** (1972), *After the Turn On, What?: Learning Perspectives on Humanistic Groups.* Champaign, IL: Research Press.
05493 **HOUTS, P. S.**, and **WITTNER, W. K.** (1968), Patients' recognition memory for statements made in ward community meetings. *J. Consult. & Clin. Psychol.*, 32:130-133.
05494 **HOVER, D. E.** (1968), The theory of the interdependence of family members and its application in an emotionally disturbed family. *ANA Clin. Sessions*, pp. 46-52.
05495 **HOWARD, G.** (1948), The principal speaks. *Sociatry*, 2:254-255.
05496 **HOWARD, J.** (1970), *Please Touch: A Guided Tour of the Human Potential Movement.* New York: McGraw-Hill.
05497 **HOWARD, J.**, and **WESLEY, W.** (1969), Group approach in nursing rehabilitation of geriatric psychiatric patients. *J. Amer. Geriat. Soc.*, 17:1147-1148.
05498 **HOWARD, R. C.** (1971), A descriptive analysis of verbal interaction in a biracial counseling group of college undergraduates. *Dissert. Abstr. Internat.*, 31:3270A.
05499 **HOWARD, W.** (1972), *Groups That Work.* Grand Rapids, MI: Zondervan.
05500 **HOWARD, W., Jr.**, and **ZIMPFER, D. G.** (1972), The findings of research on group approaches in elementary guidance and counseling. *Elem. School Guid. & Couns.*, 6:163-169.
05501 **HOWE, B. J.** (1975), The practice of psychotherapy as do-it-yourself-treatment for a beginning therapist. *Fam. Ther.*, 2:123-128.
05502 **HOWE, B. J., HOWE, S. R., ELLISON, T. R.**, and **RACKLEY, M.** (1976), The therapist and parole officer as co-therapists with involuntary patients. *Fam. Ther.*, 3:35.
05503 **HOWE, M. C.** (1968), An occupational therapy activity group. *Amer. J. Occupat. Ther.*, 22:176-179.
05504 **HOWELLS, J. G.** (1965), Child psychiatry as an aspect of family psychiatry. *Acta. Paedopsychiat.*, (Basel) 32:35-44.
05505 **HOWELLS, J. G.** (1963), Extra-interview therapy in family psychiatry. *Pub. Health*, (London) 77:368-372.
05506 **HOXWORTH, D.**, and **ALSUP, T.** (1968), Group work with parents in a day care center. *Hosp. & Community Psychiat.*, 19:256-258.
05507 **HOY, R. M.** (1969), The personality of inpatient alcoholics in relation to group psychotherapy, as measured by the 16 P. F. *Quart. J. Studies Alcohol*, 30:401-407.
05508 **HOYT, D. L., REPCIK, J. D.**, and **BROWN, B. S.** (1967), Work rehabilitation in small groups. *Hosp. & Community Psychiat.*, 18:270-271.
05509 **HUBBELL, A.** (1954), Two-persons role playing for guidance in social readjustment. *Group Psychother., Psychodrama & Sociometry*, 7:249-254.
05510 **HUBBELL, M. W.** (1973), A study of the treatment of group counseling and psychodrama at the Pre-release Center for Men. Mississippi State Penitentiary. *Dissert. Abstr. Internat.*, 33:4835.
05511 **HUBBERT, A. K.** (1970), Effect of group counseling and behavior modification on attention behavior of first grade students. *Dissert. Abstr. Internat.*, 30:3727A.
05512 **HUBER, R.** (1973), Sensory training for a fuller life. *Nursing Homes*, 22:14-15.

05513 **HUBERTY, C. E.,** and **HUBERTY, D. J.** (1976), Treating the parents of adolescent drug abusers. *Contemp. Drug Probl.*, 5:573-592.

05514 **HUCHESON, R. G.** (1972), An examination of the value system reflected by the sensitivity and encounter group movement in adult education, 1950-1970. *Dissert. Abstr. Internat.*, 6732A.

05515 **HUDDLESON, R. J.** (1972), The effects of a reinforcement counseling procedure on the social behavior and sociometric status of elementary school students. *Dissert. Abstr. Internat.*, 33:4836A.

05516 **HUDOLIN, V.,** and **MUACEVIC, V.** (1967), Die möglichkeit der psychotherapie in grosser gruppe bei alkoholikern. (The possibility of psychotherapy in larger groups with alcoholics.) *Psychother. & Psychosomat.*, (Basel) 15:31.

05517 **HUDOLIN, V., JELIC, V.,** and **KATANEC, N.** (1967), (Our experiences in group psychotherapy of children.) *Psychother. & Psychosomat.*, (Basel) 15:31.

05518 **HUEGLI, J. M.** (1972), An investigation of trustworthy group representatives' communication behavior. *Dissert. Abstr. Internat.*, 32:6586-6587A.

05519 **HUEY, F. L.** (1971), In a therapeutic community. *Amer. J. Nursing*, 71:926-933.

05520 **HUEY, K.** (1977), A remotivation institute at Philadelphia State Hospital. *Hosp. & Community Psychiat.*, 28:133-135.

05521 **HUGHES, A. E. R.** (1970), Study I: the accurate empathy ratings of therapists in telephone and face-to-face interviews. Study II: the effect of group sensitivity-training on the accurate empathy ratings of therapists. *Dissert. Abstr. Internat.*, 30:4793B.

05522 **HUGHES, A. H.,** and **DUDLEY, H. K.** (1973), An old idea for a new problem: camping as a treatment for the emotionally disturbed in our state hospitals. *Adolescence*, 8:43-50.

05523 **HUGHES, H. M.** (1979), Behavior change in children at a therapeutic summer camp as a function of feedback and individual versus group contingencies. *J. Abnorm. Child Psychol.*, 7:211.

05524 **HUGHES, P. H., FLOYD, C. M., NORRIS, G.,** and **SILVA, G.** (1970), Organizing the therapeutic potential of an addict prisoner community. *Internat. J. Addict.*, 5:205-223.

05525 **HUGHES, S. F., BERGER, M.,** and **WRIGHT, L.** (1978), The family life cycle and clinical intervention. *J. Marriage & Fam.*, 4:33.

05526 **HUGO, M. J.** (1970), The effects of group counseling on self-concepts and behavior of elementary school children. *Dissert. Abstr. Internat.*, 30:3728A.

05527 **HUICI, C.** (1980), Initial disposition and intermember perception in experiential groups. *Small Group Behav.*, 11:297-308.

05528 **HUKILL, E. L.** (1973), Toward a cybernetic model of group therapy. *Amer. J. Psychother.*, 27:251-264.

05529 **HULL, D.** (1971), Talking and body complaints in group therapy patients. *J. Psychosomat. Res.*, 15:169-177.

05530 **HULL, W. F.** (1972), Changes in world-mindedness after a cross-cultural sensitivity group experience. *J. Appl. Behav. Science*, 8:115-121.

05531 **HULL, W. F.** (1970), The influence of a random sample of international students upon American students in a sensitivity group experience. *Dissert. Abstr. Internat.*, 31:2737A.

05532 **HULSE, W.** (1954), Dynamics and techniques of group psychotherapy in private practice. *Internat. J. Group Psychother.*, 4:65-73.

05533 **HULSE, W.** (1952), Group psychotherapy at the 4th International Congress on Mental Health, Mexico City. *Internat. J. Group Psychother.*, 2:270-272.

05534 **HULSE, W.** (1947), Gruppen-psychotherapie in Amerika. (Group psychotherapy in America.) *Schweiz. Arch. Neurol, Neurochir., & Psychiat.*, (Zurich) 60:199-208.

05535 **HULSE, W.** (1959), Oneness or unification in group psychotherapy. *Acta Psychother. Psychosomat. Orthopaedagog.*, (Basel) 7:138-147.

05536 **HULSE, W.** (1952), The role of group therapy in preventive psychiatry. *Ment. Hygiene*, 36:531-547.

05537 **HULSE, W.** (1951), The role of group therapy in preventive psychiatry. *Proceed., Fourth Internat. Congr. Ment. Health*, pp. 193-205.

05538 **HULSE, W.** (1955), Transference, catharsis, insight and reality testing during concomitant individual and group psychotherapy. *Internat. J. Group Psychother.*, 5:45-53.

05539 **HULSE, W. C.** (1962), Applications and modifications of group psychotherapy in contemporary psychiatric and mental health practice. *J. Hillside Hosp.*, 12:140-144.

05540 **HULSE, W. C.** (1962), Communalization as an active psychotherapeutic group process. *Internat. J. Group Psychother.*, 12:225-229.

05541 **HULSE, W. C.** (1961), Conflict in contemporary group psychotherapy. *Comprehens. Psychiat.*, 2:60-63.

05542 **HULSE, W. C.** (1965), Curative elements in group psychotherapy. *Topical Probl. Psychol. & Psychother.*, 5:90-101.

05543 **HULSE, W. C.** (1951), Diverses expériences dans la psychothérapie de groupe. (Diverse experiences in group psychotherapy.) *Psyché*, (Stuttgart) 6:86-97.

05544 **HULSE, W. C.** (1960), The group psychotherapist looks at individual psychotherapy. *Topical Probl. Psychol. & Psychother.*, 2:64-78.

05545 **HULSE, W. C.** (1963), The healing element in group psychotherapy. *Topical Probl. Psychol. & Psychother.*, 4:133-146.

05546 **HULSE, W. C.** (1959), Einheit oder einigkeit in gruppenpsychotherapie. (Oneness or unification in group psychotherapy.) *Acta Psychother., Psychosomat. Orthopaedagog.*, (Basel) 7:138-147.

05547 **HULSE, W. C.** (1950), Group psychotherapy and the First International Congress on Psychiatry. *Group Psychother., Psychodrama & Sociometry*, 3:250-252.

05548 **HULSE, W. C.** (1948), Group psychotherapy with soldiers and veterans. *Military Surgeon*, 103:116-121.

05549 **HULSE, W. C.** (1951), International aspects of group psychotherapy. *Internat. J. Group Psychother.*, 1:172-177.

05550 **HULSE, W. C.** (1961), Multiple transferences or group neurosis. *Acta Psychother. Psychosomat. Orthopaedagog.*, (Basel) 9:348-357.

05551 **HULSE, W. C.** (1956), Private practice. In: *The Fields of Group Psychotherapy*, ed. S. R. Slavson. New York: International Universities Press, pp. 260-272.

05552 **HULSE, W. C.** (1960), Psychiatric aspects of group counseling with adolescents. *Psychiat. Quart. Suppl.*, 34:307-313.

05553 **HULSE, W. C.** (1958), Psychotherapy with ambulatory schizophrenic patients in mixed analytic groups. *Arch. Neurol. Psychiat.*, 79:681-687.

05554 **HULSE, W. C.** (1948), Report on various experiences in group psychotherapy. *Jewish Soc. Serv. Quart.*, 25:214-220.

05555 **HULSE, W. C.** (1950), The social meaning of current methods in group psychotherapy. *Group Psychother., Psychodrama & Sociometry*, 3:59-67.

05556 **HULSE, W. C.** (1960), Teaching in group psychotherapy: the auxiliary leader and normal group formation. *Topical Probl. Psychol. & Psychother.*, 1:51-55.

05557 **HULSE, W. C.** (1950), The therapeutic management of group tension. *Amer. J. Orthopsychiat.*, 20:834-838.

05558 **HULSE, W. C.** (1960), Topical problems of psychotherapy: vol. ii. sources of conflict in contemporary group psychotherapy. *Acta Psychother. Psychosomat. Orthopaedagog.*, (Basel) 7:197.

05559 **HULSE, W. C.** (1958), Training for group psychotherapy in the U.S.A. and abroad. *Internat. J. Group Psychother.*, 8:257-264.

05560 **HULSE, W. C.**, and **REENS, R. G.** (1953), Self-reporting in group psychotherapy. *Psychoanal. Rev.*, 40:117-124.

05561 **HULSE, W. C., LULOY, W. V., RINDSBERG, B. K.**, and **EPSTEIN, N. B.** (1956), Transference reactions in a group of female patients to male and female co-leaders. *Internat. J. Group Psychother.*, 6:430-435.

05562 **HULSE, W. C., DURKIN, H., GLATZER, H. T., KADIS, A. L.**, and **WOLF, A.** (1958), Acting out in group psychotherapy: a panel discussion. *Amer. J. Psychother.*, 12:87-105.

05563 **HUM, S. P. C.** (1969), An investigation of the use of focused videotape feedback in high school group counseling. *Dissert. Abstr. Internat.*, 29:4284A.

05564 **HUM, S. P. C.** (1970), Use of focused video-tape feedback in high school counseling. *Compar. Group Studies*, 1:101-127.

05565 Human relations curriculum: teaching students to care and feel and relate. (1974), *Educat. Leadership*, 32:1-60.

05566 **HUMES, C. W.** (1970), A novel group approach to school counseling of educable retardates. *Training School Bull.*, 67:164-171.

05567 **HUMES, C. W., Jr.** (1968), Group counseling with educable mentally retarded adolescents in a public school setting: a description of the process and a quantitative assessment of its effectiveness. *Dissert. Abstr. Internat.*, 29:1105-1106.

05568 **HUMES, C. W., Jr., ADAMCZYK, J. S.**, and **MYCO, R. W.** (1969), A school study of group counseling with educable retarded adolescents. *Amer. J. Ment. Deficiency*, 74:191-195.

05569 **HUMES, G. W.** (1971), A novel group approach to school counseling. *Training School Bull.*, 67:164-171.

05570 **HUNDAL, P. S.**, and **BRAR, H. S.** (1972), Measuring the impact of reformatory education on the manifest behavior and some psychosocial aspects of juvenile delinquents. *Internat. Rev. Appl. Psychol.*, (Liverpool) 20:149-156.

05571 **HUNDEVADT, E.** (1969), (Short-time group psychotherapy: an experiment with treatment groups in a psychiatric clinic.) *Nordisk Psychiat. Tidsskr.*, (Kungsbacha) 23:179-188.

05572 **HUNSICKER, A. L., HURD, D. E.**, and **MORSE, D.** (1967), Group therapy with alcoholic tuberculous patients. *Amer. Rev. Respirat. Disease*, 95:313-316.

05573 **HUNT, J. McV.** (1964), Concerning the impact of group psychotherapy on psychology. *Internat. J. Group Psychother.*, 14:3-31.

05574 **HUNT, J. McV.** (1969), Parent and child centers: one alternative model. *Clin. Psychologist*, 22:71-77.

05575 **HUNT, L., HARRISON, K.**, and **ARMSTRONG, M.** (1974), Integrating group dynamics training and the education and development of social work students. *Brit. J. Soc. Work*, (Birmingham) 4:405-423.

05576 **HUNT, W.**, and **ISSACHAROFF, A.** (1975), History and analysis of a leaderless group of professional therapists. *Amer. J. Psychiat.*, 132:1164-1167.

05577 **HUNTER, A.** (1975), An assessment of a group counseling program in the secondary schools. *Dissert. Abstr. Internat.*, 36:3510A.

05578 **HUNTER, G. P.** (1977), An interpersonal relations and group process approach to affective education for young children. *J. School Psychol.*, 15:141-151.

05579 **HUNTER, E.** (1972), *Encounter in the Classroom.* New York: Holt, Rinehart, and Winston.

05580 **HUNTER, E.** (1971), Sharing and caring: microlabs. *Today's Educat.*, 60:73.

05581 **HUNTER, G. F.**, and **STERN, H.** (1968), The training of mental health workers. *Internat. J. Group Psychother.*, 18:104-109.

05582 **HUNTER, I.** (1967), The effects of pre-sleep group therapy upon subsequent dream content. *Dissert. Abstr. Internat.*, 27:3672B.

05583 **HUNTER, M. L.** (1974), Group effect on self-concept and math performance. *Dissert. Abstr. Internat.*, 34:5169B.

05584 **HUNTLEY, A. C.** (1964), Day patients' reactions to vacation closure. *Ment. Hosp.*, 51:663-664.

05585 **HUNZIKER, J. C.** (1977), A comparison of group and individual assertive training. *Dissert. Abstr. Internat.*, 38:1404B.

05586 **HUREWITZ, P.** (1970), Ethical considerations in leading therapeutic and quasi-therapeutic groups: encounter and sensitivity groups. *Group Psychother., Psychodrama & Sociometry*, 23:17-20.

05587 **HUREWITZ, P.** (1962), The neutral isolate: an operational definition. *Internat. J. Sociometry & Sociatry*, 2:155-157.

05588 **HURLEY, J. R.** (1973), Conflicting interpretations of the effects of trainers on t-groups. *Proceed., 81st Annual Convention,* Amer. Psychological Association, Montreal, Canada, 8:525-526.

05589 **HURLEY, J. R.** (1976), Helpful behaviors in groups of mental health professionals and undergraduates. *Internat. J. Group Psychother.*, 26:173-189.

05590 **HURLEY, J. R.** (1969), Intergenerational sensitivity training: a follow-up study. *Michigan J. Second. Educat.*, 11:27-30.

05591 **HURLEY, J. R.** (1969), Intergenerational sensitivity training and preferred personal attributes. *Mich. J. Secondary Educat.*, 11:14-26.

05592 **HURLEY, J. R.** (1971), The neglected effects of trainers on t-groups. *J. Appl. Behav. Science*, 7:647-649.

05593 **HURLEY, J. R.** (1975), "Some effects of trainers on their t-groups" reconsidered. *J. Appl. Behav. Science*, 11:190-196.

05594 **HURLEY, J. R.** (1978), Toward seeing ourselves as others see us. In: *Group Therapy 1978: An Overview*, eds. L. R. Wolberg and M. L. Aronson. New York: Stratton Intercontinental Medical Books.

05595 **HURLEY, J. R.** (1976), Two prepotent interpersonal dimensions and the effects of trainers on t-groups. *Small Group Behav.*, 7:77-98.

05596 **HURLEY, J. R.**, and **FORCE, E. J.** (1973), T-group gains in acceptance of self and others. *Internat. J. Group Psychother.*, 23:166-176.

05597 **HURLEY, J. R.**, and **HURLEY, S. J.** (1969), Toward authenticity in measuring self-disclosure. *J. Couns. Psychol.*, 15:271-274.

05598 **HURLEY, J. R.**, and **PINCHES, S. K.** (1978), Interpersonal behavior and effectiveness of t-group leaders. *Small Group Behav.*, 9:329-339.

05599 **HURLEY, J. R.**, and **ROSENTHAL, M.** (1978), Interpersonal perceptions within AGPA's annual institute groups. *Group*, 2:220-238.

05600 **HURLEY, J. R.**, and **ROSENTHAL, M.** (1978), Interpersonal rating shifts during and after AGPA's institute groups. *Internat. J. Group Psychother.*, 28:115-121.

05601 **HURLEY, S. J.** (1968), Self-disclosure in counseling groups as influenced by structured confrontation and interpersonal process recall. *Dissert. Abstr. Internat.*, 29:123.

05602 **HURST, A. G.** (1978), Leadership style determinants of cohesiveness in adolescent groups. *Internat. J. Group Psychother.*, 28:263-277.

05603 **HURST, A. G.** (1975), Therapeutic group process: a study of leadership styles and cohesiveness with adolescents. *Dissert. Abstr. Internat.*, 36:1919B.

05604 **HURST, J. C.** (1973), Encountertapes: evaluation of a leaderless group procedure. *Small Group Behav.*, 4:476-485.

05605 **HURST, J. C.**, and **FANNER, R.** (1969), Extended-session group as a predictive technique for counselor training. *J. Couns. Psychol.*, 16:358-360.

05606 **HURT, D. J.** (1976), A group vocational experience program to facilitate narrowing of vocational choice. *Dissert. Abstr. Internat.*, 36:5247A.

05607 **HURVITZ, N.** (1961), Group counseling with expectant mothers. *Ment. Hygiene*, 45:439-449.

05608 **HURVITZ, N.** (1976), The origins of the peer self-help psychotherapy group movement. *J. Appl. Behav. Science*, 12:283-294.

05609 **HURVITZ, N.** (1970), Peer self-help psychotherapy groups and their implications for psychotherapy. *Psychother.: Theory, Res. & Pract.*, 7:41-49.

05610 **HURVITZ, N.** (1968), Shostrom's group therapy on commercial television. *Amer. Psychologist*, 23:760.

05611 **HUSBAND, D.**, and **SCHEUNEMANN, H. R.** (1972), The use of group process in teaching termination. *Child Welfare*, 51:505-513.

05612 **HUSEMANN, K.** (1978), Gruppendynamische arbeit mit dem team einer tagesklinek. (Group-dynamic work with a team in a day clinic.) *Dynam. Psychiat.*, (Berlin) 52/53:528-541.

05613 **HUSH, H.** (1969), Administrative issues in the development of group treatment. *J. Jewish Communal Serv.*, 45:236-240.

05614 **HUTCHINGS, P. B.** (1978), Comprehensive analysis of the verbal and nonverbal behavior of three psychiatric patients and a therapist in ten group therapy sessions. *Dissert. Abstr. Internat.*, 39:4034B.

05615 **HUTSON, T.**, and **OSEN, D.** (1970), A multimedia approach to gifted in a high school group psychology-counseling seminar. *Gifted Child. Quart.*, 14:186-190.

05616 **HUTTE, H. A.** (1956), Het zogenaamde creatieve spel als middel tot ontivikkeling van leidinggenende qualiteiten. (The so-called creative play as a means to develop qualities of leadership.) *Mens & Ondernening*, (Meppel) 10:120-125.

05617 **HUTTE, H. A.** (1956), *Vorming van Volwassenen door Creatief Apel.* (*Training of Adults by Creative Play.*) Purmerend: J. Muusses.

05618 **HUTTER, J.** (1970), Interpersonal themes in encounter group process as a function of style of leadership. *Dissert. Abstr. Internat.*, 3643B.

05619 **HUTTON, G. A.** (1963), It all began with talk. *Amer. J. Nursing*, 63:107-108.

05620 **HYAMS, D. E.** (1969), Psychological factors in rehabilitation of the elderly. *Gerontology*, (Basel) 11:129-136.

05621 **HYDE, R. W.** (1952), Communication of feeling in group psychotherapy. *J. Pastoral Care*, 6:26-33.

05622 **HYDE, R. W.**, and **LESLIE, R. C.** (1952), Introduction to group therapy for graduate theological students. *J. Pastoral Care*, 6:19-27.

05623 **HYDE, R. W.**, and **SOLOMON, H. C.** (1950), Patient government: a new form of group therapy. *Digest Neurol. & Psychiat.*, 18:207-218.

05624 **HYMMEN, P.** (1975), Group guidance classes: an anachronism? *Can. Counselor*, (Ottawa) 9:98-101.

05625 **HYNES, J.**, and **YOUNG, J.** (1976), Adolescent group for mentally retarded persons. *Educat. & Training Ment. Retard.*, 11:226.

05626 **HYNES, K.**, and **WERBIN, J.** (1977), Group psychotherapy for Spanish-speaking women. *Psychiat. Annals*, 7:52.

05627 **HYROOP, M. H.** (1952), Simultaneous group and insulin therapy. *Internat. J. Group Psychother.*, 2:67-70.

I

05629 **IAKOVLEVA, E. K., ZACHEPITSKIR, R. A.,** and **CHASOV, V. A.** (1959), (Experience with group psychotherapy of neurotic patients.) *Zh. Nevropat. & Psikhiat. Korsakov.*, (Moscow) 59:1201-1207.

05630 **IGERSHEIMER, W. W.** (1959), Analytically oriented group psychotherapy for patients with psychosomatic illness: part i. the selection of patients and the forming of groups. *Internat. J. Group Psychother.*, 9:71-92.

05631 **IGERSHEIMER, W. W.** (1959), Analytically oriented group psychotherapy for patients with psychosomatic illness: part ii. *Internat. J. Group Psychother.*, 9:225-238.

05632 **IGERSHEIMER, W. W.** (1959), Group psychotherapy for nonalcoholic wives of alcoholics. *Quart. J. Studies Alcohol*, 20:77-85.

05634 **IGERSHEIMER, W. W.** (1959), Part iii: the psychiatrist's and internist's evaluation of changes in psychiatric status. *Internat. J. Group Psychother.*, 9:359-375.

05635 **IHALAINEN, L.** (1976), (Nurse in group psychotherapy and therapeutic community.) *Sairaanhoitaja Sjukskoterskan*, (Helsinki) 13/14:26-28.

05636 **IHLI, K. L.,** and **GARLINGTON, W. K.** (1969), A comparison of groups vs. individual desensitization of test anxiety. *Behav. Res. & Ther.*, 7:207-209.

05637 **IKEDA, Y.** (1973), Group psychotherapists and their patients: an observation of group therapeutic sessions at a time of social crisis. *J. Ment. Health*, 21:77-124.

05638 **IKEDA, Y.** (1972), A preliminary report on group psychotherapy in a rehabilitation center for the mentally and physically handicapped. *J. Ment. Health*, 46:97.

05639 **IKEDA, Y.** (1968), Problems of the co-therapist in group psychotherapy reviewed through dream interpretation. *J. Ment. Health*, 16:29-36, 133-135.

05640 **IKEDA, Y.** (1967), (Some comments on group psychotherapy centered around interpersonal relationship and the goal of therapy.) *J. Ment. Health*, 15:1-6, 85-93.

05641 **ILGEN, D. R.,** and **O'BRIEN, G.** (1974), Leader-member relations in small groups. *Organizat. Behav. Hum. Perf.*, 12:335-350.

05642 **ILGENFRITZ, M. P.** (1961), Mothers on their own: widows and divorcees. *Marriage & Fam. Living*, 23:38-41.

05643 **ILLING, H.** (1973), Analytische gruppentherapie mit ehepaaren. (Analytic group therapy with married couples.) *Dynam. Psychiat.*, (Berlin) 21:258-264.

05644 **ILLING, H. A.** (1961), Central themes of delusional productions in group psychotherapy with schizophrenic patients. *Acta Psychotherapeut.*, 9:1-9.

05645 **ILLING, H. A.** (1957), C. G. Jung on the present trends in group psychotherapy. *Human Relat.*, 10:77-83.

05646 **ILLING, H. A.** (1963), C. G. Jung on the present trends in group psychotherapy. In: *Group Psychotherapy and Group Function*, eds. M. Rosenbaum and M. M. Berger. New York: Basic Books.

05647 **ILLING, H. A.** (1957), Critique on group psychotherapy. *Bull. Amer. Coll. Neuropsychiat.*, 11:6-7.

05648 **ILLING, H. A.** (1957), Die ethik der gruppenpsychotherapeuten. (Ethics in group psychotherapy.) *Heilkunst*, 70.

05649 **ILLING, H. A.** (1969), Die rueckkehr in die gruppe: zur dynamik der vorzeitigen beeddigung der gruppenpsychotherapie. (Returning to the group: dynamics of pseudo-termination in group therapy.) *Dynam. Psychiat.*, (Berlin) 2:164-172.

05650 **ILLING, H. A.** (1957), Discussion of H. R. Teirich on sociometry and group psychotherapy. *Group Psychother., Psychodrama & Sociometry*, 10:92-94.

05651 **ILLING, H. A.** (1959), Entwicklung und stand der amerikanschen musiktherapie. (The development and present status of American music therapy.) In: *Musik in der Medizin, (Music in Medicine)*, ed. H. R. Teirich. Stuttgart: Gustav Fischer Verlag.

05652 **ILLING, H. A.** (1975), Group psychotherapy and group work in authoritarian settings. *J. Crim. Law. & Criminol.*, 48:387-393.

05653 **ILLING, H. A.** (1957), Group psychotherapy from the points of view of various schools of psychology: iv. Jung's theory of the group as a tool in therapy. *Internat. J. Group Psychother.*, 7:392-397.

05654 **ILLING, H. A.** (1970), Group psychotherapy techniques. *Amer. J. Psychiat.*, 127:105-106.

05655 **ILLING, H. A.** (1957), Idee und praxis der gruppenpsychotherapie. (The idea and praxis of group psychotherapy.) *Der Psychologie*, (Berne) 12:465-470.

05657 **ILLING, H. A.** (1957), Jung und die moderne tendenz in der gruppenpsychotherapie. (Jung and the modern trend in group psychotherapy.) *Heilkunst*, 68:77-80.

05658 **ILLING, H. A.** (1958), Klinische erfahrungen mit ehepaaren in der gruppenpsychotherapie. (Clinical treatment of couples in group psychotherapy.) *Der Psychologie*, (Berne) 4/5:149-154.

05659 **ILLING, H. A.** (1974), Letter: questioning time-extended group therapy. *Amer. J. Psychiat.*, 131:231-232.

05660 **ILLING, H. A.** (1960), Mental hygiene in German criminology. *Arch. Crim. Psychodynam.*, 4:154-158.

05661 **ILLING, H. A.** (1952), Music as a medium of group therapy with adolescent girls. *J. Child Psychol. & Psychiat.*, 2:350-359.

05662 **ILLING, H. A.** (1971), Outpatient group psychotherapy with sex offenders. *Dynam. Psychiat.*, (Berlin) 4:7.

05663 **ILLING, H. A.** (1963), Psychoanalytische gruppenpsychotherapie. (Psychoanalytic group psychotherapy.) In: *Das Psychoanalytische Volksbuch, Vol. II (The Psychoanalytic Workbook, Vol. II)* ed. H. Meng. Berne: H. Huber.

05664 **ILLING, H. A.** (1970), Psychotherapeutic effectiveness in different social settings. *Dynam. Psychiat.*, (Berlin) 3:77-85.

05665 **ILLING, H. A.** (1960), Psychotherapeutische behandlung von ehepaaren. (The psychotherapeutic treatment of married couples.) *Heilkunst*, 73:259-261.

05667 **ILLING, H. A.** (1952), Short-contact group psychotherapy. *Internat. J. Group Psychother.*, 2:377-382.

05668 **ILLING, H. A.** (1957), Social aspects of aging. *Fortschr. Osteopsychiat.*, 32:24-26.

05669 **ILLING, H. A.** (1957), Sociometry and group psychotherapy. *Group Psychother., Psychodrama & Sociometry*, 85-94.

05670 **ILLING, H. A.** (1957), Sociometry in groups. *Internat. J. Soc. Psychiat.*, (London) 4:55-62.

05672 **ILLING, H. A.** (1951), The prisoner in his group. *Internat. J. Group Psychother.*, 1:264-277.

05673 **ILLING, H. A.** (1951), The prisoner in the group. *Group Psychother., Psychodrama & Sociometry*, 13:3-8.

05674 **ILLING, H. A.** (1956), Some aspects of authority over groups of military offenders. *California Youth Authority Quart.*, 9:27-30.

05675 **ILLING, H. A.** (1957), Einige probleme der gruppenpsychotherapie in strafenstalten. (Some problems of group therapy in penal institutions.) *Zeit. Diagnost. Psychol.*, 5:288-294.

05676 **ILLING, H. A.** (1958), A theory of the group according to C. G. Jung. *Acta Psychother., Psychosomat. Orthopaedagog.*, (Basel) 6:137-144.

05677 **ILLING, H. A.** (1957), The therapist and the group evaluate. *Ment. Hygiene*, 41:512-516.

05678 **ILLING, H. A.** (1962), Training in group counseling and group psychotherapy. *Psychoanal. Rev.*, 49:74-99.

05679 **ILLING, H. A.** (1962), Transference and countertransference in analytical group counseling. *Acta Psychother., Psychosomat. Orthopaedagog.*, (Basel) 10:13-25.

05680 **ILLING, H. A.** (1955), Transference role of the visitor in group psychotherapy. *Internat. J. Group Psychother.*, 5:204-212.

05681 **ILLING, H. A.** (1953), The "visitor" and his role of transference in group therapy. *J. Crim. Law. & Criminol.*, 44:753-758.

05682 **ILLING, H. A.** (1955), The visitor's role of transference and counter-transference in group psychotherapy. *Internat. J. Group Psychother.*, 4:1953-1954.

05683 **ILLING, H. A.**, and **BACH, G. R.** (1956), Eine historische perspektive zur gruppenpsychotherapie. (A historical perspective on group psychotherapy.) *Zeit. Psychosomat. Med. & Psychoanal.*, (Goettingen) 2:131-147.

05684 **ILLING, H. A.**, and **BROWNFIELD, B.** (1964), Central themes of delusional productions in group psychotherapy with schizophrenic patients. *Acta Psychother., Psychosomat. Orthopaedagog.*, (Basel) 9:1-9.

05685 **ILLING, H. A.**, and **BROWNFIELD, B.** (1960), Delusions of schizophrenic patients in group psychotherapy. *J. Soc. Ther.*, 6:32-36.

05686 **ILLING, H. A.**, and **MILES, J. E.** (1969), Outpatient group psychotherapy with sex offenders. *Internat. J. Soc. Psychiat.*, (London) 15:258-263.

05687 **ILLING, H. A., BACH, G. R.**, and **WELCH, E. P.** (1957), Jung's empiricism reconsidered. *Amer. J. Psychiat.*, 112:71-72.

05688 **ILLING, H. A., HACKER, F. J.**, and **BERGREEN, S. W.** (1965), Impact of different social settings on type and effectiveness of psychotherapy. *Psychoanal. Rev.*, 52:38-44.

05689 **ILLOVSKY, J.** (1962), Experiences with group hypnosis on schizophrenics. *Amer J. Med. Science*, 108:685-693.

05690 **IMBER, S. D.** (1954), Behavior patterns in later meetings of therapeutic groups. *Group Psychother., Psychodrama & Sociometry*, 7:214-217.

05691 **IMBER, S. D.** (1952), Short term group psychotherapy: an experimental investigation of its effectiveness for psychotics and a comparison of two different therapeutic methods and two different therapists. Unpublished doctoral dissertation, University of Rochester.

05692 **INDENBAUM, G. K.** (1976), The relationships among locus of control, feelings of isolation and levels of anxiety in adolescent narcotic addicts, and length of stay in therapeutic communities. *Dissert. Abstr. Internat.*, 36:7950-7951.

05693 **INDIK, B. P.** (1961), Organization size and member participation. Ph.D. thesis, University of Michigan.

05694 **INDIN, B. M.** (1966), The crisis club: a group experience for suicidal patients. *Ment. Hygiene*, 50:280-290.

05695 **INGALLS, A. S.** (1945), Analysis of psychodrama directors. *Sociometry*, 8:88-89.

05696 **INGERSOLL, B.**, and **SILVERMAN, A.** (1978), Comparative group psychotherapy for the aged. *Gerontologist*, 18:201-206.

05697 **INGERSOLL, J. W.** (1972), The effect of feedback in reducing constraining verbal behavior in small short-term training groups. *Dissert. Abstr. Internat.*, 32:5546A.

05698 **INGHAM, R. J., ANDREWS, G.,** and **WINKLER, R.** (1972), Stuttering: a comparative evaluation of the short-term effectiveness of four treatment techniques. *J. Communicat. Disorders*, 5:91-117.

05699 **INGILS, C. R.** (1968), Group dynamics: boon or bane? *Personnel & Guid. J.*, 46:744-748.

05700 **INGLIS, S.** (1979), Group meditation therapy. In: *Hypnosis: 1979*, eds. G. D. Burrows, D. R. Collison, and L. Dennerstein. Amsterdam: Elseview/North Holland Biomedical Press.

05701 **INSEL, P.,** and **MOOS, R.** (1972), An experimental investigation of process and outcome in an encounter group. *Hum. Relat.*, 25:441-448.

05702 **INTAGLIATA, J. C.** (1977), Increasing the interpersonal problem-solving skills of an alcoholic population. *Dissert. Abstr. Internat.*, 37:4146.

05703 **INTAGLIATA, J. C.** (1978), Increasing the interpersonal problem-solving skills of an alcoholic population. *J. Consult. Clin. Psychol.*, 46:489-498.

05704 **IONEDES, N. S.** (1979), Adlerian psychotherapy in practice: the case of Mr. and Mrs. T. *J. Individ. Psychol.*, 35:70-78.

05705 **IONEDES, N. S.** (1962), Group methods and the adult offender. *Group Psychother., Psychodrama & Sociometry*, 15:144-146.

05706 **IRONS, L.,** and **GANTER, G.** (1955), Coordination of group work and casework to promote effective treatment in child guidance clinic. *Amer. J. Orthopsychiat.*, 25:138-147.

05707 **IRVIN, A. M.** (1960), Regression in a children's activity therapy group. *Smith Coll. Studies Soc. Work*, 31:22-37.

05708 **IRVINE, L. S.,** and **PALMER, M. B.** (1961), The psychiatric social worker as leader of a group. *Ment. Hosp.*, 12:29-32.

05709 **IRWIN, E., LEVY, P.,** and **SHAPIRO, M.** (1972), Assessment of drama therapy in a child guidance setting. *Group Psychother., Psychodrama & Sociometry*, 25:105-116.

05710 **IRWIN, E. C.** (1977), Play, fantasy, and symbols: drama with emotionally disturbed children. *Amer. J. Psychother.*, 31:426-436.

05711 **IRWIN, E. C.,** and **McWILLIAMS, B. G.** (1973), Parents working with parents: the cleft palate program. *Cleft Palate J.*, 10:360-366.

05712 **IRWIN, E. C., RUBIN, J. A.,** and **SHAPIRO, M. I.** (1975), Art and drama: partners in therapy. *Amer. J. Psychother.*, 29:107-116.

05713 **IRWIN, S.,** and **LLOYD-STILL, D.** (1974), The use of groups to mobilize parental strengths during hospitalization of children. *Child Welfare*, 53:305-312.

05714 **IRWIN, T. J.** (1971), An investigation of empathy of a and b therapists in a quasi-therapeutic encounter. *Dissert. Abstr. Internat.*, 31:5128-5129A.

05715 **IRWIN, T. O.** (1963), An activity-centered resocialization program. *Ment. Hosp.*, 14:405-406.

05716 **ISAACS, B.** (1967), Group therapy in the geriatric unit. *Gerontol. Clin.*, (Basel) 9:21-26.

05717 **ISAACS, L. D.** (1977), Art-therapy group for latency age children. *Soc. Work*, 22:57-59.

05718 **ISENBERG, P. L.** (1974), Medication groups for continuing care. *Hosp. & Community Psychiat.*, 25:517-519.

05719 **ISHIYAMA, T.** (1966), A new role for psychiatric aides. *Amer. J. Nursing*, 66:1590-1593.

05720 **ISLAND, D. D.** (1969), Counseling students with special problems. *Rev. Educat. Res.*, 39:239-250.

05721 **ISSACHAROFF, A.**, and **HUNT, W.** (1977), Observations on group process in a leaderless group of professional therapists. *Group*, 1:162-171.

05722 **ISSACHAROFF, A.**, **REDINGER, R.**, and **SCHNEIDER, D.** (1972), The psychiatric consultation as an experience in group process. *Contemp. Psychoanal.*, 8:260-275.

05723 **ISSROFF, J.** (1974), A group training program dealing with the problems of senior staff in custodial institutions. *Ment. Health & Soc.*, (Basel) 1:98-109.

05724 **ITO, K.** (1978), (A consideration of a therapeutic approach to school refusal in adolescence.) *Japanese J. Child Psychiat.*, (Tokyo) 19:73-90.

05725 **IVANCEVICH, J. M.** (1974), A study of a cognitive training program: trainer styles and group development. *Acad. Manag. J.*, 17:428-439.

05726 **IVANCEVICH, J. M.**, and **McMAHON, J. T.** (1976), Group development, trainer style and carry-over job satisfaction and performance. *Acad. Manag. J.*, 19:395-412.

05727 **IVANOV, N. V.** (1960), (On the problem of the theory of Soviet group psychotherapy.) *Zh. Nevropat. Psikhiat. Korsakov*, (Moscow) 60:1342-1351.

05728 **IVANOV, N. V.** (1966), A Soviet view of group therapy. *Internat. J. Psychiat. Med.*, 2:201-212.

05729 **IVANOV, N. V.** (1969), On the social foundations of group psychotherapy abroad. *Zh. Nevropat. Psikhiat. Korsakov*, (Moscow) 69:305-308.

05730 **IVANOV, N. V.**, **ZNACHENIE, A. A.** (1952), Tokarskogo v istorii otechestvennoi psikhoterapii. (The significance of A. A. Tokarskii in the history of native psychotherapy.) *Zh. Nevropat. Psikhiat. Korsakov*, (Moscow) 52:85-89.

05731 **IVERSON, D. C.**, **JURS, S. G.**, and **WENDOR, S. S.** (1976), Prediction of attrition from a therapeutic community. *Psychol. Reports*, 39:1287-1290.

05732 **IVEY, A. E.** (1974), The clinician as a teacher of interpersonal skills: let's give away what we've got. *Clin. Psychologist*, 30:6-9.

05733 **IVEY, A. E.** (1974), Counseling technology: microcounseling and systematic approaches to human relations training. *Brit. J. Educat. Technol.*, (London) 5:15-16.

05734 **IVEY, A. E.** (1973), Demystifying the group's process: adapting microcounseling procedures to counseling in groups. *Educat. Technol.*, 13:27-31.

05735 **IVEY, A. E.** (1974), Microcounseling and media therapy: the state of the art. *Counselor Educat. & Supervision*, 13:172-183.

05736 **IVEY, A. E.**, and **ROLLIN, S. A.** (1974), The human relations performance curriculum: a commitment to intentionality. *Brit. J. Educat. Technol.*, 5:21-29.

J

05737 **JACKS, I.** (1963), Accessibility to group psychotherapy among adolescent offenders in a correctional institution. *Amer. J. Orthopsychiat.*, 33:567-568.

05738 **JACKS, I.** (1964), Accessibility to group psychotherapy of incarcerated adolescent offenders. *J. Crim. Law & Criminol.*, 55:100-106.

05739 **JACKS, I.** (1960), A study of accessibility to group therapy of a group of incarcerated adolescent offenders. *Dissert. Abstr. Internat.*, 21:1254. (University Microfilms No. 60-03749.)

05740 **JACKS, J. M.** (1966), The judgment technique in the permanent theater of psychodrama. *Group Psychother., Psychodrama & Sociometry*, 19:29-31.

05741 **JACKSON, B.**, and **Van ZOOST, B.** (1974), Self-regulated teaching of others as a means of improving study habits. *J. Couns. Psychol.*, 21:489-493.

05742 **JACKSON, E. N.** (1969), *Group Counseling*. New York: Pilgrim Press.

05743 **JACKSON, E. N.** (1950), The therapeutic function in preaching. *Pastoral Psychol.*, 1:36-39.

05744 **JACKSON, J.** (1962), A family group therapy technique for a stalemate in individual treatment. *Internat. J. Group Psychother.*, 12:164-170.

05745 **JACKSON, J.**, and **GROTJAHN, M.** (1958), The reenactment of the marriage neurosis in group psychotherapy. *J. Nerv. & Ment. Diseases*, 127:503-510.

05746 **JACKSON, J.**, and **GROTJAHN, M.** (1958), The treatment of oral defenses by combined individual and group psychotherapy. *Internat. J. Group Psychother.*, 8:373-382.

05747 **JACKSON, J. D. S.** (1980), Assertion training: rational-emotive therapy vs. self-instructional coping therapy in the facilitation of refusal behavior among women. *Dissert. Abstr. Internat.*, 41:2517A. (University Microfilms No. 8024679.)

05748 **JACKSON, J. M.** (1959), Reference group processes in a formal organization. *Sociometry*, 22:307-327.

05749 **JACKSON, M.** (1964), The importance of depression emerging in a therapeutic group. *J. Anal. Psychol.*, (London) 9:51-59.

05750 **JACOBI, L.** (1952), Erfahrungen und gedanken zur gruppenbetreuung bei seelisch gestorten kendem. *Praxis Kinderpsychol. & Kinderpsychiat.*, (Goettingen) 1:310-313.

05751 **JACOBS, A.**, and **SPRADLIN, W.** (1973), *The Group as Agent of Change*. New York: Behavioral Publications.

05752 **JACOBS, A.**, and **SPRADLIN, W.** (1974), *The Group as Agent of Change: Treatment, Prevention, Personal Growth in the Family, the School, the Mental Hospital and the Community*. New York: Behavioral Publications.

05753 **JACOBS, A., JACOBS, M., CAVIOR, N.**, and **BURKE, J.** (1974), Anonymous feedback: credibility and desirability of structured emotional and behavioral feedback delivered in groups. *J. Couns. Psychol.*, 21:106-111.

05754 **JACOBS, E.** (1974), Educating group counselors: a tentative model. *Counselor Educat. & Supervision*, 13:308-310.

05755 **JACOBS, J. D.** (1964), Social action as therapy in a mental hospital. *Soc. Work*, 9:54-61.

05756 **JACOBS, M.** (1977), A comparison of publicly delivered and anonymously delivered verbal feedback in brief personal growth groups. *J. Consult. & Clin. Psychol.*, 45:385-390.

05757 **JACOBS, M.** (1973), Feedback II: the "credibility gap": delivery of positive and negative and emotional and behavioral feedback in groups. *J. Consult. & Clin. Psychol.*, 41:215-223.

05758 **JACOBS, M., GATZ, M.,** and **TRICK, L. O.** (1974), Structured versus unstructured feedback in the training of patients to be more effective participants in group psychotherapy. *Small Group Behav.*, 5:365-373.

05759 **JACOBS, M., JACOBS, A., GATZ, M.,** and **SCHAIBLE, T.** (1973), Credibility and desirability of positive and negative structured feedback in groups. *J. Consult. & Clin. Psychol.*, 40:244-252.

05760 **JACOBS, M. A.,** and **CHRIST, J.** (1967), Structuring and limit setting as techniques in the group treatment of adolescent delinquents. *Community Ment. Health J.*, 3:237-244.

05761 **JACOBS, M. A., SPILKEN, A. Z., NORMAN, M. M., WOHLBERG, G. W.,** and **KNAPP, P. H.** (1971), Interaction of personality and treatment conditions associated with success in a smoking control program. *Psychosomat. Med.*, 33:545-556.

05762 **JACOBS, M. K., TRICK, O. L.,** and **WITHERSTY, D.** (1976), Pretraining psychiatric inpatients for participation in group psychotherapy. *Psychother.: Theory, Res. & Pract.*, 13:361-367.

05763 **JACOBS, P. D.** (1972), Human relations hucksters. *Soc. Advancement Manag. J.*, 37:52-55.

05764 **JACOBSON, C., MANN, J.,** and **RAINEY, E.** (1961), Teaching group, a therapeutic group. *Group Psychother., Psychodrama & Sociometry*, 14:172-175.

05765 **JACOBSON, E.** (1971), An investigation of leader and member helpfulness in group counseling. *Dissert. Abstr. Internat.*, 32:739A.

05766 **JACOBSON, E. A.,** and **SMITH, S. J.** (1972), Effect of weekend encounter group experience upon interpersonal orientations. *J. Consult. & Clin. Psychol.*, 38:403-410.

05767 **JACOBSON, J. L.** (1970), The conceptualization and specification of target behavior and intermediate outcome criteria for prison group psychotherapy. *Dissert. Abstr. Internat.*, 32:1848B.

05768 **JACOBSON, J. L.,** and **WIRT, R. D.** (1958), Characteristics of improved and unimproved prisoners in group psychotherapy. *Group Psychother., Psychodrama & Sociometry*, 11:299-308.

05769 **JACOBSON, J. R.** (1945), Group psychotherapy in the elementary school. *Psychiat. Quart.*, 19:3-16.

05770 **JACOBSON, J. R.** (1948), Practical methods of group psychotherapy. *Psychiat. Quart.*, 22:271-286.

05771 **JACOBSON, J. R.,** and **WRIGHT, K. W.** (1944), Review of a year of group psychotherapy. *Elgin State Hosp. Papers*, 5:26-42.

05772 **JACOBSON, J. R.,** and **WRIGHT, K. W.** (1942), Review of a year of group psychotherapy. *Psychiat. Quart.*, 16:744-764.

05773 **JACOBSON, S.** (1966), A therapeutic community in an acute admission ward. *Nursing Mirror*, (London) 122: v-vii.

05774 **JACQUES, E.** (1947), Social therapy: technocracy or collaboration? *J. Soc. Issues*, 3:59-66.

05775 **JACQUES, E.** (1947), Some principles of organization of a social therapeutic institution. *J. Soc. Issues*, 3:4-10.

05776 **JAFFEE, C. L.,** and **LUCAS, R. L.** (1969), Effects of rates of talking and correctness of decisions on leader choice in small groups. *J. Soc. Psychol.*, 79:247-254.

05777 **JAFFE, J.** (1978), Review of M. Seligman's *Group Counseling and Group Psychotherapy with Rehabilitation Clients. Amer. J. Ment. Deficiency*, 83:95.

05778 **JAFFE, M.** (1976), Repatterning an ineffective mother-daughter attachment. *Perspect. Psychiat. Care*, 14:34.
05779 **JAFFE, S.** (1975), *Group Therapy M.D.* New York: Ace Books.
05780 **JAFFE, S. L.**, and **SCHERL, D. J.** (1969), Acute psychosis precipitated by t-group experiences. *Arch. Gen. Psychiat.*, 21:443-448.
05781 **JAFFE, S. L.**, and **SCHERL, D. J.** (1970), Acute psychosis precipitated by t-group experiences. *Ment. Health Digest*, 2:21-22.
05782 **JAKOBOVITS, L. A.**, and **HOGENRAAD, R.** (1967), Some suggestive evidence on the operation of semantic generation and satiation in group discussions. *Psychol. Reports*, 20:1247-1250.
05783 **JALOWSKY, H. S.** (1975), The effects of group counseling membership on mildly retarded adults. *Dissert. Abstr. Internat.*, 36:3333A.
05784 **JAMES, A.** (1968), Group therapy: a poem. *Perspect. Psychiat. Care*, 6:163.
05785 **JAMES, M. M.** (1971), Curing impotency with transactional analysis. *Transactional Anal. J.*, 1:88-93.
05786 **JAMES, R.**, and **SMITH, W. L.** (1955), Some comments on the functions of the unconscious from the Jungian point of view. *Group Psychother., Psychodrama & Sociometry*, 8:81-82.
05787 **JAMES, S. L., OSBORN, F.**, and **OETTING, E. R.** (1967), Treatment for delinquent girls: the adolescent self-concept group. *Community Ment. Health J.*, 3:377-381.
05788 **JAMES, S. R.** (1980), The individual and comparative effects of a pregroup preparation upon two different therapy groups. *Dissert. Abstr. Internat.*, 41:1919B. (University Microfilms No. 8024117.)
05789 **JANATKA, J.** (1975), To the relationship of anxiolytics and group psychotherapy in neuroses. *Activ. Nerv. Superior*, (Prague) 17:275.
05790 **JANECEK, J.**, and **MANDEL, A.** (1965), The combined use of group and pharmacotherapy by collaborative therapists. *Comprehens. Psychiat.*, 6:35-40.
05791 **JANIS, I. L.** (1972), *Victims of Groupthink: A Psychological Study of Foreign-Policy Decisions and Fiascoes.* Boston: Houghton Mifflin.
05792 **JANIS, I. L.** (1971), Groupthink. *Psychol. Today*, 5:43-46, 74-76.
05793 **JANOSIK, E.** (1977), Reachable and teachable: report on a prison alcoholism group. *J. Psychiat. Nursing*, 15:24-28.
05794 **JANOSIK, E. H.** (1972), A pragmatic approach to group therapy. *J. Psychiat. Nurs.*, 10:7-11.
05795 **JANOUCEK, J.** (1971), (Structure and typology of a group problem situation.) *Ceskoslav. Psychol.*, (Prague) 15:492-495.
05796 **JANSEN, M. A.**, and **LITWACK, L.** (1979), The effects of assertive training on counselor trainees. *Counselor Educat. & Supervision*, 19:27-34.
05797 **JANSEN, M. H.** (1964), Group counseling of hospitalized addicts. *Amer. J. Orthopsychiat.*, 34:398-399.
05798 **JANSEN, M. J.** (1965), (An experimental study on role-playing in an institution.) *Nederl. Tijdschr. Psychol.*, (Amsterdam) 18:186-219.
05799 **JANSSEN, P. L.**, and **BUSSESIMONIS, E.** (1978), (Study about role change in therapy groups.) *Gruppenpsychother. & Gruppendynam.*, (Goettingen) 13:165-171.
05800 **JANSSEN, P. L.**, and **QUINT, H.** (1977), (Analytic inpatient group psychotherapy within framework of a neuropsychiatric clinic.) *Gruppenpsychother. & Gruppendynam.*, (Goettingen) 11:221-243.
05801 **JANSSON, M.** (1974), (Alternative abstinence care.) *Tidskr. Sveriges Sjukskoterskor*, (Stockholm) 41:54-57.
05802 **JANUARY, V. C.** (1974), The comparative effects of an implosive-like technique and group "rap" sessions in training white counseling students to be effective when counseling with blacks. *Dissert. Abstr. Internat.*, 34:5631A.

05803 **JAQUES, E.** (1948), Interpretive group discussion as a method of facilitating social change. *Human Relat.*, 1:533-549.

05804 **JAQUES, M. E.**, and **PATTERSON, K. M.** (1974), The self-help group model: a review. *Rehab. Couns. Bull.*, 18:48-58.

05805 **JARVIS, P., ESTY, J.**, and **STUTZMAN, L.** (1969), Evaluation and treatment of families at the Fort Logan Mental Health Center. *Community Ment. Health*, 5:14-19.

05806 **JARVIS, P. E.**, and **ESTY, J. F.** (1968), The alternate-therapist-observer technique in group therapy training. *Internat. J. Group Psychother.*, 18:95-99.

05807 **JASPER, S. F.** (1974), The design, implementation and evaluation of a group counseling model. *Dissert. Abstr. Internat.*, 35:3425-3426.

05808 **JASTREBSKE, E. M.**, and **RULE, B. G.** (1970), Effects of group variance and advocated position on conformity. *J. Personality*, 38:550-559.

05809 **JASTROW, J.** (1929), Misery clinic. *Hygeia*, 7:692-695.

05810 **JEFFERIES, D.** (1973), Should we continue to deradicalize children through the use of counseling goups? *Educat. Technol.*, 13:45-48.

05811 **JEFFRIES, D.**, and **SCHIAFFINO, K.** (1973), Group counseling with children: an annotated bibliography. *Educat. Technol.*, 13:48-49.

05812 **JEFFERS, J. J. L.** (1971), Effects of marathon encounter groups on personality characteristics of group members and group facilitators. *Dissert. Abstr. Internat.*, 32:4153A.

05813 **JEFFERSON, R. S.** (1972), The results of group therapy with a population of black enlisted personnel in the United States Air Force. *Nat. Med. Assn. J.*, 64:414-420.

05814 **JEFFREY, W. D., KLEBAN, C. H.**, and **PAPERNIK, D. S.** (1976), Schizophrenia: treatment in therapeutic community. *N.Y. State J. Med.*, 76:384-390.

05815 **JELINEK, J. A.**, and **SCHWAB, M. T.** (1973), A model of parent involvement in programming for communicative handicapped children. *Rehab. Lit.*, 34:231-234.

05816 **JELLIFFE, S. E.** (1918), Modern art and mass psychotherapy. *Boston Med. Surg. J.*, 179:609-613.

05817 **JELLIFFE, S. E.** (1917), Psychotherapy and the drama. *N.Y. State Med. J.*, 106:442-447.

05818 **JENKINS, J. L., KEEFE, T.**, and **ROSATO, L. W.** (1971), Therapists' awareness of how group therapy patients perceive them. *Correct. Psychiat. & J. Soc. Ther.*, 17:17-24.

05819 **JENKINS, R. L.** (1979), Review of L. R. Slavson's and M. Schiffer's *Group Psychotherapies for Children. Internat. J. Soc. Psychiat.*, (London) 25:72.

05820 **JENKINS, R. L.** (1941), Treatment in an institution. *Amer. J. Orthopsychiat.*, 11:85-91.

05821 **JENKINS, S. B.** (1957), The use of group therapeutic methods in ward conferences with attendants: an aid to patients' ward adjustments. *Psychiat. Quart. Suppl.*, 31:312-317.

05822 **JENKNER, E.** (1976), (On the usefulness of cohesion and tension-measurements in sociometric tests.) *Psychother. & Med. Psychol.*, (Stuttgart) 26:12-22.

05823 **JENKNER, E.** (1976), (Sociometric test applied to hospital groups.) *Zeit. Klin. Psychol. & Psychother.*, (Freiburg) 24:256-266.

05824 **JENNER, R.**, and **JOHANSSON, R.** (1977), *Introduktion till Gruppterapi: Nagra Teorier och Begrepp.* (*Introduction to Group Therapy: Basic Theory of the Group.*) Lund: Studentlitt.

05825 **JENNI, M. A.**, and **WOOLERSHEIM, J. P.** (1980), Treatment manuals for group therapy with type and persons. *Cat. Selected Docum. Psychol.*, 10:18.

05826 **JENNINGS, H. C.** (1946), A graduate seminar in psychodrama. *Sociometry*, 9:162-165.
05827 **JENNINGS, H. C.** (1931), Experiments in impromptu analysis. *Impromptu*, 1:26-27.
05828 **JENNINGS, H. C.** (1931), Psychoanalysis and Dr. Moreno. *Impromptu*, 1:12-14.
05829 **JENNINGS, H. H.** (1936), Control study of sociometric assignment. *Sociol. Rev.*, (Keele) p. 54.
05830 **JENSEN, C. M.** (1974), The effect of parent group awareness training on intrafamily communication. *Dissert. Abstr. Internat.*, 35:261A.
05831 **JENSEN, J. L.** (1978), Eliminating self-defeating behavior in group counseling: its effects on self-concept and locus of control of economically disadvantaged high school students. *Dissert. Abstr. Internat.*, 39:3375A.
05832 **JENSEN, J. L.** (1979), The relationship of leadership techniques and anxiety level in group therapy with chronic schizophrenics. *Dissert. Abstr. Internat.*, 40:1371B.
05833 **JENSEN, J. L.** (1977), The use of group techniques to increase learning of psychiatric concepts. *J. Nursing. Educat.*, 16:33-37.
05834 **JENSEN, J. L.**, and **McGREW, W. L.** (1974), Leadership techniques in group therapy with chronic schizophrenic patients. *Nursing Res.*, 23:416-420.
05835 **JENSEN, J. S.**, and **KIRSCHBAUM, R. A.** (1961), Occupational therapy in the treatment of borderline psychiatric patients. *Amer. J. Occupat. Ther.*, 15:19-21.
05836 **JENSEN, S. E.** (1962), A treatment program for alcoholics in a mental hospital. *Quart. J. Studies Alcohol*, 23:315-320.
05837 **JENSEN, S. E., BODEN, F. K.**, and **MULTARI, G.** (1965), Treatment of severely emotionally disturbed children in a community. *Can. Psychiat. Assn. J.*, (Ottawa) 10:325-331.
05838 **JENSEN, S. E., McCREARY-JUHASZ, A., BROWN, J. S.**, and **HEPINSTALL, E. M.** (1968), Disturbed children in a camp milieu. *Can. Psychiat. Assn. J.*, (Ottawa) 13:371-373.
05839 **JENSEN, S. M.**, and **GALLANT, D. M.** (1966), Therapeutic use of the psychological report on an alcoholism treatment service. *Quart. J. Studies Alcohol*, 27:717-720.
05840 **JERNIGAN, S. W.** (1979), Motivational labs for the high school student. *Personnel & Guid. J.*, 58:67-69.
05841 **JERREMS, R. L.** (1971), Sensitivity training: Raymond School Project. *Educat. Digest*, 37:26-29.
05842 **JERSILD, E. A.** (1967), Group therapy for patients' spouses. *Amer. J. Nursing*, 67:544-549.
05843 **JERTSON, J. M.** (1975), Self-help groups. *Soc. Work*, 20:144-145.
05844 **JESKE, J. O.** (1973), Identification and therapeutic effectiveness in group therapy. *J. Couns. Psychol.*, 20:528-530.
05845 **JESSELL, J. C.**, and **BUSH, J. F.** (1973), Effects of principal actor time structuring on goal attainment in group counseling. *Counselor Educat. & Supervision*, 13:105-110.
05846 **JESSUM, K. L.** (1978), The effects of group counseling on geriatric patients institutionalized in long-term care facilities. *Dissert. Abstr. Internat.*, 39:677A.
05847 **JEW, C. C., CLANON, T. L.**, and **MATTOCKS, A. L.** (1972), The effectiveness of group psychotherapy in a correctional institution. *Amer. J. Psychiat.*, 129:602-605.
05848 **JEWELL, D. S.** (1965), Clinic needs and the open group. *Community Ment. Health J.*, 1:365-368.
05849 **JEWELL, D. S., CARRIGAN, J. F.**, and **ROBINSON, L. D.** (1966), Com-

munity clinic treatment for backward patients. *Hosp. & Community Psychiat.*, 17:20-25.
05850 **JOACHIM, M. J.** (1980), Social support, masturbatory guilt, and success of education treatment groups for primary orgasmic dysfunction. *Dissert. Abstr. Internat.*, 40:5006B. (University Microfilms No. 8008489.)
05851 **JOANNING, H. H.** (1974), Behavioral rehearsal versus traditional therapy in the group treatment of socially nonassertive individuals. *Dissert. Abstr. Internat.*, 34:4665B.
05852 **JOEL, W.** (1957), A glimpse at the group psychotherapy literature. *Internat. J. Group Psychother.*, 7:191-195.
05853 **JOEL, W.** (1953), Present trends in group psychotherapy. *First Annual Report*, Group Psychotherapy Association of Southern California, pp. 6-8.
05854 **JOEL, W.**, and **SHAPIRO, D.** (1949), A genotypical approach to the analysis of personal interaction. *J. Psychology*, 28:9-17.
05855 **JOEL, W.**, and **SHAPIRO, D.** (1950), Some principles and procedures for group psychotherapy. *J. Psychology*, 29:77-88.
05856 **JOEL, W. D.** (1955), Transference reactions of chronic regressed schizophrenic patients in group psychotherapy. *Acta Psychother. Psychosomat. Orthopaedagog.*, (Basel) 3:150-156.
05857 **JOERGENSEN, C.** (1958), The ethics of Sören Kierkegaard. *Group Psychother., Psychodrama & Sociometry*, 11:349-355.
05858 **JOHANSSON, M. A. L.** (1974), Evaluation of group therapy with children: a behavioral approach. *Dissert. Abstr. Internat.*, 34:3499B.
05859 **JOHNS, W.** (1976), Another view of the small group: a physical scientist recommends applied behavioral science. *J. Appl. Behav. Science*, 12:567-568.
05860 **JOHNSGARD, K. W.**, and **MUENCH, G. A.** (1965), Group therapy with normal college students. *Psychother.: Theory, Res. & Pract.*, 2:114-116.
05861 **JOHNSGARD, K. W.**, and **SCHUMACHER, R. M.** (1970), The experience of intimacy in group psychotherapy with male homosexuals. *Psychother.: Theory, Res. & Pract.*, 7:173-176.
05862 **JOHNSON, A. H.** (1977), Resident self-awareness through group process. *J. Fam. Practice*, 4:681-684.
05863 **JOHNSON, C.** (1974), Planning for termination of the group. In: *Individual Change Through Small Groups*, eds. P. Glasser, R. Sarri, and R. Vinter. New York: Free Press.
05864 **JOHNSON, D.**, and **JOHNSON, F.** (1975), *Joining Together: Group Theory and Group Skills*. Englewood Cliffs, NJ: Prentice-Hall.
05865 **JOHNSON, D. L.**, and **GOLD, S. R.** (1971), An empirical approach to issues of selection and evaluation in group therapy. *Internat. J. Group Psychother.*, 21:456-469.
05866 **JOHNSON, D. L.**, and **HANSON, P. G.** (1979), Locus of control and behavior in treatment groups. *J. Personality Assessment*, 43:177-183.
05867 **JOHNSON, D. L.**, and **RIDENER, L. R.** (1974), Self-disclosure, participation and perceived cohesiveness in small group interaction. *Psychol. Reports*, 35:361-363.
05868 **JOHNSON, D. L., HANSON, P. G., ROTHAUS, P., MORTON, R. B., LYLE, F. A.**, and **MOYER, R.** (1965), Human relations training for psychiatric patients: a follow-up study. *Internat. J. Soc. Psychiat.*, (London) 11:188-196.
05869 **JOHNSON, D. P.** (1979), Heraldic art as a supplement to individual psychotherapy. *Art Psychother.*, 6:185-189.
05870 **JOHNSON, D. W.** (1967), The use of role-reversal in intergroup competition. *Dissert. Abstr. Internat.*, 27:3121.

05871 **JOHNSON, D. W., KAVANAGH, J. A.,** and **LUBIN, B.** (1973), T-groups, tests, and tension. *Small Group Behav.*, 4:81-88.

05872 **JOHNSON, E. M.,** and **STARK, D. E.** (1980), A group program for cancer patients and their family members in an acute care teaching hospital. *Soc. Work & Health Care*, 5:335-349.

05873 **JOHNSON, G.** (1976), Conversion as a cure: the therapeutic community and the professional ex-addict. *Contemp. Drug Probl.*, 5:187-205.

05874 **JOHNSON, J.,** and **O'BRIEN, C. R.** (1975), Multiple therapy with the homosexual. *Psychology*, 12:23-26.

05875 **JOHNSON, J., WEEKS, G. R.,** and **L'ABATE, L.** (1979), Forced holding: a technique for treating petrified children. *Fam. Ther.*, 63:123.

05876 **JOHNSON, J. A** (1970), Comparison of group and individual counseling approaches in relation to measured changes in scholastic probation students. *Dissert. Abstr. Internat.*, 31:929A.

05878 **JOHNSON, J. A.** (1963), *Group Therapy: A Practical Approach.* New York: Blakiston Division, McGraw-Hill.

05879 **JOHNSON, J. A., Jr.** (1964), The basis and techniques of group therapy. *Diseases Nerv. System*, 25:335-343.

05880 **JOHNSON, J. D.** (1978), Review of R. V. Heckel's and H. C. Salzberg's *Group Psychotherapy: Behavioral Approach. Internat. J. Group Psychother.*, 28:281-283.

05881 **JOHNSON, K. E.** (1964), Personal religious growth through small group participation. *Dissert. Abstr. Internat.*, 25:628.

05882 **JOHNSON, M.** (1976), An approach to feminist therapy. *Psychother.: Theory, Res. & Pract.*, 13:72-76.

05883 **JOHNSON, M. H.** (1962), The development of a therapeutic community on an open ward in a general hospital. *Internat. J. Group Psychother.*, 12:99-106.

05884 **JOHNSON, M. R.,** and **RAW, G.** (1957), Sociodrama applied on a teacher-training college campus. *Peabody J. Educat.*, 35:93-96.

05885 **JOHNSON, N.** (1971), What is Al-Anon? *Nat. Cath. Guid. Conf. J.*, 15:188-191.

05886 **JOHNSON, N.,** and **JOHNSON, S. C.** (1980), A group counseling contract. *J. Special. Group Work*, 5:93-97.

05887 **JOHNSON, N. B.** (1943), Group therapy in a hospital library. *U.S. Vets Admin. Med. Bull.*, 20:207-209.

05888 **JOHNSON, P. E.** (1959), Interpersonal psychology of religion: Moreno and Buber. *Group Psychother., Psychodrama & Sociometry*, 12:211-217.

05889 **JOHNSON, P. E.** (1950), Introduction. In: *A Twenty-Year Experiment on Group Therapy*, eds. J. H. Pratt and P. E. Johnson. Boston: New England Medical Center.

05890 **JOHNSON, P. E.** (1954), Transference, tele and empathy. *Group Psychother., Psychodrama & Sociometry, 7:324-326.*

05891 **JOHNSON, R. F.** (1970), The effects of encounter groups on selected age related variables in a volunteer geriatric population. *Dissert. Abstr. Internat.*, 32:739A.

05892 **JOHNSON, R. L.,** and **CHATOWSKY, A. P.** (1969), Game theory and short-term group counseling. *Personnel & Guid. J.*, 47:758-761.

05893 **JOHNSON, S.,** and **JOHNSON, N.** (1979), Effects of various group approaches on self-actualization of graduate counseling students. *J. Couns. Psychol.*, 26:444-447.

05894 **JOHNSON, S. A.** (1970), A comparison of mothers versus child groups and traditional versus behavior modification procedures in the "treatment" of disobedient children. *Dissert. Abstr. Internat.*, 31:2989.

05895 **JOHNSON, T., TYLER, V., THOMPSON, R.,** and **JONES, E.** (1971), Systematic desensitization and assertive training in the treatment of speech anxiety in middle-school students. *Psychol. in Schools*, 8:263-267.

05896 **JOHNSON, T. F.** (1978), A contextual approach to treatment of juvenile offenders. *Offender Rehab.*, 3:171.

05897 **JOHNSON, W. G.** (1975), Group therapy: a behavioral perspective. *Behav. Ther.*, 6:30-38.

05898 **JOHNSTON, M.** (1951), An experiment in group psychotherapy with the narcotic addict. *Amer. J. Psychother.*, 5:24-31.

05899 **JOHNSTON, N.** (1965), Group reading as a treatment tool with geriatrics. *Amer. J. Occupat. Ther.*, 19:192-195.

05900 **JOHNSTONE, T.**, and **PRESLEY, A. S.** (1972), Psychiatric outpatients: some observations of a follow-up group. *Nursing Times*, (London) 68:228-230.

05901 **JOJIĆ-MILENKOVIĆ, M.** (1973), (Therapy in a large group.) *Anali Zavode Ment. Zdravlja*, 5:127-133.

05902 **JOLLES, I.** (1946), An experiment in group guidance. *J. Soc. Psychol.*, 23:55-60.

05903 **JOLLES, I.** (1946), An experiment in group therapy for adult offenders. *Fed. Probat.*, 10:16-19.

05904 **JONCKHEERE, P., EVEN, P., LAROCHE, N.**, and **FONTAINE, P.** (1973), The principles and initial results of an intensive psychotherapy center for young psychotics, centering on communication and autonomy. *Acta Neurol. & Psychiat. Belgica*, (Brussels) 73:82-100.

05905 **JONES, A. L.** (1977), Delivery of community mental health services through a five-session group therapy module. *Dissert. Abstr. Internat.*, 37:4147.

05906 **JONES, B. C.** (1978), The effects of a marathon experience upon ongoing group psychotherapy. *Dissert. Abstr. Internat.*, 38:3887B. (University Microfilms No. 7732251.)

05907 **JONES, B. S.** (1969), Functions of meaning clarification by therapists in a psychotherapy group. *Dissert. Abstr. Internat.*, 29:3706A.

05908 **JONES, D.** (1964), My experiences in a group. *Nursing Times*, (London) 60:1530-1532.

05909 **JONES, D. R.** (1970), The grief therapy project: the effects of group therapy with bereaved surviving spouses on successful coping with grief. *Dissert. Abstr. Internat.*, 39:6121B.

05910 **JONES, D. S.** (1973), Self actualization effects of marathon growth group experience. *Dissert. Abstr. Internat.*, 34:855B.

05911 **JONES, D. S.**, and **MEDVENE, A. M.** (1975), Self-actualization effects of a marathon growth group. *J. Couns. Psychol.*, 22:39-43.

05912 **JONES, F. D.** (1975), The effect of personal growth group counseling on the self-concepts and academic achievement of college freshmen. *Dissert. Abstr. Internat.*, 36:2631A.

05913 **JONES, F. D.** (1951), An evaluation of group psychotherapy. Unpublished doctoral dissertation, Washington University.

05914 **JONES, F. D.**, and **PETERS, H. N.** (1952), An experimental evaluation of group psychotherapy. *J. Abnorm. Soc. Psychol.*, 47:345-353.

05915 **JONES, F. H.**, and **EIMERS, R. C.** (1975), Role playing to train elementary teachers to use classroom management "skill package." *J. Appl. Behav. Anal.*, 8:421-435.

05916 **JONES, H.** (1958), A contribution to the evaluation of some methods of residential therapy. *Human Relat.*, 11:55-65.

05917 **JONES, H.** (1960), *Reluctant Rebels: Re-Education and Group Process in a Residential Community*. London: Tavistock Publications.

05918 **JONES, H.** (1960), *Reluctant Rebels: Re-Education and Group Process in a Residential Community*. New York: Association Press.

05919 **JONES, H.** (1979), Review of J. S. Whiteley's and T. Gordon's *Group Approaches in Psychiatry. J. Adolescence*, 2:171.

05920 **JONES, H. B.** (1969), Group therapy for mothers and children in parallel. *Amer. J. Psychiat.*, 125:1439-1442.

05921 **JONES, J.** (1977), *Group Psychotherapy as Experiencing, Interpersonal Perceiving and Developing of Values: An Integrated and Experiential Model for Practicing, Training and Researching Group Psychotherapy.* Stockholm: Almqvist & Wiksell International.

05922 **JONES, J. E.** (1974), Group studies in the classroom. *Dissert. Abstr. Internat.*, 35:2061A.

05923 **JONES, J. E.,** and **PFEIFFER, J. W.** (1977), *The 1977 Annual Handbook for Group Facilitators.* La Jolla: University Associates.

05924 **JONES, M.** (1949), Acting as an aid to therapy in a neurosis centre. *Brit. Med. J.*, (London) 1:756-758.

05925 **JONES, M.** (1948), Emotional catharsis and re-education in the neuroses with the help of group methods. *Brit. J. Med. Psychol.*, 21:104-110.

05926 **JONES, M.** (1942), Group psychotherapy. *Brit. Med. J.*, (London) 2:276-278.

05927 **JONES, M.** (1944), Group treatment with particular reference to group projective methods. *Amer. J. Psychiat.*, 101:292-299.

05928 **JONES, M.** (1966), Group work in mental hospitals. *Brit. J. Psychiat.*, (Ashford) 112:1007-1011.

05929 **JONES, M.** (1965), A passing glance at the therapeutic community in 1964. *Internat. J. Group Psychother.*, 15:5-10.

05930 **JONES, M.** (1960), Social rehabilitation with emphasis on work therapy as a form of group therapy. *Brit. J. Med. Psychol.*, (London) 33:67-71.

05931 **JONES, M.** (1953), *The Therapeutic Community: A New Treatment Method in Psychiatry.* New York: Basic Books.

05932 **JONES, M.,** and **HOLLINGSWORTH, S.** (1963), Work with large groups in mental hospitals. *J. Individ. Psychol.*, 19:61-68.

05933 **JONES, M. C.** (1968), An analysis of a family folder. *Nursing Outlook*, 16:48-51.

05934 **JONES, M. J.** (1970), Human awareness exercises in human relation groups. *Psychology*, 7:26-33.

05935 **JONES, M. S.** (1952), *Social Psychiatry: A Study of Therapeutic Communities.* London: Tavistock Publications.

05936 **JONES, R. E.** (1970), Personality, morale and rapid turnover among nurses. *J. Psychiat. Nursing*, 8:7.

05937 **JONES, R. L.** (1959), Some correlates of change following small group discussion-decision. Unpublished doctoral dissertation, Ohio State University.

05938 **JONES, R. M.** (1960), *An Application of Psychoanalysis to Education.* Springfield, IL: C. C. Thomas.

05939 **JONES, R. M.** (1965), Some educational aspects of group-leader interaction. *Topical Probl. Psychol. & Psychother.*, 5:233-242.

05940 **JONES, R. M.,** and **BONN, E. M.** (1973), From therapeutic community to self-sufficient community. *Hosp. & Community Psychiat.*, 24:675-679.

05941 **JONGERIUS, P. J.** (1968), (The clinical treatment of neuroses.) *Tijdschr. Ziekenverplaging*, (Lochem) 8:306-313.

05942 **JONGERIUS, P. J.** (1974), (Cooperating with others about yourself: group psychotherapy.) *Nederl. Tijdschr. Psychol.*, (Amsterdam) 29:377.

05943 **JONGERIUS, P. J.** (1966), (The difference between group therapy and group psychotherapy.) *Nederl. Tijdschr. Geneeskunde*, (Amsterdam) 110:1331-1336.

05944 **JONGERIUS, P. J.,** and **ARENDSEN HEIN, G. W.** (1966), Groepspsychotherapie in de Synanon-gemeenschap. (Group psychotherapy within the Synanon society.) *Nederl. Tijdschr. Geneeskunde*, (Amsterdam) 110:1244-1246.

05945 **JONGSMA, T.** (1969), (Experience of short group therapy with chronic alcoholics with social conflicts.) *Nederl. Tijdschr. Psychiat.*, (Meppel) 11:27-31.

05946 **JORDAN, C. H.** (1975), A three year follow-up evaluation of sensitivity group training offered in a graduate program in psychiatric nursing. *Dissert. Abstr. Internat.*, 36:3512A.

05947 **JORDAN, M. B.** (1972), An exploratory study of the differential effects of group experiences in relation to the multiple factors of personality, involvement and commitment. *Dissert. Abstr. Internat.*, 33:956A.

05948 **JORDAN, P. H., CAMPBELL, M.**, and **HODGE, E. J.** (1957), A therapeutically oriented group technique for the diagnostic evaluation of parents of disturbed children. *Group Psychother., Psychodrama & Sociometry*, 10:114-128.

05949 **JORDAN, T. F.** (1977), Group process in action. *Free Assn.*, 4:1-3.

05950 **JORGENSEN, F.** (1970), (Treatment of young female drug addicts in a general psychiatric department.) *Ugeskr. fer Laeger*, (Copenhagen) 132:1245-1251.

05951 **JOSEPH, B. W.** (1971), Group therapy with adolescent girls in foster care. *Adolescence*, 6:299-316.

05952 **JOSEPH, D. I.** (1975), Mental health students' reactions to a group training conference: understanding from a systems perspective. *Soc. Psychiat.*, 10:79-85.

05953 **JOSEPH, H.**, and **HEIMLICH, E. P.** (1959), The therapeutic use of music with "treatment resistant" children. *Amer. J. Ment. Deficiency*, 64:41-49.

05954 **JOSEPH, R. J., SCHER, N. H., BRICK, J., SMALLEY, R. V.**, and **JOSEPH, R. R.** (1977), Group therapy in a breast cancer clinic. *Proceed. Amer. Assn. Ca.*, 18:282.

05955 **JOSEPHSON, B.** (1972), Comparison of behaviors of pre-adolescent children in task and person oriented groups examined from transactional and symbolic interaction perspectives. *Dissert. Abstr. Internat.*, 32:4220B.

05956 **JOSSELYN, I.** (1960), Treatment of the adolescent: some psychological aspects. *Amer. J. Occupat. Ther.*, 14:191-195.

05957 **JOURE, S. A.** (1970), Influence of trainer style and participant personality on t-group change. *Dissert. Abstr. Internat.*, 31:6315B.

05958 **JOURE, S. A., FRYE, R. L., MELERHOEFER, B.**, and **VIDULICH, R. N.** (1972), Differential change among sensitivity training participants as a function of dogmatism. *J. Psychology*, 80:151-156.

05959 **JOYCE, C.** (1977), The religious as group therapists: attitudes and conflicts. *Perspect. Psychiat. Care*, 15:112-117.

05960 **JOYCE, C. R. B.**, and **WELLSON, R. M. C.** (1965), The objective efficacy of prayer: a double-blind clinical trial. *J. Chronic Diseases*, 18:367-377.

05961 **JUDGE, D. H.** (1969), Group counseling with underachieving technical college trade students. *Austral. J. Psychol.*, (Parkville) 4:89-92.

05962 **JUDGE, J. J.** (1971), Alcoholism treatment at the Salvation Army: a new men's social service center program. *Quart. J. Studies Alcohol*, 32:462-467.

05963 **JULIAN, A.**, and **KILMANN, P. R.** (1979), Group treatment of juvenile delinquents: a review of the outcome literature. *Internat. J. Group Psychother.*, 29:3-37.

05964 **JULIAN, B. M., VENTOLA, L. J.**, and **CHRIST, J.** (1968), The interaction of young hospitalized patients with their mothers in a multiple-family therapy setting. *Amer. J. Orthopsychiat.*, 38:252.

05965 **JUILLET, P.** (1964), (Reflections on the use of group psychotherapy in the armed forces.) *Rev. Internat. Serv. Santé Armées*, (Paris) 37:337-341.

05966 **JULIUS, E. K.** (1978), Family sculpting: a pilot program for a schizophrenic group. *J. Marriage & Fam.*, 4:19.
05967 **JUN, G.** (1978), Report of experience with a socio- and psychotherapeutically oriented open long-term group of parents of severely brain injured children treated in an outpatient clinic. *Psychiat., Neurol. & Med. Psychol.*, (Leipzig) 30:372-377.
05968 **JUNKER, H.** (1972), (Experiences with group therapy in married couples of the upper lower class.) *Psyche*, (Stuttgart) 26:370-388.
05969 **JURCISIN, G.** (1951), Social dancing as a therapeutic medium with long term neuropsychiatric patients. *J. Assn. Phys. Ment. Rehab.*, 11:51-55.
05970 **JURI, L. J.** (1970), Técnicas proyectivas grupales. (Group projective techniques.) *Rev. Argentina Psicol.*, (Buenos Aires) 2:81-91.
05971 **JURICH, A. P.**, and **JURICH, J. A.** (1975), The lost adolescent syndrome. *Fam. Coordinator*, 24:357-361.
05972 **JURJEVICH, R. R. M.** (1968), *No Water in My Cup: Experiences and a Controlled Study of Psychotherapy of Delinquent Girls.* New York: Libra.
05973 **JUSTICE, B.**, and **JUSTICE, R.** (1978), Evaluating outcome of group therapy for abusing parents. *Correct. & Soc. Psychiat.*, 24:45-49.
05974 **JUSTICE, R.**, and **JUSTICE, B.** (1975), TA work with child abuse. *Transactional Anal. J.*, 5:38-41.

K

05975 **KABONOFF, B.**, and **O'BRIEN, G. E.** (1979), Cooperation structure and the relationship of leader and member ability to group performance. *J. Appl. Psychol.*, 64:526-532.

05976 **KADANE, J. B.**, **LEWIS, G. H.**, and **RAMAGE, J. G.** (1969), Horvath's theory of participation in group discussions. *Sociometry*, 32:348-361.

05977 **KADIS, A.**, and **LAZARFELD, S.** (1945), The group as a psychotherapeutic factor in counseling work. *Nerv. Child*, 4:228-235.

05978 **KADIS, A. L.** (1960), Alternate meetings. *Topical Probl. Psychol. & Psychother.*, 2:164-169.

05979 **KADIS, A. L.** (1956), The alternate meeting in group psychotherapy. *Amer. J. Psychother.*, 10:275-291.

05980 **KADIS, A. L.** (1965), Application of group therapy. *Topical Probl. Psychol. & Psychother.*, 5:243-249.

05981 **KADIS, A. L.** (1975), Coordinated meetings in group psychotherapy. In: *Group Psychotherapy and Group Function*, 2d ed., eds. M. Rosenbaum and M. M. Berger. New York: Basic Books.

05982 **KADIS, A. L.** (1957), Early childhood recollections as aids in group psychotherapy. *J. Individ. Psychol.*, 13:182-187.

05983 **KADIS, A. L.** (1965), Failures in group therapy. *Topical Probl. Psychol. & Psychother.*, 5:211-218.

05984 **KADIS, A. L.** (1971), A new group supervisory technique for group therapists. *Voices*, 7:31-32.

05985 **KADIS, A. L.** (1963), *A Practicum of Group Psychotherapy.* New York: Hoeber Medical Division, Harper and Row.

05986 **KADIS, A. L.** (1974), *Practicum of Group Psychotherapy*, 2d ed. Hagerstown, MD: Harper and Row.

05987 **KADIS, A. L.** (1959), The role of coordinated group meetings in group psychotherapy. *Acta Psychother. Psychosomat. Orthopaedagog. Suppl.*, (Basel) 7:174-183.

05988 **KADIS, A. L.**, and **WINICK, C.** (1968), Fees in group therapy. *Amer. J. Psychother.*, 22:60-67.

05989 **KADIS, A. L.**, **KRASNER, J. D.**, **WINICK, C.**, and **FOULKES, S. H.** (1963), *A Practicum of Group Psychotherapy.* New York: Hoeber Medical Division, Harper and Row.

05990 **KADUSHIN, A.**, **ROSE, J.**, and **SOBEL, G. B.** (1967), The relationship between parents' expressed attitudes and their decisions. *Soc. Casework*, 48:367-371.

05991 **KADUSHIN, L.**, and **KADUSHIN, A.** (1969), The ex-addict as a member of the therapeutic team. *Community Ment. Health J.*, 5:386-393.

05992 **KAES, R.** (1974), (Conditions and applications of group psychoanalysis: a method of studying ideological results.) *Cahiers Psychol. & Reeducat.*, (Montreal) 17:169.

05993 **KAFER, N. F.** (1976), A sociometric method for identifying group boundaries. *J. Exper. Educat.*, 45:71-79.

05994 **KAFKA, H.** (1931), Impromptu express. *Impromptu*, 1:9-10.

05995 **KAFKA, J. S.** (1957), A note on the therapeutic and teaching use of projective techniques with groups. *Amer. J. Psychother.*, 11:839-840.

05996 **KAGAN, N.** (1973), Can technology help us toward reliability in influencing human interaction: *Educat. Technol.*, 13:44-51.

05997 **KAGGWA, G. H.** (1980), The effects of client centered group counseling and relaxation on the self concept and negative behavior of junior high school students who are disciplinary problems. *Dissert. Abstr. Internat.*, 40:3782A. (University Microfilms No. 8002569.)

05998 **KAHL, R. D.** (1978), The effects of awareness of the importance of confidentiality and lack of privileged communication statutes for group psychotherapy. *Dissert. Abstr. Internat.*, 39:2989B. (University Microfilms No. 7824524.)

05999 **KAHLER, T.** (1972), Let's you and him make love: a variant of kick me. *Transactional Anal. J.*, 2:131-132.

06000 **KAHLER, T.** (1975), Scripts: process and content. *Transactional Anal. J.*, 5:277-279.

06001 **KAHN, A. N.** (1978), Group education for the overweight. *Amer. J. Nursing*, 78:254.

06002 **KAHN, J., BUCHMUELLER, A. D.,** and **GILDEA, M. C. L.** (1951), Group therapy for parents of behavior problem children in public schools: failure of the method in a Negro school. *Amer. J. Psychiat.*, 108:351-357.

06003 **KAHN, J. P.** (1978), Review of M. Rosenbaum's and M. M. Berger's *Group Psychotherapy and Group Function. Amer. J. Psychiat.*, 135:396.

06004 **KAHN, L. S.** (1980), The dynamics of scapegoating: the expulsion of evil. *Psychother.: Theory, Res. & Pract.*, 17:79-84.

06005 **KAHN, M.** (1974), The I Ching as a model for a personal growth workshop. *J. Human. Psychol.*, 14:39-51.

06006 **KAHN, M. D.** (1979), Organizational consultation and the teaching of family therapy contrasting case histories. *J. Marital & Fam. Ther.*, 5:69.

06007 **KAHN, M. M. R.** (1963), Ego ideal, excitement and the threat of annihilation. *J. Hillside Hosp.*, 12:195-217.

06008 **KAHN, R.,** and **GOODMAN, H.** (1973), Successful adaptations of group therapy techniques in the treatment of socially and economically deprived mothers of school children. *Amer. J. Orthopsychiat.*, 43:262.

06009 **KAHN, S.** (1964), *Psychodrama Explained.* New York: Philosophical Library.

06010 **KAHN, S. W.,** and **PRESTWOOD, A. R.** (1954), Group therapy of parents as an adjunct to the treatment of schizophrenic patients. *Psychiatry*, 17:177-185.

06011 **KAHNE, M. J.** (1969), Psychiatrist observer in the classroom. *Med. Trial Tech. Quart.*, 15:81-98.

06012 **KAHNWEILER, W. M.** (1978), Group counseling in a correctional setting. *Personnel & Guid. J.*, 57:162.

06013 **KAHZ, M.** (1967), An education in friendship. *J. Emot. Educat.*, 7:66-72.

06014 **KAIREY, I.** (1979), Evaluating the effectiveness of relationship group therapy in an elementary school setting. *Dissert. Abstr. Internat.*, 40:2369B.

06015 **KAISER, C. A.** (1948), Current frontiers in social group work. In: *Proceed. National Conference of Social Work: Seventy-Fourth Annual Meeting, San Francisco, April 13-19, 1947*, ed. G. Springer. New York: Columbia University Press.

06016 **KAISER, C. A.** (1954), Group work. *Amer. J. Orthopsychiat.*, 25:129-132.

06017 **KALACHEV, B. P.** (1977), Efficacy of group psychotherapy practiced in polyclinic. *Soviet Med.*, 7:114-119.

06018 **KALDECK, R.** (1951), Group psychotherapy by nurses and attendants. *Diseases Nerv. System*, 12:138-142.

06019 **KALDECK, R.** (1958), Group psychotherapy with mentally defective adolescents and adults. *Internat. J. Group Psychother.*, 8:185-192.

06020 **KALIBAT, F. P., KOTIN, J.,** and **KLINE, F.** (1976), For chronic patients: the follow-up group. *Transnat. Ment. Health Res. Newsl.*, 18:2, 9-10.

06021 **KALIČANIN, P.** (1973), Socio-psychiatric methods in work with outpatients. *Anali Zavoda Ment. Zdravlja*, 5:51-57.

06022 **KALIN, K.** (1979), (Review of D. Sander's *Psychodynamics in Small Groups.*) *Der Psychologie*, (Berne) 38:174.

06023 **KALIS, B. L., HARRIS, R. E., SOKOLOW, M.,** and **CARPENTER, L.** (1957), Response to psychological stress in patients with essential hypertension. *Amer. Heart J.*, 53:572-578.

06024 **KALISKI, L.** (1959), The brain-injured child: learning by living in a structured setting. *Amer. J. Ment. Deficiency*, 63:688-695.

06025 **KALOUTSIS, A.,** and **POTAMIANOU, A.** (1958), Group psychotherapy, psychodrama and sociometry in Greece. *Group Psychother., Psychodrama & Sociometry*, 11:338-349.

06026 **KALSON, L.** (1965), The therapy of discussion. *Geriatrics*, 397-401.

06027 **KALTREIDER, N. B.,** and **LENKOSKI, L. D.** (1970), Effective use of group techniques in a maternity home. *Child Welfare*, 49:146-151.

06028 **KAMENOW, G.** (1974), On registering and assessing the dynamic structure of a small group. *Gruppenpsychother. & Gruppendynam.*, (Goettingen) 8:214-226.

06029 **KAMIN, I.** (1966), Group psychotherapy with residents. *Curr. Psychiat. Ther.*, 6:157-162.

06030 **KAMIN, I.** (1966), The resident as patient in group psychotherapy. *Internat. J. Group Psychother.*, 16:313-320.

06031 **KAMIN, S. H., LLEWELLEYN, C. J.,** and **SLEDGE, W. L.** (1958), Group dynamic in the treatment of epilepsy. *J. Pediat.*, 53:410-412.

06032 **KAMINSKI, Z.** (1975), Case report: an asthmatic adolescent and his "repressed cry" for his mother. *Brit. J. Med. Psychol.*, (London) 48:185-188.

06033 **KANAS, N., KRETH, E., ROGERS, M.,** and **PATTERSON, L.** (1978), Psychiatric research in a military setting: evolution of a study on inpatient group psychotherapy. *Military Med.*, 143:552-555.

06034 **KANAS, N., ROGERS, M., KRETH, E., PATTERSON, L.,** and **CAMPBELL, R.** (1980), The effectiveness of group psychotherapy during the first three weeks of hospitalization: a controlled study. *J. Nerv. & Ment. Diseases*, 168:487-492.

06035 **KANAS, T. E., CLEVELAND, S. E., POKORNY, A. D.,** and **MILLER, B. A.** (1976), Two contrasting alcoholism treatment programs: a comparison of outcomes. *Internat. J. Addict.*, 11:1045-1062.

06036 **KANE, F. J., WALLACE, C. D.,** and **LIPTON, M. A.** (1971), Emotional disturbance related to t-group experience. *Amer. J. Psychiat.*, 127:954-957.

06037 **KANEKAR, S.** (1975), Group performance as a function of group composition. *Psychol. Studies*, (Mysore) 20:12-15.

06038 **KANESHIGE, E.** (1973), Cultural factors in group counseling and interaction. *Personnel Guid. J.*, 51:407-412.

06039 **KANG, T. S.** (1972), Name and group identification. *J. Soc. Psychol.*, 86:159-160.

06040 **KANGAS, J. A.** (1971), Group members' self-disclosure: a function of preceding self-disclosure by leader or other group member. *Compar. Group Studies*, 2:65-70.

06041 **KANTER, R. M.** (1970), Communes. *Psychol. Today*, 4:53-57, 78.

06042 **KANTER, S. S.** (1976), The therapist's leadership in psychoanalytically oriented group psychotherapy. *Internat. J. Group Psychother.*, 26:139-147.

06043 **KANTER, S. S., BURACK, J., CASTAGNOLA, R. L., GILBERT B. D., DEN HARTOG, G., HUGHES, C.,** and **KRUGER, S. I.** (1964), A comparison of oral and genital aspects in group psychotherapy. *Internat. J. Group Psychother.*, 14:158-165.

06044 **KAPELSKA, A., KAPELSKI, Z.,** and **SEK, H.** (1976), (Short-term group psychotherapy with endogenous depression patients.) *Psychiat. Polska,* (Warsaw) 10:381-388.

06045 **KAPLAN, F.**, and **FOX, E.** (1968), Siblings of the retardate: an adolescent group experience. *Community Ment. Health J.*, 4:499-508.

06046 **KAPLAN, H.** (1968), Some aspects of parent guidance in child psychiatry. *Can. Psychiat. Assn. J.*, (Ottawa) 13:311-315.

06047 **KAPLAN, H. B.** (1967), Physiological correlates (GSR) of affect in small groups. *J. Psychosomat. Res.*, 11:173-179.

06048 **KAPLAN, H. B.** (1963), Social interaction and GSR activity during group psychotherapy. *Psychosomat. Med.*, 25:140-145.

06049 **KAPLAN, H. B.**, and **BOYD, I. H.** (1965), The social functions of humor on an open psychiatric ward. *Psychiat. Quart.*, 39:502-515.

06050 **KAPLAN, H. B., BURCH, N. R., BEDNER, T. D.**, and **TRENDA, J. D.** (1965), Physiologic (GSR) activity and perceptions of social behavior in positive, negative and neutral pairs. *J. Nerv. & Ment. Diseases*, 140:457-463.

06051 **KAPLAN, H. I.** (1973), The "group dream." *Internat. J. Group Psychother.*, 23:421-431.

06052 **KAPLAN, H. I.** (1973), Psychotherapy, encounter and sensitivity training groups. *N.Y. State J. Med.*, 73:2369-2371.

06053 **KAPLAN, H. I.**, and **SADOCK, B. J.** (1971), *Comprehensive Group Psychotherapy*. Baltimore: Williams & Wilkins.

06054 **KAPLAN, H. I.**, and **SADOCK, B. J.** (1972), *The Evolution of Group Therapy*. New York: E. P. Dutton.

06055 **KAPLAN, H. I.**, and **SADOCK, B. J.** (1972), *Groups and Drugs*. New York: E. P. Dutton.

06056 **KAPLAN, H. I.**, and **SADOCK, B. J.** (1972), *Group Treatment of Mental Illness*. New York: E. P. Dutton.

06057 **KAPLAN, H. I.**, and **SADOCK, B. J.** (1972), *New Models for Group Therapy*. New York: E. P. Dutton.

06058 **KAPLAN, H. I.**, and **SADOCK, B. J.** (1972), *The Origins of Group Psychoanalysis*. New York: E. P. Dutton.

06059 **KAPLAN, H. I.**, and **SADOCK, B. J.** (1972), *Sensitivity Through Encounter and Marathon*. New York: E. P. Dutton.

06060 **KAPLAN, H. I.**, and **SADOCK, B. J.** (1971), Structured interaction: a new technique in group psychotherapy. *Amer. J. Psychother.*, 25:418-427.

06061 **KAPLAN, H. I.**, and **SADOCK, B. J.** (1971), Structured interactional group psychotherapy: new psychiatric modality. *N.Y. State J. Med.*, 71:1632-1638.

06062 **KAPLAN, H. S., KOHL, R. N., POMEROY, W. B., OFFIT, A. K.**, and **HOGAN, B.** (1974), Group treatment of premature ejaculation. *Arch. Sexual Behav.*, 3:443-452.

06063 **KAPLAN, H. I.** (1967), Fantasies, fables and facts about groups. *J. Fort Logan Ment. Health Ctr.*, 4:149-162.

06064 **KAPLAN, L. P.** (1966), Some observations from conjoint individual and group therapy with obese women. *Internat. J. Group Psychother.*, 16:357-366.

06065 **KAPLAN, M. L.** (1978), Uses of the group in gestalt therapy groups. *Psychother.: Theory, Res. & Pract.*, 15:80.

06066 **KAPLAN, M. L.**, and **KAPLAN, N. R.** (1978), Individual and family growth: a gestalt approach. *Fam. Ther.*, 17:195.

06067 **KAPLAN, R. E.** (1974), Managing interpersonal relations in task groups: a study of two contrasting strategies. *Dissert. Abstr. Internat.*, 34:7890A.

06068 **KAPLAN, S.**, and **SADOCK, B. J.** (1971), Structured interaction: a new technique in group psychotherapy. *Amer. J. Psychother.*, 25:418-427.

06069 **KAPLAN, S.**, and **WILLIAMS, M. J.** (1972), Confrontation counseling: a new dimension in group counseling. *Amer. J. Orthopsychiat.*, 42:114-118.

06070 **KAPLAN, S. R.** (1973), Symposium: dreams and the group setting, introduction. *Internat. J. Group Psychother.*, 23:387-393.

06071 **KAPLAN, S. R.** (1967), Therapy groups and training groups: similarities and differences. *Internat. J. Group Psychother.*, 17:473-504.

06072 **KAPLAN, S. R.**, and **ROMAN, M.** (1961), Characteristic responses in adult therapy groups to the introduction of new members: a reflection on group processes. *Internat. J. Group Psychother.*, 11:372-381.

06073 **KAPLAN, S. R.**, and **ROMAN, M.** (1963), Phases of development in an adult therapy group. *Internat. J. Group Psychother.*, 13:10-26.

06074 **KAPP, F. T., GLESER, G., BRESSENDEN, A., EMERSON, R., WINGET, J. A.**, and **KASHDAN, B.** (1964), Group participation and self-perceived personality change. *J. Nerv. & Ment. Diseases*, 139:255-265.

06075 **KARDOS, G.** (1965), (Group psychological interactions in the pharmacotherapy of alcoholics.) *Pszichol. Tanulmanyok*, 7:295-302.

06076 **KARLENZIG, K.** (1973), Group guidance for anxiety relief-when traditional methods are not enough. *Can. J. Psychiat. Nursing*, (Winnipeg) 14:8-10.

06077 **KARMIOL, E.** (1962), Some observations on concomitant individual and group treatment of adolescents. *Internat. J. Group Psychother.*, 12:374-375.

06078 **KARON, B. P.**, and **VANDENBOS, G. R.** (1970), Experience, medication and the effectiveness of psychotherapy with schizophrenics. *Brit. J. Psychiat.*, (Ashford) 116:427-428.

06079 **KARP, M.** (1968), Directorial catharsis: fact or fancy. *Group Psychother., Psychodrama & Sociometry*, 21:137-139.

06080 **KARPELES, K.** (1978), Differential effectiveness of structured and nonstructured group counseling as a function of facilitation for sexual attitude change and sexual behavior change among sexually normal university students. *Dissert. Abstr. Internat.*, 39:678A.

06081 **KARPMAN, B.** (1952), Dramanalysis. *Amer. J. Orthopsychiat.*, 22:570-583.

06082 **KARPMAN, B.** (1940), Principles and aims of criminal psychopathology. *J. Crim. Psychopathol.*, 1:187-218.

06083 **KARPMAN, S.** (1971), Options. *Transactional Anal. J.*, 1:79-87.

06084 **KARPMAN, S. B.** (1972), The abcs of hooking the reader's child. *Transactional Anal. J.*, 2:8-12.

06085 **KARPMAN, S. B.** (1972), Developments in transactional analysis. *Curr. Psychiat. Ther.*, 12:132-150.

06086 **KARRAS, M.** (1978), A telephone conference group for the chronically ill homebound. *Group*, 2:239-246.

06087 **KARSON, S.** (1965), Group psychotherapy with latency age boys. *Internat. J. Group Psychother.*, 15:81-89.

06088 **KARSON, S.**, and **WIEDERSHINE, L. J.** (1961), An objective evaluation of dynamically oriented group psychotherapy. *Internat. J. Group Psychother.*, 11:166-174.

06089 **KARST, T. O.**, and **TREXLER, L. D.** (1970), Initial study using fixed-role and rational-emotive therapy in treating public-speaking anxiety. *J. Consult. & Clin. Psychol.*, 34:360-366.

06090 **KARTHA, M.**, and **ERTEL, I. J.** (1976), Short-term group therapy for mothers of leukemic children: what professional staff can do to help parents cope with chronic illness. *Clin. Pediat.*, 15:803-806.

06091 **KASCHTEN, T.** (1977), Individual spiritual care and group dynamics in the problem patients. *Rehab. Record*, 30:29-31.

06092 **KASEMAN, B. M.** (1976), An experimental use of structured techniques in group psychotherapy. *Group Psychother., Psychodrama & Sociometry*, 29:33-39.

06093 **KASHIWAGI, S.** (1977), Construction of a questionnaire based on the theory of Bradford's three component learning motivation with the purpose of diagnostic investigation of learning process in t-group. *Japanese J. Psychol.*, (Tokyo) 47:316-325.

06094 **KASS, D. J.,** and **ABROMS, G. M.** (1972), Behavioral group treatment of hysteria. *Arch. Gen. Psychiat.*, 26:42-50.

06095 **KASS, E. L.** (1970), The effect of short-term group desensitization on test anxiety. *Dissert. Abstr. Internat.*, 30:3729A.

06096 **KASSAN, M.** (1965), The counseling service: an analysis of pioneer private group resource offering mental health services. *Dissert. Abstr. Internat.*, 26:1171-1172.

06097 **KASSEBAUM, G. G., WARD, D. A.,** and **WILNER, D. M.** (1963), *Group Treatment by Correctional Personnel: A Survey of the California Department of Corrections.* Sacramento: Youth and Adult Corrections Agency.

06098 **KASSOFF, A. I.** (1958), Advantages of multiple therapists in a group of severely acting-out adolescent boys. *Internat. J. Group Psychother.*, 8:70-75.

06099 **KATAHN, M., STRENGER, S.,** and **CHERRY, N.** (1966), Group counseling and behavior therapy with test anxious college students. *J. Consult. & Clin. Psychol.*, 30:544-549.

06100 **KATANEC, N.** (1978), (Group psychotherapy in adolescence.) *Soc. Psihijat.*, (Belgrade) 6:221-226.

06101 **KATKIN, S.** (1978), Charting as a multipurpose treatment intervention for family therapy. *Fam. Process*, 17:465.

06102 **KATO, T.** (1967), (Structural analysis of small therapeutic groups composed of schizophrenic patients by means of "conversational matrix.") *Psychiat. & Neurol. Japonica*, (Tokyo) 69:1394-1428.

06103 **KATRIN, S. E.** (1974), The effects on women inmates of facilitation training provided correctional officers. *Crim. Justice & Behav.*, 1:5-12.

06104 **KATZ, A. H.** (1979), Self-help health groups: some clarification. *Soc. Science & Med.*, 13:491-494.

06105 **KATZ, A. H.** (1970), Self-help organizations and volunteer participation in social welfare. *Ment. Health Digest*, 2:6-9.

06106 **KATZ, A. H.** (1970), Self-help organizations and volunteer participation in social welfare. *Soc. Work*, 15:51-60.

06107 **KATZ, E.** (1947), Audio-visual aids for mental hygiene and psychiatry. *J. Clin. Psychol.*, 3:43-46.

06108 **KATZ, E.** (1946), A brief survey of the use of motion pictures for the treatment of neuropsychiatric patients. *Psychiat. Quart. Suppl.*, 20:204-216.

06109 **KATZ, E.** (1945), A social therapy program for neuropsychiatry in a general hospital. *Psychol. Bull.*, 42:782-788.

06110 **KATZ, M. M.** (1976), Behavioral change in the chronicity pattern of dementia in the institutional geriatric resident. *J. Amer. Geriat. Soc.*, 24:522-528.

06111 **KATZ, R.** (1974), The effects of group balance on leadership style: a field study and a laboratory experiment. *Dissert. Abstr. Internat.*, 34:5312A.

06112 **KATZ, R.** (1977), The influence of group conflict on leadership effectiveness. *Organizat. Behav. & Human Perf.*, 20:265-286.

06113 **KATZ, R. L.** (1954), "Transference and tele" by J. L. Moreno: a discussion. *Group Psychother., Psychodrama & Sociometry*, 7:326-327.

06114 **KATZ, S. I.,** and **SCHWEBEL, A. I.** (1976), The transfer of laboratory training: some issues explored. *Small Group Behav.*, 7:271-286.

06115 **KATZELL, R. A., MILLER, C. E., ROTTER, N. G.,** and **VENET, T. G.** (1970), Effects of leadership and other inputs on group process and outputs. *J. Soc. Psychol.*, 80:157-169.
06116 **KATZENSTEIN, A.** (1954), An evaluation of three types of group psychotherapy with psychotic patients. *Internat. J. Group Psychother.*, 4:409-418.
06117 **KATZMAN, L. C.** (1972), Differential effects of leader versus leaderless groups. *Dissert. Abstr. Internat.*, 33:3293A.
06118 **KAUDERS, O.** (1948), Advances in group and individual therapy. In: *International Congress on Mental Health, Vol. 3*, ed. J. C. Flugel. International Conference on Medical Psychotherapy. New York: Columbia University Press.
06119 **KAUFF, P. F.** (1979), Diversity in analytic group psychotherapy: the relationship between theoretical concepts and technique. *Internat. J. Group Psychother.*, 29:51-64.
06120 **KAUFF, P. F.** (1977), The termination process: its relationship to the separation-individuation phase of development. *Internat. J. Group Psychother.*, 27:3-18.
06121 **KAUFFMAN, J. D.** (1970), The effects of group composition on an experimental group counseling program. *Dissert. Abstr. Internat.*, 31:2685-2686.
06122 **KAUFMAN, D. N.,** and **KAUFMAN, J.** (1972), The sources of parenting behaviors: an exploratory study. *Transactional Anal. J.*, 2:191-195.
06123 **KAUFMAN, E.** (1973), Group therapy techniques used by the ex-addict therapist. *Group Process*, 5:3-19.
06124 **KAUFMAN, E.** (1975), Group therapy techniques used by the ex-addict and therapist. In: *Group Psychotherapy and Group Function*, 2d ed., eds. M. Rosenbaum and M. M. Berger. New York: Basic Books.
06125 **KAUFMAN, E.** (1978), Individualized group treatment for drug-dependent clients. *Group*, 2:22-30.
06126 **KAUFMAN, E.** (1972), A psychiatrist views an addict self-help program. *Amer. J. Psychiat.*, 128:846-852.
06127 **KAUFMAN, G.,** and **KRUPKA, J.** (1973), Integrating one's sexuality: crisis and change. *Internat. J. Group Psychother.*, 23:445-464.
06128 **KAUFMAN, M.** (1957), Readiness for, and success in group psychotherapy: a study of the ability of certain social, familial, and personality factors to permit prediction of success in group psychotherapy. *Dissert. Abstr. Internat.*, 17:896.
06129 **KAUFMAN, M.,** and **BLUESTONE, H.** (1974/1975), Patient-therapist: are we free to choose therapy? *Groups*, 6:1-13.
06130 **KAUFMAN, M. E.** (1963), Group psychotherapy in preparation for the return of mental defectives from institution to community. *Ment. Retard.*, 1:276-280.
06131 **KAUFMAN, M. L.** (1972), Transfer of laboratory experience to day-to-day use. *Training & Develop. J.*, 26:41-42.
06132 **KAUFMANN, P.** (1969), From a Balint group: history of an amenorrhea. *Gynaecologia*, (Basel) 167:128-132.
06133 **KAUFMANN, P. N.,** and **DEUTSCH, A. L.** (1967), Group therapy for pregnant unwed adolescents in the prenatal clinic of a general hospital. *Internat. J. Group Psychother.*, 17:309-320.
06134 **KAUL, T. J.,** and **BEDNAR, R. L.** (1978), Conceptualizing group research: a preliminary analysis. *Small Group Behav.*, 9:173-192.
06135 **KAVANAGH, J. J.** (1970), An investigation of the effects of sex similarities and differences on interaction and outcomes in encounter groups. *Dissert. Abstr. Internat.*, 31:3876-3877A.
06136 **KAVANAUGH, R. R.** (1977), Categories of group interaction: the effects

of leader and goal variables on the development of intimacy in t-groups. *Dissert. Abstr. Internat.*, 38:2073A.

06137 **KAY, L. W.** (1948), Psychodrama examines the doctor. *Sociometry*, 1:35-42.

06138 **KAY, L. W.** (1946), Role-playing as a teaching aid. *Sociometry*, 9:263-274.

06139 **KAY, L. W.**, and **SCHICK, J. H.** (1945), Role practice in training depth interviewers. *Sociometry*, 8:82-85.

06140 **KAYE, H.**, and **KEW, C. E.** (1973), Reactions of an on-going therapy group to the temporary introduction to a co-therapist. *Dynam. Psychiat.*, (Berlin) 6:231-237.

06141 **KAYE, H. E.** (1975), Discussion of "The effect of group therapy on compulsive homosexuality in men and women." *Amer. J. Psychoanal.*, 35:313-316.

06142 **KAYE, J. D.** (1973), Group interaction and interpersonal learning. *Small Group Behav.*, 4:424-448.

06143 **KAYSER, H.** (1965), Observations on behavior and test results in chronic schizophrenia. Methodical data on a dynamic interpretation of the "schizophrenic defect." *Schweiz. Arch. Neurol., Neurochir. & Psychiat.*, (Zurich) 95:201-204.

06144 **KAYSER, H.** (1972), (Sociometric studies on mutual relations in a group of long-term hospital patients.) *Nervenarzt*, 43:489-490.

06145 **KAZAMIAS, N.** (1974), On implications of small group research in group therapy. *Ment. Health & Soc.*, (Basel) 1:118-121.

06146 **KAZDIN, A.**, and **FORSBERG, A.** (1974), Effects of group reinforcement and punishment on classroom behavior. *Educat. & Training Ment. Retard.*, 9:50-55.

06147 **KEAN, C. D.** (1954), Some role-playing experiments with high school students. *Group Psychother., Psychodrama & Sociometry*, 6:256-265.

06148 **KEARNEY, W. J.**, and **MARTIN, D. D.** (1974), Sensitivity training: an established management development tool? *Acad. Manag. J.*, 17:755-759.

06149 **KEEFE, T. W.**, and **SMITH, T. H.** (1970), A group counseling and group counselor training program in an air force corrections setting. *Correct. Psychiat. & J. Soc. Ther.*, 16:97-102.

06150 **KEEGAN, D. L.** (1974), Adaptation to visual handicap: short-term group approach. *Psychosomatics*, 15:76-78.

06151 **KEELER, M. H.** (1960), Short-term group therapy with hospitalized nonpsychotic patients. *No. Carolina Med. J.*, 21:228-231.

06152 **KEELEY, T. D.**, **BURGIN, J. E.**, and **KENNEY, K.** (1971), The use of sensitivity training in a unit of professional education. *J. Pastoral. Care*, 25:188-195.

06153 **KEGAN, D.** (1975), Paperback images of encounter. *J. Human. Psychol.*, 15:31-38.

06154 **KEGAN, D. L.** (1976), Perceived effects of sensitivity training: samples of police officers, college students, and a group dynamics class. *Small Group Behav.*, 7:131-146.

06155 **KEGAN, D. L.**, and **RUBENSTEIN, A. H.** (1972), Measures of trust and openness. *Compar. Group Studies*, 3:179-201.

06156 **KEGELES, S. S.**, **HYDE, R. W.**, and **GREENBLATT, M.** (1952), Sociometric network on an acute psychiatric ward. *Group Psychother., Psychodrama & Sociometry*, 5:91-110.

06157 **KEHRES, M. K.** (1973), Comparative analysis of group counseling with a male-female co-counseling technique and a single counselor technique. *Dissert. Abstr. Internat.*, 33:3294A.

06158 **KEHRES, R. J.** (1972), Differential effects of group counseling methods with black male adolescents. *Dissert. Abstr. Internat.*, 33:1440A.

06159 **KEISER, S.** (1967), Freud's concept of trauma and a specific ego function. *J. Amer. Psychoanal. Assn.*, 15:781-794.

06160 **KEISLAR, E. R.**, and **ZEIGLER, J. R.** (1958), The use of mark-sense cards to obtain guess-who ratings and sociometric type data. *Group Psychother., Psychodrama & Sociometry*, 11:110-113.

06161 **KEITH, C.** (1980), Discussion group for posthysterectomy patients. *Health & Soc. Work*, 5:59-63.

06162 **KELLER, A. H.** (1975), Vicarious imaginal stimuli in group systematic desensitization of test anxiety. *Dissert. Abstr. Internat.*, 36:3515A.

06163 **KELLERMAN, H.** (1979), *Group Psychotherapy and Personality: Intersecting Structures*. New York: Grune and Stratton.

06164 **KELLERMAN, H.** (1974), Group behavior in a baboon troop: implications for human group process. In: *Group Therapy 1974: An Overview*, eds. L. R. Wolberg and M. L. Aronson. New York: Stratton Intercontinental Medical Books.

06165 **KELLERMAN, H.**, and **PLUTCHIK, R.** (1977), The meaning of tension in group therapy. In: *Group Therapy 1977: An Overview*, ed. L. R. Wolberg. New York: Stratton Intercontinental Medical Books.

06166 **KELLERMAN, H.**, and **PLUTCHIK, R.** (1978), Personality patterns of drug addicts in a therapy group: a similarity structure analysis. *Group*, 2:14-21.

06167 **KELLEY, D. M.** (1951), The use of general semantics and Korzybskian principles as an extensional method of group psychotherapy in traumatic neuroses. *J. Nerv. & Ment. Diseases*, 114:189-220.

06168 **KELLEY, F. P.** (1971), Mansfield's community group homes. *Group Process*, (London) 4:52-59.

06169 **KELLEY, J. B.** (1974), Reaching out to parents of handicapped children: a group approach in an inner city school. *J. School Health*, 44:577-579.

06170 **KELLOGG, C. R.** (1969), The vicissitudes of the male spouse around the psychiatric hospitalization of his wife. *Amer. J. Orthopsychiat.*, 39:324-325.

06171 **KELLY, B. J.**, and **GILL, J. D.** (1978), Gestalt approaches to conjoint therapy. *Texas Personnel & Guid. Assn. J.*, 6:27.

06172 **KELLY, E. E.** (1966), Member personality and group counseling interaction. *J. Psychology*, 63:89-97.

06173 **KELLY, F. D.**, and **MAIN, F. O.** (1979), Sibling conflict in a single parent family: an empirical case study. *Amer. J. Fam. Ther.*, 7:34.

06174 **KELLY, F. V.** (1972), Effects of group counseling and group coaching on academic achievement and attitude of adult part time evening students. *Dissert. Abstr. Internat.*, 33:1441A.

06175 **KELLY, G. R.** (1977), Training mental health professionals through psychodrama techniques: basic elements. *Group Psychother., Psychodrama & Sociometry*, 30:60-69.

06176 **KELLY, H. S.**, and **PHILBIN, M. K.** (1968), Sociodrama: an action-oriented laboratory for teaching interpersonal relationship skills. *Perspect. Psychiat. Care*, 6:110-115.

06177 **KELLY, J.** (1969), *Organizational Behavior*. Homewood, IL: Irwin.

06178 **KELLY, J. G.**, **BLAKE, R. R.**, and **STROMBERG, C. E.** (1957), The effect of role training on role reversal. *Group Psychother., Psychodrama & Sociometry*, 10:95-104.

06179 **KELLY, P. P.** (1979), Group approaches to cancer patients establishing a group. *Amer. J. Nursing*, 79:914.

06180 **KELLY, W. E.** (1967), Group therapy of unwed mothers. *Curr. Psychiat. Ther.*, 7:157-161.

06181 **KELLY, W. J.** (1977), The effects of facilitative communication training and group counseling on the self-concepts of young adults. *Dissert. Abstr. Internat.*, 38:1407B.

06182 **KELLY, W. L.** (1974), Group-training: perspectives of professional trainees on group dynamics. *Small Group Behav.*, 5:427-444.

06183 **KELMAN, H.** (1948), Group therapy. *Amer. J. Psychoanal.*, 8:44-54.

06184 **KELMAN, H. C.** (1963), The role of the group in the induction of therapeutic change. *Internat. J. Group Psychother.*, 13:399-432.

06185 **KELMAN, H. C.** (1952), Two phases of behavior change. *J. Soc. Issues*, 8:81-88.

06186 **KELMAN, H. C.**, and **LERNER, H. H.** (1952), Group therapy, group work, and adult education: the need for clarification. *J. Soc. Issues*, 8:3-10.

06187 **KELMAN, H. C.**, and **PARLOFF, M. B.** (1957), Interrelations among three criteria of improvement in group therapy: comfort, effectiveness and self-awareness. *J. Abnorm. Soc. Psychol.*, 54:281-288.

06188 **KELMAN, H. C., DERONIS, L. E., ROSE, S., WASSELL, B.**, and **HORNEY, K.** (1952), Group analysis: some problems and procedures. *Amer. J. Psychoanal.*, 12:78-81.

06189 **KELNAR, J.** (1948), Contribution to discussion on group psychotherapy. *Folia Psychiat. Neurol. Neurochir. Neerl.*, 51:152-160.

06190 **KELNAR, J.** (1947), Treatment of interpersonal relations in groups. *J. Soc. Issues*, 3:29-34.

06191 **KELSEY, C. E., Jr.** (1960), Group counseling: an annotated bibliography. *J. Psychol. Stud.*, 11:84-92.

06192 **KELTNER, J. W.** (1974), *Group Discussion Processes*. Westport, CT: Greenwood Press.

06193 **KEMP C. G.** (1963), Behaviors in group guidance (socio process) and group counseling (psyche process). *J. Couns. Psychol.*, 10:373-377.

06194 **KEMP, C. G.** (1970), *Foundations of Group Counseling*. New York: McGraw-Hill.

06195 **KEMP, C. G.** (1972), Love in the encounter group. *Couns. & Values*, 16:209-212.

06196 **KEMP, C. G.** (1964), *Perspectives on the Group Process: A Foundation for Counseling with Groups*. Boston: Houghton Mifflin.

06197 **KEMP, C. G.** (1970), *Perspectives on the Group Process: A Foundation for Counseling with Groups*, 2d ed. Boston: Houghton Mifflin.

06198 **KEMP, D. E.** (1972), Curing "moral masochism." *Transactional Anal. J.*, 2:169-175.

06199 **KEMP, D. E.** (1972), The "fork" in psychotherapy. *Transactional Anal. J.*, 2:28.

06200 **KEMPER, H.** (1959), Possibilities of group therapy in the psychiatric hospital. *Zeit. Psychother., Med. Psychol.*, (Stuttgart) 9:244-246.

06201 **KEMPER, H.**, and **WACHSMUTH, R.** (1954), Das Gruppenesprach. (Group Speech.) *Med. Monatsschr.*, (Stuttgart) 8:184-185.

06202 **KEMPER, W.** (1958), Zur heutigen gruppenpsychotherapie. (Group psychotherapy today.) *Psyche*, (Heidelburg) 11:707-715.

06203 **KEMPER, W. W.** (1964), (On the problem of training of group psychotherapists.) *Zeit. Psychosomat. Med. & Psychoanal.*, (Goettingen) 10:191-198.

06204 **KEMPER, W. W.** (1964), (The problem of simultaneousness of individual and group psychoanalysis.) *Psyche*, (Heidelburg) 18:314-320.

06205 **KEMPER, W. W.** (1959), Psychoanalyse und gruppenpsychotherapie. (Psychoanalysis and group psychotherapy.) *Zeit. Psychother. Med. Psychol.*, (Stuttgart) 9:125-133.

06206 **KEMPER, W. W.** (1967), (Research problems in group psychotherapy.) *Arq. Brasil. Med.*, (Rio de Janeiro) 54:335-356.

06207 **KEMPH, J. P.**, and **SCHWERIN, E.** (1966), Increased latent homosexuality

in a woman during group therapy. *Internat. J. Group Psychother.*, 16:217-224.
06208 **KENNARD, D.** (1980), Review of M. A. Lieberman's, L. D. Borman's, and associates's *Self-Help Groups of Coping with Crisis. Group Anal.*, (London) 13:223-226.
06209 **KENNEDY, D. A.**, and **SEIDMAN, S. B.** (1972), Contingency management and human relations workshops: a school intervention program. *J. School Psychol.*, 10:69-75.
06210 **KENNEDY, M. L.** (1951), The organization and administration of a group treatment program. *J. Correct. Educat.*, 3:14-19.
06211 **KENNEDY, T. F.** (1972), An exploration of the effects of sensitivity training upon selected personality traits. *Dissert. Abstr. Internat.*, 33:2813B.
06212 **KENT, E. A.** (1963), Role of admission stress in adaptation of older persons in institutions. *Geriatrics*, 18:133-138.
06213 **KENT, M. O.** (1975), The effectiveness of short-term group work treatment for mentally ill offenders in a court-study unit. *Dissert. Abstr. Internat.*, 36:2426A.
06214 **KENTSMITH, D. K.**, and **BASTANI, J. B.** (1974), Obscene telephoning by an exhibitionist during therapy: a case report. *Internat. J. Group Psychother.*, 24:352-357.
06215 **KENWARD, K.**, and **RISSOVER, J.** (1980), A family systems approach to the treatment and prevention of alcoholism: a review. *Fam. Ther.*, 7:97.
06216 **KEPHART, N. C.** (1938), A method of heightening social adjustment in an institutional group. *Amer. J. Orthopsychiat.*, 8:710-718.
06217 **KEPINSKI, A., ORWID, M.**, and **GATARSKI, J.** (1960), (Further practical considerations on group psychotherapy.) *Neurol. & Neurochir. Polska*, (Warsaw) 10:697-701.
06218 **KEPINSKI, A., ORWID, M.**, and **GATARSKI, J.** (1960), Group psychotherapy as an approach to a psychotherapeutic community. *Group Psychother., Psychodrama & Sociometry*, 13:182-187.
06219 **KERN, R.**, and **KIRBY, J. H.** (1971), Utilizing peer helper influence in group counseling. *Elem. School Guid. & Couns.*, 6:70-75.
06220 **KERN, R. M.** (1970), The comparative effectiveness of a peer helper group counseling procedure and counselor oriented group counseling procedure on the adjustment of elementary school children. *Dissert. Abstr. Internat.*, 31:3877A.
06221 **KERNBERG, O.** (1980), *Internal World and External Reality: Object Relations Theory Applied.* New York: J. Aronson and Sons.
06222 **KERNBERG, O. F.** (1975), A systems approach to priority setting of interventions in groups. *Internat. J. Group Psychother.*, 25:251-276.
06223 **KERNBERG, P. F.** (1965), Experiences with open groups on a state hospital admission ward. *Bull. Menninger Clinic*, 29:27-34.
06224 **KERNBERG, P. F.** (1978), Use of latency-age groups in the training of child psychiatrists. *Internat. J. Group Psychother.*, 28:95-108.
06225 **KERNBERG, P. F.**, and **WARE, L. M.** (1975), Understanding child development through group techniques and play. *Bull. Menninger Clinic*, 39:409-419.
06226 **KERSTEIN, M. D.** (1980), Group rehabilitation for the vascular disease amputee. *J. Amer. Geriat. Soc.*, 28:40-41.
06227 **KERSTEN, L. K.** (1979), Exchange approach to building better interpersonal relationships. In: *Building Family Strengths*, eds. N. Stinnett, B. Chesser and J. Defrain. Lincoln, NB: Lincoln University of Nebraska Press.
06228 **KERSTETTER, L. M.** (1945), Psychodramatic approach in vocational guidance. *Sociometry*, 8:88.

06229 **KERSTETTER, L. M.**, and **SARGENT, J.** (1940), Reassignment therapy in the classroom. *Sociometry*, 3:293-306.

06230 **KESSEL, E. V. S.** (1971), Interpersonal trust and attitude toward the expression of positive and negative affect within the t-group. *Dissert. Abstr. Internat.*, 32:1855-1856A.

06231 **KESSLER, J. F.**, and **FROSCHAUER, K. H.** (1978), The soap opera: a dynamic group approach for psychiatric patients. *Amer. J. Occupat. Ther.*, 32:317-319.

06232 **KESSLER, S.** (1974), Treatment of overweight. *J. Couns. Psychol.*, 21:395-398.

06233 **KESTEMBERG, J.** (1968), (Notes on the treatment by analytic psychodrama of hospitalized psychotic patients.) *Rev. Française Psychoanal.*, (Paris) 32:555-567.

06234 **KESTEMBERG, J.** (1964), (Psychoanalytic approach for comprehension of the dynamics of therapeutic groups: dynamic variants in the so-called stable and unstable groups.) *Rev. Française Psychoanal.*, (Paris) 28:393-418.

06235 **KESTEMBERG, J.**, and **DECOBERT, S.** (1969/1970), Psychoanalytic approach to the understanding of the dynamics of therapeutic groups. *Bull. de Psychol.*, (Paris) 23:802-815.

06236 **KETAI, R.** (1973), Peer-observed psychotherapy with institutionalized narcotic addicts. *Arch. Gen. Psychiat.*, 29:51-53.

06237 **KEUTZ, P. V.** (1973), (The contribution of group dynamics to academic didactics.) *Zeit. Psychother. Med. Psychol.*, (Stuttgart) 23:115-120.

06238 **KEUTZER, C. S.**, and **LINK, S. L.** (1972), "Black bag" revisited: effects of limited visual feedback on the interaction and outcome of an extended t-group. *Cat. Selected Docum: Psychol.*, 2:119.

06239 **KEUTZER, C. S.**, **LICHTENSTEIN, E.**, and **MEES, H. L.** (1968), Modification of smoking behavior: a review. *Psychol. Bull.*, 70:520-533.

06240 **KEVE, P. W.** (1967), *Imaginative Programming in Probation and Parole.* Minneapolis: University of Minnesota Press.

06241 **KEVIN, D.** (1967), Group counseling of mothers in an AFDC program. *Children*, 14:69-74.

06242 **KEW, C. E.** (1963), Counter-transference and the group therapist. *J. Pastoral Care & Couns.*, 1:9-18.

06243 **KEW, C. E.** (1965), An experiment in teaching group psychotherapy through a group experience. *J. Pastoral Care & Couns.*, 19:129-140.

06244 **KEW, C. E.** (1954), Group healing in the church. *Pastoral Psychol.*, 5:44-50.

06245 **KEW, C. E.** (1968), The hazards of establishing a group therapy program. *J. Pastoral Care & Couns.*, 6:17-23.

06246 **KEW, C. E.** (1968), A pilot study of an evaluating scale for group psychotherapy patients. *J. Pastoral Care & Couns.*, 6:9-24.

06247 **KEW, C. E.** (1973), Preliminary report on the use of a transitional object in a homogeneous group of psychotics. *Group Anal.*, (London) 6:163-166.

06248 **KEW, C. E.**, and **KEW, C. J.** (1951), Group psychotherapy in a church setting. *Pastoral Psychol.*, 1:31-37.

06249 **KEW, C. E.**, and **KEW, C. J.** (1955), Principles and values of group psychotherapy under church auspices. *Pastoral Psychol.*, 6:37-48.

06250 **KEW, C. J.**, and **KEW, C. E.** (1972), *The Therapist Responds.* New York: Philosophical Library.

06251 **KEW, C. E.**, and **KEW, C. J.** (1953), *You Can Be Healed.* New York: Prentice-Hall.

06252 **KEYS, C. B.** (1974), Group process training and small group problem-solving. *Dissert. Abstr. Internat.*, 34:4047B.

06253 **KHANNA, P.**, and **KHANNA, J.** (1958), Theories of group psychotherapy. *J. Educat. Psychol.*, 16:372-381.

06254 **KHANTZIAN, E. J.**, and **KATES, W. W.** (1978), Group treatment of unwilling addicted patients: programmatic and clinical aspects. *Internat. J. Group Psychother.*, 28:81-94.

06255 **KIBEL, H. D.** (1981), A conceptual model for short-term inpatient group psychotherapy. *Amer. J. Psychiat.*, 138:74-80.

06256 **KIBEL, H. D.** (1980), Ending human relationships: problems and potentials. *J. Religion & Health*, 19:18-23.

06257 **KIBEL, H. D.** (1973), A group member's suicide: treating collective trauma. *Internat. J. Group Psychother.*, 23:42-53.

06258 **KIBEL, H. D.** (1968), Group psychotherapy as an adjunct to milieu treatment with chronic schizophrenics. *Psychiat. Quart.*, 42:339-351.

06259 **KIBEL, H. D.** (1980), The importance of a comprehensive clinical diagnosis for group psychotherapy of borderline and narcissistic patients. *Internat. J. Group Psychother.*, 30:427-440.

06260 **KIBEL, H. D.** (1972), Interracial conflicts as resistance in group psychotherapy. *Amer. J. Psychother.*, 26:555-562.

06261 **KIBEL, H. D.** (1978), The rationale for the use of group psychotherapy for borderline patients on a short-term unit. *Internat. J. Group Psychother.*, 28:339-358.

06262 **KIDD, C. B.**, and **KINGHAM, J.** (1967), An anthropological study of the elderly patient in an adult psychiatric clinic. *Internat. J. Soc. Psychiat.*, (London) 13:115-125.

06263 **KIDD, N. V.** (1977), The effect of group counseling and mini courses on women in a community college. *Dissert. Abstr. Internat.*, 38:633A.

06264 **KIDORF, I. W.** (1963), A note on the use of a tape recording during the therapy session. *Internat. J. Group Psychother.*, 13:211-213.

06265 **KIDORF, I. W.** (1966), The Shiva: a form of group psychotherapy. *J. Religion & Health*, 5:43-46.

06266 **KIENAST, H. W.**, **FISHER, R. A.**, and **RODRIGUEZ, G.** (1965), Psychiatric treatment of tuberculous patients in a state hospital setting. *Diseases Nerv. System*, 26:284-287.

06267 **KIERNAN, J. G.** (1909), Limitations of the Emmanuel movement. *Amer. J. Clin. Med.*, 16:1088-1090.

06268 **KIERNAT, J. M.** (1979), The use of life review activity with confused nursing home residents. *Amer. J. Occupat. Ther.*, 33:306-310.

06269 **KIESEWET, M.** (1976), Why bifocal group therapy was given up. *Gruppenpsychother. & Gruppendynam.*, (Goettingen) 10:191-202.

06270 **KIEV, A.** (1972), An eight-point drug abuse plan. *J. Occupat. Med.*, 14:31-36.

06271 **KIGER, R. S.** (1971), The therapeutic community in a maximum security hospital: treatment implications. *Correct. Psychiat. & J. Soc. Ther.*, 17:34-47.

06272 **KIGER, R. S.** (1967), Treating the psychopathic patient in a therapeutic community. *Hosp. & Community Psychiat.*, 18:191-196.

06273 **KIHN, B.** (1959), Group therapy in epilepsy. *Acta Psychother. Psychosomat. Orthopaedagog. Suppl.*, (Basel) 7:183-195.

06274 **KILBANE, M. T.** (1971), Relation of quantity and quality of counselor verbal participation to outcomes of group counseling. *Dissert. Abstr. Internat.*, 32:181-182A.

06275 **KILEY, R. H.** (1977), A study of group psychotherapy with institutionalized geriatric patients. *Dissert. Abstr. Internat.*, 37:5703A.

06276 **KILGUSS, A. F.** (1977), Therapeutic use of a soap opera discussion group with psychiatric in-patients. *Clin. Soc. Work. J.*, 5:58-65.

02677 **KILLEEN, M. R.,** and **JACOBS, C. L.** (1976), Brief group therapy for women students. *Soc. Work*, 21:521-522.

06278 **KILLIAN, D. H.** (1971), The effect of instructions and social reinforcement on selected categories of behavior emitted by depressed persons in a small group setting. *Dissert. Abstr. Internat.*, 32:3640B.

06279 **KILMANN, P. R.** (1974), Anxiety reactions to marathon group therapy. *J. Clin. Psychol.*, 30:267-268.

06280 **KILMANN, P. R.** (1974), Direct and nondirect marathon group therapy and internal-external control. *J. Couns. Psychol.*, 21:380-384.

06281 **KILMANN, P. R.** (1973), The effects of structure of marathon group therapy and locus of control on therapeutic outcome. *Dissert. Abstr. Internat.*, 33:5019B.

06282 **KILMANN, P. R.** (1974), Locus of control and preference for type of group counseling. *J. Clin. Psychol.*, 30:226-227.

06283 **KILMANN, P. R.** (1976), Effects of a marathon group on self-actualization and attitudes toward women. *J. Clin. Psychol.*, 32:154-157.

06284 **KILMANN, P. R.,** and **AUERBACH, S. M.** (1974), Effects of marathon group therapy on trait and state anxiety. *J. Consult. & Clin. Psychol.*, 4:607-612.

06285 **KILMANN, P. R.,** and **HOWELL, R. J.** (1974), Effects of structure of marathon group therapy and locus of control on therapeutic outcome. *J. Consult. & Clin. Psychol.*, 42:912.

06286 **KILMANN, P. R.,** and **SOTILE, W. M.** (1976), The effects of structured and unstructured leader roles on external group participants. *J. Clin. Psychol.*, 32:848-856.

06287 **KILMANN, P. R.,** and **SOTILE, W. M.** (1976), The marathon encounter group: a review of the outcome literature. *Psychol. Bull.*, 83:827-850.

06288 **KILMANN, P. R., ALBERT, B. M.,** and **SOTILE, W. M.** (1975), Relationship between locus of control, structure of therapy, and outcome. *J. Consult. & Clin. Psychol.*, 43:588.

06289 **KILMANN, P. R., SOTILE, W. M.,** and **FRITZ, K. R.** (1978), Marathon versus weekly encounter group treatment on self-actualization: two years later. *Group & Organizat. Studies*, 3:483-488.

06290 **KILMANN, R. H.** (1974), The effect of interpersonal values on laboratory training: an empirical investigation. *Hum. Relat.*, 27:247-265.

06291 **KIMBALL, R.,** and **GELSO, C. J.** (1974), Self-actualization in a marathon growth group: do the strong get stronger? *J. Couns. Psychol.*, 21:38-42.

06292 **KIMBALL, R. L.** (1974), Effects of some pretherapy manipulations on measures of group cohesion. *Dissert. Abstr. Internat.*, 35:1051B.

06293 **KIMBER, J. A. M.** (1957), Progress in group psychotherapy as shown by decision making. *Psychol. Reports*, 3:457-458.

06294 **KIMSEY, L. R.** (1969), Out-patient group psychotherapy with juvenile delinquents. *Diseases Nerv. System*, 39:472-477.

06295 **KIMSEY, L. R.** (1969), Outpatient group psychotherapy with juvenile delinquents. *Sandoz Psychiat. Spectator*, 5:3-4.

06296 **KINCAID, M. B.** (1978), Assertiveness training from the participants' perspective. *Prof. Psychol.*, 9:153-160.

06297 **KINDER, B. N.** (1976), The relationship of pre-therapy self-disclosure, the structure of group therapy, and locus of control on therapeutic outcome. *Dissert. Abstr. Internat.*, 37:465B.

06298 **KINDER, B. N.,** and **KILMANN, P. R.** (1976), The impact of differential shifts in leader structure on the outcome of internal and external group participants. *J. Clin. Psychol.*, 32:857-863.

06299 **KING, A. P.** (1979), The conversation club. *J. Pract. Nursing*, 29:20-21, 38.

06300 **KING, C.** (1965), Activity group therapy. *Topical Probl. Psychol. & Psychother.*, 5:133-135.

06301 **KING, C. H.** (1959), Activity group therapy with a schizophrenic boy: follow up two years later. *Internat. J. Group Psychother.*, 9:184-194.

06302 **KING, C. H.** (1973), Consideration of group therapy as a treatment approach to soft drug abuse. *Group Process*, (London) 5:21-29.

06303 **KING, J. K.** (1976), The differential effects of intensive vocational orientation on a selected group of transitional services clients. *Dissert. Abstr. Internat.*, 36:7210.

06304 **KING, M.** (1976), Changes in self-acceptance of college students associated with the encounter model class. *Small Group Behav.*, 7:379-384.

06305 **KING, M.** (1973), The impact of marathon and prolonged sensitivity training on self-acceptance. *Small Group Behav.*, 4:414-423.

06306 **KING, N. A.** (1972), The effects of group bibliocounseling on selected fourth grade students who are underachieving in reading. *Dissert. Abstr. Internat.*, 33:2714A.

06307 **KING, P. D.** (1975), Life cycle in "Tavistock" study group. *Perspect. Psychiat. Care*, 13:180-184.

06308 **KING, P. D.** (1958), Regressive EST, chlorpromazine, and group therapy in treatment of hospitalized chronic schizophrenics. *Amer. J. Psychiat.*, 115:354-357.

06309 **KING, W. R.** (1970), The effects of a t-group experience on teacher self-perception and classroom behavior. *Dissert. Abstr. Internat.*, 31:4009-4010A.

06310 **KINGDON, D. R.** (1974), Team or group development: the development of dyadic relationships. *Human Relat.*, 27:169-178.

06311 **KINGSLEY, L.** (1969), The correlation of the group psychotherapy test with overt behavior. *J. Group Psychoanal. & Process*, (London) 2:79-88.

06312 **KINGSLEY, L.** (1967), Process analysis of a leaderless counter-transference group. *Psychol. Reports*, 20:555-562.

06313 **KINGSLEY, L.**, and **GOLDBERG, W.** (1971), The group psychotherapy test as a measure of interpersonal relations. *Group Process*, (London) 3:83-88.

06314 **KINSELLA, T. E.** (1972), The day hospital as part of a psychiatric service. *So. African Nursing J.*, (Pretoria) 39:23-24.

06315 **KINZIE, W. B., TOLLMAN, G. A., WEBB, R. A.**, and **BERNARD, J. L.** (1965), Some effects of a brief course in the psychology of adjustment on a psychiatric admissions ward. *J. Clin. Psychol.*, 21:322-326.

06316 **KIPPER, D. A.** (1975), The candle technique in psychodrama. *Group Psychother., Psychodrama & Sociometry*, 28:50-54.

06317 **KIPPER, D. A.** (1977), Towards a psychodramatic intake: two techniques of self-introduction. *Group Psychother., Psychodrama & Sociometry*, 30:146-154.

06318 **KIPPER, D. A.** (1978), Trends in the research on the effectiveness of psychodrama: retrospect and prospect. *Group Psychother., Psychodrama & Sociometry*, 31:5.

06319 **KIPPER, D. A.**, and **GILADI, D.** (1978), Effectiveness of structured psychodrama and systematic desensitization in reducing test anxiety. *J. Couns. Psychol.*, 25:499.

06320 **KIRBY, J. H.** (1971), Group guidance. *Personnel & Guid. J.*, 49:593-600.

06321 **KIRBY, K.**, and **PRIESTMAN, S.** (1957), Values of a daughter (schizophrenic) and mother therapy group: a preliminary report. *Internat. J. Group Psychother.*, 7:281-288.

06322 **KIRK, L.** (1971), (Psychogenic psychosis following a group course.) *Ugeskr. for Laeger.*, (Copenhagen) 133:2390-2392.

06323 **KIRK, R.** (1971), Sensitivity and sensuality. *Nat. Rev.*, (Jan. 11) 23:36.

06324 **KIRKBRIDE, V. R.** (1959), Group approaches to student personnel services in higher education. Unpublished doctoral dissertation, George Washington University.

06325 **KIRKLAND, K. D.** (1978), The effects of group assertion training on the development and maintenance of assertive skills in unassertive adolescents. *Dissert. Abstr. Internat.*, 39:4038B.

06326 **KIRN, A. G.**, and **KIRN, M. O.** (1978), *Life Work Planning*. New York: McGraw-Hill.

06327 **KIRSCH, M.** (1966), (Group therapy based upon systematic therapeutic gymnastics in psychiatric treatment.) *Zeit. Aerztl. Fortbildung*, (Jena) 60:556-559.

06328 **KIRSCHENBAUM, D. S.** (1977), Questionnaire for the process analysis of social-skills-oriented group: therapy with children. *Cat. Selected Docum. Psychol.*, 7:42.

06329 **KIRSCHENBAUM, E.**, and **GLASGOW, D.** (1964), Group work method in psychiatric nursing practice. *Amer. J. Nursing*, 64:128-132.

06330 **KIRSCHENBAUM, H.**, and **GLASER, B.** (1978), *Developing Support Groups*. La Jolla: University Associates.

06331 **KIRSHNER, L. A.** (1974), A follow-up of a freshman group counseling program. *Amer. Coll. Health Assn. J.*, 22:279-280.

06332 **KIRSHNER, L. A.** (1980), Review of M. A. Palazzoli's *Paradox and Counterparadox. Gen. Hosp. Psychiat.*, 2:326-329.

06333 **KIRTLEY, D. D.**, and **SACKS, J. M.** (1969), Reactions of a psychotherapy group to ambiguous circumstances surrounding the death of a group member. *J. Consult. & Clin. Psychol.*, 33:195-199.

06334 **KIRTLEY, D. D.**, and **SACKS, J. M.** (1968), Reactions of a psychotherapy group to ambiguous circumstances surrounding the death of a group member. *Proceed., 76th Annual Convention*, American Psychological Association, 3:523-524.

06335 **KISCHKE, M. J.** (1973), (We introduce: flattich-Haus—aid for children with behavior disorders.) *Krankenpflege*, (Frankfurt) 27:432-433.

06336 **KISELEV, V. A.** (1966), (Experience with complex methods of collective psychotherapy in an outpatient psychoneurological clinic.) *Vop. Psikhiat. & Nevropatol.*, (Leningrad) 12:427-433.

06337 **KISKER, K. P.** (1960), (Experiences with and the methodology of group organization in the psychiatric hospital.) *Nervenarzt*, 31:392-402.

06338 **KISKER, K. P.** (1967), (Out-patient psychiatry. Concerning a two year polyclinic study of the Heidelberg Clinic.) *Nervenarzt*, 38:10-15.

06339 **KISSEN, M.** (1976), *From Group Dynamics to Group Psychoanalysis*. New York: J. Wiley and Sons.

06340 **KISSEN, M.** (1976), *From Group Dynamics to Group Psychoanalysis: The Therapeutic Application of Group Dynamics Understanding*. New York: Halsted Press.

06341 **KISSEN, M.** (1976), *From Group Dynamics: Therapeutic Applications of Group Dynamic Understanding*. Washington, D.C.: Hemisphere.

06342 **KISSEN, M.** (1980), General systems theory: practical and theoretical implications for group intervention. *Group*, 4:29-39.

06343 **KISSINGER, D. R.**, and **TOLOR, A.** (1965), The attitudes of psychotherapists toward psychotherapeutic knowledge: a study in differences among the professions. *J. Nerv. & Ment. Diseases*, 140:71-79.

06344 **KITCHEN, R.** (1957), On leaving group therapy. *Psychol. Newsl.*, 9:36-40.

06345 **KJOLSTAD, T.** (1965), (Group therapy with alcoholics.) *Wiener. Med. Wochenschr.*, (Vienna) 115:146-158.

06346 **KLAF, F. S.** (1961), The power of the group leader: a contribution to the understanding of group psychology. *Psychoanal. Rev.*, 48:41-51.

06347 **KLAGSBRUN, S. C.** (1969), An analysis of groups that never were. *Internat. J. Group Psychother.*, 19:142-149.
06348 **KLAIN, E.** (1978), (Countertransference problems of the group therapist in analytical group psychotherapy.) *Psihijat. Danas*, (Belgrade) 10:95-107.
06349 **KLAPMAN, H.**, and **BAKER, R. B.** (1963), The task force treatment: intensified use of the milieu for the severely disturbed child. *Amer. J. Occupat. Ther.*, 17:239-243.
06350 **KLAPMAN, H. J.**, and **RICE, D. L.** (1965), An experience with combined milieu and family group therapy. *Internat. J. Group Psychother.*, 15:198-206.
06351 **KLAPMAN, J. W.** (1975), The case for didactic group psychotherapy. In: *Group Psychotherapy and Group Function*, 2d ed., eds. M. Rosenbaum and M. M. Berger. New York: Basic Books.
06352 **KLAPMAN, J. W.** (1951), Clinical practices of group psychotherapy with psychotics. *Internat. J. Group Psychother.*, 1:22-30.
06353 **KLAPMAN, J. W.** (1955), Common-sense group psychotherapy for mental hospitals. *Diseases Nerv. System*, 16:24-29.
06354 **KLAPMAN, J. W.** (1941), A didactic approach to group psychotherapy. *Illinois Psychiat. J.*, 1:6-10.
06355 **KLAPMAN, J. W.** (1950), Didactic group psychotherapy. *Diseases Nerv. System*, 11:35-41.
06356 **KLAPMAN, J. W.** (1956), Group psychotherapy as catalyst in mental hospital treatment. *Internat. J. Group Psychother.*, 6:80-85.
06357 **KLAPMAN, J. W.** (1951), Group psychotherapy in institutions. *Group Psychother., Psychodrama & Sociometry*, 4:181-192.
06358 **KLAPMAN, J. W.** (1957), Group psychotherapy in relation to correctional psychiatry. *J. Soc. Ther.*, 3:211-224.
06359 **KLAPMAN, J. W.** (1952), Group psychotherapy in reverse. *Diseases Nerv. System*, 13:81-85.
06360 **KLAPMAN, J. W.** (1951), Group psychotherapy: social activities as an adjunct to treatment. *Group Psychother., Psychodrama & Sociometry*, 3:327-338.
06361 **KLAPMAN, J. W.** (1948), *Group Psychotherapy: Theory and Practice*. London: W. Heinemann.
06362 **KLAPMAN, J. W.** (1946), *Group Psychotherapy: Theory and Practice*. New York: Grune and Stratton.
06363 **KLAPMAN, J. W.** (1959), *Group Psychotherapy: Theory and Practice*, 2d ed. New York: Grune and Stratton.
06364 **KLAPMAN, J. W.** (1945), An observation on the interrelationship of group and individual psychotherapy. *J. Nerv. & Ment. Diseases*, 101:242-246.
06365 **KLAPMAN, J. W.** (1954), Observations on group psychotherapy and personality resynthesis in postlobotomy patients. *Internat. J. Group Psychother.*, 4:146-153.
06366 **KLAPMAN, J. W.** (1950), Observations on "shuttle" process in individual–group psychotherapy. *Psychiat. Quart.*, 24:124-130.
06367 **KLAPMAN, J. W.** (1946), Pedagogical group psychotherapy. *Diseases Nerv. System*, 7:205-208.
06368 **KLAPMAN, J. W.** (1957), Peripheral variables of group psychotherapy techniques as milieu therapy in mental hospitals. *Psychiat. Quart. Suppl.*, 31:69-78.
06369 **KLAPMAN, J. W.** (1953), Psychiatric social club therapy. *Group Psychother., Psychodrama & Sociometry*, 6:43-49.
06370 **KLAPMAN, J. W.** (1954), Psychoanalytic or didactic group psychotherapy? *Psychiat. Quart.*, 28:279-286.

06371 **KLAPMAN, J. W.** (1950), Social adjustment: a textbook for group psychotherapy classes. Chicago: Resurgo Associates.

06372 **KLAPMAN, J. W.** (1944), Some impressions of group psychotherapy. *Psychoanal. Rev.*, 31:322-328.

06373 **KLAPMAN, J. W.** (1943), Therapeutic value of institutional journalism. *Occupat. Ther. & Rehab.*, 22:126-131.

06374 **KLAPMAN, J. W.** (1959), The unselected group in mental hospitals and group treatment of chronic schizophrenics. *Diseases Nerv. System*, 20:17-23.

06375 **KLAPMAN, J. W.** (1947), Use of autobiography in pedagogical group psychotherapy. *Diseases Nerv. System*, 8:175-181.

06376 **KLAPMAN, J. W.**, and **CORSINI, R. J.** (1955), Group psychotherapy. In: *Progress in Neurology and Psychiatry*, ed. E. A. Spiegel. New York: Grune and Stratton, pp. 556-566.

06377 **KLAPMAN, J. W.**, and **CORSINI, R. J.** (1957), Group psychotherapy. In: *Progress in Neurology and Psychiatry*, ed. E. A. Spiegel. New York: Grune and Stratton, pp. 584-594.

06378 **KLAPMAN, J. W.**, and **LUNDIN, W. H.** (1952), Objective appraisal of textbook mediated group psychotherapy with psychotics. *Internat. J. Group Psychother.*, 2:116-126.

06379 **KLAPMAN, J. W.**, and **MEYER, R. E.** (1957), The team approach in group psychotherapy. *Diseases Nerv. System*, 18:95-99.

06380 **KLARREICH, S. H.** (1979), Proposing an alternative group method of treatment for probationers. *Correct. & Soc. Psychiat.*, 25:47-55.

06381 **KLAUS, H.** (1972), Experience with teenage pregnancy. *Amer. Coll. Nurse.-Midwives Bull.*, 17:114-121.

06382 **KLEE, J. B.** (1975-76), A reflection on encounter groups. *Interpersonal Develop.*, 6:62-64.

06383 **KLEEMAN, J. A.** (1962), Dreaming for a dream course. *Psychoanal. Quart.*, 31:203-231.

06384 **KLEEMANN, J. L.** (1974), The Kendall College human potential seminar model: research. *J. Coll. Student Personnel*, 15:89-95.

06385 **KLEIN, A.** (1949), He lets them grow. *Survey Graph.*, 85:75-80.

06386 **KLEIN, A.**, and **KIELL, N.** (1953), The experiencing of group psychotherapy. *Group Psychother., Psychodrama & Sociometry*, 5:205-221.

06387 **KLEIN, A. F.** (1972), *Effective Groupwork: An Introduction to Principle and Methods.* New York: Association Press.

06388 **KLEIN, A. F.** (1963), Exploring family group counseling. *Soc. Work*, 8:23-29.

06389 **KLEIN, A. F.** (1956), *Role Playing in Leadership Training and Group Problem Solving.* New York: Association Press.

06390 **KLEIN, D. F.** (1980), Psychosocial treatment of schizophrenia or psychosocial help for people with schizophrenia. *Schiz. Bull.*, 6:122.

06391 **KLEIN, E.** (1967), Setting the stage for self understanding. *J. Emot. Educat.*, 7:108-113.

06392 **KLEIN, E. B.** (1977), Transference in training groups. *J. Personality & Soc. Systems*, 1:53-64.

06393 **KLEIN, E. B., THOMAS, C. S.**, and **BELLIS, E. C.** (1971), When warring groups meet: the use of a group approach in police-black community relations. *Soc. Psychiat.*, 6:93-99.

06394 **KLEIN, F. M.** (1972), Dynamics of a leaderless group. *Internat. J. Group Psychother.*, 22:234-242.

06395 **KLEIN, H. S.** (1952), Contribution to a symposium on group therapy. *Brit. J. Med. Psychol.*, (London) 25:223-228.

06396 **KLEIN, H. S.** (1949), Psychogenic factors in dermatitis and their treatment by group therapy. *Brit. J. Med. Psychol.*, (London) 22:32-52.

06397 **KLEIN, H. S.** (1952), Psychogenic factors in dermatitis and their treatment by group therapy. *Psychoanal. Rev.*, 39:376.

06398 **KLEIN, H. S.** (1950), The therapeutic group in hospital. *Brit. J. Med. Psychol.*, (London) 23:101-104.

06399 **KLEIN, J. G.** (1960), *Adult Education and Treatment Groups in Social Agencies*. Washington, D.C.: Catholic University of America Press.

06400 **KLEIN, J. R.** (1973), The case of Mary. *Psychiat. Opinion*, 10:31-42.

06401 **KLEIN, M.**, and **SANDER, M.** (1977), (Group therapy and group work.) *Koelner Ziet. Soziol. & Sozialpsychol.*, (Wiesbaden) 29:403-408.

06402 **KLEIN, N. K.**, and **BABCOCK, D.** (1979), Assertiveness training for moderately retarded adults. *Educat. & Training*, (London) 14:232-234.

06403 **KLEIN, R. H.** (1977), Inpatient group psychotherapy: practical considerations and special problems. *Internat. J. Group Psychother.*, 27:201-214.

06404 **KLEIN, R. H.** (1980), Review of H. B. Roback's, S. I. Abramowitz's, and D. Strassberg's *Group Psychotherapy Research: Commentaries and Selected Readings*. *Contemp. Psychol.*, 25:702-704.

06405 **KLEIN, R. H.** (1980), Review of H. Kellerman's *Group Psychotherapy and Personality: Intersecting Structures*. *Contemp. Psychol.*, 25:702.

06406 **KLEIN, R. S.** (1973), The effect of differential treatments on encounter groups. *Dissert. Abstr. Internat.*, 34:415B.

06407 **KLEIN-LIPSHUTZ, E.** (1953), Comparison of dreams in individual and group therapy. *Internat. J. Group Psychother.*, 3:143-149.

06408 **KLEINMAN, J., ROSENBERG, E.**, and **WHITESIDE, M.** (1979), Common development tasks in forming reconstituted families. *J. Marital & Fam. Ther.*, 5:79.

06409 **KLEINSON, H.** (1969), (Medical-legal problems in group therapy.) *Ther. Gegenwart*, (Munich) 108:1002-1004.

06410 **KLEINSORGE, H.** (1954), Gezieltes gruppentraining bei organfunktionsstörung. (Directed group training for functional disorders.) *Zeit. Psychother. Med. Psychol.*, (Stuttgart) 4:184-193.

06411 **KLEMES, M. A.**, and **KOLLEJIAN, V. J.** (1955), The group psychotherapist in industry: a preventive approach. *Internat. J. Group Psychother.*, 5:91-98.

06412 **KLEMES, M. A.**, and **KOLLEJIAN, V.** (1956), Industry. In: *The Fields of Group Psychotherapy*, ed. S. R. Slavson. New York: International Universities Press.

06413 **KLEMKE, L. W.** (1977), Sociological perspectives on self-concept changes in sensitivity training groups. *Small Group Behav.*, 8:135-146.

06414 **KLETT, W. G.** (1966), The effect of historically based inferences on the behavior of withdrawn psychiatric patients. *J. Clin. Psychol.*, 22:427-429.

06416 **KLINE, F.** (1976), Letter: another group heard from. *Amer. J. Psychiat.*, 133:586-587.

06417 **KLINE, F.** (1975), Personal group therapy and psychiatric training. In: *Group Therapy 1974: An Overview*, eds. L. R. Wolberg and M. L. Aronson. New York: Stratton Intercontinental Medical Books.

06418 **KLINE, F. M.** (1972), Dynamics of a leaderless group. *Internat. J. Group Psychother.*, 22:234-242.

06419 **KLINE, F. M.** (1974), Terminating a leaderless group. *Internat. J. Group Psychother.*, 24:452-459.

06420 **KLINE, M. V.** (1970), The use of extended group hypnotherapy sessions in controlling cigarette habituation. *Internat. J. Clin. & Exper. Hypnosis*, 18:270-282.

06421 **KLINE, N. S.** (1947), Psychodrama for mental hospitals. *J. Clin. Psychopathol.*, 2:817-825.

06422 **KLINE, N. S.** (1952), Some hazards in group psychotherapy. *Internat. J. Group Psychother.*, 2:111-115.

06423 **KLINE, N. S.**, and **DREYFUS, A.** (1948), Group psychotherapy in Veterans Administration hospitals. *Amer. J. Psychiat.*, 104:618-622.

06424 **KLINE, P. M.** (1967), An experience in self-discovery: problematic verbal patterns of a group psychotherapist. *Perspect. Psychiat. Care*, 5:262-265.

06425 **KLINGBERG, H. E.** (1972), An evaluation of sensitivity training effects on self-actualization, purpose in life, and religious attitudes of theological students. *Dissert. Abstr. Internat.*, 32:7312B.

06426 **KLINGLEIL, G. A.**, and **ALVANDI, O. M.** (1975), Concepts of transactional analysis and anxiety with persons in crisis. *J. Psychiat. Nursing*, 13:5-10.

06427 **KLONOFF, H.** An exploratory study of the effectiveness of short-term group psychotherapy on attitudes of tuberculous patients. Unpublished doctoral dissertation, University of Washington.

06428 **KLOPFER, W. G.** (1945), The efficacy of group therapy as indicated by group Rorschach records. *Rorschach Res. Exch.*, 9:207-209.

06429 **KLÜCKMANN, C.** (1972), (Experience of a group leader in the therapeutic educational youth hostel "Haus Sommerberg.") *Praxis Kinderpsychol. & Kinderpsychiat.*, (Goettingen) 21:67-72.

06431 **KLÜCKMANN, C., STREPPE, F.**, and **BRUNNER, H.** (1967), Erfahrungen einer gruppentherapie mit mannlichem und weiblichem therapeuten. (Experience in group therapy with male and female therapists.) *Praxis Kinderpsychol. & Kinderpsychiat.*, (Goettingen) 16:67-74.

06432 **KLUGE, E.**, and **SCHROETTER, H. V.** (1954), Gruppenpsychotherape in der anstalt: fein erfahrungsbericht. (Group psychotherapy in the institution; an experience.) *Monatsschr. Psychiat. & Neurol.*, 127:152-170.

06433 **KLUGE, K. J.** (1971), Preamble to behavior changes of depressive pupils by means of a play-therapeutic procedure. *Acta Paedopsychiat.*, (Basel) 38:221-227.

06434 **KLÜWER, K.** (1965), (Dissocial adolescents in the industrial society: a practical example of treatment.) *Praxis Kinderpsychol. & Kinderpsychiat.*, (Goettingen) 14:113-117.

06435 **KLÜWER, K.** (1970), (The therapeutic-teaching juvenile home Sommerberg: experiences with a sociotherapeutic experiment.) *Praxis Kinderpsychol. & Kinderpsychiat.*, (Goettingen) 19:223-227.

06436 **KNAPP, H.** (1959), Theorie und praxis der diskussions-gruppe. (Theory and practice of discussion groups.) *Mensch & Arbeit*, (Munich) 11:5-12.

06437 **KNAPP, J. L.** (1947), Psychotherapy in the treatment of tuberculosis patients. *W. Virginia Med. J.*, 43:12-15.

06438 **KNAPP, R. R.**, and **SHOSTROM, E. L.** (1976), POI outcomes in studies of growth groups: a selected review. *Group & Organizat. Studies*, 1:187-202.

06439 **KNAUSS, J. W.** (1978), The effects of group assertiveness training on the aggressive behavior and self-concepts of fourth grade boys. *Dissert. Abstr. Internat.*, 38:5356A.

06440 **KNEISL, C. R.** (1968), Increasing interpersonal understanding through sociodrama. *Perspect. Psychiat. Care*, 6:104-109.

06441 **KNEISL, C. R.** (1968), Parent, adult, child: identifying ego states in group therapy. *ANA Clin. Sessions*, 315-325.

06442 **KNEPLER, A. E.** (1959), Role playing in education: some problems in its use. *Group Psychother., Psychodrama & Sociometry*, 12:32-41.

06443 **KNIGHT, D. J.** (1974), Developmental stages in t-groups. *Dissert. Abstr. Internat.*, 35:4258B.

06444 **KNIGHT, M.** (1979), Comparing three group therapy approaches with Puerto Rican outpatients. *Dissert. Abstr. Internat.*, 40:5816B.

06445 **KNIGHT, M.** (1980), Comparing three group therapy approaches with Puerto Rican outpatients. *Dissert. Abstr. Internat.*, 40:5816B. (University Microfilms No. 8012674.)

06446 **KNIGHT, R. P.** (1969), Approaches and research in psychotherapy. In: *The Study of Abnormal Behavior: Selected Readings*, 2d ed., eds. M. Zax and G. Stricker. New York: MacMillan.

06447 **KNIGHT, S. W.** (1967), Group rehabilitation in chronic schizophrenia. *Nursing Times*, (London) 63:964-965.

06448 **KNITTLE, B. J.**, and **TUANA, S. J.** (1980), Group therapy as primary treatment for adolescent victims of intrafamilial sexual abuse. *Clin. Soc. Work J.*, 8:236-242.

06449 **KNOBEL, M.** (1966), On psychotherapy of adolescence. *Acta Paedopsychiat.*, (Basel) 32:168-175.

06450 **KNOBLE, P.** (1972), The on (over-nurturing) parent and the off (only faithful to father and mother) child. *Transactional Anal. J.*, 2:186-189.

06451 **KNOBLOCH, F.** (1959), The diagnostic and therapeutic community as part of a psychotherapeutic system. *Acta Psychother., Psychosomat. Orthopaedagog. Suppl.*, (Basel) 7:195-204.

06452 **KNOBLOCH, F.** (1960), On the theory of a therapeutic community for neurotics. *Internat. J. Group Psychother.*, 10:419-429.

06453 **KNOBLOCH, F.** (1963), The system of group-centered psychotherapy for neurotics in Czechoslovakia. *Amer. J. Psychiat.*, 124:1227-1231.

06454 **KNOBLOCH, F.** (1967), The systems of group-centered psychotherapy for neurotics in Prague. *Psychother. & Psychosomat.*, (Basel) 15:34.

06455 **KNOBLOCH, F.**, and **KNOBLOCHVA, J.** (1964), Psicoterapia en términos de la teoría de pequeños grupos sociales. (Psychotherapy in terms of the theory of small social groups.) *Rev. Cubana Med.*, (Havana) 3:78-91.

06456 **KNOBLOCHAVA, J.**, and **NEZKUSIL, J.** (1968), A Czechoslovak treatment project. *Internat. J. Offender Ther.*, (London) 12:19-24.

06457 **KNOEPFEL, H. K.** (1972), The effects of the Balint group on its members and leader. *Psychiat. in Med.*, 3:379-383.

06458 **KNOLL, H.** (1973), (Residential psychotherapy of adolescents and initial results with a specially assembled residential group.) *Praxis Kinderpsychol. & Kinderpsychiat.*, (Goettingen) 22:290-294.

06459 **KNOLL, J.** (1977), *Gruppentherapie und Pädagogische Praxis: Ansätze, Arbeits-Formen u. Konsequenzen für d. Arbeit mit Gruppen in Schule u. Erwachsenenbildung.* (*Group Psychotherapy and Teaching: Starting Up, Working Through and the Consequences for Group Work in the Schools and with Adults.*) Klinkhardt und Biermann.

06460 **KNOLL, R. E.** (1974), Social group work in juvenile corrections: a synthesis of clinical and group dynamics principles. *Soc. Serv. Rev.*, 48:87-95.

06461 **KNORR, N. J., CLOWER, C. G.**, and **SCHMIDT, C. W.** (1966), Mixed adult and adolescent group therapy. *Amer. J. Psychother.*, 20:323-331.

06462 **KNOWLES, J. W.** (1964), *Group Counseling*. Englewood Cliffs, NJ: Prentice-Hall.

06463 **KNOWLES, J. W.** (1967), *Group Counseling, 1967*. Philadelphia: Fortress Press.

06464 **KNOWLTON, D. D.** (1979), An examination of the therapeutic process in a juvenile probation setting and further validation of the group assessment of interpersonal traits. *Dissert. Abstr. Internat.*, 40:5408B.

06465 **KNOX, T.** (1978), Review of L. R. Wolberg's and M. L. Aronson's *Group Therapy, 1977: An Overview. Internat. J. Group Psychother.*, 28:134-135.

06466 **KNOX, T.** (1976), Review of S. de Schill's *Challenge for Group Psychotherapy: Present and Future, Contemp. Psychol.*, 21:58-59.

06467 **KNOX, W. J.** (1958), Acceptance of self, other people, and social conformity as effects of group therapeutic experiences. Unpublished doctoral dissertation, Pennsylvania State University.

06468 **KNOX, W. J.** (1974), Effects of a domiliciary restoration program on state-trait anxiety and self-ideal concepts. *Psychol. Reports*, 34:689-690.

06469 **KNOX, W. J.** (1972), Four year follow-up of veterans treated on a small alcoholism treatment ward. *Quart. J. Studies Alcohol*, 33:105.

06470 **KOBAL, M.** (1975), (Group work with dissocial juveniles.) *Anali Zavoda Ment. Zdravlju*, 7:63-66.

06471 **KOBAL, M.** (1973), (Sociotherapeutic methods in the treatment of adolescents.) *Anali Zavoda Ment. Zdravlja*, 5:59-64.

06472 **KOBAYASHI, K.** (1976), Team development in a banking corporation in Japan. *Interpersonal Develop.*, 5:181-194.

06473 **KOBOS, J. C.** (1971), An exploration of aspects of the client-therapist relationship in group psychotherapy. *Dissert. Abstr. Internat.*, 31:7601-7602B.

06474 **KOBUS, W.** (1978), *Training en Terapie in Groepen: Ordening en Beschrijving*. Alphen aan den Rijn: Samsom.

06475 **KOCH, S.** (1971), The image of man implicit in encounter group therapy. *J. Human. Psychol.*, 11:109-128.

06476 **KOCH, S.** (1973), The image of man in encounter groups. *Amer. Scholar*, 42:636-652.

06477 **KOCHENDOFER, S. A.** (1975), Group preparation: interview vs. questionnaire. *School Counselor*, 23:38-42.

06478 **KOEFFER-ULLRICH, E.** (1969), (Music therapy within the rehabilitation program of group psychotherapy.) *Zeit. Psychother. Med. Psychol.*, (Stuttgart) 19:24-27.

06479 **KOEGEL, R. L.**, and **RINCOVER, A.** (1974), Treatment of psychotic children in a classroom environment: i. learning in a large group. *J. Appl. Behav. Anal.*, 7:45-59.

06480 **KOEGLER, R. R.**, and **WILLIAMSON, E. R.** (1973), A group approach to helping emotionally disturbed Spanish-speaking patients. *Hosp. & Community Psychiat.*, 24:334-337.

06481 **KOEHLER, W. R.** (1974), Team effectiveness training. *Training & Develop. J.*, 28:3-6.

06482 **KOEHNE-KAPLAN, N. S.**, and **LEVY, K. E.** (1978), An approach for facilitating the passage through termination. *J. Psychiat. Nursing*, 16:11-14.

06483 **KOENIG, F. G.** (1949), A group therapy experiment in a city elementary school. *Understanding the Child*, 18:40-44.

06485 **KOFFER-ULLRICH, E.** (1969), (Music therapy in the group therapy rehabilitation program.) *Zeit. Psychother. Med. Psychol.*, (Stuttgart) 19:24-27.

06486 **KOFFER-ULLRICH, E.** (1967), Musiktherapie im rehabilitations programm der gruppentherapie. (Music therapy in the group therapy rehabilitation program.) *Psychother. & Psychosomat.*, (Basel) 15:35.

06487 **KOFFMANN, A.**, **GETTER, H.**, and **CHINSKY, J. M.** (1978), Social skills and the effect of a group psychotherapy analogue. *Small Group Behav.*, 9:92-101.

06488 **KOGAN, K. L.** (1978), Help seeking mothers and their children. *Child Psychiat. & Human Develop.*, 8:204.

06489 **KOGAN, N.**, and **WALLACH, M.** (1967), Group risk taking as a function of members' anxiety and defensiveness levels. *J. Personality*, 35:50-63.

06490 **KOGAN, N.**, and **WALLACH, M. A.** (1967), Effects of physical separation of group members upon group risk-taking. *Human Relat.*, 20:41-48.

06491 **KOGAN, N.**, and **WALLACH, M. A.** (1966), Modification of a judgmental

style through group interaction. *J. Personality & Soc. Psychol.*, 4:165-174.
06492 **KOGER, R. S.** (1967), Treating the psychopathic patient in a therapeutic community. *Hosp. & Community Psychiat.*, 18:191-196.
06493 **KOHLER, A. T.** (1970), Some possible effects of leader-member similarity/dissimilarity in the counseling technique of group evaluation. *Dissert. Abstr. Internat.*, 30:5240B.
06494 **KOHLER, C.** (1964), (Associations of parents of mentally ill children and the child neuropsychiatrist.) *Acta Paedopsychiat.*, (Basel) 31:162-167.
06495 **KOHUT, S.** (1976), Psychodrama techniques for inservice teacher training. *Coll. Student J.*, 10:114-115.
06496 **KOILE, E. A.**, and **DRAEGER, C.** (1969), T-group member ratings of leader and self in a human relations laboratory. *J. Psychology*, 72:11-20.
06497 **KOILE, E. A.**, and **GALLESSICH, J.** (1972), Beyond the group's mythology. *J. Psychology*, 81:129-138.
06498 **KOKANTIZIS, N. A.** (1967), Observations and conclusions on the application of group psychotherapy with psychotic patients. *Psychother. & Psychosomat.*, (Basel) 15:36.
06499 **KOLE, C.**, and **DANIELS, R. S.** (1966), An operational model for a therapeutic community. *Internat. J. Group Psychother.*, 16:279-290.
06500 **KOLJONEN, H.** (1958), Alkoholistien vaimojen ryhamatoiminta. (The group work of the wives of alcoholics.) *Alkoholikysymys*, (Helsinki) 26:69-93.
06501 **KOLODNEY, E.** (1944), Treatment of mothers in groups as a supplement to child psychotherapy. *Ment. Hygiene*, 28:437-444.
06502 **KOLODNY, R.** (1967), The impact of peer group activity on the alienated child: experiences of a specialized group work department. *Smith Coll. Studies Soc. Work*, 37:142-158.
06503 **KOLODNY, R. L.** (1957), Therapeutic group work with handicapped children. *Children*, 4:95-101.
06504 **KOLODNY, R. L.**, and **REILLY, W. V.** (1972), Group work with today's unmarried mother. *Soc. Casework*, 53:613-622.
06505 **KOMAR, M.** (1967), A "therapeutic community" for outpatients. *Ment. Hygiene*, 51:440-448.
06506 **KOMECHAK, M. G.** (1971), The activity-interaction group: a process for short-term counseling with elementary school children. *Elem. School Guid. Counselor*, 6:13-19.
06507 **KOMINS, A. S.** (1972), An analysis of trainer influence in t-group learning. *Dissert. Abstr. Internat.*, 33:1403A.
06508 **KONARGOLDBAND, E., RICE, R. W.**, and **MONKARSH, W.** (1979), Time-phased interrelationships of group atmosphere, group performance, and leader style. *J. Appl. Psychol.*, 64:401-409.
06509 **KONDAS, O.** (1967), Reduction of examination anxiety and "stage-fright" by group desensitization and relaxation. *Behav. Res. & Ther.*, 5:275-281.
06510 **KONECNY, R.** (1964), Some theoretical and practical questions in the psychotherapy of children. *Sbornik Praci Filosoficke Fakulty Brnenske University*, 13:7-16.
06511 **KONEYA, M.** (1977), Privacy regulation in small and large groups. *Group & Organizat. Studies*, 2:324-335.
06512 **KÖNIG, K.** (1975), (Factors having an influence on conflict oriented motivation for psychotherapy in a clinical setting.) *Psychother. & Med. Psychol.*, (Stuttgart) 25:103-108.
06513 **KÖNIG, K.** (1978), (Group work and working groups.) *Gruppenpsychother. & Gruppendynam.*, (Goettingen) 13:354-363.
06514 **KÖNIG, K.** (1974), (Induced but spontaneous scenic representation in

therapeutic groups.) *Gruppenpsychother. & Gruppendynam.*, (Goettingen) 8:15-21.

06515 **KÖNIG, K.** (1975), (Reconstructive interpretations in analytic group psychotherapy.) *Gruppenpsychother. & Gruppendynam.*, (Goettingen) 9:26-31.

06516 **KÖNIG, K.** (1975), (Silent schizoid patient in an analytic group.) *Gruppenpsychother. & Gruppendynam.*, (Goettingen) 9:185-190.

06517 **KÖNIG, K.** (1977), (Structuring factors in group psychotherapy and group work: who or what gives structure to a group process.) *Gruppenpsychother. & Gruppendynam.*, (Goettingen) 11:211-220.

06518 **KÖNIG, K.** (1980), (The therapeutic function in group analysis.) *Connexions*, (Paris) 31:25-34.

06519 **KÖNIG, K.** (1977), (Therapist as observer, interpreter, pacemaker and participant in group psychotherapy.) *Praxis der Psychother.*, 22:249-255.

06520 **KÖNIG, K.** (1974), (Working relationship in analytic group therapy: concept and technique.) *Gruppenpsychother. & Gruppendynam.*, (Goettingen) 8:152-166.

06521 **KONOPKA, G.** (1944), Group therapy at the Pittsburgh Child Guidance Center. *Federator*, 19:8-11.

06522 **KONOPKA, G.** (1947), Group therapy in overcoming racial and cultural tensions. *Amer. J. Orthopsychiat.*, 17:693-699.

06523 **KONOPKA, G.** (1967), Group treatment of the mentally ill: education for life. *Can. Ment. Health Suppl.*, (Ottawa) 54:11.

06524 **KONOPKA, G.** (1950), Group work and group therapy in a psychiatric setting. In: *Education for Psychiatric Social Work, Proceed., Dartmouth Conference*, Hanover, New Hampshire, August 26 to September 9, 1949. New York: American Association of Psychiatric Social Workers.

06525 **KONOPKA, G.** (1948), Group work and therapy. In: *A Decade of Group Work*, ed. C. E. Hendry. New York: Association Press.

06526 **KONOPKA, G.** (1954), *Group Work in the Institution: A Modern Challenge*, New York: Whiteside.

06527 **KONOPKA, G.** (1961), A healthy group life-social group work's contribution to mental health. *Ment. Hygiene*, 45:327-335.

06528 **KONOPKA, G.** (1949), Knowledge and skill of the group therapist. *Amer. J. Orthopsychiat.*, 19:56-60.

06529 **KONOPKA, G.** (1952), The role of the social group worker in the psychiatric setting. *Amer. J. Orthopsychiat.*, 22:176-185.

06530 **KONOPKA, G.** (1949), *Therapeutic Group Work with Children*, Minneapolis: University of Minnesota Press.

06531 **KONOPKA, G.** (1947), Therapy through social group work. *Proceed. Nat. Conf. Soc. Workers*, pp. 228-236.

06532 **KOPEL, K.**, and **MOCK, L. A.** (1978), The use of group sessions for the emotional support of families of terminal patients. *Death Educat.*, 1:409-422.

06533 **KOPEL, K.**, **O'CONNELL, W.**, **PARIS, J.**, and **GIRARDIN, P.** (1975), A human relations laboratory approach to death and dying. *Omega: J. Death & Dying*, 6:219-222.

06534 **KOPELKE, C. E.** (1975), Group education to reduce overweight in a blue-collar community. *Amer. J. Nursing*, 75:1993-1995.

06535 **KOPFF, R. G.**, and **KRAMER, J.** (1969), A college student center: a new concept in community psychiatry. *Amer. J. Orthopsychiat.*, 39:343-344.

06536 **KOPPLE, H.** (1974), Head start parents in participant groups: ii. practical, yes; sufficient, no. *J. Appl. Behav. Science*, 10:256-259.

06537 **KORAN, L. M.**, and **COSTELL, R. M.** (1973), Early termination from group psychotherapy. *Internat. J. Group Psychother.*, 23:346-359.

06538 **KORB, M. P.**, and **THEMIS, S.** (1980), The importance of group process in gestalt therapy *J. Special. Group Work*, 5:36-40.

06539 **KORDINAK, S. T.** (1974), The relationship between cognitive rehearsal and the reduction of measured anxiety in college students. *Dissert. Abstr. Internat.*, 34:3501.

06540 **KORN, E. J.** (1973), The effectiveness of induced anxiety in group counseling as a preventive intervention procedure for freshmen. *Dissert. Abstr. Internat.*, 34:2937B.

06541 **KORNBLIT, A.**, and **GASPARINO, A.** (1967), Test grupal para la evalucíon de la dinámica de grupos psicoterapéuticos. (Test administration for the evaluation of therapeutic group dynamics.) *Acta Psiquiat. Psicol. Amer. Latina*, (Buenos Aires) 13:215-220.

06542 **KORNFELD, M., PUNTIL, J., DUEHN, W., LANE, B., MORRISON E.**, and **PEPPER, S.** (1967), Community mental health project as a part of training in a traditional child guidance clinic. *Amer. J. Orthopsychiat.*, 37:364-365.

06543 **KORNFELD, M. S.** (1980), Parental group therapy in the management of two fatal childhood diseases: a comparison . . . spinal muscular atrophy . . . Duchenne muscular dystrophy. *Health & Soc. Work*, 5:28-34.

06544 **KORNFELD, M. S.**, and **DIEGEL, I. M.** (1979), Parental group therapy in the management of a fatal childhood disease. *Health & Soc. Work*, 4:99-118.

06545 **KORNHABER, A.** (1968), Group treatment for obesity. *Group Psychother., Psychodrama & Sociometry*, 38:116-120.

06546 **KOROB, A.** (1964), (Technique of psychotherapy of a group of psychotics centered on analysis of the constraints.) *Rev. Argentina Neurol. Psiquiat.*, (Rio de Janeiro) 1:316-318.

06547 **KORS, P. C.** (1964), Unstructured puppet shows as group procedure in therapy with children. *Psychiat. Quart. Suppl.*, 38:56-75.

06548 **KORTE, J. D.** (1976), (Group psychotherapy with psoriasis patients.) *Nederl. Tijdschr. Psychol.*, (Amsterdam) 18:528-534.

06549 **KOSBAB, F.**, and **KOSBAB, M. E.** (1962), A buddy system for hospitalized geriatric patients. *Arch. Gen. Psychiat.*, 7:135-139.

06550 **KOSCH-GRAHAM, S. J.** (1973), Psychotherapeutic interaction in multiple and individual therapy. *Dissert. Abstr. Internat.*, 34:2938B.

06551 **KOSEMIHAL, N. S.** (1959), Sociometry and cybernetics. *Group Psychother., Psychodrama & Sociometry*, 12:97-109.

06552 **KOSOFSKY, S.** (1957), An attempt at weight control through group psychotherapy. *J. Individ. Psychol.*, 13:68-71.

06553 **KOSTECKA, M.** (1970), (Group therapy in a day care hospital.) *Psychiat. Polska*, (Warsaw) 4:661-665.

06554 **KOSTECKA, M.** (1974), (Use of sensitizing technics in group psychotherapy of schizophrenics.) *Psychiat. Polska*, (Warsaw) 8:477-483.

06555 **KOSTER, A.**, and **KOOGER, J.** (1979), *Relatietraining in het Bedrijf: Of Wat Denk Je er Zelf Van?* Deventer: Kluwer.

06556 **KOSTIĆ, M.** (1975), (Group psychotherapy of inpatient adolescents.) *Anali Zavoda Ment. Zdravlje*, 7:157-162.

06557 **KOSTIĆ, M.** (1979), (Group therapist in Gestalt therapy.) *Psihijat. Danas*, (Belgrade) 11:59-65.

06558 **KOSTKA, M. P.** (1974), The effectiveness of group systematic desensitization vs. covert positive reinforcement as utilized by paraprofessionals in the reduction of test anxiety in college students. *Dissert. Abstr. Internat.*, 34:4747A.

06559 **KOSTKA, M. P.**, and **GALASSI, J. P.** (1974), Group systematic desensitization versus covert positive reinforcement in the reduction of text anxiety. *J. Couns. Psychol.*, 21:464-468.

06560 **KOTILAINEN, M.** (1963), (Group therapy for obesity: a study of results obtained at weight-reducing courses in Finland.) *Annales Med. Internal Fennial*, (Helsinki) 52:155-161.
06561 **KOTIS, J. P.** (1968), Initial sessions of group counseling with alcoholics and their spouses. *Soc. Casework*, 49:228-232.
06562 **KOTKOV, B.** (1953), Analytically oriented group therapy. *Psychoanal. Rev.*, 40:333-350.
06563 **KOTKOV, B.** (1947), *A Bibliography for the Student of Group Therapy.* Boston: V.A. Boston Regional Office.
06564 **KOTKOV, B.** (1950), A bibliography for the student of group therapy. *J. Clin. Psychol.*, 6:77-91.
06565 **KOTKOV, B.** (1957), Common forms of resistance in group psychotherapy. *Psychoanal. Rev.*, 44:88-96.
06566 **KOTKOV, B.** (1955), The effect of individual psychotherapy on group attendance: a research study. *Internat. J. Group Psychother.*, 5:280-285.
06567 **KOTKOV, B.** (1951), Experiences in group psychotherapy with the obese. *Internat. Rev. Med. Gen. Pract. Clin.*, 164:566-576.
06568 **KOTKOV, B.** (1953), Experiences in group psychotherapy with the obese. *Psychosomat. Med.*, 15:243-251.
06569 **KOTKOV, B.** (1958), Favorable clinical indications for group attendance. *Internat. J. Group Psychother.*, 8:419-427.
06570 **KOTKOV, B.** (1956), Goals of short-term group psychotherapy. *J. Nerv. & Ment. Diseases*, 123:546-552.
06571 **KOTKOV, B.** (1954), The group as a training device for a girl's training school staff. *Internat. J. Group Psychother.*, 4:193-198.
06572 **KOTKOV, B.** (1952), Group psychotherapy with an obsessive compulsive. *Delaware State Med. J.*, 24:215-218.
06573 **KOTKOV, B.** (1962), Group psychotherapy with six-year-old boys. *Internat. J. Sociometry & Sociatry*, 2:146-150.
06574 **KOTKOV, B.** (1953), Group psychotherapy with wayward girls. *Diseases Nerv. System*, 14:308-312.
06575 **KOTKOV, B.** (1961), Power factors in psychotherapy groups. *Psychoanal. Rev.*, 48:68-76.
06576 **KOTKOV, B.** (1958), Psychoanalytic application to levels of group psychotherapy with adults. *Diseases Nerv. System*, 19:379-385.
06577 **KOTKOV, D.** (1940), Technique and explanatory concepts of short term group psychotherapy. *J. Clin. Psychopathol.*, 10:304-316.
06578 **KOTKOV, B.** (1957), Unresolved sexual fantasies in group psychotherapy. *Psychoanal. Rev.*, 44:313-322.
06579 **KOTKOV, B.** (1956), Vicissitudes of student group psychotherapists. *Internat. J. Group Psychother.*, 6:48-52.
06580 **KOTKOV, B.,** and **MEADOW, A.** (1952), Rorschach criteria for continuing group psychotherapy. *Internat. J. Group Psychother.*, 2:324-333.
05681 **KOUSHAN, K.** (1978), (Review of L. Grinberg's, M. Langer's, and E. Rodrigue's *Psychoanalytic Group-Therapy: Practice and Theoretical Basis.*) *Zeit. Klin. Psychol. & Psychother.*, (Freiburg) 26:185-186.
06582 **KOVAN, R. A.** (1968), Resistance of the marathon facilitator to becoming an intimate member of the group. *Psychosomatics*, 9:286-288.
06583 **KOVENOCK, E.** (1966), *Informal Group Process in Social Work: An Account of a Series of Discussions on Parent Education.* Milwaukee: Wisconsin State Board of Health.
06584 **KOWALSKI, W. J.** (1970), Structuring of feedback information within sensitivity training: a group process analysis. *Dissert. Abstr. Internat.*, 31:2614-2615.
06585 **KOWERT, E. H.** (1948), A demonstration of the laboratory method in the

investigation and teaching of group psychotherapy. *J. Clin. Psychopathol.*, 3:426-432.
06586 **KOZ, G.**, and **CHRIST, J.** (1970), Group psychotherapy with lower socioeconomic classes, in a metropolitan hospital setting. *Internat. J. Soc. Psychiat.*, (London) 16:306-313.
06587 **KOZNAR, J.** (1979), (Experience with group psychotherapy of adolescents in advisory centers.) *Ceskoslov. Psychol.*, (Prague) 23:303-311.
06588 **KOZNAR, J.** (1979), (Interpersonal dimensions of a psychotherapeutic group.) *Ceskoslov. Psychiat.*, (Prague) 75:46.
06589 **KRAAK, B.** (1961), Nichtdirektive gruppentherapie mit heimkindern. (Nondirective group therapy with institutionalized children.) *Zeit. Exper. & Angewandte Psychol.*, (Goettingen) 8:595-622.
06590 **KRAEMER, W. P.** (1951), Group psychotherapy at the Davidson Clinic, Edinburgh, Scotland. *Internat. J. Group Psychother.*, 1:281-284.
06591 **KRAFT, H.** (1977), Indirect portraits: the attempt at a nonverbal communication in an analytic group. *Confinia Psychiat.*, (Basel) 20:26-60.
06592 **KRAFT, I. A.** (1972), Group therapy. In: *The Child: His Psychological and Cultural Development: II. The Major Psychological Disorders and Their Treatment*, eds. A. M. Freedman and H. I. Kaplan. New York: Atheneum.
06593 **KRAFT, I. A.** (1960), The nature of sociodynamics and psychodynamics in a therapy group of adolescents. *Internat. J. Group Psychother.*, 10:313-320.
06594 **KRAFT, I. A.** (1968), An overview of group therapy with adolescents. *Internat. J. Group Psychother.*, 18:461-480.
06595 **KRAFT, I. A.** (1961), Some special considerations in adolescent group psychotherapy. *Internat. J. Group Psychother.*, 11:196-203.
06596 **KRAIDMAN, M.** (1980), Group therapy with Spanish-speaking clinic patients to enhance ego functioning. *Group*, 4:59-64.
06597 **KRAININ, J. M.** (1972), Counter-playing: a group therapy technique. *Amer. J. Psychiat.*, 129:600-601.
06598 **KRAMER, C. H.**, and **DUNLOP, H. E.** (1967), If wishing could make it so. *Geriat. Nursing*, 3:8.
06599 **KRAMER, C. H.**, and **KRAMER, J. R.** (1976), *Basic Principles of Longterm Patient Care: Developing a Therapeutic Community*. Springfield, MA: C. C. Thomas, pp. xiv, 375.
06600 **KRAMER, E.** (1966), Group induction of hypnosis with institutionalized patients. *Internat. J. Clin. & Exper. Hypnosis*, 14:243-246.
06601 **KRAMER, H. C.** (1968), Effects of conditioning several responses in a group setting. *J. Couns. Psychol.*, 15:58-62.
06602 **KRAMER, M.** (1967), Group milieu in a hospital. *J. Asthma Res.*, 4:241-246.
06603 **KRAMER, H. C.** (1957), Group psychotherapy with psychotic patients. *J. Nerv. & Ment. Diseases*, 125:36-43.
06604 **KRAMER, H. C.** (1945), A medical approach to group therapy. *Nerv. Child*, 4:236-242.
06605 **KRAMER, H. C.** (1972), The microlab-uses in student personnel. *Coll. Student J.*, 6:62-65.
06606 **KRAMER, M.**, and **DANIELS, R. S.** (1959), A group psychotherapeutic rehabilitation program for chronic psychotics. *Psychiat. Quart. Suppl.*, 33:119-127.
06607 **KRAMISH, A. A.** (1958), Former patients report on letter reading technique. *Group Psychother., Psychodrama & Sociometry*, 11:320-323.
06608 **KRAMISH, A. A.** (1956), Letter reading in group psychotherapy. *Group Psychother., Psychodrama & Sociometry*, 9:40-43.

06609 **KRANZ, P. L.** (1972), A racial confrontation group implemented within a junior college. *Negro Educat. Rev.*, 23:70-80.

06610 **KRANZ, P. L.** (1972), Using confrontation groups to lessen community racial tensions. *Hosp. & Community Psychiat.*, 23:47-48.

06611 **KRASNER, J., FELDMAN, B., LIFF, Z., MERMELSTEIN, I., ARONSON, M. L.**, and **GUTTMANN, O.** (1964), Observing the observers. *Internat. J. Group Psychother.*, 14:214-217.

06612 **KRASNER, J. D.** (1974), Analytic group psychotherapy with the aged. In: *The Challenge for Group Psychotherapy: Present and Future*, ed. S. de Schill. New York: International Universities Press.

06613 **KRASNER, J. D.** (1959), The psychoanalytic treatment of the elder person via group psychotherapy. *Acta Psychother. Psychosomat. Orthopaedagog. Suppl.*, (Basel) 7:205-223.

06614 **KRATOCHVÍL, S.** (1976), (Effect of therapist's qualities on cohesion and tension in group session.) *Ceskoslov. Psychiat.*, (Prague) 72:332-336.

06615 **KRATOCHVÍL, S.** (1975), (Interaction groups for therapy and training: ii. elements and examples of interaction.) *Ceskoslov. Psychiat.*, (Prague) 71:120.

06616 **KRATOCHVÍL, S.** (1977), (Review of B. D. Karvasarskij's *Group Psychotherapy in Neuroses and Psychoses.*) *Ceskoslov. Psychol.*, (Prague) 21:381.

06617 **KRATOCHVÍL, S.** (1979), (Review of I. A. Greenberg's *Group Hypnotherapy and Hypnodrama). Ceskoslov. Psychol.*, (Prague) 23:360.

06618 **KRATOCHVÍL, S.** (1979), (Review of J. C. Hansen's, R. W. Warner's and E. M. Smith's *Group Counseling: Theory and Process.*) *Ceskoslov. Psychol.*, (Prague) 23:256.

06619 **KRATOCHVÍL, S.** (1979), (Review of J. L. Shapiro's *Methods of Group Psychotherapy and Encounter.*) *Ceskoslov. Psychol.*, (Prague) 23:360.

06620 **KRATOCHVÍL, S.** (1977), (Review of K. Hock's *Study on Group Psychotherapy.*) *Ceskoslov. Psychol.*, (Prague) 21:285-286.

06621 **KRATOCHVÍL, S.** (1980), Sex therapy in an inpatient and outpatient setting. *J. Sex & Marital Ther.*, 6:135.

06622 **KRATOCHVÍL, S.** (1975), (Therapeutic and training interaction group.) *Ceskoslov. Psychol.*, (Prague) 71:38-44.

06623 **KRATOCHVÍL, S.** (1974), (Training in constructive controversy as a supportive method in group psychotherapy.) *Psychiat. Neurol. & Med. Psychol.*, (Leipzig) 26:358-363.

06624 **KRATOCHVÍL, S.** (1960), (Use of mental hygiene films in group psychotherapy.) *Ceskoslov. Psychiat.*, (Prague) 56:299-302.

06625 **KRATOCHVÍL, S., MANDLOVÁ, M.**, and **MIKŠOVIČOVÁ, M.** (1975), (Influence of group size on process of group therapy in a therapeutic community.) *Ceskoslov. Psychol.*, (Prague) 19:149-156.

06626 **KRATOCHVÍL, S.**, and **PATUČKOVÁ, M.** (1974), (The effects of initial warm-up period upon the course of group psychotherapy sessions.) *Ceskoslov. Psychol.*, (Prague) 18:411-418.

06628 **KRATOCHVÍL, S.** (1977), Open and closed groups in therapeutic community. *Ceskoslov. Psychiat.*, 23:145-149.

06629 **KRAUFT, C.**, and **BOZARTH, J.** (1971), Democratic, authoritarian, and laissez-faire leadership with institutionalized mentally retarded boys. *Ment. Retard.*, 9:7-10.

06630 **KRAUFT, V. R.** (1974), Transactional analysis group interaction with sixth grade behavioral problem boys. *Dissert. Abstr. Internat.*, 34:3874A.

06631 **KRAÜPL, F.** (1947), Emotional interplay and dominant personalities in therapeutic groups: observations on combined schizophrenic-neurotic groups. *J. Ment. Science*, (London) 93:613-630.

06632 **KRAÜPL, F.** (1948), Some observations on the analytical group treatment of a phobic patient. *J. Ment. Science*, (London) 94:77-88.
06633 **KRAUS, A. R.** (1959), Experimental study of the effect of group psychotherapy with chronic psychotic patients. *Internat. J. Group Psychother.*, 9:293-302.
06634 **KRAUS, R. F.** (1970), Informal social groupings on psychiatric wards. *Hosp. & Community Psychiat.*, 21:27-30.
06635 **KRAUS, R. F.** (1970), The use of symbolic technique in the group psychotherapy of chronic schizophrenia. *Psychiat. Quart.*, 44:143-157.
06636 **KRAUS, W. A.** (1970), Laboratory groups: effect on the tolerance scale of the California psychological inventory. *Dissert. Abstr. Internat.*, 31:2686-2687.
06637 **KRAUSE, L. F., GLAD, D. D.,** and **SMITH, W. L.** (1954), An inverse factor analysis of the relationships between overt and projective test behavior in experimental group psychotherapy. *Colorado-Wyoming Acad. Sci. J.*, 4:53-54.
06638 **KRAUSE, M. S.** (1968), Clarification at intake and motivation for treatment. *J. Couns. Psychol.*, 15:576-577.
06639 **KRAUSE, R.** (1979), (Review of A. Franke's *Patient-Oriented Group Psychotherapy.*) *Der Psychologie*, (Berne) 38:175.
06640 **KRAUSE, R.** (1979), (Review of S. H. Foulkes' *Praxis of Group-Analytical Psychotherapy.*) *Der Psychologie*, (Berne) 38:175.
06641 **KRAUSE, R., EBERT, B., CZESCHICK, E. R.,** and **MÜLLER, K.** (1977), (A behavior-therapeutic concept of the group: treatment of psychosomatic disorders.) *Zeit. Klin. Psychol. & Psychother.*, (Freiburg) 25:64-79.
06642 **KRAUSE, C.** (1978), Characteristics of group psychotherapy with adolescents.) *Psychiat., Neurol. & Med. Psychol.*, (Leipzig) 30:608-612.
06643 **KRAUSE, C.** (1977), (Conflict play and its modification in the course of treating children.) *Psychiat., Neurol. & Med. Psychol.*, (Leipzig) 29:606-609.
06644 **KRAUSE, R.** (1977), (A group behavior psychotherapy concept: treatment of psychosomatic disorders.) *Zeit. Klin. Psychol. & Psychother.*, (Freiburg) 25:64-79.
06645 **KRAUSER, W.** (1969), (Unintended action of resolution formula with autogenic training.) *Praxis der Psychother.*, 14:236-237.
06646 **KRAUSZ, S. L.** (1980), Group psychotherapy with legally blind patients. *Clin. Soc. Work J.*, 8:37-49.
06647 **KRAVETZ, D. F.** (1976), Consciousness-raising groups and group psychotherapy: alternative mental health resources for women. *Psychother.: Theory, Res. & Pract.*, 13:66-71.
06648 **KRAWITZ, M.,** and **WOLMAN, T.** (1979), Goup therapy in rheumatoid arthritis. *Pennsylvania Med.*, 82:35.
06649 **KREEGER, L.** (1975), *The Large Group: Dynamics and Therapy.* Itasca, IL: Peacock.
06650 **KREINIK, P. S.,** and **COLARELLI, R. J.** (1971), Managerial grid human relations training for mental hospital personnel. *Human Relat.*, 24:91-104.
06651 **KREITLER, H.** (1960), Psychodrama: a tool for teaching the psychology of personality. *Internat. J. Sociometry & Sociatry*, 2:23-27.
06652 **KREITLER, H.** (1960), Psychodrama in Israel. *Internat. J. Sociometry & Sociatry*, 2:104.
06653 **KREITLER, H.,** and **BORNSTEIN, I. I.** (1958), Some aspects of the interaction of psychodrama and group psychotherapy. *Group Psychother., Psychodrama & Sociometry*, 11:332-337.
06654 **KREITLER, H.,** and **ELBLINGER, S.** (1960), Hapsikhodrama behoraat

hapsikhologia shel haishiyut. (Psychodrama in teaching the psychology of personality.) *Ofakim*, (Tel Aviv) 14:249-252.
06655 **KREITLER, H.,** and **ELBLINGER, S.** (1960), Individual psychotherapy, group psychotherapy, psychodrama: a report from Israel. *Prog. Psychother.*, 5:212-217.
06656 **KREITLER, H.,** and **ELBLINGER, S.** (1961), (Psychiatric and cultural aspects of resistance to psychodrama.) *Psyche*, (Stuttgart) 15:155-161.
06657 **KREITLER, H.,** and **KREITLER, S.** (1964), Modes of action in the psychodramatic role test. *Internat. J. Sociometry & Sociatry*, 4:10-25.
06658 **KREITLER, H.,** and **KREITLER, S.** (1968), Validation of psychodramatic behavior against behavior in life. *Brit. J. Med. Psychol.*, (London) 41:185-192.
06659 **KREMEN, I.** (1970), Recent innovations in the clinical psychology training program at Duke University. *Prof. Psychol.*, 1:402.
06660 **KREUGER, J. R.,** and **CONNELLY, E. J.** (1973), Motivation of the hospital-dependent patient: a group therapy approach to discharge. *Newsl. Res. Ment. Health & Behav. Science*, 15:12-18.
06661 **KREVELEN, D. A.** (1962), (Group psychological aspects in the treatment of neurotic youngsters.) *Zeit. Psychother. & Med. Psychol.*, (Stuttgart) 12:186-194.
06662 **KREVELEN, D. A.** (1962), (On the problem of therapeutic pairing in neurotic youngsters.) *Acta Psychother., Psychosomat. Orthopaedagog.*, (Basel) 10:233-245.
06663 **KRIEGER, G. W.** (1972), The client-in-prison: a rehabilitation dilemma. *J. Appl. Behav. Couns.*, 2:161-164.
06664 **KRIEGER, M. H.,** and **KOGAN, W. S.** (1964), A study of group processes in the small therapeutic group. *Internat. J. Group Psychother.*, 14:178-188.
06665 **KRIEGHBAUM, H.** (1948), Rehabilitation by self-help. *Survey Graphics*, 37:15-18, 36.
06666 **KRISCH, M.,** and **SEIDEL, K.** (1966), Gruppentherapeutische fundierte systematische krankengynastik in der psychiatrischen therapie. (Group therapy based upon systematic therapeutic gymnastics in psychiatric treatment.) *Zeit. Aerztl. Fortbildung*, (Jena) 60:556-559.
06667 **KRISE, M.** (1952), Creative dramatics and group psychotherapy. *J. Child Psychol. & Psychiat.*, 2:337-342.
06668 **KRISE, N. W.,** and **ROTH, M. J.** (1948), Group dynamics and the mentally ill. *Hosp. Prog.*, 29:384-387.
06669 **KRITKAVSKY, R. P.** (1976), A comparative analysis of the short-term effects of three group approaches used in the treatment of drug abuse. *Dissert. Abstr. Internat.*, 37:466B.
06670 **KRITZER, H.,** and **PHILLIPS, C. A.** (1966), Observing group psychotherapy: an affective learning experience. *Amer. J. Psychother.*, 20:471-476.
06671 **KRIVATSY-O'HARA, S., REED, P.,** and **DAVENPORT, J.** (1978), Group counseling with potential high school dropouts. *Personnel & Guid. J.*, 56:510.
06672 **KRÖBER, E.** (1968), (Alcoholics.) *Schwestern Rev.*, (Wuerzburg) 6:40-41.
06673 **KROEKER, L. L.** (1974), Pretesting as a confounding variable in evaluating an encounter group. *J. Couns. Psychol.*, 21:548-552.
06674 **KROJANKER, R.** (1961), Patient participation in the national election. *Group Psychother., Psychodrama & Sociometry*, 14:82-84.
06675 **KROJANKER, R.** (1962), Training of the unconscious by hypnodramatic reenactment of dreams. *Group Psychother., Psychodrama & Sociometry*, 15:134-143.

06676 **KROJANKER, R. J.** (1966), Leuner's symoblic drama. *Amer. J. Hypnosis*, 9:56-61.

06677 **KROMBERG, C. J.**, and **PROCTOR, J. B.** (1970), Methadone maintenance in heroin addiction: evolution of a day program. *Amer. J. Nursing*, 70:2575-2577.

06678 **KROMKA, F.** (1979), Establishing of the criteria for measuring the effectiveness of state counseling of farmers. *Sociol. Ruralis*, (Assen) 19:160.

06679 **KRONICK, D.** (1978), Educational and counseling groups for parents. *Acad. Ther.*, 13:355-359.

06680 **KROTH, J. A.** (1973), *Counseling Psychology and Guidance: An Overview in Outline*. Springfield, IL: C. C. Thomas.

06681 **KROTKIEWSKI, M.** (1965), (Group therapy for obesity in a sanitarium.) *Wiad. Lekarski*, (Warsaw) 18:1845-1847.

06682 **KRUDER, H.**, and **HEFTNER, E.** (1975), (Free application as client-centered group therapy.) *Gruppenpsychother. & Gruppendynam.*, (Goettingen) 9:118-124.

06683 **KRUEGER, D. E.** (1971), Operant group therapy with delinquent boys using therapist's versus peer's reinforcement. *Dissert. Abstr. Internat.*, 31:6877B.

06684 **KRUEGER, D. W.** (1979), Clinical considerations in the prescriptions of group, brief, long-term and couples therapy. *Psychiat. Quart.*, 51:92.

06685 **KRUGER, H.** (1972), (Leadership styles and therapy concepts in social psychiatry.) *Nervenartz*, 43:181.

06686 **KRUGER, R. T.** (1978), (Dream-mechanisms and techniques of psychodrama-comparison.) *Gruppenpsychother. & Gruppendynam.*, (Goettingen) 13:172-200.

06687 **KRUGMAN, M.** (1953), The psychocultural approach in the Three Schools Project, Bronx: round table, 1952. *Amer. J. Orthopsychiat.*, 23:369-390.

06688 **KRUMBOLTZ, J. D.**, and **POTTER, B.** (1973), Behavioral techniques for developing trust, cohesiveness and goal accomplishment. *Educat. Technol.*, 13:26-30.

06689 **KRUSE, G.** (1961), (Experiences with autogenous group training in the outpatient department.) *Zeit. Aerztl. Fortbildung*, (Jena) 55:245-246.

06690 **KRUSE, W.** (1978), (Application of intentional formulas in therapy of children with autogenic training.) *Psychother. & Med. Psychol.*, (Stuttgart) 28:171-173.

06691 **KUBANY, A. J.** (1956), Peer nomination vs. sociometric choice. *Internat. J. Sociometry & Sociatry*, 1:99-100.

06692 **KUBIE, L. S.** (1958), Some theoretical concepts underlying the relationship between individual and group psychotherapies. *Internat. J. Group Psychother.*, 8:3-43.

06693 **KUBIE, L. S.** (1973), Unsolved problems in the use of group processes in psychotherapy. *J. Nerv. & Ment. Diseases*, 157:434-441.

06694 **KUBIE, S. H.**, and **LANDAU, G.** (1953), *Group Work with the Aged*. New York: International Universities Press.

06695 **KUCEK, P.** (1976), (The character of therapy and a number of underwent antialcoholic therapies as determinants of group interaction.) *Ceskoslov. Psychiat.*, (Prague) 72:390-396.

06696 **KUCH, K.**, **HARROWER, M.**, and **RENICK, J. T.** (1972), Observations on a time-extended group with campus volunteers. *Internat. J. Group Psychother.*, 22:471-487.

06697 **KUCHAN, A. M., JR.** (1965), Psychiatric nursing experience and group discussion as variables affecting attitudes toward the mentally ill. *Dissert. Abstr. Internat.*, 26:2870.

06698 **KUEHN, J.** (1974), Group counseling with undecided college students. *Vocat. Guid. Quart.*, 22:232-234.

06699 **KUEHN, J. L.**, and **CRINELLA, F. M.** (1969), Sensitivity training: interpersonal "overskill" and other problems. *Amer. J. Psychiat.*, 126:840-845.

06700 **KUESTER-GINSBERG, C.** (1972), How one's choice (of a way of life) may become a repressive authority. *Psychother. & Psychosomat.*, (Basel) 20:212-217.

06701 **KUGEL, L.** (1974), Combining individual and conjoint sessions in group therapy. *Hosp. & Community Psychiat.*, 25:795.

06702 **KUGELMASS, S.**, and **SCHOSSBERG, J.** (1958), Problems of initial training for group psychotherapy in Israel. *Internat. J. Group Psychother.*, 8:179-184.

06703 **KUHNE, G. E.** (1970), (Experiences with the patient group in the system of a flexible rehabilitation program in psychiatry.) *Psychiat., Neurol. & Med. Psychol.*, (Leipzig) 22:25-29.

06704 **KUIKEN, D., RASMUSSEN, R. V.**, and **CULLEN, D.** (1974), Some predictors of volunteer participation in human relations training groups. *Psychol. Reports*, 35:499-505.

06705 **KUIKEN, D. L.** (1972), Mythological parallels in t-groups. *Dissert. Abstr. Internat.*, 32:6538-6539A.

06706 **KUIPER, P. C.** (1969), Psychoanalytic group therapy. *Soc. Psychiat.*, 4:120-125.

06707 **KUIPER, P. C.** (1977), (Purpose of individual and group therapy.) *Praxis der Psychother.*, 22:145-151.

06708 **KULCAR, Z., SESO, M. E.**, and **MAJNARIC, V.** (1966), Group therapy of chronic patients in general medicine. *J. Med.*, 88:14-24.

06709 **KUNIHOLM, P. I.** (1967), Role of a psychotic member in a mothers' group at a child guidance clinic. *Sandoz Psychiat. Spectator*, 4:14-15.

06710 **KUNEMOTO, E. N.** (1972), Effects of nonverbal experiences on interpersonal communication. *Dissert. Abstr. Internat.*, 32:4954A.

06711 **KUNTZ, A. B.** (1967), An experimental evaluation of short term counseling with nonconforming adolescents. *Dissert. Abstr. Internat.*, 27:3290A.

06712 **KURASIK, S.** (1967), Group dynamics in the rehabilitation of hemiplegic patients. *J. Amer. Geriat. Soc.*, 15:852-855.

06713 **KUREGER, W. P.** (1973), Maximizing expectancy in psychotherapy: the role induction interview and verbalized expectations in behaviorally oriented group therapy. *Dissert. Abstr. Internat.*, 33:4513B.

06714 **KURILOFF, A. H.**, and **ATKINS, S.** (1966), T-group for a work team. *J. Appl. Behav. Science*, 2:63-93.

06715 **KURLAND, A. A.** (1952), Evaluation of drama therapy. *Psychiat. Quart. Suppl.*, 26:210-229.

06716 **KURLAND, A. A.** (1966), The narcotic addict: some reflections on treatment, *Maryland Med. J.*, 15:37-39.

06717 **KURODA, K.** (1973), Therapeutic camp with school phobic children. *Japanese J. Child Psychiat.*, (Tokyo) 14:254-257.

06718 **KURSH, A. J.** (1979), Changes in self concept and locus of control as a function of personal growth group design. *Dissert. Abstr. Internat.*, 41:409B.

06719 **KURSH, A. J.** (1980), Changes in self concept and locus of control as a function of personal growth group design. *Dissert. Abstr. Internat.*, 41:409B. (University Microfilms No. 8014497.)

06720 **KURT, H.** (1974), (Development, forms and aims of group psychotherapy.) *Orvosi Hetilop*, (Budapest) 115:123-129.

06721 **KURTZ, R. R.** (1974), Using a transactional analysis format in vocational group counseling. *J. Coll. Student Personnel*, 15:447-451.

06722 **KURZMAN, T. A.** (1975), Communication skills seminar: a nondrug approach to drug education. *Contemp. Drug Probl.*, 3:187-196.

06723 **KUSCH, E. H.**, and **LUCAS, L.** (1949), Group guidance in preparation for convalescent care. *Psychiat. Quart. Suppl.*, 23:345-362.
06724 **KUSH-GOLDBERG, C.** (1979), The health self-help group as an alternative source of health care for women. *Internat. J. Nursing Studies*, 16:283.
06725 **KUTASH, S. B.** (1968), Group psychotherapy and the educative process. *J. Group Psychoanal. & Process*, (London) 1:83-87.
06726 **KUTASH, S. B.** (1971), Values and dangers in group process experiences. *Group Process*, 3:7-11.
06727 **KUTNER, B.** (1968), Milieu therapy in rehabilitation medicine. *J. Rehab.*, 34:14-17.
06728 **KUTTER, D.** (1970), Aspekte der gruppentherapie. (Aspects of group therapy.) *Psyche*, (Stuttgart) 24:721-738.
06729 **KUTTER, P.** (1978), (Applied psychoanalysis in group therapy.) *Praxis der Psychother.*, 23:181-190.
06730 **KUTTER, P.** (1970), Aspects of group therapy. *Psyche*, 24:721-738.
06731 **KUTTER, P.** (1979), (Interactions of the group leader in the analytical self-experience group.) *Gruppenpsychother. & Gruppendynam.*, (Goettingen) 14:132-145.
06732 **KUTTER, P.** (1973), (Methods of psychoanalytic group work: part i.) *Zeit. Psychother. Med. Psychol.*, (Stuttgart) 23:15-23.
06733 **KUTTER, P.** (1973), Methods in psychoanalytic group work: part ii. *Zeit. Psychother. Med. Psychol.*, (Stuttgart) 23:51-54.
06734 **KUTTER, P.** (1978), Modelle psychoanalytischer gruppenpsychotherapie und das verhältnis von individuum und gruppe. (Models of psychoanalytic group psychotherapy and the relationship between individual and group.) *Gruppenpsychother. & Gruppendynam.*, (Goettingen) 13:134-151.
06735 **KUTTER, P.** (1971), (Transfer and process in psychoanalytic group therapy.) *Psyche*, (Stuttgart) 25:856-873.
06736 **KYLE, J. K.** (1976), Effects of the EPI-C model upon self-actualization of clients in group counseling. *Dissert. Abstr. Internat.*, 36:5049A.
06737 **KYMISSIS, P.** (1977), The use of paintings in analytic group psychotherapy. In: *Group Therapy 1977: An Overview*, ed. L. R. Wolberg. New York: Stratton Intercontinental Medical Books.
06738 **KYSER, M. L.** (1972), An explanatory study of the effects of group counseling upon community college students who are living at home. *Dissert. Abstr. Internat.*, 32:6133A.

L

06739 **LABARBERA, J. D.** (1980), Fathers who undermine children's treatment: a challenge for the clinician. *J. Clin. Child Psychol.*, 9:204.

06740 **L'ABATE, L.** (1977), *Enrichment: Structured Interventions with Couples, Families, and Groups*. Washington: University Press of America.

06741 **L'ABATE, L.**, and **ALLISON, M. Q.** (1977), Planned change intervention: the enrichment model with couples, families and groups. *Trans. Ment. Health Res. Newsl.*, 19:11-15.

06742 **L'ABATE, L., WEEKS, G. R.**, and **WEEKS, K. G.** (1978), Psychopathology as transaction: a historical note. *Internat. J. Fam. Couns.*, 6:60-65.

06743 **LABERD, W. G.** (1965), A therapeutic community in a general hospital psychiatric ward. *Med. Serv. J. Can.*, 21:389-397.

06744 **LABOURDETTE, I.**, and **ROCKLAND, L.** (1975), Developing a psychiatric residency program: focus on the community. *Hosp. & Community Psychiat.*, 26:279-282.

06745 **LABOVITZ, D. R.** (1978), The returning therapist: a group approach. *Amer. J. Occupat. Ther.*, 3:580-585.

06746 **LABOVITZ, S.**, and **HAGEDORN, R.** (1975), A structural-behavioral theory of intergroup antagonism. *Soc. Forces*, 53:444-448.

06747 **LaCALLE, J. J.** (1973), Group psychotherapy with Mexican-American drug addicts. *Dissert. Abstr. Internat.*, 34:1753B.

06748 **LACHENMEYER, C. W.** (1971), The effectiveness of "recreational" and "therapeutic" encounter with psychiatric patients. *J. Psychology*, 79:295-297.

06749 **LACHMANN, E. R.** (1949), Interview group therapy: process and effects. *Smith Coll. Studies Soc. Work*, 20:33-66.

06750 **LACHMANN, E. R.** (1949), Value of interview group therapy. *Smith Coll. Studies Soc. Work*, 19:113-114.

06751 **LaCOURSIERE, R.** (1980), *The Life Cycle of Groups: Group Developmental Stage Theory*. New York: Human Sciences Press.

06752 **LAEDER, R.**, and **FRANCIS, W. C.** (1968), Stuttering workshops: group therapy in a rural high school setting. *J. Speech & Hearing Disorders*, 33:38-41.

06753 **LaFAVE, H. G.**, and **BURKE, J. L.** (1965), Two intensive treatment programmes: nursing attitudes and evaluations. *Brit. J. Psychiatry*, 3:541-543.

06754 **LAFEBER, C.** (1967), (Group therapy of patients with anorexia nervosa.) *Voordrachtent. Nederl. Ver. Psychiat. Dienstverb*, 9:65-80.

06755 **LAFEBER, C., LANSEN, J.**, and **JONGERIUS, P. J.** (1967), Group therapy with anorexia nervosa patients. *Psychother. & Psychosomat.*, (Basel) 15:38.

06756 **LAFFAL, J., GROSSMAN, G., SAMEROFF, A. J.**, and **WINER, J.** (1967), Individual and group in group therapy. *J. Gen. Psychol.*, 76:113-123.

06757 **LAFFAL, J.**, and **SARASON, I. G.** (1957), Limited goal group psychotherapy on a locked service. *Diseases Nerv. System*, 18:63-66.

06758 **LATORGUE, R.** (1960), Familienneurosen in psychoanalystischer sicht. (Family neuroses in psychoanalytic view.) *Zeit. Psychosomat. Med. & Psychoanal.*, (Goettingen) 7:1-9.

06759 **LaFRANCE, S. C.** (1971), Developing ego strength in drug dependent persons through group therapy. *Correct. & Soc. Psychol.*, 4:171-182.

06760 **LAGO, D.**, and **HOFFMAN, S.** (1978), Structured group interaction: an intervention strategy for the continued development of elderly populations. *Internat. J. Aging & Human Develop.*, 8:311-324.

06761 **LAI, G.** (1964), Quelques considerations sur la psychothérapie de groupe de psychotiques. (Observations on group psychotherapy for psychotics.) *Acta Psychother., Psychosomat. Orthopaedagog.*, (Basel) 12:354-368.

06762 **LAI, G.** (1969), (Training of a psychiatrist: various considerations on training in the relational aspect of professional activity of social operators according to the method of human sciences.) *Evolut. Psychiat.*, (Toulouse) 34:775-788.

06763 **LAI, G., de PERROT, E.,** and **LAVANCHY, P.** (1966), La bifocalisation transferale dans l'association de la psychothérapie de groupe a la psychothérapie individuelle. (Bifocal transfer in combined group and individual psychotherapy.) *Evolut. Psychiat.*, (Toulouse) 31:33-50.

06764 **LAI, G.,** and **LAI, P.** (1968), Role du sexe des cotherapeutes dans la structuration dynamique des groups. (The sex of cotherapist and its role in the dynamic structure of groups.) *Annales Medico-Psychol.*, (Paris) 2:1-23.

06765 **LAINE, C. R.** (1974), A study of the impact of the Dreikurs parent study group method on parental attitudes toward and behavioral interaction with the school. *Dissert. Abstr. Internat.*, 34:6386A.

06766 **LAING, M. M.,** and **SCHULZ, E. D.** (1977), The planning and implementation of a psychiatric self-care unit, Mounds Park Hospital, St. Paul, Minnesota. *J. Psychiat. Nursing*, 15:30-34.

06767 **LAING, R. D.,** and **ESTERSON, A.** (1958), The collusion function of pairing in analytic groups. *Brit. J. Med. Psychol.*, (London) 31:117-123.

06768 **LAIR, C. V., SMITH, J. D.,** and **DEATON, A. N.** (1961), Combined group recreation and psychotherapy for hospitalized geriatric patients. *Geriatrics*, 16:598-603.

06769 **LAITMON, E.** (1979), Group counseling: sexuality and the hearing impaired adolescent. *Sex. Disabil.*, 2:169-177.

06770 **LAKE, R.** (1970), The varieties of communicative experience. *Compar. Group Studies*, 1:305-314.

06771 **LAKIN, M.** (1970), Group sensitivity training and encounter: uses and abuses of a method. *Couns. Psychologist*, 2:66-70.

06772 **LAKIN, M.** (1972), *Interpersonal Encounter: Theory and Practice in Sensitivity Training*. Hightstown, NJ: McGraw-Hill.

06773 **LAKIN, M.** (1969), Some ethical issues in sensitivity training. *Amer. Psychologist*, 24:923-928.

06774 **LAKIN, M.** (1979), What's happened to small group research: introduction. *J. Appl. Behav. Science*, 15:265-271.

06775 **LAKIN, M.,** and **CARSON, R. C.** (1964), Participant perception of group process in group sensitivity training. *Internat. J. Group Psychother.*, 14:116-122.

06776 **LAKIN, M.,** and **CARSON, R. C.** (1966), A therapeutic vehicle in search of a theory of therapy. *J. Appl. Behav. Science*, 2:27-40.

06777 **LAKIN, M.,** and **DOBBS, W. H.** (1962), The therapy group promotes an hypothesis of psychogenesis: a study in group process. *Internat. J. Group Psychother.*, 12:64-74.

06778 **LAKIN, M., LIEBERMAN, M. A.,** and **WHITAKER, D. S.** (1969), Issues in the training of group psychotherapists. *Internat. J. Group Psychother.*, 19:307-325.

06779 **LAKIN, M., LOMRANZ, J.,** and **LIEBERMAN, M. A.** (1969), *Arab and Jew in Israel: A Case Study in a Human Relations Approach to Conflict*. Washington, D.C.: National Institute for Applied Behavioral Science.

06780 **LAKIN, M.** (1977), Interactions among aged and group therapy intervention. *Gerontologist*, 17:85.

06781 **LAMB, D. W.** (1969), Demonstrated internal, external reward expectancies as a variable in group counseling. *Dissert. Abstr. Internat.*, 29:2568A.

06782 **LAMB, H. R.** (1967), Aftercare for former day hospital patients. *Hosp. & Community Psychiat.*, 18:342-344.
06783 **LAMB, H. R.**, and **GOERTZEL, V.** (1972), Evaluating aftercare for former day treatment centre patients. *Internat. J. Soc. Psychiat.*, (London) 18:67-78.
06784 **LAMBERT, C. S.** (1971), A video-modeling approach to group counseling. *Dissert. Abstr. Internat.*, 32:1275A.
06785 **LAMBERT, J. M.** (1979), Converting denial systems into personal power. *Fam. Ther.*, 6:65-69.
06786 **LAMM, H.** (1967), The effect of conceptual complexity and group discussion on risk taking and judgemental behavior. *Dissert. Abstr. Internat.*, 27:4144.
06787 **LAMOTT, K.** (1968), The year of group: eavesdropping on some highly intelligent neurotics. *New York Times Magazine* (Nov. 10) 28:87-104.
06788 **LAMPER, N.** (1967), Growing pains. *Voices*, 3:114, 130.
06789 **LANCASTER, J.** (1976), Working with schizophrenic patients. Activity groups as therapy: part 3. *Amer. J. Nursing*, 76:947-949.
06790 **LAND, E. C.** (1964), A comparison of patient improvement resulting from two therapeutic techniques. *Dissert. Abstr. Internat.*, 25:628-629.
06791 **LANDAU, M. E.** (1968), Group psychotherapy with deaf retardates. *Internat. J. Group Psychother.*, 18:345-351.
06792 **LANDER, N. R.** (1974), Levels of functioning of group members and the group process. *Dissert. Abstr. Internat.*, 34:7536A.
06793 **LANDERS, J. J.** (1957), Group therapy in H.M. Prison, Wormwood Scrubs. *Howard J. Penol. & Crime Prevention*, (London) 9:328-337.
06794 **LANDERS, J. J.**, **McPHAIL, D. S.**, and **SIMPSON, R. C.** (1954), Group theory in H.M. Prison, Wormwood Scrubs: the application of analytic psychology. *J. Ment. Science*, 100:953-960.
06795 **LANDGARTEN, H.** (1975), Group art therapy for mothers and daughters. *Amer. J. Art. Ther.*, 14:31-35.
06796 **LANDRETH, G. E.** (1966), Group counseling and varied time effects. *Dissert. Abstr. Internat.*, 27:1660A.
06797 **LANDRETH, G. C.** (1973), Group counseling: to structure or not to structure. *School Counselor*, 20:371-374.
06798 **LANDRETH, G. L.**, and **BERG, R. C.** (1979), Overcoming initial group leader anxiety: skills plus experience. *Personality & Guid. J.*, 58:65-66.
06799 **LANDSMAN, T.**, and **SHELDON, W. D.** (1949), Nondirective group psychotherapy with failing college students. *Amer. Psychologist*, 4:287.
06800 **LANDY, D.** (1965), Study of a halfway house. *Rehab. Record*, 6:14-16.
06801 **LANDY, E. E.** (1970), Attitude and attitude change toward interaction as a function of participation versus observation. *Compar. Group Studies*, 1:128-155.
06802 **LANG, E. F.** (1976), The effects of group counseling on selected culturally disadvantaged children. *Dissert. Abstr. Internat.*, 37:2638A.
06803 **LANG, F. A.** (1975), Effects of maternal group counseling on the academic achievement of high risk grade children. *Dissert. Abstr. Internat.*, 36:1309A.
06804 **LANG, N. C.** (1980), Review of B. Levine's *Group Psychotherapy: Practice and Development. Soc. Serv. Rev.*, 54:145-146.
06805 **LANG, N. C.** (1972), Social worker actions in response to group conditions representing three group forms. *Dissert. Abstr. Internat.*, 33:1842A.
06806 **LANGE, B. U.** (1970), Language: a bond in group therapy. *ANA Clin. Sessions*, 70:70-74.
06807 **LANGE, S.** (1970), Esalen: and afterward. *Nursing Outlook*, 18:33-35.
06808 **LANGE, S.** (1968), Nurse participation in action techniques. *ANA Clin. Sessions*, 279-285.

06810 **LANGEN, D.** (1965), (Clinical psychotherapy, methods and goals.) *Nervenarzt*, 36:254-257.

06811 **LANGEN, D.** (1958), Comments on "Code of ethics of group psychotherapists." *Group Psychother., Psychodrama & Sociometry*, 11:356-360.

06812 **LANGEN, D.** (1968), (Development towards modern group psychotherapy.) *Munchen Med. Wochenschr.*, (Munich) 110:2341-2347.

06813 **LANGEN, D.** (1957), Die besonderheiten der gruppenbehandlung bei klinischer psychotherapie. (Special aspects of group treatment with inpatient Psychotherapy. *Zeit. Diagnost. Psychol.*, 5:219-226.

06814 **LANGEN, D.** (1954), Die gruppentherapie in der Klinik. (Clinical group therapy.) *Arch. Psychiat. & Nervenkrankheiten*, 192:101-114.

06815 **LANGEN, D.** (1953), Die stationäre gruppenpsychotherapie. (The group psychotherapy unit.) *Zeit. Psychother. Med. Psychol.*, (Stuttgart) 3:193-204.

06816 **LANGEN, D.** (1960), (Difficulties at the beginning of group therapy: an experience report on group demonstrations.) *Zeit. Psychother. Med. Psychol.*, (Stuttgart) 10:65-70.

06817 **LANGEN, D.** (1963), (Difficulties in the training of group psychotherapists.) *Zeit. Psychother. Med. Psychol.*, (Stuttgart) 13:125-127.

06818 **LANGEN, D.** (1957), Gruppentherapeutischer indikationsbereich. (The scope of indications for group therapy.) *Zeit. Psychother. Med. Psychol.*, (Stuttgart) 7:116-125.

06819 **LANGEN, D.** (1953), La psicoterapia en grupo en el tratamiento sahatorial de las neurosis. *Folia Clin. Internac.*, (Barcelona) 3:114-115.

06820 **LANGEN, D.** (1980), (Review of D. Sander's *Psychodynamics in Small Groups.*) *Psychother. & Med. Psychol.*, (Stuttgart) 30:136.

06821 **LANGEN, D.** (1978), (Review of G. A. Leutz's *Classic Psychodrama According to J. L. Moreno.*) *Psychother. & Med. Psychol.*, (Stuttgart) 28:73.

06822 **LANGEN, D.** (1980), (Review of H. Christ's *Psychoanalytic Group Therapy in a Youth Detention Center.*) *Psychother. & Med. Psychol.*, (Stuttgart) 30:192.

06823 **LANGEN, D.** (1980), (Review of R. Battegay's *Humans in Group Psychotherapy, Vol. 3: Group Dynamics and Group Psychotherapy.*) *Psychother. & Med. Psychol.*, (Stuttgart) 30:136.

06824 **LANGEN, D.** (1980), (Review of R. Battegay's *Individual in the Group, Vol. 3: Group Dynamics and Group Therapy.*) *Psychother. & Med. Psychol.*, (Stuttgart) 30:45.

06826 **LANGEN, D.** (1958), (Sociometry in clinical group psychotherapy.) *Zeit. Psychother. Med. Psychol.*, (Stuttgart) 8:185-188.

06827 **LANGE-NIELSEN, F.**, and **RETTERSTOL, N.** (1959), Group psychotherapy in bronchial asthma. *Acta Psychiat. Scand. Suppl.*, (Copenhagen) 34:187-204.

06828 **LANGER, M.**, and **PUGET, J.** (1961), (A theoretic-scientific frame of reference of group therapy.) *Zeit. Psychother. Med. Psychol.*, (Stuttgart) 11:1-10.

06829 **LANGLOIS, P.**, and **TERAMOTO, V.** (1971), Helping patients cope with hospitalization. *Nursing Outlook*, 19:334-336.

06830 **LANGMAN-DORWART, N.** (1976), Planning and organizing a young adult social club. *J. Psychiat. Nursing*, 14:22-26.

06831 **LANGROD, J.**, and **LOWINSON, J.** (1972), Group therapy in the treatment of the juvenile narcotic addict. *Internat. Pharmacopsychiat.*, (Basel) 7:44-52.

06832 **LANGSLEY, D. G.** (1971), Avoiding mental hospital admission: a follow-up study. *Amer. J. Psychiat.*, 127:1391-1394.

06833 **LANKFORD, V.** (1972), Rapid identification of symbiosis. *Transactional Anal. J.*, 2:165-167.

06834 **LANNING, F. W.** (1956), Selected factors of group interaction and their relation with leadership performance. *Internat. J. Sociometry & Sociatry*, 1:170-175.
06835 **LANNING, W. L.** (1971), A study of the relation between group and individual supervision and three relationship measures. *J. Couns. Psychol.*, 18:401-406.
06836 **LANSEN, J.** (1977), Review of J. Huinck's *Getting Acquainted with Group Therapy. Tijdschr. Psychol.*, 19:814-815.
06837 **LANSKY, M. R.** (1977), Establishing a family-oriented inpatient unit. *J. Operat. Psychiat.*, 8:66-74.
06838 **LANTZ, J. E.** (1975), The rational treatment of parental adjustment reaction to adolescence. *Clin. Soc. Work J.*, 3:100-108.
06839 **LANTZ, J. E.**, and **WODARSKI, J. S.** (1974), Adolescent group therapy membership selection. *Clin. Soc. Work J.*, 2:172-181.
06840 **LAPIERRE, Y. D., LAVALLEE, J.**, and **TETREAULT, L.** (1973), Simultaneous mesoridazine and psychodrama in neurotics. *Internat. J. Clin. Pharmacol. & Biopharmacy*, (Munich) 7:62-66.
06841 **LAPINSKI, M.** (1973), (Group psychotherapy in the treatment of neuroses.) *Polski Tygodnik Lekarski*, (Warsaw) 28:368-371.
06842 **LAPINSKI, M.** (1972), (Method of treatment of neuroses based on group psychotherapy.) *Przeglad Lekarski*, (Warsaw) 29:775-779.
06843 **LaPOINTE, K. A.**, and **RIMM, D. C.** (1980), Cognitive, assertive, and insight-oriented group therapies in the treatment of reactive depression in women. *Psychother.: Theory, Res. & Pract.*, 17:312-321.
06844 **La PORTA, E.** (1964), (Group psychotherapy in psychotics.) *J. Brasil. Psiquiat.*, (Rio de Janeiro) 13:317-329.
06845 **LAPP, E. A.** (1962), Sociometry and group therapeutic experience in psychiatric occupational therapy. *Group Psychother., Psychodrama & Sociometry*, 15:36-39.
06846 **LAPP. E. A.** (1960), Sociometry and group therapy in the mental hospital. *Group Psychother., Psychodrama & Sociometry*, 13:135-152.
06847 **LAQUEUR, H. P.**, and **LEBOVIC, D.** (1968), Correlation between multiple family therapy, acute crises in a therapeutic community and drug levels. *Diseases Nerv. System*, 29:188-192.
06848 Large group therapy seen as an improvement over ward meetings (1970), *Roche Report: Front. Hosp. Psychiat.*, 7:1-2, 11.
06849 **LARGE, R. G.** (1976), The use of the role construct repertory grid in studying changes during psychotherapy. *Austral. & New Zeal. J. Psychiat.*, (Carlton) 10:315-320.
06850 **LaROCCO, J. M., BIERSNER, R. J.**, and **RYMAN, D. H.** (1975), Mood effects of large group counseling among navy recruits. *J. Consult. & Clin. Psychol.*, 22:127-131.
06851 **LaROSA, J. C., LIPSIUS, S. H.**, and **LAROSA, J. H.** (1974), Experiences with a combination of group therapy and methadone maintenance in the treatment of heroin addiction. *Internat. J. Addict.*, 9:605-609.
06852 **LARSEN, K. S.** (1971), Dogmatism and sociometric status as determinants of interaction in a small group. *Psychol. Reports*, 29:449-450.
06853 **LARSEN, P. T.** (1976), A study of the effects of group counseling on absentee prone high school sophomores. *Dissert. Abstr. Internat.*, 37:3311A.
06854 **LARSON, D., EASTER, P.**, and **WARD, B.** (1974), A group treatment program for masochistic patients. *Hosp. & Community Psychiat.*, 25:525-528.
06855 **LARSON, M. L.** (1973), From psychiatric to psychosocial nursing. *Nursing Outlook*, 21:520-523.
06856 **LaSALLE, A. J.** (1971), The effect of encounter and programmed group treatments on self-concept. *Dissert. Abstr. Internat.*, 32:1857A.

06857 **LASCHINSKY, D.**, and **KOCH, U.** (1975), T-groups: Origin, participants and goals. *Psychother. & Psychosomat.*, (Basel) 26:39-48.

06858 **LASH, M.**, and **SCHMITT, M. A.** (1978), Group-therapy with outpatients to facilitate functional communication and psychosocial adjustment. *Arch. Physical Med. & Rehab.*, 59:539.

06859 **LASKY, R. G.**, and **DELL ORTO, A. E.** (1979), *Group Counseling and Physical Disability: Rehabilitation and Health Care Perspectives*, North Scituate, MA: Duxbury Press.

06860 **LASSAR, B. T.** (1957), A study of the effects of group discussion on the attitudes of mothers toward their cerebral palsied children. Unpublished doctoral dissertation, New York University.

06861 **LASSITER, R. E.**, and **WILLETT, A. B.** (1973), Interaction of group co-therapists in the multidisciplinary team treatment of obesity. *Internat. J. Group Psychother.*, 23:82-92.

06862 **LASSNER, R.** (1947), Playwriting and acting as diagnostic therapeutic techniques with delinquents. *J. Clin. Psychol.*, 3:349-356.

06863 **LASSNER, R.** (1950), Psychodrama in prison. *Group Psychother., Psychodrama & Sociometry*, 3:77-91.

06864 **LASSNER, R.**, and **DEWEES, M.** (1955), Group psychotherapy as a form of rehabilitation service. *Delaware State Med. J.*, 27:194-198.

06865 **LATENDRESSE, J. D.**, and **KENNEDY, D. F.** (1961), Free discussion in teaching group therapy to residents. *Diseases Nerv. System*, 22:527-529.

06866 **LATHEY, R. K.** (1972), A comparison of change toward self-actualization in marathon group counseling and traditional group counseling. *Dissert. Abstr. Internat.*, 32:3692.

06867 **LATHROP, D. D.** (1968), Acting out in supportive group psychotherapy. *Voices*, 4:42-43.

06868 **LATORRE, R. A.** (1977), Protherapy role induction procedures. *Can. Psychol. Rev.*, 18:308-321.

06869 **LAU, J. B.** (1979), *Behavior in Organizations*. Homewood, IL: Richard D. Irwin.

06870 **LAUER, R.** (1972), Creative writing as a therapeutic tool. *Hosp. & Community Psychiat.*, 23:55-56.

06871 **LAUER, R.**, and **GOLDFIELD, M.** (1970), Creative writing in group therapy. *Psychother.: Theory, Res. & Pract.*, 7:248-252.

06872 **LAUFER, L. G.** (1968), Group therapy, sensitivity training groups and the industrial physician. *J. Occupat. Med.*, 10:124-126.

06873 **LAUGHLIN, H. P.** (1954), Approach to executive development: 5 years experience with analytically oriented groups of executives. *Diseases Nerv. System*, 15:12-22.

06874 **LAUGHLIN, H. P.** (1954), A group approach to management improvement. *Internat. J. Group Psychother.*, 4:165-171.

06875 **LAUGHLIN, H. P.**, and **HALL, M.** (1951), Psychiatry for executives: an experiment in the use of group analysis to improve relationships in an organization. *Amer. J. Psychiat.*, 107:493-497.

06876 **LAUGHLIN, K. D.** (1979), Effects of three different behavior therapies in the treatment of essential hypertension. *Dissert. Abstr. Internat.*, 40:5817B.

06877 **LAUGHLIN, P. R.**, and **DOHERTY, M. A.** (1967), Discussion versus memory in cooperative group concept attainment. *J. Educat. Psychol.*, 58:123-128.

06878 **LAVALLÉE, J.**, and **LAPIERRE, Y. D.** (1973), Free psychodrama or an introduced theme. *Can. Psychiat. Assn. J.*, (Ottawa) 18:505-509.

06879 **LAVIN, P. J.** (1972), The use of anecdotes in group counseling with socially maladjusted fourth, fifth, and sixth grade boys. *Dissert. Abstr. Internat.*, 32:5549-5550A.

06880 **LAVIOLETTE, J.** (1970), Experiences in group therapy. *Can. Nurse,* (Ottawa) 43:217-220.

06881 **LAVITOLA, G.** (1965), (Psychotherapy in the psychiatric hospitals.) *Arch. Neurobiol.,* (Madrid) 28:677-713.

06882 **LAVOIE, D.** (1973), The phenomenological transformation of the self-concept towards self-actualization through sensitivity training laboratory. *Interpersonal Develop.,* 2:201-212.

06883 **La VORGNA, D.** (1979), Group treatment for wives of patients with alzheimers disease. *Soc. Work & Health Care,* 5:219.

06884 **LAWANI, A. A.** (1967), First attempts at group therapy in a Nigerian mental hospital. *Brit. J. Psychiat. Soc. Work,* 9:3-7.

06885 **LAWLER, M. H.** (1980), Termination in a work group: four models of analysis and intervention. *Group,* 4:3-27.

06886 **LAWLOR, G.** (1946), Psychodrama in group therapy. *Sociometry,* 9:275-281.

06887 **LAWLOR, G. W.** (1947), Problems connected with setting up a psychodramatic unit. *Sociometry,* 9:168.

06888 **LAWLOR, G. W.** (1947), Role therapy. *Sociatry,* 1:51-55.

06889 **LAWLOR, G. W.** (1948), Two aids to the analysis of role behavior. *Sociatry,* 2:403-406.

06890 **LAWRENCE, H.,** and **SUNDEL, J.** (1972), Behavior modification in adult groups. *Soc. Work,* 17:34-43.

06891 **LAWRENCE, H.,** and **SUNDEL, M.** (1975), Self-modification in groups: a student training method for social groupwork. *J. Educat. Soc. Work,* 11:76-83.

06892 **LAWRENCE, R. M.,** and **KIELL, N.** (1961), Group guidance with college students. *Internat. J. Group Psychother.,* 11:78-87.

06893 **LAWRENCE, S. B.** (1969), Video tape and other therapeutic procedures with nude marathon groups. *Amer. Psychologist,* 24:476-479.

06894 **LAWTON, J. J., JR.** (1951), The expanding horizon of group Psychotherapy in schizophrenic convalescence. *Internat. J. Group Psychother.,* 1:218-224.

06895 **LAWTON, M. P.** (1967), Group methods in smoking withdrawal. *Arch. Environ. Health,* 14:258-265.

06896 **LAXENAIRE, M.** (1978), Introduction a l'ouverture de la table ronde sur le psychodrame. (Introduction to work of the round table on psychodrama.) *Psychother. & Psychosomat.,* (Basel) 29:262.

06897 **LAXENAIRE, M.,** and **PICARD, F.** (1969/1970), (Transference in group psychotherapy and psychodrama.) *Bull. de Psychol.,* (Paris) 23:715-725.

06898 **LAYCOCK, S. R.** (1947), The mental hygiene of classroom teaching. *Understanding the Child,* 16:39-43.

06899 **LAZARUS, A. A.** (1966), Behaviour rehearsal vs. non-directive therapy vs. advice in effecting behaviour change. *Behav. Res. & Ther.,* 4:209-212.

06900 **LAZARUS, A. A.** (1961), Group therapy of phobic disorders by systematic desensitization. *J. Abnorm. & Soc. Psychol.,* 63:504-510.

06901 **LAZARUS, H. R.,** and **BIENLEIN, D. K.** (1967), Soap opera therapy. *Internat. J. Group Psychother.,* 17:252-256.

06902 **LAZARUS, L. W.** (1976), A program for the elderly at a private psychiatric hospital. *Gerontologist,* 16:125-131.

06903 **LAZELL, E. W.** (1930), The group psychic treatment of dementia praecox by lectures in re-education. *U.S. Veterans' Admin. Med. Bull.,* 6:733-747.

06904 **LAZELL, E. W.** (1945), Group psychotherapy. *Sociometry,* 8:339-345.

06905 **LAZELL, E. W.** (1921), The group treatment of dementia praecox. *Psychoanal. Rev.,* 8:168-179.

06906 **LEADER, A. L.** (1947), The use of psychiatric social workers in conjunction with group therapy. *J. Soc. Casework,* 28:269-275.

06907 **LEAL, M. R. M.** (1966), Group-analytic play therapy with pre-adolescent girls. *Internat. J. Group Psychother.*, 16:58-64.

06908 **LEAR, T.** (1980), Unstructured large group learning of boundary phenomena. *Group Anal.*, (London) 13:164-168.

06909 **LEARD, H. M.** (1969), Group counseling: a study of changes that accompany operant reinforcement. *Dissert. Abstr. Internat.*, 29:2123A.

06910 **LEARNER, L.** (1955), A comparative study of the effects of individual and group wage incentive plans upon productivity and interpersonal relations. *Dissert. Abstr. Internat.*, 15:869.

06911 **LEARY, T.** (1955), The theory and measurement of interpersonal communication. *Psychiatry*, 18:147-161.

06912 **LEARY, T.**, and **COFFEY, H. S.** (1954), The prediction of interpersonal behavior in group psychotherapy. *Group Psychother., Psychodrama & Sociometry*, 7:7-51.

06913 **LEARY, T. F.** (1957), *Interpersonal Diagnosis of Personality*, New York: Ronald Press.

06914 **LEARY, T. F.**, and **HARVEY, J. S.** (1956), A methodology for measuring personality changes in psychotherapy. *J. Clin. Psychol.*, 12:123-132.

06915 **LEBEDINSKI, M. S.** (1960), Psychotherapy in the Soviet Union. *Group Psychother., Psychodrama & Sociometry*, 13:170-172.

06916 **LEBEDUN, M.** (1970), A technique for insuring good group attendance. *Psychother.: Theory, Res. & Pract.*, 7:138.

06917 **LeBLANC, A. F.** (1966), Making small groups more effective. *Pastoral Couns.*, 4:31-33.

06918 **LEBO, D.** (1953), The present status of research on nondirective play therapy. *J. Psychol., Couns.*, 17:177-183.

06919 **LEBOVICI, S.** (1974), A combination of psychodrama and group psychotherapy. In: *The Challenge for Group Psychotherapy: Present and Future*, 2d ed., ed. S. deSchill. New York: International Universities Press.

06920 **LEBOVICI, S.** (1955), A few remarks about the points proposed for discussion by Dr. Moreno. *Group Psychother., Psychodrama & Sociometry*, 8:173-177.

06921 **LEBOVICI, S.** (1969/1970), (A ledger of ten years practice of psychodrama with children and adolescents.) *Bull. de Psychol.*, (Paris) 23:839-888.

06922 **LEBOVICI, S.** (1953), A propos de la psychoanalyse de groupe. (On psychoanalysis in groups.) *Rev. Française Psychoanal.*, (Paris) 17:266-278.

06923 **LEBOVICI, S.** (1952), Ce que la psychotherapie apporte a la comprehension psychologique des groupes. (On the use of psychotherapy in the psychological understanding of groups.) *Bull. Grad. Studies Psychol. Univ. Paris*, 4:101-104.

06924 **LEBOVICI, S.** (1958), Group psychotherapy in France. *Internat. J. Group Psychother.*, 8:471-472.

06925 **LEBOVICI, S.** (1956), Psychoanalytical applications of psychodrama. *J. Soc. Ther.*, 2:280-291.

06926 **LEBOVICI, S.** (1956), Psychoanalytical group psychotherapy. *Group Psychother., Psychodrama & Sociometry*, 9:282-289.

06927 **LEBOVICI, S.** (1961), Psychodrama as applied to adolescents. *J. Child Psychol. & Psychiat.*, 1:298-305.

06928 **LEBOVICI, S.** (1956), Uses of psychodrama in psychiatric diagnosis. *Internat. J. Sociometry & Sociatry*, 1:175-180.

06929 **LEBOVICI, S., DIATKINE, R.**, and **KESTENBERG, E.** (1952), Applications of psychoanalysis to group psychotherapy and psychodrama therapy in France. *Group Psychother., Psychodrama & Sociometry*, 5:38-50.

06930 **LEBOVICI, S., DIATKINE, R.**, and **KESTENBERG, E.** (1958), *Bilan de Dix Ans de Therapeutique par le Psychodrame Chez l'Enfant et l'Adolescent.*

(*A Tally Sheet of Ten Years of Psychodrama Therapy at a Home for Children and Adolescents.*) Paris: Presses Universitares de France.
06931 **LEBOU, M. D.** (1973), The behavior modification process for parent-child therapy. *Fam. Coordinator*, 22:313-319.
06932 **LEBRAY, P. R.** (1979), Geropsychology in long-term care settings. *Prof. Psychol.*, 10:475-484.
06933 **LECHOWICZ, J.**, and **GAZDA, G.** (1975), Group counseling instruction: objectives established by experts. *Counselor Educat. & Supervision*, 15:21-27.
06934 **LEDEBUR, G. W.** (1977), The elementary learning disability process group and the school psychologist. *Psychol. in Schools*, 14:62-66.
06935 **LEDER, S.** (1963), (Apropos of group psychotherapy.) *Neurol. & Neurochir. Polska*, (Warsaw) 13:929-934.
06936 **LEDER, S.** (1963), (Group psychotherapy on psychiatric wards.) *Neurol. & Neurochir. Polska*, (Warsaw) 13:405-414.
06937 **LEDER, S.** (1970), Zum zusammenhang zwischentherapeutischen techniken und charakter und zusammensetzung der psychotherapeutischen gruppen. (On the relationship between therapeutic techniques and character and composition of the psychotherapeutic groups.) *Psychiat., Neurol. & Med. Psychol.*, (Leipzig) 22:369-373.
06938 **LEDERER, W.** (1971), Some moral dilemmas encountered in psychotherapy. *Psychiatry*, 34:75-85.
06939 **LEDERMAN, D. G.** (1958), Small group observation as a diagnostic technique. *Amer. J. Ment. Deficiency*, 63:64-71.
06940 **LEDERMAN, S.** (1974), Some ideas and gains in training paraprofessionals as group therapists. *J. Bronx State Hosp.*, 2:86.
06941 **LEDORT, S.**, and **GRUNEBAUM, H.** (1969), Group psychotherapy on alien turf. *Psychiat. Quart.*, 43:512-524.
06942 **LEE, D. Y.** (1977), Evaluation of a group counseling program designed to enhance social adjustment of mentally retarded adults. *Amer. J. Psychol.*, 24:318-323.
06943 **LEE, F.**, and **BEDNAR, R. L.** (1977), Effects of group structure and risk-taking disposition on group behavior, attitudes, and atmosphere. *J. Couns. Psychol.*, 24:191-199.
06944 **LEE, F. T.** (1976), The effects of sex, risk-taking, and structure on prescribed group behavior, cohesion, and evaluative attitudes in a simulated early training phase of group psychotherapy. *Dissert. Abstr. Internat.*, 36:4695-4696.
06945 **LEE, G. M.** (1963), Help for the helpers: a new role for community mental health centers. *J. Hillside Hosp.*, 12:134-139.
06946 **LEE, G. M.** (1964), Help for the helpers: a new role for community mental health centers. *J. Kansas Med. Soc.*, 65:24-26.
06947 **LEE, J. A.** (1977), Group work with mentally retarded foster adolescents. *Soc. Casework*, 58:164-173.
06948 **LEE, J. A.**, and **PARK, D. N.** (1978), A group approach to the depressed adolescent girl in foster care. *Amer. J. Orthopsychiat.*, 48:516-527.
06949 **LEE, W. G.** (1971), Differences in self-concept changes among three educative treatments. *Dissert. Abstr. Internat.*, 32:6622B.
06950 **LEEDY, J. J.** (1962), Charlie's wife. *Group Psychother., Psychodrama & Sociometry*, 15:89-90.
06951 **LEEDY, J. J.** (1969), *Poetry Therapy: The Use of Poetry in the Treatment of Emotional Disorders.* Philadelphia: J. B. Lippincott.
06952 **LEEMAN, C. P.** (1970), Dependency, anger, and denial in pregnant diabetic women: a group approach. *Psychiat. Quart.*, 44:1-12.
06953 **LEEPSON, R. E.** (1980), Psychodramatic treatment of the schizoid personality. *Group Psychother., Psychodrama & Sociometry*, 33:121-127.

06954 **LEFFINGWELL, R. J.** (1972), A study of the generalization of the effects of group, systematic desensitization of test anxiety on co-existent anxiety in college students. *Dissert. Abstr. Internat.*, 7313B.

06955 **LEGER, L.** (1979), Review of A. S. Goldstein's, R. P. Sprafkin's and N. J. Gershaw's *Skill Training for Community Living: Applying Structural Learning Therapy. Brit. J. Soc. & Clin. Psychol.*, (London) 18:259.

06956 **LEGO, S.** (1973), Continuing education by mail. *Amer. J. Nursing*, 73:840-841.

06957 **LEGO, S.** (1979), Division on psychiatric and mental health nursing practice: treatment of the acting out borderline patient in private practice—clinical and scientific sessions. *Ana. Publ. Div. Pract.*, 333-341.

06958 **LEGO, S.** (1966), Five functions of the group therapist: twenty sessions later. *Amer. J. Nursing*, 66:795-797.

06959 **LEGO, S.** (1979), Treatment of the acting out borderline patient in private practice. *ANA Clin. Sessions*, 59:333-341.

06960 **LEHMAN-OLSON, P. J.** (1975), Cognitive-behavioral approaches to the reduction of anger and aggression. *Dissert. Abstr. Internat.*, 35:5118-5119.

06961 **LEHMANN, L.**, and **TOURLENTES, T. T.** (1963), The drama workshop. *Ment. Hosp.*, 14:158-162.

06962 **LEHMENKUHLER, R.**, and **LEUSCHNER, G.** (1977), (Conflict analysis and conflict management in a large group.) *Gruppenpsychother. & Gruppendynam.*, (Goettingen) 11:171-183.

06963 **LEHNHARDT, K.** (1965), (Practical experiences with open groups of parents in a child guidance center: report based on a catamnestic interview with parents.) *Praxis Kinderpsychol. & Kinderpsychiat.*, (Goettingen) 14:125-140.

06964 **LEHRER-CARLE, I.** (1971), Group music with schizophrenics. *J. Contemp. Psychother.*, 2:111-116.

06965 **LEHRMAN, N. S.**, and **FRIEDMAN, J. H.** (1970), A treatment-focused geriatric program in a state mental hospital. *Ment. Health Digest*, 2:8-10.

06966 **LEIB, J. W.** (1971), The effects of group relaxation training and group discussion on verbal productivity: some implications for group therapy. *Dissert. Abstr. Internat.*, 31:5000-5001B.

06967 **LEIB, J. W.**, and **SNYDER, W. V.** (1967), Effects of group discussions on under-achievement and self-actualization. *J. Couns. Psychol.*, 14:282-285.

06968 **LEIBERMAN, F.** (1964), Transition from latency to prepuberty in girls: an activity group becomes an interview group. *Internat. J. Group Psychother.*, 14:455-463.

06969 **LEIBL, R. D.** (1972), Treating schizophrenia. *Transactional Anal. J.*, 2:177-179.

06970 **LEIBLUM, S. R.**, and **ERSNER-HERSCHFIELD, R.** (1977), Sexual enhancement groups for dysfunctional women: an evaluation. *J. Sex & Marital Ther.*, 3:139-152.

06971 **LEIBLUM, S. R., ROSEN, R. C.**, and **PIERCE, D.** (1976), Group treatment format: mixed sexual dysfunctions. *Arch. Sexual Behav.*, 5:313-322.

06972 **LEICHTER, E.** (1966), The interrelationship of content and process in therapy groups. *Soc. Casework*, 47:302-306.

06973 **LEICHTER, E.** (1977), (Multi-family group therapy: a multidimensional solution.) *Praxis Kinderpsychol. & Kinderpsychiat.*, (Goettingen) 26:169-176.

06974 **LEICHTER, E.** (1963), Use of group dynamics in the training and supervision of group therapists in a social agency. *Internat. J. Group Psychother.*, 13:74-79.

06975 **LEICHTER, E.**, and **SCHULMAN, G. L.** (1972), Interplay of group and family treatment techniques in multifamily group therapy. *Internat. J. Group Psychother.*, 22:167-176.

06976 **LEICHTER, E.**, and **SCHULMAN, G. L.** (1968), Emerging phenomena in multi-family group treatment. *Internat. J. Group Psychother.*, 18:59-69.

06977 **LEIGH, K. B.** (1975), The effectiveness of a parent group training program with-and-without social models. *Dissert. Abstr. Internat.*, 36:2109A.

06978 **LEIK, R. K.** (1967), The distribution of acts in small groups. *Sociometry*, 30:280-299.

06979 **LEINHARDT, S.** (1972), Developmental change in the sentiment structure of children's groups. *Amer. Sociol. Rev.*, 37:202-212.

06980 **LEITERMAN, P. H.** (1970), Attitudinal and behavioral changes in self-directed and leader-directed personal growth groups. *Dissert. Abstr. Internat.*, 32:741A.

06981 **LEITH, W. R.**, and **UHLEMANN, M. R.** (1972), The shaping group approach to stuttering: a pilot study. *Compar. Group Studies*, 3:175-199.

06982 **LELAND, H.**, and **SMITH, D.** (1962), Unstructured material in play therapy for emotionally disturbed, brain damaged mentally retarded children. *Amer. J. Ment. Deficiency*, 66:621-628.

06983 **LELAND, H.**, **WALKER, J.**, and **TABOADA, A. N.** (1959), Group play therapy with a group of post-nursery male retardates. *Amer. J. Ment. Deficiency*, 63:848-851.

06984 **LeMAY, M.** (1969/1970), (Reflections on triadic psychodrama with children and adolescents in a medico-psycho-pedagogical treatment center.) *Bull. de Psychol.*, (Paris) 23:784-792.

06985 **LeMAY, M. L.**, and **CHRISTENSEN, O. C., JR.** (1968), The uncontrollable nature of control groups. *J. Couns. Psychol.*, 15:63-67.

06986 **LEMERT, E. M.**, and **van RIPER, C.** (1944), The use of psychodrama in the treatment of speech defects. *Sociometry*, 7:190-195.

06987 **LEMLIJ, M.** (1978), Primitive group treatment. *Psychiat. Clin.*, (Basel) 11:10-14.

06988 **LEMOINE, G.** (1969/1970), (The imagined, the symbolic and the real confronted in the psychodrama experience.) *Bull. de Psychol.*, (Paris) 23:895-903.

06989 **LEMOINE, P.** (1969/1970), (Oedipus and its referents in psychodrama.) *Bull. de Psychol.*, (Paris) 23:904-907.

06990 **LENERT, M. H.** (1947), Eight original monodramas for speech personality therapy and development. *Speech Monogr.*, 4:211.

06991 **LENN, T. I.**, **LANE, P. A.**, **MERRIT, E. T.**, and **SILVERSTONE, L.** (1967), Parent group therapy for adolescent rehabilitation: an exploratory study. *J. Educat.*, 7:17-26.

06992 **LENNARD, H. L.**, and **BERNSTEIN, A.** (1969), *Patterns in Human Interaction*, San Francisco: Jossey-Bass.

06993 **LENNARD, H. L.**, **EPSTEIN, L. J.**, and **KATZUNG, B. G.** (1967), Psychoactive drug action and group interaction process. *J. Nerv. & Ment. Diseases*, 145:69-78.

06994 **LENNEER-AZELSON, B.**, and **THYLEFORS, I.** (1979), *Arbetsgruppens Psykologi. (Groupwork Psychology.)* Stockholm: Natur och kultur.

06995 **LENNHOFF, F. G.** (1960), *Exceptional Children: Residential Treatment of Emotionally Disturbed Boys at Shotton Hall*, London: Allen and Unwin.

06996 **LENNON, P.** (1964), The first international congress of psychodrama, press reports: the truth bringers. *Group Psychother., Psychodrama & Sociometry*, 17:89-91.

06997 **LENNUNG, S.** (1974/1975), Implicit theories in experiential group practices: a pedagogical approach. *Interpersonal Develop.*, 5:37-49.

06998 **LENNUNG, S.**, and **AHLBERG, A.** (1975), The effects of laboratory training: a field experiment. *J. Appl. Behav. Science*, 11:177-188.

06999 **LENNUNG, S. A.** (1974), *Meta-Learning, Laboratory Training, and Individually Different Change: A Study on the Effects of Laboratory Training*, Sturegatan: Swedish Council for Personnel Administration.

07000 **LENTCHNER, L. H.** (1968), Group behavior therapy in a workshop setting. *Correct. Psychiat. & J. Soc. Ther.*, 14:84-95.

07001 **LEO, P. F.** (1972), The effects of two types of group counseling upon the academic achievement and self-concept of Mexican-American pupils in the elementary schools. *Dissert. Abstr. Internat.*, 33:1442A.

07002 **LEON, H. V.** (1968), Reciprocal inhibition: an evaluation of group procedures with "normal" snake phobic subjects. *Dissert. Abstr. Internat.*, 28:3878-3879.

07003 **LEON, L. E.** (1972), Attitude change, as a result of t-group sessions in a pre-teaching population. *Dissert. Abstr. Internat.*, 33:1442A.

07004 **LEON, R.** (1973), An experiment with early group counseling practicum in a Chicano counselor training program. *Dissert. Abstr. Internat.*, 33:4840A.

07005 **LEONARD, A. R.**, and **HEIMAN, E. M.** (1972), Small group discussions in a neighborhood health center as a teaching aid. *J. Med. Educat.*, 47:294-296.

07006 **LEONARD, G. B.** (1969), How to have a bloodless riot. *Look*, 33:24-28.

07007 **LEONE, D.**, and **ZAHOUREK, R.** (1974), "Aloneness" in a therapeutic community. *Perspect. Psychiat. Care*, 12:60-63.

07008 **LEOPOLD, H.** (1961), The new member in the group: some specific aspects of the literature. *Internat. J. Group Psychother.*, 11:367-371.

07009 **LEOPOLD, H.** (1957), Selection of patients for group psychotherapy. *Amer. J. Psychother.*, 11:634-637.

07010 **LEOPOLD, H. S.** (1959), The problem of working through in group psychotherapy. *Internat. J. Group Psychother.*, 9:287-292.

07011 **LEOPOLD, H. S.** (1976), Selective group approaches with psychotic patients in hospital settings. *Amer. J. Psychother.*, 30:95-103.

07012 **LePAGE, H. L.** (1974), Group process and outcome: a study of interaction patterns and changes in self-actualization among three marathon encounter groups varying in levels of self-actualization. *Dissert. Abstr. Internat.*, 35:5027A.

07013 **LePONTOIS, J.** (1975), Adolescents with sickle-cell anemia deal with life and death. *Soc. Work & Health Care*, 1:71-80.

07014 **LEPPER, M.** (1972), (Group therapy with smokers.) *Der Rehab.*, (Bonn) 25:95-97.

07015 **LERER, I.** (1964), Psicodrama aplicado a la pedagogia educacional. (Psychodrama applied to educational pedagogy.) *Rev. Mexicana Pedagog.*, 1:363-367.

07016 **LERER, I. E.**, and **COLOSIMO, E.** (1966), Psicodrama aplicado a la labor educacional. *(Psychodrama used in education.) Rev. Mexicana Psicol.*, (Jalisco) 2:847-853.

07017 **LERMAN, C. A.**, and **BARON, A.** (1981), Depression management training: a structured group approach. *Personnel & Guid. J.*, 60:86-88.

07018 **LERNER, A.** (1954), Considerations of content material of group counseling sessions with jailed alcoholics. *Quart. J. Studies Alcohol*, 15:432-452.

07019 **LERNER, A.** (1953), An experiment in group counseling with male alcoholic inmates. *Fed. Probat.*, 17:37-39.

07020 **LERNER, A.** (1953), An exploratory approach in group counseling with male alcoholic inmates in a city jail. *Quart. J. Studies Alcohol*, 14:427-467.

07021 **LERNER, A.** (1954), Interaction among male alcoholic inmates. *Soc. Serv. Res.*, 38:313-319.
07022 **LERNER, A.** (1973), Poetry therapy. *Amer. J. Nursing*, 73:1336-1338.
07023 **LERNER, A.** (1958), Research and the group method in a city jail setting. *Group Psychother., Psychodrama & Sociometry*, 11:150-152.
07024 **LERNER, A.** (1955), Self-evaluation in group counseling with male alcoholic inmates. *Internat. J. Group Psychother.*, 5:286-298.
07025 **LERNER, R. D.** (1975), (Combined individual and group psychotherapy.) *Acta Psiquiat. Psicol. Amer. Latina*, (Buenos Aires) 21:118-128.
07026 **LERNER, H. E.** (1980), One therapist's absence in cotherapy work: facilitative effects. *Small Group Behav.*, 11:193-208.
07027 **LERNER, H. E., HORWITZ, L.,** and **BURSTEIN, E. D.** (1978), Teaching psychoanalytic group-psychotherapy: combined experiential-didactic workshop. *Internat. J. Group Psychother.*, 28:453-466.
07028 **LERNER, S.** (1966), Discussion: group therapy from the perspective of a large family agency. *J. Jewish Communal Serv.*, 42:255-258.
07029 **LERO, A.** (1969), (Family group therapy: a preliminary report.) *Ugeskr. for Laeger*, 131:851-852.
07030 **LESHNER, M.** (1967), Attitude change: a comparison study of multiple role-playing and group discussion under conditions of effort, exposure, and direction. *Dissert. Abstr. Internat.*, 28:1166-1167.
07031 **LESKIN, L.** (1965), Training experiences in psychodrama. *Group Psychother., Psychodrama & Sociometry*, 18:166-170.
07032 **LESLIE, R. C.** (1955), Group therapy: a new approach for the church. *Pastoral Psychol.*, 6:9-14.
07033 **LESLIE, R. C.** (1956), *Group Therapy as a Method for Church Work.* Madison, WI: Microcard Foundation for the American Theological Library Association.
07034 **LESLIE, R. C.** (1949), Group therapy for emotional re-education. *J. Pastoral Care & Couns.*, 3:1-5.
07035 **LESLIE, R. C.** (1950), Pastoral group psychotherapy. *Group Psychother., Psychodrama & Sociometry,* 3:68-73.
07036 **LESLIE, R. C.** (1951), Pastoral group psychotherapy. *J. Pastoral Care & Couns.*, 6:56-61.
07037 **LESSER, I. M.,** and **FRIEDMANN, C. T. H.** (1980), Beyond medications: group therapy for the chronic psychiatric patient. *Internat. J. Group Psychother.*, 30:187-199.
07038 **LESSIN, S., FINNILA, M.,** and **GORELICK, M. C.** (1969), A marathon workshop: help for the retarded child with management problems. *Child Welfare*, 48:560-563.
07039 **LESSING, R. A.** (1976), Staff perceptions of treatment benefits & treatment failures at a Synanon-oriented therapeutic community. *Dissert. Abstr. Internat.*, 36:7869-7870.
07040 **LESSMAN, S. E.** (1978), Group treatment of epileptics. *Health & Soc. Work*, 3:105-121.
07041 **LESSNER, J. W.** (1974), The poem as catalyst in group counseling. *Personnel & Guid. J.*, 53:33-38.
07042 **LESSOFF, B.** (1977), What to say when . . . *Clin. Soc. Work J.*, 5:66-76.
07043 **LESSOR, L. R.** (1971), Time-extended group treatment sessions. *Soc. Casework*, 52:97-103.
07044 **LETNER, R. C.** (1970), The effect of group counseling on the self-concept as measured by the Tennessee self-concept scale. *Dissert. Abstr. Internat.*, 30:2803A-2804A.
07045 **LETON, D. A.** (1957), An evaluation of group methods in mental hygiene. *Ment. Hygiene*, 41:525-533.

07046 **LETT, W. R.** (1973), The relevance and structure of human relations training in Teacher Education. *Austral. J. Psychol.*, (Parkville) 8:17-27.
07047 **LEUNER, H.** (1960), (The performance, indications and limitations of the symbol drama: results with the experimental catathymic life picture.) *Zeit. Psychother. Med. Psychol.*, (Stuttgart) 10:45-52.
07048 **LEUNER, H. C.** (1969), (The stage of development of guided affective imagery.) *Zeit. Psychother. Med. Psychol.*, (Stuttgart) 19:177-187.
07049 **LEUTZ, G. A.** (1975), (Imagination and psychodrama.) *Gruppendynamik*, (Stuttgart) 2:97-104.
07050 **LEUTZ, G. A.** (1977), The integrative force of psychodrama in present-day psychotherapy. *Group Psychother., Psychodrama & Sociometry*, 30:163-172.
07051 **LEUTZ, G. A.** (1959), Sociometry in its relation to psychodrama. *Acta Psychother., Psychosomat. Orthopaedagog. Suppl.*, (Basel) 7:224-231.
07052 **LEUTZ, G.**, and **TEIRICH, H.** (1958), Group psychotherapy in Germany. *Group Psychother., Psychodrama & Sociometry*, 11:177-186.
07053 **LeVAY, A. N.**, and **KAGLE, A.** (1978), Recent advances in sex therapy: integration with the dynamic therapies. *Psychiat. Quart.*, 50:5-16.
07054 **LeVAY, M.**, and **RATHOD, N. H.** (1963), Concurrent treatment groups of mothers and children. *Amer. J. Psychiat.*, 119:1169-1171.
07055 **LEVENE, R. I.** (1980), The effects of microcounseling-personal growth groups and microcounseling-only groups on the self-actualization of community college students. *Dissert. Abstr. Internat.*, 41:2455A. (University Microfilms No. 8026341.)
07056 **LEVENSTEIN, J., JACOBS, A.**, and **COHEN, S. H.** (1977), The effects of feedback as interpersonal reciprocities. *Small Group Behav.*, 8:415-432.
07057 **LEVEQUE, J.**, and **LEVEQUE, M.** (1963), (Attempt at a didactic form of group psychotherapy in the treatment of chronic alcoholism.) *J. Med. Bordeaux*, 140:731-737.
07058 **LeVIEGE, R. O.** (1973), *Group Relations: Group Therapy with Mentally Ill Offenders.* New York: Vantage.
07059 **LEVIN, E. M.** (1974), Effects of a structured and nonstructured small group experience on counselor candidates' self-concept, interpersonal orientation, and perceptions of the group experience. *Dissert. Abstr. Internat.*, 34:5635A.
07060 **LEVIN, E. M.**, and **KURTZ, R. R.** (1974), Structured and nonstructured human relations training. *J. Couns. Psychol.*, 21:526-531.
07061 **LEVIN, P.**, and **BERNE, E.** (1972), Games nurses play. *Amer. J. Nursing*, 72:483-487.
07062 **LEVÍN, R.**, and **RIVELISDEPAZ, L.** (1970), Aportes para una teoria de la técnica en psicoterapia grupal: grupos de duración limitadade niños en edad de latencia. (Contributions to the theory of the technique for group psychotherapy: short-term groups for children in latency age.) *Acta Psiquiat. Psicol. Amer. Latina*, (Buenos Aires) 16:265-268.
07063 **LEVIN, S.** (1963), Some comparative observations of psychoanalytically oriented group and individual psychotherapy. *Amer. J. Orthopsychiat.*, 33:148-160.
07064 **LEVIN, S.**, and **KANTER, S. S.** (1964), Some general considerations in the supervision of beginning group psychotherapists. *Internat. J. Group Psychother.*, 14:318-331.
07065 **LEVINE, B.** (1979), *Group Psychotherapy: Practice and Development.* Englewood Cliffs, NJ: Prentice-Hall.
07066 **LEVINE, B.**, and **SCHILD, J.** (1969), Group treatment of depression. *Soc. Work*, 14:46-52.
07067 **LEVINE, B. E.**, and **POSTON, M.** (1980), A modified group treatment for elderly narcissistic patients. *Internat. J. Group Psychother.*, 30:153-167.

07068 **LEVINE, F. M., FASNACHT, G., FUNABIKI, D.,** and **BURKART, M. R.** (1979), Methodological considerations regarding the evaluations of maintenance of gains due to token programs. *Psychol. in Schools*, 16:568.
07069 **LEVINE, H. B.** (1980), Milieu biopsy: the place of the therapy group on the inpatient ward. *Internat. J. Group Psychother.*, 30:77-93.
07070 **LEVINE, H. B.** (1978), Review of L. R. Wolberg's and M. L. Aronson's *Group Therapy 1977: An Overview. Internat. J. Group Psychother.*, 28:565-567.
07071 **LEVINE, M.,** and **BUNKER, B. B.** (1975), *Mutual Criticism*. Syracuse, NY: Syracuse University Press.
07072 **LEVINE, N.,** and **COOPER, C. L.** (1976), T-groups: twenty years on a prophecy. *Human Relat.*, 29:1-23.
07073 **LEVINE, S. D.** (1974), A study of the effects of group counseling on religious attitudes and verbal behaviors of members of a conservative synagogue. *Dissert. Abstr. Internat.*, 35:1982.
07074 **LEVINSON, B. L., SHAPIRO, D., SCHWARTZ, G. E.,** and **TURSKY, B.** (1971), Smoking elimination by gradual reduction. *Behav. Ther.*, 2:477.
07075 **LEVINSON, D. A.,** and **JENSEN, S. M.** (1967), Assertive versus passive group therapist behavior with Southern White and Negro schizophrenic hospital patients. *Internat. J. Group Psychother.*, 17:328-335.
07076 **LEVINSON, H. M.** (1973), Use and misuse of groups. *Soc. Work*, 18:66-73.
07077 **LEVINSON, R. B., INGRAM, G. L.,** and **AZCARATE, E.** (1968), "Aversive" group therapy. *Crime & Delinquency*, 14:336-339.
07078 **LEVINSON, V. R.** (1979), The decision group: beginning treatment in an alcoholism clinic. *Health & Soc. Work*, 4:199.
07079 **LEVITT, L.** (1968), Rehabilitation of narcotic addicts among lower-class teenagers. *Amer. J. Orthopsychiat.*, 38:56-62.
07080 **LEVITT, M.,** and **RUBENSTEIN, B. O.** (1959), Acting out in adolescence: a study in communication. *Amer. J. Orthopsychiat.*, 29:622-632.
07081 **LEVY, D. M.** (1966), *Maternal Overprotection*. New York: W. W. Norton.
07082 **LEVY, E., FALTICO, G.,** and **BRATTER, T. E.** (1977), The development and structure of the drug-free therapeutic community. *Addict. Ther.*, 2:40-52.
07083 **LEVY, E. E.** (1972), Activate: don't vegetate. *Nursing Homes*, 21:29-30.
07084 **LEVY, G.,** and **DERRIEN, J.** (1975), (Concerning a trial of group therapy with games for children from eight to eleven years of age, organized by two therapists.) *Rev. Neuropsychiat. Infantile*, (Paris) 23:313-328.
07085 **LEVY, J.** (1971), Group responses to simulated erotic experiences in a theatrical production. *Internat. J. Group Psychother.*, 21:275-287.
07086 **LEVY, J., TROSSMAN, B., KRAVITZ, H., ROBERTSON, B.,** and **DOW, T.** (1973), Inpatients in love: conjoint therapy of two adolescents. *Can. Psychiat. Assn. J.*, (Ottawa) 18:435-438.
07087 **LEVY, J. S.** (1979), Factors bearing on role definition and dilemmas of therapists in training. *Dissert. Abstr. Internat.*, 41:356B.
07088 **LEVY, L. H.** (1964), Group variance and group attractiveness. *J. Abnorm. & Soc. Psychol.*, 68:661-664.
07089 **LEVY, L. H.** (1976), Self-help groups: types and psychological processes. *J. Appl. Behav. Science*, 12:310-322.
07090 **LEVY, M. M.** (1950), Outdoor group therapy with preadolescent boys. *Psychiatry*, 13:333-347.
07091 **LEVY, R. B.** (1969), *Human Relations: A Conceptual Approach*. Scranton: International Textbooks.
07092 **LEVY, R. B.** (1948), Psychodrama and the philosophy of cultural education. *Sociatry*, 2:225-234.

07093 **LEVY, S. J.** (1972), An empirical study of disclosing behavior in a verbal encounter group. *Dissert. Abstr. Internat.*, 5896A.

07094 **LEVY-LeBOYER, C.** (1963), Comportement social et caracteristiques individuelles: etude des participants a un groupe restreint. (Social behavior and individual characteristics: a study of members of a controlled group.) *Monogr. Francaise Psychol.*, 10.

07095 **LEWIN, B.** (1963), (Group therapy of chronic alcoholism.) *Zeit. Psychother. Med. Psychol.*, (Stuttgart) 13:101-107.

07096 **LEWIN, H. S.** (1950), The use of religious elements in modern psychotherapy. *J. Pastoral Care*, 4:9-16.

07097 **LEWIN, K., LIPPITT, R.,** and **WHITE, R.** (1939), Patterns of aggressive behavior in experimentally created "social climates." *J. Soc. Psychol.*, 10:271-299.

07098 **LEWIN, K. K.** (1970), *Brief Encounters: Brief Psychotherapy*. St. Louis: Green.

07099 **LEWIN, M. H.** (1961), Change in social desirability responses as a function of direct instructions, verbal reinforcement, role playing and counterconditioning. Ph.D. thesis, University of Wisconsin.

07100 **LEWINSOHN, P. M., WEINSTEIN, M. S.,** and **ALPER, T.** (1970), A behavioral approach to the group treatment of depressed persons: a methodological contribution. *J. Clin. Psychol.*, 26:525-532.

07101 **LEWIS, A.** (1963), Attitudes of geriatric patients toward planned activity. *Geriatrics*, 18:725-728.

07102 **LEWIS, B.** (1958), Report: a demonstration by J. L. and Zerka Moreno. *Group Psychother., Psychodrama & Sociometry*, 11:87-88.

07103 **LEWIS, B. F.** (1977), Group silences. *Small Group Behav.*, 8:109-120.

07104 **LEWIS, D. J.** (1971), Some approaches to the evaluation of milieu therapy. *Can. Psychiat. Assn. J.*, (Ottawa) 16:203-208.

07105 **LEWIS, G. H.** (1970), Bales' Monte Carlo model of small group discussions. *Sociometry*, 33:20-36.

07106 **LEWIS, G. H.** (1971), Organization in communication networks. *Compar. Group Studies*, 2:149-160.

07107 **LEWIS, J.** (1972), Effects of group procedure with parents of MR children. *Ment. Retard.*, 10:14-15.

07108 **LEWIS, J.,** and **MIDER, P. A.** (1973), Effects of leadership style on content and work styles of short-term therapy groups. *Couns. Psychologist*, 20:137-141.

07109 **LEWIS, J. A.** (1972), Counselors and women: finding each other. *Personnel & Guid. J.*, 51:147-150.

07110 **LEWIS, J. E.** (1976), Relationships of a-b type and other therapist personality characteristic to leadership styles in short-term therapy groups. *Dissert. Abstr. Internat.*, 36:5266.

07111 **LEWIS, J. H.** (1970), The effect of a group procedure on selected parents of mentally retarded children. *Dissert. Abstr. Internat.*, 31:4553A.

07112 **LEWIS, J. M.,** and **OSBERG, J. W.** (1958), Treatment of the narcotic addict: ii. observations on institutional treatment of character disorders. *Amer. J. Orthopsychiat.*, 28:730-749.

07113 **LEWIS, M. I.,** and **BUTLER, R. N.** (1974), Life-review therapy: putting memories to work in individual and group psychotherapy. *Geriatrics*, 29:165-173.

07114 **LEWIS, N. D. C.** (1948), Review of psychiatric progress, 1947: general clinical psychiatry, psychosomatic medicine, psychotherapy, group therapy, and psychosurgery. *Amer. J. Psychiat.*, 104:465-470.

07115 **LEWIS, P., DAWES, S. A.,** and **CHENEY, T.** (1974), Effects of sensitivity training on belief in internal control of interpersonal relationships. *Psychother.: Theory, Res. & Pract.*, 11:282-284.

07116 **LEWIS, P., LISSITZ, R. W.,** and **JONES, C. L.** (1974), Assessment of change in interpersonal perception in a t-group using individual differences multidimensional scaling. *J. Couns. Psychol.*, 22:44-48.

07117 **LEWIS, P.,** and **McCANTS, J.** (1973), Some current issues in group psychotherapy research. *Internat. J. Group Psychother.*, 23:268-278.

07118 **LEWIS, R. T.** (1953), An analysis of group cohesiveness as a function of different types of group therapy focus. Unpublished doctoral dissertation, Cornell University.

07119 **LEWIS, R. W.** (1968), The effect of long group therapy sessions on participant perceptions of self and others. *Dissert. Abstr. Internat.*, 28:3879.

07120 **LEWIS, T. H.** (1980), Group-therapy with large groups. *Group Psychother., Psychodrama & Sociometry*, 33:156-161.

07121 **LEWIS, W.** (1980), A structured group counseling program for reading disabled elementary students. *Dissert. Abstr. Internat.*, 40:4493A. (University Microfilms No. 8004457.)

07122 **LEZENKO, V. N.** (1968), K metodike kollektivnoi psikhoterapii nekotorykh form funktsional noi impotentsii u muzhchin. (On a method of collective psychotherapy of some forms of functional impotence in men.) *Zh. Nevropat. Psikhol.*, 68:775-778.

07124 **L'HERISSON, L. A.** (1978), Effects of the sex of group leaders on women participants in assertion training. *Dissert. Abstr. Internat.*, 39:4041B.

07125 **LHOTELLIER, A.** (1963), La conduite des réunions. (Leading group discussion.) *Inform. Psychol.*, 9:57-69.

07126 **LIBBY, H. E.** (1966), Group therapy: an aid to the alcoholic. *J. Maine Med. Assn.*, 57:8-11.

07127 **LIBERMAN, M. A., LAKIN, M.,** and **WHITAKER, D. S.** (1969), Problems and potential of psychoanalytic and group-dynamic theories for group psychotherapy. *Internat. J. Group Psychother.*, 19:131-141.

07128 **LIBERMAN, R.** (1970), A behavioral approach to group dynamics: 1. reinforcement and prompting of cohesiveness in group therapy. *Behav. Ther.*, 1:141-175.

07129 **LIBERMAN, R. P.** (1971), Behavioral group therapy: a controlled clinical study. *Brit. J. Psychiat.*, (Ashford) 119:535-544.

07130 **LIBERMAN, R. P.** (1972), Behavioral methods in group and family therapy. *Sem. Psychiat.*, 4:145-156.

07131 **LIBERMAN, R. P.** (1975), Behavioral methods in group and family therapy. In: *Group Psychotherapy and Group Function*, 2d ed., eds. M. Rosenbaum and M. M. Berger. New York: Basic Books.

07132 **LIEBERMAN, R. P.** (1975), *Personal Effectiveness: Guiding People to Assert Themselves and Improve Their Social Skills.* Champaign, IL: Research Press.

07133 **LIBERMAN, R. P.** (1971), Reinforcement of cohesiveness in group therapy. *Arch. Gen. Psychiat.*, 25:168-177.

07134 **LIBERTO, M.,** and **BARCH, J. M. P.** (1978), Group-psychotherapy with amputees: cycles of issues and their implications. *Arch. Physical Med. & Rehab.*, 59:539.

07135 **LIBO, L.** (1977), *Is There Life after Group?* Garden City, NY: Anchor.

07136 **LICHTENBERG, J. D.** (1954), Study of changing role of psychiatrist in state hospital. *Psychiat. Quart.*, 28:428-441.

07137 **LICHTER, C.** (1967), (Considerations on psychotherapy of marginal states in psychiatry.) *Neurologia*, (Bucharest) 12:315-320.

07138 **LIDEN, D. J.** (1970), The effect of visual and tactile bodily stimulation on the task performance of chronic schizophrenics. *Dissert. Abstr. Internat.*, 30:4375.

07139 **LIEBENTHAL, D. M.** (1980), The experience of patients in group psychotherapy. *Dissert. Abstr. Internat.*, 41:2330B. (University Microfilms No. 8026857.)

07140 **LIEBER, A. L.** (1978), Group-therapy with hemodialysis patients. *Dialysis & Transplantation*, 7:464.

07141 **LIEBERMAN, F.** (1964), Transition from latency to prepuberty in girls: an activity group becomes an interview group. *Internat. J. Group Psychother.*, 14:455-463.

07142 **LIEBERMAN, F.**, and **TAYLOR, S. S.** (1964), Combined group and individual treatment of a schizophrenic child. *Soc. Casework*, 45:2, 80-85.

07143 **LIEBERMAN, M. A.** (1976), Change induction in small groups. In: *Annual Review of Psychology*, 27:217-250. Palo Alto: Annual Reviews.

07144 **LIEBERMAN, M. A.** (1971/1972), Encounter leaders: their behavior and impact. *Interpersonal Develop.*, 2:21-49.

07145 **LIEBERMAN, M. A.** (1975), Group therapies. In: *Overview of the Psychotherapies*, ed. G. Usdin. New York: Brunner/Mazel.

07146 **LIEBERMAN, M. A.** (1980), Group therapy beyond the therapy group. *Group Anal. Suppl.*, (London) 13:1-14.

07147 **LIEBERMAN, M. A.** (1967), The implications of total group phenomena analysis for patients and therapists. *Internat. J. Group Psychother.*, 17:71-81.

07148 **LIEBERMAN, M. A.** (1975), Joy less facts? a response to Schutz, Smith, and Rowan. *J. Human. Psychol.*, 15:49-54.

07149 **LIEBERMAN, M. A.** (1977), Problems in integrating traditional group therapies with new group forms. *Internat. J. Group Psychother.*, 27:19-33.

07150 **LIEBERMAN, M. A.** (1958), The relationship between emotional cultures of groups and individual change. Unpublished doctoral dissertation, University of Chicago.

07151 **LIEBERMAN, M. A.** (1975), Some limits to research on t-groups. *J. Appl. Behav. Science*, 11:241-249.

07152 **LIEBERMAN, M. A.** (1974), Up the right mountain down the wrong path: theory development for people-changing groups. *J. Appl. Behav. Science*, 10:166-174.

07153 **LIEBERMAN, M. A.**, and **BOND, G. R.** (1976), The problem of being a woman: a survey of 1700 women in consciousness-raising groups. *J. Appl. Behav. Science*, 12:363-379.

07154 **LIEBERMAN, M. A.**, and **BOND, G. R.** (1978), Self-help groups: problems of measuring outcome. *Small Group Behav.*, 9:221-242.

07155 **LIEBERMAN, M. A.**, and **GARDNER, J. R.** (1976), Institutional alternatives to psychotherapy: a study of growth center users. *Arch. Gen. Psychiat.*, 33:157-162.

07156 **LIEBERMAN, M. A.**, and **GOURASH, N.** (1979), Evaluating the effects of change groups on the elderly. *Internat. J. Group Psychother.*, 29:283-304.

07157 **LIEBERMAN, M. A., LAKIN, M. E.**, and **WHITAKER, D. S.** (1968), The group as a unique context for therapy. *Psychother.: Theory, Res. & Pract.*, 5:29-36.

07158 **LIEBERMAN, M. A., MEYER, G. G.**, and **McFARLAND, R.** (1966), Group psychotherapy. *Progr. Neurol. Psychiat.*, 21:579-585.

07159 **LIEBERMAN, M. A., SALOW, N., BOND, G. R.**, and **REIBSTEIN, J.** (1979), The psychotherapeutic impact of women's consciousness raising groups. *Arch. Gen. Psychiat.*, 36:161.

07160 **LIEBERMAN, M. A., YALOM, I. D.**, and **MILES, M. B.** (1972), The impact of encounter groups on participants: some preliminary findings. *J. Appl. Behav. Science*, 8:29-50.

07161 **LIEBERMAN, M. A.** (1973), *Encounter Groups: First Facts*. New York: Basic Books.

07162 **LIEBERMAN, P. C.**, and **GREEN, R.** (1965), Geriatric outpatient group therapy. *Comprehens. Psychiat.*, 6:51-60.
07163 **LIEBERMAN, R.** (1971), Reinforcement of cohesiveness in group therapy. *Arch. Gen. Psychiat.*, 25:168-177.
07164 **LIEBERMAN, R. P.** (1976), *Marital Therapy in Groups: A Comparative Evaluation of Behavioral and Interactional Formats.* Copenhagen: Munksgaard.
07165 **LIEBERMAN, S.** (1975), (Psychoanalytical group therapy: experience in a group of psychotics.) *Neurol.-Neurocir.-Psiquiat.*, (Mexico City) 16:91-100.
07166 **LIEBERMANN, L. P.** (1957), Joint-interview technique: an experiment in group therapy. *Brit. J. Med. Psychol.*, (London) 30:202-207.
07167 **LIEBHART, E. H.** (1972), (Variation in attitude during change of group membership: authoritarianism and alienation as determinant factors in alteration of prejudiced and anti-social attitude.) *Zeit. Exper. & Argewandte Psychol.*, (Goettingen) 19:563-579.
07168 **LIEBLUM, S. R., ROSEN, C.**, and **PIERCE, D.** (1976), Group treatment format: mixed sexual dysfunctions. *Arch. Sexual Behav.*, 5:313-322.
07169 **LIEBOWITZ, B.** (1972), A method for the analysis of the thematic structure of t-groups. *J. Appl. Behav. Science*, 8:149-173.
07170 **LIEBRODER, M. N.** (1963), Effects of therapy style on interaction in psychotherapy groups. *Dissert. Abstr. Internat.*, 23:3976.
07171 **LIEDER, S.**, and **MARGULIES, N.** (1971), A sensitivity training design for organizational development. *Soc. Change*, 1:6-7.
07172 **LIEDERMAN, P. C.** (1967), Music and rhythm group therapy for geriatric patients. *J. Music Ther.*, 4:126-127.
07173 **LIEDERMAN, P. C.** (1964), Non-symptomatic treatment for the geriatric patient. *Western Med.*, 5:263-266.
07174 **LIEDERMAN, P. C.**, and **GREEN, R.** (1965), Geriatric outpatient group therapy. *Comprehens. Psychiat.*, 6:51-60.
07175 **LIEDERMAN, P. C., GREEN, R.**, and **LIEDERMAN, V. R.** (1967), Outpatient group therapy with geriatric patients. *Geriatrics*, 22:148-153.
07176 **LIEDERMAN, P. C.**, and **LIEDERMAN, V. R.** (1967), Group therapy: an approach to problems of geriatric outpatients. *Curr. Psychiat. Ther.*, 7:179-185.
07177 **LIETAER, G.** (1972), (The client-centered viewpoint on the role of the group therapist.) *Nederl. Tijdschr. Psychol.*, (Amsterdam) 27:249-265.
07178 **LIEVANO, U.** (1970), Group psychotherapy with adolescents in an industrial school for delinquent boys. *Adolescence*, 5:231-252.
07179 **LIFF, Z. A.** (1978), Group psychotherapy for the 1980s: psychoanalysis of pathological boundary structuring. *Group Psychother., Psychodrama & Sociometry*, 2:184-192.
07180 **LIFF, Z. A.** (1970), Impasse: interpersonal, intergroup and international. *Group Process*, (London) 3:7-30.
07181 **LIFF, Z. A.** (1975), *The Leader in the Group.* New York: J. Aronson.
07182 **LIFTON, N.**, and **SMOLEN, E. M.** (1966), Group psychotherapy with schizophrenic children. *Internat. J. Group Psychother.*, 16:23-41.
07183 **LIFTON, W.** (1972), *Groups: Facilitating Individual Growth and Societal Change.* New York: J. Wiley and Sons.
07184 **LIFTON, W.** (1961), *Working with Groups: Group Process and Individual Growth.* New York: J. Wiley and Sons.
07185 **LIFTON, W. M.** (1973), Applying group counseling techniques to future social problem-solving. *Educat. Technol.*, 13:50-52.
07186 **LIFTON, W. M.** (1954), Group therapy in educational institutions. *Rev. Educat. Res.*, 24:156-165.

07187 **LIFTON, W. M.** (1966), *Working with Groups: Group Process and Individual Growth*, 2d ed. New York: J. Wiley and Sons.
07188 **LIGHT, N.** (1974), The "chronic helper" in group therapy. *Perspect. Psychiat. Care*, 12:129-134.
07189 **LILIENTHAL, R. A.**, and **HUTCHISON, S. L.** (1979), Group polarization (risky-shift) in led and leaderless group discussions. *Psychol. Reports*, 45:168.
07190 **LILLESKOV, R. K., GILBERT, M. L., MINALOV, T.**, and **BARKSDALE, C.** (1970), Planning an infant care unit with community participation. *Amer. J. Orthopsychiat.*, 40:281-282.
07191 **LILLESKOV, R. K., HARRIS, S., HUGHSON, H.**, and **WILLIG, C.** (1969), A therapeutic club for severely disturbed prepubertal boys. *Amer. J. Orthopsychiat.*, 39:262-263.
07192 **LIMA, D. R.** (1969), Social group work with dependent children. *Hosp. & Community Psychiat.*, 20:122-123.
07193 **de LIMA, O. R.** (1963), (Genetico-historical interpretations in group psychotherapy.) *Rev. Paulista Med.*, (Sao Paulo) 63:339-341.
07194 **de LIMA, O. R.** (1962), (Group psychotherapy technic.) *Rev. Paulista Med.*, (Sao Paulo) 61:260-264.
07195 **de LIMA, O. R.** (1961), (Psychogenic aspects of somatic symptomatology: study in group psychotherapy, of a case of schistosomiasis.) *Rev. Paulista Med.*, (Sao Paulo) 59:195-198.
07196 **LIMBEKNÉ IGNÁCZ, P.** (1976), (Brainstorming as group therapy for psychotics.) *Magyar Pszichol. Szemle*, (Budapest) 33:32-41.
07197 **LIMENTANI, D., GELLER, M.**, and **DAY, M.** (1960), A group leader-recorder relationship in a state hospital: a learning tool. *Internat. J. Group Psychother.*, 10:333-345.
07198 **LINARES, J. O.** (1974), (Group psychotherapy and group phenomenology.) *Riv. Sper. Freniatria*, (Emilia) 98:983-992.
07199 **LINDELL, A. R.** (1979), Congruence: a necessary behavior in the nurse-patient relationship. *Issues Ment. Health Nursing*, 2:27-40.
07200 **LINDELL, A. R.** (1978), Group therapy for the institutionalized aged. *Issues Ment. Health Nursing*, 1:76-86.
07201 **LINDELL, A. T.** (1979), Congruence—a necessary behavior in the nurse-patient relationship. *Issues Ment. Health Nursing*, 2:27-40.
07202 **LINDEMANN, J. E.** (1955), *The Process and Efficacy of Short-Term Nondirective Group Psychotherapy with Hospitalized Schizophrenic Patients*. Ann Arbor: University Microfilms.
06203 **LINDEMANN, J. E.** (1954), The process and efficacy of short-time nondirective group psychotherapy with hospitalized schizophrenic patients. Unpublished doctoral dissertation, University of Pennsylvania.
07204 **LINDEMANN, C.** (1977), A review of P. L. Wachtel's *Psychoanalysis & Behavior Therapy: Toward an Integration. Group*, 1:201-202.
07205 **LINDEN, M. E.** (1956), Geriatrics. In: *The Fields of Group Psychotherapy*, ed. S. R. Slavson. New York: International Universities Press.
07206 **LINDEN, M. E.** (1953), Group psychotherapy with institutionalized senile women: study in gerontologic human relations. *Internat. J. Group Psychother.*, 3:150-170.
07207 **LINDEN, M. E.** (1960), Our heritage in prospect. *Internat. J. Group Psychother.*, 10:131-135.
07208 **LINDEN, M. E.** (1954), The significance of dual leadership in gerontologic group psychotherapy: studies in gerontologic human relations, iii. *Internat. J. Group Psychother.*, 4:262-273.
07209 **LINDEN, M. E.** (1955), Transference in gerontologic group psychotherapy: studies in gerontologic human relations, iv. *Internat. J. Group Psychother.*, 5:61-79.

07210 **LINDENAUER, G. G.** (1971), Marriage education in a group therapy setting. *J. Emot. Educat.*, 11:165-177.
07211 **LINDENBERG, S. P.** (1977), The effects of an existential type of group psychotherapy on a time-limited group of members for whom the imminence of death is a pressing reality. *Dissert. Abstr. Internat.*, 38:3404.
07212 **LINDER, L.** (1963), (Group therapy in the treatment of obesity.) *Svenska Lakartidningen*, (Stockholm) 60:2612-2619.
07213 **LINDER, R.** (1970), Mothers of disabled children: the value of weekly group meetings. *Develop. Med. & Child Neurol.*, (London) 12:202-206.
07214 **LINDERES, L. F.** (1979), Educative/psychotherapeutic rehabilitation groups following myocardial infarction: a study of denial and depression in the post infarct patient. *Dissert. Abstr. Internat.*, 39:5556.
07215 **LINDINGER, H.** (1964), (From the activity of a psychotherapy center in a psychiatric clinic.) *Wiener Zeit. Nervenheilk.*, (Vienna) 21:419-428.
07216 **LINDINGER, H.** (1964), (Group psychotherapy combined with occupational therapy in an institution.) *Med. Klinik*, (Munich) 59:983-985.
07217 **LINDINGER, H.** (1968), (On the changing "mirror-image-like" termination of a resistance phenomenon in the group.) *Zeit. Psychosomat. Med. & Psychoanal.*, (Goettingen) 14:200-204.
07218 **LINDINGER, H.** (1965), (On the formation of a psychotherapeutic group.) *Arch. Psychiat. & Nervenkrankheiten*, 207:45-51.
07219 **LINDINGER, H.** (1967), (On the problems of short-term instruction groups.) *Z. Psychother. Med. Psychol.*, (Stuttgart) 17:23-27.
07220 **LINDINGER, H.** (1965), (Self-interpretation in group therapy.) *Psyche*, (Stuttgart) 19:398-402.
07221 **LINDINGER, H.** (1966), Zur frage der prinzipien einer psychotherapie schizophrener psychosen. (The guiding principles of psychotherapy for schizophrenic psychoses.) *Nervenarzt*, 37:168-173.
07222 **LINDINGER, H. C.** (1965), "Gruppenschicksal" und individuelle prognose bei der gruppenpsychotherapie. ("Group destiny" and individual prognosis in group psychotherapy.) *Zeit. Psychother. Med. Psychol.*, (Stuttgart) 15:195-202.
07223 **LINDINGER, H. C.** (1963), (On environmental and social therapy of schizophrenic psychoses following their psychodynamic aspects.) *Med. Klinik*, (Munich) 58:1891-1896.
07224 **LINDINGER, H. C.** (1964), Psychodrama mit einer gruppe neurotischer patienten. (Psychodrama with a group of neurotic patients.) *Praxis der Psychother.*, 9:117-127.
07225 **LINDNER, M.** (1965), A social experiment in masked group therapy. *Internat. J. Soc. Psychiat.*, (London) 11:167-172.
07226 **LINDNER, T.** (1977), (Hernstein questionnaire of subjects having completed group therapy.) *Gruppendynamik*, (Stuttgart) 8:358-363.
07227 **LINDSAY, D.** (1963), Social group work in a day treatment center. *Ment. Hosp.*, 14:498-502.
07228 **LINDSAY, D. G.** (1955), Group therapy at an army mental hygiene center. *U.S. Forces Med. J.*, 6:633-644.
07229 **LINDSAY, J. S.** (1967), The structure within groups. *Brit. J. Soc. & Clin. Psychol.*, (London) 6:195-203.
07230 **LINDSAY, J. S. B.** (1972), On the number in a group. *Human Relat.*, 25:47-64.
07231 **LINDSAY, W. R., SYMONS, R. S.,** and **SWEET, T.** (1979), Programs for teaching social skills to socially inept adolescents: description and evaluation. *J. Adolescence*, 2:215.
07232 **LINDSTEPT, E.** (1979), Assessment, counseling and training of integrated visually impaired children. *J. Visual Impair. & Blindness*, 73:351-358.

07233 **LINDT, H.** (1958), The nature of therapeutic interaction of patients in groups. *Internat. J. Group Psychother.*, 8:55-69.

07234 **LINDT, H.** (1948), Reactivation of mother-child relationships in hospital group therapy. *Amer. Psychologist*, 3:346.

07235 **LINDT, H.** (1959), The "rescue fantasy" in group treatment of alcoholics. *Internat. J. Group Psychother.*, 9:43-52.

07236 **LINDT, H.,** and **LEVENTHAL, G.** (1950), Group therapy and hospital administration. *Amer. Psychologist*, 5:470.

07237 **LINDT, H.,** and **PENNAL, H. A.** (1962), On the defensive quality of groups: a commentary on the use of the group as a tool to control reality. *Internat. J. Group Psychother.*, 12:171-179.

07238 **LINDT, H.,** and **SHERMAN, M. A.** (1952), "Social incognito" in analytically oriented group psychotherapy. *Internat. J. Group Psychother.*, 2:209-220.

07239 **LINDT, H.,** and **SHERMAN, M. A.** (1965), Use of an intermission as a partial answer to the "alternate session" dilemma. *Internat. J. Group Psychother.*, 15:345-349.

07240 **LINDZEY, G.,** and **ARONSON, E.** (1969), *The Handbook of Social Psychology, Vol. IV: Group Psychology and Phenomena of Interaction*, 2nd ed. Reading, MA: Addison-Wesley.

07241 **LINEHAN, E. J.** (1980), The effect of subliminal stimulation of symbiotic fantasies on college student self-disclosure in group counseling. *Dissert. Abstr. Internat.*, 41:108A. (University Microfilms No. 8014085.)

07242 **LINEHAN, M. M., WALKER, R. O., BRENHEIMS, S., HAYNES, K. F.,** and **YEUZEROFF, H.** (1979), Group versus individual assertion training. *J. Consult. & Clin. Psychol.*, 47:1000.

07243 **LINK, M.** (1978), Review of K. Hock's *Group Psychotherapy. Dynam. Psychiat.*, (Berlin) 11:79-81.

07244 **LINK, S. L.** (1971), A study of degree of change in self-concept as a result of participation in a marathon t-group. *Dissert. Abstr. Internat.*, 32:6622-6623B.

07245 **LINOFF, M. G.** (1972), An investigation of attitudes of teachers toward student problem behavior using behavior modification and consultation groups. *Dissert. Abstr. Internat.*, 33:1517-1518A.

07246 **LINZER, N.** (1967), Deepening the Jewish understanding of teenagers: a study of group process affected by group worker's role. *Jewish Community Ctr. Prog. Aids*, 28:7-10.

07247 **LION, J. R.,** and **BACH-Y-RITA, G.** (1970), Group psychotherapy with violent outpatients. *Internat. J. Group Psychother.*, 20:185-191.

07248 **LION, J. R.,** and **MADDEN, D. J.** (1977), A group approach with violent outpatients. *Internat. J. Group Psychother.*, 27:67-75.

07249 **LIPGAR, R.** (1952), An evaluation of the group psychotherapist's role in the therapeutic process. *Group Psychother., Psychodrama & Sociometry*, 5:54-58.

07250 **LIPGAR, R. M.** (1968), Evolution from a locked to an open ward through therapeutically guided group meetings. *Community Ment. Health J.*, 4:221-228.

07251 **LIPKIN, K. M.,** and **DANIELS, R. S.** (1968), Programs for discharged patients: i. community activities help readjustment. *Hosp. & Community Psychiat.*, 19:76-77.

07252 **LIPKIN, S.** (1948), Notes on group psychotherapy. *J. Nerv. Ment. Disorders*, 107:459-479.

07253 **LIPMAN, R. S.** (1976), Outpatient treatment of neurotic depression: medication and group psychotherapy. In: *Evaluation of Psychological Therapies*, eds. R. L. Spitzer and D. F. Klein. Baltimore: Johns Hopkins University Press.

07254 **LIPNITZKI, S. J.** (1940), Psychotherapy in an institution for mental defective patients. *Lost & Found*, 3:68-70.
07255 **LIPP, M. R.**, and **MALONE, S. T.** (1976), Group rehabilitation of vascular surgery patients. *Arch. Phys. Med. & Rehab.*, 57:180-183.
07256 **LIPPITT, G. L.** (1959), Effects of information about group desire for change on members of a group. Unpublished doctoral dissertation, American University.
07257 **LIPPITT, R.** (1947), Administrator perception and administrative approval: a communication problem. *Sociatry*, 1:209-219.
07258 **LIPPITT, R.** (1958), The auxiliary chair technique. *Group Psychother., Psychodrama & Sociometry*, 11:8-23.
07259 **LIPPITT, R.** (1958), Professional training and experience: affiliations and publications. *Group Psychother., Psychodrama & Sociometry*, 11:24-26.
07260 **LIPPITT, R.** (1943), The psychodrama in leadership training. *Sociometry*, 6:286-292.
07261 **LIPPITT, R.** (1947), Psychodrama in the home. *Sociatry*, 1:148-167.
07262 **LIPPITT, R.**, and **CLANCY, C.** (1954), Psychodrama in the kindergarten and nursery school. *Group Psychother., Psychodrama & Sociometry*, 7:262-290.
07263 **LIPPITT, R.**, and **HUBBELL, A.** (1956), Role playing for personnel and guidance workers: review of the literature with suggestions for application. *Group Psychother., Psychodrama & Sociometry*, 9:89-114.
07264 **LIPPITT, R., BRADFORD, L. P.**, and **BENNE, K. D.** (1947), Sociodramatic clarification of leader and group roles as a starting point for effective group functioning. *Sociatry*, 1:82-91.
07265 **LIPSCHUTZ, D. M.** (1957), Combined group and individual psychotherapy. *Amer. J. Psychother.*, 11:336-344.
07266 **LIPSHUTZ, D. M.** (1960), Combined group psychotherapy. *Topical Probl. Psychol. & Psychother.*, 2:79-85.
07267 **LIPSHUTZ, D. M.** (1952), Group psychotherapy as an aid in psychoanalysis. *Internat. J. Group Psychother.*, 2:316-323.
07268 **LIPSHUTZ, D. M.** (1952), Psychoanalytical group therapy. *Amer. J. Orthopsychiat.*, 22:718-737.
07269 **LIPSCHUTZ, L. S.** (1945), A mental hygiene program for the military hospital. *Amer. J. Psychiat.*, 101:614-618.
07270 **LIPSITT, P. D.**, and **STEINBRUNER, M.** (1969), An experiment in police-community relations: a small group approach. *Community Ment. Health J.*, 5:172-179.
07271 **LIPSON, J. G.** (1980), Consumer activism in two women's self-help groups. *Western J. Nursing Res.*, 2:393-405.
07272 **LIPTON, A.**, and **FEINER, A. H.** (1956), Group therapy and remedial reading. *J. Educat. Psychol.*, 47:330-334.
07273 **LIPTON, M. I.** (1970), Effective day center treatment. *Psychosomatics*, 11:55-56.
07274 **LIPTON, S. M., FIELDS, F. R.**, and **SCOTT, R. A.** (1968), Effects of group psychotherapy upon types of patient movement. *Diseases Nerv. System*, 29:603-605.
07275 **LIPTZIN, M. B.**, and **REIFLER, C. B.** (1970), Sensitivity training and the university. *J. Amer. College Health Assn.*, 19:136-139.
07276 **LISS, J.** (1974), *Free to Feel: Finding Your Way Through the New Therapies*. New York: Praeger.
07277 **LIST, M. D.**, and **STRACHSTEIN, H.** (1978), Other voices—other groups: an interview with Paul Sorvino. *Group Psychother., Psychodrama & Sociometry*, 2:118-125.
07278 **LISTELLA, G. M., PANKRATZ, L. D.**, and **JETMALANI, N. B.** (1965), Defective delinquents can be reached. *Ment. Hosp.*, 16:333-337.

07279 **LISTER, H. L.,** and **LAZAR, A.** (1974), Group work with disabled young men. *Soc. Work*, 19:489-494.

07280 **LISTON, C. T.** (1973), Level of manifest anxiety as a predictor of attitude change, through group vocational counseling. *Dissert. Abstr. Internat.*, 34:1621A.

07281 **LISTWAN, I. A.** (1955), Psychodrama. *Med. J. Austral.*, (Glebe) 1:524-527.

07282 **LITMAN, R. E.** (1961), Psychotherapy of a homosexual man in a heterosexual group. *Internat. J. Group Psychother.*, 11:440-448.

07283 **LITOVSKYDEEIGUE, R. D.** (1980), An attempt to reconcile systems theory with group psychoanalytic theory within the context of their application in family therapy. *Neuropsychiat. Enfantile Adoles.*, 28:375-382.

07284 **LITOW, L.,** and **PUMROY, D. K.** (1975), A brief review of classroom group-oriented contingencies. *J. Appl. Behav. Anal.*, 8:341-347.

07285 **LITTLE, F. W.** (1972), The effect of a personal growth group experience upon measured self concept of a selected group of black college freshmen. *Dissert. Abstr. Internat.*, 32:4957A.

07286 **LITTLE, H. M.,** and **KONOPKA, G.** (1947), Group psychotherapy in a child guidance center. *Amer. J. Orthopsychiat.*, 17:303-311.

07287 **LITTLE, M. L.** (1946), Psychiatric and psychological group therapy: i. *Elem. School J.*, 46:369-374.

07288 **LITTLE, M. L.** (1946), Psychiatric and psychological group therapy: ii. *Elem. School J.*, 46:453-460.

07289 **LITTLE, W.** (1972), Integrity groups: a pastoral counselor's reaction. *Couns. Psychol.*, 3:63-67.

07290 **LITTMANN, F.** (1980), *Der "Normale" Mittelweg zum "Wahren" Selbst: Analyse und Kritik Grundlegender Denkfiguren der Gruppendynamik.* Marburg/Lahn: Guttandin und Hoppe.

07291 **LITTMANN, S. K.,** and **GOERING, P.** (1976), Group therapy training in a mental hospital. *Can. Ment. Health*, (Ottawa) 24:15.

07292 **LITVAK, S. B.** (1969), A comparison of two brief group behavior therapy techniques on the reduction of avoidance behavior. *Psychol. Record*, 19:329-334.

07293 **LIVERGOOD, N. D.** (1968), Roles people over-act. *Psychother.: Theory, Res. & Pract.*, 5:248-253.

07294 **LIVINGSTON, D. D.** (1977), The effect of verbal feedback and verbal self-disclosure on self-perceived change in a small group setting. *Dissert. Abstr. Internat.*, 37:4152.

07295 **LIVINGSTON, L. B.** (1971), Self-concept change of black college males as a result of a weekend black experience encounter workshop. *Dissert. Abstr. Internat.*, 32:2423B.

07296 **LIVINGSTON, M. S.** (1975), On barriers, contempt, and the "vulnerable moment" in group psychotherapy. In: *Group Therapy 1975: An Overview*, eds. L. R. Wolberg and M. L. Aronson. New York: Stratton Intercontinental Medical Books.

07297 **LIVINGSTON, M. S.** (1971), Working through in analytic group psychotherapy in relation to masochism as a refusal to mourn. *Internat. J. Group Psychother.*, 21:339-344.

07298 **LLANES, A. S.** (1975), (Analogies between psychotic experiences and those lived during respiratory autogenic training relaxation.) *Minerva Med.*, (Turin) 66:262-264.

07299 **LLANOS, Z. R.** (1973), (Experiences in psychodrama with adults.) *Rev. Neuro-Psiquiat.*, (Lima) 36:117-126.

07300 **LLOYD, W.** (1950), Group work with mothers in a child development center. *Ment. Hygiene*, 34:620-640.

07301 **LOBITZ, W. C.**, and **BAKER, E. L.** (1979), Group treatment of single males with erectile dysfunction. *Arch. Sexual Behav.*, 8:127-138.
07302 **LOBOVIVI, S.** (1957), L'utilisation du psychodrame dans le diagnostic in psychiatrie. (The utilization of psychodrama in psychiatric diagnosis.) *Ziet. Diagnost. Psychol.*, 5:197-205.
07303 **LOBROT, M.** (1971), Die selbstbestimmung schulischer gruppen. (The self-regulation of t-group.) *Gruppendynamik*, (Stuttgart) 2:166-183.
07304 **LOCICERO, V. J.** (1964), Teaching of psychotherapy and group therapy. *Internat. Psychiat. Clinics*, 1:417-430.
07305 **LOCKE, B. J.**, and **GATES, J. J.** (1971), Verbal conditioning with retarded subjects: experimental control of vocal duration in dyadic assemblies. *Amer. J. Ment. Deficiency*, 76:53-59.
07306 **LOCKE, C. K.** (1970), Small group counseling compared with freshman orientation classes in reducing attrition of freshmen junior college students. *Dissert. Abstr. Internat.*, 31:1576A.
07307 **LOCKE, N.** (1954), *Bibliography on Group Psychotherapy*. New York: American Group Psychotherapy Association, pp. 29.
07308 **LOCKE, N.** (1961), Emotional factors in the analyst's attitude to group psychoanalysis. *Amer. J. Psychother.*, 15:436-441.
07309 **LOCKE, N.** (1961), *Group Psychoanalysis: Theory and Technique*. New York: New York University Press.
07310 **LOCKE, N.** (1952), The psychologist in group therapy. *Internat. J. Group Psychother.*, 2:34-39.
07311 **LOCKE, N.** (1957), Remarks on the psychology and the group psychotherapy of the hard of hearing. *J. Hillside Hosp.*, 6:100-106.
07312 **LOCKE, N.** (1955), Trends in the literature on group psychotherapy. *Internat. J. Group Psychother.*, 5:181-184.
07313 **LOCKE, N.** (1957), The use of dreams in group psychoanalysis. *Amer. J. Psychother.*, 11:98-110.
07314 **LOCKE, N. M.** (1960), *A Decade of Group Psychotherapy: The Bibliography for 1950-1959*. New York: Group Psychotherapy Center.
07315 **LOCKE, N. M.** (1961), *Group psychoanalysis: Theory and Technique*. New York: New York University Press.
07316 **LOCKWOOD, G. E.** (1977), Effects of videotaped feedback on self concept, role playing ability and growth in group therapy. *Dissert. Abstr. Internat.*, 37:5363B.
07317 **LOCKWOOD, G., SALZBERG, H. C.**, and **HECKEL, R. V.** (1978), The effects of videotape feedback on self-concept, role-playing ability, and growth in a leaderless therapy group. *J. Clin. Psychol.*, 34:718-721.
07318 **LODATO, F. J.**, and **KOSKY, E. M.** (1967), A multileader approach in group counseling as a method of modifying attitudes toward school in slow learners. *Proceed., 75th Annual Convention*, American Psychological Association, 343-344.
07319 **LODEWEGENS, F. J.** (1980), (The narrow margins of the hierarchy: therapeutic possibilities and limits of the hierarchically structured therapeutic community.) *Tijdschr. voor Psychother.*, 6:270-281.
07320 **LOEB, R. C.** (1977), Group therapy for parents of mentally retarded children. *J. Marriage & Fam. Couns.*, 3:77-82.
07321 **LOEBLOWITZ-LENNARD, H.** (1945), The meaning of laughter in the psychodramatic audience. *Sociometry*, 8:86.
07322 **LOEFFLER, F. J.**, and **WEINSTEIN, H. M.** (1954), The co-therapist method: special problems and advantages. *Group Psychother., Psychodrama & Sociometry*, 6:189-192.
07323 **LOESER, L. H.** (1975), Editorial. *Internat. J. Group Psychother.*, 25:127-130.

07324 **LOESER, L. H.** (1956), The role of group therapy in private practice: a clinical evaluation. *J. Hillside Hosp.*, 5:460-467.

07325 **LOESER, L. H.** (1957), Some aspects of group dynamics. *Internat. J. Group Psychother.*, 7:5-19.

07326 **LOESER, L. H.,** and **BRY, T.** (1953), The position of the group therapist in transference and countertransference: an experimental study. *Internat. J. Group Psychother.*, 3:389-406.

07327 **LOESER, L. H.,** and **PARLOFF, M. B.** (1963), Introduction: symposium on the relationship of group psychotherapy to group dynamics. *Internat. J. Group Psychother.*, 13:391-392.

07328 **LOESER, L. H., FURST, W., ROSS, I. S.,** and **BRY, T.** (1949), Group therapy in private practice: preliminary evaluation. *Amer. J. Psychother.*, 3:213-233.

07329 **LOESSER, L. H.,** and **BRY, T.** (1960), The role of death fears in the etiology of phobic anxiety as revealed in group psychotherapy. *Internat. J. Group Psychother.*, 10:287-297.

07330 **LOEWENBERG, F. M.** (1968), The directors: a pilot study of volunteer participation in decision-making in voluntary group service agencies. *Dissert. Abstr. Internat.*, 28:4720.

07331 **LOEWENSTEIN, S.** (1979), Review of H. Mullan's and M. Rosenbaum's *Group Psychotherapy: Theory and Practice. Amer. J. Psychother.*, 33:628.

07332 **LOFGREN, L. B.** (1976), A process-oriented group approach to schizophrenia. In: *Treatment of Schizophrenia: Progress and Prospects*, eds. L. J. West and D. E. Flinn. New York: Grune and Stratton.

07333 **LOGAN, D.** (1980), Review of M. Seligman's *Group Counseling and Group Psychotherapy with Rehabilitation Clients. Fam. Relat.*, 29:137.

07334 **LOGAN, D. G.** (1972), A pilot methadone program to introduce comprehensive addiction treatment. *Hosp. & Community Psychiat.*, 23:76-79.

07335 **LOGAN, D. L.** (1969), Action-oriented group therapy as a training method for psychiatric student nurses. *J. Psychiat. Nursing*, 7:201-206.

07336 **LOGAN, J. C.** (1971), Use of psychodrama and sociodrama in reducing excessive Negro aggression. *Group Psychother., Psychodrama & Sociometry*, 24:138-149.

07337 **LOGAN, N. S.** (1974), Effective use of small-group discussion: part i. the teacher (facilitator). *J. Dental Educat.*, 38:436-440.

07338 **LOGIE, I. R.,** and **BALLIN, M. R.** (1952), Group guidance for adults: an evaluation. *Occupat. Ther. & Rehab.*, 30:530-533.

07339 **LOHMANN, G.** (1971), (Contact establishing manifestations of group members to their male and female leaders in group therapy.) *Praxis Kinderpsychol. &Kinderpsychiat.*, 20:91-97.

07340 **LOMAX-SIMPSON, J. M.** (1980), The large group as a vehicle for change, maturation and therapy for predominantly unsupported mothers and their children. *Internat. J. Soc. Psychiat.*, (London) 25:306-308.

07341 **LOMONT, J. F.** (1969), Group assertion training and group insight therapies. *Psychol. Reports*, 25:463-470.

07342 **LOMONT, J. F.,** and **SHERMAN, L. J.** (1971), Group systematic desensitization and group insight therapies for test anxiety. *Behav. Res. & Ther.*, 2:511-518.

07343 **LOMRANZ, J.** (1971), Variants in group sensitivity training and encounter. Unpublished Ph.D. dissertation, Duke University.

07344 **LOMRANZ, J., LAKIN, M.,** and **SCHIFFMAN, H.** (1972), Variants of sensitivity training and encounter: diversity or fragmentation? *J. Appl. Behav. Science*, 8:399-420.

07345 **LONDON, A. M.,** and **SCHREIBER, E. D.** (1966), A controlled study of the effects of group discussions and an anorexiant in outpatient treatment of obesity: with attention to the psychological aspects of dieting. *Annals Internal Med.*, 65:80-92.

07346 **LONDON COUNCIL OF SOCIAL SERVICE. FAMILY SERVICES COMMITTEE** (1975), *Family Groups: A Report by the LCSS Family Services Committee on Work with Disadvantaged Parents and Their Children.* London: L.C.S.S.

07347 **LONDON, M.** (1975), Effects of shared information and participation on group process and outcome. *J. Appl. Psychol.*, 60:537-543.

07348 **LONDON, P.**, and **BOWER, R. K.** (1968), Effect of role playing on hypnotic susceptibility in children. *J. Personality*, 10:66-68.

07349 **LONERGAN, E. C.** (1980), Group intervention for medical patients: a treatment for damaged self-esteem. *Group*, 4:36-45.

07350 **LONERGAN, E. C.** (1980), Humanizing the hospital experience: report of a group program for medical patients. *Health & Soc. Work*, 5:53-63.

07351 **LONERGAN, W. G.** (1957), Role playing in industrial conflict. *Group Psychother., Psychodrama & Sociometry*, 10:105-110.

07352 **LONG, H. B.** (1968), Factors influencing the relationship between dogmatism and conformity in an employee group. *J. Soc. Psychol.*, 74:209-213.

07353 **LONG, L. D.**, and **COPE, C. A.** (1980), Curative factors in a male felony offender group. *Small Group Behav.*, 11:389-398.

07354 **LONG, T.**, and **SCHULTZ, E. W.** (1973), Empathy: a quality of an effective group leader. *Psychol. Reports*, 32:699-705.

07355 **LONG, T. J.**, and **BOSSHART, D.** (1974), The facilitator behavior index. *Psychol. Reports*, 34:1059-1068.

07356 **LONGABAUGH, R.** (1963), A category system for coding interpersonal behavior as social exchange. *Sociometry*, 26:319-344.

07357 **LONGIN, H.**, and **ROONEY, W.** (1975), Teaching denial assertion to chronic hospitalized patients. *J. Behav. Ther. & Exper. Psychiat.*, 6:219-223.

07358 **LONGKER, C. E.** (1973), The effect of selected group counseling approaches on the self concept of student teachers. *Dissert. Abstr. Internat.*, 34:1763A.

07359 **LOOMIS, E. A.** (1955), Child psychiatry and religion. *Group Psychother., Psychodrama & Sociometry*, 8:291-297.

07360 **LOOMIS, E. A.** (1955), Comments, appreciation and critique of J. L. Moreno's "Interpersonal therapy and the function of the unconscious." *Group Psychother., Psychodrama & Sociometry*, 8:67-69.

07361 **LOOMIS, E. A.** (1954), Comments, appreciation, and critique of J. L. Moreno's "Transference, countertransference, and tele: their relations to group research and group psychotherapy." *Group Psychother., Psychodrama & Sociometry*, 7:310-313.

07362 **LOOMIS, E. A., JR.** (1953), Group psychotherapy in a naval psychiatric service. *Group Psychother., Psychodrama & Sociometry*, 5:240-252.

07363 **LOOMIS, M. E.** (1973), Use of group contingencies with psychiatric patients. *ANA Clin. Sessions*, 208-216.

07364 **LOOMIS, M. E.**, and **DODENHOFF, J. T.** (1970), Working with informal patient groups. *Amer. J. Nursing*, 70:1939-1944.

07365 **LOPEZ, D.** (1965), Alcune perplessita sulla psicoterapia di gruppo. (Some perplexity in group psychotherapy.) *Rev. de Psicoanal.*, (Buenos Aires) 11:57-65.

07366 **LOPEZ IBOR, J.** (1973), (Editorial: group psychotherapy.) *Actas Luso Espanolas Neurol. Psiquiat.*, (Madrid) 1:415-416.

07367 **LOPICCOLO, J.**, and **MILLER, V. H.** (1975), Procedural outline: sexual enrichment groups. *J. Couns. Psychol.*, 5:46-49.

07368 **LOPRIENO, M.** (1961), (Preliminary experiences with an application of the technique of analysis relative to a group of mental patients.) *Rass. Studi Psichiat.*, (Siena) 50:36-38.

07369 **LORANGER, P. D.** (1973), An analysis of problem drinkers undergoing treatment through educational therapy, group therapy and family orientation. *Dissert. Abstr. Internat.*, 33:4350B.

07370 **LORBER, N. M.** (1976), The group as a medium for change. *J. Psychology*, 13:30-32.

07371 **LORDI, W. M.** (1975), Group psychotherapy in an adolescent therapeutic community. *Amer. J. Orthopsychiat.*, 45:224-225.

07372 **LORDI, W. M.** (1963), Group psychotherapy with children: a five-year experience. *Virginia Med. Monthly*, 90:577-579.

07373 **LORING, R. K.** (1958), Using group process in in-service training. *Group Psychother., Psychodrama & Sociometry*, 11:144-149.

07374 **LORR, M.** (1966), Dimensions of interaction in group therapy. *Multivar. Behav. Res.*, 1:67-73.

07375 **LOTHSTEIN, L. M.** (1977), Countertransference reactions to gender dysphoric patients: implications for psychotherapy. *Psychother.: Theory, Res. & Pract.*, 14:21-31.

07376 **LOTHSTEIN, L. M.** (1978), The group psychotherapy dropout phenomenon revisited. *Amer. J. Psychiat.*, 135:1492-1495.

07377 **LOTHSTEIN, L. M.** (1979), Group therapy with gender-dysphoria patients. *Amer. J. Psychother.*, 33:67.

07378 **LOTHSTEIN, L. M.** (1978), Human territoriality in group psychotherapy. *Internat. J. Group Psychother.*, 28:55-71.

07379 **LOTT, G. M.** (1957), Multiple psychotherapy: The efficient use of psychiatric treatment and training time. *Psychiat. Quart. Suppl.*, 31:277-294.

07380 **LOUCKES, S.** (1979), Review of A. S. Gurman's *Handbook of Research. Contemp. Psychol.*, 24:859.

07381 **LOVASDAL, S.** (1976), A multiple therapy approach in work with children. *Internat. J. Group Psychother.*, 26:475-486.

07382 **LOVETT, T. M.** (1975), Influencing the success and attitudes toward success of disadvantaged college students through the use of group goal setting training. *Dissert. Abstr. Internat.*, 36:3409A.

07383 **LOW, A. A.** (1945), The combined system of group psychotherapy and self help as practiced by Recovery Inc. *Sociometry*, 8:332-337.

07384 **LOW, A. A.** (1941), Group psychotherapy. *Illinois Psychiat. J.*, 1:3-4.

07385 **LOW, A. A.** (1943), *Group Psychotherapy: A Record of Class Interviews with Patients Suffering from Mental and Nervous Ailments*. Chicago: Recovery.

07386 **LOW, A. A.** (1949), Recovery, Inc.: a project for rehabilitating postpsychotic and long-term psychoneurotic patients. In: *Rehabilitation of the Handicapped: A Survey of Means and Methods*, ed. W. H. Soden. New York: Ronald Press.

07387 **LOW, A. A.** (1943), *Recovery's Self-Help Techniques, History and Description*. Chicago: Recovery.

07388 **LOW, A. A.** (1943), *The Technique of Self-Help in Psychiatric After-Care*. Chicago: Recovery.

07389 **LOWE, W. R.** (1973), A comparison of personality changes in ex-drug users living in a communal setting and non-drug users from a therapy group. *Dissert. Abstr. Internat.*, 33:6179A.

07390 **LOWNAU, H. W.** (1969), (Association-drawing in the psychotherapeutic treatment of children and youths.) *Praxis Kinderpsychol. & Kinderpsychiat.*, (Goettingen) 18:241-254.

07391 **LOWREY, L.** (1954), Group treatment of mothers. *Amer. J. Orthopsychiat.*, 14:589.

07392 **LOWREY, L. G.** (1942), *Group Therapy: A Survey of Practices at the Jewish Board of Guardians.* Annual Report, Jewish Board of Guardians, New York.

07393 **LOWREY, L. G.** (1943), Group therapy at the Brooklyn Child Guidance Center. *Newsl. Amer. Assn. Psychiat. Soc. Workers*, 13:72-74.

07394 **LOWREY, L. G.** (1944), Group therapy for mothers. *Amer. J. Orthopsychiat.*, 14:589-592.

07395 **LOWREY, L. G.** (1943), Group therapy: special section meeting. *Amer. J. Orthopsychiat.*, 13:648-691.

07396 **LOWREY, L. G.** (1939), Trends in treatment. *Amer. J. Orthopsychiat.*, 9:669-760.

07397 **LOWS, A. A.** (1952), *Mental Health Through Will-Training.* Boston: Christopher Publishing House.

07398 **LUBAN-PLOZZA, B.**, and **ANTONELLI, F.** (1974), *Praxis der Balint-Gruppen: Beziehungsdiagnostik und Therapie.* (*Balint-Group Practice: Diagnostic Relations and Therapy.*) Munich: Lehmann.

07399 **LUBELL, D.** (1976), Group work with patients on peritoneal dialysis. *Health Soc. & Work*, 1:158-176.

07400 **LUBER, R. F., JR.** (1978), Recurrent spontaneous themes in group poetry therapy. *Art Psychother.*, 5:55-60.

07401 **LUBIN, B.** (1963), Characteristics of clinical psychologists in various work settings. *Diseases Nerv. System*, 24:1-4.

07402 **LUBIN, B.** (1976), Group therapy. In: *Clinical Methods in Psychology*, ed. I. B. Weiner. New York: J. Wiley and Sons.

07403 **LUBIN, B.** (1962), Survey of psychotherapy training and activities of psychologists. *J. Clin. Psychol.*, 18:252-256.

07404 **LUBIN, B.** (1968), Which figure is correct? concerning Shostrom's article. *Amer. Psychologist*, 23:759-760.

07405 **LUBIN, B.**, and **EDDY, W. B.** (1970), The laboratory training model: rationale, method, and some thoughts for the future. *Internat. J. Group Psychother.*, 20:305-339.

07406 **LUBIN, B.**, and **HARRISON, R. L.** (1964), Predicting small group behavior with the Self-Disclosure Inventory. *Psychol. Reports*, 15:77-78.

07407 **LUBIN, B.**, and **LUBIN, A. W.** (1964), Bibliography of group psychotherapy: 1956-1963. *Group Psychother., Psychodrama & Sociometry*, 17:177-230.

07408 **LUBIN, B.**, and **LUBIN, A. W.** (1966), *Group Psychotherapy: A Bibliography of the Literature from 1956 through 1964.* East Lansing: Michigan State University Press.

07409 **LUBIN, B.**, and **LUBIN, A. W.** (1973), The group psychotherapy literature: 1972. *Internat. J. Group Psychother.*, 23:474-513.

07410 **LUBIN, B.**, and **LUBIN, A. W.** (1971), Laboratory stress compared with college examination stress. *J. Appl. Behav. Science*, 7:502-507.

07411 **LUBIN, B.**, and **SLOMINSKI, A.** (1960), A counseling program with adult, male cerebral palsied patients. *Cerebral Palsy Rev.*, 21:3-5, 11.

07412 **LUBIN, B.**, and **SMITH, P. B.** (1979), Affect levels in one-day experiential groups. *Psychol. Reports*, 45:117-118.

07413 **LUBIN, B., LUBIN, A. W.**, and **SARGENT, C. W.** (1972), The group psychotherapy literature: 1971. *Internat. J. Group Psychother.*, 22:492-529.

07414 **LUBIN, B., REDDY, W. B., STANSBERRY, C.**, and **LUBIN, A. W.** (1977), Group psychotherapy literature: 1976. *Internat. J. Group Psychother.*, 27:521-552.

07415 **LUBIN, B., REDDY, W. B., TAYLOR, A.**, and **LUBIN, A. W.** (1978), Group psychotherapy literature: 1977. *Internat. J. Group Psychother.*, 28:509-555.

07416 **LUBORSKY, L.** (1959), Psychotherapy. In: *Annual Review of Psychology, 10*, eds. P. R. Farnsworth and Q. McNemar. Palo Alto: Annual Reviews.

07417 **LUCAS, A. R., DUNCAN, J. W.,** and **PIENS, V.** (1976), The treatment of anorexia nervosa. *Amer. J. Psychiat.*, 133:1034.

07418 **LUCAS, D.,** and **LUDWIK, R. G.** (1964), Group psychotherapy with depressed patients incorporating "mood" music. *Amer. J. Psychother.*, 18:126-137.

07419 **LUCAS, L.** (1943), Treatment of young children in a group, a supplement to individual treatment. *Newsl. Amer. Assn. Psychiat. Soc. Workers*, 13:59-65.

07420 **LUCAS, R. L.,** and **JAFFEE, C. L.** (1969), Effects of high-rate talkers on group voting behavior in the leaderless-group problem solving situation. *Psychol. Reports*, 25:471-477.

07421 **LUCERO, K. F.** (1980), The effects of group counseling on self-concept and academic performance of a select group of seventh grade students in a remedial reading program. *Dissert. Abstr. Internat.*, 41:1406A. (University Microfilms No. 8022817.)

07422 **LUCHINA, I. L.,** and **MEREA, E. C.** (1973), (Group therapy for medical practice.) *Acta Psiquiat. Psicol. Amer. Latina*, (Buenos Aires) 19:462-469.

07423 **LUCHINS, A. S.** (1960), An approach to evaluating the achievements of group psychotherapy. *J. Soc. Psychol.*, 52:345-353.

07424 **LUCHINS, A. S.** (1946), A course in group psychotherapy: method, content and results. *J. Clin. Psychol.*, 2:231-239.

07425 **LUCHINS, A. S.** (1947), Experience with closed ward group psychotherapy. *Amer. J. Orthopsychiat.*, 17:511-520.

07426 **LUCHINS, A. S.** (1947), Group structures in group psychotherapy. *J. Clin. Psychol.*, 3:269-273.

07427 **LUCHINS, A. S.** (1964), *Group Therapy: A Guide*. New York: Random House.

07428 **LUCHINS, A. S.** (1972), *Group Therapy*. Westminster, MD.: Random House.

07429 **LUCHINS, A. S.** (1947), Methods of studying the progress and outcomes of a group psychotherapy program. *J. Couns. Psychol.*, 11:173-183.

07430 **LUCHINS, A. S.** (1967), Practice and levels of theory. *Internat. J. Psychiat.*, 4:344-348.

07431 **LUCHINS, A. S.** (1950), Restructuring social perceptions: a group psychotherapy technique. *J. Couns. Psychol.*, 14:446-451.

07432 **LUCHINS, A. S.** (1948), The role of the social field in psychotherapy. *J. Couns. Psychol.*, 12:417-425.

07433 **LUCHINS, A. S.** (1955), A social-experimental approach to group psychotherapy. *J. Soc. Psychol.*, 42:121-127.

07434 **LUCHINS, A. S.** (1948), Specialized audio-aids in a group psychotherapy program for psychotics. *J. Couns. Psychol.*, 12:313-320.

07435 **LUCHINS, A. S., AUMACK, L.,** and **DICKMAN, H. R.** (1960), *Manual of Group Therapy*. Roseburg, OR: Veterans Administration Hospital Psychology Service.

07436 **LUCIA MOTO do PRADO, R.** (1980), (Effect of psychotherapy on exceptional children.) *Arq. Brasil. Psicol. Apl.*, (Rio de Janeiro) 32:11-35.

07437 **LUCK, J. M.** (1954), A study of peer relationships which children in their latency years are observed to form during 25 group therapy sessions. *Dissert. Abstr. Internat.*, 14:2145-2146.

07438 **LUDLOW, B.,** and **EPSTEIN, N.** (1972), Groups for foster children. *Soc. Work*, 17:95-99.

07439 **LUDWIG, A. M.** (1967), Forced small group responsibility in the treatment of chronic schizophrenics. *Psychiat. Quart. Suppl.*, 41:262-280.

07440 **LUDWIG, A. M.** (1976), Group treatment methods for chronic schizophrenics. In: *Treatment of Schizophrenia: Progress and Prospects*, eds. L. J. West and D. E. Flinn. New York: Grune and Stratton.

07441 **LUDWIG, A. M.**, and **MARX, A. J.** (1968), Influencing techniques of chronic schizophrenics. *Arch. Gen. Psychiat.*, 18:681-688.

07442 **LUDWIG, A. M., LYLE, W. H.**, and **MILLER, J. S.** (1964), Group hypnotherapy techniques with drug addicts. *Internat. J. Clin. & Hypnosis*, 12:53-66.

07443 **LUFT, J.** (1965), *Group Processes*. Palo Alto: National Press Publications.

07444 **LUFT, J.** (1970), *Group Processes: An Introduction to Group Dynamics*. Palo Alto: Mayfield Publishing.

07445 **LUFT, J.** (1969), *Of Human Interaction*. Palo Alto: National Press Books.

07446 **LUKAS, K. H.** (1959), Psychological preparation for labor in groups. *Acta Psychother., Psychosomat. Orthopaedagog. Suppl.*, (Basel) 7:231-233.

07447 **LUKE, R. A.** (1972), The institution of sensitivity training on the cultural island. *Dissert. Abstr. Internat.*, 32:4127A.

07448 **LUKE, R. A.** (1972), The internal normative structure of sensitivity training groups. *J. Appl. Behav. Science*, 8:421-437.

07449 **LULLER, J. B.** (1971), An investigation of self-disclosing behavior and the affective response within a t-group setting. *Dissert. Abstr. Internat.*, 32:1852A.

07450 **LULOW, W. V.** (1951), An experimental approach toward the prevention of behavior disorders in a group of nursery school children. *Internat. J. Group Psychother.*, 1:144-153.

07451 **LUMPKIN, M. A.** (1971), The effect of an encounter group experience on the role anxiety and therapeutic competence of student therapists. *Dissert. Abstr. Internat.*, 32:5448B.

07452 **LUND, M. A.** (1965), (A vacation trip with psychotic patients.) *Nordisk Med.*, (Copenhagen) 73:558-560.

07453 **LUNDBERG, C. C.** (1973/1974), Toward explicating effective interventions: an emphasis on reducing incongruities. *Interpersonal Develop.*, 4:42-50.

07454 **LUNDBERG, C. C.**, and **LUNDBERG, J.** (1974), Encounter co-training: benefits and pitfalls. *Training Develop. J.*, 28:20-27.

07455 **LUNDGREN, D. C.** (1973), Attitudinal and behavioral correlates of emergent status in training groups. *J. Soc. Psychol.*, 90:141-153.

07456 **LUNDGREN, D. C.** (1979), Authority and group formation. *J. Appl. Behav. Science*, 15:330-345.

07457 **LUNDGREN, D. C.** (1977), Developmental trends in the emergence of interpersonal issues. *Small Group Behav.*, 8:179-200.

07458 **LUNDGREN, D. C.** (1975), Interpersonal needs and member attitudes toward trainer and group. *Small Group Behav.*, 6:371-388.

07459 **LUNDGREN, D. C.** (1976), Member attitudes towards the leaders and interpersonal attraction in short-term training groups. *Group Process*, (London) 6:141-148.

07460 **LUNDGREN, D. C.** (1974), Trainer-member influence in t-groups: one-way or two-way? *Human Relat.*, 27:755-766.

07461 **LUNDGREN, D. C.**, and **KNIGHT, D. J.** (1977), Trainer style and member attitudes toward trainer and group in t-groups. *Small Group Behav.*, 8:47-64.

07462 **LUNDGREN, D. C.**, and **SCHAEFER, C.** (1976), Feedback processes in sensitivity training groups. *Human Relat.*, 29:763-782.

07463 **LUNDGREN, K. D., SCOTT, G.**, and **GRABSKI, D. A.** (1977), Enhancing the outcome of jejunoileal bypass in poor-risk patients through post-operative group counseling. *Amer. Surgeon*, 43:534-537.

07464 **LUNDIN, W. H.** (1951), Group therapy in mental institutions. *Group Psychother., Psychodrama & Sociometry*, 4:193-196.

07465 **LUNDIN, W. H.**, and **ARONOV, B. M.** (1952), The use of co-therapists in group psychotherapy. *J. Couns. Psychol.*, 16:76-80.
07466 **LUNDQVIST, B.** (1961), (Occupational therapy: group therapy and sociotherapy.) *Socialmed. Tidskr.*, (Copenhagen) 38:131-137.
07467 **LUNSKY, L.** (1957), A psychotic episode precipitated by group psychotherapy. *Psychiat. Quart. Suppl.*, 31:65-68.
07468 **LURIA, Z.** (1959), A semantic analysis of a normal and a neurotic therapy group. *J. Abnorm. & Soc. Psychol.*, 58:216-220.
07469 **LURIE, A.**, and **RON, H.** (1970), Utilization of groups in rehabilitating young discharged schizophrenic patients. *Proceed., 78th Annual Convention*, American Psychology Association, 505-506.
07470 **LUST, I.** (1976), (Group models and the issue of latent content in group therapy.) *Magyar Pszichol. Szemle*, (Budapest) 33:364-374.
07471 **LUTTIKHOLT, A.** (1980), *Van Huis Uit: Werken in Vrouwengroepen*. Amsterdam: Feministische Uitgeverj Sara.
07472 **LUZES, P.**, and **CABBABE, G.** (1962), (Psychiatric hospitalism seen in the light of ward psychotherapy.) *Hygiene Ment. Can.*, (Ottawa) 51:273-282.
07473 **LYAPIN, E. S.** (1971), *Exercises in Group Theory*. New York: Plenum.
07474 **LYLE, J.**, and **HOLLY, S.** (1941), The therapeutic value of puppets. *Bull. Menninger Clinic*, 5:223-226.
07475 **LYNCH, C. C.** (1973), Management of nursing care on a psychiatric service. *Nursing Clinics North Amer.*, 8:293-303.
07476 **LYNCH, K. A. B.** (1975), The effects of group therapy on self concept and behaviors of male prisoners. *Dissert. Abstr. Internat.*, 36:1442B.
07477 **LYNCH, L.** (1970), Leadership training in the west. *Nursing Outlook*, 18:38-39.
07478 **LYNCH, M.**, and **GARDNER, E. A.** (1970), Some issues raised in the training of paraprofessional personnel as clinic therapists. *Amer. J. Psychiat.*, 226:1473-1479.
07479 **LYNN, A. W.** (1972), Measures of self-actualization changes and their relationship to interaction preferences among encounter group participants. *Dissert. Abstr. Internat.*, 33:1443A.
07480 **LYNN, R.** (1980), Why did I choose group analysis? *Group Anal.*, (London) 13:46-47.
07481 **LYON, G. G.** (1970), Trust in the non-hospitalized group. *Perspect. Psychiat. Care*, 8:64-72.
07482 **LYON, H. C.** (1974), *It's Me and I'm Here! From West Point to Esalen: The Struggles of an Overachiever to Revitalize His Life Through the Human Potential Movement*. New York: Delacorte Press.
07483 **LYON, V.** (1953), The case worker as group therapist. *Internat. J. Group Psychother.*, 3:198-203.
07484 **LYON, W.** (1956), Group therapy for students in clinical psychology. *Amer. Psychologist*, 11:290-291.

M

07485 **MAAS, H. S.** (1951), Applying group therapy to classroom practice. *Ment. Hygiene*, 35:250-259.

07486 **MAAS, H. S.** (1956), Cultural elements in group psychotherapy: some problems for study. *Ment. Hygiene*, 40:44-52.

07487 **MAAS, J.** (1966), The use of actional procedures in group psychotherapy with sociopathic women. *Internat. J. Group Psychother.*, 16:190-197.

07488 **MAAS, J. P.** (1964), Ego diffusion in women with behavioral disorders and the integrating effects of psychodrama in identity consolidation. *Dissert. Abstr. Internat.*, 25:3689.

07489 **MAASS, V. S.** (1978), The effects of three types of physical structure upon clients' risk-taking change in beliefs, and selected perceptions in rational-emotive/rational group therapy. *Dissert. Abstr. Internat.*, 39:3378A.

07490 **MACASKILL, N. D.** (1980), The narcissistic core as a focus in the group therapy of the borderline patient. *Brit. J. Med. Psychol.*, (London) 53:137-144.

07491 **MacDONALD, A. P., GAMEO, R. G.,** and **MINK, O. G.** (1972), Film-mediated facilitation of self-disclosure and attraction to sensitivity training. *Psychol. Reports*, 30:847-857.

07492 **MacDONALD, B. L.** (1978), An investigation of therapist pathogenesis. *Dissert. Abstr. Internat.*, 40:5411B.

07493 **MacDONALD, C.** (1968), Treatment of the mentally disturbed geriatric patient. *Geriatrics*, 23:168-176.

07494 **MacDONALD, D. E.** (1974), Group characteristics of alcoholics: a videotape demonstration. *Ann. N.Y. Acad. Science*, 233:128-134.

07495 **MacDONALD, D. E.** (1958), Group psychotherapy with wives of alcoholics. *Quart. J. Studies Alcohol*, 19:125-132.

07496 **MacDONALD, G. H.,** and **DiFURI, A. G.** (1971), A guided self-help approach to the treatment of the habitual sex offender. *Hosp. & Community Psychiat.*, 22:310-313.

07497 **MacDONALD, M. L.** (1975), Social skills training: behavior rehearsal in groups and dating skills. *J. Couns. Psychol.*, 22:224-230.

07498 **MacDONALD, W. S.** (1966), Small group treatment of chronic mental patients: the problem of applicability. *Amer. J. Psychiat.*, 122:1298-1301.

07499 **MacDONALD, W. S., BLOCHBERGER, C. W.,** and **MAYNARD, H. M.** (1964), Group therapy: a comparison of patient-led and staff-led groups on an open hospital ward. *Psychiat. Quart. Suppl.*, 38:290-303.

07500 **MacDONALD, W. S., SANDERS, D. H., CARLIN, A.,** and **TROFFER, S.** (1965), Assimilation of new members into problem-solving groups of patients. *J. Nerv. & Ment. Diseases*, 141:371-377.

07501 **MacDOUGALL, A. A.** (1958), Group therapy for alcoholics and addicts. *Brit. J. Addict.*, (Edinburgh) 54:127-132.

07502 **MacDOUGALL, D. B.** (1970), The effects of group counseling and improved student-teacher communications on the anxiety level of students entering junior high school. *Dissert. Abstr. Internat.*, 30:5241A-5242A.

07503 **MACE, D. L.** (1970), College volunteers as group leaders with chronic patients: effects of ward personnel involvement on ward behavior change. *Dissert. Abstr. Internat.*, 31:2287.

07504 **MACE, D. R.** (1975), We call it ACME. *Small Group Behav.*, 6:31-44.

07505 **MacGREGOR, R.** (1970), Group and family therapy: moving into the present and letting go of the past. *Internat. J. Group Psychother.*, 20:495-515.

07506 **MacELVER, R. M.** (1972), *Group Relations and Group Antagonisms*. New York: P. Smith.

07507 **MACK, J. E.** (1963), From a night hospital unit: the evolution of patient ward meetings into group psychotherapy. *Internat. J. Soc. Psychiat.*, (London) 9:51-57.

07508 **MACK, J. E.**, and **BARNUM, M. C.** (1966), Group activity and group discussion in the treatment of hospitalized psychiatric patients. *Internat. J. Group Psychother.*, 16:452-462.

07509 **MacKEEN, B. A.**, and **HERMAN, A.** (1974), Effects of group counseling on self-esteem. *J. Couns. Psychol.*, 21:210-214.

07510 **MacKENZIE, K. R.** (1979), Group norms: importance and measurement. *Internat. J. Group Psychother.*, 29:471.

07511 **MacKENZIE, K. R.** (1980), Review of H. Kellerman's *Group Psychotherapy and Personality: Intersecting Structures*. *Group*, 4:62-64.

07512 **MacKENZIE, K. R.**, and **ANDERSON, J.** (1974), Holding tea groups: a home visiting program for chronic schizophrenics. *Hosp. & Community Psychiat.*, 25:509.

07513 **MACKEY, R. A.**, and **HASSLER, F. R.** (1966), Group consultation with school personnel. *Ment. Hygiene*, 50:416-420.

07514 **MACKIE, R. E.**, and **WOOD, J.** (1968), Observations on two sides of a one-way screen. *Internat. J. Group Psychother.*, 18:177-185.

07515 **MacLEAN, B.** (1971), Simulated situations in group psychotherapy training. *Internat. J. Group Psychother.*, 21:330-332.

07516 **MacLENNAN, B. W.** (1965), Co-therapy. *Internat. J. Group Psychother.*, 15:154-166.

07517 **MacLENNAN, B. W.** (1968), Group approaches to the problems of socially deprived youths: the classical psychotherapeutic model. *Internat. J. Group Psychother.*, 18:481-494.

07518 **MacLENNAN, B. W.** (1967), The group as a reinforcer of reality: a positive approach in the treatment of adolescents. *Amer. J. Orthopsychiat.*, 37:272-273.

07519 **MacLENNAN, B. W.** (1970), Groups for teenagers in the everyday world. In: *Understanding and Aiding Disturbed Youth*, eds. S. J. Shamsic and J. Unwin. Philadelphia: Lea and Febiger.

07520 **MacLENNAN, B. W.** (1977), Modifications of activity group therapy for children. *Internat. J. Group Psychother.*, 27:85-96.

07521 **MacLENNAN, B. W.** (1975), The personalities of group leaders: implications for selection and training. *Internat. J. Group Psychother.*, 25:177-183.

07522 **MacLENNAN, B. W.** (1972), Selected annotated reading list in group work (1951-71). *Psychiat. Annals*, 2:63-73.

07523 **MacLENNAN, B. W.** (1971), Simulated situations in group psychotherapy training. *Internat. J. Group Psychother.*, 21:330-332.

07524 **MacLENNAN, B. W.** (1969), Therapeutic group approaches with ghetto youth. *Newsl. Amer. Orthopsychiat. Assn.*, 13:40.

07525 **MacLENNAN, B. W.** (1969), Training for new careers. In: *The Study of Abnormal Behavior: Selected Readings*, 2d ed., eds. M. Zax and G. Stricker. New York: Macmillan.

07526 **MacLENNAN, B. W.**, and **FELSENFELD, N.** (1968), *Group Counseling and Psychotherapy with Adolescents*. New York: Columbia University Press.

07527 **MacLENNAN, B. W.**, and **MORSE, V.** (1966), *Readings on Group Approaches in the Treatment of Adolescent Problems*. Washington, D.C.: Howard University Institute for Youth Studies.

07528 **MacLENNAN, B. W.**, and **LEVY, W.** (1971), The group psychotherapy literature, 1970. *Internat. J. Group Psychother.*, 21:345-359.

07529 **MacLENNAN, B. W.**, and **LEVY, N.** (1970), Group psychotherapy literature, 1969. *Internat. J. Group Psychother.*, 20:380-411.

07530 **MacLENNAN, B. W.**, and **LEVY, N.** (1969), The group psychotherapy literature, 1968. *Internat. J. Group Psychother.*, 19:382-408.

07531 **MacLENNAN, B. W.**, and **LEVY, N.** (1968), The group psychotherapy literature, 1967. *Internat. J. Group Psychother.*, 18:375-401.

07532 **MacLENNAN, B. W.**, and **LEVY, N.** (1967), The group psychotherapy literature, 1966. *Internat. J. Group Psychother.*, 17:378-398.

07533 **MacLENNAN, B. W.**, and **ROSEN, B.** (1963), Female therapists in activity group psychotherapy with boys in latency. *Internat. J. Group Psychother.*, 13:34-42.

07534 **MacLENNAN, B. W.**, **MORSE, V.**, and **GOODE, P.** (1966), The group psychotherapy literature, 1965. *Internat. J. Group Psychother.*, 16:225-241.

07535 **MacLENNAN, B. W.**, **FELENSFELD, N. S.**, **BELTON, S.**, and **BURKE, K.** (1965), The group psychotherapy literature, 1964. *Internat. J. Group Psychother.*, 15:251-269.

07536 **MacMILLAN, M.** (1980), Madness: or just a case of sadness? Psychodrama with a group of psychiatric patients. *Nursing Times*, (London) 76:1310-1313.

07537 **MacNAMARA, M.** (1972), Group dynamics in university tutorials. *Univ. Quart.*, 26:231-253.

07538 **MacNEIL, M. K.** (1975), Group status displacement under stress: a serendipitous finding. *Sociometry*, 38:293-307.

07539 **MACOMBER, M. V.** (1975), The comparative effectiveness of group therapy and inmate group activities at a correctional facility. *Dissert. Abstr. Internat.*, 35:4655B.

07540 **MACOMBER, W.** (1908), *History of the Emmanuel Movement from the Standpoint of a Patient.* Boston: Moffat, Yard.

07541 **MacPHAIL, D.** (1965), Personal experience of group therapy for alcoholism: a critical examination. *Lancet*, 2:75-77.

07542 **MacRAE-GIBSON, N.** (1972), Failure of therapeutic communities. *New Era*, (London) 53:122-128.

07543 **MADDEN, D. J.** (1977), Voluntary and involuntary treatment of aggressive patients. *Amer. J. Psychiat.*, 134:553-555.

07544 **MADDEN, J. S.** (1977), Programme of group counseling for alcoholics. In: *Alcoholism and Drug Dependence: A Multidisciplinary Approach*, eds. J. S. Madden, R. Walker, W. H. Kenyon. New York: Plenum Press.

07545 **MADDEN, J. S.**, and **KENYON, W. H.** (1975), Group counseling of alcoholics by a voluntary agency. *Brit. J. Psychiat.*, (Ashford) 126:289-291.

07546 **MADDISON, B.** (1978), Personal story of mental decline and return. *Australasian Nurses J.*, (Port Adelaide) 7:23-24.

07547 **MADDISON, D.**, and **WALKER, W. L.** (1967), Factors affecting the outcome of conjugal bereavement. *Brit. J. Psychiat.*, (Ashford) 113:1057-1067.

07548 **MADDOCKS, P. D.** (1967), A group personality measure and relationship to prognosis. *Brit. J. Psychiat.*, (Ashford) 113:143-148.

07549 **MADISON, P.** (1972), Have group, will travel. *Psychother.: Theory, Res. & Pract.*, 9:324-327.

07550 **MADURO, R.** (1976), Journey dreams in Latino group psychotherapy. *Psychother.: Theory, Res. & Pract.*, 13:148.

07551 **MAEDA, E.** (1960), Activity programming for the aggressive child. *Amer. J. Occupat. Ther.*, 14:223-226.

07552 **MAFFEO, P. A.** (1979), Thoughts on Strüchess' "Implications of research for psychotherapeutic treatment of women." *Amer. Psychologist*, 34:690-695.

07553 **MAFFEZZONI, G.**, and **COLUCCI-D'AMATO, F.** (1966), Aspetti psicoterapeutici del disegno in un gruppo di ricoverate. (Psychotherapeutic aspects of drawing in a group of female patients.) *Ospedale Psichiat.*, (Naples) 34:75-94.

07554 **MAGAZU, P.**, **GOLNER, J.**, and **ARSENIAN, J.** (1964), Reactions of a group of chronic psychotic patients to the departure of the group therapist. *Psychiat. Quart.*, 38:292-303.

07555 **MAGDEN, R. F.** (1975), Eight dimensions of group psychotherapy as they relate to three approaches to group therapy. *Dissert. Abstr. Internat.*, 36:1412B.

07556 **MAGEL, D. G.** (1976), The development of an inventory for determining the relationship of agreement among related groups concerning those facets of group leader behavior which tend to promote effective group counseling. *Dissert. Abstr. Internat.*, 36:5830A.

07557 **MAGEN, Z.** (1980), Encounter group effects on soccer team performance. *Small Group Behav.*, 11:339-344.

07558 **MAGERS, B. D.** (1978), Cognitive-behavioral short-term group therapy with depressed women. *Dissert. Abstr. Internat.*, 38:4468B. (University Microfilms No. 7801687.)

07559 **MAGHERINI, G.**, and **ZELONI, G.** (1961), (Combination of neuroplegic, end group, and occupational therapy in the treatment of chronic psychotics.) *Rass. Studi Psichiat.*, (Siena) 50:305-308.

07560 **MAGINNIS, M.** (1958), Gesture and status. *Group Psychother., Psychodrama & Sociometry*, 11:105-109.

07561 **MAGNY, C.** (1971), (Theoretical and technical elements for group analysis.) *Evolut. Psychiat.*, (Toulouse) 36:399-411.

07562 **MAGYAR, C. W.** (1974), The effects of interpersonal growth contracts and leader experience on the process and outcome of encounter groups. *Dissert. Abstr. Internat.*, 35:193A.

07563 **MAHLER, C. A.** (1969), *Group Counseling in the Schools*. Boston: Houghton-Mifflin.

07564 **MAHLER, C. A.** (1971), Group counseling. *Personnel & Guid. J.*, 49:601-610.

07565 **MAHLER, C. A.** (1973), Minimal necessary conditions in schools for effective group counseling. *Educat. Technol.*, 13:21-23.

07566 **MAHLER, C. A.**, and **CALDWELL, E.** (1961), *Group Counseling in Secondary Schools*. Chicago: Science Research Associates.

07567 **MAHLER, E.** (1976), (Interdependence of group processes between small groups and a large group from a psychoanalytic point of view.) *Gruppenpsychother. & Gruppendynam.*, (Goettingen) 10:25-49.

07568 **MAHLER, E.** (1969), (Observed collective ego reactions as demonstrated by a psychoanalytic group session and by theater audience.) *Psyche*, (Stuttgart) 23:506-515.

07569 **MAHLER, E.** (1974), (Psychoanalytically oriented thematic self-experience in groups: a preliminary report on the applicability of psychoanalytic group concepts to work with teachers in training.) *Psyche*, (Stuttgart) 28:97-115.

07570 **MAHOLICK, L. T.**, and **BAKER, F. P.** (1953), The resolution of professional cloaks through an interagency group experience. *Group Psychother., Psychodrama & Sociometry*, 5:226-232.

07571 **MAHRER, A. R.**, and **PEARSON, L.** (1971), *Creative Developments in Psychotherapy: I*. Cleveland: Case Western Reserve University Press.

07572 **MAHRLEIN, W.**, **SCHNABL, S.**, and **BOTHE, E.** (1961), (Psychotherapeutic aspects of the treatment of obesity.) *Deutsche Gesundh.*, (Berlin) 16:194-197.

07573 **MAIER, G. J.** (1976), Review of T. Verny's *Inside Groups: A Practical*

Guide to Encounter Groups and Therapy Groups. Can. Psychiat. Assn. J., (Ottawa) 21:127-128.
07574 **MAIER, H. W.**, and **LOOMIS, E. A.** (1954), Effecting impulse control in children through group therapy. *Internat. J. Group Psychother.*, 4:312-320.
07575 **MAIER, N. R.** (1972), Effects of training on decision-making. *Psychol. Reports*, 30:159-164.
07576 **MAIER, N. R. F.** (1953), Dramatized case material as a springboard for role playing. *Group Psychother., Psychodrama & Sociometry*, 6:30-42.
07577 **MAIER, N. R. F.** (1970), *Problem Solving and Creativity: In Individuals and Groups*. Belmont, CA: Brooks/Cole.
07578 **MAIERHOFER, R. A.** (1970), Pupil behavior change through group counseling and teacher consultation. *Dissert. Abstr. Internat.*, 31:3879A.
07579 **MAILHIOT, B.** (1967), La psychologie des relations interethniques: implications pour la psychiatrie sociale. (The psychology of interethnic relations: implications for social psychiatry.) *Can. Psychiat. Assn. J. Suppl.*, (Ottawa) 12:53-69, 82-85.
07580 **MAILLOUX, N.** (1964), Delinquency and repetition compulsion. *Arch. Psicol., Neurol. & Psichiat.*, (Milan) 25:7-17.
07581 **MAIN, T.** (1975), Some psychodynamics of large groups. In: *The Large Group: Dynamics and Therapy*, ed. L. Kreeger. London: Constable.
07582 **MAIN, T. F.** (1974), Some psychodynamic aspects of large groups. *Arch. Psicol. Neurol. & Psichiat.*, (Milan) 35:453-479.
07583 **MAINORD, W. A., BURK, H. W.**, and **COLLINS, L. G.** (1965), Confrontation versus diversion in group therapy with chronic schizophrenics are measured by a "positive incident" criterion. *J. Clin. Psychol.*, 21:222-225.
07584 **MAIZLER, J. S.**, and **SOLOMON, J. R.** (1976), Therapeutic group process with the institutional elderly. *J. Amer. Geriat. Soc.*, 24:542-546.
07585 **MAIZLISH, I. L.**, and **HURLEY, J. R.** (1963), Attitude changes of husbands and wives in time-limited group psychotherapy. *Psychiat. Quart. Suppl.*, 37:230-249.
07586 **MAKO, A. E.** (1961), Patient government: development and outgrowths. *Ment. Hosp.*, 12:30-32.
07587 **MAKOWSKY, B.**, and **OKEN, D.** (1969), The contributions of social group work to the therapeutic milieu. *Hosp. & Community Psychiat.*, 20:119-122.
07588 **MALAMUD, D. I.** (1975), Communication training in the second-chance family. *Small Group Behav.*, 6:72-90.
07589 **MALAMUD, D. I.** (1980), The laughing game: an exercise for sharpening awareness of self-responsibility. *Psychother.: Theory, Res. & Pract.*, 17:69-73.
07590 **MALAMUD, D. I.** (1974), One step at a time. *Voices*, 6:54-59.
07591 **MALAMUD, D. I.**, and **MACHOVER, S.** (1965), *Toward Self-Understanding: Group Techniques in Self-Confrontation*. Springfield, IL: C. C. Thomas.
07592 **MALAN, D. H., BALFOUR, F. H. G., HOOD, V. G.**, and **SHOOTER, A. M.** (1976), Group psychotherapy: long term follow-up study. *Arch. Gen. Psychiat.*, 33:1303-1315.
07593 **MALCOLM, A. I.** (1973), *The Tyranny of the Group*. Toronto: Clarke, Irwin.
07594 **MALDONADO-SIERRA, E., TRENT, R. D., FERNANDEZ-MARINA, R., FLORES-GALLARDO, A., VIGOREAUX-RIVERA, J.**, and **DE COLON, L. S.** (1960), Cultural factors in the group-psychotherapeutic process for Puerto Rican schizophrenics. *Internat. J. Group Psychother.*, 10:373-382.
07595 **MALDONADO-SIERRA, E. D.**, and **TRENT, R. D.** (1960), The sibling re-

lationship in group psychotherapy with Puerto Rican schizophrenics. *Amer. J. Psychiat.*, 117:239-244.

07596 **MALEK, Z. B.** (1961), The effects of group experiences on the aged. *Dissert. Abstr. Internat.*, 21:3525.

07597 **MALER, J. S.**, and **MEYEROWITZ, J. H.** (1973), An interesting fifteen-month experience in group process with chronic schizophrenics. *Newsl. Res. Ment. Health & Behav. Sciences*, 15:13-15.

07598 **MALHOTRA, K. H.**, and **OLGIATI, S. G.** (1977), Fluphenazine therapy in groups. *Comprehens. Psychiat.*, 18:89-92.

07599 **MALIKOVIC, B., DIVAC, M., BLAGOJEVIC, M.**, and **KIRKOVIC, M.** (1976), (Special features of group psychotherapy of elderly alcoholics.) *Soc. Psihijatr.*, 4:67-76.

07600 **MALIVER, B. L.** (1973), *Encounter Game.* New York: Stein and Day.

07601 **MALIVER, B. L.** (1971), Encounter groupers up against the wall. *N.Y. Times Magazine*, (Jan. 3) 4-5.

07602 **MALIVER, B. L.** (1972), How valuable are encounter techniques in analytic group psychotherapy. *Psychiat. Annals*, 2:34-37.

07603 **MALIVER, R. R.** (1971), Encounter groups: a dangerous game? *Current*, 126:3-12.

07604 **MALLINSON, T. J.** (1965), Applications of group processes to a clinical (psychiatric) setting. *Internat. J. Soc. Psychiat.*, (London) 11:32-37.

07605 **MALLY, M. A.**, and **OGSTON, W. D.** (1964), Treatment of the "untreatables." *Internat. J. Group Psychother.*, 14:369-374.

07606 **MALLY, M. A.**, and **STREHL, C. B.** (1963), Evaluation of a three-year group therapy program for multiple sclerosis patients. *Internat. J. Group Psychother.*, 13:328-334.

07607 **MALNATI, R. J.**, and **PASTUSHAK, R.** (1980), Conducting group practice with the aged. *Psychother.: Theory, Res. & Pract.*, 17:352.

07608 **MALNATI, R. J.**, and **TREMBLY, E. L.** (1974), *Group Procedures for Counselors in Educational and Community Settings.* New York: Mss Information.

07609 **MALONE, T. P.** (1948), Analysis of the dynamics of group psychotherapy based on observations in a twelve-month experimental program. *J. Personality*, 16:245-277.

07610 **MALONE, T. P.**, and **WHITAKER, C. A.** (1965), A community of psychotherapists. *Internat. J. Group Psychother.*, 15:23-28.

07611 **MALONEY, W. P.** (1970), A review and analysis of the reported experimental research on group counseling in higher education between 1955 and 1967. *Dissert. Abstr. Internat.*, 31:4467A.

07612 **MALOTT, R. W.**, and **ROLLOFSON, R. L.** (1972), An empirical evaluation of student-led discussions. *Psychol. Reports*, 30:531-535.

07613 **MAMOLA, C.** (1979), Women in mixed groups. *Small Group Behav.*, 10:431.

07614 **MANASTER, A.** (1971), Theragnostic group in a rehabilitation center for visually handicapped persons. *New Outlook Blind*, 65:261-264.

07615 **MANASTER, A.** (1972), Therapy with the "senile" geriatric patient. *Internat. J. Group Psychother.*, 22:250-257.

07616 **MANASTER, A.**, and **KUCHARIS, S.** (1972), Experiential methods in a group counseling program with blind children. *New Outlook Blind*, 66:15-19.

07617 **MANDEL, R.** (1971), A comparison of short-term leaderless guidance groups and counselor-led groups with hospitalized physically disabled veterans. *Dissert. Abstr. Internat.*, 32:3693A.

07618 **MANDELBAUM, A.** (1967), The group process in helping parents of retarded children. *Children*, 14:227-232.

07619 **MANDELBAUM, A.** (1969), Group processes with parents of retarded children. *Ment. Retard. Abstr.*, 6:726.
07620 **MANDELBAUM, A.** (1973), Intergenerational groups in a drop-in mental health center. *Soc. Casework*, 54:154-161.
07621 **MANDELBROTE, B.**, and **FREEMAN, H.** (1963), The closed group concept in open psychiatric hospitals. *Amer. J. Psychiat.*, 119:763-767.
07622 **MANDERINO, M. A.** (1974), Effects of a group assertive training procedure on undergraduate women. *Dissert. Abstr. Internat.*, 35:1389B.
07623 **MANDERSHEID, R. W., KOENIG, G. R.**, and **SILBERGELD, S.** (1978), Psychosocial factors for classroom, group, and ward. *Psychol. Reports*, 43:555-561.
07624 **MANGHAM, I.** (1977), Definitions, interactions, and disengagement: notes towards a theory of intervention processes in t-groups. *Small Group Behav.*, 8:487-510.
07625 **MANGHAM, I.** (1966), Group dynamics and educational drama. *Educat. Rev.*, (Birmingham) 19:45-55.
07626 **MANHAES, M. P.** (1960), (The artist and the initial situation in group therapy.) *Med. Cir. For.*, 288:175-186.
07627 **MANIS, L. G.** (1977), *Womanpower*. Cranston, RI: Carroll Press.
07628 **MANLEY, S.** (1973), A definitive approach to group counseling. *J. Rehab.*, 39:38-40.
07629 **MANN, A.** (1955), Group therapy: irradiation. *J. Crim. Law & Criminol.*, 46:50-66.
07630 **MANN, H.** (1961), *The Use of Psychodrama in Health Education*. New York: Carlton.
07631 **MANN, C. H.** (1955), The effect of role playing on role playing ability and interpersonal adequacy. *Dissert. Abstr. Internat.*, 18:665.
07632 **MANN, J.** (1951), An analytically oriented study of groups. *J. Psychiat. Soc. Work*, 20:137-143.
07633 **MANN, J.** (1954), Didactic use of sociometry and psychodrama. *Group Psychother., Psychodrama & Sociometry*, 7:242-248.
07634 **MANN, J.** (1970), *Encounter: A Weekend with Intimate Strangers*. New York: Grossman.
07635 **MANN, J.** (1953), Group therapy with adults. *Amer. J. Orthopsychiat.*, 23:332-337.
07636 **MANN, J.** (1974), *Learning To Be: The Education of Human Potential*. New York: Free Press.
07637 **MANN, J.** (1962), Psychoanalytic observations regarding conformity in groups. *Internat. J. Group Psychother.*, 12:3-13.
07638 **MANN, J.** (1955), Some theoretic concepts of the group process. *Internat. J. Group Psychother.*, 5:235-241.
07639 **MANN, J.**, and **MANN, H.** (1948), Organization and technique of group treatment of psychoses. *Diseases Nerv. System*, 9:46-51.
07640 **MANN, J.**, and **ROSENTHAL, T. L.** (1969), Vicarious and direct counterconditioning of test anxiety through individual and group desensitization. *Behav. Res. & Ther.*, 7:359-367.
07641 **MANN, J.**, and **SEMRAD, E. V.** (1948), The use of group therapy in psychoses. *J. Soc. Casework*, 29:176-181.
07642 **MANN, J. H.** (1970), *Encounter: A Weekend with Intimate Strangers*. New York: Grossman Publishers.
07643 **MANN, J. H.** (1956), The experimentalist vs. the clinician: a dialogue. *Internat. J. Sociometry & Sociatry*, 1:159-163.
07644 **MANN, J. H.** (1960), The relation between role playing ability and interpersonal adjustment. *J. Gen. Psychol.*, 62:177-183.
07645 **MANN, J. H.**, and **MANN, C. H.** (1958), The effect of role playing expe-

rience on self ratings of interpersonal adjustment. *Group Psychother., Psychodrama & Sociometry*, 11:27-34.

07646 **MANN, J. H.**, and **MANN, C. H.** (1960), The relative effectiveness of role playing and task oriented group experience in producing personality and behavior change. *J. Soc. Psychol.*, 51:313-317.

07647 **MANN, L.**, and **JANIS, I. L.** (1968), A follow-up study on the long-term effects of emotional role playing. *J. Personality*, 8:339-342.

07648 **MANN, P. H., BEABER, J. D.**, and **JACOBSON, M. D.** (1969), The effect of group counseling on educatable mentally retarded boys' self-concept. *Except. Children*, 35:359-366.

07649 **MANN, R. D.** (1966), The development of the member-trainer relationship in self-analytic groups. *Human Relat.*, 19:85-115.

07650 **MANNE, S. H.** (1962), An investigation of the effects of group therapy on some personality characteristics of adult male offenders: the effects of group therapy on anxiety, impulse control, and overt behavior of adults legally classified as defective delinquents. *Dissert. Abstr. Internat.*, 23:2206-2207.

07651 **MANN, W., GODFREY, M. E.**, and **DOWD, E. T.** (1973), The use of group counseling procedures in the rehabilitation of spinal cord injured patients. *Amer. J. Occupat. Ther.*, 27:73-77.

07652 **MANNING, N. P.** (1976), Innovation in social policy: the case of the therapeutic community. *J. Soc. Policy*, (London) 5:265-279.

07653 **MANNING, N. D.** (1976), Values and practice in the therapeutic community. *Human Relat.*, 29:125-138.

07654 **MANNO, A. O.** (1969), Group interaction as a means of inducing innovative teaching in elementary schools. *Dissert. Abstr. Internat.*, 30:1023A-1024A.

07655 **MANSFIELD, E.** (1977), Teaching group leadership: concept, illustration, analogy and role model. *J. Nursing Educat.*, 16:3-8.

07656 **MANTHEI, M.** (1979), *Positively Me: An Assertive Training Guide*. Auckland: Methuen.

07657 **MANTIONE, F. F.** (1976), A comparison of the effects of muscular relaxation and rest on the behavior of grammar school children described as hyperactive. *Dissert. Abstr. Internat.*, 36:5268.

07658 **MAO, C. L.** (1980), Theory and practice of group therapy. *Hu Li Tsa Chih*, (Hong Kong) 27:1-8.

07659 **MARACER, J., KRAVETZ, D.**, and **FINN, S.** (1979), Comparison of women who enter feminist therapy and women who enter traditional therapy. *J. Consult. & Clin. Psychol.*, 47:734-742.

07660 **MARCHAND, H.** (1961), (Group therapy at a health resort.) *Psychiat., Neurol. & Med. Psychol.*, (Leipzig) 13:169-172.

07661 **MARCHAND, R. H.** (1972), A comparison of t-group and practicum approaches to the training of undergraduate resident assistants. *Dissert. Abstr. Internat.*, 33:973A.

07662 **MARCHIORI, H.** (1975), *Psicologia Criminal.* (*Criminal Psychology.*) México: Editorial Porrúa.

07663 **MARCONDES, E.** (1977), Training drama. *Rev. Hosp. Clin. Fac. Med. São Paulo*, 32:377-378.

07664 **MARCUS, A. M.**, and **CONWAY, C.** (1971), A Canadian group approach study of dangerous sexual offenders. *Internat. J. Offender Ther.*, (London) 15:59-66.

07665 **MARCUS, I. M.** (1951), Analytic group psychotherapy: its pertinence to family disorders. *Bull. Tulane Univ. 11.*

07666 **MARCUS, I. M.** (1966), Costume play therapy: the exploration of a method for stimulating imaginative play in older children. *J. Amer. Acad. Child. Psychiat.*, 5:441-452.

07667 **MARCUS, I. M.** (1956), Psychoanalytic group therapy with fathers of emotionally disturbed preschool children. *Internat. J. Group Psychother.*, 6:61-79.

07668 **MARCY, M. R.**, and **FROMME, O. K.** (1979), Group modification of affective verbalizations. *Small Group Behav.*, 10:547.

07669 **MARGOLIN, J. B.** (1952), The use of an interaction matrix to validate patterns of group behavior. *Human Relat.*, 5:407-416.

07670 **MARGOLIN, R. J.**, and **ROSE, C. L.** (1951), A dynamic group experience in a military hospital paraplegic unit. *Military Surg.*, 109:712-720.

07671 **MARGOLIS, H.** (1946), The psychodramatic approach to medical diagnosis in treatment. *J. Soc. Casework*, 27:291-299.

07672 **MARGOLIS, J.** (1977), (Group psychotherapy: operative groups at ISSSTE.) *Neurol.-Neurocir.-Psiquiat.*, (Mexico City) 18:117-120.

07673 **MARGOLIS, L.** (1946), Criteria for selection of children for activity group therapy. *Smith Coll. Studies Soc. Work*, 17:32-49.

07674 **MARGOLIS, P. M.**, and **BONSTEDT, T.** (1970), What is community psychiatry? *Diseases Nerv. System*, 31:251-258.

07675 **MARGRO, A. L.** (1973), The effectiveness of peer-led and adult-led group counseling of behavioral problem girls in a middle school. *Dissert. Abstr. Internat.*, 34:137A.

07676 **MARGULIES, N.** (1973), The effects of an organizational sensitivity training program on a measure of self-actualization. *Studies Personnel Psychol.*, (Ottawa) 5:67-74.

07677 **MARHOLIN, D.**, and **MCINNIS, E. T.** (1978), Treating children in group settings: techniques for individualizing behavioral programs. In: *Child Behavior Therapy*, ed. D. Marholin. New York: Gardner Press.

07678 **MARIC, J.**, and **VELEL, J.** (1976), (The athymohormic patient in the therapeutic community.) *Soc. Psihijat.*, (Belgrade) 4:39-46.

07679 **MARKENSON, D. J.** (1969), New approaches to the symptomatic treatment of multiple-problem predelinquent and delinquent teenage girls. *Amer. J. Orthopsychiat.*, 39:309-310.

07680 **MARKHAM, C.** (1974), Letter: the cons of group psychotherapy. *Lancet*, 2:518-523.

07681 **MARKHAM, D. J.** (1980), Behavioral rehearsal vs. group systematic desensitization in assertiveness training. *Dissert. Abstr. Internat.*, 41:357B. (University Microfilms No. 8014030.)

07682 **MARKHAM, D. J.** (1979), Behavioral rehearsal vs. group systematic desensitization in assertiveness training. *Dissert. Abstr. Internat.*, 41:357B.

07683 **MARKOFF, E. L.** (1969), Synanon in drug addiction. In: *Current Psychiatric Therapies*, ed. J. H. Masserman. New York: Grune and Stratton.

07684 **MARKOWITZ, I.** (1967), Confidentiality in group therapy. *Ment. Hygiene*, 51:601-603.

07685 **MARKOWITZ, I.** (1975), Making meaningful advice to parents acceptable. *Internat. J. Group Psychother.*, 25:323-329.

07686 **MARKOWITZ, I.** (1965), The therapist in the nonpatient group. *Internat. J. Group Psychother.*, 15:358-365.

07687 **MARKOWITZ, M.** (1965), Narcissism and the development of self from dyadic to group relatedness. *Topical Probl. Psychol. & Psychother.*, 5:59-66.

07688 **MARKOWITZ, M., SCHWARTZ, E. K.**, and **LIFF, Z. A.** (1965), Nondidactic methods of group psychotherapy training based on frustration experience. *Internat. J. Group Psychother.*, 15:220-227.

07689 **MARKS, I.** (1971), The future of the psychotherapies. *Brit. J. Psychiat.*, (Ashford) 118:69-73, 542.

07690 **MARKS, J. B.** (1952), Special problems in group work with tuberculosis patients. *Internat. J. Group Psychother.*, 2:150-158.

07691 **MARKS, M. J.** (1965), The personal impact of group training experience. *Topical Probl. Psychol. & Psychother.*, 5:39-47.
07692 **MARKS, M. W.** (1975), The effects of encounter groups on participants' levels of moral reasoning. *Dissert. Abstr. Internat.*, 36:916B.
07693 **MARKS, M. W.**, and **VESTRE, N. D.** (1974), Self-perception and interpersonal behavior changes in marathon and time-extended encounter groups. *J. Consult. & Clin. Psychol.*, 42:729-733.
07694 **MARKS, S. E.** (1973), The marathon group hypothesis: an unanswered question. *Couns. Psychologist*, 20:185-187.
07695 **MARKS, S. E.** (1975), Videotape recording in counseling: "what we know and where to find it." *Can. Counselor*, (Ottawa) 9:31-44.
07696 **MARLER, D. C.** (1964), A follow-up study of a weekend hospital program. *Ment. Hosp.*, 15:204.
07697 **MARLER, D. C.**, and **STRAIGHT, E. M.** (1965), Evaluation of the weekend hospital program: a follow-up study. *Diseases Nerv. System*, 26:485-489.
07698 **MARLOWE, R. H.** (1972), A comparison of teacher use of behavior modification and two group counseling techniques in change of inappropriate classroom behavior of low achieving seventh grade students. *Dissert. Abstr. Internat.*, 32:6273A.
07699 **MARMOR, J.** (1971), Dynamic psychotherapy and behavior therapy: are they irreconcilable? *Arch. Gen. Psychiat.*, 24:22-28.
07700 **MARMOR, J.** (1971), Limitations of dyadic therapy: S. R. Slavson Lecture. Annual Meeting of the American Group Psychotherapy Association, Los Angeles, California.
07701 **MAROHN, R. C.** (1969), The similarity of therapy and supervisory themes. *Internat. J. Group Psychother.*, 19:176-184.
07702 **MAROHN, R. C.** (1970), The therapeutic milieu as an open system. *Arch. Gen. Psychiat.*, 22:360-364.
07703 **MAROHN, R. C.** (1967), The unit meeting: its implications for a therapeutic correctional community. *Internat. J. Group Psychother.*, 17:159-167.
07704 **MAROHN, R. C.** (1970), The ward meetings as an open system. *Sandoz Psychiat. Spectator*, 6:9-10.
07705 **MAROON, E. C.** (1977), The effects of the tenth grade administration of the PSAT/NMSQT and a group counseling experience on eleventh grade performance on the PSAT/NMSQT. *Dissert. Abstr. Internat.*, 38:2559A.
07706 **MAROUN, T. J.** (1970), Differential effects of two methods of encounter group training on the personal growth of counselor candidates. *Dissert. Abstr. Internat.*, 31:5134A.
07707 **MARRAM, G.** (1972), Coalition attempts in group therapy: indicators of inclusion and group cohesion problems. *J. Psychiat. Nursing*, 10:21-23.
07708 **MARRAM, G. D.** (1978), *The Group Approach in Nursing Practice*. St. Louis: C. B. Mosby.
07709 **MARRAM, G. D.** (1971), Latent content and covert group forces in therapy with acute psychiatric patients. *J. Psychiat. Nursing*, 9:24-27.
07710 **MARRONE, M.** (1980), Review of A. Dellarossa's *Reflexion Groups. Group Anal.*, (London) 13:147.
07711 **MARRONE, M.** (1980), Review of T. Saretsky's *Active Techniques and Group Psychotherapy. Group Anal.*, (London) 13:147-148.
07712 **MARRONE, R. L.**, **MERKSAMER, M. A.**, and **SALZBERG, P. M.** (1970), A short duration group treatment of smoking behavior by stimulus saturation. *Behav. Res. & Ther.*, 8:347-352.
07713 **MARRONE, R. T.**, and **ANDERSON, N.** (1970), Innovative public school programming for emotionally disturbed children. *Amer. J. Orthopsychiat.*, 40:694-701.

07714 **MARSH, C.**, and **DRENNAN, B.** (1976), Ego states and egogram therapy. *Transactional Anal. J.*, 6:135-137.

07715 **MARSH, J. C.** (1977), Review of S. D. Rose's *Group Therapy: Behavioral Approach. Soc. Work*, 22:437.

07716 **MARSH, L. C.** (1933), An experiment in the group treatment of patients at Worchester State Hospital. *Ment. Hygiene*, 17:396-416.

07717 **MARSH, L. C.** (1935), Group therapy and the psychiatric clinic. *J. Nerv. & Ment. Diseases*, 82:381-393.

07718 **MARSH, L. C.** (1975), Group therapy and the psychiatric clinic. In: *Group Psychotherapy and Group Function*, 2d ed., eds. M. Rosenbaum and M. M. Berger. New York: Basic Books.

07719 **MARSH, L. C.** (1931), Group treatment of the psychoses by the psychological equivalent of the revival. *Ment. Hygiene*, 15:328-349.

07720 **MARSHALL, E. K.** (1972), Trainee preparation for group counseling: attitudinal and goal-setting effects of video taped counseling groups modeling different levels of goal specificity. *Dissert. Abstr. Internat.*, 33:973A.

07721 **MARSHALL, K. E.**, and **COLMAN, A. D.** (1974), Operant analysis of encounter groups: a pilot study. *Internat. J. Group Psychother.*, 24:42-54.

07722 **MARSHALL, P.** (1974), Career guidance through group dynamics. *Manpower*, 6:14-18.

07723 **MARSHALL, P. H., COLEMAN, L. S., DAEHLER, R. T.**, and **LABAW, W. L.** (1970), Rural community consultation in child psychiatric training. *Amer. J. Orthopsychiat.*, 40:294-295.

07724 **MARSHALL, R. J.** (1965), A guide toward establishing patient government. *Ment. Hygiene*, 49:230-237.

07725 **MARSHALL, R. J.** (1977), Review of A. Rachman's *Identity Group Psychotherapy with Adolescents. Amer. J. Psychiat.*, 31:153-154.

07726 **MARTENSEN-LARSEN, O.** (1956), Group psychotherapy with alcoholics in private practice. *Internat. J. Group Psychother.*, 6:28-37.

07727 **MARTENSEN-LARSEN, O.** (1963), The importance of the treatment of both spouses with special reference to group therapy of alcoholism. *Acta. Psychiat. Scand. Suppl.*, 39:134-135.

07728 **MARTH, D. R.** (1970), The effect of group counseling on visual imagery and selected personality factors for junior and senior level high school students. *Dissert. Abstr. Internat.*, 31:5134A.

07729 **MARTIN, A. B.** (1968), A prescription for success. *Amer. J. Nursing*, 68:525-526.

07730 **MARTIN, C. V.**, and **BANKS, F. M.** (1972), Marathon group therapy. *Psychother. & Psychosomat.*, (Basel) 20:191-199.

07731 **MARTIN, C. V.**, and **PARRISH, M. J.** (1973), The application of closed circuit television instant replay as a self-confrontation method in children's group therapy. *Correct. Psychiat. & J. Soc. Ther.*, 19:31-36.

07732 **MARTIN, D.** (1965), The beginnings of the growth and development of an adolescent unit in the Cassel Hospital. *Psychother. & Psychosomat.*, (Basel) 13:309-313.

07733 **MARTIN, D. V.**, and **CAINE, T. M.** (1963), Personality change in the treatment of chronic neurosis in a therapeutic community. *Brit. J. Psychiat.*, (Ashford) 109:267-272.

07734 **MARTIN, D. W.**, and **BEAVER, N.** (1951), A preliminary report on the use of the dance as an adjuvant in the therapy of schizophrenics. *Psychiat. Quart. Suppl.*, 25:176-190.

07735 **MARTIN, E. A., JR.**, and **HILL, W. F.** (1957), Toward a theory of group development: six phases of therapy group development. *Internat. J. Group Psychother.*, 7:20-30.

07736 **MARTIN, H.**, and **SHEWMAKER, K.** (1962), Written instructions in group psychotherapy. *Group Psychother., Psychodrama & Sociometry*, 15:24-29.

07737 **MARTIN, L.**, and **JACOBS, M.** (1980), Structured feedback delivered in small groups. *Small Group Behav.*, 11:88-107.

07738 **MARTIN, P. A., TORNGA, M., McGLOIN, J. F. JR.**, and **BOLES, S.** (1977), Observing groups as seen from both sides of the looking glass. *Group*, 1:147-161.

07739 **MARTIN, P. J.** (1973), The effects of group counseling on self-concept and achievement of selected educationally disadvantaged elementary school children. *Dissert. Abstr. Internat.*, 33:3297A.

07740 **MARTIN, R. B.** (1971), The effect of vocational training and group counseling on selected vocational attitudes. *Dissert. Abstr. Internat.*, 32:182-183A.

07741 **MARTIN, R. D.** (1971), Videotape self-confrontation in human relations training. *J. Couns. Psychol.*, 18:340-347.

07742 **MARTIN, R. D.**, and **FISCHER, D. G.** (1974), Encounter-group experience and personality change. *Psychol. Reports*, 35:91-96.

07743 **MARTIN, R. D.**, and **WILSON, J. D.** (1969), Community psychiatry as practiced in the U.S. Navy. *Military Med.*, 134:274-280.

07744 **MARTIN, R. D.**, and **ZINGLE, H. W.** (1970), Videotape equipment and procedures in group settings. *Internat. J. Group Psychother.*, 20:230-234.

07745 **MARTIN, S. D.** (1973), The effects of group counseling on selected senior high school students who demonstrate negative attitudes and behaviors. *Dissert. Abstr. Internat.*, 34:3996.

07746 **MARTINDALE, B.**, and **BOTTOMLEY, V.** (1980), The management of families with Huntington's chorea: a case study to illustrate some recommendations. *J. Child Psychol. & Psychiat.*, 21:343-351.

07747 **MARTINEZ, C.** (1977), Group process and the Chicano: clinical issues. *Internat. J. Group Psychother.*, 27:225-232.

07748 **MARTINEZ BOUQUET, C.**, and **BUCHBINDER, M. J.** (1978), (Reflections about a group after its dissolution.) *Acta Psiciat. Psicol. Amer. Latina*, (Buenos Aires) 24:132.

07749 **MARTINEZ BOUQUET, C., MOCCIO, F.**, and **PAVLOVSKY, E.** (1979), *Psicodrama Psicoanaltico en Grupos.* (*Psychoanalytic Psychodrama in Groups.*) Madrid: Fundamentos.

07750 **MARTINEZ PÉREZ, A.** (1977), Rehabilitation of cardiac patients and of semiphlegics. *Neurol.-Neurocir.-Psiquiat.*, (Mexico City) 18:109-112.

07751 **MARTINS, C.** (1976), (Community psychiatry programs.) *Acta Psiciat. & Psicol. Amer. Latina*, (Buenos Aires) 22:56-62.

07752 **MARTINSON, I.** (1976), The child with leukemia: parents help each other: part 3. *Amer. J. Nursing*, 76:1120-1122.

07753 **MARTI-TUSQUETS, J. L.**, and **CABRESO, A. L.** (1973), (Experience in group psychotherapy.) *Rev. Psiquiat. Psicol. Med.*, 11:225.

07754 **MARTI-TUSQUETS, J. L.** (1958), Psychodrama in Spain. *Group Psychother., Psychodrama & Sociometry*, 11:325-329.

07755 **MARTI-TUSQUETS, J. L.**, and **MOLL, P. S.** (1966), (Basic levels of control for the investigation of small groups.) *Rev. Psiquiat. Psicol. Med.*, 7:540-543.

07756 **MARTI-TUSQUETS, J. L.**, and **MOLL, P. P.** (1966), Identification and leadership in group psychotherapy. *Internat. J. Group Psychother.*, 16:442-451.

07757 **MARTI-TUSQUETS, J. L., TURÓ, P.**, and **GONZÁLEZ MONCLÚS, E.** (1955), (Psychodrama in diagnosis and therapy of mental diseases.) *Rev. Psiquiat. Psicol. Med.*, 2:326-336.

07758 **MARUCCO, N. C.** (1973), (Some reflections about group psychotherapy's theory.) *Acta Psiciat. Psicol. Amer. Latina*, (Buenos Aires) 19:355-361.

07759 **MARVIT, R. C.** (1972), Improving behavior of delinquent adolescents through group therapy. *Hosp. & Community Psychiat.*, 23:239-241.
07760 **MARVIT, R. C., LIND, J.,** and **MCLAUGHLIN, D. G.** (1974), Use of videotape to induce attitude change in delinquent adolescents. *Amer. J. Psychiat.*, 131:996-999.
07761 **MARWELL, G.** (1968), Role allocation and differentiation through time in medium-sized groups. *J. Soc. Psychol.*, 74:225-231.
07762 **MARX, J. H.,** and **ELLISON, D. L.** (1975), Sensitivity training and communes: contemporary quests for community. *Pacific Sociol. Rev.*, 18:442-462.
07763 **MASCIA, A. V.,** and **REITER, S. R.** (1971), Group therapy in rehabilitation of severe chronic asthmatic children. *Annual Children*, 29:223.
07764 **MASCIA, A. V.,** and **REITER, S. R.** (1971), Group therapy in the rehabilitation of the severe chronic asthmatic child. *J. Asthma Res.*, 9:81-85.
07765 **MASE, B. F.** (1971), Changes in self-actualization as a result of two types of residential group experience. *Dissert. Abstr. Internat.*, 32:3643B.
07766 **MASH, E. J., LAZERE, R., TERCHL, C.,** and **GARNER, A.** (1973), Modification of mother-child interactions: a modeling approach for groups. *Child Study J.*, 3:131-143.
07767 **MASIAK, M.** (1974), (Effect of group psychotherapy and therapeutic community on the rehabilitation process in chronic schizophrenics.) *Psychiat. Polska*, (Warsaw) 8:175-180.
07768 **MASLER, E. G.** (1969), The interpretations of projective identification in group psychotherapy. *Internat. J. Group Psychother.*, 19:441-447.
07769 **MASLOWSKI, R. M.,** and **MORGAN, L. B.** (1973), *Interpersonal Growth and Self Actualization in Groups*. New York: Mss. Information.
07770 **MASNIK, R., OLAARTE, S. W.,** and **ROSEN, A.** (1980), "Coffee groups": a nine-year follow-up study. *Amer. J. Psychiat.*, 137:91-93.
07771 **MASS, P.,** and **O'DANIELL, J.** (1968), Group casework with relatives of adult schizophrenic patients. *Ment. Hygiene*, 42:504-510.
07772 **MASS, P.,** and **O'DANIELL, J.** (1958), Group casework with relatives of adult schizophrenic patients. *Ment. Hygiene*, 42:504-510.
07773 **MASSARIK, F.** (1971), *Sensitivity Training Around the World*. White Plains: NY: Phiebig.
07774 **MASSERMAN, J.** (1955), Comments on Moreno's "Interpersonal therapy, the function of the unconscious." *Group Psychother., Psychodrama & Sociometry*, 8:62-64.
07775 **MASSERMAN, J. H.** (1954), A comment on Moreno's "transference, countertransference and tele." *Group Psychother., Psychodrama & Sociometry*, 7:309-310.
07776 **MASSERMAN, J. H.** (1969), *Current Psychiatric Therapies, Vol. 9*. New York: Grune and Stratton.
07777 **MASSERMAN, J. H.,** and **MORENO, J. L.** (1958), *Progress in Psychotherapy, Vol. 3: Techniques of Psychotherapy*. New York: Grune and Stratton.
07778 **MASSIE, H. R.** (1971), Bedlam in the therapeutic community: the disruption of a hospital therapeutic community as a pattern of social conflict. *Psychiat. in Med.*, 2:278-293.
07779 **MASSMAN, B. M.,** and **ZILLER, R. C.** (1968), Self-esteem and consistency of social behavior. *J. Abnorm. Psychol.*, 73:363-367.
07780 **MAST, G. R.** (1968), (The group process in therapy groups of socially retarded children.) *Nederl. Tijdschr. Geneeskunde*, (Amsterdam) 112:727-729.
07781 **MASTERS, G.** (1978), Psychodrama: learning to communicate. part 1. *Nursing Times*, (London) 74:350-352.
07782 **MASTERSON, J. F., JR.** (1958), Psychotherapy of the adolescent: a com-

parison with psychotherapy of the adult. *J. Nerv. & Ment. Diseases*, 127:511-517.

07783 **MASTROPAOLO, C.**, and **VANNUCCI, L.** (1968), (Indications, limits, and primary personal experiences on the subject of group therapy in the dissociation of minors.) *Riv. Psichiat.*, (Rome) 3:337-343.

07784 **MASUMURA, M.** (1975), (Group therapy of autistic children at an outpatient clinic.) *Japanese J. Child Psychiat.*, (Tokyo) 16:316-324.

07785 **MATARAZZO, R. G.**, and **SMALL, I. F.** (1963), An experiment in teaching group psychotherapy. *J. Nerv. & Ment. Diseases*, 136:252-262.

07786 **MATERAZZI, M. A.** (1980), Psychocinema: a creative psychotherapeutic technique. *Confinia Psychiat.*, (Basel) 23:88-92.

07787 **MATES, M. E.** (1972), The effects of trainer personality on trainer behavior and on participant personality change in a sensitivity training experience. *Dissert. Abstr. Internat.*, 33:1767-1768B.

07788 **MATHE, A.** (1969/1970), (Group psychotherapy with delinquents.) *Bull. de Psychol.*, (Paris) 23:820-825.

07789 **MATHE, A.** (1967), Psychotherapie de groupe des delinquants. (Group psychotherapy of delinquents.) *Psychother. & Psychosomat.*, (Basel) 15:45.

07790 **MATHESON, W. E.** (1975), Group therapy as theatre. *J. Psychiat. Nursing*, 13:16-19.

07791 **MATHESON, W. E.** (1974), Which patient for which therapeutic group? *J. Psychiat. Nursing*, 12:10-13.

07792 **MATTHEWS, A.** (1977), Review of J. C. Brengelmann's, P. J. Graham's, J. J. M. Harbison's, H. McAllister's and J. C. Quinn's *Progress in Behavior Therapy*. *Behav. Res. & Ther.*, 15:510-511.

07793 **MATHIAS, J. L.**, and **COLLINS, M.** (1970), Mandatory group therapy for exhibitionists. *Amer. J. Psychiat.*, 126:1162-1167.

07794 **MATHIAS, J. L.**, and **COLLINS, M.** (1970), Progressive phases in the group therapy of exhibitionists. *Internat. J. Group Psychother.*, 20:163-169.

07795 **MATHIEU, M.** (1971), (A group analytic psychotherapy experiment in the army.) *Rev. Med. Psychosomat.*, (Toulouse) 13:47-52.

07796 **MATHIEU, P. L.** (1965), An investigation to determine the relationship between counselor preparation and positive personality growth in individuals participating in a group counseling situation. *Dissert. Abstr. Internat.*, 26:5549.

07797 **MATHIEU, P. L.**, and **MOURSUND, J. P.** (1962), *Relationship of Group Counseling to Subsequent Academic Performance at the College Level*. Madison: University of Wisconsin Press.

07799 **MATHIS, J. L.**, and **COLLINS, M.** (1971), Enforced group treatment of exhibitionists. *Curr. Psychiat. Ther.*, 11:139-145.

07800 **MATIS, E. E.** (1961), Psychotherapeutic tools for parents. *J. Speech & Hearing Disorders*, 26:164-170.

07801 **MATKOM, A. J.** (1967), Community meetings on the admission ward. *Hosp. & Community Psychiat.*, 18:206-209.

07802 **MATOVŠEK, O.** (1978), (Groups of relatives in psychotherapeutic system of a day hospital.) *Ceskoslov. Psychiat.*, (Prague) 74:183-188.

07803 **MATOVSEK, O.** (1979), (The results of group psychotherapy in patients with disorders of interpersonal relations.) *Ceskoslov. Psychiat.*, (Warsaw) 75:26.

07804 **MATSUMURA, K.** (1964), A new journal of psychodrama in Japan. *Internat. J. Sociometry & Sociatry*, 4:60.

07805 **MATTA, J. E.** (1975), *Dinâmica de Grupo e Desenvolvimento de Organizações*. (*Group Dynamics and Organizational Apathy*.) São Paulo: Pioneira.

07806 **MATTHEWS, C. G.** (1963), Problem-solving and experiential background determinants of test performances in mentally retarded subjects. *Psychol., Reports*, 13:391-401.

07807 **MATTHEWS, G. N.** (1974), Changes in internal-external control related to membership in therapy and learning groups. *Dissert. Abstr. Internat.*, 35:4186B.

07808 **MATTHEWS, M. F.** (1978), Personality variants of group and encounter group selectors and group non-selectors. *Dissert. Abstr. Internat.*, 38:6622A.

07809 **MATTHEWS, P. B.** (1973), The effects of reality therapy on reported self-concept, adjustment, reading achievement, and discipline of fourth and fifth graders in two elementary schools. *Dissert. Abstr. Internat.*, 33:4842A.

07810 **MATTHEWS, V.** (1949), An experiment in case work by the group process. *Soc. Serv. Rev.*, 23:315-321.

07811 **MATTESON, A.**, and **AGLE, D. P.** (1972), Group therapy with parents of hemophiliacs: therapeutic process and observations of parental adaptation to chronic illness in children. *J. Amer. Acad. Child Psychiat.*, 11:558-571.

07812 **MATULICH, W. J.** (1978), An investigation of the effectiveness of group biofeedback as a treatment for tension headaches. *Dissert. Abstr. Internat.*, 38:3896B-3897B. (University Microfilms No. 7732445.)

07813 **MAUCH, G.** (1970), Sozialtherapie im strafvollzug. (Social therapy in the penal institute.) *Zeit. Psychother. Med. Psychol.*, (Stuttgart) 20:66-75.

07814 **MAUGILE, D.** (1967), (The concept of the couples as a unit during group psychotherapy of married couples.) *Loval Med.*, (Quebec) 38:113-118.

07815 **MAUGILE, D.**, and **FERRON, L. P.** (1967), Les phases fondamentales de la psychotherapie collective des schizophrenes. (Fundamental phases of collective psychotherapy of schizophrenics). *Can. Psychiat. Assn. J.*, (Ottawa) 12:205-206.

07816 **MAUL, P.** and **THOMAS, L.** (1974), The cinderella syndrome: young women in crisis. *J. Psychiat. Nursing*, 12:10-13.

07817 **MAULTSBY, M. C.** (1974), Teaching self-help in the classroom with rational self-counseling. *J. School Health*, 44:445-448.

07818 **MAURER-GROELI, Y. A.** (1976), Body-centered group psychotherapy in acute schizophrenics: evaluation by rating of ego functions. *Arch. Psychiat. & Nervenkrankheiten*, 221:259-271.

07819 **MAURER-GROELI, Y. A.** (1975), Group psychotherapy with schizophrenic patients. *Schweiz. Arch. Neurol., Neurochir. & Psychiat.*, (Zurich) 117:305-324.

07820 **MAURIN, J. T.** (1970), Regressed patients in group therapy. *Perspect. Psychiat. Care*, 8:131-135.

07821 **MAXMEN, J. S.** (1978), An educative model for inpatient group therapy. *Internat. J. Group Psychother.*, 28:321-338.

07822 **MAXMEN, J. S.** (1973), Group therapy as viewed by hospitalized patients. *Arch. Gen. Psychiat.*, 28:404-408.

07823 **MAXWELL, M. G.** (1973), The effects of focused videotape feedback in marathon therapy groups. *Dissert. Abstr. Internat.*, 34:2307A.

07824 **MAY, E. P.** (1972), Critique of integrity therapy. *Couns. Psychol.*, 3:50-63.

07825 **MAY, J. G.**, and **MAIN, W.** (1969), "We just want to help you": a note on anger in adolescent group therapy. *Ment. Hygiene*, 53:638-640.

07826 **MAY, O. P.** (1973), Self-disclosure and mental health: a study of encounter group members' perceptions of group leaders. *Dissert. Abstr. Internat.*, 33:4092A.

07827 **MAY, O. P.**, and **THOMPSON, C. L.** (1973), Perceived levels of self-disclosure, mental health, and helpfulness of group leaders. *J. Couns. Psychol.*, 20:349-352.

07828 **MAY, P.** (1971), Cost efficiency of treatments for the schizophrenic patient. *Amer. J. Psychiat.*, 127:1382-1385.

07829 **MAY, P. R., TUMA, H.,** and **DIXON, W. J.** (1976), Schizophrenia: a follow-up study of results of treatment. i. design and other problems. *Arch. Gen. Psychiat.*, 33:474-478.

07830 **MAY, P. R., TUMA, H., YALE, C., POTEPAN, C.,** and **DIXON, W. J.** (1976), Schizophrenia: a follow-up study of results of treatment. ii. hospital stay over two to five years. *Arch. Gen. Psychiat.*, 33:481-486.

07831 **MAY, R. J.,** and **TIERNEY, D. E.** (1976), Personality changes as a function of group transactional analysis. *J. Coll. Student Personnel*, 17:485-488.

07832 **MAYADAS, N. S.,** and **HINK, D. L.** (1974), Group work with the aging: an issue for social work education. *Gerontologist*, 14:440-445.

07833 **MAYADAS, N. S.,** and **OBRIEN, D. E.** (1978), Use of videotape in group psychotherapy. In: *Videotape Techniques in Psychiatric Training and Treatment*, ed. M. M. Berger. New York: Brunner/Mazel.

07834 **MAYER, G. R., ROHEN, T. M.,** and **WHITLEY, A. D.** (1969), Group counseling with children: a cognitive-behavioral approach. *J. Couns. Psychol.*, 16:142-149.

07835 **MAYER, J.,** and **GREEN, M.** (1967), Group therapy of alcoholic women ex-prisoners. *Quart. J. Studies Alcohol*, 28:493-504.

07836 **MAYER, L.,** and **ISBISTER, C.** (1970), Report on group therapy for mothers of children with intractable asthma. *Med. J. Austral.*, (Glebe) 1:887-889.

07837 **MAYER, M. F.** (1972), The group in residential treatment of adolescents. *Child Welfare*, 51:482-493.

07838 **MAYERS, A. N.** (1950), A psychiatric evaluation of discussion groups. *J. Nerv. & Ment. Diseases*, 111:499-509.

07839 **MAYERS, F.** (1970), Differential use of group teaching in first-year field work. *Soc. Serv. Rev.*, 44:63-75.

07840 **MAYERS, K. S.** (1978), Sexual and social concerns of the disabled: group counseling approach. *Sexual Disabil.*, 1:100-111.

07841 **MAYHEW, B. H., JR.,** and **GRAY, L. N.** (1971), The structure of dominance relations in triadic interaction systems. *Compar. Group Studies*, 2:161-190.

07842 **MAYNARD, L.,** and **HOGAN, K.** (1980), A socialization group for clients in a partial hospitalization program. *Hosp. & Community Psychiat.*, 31:705-706.

07843 **MAYNARD, M.** (1971), One day experience in group dynamics in an occupational therapy assistant course. *Amer. J. Occupat. Ther.*, 25:170-171.

07844 **MAYNARD, R. E.** (1971), Disturbance and group interaction. *Amer. J. Correct.*, 33:35.

07845 **MAYO, P. R., WALTON, H. J.,** and **LITTMANN, S. K.** (1971), Relevance of repression–sensitization to neurotic patients in milieu treatment. *Psychol. Reports*, 28:794.

07846 **MAYTON, D. M., II,** and **ATKINSON, D. R.** (1974), Systematic desensitization in group counseling settings: an overview. *J. Coll. Student Personnel*, 15:83-88.

07847 **MAZZOLENI, A.** (1979), (Theory and practice in a group of alcoholics.) *Krankenpflege*, (Frankfurt) 72:379-382.

07848 **MAZZONIS, E.** (1967), (The film "Marat-Sade": an attempted therapy with psychodrama.) *Minerva Med.*, (Turin) 58:1586.

07849 **MAZZONIS, E.** (1965), (Group psychotherapy and psychodrama: observations in children's therapeutic group with totally open character.) *Minerva Med.*, (Turin) 56:165-166.

07850 **McALLISTER, R. J.** (1967), Open-door group therapy in a community hospital. *Curr. Psychiat. Ther.*, 7:162-163.
07851 **McBRIDE, H. S.** (1976), An application of the Adlerian group counseling approach to nursing home staff members. *Dissert. Abstr. Internat.*, 37:1409A.
07852 **McBRIEN, D. E.** (1976), An evaluation of a systematic career decision-making program administered in a group and individual counseling context. *Dissert. Abstr. Internat.*, 36:6978A.
07853 **McBRIEN, R. J.**, and **NELSON, R. J.** (1972), Experimental group strategies with primary grade children. *Elem. School Guid. Couns.*, 6:170-174.
07854 **McCAFFERY, M.**, and **JOHNSON, D. E.** (1967), Effect of parent group discussion upon epistemic responses. *Nursing Res.*, 16:352-358.
07855 **McCAFTHY, B. W.** (1973), A modification of Masters and Johnson's sex therapy in a clinical setting. *Psychother.: Theory, Res. & Pract.*, 10:290-293.
07856 **McCALL, R. J.** (1974), Group therapy with obese women of varying MMPI profiles. *J. Clin. Psychol.*, 30:466-470.
07857 **McCALL, R. J.** (1977), Differential effectiveness of informal group procedures in weight control. *J. Clin. Psychol.*, 33:351-360.
07858 **McCANCE, C.**, and **McCANCE, P. F.** (1969), Alcoholism in North-East Scotland: its treatment and outcome. *Brit. J. Psychiat.*, (Ashford) 115:189-198.
07859 **McCANN, J. R.** (1956), A technique to facilitate acceptance and its relationship to interaction during group psychotherapy. *Dissert. Abstr. Internat.*, 16:576.
07860 **McCANN, M. E.** (1966), Group reconstruction: a technique for studying the why's of behavior. *Amer. J. Nursing*, 66:1995-1998.
07861 **McCANN, W. H.** (1953), The round table technique in group psychotherapy. *Group Psychother., Psychodrama & Sociometry*, 5:233-239.
07862 **McCANN, W. H.**, and **ALMADA, A. A.** (1950), Round-table psychotherapy: a technique in group psychotherapy. *J. Consult. & Clin. Psychol.*, 14:421-435.
07863 **McCANNE, L.** (1977), Dimensions of participant goals, expectations, and perceptions in small group experiences. *J. Appl. Behav. Science*, 13:533-542.
07864 **McCANTS, A. J. F.** (1971), An experimental case study of a group process dimension and its impact on individually diagnosed social behavior problems of members of a quasi-therapeutic group. *Dissert. Abstr. Internat.*, 32:5450B.
07865 **McCARDEL, J.**, and **MURRAY, E. J.** (1974), Nonspecific factors in weekend encounter groups. *J. Consult. & Clin. Psychol.*, 42:337-345.
07866 **McCARTHY, B. W.** (1971), Comparison of effectiveness of group counseling procedures. *Psychol. Reports*, 28:283-286.
07867 **McCARTHY, K.** (1963), Experience with supportive group therapy with the adolescent children of psychiatric patients. *J. Fort Logan Ment. Health Ctr.*, 1:37-42.
07868 **McCARTHY, M. A., YOUNG, G. C.**, and **RODMAN, N.** (1968), A dynamic educative experience for a group of mothers and their two-year-old children coping with development stresses. *Amer. J. Orthopsychiat.*, 38:339-340.
07869 **McCARTHY, M. L.** (1976), Life issues and group psychotherapy with terminal cancer patients. *Dissert. Abstr. Internat.*, 36:3615-3616.
07870 **McCARTHY, R. G.** (1949), Group therapy in alcoholism: transcriptions of a series of sessions recorded in an outpatient clinic: i. introduction and first two sessions. *Quart. J. Studies Alcohol*, 10:63-108.

07871 **McCARTHY, R. G.** (1949), Group therapy in alcoholism: transcriptions of a series of sessions recorded in an outpatient clinic: ii. third session. *Quart. J. Studies Alcohol*, 10:217-250.

07872 **McCARTHY, R. G.** (1949), Group therapy in alcoholism: transcriptions of a series of sessions recorded in an outpatient clinic: iii. fourth session. *Quart. J. Studies Alcohol*, 10:479-500.

07873 **McCARTHY, R. G.** (1950), Group therapy in alcoholism: transcriptions of a series of sessions recorded in an outpatient clinic: iv. fifth session. *Quart. J. Studies Alcohol*, 11:119-140.

07874 **McCARTHY, R. G.** (1950), Group therapy in alcoholism: transcriptions of a series of sessions recorded in an outpatient clinic: vi. seventh session. *Quart. J. Studies Alcohol*, 11:630-653.

07875 **McCARTHY, R. G.** (1951), Group therapy in alcoholism: transcriptions of a series of sessions recorded in an outpatient clinic: vii. eighth session. *Quart. J. Studies Alcohol*, 12:103-117.

07876 **McCARTHY, R. G.** (1951), Group therapy in alcoholism: transcriptions of a series of sessions recorded in an outpatient clinic: viii. ninth session. *Quart. J. Studies Alcohol*, 12:273-296.

07877 **McCARTHY, R. G.** (1952), Group therapy in alcoholism: transcriptions of a series of sessions recorded in an outpatient clinic. *Quart. J. Studies Alcohol*, 13:95-126.

07878 **McCARTHY, R. G.** (1946), Group therapy in an outpatient clinic for the treatment of alcoholism. *Quart. J. Studies Alcohol*, 7:98-109.

07879 **McCARTNEY, J. L.** (1961), Suicide as a complication to group psychotherapy. *Military Med.*, 126:895-898.

07880 **McCARTNEY, J. L.** (1952), The use of group psychotherapy in shortening individual treatment in private practice. *Internat. J. Group Psychother.*, 2:262-269.

07881 **McCARTY, P. T.** (1972), Effects of sub-professional group counseling with probationers and parolees. *Dissert. Abstr. Internat.*, 5550A.

07882 **McCLAIN, A. D.** (1970), The effect of group counseling upon the self-concepts of disabled readers at the elementary school level. *Dissert. Abstr. Internat.*, 31:5770A.

07883 **McCLAIN, G. R.** (1974), The individual within: an instrumented case study analysis of a marathon encounter group. *Dissert. Abstr. Internat.*, 34:4752A.

07884 **McCLEAN, P. D.**, and **CRAIG, K. D.** (1975), Evaluating treatment effectiveness by monitoring changes in problematic behaviors. *J. Consult. & Clin. Psychol.*, 43:105.

07885 **McCLELLAN, M. S.** (1972), Crisis groups in special care areas. *Nursing Clin. North Amer.*, 7:363-371.

07886 **McCLENDON, R.**, and **McCLENDON, G.** (1976), Review of A. L. Kadis's *Practicum of Group Psychotherapy*. *Internat. J. Group Psychother.*, 26:253-254.

07887 **McCLINTOCK, C. G.** (1965), Group support, satisfaction, and the behaviour profiles of group members. *Brit. J. Sociol. & Clin. Psychol.*, (London) 4:169-174.

07888 **McCOLLUM, E. E.** (1979), A family-oriented admission procedure on an inpatient psychiatric unit. *Soc. Work & Health Care*, 4:423-430.

07889 **McCOLLUM, P. S.** (1971), Group counseling as an adjunctive remediation technique for learning disabilities. *Dissert. Abstr. Internat.*, 32:2404B.

07890 **McCOLLUM, P. S.**, and **ANDERSON, R. P.** (1974), Group counseling with reading disabled children. *J. Couns. Psychol.*, 21:150-155.

07891 **McCONNELL, H. K.** (1971), Individual differences as mediators of participant behavior and self-descriptive change in two human relations training programs. *Organizat. Behav. & Human Perf.*, 6:550-572.

07892 **McCORKLE, L. W.** (1951), Group therapy. In: *Contemporary Correction*, ed. P. W. Tappan. New York: McGraw Hill.
07893 **McCORKLE, L. W.** (1949), Group therapy in correctional institutions. *Fed. Probat.*, 13:34-37.
07894 **McCORKLE, L. W.** (1952), Group therapy in the treatment of offenders. *Fed. Probat.*, 16:22-27.
07895 **McCORKLE, L. W.** (1954), Guided group interaction in a correctional setting. *Internat. J. Group Psychother.*, 4:199-203.
07896 **McCORKLE, L. W.** (1953), The present status of group therapy in United States correctional institutions. *Internat. J. Group Psychother.*, 3:79-87.
07897 **McCORKLE, L. W.**, and **KORN, R.** (1954), Resocialization within walls. *Annual Amer. Acad. Polit. & Soc. Sciences*, 293:88-98.
07898 **McCORKLE, L. W.**, **ELIAS, A.**, and **BIXBY, F. L.** (1958), *The Highfields Story: An Experimental Treatment Project for Youthful Offenders*. New York: H. Holt.
07899 **McCORMACK, E. J.** (1945), The effectiveness of group systematic desensitization for the reduction of anxiety in counselor trainees in the individual practicum setting. *Dissert. Abstr. Internat.*, 36:3411A.
07900 **McCORMICK, C. G.** (1957), Group dynamics: homeopathic treatment. *Internat. J. Group Psychother.*, 7:103-112.
07901 **McCORMICK, C. G.** (1953), Objective evaluation of the process and effects of analytic group psychotherapy with adolescent girls. *Internat. J. Group Psychother.*, 3:181-190.
07902 **McCOURT, W.**, and **GLANTZ, M.** (1980), Cognitive behavior therapy in groups for alcoholics. *J. Studies Alcohol*, 41:338-346.
07903 **McCOWAN, R. J.** (1965), A study of the effectiveness of group counseling with underachievers and their parents. Unpublished doctoral dissertation, St. John's University.
07904 **McCRINNON, J. K.** (1975), Variables influencing increased cognitive complexity in the t-group setting. *Dissert. Abstr. Internat.*, 36:2478B.
07905 **McCUE, A. E.** (1980), Multi-media approach to group counseling with preadolescent girls. *J. School Health*, 50:156-160.
07906 **McCULLOUGH, W. E.** (1955), Integrated therapeutic (group) program: 3 year ward experiment. *Psychiat. Quart.*, 29:280-309.
07907 **McDANIEL, J.** (1960), Group action in the rehabilitation of the mentally retarded. *Group Psychother., Psychodrama & Sociometry*, 13:5-13.
07908 **McDANIEL, J.** (1962), Group psychotherapy and vocational rehabilitation: a state program. *Group Psychother., Psychodrama & Sociometry*, 15:80-83.
07909 **McDANIEL, W.** (1963), Evaluation of the use of group therapeutic techniques for vocational rehabilitation. *Group Psychother., Psychodrama & Sociometry*, 16:255-259.
07910 **McDAVID, J. W.** (1964), Immediate effects of group therapy upon response to social reinforcement among juvenile delinquents. *J. Cons. Psychol.*, 28:409-412.
07911 **McDONALD, E. C., JR.** (1951), The masking function of self-revelation in group therapy. *Internat. J. Group Psychother.*, 1:59-63.
07912 **McDONALD, M. A.** (1947), Psychodrama explores a private world. *Sociatry*, 1:97-118.
07913 **McDONALD, T.** (1975), Group psychotherapy with Native-American women. *Internat. J. Group Psychother.*, 25:410-420.
07914 **McDONOUGH, J. J.** (1975), *One Day in the Life of Ivan Denisovich*: a study of the structural requisites of organization. *Human Relat.*, 28:295-328.
07915 **McDONOUGH, T. J.** (1980), A comparison of self-instruction and play group therapy in lessening impulsivity and subsequent hyperaggressiv-

ity in fourth, fifth, and sixth grade boys. *Dissert. Abstr. Internat.*, 40:4493B. (University Microfilms No. 8005255.)

07916 **McELROY, D. M.** (1976), A modified marathon with voluntarily institutionalized substance abusers: effects on psychopathology, self-actualization and ward behavior. *Dissert. Abstr. Internat.*, 36:7213-7214.

07917 **McENERY, R. F.** (1972), The existential approach to encounter in Rollo May. *Dissert. Abstr. Internat.*, 33:1768B.

07918 **McFARLAND, R. L., DANIELS, R. S.**, and **LIEBERMAN, M.** (1963), Group psychotherapy. In: *Progress in Neurology and Psychiatry, Vol. 18*. New York: Grune and Stratton, pp. 622-630.

07919 **McFARLAND, R. L., DANIELS, R. S.**, and **SOLON, E.** (1961), Group psychotherapy. *Progress in Neurol. & Psychiat., Vol. 16*, New York: Grune and Stratton, pp. 527-538.

07920 **McFARLAND, R. L., NELSON, C. L.**, and **ROSSI, A. M.** (1962), Prediction of participation in group psychotherapy from measures of intelligence and verbal behavior. *Psychol. Reports*, 11:291-298.

07921 **McGAUGH, J. D.** (1974), The relevance of a social psychological model to growth groups. *Dissert. Abstr. Internat.*, 35:1440B.

07922 **McGEE, T. F.** (1969), Comprehensive preparation for group psychotherapy. *Amer. J. Psychother.*, 23:303-312.

07923 **McGEE, T. F.** (1968), Supervision on group psychotherapy: a comparison of four approaches. *Internat. J. Group Psychother.*, 18:165-176.

07924 **McGEE, T. F.** (1974), Therapist termination in group psychotherapy. *Internat. J. Group Psychother.*, 24:3-12.

07925 **McGEE, T. F.** (1980), Transition in the cotherapy dyad: to wait or not to wait. *Group*, 4:65-71.

07926 **McGEE, T. F.** (1974), The triadic approach to supervision in group psychotherapy. *Internat. J. Group Psychother.*, 24:471-476.

07927 **McGEE, T. F.**, and **LARSEN, V. B.** (1967), An approach to waiting list therapy groups. *Amer. J. Orthopsychiat.*, 37:594-597.

07928 **McGEE, T. F.**, and **RACUSEN, F. R.** (1967), Alumni group psychotherapy as a form of aftercare program. *Internat. J. Group Psychother.*, 17:243-247.

07929 **McGEE, T. F.**, and **RACUSEN, F. R.** (1968), An evaluation of alumni group psychotherapy: for patients discharged from a group living program. *Arch. Gen. Psychiat.*, 18:420-427.

07930 **McGEE, T. F.**, and **SCHUMAN, B. N.** (1970), The nature of the co-therapy relationship. *Internat. J. Group Psychother.*, 20:25-36.

07931 **McGEE, T. F.**, and **WILLIAMS, M.** (1971), Time-limited and time-unlimited group psychotherapy: a comparison with schizophrenic patients. *Compar. Group Studies*, 2:71-84.

07932 **McGEE, T. F., SCHUMAN, B. N.**, and **RACUSEN, F.** (1972), Termination in group psychotherapy. *Amer. J. Psychother.*, 26:521-532.

07933 **McGEE, T. F., WILLIAMS, M., RACUSEN, F. R.**, and **COWEN, J.** (1968), Further evaluation of small group living program with schizophrenics. *Arch. Gen. Psychiat.*, 19:717-726.

07934 **McGEE, T. F., STARR, A., POWERS, J., RACUSEN, F. R.**, and **THORNTON, A.** (1965), Conjunctive use of psychodrama in schizophrenic patients. *Group Psychother., Psychodrama & Sociometry*, 18:127-135.

07935 **McGHAN, W. F.** (1979), Pharmacist-conducted reviews of drug therapy in nursing homes: an analysis with medicaid data. *Dissert. Abstr. Internat.*, 40:5617B.

07936 **McGINNIS, E.**, and **ALTMAN, I.** (1959), Discussion as a function of attitudes and content of a persuasive communication. *J. Appl. Psychol.*, 43:53-59.

07937 **McGLYNN, D., REYNOLDS, E. J.**, and **LINDER, L. H.** (1971), Systematic desensitization with pre-treatment and intra-treatment therapeutic instructions. *Behav. Res. & Ther.*, 9:57-63.

07939 **McGRATH, J., O'BRIEN, J.,** and **LIFTIK, J.** (1977), Coercive treatment for alcoholic "driving under the influence of liquor" offenders. *Brit. J. Addict.*, (Edinburgh) 72:223-229.

07940 **McGRATH, J. E.** (1963), Systems of information in small group research studies. *Human Relat.*, 16:263-277.

07941 **McGRATH, L. P.,** and **SCOBEY, J.** (1969), Marathon assault on your hang-ups. *Family Circle*, 75:31, 75, 81-83.

07942 **McGRATH, M. M.** (1979), Group preparation of pediatric surgical patients. *Image*, 11:52-62.

07943 **McGREW, W. L.,** and **JENSEN, J. L.** (1972), A technique for facilitating therapeutic group interaction. *J. Psychiat. Nursing*, 10:18-21.

07944 **McGRIFF, D.** (1965), A coordinated approach to discharge planning. *Soc. Work*, 10:45-50.

07945 **McGRIFF, D.** (1960), Working with a group of authoritative mothers. *Soc. Work*, 5:63-68.

07946 **McHUGH, J. P.** (1976), The use of behavioral techniques in group therapy. *Dissert. Abstr. Internat.*, 36:5808.

07947 **McINTIRE, W. G.** (1973), The impact of t-group experience on level of self-actualization. *Small Group Behav.*, 4:459-465.

07948 **McKAY, C.** (1972), Health education: mental health education and quality of life. part 4. *Health Servs. Reports*, 87:941-946.

07949 **McKAY, L. A.** (1945), Music as a group therapeutic agent in the treatment of convalescents. *Sociometry*, 8:471-476.

07950 **McKELVIE, W. H.** (1974), An evaluation of a model to train high school students as leaders of Adlerian guidance groups. *Individ. Psychol.*, 11:7-14.

07951 **McKENDRY, A. W.** (1965), The effects of group counseling on the educational planning of college bound high school seniors. *Dissert. Abstr. Internat.*, 25:3978.

07952 **McKINLEY, J.** (1980), *Group Development Through Participation Training: A Trainer's Resource for Teambuilding*. New York: Paulist Press.

07953 **McKINNON, D. W.** (1968), Some effects of concomitant group counseling experience on students in the counseling practicum. *Dissert. Abstr. Internat.*, 28:2561A.

07954 **McKNEW, D. H., JR.,** and **EASTERLY, J.** (1969), Psychosocial seminars for nursing students. *Nursing Outlook*, 17:44-46.

07955 **McLACHLAN, F. J. C.** (1973), Patient and therapist: correlates of change during group psychotherapy. *Dissert. Abstr. Internat.*, 33:5023B.

07956 **McLACHLAN, J. F.** (1972), Benefit from group therapy as a function of patient therapist match on the conceptual level. *Psychother.: Theory, Res. & Pract.*, 9:317.

07957 **McLACHLAN, J. F.** (1974), Social competence and response to group therapy. *J. Community Psychol.*, 2:248-250.

07958 **McLACHLAN, J. F.** (1974), Therapy strategies, personality orientation and recovery from alcoholism. *Can. Psychiat. Assn. J.*, (Ottawa) 19:25-30.

07959 **McLAUGHLIN, F.** (1971), Personality changes through alternate group leadership. *Nursing Res.*, 2:123-130.

07960 **McLAUGHLIN, F. E., WHITE, E.,** and **BYFIELD, B.** (1974), Modes of interpersonal feedback and leadership structure in six small groups. *Nursing Res.*, 23:307-318.

07961 **McLAUGHLIN, G. M.** (1972), The effect of group counseling upon students' achievement in a baccalaureate program in nursing. *Dissert. Abstr. Internat.*, 33:974A.

07962 **McLAUGHLIN, T. F.** (1974), Review of applications of group contingency procedures used in behavior modification in the regular classroom: some recommendations for school personnel. *Psychol. Reports*, 35:1299-1303.

07963 **McLAUGHLIN, T. F.**, and **WAKABAYASHI, L.** (1980), Review of M. C. Collins's *Child Abuser: A Study of Child Abusers in Self-Help Group Therapy. Behav. Engineering*, 6:41.

07964 **McLEAN, C.** (1974), Undergraduate students as peer group counselors: effects on group members and counselors. *Dissert. Abstr. Internat.*, 35:3024B.

07965 **McLEAN, H.** (1968), First lesson in psychodrama. *Group Psychother., Psychodrama & Sociometry*, 21:26-37.

07966 **McLEISH, J.**, and **PARK, J.** (1972), Outcomes associated with direct and vicarious experience in training groups: i. personality changes. *Brit. J. Social. & Clin. Psychol.*, (London) 11:333-341.

07967 **McMANUS, J. E.** (1962), Group techniques in a child welfare agency. *Group Psychother., Psychodrama & Sociometry*, 15:63-68.

07968 **McMANUS, M.** (1971), Group desensitization of test anxiety. *Behav. Res. & Ther.*, 9:51-56.

07969 **McMILLAN, O. D.** (1972), The development and use of the McMillan affective relationship scale in measuring the effects of verbal interaction and of selected nonverbal techniques of communication on synthesized desirable outcomes of group dynamics procedures in sensitivity training. *Dissert. Abstr. Internat.*, 5551A.

07970 **McMILLAN, R. L.** (1978), The effect of group counseling on the self-concept of Black college students. *Dissert. Abstr. Internat.*, 39:2067A.

07971 **McMINNIS, C. A.** (1963), The effect of group-therapy on the ego-strength scale scores of alcoholic patients. *J. Clin. Psychol.*, 19:346-347.

07972 **McMORDLE, W. R.**, and **BIOM, S.** (1979), Life review therapy: psychotherapy for the elderly. *Perspect. Psychiat. Care*, 17:162-166.

07973 **McMULLEN, H. M.** (1973), The listening team: a venture in counseling. *Christian Cent.*, 90:855-857.

07974 **McMULLEN, R. S.** (1973), The achievement motivation workshop. *Personnel Guid. J.*, 51:642-645.

07975 **McMURRAIN, T. T.** (1970), Levels of interpersonal functioning in counseling group interactions. *Dissert. Abstr. Internat.*, 31:5771A.

07976 **McMURRAIN, T. T.**, and **GAZDA, G. M.** (1974), Extended group interaction: interpersonal functioning as a developmental process variable. *Small Group Behav.*, 5:393-403.

07977 **McNASSOR, D., WILLIAMS, L.**, and **ROUMAN, J.** (1958), A small activity group project. *Group Psychother., Psychodrama & Sociometry*, 11:137-143.

07978 **McNEEL, J. R.** (1976), Redecisions in psychotherapy: a study of the effects of an intensive weekend group workshop. *Dissert. Abstr. Internat.*, 36:4700.

07979 **McNEIL, J. N.**, and **VERWOERDT, A.** (1972), A group treatment program combined with a work project on the geriatric unit of a state hospital. *J. Amer. Geriat. Soc.*, 20:259-264.

07980 **McNEIL, J. N.**, and **VERWOERDT, A.** (1973), Group treatment program combined with work project on geriatric unit of state hospital. *Psychiat. Digest*, 34:11-17.

07981 **McNEIL, J. S.**, and **McBRIDE, M. L.** (1979), Group therapy with abusive parents. *Soc. Casework*, 60:36-42.

07982 **McNEILLY, G.** (1980), Learning from experience in therapeutic community living: training weekend. *Group Anal.*, (London) 13:67-70.

07983 **McPHERSON, F. M.**, and **WALTON, H. J.** (1970), The dimensions of psychotherapy group interaction: an analysis of clinicians' constructs. *Brit. J. Med. Psychol.*, (London) 43:281-289.

07984 **McPHERSON, R.** (1972), *Small Group Psychotherapy.* Baltimore: Penguin.

07985 **McPHERSON, S. B.**, and **SAMUELS, C. R.** (1971), Teaching behavioral methods to parents. *Soc. Casework*, 52:148-153.

07986 **McREYNOLDS, J. E.** (1972), A study of the relationship of sensitivity group insights to the preaching ministry of the church. *Dissert. Abstr. Internat.*, 33:1822A.

07987 **McREYNOLDS, W. T.** (1969), A note on relaxation treatment groups in studies of systematic desensitization. *J. Abnorm. & Soc. Psychol.*, 74:561-562.

07988 **McWHINNEY, W. H.** (1963), Isolating organizational dynamics in a small group experiment. *Sociometry*, 26:354-372.

07989 **McWHIRTER, J. J.** (1974), Counselor preparation through small group interaction. *Small Group Behav.*, 5:23-29.

07990 **McWHIRTER, J. J.** (1970), Small group process in training effective counselors. *Dissert. Abstr. Internat.*, 30:3282A.

07991 **McWHIRTER, J. J.**, and **KAHN, S. E.** (1974), A parent communication group. *Elem. School Guid. & Couns.*, 9:116-122.

07992 **McWHIRTER, J. J.**, and **MARKS, S. E.** (1972), An investigation of the relationship between the facilitative conditions and peer and group leader ratings of perceived counseling effectiveness. *J. Clin. Psychol.*, 28:116-117.

07993 **MEAD, E.**, and **CRANE, D. R.** (1978), Empirical approach to supervision and training of relationship therapists. *J. Marriage & Fam. Ther.*, 4:67-76.

07994 **MEAD, M.** (1951), Group psychotherapy in the light of social anthropology. *Internat. J. Group Psychother.*, 1:193-199.

07995 **MEADOR, B. D.** (1970), An analysis of process movement in a basic encounter group. *Dissert. Abstr. Internat.*, 30:3872B.

07996 **MEADOR, B. D.** (1971), Individual process in a basic encounter group. *J. Couns. Psychol.*, 18:70-76.

07997 **MEALEY, A. R.** (1977), Sculpting as a group technique for increasing awareness. *Perspect. Psychiat. Care*, 15:118-121.

07998 **MEALS, D. W.**, and **SUMMERSKILL, J.** (1951), A technique for dealing with hostility in activity therapy. *J. Clin. Psychol.*, 7:376-378.

07999 **MEARES, A.** (1972), Group relaxing hypnosis. *J. Amer. Soc. Psychosomat. Dent. & Med.*, 19:137.

08000 **MEARES, A.** (1973), A psychiatric experiment in community service. *Med. J. Austral.*, (Glebe) 1:733-734.

08001 **MEARES, R.** (1973), Two kinds of groups. *Brit. J. Med. Psychol.*, (London) 46:373-379.

08002 **MECHANIC, D.** (1962), Factors associated with attitudes favorable to rehabilitation among committed alcoholic patients. *Quart. J. Studies Alcohol*, 23:624-633.

08003 **MECHANIC, D.** (1961), Relevance of group atmosphere and attitudes for the rehabilitation of alcoholics. *Quart. J. Studies Alcohol*, 22:634-645.

08004 **MECK, D. S.**, and **BALL, J. D.** (1979), Teaching adjunctive coping skills in a personality adjustment course. *Teaching Psychol.*, 6:185.

08005 **MECKER, A. E.** (1972), Some reflections of Steiner's *Games Alcoholics Play. Transactional Anal. J.*, 2:122-123.

08006 **MEDINA, G.** (1972), (Technical use of drawings in psychotherapy of children and various group phenomena.) *Actas Luso Espanolas Neurol. Psiquiat.*, (Madrid) 1:197-201.

08007 **MEDINA, G. S.** (1965), Psychotrial: a new type of group psychotherapy. *Correct. Psychiat. & J. Soc. Ther.*, 11:157-162.

08008 **MEDVENE, A. M.**, and **Del BEATO, D.** (1972), A no-wait group counseling program. *Personnel & Guid. J.*, 50:397-398.

08009 **MEDVIN, D.** (1970), A study comparing the effects of individual counseling, multiple counseling, and non-counseling procedures on students enrolled in an experimental teacher certification program. *Dissert. Abstr. Internat.*, 30:4281.

08010 **MEEKS, J. E.** (1973), Structuring the early phase of group psychotherapy with adolescents. *Internat. J. Child Psychother.*, 2:391.

08011 **MEEKS, J. E.** (1980), What did the therapists say? What did the therapists do? *Internat. J. Psychoanal. & Psychother.*, 81:233.

08012 **MEERLOO, J. A.** (1970), Saltwater-, air-, and grass-neuroses: a war memory. *Psychiat. Neurol. Neurochir.*, 73:221-223.

08013 **MEES, H. L.**, and **KEUTZER, C. S.** (1967), Short-term group psychotherapy with obese women: a pilot project. *Northwestern Med.*, 66:548-550.

08014 **MEHL, R. F., III** (1979), Locus of problem and locus of solution attributions in patients and therapists. *Dissert. Abstr. Internat.*, 40:5820B.

08015 **MEHLE, M.** (1977), (Transference in group psychotherapy of schizophrenic patients.) *Psihijat. Danas*, (Belgrade) 9:87-90.

08016 **MEHLMAN, B.** (1953), Group play therapy with mentally retarded children. *J. Abnorm. & Soc. Psychol.*, 48:53-60.

08017 **MEHR, L. M.** (1973), Effects of a rehabilitation program including group counseling on the personality constructs of internal/external control of patients in a methadone treatment program. *Dissert. Abstr. Internat.*, 33:3300A.

08018 **MEICHENBAUM, D. H., GILMORE, J. B.**, and **FEDORAVICIUS, A.** (1971), Group insight versus group desensitization in treating speech anxiety. *J. Consult. & Clin. Psychol.*, 36:410-421.

08019 **MEIER, C. A.** (1948), Advances in group and individual therapy. In: *International Congress on Mental Health, Vol. 3, Proceedings of the International Conference on Medical Psychotherapy*, ed. J. C. Flugel. New York: Columbia University Press.

08020 **MEIER, G.** (1975), A health-oriented program for emotionally disturbed women. *Soc. Casework*, 56:411-417.

08021 **MEIERS, J.** (1957), Scandinavian myth about the psychodrama: a counter-statement to S. R. Slavson's "Preliminary note." *Group Psychother., Psychodrama & Sociometry*, 10:349-352.

08022 **MEIERS, J. I.** (1945), Origins and development of group psychotherapy. *Sociometry*, 8:499-534.

08023 **MEIERS, J. I.** (1947), Reaching out for the psychodrama. *Sociatry*, 1:64-69.

08024 **MEIERS, J. I.** (1956), Therapy at a distance. *Internat. J. Sociometry & Sociatry*, 1:109-111.

08025 **MEIERS, J. I.** (1950), Thoughts on recent advances in group psychotherapy. *Group Psychother., Psychodrama & Sociometry*, 3:241-245.

08026 **MEIERS, J. I.** (1947), Three word histories important in psychodrama. *Sociatry*, 1:239-242.

08027 **MEIGNIEZ, R.** (1967), *L'Analyses de Groupe, Regards Existentiels.* (*Group Analysis and Existentialism.*) Paris: Éditions Universitaires.

08028 **MEIGNIEZ, R.** (1967), (The nature of individual and group psychotherapy.) *Evolut. Psychiat.*, (Toulouse) 32:941-959.

08029 **MEIGNIEZ, R.** (1963), (Outline of a presentation of the stage of development of the "restricted group" or t group.) *Evolut. Psychiat.*, (Toulouse) 28:305-317.

08030 **MEIJERING, W. L.** (1960), The interrelation of individual, group, and hospital community psychotherapy. *Internat. J. Group Psychother.*, 10:46-62.

08031 **MEIJERING, W. L.** (1955), The use of multiple transference in community psychotherapy. *Acta Psychother., Psychosomat. Orthopaedagog.*, (Basel) 3:246-252.

08032 **MEISS, R., LICHTE-SPRAUGER, W.,** and **PETERSEN, P.** (1971), (Chronic mental patients shape their vacation: the group approach to the democratic style of the social psychiatrist's contribution to extramural therapy.) *Praxis der Psychother.*, 16:142-152.

08033 **MEISSNER, W. W.** (1965), *Group Dynamics in the Religious Life.* Notre Dame, IN: University of Notre Dame Press.

08034 **MEISTER, A.** (1956), Perception and acceptance of power relations in children. *Group Psychother., Psychodrama & Sociometry*, 9:153-163.

08035 **MEISTERMANN-SEEGER, E. M.** (1967), Gruppentherapie in der ausbildung fur caseworkarbeit. (Group therapy in the training of case workers.) *Psychother. & Psychosomat.*, (Basel) 15:46.

08036 **MEIZER, M.** (1979), Group treatment to combat loneliness and mistrust in chronic schizophrenics. *Hosp. & Community Psychiat.*, 30:18.

08037 **MELBY, D. J.** (1973), Individual and common goals: an analysis of the criterion problem in group counseling. *Dissert. Abstr. Internat.*, 33:4520B.

08038 **MELCHERT, P. A.** (1969), An investigation of the efficacy of vicarious group counseling. *Dissert. Abstr. Internat.*, 30:1024A-1025A.

08039 **MELDMAN, M. J., MCGOWAN, M., HIGGINS, J.,** and **SCHALLER, D.** (1969), Nurse psychotherapists in a private practice. *Amer. J. Nursing*, 69:2412-2415.

08040 **MELIKER, M. L.** (1974), The role of the subject's perception of control of therapy in analogue group systematic desensitization. *Dissert. Abstr. Internat.*, 34:3503B.

08041 **MELKUS, R. A.** (1977), The effects of a group vocational counseling method on selected variables among community college students. *Dissert. Abstr. Internat.*, 37:6955A.

08042 **MELLAN, J.** (1968), (Psychotherapy of sexual disturbances in single men.) *Psychiat., Neurol., & Med. Psychol.*, (Leipzig) 20:19-21.

08043 **MELLOR, J.** (1977), Re-activation: part 9. *Australasian Nurses J.*, (Port Adelaide) 7:19-20.

08044 **MELNICK, J.,** and **TIMS, A. R., Jr.** (1974), Application of videotape equipment to group therapy. *Internat. J. Group Psychother.*, 24:199-206.

08045 **MELNICK, J.,** and **WOODS, M.** (1976), Analysis of group composition research and theory for psychotherapeutic and growth-oriented groups. *J. Appl. Behav. Science*, 12:493-512.

08046 **MELTZER, H.** (1980), The impact of encounter groups: actualizing differences between a t-lab group and a humanistic psychology group. *Small Group Behav.*, 11:23-34.

08047 **MELTZOFF, J.,** and **KORNREICH, M.** (1970), *Research in Psychotherapy.* New York: Atherton Press.

08048 **MENCKE, R. A.,** and **COCHRAN, D. J.** (1974), Impact of a counseling outreach workshop on vocational development. *J. Couns. Psychol.*, 21:185-190.

08049 **MENDEL, W. M., WEXLER, M.,** and **BROTMAN, S.** (1964), Group psychotherapy as a technique for teaching psychiatry to medical students. *J. Med. Educat.*, 39:497-501.

08050 **MENDELL, D.** (1975), Combined family and group therapy for problems of adolescents: a synergistic approach. In: *The Adolescent in Group and Family Therapy*, ed. M. Sugar. New York: Brunner/Mazel.

08051 **MENDELL, D.** (1968), Group therapy modes at scientific meetings: an

approach to creative communication. *Internat. J. Group Psychother.*, 18:369-374.
08052 **MENDELL, D.** (1977), Review of P. A. Martin's *Marital Therapy Manual. Amer. J. Psychiat.*, 134:337.
08053 **MENDELL, P.** (1975), A paratherapeutic system: southwest group therapy model. *Internat. J. Group Psychother.*, 25:291-304.
08054 **MENDELSOHN, A. S.** (1978), Video-taped modeling as a determinant of verbal communication in encounter groups. *Dissert. Abstr. Internat.*, 39:2510B.
08055 **MENDES LEAL, M. R.** (1966), Group-analytic play therapy with preadolescent girls. *Internat. J. Group Psychother.*, 16:58-64.
08056 **MENDES, L. R.** (1969/1970), (Analytic transference of group analysis.) *Bull. de Psychol.*, (Paris) 23:760-764.
08057 **MENEFEE, M. M.** (1974), Influence of the creative process in producing significant behavior change in the intensive small group. *Dissert. Abstr. Internat.*, 34:4670B.
08058 **MENGES, R. J.,** and **McGAHIE, W. C.** (1974), Learning in group settings: toward a classification of outcomes. *Educat. Technol.*, 14:56-60.
08059 **MENKS, F., SITTLER, S., WEAVER, D.,** and **YANOW, B.** (1977), A psychogeriatric activity group in a rural community. *Amer. J. Occupat. Ther.*, 31:376.
08060 **MENNINGER, K., PRUYSER, P. W., MAYMAN, M.,** and **HOUSTON, M.** (1960), The prescription of treatment. *Bull. Menninger Clinic*, 24:217-249.
08061 **MENNINGER, R. W.** (1972), The impact of group relations conferences on organizational growth. *Internat. J. Group Psychother.*, 22:415-432.
08062 **MENNINGER, R. W.** (1959), Observations on absences of member patients in group psychotherapy. *Internat. J. Group Psychother.*, 9:195-203.
08063 **MENNINGER, W. C.** (1942), Experiments and educational treatment in a psychiatric institution. *Bull. Menninger Clinic*, 6:38-45.
08064 **MENTZ, A.,** and **SPITTLER, H-D.** (1975), (Ambulant client-centered group therapy: concept and application.) *Gruppendynamik*, (Stuttgart) 6:261-270.
08065 **MENTZEL, G.** (1965), (Alcoholics anonymous and the treatment of the chronic alcoholic patients.) *Nervenarzt*, 36:257-261.
08066 **MENTZER, R. T.** (1965), Early experiences with a mixed-sex ward. *Ment. Hosp.*, 16:267-271.
08067 **MENZER, D., IRVINE, L. S.,** and **SEMRAD, E. V.** (1951), The role of the social worker in group therapy. *J. Psychiat. Soc. Work*, 20:158-166.
08068 **MERCHANT, F. C.** (1941), The place of psychodrama in training the clinician. *Psychol. Bull.*, 38:748.
08069 **MERGUET, H.** (1950), Discussion on group psychotherapy. International Congress on Psychiatry, Paris.
08070 **MERMELSTEIN, M. D.,** and **VOTH, A. C.** (1954), Round table group therapy with psychotic patients. *Proceed. Iowa Acad. Science*, 61:387-393.
08071 **MERMIS, W. L.** (1970), Bibliography. *Compar. Group Studies*, 1:199-207.
08072 **MERRILL, A. D.** (1949), Occupational treatment with maximum security patients: an adjunct to group psychotherapy. *Psychiat. Quart. Suppl.*, 23:205-223.
08073 **MERRILL, O. W., JR.** (1974), Group psychotherapy with American-Indian adolescents: a study of reported changes. *Dissert. Abstr. Internat.*, 35:1392B.
08074 **MERRY, J.** (1953), Excitatory group psychotherapy. *J. Ment. Science*, (London) 99:513-520.
08075 **MERRY, J.** (1954), Participation of patient in treatment. *Brit. J. Phys. Med.*, 17:227-232.

08076 **MERRY, J.** (1953), The relative roles of individual psychotherapy and group psychotherapy in the individual neurosis unit. *J. Ment. Science*, 99:301-307.

08077 **MERZBACH, U.** (1975), *Verhaltensmodifikation in Einer Gruppe Verhaltensauffälliger Kinder.* (*Behavior Modification in a Group for Delinquent Children.*) Dortmund: Verlag Modernes Lernen.

08078 **MESHANU, R. W.** (1972), An experimental investigation into the training of empathic skills in groups of resistant assistants. *Dissert. Abstr. Internat.*, 32:4958A.

08079 **MESSÉ, L. A.** (1972), Motivation as a mediator of the mechanisms underlying role assignments in small groups. *Personality & Soc. Psychol. Bull.*, 24:84-90.

08080 **MESSER, S. B.**, and **LEHRER, P. M.** (1976), Short-term groups with female welfare clients in a job-training program. *Prof. Psychol.*, 7:352-358.

08081 **MESSING, S. D.** (1958), Group therapy and social status in the Zar cult of Ethiopia. *Amer. Anthropol.*, 60:1120-1126.

08082 **MESSMORE, D. W.** (1973), An experimental study on the effects of 24 hour marathon encounter groups on self concept. *Dissert. Abstr. Internat.*, 34:174A.

08083 **MESTER, R.**, **KLEIN, H.**, and **LOWENTAL** (1975), Conjoint hospitalization of mother and baby in post-partum syndromes: why and how? *Israel Annals Psychiat.*, (Jerusalem) 13:124-136.

08084 **METZ, A. S.** (1965), A comparison of the use of the sound recording and the written transcript in the coding of verbal interaction. *J. Soc. Psychol.*, 65:325-335.

08085 **METZL, J.** (1927), Die arbeitsmethoden der trinkfuersorgestelle brigittenau. *Internat. Zeit. Alkoholismus*, 35:65-80, 222-243, 293-305.

08086 **MEYER, A.** (1940), Spontaneity. *Sociometry*, 4:150-167.

08087 **MEYER, C. H.** (1966), The changing concept of individualized services. *Soc. Casework*, 47:279-285.

08088 **MEYER, E.**, and **ALBISSER, S.** (1978), (Review of *Introduction to Praxis of Scholastic Group Work.*) *Der Psychol.*, (Berne) 37:165.

08089 **MEYER, G. G.** (1969), Psychiatric consultation for blind students preparing to enter college. *Amer. J. Orthopsychiat.*, 39:303-304.

08090 **MEYER, G. G.** (1967), Group psychotherapy. *Progr. Neurol. Psychiat.*, 22:501-508.

08091 **MEYER, G. G.** (1971), Group psychotherapy. In: *Progress in Neurology and Psychiatry*, ed. E. A. Spiegel. New York: Grune and Stratton.

08092 **MEYER, J. B.**, and **STROWIG, W.** (1970), Behavioral-reinforcement counseling with rural high school youth. *J. Couns. Psychol.*, 17:127-132.

08093 **MEYER, J. E.** (1972), (Psychiatric compulsive syndromes and their delineation from compulsive neurosis.) *Praxis der Psychother.*, 17:204.

08094 **MEYER, M. S.**, and **POWER, E. J.** (1953), The family case-worker's contribution to parent education through the medium of the discussion group. *Amer. J. Orthopsychiat.*, 23:621-628.

08095 **MEYER, P.** (1964), Effect of group counseling upon certain educative and emotional factors of first year nursing students. *Dissert. Abstr. Internat.*, 25:1009.

08096 **MEYER, R.**, and **SUSMANN, I.** (1956), Psihoterapia k'vutsatit etsel holim psihotiyim. (Group psychotherapy with psychotic patients.) *Harefuah*, (Tel Aviv) 51:197-199.

08097 **MEYER, R. G.**, and **SMITH, S. R.** (1977), Crisis in group therapy. *Amer. Psychologist*, 32:638-643.

08098 **MEYERHOFF, H.** (1977), Art as therapy in a group setting: the stories of Batja and Rina. *Amer. J. Art Ther.*, 16:135-144.

08099 **MEYERING, W. L.** (1955), Group psychotherapy and the "frame of reference." *Internat. J. Group Psychother.*, 5:242-248.

08100 **MEYERING, W. L.** (1964), (The place of group therapy in the treatment of schizophrenia.) *Psychiat. Neurol., Neurochir.*, (Amsterdam) 67:137-142.

08101 **MEYERS, S. J.** (1978), The disorders of the self: developmental and clinical considerations. *Group*, 2:131-140.

08102 **MEZQUITA, J.** (1977), (Structure, organization, and results of a specialized unit for alcoholics.) *Arch. Neurobiol.*, (Madrid) 40:79-104.

08103 **MEZZANO, J.** (1967), Group counseling with low motivated male high school students: comparative effects of two users of counselor time. *Dissert. Abstr. Internat.*, 27:2893A.

08104 **MEZZANO, J.** (1968), Group counseling with low-motivated male high school students: comparative effects of two uses of counselor time. *J. Educat. Res.*, 61:222-224.

08105 **MEZZANOTTE, E. J.** (1970), Group instruction in preparation for surgery. *Amer. J. Nursing*, 70:89-91.

08106 **MICATI, L.** (1977), *Dinamica Degli Inconsci: La Psicoterapia Analitica di Gruppo.* (*Dynamics of the Unconscious: Analytic Group Psychotherapy.*) Bari: Dedalo Libri.

08107 **MICHAELS, F.** (1977), The effects of discussing grief, loss, death, and dying on depression levels in a geriatric outpatient therapy group. *Dissert. Abstr. Internat.*, 38:910B.

08108 **MICHAELS, J. J.** (1963), Some psychoanalytic aspects of group therapy: the psychoanalytic contributions of Leo Berman. *Amer. J. Orthopsychiat.*, 33:132-135.

08109 **MICHAELS, J. J.**, and **MILTON, E. O.** (1946), Group psychotherapy for neuropsychiatric patients being discharged from the army. *Occupat. Med.*, 1:60-74.

08110 **MICHAELS, J. J., REDL, F.**, and **LEVIN, S.** (1963), Leo Berman memorial meeting: some psychoanalytic aspects of group therapy. *Amer. J. Orthopsychiat.*, 33:132-160.

08111 **MICHAL-SMITH, H., GOTTSEGEN, M.**, and **GOTTSEGEN, G.** (1955), A group technique for mental retardies. *Internat. J. Group Psychother.*, 5:84-90.

08112 **MICHAUX, W. W.** (1961), Note on a projective technique for studying group dynamics. *Group Psychother., Psychodrama & Sociometry*, 14:48-49.

08113 **MICHAUX, W. W.** (1962), Note on a projective technique for studying group dynamics. *Group Psychother., Psychodrama & Sociometry*, 15:334-335.

08114 **MICK, R. M.**, and **HEINE, R. W.** (1957), Group therapy program for chronically unemployed psychiatric patients. *Psychol. Reports*, 3:607-612.

08115 **MICKOW, G.**, and **BENSON, M.** (1973), Group therapy for sex offenders. *Soc. Work*, 18:98-100.

08116 **MIDDLEMAN, R. R.** (1970), A service pattern for helping unmarried pregnant teenagers. *Children*, 17:108-112.

08117 **MIDDLEMAN, R. R.**, and **GOLDBERG, G.** (1972), The interactional way of presenting generic social work concepts. *J. Educat. Soc. Work*, 8:48-57.

08118 **MIDDLETON, P.** (1978), A test of Sarbin's self-role congruency therapy within a role-playing therapy analogue situation. *J. Clin. Psychol.*, 34:505-511.

08119 **MIEZIO, S.** (1967), Group therapy with mentally retarded adolescents in institutional settings. *Internat. J. Group Psychother.*, 17:321-327.

08120 **MIFLIN, A. B.**, and **BAUM, Z. E.** (1954), A settlement house uses role-playing. *Group Psychother., Psychodrama & Sociometry*, 7:227-237.

08121 **MIGLIONICO, L. R.** (1978), The relative efficacy of gestalt and human relations training group treatment. *Dissert. Abstr. Internat.*, 39:4044B.

08122 **MIKAWA, J. K., CLAPP, W.**, and **FREMLIN, R.** (1972), Group participation procedures for improving ethnic minority job opportunities. *Internat. J. Group Tensions*, 2:63-76.

08123 **MIKLICH, D. R.** (1979), Health psychology practice with asthmatics. *Prof. Psychol.*, 10:580-583.

08124 **MILANI, B.** (1960), (Present trends in group psychotherapy: a new psychodramatic experiment.) *Rass. Studi Psichiat.*, (Siena) 49:129-149.

08125 **MILASAVLIJEVIC, P.** (1976), (Emotional attitudes of parents of schizophrenic patients during family psychotherapy.) *Soc. Psihijat.*, (Belgrade) 43:309.

08126 **MILBERG, I. L.** (1963), Group therapy in the treatment of some dermatoses. *Skin*, 2:307-310.

08127 **MILBERG, I. L.** (1956), Group psychotherapy in the treatment of some neurodermatoses. *Internat. J. Group Psychother.*, 6:53-60.

08128 **MILES, A.** (1969), Changes in the attitudes to authority of patients with behavior disorders in a therapeutic community. *Brit. J. Psychiat.*, 115:1049-1057.

08129 **MILES, A. E.** (1969), The effects of a therapeutic community on the interpersonal relationship of a group of psychopaths. *Brit. J. Criminol.*, (London) 9:22-38.

08130 **MILES, D. G.**, and **HARRIS, F. E.** (1966), An overview of vocational rehabilitation in the modern mental health center. *J. Rehab.*, 32:34-35.

08131 **MILES, H.** (1968), Implications of intermediary group treatment for readying unmarried mothers for continued casework. *Smith Coll. Studies Soc. Work*, 39:80-81.

08132 **MILES, H. S.**, and **HAYS, D. R.** (1975), Widowhood. *Amer. J. Nursing*, 75:280-282.

08133 **MILES, M. B.** (1959), *Learning to Work in Groups: A Program Guide for Education Leaders*. New York: Columbia University Teachers College.

08134 **MILES, M. B.** (1975), Rejoinder to Schutz, Smith, and Rowan. *J. Human. Psychol.*, 15:55-58.

08135 **MILES, M. S.** (1977), The effects of small group education/counseling experience on the attitudes of nurses toward death and toward dying patients. *Dissert. Abstr. Internat.*, 33:636A.

08136 **MILINE, A.** (1967), Out-patient group therapy follow-up of treated chronic schizophrenics. *Psychother. & Psychosomat.*, (Basel) 15:73.

08137 **MILL, C. R.** (1980), *Activities for Trainers: 50 Useful Designs*. San Diego: University Associates.

08138 **MILL, C. R.** (1971), A new technology. *Internat. J. Psychiat.*, 9:193-196.

08139 **MILL, C. R.** (1969), *Selections from Human Relations Training News*. Washington: National Institute for Applied Behavioral Science.

08140 **MILLAR, W. M., MACKIE, R. E.**, and **GOMERSALL, J. D.** (1968), Training in psychotherapy: the Aberdeen diploma course. *Brit. J. Psychiat.*, (Ashford) 114:1425-1428.

08141 **MILLARD, J.**, and **McLAGAN, J. R.** (1972), Multifamily group work: a hopeful approach to the institutionalized delinquent and his family. *Compar. Group Studies*, 3:117-127.

08142 **MILLER, A.** (1972), Role playing with large and small groups. *Couns. & Values*, 17:62-68.

08143 **MILLER, A. B.**, and **MALONEY, D.** (1972), Turn over. *Transactional Anal. J.*, 2:117-121.

08144 **MILLER, A. H.** (1973), The spontaneous use of poetry in an adolescent girl's group. *Internat. J. Group Psychother.*, 23:223-227.
08145 **MILLER, B. A., POKORNEY, A. D.,** and **KANAS, T. E.** (1970), Problems in treating homeless, jobless alcoholics. *Hosp. & Community Psychiat.*, 21:98-99.
08146 **MILLER, C.,** and **SLAVSON, S. R.** (1939), Integration of individual and group therapy in the treatment of a problem boy. *Amer. J. Orthopsychiat.*, 9:792-797.
08147 **MILLER, C. B.** (1978), The impact of group career counseling on career maturity and on stereotypical occupational choice of high school girls. *Dissert. Abstr. Internat.*, 39:5330A.
08148 **MILLER, D.** (1970), The effect of immediate and delayed audiotape and videotape playback of group counseling. *Dissert. Abstr. Internat.*, 30:3872B.
08149 **MILLER, D.** (1972), Psychodramatic ways of coping with potentially dangerous situations in psychotic and non-psychotic populations. *Group Psychother., Psychodrama & Sociometry,* 25:57-68.
08150 **MILLER, D. C.** (1953), A role playing workshop for business and government administrators; its research implications. *Group Psychother., Psychodrama & Sociometry*, 6:50-62.
08151 **MILLER, D. H.** (1957), The treatment of adolescents in an adult hospital by preliminary report. *Bull. Menninger Clinic*, 21:189-198.
08152 **MILLER, D. K.** (1978), Poetry therapy with psychotic patients. *J. Contemp. Psychother.*, 9:135-138.
08153 **MILLER, D. L.** (1978), Helping parents to be parents: a special center. *MCN: Amer. J. Maternal Child Nursing*, 3:117-120.
08154 **MILLER, D. L.,** and **WILDER, J. F.** (1978), Multimodal outpatient group treatment for the psychiatrically disabled. *Community Ment. Health J.*, 14:209-215.
08155 **MILLER, E. C., DVORAK, B. A.,** and **TURNER, D. W.** (1960), A method of creating aversion to alcohol by reflex conditioning in a group setting. *Quart. J. Studies Alcohol*, 21:424-431.
08156 **MILLER, E. G.** (1976), Conjecturing about the future of t-groups. *Pub. Admin. Rev.*, 36:688.
08157 **MILLER, E. R.,** and **SHASKAN, D. A.** (1963), A note on the group management of a disgruntled, suicidal patient. *Internat. J. Group Psychother.*, 13:216-218.
08158 **MILLER, F. D.** (1976), The problem of transfer of training in learning groups: group cohesion as an end in itself. *Small Group Behav.*, 7:221-236.
08159 **MILLER, F. E.** (1973), The effects of pretraining in openness on depth of interaction and behavioral change in group therapy. *Dissert. Abstr. Internat.*, 33:5521B.
08160 **MILLER, F. T.** (1974), Youth talk it over: solving mutual problems. *Personnel & Guid. J.*, 52:478-482.
08161 **MILLER, G. D.,** and **ZORADI, S. D.** (1977), Roommate conflict resolution. *J. Coll. Student Personnel*, 18:228-230.
08162 **MILLER, H.,** and **BARUCH, D.** (1956), Allergies. In: *The Fields of Group Psychotherapy*, ed. S. R. Slavson. New York: International Universities Press.
08163 **MILLER, H.,** and **BARUCH, D. W.** (1948), Psychological dynamics in allergic patients as shown in group and individual psychotherapy. *J. Consult. & Clin. Psychol.*, 12:111-115.
08164 **MILLER, H.,** and **BARUCH, D. W.** (1952), Some paintings by allergic patients in group psychotherapy and their dynamic implications in the practice of allergy. *Internat. Arch. Allergy*, 1:60-71.
08165 **MILLER, H. R.,** and **MALEY, R. G.** (1969), The accuracy of sampling

procedures in studying recorded group psychotherapy sessions. *J. Clin. Psychol.*, 25:228-230.
08166 **MILLER, I.**, and **SOLOMON, R.** (1979), Development of group services for the elderly. In: *Social Work Practice*, ed. C. B. Germain. New York: Columbia University Press.
08167 **MILLER, J.** (1978), Attaining freedom in existential group therapy. *Amer. J. Psychoanal.*, 38:179-183.
08168 **MILLER, J. C.**, and **JANIS, I. L.** (1973), Dyadic interaction and adaptation to the stresses of college life. *J. Couns. Psychol.*, 20:258-264.
08169 **MILLER, J. G.** (1965), Living systems: basic concepts. *Behav. Science Res.*, 10:193-237.
08170 **MILLER, J. G.** (1971), Living systems: the group. *Behav. Science Res.*, 16:302-398.
08171 **MILLER, J. G.** (1964), Psychodivorce: a psychodramatic technique. *Group Psychother., Psychodrama & Sociometry*, 17:129-133.
08172 **MILLER, J. H.** (1972), Sensitivity training with incarcerated criminals: personality correlates of participant duration and assessment of therapeutic value. *Dissert. Abstr. Internat.*, 32:3794A.
08173 **MILLER, J. P.** (1976), *Humanizing the Classroom*. New York: Praeger.
08174 **MILLER, J. S. A.**, **KWALWASSER, S.**, and **STEIN, A.** (1954), Observations concerning the use of group psychotherapy in a voluntary mental hospital: effects of group psychotherapy on the training of residents. *Internat. J. Group Psychother.*, 4:86-94.
08175 **MILLER, M. A.** (1975), Remotivation therapy: a way to reach the confused elderly patient. *J. Gerontol. Nursing*, 1:28-31.
08176 **MILLER, M. B.** (1966), Synthesis of a therapeutic community for the aged ill. *Geriatrics*, 21:151-163.
08177 **MILLER, M. M.** (1957), A group therapeutic approach to a case of bed wetting and fire setting with the aid of hypnoanalysis. *Group Psychother., Psychodrama & Sociometry*, 10:181-190.
08178 **MILLER, M. M.** (1960), Psychodrama in the treatment program of a juvenile court. *J. Crim. Law & Criminol.*, 50:453-459.
08179 **MILLER, M. M.** (1956), A sociometric approach to living. *Internat. J. Sociometry & Sociatry*, 1:155-158.
08180 **MILLER, N.**, and **BUTLER, D. C.** (1969), Social power and communication in small groups. *Behav. Science Res.*, 14:11-18.
08181 **MILLER, N. R.** (1974), The efficacy of using the Masters and Johnson method, with modification, to rapidly treat sexually dysfunctional couples in a group. *Dissert. Abstr. Internat.*, 35:824A.
08182 **MILLER, P. M.**, **HERSEN, M.**, **EISLER, B. M.**, and **HEMPHILL, D. P.** (1973), Electrical aversion therapy with alcoholics: an analogue study. *Behav. Res. & Ther.*, 11:491-497.
08183 **MILLER, P. M.**, **STANFORD, A. G.**, and **HEMPHILL, D. P.** (1974), A social-learning approach to alcoholism treatment. *Soc. Casework*, 55:279-284.
08184 **MILLER, P. R.**, and **FERONE, L.** (1966), Group psychotherapy with depressed women. *Amer. J. Psychiat.*, 123:701-703.
08185 **MILLER, R. A.** (1964), Alcoholism in the services. *Royal Army Med. Corps J.*, (Liverpool) 110:105-109.
08186 **MILLER, R. S.** (1973), A comparative study of the marathon group experience in a university counseling center. *Dissert. Abstr. Internat.*, 33:5497A.
08187 **MILLER, S.** (1973), *Hot Springs*. New York: Bantam Books.
08188 **MILLER, S.** (1979), Strategy: patient leader for group therapy. *Free Assn.*, 6:1-2.
08189 **MILLER, S. E.** (1980), The effects of two group approaches, psychodrama

and encounter, on levels of self-actualization: a comparative study. *Dissert. Abstr. Internat.*, 41:2456A. (University Microfilms No. 8021154.)
08190 **MILLER, V. H.** (1974), An evaluation of the effect of a sexual enrichment group experience on the sexual satisfaction and sexual pleasure of married couples. *Dissert. Abstr. Internat.*, 34:6218B.
08191 **MILLER, W. R.,** and **TAYLOR, C. A.** (1980), Relative effectiveness of bibliotherapy, individual and group self-control training in the treatment of problem drinkers. *Addict. Behav.*, 5:13-24.
08192 **MILLER de PAIVA, L.** (1973), Defense mechanisms in group therapy: introjective identification of the thanototic project, the false ego, and beta-screen. *Dynam. Psychiat.*, (Berlin) 6:238-248.
08193 **MILLIN, B.** (1975), Drama as therapy for the psychopathic personality. *Nursing Times*, (London) 71:69-71.
08194 **MILLON, T., GREEN, C. J.,** and **MEAGHER, R. B., JR.** (1979), The MHBI: a new inventory for the psychodiagnostician in medical settings. *Prof. Psychol.*, 10:529-539.
08195 **MILLS, C. L.** (1978), The use of modeling, coaching, and behavior rehearsal in assertive training as therapy with a group of men at a correctional institution. *Dissert. Abstr. Internat.*, 39:2511B. (University Microfilms No. 7821876.)
08196 **MILLS, R. B.** (1969), Use of diagnostic small groups in police recruit selection and training. *J. Crim. Law & Criminol.*, 60:238-241.
08197 **MILLS, T. M.** (1979), Changing paradigms for studying human groups. *J. Appl. Behav. Science*, 15:407-423.
08198 **MILLS, T. N.** (1978), Seven steps in developing group awareness. *J. Personality & Soc. Systems*, 1:15-29.
08199 **MILMAN, D. H.** (1952), Group therapy with parents: an approach to the rehabilitation of physically disabled children. *J. Pediat.*, 41:113-116.
08200 **MILMAN, D. S.,** and **GOLDMAN, G. D.** (1974), *Group Processes Today.* Springfield, IL: C. C. Thomas.
08201 **MILNE, A.** (1967), Outpatient group therapy follow-up of treated chronic schizophrenics. *Psychother. & Psychosomat.*, (Basel) 15:73.
08202 **MILOSAVLJEVIĆ, P.** (1975), (Difficulties in group work with the parents of schizophrenic patients.) *Anali Zavoda Ment. Zdravlje*, 7:151-156.
08203 **MILSTEAD, J. W.** (1972), The effects of group work on the school adjustment of "pre-delinquent" male adolescent peer groups. *Dissert. Abstr. Internat.*, 2527A.
08204 **MILSTONE, S.** (1976), Group therapy (letter). *J. Amer. Med. Assn.*, 235:2476.
08205 **MILTON, R.,** and **AGRIN, A.** (1966), Resolution of a crisis in a therapeutic community for alcoholics. *Quart. J. Studies Alcohol*, 27:517-524.
08206 **MIMS, F. H.** (1974), Experiential learning in groups. *J. Nursing Educat.*, 13:30-38.
08207 **MIMS, F. H.** (1971), The need to evaluate group therapy. *Nursing Outlook*, 19:776-778.
08208 **MINDE, K. K.,** and **WERRY, J. S.** (1969), Intensive psychiatric teacher counseling in a low socioeconomic area: a controlled evaluation. *Amer. J. Orthopsychiat.*, 39:595-608.
08209 **MINDLIN, D. F.** (1960), Evaluation of therapy for alcoholics in a workhouse setting. *Quart. J. Studies Alcohol*, 21:90-112.
08210 **MINDLIN, D. F.** (1965), Group therapy for alcoholics: a study of the attitude and behavior changes in relation to perceived group norms. *Dissert. Abstr. Internat.*, 26:2323-2324.
08211 **MINDLIN, D. F.,** and **BELDEN, E.** (1965), Attitude changes with alcoholics in group therapy. *California Ment. Health Res. Digest*, 3:102-103.
08212 **MINEAR, V.** (1953), An initial venture in the use of television as a me-

dium for psychodrama. *Group Psychother., Psychodrama & Sociometry*, 6:115-117.

08213 **MINICHIELLO, W. E.** (1972), An analysis of the effects of group counseling on the reduction of transfer-shock on community college students transferring to the University of Massachusetts. *Dissert. Abstr. Internat.*, 32:4958A.

08214 **MINNIGH, E. C.** (1971), The changing picture of Parkinsonism: ii. the Northwestern University concept of rehabilitation through group physical therapy. *Rehab. Lit.*, 32:38-39, 50.

08215 **MINOR, H. D.** (1972), *Techniques and Resources for Guiding Adult Groups*. Nashville: Abingdon.

08216 **MINTON, H. L.**, and **MILLER, A. G.** (1970), Group risk taking and internal-external control of group members. *Psychol. Reports*, 26:431-436.

08217 **MINTURN, E. B.**, and **LANSKY, L. M.** (1972), The trainerless laboratory. *J. Appl. Behav. Science*, 8:277-284.

08218 **MINTZ, A. L.** (1973), Encounter groups and other panaceas. *Commentary*, 56:42-49.

08219 **MINTZ, A. L.** (1974), Encounter groups and other panaceas. *Nursing Digest*, 2:78-86.

08220 **MINTZ, E.** (1971), *Marathon Groups: Reality and Symbol*. New York: Appleton-Century-Crofts.

08221 **MINTZ, E. E.** (1978), Group supervision: an experiential approach. *Internat. J. Group Psychother.*, 28:467-469.

08222 **MINTZ, E. E.** (1969), Group supervision for mature therapists. *J. Group Psychoanal. & Process*, (London) 1:63-70.

08223 **MINTZ, E. E.** (1965), Male-female co-therapists: some values and some problems. *Amer. J. Psychother.*, 19:293-301.

08224 **MINTZ, E. E.** (1969), Marathon groups: a preliminary evaluation. *J. Contemp. Psychother.*, 1:91-94.

08225 **MINTZ, E. E.** (1971), *Marathon Groups: Reality and Symbol*. New York: Irvingon Publishers.

08226 **MINTZ, E. E.** (1970), The marathon on wings. *Voices*, 5:23-27.

08227 **MINTZ, E. E.** (1976), New life styles: should they influence our group goals and values? *Internat. J. Group Psychother.*, 26:225-233.

08228 **MINTZ, E. E.** (1974), On the dramatization of psychoanalytic interpretations. In: *Group Therapy 1974: An Overview*, eds. L. R. Wolberg and M. L. Aronson. New York: Stratton Intercontinental Medical Books.

08229 **MINTZ, E. E.** (1969), On the rationale of touch in psychotherapy. *Psychother.: Theory, Res. & Pract.*, 6:232-234.

08230 **MINTZ, E. E.** (1966), Overt male homosexuals in combined group and individual treatment. *J. Consult. & Clin. Psychol.*, 30:193-198.

08231 **MINTZ, E. E.** (1963), Special values of co-therapists in group psychotherapy. *Internat. J. Group Psychother.*, 13:127-132.

08232 **MINTZ, E. E.** (1971), Therapy techniques and encounter techniques: comparison and rationale. *Amer. J. Psychother.*, 25:104-109.

08233 **MINTZ, E. E.** (1967), Time-extended marathon groups. *Psychother.: Theory, Res. & Pract.*, 4:65-70.

08234 **MINTZ, E. E.** (1963), Transference in co-therapy groups. *J. Consult. & Clin. Psychol.*, 27:34-39.

08235 **MINTZ, E. E.** (1974), What do we owe today's woman? *Internat. J. Group Psychother.*, 24:273-287.

08236 **MINTZ, J., O'BRIEN, C. P.**, and **LUBORSKY, L.** (1976), Predicting the outcome of psychotherapy for schizophrenics: relative contributions of patient, therapist, and therapist and treatment characteristics. *Arch. Gen. Psychiat.*, 33:1183-1186.

08237 **MIRROW, G. S.** (1978), A study of the effect of group counseling on the

self-concept and level of self-actualization of high school students. *Dissert. Abstr. Internat.*, 38:5928A.
08238 **MIRSKY, A.** (1972), "Jiffy stage" makes learning exciting. *Hosp. & Community Psychiat. Suppl.*, 23:11.
08239 **MISEL, L. T.** (1975), Stages of group treatment. *Transactional Anal. J.*, 5:385-391.
08240 **MISHNE, J.** (1971), Group therapy in an elementary school. *Soc. Casework*, 52:18-25.
08241 **MISTILIS, B. A.** (1978), An investigation of goal attainment scaling as an adjunct in group counseling with high school students. *Dissert. Abstr. Internat.*, 39:3477A.
08242 **MISTUR, R. J.** (1978), Behavioral group counseling with elementary school children: a model. *Dissert. Abstr. Internat.*, 38:7456A.
08243 **MITCHELL, B. A.** (1980), An investigation of therapist and patient self-disclosure in an outpatient therapy group. *Dissert. Abstr. Internat.*, 41:1119B. (University Microfilms No. 8021155.)
08244 **MITCHELL, B. D.** (1962), Role reversal in musical training. *Group Psychother., Psychodrama & Sociometry*, 15:154-158.
08245 **MITCHELL, G. W.** (1973), Effectiveness of short-term group counseling led by disadvantaged peer counselors on a group of disadvantaged freshmen at Oakland Community College. *Dissert. Abstr. Internat.*, 34:3882A.
08246 **MITCHELL, K. R.** (1971), Effects of neuroticism on intra-treatment responsivity to group desensitization of test anxiety. *Behav. Res. & Ther.*, 9:371-374.
08247 **MITCHELL, K. R.** (1975), A group program for the treatment of failing college students. *Behav. Ther.*, 6:324-336.
08248 **MITCHELL, K. R.** (1975), A group program for bright failing underachievers. *J. Coll. Student Personnel*, 16:306-312.
08249 **MITCHELL, K. R.**, and **INGHAM, R. J.** (1970), The effects of general anxiety on group desensitization of test anxiety. *Behav. Res. & Ther.*, 8:69-78.
08250 **MITCHELL, K. R.**, and **NG, K. T.** (1972), Effects of group counseling and behavior therapy on the academic achievement of test-anxious students. *J. Couns. Psychol.*, 19:491-497.
08251 **MITCHELL, K. R.**, and **PIATKOWSKA, O. E.** (1974), Effects of group treatment for college underachievers and bright failing underachievers. *J. Couns. Psychol.*, 21:494-502.
08252 **MITCHELL, L. E.** (1967), Psychotherapy with the culturally and economically deprived youth. *Adolescence*, 2:345-358.
08253 **MITCHELL, L. E., MacLENNAN, B. W., GIBBONS, I., YATES, E.**, and **JUSTISON, G.** (1965), A mobile therapeutic community for adolescents. *Amer. J. Orthopsychiat.*, 35:372-373.
08254 **MITCHELL, R.** (1978), Establishing a therapy group: part 2. *Nursing Times*, (London) 73:352-354.
08255 **MITCHELL, R. A.** (1972), The effects of group counseling experiences in a didactic classroom setting on selected personality variables and counseling effectiveness. *Dissert. Abstr. Internat.*, 32:6765A.
08256 **MITCHELL, R. R.** (1975), Relationships between personal characteristics and change in sensitivity training groups. *Small Group Behav.*, 6:414-420.
08257 **MITCHELL, S. D.**, and **ZANKER, A.** (1948), The use of music in group therapy. *J. Ment. Science*, 94:737-748.
08258 **MITCHELL, T. R.** (1970), Leader complexity, leadership style and group performance. *Dissert. Abstr. Internat.*, 30:3375B.
08259 **MITCHUM, N. T.** (1978), The effects of group counseling on the self-es-

teem, achievement and sex role awareness of children. *Dissert. Abstr. Internat.*, 39:4062A.

08260 **MITSCHERLICH, A.** (1971), Psycho-analysis and the aggression of large groups. *Internat. J. Psycho-Anal.*, (London) 52:161-167.

08261 **MITTWOCH, A.** (1980), Review of M. L. Moeller's *Self Help Groups. Group Anal.*, (London) 13:226-227.

08262 **MLOTT, S. R.** (1975), A group therapy approach with hemodialysis patients and their families. *J. Amer. Assn. Nephrol. Nursing Tech.*, 2:105-108.

08263 **MLYNARCZYK, R. K.** (1973), Higher horizons for the handicapped. *Parents*, 48:42-43.

08264 **MOACANIN, R.**, and **YAMAMOTO, J.** (1967), New roles for mental health personnel: i. the social worker as therapist. *Hosp. & Community Psychiat.*, 18:19-20.

08265 **MOADEL, Y.** (1970), Adolescent group psychotherapy in a hospital setting. *Amer. J. Psychoanal.*, 30:68-72.

08266 **MOATES, H. L.** (1970), The effects of activity group counseling on the self-concept, peer acceptance and grade-point average of disadvantaged seventh grade Negro boys and girls. *Dissert. Abstr. Internat.*, 30:3795A-3796A.

08267 **MOE, M., WAAL, N.**, and **URDAHL, B.** (1960), Group psychotherapy with parents of psychotic and neurotic children. *Acta Psychother., Psychosomat. Orthopaedagog.*, (Basel) 8:134-146.

08268 **MOELLER, M. L.** (1978), *Selbsthilfegruppen: Selbstbehandlung und Selbsterkenntnis in Eigenverantwortl Kleingruppen.* Reinbek bei Hamburg: Rowohlt.

08269 **MOELLER, M. L.** (1975), (Self-help groups and psychotherapy.) *Praxis der Psychother.*, 20:181.

08270 **MOERK, E. L.** (1972), Effects of personality structure on individual activities in a group and on group processes. *Human Relat.*, 25:505-514.

08271 **MOFFETT, L. A.**, and **STOKLOSA, J. M.** (1976), Group therapy for socially anxious and unassertive young veterans. *Internat. J. Group Psychother.*, 26:421-430.

08272 **MOGLICH, H.-J.** (1958), Kasuistischer beitrag zur frage fehlgeleiteter kindlicher gewissensreaktionen. (Contribution of a case study on the problem of misdirected infantile conscience reactions.) *Praxis Kinderpsychol. & Kinderpsychiat.*, (Goettingen) 7:64-68.

08273 **MOHR, K. E.** (1970), An evaluation of marathon group procedures and leaders as measured by the Structured Objective Rorschach Test (S.O.R.T.). *Dissert. Abstr. Internat.*, 31:2741A.

08274 **MOLDENHAUER, P.** (1974), The interdependence of behavior and the psychosomatic symptom. *Psychother. & Psychosomat.*, (Basel) 24:146-150.

08275 **MOLDENHAUER, P.** (1973), Psychosomatisches syndrom, verhalten in der gruppe und selbst. (Psychosomatic syndrome, group behavior, and self.) *Dynam. Psychiat.*, (Berlin) 6:33-56.

08276 **MOLDOWSKY, S.** (1950), Sociodrama session at the Mansfield Theater. *Group Psychother., Psychodrama & Sociometry*, 3:102-105.

08277 **MOLES, A.** (1956), L'homme futur, sociométrie et sociatrie: modèles de l'égo et impact de la technologie. (Future man, sociometry and sociatry: ego models and the impact of technology.) *Internat. J. Sociometry & Sociatry*, 1:48-51.

08278 **MOLL, A. E.**, and **SHANE, S. G.** (1951), Short term group psychotherapy: i. *Treatment Serv. Bull.*, 6:521-528.

08279 **MOLL, A. E.**, and **SHANE, S. G.** (1952), Short term group psychotherapy: ii. *Treatment Serv. Bull.*, 7:7-14.

08280 **MOLLOY, B.** (1979), Review of A. Jones's *Counseling Adolescents in School. J. Adolescence*, 2:177.
08281 **MOLLOY, G. N.** (1980), Wanted: some guidelines for investigating reporting and evaluating parent training interventions. *Austral. J. Develop. Disabil.*, 6:71-77.
08282 **MOLNAR, G.**, and **CAMERON, P.** (1975), Incest syndromes: observations in a general hospital psychiatric unit. *Can. Psychiat. Assn. J.*, (Ottawa) 20:373-377.
08283 **MOLNOS, A.** (1980), Healing "hidden dependence" through holding in the group. *Group Anal.*, (London) 13:183-191.
08284 **MONE, L. C.** (1970), Short-term group psychotherapy with postcardiac patients. *Internat. J. Group Psychother.*, 20:99-108.
08285 **MONE, L. C.** (1970), Short-term group psychotherapy with postcardiac patients. *Sandoz Psychiat. Spectator*, 6:20-21.
08286 **MONOD, G. T.**, and **WIDLUCKER, D.** (1971), (Psychotherapy of children and adolescents by means of psychodrama.) *Rev. Neuropsychiat. Infantile*, (Paris) 19:485-495.
08287 **MONOD, M.** (1948), First French experience with psychodrama. *Sociatry*, 1:400-403.
08288 **MONOD, M.** (1968), (Group psychotherapy of adolescents: parents and the psychotherapist couple.) *Rev. Neuropsychiat. Infantile*, (Paris) 16:511-524.
08289 **MONOD, M.** (1965), (Group psychotherapy of adolescents presenting disorders of expression.) *Rev. Neuropsychiat. Infantile*, (Paris) 13:867-872.
08290 **MONOD, M.**, and **BOSSE, J.** (1978-79), (Group psychotherapy with adolescents.) *Bull. de Psychol.*, (Paris) 32:253-261.
08291 **MONOD, M. E.**, and **MONTGRAIN, N. H.** (1966), Une experience de groupe aupres d'eleves infirmieres et eleves assistantes sociales. (Professional adaptation of student nurses and of social workers.) *Rev. Med. Psychosomat.*, (Toulouse) 8:57-64.
08292 **MONSERRAT-VALLE, L.** (1953), Psicoterapia de grupo. (Group psychotherapy.) *Rev. Psiquiat. & Psicol. Méd.*, 1:204-220.
08293 **MONTAGUE, H. C.** (1951), A case of regression in activity group therapy. *Internat. J. Group Psychother.*, 1:225-234.
08294 **MONTANELLI, R. P.**, and **CASAGRANDE, S.** (1971), Encuadre y contrato para pacientes de psicoterapia de grupo en la direccion de psicologia y orientacion vocacional. (Frame and contrast for group psychotherapy patients in the department of psychology and vocational counseling.) *Acta Psiquiat. Psicol. Amer. Latina* (Buenos Aires) 17:113-116.
08295 **MONTEIRO, M. G.**, and **SNYDER, L. M.** (1961), Social therapy through hospital ward discussions. *Ment. Hygiene*, 45:519-527.
08296 **MONTGOMERY, E. F.** (1975), A study of the effects of career and personal group counseling on retention rates and self-actualization. *Dissert. Abstr. Internat.*, 36:2028A.
08297 **MONTGOMERY, J.**, and **McBURNEY, R. D.** (1970), Problems and pitfalls of establishing an operant conditioning-token economy program. *Ment. Hygiene*, 54:382-387.
08298 **MONTGOMERY, J. L.** (1970), The effects of awareness training in a modified encounter group on selected aspects of personality with kindergarten children. *Dissert. Abstr. Internat.*, 31:5773A.
08299 **MONTGOMERY, J. S.** (1971), Treatment management of passive-dependent behavior. *Internat. J. Soc. Psychiat.*, (London) 17:311.
08300 **MONTGOMERY, L. J.** (1973), The sensitivity movement: questions to be researched. *Small Group Behav.*, 4:387-406.
08301 **MONTI, P. M.** (1979), Effect of social skills training groups and social

skills bibliotherapy with psychiatric patients. *J. Consult. & Clin. Psychol.*, 47:189.

08302 **MONTIONE, F. F.** (1976), A comparison of the effects of muscular relaxation and rest on the described as hyperactive. *Dissert. Abstr. Internat.*, 36:5268.

08303 **MOORE, C. D.** (1975), Discussion group for "intermediate care" patients. *Amer. Arch. Rehab. Ther.*, 23:36-38.

08304 **MOORE, J. C.** (1978), Relationship of group counseling and personality factors to attrition of freshman nursing students. *Dissert. Abstr. Internat.*, 38:6540A.

08305 **MOORE, K. B.**, and **QUERY, W. T.** (1963), Group psychotherapy as a means of approaching homosexual behavior among hospitalized psychiatric patients. *J. Kentucky Med. Assn.*, 61:403-407.

08306 **MOORE, M.** (1970), An account of a nurse's role and functions in an alcoholic treatment program. *J. Psychiat. Nursing*, 8:21-27.

08307 **MOORE, R. A.**, and **BUCHANAN, T. K.** (1966), State hospitals and alcoholism: a nation-wide survey of treatment techniques and results. *Quart. J. Studies Alcohol*, 27:459-468.

08308 **MOORE, R. A.**, and **RAMSEUR, F.** (1960), Effects of psychotherapy in an open ward hospital on patients with alcoholism. *Quart. J. Studies Alcohol*, 21:233-252.

08309 **MOORE, R. L.** (1978), Review of C. L. Cooper's *Theories of Group Processes. J. Communicat.*, 28:216.

08310 **MOORE, R. L., JR., ZIMMERMAN, R. R.**, and **ESTELLE, J.** (1972), Program of psychotherapy for inmates at the Montana State Prison. *Psychol. Reports*, 30:756-758.

08311 **MOORE, S.** (1970), Group supervision: forerunner or trend reflector? *Soc. Worker*, (Ottawa) 38:16-20.

08312 **MOORE, S. L.** (1971), The effect of group counseling on student teachers toward interpersonal relationships with children. *Dissert. Abstr. Internat.*, 32:184A.

08313 **MOORE, W. E.** (1954), Introduction of new patients into individual-centered psychodrama within a group-setting. *Group Psychother., Psychodrama & Sociometry*, 6:174-182.

08314 **MOOSBROKER, J.** (1973), Effects of t-group experiences on some attitudinal and personality dimensions. *Interpersonal Develop.*, 2:173-174.

08315 **MORA, G., TALMADGE, M., BRYANT, F. I.**, and **HAYDEN, B. S.** (1969), A residential treatment center moves toward the community mental health model. *Child Welfare*, 48:585-590, 628-629.

08316 **MORACCO, J.**, and **BUSHWAR, A.** (1976), The effects of human relations training on dogmatic attitudes of educational administration students. *J. Exper. Educat.*, 44:32-34.

08317 **MORAN, G.**, and **KLOCKARS, A. J.** (1968), Favorability of group atmosphere and group dimensionality. *Psychol. Reports*, 22:3-6.

08318 **MORAN, J. A., JR.** (1978), The effects of insight-oriented group therapy and task-oriented group therapy on the coping style and life satisfaction of nursing home elderly. *Dissert. Abstr. Internat.*, 40:1377B.

08319 **MORDOCK, J. B., ELLIS, M. H.**, and **GREENSTONE, J. L.** (1969), The effects of group and individual therapy on sociometric choice of disturbed institutionalized adolescents. *Internat. J. Group Psychother.*, 19:510-517.

08320 **MOREAU, A.** (1976), A kibbutz group. *Acta Psychiat. Belgica*, (Brussels) 76:617-631.

08322 **MOREAU, A.** (1972), Transcript of a Balint group session. *Psychiat. in Med.*, 3:389-394.

08323 More Highlights: American Group Psychotherapy Association meeting (1968), *Roche Report: Front. Hosp. Psychiat.*, 5:5-6, 8, 11.

08324 **MOREHOUSE, K. J.** (1973), The process of development of interracial encounter groups. *Dissert. Abstr. Internat.*, 34:570A.

08325 **MORELAND, R. L.** (1978), Social categorization and the assimulation of "new" group members. *Dissert. Abstr. Internat.*, 39:5145B.

08326 **MORENO, F.** (1948), The learning process in nurses' training. *Sociatry*, 2:207-215.

08327 **MORENO, F. B.** (1947), Psychodrama in the neighborhood. *Sociatry*, 1:168-178.

08328 **MORENO, F. B.** (1948), Sociodrama in the sociology classroom. *Sociatry*, 1:404-413.

08329 **MORENO, F. B.,** and **MORENO, J. L.** (1945), Role tests and role diagrams of children. *Sociometry*, 8:426-441.

08330 **MORENO, J. D.** (1975), Notes on the concept of role playing. *Group Psychother., Psychodrama & Sociometry*, 28:105-107.

08331 **MORENO, J. L.** (1963), The actual trends in group psychotherapy. *Group Psychother., Psychodrama & Sociometry*, 16:117-131.

08332 **MORENO, J. L.** (1968), Address of the honorary president of the Fourth International Congress of Group Psychotherapy. *Group Psychother., Psychodrama & Sociometry*, 21:95-99.

08333 **MORENO, J. L.** (1950), The ascendance of group psychotherapy and the declining influence of psychoanalysis. *Group Psychother., Psychodrama & Sociometry*, 3:121-125.

08334 **MORENO, J. L.** (1963), Behaviour therapy. *Amer. J. Psychiat.*, 120:194-195.

08335 **MORENO, J. L.** (1956), Bibliography. *Group Psychother., Psychodrama & Sociometry*, 9:177-249.

08336 **MORENO, J. L.** (1931), Case of Miss X. *Impromptu*, 1:27-29.

08337 **MORENO, J. L.** (1945), *Case of Paranoia Treated through Psychodrama.* New York: Beacon House.

08338 **MORENO, J. L.** (1944), A case of paranoia treated through psychodrama. *Sociometry*, 7:312-327.

08339 **MORENO, J. L.** (1955), Clarification and summary. *Group Psychother., Psychodrama & Sociometry*, 8:87-91.

08340 **MORENO, J. L.** (1957), Code of ethics of group psychotherapists. *Group Psychother., Psychodrama & Sociometry*, 10:143-144.

08341 **MORENO, J. L.** (1962), *Code of Ethics for Group Psychotherapy and Psychodrama: Relationship to the Hippocratic Oath.* New York: Beacon House.

08342 **MORENO, J. L.** (1955), Comments on "The discovery of the spontaneous man." *Group Psychother., Psychodrama & Sociometry*, 8:351-352.

08343 **MORENO, J. L.** (1962), Common ground for all forms of group psychotherapy. *Group Psychother., Psychodrama & Sociometry*, 15:345-347.

08344 **MORENO, J. L.** (1943), The concept of sociodrama. *Sociometry*, 6:434-449.

08345 **MORENO, J. L.** (1959), Concerning the origin of the terms group therapy and group psychotherapy. *Amer. J. Psychiat.*, 116:176-177.

08346 **MORENO, J. L.** (1960), Concerning the origin of the terms group therapy and group psychotherapy. *Group Psychother., Psychodrama & Sociometry*, 13:58-59.

08347 **MORENO, J. L.** (1947), Contributions of sociometry to research methodology in sociology. *Amer. Soc. Rev.*, 12:287-292.

08348 **MORENO, J. L.** (1960), Cover and title page (photograph) of J. L. Moreno's "Sociometry experimental method and the science of society" in Russian translation. *Internat. J. Sociometry & Sociatry*, 2:59-62.

08349 **MORENO, J. L.** (1950), Cradle of group psychotherapy. *Group Psychother., Psychodrama & Sociometry*, 3:126-141.

08350 **MORENO, J. L.** (1931), The creative act. *Impromptu*, 1:18-19.
08351 **MORENO, J. L.** (1948), Current trends in clinical psychology: psychodrama and group psychotherapy. *Annals New York Acad. Science*, 49:902-903.
08352 **MORENO, J. L.** (1960), Czechoslovak Psychiatric Congress with photographs. *Internat. J. Sociometry & Sociatry*, 2:48-55.
08353 **MORENO, J. L.** (1923), *Das stegreiftheater.* (*The Free Association Theater.*) Potsdam: Kiepenheuer.
08354 **MORENO, J. L.** (1960), Definitions of group psychotherapy. *Group Psychother., Psychodrama & Sociometry*, 13:56.
08355 **MORENO, J. L.** (1960), Definitions of the transference-tele relation. *Group Psychother., Psychodrama & Sociometry*, 13:57.
08356 **MORENO, J. L.** (1957), Die epochale bedeutung der gruppentherapie. (The epochal significance of group psychotherapy.) *Zeit. Diagnost. Psychol.*, 5:139-150.
08357 **MORENO, J. L.** (1918), Die gottheit als autor. (The divine author.) *Daimon*, 1:3-21.
08358 **MORENO, J. L.** (1911), *Die gottheit als Komodiant.* (*The divine comedian.*) Vienna: Anzengruber Verlag.
08359 **MORENO, J. L.** (1919), Die gottheit als redner. (The divine speaker.) *Daimon*, 2:1-19.
08360 **MORENO, J. L.** (1956), The dilemma of existentialism, daseinsanalyses and the psychodrama, with special emphasis upon existential validation. *Internat. J. Sociometry & Sociatry*, 1:55-63.
08361 **MORENO, J. L.** (1954), Discussion and summary. *Group Psychother., Psychodrama & Sociometry*, 7:327-333.
08362 **MORENO, J. L.** (1960), Discussion of Ehrenwald's dialogue "Psychoanalyst vs. psychodramatist." *Group Psychother., Psychodrama & Sociometry*, 13:74-75.
08363 **MORENO, J. L.** (1964), Discussion of J. D. Sutherland's address "Recent advances in the understanding of small groups, their disorders and treatment." *Internat. J. Sociometry & Sociatry*, 4:56-59.
08364 **MORENO, J. L.** (1947), Discussion of Snyder's "The present status of psychotherapeutic counseling." *Psychol. Bull.*, 44:564-567.
08365 **MORENO, J. L.** (1958), Earliest definitions of group psychotherapy. *Group Psychother., Psychodrama & Sociometry*, 11:361.
08366 **MORENO, J. L.** (1959), Earliest definitions of group psychotherapy. *Group Psychother., Psychodrama & Sociometry*, 12:110.
08367 **MORENO, J. L.** (1959), Earliest definitions of the transference-tele relation. *Group Psychother., Psychodrama & Sociometry*, 12:111.
08368 **MORENO, J. L.** (1914), *Einladung zu einer begegnung.* (*An Invitation to a Celebration.*) Vienna: Anzengruber Verlag.
08370 **MORENO, J. L.** (1957), *The first book on group psychotherapy.* (3rd ed.) Beacon, N.Y.: Beacon House, xxiv, 138p.
08371 **MORENO, J. L.** (1960), The First National Cuban Neuro-Psychiatric Congress. *Internat. J. Sociometry & Sociatry*, 2:104.
08372 **MORENO, J. L.** (1948), Forms of psychodrama. *Sociatry*, 1:447-448.
08373 **MORENO, J. L.** (1947), Foundations of sociatry: an introduction. *Sociatry*, 1:10-15.
08374 **MORENO, J. L.** (1951), Fragments from the psychodrama of a dream. *Group Psychother., Psychodrama & Sociometry*, 3:344-365.
08375 **MORENO, J. L.** (1947), The Future of Man's World, *Psychodrama Monogr.*, 21. New York: Beacon House.
08376 **MORENO, J. L.** (1963), Genesis of sociometry. *Internat. J. Sociom. Soc.*, 3:21-24.

08377 **MORENO, J. L.** (1932), Group Method and Group Psychotherapy, *Sociometry Monogr.* 5. New York: Beacon House.

08378 **MORENO, J. L.** (1961), Group oath. *Group Psychother., Psychodrama & Sociometry*, 14:242.

08379 **MORENO, J. L.** (1972), *Group Psychotherapy: A Symposium.* Boston: Beacon Press.

08380 **MORENO, J. L.** (1945), *Group Psychotherapy: A Symposium.* New York: Beacon House.

08381 **MORENO, J. L.** (1946), *Group Psychotherapy.* New York: Beacon House.

08382 **MORENO, J. L.** (1962), The group psychotherapy movement: past, present and future. *Group Psychother., Psychodrama & Sociometry*, 15:21-23.

08383 **MORENO, J. L.** (1950), Group psychotherapy, theory and practice: recommendations presented at the A.P.A. Philadelphia conference on group method, June, 1932. *Group Psychother., Psychodrama & Sociometry*, 3:142-188.

08384 **MORENO, J. L.** (1959), *Gruppenpsychotherapie und Psychodrama: Einleitung in die Theorie und Praxis.* (*Group Psychotherapy and Psychodrama: An Introduction to Its Theory and Practice.*) Stuttgart: G. Thieme Verlag.

08385 **MORENO, J. L.** (1950), Hypnodrama and psychodrama. *Group Psychother., Psychodrama & Sociometry*, 3:1-10.

08386 **MORENO, J. L.** (1928), *The Impromptu School.* New York: Plymouth Institute.

08387 **MORENO, J. L.** (1931), The impromptu state. *Impromptu*, 1:9.

08388 **MORENO, J. L.** (1929), *Impromptu vs. Standardization.* New York: Moreno Laboratories.

08389 **MORENO, J. L.** (1961), Interpersonal therapy and co-unconscious states: a progress report in psychodramatic theory. *Group Psychother., Psychodrama & Sociometry*, 14:234-241.

08390 **MORENO, J. L.** (1937), Interpersonal therapy and psychopathology of interpersonal relations. *Sociometry*, 1:9-76.

08391 **MORENO, J. L.** (1954), Interpersonal therapy and the function of the unconscious. *Group Psychother., Psychodrama & Sociometry*, 7:191-204.

08392 **MORENO, J. L.** (1975), Mental catharsis and the psychodrama. *Group Psychother., Psychodrama & Sociometry*, 28:105-132.

08393 **MORENO, J. L.** (1944), Mental catharsis and the psychodrama. *Psychodrama Monogr.*, 6:209-244.

08394 **MORENO, J. L.** (1940), Mental catharsis and psychodrama. *Sociometry*, 3:209-244.

08395 **MORENO, J. L.** (1950), Note as to the possible meaning of group psychotherapy for the people of the United States. *Group Psychother., Psychodrama & Sociometry*, 3:256-257.

08396 **MORENO, J. L.** (1961), Note on psychodrama of the blind. *Group Psychother., Psychodrama & Sociometry*, 14:54.

08397 **MORENO, J. L.** (1958), On the history of psychodrama. *Group Psychother., Psychodrama & Sociometry*, 11:257-260.

08398 **MORENO, J. L.** (1957), Ontology of group formation. *Group Psychother., Psychodrama & Sociometry*, 10:346-348.

08399 **MORENO, J. L.** (1961), The "open door" policy in mental hospitals vs. the "closed door" policy in the community. (Discussion of Dr. Pearse's Paper.) *Group Psychother., Psychodrama & Sociometry*, 14:18-19.

08400 **MORENO, J. L.** (1947), Open letter to group therapists. *Sociatry*, 1:16-30.

08401 **MORENO, J. L.** (1968), Open letter to the members of the International Council of Group Psychotherapy. *Group Psychother., Psychodrama & Sociometry*, 21:89-90.

08402 **MORENO, J. L.** (1936), Organization of the social atom. *Sociometric Rev.*, p. 11.
08403 **MORENO, J. L.** (1941), The philosophy of the moment and the spontaneity theatre. *Sociometry*, 4:205-226.
08404 **MORENO, J. L.** (1962), The place of group psychotherapy, psychodrama and psychoanalysis in the framework of creativity and destruction. *Group Psychother., Psychodrama & Sociometry*, 15:339-341.
08405 **MORENO, J. L.** (1936), A plan for regrouping of communities. *Sociometric Rev.*, p. 58.
08406 **MORENO, J. L.** (1955), Plan of discussion. *Group Psychother., Psychodrama & Sociometry*, 8:168-169.
08407 **MORENO, J. L.** (1960), Political prospects of sociometry. *Internat. J. Sociometry & Sociatry*, 2:3-5.
08408 **MORENO, J. L.** (1960), Psychiatric encounter in Soviet Russia. *Internat. J. Sociometry & Sociatry*, 2:63-87.
08409 **MORENO, J. L.** (1955), Psychodrama. In: *Six Approaches to Psychotherapy*, eds. J. L. McCary and D. E. Sheer. New York: Dryden Press.
08410 **MORENO, J. L.** (1961), (Psychodrama.) *Resen. Clin. Client.*, 30:255-260.
08411 **MORENO, J. L.** (1946), *Psychodrama, Vol. 1.* New York: Beacon House.
08412 **MORENO, J. L.** (1964), *Psychodrama, Vol. 1*, 3d ed. New York: Beacon House.
08413 **MORENO, J. L.** (1957), Psychodrama and group psychotherapy. *Psychotherapy*, 2:177-181.
08414 **MORENO, J. L.** (1964), Psychodrama and group psychotherapy. *Sociometry*, 9:249-253.
08415 **MORENO, J. L.** (1955), Psychodrama and sociatry. In: *Present Day Psychology*, ed. A. A. Roback. New York: Philosophical Library, pp. 679-686.
08416 **MORENO, J. L.** (1945), Psychodrama and the psychopathology of interpersonal relations. *Psychodrama Monogr.* 16. New York: Beacon House.
08417 **MORENO, J. L.** (1944), Psychodrama and therapeutic motion pictures. *Sociometry*, 7:230-244.
08418 **MORENO, J. L.** (1959), *Psychodrama: Foundations of Psychotherapy, Vol. 2.* New York: Beacon House.
08419 **MORENO, J. L.** (1965), Psychodrama in action. *Group Psychother., Psychodrama & Sociometry*, 18:87-117.
08420 **MORENO, J. L.** (1957), Psychodrama of Adolph Hitler. *Internat. J. Sociometry & Sociatry*, 1:71-80.
08421 **MORENO, J. L.** (1956), Psychodrama of "Adolf Hitler": summary and evaluation of the significance of the psychotic Hitler drama. *Internat. J. Sociometry & Sociatry*, 1:80-82.
08422 **MORENO, J. L.** (1948), Psychodrama of an adolescent. *Sociatry*, 2:7-26.
08423 **MORENO, J. L.** (1961), Psychodrama of Judaism and the Eichmann trial. *Group Psychother., Psychodrama & Sociometry*, 14:114-116.
08424 **MORENO, J. L.** (1964), Psychodrama of murder: a joint trial of Lee Harvey Oswald and Jack Ruby. *Group Psychother., Psychodrama & Sociometry*, 17:61-62.
08425 **MORENO, J. L.** (1954), Psychodramatic frustrations test. *Group Psychother., Psychodrama & Sociometry*, 6:137-167.
08426 **MORENO, J. L.** (1944), Psychodramatic shock therapy: a sociometric approach to the problem of mental disorders. *Psychodrama Monogr.*, 5:1-30.
08427 **MORENO, J. L.** (1939), Psychodramatic shock therapy: a sociometric approach to the problem of mental disorders. *Sociometry*, 2:1-30.
08428 **MORENO, J. L.** (1944), Psychodramatic treatment of a performance neurosis: case history of a musician. *Psychodrama Monogr.* 2. New York: Beacon House.

08429 **MORENO, J. L.** (1945), *Psychodramatic Treatment of Marriage Problems.* New York: Beacon House.

08430 **MORENO, J. L.** (1945), Psychodramatic treatment of psychoses, *Psychodrama Monogr. 15.* New York: Beacon House.

08431 **MORENO, J. L.** (1940), Psychodramatic treatment of the psychoses. *Sociometry,* 3:115-132.

08432 **MORENO, J. L.** (1963), Reflections on my method of group psychotherapy and psychodrama. *Ciba Symp.,* 11:148-157.

08433 **MORENO, J. L.** (1956), Replies to Medard Boss, Jiri Kojala and Jiri Nehnevajsa on existentialism. *Internat. J. Sociometry & Sociatry,* 1:117-121.

08434 **MORENO, J. L.** (1958), Research note on transference and tele. *Group Psychother., Psychodrama & Sociometry,* 11:362.

08436 **MORENO, J. L.** (1962), (The role concept: a tie between psychiatry and sociology.) *Evolut. Psychiat.,* (Toulouse) 27:327-337.

08437 **MORENO, J. L.** (1962), Role theory and the emergence of the self. *Group Psychother., Psychodrama & Sociometry,* 15:114-117.

08438 **MORENO, J. L.** (1966), The roots of psychodrama: autobiographical notes—a reply to Sarro. *Group Psychother., Psychodrama & Sociometry,* 19:140-145.

08439 **MORENO, J. L.** (1945), Scientific foundations of group psychotherapy. *Sociometry,* 8:315-322.

08440 **MORENO, J. L.** (1959), The scientific meaning and the global significance of group psychotherapy. *Acta Psychother., Psychosomat. Orthopaedagog.,* (Basel) 7:148-167.

08441 **MORENO, J. L.** (1967), Scientific validation of group psychotherapy. *Internat. J. Psychiat. Med.,* 4:349.

08442 **MORENO, J. L.** (1955), The significance of the therapeutic format and the place of acting out in psychotherapy. *Group Psychother., Psychodrama & Sociometry,* 8:7-19.

08443 **MORENO, J. L.** (1951), The situation of group psychotherapy. *Group Psychother., Psychodrama & Sociometry,* 3:281-283.

08444 **MORENO, J. L.** (1946), Situation test. *Sociometry,* 9:166-167.

08445 **MORENO, J. L.** (1952), Sociodrama of a family conflict. *Group Psychother., Psychodrama & Sociometry,* 5:20-37.

08446 **MORENO, J. L.** (1948), The sociodrama of Mahandas Gandhi. *Sociatry,* 1:357-358.

08447 **MORENO, J. L.** (1952), Sociodramatic approach to minority problems. *Group Psychother., Psychodrama & Sociometry,* 5:7-19.

08448 **MORENO, J. L.** (1948), Sociology and sociodrama. *Sociatry,* 2:67-68.

08449 **MORENO, J. L.** (1956), Sociometry of the Soviet purges: a discussion. *Internat. J. Sociometry & Sociatry,* 1:121-123.

08450 **MORENO, J. L.** (1959), *The Sociometry Reader.* Glencoe, IL: The Free Press.

08451 **MORENO, J. L.** (1952), Some comments to the trichotomy, tele–transference–empathy. *Group Psychother., Psychodrama & Sociometry,* 5:87-90.

08452 **MORENO, J. L.** (1951), Some misunderstandings in the terminology of group psychotherapy and psychodrama. *Group Psychother., Psychodrama & Sociometry,* 4:112-113.

08453 **MORENO, J. L.** (1944), Spontaneity test and spontaneity training. *Psychodrama Monogr.,* 4.

08454 **MORENO, J. L.** (1948), The spontaneity theory of learning. *Sociatry,* 2:191-196.

08455 **MORENO, J. L.** (1956), Sputnick and the psychodramatic space traveler. *Internat. J. Sociometry & Sociatry,* 1:193-195.

08456 **MORENO, J. L.** (1956), The story of Johnny Psychodramatist. *Internat. J. Sociometry & Sociatry*, 1:3-4.
08457 **MORENO, J. L.** (1955), Summary and evaluation. *Group Psychother., Psychodrama & Sociometry*, 8:191-196.
08458 **MORENO, J. L.** (1947), *The Theatre of Spontaneity*. New York: Beacon House.
08459 **MORENO, J. L.** (1964), The third psychiatric revolution and the scope of psychodrama. *Group Psychother., Psychodrama & Sociometry*, 17:149-171.
08460 **MORENO, J. L.** (1954), Transference, countertransference and tele: their relation to group research and group psychotherapy. *Group Psychother., Psychodrama & Sociometry*, 7:107-117.
08461 **MORENO, J. L.** (1970), The triadic system: psychodrama–sociometry–group psychotherapy. *Group Psychother., Psychodrama & Sociometry*, 23:16.
08462 **MORENO, J. L.** (1962), The "united role theory" and the drama. *Group Psychother., Psychodrama & Sociometry*, 15:253-254.
08463 **MORENO, J. L.** (1953), *Who Shall Survive? Foundations of Sociometry, Group Psychotherapy and Sociodrama*. 2d ed. New York: Beacon House.
08464 **MORENO, J. L.** (1934), *Who Shall Survive*. Washington: Nervous and Mental Disease Publishing.
08465 **MORENO, J. L.** (1947), Workshop in sociodrama: papers, projects and evaluations. *Sociatry*, 1:333.
08466 **MORENO, J. L.**, and **DUNKIN, W. S.** (1941), The function of the social investigator in experimental psychodrama. *Sociometry*, 4:392-417.
08467 **MORENO, J. L.**, and **ENNEIS, J. M.** (1950), *Hypnodrama and Psychodrama. Psychodrama Monogr.* 27. New York: Beacon House.
08468 **MORENO, J. L.**, and **JENNINGS, H. H.** (1936), Advances in sociometric technique. *Sociometric Rev.*, p. 26.
08469 **MORENO, J. L.**, and **JENNINGS, H. H.** (1936), Spontaneity training: a method of personality development. *Sociometric Rev.*, p. 17.
08470 **MORENO, J. L.**, and **MORENO, F. B.** (1944), Spontaneity theory in its relation to problems of interpretation and measurement. *Sociometry*, 7:339-355.
08471 **MORENO, J. L.**, and **MORENO, Z. T.** (1960), An objective analysis of the group psychotherapy movement. *Group Psychother., Psychodrama & Sociometry*, 13:233-237.
08472 **MORENO, J. L.**, and **MORENO, Z. T.** (1969), *Psychodrama: III. Action Therapy and Principles of Practise*. New York: Beacon House.
08473 **MORENO, J. L.**, and **SCHWARTZ, M.** (1948), Psychodrama combined with insulin in the treatment of psychoses. *Psychiat. Quart.*, 22:621-633.
08474 **MORENO, J. L.**, and **TOEMAN, Z.** (1942), The group approach in psychodrama. *Sociometry*, 5:191-196.
08475 **MORENO, J. L.** (1943), Discussion of sociometry: symposium. *Sociometry*, 6:197-344.
08476 **MORENO, J. L.** (1966), *The International Handbook of Group Psychotherapy*. New York: Philosophical Library.
08477 **MORENO, J. L.**, and **WHITIN, E. S.** (1932), *Application of the Group Method to Classification*, 2d ed. New York: National Committee on Prisons and Prison Labor.
08478 **MORENO, J. L.**, and **WHITIN, E. S.** (1932), *Plan and Technique of Developing a Prison into a Socialized Community*. New York: National Committee on Prisons and Prison Labor.
08479 **MORENO, J. L., MORENO, Z. T.**, and **MORENO, J.** (1964), New Moreno legends. *Group Psychother., Psychodrama & Sociometry*, 17:1-35.
08480 **MORENO, J. L., MORENO, Z. T.**, and **MORENO, J. F.** (1955), The discovery of the spontaneous man, with special emphasis upon the technique

of role reversal. *Group Psychother., Psychodrama & Sociometry*, 8:103-129.

08481 **MORENO, J. L., FRIEDEMANN, A., BATTEGAY, R.**, and **MORENO, Z.** (1966), *The International Handbook of Group Psychotherapy*. New York: Philosophical Library.

08482 **MORENO, Z. T.** (1954), International committee on group psychotherapy and the First International Congress on Group Psychotherapy. *Group Psychother., Psychodrama & Sociometry*, 7:91-92.

08483 **MORENO, Z. T.** (1958), Note on spontaneous learning "in situ" versus learning the academic way. *Group Psychother., Psychodrama & Sociometry*, 11:50-51.

08484 **MORENO, Z. T.** (1969), Practical aspects of psychodrama. *Group Psychother., Psychodrama & Sociometry*, 22:213-219.

08485 **MORENO, Z. T.** (1951), Psychodrama in a well-baby clinic. *Group Psychother., Psychodrama & Sociometry*, 4:100-106.

08486 **MORENO, Z. T.** (1954), Psychodrama in the crib. *Group Psychother., Psychodrama & Sociometry*, 7:291-302.

08487 **MORENO, Z. T.** (1969/1970), Psychodrama of infants in a baby consultation. *Bull. de Psychol.*, (Paris) 23:826-828.

08488 **MORENO, Z. T.** (1957), Psychodrama of young mothers. *Zeit. Diagnost. Psychol.*, 5:270-282.

08489 **MORENO, Z. T.** (1968), Psychodrama on closed and open circuit television. *Group Psychother., Psychodrama & Sociometry*, 21:106-109.

08490 **MORENO, Z. T.** (1965), Psychodramatic rules, techniques and adjunctive methods. *Group Psychother., Psychodrama & Sociometry*, 18:73-86.

08491 **MORENO, Z. T.** (1959), Psychodramatic techniques. *Acta Psychother., Psychosomat. Orthopaedagog.*, (Basel) 7:197-206.

08492 **MORENO, Z. T.** (1958), The "reluctant therapist" and the "reluctant audience" technique in psychodrama. *Group Psychother., Psychodrama & Sociometry*, 11:278-282.

08493 **MORENO, Z. T.** (1975), The significance of doubling and role reversal for cosmic man. *Group Psychother., Psychodrama & Sociometry*, 28:55-59.

08494 **MORENO, Z. T.** (1963), Sociogenesis of individuals and groups. *Internat. J. Sociometry & Sociatry*, 3:29-39.

08495 **MORENO, Z. T.** (1959), A survey of psychodramatic techniques. *Group Psychother., Psychodrama & Sociometry*, 12:5-14.

08496 **MORENO, Z. T., STEVENSON, G. S., STEIN, C., GARDNER, M., HARTLEY, E., YABLONSKY, L., HASKELL, M. R., TWITCHELL-ALLEN, D., MEIERS, J. I.**, and **WEINER, H. B.** (1962), The twenty-fifth anniversary of the American Theater of Psychodrama. *Group Psychother., Psychodrama & Sociometry*, 15:5-20.

08497 **MORGAN, D. W.** (1973), Analytische gruppen-therapie für therapeuten und deren ehe-frauen. (Analytic group therapy for therapists and their wives.) *Dynam. Psychiat.*, (Berlin) 6:249-257.

08498 **MORGAN, D. W.** (1971), A note on analytic group psychotherapy for therapists and their wives. *Internat. J. Group Psychother.*, 21:244-247.

08499 **MORGAN, M. D.** (1978), Must the group get up and testify? an examination of group therapy privilege. *Group*, 2:67-87.

08500 **MORGAN, P. K.** (1960), Attitude change and group conformity in the psychopathic personality. Ph. D. thesis, Louisiana State University.

08501 **MORI, F.** (1960), A report on play therapy with a boy of long-term hospitalization. *Japanese J. Child Psychiat.*, (Tokyo) 1:328-339.

08502 **MORIARTY, J.** (1973), College group therapy with female chronic schizophrenic inpatients. *Psychother.: Theory, Res. & Pract.*, 10:153-154.

08503 **MORIARTY, J.** (1976), Combining activities and group psychotherapy in treatment of chronic schizophrenics. *Hosp. & Community Psychiat.*, 27:574-576.

08504 **MORLEY, R. E.**, and **KOKASKA, C.** (1979), Guidance and counseling practices with mentally retarded youth. *Ment. Retard.*, 17:201.

08505 **MORO, L.** (1978), (The therapist and here and now situation.) *Psihijat. Danas*, (Belgrade) 10:117-122.

08506 **MOROKOFF, P. J.**, and **HEIMAN, J. R.** (1980), Effects of erotic stimuli on sexually functional and dysfunctional women: multiple measures before and after sex therapy. *Behav. Res. & Ther.*, 18:127-137.

08507 **MORRA, M.** (1965), Valore diagnostico della psicodramma nell eta evolutiva. (Diagnostic value of psychodrama in the development age.) *Rev. de Psicoanal.*, (Buenos Aires) 11:45-55.

08508 **MORRAN, D. K.** (1980), The effects of valence and session of presentation on receiver acceptance of verbal feedback in personal growth groups. *Dissert. Abstr. Internat.*, 41:945A. (University Microfilms No. 8020034.)

08509 **MORRAN, D. K.**, and **STOCKTON, R. A.** (1980), Effect of self-concept on group member reception of positive and negative feedback. *J. Couns. Psychol.*, 27:260-267.

08510 **MORRICE, J. K.** (1965), Permissiveness. *Brit. J. Med. Psychol.*, (London) 38:247-251.

08511 **MORRICE, J. K.** (1975), The psychotherapeutic role of the nurse. *Nursing Times*, (London) 71:1634-1635.

08512 **MORRICE, J. K.** (1964), The ward as a therapeutic group. *Brit. J. Med. Psychol.*, (London) 37:157-165.

08513 **MORRILL, C. M.** (1974), A behavioral group method for teaching interpersonal skills to children. *Dissert. Abstr. Internat.*, 35:825A.

08514 **MORRIS, C. C., II, NELLIS, B.**, and **STROMBERG, C. E.** (1959), The development of an interdisciplinary psychotherapeutic program in an institution for the mentally retarded. *Amer. J. Ment. Deficiency*, 63:605-610.

08515 **MORRIS, J.** (1973), Career counseling: does group guidance have a role to play in it? *School Guid. Worker*, (Toronto) 29:4-10.

08516 **MORRIS, K. L.** (1980), The effects of cognitive restructuring on assertion group training. *Dissert. Abstr. Internat.*, 41:1144B. (University Microfilms No. 8018671.)

08517 **MORRIS, K. T.**, and **CINNAMON, K. M.** (1976), *Controversial Issues in Human Relations Training Groups*. Springfield, IL: C. C. Thomas.

08518 **MORRIS, K. T.**, and **CINNAMON, K. M.** (1975), *A Handbook of Non-Verbal Group Exercises*. Springfield, IL: C. C. Thomas.

08519 **MORRIS, K. T.**, and **CINNAMON, K. M.** (1974), *A Handbook of Verbal Group Exercises*. Springfield, IL: C. C. Thomas.

08520 **MORRIS, N. E.** (1975), A group self-instruction method for the treatment of depressed outpatients. Unpublished doctoral dissertation, University of Toronto.

08521 **MORRISON, A. P.** (1970), Consultation and group process with indigenous neighborhood workers. *Community Ment. Health J.*, 6:3-12.

08522 **MORRISON, J. K., LIBOW, J. A., SMITH, F. J.**, and **BECKER, R. E.** (1978), Comparative effectiveness of directive vs. nondirective group therapist style on client problem resolution. *J. Clin. Psychol.*, 34:186-187.

08523 **MORRISON, T. L.**, and **THOMAS, M. D.** (1976), Judgements of educators and child care personnel about appropriate treatment for mentally retarded or normal, overactive or withdrawn, boys. *J. Clin. Psychol.*, 32:449-452.

08524 **MORRISON, T. L.**, and **THOMAS, M. D.** (1976), Participants' perceptions of themselves and leaders in two kinds of group experience. *J. Soc. Psychol.*, 98:103-110.

08525 **MORROW, T. F., LAUCKS, S. P.,** and **McKNIGHT, W. K.** (1952), Insulin coma and group psychotherapy. *Arch. Neurol. Psychiat.*, 68:491-497.

08526 **MORSE, P. W.** (1953), A proposed technique for the evaluation of psychotherapy. *Amer. J. Orthopsychiat.*, 23:716-731.

08527 **MORSE, P. W., GESSAY, L. H.,** and **KARPE, R.** (1955), The effect of group psychotherapy in reducing resistance to individual psychotherapy: a case study. *Internat. J. Group Psychother.*, 5:261-269.

08528 **MORTON, J. E.** (1966), Intensive milieu therapy: a plan of attack upon all forms of mental and emotional illness. *J. Kansas Med. Soc.*, 67:79-80.

08529 **MORVIT, R. C.** (1972), Improving behavior of delinquent adolescents through group therapy. *Hosp. & Community Psychiat.*, 23:239.

08530 **MOSAK, H. H.,** and **POLLACK, H.** (1975), *Group Psychotherapy: A Syllabus.* New York: Adler Institute.

08531 **MOSCOVICI, F.** (1972), (Sensitivity training: a study of perceptions.) *Arq. Brasil. Psicol. Apl.*, (Rio de Janeiro) 24:63-72.

08532 **MOSCOVICI, F.** (1970), Treinamento de sensibilidade: o grupo te os metodos de laboratorio. (Sensitivity training: the t-group and the laboratory approach.) *Arq. Brasil. Psicol. Apl.*, (Rio de Janeiro) 22:151-162.

08533 **MOSCOVICI, F.** (1973), A study of perceptions in sensitivity training in Brazil. *Interpersonal Develop.*, 2:130-136.

08534 **MOSCOVICI, S.,** and **ZAVALLONI, M.** (1969), The group as a polarizer of attitudes. *J. Personality & Soc. Psychol.*, 12:125-135.

08535 **MOSCOVICI, S., ZAVALLONI, M.,** and **WEINBERGER, M.** (1972), Studies on polarization of judgements: ii. person perception, ego involvement and group interaction. *European J. Soc. Psychol.*, (The Hague) 2:92-94.

08536 **MOSCOW, D.** (1971), T-group training in the Netherlands: an evaluation and cross-cultural comparison. *J. Appl. Behav. Science*, 7:427-448.

08537 **MOSER, A. J.** (1975), Structured group interaction: a psychotherapeutic technique for modifying locus of control. *J. Contemp. Psychother.*, 7:23-28.

08538 **MOSER, T.** (1977), *Verstehen, Urteilen, Verurteilen: Psychoanalyt Gruppendynamik mit Jurastudenten.* (*Hearing, Judging, Sentencing: Psychoanalytic Group Dynamics with Law Students.*) Frankfurt am Main: Suhrkamp.

08539 **MOSES, R.** (1965), Hitpashtat hapsikhoterapia hakevutsatit baarets vesakanoteha. (Growth of group psychotherapy in Israel and its dangers.) *Megamot*, (Jerusalem) 13:204-206.

08540 **MOSES, R.** (1961), Problems in introducing group psychotherapy in a psychiatric outpatient clinic. *Acta Psychother., Psychosomat. Orthopaedagog.*, (Basel) 9:277-280.

08541 **MOSES, R.,** and **SCHWARTZ, D. P.** (1958), A crisis in a prison therapy group. *Internat. J. Group Psychother.*, 8:445-458.

08542 **MOSEY, A. C.** (1970), The concept and use of developmental groups. *Amer. J. Occupat. Ther.*, 24:272-275.

08543 **MOSHER, D. L.** (1979), Negative attitudes toward masturbation in sex therapy. *J. Sex & Marital Ther.*, 5:315-333.

08544 **MOSHER, L. R.,** and **KEITH, S. J.** (1980), Psychosocial treatment: individual, group, family and community support approaches. *Schiz. Bull.*, 6:10-41.

08545 **MOSHER, L. R.,** and **KEITH, S. J.** (1979), Research on the psychosocial treatment of schizophrenia: a summary report. *Amer. J. Psychiat.*, 136:623.

08546 **MOSKOWITZ, J. A.,** and **DEFRIES, Z.** (1973), The coup: activist students take over a psychotherapy group in a university. *Adolescence*, 8:155-164.

08547 **MOSS, C. J.** (1976), Effects of leader behavior in personal growth groups: self-disclosure and experiencing. *Dissert. Abstr. Internat.*, 36:6361B.

08548 **MOSS, C. J.,** and **HARREN, V. A.** (1978), Member disclosure in personal growth groups: effects of leader disclosure. *Small Group Behav.*, 9:64-79.

08549 **MOSS, C. R.** (1946), Integrating casework and recreation in a military hospital. *J. Soc. Casework*, 27:307-313.

08550 **MOSS, E. P.** (1976), A study of the relationship between group counseling, social activities and aspects of life adjustment of older sheltered workshop clients. *Dissert. Abstr. Internat.*, 37:979B.

08551 **MOSS, E. P.** (1945), A vacation experiment with a group of psychoanalytic patients. *Psychoanal. Rev.*, 32:219-224.

08552 **MOSS, M. C.,** and **HUNTER, P.** (1963), Community methods of treatment. *Brit. J. Med. Psychol.*, (London) 36:85-91.

08553 **MOSSMAN, B. M.,** and **ZILLER, R. C.** (1968), Self-esteem and consistency of social behavior. *J. Abnorm. & Soc. Psychol.*, 73:363-367.

08554 **MOSVICK, R. K.** (1971), Human relations training for scientists, technicians, and engineers: a review of relevant experimental evaluations of human relations training. *Personnel Psychol.*, 24:275-292.

08555 **MOTE, A. O.** (1974), A comparison of the effects of a marathon group and an encounter group on personal growth in college students. *Dissert. Abstr. Internat.*, 35:3431A.

08556 **MOTTA, E.** (1970), (Role of sociotherapy and amateur acting in the present challenging conditions characteristic of psychiatry and psychiatric institutions.) *Riv. Sper. Freniatria*, (Emilia) 94:796-800.

08557 **MOTTO, J. A.** (1979), Starting a therapy group in a suicide prevention and crisis center. *Suicide & Life-Threatening Behav.*, 9:47-56.

08558 **MOTTRAM, E. M.** (1980), Psychotherapy: the sister's role in group therapy in a general practice. *Nursing Times*, (London) 76:253-254.

08559 **MOULIN, E. K.** (1968), The effects of client-centered group counseling utilizing play media on the intelligence, achievement and psycholinguistic abilities of under-achieving primary school children. *Dissert. Abstr. Internat.*, 29:1425-1426.

08560 **MOUSTAKAS, C.** (1951), Situational play therapy with normal children. *J. Consult. & Clin. Psychol.*, 15:225-230.

08561 **MOUSTAKAS, C.** (1960), Sociometric study of a Greek school. *Internat. J. Sociometry & Sociatry*, 2:35-38.

08562 **MOUSTAKAS, C. E.** (1968), *Individuality and Encounter: A Brief Journey into Loneliness and Sensitivity Groups*. Cambridge, MA: H. A. Doyle.

08563 **MOUTON, J. S.,** and **BLAKE, R. R.** (1955), Conflicting careers. *Group Psychother., Psychodrama & Sociometry*, 8:130-141.

08564 **MOUTON, J. S.** (1957), Training for decision-making in groups in a university laboratory. *Group Psychother., Psychodrama & Sociometry*, 10:342-345.

08565 **MOUTON, J. S.,** and **BLAKE, R. R.** (1961), University training in human relations skills. *Group Psychother., Psychodrama & Sociometry*, 14:140-153.

08566 **MOUTON, J. S., BELL, R. L., Jr.,** and **BLAKE, R. R.** (1956), Role playing skill and sociometric peer status. *Group Psychother., Psychodrama & Sociometry*, 9:7-17.

08567 **MOUW, M. L.,** and **HAYLETT, C. H.** (1967), Mental health consultation in a public health nursing service. *Amer. J. Nursing*, 67:1447-1450.

08568 **MOWATT, M. H.** (1965), Emotional conflicts of handicapped young adults and their mothers. *Cerebral Palsy J.*, 26:6-8.

08569 **MOWATT, M. H.** (1972), Group psychotherapy for stepfathers and their wives. *Psychother.: Theory, Res. & Pract.*, 9:328-331.

08570 **MOWBRAY, R. M.,** and **TIMBURY, G. C.** (1966), Opinions on psychotherapy: an enquiry. *Brit. J. Psychiat.*, (Ashford) 112:351-361.

08571 **MOWRER, O. H.** (1976), Changing conceptions of neurosis and the small-groups movement. *Education*, 97:24-62.

08572 **MOWRER, O. H.** (1972), Integrity groups: principles and procedures. *Couns. Psychologist*, 3:7-32.

08573 **MOWRER, O. H.** (1971), Is the small-group movement a religious revolution? *Voices*, 7:17-20.

08574 **MOWRER, O. H.** (1973), My philosophy of psychotherapy. *J. Contemp. Psychother.*, 6:35-42.

08575 **MOWRER, O. H.** (1964), *The New Group Therapy*. Princeton: Van Nostrand.

08576 **MOWRER, O. H.,** and **VALLANO, A. J.** (1976), Integrity Groups: a context for growth in honesty, responsibility, and involvement. *J. Appl. Behav. Science*, 12:419-431.

08577 **MOXNES, P.** (1974), Verbal communication level and anxiety in psychotherapeutic groups. *J. Couns. Psychol.*, 21:399-403.

08578 **MOXNES, P. A.,** and **ENGVIK, H. A.** (1973/1974), Diagnosing the organization: the psychogram. *Interpersonal Develop.*, 4:177-189.

08579 **MOZDZIERZ, G. J.,** and **FRIEDMAN, K.** (1978), The superiority–inferiority spouses syndrome: diagnostic and therapeutic considerations. *J. Individ. Psychol.*, 34:232-243.

08580 **MOZDZIERZ, G. J., ELBAUM, P. L.,** and **HOUDA, A. J.** (1974), Changing patterns in the use of an intake–diagnostic–orientation group. *Amer. J. Psychother.*, 28:129-136.

08581 **MSYZKA, M. A. F.,** and **JOSEFIAK, D.** (1973), Development of the co-therapy relationship. *J. Psychiat. Nursing*, 11:27-31.

08582 **MUAČEVIĆ, V.** (1973), (Acute psychotic patients in a therapeutic community.) *Anali Zavoda Ment. Zdravlje*, 5:121-125.

08583 **MUAČEVIĆ, V.** (1975), (Group psychotherapy in inpatient treatment.) *Anali Zavoda Ment. Zdravlje*, 7:81-87.

08584 **MUACEVIC, V.,** and **HUDOLIN, V.** (1968), (Psychotherapy of neurotics with actual family conflicts.) *Psychother. & Psychosomat.*, (Basel) 16:357-365.

08585 **MUAČEVIĆ, V.,** and **MARANGUNIĆ, M.** (1979), (Group psychotherapy of schizophrenics.) *Soc. Psihijat.*, (Belgrade) 7:361-367.

08586 **MUAČEVIĆ, V.,** and **TRBOVIC, M.** (1973), (The therapeutic community and the isolated family of the patient.) *Soc. Psihijat.*, (Belgrade) 1:75-81.

08587 **MUDD, S. A.** (1968), Group sanction severity as a function of degree of behavior deviation and relevance of norm. *J. Personality & Soc. Psychol.*, 8:258-260.

08588 **MUDGETT, W. C., HUNSAKER, P. L.,** and **WYNNE, B. E.** (1975), A tactical pacification game for leadership development. *Psychol. Reports*, 36:439-445.

08589 **MUELLER, B.,** and **MACELVEEN-HOEHN, P.** (1979), The use of network concepts in an educational model. *Group Psychother., Psychodrama & Sociometry*, 32:165-172.

08590 **MUELLER, E. E.** (1950), An experience with group psychotherapy in Japan. *Amer. J. Psychother.*, 4:293-302.

08591 **MUELLER, E. E.** (1967), Feeler phrases in group psychotherapy and mental patients' families. *Correct. Psychiat. & J. Soc. Ther.*, 13:142-151.

08592 **MUELLER, E. E.** (1949), Group therapy with alcoholism in a hospital setting. *Diseases Nerv. System*, 10:298-303.

08593 **MUELLER, E. E.** (1954), A psychiatric social worker's experience in group psychotherapy with discharged patients. *Amer. J. Psychother.*, 8:276-292.

08594 **MUELLER, E. E.** (1971), Psychodrama with delinquent siblings. *Correct. Psychiat. & J. Soc. Ther.*, 17:18-22.

08595 **MUELLER, E. E.** (1964), Rebels—with a cause. *Amer. J. Psychother.*, 18:272-284.

08596 **MULLAN, H.** (1953), Conflict avoidance in group psychotherapy. *Internat. J. Group Psychother.*, 3:243-253.

08597 **MULLAN, H.** (1953), Countertransference in groups. *Amer. J. Psychother.*, 7:680-688.

08598 **MULLAN, H.** (1965), The existential change in a woman in group psychotherapy. *Topical Probl. Psychol. & Psychother.*, 5:136-145.

08599 **MULLAN, H.** (1961), Existential factors in group psychodrama. *Internat. J. Group Psychother.*, 11:449-455.

08600 **MULLAN, H.** (1979), An existential group psychotherapy. *Internat. J. Group Psychother.*, 39:163.

08601 **MULLAN, H.** (1955), The group analysts' creative functions. *Amer. J. Psychother.*, 9:320-334.

08602 **MULLAN, H.** (1957), The group patient as a therapist. *Psychiat. Quart. Suppl.*, 31:90-101.

08603 **MULLAN, H.** (1957), The group psychotherapeutic experience. *Amer. J. Psychother.*, 11:830-838.

08604 **MULLAN, H.** (1957), Group psychotherapy in private practice: practical considerations. *J. Hillside Hosp.*, 6:34-42.

08605 **MULLAN, H.** (1963), Group psychotherapy with the alcoholic. *Curr. Psychiat. Ther.*, 3:234-243.

08606 **MULLAN, H.** (1969), Interaction in group psychotherapy. *Can. Psychiat. Assn. J.*, (Ottawa) 14:15-19.

08607 **MULLAN, H.** (1956), The nonteleological in dreams in group psychotherapy. *J. Hillside Hosp.*, 5:480-487.

08608 **MULLAN, H.** (1968), The potentiality of the small experiential group. *Psychiat. Digest*, 29:38-42.

08609 **MULLAN, H.** (1952), Some essentials in group psychotherapy. *Group Psychother., Psychodrama & Sociometry*, 5:68-69.

08610 **MULLAN, H.** (1955), Status denial in group psychoanalysis. *J. Nerv. & Ment. Diseases*, 122:345-352.

08611 **MULLAN, H.** (1958), Training in group psychotherapy: a symposium. (ii) The training of group psychotherapists. *Amer. J. Psychother.*, 12:495-500.

08612 **MULLAN, H.** (1955), Transference and countertransference: new horizons. *Internat. J. Group Psychother.*, 5:169-180.

08613 **MULLAN, H.** (1957), Trends in group psychotherapy in the United States. *Internat. J. Soc. Psychiat.*, (London) 3:224-230.

08614 **MULLAN, H.** (1968), The use of dynamic groups in psychiatric staff reorganization. *Psychother. & Psychosomat.*, (Basel) 16:146-151.

08615 **MULLAN, H.**, and **ROSENBAUM, M.** (1978), *Group Psychotherapy*, 2d ed. New York: Macmillan.

08616 **MULLAN, H.**, and **ROSENBAUM, M.** (1962), *Group Psychotherapy: Theory and Practice*. New York: Free Press.

08617 **MULLAN, H.**, and **ROSENBAUM, M.** (1975), The suitability for the group experience. In: *Group Psychotherapy and Group Function*, 2d ed., eds. M. Rosenbaum and M. M. Berger. New York: Basic Books.

08618 **MULLAN, H.**, and **SANGIULIANO, T.** (1966), *Alcoholism: Group Psychotherapy and Rehabilitation*. Springfield, IL: C. C. Thomas.

08619 **MULLAN, H.**, and **SANGIULIANO, I.** (1960), Multiple psychotherapeutic practice: preliminary report. *Amer. J. Psychother.*, 14:550-565.

08620 **MULLEN, E. J.** (1968), Casework communication. *Soc. Casework*, 49:546-551.

08621 **MULLER, A.** (1978), (Inclusion of psychotherapeutic methods in group work with schoolchildren.) *Praxis Kinderpsychol. & Kinderpsychiat.*, (Goettingen) 27:216-220.

08622 **MULLER, A.** (1952), Le psychodrama selon Moreno. (Psychodrama according to Moreno.) *Rev. Francaise Psychoanal.*, (Paris) 16:416-429.

08623 **MULLER, C.,** and **BADER, A.** (1968), The cinema and the mental patient: a new form of group therapy. In: *Current Psychiatric Therapies*, ed. J. H. Masserman. New York: Grune and Stratton.

08624 **MÜLLER, H.** (1965), (The promotion of the physician's self-understanding as a function of group–dynamic correlations.) *Zeit. Psychother. Med. Psychol.*, (Stuttgart) 15:256-260.

08625 **MÜLLER, M.** (1949), *Prognose und Therapie der Geisteskrankheiten.* (*Prognosis and Therapy of Mental Diseases.* 2d. ed.) Stuttgart: G. Thieme.

08626 **MÜLLER, R.** (1931), The impromptu theatre in Vienna. *Impromptu*, 1:23-25.

08627 **MULLER, R. G. E.** (1977), (Review of H. Walton's *Small Group Psychotherapy.*) *Psychol. Rundschau*, (Goettingen) 28:310.

08628 **MULLER, T. G.** (1959), Psychotherapeutic elements in the teaching process. *Acta Psychother. Psychosomat. Orthopaedagog. Suppl.*, (Basel) 7:246-254.

08629 **MULTARI, G.** (1975), A psychotherapeutic approach with elementary school teachers. *Community Ment. Health J.*, 11:122-128.

08630 Multiple Group sessions aid young patients and parents (1969), *Roche Report: Front. Hosp. Psychiat.*, 6:3.

08631 **MULVANEY, J. J.** (1970), Short-term treatment of adolescents on an adult psychiatric unit. *Hosp. & Community Psychiat.*, 21:255-257.

08632 **MUMFORD, M. S.** (1974), A comparison of interpersonal skills in verbal and activity groups. *Amer. J. Occupat. Ther.*, 28:281-283.

08633 **MUMMA, F. S.** (1978), The relevance of identity statuses in the development of a t-group. *Dissert. Abstr. Internat.*, 9:2152A.

08634 **MÜNCH, F.** (1971), Intensivierte gruppenpsychotherapie in der freien praxis. (Intensified group psychotherapy in private practice.) *Praxis der Psychother.*, 16:109-117.

08635 **MUNDY, L.** (1958), Psychotherapy with children having little or no speech. *Brit. Psychol. Soc. Bull.*, (London) 35:6A-7A.

08636 **MUNDY, W. L.** (1972), Physical exam and script decision: one hour. *Transactional Anal. J.*, 2:109-112.

08637 **MUNOZ, D. G.** (1971), The effects of simulated affect films and videotape feedback in group psychotherapy with alcoholics. *Dissert. Abstr. Internat.*, 32:1854B.

08638 **MUNZER, J.** (1966), Acting out: communication or resistance? *Internat. J. Group Psychother.*, 16:434-441.

08639 **MUNZER, J.** (1972), Discussion. *Internat. J. Group Psychother.*, 22:464-466.

08640 **MUNZER, J.** (1962), The effect of analytic therapy groups of the experimental introduction of special "warm-up" procedures during the first five sessions. *Dissert. Abstr. Internat.*, 22:2896-2897.

08641 **MUNZER, J.** (1964), The effect on analytic therapy groups of the experimental introduction of special "warm-up" procedures during the first five sessions. *Internat. J. Group Psychother.*, 14:60-71.

08642 **MUNZER, J.** (1962), Group therapy with parents of psychotic children in a coordinated research program. *Internat. J. Group Psychother.*, 12:107-112.

08643 **MUNZER, J.** (1965), Treatment of the homosexual in group psychotherapy. *Topical Probl. Psychol. & Psychother.*, 5:164-169.

08644 **MUNZER, J.**, and **GREENWALD, H.** (1957), Interaction process analysis of a therapy group. *Internat. J. Group Psychother.*, 7:175-190.

08645 **MURATA, T.** (1973), (A group therapy of autistic children: the result of four year Saturday class treatment at Kyusho University Psychiatric Hospital.) *Kyusho Neuro-Psychiat.*, (Fukuoka) 19:170-177.

08646 **MURI, S.** (1979), (Practice in child group psychotherapy.) *Gruppenpsychother. & Gruppendynam.*, (Goettingen) 14:166-182.

08647 **MURICA–VALCARCEL, E.** (1967), Rehabilitación psiquica, social, familiar y laboral del enfermo alcohólico por la psicoterapía de grupo, sin la reflexoterapía. (Psychological, social, familial, and occupational rehabilitation of the alcoholic through group psychotherapy without reflex therapy.) *Psychother. & Psychosomat.*, (Basel) 15:50.

08648 **MURO, J. J.**, and **BROWN, D. B.** (1973), Group dynamics in the classroom. *Amer. Vocat. J.*, 48:20-22.

08649 **MURO, J. J.**, and **ENGELS, D. W.** (1980), Life coping skills through developmental group counseling. *J. Special. Group Work*, 5:127-130.

08650 **MURO, J. J.**, and **FREEMAN, S. L.** (1968), *Readings in Group Counseling.* Unt. textbook.

08651 **MURPHY, A., PUESCHEL, S. M.**, and **SCHNEIDER, J.** (1973), Group work with parents of children with Down's syndrome. *Soc. Casework*, 54:114-119.

08652 **MURPHY, B. C.** (1967), Pioneering narcotic addiction treatment research: the role of the pilot treatment unit at Matsqui Institution. *Can. J. Psychiat. Nursing*, (Winnipeg) 8:6-9.

08653 **MURPHY, F. J.** (1975), A study of the effects of group counseling on attendance at the senior high school level. *Dissert. Abstr. Internat.*, 36:2549A.

08654 **MURPHY, G.** (1975), Group psychotherapy in our society. In: *Group Psychotherapy and Group Function*, 2d ed., eds. M. Rosenbaum and M. M. Berger. New York: Basic Books.

08655 **MURPHY, G.** (1937), The mind is a stage: adjusting mental problems in a "spontaneity theater." *Forum*, 97:277-280.

08656 **MURPHY, M. M.** (1958), A large scale music therapy program for institutionalized low grade and middle grade defectives. *Amer. J. Ment. Deficiency*, 63:268-273.

08657 **MUPRHY, P. L.**, and **SCHULZ, E. D.** (1978), Passive-aggressive behavior in patients and staff. *J. Psychiat. Nursing*, 16:43-45.

08658 **MURPHY, W. D., COLEMAN, E. HOON, E.**, and **SCOTT, C.** (1980), Sexual dysfunction and treatment in alcoholic women. *Sexual Disabil.*, 3:240-255.

08659 **MURRAY, D. C.**, and **BROWN, J.** (1961), A consistent pattern in variations in amount of talking by patients during group therapy sessions. *Internat. J. Group Psychother.*, 11:456-461.

08660 **MURRAY, D. C., BROWN, J.**, and **KNOX, W.** (1964), Verbal participation of Negro psychotics in combined as contrasted to all-Negro groups. *Internat. J. Group Psychother.*, 14:221-223.

08661 **MURRAY, D. C., DAVIDOFF, L.**, and **HARRINGTON, G.** (1975), In vivo self-control training: ii. *Psychol. Reports*, 37:249-258.

08662 **MURRAY, E.** (1948), Combining general semantics with sociodrama: for a laboratory method in the social sciences. *Sociatry*, 2:69-72.

08663 **MURRAY, E.** (1946), Several relationships of psychodrama and general semantics. *Sociometry*, 9:184-185.

08664 **MURRAY, E.** (1948), Sociodrama and psychodrama in the college basic communication class. *Sociatry*, 2:322-329.

08665 **MURRAY, E.** (1948), Sociodrama in a special pilot course on intercultural communication. *Sociatry*, 2:330-333.

08666 **MURRAY, E. R.**, and **SMITSON, W. S.** (1963), Brief treatment of parents in a military setting. *Soc. Work*, 8:57-64.

08667 **MURRAY, N.** (1961), Diagnostic use of psychodrama in forensic psychiatry. *Group Psychother., Psychodrama & Sociometry*, 14:138-139.

08668 **MURRAY, N.** (1962), Malunion of the femur treated by group psychotherapy and psychodrama: case report. *Southern Med. J.*, 55:921-926.

08669 **MURRAY, N.**, and **MURRAY, B.** (1962), Recognition and management of group self destruction in psychodrama. *Group Psychother., Psychodrama & Sociometry*, 15:200-202.

08670 **MURRAY, N.**, and **MURRAY, B.** (1962), The West Texas syndrome in psychodrama. *Group Psychother., Psychodrama & Sociometry*, 15:52-54.

08671 **MURTHY, H. N.** (1959), Group therapy with schizophrenics. *J. All-India Inst. Ment. Health*, (New Delhi) 2:14-19.

08672 **MURUA, C. W., OLKIES, A., GUALBERT, B.**, and **CORMILLO, A. E.** (1978), Group-therapy of multiple impact for treatment of 800 obese patients. *Internat. J. Obesity*, 2:487.

08673 **MURY, G.** (1972), Do Rogerian groups exist? *Informat. Psychol.*, 48:15.

08674 **MUSANTE, G.**, and **GALLEMORE, J. L., JR.** (1973), Utilization of a staff development group in prison consultation. *Community Ment. Health J.*, 9:224-232.

08675 **MUSHOLT, E. A.** (1980), Evaluation of a gestalt oriented group art experience. *Dissert. Abstr. Internat.*, 40:4465B. (University Microfilms No. 8006545.)

08676 **MUSKATEVC, L. C.** (1961), Principles of group psychotherapy and psychodrama as applied to music therapy. *Group Psychother., Psychodrama & Sociometry*, 14:176-185.

08677 **MUSTO, D. F.**, and **ASTRACHAN, B. M.** (1968), Strange encounter: the use of study groups with graduate students in history. *Psychiatry*, 31:264-276.

08678 **MUZEKARI, L. H.** (1970), The induction process: a method of choice in intrainstitutional transfer. *J. Nerv. & Ment. Diseases*, 150:419-422.

08679 **MUZEKARI, L. H., HAMILTON, M.**, and **LEVITT, C.** (1967), Gradual introduction of chronic schizophrenics to intensive social therapy. *Proceed., 75th Annual Convention*, American Psychological Association, 2:229-230.

08680 **MYERHOFF, H. L., JACOBS, A.**, and **STOLLER, F.** (1970), Emotionality in marathon and traditional psychotherapy groups. *Psychother.: Theory, Res. & Pract.*, 7:33-36.

08681 **MYERS, D. G.** (1970), A comparison of the effects of group puppet therapy and group activity with mentally retarded children. *Dissert. Abstr. Internat.*, 31:5234.

08682 **MYERS, D. G.** (1975), Discussion-induced attitude polarization. *Human Relat.*, 28:699-714.

08683 **MYERS, D. G.** (1968), Enhancement of initial risk taking tendencies in social situations. *Dissert. Abstr. Internat.*, 28:3265.

08684 **MYERS, D. G.**, and **LAMM, H.** (1975), The polarizing effect of group discussion. *Amer. Scientist*, 63:297-303.

08685 **MYERS, E. D.** (1975), Age, persistence and improvement in an open outpatient group. *Brit. J. Psychiat.*, (Ashford) 27:157-159.

08686 **MYERS, K.**, and **CLARK, D. H.** (1972), Results in a therapeutic community. *Brit. J. Psychiat.*, (Ashford) 120:51-58.

08687 **MYERS, P. A.** (1977), Working with parents of children with profound developmental retardation: a group approach. *Clin. Pediat.*, 16:367-370.

08688 **MYERSON, D. J.** (1965), The study and treatment of alcoholism. *Philippine Federat. Priv. Med. Pract. J.*, (Manila) 14:512-523.

08689 **MYKEL, N.** (1971), The application of ethical standards to group psychotherapy in a community. *Internat. J. Group Psychother.*, 21:248-254.

08690 **MYRICK, R. D.,** and **HAIGHT, D. A.** (1972), Growth groups: an encounter with underachievers. *School Counselor*, 20:115-121.
08691 **MYRICK, R. D.,** and **KELLY, F. D.** (1971), Group counseling with primary school-age children. *J. School Psychol.*, 9:137-143.

N

08692 **NAAR, R.** (1977), Psychodramatic intervention within a t.a. framework in individual and group psychotherapy. *Group Psychother., Psychodrama & Sociometry,* 30:127-134.
08693 **NAAR, R.** (1975), A theoretical framework for group psychotherapy. *J. Contemp. Psychother.,* 7:50-55.
08694 **NAGEL, G. S.** (1973), Can the chain be broken? *J. Bronx State Hosp.,* 1:161-167.
08695 **NAGELBERG, L.,** and **ROSENTHAL, L.** (1955), Validation of selection of patients for activity group therapy through the Rorschach and other tests. *Internat. J. Group Psychother.,* 5:380-391.
08696 **NAHINSKY, I. D.** (1969), A group interaction stochastic model based on balance: theoretical considerations. *Behav. Science Res.,* 14:289-302.
08697 **NAHOR, A.,** and **FELTHOUS, A. R.** (1976), Therapeutic economy: an effective model for residential psychiatric treatment. *J. Psychiat.,* 7.
08698 **NAMER, A.** (1968), An experiment with children: group psychotherapy through activity. *Rev. Psiquiat. Psichol. Med.,* 8:328-337.
08699 **NAMER, A.,** and **MARTINEZ, Y.** (1967), Case study: the use of painting in group psychotherapy with children. *Bull. Art Ther.,* 6:73-78.
08700 **NAPIER, R. W.,** and **GERSHENFELD, M. K.** (1973), *Groups: Therapy and Experience.* Boston: Houghton Mifflin.
08701 **NAPOLITANI, D.** (1980), Beyond the individual. *Group Anal.,* (London) 13:12-16.
08702 **NAPOLITANI, D.** (1974), Maturational phases of the psychoanalytic group: reciprocal phantomatic inductions between analyst and group. *Arch. Psicol. Neurol., & Psichiat.,* (Milan) 35:536-552.
08703 **NAPOLITANI, F.** (1963), (Experiment of a psychotherapy of psychoses performed in a hospital department with self-administration by the patients.) *Bibl. Psychiat. Neurol.,* (Basel) 118:23-29.
08704 **NAPOLITANI, F.** (1974), The group as a therapeutic instrument. *Arch. Psicol., Neurol. & Psichiat.,* (Milan) 35:480-506.
08705 **NAPOLITANI, F.,** and **ANCONA, L.** (1974), Internal processes of a psychoanalytically-led group in terms of Klein's identifications. *Arch. Psicol., Neurol. & Psichiat.,* (Milan) 35:553-576.
08706 **NARAYANAN, H. S.** (1977), Experiences with group and family therapy in India. *Internat. J. Group Psychother.,* 27:517-519.
08707 **NARAYAN, H. S.,** and **EMBAR, P.** (1968), Review of group psychotherapy work done in the mental hospitals and the Victoria Hospital Psychiatric Outpatient Clinic, Bangalore. *Trans. All-India Inst. Ment. Health,* (New Delhi) 8:25-26.
08708 **NARUSE, G.** (1959), Recent development of psychodrama and hypnodrama in Japan. *Group Psychother., Psychodrama & Sociometry,* 12:258-262.
08709 **NARUSE, G.** (1960), Recent development of psychodrama and hypnodrama in Japan. *Internat. J. Sociometry & Sociatry,* 2:18-22.
08710 **NASH, E. H., JR., FRANK, J. D., GLIEDMAN, L. H., IMBER, S. D.,** and **STONE, H. R.** (1957), Some factors related to patients remaining in group psychotherapy. *Internat. J. Group Psychother.,* 7:264-274.
08711 **NASH, H. T.,** and **STONE, A. R.** (1951), Collaboration of therapist and observer in guiding group psychotherapy. *Group Psychother., Psychodrama & Sociometry,* 4:85-93.
08712 **NASH, K. B.** (1968), Group guidance and counseling programs: a vehicle

for the introduction of sex education for adolescents in the public school. *J. School Health*, 38:577-583.

08713 **NASH, K. B.** (1974), The group psychotherapist and the training of the new mental health worker: what else is new? *Internat. J. Group Psychother.*, 24:32-41.

08714 **NASH, P. H.** (1970), Treatment of math anxiety through systematic desensitization and insight oriented therapy groups. *Dissert. Abstr. Internat.*, 31:1018A.

08715 **NASH, W. F.**, and **PHILLIPS, L.** (1979), A venture in community care: a social work scheme involving young mothers suffering from depression. *Midwife*, (London) 15:12-13.

08716 **NASON, J. D.** (1977), Teaching psychotherapy in a community mental health center. *Amer. J. Psychiat.*, 134:14-19.

08717 **NASS, M. L.** (1959), Characteristics of a psychotherapeutically oriented group for beginning teachers. *Ment. Hygiene*, 43:562-567.

08718 **NATH, C.**, and **RINEHART, J.** (1979), Effects of individual and group relaxation therapy on blood pressure in essential hypertension. *Res. Nursing & Health*, 2:119-126.

08719 **NATHAN, P. E.** (1977), Review of R. V. Heckel's and H. C. Salzberg's *Group Psychotherapy: Behavioral Approach. Contemp. Psychol.*, 22:807-808.

08720 **NATHAN, T. S.**, and **HESSE, P. P.** (1978), Developmental and interactional aspects of creative expression in course of group psychotherapy. *Confinia Psychiat.*, (Basel) 21:119-132.

08721 **NAUMBURG, M.** (1966), *Dynamically Oriented Art Therapy: Its Principles and Practice*. New York: Grune and Stratton.

08722 **NAUMBURG, M.**, and **CALDWELL, J.** (1959), The use of spontaneous art in analytically oriented group therapy of obese women. *Acta Psychother., Psychosomat. Orthopaedagog. Suppl.*, (Basel) 7:254-287.

08723 **NAUN, R. J.** (1971), Comparison of group counseling approaches with Puerto Rican boys in an inner city high school. *Dissert. Abstr. Internat.*, 32:742A.

08724 **NAUN, R. A. S.** (1972), An investigation of the effectiveness of two approaches to group work with the educable mentally retarded in a public high school. *Dissert. Abstr. Internat.*, 33:160A.

08725 **NAVARRE, E.** (1974), An evaluation of group work practice with AFDC mothers. In: *Individual Change Through Small Groups*, ed. P. Glasser, R. Sarri, and R. Vinter. New York: Free Press.

08726 **NAWAS, M. M.**, and **PUCEL, J. C.** (1971), Relationship factors in desensitization: a persistent trend. *J. Couns. Psychol.*, 18:239-243.

08727 **NAWAS, M. M.**, **FISHMAN, T.**, and **PURCEL, J. C.** (1970), A standardized desensitization program applicable to group and individual treatments. *Behav. Res. & Ther.*, 8:49-56.

08728 **NEAL, R. B.** (1977), The effect of group counseling and physical fitness programs on self-esteem and cardio-vascular fitness. *Dissert. Abstr. Internat.*, 38:1911A.

08729 **NEDD, A. N. B.**, and **SHIHADEH, E. S.** (1974), The impact of group therapy on penitentiary vocational and academic education program. *J. Psychol.*, 18:215-222.

08730 **NEEDHAM-GREISCHAR, M.** (1975), Behavioral change through self appraisal and group interaction. *Dissert. Abstr. Internat.*, 36:2030A.

08731 **NEFF, R.** (1974), The group constellation. *Psychother.: Theory, Res. & Pract.*, 11:80-82.

08732 **NEGELE, R. A.** (1976), A study of the effectiveness of brief time-limited psychotherapy with children and their parents. *Dissert. Abstr. Internat.*, 36:4172.

08733 **NEHNEVAJSA, J.** (1956), Review of J. L. Moreno's "Dilemma of Existentialism." *Internat. J. Sociometry & Sociatry*, 1:113-115.

08734 **NEHNEVAJSA, J.** (1955), Notes on "The discovery of the spontaneous man." *Group Psychother., Psychodrama & Sociometry*, 8:338-346.

08735 **NEHNEVAJSA, J.** (1956), Psychodrama of "Adolph Hitler." *Internat. J. Sociometry & Sociatry*, 1:80.

08736 **NEHNEVAJSA, J.** (1956), Reflections on theories and sociometric systems. *Internat. J. Sociometry & Sociatry*, 1:8-15.

08737 **NEHNEVAJSA, J.** (1956), Socio-cultural models in psychiatry. *Group Psychother., Psychodrama & Sociometry*, 9:268-273.

08738 **NEIBERG, N. A.** (1980), Presidential address: group psychotherapy: retrospect, current status and prospects. *Internat. J. Group Psychother.*, 30:259-272.

08739 **NEIBERG, N. A.** (1976), Symposium: contrasting models of leadership in group psychotherapy: introduction. *Internat. J. Group Psychother.*, 26:135-138.

08740 **NEIGHBOR, J. E., BEACH, M., BROWN, D. T., KEVIN, D.,** and **VISHER, J. S.** (1958), An approach to the selection of patients for group psychotherapy. *Ment. Hygiene*, 42:243-254.

08741 **NELL, J. E.** (1965), The use of music in group psychotherapy. *Curr. Psychiat. Ther.*, 5:145-149.

08742 **NELLESSEN, L.** (1975), (Institutional requirements of social therapy in penal settings: an attempt to simulate models and methods of sociodrama.) *Gruppendynamik*, (Stuttgart) 6:50-72.

08743 **NELLESSEN, L.,** and **SVENSSON, A.** (1972), (A factor analytical description of the t-group.) *Gruppendynamik*, (Stuttgart) 3:92-110.

08744 **NELSEN, J. W.** (1980), The effectiveness of Adlerian parent and teacher study groups in changing child maladaptive behavior in a positive direction. *Dissert. Abstr. Internat.*, 41:601A. (University Microfilms No. 8017442.)

08745 **NELSON, K. F.,** and **HASBACHER, P.** (1972), Sensitivity training in psychiatric nursing: evolution and evaluation of a student group experience. *J. Psychiat. Nursing*, 10:21-26.

08746 **NELSON, K. O.** (1972), The effect of two parent group counseling models in the behavior of educationally handicapped children. *Dissert. Abstr. Internat.*, 33:2110A.

08747 **NELSON, R. C.** (1980), Coping and beyond: choice awareness as a structured group process. *J. Special. Group Work*, 5:148-156.

08748 **NELSON, R. C.** (1971), Organizing for group counseling. *Personnel & Guid. J.*, 50:25-28.

08749 **NELSON, R. E.** (1976), A comparison of the effects of three career group counseling techniques on measures of self information, cognitive self-information seeking behavior, and group process factors. *Dissert. Abstr. Internat.*, 36:6560A.

08750 **NELSON, R. H.** (1970), The involved therapists: to be or not to be? *Voices*, 6:60-64.

08751 **NEMETH, G. A.** (1974), Arousal and orienting response in psychopathological groups. *Dissert. Abstr. Internat.*, 34:5202B.

08752 **NERVRUS, N.** (1968), Unstructured and structured group psychotherapy, geriatric patients, and decision to leave the hospital. *Dissert. Abstr. Internat.*, 28:4879.

08753 **NESBIT, M.** (1978), The treatment of chronic pain patients via a structured group counseling approach. *Dissert. Abstr. Internat.*, 39:5331A.

08754 **NESS, J. M.** (1979), Competing reinforcement systems in a small group setting. *Dissert. Abstr. Internat.*, 40:5795B.

08755 **NETO, B. B.** (1968), (Frequency of sessions in group psychotherapy.) *Rev. Paulista Med.*, (Sao Paulo) 72:18-22.

08756 **NETO, B. B.** (1975), Greetings. *Internat. J. Group Psychother.*, 25:173-174.

08757 **NETO, B. B.** (1971), Some aspects of countertransference in group psychotherapy. *Internat. J. Group Psychother.*, 21:95-98.

08758 **NETO, B. B.** (1970), Some aspects of countertransference in group psychotherapy. *Sandoz Psychiat. Spectator*, 6:14-15.

08759 **NETO, B. B.** (1966), Zur gegenübertragung in der gruppentherapie. (On countertransference in group therapy.) *Zeit. Psychosomat. Med. & Psychoanal.*, (Stuttgart) 12:138-143.

08760 **NETO, D. A.,** and **DAVANZO, H. C.** (1964), Alguns aspectos relativos à localizacão como forma de comunicacão não verbal num grupo terapêutico. (Some aspects of seating positions as a form of nonverbal communication in a therapeutic group.) *J. Brasil. Psiquiat.*, (Sao Paulo) 13:331-338.

08761 **NETTER, M.** (1974), Homogeneity of the psychoanalytic method in training groups. *Cahiers de Psychol.*, (Paris) 17:199.

08762 **NETTLETON, M. A.** (1970), Differential effects of goal structuring in counseling groups identified on the variable of internal-external control. *Dissert. Abstr. Internat.*, 32:186A.

08763 **NEUBAUER, P. B.** (1953), Basic considerations in the application of therapy and education to parent groups. *Internat. J. Group Psychother.*, 3:315-319.

08764 **NEUMAN, D. R.** (1968), Professional and subprofessional counselors using group desensitization and insight procedures to reduce examination anxiety. *Dissert. Abstr. Internat.*, 29:1757A.

08765 **NEUMANN, M.,** and **GAOMI, B.** (1974), Types of patients especially suitable for analytically oriented group psychotherapy: some clinical examples. *Isr. Annals Psychiat.*, (Jerusalem) 12:303-307.

08766 **NEVALAINEN, O.** (1966/1967), Alcoholism and group therapy. *Sairaan Vuosik*, 4:108-140.

08767 **NEVILLE, W. G.** (1971), An analysis of personality types and their differential response to marital enrichment groups. *Dissert. Abstr. Internat.*, 32:6766A.

08768 **NEVRUZ, N.** (1968), Unstructured and structured group psychotherapy: geriatric patients, and decision to leave the hospital. *Dissert. Abstr. Internat.*, 28:4879.

08769 **NEVRUZ, N.,** and **HRUSHKA, M.** (1969), The influence of unstructured and structured group psychotherapy with geriatric patients on their decision to leave the hospital. *Internat. J. Group Psychother.*, 19:72-78.

08770 New Alcoholism treatment program (1969), *Illinois Med. J.*, 135:393 passim.

08771 **NEWBURGER, H. M.** (1963), Psychotherapy and anxiety: a sociometric study. *Group Psychother., Psychodrama & Sociometry*, 16:1-7.

08772 **NEWBURGER, H. M.,** and **SCHAUER, G.** (1953), Sociometric evaluation of group psychotherapy. *Group Psychother., Psychodrama & Sociometry*, 6:7-20.

08773 **NEWMAN, B. M.** (1976), The development of social interaction from infancy through adolescence. *Small Group Behav.*, 7:19-32.

08774 **NEWMAN, C.,** and **GLOVER, L.** (1967), Group psychotherapy and social group work. *Ment. Hygiene*, 51:593-600.

08775 **NEWMAN, G.,** and **HALL, R. C. W.** (1971), Acting out: an indication for psychodrama. *Group Psychother., Psychodrama & Sociometry*, 24:87-96.

08776 **NEWMAN, L. E.** (1976), Treatment for the parents of feminine boys. *Amer. J. Psychiat.*, 133:683-687.

08777 **NEWMAN, L. E.**, and **STEINBERG, J. L.** (1970), Consultation with police on human relations training. *Amer. J. Psychiat.*, 126:1421-1429.

08778 **NEWMAN, P. R.** (1976), Analysis of social interaction as an environmental variable. *Small Group Behav.*, 7:33-46.

08779 **NEWMAN, R. G.** (1959), The assessment of progress in the treatment of hyperaggressive children with learning disturbances within a school setting. *Amer. J. Orthopsychiat.*, 29:633-643.

08780 **NEWMAN, R. G.** (1969), Effects and interrelationship of adolescent crisis on significant adults as seen and handled through group work. *Amer. J. Orthopsychiat.*, 39:306-307.

08781 **NEWMAN, R. G.** (1974), *Groups in Schools.* New York: Simon and Schuster.

08782 **NEWNHAM, W. H.** (1967), Music therapy in a neurosis centre. *Nursing Times*, (London) 63:146-148.

08783 **NEWSTETTER, W. I., FELDSTEIN, M. J.**, and **NEWCOMB, T. M.** (1938), *Group Adjustment: A Study in Experimental Sociology.* Cleveland: Western Reserve University.

08784 **NEWSTROM, J. W.** (1973), Human relations training. *Training & Develop. J.*, 27:3-6.

08785 **NEWSTROM, J. W.**, and **SCANNELL, E. E.** (1980), *Games Trainers Play: Experimental Learning Exercises.* New York: McGraw-Hill.

08786 **NEWTON, H. J.**, and **SOVAK, R. J.** (1968), A therapeutic community for adolescents. *Hosp. & Community Psychiat.*, 19:106-107.

08787 **NEWTON, P. M.** (1971), Abstinence as a role requirement in psychotherapy. *Psychiatry*, 34:391-400.

08788 **NEWTON, P. M.**, and **LEVINSON, D. J.** (1973), The work group within the organization: a socio-psychological approach. *Psychiatry*, 36:115-142.

08789 New volume integrates group and behavior therapy as new psychotherapy approach (1978), *Correct. Soc. Psychiat. & J. Appl. Behav. Ther.*, 24:15-16.

08790 **NICHOL, J. S.** (1970), The use of vocational discussion in small groups to increase vocational maturity. *Dissert. Abstr. Internat.*, 30:3733A.

08791 **NICHOLL, G. M.** (1975), The effect of advanced organizers on a cognitive social learning group. Unpublished doctoral dissertation, University of Toronto.

08792 **NICHOLLS, G.** (1975), Treatment of dependence on alcohol and drugs at St. Anthony's Hospital. *Australasian Nurses J.*, (Port Adelaide) 4:8-9.

08793 **NICHOLS, F. L.** (1962), Psychiatrist and nurse as co-therapists in a psychodrama group. *Group Psychother., Psychodrama & Sociometry*, 15:197-199.

08794 **NICHOLS, H.** (1954), Role-playing in primary grades. *Group Psychother., Psychodrama & Sociometry*, 7:238-241.

08795 **NICHOLS, H.**, and **WILLIAMS, L.** (1960), *Learning About Role-Playing for Children and Teachers.* Washington, D.C.: Association for Childhood Education.

08796 **NICHOLS, M. P.** (1977), The delayed impact of group therapists' intervention. *J. Clin. Psychol.*, 33:258-262.

08797 **NICHOLS, M. P.** (1975), Methodology for evaluating the therapists' influence on the process of group psychotherapy. *Am. Coll. Health Assn. J.*, 24:8-12.

08798 **NICHOLS, M. P.**, and **TAYLOR, T. Y.** (1975), Impact of therapist interventions on early sessions of group therapy. *J. Clin. Psychol.*, 31:726-729.

08799 **NICHOLS, P. W.** (1975), The comparative effects of human potential counseling, and group guidance on achievement and academic behaviors of "high risk" junior college students. *Dissert. Abstr. Internat.*, 36:3414A.

08800 **NICOLE, J. E.** (1949), Psychiatric rehabilitation in a hospital. *Practitioner*, 163:533-540.
08801 **NIEHAUS, J. T.** (1967), Group social work with children. *J. Asthma Res.*, 4:247-249.
08802 **NIELSEN, G. H.** (1970), A project in parent education. *Can. J. Pub. Health*, (Ottawa) 61:210-214.
08803 **NIELSON, D.** (1948), A student's observations on Beacon as a setting for self-therapy. *Sociatry*, 2:399-403.
08804 **NIEROJEWSKI, W.** (1975), (The role of group psychotherapy in the treatment of alcoholism in an outpatient clinic.) *Psychiat. Polska*, (Warsaw) 9:351-357.
08805 **NIETO, G. M.** (1957), (Group psychotherapy: an experiment with a group of mothers whose children were under treatment.) *Arch. Pediat. Uruguay*, (Montevideo) 28:798-802.
08806 **NIETZEL, M. T.**, and **BERNSTEIN, D.** (1976), Effects of instructionally mediated demand on the behavioral assessment of assertiveness. *J. Couns. Psychol.*, 44:500.
08807 **NIEWOEHNER, G. J.** (1973), Effects of group counseling on vocational decision of workshop clients: an incidental finding. *Rehab. Lit.*, 34:235-236.
08808 **NIEWOEHNER, G.** (1972), The use of group methods in facilitating work adjustment. *Dissert. Abstr. Internat.*, 32:436A.
08809 **NIKELLY, A. G.** (1963), Democratic assumptions in Adler's psychology. *J. Individ. Psychol.*, 19:161-166.
08810 **NIKOLIĆ, S.** (1975), (Analytical psychodrama as a psychotherapeutic technique.) *Anali Zavoda Ment. Zdravlje*, 7:97-117.
08811 **NISHIYAMA, M.** (1980), (Psychotherapy of alcohol-dependent patients: group therapy and beyond.) *Japanese J. Nursing*, (Tokyo) 26:2134-2139.
08812 **NISHPITZ, J.** (1960), Milieu therapy. *Amer. J. Occupat. Ther.*, 14:221-222.
08813 **NITZBERG, J.** (1971), Group work with mentally retarded adolescents and young adults in a vocational habilitation center. *Group Process*, (London) 4:18-31.
08814 **NIVER, E. O.**, **ADAM, A. B.**, **STERLING, V.**, and **COULTER, G.** (1965), Exercise as group therapy. *Ment. Hosp.*, 16:112-113.
08815 **NOBEL, F. C.** (1959), A method for the quantification of interaction in psychotherapeutic groups. Ann Arbor: University Microfilms.
08816 **NOBLE, F.**, **OHLSEN, M.**, and **PROFF, F.** (1961), A method for the quantification of psychotherapeutic interaction in counseling groups. *J. Couns. Psychol.*, 8:54-61.
08817 **NOBLE, P. F.** (1974), Effects of leader verbal behaviors on patterns of small group interaction. *Dissert. Abstr. Internat.*, 35:2777A.
08818 **NOBLER, H.** (1972), Group therapy with male homosexuals. *Compar. Group Studies*, 3:161-178.
08819 **NODIOT, S.** (1969/1970), (Some thoughts concerning psychodrama.) *Bull. de Psychol.*, (Paris) 23:771-774.
08820 **NOLAN, B.** (1972), The effects of selected types of feedback on self-perceived changes in sensitivity training. *Dissert. Abstr. Internat.*, 32:4357A.
08821 **NOLAN, J. J.** (1974), The effectiveness of the self-directed search compared with group counseling in promoting information-seeking behavior and realism of vocational choice. *Dissert. Abstr. Internat.*, 35:195A.
08822 **NOLAN, K. J.**, and **COOKE, E. T.** (1970), The training and utilization of the mental health paraprofessional within the military: the social work/psychology specialist. *Amer. J. Psychiat.*, 127:74-79.
08823 **NOLL, G. A.**, and **WATKINS, J. T.** (1974), Differences between persons

seeking encounter group experiences and others on the Personal Orientation Inventory. *J. Couns. Psychol.*, 21:206-209.
08824 **NOLTE, J., SMALLWOOD, C.**, and **WEISTART, J.** (1975), Role reversal with God. *Group Psychother., Psychodrama & Sociometry*, 28:70-76.
08825 **NOLTE, J., WEISTART, J.**, and **WYATT, J.** (1977), Psychodramatic production of dreams: "The end of the road." *Group Psychother., Psychodrama & Sociometry*, 30:37-48.
08826 Nonverbal co-leader works "miracle" in a training group (1968), *Roche Report: Front. Hosp. Psychiat.*, 5:3, 8.
08827 **NOONAN, J.** (1971), Sensitivity nonsense: cartoons. *Christian Cent.*, (Jan. 6) 88:22.
08828 **NOORDZIJ, J. C.** (1964), (The promotion of the tie of the nursing personnel with the psychiatric institution: self-realization in a therapeutic community.) *Ziekenhuis*, (Lochem) 37:172-189.
08829 **NORDEN, H.** (1953), Social group work with delinquent groups. *Group Psychotherapy Association of Southern California, First Annual Report*, pp. 9-11.
08830 **NORDLAND, E.** (1951), Synsmåter innen psykoterapien. (Viewpoints within psychotherapy.) *Norsk Pedagog. Tidsskr.*, (Kungsbacha) 35:161-176.
08831 **NORDMEYER, B.** (1975), *Lebenskrisen und Ihre Bewältigung: Psychoanalyse, Gruppentherapie, Seelsorge.* Stuttgart: Verlag Urachhaus.
08832 **NORDON, A.** (1964), Le premier congrès international du psychodrame. (The First International Psychodrama Congress.) *Group Psychother., Psychodrama & Sociometry*, 17:92-93.
08833 **NORMAN, A.** (1972), Double messages in a therapeutic community. *Psychother. & Psychosomat.*, (Basel) 20:143-147.
08834 **NORMAND, W. C., IGLESIAS, J.**, and **PAYNE, S.** (1974), Brief group therapy to facilitate utilization of mental health services by Spanish-speaking patients. *Amer. J. Orthopsychiat.*, 44:37-42.
08835 **NORRIS, C. M.** (1964), The relationship of medicine and nursing in psychiatric hospitals. *Perspect. Psychiat. Care*, 2:32-39.
08836 **NORRIS, J. W.** (1976), The use of spontaneous drawing with chromatic colors as a facilitator for group psychotherapy: the development and exploration of a technique. *Dissert. Abstr. Internat.*, 36:5054-5055.
08837 **NORTH, A. J.** (1957), Language and communication in group functioning. *Group Psychother., Psychodrama & Sociometry*, 10:308-318.
08838 **NORTHEN, H.** (1969), *Social Work with Groups.* New York: Columbia University Press.
08839 **NORTHWAY, M. L.** (1954), Comments on Moreno's "Transference and tele." *Group Psychother., Psychodrama & Sociometry*, 7:313-315.
08840 **NORTHWAY, M. L.** (1956), A sociometric basis for a science of man. *Internat. J. Sociometry & Sociatry*, 1:6-8.
08841 **NORTON, F. H.** (1976), Counseling parents of the mentally retarded child. *School Counselor*, 23:200-205.
08842 **NORTON, R. W.** (1979), Identifying coalitions. *Small Group Behav.*, 10:343-354.
08843 **NOSZLOPI, L.** (1963), Note on the dream from the point of view of the psycho- and sociodrama. *Internat. J. Sociometry & Sociatry*, 3:3-4.
08844 **NOVAK, T.**, and **STEPANIK, J.** (1975), The use of group psychagogics in children and parents to solve educational problems. *Psychol. Patopsychol. Dietala*, 10:351-357.
08845 **NOVAK, T.** (1976), (Group counseling with single adults.) *Ceskoslov. Psychol.*, (Prague) 20:528-532.
08846 **NOVAK, T., ROLLEROVA, V.**, and **STEPANIK, J.** (1976), (Group coun-

seling in person without partner relationships.) *Ceskoslov. Psychol.*, (Prague) 20:528-532.

08847 **NOVICK, J. I.** (1965), Comparison between short-term group and individual psychotherapy in effecting change in nondesirable behavior in children. *Internat. J. Group Psychother.*, 15:366-373.

08848 **NOY, P.** (1967), Resistance to a change in group psychotherapy. *Internat. J. Group Psychother.*, 17:371-377.

08849 **NOY, P.**, and **SHANAN, J.** (1964), A method for the assessment of personality changes in group psychotherapy. *Internat. J. Group Psychother.*, 14:139-157.

08850 **NUGENT, S. M.** (1965), The treatment of addictive smokers. *Brit. J. Addict.*, (Edinburgh) 61:125-128.

08851 **NUNNELLY, K. G.** (1969), The use of multiple therapy in group counseling and psychotherapy. *Dissert. Abstr. Internat.*, 30:387B-388B.

08852 **NURSE, J.** (1972), Retarded infants and their parents: a group for fathers and mothers. *Brit. J. Soc. Work*, (Birmingham) 2:159-174.

08853 **NYDEGGER, R. V.** (1975), Leadership in small groups: a rewards-costs analysis. *Small Group Behav.*, 6:353-368.

08854 **NYLEN, D., MITCHELL, J. R.**, and **STOUT, A.** (1967), *Handbook of Staff Development and Human Relations Training: Materials Developed for Use in Africa*. Copenhagen: European Institute for Trans-National Studies in Group and Organizational Development; Washington: National Training Laboratories, National Education Association.

O

08855 **OAKES, W. F., DROGE, H. E.,** and **AUGUST, B.** (1960), Reinforcement effects on participation in group discussion. *Psychol. Reports*, 7:503-514.
08856 **O'BANNON, T.,** and **O'CONNELL, A.** (1970), *The Shared Journey*. Englewood Cliffs, NJ: Prentice-Hall.
08857 **OBITZ, F. W., WOOD, J. D.,** and **CANTERGIANI, N.** (1977), Alcoholics' perceptions of group therapy and Alcoholics Anonymous. *Brit. J. Addict.*, (Edinburgh) 72:321-324.
08858 **OBLER, M.** (1975), Multivariate approaches to psychotherapy with sexual dysfunctions. *Couns. Psychol.*, 5:55-60.
08859 **OBLER, M.** (1973), Systematic desensitization in sexual disorders. *J. Behav. Ther. & Exper. Psychiat.*, 4:93-101.
08860 **O'BRIEN, C. P.** (1975), Group therapy for schizophrenia: a practical approach. *Schizo. Bull.*, 13:119-130.
08861 **O'BRIEN, C. P., HAMM, K. B., RAY, B. A., PIERCE, J. F., LUBORSKY, L.,** and **MINTZ, J.** (1972), Group vs. individual psychotherapy with schizophrenics. *Arch. Gen. Psychiat.*, 27:474-478.
08862 **O'BRIEN, G. E.,** and **HARARY, F.** (1977), Measurement of the interactive effects of leadership style and group structure upon group performance. *Austral. J. Psychol.*, (Parkville) 29:59-64.
08863 **O'BRIEN, H. P.** (1950), The use of group methods in correctional treatment. *Proceed. Amer. Prison Assn.*, 80:263-268.
08864 **O'BRIEN, W. J.** (1963), *Participation and Response: How Delinquents Saw Their Experience in an Experimental Group Therapy Program*. Sacramento: Institute for the Study of Crime and Delinquency and the California Youth Authority.
08865 **O'BRIEN, W. J.** (1961), *Personality Assessment as a Measure of Change Resulting from Group Psychotherapy with Male Juvenile Delinquents*. Sacramento: Institute for the Study of Crime and Delinquency and the California Youth Authority.
08866 **O'CONNELL, R. A., GOLDER, J. M.,** and **SENONSKY, C. J.** (1972), Which adolescent stays in group psychotherapy? *Adolescence*, 6:51-60.
08867 **O'CONNELL, W.** (1966), Psychotherapy for everyman: a look at action therapy. *J. Existentialism*, 7:85-91.
08868 **O'CONNELL, W. E.** (1972), Adlerian action therapy technique. *J. Individ. Psychol.*, 28:184-191.
08869 **O'CONNELL, W. E.** (1963), Adlerian psychodrama with schizophrenics. *J. Individ. Psychol.*, 19:69-76.
08870 **O'CONNELL, W. E.** (1969), Community confrontations: a challenge to psychotherapeutic practice. *J. Individ. Psychol.*, 25:38-47.
08871 **O'CONNELL, W. E.** (1975), Encouragement labs: a didactic-experiential approach to courage. *Individ. Psychologist*, 12:8-12.
08872 **O'CONNELL, W. E.** (1971), Equality in encounter groups. *Individ. Psychologist*, 8:15-17.
08873 **O'CONNELL, W. E.** (1967), Psychodrama: involving the audience. *Rational Living*, 2:22-25.
08874 **O'CONNELL, W. E.** (1971), Sensitivity training and Adlerian therapy. *J. Individ. Psychol.*, 1:65-72.
08875 **O'CONNELL, W. E.,** and **HANSON, P. G.** (1970), Patients' cognitive changes in human relations training. *J. Individ. Psychol.*, 26:57-63.
08876 **O'CONNELL, W. E., ROTHAUS, P., HANSON, P. G.,** and **MOYER, R.** (1969), Jest appreciation and interaction in leaderless groups. *Internat. J. Group Psychother.*, 19:454-462.

08877 **O'CONNOR, F.** (1969), A group therapy experience with regressed patients. *J. Psychiat. Nursing*, 7:226-229.

08878 **O'CONNOR, G.,** and **ALDERSON, J.** (1974), Human relations groups for human services practitioners. *Small Group Behav.*, 5:495-505.

08879 **O'CONNOR, N.,** and **YONGE, K. A.** (1955), Methods of evaluating the group psychotherapy of unstable defective delinquents. *J. Genetic Psychol.*, 87:89-101.

08880 **O'CONNOR, W. H.,** and **MORGAN, D. W.** (1968), Multidisciplinary treatment of alcoholism: a consultation program for team coordination. *Quart. J. Studies Alcohol*, 29:903-908.

08881 **O'DAY, R.** (1976), Individual training styles: an empirically derived typology. *Small Group Behav.*, 7:147-182.

08882 **O'DELL, J. W.** (1968), Group size and emotional interaction. *J. Personality & Soc. Psychol.*, 8:75-78.

08883 **O'DELL, S.,** and **SEILER, G.** (1975), The effects of short-term personal growth groups on anxiety and self-perception. *Small Group Behav.*, 6:251-271.

08884 **ODEN, T. C.** (1972), *The Intensive Group Experience*. Philadelphia: Westminster Press.

08885 **ODENWALD, R. P.** (1961), Outline of group psychotherapy for juvenile delinquents and criminal offenders. *Group Psychother., Psychodrama & Sociometry*, 14:50-53.

08886 **ODHNER, F.** (1970), Group dynamics of the interdisciplinary team. *Amer. J. Occupat. Ther.*, 24:484-487.

08887 **ODHNER, F.** (1970), A study of group tasks as facilitators of verbalization among hospitalized schizophrenic patients. *Amer. J. Occupat. Ther.*, 24:7-i2.

08888 **O'DONNELL, C. R.** (1972), Group behavior modification with chronic inpatients: a case study. *Psychother.: Theory, Res. & Pract.*, 9:120-122.

08889 **O'DONNELL, C. R.** (1973), Predicting success in a group treatment program for delinquent males. *Proceed., 81st Annual Convention*, American Psychological Association, Montreal, Canada, 8:951-952.

08890 **O'DONNELL, J. N.** (1973), Marathon group therapy and marathon *in vivo* group desensitization. *Dissert. Abstr. Internat.*, 33:5024B.

08891 **O'DONNELL, W. E.** (1978), The relative effectiveness of transactional analysis group counseling vs. gestalt group counseling in effecting change in male junior high school truants. *Dissert. Abstr. Internat.*, 38:6042B.

08892 **OECHEL, S.** (1977), (Group therapy in gerontopsychiatry: limits and possibilities.) *Psychiat., Neurol. & Med. Psychol.*, (Leipzig) 29:31-38.

08893 **OEHLER-GIARRATANA, J.,** and **FITZGERALD, R. G.** (1980), Group therapy with blind diabetics. *Arch. Gen. Psychiatry*, 37:463-467.

08894 **OEI, P.,** and **JACKSON, P.** (1980), Long-term effects of group and individual social skills training with alcoholics. *Addict. Behav.*, 5:129-136.

08895 **OFMAN, W.** (1964), Evaluation of a group counseling procedure. *Dissert. Abstr. Internat.*, 24:5549.

08896 **OFMAN, W.** (1964), Evaluation of a group counseling procedure. *J. Couns. Psychol.*, 11:152-159.

08897 **OFMAN, W. V.** (1978), Review of M. M. Ohlsen's *Group Counseling*, 2d ed. *Contemp. Psychol.*, 23:757-758.

08898 **OFSHE, R. J.** (1973), *Interpersonal Behavior in Small Groups*. Englewood, NJ: Prentice-Hall.

08899 **OGARA, C. R.** (1959), Principles of group psychotherapy with schizophrenic patients. *Internat. J. Group Psychother.*, 9:53-61.

08900 **OGBORNE, A. C.,** and **MELOTTE, C.** (1977), An evaluation of a thera-

peutic community for former drug users. *Brit. J. Addict.*, (Edinburgh) 72:75-82.
08901 **OGILVIE, V. N.** (1976), Evaluation of a group career counseling program for women. *Dissert. Abstr. Internat.*, 36:4266A.
08902 **OGLE, M. G.** (1973), The effect of group counseling mode upon internally versus externally oriented counselors. *Dissert. Abstr. Internat.*, 33:4184A.
08903 **OGNYANOV, V.**, and **COWEN, L.** (1974), A day hospital program for patients in crisis. *Hosp. & Community Psychiat.*, 25:209.
08904 **O'GORMAN, E. C.** (1978), The treatment of frigidity: a comparative study of group and individual desensitization. *Brit. J. Psychiat.*, (Ashford) 132:580-584.
08905 **OGSTON, D. G.**, and **OGSTON, K. M.** (1970), Counseling students in a hospital school of nursing. *Can. Nurse*, (Ottawa) 66:52-53.
08906 **O'HARA, B.** (1972), Working with small groups: a foreward. *Nursing Times Suppl.*, (London) 68:153.
08907 **O'HEARNE, J. J.** (1976), How and why do transactional-gestalt therapists work as they do? *Internat. J. Group Psychother.*, 26:163-172.
08908 **O'HEARNE, J. J.** (1972), How can we reach patients most effectively? *Internat. J. Group Psychother.*, 22:446-454.
08909 **O'HEARNE, J. J.** (1974), Presidential address: we've come a long way—now what? *Internat. J. Group Psychother.*, 24:151-158.
08910 **O'HEARNE, J. J.** (1962), Some methods of dealing with delusions in group psychotherapy. *Internat. J. Group Psychother.*, 12:35-40.
08911 **O'HEARNE, J. J.**, and **GLAD, D. D.** (1969), The case for interaction. *Internat. J. Group Psychother.*, 19:268-278.
08912 **OHLMEIER, D.** (1973), Psychoanalytic group interviews and short-term group psychotherapy with post-myocardial infarction patients. *Psychiat. Clin.*, (Basel) 6:240-249.
08913 **OHLSEN, M. M.** (1964), *Appraisal of Group Counseling for Underachieving Bright 5th Graders and Their Parents.* Urbana, IL: University of Illinois College of Education.
08914 **OHLSEN, M. M.** (1973), *Counseling Children in Groups: A Forum.* New York: Holt, Rinehart & Winston.
08915 **OHLSEN, M. M.** (1970), *Group Counseling.* New York: Holt, Rinehart and Winston.
08916 **OHLSEN, M. M.** (1973), Readiness for membership in a counseling group. *Educat. Technol.*, 13:58-60.
08917 **OHLSEN, M. M.**, and **OELKE, M. C.** (1962), An evaluation of discussion topics in group counseling. *J. Clin. Psychol.*, 18:317-322.
08918 **OHLSEN, M. M.**, and **PEARSON, R. E.** (1965), A method for the classification of group interaction and its use to explore the influence of individual and role factors in group counselling. *J. Clin. Psychol.*, 21:436-441.
08919 **OHLSEN, M. M.**, and **PROFF, F. C.** (1960), *Response Patterns Associated with Group Counseling.* Urbana, IL: College of Education, University of Illinois.
08920 **O'KEEFE, E. A.** (1973), A comparison of group counseling approaches with behavior-problem boys in an urban elementary school. *Dissert. Abstr. Internat.*, 34:1625A.
08921 **OLBRISH, M. E.**, and **SECHREST, L.** (1979), Educating health psychologists in traditional graduate training programs. *Prof. Psychol.*, 10:589-595.
08922 **OLCH, D.**, and **SNOW, D. L.** (1970), Personality characteristics of sensitivity group volunteers. *Personnel & Guid. J.*, 48:848-850.
08923 Older, younger patients alternate as observers in group therapy (1970). *Roche Report: Front. Hosp. Psychiat.*, 7:5-6, 8.

08924 **O'LEARY, K. D.**, and **BORKOVEC, T. D.** (1978), Conceptual, methodological, and ethical problems of placebo groups in psychotherapy research. *Amer. Psychologist*, 33:821-830.

08925 **OLEO, H. J.**, and **ZANKER, V. G.** (1975), Need for establishing desensitization programs on university campuses. *Psychol. Reports*, 35:885-886.

08926 **OLINICK, S. L.**, and **FRIEND, M. R.** (1945), Indirect group therapy of psychoneurotic soldiers. *Psychiatry*, 8:147-153.

08927 **de OLIVEIRA, L.** (1970), (Social treatment of alcoholic patients in the Olavo Rocha section of the Hospital Odilon Galotti do CPP II [SNDM].) *J. Brasil. Psiquiat.*, (Rio de Janeiro) 19:47-50.

08928 **de OLIVEIRA, W. I.** (1964), (Notes on the termination of group analysis.) *J. Brasil. Psiquiat.*, (Rio de Janeiro) 13:21-52.

08929 **de OLIVEIRA, W. I.** (1963), The psycho-analytic approach to group psychotherapy. *J. Hillside Hosp.*, 12:156-166.

08930 **de OLIVEIRA, W. I.**, **AZULAY, J. D.**, and **CORREA, P. D.** (1966), (Principles and technique of group interpretation.) *J. Brasil. Psiquiat.*, (Rio de Janeiro) 15:145-161.

08931 **de OLIVEIRA, W. I.** (1965), (Basic phantasies and anxieties in the therapeutic group.) *J. Brasil. Psiquiat.*, (Rio de Janeiro) 14:5-22.

08932 **OLIVER, C. M.** (1970), A study of the effects of behavioral group counseling on self-actualization. *Dissert. Abstr. Internat.*, 31:3881A.

08933 **OLIVERSON, L. R.** (1976), Identification of dimensions of leadership and leader behavior and cohesion in encounter groups. *Dissert. Abstr. Internat.*, 37:136A.

08934 **OLLERMAN, T. E.** (1975), The effect of group counseling upon self–actualization, self–disclosure, and the development of interpersonal trust among prison inmates. *Dissert. Abstr. Internat.*, 36:3415A.

08935 **OLMSTED, D. W.** (1955), Assessment of leader adequacy from structured questionnaire responses of voluntary group members. *Dissert. Abstr. Internat.*, 15:1130-1131.

08936 **OLSEN, L. E.** (1971), Ethical standards for working with groups. *Personnel & Guid. J.*, 50:288.

08937 **OLSON, E. H.** (1969), A social rehabilitation program in a county hospital. *Hosp. & Community Psychiat.*, 20:173-174.

08938 **OLSON, J. K.** (1974), The effects of instructions and positive feedback on quality and quantity of patient verbalizations in group psychotherapy. *Dissert. Abstr. Internat.*, 35:4192B.

08939 **OLSON, R. P.**, and **GREENBERG, D. J.** (1972), Effects of contingency–contracting and decision–making groups with chronic mental patients. *J. Consult. & Clin. Psychol.*, 38:376-383.

08940 **OLSON, R. W.** (1962), An experimental program for alcoholic patients. *Ment. Hosp.*, 13:28-29.

08941 **OLSSON, P. A.** (1972), Psychodrama and group therapy with young heroin addicts returning from duty in Vietnam. *Group Psychother., Psychodrama & Sociometry*, 25:141.

08942 **OLSSON, P. A.**, and **MYERS, I. L.** (1972), Nonverbal techniques in an adolescent group. *Internat. J. Group Psychother.*, 22:186-191.

08943 **O'MALLEY, J. E.**, **ANDERSON, W. H.**, and **LAZARE, A.** (1972), Failure of outpatient treatment of drug abuse: i. heroin. *Amer. J. Psychiat.*, 128:865-868.

08944 **OMAN, J. B.** (1972), *Group Counseling in the Church: A Practical Guide for Lay Counselors*. Minneapolis: Augsburg Press.

08945 **ONDARAZA LINARES, J.** (1969), (Some group phenomena in borderline patients: introductory considerations.) *Riv. Psichiat.*, (Rome) 4:381-388.

08946 **O'NEIL, D. G.**, and **HOWELL, R. J.** (1969), Three modes of hierarchy

presentation in systematic desensitization therapy. *Behav. Res. & Ther.*, 7:289-294.
08947 **O'NEIL, M. B.** (1974), The effect of glasser peer group counseling upon academic performance, self satisfaction, personal worth, social interaction and self esteem of low achieving female college freshmen. *Dissert. Abstr. Internat.*, 34:6389A.
08948 **OPLER, M. K.** (1956), Entities and organization in individual and group behavior: a conceptual framework. *Group Psychother., Psychodrama & Sociometry*, 9:290-300.
08949 **OPLER, M. K.** (1957), Group psychotherapy: individual and cultural dynamics in a group process. *Amer. J. Psychiat.*, 114:433-438.
08950 **OPLER, M. K.** (1959), Values in group psychotherapy. *Int. J. Soc. Psychiat.*, (London) 4:296-298.
08951 **ORADEI, D. M.**, and **WAITE, N. S.** (1974), Group psychotherapy with stroke patients during the immediate recovery phase. *Amer. J. Orthopsychiat.*, 44:386-395.
08952 **ORADEI, D. M.**, and **WAITE, N. S.** (1975), Group psychotherapy with stroke patients during the immediate recovery phase. *Nursing Digest*, 3:26-29.
08953 **ORANGE, A. J.** (1955), A note on brief group psychotherapy with psychotic patients. *Internat. J. Group Psychother.*, 5:80-83.
08954 **ORCUTT, T. L.** (1977), Roles and rules: the kinship and territoriality of psychodrama and gestalt therapy. *Group Psychother., Psychodrama & Sociometry*, 30:97-107.
08955 **ORCUTT, T. L.**, and **WILLIAMS, G. A.** (1974), Toward a facilitative ethic in the human potential movement. *Interpersonal Develop.*, 4:77-84.
08956 **O'REAR, J. M.** (1976), Characteristics of volunteers and non-volunteers for personal growth groups and of joiners and nonjoiners in extracurricular activities. *Dissert. Abstr. Internat.*, 36:5156A.
08957 **O'REILLY, E. P.**, and **TUDYMAN, A.** (1948), A psychodramatic measure of administrator success. *Sociatry*, 2:99-102.
08958 **ORGEL, S. Z.** (1955), Clinical symposium on group psychotherapy: a problem of oral aggression experienced in group psychotherapy. *J. Hillside Hosp.*, 4:32-58.
08959 **ORIGENES, M. V. L.** (1972), The use of unstructured group discussions in helping basic psychiatric nursing students gain beginning self-awareness. *ANPHI Papers*, 7:9-20.
08960 **ORLOV, L. G.** (1972), An experimental study of the effects of group counseling with behavior problem children at the elementary school level. *Dissert. Abstr. Internat.*, 32:6766A.
08961 **ORMONT, L. R.** (1969), Acting in and the therapeutic contract in group psychoanalysis. *Internat. J. Group Psychother.*, 19:420-432.
08962 **ORMONT, L. R.** (1970), Acting in and the therapeutic contract in group psychoanalysis. *Ment. Health Digest*, 2:27-30.
08963 **ORMONT, L. R.** (1962), Establishing the analytic contract in a newly formed therapeutic group. *Brit. J. Med. Psychol.*, (London) 35:333-337.
08964 **ORMONT, L. R.** (1968), Group resistance and the therapeutic contract. *Internat. J. Group Psychother.*, 18:147-154.
08965 **ORMONT, L. R.** (1959), The opening session in group psychoanalysis. *Acta Psychother., Psychosomat. Orthopaedagog. Suppl.*, (Basel) 7:288-294.
08966 **ORMONT, L. R.** (1957), The preparation of patients for group psychoanalysis. *Amer. J. Psychother.*, 11:841-848.
08967 **ORMONT, L. R.** (1964), The resolution of resistances by conjoint psychoanalysis. *Psychoanal. Rev.*, 57:425-437.

08968 **ORMONT, L. R.** (1980), Training group therapists through the study of countertransferences. *Group*, 4:17-26.

08969 **ORMONT, L. R.** (1974), The treatment of preoedipal resistances in the group setting. *Psychoanal. Rev.*, 61:429-442.

08970 **ORMONT, L. R.** (1971), The use of the objective countertransference to resolve group resistances. *Group Process*, (London) 3:95-111.

08971 **ORMONT, L. R.,** and **STREAN, H. S.** (1978), *The Practice of Conjoint Therapy: Combining Individual and Group Treatment.* New York: Human Sciences Press.

08972 **ORNER, M.** (1972), Experiential awareness: an integration of behavioral principles in an existential approach to interpersonal relations. *Dissert. Abstr. Internat.*, 32:4961A.

08973 **O'ROURKE, H.,** and **CHAVERS, F.** (1968), The use of groups with unmarried mothers to facilitate casework. *Child Welfare*, 47:17-25.

08974 **OROZCO, E.** (1976), (Review of M. A. Materazzi's *Group Psychotherapy in Psychosis: Psychocinema.) Acta Psiquiat. Psicol. Amer. Latina*, (Buenos Aires) 22:239-240.

08975 **ORTEGA, M. S.** (1969), (Present state of psychodrama.) *Acta Psiq. Psicol. Med.*, (Buenos Aires) 9:107-121.

08976 **ORTEN, J. D.** (1972), Contributions to stroke vocabulary. *Transactional Anal. J.*, 2:104-106.

08077 **ORTEN, J. D.** (1972), Transactional analysis in a public welfare setting. *Pub. Welfare*, 30:48-52.

08978 **ORTMAN, H. L.** (1966), How psychodrama fosters creativity. *Group Psychother., Psychodrama & Sociometry*, 19:201-212.

08979 **ORTMAN, H. L.** (1965), Psychodramatic analysis and treatment of stage-fright. *Group Psychother., Psychodrama & Sociometry*, 18:199-203.

08980 **ORVAL, J.** (1973), An experimental group therapy technique aimed at teaching social skills to children and character disordered adolescents. *Acta Psychiat. Belgica*, (Brussels) 73:620.

08981 **ORVAL, J.** (1973), Trial of group therapy aimed at the assumption of sociocultural behavior patterns in difficult children and adolescents. *Acta Psychiat. Belgica*, (Brussels) 73:620-629.

08982 **ORVIK, J. M.** (1972), Social desirability for the individual, his group, and society. *Multivar. Behav. Res.*, 7:3-32.

08983 **OSBERG, J. W.,** and **BERLINER, A.** (1956), The developmental stages in group psychotherapy with hospitalized narcotic addicts. *Internat. J. Group Psychother.*, 6:436-446.

08984 **OSBORN, S. M.,** and **HARRIS, G. G.** (1975), *Assertive Training for Women.* Springfield, IL: C. C. Thomas.

08985 **OSBORNE, D.,** and **SWENSON, W. M.** (1972), Counseling readiness and changes in self-evaluation during intensive group psychotherapy. *Psychol. Reports*, 31:646.

08986 **OSBORNE, D., SWENSON, W. M.,** and **HARDMAN, J. B.** (1972), Counseling readiness and changes in perception of spouse during intensive group therapy. *Psychol. Reports*, 31:208-210.

08987 **O'SHEA, C.** (1975), "Two gray cats learn how it is" in a group of black teenagers. In: *Adolescents Grow in Groups*, ed. I. Berkovitz. New York: Brunner/Mazel.

08988 **O'SHEA, J. J.** (1967), A six-year experience with nontraditional methods in a child clinic setting. *Amer. J. Orthopsychiat.*, 37:56-63.

08989 **OSHERSON, S.** (1968), Self-acceptance through psychodrama. *Group Psychother., Psychodrama & Sociometry*, 21:12-19.

08990 **OSLIN, Y. D.** (1974), An assessment of the differential effects of race on small decision-making groups. *Dissert. Abstr. Internat.*, 34:5660B.

08991 **OSMAN, M. P.,** and **HOBBS, D. B.** (1966), Considerations of group therapy for recently released offenders. *Correct. Psychiat. & Soc. Ther.*, 12:363-370.

08992 **OSNES, R. E.** (1972), Santa Claus scores again. *Transactional Anal. J.*, 2:29.

08993 **OSORIO, L. C.** (1970), Milieu therapy for child psychosis. *Amer. J. Orthopsychiat.*, 40:121-129.

08994 **OSORIO, L. C.** (1970), Therapeutic agents in an impatient community for children. *Acta Paedopsychiat.*, (Basel) 37:56-61.

08995 **OSSENDORF, K.** (1953), Das familiare milieu bei der gruppenspieltherapie. (The familiar setting in group play therapy.) *Heilpädagog. Werkbl.*, 22:51-54.

08996 **OSSORIO, A. G.**, and **FINE, L.** (1960), Psychodrama as a catalyst for social change in a mental hospital. *Prog. Psychother.*, 5:122-131.

08997 **OSSORIO, A. G.**, and **FINE, L.** (1969/1970), (Psychodrama in a psychiatric hospital.) *Bull. Psychol.*, (Paris) 23:934-939.

08998 **OSTBY, C. H.** (1968), Conjoint group therapy with prisoners and their families. *Fam. Process.*, 7:184-201.

08999 **OSTERBERG, E.** (1968), Gruppendynamiska aspekter pa personalarbete. (Aspect of group dynamics in personality work.) *Nordisk Psykol.*, (Copenhagen) 20:389-400.

09000 **O'SULLIVAN, T.** (1980), The effect of short-term behavioral group counseling on academic achievement and behavior with adolescent boys in a residential treatment program. *Dissert. Abstr. Internat.*, 41:109A. (University Microfilms No. 8014090.)

09001 **OTAKE, T.**, **UEYAMA, Y.**, **SUZUKI, A.**, **HARADA, A.**, and **AMEMORI, T.** (1965), (The observation of "early infantile autism" through group therapy.) *Japanese J. Child Psychol.*, (Tokyo) 6:90-96.

09002 **OTAOLA, J. R.** (1967), (Actual state of group therapy.) *Actas Luso-Espanolas Neurol. Psiquiat.*, (Barcelona) 26:46-51.

09003 **OTT, J.**, and **GEYER, M.** (1972), (Report on a self–actualization group after 16 months.) *Psychiat., Neurol. & Med. Psychol.*, (Leipzig) 24:210-215.

09004 **OTT, J.**, **GEYER, M.**, and **SCHNEEMANN, K.** (1972), (Multidimensional clinical psychotherapy of a group of children and adolescents after attempted suicide.) *Psychiat., Neuro. & Med. Psychol.*, (Leipzig) 24:104-110.

09005 **OTTAWAY, A. K. C.** (1966), *Learning Through Group Experience*. London: Routledge & K. Paul.

09006 **OTTAWAY, A. K. C.** (1966), *Learning Through Group Experience*. London: Routledge & K. Paul.

09007 **OTTENBERG, D. J.** (1975), Drug spotlight: help for young alcoholics who want help—part 2. *Patient Care*, 9:106-108.

09008 **OTTENBERG, D. J.**, and **ROSEN, A.** (1971), Merging the treatment of drug addicts into an existing program for alcoholics. *Quart. J. Studies Alcohol*, 32:94-103.

09009 **OTTESON, J. P.** (1979), Curative caring: the use of buddy groups with chronic schizophrenics. *J. Consult. & Clin. Psychol.*, 4:649.

09010 **OTTO, H. A.** (1974), *Fantasy Encounter Games*. Scranton: Barnes & Noble.

09011 **OTTO, H. A.** (1973), *Group Methods to Actualize Human Potential: A Handbook*, 3d ed. Beverly Hills, CA: Holistic Press.

09012 **OTTO, H. A.** (1964), Personal and family strength research and spontaneity training. *Group Psychother., Psychodrama & Sociometry*, 17:143-148.

09013 **OTTO, H. A.** (1962), Spontaneity training with teachers. *Group Psychother., Psychodrama & Sociometry*, 15:74-79.

09014 **OTTO, S. T.**, and **MAHOLICK, L. T.** (1972), Sensitivity training in a psychotherapeutic milieu. *Hosp. & Community Psychiat.*, 23:170-173.

09015 **OULES, J., SAUCET, D.**, and **LABORDE, P.** (1953), Une experience de psychotherapie de groupe chez des alcooliques internes. (Group psychotherapy with institutionalized alcoholics.) *Annales Medico-Psychol.*, (Paris) 111:72-74.

09016 **OURTH, L.**, and **LANDFIELD, A. W.** (1965), Interpersonal meaningfulness and nature of termination in psychotherapy. *J. Couns. Psychol.*, 12:366-371.

09017 **OURY, J.**, and **ZENNER, W.** (1959), Analysis of the immediate environment of the patient in connection with institutional therapy. *Acta Psychother., Psychosomat. Orthopaedagog. Suppl.*, (Basel) 7:295-302.

09018 Outcome of group therapy for sex offenders to be studied (1969), *Roche Report: Front. Hosp. Psychiat.*, 6:1-11.

09019 Outpatient group therapy found feasible for schizophrenics (1967). *Roche Report: Front. Hosp. Psychiat.*, 4:8.

09020 Overcoming resistances to group therapy: supervised leaderless groups (1970). *Roche Report: Front. Hosp. Psychiat.*, 7:5-6.

09021 **OVERHOLSER, W.**, and **ENNEIS, J. M.** (1959), Twenty years of psychodrama at Saint Elizabeths Hospital. *Group Psychother., Psychodrama & Sociometry*, 12:283-292.

09022 **OVERTON, A.** (1968), The issue of integration of casework and group work. *Soc. Work Educat. Reporter*, 16:25-27, 47.

09023 **OWEN, C.**, and **NEWMAN, N.** (1965), Utilizing films as a therapeutic agent in group interaction. *Amer. J. Occupat. Ther.*, 19:205-207.

09024 **OWEN, C. M.** (1970), Effects of activity oriented group counseling with selected outpatients. *Dissert. Abstr. Internat.*, 31:2743-2744A.

09025 **OWENS, J. M.** (1973), Personal orientation inventory real-ideal response set measures of self–actualization and congruency in an encounter and marathon group. *Dissert. Abstr. Internat.*, 33:5498A.

09026 **OWEN, S.**, and **BOCHNER, S.** (1968), Social factors in the hospital treatment of leprosy. *Med. J. Austral.*, (Glebe) 2:351-353.

09027 **OWEN, S. M.** (1972), Is group counseling neglected? *J. Rehab.*, 38:12-15.

09028 **OXFORD, H. O.** (1980), The effect of a classroom group counseling component on classroom behavior and self-concept of elementary school students. *Dissert. Abstr. Internat.*, 40:5310A. (University Microfilms No. 8008063.)

09029 **OXLEY, G. B.** (1977), A modified form of residential treatment. *Soc. Work*, 22:493-498.

09030 **ÖZBEK, G.** (1975), The use of hypnosis and deprivation for the control of cigarette smoking in an extended group session. *Dissert. Abstr. Internat.*, 36:2482B.

09031 **OZERTZOVSKY, D. S.** (1927), Treatment of the neuroses by the method of collective therapy. *Zh. Neuropat. & Psikiat. Korsakov*, (Moscow) 20:587-594.

09032 **OZSVATH, K.** (1978), (Behavior analyzing: group therapy in the rehabilitation of neurotic executives.) *Orvosi Hetilap,* (Budapest) 119:439-444.

P

09033 **PADBERG, J.** (1972), Nursing and forensic psychiatry. *Perspect. Psychiat. Care*, 10:163-167.

09034 **PADEN, R. C., HIMELSTEIN, H. C.,** and **PAUL, G. L.** (1974), Videotape versus verbal feedback in the modification of meal behavior of chronic mental patients. *J. Consult. & Clin. Psychol.*, 42:623-628.

09035 **PADOVANI, G.** (1971), (Basic principles of modern psychiatric ergotherapy.) *Riv. Sper. Freniatria*, (Emilia) 95:423-428.

09036 **PADOVANI, G., CECCARELLI, G.,** and **DAMONTE, C.** (1965), Il ruolo della psicoterapia di gruppo in ospedale psichiatrico. (The role of group psychotherapy in a psychiatric hospital.) *Neuropsichiatria*, (Genoa) 21:679-691.

09037 **PAGE, C. W.** (1953), A comparative study of three types of group psychotherapy formulations. Unpublished doctoral dissertation, Cornell University.

09038 **PAGE, H. A.,** and **HENDRICK, C.** (1972), The encounter movement. *Acta Symbol.*, 3:6-11.

09039 **PAGE, R. C.** (1979), Developmental stages of unstructured counseling groups with prisoners. *Small Group Behav.*, 10:271-283.

09040 **PAGE, R. C.** (1980), Marathon groups: counseling the imprisoned drug abuser. *Internat. J. Addict.*, 15:765-770.

09041 **PAGE, R. C.** (1978), The social learning process of severely disabled group counseling participants. *Psychosocial Rehab. J.*, 2:28-35.

09042 **PAGE, R. C.,** and **KUBIAK, L.** (1978), Marathon groups: facilitating the personal growth of imprisoned, black female heroin abusers. *Small Group Behav.*, 9:409-416.

09043 **PAGE, R. C.,** and **MANNION, J.** (1980), Marathon group therapy with former drug users. *J. Employment Couns.*, 17:307-313.

09044 **PAGE, R. C., MANNION, J.,** and **WATTENBARGER, W.** (1980), Marathon group counseling: A study with imprisoned male former drug users. *Small Group Behav.*, 11:399-410.

09045 **PAGE, S.,** and **COPELAND, E. V.** (1972), Reinforcement of conservation "operants" in psychiatric patients. *Can. J. Behav. Science*, (Montreal) 4:348-357.

09046 **PAGES, M.** (1969/1970), (The languages of the feelings.) *Bull. de Psychol.*, 23:779-783.

09047 **PAGÈS, M.** (1975), *La Vie Affective des Groupes: Esquisse d'Une Théorie de la Relation Humanine. (The Affective Life of Groups: Toward a Theory of Human Relations.)* Paris: Dunod.

09048 **PAGES, M.** (1965), L'Orientation non-directive et ses applications en psychologie sociale. (Non-directive orientation and its application in social psychology.) *Bull. de Psychol.*, (Paris) 19:345-350.

09049 **PAGÈS, M.** (1971), (Nondirective orientation in social psychology.) *Gruppendynamik*, (Stuttgart) 2:153-160.

09050 **PAHL, J.** (1979), The clinic as an interpersonal field of dynamic psychiatric treatment of psychosomatic diseases. *Psychother. & Psychosomat.*, (Basel) 31:190.

09051 **PAINTER, G.** (1970), Remediation of maladaptive behavior and psycholin deficits in a group sensory-motor activity program. *Ment. Retard.*, 7:133.

09052 **PAISLEY, J. D.** (1971), Verbal interaction and member acceptance of associates and nonassociates in encounter groups. *Dissert. Abstr. Internat.*, 32:1757A.

09053 **PAKESCH, E.** (1974), Position of the depressive patient in the therapeutic group. In: *Zur Systematik, Provokation und Therapie depressiver Psychosen*, ed. W. Walcher. Vienna: Hollinke.

09054 **PAKESCH, E. F.** (1950), (Contribution to group therapy.) *Comptes Rendus*, Premier Congres Mondial de Psychiatrie, 269-273.

09055 **PALAU, J., LEITNER, L., DRASGOW, F.,** and **DRASGOW, J.** (1974), Further improvement following therapy. *Group Psychother., Psychodrama & Sociometry*, 27:42-47.

09056 **PALEY, A.** (1952), Hypnotherapy in the treatment of alcoholism. *Bull. Menninger Clinic*, 16:14-19.

09057 **PALEY, A. M.** (1974), Dance therapy: an overview. *Amer. J. Psychoanal.*, 34:81-83.

09058 **PALME, G.** (1974), (Psychologic–pedagogical treatment of overweight.) *Svenska Lakartidningen*, (Stockholm) 71:4960-4962.

09059 **PALMER, A. J.** (1974), An experimental evaluation of the therapist role, peer interactions, and self–motivation in the treatment of depressed female psychiatric patients. *Dissert. Abstr. Internat.*, 34:3886.

09060 **PALMER, D. S.** (1966), Group work on probation. *Probation*, (Surrey) 12:18-20.

09061 **PALMER, J. D.** (1976), Group psychotherapy in a state mental hospital: who needs it? *J. Psychiat. Nursing*, 14:19-22.

09062 **PALMO, A. J.** (1971), The effect of group counseling and parent–teacher consultations on the classroom behavior of elementary school children. *Dissert. Abstr. Internat.*, 32:1863-1864A.

09063 **PALMO, A. J.,** and **KUZNIAR, J.** (1972), Modification of behavior through group counseling and consultation. *Elem. School Guid. & Couns.*, 6:258-262.

09064 **PANKRATZ, L. D.,** and **BUCHAN, G.** (1965), Exploring psychodramatic techniques with defective delinquents. *Group Psychother., Psychodrama & Sociometry*, 18:136-141.

09065 Panel discussion (1968), the nurse as a therapist. *Perspect. Psychiat. Care*, 6:273-289.

09066 **PANETH, G.** (1978), (Review of C. Lutz's *Group-Therapy With Children.*) *Analyt. Psychol.*, (Basel) 9:313-315.

09067 **PANKOWSKI, M. L.** (1972), The relationship between group process training and group problem solving. *Dissert. Abstr. Internat.*, 2683A.

09068 **PANKOWSKI, M. L.** (1973), The relationship between group process and group problem-solving. *Adult Educat.*, 24:20-42.

09069 **PANKRATZ, L. D.** (1971), Extended doubling and mirroring 'in situ' in the mental hospital. *Group Psychother., Psychodrama & Sociometry*, 24:150-151.

09070 **PANKRATZ, L. D.,** and **BUCHAN, L. G.** (1966), Techniques of "warm-up" in psychodrama with the retarded. *Mental Retard.*, 4:12-15.

09071 **PANNABEKER, W. J.** (1975), An evaluation of group vocational counseling with hospitalized psychiatric patients. *Dissert. Abstr. Internat.*, 36:1928B.

09072 **PANNER, R.,** and **NERLOVE, E. A.** (1977), Fostering understanding between adolescents and adoptive parents through group experiences. *Child Welfare*, 56:532-545.

09073 **PANYARD, C. M.,** and **WOLF, K. L.** (1979), Attitudinal differences affecting participation in group counseling in out-patient drug treatment centers. *Internat. J. Addict.*, 14:987-992.

09074 **PAPAGEORGIOU, M. G.** (1969), Forms of psychotherapy in use in ancient Greece and among the population of modern Greece. *Psychother. & Psychosomat.*, (Basel) 17:114-118.

09075 **PAPANEK, E.** (1945), Treatment by group work. *Amer. J. Orthopsychiat.*, 15:223-229.
09076 **PAPANEK, H.** (1970), Adler's psychology and group psychotherapy. *Amer. J. Psychiat.*, 127:783-786.
09077 **PAPANEK, H.** (1964), Bridging dichotomies through group psychotherapy. *J. Individ. Psychol.*, 20:38-47.
09078 **PAPANEK, H.** (1958), Change of ethical values in group psychotherapy. *Internat. J. Group Psychother.*, 8:435-444.
09079 **PAPANEK, H.** (1954), Combined group and individual therapy in private practice. *Amer. J. Psychother.*, 8:679-686.
09080 **PAPANEK, H.** (1956), Combined group and individual therapy in the light of Adlerian psychology. *Internat. J. Group Psychother.*, 6:136-146.
09081 **PAPANEK, H.** (1962), Expression of hostility: its value in the psychotherapy group. *J. Individ. Psychol.*, 18:62-67.
09082 **PAPANEK, H.** (1970), Group psychotherapy interminable. *Internat. J. Group Psychother.*, 20:219-223.
09083 **PAPANEK, H.** (1965), Group psychotherapy with married couples. *Curr. Psychiat. Ther.*, 5:157-163.
09084 **PAPANEK, H.** (1970), Group therapy with married couples. *Sandoz Psychiat. Spectator*, 6:8-9.
09085 **PAPANEK, H.** (1962), The hysterical personality in combined individual and group psychotherapy: a case report. *Internat. J. Group Psychother.*, 12:89-98.
09086 **PAPANEK, H.** (1960), Projective test evaluation of changes effected by group psychotherapy. *Internat. J. Group Psychother.*, 10:446-455.
09087 **PAPANEK, H.** (1969), Therapeutic and antitherapeutic factors in group relations. *Amer. J. Psychother.*, 23:396-404.
09088 **PAPANEK, H.** (1958), Training in group psychotherapy: a symposium. (iii) satisfactions and frustrations of a supervisor of group psychotherapists. *Amer. J. Psychother.*, 12:500-503.
09089 **PAPANTONES, M.** (1978), A transactional analysis group program designed to increase the self-actualization of adolescent males in a resident camp setting as measured by the personal orientation inventory. *Dissert. Abstr. Internat.*, 38:6542A.
09090 **PAPELL, C.** (1972), Sensitivity training: relevance for social work education. *J. Educat. Soc. Work*, 8:42-55.
09091 **PAPENEK, G. O.** (1967), The researcher's dilemma: wresting comparable units from a unitary process. *Internat. J. Group Psychother.*, 4:350-352.
09092 **PAPPACHRISTON, J.** (1974), The effectiveness of modeling a socially approved and a socially disapproved behavior with a group of delinquent and non-delinquent boys. *Dissert. Abstr. Internat.*, 35:1059B.
09093 **PARAD, H. J.**, and **YOUNG, R. A.** (1953), Recording practices in a therapeutic camp. *Amer. J. Orthopsychiat.*, 23:358-368.
09094 **PARAD, L. G.** (1968), Planned short-term treatment: a study of 1656 family service and child guidance cases. *Dissert. Abstr. Internat.*, 29:3672.
09095 **PARADIS, A. P.** (1973), Brief out–patient group psychotherapy with older patients in the treatment of age-related problems. *Dissert. Abstr. Internat.*, 34:2947B.
09096 **PARADISE, R.** (1968), The factor of timing in the addition of new members to established groups. *Child Welfare*, 47:524-529, 553.
09097 **PAREEK, U.**, and **MOULIK, T. K.** (1963), Sociometric study of a north Indian village. *Internat. J. Sociometry & Sociatry*, 3:6-16.
09098 **PARIENTE, —.** (1963), (The treatment of chronic alcoholism and the pitfalls of statistics.) *Annales Medico-Psychol.*, (Paris) 121:377-396.
09099 **PARISI, E. M.** (1972), The t-group and accurate self-perception: a time trend and process analysis. *Dissert. Abstr. Internat.*, 33:4950A.

09100 **PARISI, J. A.** (1977), An evaluation of an anticipatory socialization interview to prepare drug abusers for group psychotherapy. *Dissert. Abstr. Internat.*, 38:3900.

09101 **PARKER, B.** (1958), *Psychiatric Consultation for Nonpsychiatric Professional Workers: A Concept of Group Consultation Developed from a Training Program for Nurses.* Washington, D.C.: Dept. Health, Education, and Welfare.

09102 **PARKER, C. C.** (1972), The effects of the group process experience on rigidity as a personality parable. *Dissert. Abstr. Internat.*, 32:4962A.

09103 **PARKER, C. C.**, and **VAUGHN, E. H.** (1975), The effects of group counseling on rigidity. *Small Group Behav.*, 6:402-414.

09104 **PARKER, C. L.** (1975), A desensitization group for adult community leaders. *Personnel & Guid. J.*, 54:48-49.

09105 **PARKER, C. P., BUNCH, S.**, and **HAGBERG, R.** (1974), Group vocational guidance with college students. *Vocat. Guid. Quart.*, 23:168-172.

09106 **PARKER, G. M.** (1974), Human relations training: improving police/community relations. *Training & Develop. J.*, 28:7-12.

09107 **PARKER, R. S.** (1975), Adaptation as an integrating principle in psychotherapy. *J. Clin. Issues Psychol.*, 6:11-13.

09109 **PARKER, R. S.** (1972), Can group therapy be harmful to the individual? *J. Clin. Issues Psychol.*, 3:22-24.

09110 **PARKER, R. S.** (1977), *Effective Decisions and Emotional Fulfillment.* Chicago: Nelson-Hall, Chap. 12.

09111 **PARKER, R. S.** (1973), *Emotional Common Sense.* New York: Harper and Row.

09112 **PARKER, R. S.** (1972), *The Emotional Stress of War, Violence and Peace.* Proceed., Symposium on Nov. 14-15, 1968. Pittsburgh: Stanwix House.

09113 **PARKER, R. S.** (1976), Ethical and professional considerations concerning high risk groups. *J. Clin. Issues Psychol.*, 7:4-19.

09114 **PARKER, R. S.** (1978), *Living Single Successfully.* New York: Franklin Watts.

09115 **PARKER, R. S.** (1965), Patient variability as a factor in group activities on a maximum security ward. *Psychiat. Quart.*, 39:264-277.

09116 **PARKER, R. S.** (1963), The perceivers' identification of the figure in their own Rorschach human movement (M). *J. Project. Tech., & Personality Assessment*, 27:214-219.

09117 **PARKER, R. S.** (1969), Poetry: a therapeutic art in the resolution of psychotherapeutic resistance. In: *Poetry Therapy*, ed. J. Leedy. Philadelphia: Lippincott, pp. 155-170.

09118 **PARKER, R. S.** (1975), Review of G. Claridge's *Drugs and Human Behavior. J. Personality Assessment*, 30:643-644.

09119 **PARKER, R. S.** (1974), Review of H. V. Dicks's *Licensed Mass Murder: A Socio-Psychological Study of Some S. S. Killers. J. Personality Assessment*, 38:283-285.

09120 **PARKER, R. S.** (1975), Review of J. Bowlby's *Attachment and Loss. I Separation, Anxiety and Anger. J. Personality Assessment*, 39:180-181.

09121 **PARKER, R. S.** (1977), Review of J. J. Piotrofesa's and H. Splete's *Career Development: Theory and Research. J. Personality Assessment*, 41:442-443.

09122 **PARKER, R. S.** (1977), Review of L. A. Hart's *How the Brain Works. J. Personality Assessment*, 41:103-104.

09123 **PARKER, R. S.** (1978), Review of L. Ehrman's and P. A. Parsons' *The Genetics of Behavior. J. Personality Assessment*, 2:188-189.

09124 **PARKER, R. S.** (1979), Review of Shingleton's *College to Career: Finding Yourself in the Job Market. J. Personality Assessment.*

09125 **PARKER, R. S.** (1975), Review of T. Dobzhansky's *Genetic Diversity and Human Equality. J. Personality Assessment*, 39:180-181.

09126 **PARKER, R. S.** (1978), Review of W. W. Burke's *Current Issues and Strategies in Organization Development. J. Personality Assessment.*

09127 **PARKER, R. S.** (1972), Some personal qualities enhancing group therapist effectiveness. *J. Clin. Issues Psychol.*, 4:25-28.

09128 **PARKER, R. S.** (1967), Therapists' activity in the resolution of resistance in outpatient group psychotherapy. *Psychiat. Quart. Suppl.*, 41:86-98.

09129 **PARKER, R. S.** (1967), The varieties of resistance in group psychotherapy considered from the viewpoint of adaptation. *Psychiat. Quart.*, 41:525-535.

09130 **PARKER, R. S.**, and **DAVIDSON, N. L.** (1963), A comparison of students of nursing and hospitalized patients on scores derived from an intelligence test (WAIS). *Psychiat. Quart. Suppl.*, 37:297-306.

09131 **PARKER, R. S.**, and **PIOTROWSKI, Z. A.** (1968), The significance of varieties of actors of the Rorschach human movement response (M). *J. Project. Tech. & Personality Assessment*, 32:32-44.

09132 **PARKS, J. C.** (1971), An interaction process analysis of a modified marathon with voluntary institutionalized alcoholics. *Dissert. Abstr. Internat.*, 31:3883.

09133 **PARKS, J. C.**, and **ANTENEN, W. W.** (1970), A modified marathon with voluntarily institutionalized alcoholics: an interaction process analysis. *Compar. Group Stud.*, 1:357-371.

09134 **PARKS, J. H.** (1967), Group psychotherapy with married couples: new variations in technique. *Pastoral Couns.*, 3:4-11.

09135 **PARLEE, M. B.** (1979), Who needs groups (besides social psychologists)? *Psychol. Today*, 13:95-107.

09136 **PARLOFF, M. B.** (1953), An analysis of therapeutic relationships in a group therapy setting. Unpublished doctoral dissertation, Western Reserve University.

09137 **PARLOFF, M. B.** (1970), Assessing the effects of headshrinking and mind-expanding. *Internat. J. Group Psychother.*, 20:15-24.

09138 **PARLOFF, M. B.** (1968), Discussion of F. H. Stoller's "Accelerated interaction." *Internat. J. Group Psychother.*, 18:239-244.

09139 **PARLOFF, M. B.** (1976), Discussion: the narcissism of small differences—and some big ones. *Internat. J. Group Psychother.*, 26:311-321.

09140 **PARLOFF, M. B.** (1956), Factors affecting quality of therapeutic relationships. *J. Abnorm. & Soc. Psychol.*, 52:5-10.

09141 **PARLOFF, M. B.** (1963), Group dynamics and group psychotherapy: the state of the union. *Internat. J. Group Psychother.*, 13:393-398.

09142 **PARLOFF, M. B.** (1970), Group therapy and the small-group field: an encounter. *Internat. J. Group Psychother.*, 20:267-304.

09143 **PARLOFF, M. B.** (1967), Group therapy evaluation: much to do about nothing. *Internat. J. Group Psychother.*, 4:352-358.

09144 **PARLOFF, M. B.** (1960), The impact of ward milieu philosophies on nursing-role concepts. *Psychiatry*, 23:141-151.

09145 **PARLOFF, M. B.** (1971), Sheltered workshops for the alienated. *Internat. J. Psychiat.*, 9:197-204.

09146 **PARLOFF, M. B.** (1961), Therapist-patient relationships and outcome of psychotherapy. *J. Consult. & Clin. Psychol.*, 25:29-38.

09147 **PARLOFF, M. B.** (1967), A view from the incompleted bridge: group process and outcome. *Internat. J. Group Psychother.*, 17:236-242.

09148 **PARLOFF, M. B.**, and **DIES, R. R.** (1977), Group psychotherapy outcome research 1966-1975. *Internat. J. Group Psychother.*, 27:281-319.

09149 **PARLOFF, M. B.**, and **DIES, R. R.** (1978), Group therapy outcome instrument: guidelines for conducting research. *Small Group Behav.*, 9:243-285.

09150 **PARLOFF, M. B.**, and **HANDLON, J. H.** (1964), The influence of criticalness on creative problem solving in dyads. *Psychiatry*, 27:17-27.

09151 **PARRISH, J. M.** (1961), Effects of external control and ambiguous information on generalized expectancy changes for self and others. Ph.D. thesis, Indiana University.

09152 **PARRISH, M. M.** (1958), The development of a psychodrama program in a state hospital setting. *Group Psychother., Psychodrama & Sociometry*, 11:63-68.

09153 **PARRISH, M. M.** (1959), The effect of short term psychodrama on chronic schizophrenic patients. *Group Psychother., Psychodrama & Sociometry*, 12:15-26.

09154 **PARRISH, M. M.** (1961), Group techniques with teenage emotionally disturbed girls. *Group Psychother., Psychodrama & Sociometry*, 14:20-25.

09155 **PARRISH, M. M.** (1953), Psychodrama: description of application and review of techniques. *Group Psychother., Psychodrama & Sociometry*, 6:63-89.

09156 **PARRISH, M. M.**, and **MITCHELL, J.** (1952), Psychodrama in a state hospital. *Ment. Hygiene*, 36:33-43.

09157 **PARRISH, M. M.**, and **MITCHELL, J.** (1951), Psychodrama in Pontiac State Hospital. *Group Psychother., Psychodrama & Sociometry*, 4:80-84.

09158 **PARRISH, V.**, and **HESTER, P.** (1980), Controlling behavioral techniques in an early intervention program. *Community Ment. Health J.*, 16:169.

09159 **PARSELL, S.**, and **TAGLIARENI, E. M.** (1974), Cancer patients help each other. *Amer. J. Nursing*, 74:650-651.

09160 **PARSLOE, P.** (1969), Some thoughts on social group work. *Brit. J. Psychiat. Soc. Work*, 10:3-11.

09161 **PARSLOE, P.** (1967), Summing up of the study course: thinking about the future of child guidance. *Brit. J. Psychiat. Soc. Work*, 9:90-96.

09162 **PARSONS, E.** (1954), Group psychotherapy in private practice. *Diseases Nerv. System*, 15:9-11.

09163 **PARSONS, E.** (1955), Some problems encountered in the private practice of group therapy. *Internat. J. Group Psychother.*, 5:422-432.

09164 **PARSONS, J.**, and **WARREN, D. H.** (1974), How mature is your learning group? *Contin. Educat.*, 7:64-65.

09165 **PARSONS, J. A.** (1980), Effects of therapist modeling of feedback delivery on member feedback and self-concept in group therapy with students. *Dissert. Abstr. Internat.*, 41:1122B. (University Microfilms No. 8020360.)

09166 **PARSONS, J. B.** (1977), A descriptive study of intermediate stage terminally ill cancer patients at home. *Nursing Digest*, 5:1-26.

09167 **PASCAL, G. R., COTTRELL, T. B.**, and **BAUGH, J. R.** (1967), A methodological note on the use of video tape in group psychotherapy with juvenile delinquents. *Internat. J. Group Psychother.*, 17:248-251.

09168 **PASCHAL, J. A.** (1977), The effects of activity group counseling and tutoring on changing attitudes, reading ability, and grade point averages of academically deficient veteran students. *Dissert. Abstr. Internat.*, 38:2467A.

09169 **PASCALE, J. R.** (1970), Increasing classroom participation of college students: a comparison of group systematic desensitization with group discussion-counseling and group reading. *Dissert. Abstr. Internat.*, 30:3331A.

09170 **PASCOE, H. R.** (1963), Group therapy with student nurses. *Can. Psychiat. Assn. J.*, (Ottawa) 8:205-210.

09171 **PASEWARK, R. A.** (1969), Patients' perception of clergy as group psychotherapist. *Pastoral Couns.*, 7:18-19.

09172 **PASEWARK, R. A., HALL, W. T., and GRICE, J. E.** (1970), The mental hospital patient's perception of the aide as a psychotherapist. *J. Psychiat. Nursing*, 8:28-29.
09173 **PASEWARK, R. A., HALL, W. T., and GRICE, J. E.** (1969), Patients' perception of clergy as group psychotherapists. *Pastoral Couns.*, 7:18-19.
09174 **PASLONE, C. J.** (1971), A large-scale group therapy program in a state hospital. *Hosp. & Community Psychiat.*, 22:33-35.
09175 **PASNAU, R. D., MEYER, M., DAVIS, L. J., LLOYD, R., and KLINE, G.** (1976), Coordinated group psychotherapy of children and parents. *Internat. J. Group Psychother.*, 26:89-103.
09176 **PASNAU, R. O., WILLIAMS, L., and TALLMAN, F. F.** (1971), Small activity groups in the school: report of a twelve year research project in community psychiatry. *Community Ment. Health J.*, 7:303-311.
09177 **PASRICHA, P.** (1953), Play therapy. *J. Ed. Psychol.*, 11:20-28.
09178 **PASSONS, W. R.** (1972), Gestalt therapy interventions for group counseling. *Personnel & Guid. J.*, 51:183-189.
09179 **PASSONS, W. R., and GARRETT, L. D.** (1974), An in-service workshop on group counseling. *Personnel & Guid. J.*, 52:482-486.
09180 **PASTER, S.** (1945), Group psychotherapy and combat neuroses. *Amer. J. Orthopsychiat.*, 15:472-482.
09181 **PASTER, S.** (1944), Group psychotherapy in an army general hospital. *Ment. Hosp.*, 28:529-536.
09182 **PASTUSHAK, R. J.** (1978), The effects of videotaped pretherapy training on interpersonal openness, self-disclosure, and group psychotherapy outcome measures. *Dissert. Abstr. Internat.*, 39:993B. (University Microfilms No. 7812232.)
09183 **PATALANO, F.** (1976), Psychodiagnostic testing in a therapeutic community for drug abusers. *Psychol. Reports*, 39:1279-1285.
09184 **PATALANO, F. P.** (1976), Personality differences in young multiple drug abusers who enter a drug-free therapeutic community. *Dissert. Abstr. Internat.*, 36:4174.
09185 **PATE, J. E.** (1966), Psychodrama for disturbed children. *Hosp. & Community Psychiat.*, 17:96-97.
09186 **PATELLA, V.** (1975), (Archetypic and mythological images detectable in respiratory autogenic training relaxation.) *Minerva Med.*, (Turin) 66:273-275.
09187 **PATERSON, E. S.** (1978), Comparison of group marital treatments: behavior modification, communication, and combined communication and behavior modification. *Dissert. Abstr. Internat.*, 38:5037B. (University Microfilms No. 7802840.)
09188 **PATERSON, J. G.** (1966), Group supervision: a process and philosophy. *Community Ment. Health*, 2:315-318.
09189 **PATTEN, B. B.** (1968), Group counseling with teachers and teacher-student perceptions of behavior. *Dissert. Abstr. Internat.*, 29:1455-1456.
09190 **PATTEN, T. H., JR., and DOREY, L. E.** (1972), An equal employment opportunity. *Training & Develop. J.*, 26:42-55.
09191 **PATTERSON, C. H.** (1969), What is counseling psychology? *J. Couns. Psychol.*, 16:23-29.
09192 **PATTERSON, D. L., and SMIT, S. J.** (1974), Communication bias in Black-White groups. *J. Psychol.*, 88:9-25.
09193 **PATTERSON, G.** (1973), A historical review and classification system of the new group therapies. *Western Psychol.*, 4:79.
09194 **PATTERSON, G., SCHWARTZ, R., and VAN DER WART, E.** (1956), The integration of group and individual therapy. *Amer. J. Orthopsychiat.*, 26:618-629.
09195 **PATTERSON, G. R.** (1974), Interventions for boys with conduct problems:

multiple settings, treatments, and criteria. *J. Consult. & Clin. Psychol.*, 42:471-481.

09196 **PATTERSON, M. L.**, and **SCHAEFFER, R. E.** (1977), Effects of size and sex composition on interaction, distance, participation, and satisfaction in small groups. *Small Group Behav.*, 8:433-442.

09197 **PATTERSON, R. M.** (1950), Psychiatric treatment of institutionalized delinquent adolescent girls. *Diseases Nerv. System*, 11:227-232.

09198 **PATTISON, E.** (1973), Social system psychotherapy. *Amer. J. Psychother.*, 27:396-409.

09199 **PATTISON, E.**, and **RHODES, R. J.** (1974), Clinical prediction with the NOSIE-30 scale. *J. Clin. Psychol.*, 30:200-201.

09200 **PATTISON, E., RHODES, R. J.**, and **DUDLEY, D. L.** (1971), Response to group treatment in patients with severe chronic lung disease. *Internat. J. Group Psychother.*, 2:214-225.

09201 **PATTISON, E. M.** (1966), Evaluation of group psychotherapy. *Curr. Psychiat. Ther.*, 6:211-218.

09202 **PATTISON, E. M.** (1967), Evaluation studies of group psychotherapy. *Internat. J. Group Psychother.*, 4:333-343.

09203 **PATTISON, E. M.** (1970), Group psychotherapy and group methods in community mental health programs. *Internat. J. Group Psychother.*, 20:516-539.

09204 **PATTISON, E. M.** (1974), The place of new professionals in the practice of group skills: an overview. *Internat. J. Group Psychother.*, 24:409.

09205 **PATTISON, E. M.** (1974), Training new mental health personnel in group methods: iv. the place of new professionals in the practice of group skills—an overview. *Internat. J. Group Psychother.*, 24:409-416.

09206 **PATTISON, E. M., BRISSENDEN, A.**, and **WOHL, T.** (1967), Assessing specific effects of inpatient group psychotherapy. *Internat. J. Group Psychother.*, 17:283-297.

09207 **PATTISON, E. M., COURLAS, P. G., PATTI, R., MANN, B.**, and **MULLEN, D.** (1965), Diagnostic-therapeutic intake groups for wives of alcoholics. *Quart. J. Studies Alcohol*, 26:605-616.

09208 **PATTISON, E. M.** (1969), Evaluation of alcoholism treatment: a comparison of three facilities. *Ment. Health Digest*, 1:1-3.

09209 **PATTISON, M. E.** (1965), Evaluation studies of group psychotherapy. *Internat. J. Group Psychother.*, 15:382-393.

09210 **PATTISON, M. E., BRISSENDEN, A.**, and **WOHL, T.** (1967), Assessing specific effects of inpatient group psychotherapy. *Internat. J. Group Psychother.*, 17:283-297.

09211 **PATTON, E. R.** (1974), A comparison of transactional analysis group counseling and client–centered individual counseling of admissions risk college freshmen. *Dissert. Abstr. Internat.*, 34:5640A.

09212 **PATTON, J. D.** (1954), The group as a training device and treatment method in a private psychiatric hospital. *Internat. J. Group Psychother.*, 4:419-428.

09213 **PATTON, J. H., WIMBERLEY, E. J.**, and **FADDIS, J. D.** (1968), Ministering to parents' groups. *Amer. J. Nursing*, 68:1290-1292.

09214 **PAUL, G. L.** (1968), Two-year follow-up systematic desensitization in therapy groups. *J. Abnorm. & Soc. Psychol.*, 73:119-130.

09215 **PAUL, G. L.**, and **SHANNON, D. T.** (1966), Treatment of anxiety through systematic desensitization in therapy groups. *J. Abnorm. & Soc. Psychol.*, 71:124-135.

09216 **PAUL, H.** (1959), Military group psychohygiene in war and war captivity. *Acta Psychother. Psychosomat. Orthopaedagog. Suppl.*, (Basel) 7:302-319.

09217 **PAUL, J. H.** (1973), *Letters to Simon: On the Conduct of Psychotherapy.* New York: International Universities Press.

09218 **PAULSON, H. B.** (1969), Hope for the chronic patient in the community mental health center. *ANA Clin. Conf.*, 274-280.
09219 **PAULSON, I., BURROUGHS, J. C.,** and **GELB, C. G.** (1976), Cotherapy: what is the crux of the relationship? *Internat. J. Group Psychother.*, 26:213-224.
09220 **PAULSON, M. J.,** and **CHALEFF, A.** (1973), Parent surrogate roles: a dynamic concept in understanding and treating elusive parents. *J. Clin. Child Psychol.*, 2:38-40.
09221 **PAULSON, H. J., STROUSE, L.,** and **CHALEFF, A.** (1980), Further observations on child abuse: an a-posteriori examination of group therapy notes. *J. Clin. Child Psychol.*, 9:241-246.
09222 **PAULSON, M. J.** (1974), Parents of the battered child: a multidisciplinary group therapy approach to life-threatening behavior. *Life-Threatening Behav.*, 4:18-31.
09223 **PAULSON, T.** (1975), Short term group assertion training with token feedback as an adjunct to ongoing group psychotherapy. *Couns. Psychol.*, 15:60-64.
09224 **PAULY, I. B.,** and **SASLOW, G.** (1968), Group learning process. *Sandoz Psychiat. Spectator*, 5:17.
09225 **PAUSER, H.** (1962), (Experiment with group and insulin treatment in an outpatient clinic.) *Nordisk Psykiat. Tidsskr.*, (Kungsbacha) 16:362-365.
09226 **PAVAN, L., AGIUS, S.,** and **BAGGIO, M.** (1969), (On some institutional and dynamic aspects of group therapy in short-term hospitalization.) *Riv. Psichiat.*, (Rome) 4:403-420.
09227 **PAVEL, F. G.,** and **SANDER, K.** (1975), (Client centered psychotherapy groups with emphasis on self-experience.) *Gruppendynamik*, (Stuttgart) 6:237-250.
09228 **PAVLOV, M., HARTINGS, M.,** and **DAVIS, F. A.** (1978), Discussion groups for medical patients: a vehicle for improved coping. *Psychother. & Psychosomat.*, (Basel) 30:105.
09229 **PAVLOV, M., JOHNSON, P., DAVIS, F. A.,** and **LEFEVRE, K.** (1979), A program of psychologic service delivery in a multiple sclerosis center. *Prof. Psychol.*, 10:503-510.
09230 **PAVLOVSKY, E. A.** (1968), *Psicoterapia de Grupo en Niños y Adolescentes.* (*Group Psychotherapy with Children and Adolescents.*) Buenos Aires, Centro Editor de America Latina.
09231 **PAYMAN, D. A. R.** (1956), An investigation of the effects of group psychotherapy on chronic schizophrenic patients. *Group Psychother., Psychodrama & Sociometry*, 9:35-39.
09232 **PAYN, S. B.** (1965), Group methods in the pharmacotherapy of chronic psychotic patients. *Psychiat. Quart.*, 39:258-263.
09233 **PAYN, S. B.** (1975), Group pharmacotherapy for chronic schizophrenic patients. *Curr. Psychiat. Ther.*, 15:237-240.
09234 **PAYN, S. B.** (1978), Group pharmacotherapy for withdrawn schizophrenic patients. *Can. Psychiat. Assn. J.*, (Ottawa) 23:97-100.
09235 **PAYN, S. B.** (1965), Group psychotherapy approach to discord among performing artists. *Internat. J. Group Psychother.*, 15:350-357.
09236 **PAYN, S. B.** (1974), Reaching chronic schizophrenic patients with group pharmacotherapy. *Internat. J. Group Psychother.*, 24:25-31.
09237 **PAYNE, B. F.** (1970), The effects of group counseling upon the self-concept of disadvantaged elementary school students. *Dissert. Abstr. Internat.*, 31:1019A.
09238 **PAYNE, B. F.,** and **DUNN, C. J.** (1972), An analysis of the change in self concept by racial dissent. *J. Negro Educat.*, 41:156-163.
09239 **PAYNE, I. R., RASMUSSEN, D. M.,** and **SHINEDLING, M.** (1970), Char-

acteristics of obese university females who lose weight. *Psychol. Reports*, 27:567-570.

09240 **PAYNE, J. E., and WILLIAMS, M.** (1971), Practical aspects of group work with the mentally retarded. *Group Process*, (London) 4:9-17.

09241 **PAYNE, J. E., and WILLIAMS, M.** (1975), Practical aspects of group work with the mentally retarded. In: *Group Psychotherapy and Group Function*, 2d ed., ed. M. Rosenbaum and M. M. Berger. New York: Basic Books.

09242 **PAYNE, W.** (1972), The study of an informational component designed to modify participation within an obesity reduction program. *Dissert. Abstr. Internat.*, 32:4683-4684A.

09243 **PAZDUR, H. C.** (1969), Group work with children: a child psychiatric nurse's experience. *ANA Clin. Conf.*, 281:287.

09244 **PEAKE, T., and BORDUIN, C.** (1977), Combining systems behavioral and analytical approaches to the treatment of anorexia nervosa: a case study. *Fam. Ther.*, 4:49-56.

09245 **PEAKE, T. H.** (1976), Relationship, ambiguity, therapist-patient agreement, and therapeutic outcome: a study of group therapy. *Dissert. Abstr. Internat.*, 37:3089.

09246 **PEAKE, T. H.** (1979), Therapist–patient agreement and outcome in group therapy. *J. Clin. Psychol.*, 35:637-646.

09247 **PEARCE, S. S.** (1978), The effect of structured group counseling on levels of depression among retired women in institutional and non-institutional settings. *Dissert. Abstr. Internat.*, 39:4064A.

09248 **PEARL, D.** (1955), Psychotherapy and ethnocentrism. *J. Abnorm. & Soc. Psychol.*, 20:227-229.

09249 **PEARNE, S. A.** (1972), The development of a structured group procedure and the evaluation of its effects on the self concepts of group participants. *Dissert. Abstr. Internat.*, 32:6657-6658B.

09250 **PEARSE, J. J.** (1961), Influence of open door policy in mental hospitals. *Group Psychother., Psychodrama & Sociometry*, 14:13-17.

09251 **PEARSON, D. T.** (1970), The effects of a combined reading and group counseling program on community college students. *Dissert. Abstr. Internat.*, 31:2690A.

09252 **PEARSON, J. W.** (1970), A differential use of group homes for delinquent boys. *Children*, 17:143-148.

09253 **PEARSON, M. M.** (1947), Group psychotherapy. *Diseases Nerv. System*, 8:163-165.

09254 **PEARSON, M. M., and COHEN, R. A.** (1946), Psychotherapy in a naval convalescent hospital. *Res. Pub. Assn. Nerv. & Ment. Diseases*, 25:181-187.

09255 **PEASE, J. J.** (1979), Social skills training group for early adolescents. *J. Adolescence*, 2:229.

09256 **PEBERDY, G. R.** (1961), Group resort to fantasy: a field study. *J. Ment. Science*, (London) 107:787-794.

09257 **PEBERDY, G. R.** (1960), Hypnotic methods in group psychotherapy. *J. Ment. Science*, (London) 106:1016-1020.

09258 **PECK, B. B., HOWE, B. J., and STOCKHOUSE, T. W.** (1978), Network psychotherapy as a community consultation technique. *Psychother.: Theory, Res. & Pract.*, 15:95.

09259 **PECK, H. B.** (1953), An application of group therapy to the intake process. *Amer. J. Orthopsychiat.*, 3:338-349.

09260 **PECK, H. B.** (1967), Approaches to training through the small group. *Internat. J. Group Psychother.*, 17:419-420.

09261 **PECK, H. B.** (1968), Editor's preamble to Dr. Anthony's anniversary reflections. *Internat. J. Group Psychother.*, 18:275-276.

09262 **PECK, H. B.** (1970), Encounter and t-groups: the current use of the group for personal growth and development—introduction. *Internat. J. Group Psychother.*, 20:263-266.

09263 **PECK, H. B.** (1965), Group approaches in programs for socially deprived populations. *Internat. J. Group Psychother.*, 15:423.

09264 **PECK, H. B. CHMN.** (1954), The group in education, group work and psychotherapy. *Amer. J. Orthopsychiat.*, 25:128-152.

09265 **PECK, H. B.** (1951), Group psychotherapy and mental health. *Internat. J. Group Psychother.*, 1:301-310.

09266 **PECK, H. B.** (1966), Group-therapeutic approaches within the hospital community. *Internat. J. Group Psychother.*, 16:267-279.

09267 **PECK, H. B.** (1943), Group therapy as social prophylaxis. *Amer. J. Orthopsychiat.*, 13:664-671.

09268 **PECK, H. B.** (1962), Group treatment approaches to the family. *Internat. J. Group Psychother.*, 12:131.

09269 **PECK, H. B.** (1978), Integrating transactional analysis and group process approaches in treatment. *Transactional Anal. J.*, 8:328-331.

09270 **PECK, H. B.** (1975), Reflections on 25 years of the *International Journal of Group Psychotherapy. Internat. J. Group Psychother.*, 25:153-157.

09271 **PECK, H. B.** (1963), The role of the psychiatric day hospital in a community mental health program: a group process approach. *Amer. J. Orthopsychiat.*, 33:482-493.

09272 **PECK, H. B.** (1970), A small-group approach to individual and institutional change. *Internat. J. Group Psychother.*, 20:435-449.

09273 **PECK, H. B.** (1968), The small group: core of the community mental health center. *Community Ment. Health J.*, 4:191-200.

09274 **PECK, H. B.** (1963), Some relationships between group process and mental health phenomena in theory and practice. *Internat. J. Group Psychother.*, 13:269-289.

09275 **PECK, H. B.**, and **BELLSMITH, V.** (1954), *Treatment of the Delinquent Adolescent: Group and Individual Therapy with Parent and Child.* New York: Family Service Assn.

09276 **PECK, H. B.**, and **KAPLAN, S. R.** (1966), Crisis theory and therapeutic change in small groups: some implications for community mental health programs. *Internat. J. Group Psychother.*, 16:135-149.

09277 **PECK, H. B.**, and **RABBAN, M.** (1964), An approach to the correction of reading disability through the combined use of family and teacher groups. *Amer. J. Orthopsychiat.*, 34:258-259.

09278 **PECK, H. B.**, and **SCHEIDLINGER, S.** (1968), Group therapy with the socially disadvantaged. In: *Current Psychiatric Therapies*, ed. J. H. Masserman. New York: Grune and Stratton.

09279 **PECK, H. B., RABINOVITCH, R. D.**, and **CRAMER, J. B.** (1949), A treatment program for parents of schizophrenic children. *Amer. J. Orthopsychiat.*, 19:592-598.

09280 **PECK, H. B., ROMAN, M., KAPLAN, S. R.**, and **BAUMAN, G.** (1965), An approach to the study of the small group in a psychiatric day hospital. *Internat. J. Group Psychother.*, 15:207-219.

09281 **PECK, M. L.**, and **STEWART, R. H.** (1964), Current practices in selection criteria for group play-therapy. *J. Clin. Psychol.*, 20:146.

09282 **PECK, R. E.** (1949), Comparison of adjunct group therapy with individual psychotherapy. *Arch. Neurol. Psychiat.*, 62:173-177.

09283 **PECK, R. E.** (1951), Observations of group therapy in an army general hospital. *Internat. J. Group Psychother.*, 1:365-373.

09284 **PEDERSON-KRAG, G.** (1956), Similarities in the dynamic functioning of industrial and therapeutic groups. *Internat. J. Group Psychother.*, 6:280-285.

09285 **PEDERSON-KRAG, G.** (1946), Unconscious factors in group therapy. *Psychiat. Quart.*, 15:180-189.

09286 **PEDLEY, D.** (1968), The psychodynamics involved in an occupational therapist's use of creative activities and discussion groups in physical and psychiatric rehabilitation. *Austral. Occupat. Ther. J.*, 15:37-46.

09287 **PEDRAZZI, G.** (1967), (A pedagogic and psychotherapeutic experiment performed by the institute psychologist in cooperation with a group educator.) *Riv. Sper. Freniatria*, (Emilia) 91:1637-1645.

09288 **PEEBLER, D.**, and **SHIPPY, H.** (1975), Cancer update: how patients help each other. part 7. *Amer. J. Nursing*, 75:1354.

09289 **PEELE, R.** (1978), Review of A. Starr's *Psychodrama: Rehearsal for Living—Illustrated Therapeutic Techniques. Amer. J. Psychiat.*, 135:398.

09290 **PEELE, R.** (1977), Review of L. Yablonsky's *Psychodrama: Resolving Emotional Problems Through Role-Playing. Amer. J. Psychiat.*, 134:342.

09291 **PEET, D. S.** (1964), Children reborn. *Amer. J. Nursing*, 64:102-106.

09292 **PEET, D. S.** (1962), Learning to play. *Amer. J. Nursing*, 62:79.

09293 **PEIRCE, F. J.** (1963), Social group work in a women's prison. *Fed. Probat.*, 27:37-43.

09294 **PEITLER, E. J.** (1980), A comparison of the effectiveness of group counseling and Al-Ateen on the psychological adjustment of two groups of adolescent sons of alcoholic fathers. *Dissert. Abstr. Internat.*, 41:1520B. (University Microfilms No. 8021807.)

09295 **PEIZER, S. B.** (1957), Rebuttal to Armegeddon. *J. Correct. Psychol.*, 2:10-16.

09296 **PELED, E.** (1958), Psikhoterapia kevutsatit besherut harefuah vehahinukh. (Group psychotherapy in service of medicine and education.) *Harefuah*, (Tel Aviv) 55:34-40.

09297 **PELHAM, L. E.** (1972), Self-directive play therapy with socially immature kindergarten students. *Dissert. Abstr. Internat.*, 32:3798A.

09298 **PELLEGRENO, D. D.** (1971), The class is a group. *Nat. Cath. Guid. Conf. J.*, 15:157-162.

09299 **PELLMAN, D. R.** (1977), Learning to live with dying: Make Today Count—a national self–help organization for cancer patients. *Nursing Digest*, 5:27-31.

09300 **PELOSI, A. A.**, and **FRIEDMAN, H.** (1974), The activity period in group psychotherapy. *Psychiat. Quart.*, 48:223-229.

09301 **PELSER, H. E., GROEN, J. J., STUYLING de L.**, and **DIT, P. C.** (1979), Experiences in group discussion with diabetic patients. *Psychother. & Psychosomat.*, 32:257-269.

09302 **PELTZ, W., STEEL, E. H., SAMUEL, M. S., HADDEN, S. B., SCHWAB, M. L.**, and **NICHOLS, F.** (1955), A group method of teaching psychiatry to medical students. *Internat. J. Group Psychother.*, 5:270-279.

09303 **PELTZ, W. L.**, and **GOLDBERG, M.** (1959), A dynamic factor in group work with post-adolescents and its effects on the role of the leader. *Ment. Hygiene*, 43:71-75.

09304 **PELZMAN, O.** (1952), Some problems in the use of psychotherapy. *Psychiat. Quart. Suppl.*, 26:53-58.

09305 **PELZMAN, O.**, and **BELLSMITH, E. B.** (1949), A group therapy service in a psychiatric hospital: the place of social service in the program. *Psychiat. Quart. Suppl.*, 23:332-344.

09306 **PENA y LILLO, S.** (1972), (Magnetophonic systematic desensitization in the collective treatment of phobic symptoms.) *Rev. Med. Chile*, (Santiago) 100:1244-1251.

09307 **PENA y LILLO, S.** (1972), Method for tape recorder deconditioning for collective use. *Annales Medico-Psychol.*, (Paris) 2:375-388.

09308 **PEÑA y LILLO, S., LECLERC, C.**, and **ALESSANDRI, A. M.** (1972), De-

conditioning by tape-recorder: group application. *Annales Médico-Psychol.*, (Paris) 2:375-388.
09309 **PENLAND, P. R.**, and **FINE, S.** (1974), *Group Dynamics and Individual Development.* New York: M. Dekker.
09310 **PENNOCK, M. E.**, and **WEYKER, G.** (1953), Some developments in the integration of case work and group work in a child guidance clinic. *J. Psychiat. Social Work*, 22:75-81.
09311 **PEPINSKY, H. B.** (1949), Brief group psychotherapy and role and status: a case-study. *Amer. Psychologist*, 4:294-295.
09312 **PEPINSKY, H. B.** (1951), Counseling methods: therapy. *Annual Rev. Psychol.*, 2:317-344.
09313 **PEPINSKY, H. B.** (1949), An experimental approach to group therapy in a counseling center. *Occupat. & Vocat. Guid. J.*, 28:35-40.
09314 **PEPINSKY, H. B.** (1947), Measuring outcomes of classroom therapy. *Educat. Psychol. Measurement*, 7:713-724.
09315 **PEPINSKY, H. B.** (1953), The role of group procedures in the counseling programs. In: *Roles and Relationships in Counseling*, ed. R. F. Berdie. Minneapolis: University of Minnesota Press.
09316 **PEPINSKY, H. B.**, and **PEPINSKY, P. N.** (1942), Implication of social dynamics for methods of therapy with college students. *Amer. Psychologist*, 2:292-293.
09317 **PEPINSKY, H. B., SIEGEL, L.**, and **VANATTA, E. L.** (1952), The criterion in counseling: a group participation scale. *J. Abnorm. & Soc. Psychol.*, 47:415-419.
09318 **PERCELL, L. P.** (1974), The relationship among assertiveness, self-acceptance and anxiety, and their systematic responsiveness to group assertive training. *Dissert. Abstr. Internat.*, 35:3030B.
09319 **PERCELL, L. P., BERWICK, P. T.**, and **BEIGEL, A.** (1974), The effects of assertive training on self-concept and anxiety. *Arch. Gen. Psychiat.*, 31:502-504.
09320 **PERELMAN, M. A.** (1977), The treatment of premature ejaculation by time limited group sex therapy. *Dissert. Abstr. Internat.*, 37:6373B.
09321 **PERESTRELLO, D.** (1963), Abandono, ódio, culpa e nevus vistos numa sessão de psicoterapia de grupo. (Abandonment, hate, guilt observed during a group psychotherapy session.) *J. Brasil. Psiquiat.*, (Rio de Janeiro) 12:343-349.
09322 **PERES, H.** (1947), An evaluation of non-directive group therapy. Unpublished masters thesis, University of Chicago.
09323 **PERES, H.** (1947), An investigation of nondirective group therapy. *J. Consult. & Clin. Psychol.*, 11:159-172.
09325 **PERETZ, M.**, and **GLASER, F. B.** (1975), Value change in drug education: the role of encounter groups. *Internat. J. Addict.*, 9:637-652.
09326 **PÉREZ MORALES, F.** (1963), Psicoterapia y LSD 25. iii. (Psychotherapy and LSD 25. iii) *Acta Psiquiat. Psicol. Argentina*, 9:226-232.
09327 **PERKINS, I. H.** (1972), A unique approach to hospital treatment of narcotic addicts. *Adolescence*, 6:29-50.
09328 **PERKINS, J. A.** (1970), Group counseling with bright underachievers and their mothers. *Dissert. Abstr. Internat.*, 30:2809A.
09329 **PERKINS, J. A.**, and **WICAS, E. A.** (1971), Group counseling of bright underachievers and their mothers. *J. Couns. Psychol.*, 18:273-278.
09330 **PERKINS, S. R.**, and **ATKINSON, D. R.** (1973), Effect of selected techniques for training resident assistants in human relations skills. *J. Couns. Psychol.*, 20:84-90.
09331 **PERL, W. R.** (1958), American communities in foreign settings: group problems and an American therapy programme in Germany. *Internat. J. Soc. Psychiat.*, (London) 3:278-286.

09332 **PERL, W. R.** (1956), Benefits from including one psychopath in a group of mildly delinquent patients. *Internat. J. Group Psychother.*, 6:77-79.

09333 **PERL, W. R.** (1963), Use of fantasy for a breakthrough in psychotherapy groups of hard-to-reach delinquent boys. *Internat. J. Group Psychother.*, 13:27-33.

09334 **PERL, W. R.** (1954), Utilization in group therapy of disadvantages of the prevailing prison system. *Group Psychother., Psychodrama & Sociometry*, 7:159-166.

09335 **PERLMAN, B.** (1949), Group work with psychotic veterans. *Amer. J. Orthopsychiat.*, 19:69-78.

09336 **PERLMUTTER, J., LIEBERMAN, M. A.,** and **MEYER, G. G.** (1968), Group psychotherapy. *Prog. Neurol. Psychiat.*, 23:548-558.

09337 **PERLMUTTER, M. S.,** and **HATFIELD, E.** (1980), Intimacy, intentional metacommunication and second order change. *Amer. J. Fam. Ther.*, 8:17-23.

09338 **PERLS, F. S.** (1967), Workshop vs. individual therapy. *J. Long Island Consult. Ctr.*, 5:30-37.

09339 **PERLS, R. D.** (1974), Experimental awareness: an existential approach to group psychotherapy with adolescents. *Dissert. Abstr. Internat.*, 34:5203-5204.

09340 **PERREAULT, R., WRIGHT, J.,** and **MATHIEU, M.** (1979), The directive sex therapies in psychiatric outpatient settings. *Can. Psychiat. Assn. J.*, (Ottawa) 24:47-54.

09341 **PERRIER, N.** (1965), (Place of psychotherapy: gear wheel or pillar.) *Inform. Psychiat.*, 41:559-563.

09342 **PERRINO, C. A.** (1969), Effects of two types of group counseling approaches on selected variables of a junior high school population. *Dissert. Abstr. Internat.*, 29:2969A.

09343 **PERRIS, C.** (1964), (Reflections concerning activities in a "therapeutic community.") *Nordisk Psykiat. Tidsskr.*, (Kungsbacha) 18:386-396.

09344 **PERROTT, L. A.** (1975), Doubling from an existential–phenomenological viewpoint. *Group Psychother., Psychodrama & Sociometry*, 28:66-69.

09345 **PERSONS, R. W.** (1966), Psychological and behavioral change in delinquents following psychotherapy. *J. Clin. Psychol.*, 22:337-340.

09346 **PERSONS, R. W.** (1965), Psychotherapy with sociopathic offenders: an empirical evaluation. *J. Clin. Psychol.*, 21:205-207.

09347 **PERSONS, R. W.** (1967), Relationship between psychotherapy with institutionalized boys and subsequent community adjustment. *J. Consult. & Clin. Psychol.*, 31:137-141.

09348 **PERSONS, R. W.,** and **PEPINSKY, H. B.** (1966), Convergence in psychotherapy with delinquent boys. *J. Couns. Psychol.*, 13:329-334.

09349 **PESHKIN, M. M.,** and **ABRAMSON, H. A.** (1974), Psychosomatic group therapy with parents of children with intractable asthma: vi. the Temple family: 2. *J. Asthma Res.*, 12:95-122.

09350 **PESHKIN, M. M.,** and **ABRAMSON, H. A.** (1974), Psychosomatic group therapy with parents of children with intractable asthma: v. the Temple family: 1. *J. Asthma Res.*, 12:27-63.

09351 **PESHKIN, M. M., MAYER, L. C.,** and **ABRAMOSON, H. A.** (1976), Psychosomatic group therapy with parents of children with intractable asthma. *J. Asthma Res.*, 13:151-157.

09352 **PESSIN, N. H.** (1980), The effects of audiovisual modeling on verbal behavior in group therapy. *Dissert. Abstr. Internat.*, 40:5825B. (University Microfilms No. 8012686.)

09353 **PESSO, A.** (1969), *Movement in Psychotherapy: Psychomotor Techniques and Training*. New York: New York University Press.

09354 **PETERNEL, F.** (1979), (Cotherapist in group psychotherapy.) *Psihijat. Danas*, (Belgrade) 11:21-29.

09355 **PETEROY, E. T.** (1979), Effects of member and leader expectations on group outcome. *J. Couns. Psychol.*, 26:534.

09356 **PETERS, C. B.**, and **GRUNEBAUM, H.** (1977), It could be worse: effective group psychotherapy with help-rejecting complainers. *Internat. J. Group Psychother.*, 27:471-480.

09357 **PETERS, D. R.** (1973), Identification and personal learning in t-groups. *Human Relat.*, 26:1-21.

09358 **PETERS, D. R.** (1970), Self-ideal congruence as a function of human relations training. *J. Psychology*, 76:199-207.

09359 **PETERS, G. A.**, and **GARDNER, S.** (1959), Inducing creative productivity in industrial research scientists. *Group Psychother., Psychodrama & Sociometry*, 12:179-186.

09360 **PETERS, G. A.**, and **PHELAN, J. G.** (1957), Practical group psychotherapy reduces supervisors' anxiety. *Personnel J.*, 35:376-378.

09361 **PETERS, G. A.**, and **PHELAN, J. G.** (1959), Practical group psychotherapy and role playing for the industrial supervisor. *Group Psychother., Psychodrama & Sociometry*, 12:143-147.

09362 **PETERS, G. A.**, and **PHELAN, J. G.** (1957), Relieving personality conflicts by a kind of group therapy. *Personnel J.*, 36:61-64.

09363 **PETERS, G. A.**, and **PHELAN, J. G.** (1959), Role playing technique in industrial situations. *Group Psychother., Psychodrama & Sociometry*, 12:148-155.

09364 **PETERS, H. N.**, and **JONES, F. D.** (1951), Evaluation of group psychotherapy by means of performance tests. *J. Consult. & Clin. Psychol.*, 15:363-367.

09365 **PETERS, J. J.** (1973), Do encounter groups hurt people? *Psychother.: Theory, Res. & Pract.*, 10:33-35.

09366 **PETERS, J. J., PEDIGO, J. M., STEG, J.**, and **MCKENNA, J. J.** (1968), Group psychotherapy of the sex offender. *Fed. Probat.*, 32:41-45.

09367 **PETERS, N. C.** (1974), A study of interpersonal behavior and personality of members of a self-analytic group. *Dissert. Abstr. Internat.*, 35:521B.

09368 **PETERS, R. W.** (1973), The facilitation of change in group counseling by group composition. *Dissert. Abstr. Internat.*, 33:3319B.

09369 **PETERSEN, D. J.** (1972), The relationship between self-concept and self-disclosure of underachieving college students in group counseling. *Dissert. Abstr. Internat.*, 33:2354B.

09370 **PETERSEN, P.** (1967), Sitzordnung und gruppendynamik in therapeutischen gruppen. (Seating order and group dynamics in therapeutic groups.) *Zeit. Psychother. Med. Psychol.*, (Stuttgart) 17:216-219.

09371 **PETERSEN, P.**, and **UCHTENHAGEN, A.** (1967), Gruppentherapien an der zuricher psychiatrischen Universitäts-klinik. (Group therapy at the University of Zurich Psychiatric Clinic.) *Psychother. & Psychosomat.*, (Basel) 15:52.

09372 **PETERSEN, R. C.** (1965), Group therapy and the traffic violators. *Group Psychother., Psychodrama & Sociometry*, 18:65-68.

09373 **PETERSON, C. E., PETERSON, B. M.**, and **CAMERON, C.** (1977), Pyramid groups: a new model for therapy and intern training. *Prof. Psychol.*, 8:214-221.

09374 **PETERSON, D. M.**, and **YARVIS, R. M.** (1969), The federal bureau of prisons treatment program for narcotic addicts. *Fed. Probat.*, 33:35-40.

09375 **PETERSON, E. R.** (1970), Comparative effects of group counseling and a program of social interaction combined with group counseling on university students. *Dissert. Abstr. Internat.*, 30:4231A-4232A.

09376 **PETERSON, N. L.** (1962), Group dynamics found in scriptures. *Group Psychother., Psychodrama & Sociometry*, 15:126-128.

09377 **PETERSEN, P.** (1968), Motivations behind the formation of psychotherapeutic groups in a psychiatric institution. *Psychother. & Psychosomat.*, (Basel) 16:152-158.

09378 **PETERSON, R. L.** (1973), *Small Groups: Selected Bibliography Cat. Selected Docum. Psychol.*, 3:47.

09379 **PETERSON, S.** (1969), The psychiatric nurse specialist in a general hospital. *Nursing Outlook*, 17:56-58.

09380 **PETRI, H.** (1969), (Exhibitionism: theoretical and social aspects and treatment with artiandrogeus.) *Nervenarzt*, 40:220-228.

09381 **PETROV, I. H.** (1972), Cultural therapy in the old people's home. *Child Welfare*, 12:429-434.

09382 **PETROVIĆ, D.** (1977), (The principles of social group work.) *Psihijat. Danas*, (Belgrade) 9:131-135.

09383 **PETROVIĆ, V.** (1975), (Encounter groups and group psychotherapy.) *Anali Zavoda Ment. Zdravlje*, 7:43-48.

09384 **PETROVSKII, A. V.** (1973), (Experimental development of a social-psychological concept of group activity.) *Vop. Psikhol.*, (Moscow) 19:3-17.

09385 **PETTERA, R. L.**, and **FECENKO, H.** (1972), Hale Nui, Schofield Barracks: a community mental health program. *Amer. J. Psychiat.*, 128:1257-1261.

09386 **PETTIFOR, R. E.** (1973), Integration of treatment modalities through evaluation. *West. Psychol.*, 4:27-30.

09387 **PETTY, B. J., MOELLER, T. P.**, and **CAMPBELL, R. Z.** (1976), Support groups for elderly persons in the community. *Gerontologist*, 16:522-528.

09388 **PETTY, M. M.** (1972), The effects of assigned position, experience and training upon performance in a leaderless group discussion. *Dissert. Abstr. Internat.*, 1838B.

09389 **PETTY, M. M.** (1974), A multivariate analysis of the effects of experience and training upon performance in a leaderless group discussion. *Personnel Psychol.*, 27:271-282.

09390 **PETTY, R. E.** (1977), Effects of group size on cognitive effort and evaluation. *Personality & Soc. Psychol. Bull.*, 3:579.

09391 **PETZOLD, H.** (1974), The diagnostic and therapeutic possibilities of psychodrama in the "tetradic system." *Dynam. Psychiat.*, (Berlin) 7:151-181.

09392 **PETZOLD, H. G.** (1975), (The "therapeutic theater" of Illiine.) *Gruppendynamik*, (Stuttgart) 2:117-126.

09393 **PEW, M. L., SPEER, D. C.**, and **WILLIAMS, J.** (1973), Group counseling for offenders. *Soc. Work*, 18:74-79.

09394 **PFEFFER, A. Z., FRIEDLAND, P.**, and **WORTIS, S. B.** (1949), Group psychotherapy with alcoholics: preliminary report. *Quart. J. Studies Alcohol*, 10:198-210.

09395 **PFEFFER, A. Z., FELDMAN, D. J., FEIBEL, C., FRANK, J. A. A., COHEN, M., BERGER, A., FLEETWOOD, M. F.**, and **GREENBERG, S. S.** (1956), A treatment program for the alcoholic in industry. *J. Amer. Med. Assn.*, 161:827-836.

09396 **PFEIFFER, J. W.** (1975), *The 1975 Annual Handbook for Group Facilitators*. San Diego: University Associates.

09397 **PFEIFFER, J. W.**, and **HESLIN, R.** (1973), *Instrumentation in Human Relations Training: A Guide to 75 Instruments with Wide Application to the Behavioral Sciences*. Iowa City: University Associates.

09398 **PFEIFFER, J. W.**, and **JONES, J. E.** (1980), *The Annual Handbook for Group Facilitators, 1980*. San Diego: University Associates.

09399 **PFEIFFER, J. W.**, and **JONES, J. E.** (1975), *A Handbook of Structured Experiences for Human Relations Training*. La Jolla: University Associates.

09400 **PFEIFFER, J. W.**, and **JONES, J. E.** (1977), *A Handbook of Structured Experiences in Human Relations Training*, VI. La Jolla: University Associates.

09401 **PFEIFFER, J. W.**, and **JONES, J. E.** (1974), *The 1974 Annual Handbook for Group Facilitators*. La Jolla: University Associates.

09402 **PFEIFFER, J. W.**, and **JONES, J. E.** (1976), *The 1976 Annual Handbook for Group Facilitators*. La Jolla: University Associates.

09403 **PFEIFFER, V. M.** (1965), (Puppet shows in the therapy of psychoses.) *Zeit. Psychother. Med. Psychol.*, (Stuttgart) 15:135-139.

09404 **PFISTER, G.** (1975), Outcomes of laboratory training for police officers. *J. Soc. Issues*, 31:115-121.

09405 **PHARES, L. G.**, and **CAMPBELL, J. P.** (1971), Sensitivity training in industry: issues and research. In: *Progress in Clinical Psychology*, eds. L. E. Abt and B. F. Riess. New York: Grune and Stratton, 9:176-190.

09406 **PHELAN, J. F., Jr.** (1960), Recent observations on group psychotherapy with adolescent delinquent boys in residential treatment: introduction. *Internat. J. Group Psychother.*, 10:174-179.

09407 **PHELAN, J. R. M.** (1974), Parent, teacher, or analyst: the adolescent-group therapist's trilemma. *Internat. J. Group Psychother.*, 24:238-244.

09408 **PHIEBIG, A. J.** (1959), International congress of group psychotherapy: proceedings, 1957. Basel: S. Karger.

09409 **PHIEBIG, A. J.** (1963), *Phyloanalysis: Theoretical and Practical Considerations on Burrow's Group-Analytic and Socio–Therapeutic Method*. Basel: S. Karger.

09410 **PHILBRICK, J. L.** (1965), *Readings in Psychodynamics of Group Psychotherapy*. New York: Selected Academic Readings.

09411 **PHILIP, B. R.**, and **PEIXOTTO, H. E.** (1959), An objective evaluation of brief group psychotherapy on delinquent boys. *Can. J. Psychol.*, (Toronto) 13:273-280.

09412 **PHILIP, H.**, and **DUNPHY, D.** (1959), Developmental trends in small groups. *Sociometry*, 22:162-174.

09413 **PHILIPS, S. L.**, and **FIELDS, J.** (1975), An experiment in activity groups for juvenile offenders. *Correct. & Soc. Psychiat.*, 21:4-6.

09414 **PHILIPSEN, G. F.**, and **SAINE, T. J.** (1973), The effect of reward criteria on verbal participation in group discussion. *Speech Monogr.*, 40:151-153.

09415 **PHILLIP, R., ROSENBERG, S., MOORE, S.**, and **SHOOM–KIRSCH, D.** (1979), Parent–training groups: similarities and differences. *Can. Ment. Health*, (Ottawa) 27:15-18.

09416 **PHILLIPS, E. L.** (1960), Parent-child psychotherapy: a follow-up study comparing two techniques. *J. Psychology*, 49:195-202.

09417 **PHILLIPS, E. L., WOLF, M. M., FIXEN, D. L.**, and **BAILEY, J. S.** (1976), The achievement place model: a community-based, family-style, behavior modification program for delinquents. In: *Analysis of Delinquency and Aggression*, eds. E. Ribes-Inesta and A. Bandura. Hillsdale, NJ: Lawrence Erlbaum, pp. 171-202.

09418 **PHILLIPS, J. G.** (1978), A study of psychodrama as a teaching technique in psychology of personality and adjustment. *Dissert. Abstr. Internat.*, 39:3054B-3055B. (University Microfilms No. 7824149.)

09419 **PHILLIPS, P. B.** (1974), Head start parents in participant groups: iii. community trainer as link to social change. *J. Appl. Behav. Science*, 10:259-263.

09420 **PHILLIPS, R. D.** (1972), Group psychotherapy: current concepts and styles. *North Carolina Med. J.*, 33:953-956.

09421 **PHILLIPSON, H.** (1958), The assessment of progress after at least two years of group psychotherapy. *Brit. J. Med. Psychol.*, (London) 31:32-42.

09422 **PHILLIPSON, H.** (1953), Unconscious object relations and the techniques

of the clinical psychologist: some reflections on experiences with therapeutic groups. *Brit. J. Med. Psychol.*, (London) 26:49-57.
09423 **PHOLEN, M.** (1973), (The Munchin cooperation model: group therapy in a new clinical organizational model.) *Nervenarzt*, 44:476-483.
09424 **PICKHARDT, C. E.** (1970), Perceptions by self and others of female black and white teachers from segregated and desegregated schools before and after a six week training institute. *Dissert. Abstr. Internat.*, 31:3348A.
09425 **PIERCE, C. M., DOWNING, M. J.,** and **DeBROUX, K.** (1964), Why a nurse in a day center? *Ment. Hosp.*, 15:446-447.
09426 **PIERCE, C. M., SCHWARTZ, D.,** and **THOMAS, E. M.** (1964), Music therapy in a day care center. *Diseases Nerv. System*, 25:29-32.
09427 **PIERCE, R. A.,** and **WOLFF, T.** (1970), Modification of group therapy for use on the college campus. *J. Amer. Coll. Health Assn.*, 18:234-237.
09428 **PIERCE, R. M.,** and **DRASGOW, J.** (1969), Teaching facilitative interpersonal functioning to psychiatric inpatients. *J. Couns. Psychol.*, 16:295-298.
09429 **PIERCE, W. D., TRICKETT, E. J.,** and **MOOS, R. H.** (1972), Changing ward atmosphere through staff discussion of the perceived ward environment. *Arch. Gen. Psychiat.*, 26:35-41.
09430 **PIERCY, F. P.,** and **PIERCY, S. K.** (1972), Interpersonal attraction as a function of propinquity in two sensitivity groups. *Psychology*, 9:27-30.
09431 **PIERSON, D. F.** (1980), Self-injurious behavior: sensory awareness training as group treatment and an etiological analysis. *Dissert. Abstr. Internat.*, 40:4499B.
09432 **PIETERS, H.** (1973), The Transvaal Memorial Hospital for Children: socialization of the child by peer group. *South African Nursing J.*, (Pretoria) 40:19-20 passim.
09433 **PIETROPINTO, A.** (1975), Poetry therapy in groups. *Curr. Psychiat. Ther.*, 15:221-232.
09434 **PILE, E.** (1958), A note on a technique designed to aid in studying the process of group psychotherapy. *Group Psychother., Psychodrama & Sociometry*, 11:211-212.
09435 **PILKEY, L., GOLDMAN, M.,** and **KLEINMAN, B.** (1961), Psychodrama and emphatic ability in the mentally retarded. *Amer. J. Ment. Deficiency*, 65:595-605.
09436 **PILKINGTON, T. L.** (1972), Symposium on the treatment of behavioral problems: i. psychiatric needs of the subnormal. *Brit. J. Ment. Subnorm.*, (Birmingham) 28:66-70.
09437 **PILKONIS, P. A., LEWIS, P., CALPIN, J., SENATORE, V.,** and **HERSEN, M.** (1980), Training complex social skills for use in a psychotherapy group: a case study. *Internat. J. Group Psychother.*, 30:347-356.
09438 **PILNICK, S., ELIAS, A.,** and **CLAPP, N. W.** (1966), The Essexfields concept: a new approach to the social treatment of juvenile delinquents. *J. Appl. Behav. Science*, 2:109-125.
09439 **PILON-PODHORSKI, A.** (1976), (Some reflections on extraverbal dimensions in analytic psychodrama.) *Persp. Psychiat.*, (Paris) 57:224-234.
09440 **PINE, I., GARDNER, M.,** and **TIPPETT, D. L.** (1958), Experiences with short-term group psychotherapy. *Internat. J. Group Psychother.*, 8:276-284.
09441 **PINE, I., TODD, W. E.,** and **BOENHEIM, C.** (1965), Signs of countertransference problems in co-therapy groups. *Psychosomatics*, 6:79-83.
09442 **PINE, I., TODD, W. E.,** and **BOENHEIM, C.** (1963), Special problems of resistance in cotherapy groups. *Internat. J. Group Psychother.*, 13:354-362.
09443 **PINES, M.** (1980), The frame of reference of group psychotherapy. *Group Anal.*, (London) 13:16-21.

09444 **PINES, M.** (1980), Group psychotherapy: frame of reference for training. In: *Psychotherapy: Research and Training*, eds. W. Demoor and H. R. Wijngaarden. Amsterdam: Elsevier.

09445 **PINES, M.** (1975), Group therapy with "difficult" patients. In: *Group Therapy 1975: An Overview*, eds. L. R. Wolberg and M. L. Aronson. New York: Stratton Intercontinental Medical Books.

09446 **PINES, M.** (1980), Review of M. Kissen's "From group dynamics to group psychoanalysis." *Group Anal.*, (London) 13:77-78.

09447 **PINES, M.** (1980), Review of S. Scheidlinger's *Psychoanalytic Group Dynamics: Basic Readings. Group Anal.*, (London) 13:77-78.

09448 **PINES, M.** (1980), (Therapeutic factors in group analytic psychotherapy.) *Connexions*, (Paris) 31:11-24.

09449 **PINES, M.** (1980), What to expect in the psychotherapy of the borderline patient. *Group Anal.*, (London) 13:168-177.

09450 **PINKNEY, J. W.** (1974), A comparison of structured and non-structured group and individual vocational counseling using client satisfaction and an individualized measure of counseling effectiveness. *Dissert. Abstr. Internat.*, 35:196A.

09451 **PINNEY, E. L.** (1970), *A First Group Psychotherapy Book*. Springfield, IL: C. C. Thomas.

09452 **PINNEY, E. L.** (1978), Paul Schilder and group psychotherapy: the development of psychoanalytic group psychotherapy. *Psychiat. Quart.*, 50:133-143.

09453 **PINNEY, E. L., Jr.** (1965), The psychiatric indications for group psychotherapy. *Psychosomatics*, 6:139-144.

09454 **PINNEY, E. L.,** and **WEIDENBACHER, R.** (1970), The outcome of group psychotherapy in a group used for teaching. *Psychiat. Quart.*, 44:271-280.

09455 **PINNEY, E. L., SCHIMIZZI, G. F.,** and **JOHNSON, N.** (1979), Group psychotherapy for substance abuse: patients' development of a technique. *Internat. J. Addict.*, 14:437.

09456 **PINNEY, E. L., WELLS, S. H.,** and **FISHER, B.** (1978), Group–therapy training in psychiatric residency programs: a national survey. *Amer. J. Psychiat.*, 135:1505-1508.

09457 **PINNEY, E. L., Jr.** (1978), The beginning of group psychotherapy: Joseph Henry Pratt, M.D., and the Reverend Dr. Elwood Worcester. *Internat. J. Group Psychother.*, 28:109-114.

09458 **PINNEY, E. L., Jr.** (1956), Reactions of outpatient schizophrenics to group psychotherapy. *Internat. J. Group Psychother.*, 6:147-151.

09459 **PINNEY, E. L., Jr.** (1955), Use of recorded minutes of group meetings: preliminary report on new technic. *Psychiat. Quart. Suppl.*, 29:248-255.

09460 **PINNEY, E. L., Jr.** (1963), The use of recorded minutes in group psychotherapy: the development of a "readback" technique. *Psychiat. Quart.*, 37:263-269.

09461 **PINO, C. J.** (1971), Relation of a trainability index to t-group outcomes. *J. Appl. Psychol.*, 55:439-442.

09462 **PINO, C. J.,** and **COHEN, H.** (1971), Trainer style and trainee self–disclosure. *Internat. J. Group Psychother.*, 21:202.

09463 **PINSKER, H.** (1966), Fallacies in hospital community therapy. *Curr. Psychiat. Ther.*, 6:344-352.

09464 **PINSKY, J. J.** (1978), Chronic, intractable, benign pain: a syndrome and its treatment with intensive short–term group psychotherapy. *J. Human Stress*, 4:17-21.

09465 **PINSKY, S.** (1965), Resocializing expatients in a neighborhood center. *Ment. Hygiene*, 16:260-263.

09466 **PINSKY, S.** (1964), Social group work in a private hospital. *Ment. Hosp.*, 15:516-524.

09467 **PINTO, R.,** and **D'ELIA, A.** (1980), The therapeutic role of the observer. *Group Anal.*, (London) 13:21-24.
09468 **PINZÓN UMAÑA, E.** (1975), *Grupos e Individuos: Dimensión Dialéctico Psicoanaltica. (Group and Individual: Dialectic Dimensions of Psychoanalysis.)* Salamanca: Instituto Pontificio San Pió X.
09469 **PIOKHARDT, C. E.** (1971), Perceptions by self and others of female Black and White teachers from segregated and desegregated schools before and after a six-week training institute. *Dissert. Abstr. Internat.*, 31:3348.
09470 **PION, R. J., GOLDEN, J. S.,** and **CALDWELL, A. B., Jr.** (1969), Prenatal care: a group psychotherapeutic approach. *California Med.*, 97:281-285.
09471 Pioneering Mental Health Services to the Deaf (1967), *Roche Report: Front. Hosp. Psychiat.*, 4:2-11.
09472 Pioneers in group psychotherapy: Joseph Hersey Pratt, M.D. (1951), *Internat. J. Group Psychother.*, 1:95-99.
09473 **PIPER, W. E.** (1972), Evaluation of the effects of sensitivity training and the effects of varying group composition according to interpersonal trust. *Dissert. Abstr. Internat.*, 33:2819B.
09474 **PIPER, W. E.** (1977), Outcome study of group therapy. *Arch. Gen. Psychiat.*, 34:1027-1032.
09475 **PIPER, W. E., DEBBANE, E. G.,** and **GARANT, M. D.** (1977), Group psychotherapy outcome research: problems and prospects of a first year project. *Internat. J. Group Psychother.*, 27:321-341.
09476 **PIPER, W. E., DEBBANE, E. G., GARANT, J.,** and **BIENVENU, J. P.** (1979), Pretraining for group psychotherapy: a cognitive-experiential approach. *Arch. Gen. Psychiat.*, 36:1250-1256.
09477 **PIPER, W. E., DOAN, B. D., EDWARDS, E. M.,** and **JONES, B. D.** (1979), Cotherapy behavior, group therapy process and treatment outcome. *J. Consult. & Clin. Psychol.*, 47:1081.
09478 **PIPINELI-POTAMIANOU, A.** (1973), Listening to the family interplay: a parent–child interview. *Internat. J. Group Psychother.*, 23:338-345.
09479 **PIRO, L. J.** (1958), Group therapy with mothers. *Internat. J. Group Psychother.*, 8:301-312.
09480 **PISA, A.,** and **LUKENS, H.** (1975), A multifaceted approach to psychodrama in a day treatment center. *Hosp. & Community Psychiat.*, 26:444-447.
09481 **PISANI, V. D.,** and **MOTANKY, G. U.** (1970), Predictors of premature termination of out–patient follow-up group psychotherapy among male alcoholics. *Internat. J. Addict.*, 5:731-737.
09482 **PISCICELLI, U.** (1975), (Respiratory autogenic training (RAT) in the psychosomatic training of physicians.) *Minerva Med.*, (Turin) 66:257-261.
09483 **PISETSKY, M. M.** (1978), Review of H. M. Rabin's and M. Rosenbaum's *How to Begin a Psychotherapy Group: 6 Approaches. Amer. J. Psychiat.*, 135:394.
09484 **PISKOR, B. K.,** and **PALEOS, S.** (1968), The group way to banish after-stroke blues. *Amer. J. Nursing*, 68:1500-1503.
09485 **PITTMAN, D. J.,** and **TATE, R. L.** (1969), A comparison of two treatment programs for alcoholics. *Quart. J. Studies Alcohol*, 30:888-899.
09486 **PITTMAN, F. S.,** and **De YOUNG, C. D.** (1971), The treatment of homosexuals in heterogeneous groups. *Internat. J. Group Psychother.*, 21:62-73.
09487 **PITZELE, M. S.** (1980), Moreno's chorus: the audience in psychodrama. *Group Psychother., Psychodrama & Sociometry*, 33:139-141.
09488 **PIUCK, C. L.** (1970), Evolution of a treatment method for disadvantaged children. *Amer. J. Psychother.*, 24:112-123.
09489 **PIVNICK, H.** (1951), *Group Discussion and Its Relationship to Social Ac-*

ceptability and Personality Adjustment in Normal Adolescent Girls. Ann Arbor: University Microfilms.

09490 **PIXAKETTNER, U., AHRBECK, B., SCHEIBEL, B.,** and **TAUSCH, A. M.** (1978), (Client-centered individual and group-therapy with mentally disturbed intermediate students in their years 5 and 6.) *Zeit. Klin. Psychol.-Forschung & Praxis,* (Goettingen) 7:28-40.

09491 **PIXLEY, J. M.,** and **STIEFEL, J. R.** (1963), Group therapy designed to meet the needs of the alcoholic's wife. *Quart. J. Studies Alcohol,* 24:304-314.

09492 **PLACH, T.** (1980), *The Creative Use of Music in Group Therapy.* Springfield, IL: C. C. Thomas.

09493 **PLANK, R.** (1951), An analysis of a group therapy experiment. *Human Organizat.,* 10:5-21.

09494 **PLANK, R.** (1951), An analysis of a group therapy experiment. *Human Organizat.,* 10:26-36.

09495 **PLANT, M. A.,** and **REEVES, C. E.** (1974), The group dynamics of becoming a drug taker. *Interpersonal Develop.,* 4:99-106.

09496 **PLANTE, G.** (1973), (Inhibited children and free printing.) *Vie Méd. Can. Française,* (Quebec) 2:832-838.

09497 **PLANTE, N.,** and **ROBERT, G.** (1966), La remotivation: auxiliare thérapeutique. (Remotivation: a therapeutic aid.) *Laval Med.,* (Quebec) 37:151-155.

09498 **PLASKA, T.,** and **RAGEE, G.** (1979), Intensive training project: program to prepare aggressive and disruptive residents for community placement. In: *Behavioral Systems for the Developmentally Disabled II,* ed. L. A. Hamerlynck. New York: Brunner/Mazel.

09499 **PLATZER, O.** (1955), Das biodrama als hilfsmittel zur umstrukturierung entwicklungsgtorter kinder. (Biodrama as an aid in re-education of children with disturbed development.) *Praxis Kinderpsychol. & Kinderpsychiat.,* (Goettingen) 4:127-131.

09500 **PLECK, J. H.** (1972), Self-referent accuracy in self-analytic groups. *J. Soc. Psychol.,* 88:289-296.

09501 **PLENK, A. M.** (1978), Activity group therapy for emotionally disturbed pre-school children. *Behav. Disorders,* 3:210.

09502 **PLENK, A. M.** (1969), Group therapy with young nonfunctioning children. *Newsl. Amer. Orthopsychiat. Assn.,* 13:22.

09503 **PLOEGER, A.** (1969), (The activation technique: a way to stimulation and deepening of therapy in psychodrama.) *Praxis der Psychother.,* 14:73-80.

09504 **PLOEGER, A.** (1964), (Clinical group psychotherapy.) *Med. Welt,* (Stuttgart) 36:1909-1915.

09505 **PLOEGER, A.** (1974), (Defective developments in psychodrama groups.) *Psychother. & Med. Psychol.,* (Stuttgart) 24:50-54.

09507 **PLOEGER, A.** (1967), (Indications for group psychotherapy in the clinic.) *Zeit. Psychosomat. Med. & Psychoanal.,* (Goettingen) 13:38-42.

09508 **PLOEGER, A.** (1975), (In-hospital and outpatient group therapy and sociotherapy.) *Nervenarzt,* 46:18-23.

09509 **PLOEGER, A.** (1971), (Milestone in the history of group psychotherapy: on the second edition of the *Improving Theatre* by J. K. Moreno.) *Zeit. Psychother. Med. Psychol.,* (Stuttgart) 21:228-230.

09510 **PLOEGER, A.** (1964), Program, 24th annual meeting, American Society of Group Psychotherapy and Psychodrama, March 19-21, 1965. *Group Psychother., Psychodrama & Sociometry,* 17:236-243.

09511 **PLOEGER, A.** (1965), (Psychodrama in clinical psychotherapy.) *Zeit. Psychother. Med. Psychol.,* (Stuttgart) 15:202-207.

09512 **PLOEGER, A.** (1967), (Sociometry and clinical group psychotherapy.) *Landarzt*, (Stuttgart) 43:1569-1575.

09513 **PLOEGER, A.** (1964), Unterschiede der therapie auf grund der psychologischen bedingen in männer- und frauengruppen. (Differences in therapy of male and female groups due to psychological conditions.) *Zeit. Psychother. Med. Psychol.*, (Stuttgart) 14:240-249.

09514 **PLOEGER, A., and SCHLUNK, J.** (1967), Gesprachsverhalten und soziometrische position: untersuchungen in stationären therapie-gruppen. (Conversational restraint and sociometric position: research on stationary therapy groups.) *Psychother. & Psychosomat.*, (Basel) 15:53-54.

09515 **PLOEGER, A., and SCHLUNK, P.** (1968), Sociometric position and conversational behavior in male and female groups of hospitalized patients. *Psychother. & Psychosomat.*, (Basel) 16:159-166.

09516 **PLOEGER, A., SEELBACK, G., and STEINMEYER, E.** (1972), (Changes in social perception and group structure during ambulatory group psychotherapy and sociometric analysis.) *Zeit. Psychother. Med. Psychol.*, (Stuttgart) 22:112-116.

09517 **PLON, H. B.** (1973), The establishment and evaluation of a group counseling program for ninth and tenth grade students: transferring from parochial to public school. *Dissert. Abstr. Internat.*, 34:3887A.

09518 **PLOWITZ, P. E.** (1950), Psychiatric service and group therapy in the rehabilitation of offenders. *J. Correct. Educat.*, 2:78-80.

09519 **PLUMMER, A. L. R.** (1972), Future predictions in therapy. *Transactional Anal. J.*, 2:107-108.

09520 **PODEL, B. M.** (1973), An investigation of the relationship between group counselor functioning and the group participants' perception of the college environment. *Dissert. Abstr. Internat.*, 134:4758A.

09521 **PODESTA, B.** (1970), Notes on re-entry. *Voices*, 6:76-80.

09522 **PODIETZ, L.** (1971), Activity group therapy for adolescents with orthopedic handicaps. *Proceed. 79th Annual Convention*, American Psychological Association, 6:639-640.

09523 **PODNOS, B., and ROBINSON, L.** (1967), A dynamic approach to supervision of trainees for group psychotherapy. *Internat. J. Group Psychother.*, 17:257-260.

09524 **POE, B. J.** (1972), The effect of sensitivity training on the relationship between risk taking and other selected behavioral factors. *Dissert. Abstr. Internat.*, 32:6037-6038B.

09525 **POETTER, G., and STEWART, H.** (1975), Fundamental values, the work ethic, and spirituality are basic for the therapeutic program at Annee Wakee. *Adolescence*, 10:247-252.

09526 **POHLEN, M.** (1972), Group analysis in the clinical field. *Psychother. & Psychosomat.*, 20:117-129.

09527 **POHLEN, M., and BAUTZ, M.** (1974), (Group-analysis as short psychotherapy: empiric comparative study in specific inhomogenic groups of psychotic and neurotic patients.) *Nervenarzt*, 45:514-533.

09528 **POHLEN, M., and WITTMAN, L.** (1979), (Concerning the concept-depending model of perception in group analysis.) *Gruppenpsychother. & Gruppendynam.*, (Goettingen) 14:105-116.

09529 **POHLMANN, K. E.** (1951), Group techniques in rehabilitation counseling. *J. Rehab.*, 17:7-9.

09530 **POINDEXTER, W. R.** (1972), The excluded parent and child in game theory. *Transactional Anal. J.*, 2:124-217.

09531 Points of View (1971), Human relations groups and the mental health professions. *Can. Ment. Health*, (Ottawa) 19:24-26.

09532 **POIRIER, J. G., and JONES, F. D.** (1977), A group operant approach to

drug dependence in the military that failed: retrospect. *Military Med.*, 142:366-369.
09533 **POKORNY, A. D., MILLER, B. A.,** and **CLEVELAND, S. E.** (1968), Response to treatment of alcoholism: a follow-up study. *Quart. J. Studies Alcohol*, 29:364-381.
09534 **POKORNY, A. D., MILLER, B. A., KANAS, T.,** and **VALLES, J.** (1973), Effectiveness of extended aftercare in the treatment of alcoholism. *Quart. J. Studies Alcohol*, 34:435-443.
09535 **POKORNY, A. D., RUMBAUT, R. D., WIGGINS, G. E.,** and **KYLE-VEGA, A.** (1973), Joint treatment of drug addicts and other psychiatric patients. *Hosp. & Community Psychiat.*, 24:234-235.
09536 **POLAN, S.,** and **SPARK, I.** (1950), Group psychotherapy of schizophrenics in an out-patient clinic. *Amer. J. Orthopsychiat.*, 20:382-396.
09537 **POLAND, W. D.,** and **JONES, J. E.** (1973), Personal orientations and perceived benefit from a human relations laboratory. *Small Group Behav.*, 4:496-502.
09538 **POLANSKY, N. A.,** and **HARKINS, E. B.** (1969), Psychodrama as an element in hospital treatment. *Psychiatry*, 32:74-87.
09539 **POLDRUGO, F.** (1980), (Experience in treating a group of alcoholics: preliminary notes after six months of treatment.) *Minerva Psichiat.*, (Turin) 21:391.
09540 **POLGAR, S.,** and **ARONSON, J.** (1964), The group interview in mental health research: methodological aspects of an inquiry among prehospitalization associates of schizophrenics. *Ment. Hygiene*, 48:85-92.
09541 **POLKE, R.** (1978), Processes of creative ego-development and ego-expansion within frame of a group dynamical workshop. *Dynam. Psychiat.*, (Berlin) 11:30-39.
09542 **POLLACK, D.** (1971), A sensitivity-training approach to group therapy with children. *Child Welfare*, 50:86-89.
09543 **POLLACK, D.,** and **STANLEY, G.** (1971), Coping and marathon sensitivity training. *Psychol. Reports*, 29:379-385.
09544 **POLLACK, H. B.** (1971), Change in homogeneous and heterogeneous sensitivity training groups. *J. Consult. & Clin. Psychol.*, 37:60-66.
09545 **POLLAK, G. K.** (1976), *Leadership of Discussion Groups*. New York: J. Wiley and Sons.
09546 **POLLAK, O.** (1976), Group psychotherapy and changing social values. *Internat. J. Group Psychother.*, 26:411-419.
09547 **POLLAK, S. W.** (1969), Theory and techniques for a therapeutic milieu. *J. Individ. Psychol.*, 25:164-173.
09548 **POLLARD, R. A.** (1960), A clergyman's first psychodramatic experience. *Group Psychother., Psychodrama & Sociometry*, 13:206-207.
09549 **POLLARD, T. D.** (1974), Influencing belief systems through teachers in service training and student group counseling. *Dissert. Abstr. Internat.*, 34:6503A.
09550 **POLLOCK, A.** (1968), Characteristics of patients recommended for individual or group treatment. *Smith Coll. Studies Soc. Work*, 39:81-82.
09551 **POLONSKY, N. A., MILLER, S. C.,** and **WHITE, R. B.** (1955), Some reservations regarding group psychotherapy in inpatient psychiatric treatment. *Group Psychother., Psychodrama & Sociometry*, 8:254-262.
09552 **POLOWAIAK, W. A.** (1973), The mediation-encounter-growth group. *Dissert. Abstr. Internat.*, 34:1732B.
09553 **POLSKY, H. W.** (1962), *Cottage Six: The Social System of Delinquent Boys in Residential Treatment*. New York: Russell Sage Foundation.
09555 **POLSKY, H. W.,** and **CLASTER, D. S.** (1968), *The Dynamics of Residential Treatment: A Social System Analysis*. Chapel Hill: University of North Carolina Press.

09556 **POLSTER, E.**, and **POLSTER, M.** (1973), *Gestalt Therapy Integrated: Contours of Theory and Practice.* New York: Brunner/Mazel.

09557 **POMERLEASE, O. F., BOBROVE, P. H.**, and **HARRIS, L. C.** (1972), Some observations on a controlled social environment for psychiatric patients. *J. Behav. Ther. & Exper. Psychiat.*, 3:15-21.

09558 **POMPILO, P. T.**, and **KREBS, R.** (1972), A time-limited group experience with a religious teaching order. *J. Religion & Health*, 11:139-152.

09559 **PONTALTI, C.** (1974), Metapsychological reflections on the first session of group analysis. *Arch. Psicol. Neurol. & Psichiat.*, (Milan) 35:577-588.

09560 **PONTALTI, C.** (1979), Sexual intervention: amplifying diagnostic functions for psychotherapeutic strategies. *Arch. Psicol., Neurol. & Psichiat.*, (Milan) 40:304-309.

09561 **POOLE, P. S.** (1973), A study of short-term group counseling with educable mentally retarded students in a junior high school. *Dissert. Abstr. Internat.*, 34:3068A.

09562 **POPE, B.** (1956), Attitudes toward group therapy in a psychiatric clinic for alcoholics. *Quart. J. Studies Alcohol*, 17:233-254.

09563 **POPE, B.** (1953), Sociometric structure and group psychotherapy on a mental hospital service for criminally insane. *Group Psychother., Psychodrama & Sociometry*, 5:183-198.

09564 **POPIEL, E.** (1971), Intrapersonal factors as correlates of interpersonal awareness in training groups. *Nursing Res.*, 20:165-167.

09565 **POPOVIĆ, M.** (1977), (Clinical inpatient therapy.) *Psihijat. Danas*, (Belgrade) 9:91-97.

09566 **POPOVIĆ, M.** (1978), (Development of group psychotherapy.) *Psihijat. Danas*, (Belgrade) 10:5-14.

09567 **POPOVIĆ, M.** (1975), (Group therapy.) *Anali Zavoda Ment. Zdravlje*, 7:7-23.

09568 **POPOVIĆ, M.** (1978), La psychothérapie de groupe des schizophrènes par l'image. (Group psychotherapy with schizophrenics using imagery.) *Psychother. & Psychosomat.*, (Basel) 29:137-142.

09569 **POPOVIĆ, M.** (1964), (Some problems in group psychotherapy of mental patients under clinical conditions.) *Med. Glasnik*, (Belgrade) 18:422-426.

09570 **POPOVIC, M.** (1973), Sociotherapeutic work with large groups of inpatients. *Anali Zavoda Ment. Zdrovlge*, 5:39-46.

09571 **PORPOTAGE, F. M. II** (1972), Sensitivity training. *Police Chief*, 39:60-61.

09572 **la PORTA, E.** (1964), (Group psychotherapy of psychotics.) *J. Brasil. Psiquiat.*, (Rio de Janeiro) 13:317-329.

09573 **PORTA, J. M.** (1975), (The Manga ceremony as an example of group therapy in a primitive tribe: Manga ritual ceremony of the Ngovayang village, South wilderness of Cameroon.) *Actas Luso.-Espanoles Neurol. Psiquiat.*, (Madrid) 3:195-199.

09574 **PORTER, B. L.** (1977), The effects of behavioral group counseling method on the study habits, attitudes and academic achievement of some differently qualified students. *Dissert. Abstr. Internat.*, 38:184A.

09575 **PORTER, K.** (1980), Combined individual and group psychotherapy: review of the literature 1965-1978. *Internat. J. Group Psychother.*, 30:107-114.

09576 **PORTER, K.** (1980), Review of L. R. Wolberg's and M. L. Aronson's *Group Therapy 1979: An Overview. Group*, 4:57-58.

09577 **PORTER, N.** (1975), Functional analysis. *Transactional Anal. J.*, 5:272-273.

09578 **PORTER, R. M.** (1965), Relationship of participation to satisfaction is small group discussions. *J. Educat. Res.*, 59:128-132.

09579 **PORTO, A.** (1958), The various approaches to group therapy. *Arch. Neuro-Psiquiat.*, 16:5-18.
09580 **POSER, E. G.** (1966), The effect of therapists' training on group therapeutic outcome. *J. Clin. Psychol.*, 30:283-289.
09581 **POSER, E. G.** (1969), The effect of therapists' training on group therapeutic outcome. In: *The Study of Abnormal Behavior: Selected Readings*, 2d ed., eds. M. Zax and G. Stricker. New York: Macmillan.
09582 **POSER, E. G.** (1966), Group therapy in Canada: a national survey. *Can. Psychiat. Assn. J.*, (Ottawa) 11:20-25.
09583 Position Statement by ACPA (1976), The use of group procedures in higher education. *J. Coll. Student Personnel*, 17:161-165.
09584 **POSNER, K. M.** (1976), The effect of two modalities of group counseling for secondary school seniors upon their locus of control expectancies. *Dissert. Abstr. Internat.*, 36:6483A.
09585 **POST, J. M.**, and **SOLOMON, L.** (1965), Group drug supervision saves staff time. *Ment. Hosp.*, 16:241-242.
09586 **POST, M. T.** (1969), Anxiety as a factor in discontinuance from group psychotherapy. *Smith Coll. Studies Soc. Work*, 50:80-81.
09587 **POSTHUMA, A. B.**, and **POSTHUMA, B. W.** (1973), Some observations on encounter group casualties. *J. Appl. Behav. Science*, 9:595-608.
09588 **POSTHUMA, B. W.**, and **POSTHUMA, A. B.** (1972), The effect of a small-group experience on occupational therapy students. *Amer. J. Occupat. Ther.*, 26:415-418.
09589 **POTHIER, P. C.** (1970), Marathon encounter groups: rationale, techniques, and crucial issues. *Perspect. Psychiat. Care*, 8:153-159.
09590 **POTHIER, P. C.** (1968), A thing called hope: creative ways of stimulating mental health. *J. Psychiat. Nursing*, 6:15-19.
09591 **POTTER, H. W.** (1952), Group psychotherapy in psychiatric practice. *Internat. J. Group Psychother.*, 2:207-208.
09592 **POTTER, M. C.** (1969), The nurse as community crisis counselor. *Nurs. Outlook*, 17:39-42.
09593 **POTTS, F.** (1954), Dr. Moreno's paper, "Transference, countertransference and tele: their relation to group research and group psychotherapy": a commentary. *Group Psychother., Psychodrama & Sociometry*, 7:323-324.
09594 **POTTS, F.** (1958), Relief of an anxiety state by a single psychodramatic session. *Group Psychother., Psychodrama & Sociometry*, 11:330-331.
09595 **POTTS, F. J.** (1960), Psychodrama of a chronic catatonic. *Internat. J. Sociometry & Sociatry*, 2:91-96.
09596 **POTTS, J. R.** (1970), Subjective effects of required group counseling in the regular curriculum for disadvantaged ninth grade students. *Dissert. Abstr. Internat.*, 30:3736A.
09597 **POTTS, L.** (1980), Considering parenthood: group support for a critical decision. *Amer. J. Orthopsychiat.*, 50:629-638.
09598 **POTTS, L. R.** (1958), Two picture series showing emotional changes during art therapy. *Internat. J. Group Psychother.*, 8:383-394.
09599 **POTTS, L. R.** (1956), The use of art in group psychotherapy. *Internat. J. Group Psychother.*, 6:115-135.
09600 **POWDERMAKER, F.**, and **FRANK, J. D.** (1972), *Group Psychotherapy: Studies in Methodology of Research and Therapy—Report of a Group Psychotherapy Research Project of the U.S. Veterans Administration.* Westport, CT: Greenwood Press.
09601 **POWDERMAKER, F.**, and **FRANK, J. D.** (1948), Group psychotherapy with neurotics. *Amer. J. Psychiat.*, 105:449-455.
09602 **POWDERMAKER, F. B.** (1951), Psychoanalytic concepts in group psychotherapy. *Internat. J. Group Psychother.*, 1:16-21.

09603 **POWDERMAKER, F. B.**, and **FRANK, J. D.** (1953), *Group Psychotherapy: Studies in Methodology of Research and Therapy—Report of a Group Psychotherapy Research Project of the U.S. Veterans Administration*, Cambridge, MA: Harvard University Press.

09604 **POWELL, C.** (1979), The induction of acute psychosis in a group setting. *Can. Psychiat. Assn. J.*, (Ottawa) 24:237-241.

09605 **POWELL, J. P.**, and **JACKSON, P.** (1964), A note on the simplified technique for recording interaction. *Human Relat.*, 17:289-291.

09606 **POWELL, J. W.** (1950), Group reading in mental hospitals. *Psychiatry*, 13:213-226.

09607 **POWELL, J. W.** (1952), Process analysis as content: a suggested basis for group classification. *J. Soc. Issues*, 8:54-64.

09608 **POWELL, J. W., STON, A. R.**, and **FRANK, J. D.** (1952), Group reading and group therapy. *Psychiatry*, 15:33-51.

09609 **POWELL, M., TAYLOR, J.**, and **SMITH, R.** (1967), Parents and child in a child guidance clinic: should they share the same therapist? *Internat. J. Group Psychother.*, 17:25-34.

09610 **POWELL, M. F.**, and **CLAYTON, M. S.** (1980), Efficacy of human relations training on selected coping behaviors of veterans in a psychiatric hospital. *J. Special. Group Work*, 5:170-176.

09611 **POWELL, R. R.** (1972), Psychological effects of exercise therapy upon institutionalized geriatric mental patients. *Dissert. Abstr. Internat.*, 33:2771A.

09612 **POWELL, T. A.** (1972), An investigation of the t-group and its effect upon group decision-making skills. *Dissert. Abstr. Internat.*, 6084A.

09613 **POWERS, R. J.** (1976), The effects of structured group counseling on the career development of ex–drug abusers. *Dissert. Abstr. Internat.*, 37:959B.

09614 **POWERS, R. J.** (1978), Enhancement of former drug abusers' career development through structured group counseling. *J. Couns. Psychol.*, 25:585.

09615 **POWLES, W. E.** (1959), Psychosexual maturity in a therapy group of disturbed adolescents. *Internat. J. Group Psychother.*, 9:429-441.

09616 **POWLES, W. E.** (1978), Review of H. M. Rabin's and M. Rosenbaum's *How to Begin a Therapy Group: 6 Approaches. Internat. J. Group Psychother.*, 28:567.

09617 **POWLES, W. E.** (1964), Varieties and uses of group psychotherapy. *Can. Psychiat. Assn. J.*, (Ottawa) 9:196-201.

09618 **POŽARNIK, H.** (1975), (Some problems of analytic group psychotherapy of suicidal patients in the department for urgent psychiatric help.) *Anali Zavoda Ment. Zdravlje*, 7:145-150.

09619 **PRABHU, P. H.** (1960), Military applications of sociometry and psychodrama. *Internat. J. Sociometry & Sociatry*, 2:104.

09620 **PRABHU, P. H.** (1959), Sociometry and psychodrama in India. *Group Psychother., Psychodrama & Sociometry*, 12:329-341.

09621 **PRABHU, P. H.** (1960), Sociometry and psychodrama in India. *Internat. J. Sociometry & Sociatry*, 2:6-17.

09622 **PRADOS, M.** (1953), Some technical aspects of group psychotherapy. *Internat. J. Group Psychother.*, 3:131-142.

09623 **PRADOS, M.** (1951), The use of films in psychotherapy. *Amer. J. Orthopsychiat.*, 21:36-46.

09624 **PRADOS, M.** (1951), The use of pictorial images in group therapy. *Amer. J. Psychother.*, 5:196-214.

09625 **PRADOS y SUCH, M.** (1965), (The audio-visual or cinematographic technic in group psychotherapy.) *Arch. Neurobiol.*, (Madrid) 28:546-561.

09626 **PRANGE, F. B.** (1963), The self-improvement group at the McNeil Island Penitentiary. *Fed. Probat.*, 27:34-36.

09627 **PRATT, J. H.** (1911), The Glass Method in the home treatment of tuberculosis and what it has accomplished. *Trans. Amer. Climat. Assn.*, 27:87-118.

09628 **PRATT, J. H.** (1907), The class method of treating consumption in the homes of the poor. *J. Amer. Med. Assn.*, 49:755-757.

09629 **PRATT, J. H.** (1946), The group method in the treatment of psychosomatic disorders. *Psychodrama Monogr.* No. 19. New York: Beacon House.

09630 **PRATT, J. H.** (1945), The group method in the treatment of psychosomatic disorders. *Sociometry*, 8:323-331.

09631 **PRATT, J. H.** (1906), The "home sanatorium" treatment of consumption. *Bost. Med. Surg. J.*, 154:210-216.

09632 **PRATT, J. H.** (1906), The "home sanatorium" treatment of consumption. *Johns Hopkins Hosp. Bull.*, 17:140-144.

09633 **PRATT, J. H.** (1934), The influence of emotions in the causation and cure of psychoneuroses. *Internat. Clin.*, 4:1-16.

09634 **PRATT, J. H.** (1907), The organization of tuberculosis classes. *Med. Communicat. Mass. Med. Soc.*, 20:475-492.

09635 **PRATT, J. H.** (1922), The principles of class treatment and their application to various chronic diseases. *Hosp. Soc. Serv. Quart.*, 6:401-411.

09636 **PRATT, J. H.** (1908), Results obtained in treatment of pulmonary tuberculosis and the class method. *Brit. Med. J.*, (London) 2:1070-1071.

09637 **PRATT, J. H.** (1917), The tuberculosis class: an experiment in home treatment. *Proceed. N.Y. Conf. Hosp. Soc. Serv.*, 4:49-68.

09638 **PRATT, J. H.** (1953), The use of Dejerine's methods in the treatment of the common neuroses. *Bull. New Engl. Med. Ctr.*, 15:1-9.

09639 **PRATT, J. H.** (1975), The use of Dejerine's methods in the treatment of the common neuroses by group psychotherapy. In: *Group Psychotherapy and Group Function*, 2d ed., eds. M. Rosenbaum and M. M. Berger. New York: Basic Books.

09640 **PRATT, J. H.**, and **JOHNSON, P. E.** (1950), *A Twenty Year Experiment in Group Therapy*. Boston: New Engl. Med. Ctr.

09641 **PRATT, S.**, and **DELANGE, W.** (1963), The admission therapy group treatment of choice at a state hospital. *Ment. Hosp.*, 14:222-224.

09642 **PRATT, S. J.**, and **FISCHER, J.** (1975), Behavior modification: changing hyperactive behavior in a children's group. *Perspect. Psychiat. Care*, 8:37-42.

09643 **PRATT, W. M.** (1970), The effectiveness of the use of the t-group laboratory method as an adjunct to a developmental approach to teaching. *Dissert. Abstr. Internat.*, 31:234A-235A.

09644 **PRAŽIĆ, B.** (1969), (Proverbs and sayings in group therapy.) *Neuropsihijatrija*, (Zagreb) 17:99-105.

09645 **PREDESCU, V.** (1970), (Group psychotherapy: ii. psychological dynamics in group therapy.) *Neurologia*, (Bucharest) 15:243-249.

09646 **PREDESCU, V.**, and **IONESCU, G.** (1970), (Group psychotherapy: iii.) *Neurologia*, (Bucharest) 15:289-300.

09647 **PREDESCU, V.**, and **IONESCU, G.** (1970), Psihoterapia in grup: i. probleme de metodologie psihoterapuetica. (Group psychotherapy: i. problems of psychotherapeutic methods.) *Neurologia*, (Bucharest) 15:49-59.

09648 **PREDIGER, D. J.**, and **BAUMANN, R. R.** (1970), Developmental group counseling: an outcome study. *J. Couns. Psychol.*, 17:527-533.

09649 **PRENTICE, P. S.** (1972), The process effects of trust destroying behavior on the quality of communication in the small group. *Dissert. Abstr. Internat.*, 33:1871A.

09650 **PRENTICE, N. M.** (1977), Issues in the transfer of children in dynamic psychotherapy. *J. Amer. Acad. Child Psychol.*, 16:693.

09651 **PRESCOTT, P. S.** (1970), The theater of neurosis presents: "Let it all hang out." *Look*, (May 19) 34.
09652 **PRESTON, B. H.** (1957), The alcoholic in group psychotherapy with psychotic patients. *Ohio State Med. J.*, 53:656-658.
09653 **PRESTON, B. H.** (1954), The class method in the treatment of psychotic patients. *Internat. J. Group Psychother.*, 4:321-330.
09654 **PRESTON, B. H.** (1958), Group activities with patients in a mental hospital. *Internat. J. Group Psychother.*, 8:459-465.
09655 **PRESTON, F. B.** (1960), Combined individual, joint and group therapy in the treatment of alcoholism. *Ment. Hygiene*, 44:522-528.
09656 **PREUSS, H. G.** (1966), *Analytische Gruppenpsychotherapie: Grundlagen und Praxis.* (*Analytic Group Psychotherapy: Principles and Practice.*) Munich: Urban & Schwarzenberg.
09657 **PREUSS, H. G.** (1975), (Group psychotherapy and psychosomatic medicine.) *Gruppenpsychother. & Gruppendynam.*, (Goettingen) 9:191-211.
09658 **PREWITT, C. B.** (1975), The use of third-force psychology and small growth group in the air force chaplain ministry. *Dissert. Abstr. Internat.*, 36:3796A.
09659 **PRICE, E. A.** (1971), Parent discussion groups. *Elem. School Guid. & Couns.*, 6:92-97.
09660 **PRICE, J. V.** (1971), Adolescents/youth. *Amer. J. Orthopsychiat.*, 41:293-306.
09661 **PRICE, N. I.** (1980), The effects of activity-interview group counseling on the self-esteem and classroom behavior of selected middle school students. *Dissert. Abstr. Internat.*, 41:111A. (University Microfilms No. 8016235.)
09662 **PRIDHAM, K. F.** (1975), Acts of turning as stress-resolving mechanisms in work groups: with special reference to the work of W. R. Bion. *Human Relat.*, 28:229-248.
09663 **PRIEN, E. P.**, and **CULLER, A. R.** (1964), Leaderless group discussion participation and interobserver agreements. *J. Soc. Psychol.*, 62:321-328.
09664 **PRIEN, E. P.**, and **LEE, R. J.** (1965), Peer ratings and leaderless group discussions for evaluation of classroom performance. *Psychol. Reports*, 16:59-64.
09665 **PRILL, H. J.** (1960), Gruppentherapeutische erfahrungen in der geburtshilfe und gynakologie. (Group therapy experience in obstetrics and gynecology.) *Praxis der Psychother.*, 5:208-216.
09666 **PRINCE, R. M., ACKERMAN, R. E.**, and **BARKSDALE, D. S.** (1973), Collaborative provision of aftercare services. *Amer. J. Psychiat.*, 130:930-932.
09667 **PRINCE, R. M., ACKERMAN, R. E., CARTER, N. C.**, and **HARRISON, A.** (1977), Group aftercare: impact on a statewide program. *Diseases Nerv. Systems*, 38:793-796.
09668 **PROBSTEIN, I.**, and **KUSUDA, P.** (1962), Use of group techniques in the preadmission process. *Amer. J. Ment. Deficiency*, 67:227-231.
09669 **PROCHASKA, J. O.**, and **MARZILLI, R.** (1973), Modifications of the Masters and Johnson approach to sexual problems. *Psychother.: Theory, Res. & Pract.*, 10:294-296.
09670 **PROEDROU, R. D.** (1975), The adjunctive use of videotape feedback in group psychotherapy. *Dissert. Abstr. Internat.*, 35:6519.
09671 Program, 24th Annual meeting, American Society of Group Psychotherapy and Psychodrama (1964), March 19-21, 1965. *Group Psychother., Psychodrama & Sociometry*, 17:236-243.
09672 **PROKOP, H.** (1967), (Psychotherapeutic methods for alcoholics.) *Ther. Gegenwart*, (Munich) 106:1394.
09673 **PROKOP, H.**, and **FELLNER, F.** (1963), (Experience with group psycho-

therapy at the Universitaets-Nervenklinik Innsbruck.) *Wiener Med. Wochenschr.*, (Vienna) 113:436-439.
09674 **PROPPER, V.** (1980), Psychodrama in rehearsals of Moliere's "Tartuffe." *Group Psychother., Psychodrama & Sociometry*, 33:71-87.
09675 **PROSEN, H.**, and **LAMBERD, W. G.** (1966), Movement in a ward community group as a reflection of patient change. *Internat. J. Group Psychother.*, 16:291-303.
09676 **PROSSER, K. B.** (1954), A survey of practices in group therapy. Unpublished masters thesis, University of Southern California.
09677 **PRUITT, W. A.** (1963), Satiation effect in vocationally oriented group therapy as determined by the Palo Alto group psychotherapy scale. *Group Psychother., Psychodrama & Sociometry*, 16:55-58.
09678 **PSATHAS, G.** (1960), Interaction process analysis of two psychotherapy groups. *Internat. J. Group Psychother.*, 10:430-445.
09679 **PSATHAS, G.** (1967), Overview of process studies in group psychotherapy. *Internat. J. Group Psychother.*, 17:225-235.
09680 **PSATHAS, G.** (1960), Phase movement and equilibrium tendencies in interaction process in psychotherapy groups. *Sociometry*, 23:177-194.
09681 **PSATHAS, G.**, and **IGERSHEIMER, W.** (1966), Interaction processes in two psychotherapy groups: therapist and patient differences. *J. Nerv. & Ment. Diseases*, 142:340-354.
09682 Psychiatry residents undergo 3-year group psychotherapy (1970). *Roche Report: Front. Hosp. Psychiat.*, 7:3.
09683 Psychoanalytic group therapy found to benefit elderly (1967). *Roche Report: Front. Hosp. Psychiat.*, 4:1-2.
09684 **PTHIER, P. C.** (1968), A clinical application of child psychiatric nursing concepts to expand the scope of community health nursing practice. *ANA Clin. Sessions*, 125-130.
09685 **PUCKETT, D. E. W.** (1976), Educational counseling groups for black adolescent females from a low income housing area. *Dissert. Abstr. Internat.*, 37:1472A.
09686 **PUESCHEL, S. M.**, and **YEATMAN, S.** (1977), An educational and counselling program for phenylketonuric adolescent girls and their parents. *Soc. Work & Health Care*, 3:29-36.
09687 **PUGH, H. W.** (1980), The use of role theory in training the unemployed disadvantaged in job seeking skills: a group approach. *Dissert. Abstr. Internat.*, 40:4902A. (University Microfilms No. 8005198.)
09688 **PULLEN, G.** (1975), Social therapy. *Brit. J. Psychiat.*, (Ashford) 135:379.
09689 **PULLINGER, W. F.** (1968), A twelve-week discharge program. *Hosp. & Community Psychiat.*, 19:21-23.
09690 **PULOS, L.** (1971), The human potential movement: a new frontier. *Can. Ment. Health*, (Ottawa) 19:4-9.
09691 **PUMPIAN-MINDLIN, E.** (1955), The psychoanalytic concept of resistance and its relation to group psychotherapy. *J. Couns. Psychol.*, 2:58-61.
09692 **PUNDIK, J.**, and **DAVIDOVICH de PUNDIK, M. A.** (1974), *Introducción al Psicodrama y a las Nuevas Experiencias Grupales: Entrenamiento Sensorial, Grupos de Encuentros, Grupos Marathón, Laboratorios Intensivos, Roleplaying.* (*Introduction to Psychodrama and the New Group Experiences: Sensory Awareness, Encounter Groups, Marathon Groups, Intensive Laboratories and Roleplaying.*) Buenos Aires: Editorial Paidós.
09693 **PURINTON, M., HEALY, J.**, and **WHITNEY, B.** (1974), Layers of self: a group fantasy technique. *Psychother.: Theory, Res. & Pract.*, 11:83-86.
09694 **PUTMAN, A. O.** (1974), Effects of marathon encounter groups on self-reported behavior in interpersonal contexts. *Dissert. Abstr. Internat.*, 34:3506B.

09695 **PUTTER, Z. H.** (1967), Group approaches in the care of the chronically ill. *J. Jewish Communal Serv.*, 45:177-183.
09696 **PYKE, S. W.**, and **NEELY, C. A.** (1970), Evaluation of a group training program. *J. Communicat.*, 20:291-304.
09697 **PYKE, S. W.**, and **NEELY, C. A.** (1975), Training and evaluation of communication skills. *Can. Counselor*, (Ottawa) 9:20-30.
09698 **PYLE, R. R.** (1973), An intervention study of behavioral counseling for interpersonal problems. *Dissert. Abstr. Internat.*, 34:422B.
09699 **PYRON, H. C.** (1964), An experimental study of the role of reflective thinking in business and professional conferences and discussions. *Speech Monogr.*, No. 31, 157-161.

Q

09700 **QUARLES van UFFORD, W. J.** (1965), (Experiences with sending asthmatic children to so-called "therapeutic summer camps.") *Allerg. Asthma*, (Leipzig) 11:129-134.

09701 **QUATRANO, L. A.** (1973), Teaching elementary students to plan: a comparison of simulation and group counseling procedures. *Dissert. Abstr. Internat.*, 33:3402A.

09702 **QUATTLEBAUM, J. T.** (1967), A therapeutic community on a short-term psychiatric unit. *Hosp. & Community Psychiat.*, 18:353-360.

09703 **QUAYTMAN, W.** (1969), Impressions of the Esalen (Schutz) phenomenon. *J. Contemp. Psychother.*, 2:57-64.

09704 **QUEKELBERGHE, R.**, and **DROSTE, G.** (1976), Bibliography of marathon group research, 1966-1975. *Interpersonal Develop.*, 6:42-47.

09705 **QUERY, W. T.** (1961), An experimental investigation of self-disclosure and its effect upon some properties of psychotherapeutic groups. *Dissert. Abstr. Internat.*, 31:2263B.

09706 **QUERY, W. T.** (1964), Self-disclosure as a variable in group psychotherapy. *Internat. J. Group Psychother.*, 14:107-115.

09707 **QUEVEDO, S. S.** (1977), (Group psychotherapy: working team in community psychiatry.) *Neurol.-Neurocir.-Psiquiat.*, (Mexico City) 18:121-126.

09708 **QUIMBY, S. L.** (1975), An experimental analysis of a proposed methodology for investigating self-disclosure, feedback, leads, and impersonal communication in a t-group setting. *Dissert. Abstr. Internat.*, 36:6484A.

09709 **QUINN, D. C.** (1969), Preadolescent girls in "transitional" group therapy. *Amer. J. Orthopsychiat.*, 39:263-264.

09710 **QUINN, J.** (1959), Emotional aspects of training discussion leaders. *Personnel J.*, 36:68-77.

09711 **QUINTANO, J. H.** (1974), Effects of content centered group counseling on memory recall in alcoholic brain damaged subjects. *Dissert. Abstr. Internat.*, 35:1988-1989.

09712 **QUINTART, J. C.** (1972), Problems of treating patients by group and individual therapy concurrently. *Feuillets Psychiat. Liège*, 5:445-456.

09713 **QUINTEROS, L. H.** (1966), El aprendizaje en el grupo de discusion y la perception. (Learning in discussion groups and perception.) *Acta Psiquiat. Psicol. Amer. Latina*, (Buenos Aires) 12:263-267.

09714 **QUIRK, M. P.** (1976), Training in human relations for dormitory resident assistants. *Psychol. Reports*, 39:123-129.

R

09715 **RABBAN, M.** (1973), Group effectiveness. *Camp. Mag.*, 45:8-9.

09716 **RABE, W.** (1968), (The alcoholic and his treatment.) *Deutsche Schwesternzeit.*, (Stuttgart) 21:269-272.

09717 **RABEN, C. S.** (1974), Participation and member power base in group decision making. *Dissert. Abstr. Internat.*, 34:4109A.

09718 **RABIN, H. M.** (1967), The benefits of co-therapy. *Sandoz Psychiat. Spectator*, 4:13-14.

09719 **RABIN, H. M.** (1974), Countertransference in analytic group psychotherapy. In: *Group Therapy 1974: An Overview*, eds. L. R. Wolberg and M. L. Aronson. New York: Stratton Intercontinental Medical Books.

09720 **RABIN, H. M.** (1967), How does co-therapy compare with regular group therapy? *Amer. J. Psychother.*, 21:244-255.

09721 **RABIN, H. M.** (1970), Preparing patients for group psychotherapy. *Internat. J. Group Psychother.*, 20:135-145.

09722 **RABIN, H. M.** (1977), The use of role playing to further working through an analytic group psychotherapy. In: *Group Therapy 1977: An Overview*, ed. L. R. Wolberg. New York: Stratton Intercontinental Medical Books.

09723 **RABIN, H. M.**, and **ROSENBAUM, M.** (1976), *How to Begin a Psychotherapy Group: Six Approaches.* New York: Gordon and Breach.

09724 **RABINER, C. J.**, and **DRUCKER, M.** (1967), Use of psychodrama with hospitalized schizophrenic patients. *Diseases Nerv. System*, 28:34-38.

09725 **RABINER, E. K.**, **WELLS, C. F.**, and **ZAWEL, D.** (1975), The assessment of individual coping capacities in a group therapy setting. *Amer. J. Orthopsychiat.*, 45:399-413.

09726 **RABKIN, R.** (1979), Discussion: of scapegoats, strawmen, and scarecrows. *Internat. J. Fam. Ther.*, 1:97-99.

09727 **RABON, J.**, **MANOS, J. J.**, and **ENGELBERG, L.** (1979), Separate realities. *Small Group Behav.*, 10:445-474.

09728 **RABOW, J.** (1965), Quantitative aspects of the group psychotherapist's role behavior: a methodological note. *J. Soc. Psychol.*, 67:31-37.

09729 **RACHMAN, A. W.** (1977), A biography of S. R. Slavson: a personal reaction. *Group*, 1:56-64.

09730 **RACHMAN, A. W.** (1971), Encounter techniques in analytic group psychotherapy with adolescents. *Internat. J. Group Psychother.*, 21:319-329.

09731 **RACHMAN, A. W.** (1972), Group psychotherapy in treating the adolescent identity crisis. *Internat. J. Child Psychother.*, 1:97-119.

09732 **RACHMAN, A. W.** (1975), *Identity Group Psychotherapy with Adolescents.* Springfield, IL: C. C. Thomas.

09733 **RACHMAN, A. W.** (1975), The issue of countertransference in encounter and marathon group psychotherapy. In: *Group Therapy 1975: An Overview*, eds. L. R. Wolberg and M. L. Aronson. New York: Stratton Intercontinental Medical Books.

09734 **RACHMAN, A. W.** (1970), Marathon group psychotherapy: from where did it come? what does it mean? where is it taking us? *Sandoz Psychiat. Spectator*, 6:2-3.

09735 **RACHMAN, A. W.** (1970), Marathon group psychotherapy: its origins, significance, and direction. *J. Group Psychoanal. Process*, 2:57-74.

09736 **RACHMAN, A. W.** (1974), The role of "fathering" in group psychotherapy with adolescent delinquent males. *Correct. & Soc. Psychiat.*, 20:11-22.

09738 **RACHMAN, A. W.** (1969), Talking it out rather than fighting it out: prevention of a delinquent gang war by group therapy intervention. *Internat. J. Group Psychother.*, 19:518-521.

09739 **RACHMAN, A. W.,** and **HELLER, M. E.** (1976), Peer group psychotherapy with adolescent drug–abusers. *Internat. J. Group Psychother.*, 26:373-383.
09740 **RACKOW, L. L.** (1951), Modified insulin, psychodrama, and rehabilitation techniques in the treatment of anxiety and tension states. *Group Psychother., Psychodrama & Sociometry*, 4:215-222.
09741 **RACY, J.** (1969), How a group grows. *Amer. J. Nursing*, 69:2396-2402.
09742 **RADEBOLD, H.** (1976), (Psychoanalytic group psychotherapy with older adults.) *Zeit. Gerontol.*, (Darmstadt) 9:128-142.
09743 **RADER, B. B.** (1970), Koinonia and the therapeutic relationship. *Pastoral Psychol.*, 21:39-44.
09744 **RADER, F. C.** (1971), Group counseling with secondary school norm violators. *Dissert. Abstr. Internat.*, 32:797A.
09745 **RADER, G. E.** (1960), Rorschach productivity and participation in group psychotherapy. *J. Clin. Psychol.*, 16:422-424.
09746 **RAFAEL PAZ, J.** (1962), La psicoterapia del grupo en pacientes hospitalizados. (Group psychotherapy with hospitalized patients.) *Acta Psiquiat. Psicol. Argentina*, 8:231-234.
09747 **RAFFERS, T.** (1969), Conditioning a style of interaction in counseling groups and its effects on behavior and attitude change in college students. *Dissert. Abstr. Internat.*, 30:2915B.
09748 **RAHE, R. H., WARD, H. W.,** and **HAYES, V.** (1979), Brief group therapy in myocardial infarction rehabilitation: three-to-four-year follow-up of a controlled trial. *Psychosomat. Med.*, 41:229-242.
09749 **RAHE, R. H., O'NEILL, T., HAGAN, A.,** and **ARTHUR, R. J.** (1975), Brief group therapy following myocardial infarction: eighteen-month follow-up of a controlled trial. *Internat. J. Psychiat. Med.*, 6:349-358.
09750 **RAHE, R. H., TUFFLI, C. F., SUCHOR, R. J.,** and **ARTHUR, R. J.** (1973), Group therapy in the outpatient management of post-myocardial infarction patients. *Psychiat. Med.*, 4:77-88.
09751 **RAINEY, J. D.** (1976), Q-therapy and schizophrenic gaze. *New Zeal. Psychologist*, (Wellington) 5:11-15.
09752 **RAJAN, K. V.** (1956), Psychotherapy in India. *Internat. J. Sociometry & Sociatry*, 1:33-37.
09753 **RAJOKOVICH, M.** (1969), Meeting the needs of parents with a mentally retarded child. *J. Psychiat. Nursing*, 7:207-211.
09754 **RAKHAVRY, Y. T.** (1979), The phenomenon of dependency in group therapy. *Egyptian J. Psychiat.*, (Cairo) 2:205-220.
09755 **RAKIĆ, Z.** (1979), (Dynamic approach possibilities in psychotherapy of secondary impotence.) *Psihijat. Danas*, (Belgrade) 11:345-350.
09756 **RALPH, G. S.** (1974), The t-group trainer in task and socio-emotional leadership roles. *Dissert. Abstr. Internat.*, 34:5642A.
09757 **RAMIREZ, E.** (1967), Help for the addict. *Amer. J. Nursing*, 67:2348-2353.
09758 **RAMIREZ, F.** (1970), (Integration of a dynamic–behavioral psychotherapeutic method.) *Acta Psiquiat. Psicol. Amer. Latina*, (Buenos Aires) 16:125-134.
09759 **RAMIREZ, F.** (1970), La psicotherapia grupal dinamico-conductual en los alcholistas. (Dynamic behavioral group therapy among alcohol drinkers.) *Acta Psiquiat. Psicol. Amer. Latina*, (Buenos Aires) 16:345-349.
09760 **RAMIREZ-CANCEL, C. M.** (1975), Effects of verbal reinforcement and modeling in group counseling on the career–information seeking behavior of college freshmen. *Dissert. Abstr. Internat.*, 36:2719A.
09761 **RAMPAGE, C. R.** (1979), Review of L. R. Ormont's and H. S. Strean's *Practice of Conjoint Therapy: Combining Individual and Group Treatment. Contemp. Psychol.*, 24:335.

09762 **RAMPLING, D. J.**, and **WILLIAMS, R. A.** (1977), Evaluation of group process using visual analogue scales. *Austral. & New Zeal. J. Psychiat.*, (Carlton) 11:189-191.

09763 **RAMSEY, G. V.** (1967), Review of group methods with parents of the mentally retarded. *Amer. J. Ment. Deficiency*, 71:857-863.

09764 **RAMSEY, G. V.** (1964), Sociotherapeutic camping for the mentally ill. *Soc. Work*, 9:45-53.

09765 **RAMSHORN, M. T.** (1970), The group as a therapeutic tool. *Perspect. Psychiat. Care*, 8:104-105.

09766 **RANCE, C.**, and **PRICE, A.** (1973), Poetry as a group project. *Amer. J. Occupat. Ther.*, 27:252-255.

09767 **RAND, L. P.**, and **CAREW, D. K.** (1970), Comparison of t-group didactic approaches to training undergraduate resident assistants. *J. Coll. Student Personnel*, 11:432-438.

09768 **RAND, M. E.** (1970), The use of didactic group therapy with academic underachievers in a college setting. *Dissert. Abstr. Internat.*, 30:4379B.

09769 **RANDALL, G. C.**, and **ROGERS, W. C.** (1950), Group therapy for epileptics. *Amer. J. Psychiat.*, 107:422-427.

09770 **RANDAR, M. A.** (1973), Systems of group work: Roger's and Johnson's—a comparison with implications for an integrated model. *Internat. J. Soc. Psychiat.*, (London) 18:280-286.

09771 **RANDELL, B. P.** (1971), Short-term group therapy with the adolescent drug offender. *Perspect. Psychiat. Care*, 9:123-128.

09772 **RANDOLPH, D. L.** (1974), Training the counselor as a behavioral consultant: a workshop model. *Counselor Educat. & Supervision*, 14:147-150.

09773 **RANDOLPH, D. L.**, and **HARDAGE, NELL C.** (1973), Behavioral consultation and group counseling with potential dropouts. *Elem. School Guid. & Couns.*, 7:204-209.

09774 **RANDOLPH, J. L.**, and **WEINBACH, R. W.** (1979), Career counseling for the rejected professional school applicant. *Coll. Nirv.*, 55:60-68.

09775 **RANGELL, M.** (1962), Random thoughts on spontaneity. *Group Psychother., Psychodrama & Sociometry*, 15:132-133.

09776 **RANIER, J. D., FARKAS, T., ALTSCHULER, K. Z.**, and **VOLLENWELDER, J. A.** (1965), Psychiatric services for deaf patients: i. a comprehensive program in a special unit. *Ment. Hosp.*, 16:170-172.

09777 **RANIERI, R. F.**, and **PRATT, T. C.** (1978), Sibling therapy. *Soc. Work*, 23:418-419.

09778 **RANK, R. C.** (1972), Encouraging counselor trainee affective group behavior by social modeling. *Counselor Educat. & Supervision*, 11:270-278.

09779 **RANKIN, J. E.** (1957), A group therapy experiment with mothers of mentally deficient children. *Amer. J. Ment. Deficiency*, 62:49-55.

09780 **RANSBERG, M.** (1951), Integration of group therapy and individual therapy. *Internat. J. Group Psychother.*, 1:115-118.

09781 **RAPOPORT, R.**, and **RAPOPORT, R.** (1959), Permissiveness and treatment in a therapeutic community. *Psychiatry*, 22:57-64.

09782 **RAPP, H. M.** (1975), The roles of a parent discussion group leader. *Personnel & Guid. J.*, 54:110-112.

09783 **RAPPAPORT, E.** (1979), General versus situation specific trait anxiety in prediction of state anxiety during group therapy. *Psychol. Reports*, 44:715-718.

09785 **RAPPAPORT, H.** (1977), Psychotherapy with natural groups: an adoption of pre-scientific healing. *Psychother.: Theory, Res. & Pract.*, 14:181-187.

09786 **RAPPAPORT, H. R.** (1979), Is there hope in psychotherapy? Toward the specification of one nonspecific factor in effective psychotherapy and behavior change. *Dissert. Abstr. Internat.*, 40:5416B.

09787 **RAPPAPORT, J.** (1969), Nonprofessionals in a mental hospital: college students as group leaders with chronic patients. *Dissert. Abstr. Internat.*, 30:1365B.

09788 **RAPPAPORT, J., GROSS, T.,** and **LEPPER, C.** (1973), Modeling, sensitivity training, and instruction: implications for the training of college student volunteers and for outcome research. *J. Consult. & Clin. Psychol.*, 40:99-107.

09789 **RAPPAPORT, R. G.** (1971), Group therapy in prison. *Internat. J. Group Psychother.*, 21:489-496.

09790 **RAPPARD, P.** (1955), Psychopathologie et clubs psychotherapiques. (Psychopathology and group psychotherapy.) *Evolut. Psychiat.*, (Toulouse) 2:349-357.

09791 **RASHKIS, H. A.** (1959), The development of group psychotherapy in a clinical research setting. *Internat. J. Group Psychother.*, 9:504-509.

09792 **RASHKIS, H. A.** (1967), The principle of organization and the treatment of individual and multiple patients. *Comprehens. Psychiat.*, 8:135-140.

09793 **RASHKIS, H. A.** (1946), Some phenomena of group psychotherapy. *J. Nerv. & Ment. Diseases*, 104:187-191.

09794 **RASHKIS, H. A.,** and **SHASKAN, D. A.** (1946), The effects of group psychotherapy on personality inventory scores. *Amer. J. Orthopsychiat.*, 16:345-349.

09795 **RASHMAN, S.** (1961), Sexual disorders and behavior therapy. *Amer. J. Psychiat.*, 118:235-240.

09796 **RASKIN, N. J.** (1965), The psychotherapy research project of the American Academy of Psychotherapists. *Proceed., 73rd Annual Convention*, American Psychological Association, 253-254.

09797 **RASMUSSEN, D. M.** (1968), A comparison of the effects of commitment-action group therapy with two other weight reduction programs and a no-treatment control group on obese university females. *Dissert. Abstr. Internat.*, 29:1136-1137.

09798 **RASMUSSEN, J. L.** (1968), The effect of five discussion procedures on the development of sentiments of competition and cooperation. *Dissert. Abstr. Internat.*, 28:3286-3287.

09799 **RASSIDAKIS, N. C., YANNACOPOULOS, J.,** and **MALLIARA, A.** (1959), On the application of sociometry to three psychotherapeutic groups of chronic schizophrenic patients. *Group Psychother., Psychodrama & Sociometry*, 12:69-85.

09800 **RATH, R.,** and **MISRA, S. K.** (1963), Change of attitudes as a function of size of discussion groups. *J. Soc. Psychol.*, 59:247-257.

09801 **RATHBONE-McCUAN, E.,** and **LEVENSON, J.** (1975), Impact of socialization therapy in a geriatric day-care setting. *Gerontologist*, 15:338-342.

09802 **RATHBUN, C.,** and **KOLODNY, R. L.** (1967), A group work approach in cross–cultural adoptions. *Children*, 14:117-121.

09803 **RATHOD, N. H., GREGORY, E., BLOWS, D.,** and **THOMAS, G. H.** (1966), A two-year follow-up study of alcoholic patients. *Brit. J. Psychiat.*, (Ashford) 112:683-692.

09804 **RATHUS, S. A.** (1972), An experimental investigation of assertive training in a group setting. *J. Behav. Ther. & Exper. Psychiat.*, 3:81-86.

09805 **RATNAVALE, D. N.** (1973), Psychiatry in Shanghai, China: observations in 1973. *Amer. J. Psychiat.*, 130:1082-1087.

09806 **RATNER, R. S.** (1969), The use of interaction process analysis in nondirective group psychotherapy. *Dissert. Abstr. Internat.*, 30:1654-1655.

09807 **RATTRAY, P. R.** (1973), A student-parent retreat. *Personnel & Guid. J.*, 52:114-115.

09808 **RATUSNIK, C. M.,** and **RATUSNIK, D. L.** (1976), A therapeutic milieu for establishing and expanding communicative behaviors in psychotic children. *J. Speech & Hearing Disorders*, 41:70-92.

09809 **RATZLAFF, C. N.** (1970), Effects of relaxation on self-report measures of a basic-encounter group experience. *Dissert. Abstr. Internat.*, 31:2116A.

09810 **RATZLOFF, L. W.** (1976), Salvation: individualistic or communal? *J. Psychol. & Theology*, 4:108-117.

09811 **RAUBOLT, R.** (1977), Review of A. W. Rachman's *Identity Group Psychotherapy with Adolescents. Psychol. in Schools*, 14:125.

09812 **RAUBOLT, R.**, and **BRATTER, T. E.** (1976), Beyond adolescent group psychotherapy: the caring community. *Addict. Ther.*, 1:10-16.

09813 **RAUBOLT, R., STRAUSS, M.**, and **BRATTER, T. E.** (1976), Evolution of an adolescent caring community. *Together: J. Special. Group Work*, 1:32-39.

09814 **RAUBOLT, R. R.** (1975), Adolescent peer networks: an alternative to alienation. *Correct. Psychiat. & J. Soc. Ther.*, 21:1-3.

09815 **RAUBOLT, R. R.**, and **RACHMAN, A. W.** (1980), A therapeutic group experience for fathers. *Internat. J. Group Psychother.*, 30:229-239.

09816 **RAVEN, B. H.**, and **SHAW, J. I.** (1970), Interdependence and group problem–solving in the triad. *J. Personality & Soc. Psychol.*, 14:157-165.

09817 **RAVE-SCHWANK, M.** (1976), (Social learning for mentally ill through role playing in a group.) *Psychiat. Praxis*, (Stuttgart) 3:58-62.

09818 **RAVID, R. S.** (1969), Effect of group therapy on long term individual patients. *Dissert. Abstr. Internat.*, 30:2427B.

09819 **RAVSTEN, L. A.** (1967), Mood–judgement from vocal cues and its relationship to personality variables and group psychotherapy. *Dissert. Abstr. Internat.*, 27:2876-2877.

09820 **RAWLINGS, E. I.**, and **CARTER, D. K.** (1977), *Psychotherapy for Women: Treatment toward Equality*. Springfield, IL: C. C. Thomas.

09821 **RAWLINGS, E. I.**, and **GAVRON, E. F.** (1973), Responders and non-responders to an accelerated time-limited group: a case history. *Perspect. Psychiat. Care*, 11:65-69.

09822 **RAWSON, M. B.** (1971), Teaching children with language disabilities in small groups. *J. Learning Disabil.*, 4:17-25.

09823 **RAY, M. L.** (1967), The effect of choice, controversy and selectivity on the effectiveness of various defenses to persuasion. *Dissert. Abstr. Internat.*, 28:2340-2341.

09824 **RAYNER, P.** (1977), Psycho–drama as a medium for intermediate treatment. *Brit. J. Soc. Work*, (Birmingham) 7:443-453.

09825 **RAZZELL, M.** (1975), "No thanks, I've quit smoking." *Can. Nurse*, (Ottawa) 71:23-25.

09826 **READ, P. B.** (1974), Source of authority and the legitimation of leadership in small groups. *Sociometry*, 37:189-193.

09827 **READER, D.** (1969), *Designing and Conducting Sensitivity Training Laboratories for Management.* Pretoria: National Institute for Personnel Research.

09828 **READER, D. H.**, and **von MAYER, B.** (1966), T-groups and a process–oriented model of their development. *Psychol. Africaine*, 11:74-89.

09829 **REAKES, J. C.** (1979), Behavior rehearsal revisited: a multi-faceted tool for the instructor. *J. Nursing Educat.*, 18:48-51.

09830 **REARDON, R. C.**, and **BURCK, H. D.** (1972), An encounter group and changes in counselors' values. *J. Employment Couns.*, 9:140-150.

09831 **RECHENBERGER, H. G.** (1963), (The symbol drama in psychotherapeutic practice: a case report.) *Zeit. Psychother. Med. Psychol.*, (Stuttgart) 13:239-248.

09832 **RECKEL, K.** (1972), Man in a group: group relations in psychiatry. *Schweiz. Arch. Neurol., Neurochir. & Psychiat.*, (Zurich) 110:131-142.

09833 **RECKLESS, J.**, and **BYRD, P.** (1980), A system of group therapy for the treatment of marital and sexual dysfunction. *J. Sex & Marital Ther.*, 6:199-204.

09834 **RECKLESS, J.**, and **FAUNTLEROY, A.** (1972), Groups, spouses and hospitalization as a trial of treatment in psychosomatic illness. *Psychosomatics*, 13:353.

09835 **RECKLESS, J., HAWKINS, D.**, and **FAUNTLEROY, A.** (1973), Time extended group therapy sessions in a remote setting. *Amer. J. Psychiat.*, 130:1024-1026.

09836 **RECKLESS, J. B.** (1972), Audio-visual feedback in group psychotherapy: a method using tape recordings and full colour photographs. *Can. Psychiat. Assn. J.*, (Ottawa) 17:331-332.

09837 **RECKLESS, J. B.** (1971), A behavioral treatment of bronchial asthma in modified group therapy. *Psychosomatics*, 12:168-173.

09838 **RECKLESS, J. B.** (1970), Enforced outpatient treatment of advantaged pseudosociopathic neurotically disturbed young women. *Can. Psychiat. Assn. J.*, (Ottawa) 15:335-345.

09839 **RECKLESS, J. B.** (1972), Hysterical behavior treated by psychotherapy and conditioning procedures in a group setting. *Psychosomatics*, 13:263-264.

09840 **REDDICK, S. K.**, and **COBLE, P. A.** (1973), Discharge and discharge group. *J. Psychiat. Nursing*, 11:12-15.

09841 **REDDY, W. B.** (1975), Diagnosing team problem-solving effectiveness: a comparison of four populations. *Small Group Behav.*, 6:174-186.

09842 **REDDY, W. B.** (1973), The impact of sensitivity training on self-actualization: a one-year follow-up. *Small Group Behav.*, 4:407-413.

09843 **REDDY, W. B.** (1972), Interpersonal compatibility and self-actualization in sensitivity training. *J. Appl. Behav. Science*, 8:237-240.

09844 **REDDY, W. B.** (1972), On affection, group composition, and self-actualization in sensitivity training. *J. Consult. & Clin. Psychol.*, 38:211-214.

09845 **REDDY, W. B.** (1976), On thinking—and not writing—about the small group for awhile. *J. Appl. Behav. Science*, 12:563-566.

09846 **REDDY, W. B.** (1970), Sensitivity training or group psychotherapy: the need for adequate screening. *Internat. J. Group Psychother.*, 20:366-371.

09847 **REDDY, W. B.**, and **BEERS, T.** (1977), Sensitivity training—and the healthy become self-actualized. *Small Group Behav.*, 8:525-532.

09848 **REDDY, W. B.**, and **LANSKY, L. M.** (1974), The group psychotherapy literature, 1973. *Internat. J. Group Psychother.*, 24:477-517.

09849 **REDDY, W. B.**, and **LANSKY, L. M.** (1975), Nothing but the facts: and some observations on norms and values—the history of a consultation with a metropolitan police division. *J. Soc. Issues*, 31:123-128.

09850 **REDDY, W. B.**, and **LIPPERT, K. M.** (1977), A bibliography of small group training: 1974-1976. In: *The 1977 Annual Handbook for Group Facilitators*, eds. J. E. Jones and J. W. Pfeiffer. La Jolla: University Associates.

09851 **REDDY, W. B., COLSON, D. B.**, and **KEYS, C. B.** (1975), The group psychotherapy literature, 1974. *Internat. J. Group Psychother.*, 25:429-479.

09852 **REDDY, W. B., COLSON, D. B.**, and **KEYS, C. B.** (1976), The group psychotherapy literature, 1975. *Internat. J. Group Psychother.*, 24:487-545.

09853 **REDER, P.** (1978), An assessment of the Group Therapy Interaction Chronogram. *Internat. J. Group Psychother.*, 28:185-194.

09854 **REDFERING, D. L.** (1975), Differential effects of group counseling with Black and White female delinquents: one year later. *J. Negro Educat.*, 44:530-537.

09855 **REDFERING, D. L.** (1971), Differential effects of group counseling with

Negro and White delinquent females. *Correct. Psychiat. & J. Soc. Ther.*, 17:29-34.

09856 **REDFERING, D. L.** (1973), Durability of effects of group counseling with institutionalized delinquent females. *J. Abnorm. & Soc. Psychol.*, 82:85-86.

09857 **REDFERING, D. L.** (1971), The effect of group counseling on the connotative meanings of selected concepts held by delinquent adolescent girls in a state training school. *Dissert. Abstr. Internat.*, 31:4473A.

09858 **REDICK, R. J.** (1974), Behavioral group counseling and death anxiety in student nurses. *Dissert. Abstr. Internat.*, 35:1989.

09859 **REDINGER, R. A.** (1971), Group therapy in the rehabilitation of the severely aphasic and hemiplegic in the late stages. *Scand. J. Rehab. Med.*, (Stockholm) 3:89-91.

09860 **REDL, F.** (1959), The concept of a "therapeutic milieu." *Amer. J. Orthopsychiat.*, 29:721-736.

09861 **REDL, F.** (1944), Diagnostic group work. *Amer. J. Orthopsychiat.*, 14:53-67.

09862 **REDL, F.** (1947), Discipline and group psychology. *J. Nat. Assn. Deans Women*, 11:3-15.

09863 **REDL, F.** (1942), Group emotion and leadership. *Psychiatry*, 5:573-596.

09864 **REDL, F.** (1949), New ways of ego support in residential treatment of disturbed children. *Bull. Menninger Clinic*, 13:60-66.

09865 **REDL, F.** (1949), The phenomenon of contagion and "shock effect" in group therapy. In: *Searchlights on Delinquency: New Psychoanalytic Studies*, ed. K. R. Eissler. New York: International Universities Press.

09866 **REDL, F.** (1963), Psychoanalysis and group therapy: a developmental point of view. *Amer. J. Orthopsychiat.*, 33:135-147.

09867 **REDL, F.** (1945), The psychology of gang formation and the treatment of juvenile delinquents. *The Psychoanalytic Study of the Child*, 1:367-377. New York: International Universities Press.

09868 **REDL, F.** (1948), Resistance in therapy groups. *Human Relat.*, 1:307-313.

09869 **REDLICH, F. C.**, and **ASTRACHAN, B.** (1969), Group dynamics training. *Amer. J. Psychiat.*, 125:1501-1507.

09870 **REDSTONE, J. F.** (1980), Concurrent individual and group psychotherapy: theoretical considerations. *Smith Coll. Studies Soc. Work*, 51:1-8.

09871 **REDWIN, E.**, and **GREVEN, G.** (1967), Discussion group of small children. *Individ. Psychol.*, 5:26-29.

09872 **REED, A. W., JR.** (1965), Activity group therapy. *Topical Probl. Psychol. & Psychother.*, 5:126-132.

09873 **REED, J. W.** (1962), Group therapy with asthmatic patients. *Geriatrics*, 17:823-830.

09874 **REED, R. B.** (1977), A comparison of massed versus spaced encounter group experiences as measured by predetermined behavior change criteria. *Dissert. Abstr. Internat.*, 37:4162-4163.

09875 **REED, W. H.** (1977), The differential effect of a vocational training program and a group therapy program on the frequency of misconduct of inmates in a state correctional institution. *Dissert. Abstr. Internat.*, 38:7295A.

09876 **REEDER, S. R.** (1963), Nurses' participation in a group psychotherapeutic approach to antepartal management. *Nursing Forum*, 2:81-92.

09877 **REES, T. P.**, and **GLATT, M. M.** (1956), Mental hospitals. In: *The Fields of Group Psychotherapy*, ed. S. R. Slavson. New York: International Universities Press.

09878 **REES, T. P.**, and **GLATT, M. M.** (1955), The organization of a mental hospital on the basis of group participation. *Internat. J. Group Psychother.*, 5:157-161.

09879 **REEVE, G. H.** (1939), A method of coordinated treatment. *Amer. J. Orthopsychiat.*, 9:743-747.
09880 **REGAN, J. R.** (1979), A comparative study of three different orientations to group psychotherapy with alcoholics. *Dissert. Abstr. Internat.*, 40:2384B.
09881 **REICH, M.** (1977), (Report from the Hauptkinderheim [HKH] Berlin.) *Praxis Kinderpsychol. & Kinderpsychiat.*, (Goettingen) 26:70-79.
09882 **REICH, S. K.** (1973), The effects of group systematic desensitization on the symptoms of primary dysmenorrhea. *Dissert. Abstr. Internat.*, 33:5499A.
09883 **REICHENFELD, H. F., CSAPO, K. G., CARRIERE, L.,** and **GARDNER, R. C.** (1973), Evaluating the effect of activity programs on a geriatric ward. *Gerontologist*, 13:305-310.
09884 **REID, F. T., JR.** (1970), Impact of leader style on the functioning of a decision–making group. *Arch. Gen. Psychiat.*, 23:268-276.
09885 **REID, F. T.** (1977), Review of J. B. Schaffer's and M. D. Galinsky's *Models of Group Therapy and Sensitivity Training. Internat. J. Group Psychother.*, 27:119-121.
09886 **REID, K. E.** (1968), Social group work enhances milieu therapy. *Hosp. & Community Psychiat.*, 19:26-29.
09887 **REIDER, N., OLINGER, D.,** and **LYLE, J.** (1939), Amateur dramatics as a therapeutic agent in a psychiatric hospital. *Bull. Menninger Clinic*, 3:20-28.
09888 **REIDY, J. J.** (1972), *The Sensitivity Phenomenon.* St. Meinrad, IN: Abbey Press.
09889 **REILLY, M.** (1960), Research potentiality of occupational therapy. *Amer. J. Occupat. Ther.*, 14:206-209.
09890 **REIMER, M. K.** (1971), Critique of sensitivity training. *School & Society*, 99:356-357.
09891 **REINER, E. R.,** and **QUIST, C. C.** (1964), Using psychotherapy groups to observe and supervise personnel relationships with adolescent offenders. *Psychiat. Studies Proj.*, 2:14.
09892 **REINFELD, W. V.** (1976), The effects of a group psychotherapy intervention on clients with an external locus of control. *Dissert. Abstr. Internat.*, 36:5056.
09893 **REINSTEIN, M.** (1970), Group therapy for basic trainees: a means of coping with adjustment problems. *Military Med.*, 135:760-764.
09894 **REISER, M.** (1975), A drop–in group for teenagers in a poverty area. In: *Adolescents Grow in Groups*, ed. I. Berkovitz. New York: Brunner/Mazel.
09895 **REISER, M.** (1961), The effects of group counseling on interpersonal relationships, anxiety level, intellectual functioning, and certain personality characteristics in a planned workshop experience. *Dissert. Abstr. Internat.*, 22:325.
09896 **REISER, M.,** and **SPERBER, Z.** (1969), Utilizing nonprofessional case aides in the treatment of psychotic children at an outpatient clinic. *Amer. J. Orthopsychiat.*, 39:356-357.
09897 **REISER, M.,** and **WALDMAN, M.** (1963), Group therapy in a work adjustment center. *Internat. J. Group Psychother.*, 13:300-307.
09898 **REISER, M.,** and **WALDMAN, M.** (1961), Views differ on group therapy technique. *J. Rehab.*, 27:23-24.
09899 **REISER, M. F.,** and **ROSENBAUM, M.** (1954), Supervision of residents in psychotherapy: comparison of problems of residents in psychiatry and medicine. *Amer. J. Psychiat.*, 110:835-839.
09900 **REISMAN, E. F.,** and **BEYER, L. M.** (1973), Group counseling in an elementary school setting. *Child Welfare*, 52:192-195.
09901 **REISMAN, S. D.,** and **LEE, M.** (1956), Use of material from group treatment of child in casework with parents. *Amer. J. Orthopsychiat.*, 26:630-634.

09902 **REISS, A. J., JR.** (1961), The social integration of queers and peers. *Soc. Probl.*, 9:102-120.
09903 **REISS, W. F.** (1964), The effect of psychotherapy like interviews upon adaptation to psychological issues. *Dissert. Abstr. Internat.*, 25:2054-2055.
09904 **REISSENBERGER, K.**, and **VOSSKUHLER, K.** (1978), (Music and movement therapy: group-therapy with schizophrenic psychotics.) *Praxis der Psychother.*, 23:287-291.
09905 **REISTER, B. W.** (1976), A treatment outcome study: two group treatments and their outcomes in relation to state and trait anxiety. *Dissert. Abstr. Internat.*, 36:5835A.
09906 **REITER, P. J.** (1952), Differential reactions of men and women patients to group psychotherapy. *Internat. J. Group Psychother.*, 2:103-110.
09907 **REIVICH, R. S.** (1966), Teaching, treatment, and research in a therapeutic community. *Hosp. & Community Psychiat.*, 17:59-62.
09908 **REMER, P. A. P.** (1973), The multiple effects of career group counseling on university students. *Dissert. Abstr. Internat.*, 33:4099A.
09909 **REMMERSWAAL, J.** (1975), *Inleiding tot de Groepsdynamika.* (*Introduction to Group Dynamics.*) Bloemondaal: Nelissen.
09910 **REMNET, V. L.** (1974), A group program for adaptation to a convalescent hospital. *Gerontologist*, 14:336-341.
09911 **REMOCKER, A. J.**, and **STORCH, E. T.** (1979), *Action Speaks Louder: A Handbook of Nonverbal Group Techniques.* New York: Longman.
09912 **RENNIE, T. A. C.** (1947), Psychotherapy for the general practitioner: a program for training. *Amer. J. Psychiat.*, 103:653-660.
09913 **RENOUVIER, P.** (1948), Group psychotherapy in the United States. *Sociatry*, 2:75-83.
09914 **RENOUVIER, P.** (1958), *Group Psychotherapy Movement.* Boston: Beacon House.
09915 **RENOUVIER, P.** (1958), The group psychotherapy movement and J. L. Moreno, its pioneer and founder. *Group Psychother., Psychodrama & Sociometry*, 11:69-86.
09916 **RENOUVIER, P.** (1957), Open letter to all group psychotherapists. *Group Psychother., Psychodrama & Sociometry*, 10:1-2.
09917 **RERES, M. E.** (1969), A survey of the nurse's role in psychiatric out–patient clinics in America. *Community Ment. Health J.*, 5:382-385.
09918 **RESNIK, H. L.**, and **PETERS, J. J.** (1968), Group psychotherapy with sexual offenders. In: *Current Psychiatric Therapies*, ed. J. H. Masserman. New York: Grune and Stratton.
09919 **RESNIK, H. L.**, and **PETERS, J. J.** (1967), Outpatient group therapy with convicted pedophiles. *Internat. J. Group Psychother.*, 17:151-158.
09920 **RESNICK, H. L.**, and **WOLFGANG, M. E.** (1972), *Sexual Behavior: Social, Clinical and Legal Aspects.* Boston: Little, Brown.
09921 **RESNIK, S.** (1963), Experience with a group of chronic psychotics. *Brit. J. Med. Psychol.*, (London) 36:327-330.
09922 **REST, W. G.**, and **RYAN, E. J.** (1970), Group vocational counseling for the probationer and parolee. *Fed. Probat.*, 34:49-54.
09923 **RETTERSTOL, N.** (1964), (General remarks on group psychotherapy.) *Nordisk Med.*, (Copenhagen) 72:1407-1411.
09924 **RETTIG, J. L.**, and **AMANO, M. M.** (1976), A survey of ASPA experience with management by objectives, sensitivity training and transactional analysis. *Personnel J.*, 55:26-29.
09925 **RETTIG, S.** (1966), Ethical risk-taking in group and individual conditions. *J. Personality & Soc. Psychol.*, 4:648-654.
09926 **RETTIG, S.** (1966), Group discussion and predicted ethical risk taking. *J. Personality & Soc. Psychol.*, 3:629-633.

09927 **RETTIG, S.**, and **SABENA, P.** (1977), Instrumental learning in the small group. *Group*, 1:184-193.

09928 **RETTIG, S.**, and **TUROFF, S. J.** (1967), Exposure to group discussion and predicted ethical risk taking. *J. Personality & Soc. Psychol.*, 7:177-180.

09929 **REVELES, E.** (1969), *The Accelerated Groups*. Albuquerque: New Mexico Press.

09930 (Review of M. Grotjahn's *Art and Technique of Group Therapy* (1980).) *Acta Psiquiat. Psicol. Amer. Latina*, (Rio de Janeiro) 26:171.

09931 Review of M. Seligman's *Group–Counseling and Group–Psychotherapy with Rehabilitation Clients* (1978). *Rehab. Lit.*, 39:82.

09932 Review of S. E. Rose's *Group Therapy: A Behavioral Approach* (1978). *Manag. Internat. Rev.*, (Wiesbaden) 18:116.

09933 **REW, K. G.** (1949), The patient's evaluation of group therapy. *Military Surg.*, 105:389-399.

09934 **REXFORD, E. N.** (1977), *A Developmental Approach to Problems of Acting Out: A Symposium*. New York: International Universities Press.

09935 **REY, J. H.** (1975), Intrapsychic object relations: the individual and the group. In: *Group Therapy 1975: An Overview*, eds. L. R. Wolberg and M. L. Aronson. New York: Stratton Intercontinental Medical Books.

09936 **RHOADES, W.** (1935), Group training in thought control for relieving nervous disorders. *Ment. Hygiene*, 19:373-386.

09937 **RHODES, S. L.** (1973), Short-term groups of latency-age children in a school setting. *Internat. J. Group Psychother.*, 23:204-216.

09938 **RIBNER, N. G.** (1974), Effects of an explicit group contract on self-disclosure and group cohesiveness. *J. Couns. Psychol.*, 21:116-120.

09939 **RICCIARDI-von PLATEN, A.** (1971), Bericht uber psychotherapeutische gruppenfahrten mit je zwei parallelgruppen. (Report of psychotherapeutic group trips with two parallel groups.) *Praxis der Psychother.*, 16:117-124.

09940 **RICE, C. A.** (1977), Observations on the unexpected and simultaneous termination of leader and group. *Group*, 1:100-117.

09941 **RICE, D. G.** (1972), Therapist experience and "style" as factors in co-therapy. *Fam. Process*, 11:1-12.

09942 **RICE, D. G.**, and **RICE, J. K.** (1977), Non-sexist marital therapy. *J. Marriage & Fam. Couns.*, 3:3-11.

09943 **RICE, K. K.** (1952), The importance of including fathers. *Internat. J. Group Psychother.*, 2:232-238.

09944 **RICE, M. E.**, and **CHAPLIN, T. C.** (1979), Social skills training for hospitalized male arsonists. *J. Behav. Ther. & Exper. Psychiat.*, 10:105-108.

09945 **RICH, A. R.**, and **SCHROEDER, H. E.** (1976), Research issues in assertiveness training. *Psychol. Bull.*, 83:1081-1096.

09946 **RICHARD, M.** (1978), (Review of A. Heiglevers' *Concept of Analytical Group Psychotherapy.*) *Praxis Kinderpsychol. & Kinderpsychiat.*, (Goettingen) 27:275-276.

09947 **RICHARDS, C. S.** (1975), Behavior modification of studying through study skills advice and self-control procedures. *J. Couns. Psychol.*, 22:431-436.

09948 **RICHARDS, H.** (1967), The role of the nurse in the therapy of the lower socioeconomic psychiatric patient. *Perspect. Psychiat. Care*, 5:82-91.

09949 **RICHARDS, H.**, and **DANIELS, M. S.** (1969), Sociopsychiatric rehabilitation in a black urban ghetto: ii. innovative treatment roles and approaches. *Amer. J. Orthopsychiat.*, 39:662-676.

09950 **RICHARDS, L.** (1966), Group therapy in a rehabilitation centre. *Can. J. Occupat. Ther.*, (Ottawa) 33:141-147.

09951 **RICHARDS, L. D.**, and **LEE, K. A.** (1972), Group process in social habilitation of the retarded. *Soc. Casework*, 53:30-37.

09952 **RICHARDS, S. A.**, and **CUFFE, J. U.** (1972), Behavioral correlates of leadership effectiveness in interacting and counteracting groups. *J. Appl. Psychol.*, 56:377-381.

09953 **RICHARDS, S. A.**, and **JAFEE, C. L.** (1972), Blacks supervising whites: a study of interracial difficulties in working together in a simulated organization. *J. Appl. Psychol.*, 56:234-240.

09954 **RICHARDS, W. A.** (1975), Counseling, peak experiences and the human encounter with death: an empirical study of the efficacy of DPT-assisted counseling in enhancing the quality of life of persons with terminal cancer and their closest family members. *Dissert. Abstr. Internat.*, 36:1314A.

09955 **RICHARDSON, C.**, and **MEYER, R. G.** (1972), Techniques in guided group interaction programs. *Child Welfare*, 51:519-527.

09956 **RICHARDSON, E. A.** (1971), Behavioral and existential interpretations of an experiment in altered perception of roles used in a counseling group. *Correct. Psychiat. & J. Soc. Ther.*, 17:57-64.

09957 **RICHARDSON, E. A.** (1973), The effects of videotape recording as an extension of group therapy with children who have learning disabilities. *Dissert. Abstr. Internat.*, 34:1086A.

09958 **RICHARDSON, F. D.**, and **ISLAND, D.** (1975), A model for training workshops and labs. *Personnel & Guid. J.*, 53:592-597.

09959 **RICHARDSON, G. A.** (1969), Problems concerning acting out. *Psychiat. Quart.*, 43:285-300.

09960 **RICHARDSON, G. A., MILLER, I., McNEELEY, J. D.**, and **PEDERSON, W. M.** (1969), Problems concerning acting out. *Psychiat. Quart.*, 43:285-300.

09961 **RICHARDSON, H.** (1951), The efficacy of group preparation for counseling. Unpublished doctoral dissertation, University of Minnesota.

09962 **RICHER, L. H.** (1969), A comparison of three approaches to group counseling involving motion pictures with mentally retarded young adults. *Ment. Retard. Abstr.*, 6:453.

09963 **RICHMAN, A. P.**, and **WHITE, P. A.** (1969), Thursday's child. *Nursing Outlook*, 17:47-49.

09964 **RICHMAN, D. R.** (1980), A comparison of cognitive and behavioral group counseling techniques for job finding with welfare women. *Dissert. Abstr. Internat.*, 40:5416B. (University Microfilms No. 8007670.)

09965 **RICHMAN, J.** (1977), Art therapy and group process. *Art Psychother.*, 4:5-9.

09966 **RICHMAN, J.**, and **DAVIDOFF, I. F.** (1971), Interaction testing and counseling as a form of crisis intervention during marital therapy. *Proceed. Annual Convention*, American Psychological Association, 6:439-440.

09967 **RICHMOND, A. H.** (1965), Group therapy for the hard-to-treat, poorly motivated patient in the community. *Amer. J. Orthopsychiat.*, 35:259-260.

09968 **RICHMOND, A. H.**, and **SCHECTER, S.** (1964), A spontaneous request for treatment by a group of adolescents. *Internat. J. Group Psychother.*, 14:97-106.

09969 **RICHMOND, A. H.**, and **SLAGLE, S.** (1971), Some notes on the inhibition of aggression in an inpatient psychotherapy group. *Internat. J. Group Psychother.*, 21:333-338.

09970 **RICHMOND, C.** (1968), Programs for discharged patients: ii. halfway house and day hospital complement each other. *Hosp. & Community Psychiat.*, 19:78-79.

09971 **RICHMOND, J.** (1960), Behavior, occupation and treatment of children. *Amer. J. Occupat. Ther.*, 14:183-186.

09972 **RICHMOND, L. H.** (1978), The effects of group counseling combined with audiotaped and videotaped feedback upon fourth and sixth grade children. *Dissert. Abstr. Internat.*, 39:5956A.

09973 **RICHMOND, L. H.** (1977), Review of A. W. Rachman's *Identity Group Psychotherapy with Adolescents. Psychiatry*, 40:290-291.

09974 **RICHMOND, L. H.** (1978), Review of L. R. Wolberg's, M. L. Aronson's, and A. R. Wolberg's *Group-Therapy 1977: An Overview. Amer. J. Psychiat.*, 135:394-395.

09975 **RICHMOND, L. H.** (1980), Review of S. R. Slavson's and M. Schiffer's *Dynamics of Group Psychotherapy. Amer. J. Psychiat.*, 137:640.

09976 **RICHMOND, L. H.** (1978), Some further observations on private practice and community clinic adolescent psychotherapy groups. *Correct. & Soc. Psychiat.*, 24:57-61.

09977 **RICHMOND, L. H.**, and **GAINES, T.** (1979), Factors influencing attendance in group psychotherapy with adolescents. *Adolescence*, 14:715-720.

09978 **RICHMOND, R. D.**, and **OSTLUND, L. A.** (1966), Relationship between academic preference and group discussion performance. *J. Human Relat.*, 14:207-216.

09979 **RICHMOND, W.** (1936), Sociometric tests in a training school for nurses. *Sociometric Rev.*, 41.

09980 **RICK, M.** (1964), The effect of time limited group psychotherapy on underachieving male college freshmen: i. academic achievement, anxiety, and attitudes. Unpublished doctoral dissertation, Adelphi University.

09981 **RICKABAUGH, K. R.** (1975), Correlates of differential achievement among student-clients receiving group counseling for academic improvement. *Dissert. Abstr. Internat.*, 36:2033A.

09982 **RICKARD, H. C.** (1962), Selected group psychotherapy evaluation studies. *J. Gen. Psychol.*, 67:35-50.

09983 **RICKARD, H. L.**, and **LATTAL, K. A.** (1969), Group problem-solving in therapeutic summer camp: an illustration. *Adolescence*, 4:320-332.

09984 **RICKMAN, J.** (1950), The factor of number in individual- and group-dynamics. *J. Ment. Science*, (London) 96:770-773.

09985 **RIDEOUT, T. M.** (1980), A comparison of individual biofeedback training and group relaxation/imagery tapes on self-concept, level of muscle tension and classroom behavior of fifth-grade students. *Dissert. Abstr. Internat.*, 41:1410A. (University Microfilms No. 8021833.)

09986 **RIEGEL, B.** (1968), Group meetings with adolescents in child welfare. *Child Welfare*, 47:417-418, 427.

09987 **RIEGERT, F. J.** (1969), The effect of group counseling on the academic performance of marginal risk college freshmen. *Dissert. Abstr. Internat.*, 30:139A.

09988 **RIEGESTIN, Q. R.**, and **HOWE, L. P.** (1972), A psychotherapy group for skid-row alcoholics. *Mass. J. Ment. Health*, 2:4-24.

09989 **RIESE, H.** (1959), Educational therapy: a methodical approach to the problem of the "untreatable" child. *Group Psychother., Psychodrama & Sociometry*, 12:58-66.

09990 **RIESE, W.** (1951), Outline of history of ideas in psychotherapy. *Bull. Hist. Med.*, 25:442-456.

09991 **RIESE, W.** (1963), Psychoanalysis: its historical and philosophical implications. *Acta Psychother., Psychosomat. Orthopaedagog. Suppl.*, 11:5-36.

09992 **RIESMAN, D.** (1959), Some observations on interviewing in a state mental hospital. *Bull. Menninger Clinic*, 23:7-19.

09993 **RIESSMAN, C. K.** (1970), The supply-demand dilemma in community mental health centers. *Amer. J. Orthopsychiat.*, 40:276-277.

09994 **RIESSMAN, F.** (1964), Role-playing and the lower socio-economic group. *Group Psychother., Psychodrama & Sociometry*, 17:36-48.

09995 **RIESSMAN, F.** (1967), Strategies and suggestions for training nonprofessionals. *Community Ment. Health J.*, 3:103-110.

09996 **RIESSMAN, F., COHEN, J.,** and **PEARL, A.** (1964), *Mental Health of the Poor: New Treatment Approaches for Low Income People.* New York: Free Press.

09997 **RIESTER, A.** (1975), The leadership laboratory: A group counseling intervention model for schools. In: *Group Psychotherapy from the Southwest,* ed. M. Rosenbaum. New York: Gordon/Breach.

09998 **RIESTER, A. E.,** and **TANNER, D. L.** (1974), The leadership laboratory: a group counseling intervention model for schools. *Group Process,* (London) 6:49-57.

09999 **RIGGS, R. L.** (1979), Evaluations of counselor effectiveness. *Personnel & Guid. J.*, 58:54-60.

10000 **RIGO, L.** (1970), Group mental imagery in adults. *Riv. Sper. Freniatr.*, (Florence) 94:1231-1247.

10001 **RIGO, L.** (1970), Notes on a t-group conducted with "mental imagery" technics and non-verbal psychotherapy. *Riv. Sper. Freniatr.*, (Florence) 94:589-636.

10002 **RIHANI, S. J.** (1972), The comparative effects of implosive therapy and systematic desensitization upon counselor trainees' anxiety and ability to communicate emotions. *Dissert. Abstr. Internat.*, 33:4847A.

10003 **RIJKEN, H.,** and **de WILDT, A.** (1978), (Structured therapy groups for women with social/assertiveness problems.) *Tijdsch. voor Psychother.*, 4:155-163.

10004 **RIJKERS, T.** (1979), *Opleider, Het Zal je Vak Maar Wezen: Ervaringen, Theorieën, Visies en Methoden.* Bloemendaal: H. Nelissen.

10005 **RILEY, R.** (1970), An investigation of the influence of group compatibility of group cohesiveness and change in self-concept in a t-group setting. *Dissert. Abstr. Internat.*, 31:3277A.

10006 **RIMM, D. C., HILL, G. A., BROWN, N. N.,** and **STUART, J. E.** (1974), Group-assertive training in treatment of expression of inappropriate anger. *Psychol. Reports,* 34:791-798.

10007 **RING, B.** (1972), Recognized similarity: an investigation of significant events reported by encounter group participants. *Dissert. Abstr. Internat.*, 33:1527A.

10008 **RINGEL, S.** (1969), Risk, performance, and confidence of individuals and groups. *Dissert. Abstr. Internat.*, 30:2153A.

10009 **RINGELHEIM, D.,** and **POLATSEK, I.** (1955), Group therapy with a male mental defective group. *Amer. J. Ment. Deficiency,* 60:157-162.

10010 **RINGWALD, J. W.** (1974), An investigation of group reaction to central group figures. *Dissert. Abstr. Internat.*, 35:488B.

10011 **RINK, J. E.** (1976), *Residentiele Hulpverlening aan Gedetineerde Adolescenten: De Ontwikkeling van de Confrontatiemethodiek.* Bloemendaal: H. Nelissen.

10012 **RINN, R.** (1968), The selection of boys for activity group therapy. *Smith Coll. Studies Soc. Work,* 39:82-83.

10013 **RINN, R. C., VERNON, J. C.,** and **WISE, M. J.** (1975), Training parents of behaviorally disordered children in groups: a three year program evaluation. *Behav. Ther.*, 6:378-387.

10014 **RIOCH, D. M.,** and **STANTON, A. H.** (1951), Milieu therapy. *Res. Publicat. Assess. Nerv. & Ment. Diseases,* 31:94-105.

10015 **RIOCH, M. J.** (1977), The A. K. Rice group relation conferences as a reflection of society. *J. Personality & Soc. Systems,* 1:1-16.

10016 **RIOCH, M. J.** (1970), Group relations: rationale and technique. *Internat. J. Group Psychother.*, 20:340-355.

10017 **RIOCH, M. J.** (1970), The work of Wilfred Bion on groups. *Psychiatry,* 33:56-66.

10018 **RIORDAN, C. E., RICHMAN, E. L.,** and **RICHMAN, A.** (1969), Psychosocial function and staff decentralization on an inpatient ward. *Amer. J. Orthopsychiat.*, 39:348-349.

10019 **RIORDAN, R. J.,** and **MATHENY, K. B.** (1972), Dear diary: logs in group counseling. *Personnel & Guid. J.*, 379-382.

10020 **RIOS, R. M.** (1972), The comparative effects of tape-led, led, and leaderless groups. *Dissert. Abstr. Internat.*, 32:6769A.

10021 **RIQUELME, E.** (1977), (Psychotherapy for children: theoretical and practical approach.) *Neurol.-Neurocir.-Psiquiat.*, (Mexico City) 18:167-172.

10022 **RITCHEY, M.** (1971), Seeds of social change: laboratory techniques in a traditional society. *Soc. Change*, 3:1-2.

10023 **RITCHEY, R. E.** (1971), Activity groups help long-term patients solve everyday problems. *Hosp. & Community Psychiat.*, 22:335-336.

10024 **RITCHIE, A.** (1960), Multiple impact therapy: an experiment. *Soc. Work,* 5:16-21.

10025 **RITSON, E. B.,** and **SMITH, C. G.** (1967), The development of treatment skills in contrasted therapeutic communities. *Brit. J. Psychiat.*, (Ashford) 113:159-165.

10026 **RITTER, B.** (1968), The group desensitization of children's snake phobias using vicarious and contact desensitization procedures. *Behav. Res. & Ther.*, 6:1-6.

10027 **RITTER, K. Y.** (1978), Group psychotherapy research and personality change: a discussion. *Small Group Behav.*, 9:319-323.

10028 **RITTER, K. Y.** (1977), Growth groups and the personal orientation inventory. *Group Organizat. Studies*, 2:234-241.

10029 **RITTER, K. Y.** (1978), The use of growth groups as a critical ingredient in counselor training. *Internat. J. Adv. C.*, 1:295-302.

10030 **RIVERA, G., JR.** (1972), Nosotros venceremos: Chicano consciousness and change strategies. *J. Appl. Behav. Science*, 8:56-72.

10031 **RIZZO, N. D.** (1980), Group therapy: possibilities and pitfalls. *Internat. J. Offend. Ther.*, (London) 24:27-31.

10032 **RIZZO, P.** (1972), Three new variations of FOOJY with a double switch. *Transactional Anal. J.*, 2:30-33.

10033 **RIZZO, S. J.** (1977), A comparison of the effects of variations in microcounseling training with groups of parents of the developmentally disabled. *Dissert. Abstr. Internat.*, 37:7547A.

10034 **ROBACK, H. B.** (1976), An experimental comparison of outcomes in insight and non-insight oriented therapy groups. *Dissert. Abstr. Internat.*, 36:5280.

10035 **ROBACK, H. B.** (1972), Experimental comparisons of outcomes in insight- and non-insight-oriented therapy groups. *J. Consult. & Clin. Psychol.*, 38:411-417.

10036 **ROBACK, H. B.** (1979), *Group Psychotherapy Research.* Melbourne, FL: Krieger.

10037 **ROBACK, H. B.** (1974), The role of content in intragroup interaction. *Internat. J. Group Psychother.*, 24:288-299.

10038 **ROBACK, H. B.** (1976), Use of patient feedback to improve the quality of group therapy training. *Internat. J. Group Psychother.*, 26:243-247.

10039 **ROBACK, H. B.,** and **STRASSBERG, D. S.** (1975), Relationship between perceived therapist-offered conditions and therapeutic movement in group psychotherapy. *Small Group Behav.*, 6:352-354.

10040 **ROBAR, D. E.** (1978), The comparative effectiveness of live, video-taped and audio-taped group relaxation training on the ability to reduce physiological arousal and self-report measures of anxiety. *Dissert. Abstr. Internat.*, 39:2517B-2518B. (University Microfilms No. 7820364.)

10041 **ROBBINS, D. B.** (1967), Innovations in military corrections. *Amer. J. Psychiat.*, 123:828-35.

10042 **ROBBINS, J. G.** (1969), Correlates between effective communication and wellness in a psychotherapy group. *Dissert. Abstr. Internat.*, 29:3709A.

10043 **ROBBINS, J. J.** (1931), Impromptu for America. *Impromptu*, 1:23-25.

10044 **ROBBINS, L. L.** (1963), The contributions of psychoanalysis in psychiatric hospital treatment. *J. Hillside Hosp.*, 12:232-238.

10045 **ROBBINS, R. H.** (1968), The re-acting barrier in psychodrama settings. *Group Psychother., Psychodrama & Sociometry*, 21:140-143.

10046 **ROBERSON, A. B.** (1978), An elementary school cross-age group counseling program: changes in self-concept, career goals, and career-related activities preference. *Dissert. Abstr. Internat.*, 40:681A.

10047 **ROBERTIELLO, R. C.** (1972), After the sexual revolution and the women's liberation movement. *J. Contemp. Psychother.*, 5:31.

10048 **ROBERTIELLO, R. C.** (1970), Encounter techniques: ridiculous or sublime? *Voices*, 5:89-90.

10049 **ROBERTIELLO, R. C.** (1972), The leader in a leaderless group. *Psychother.: Theory, Res. & Pract.*, 9:259-261.

10050 **ROBERTS, A. L.** (1976), Review of G. M. Gazda's *Basic Approaches to Group Psychotherapy and Group Counseling. Personnel & Guid. J.*, 54:334.

10051 **ROBERTS, B. H.** (1954), Applications of group psychotherapy techniques in non clinical settings: a symposium. *Internat. J. Group Psychother.*, 4:163-164.

10052 **ROBERTS, B. H.**, and **STRODTBECK, F. L.** (1953), Interaction processes differentiating between groups of paranoid schizophrenic and depressed patients. *Internat. J. Group Psychother.*, 3:29-41.

10053 **ROBERTS, C.** (1972), The effects of self-confrontation, role playing, and response feedback on the level of self-esteem. *Speech Teacher*, 21:22-38.

10054 **ROBERTS, D. M.** (1959), *How to Work with Teenage Groups*. New York: Association Press.

10055 **ROBERTS, L. A. M.** (1977), Obsessional compulsive (psycho) neurosis. *Nursing Times*, (London) 73:1789-1793.

10056 **ROBERTS, H.**, and **WHITING, M.** (1973), Encounter groups in adult education. *Austral. J. Adult Educat.*, (Sydney) 13:19-26.

10057 **ROBERTS, J.**, **BESWICK, K.**, **LEXERTON, B.**, and **LYNCH, M. A.** (1977), Prevention of child abuse: group therapy for mothers and children. *Practitioner*, 219:111-115.

10058 **ROBERTS, J. P.** (1977), Problems of group psychotherapy for psychosomatic patients. *Psychother. & Psychosomat.*, (Basel) 28:305-315.

10059 **ROBERTSON, M. H.** (1955), The relationship between the concept of change and certain psychotherapeutic variables. *Dissert. Abstr. Internat.*, 15:871-872.

10060 **ROBERTSON, W.**, **FORD, M.**, and **PITT, B.** (1965), The role of a day hospital in geriatric psychiatry. *Brit. J. Psychiat.*, (Ashford) 3:635-640.

10061 **ROBIN, A. L.** (1979), Problem-solving communication training: a behavioral approach to the treatment of parent-adolescent conflict. *Amer. J. Fam. Ther.*, 7:69-82.

10062 **ROBIN, S. S.** (1967), Three approaches to role theory. *Rocky Mtn. Soc. Science J.*

10063 **ROBINAULT, I. P.**, and **WEISINGER, M.** (1973), Leaderless groups: a tape cassette technique for vocational education. *Rehab. Lit.*, 34:80-84, 87.

10064 **ROBINE, J. M.** (1971), (Psychodramatic festivals: psychodrama in a group of pre–adolescents.) *Rev. Neuropsychiat. Infantile*, (Paris) 19:549-563.

10065 **ROBINS, A. J.** (1953), Group therapy with pre-convalescent patients. *J. Psychiat. Soc. Work*, 22:153-158.

10066 **ROBINSON, C.**, and **SUINN, R. M.** (1969), Group desensitization of a phobia in massed sessions. *Behav. Res. & Ther.*, 7:319-321.

10067 **ROBINSON, E. H.** (1980), Life coping skills through the group medium. *J. Special. Group Work*, 5:117-119.

10068 **ROBINSON, E. H.**, and **WILSON, E. S.** (1980), Effects of human relations training on indices of skill development and self-concept changes in classroom teachers. *J. Special. Group Work*, 5:163-169.

10069 **ROBINSON, J. F.** (1951), Therapeutic values of group experiences in a children's institution. *Ment. Hygiene*, 35:439-447.

10070 **ROBINSON, J. T.** (1948), Group therapy and its application in the British army today. *Royal Army Med. Corps J.*, (Liverpool) 91:66-79.

10071 **ROBINSON, L.** (1970), Role play with retarded adolescent girls: teaching and therapy. *Mental Retard.*, 8:36-37.

10072 **ROBINSON, L. D.** (1966), Group psychotherapy for deaf psychiatric patients. *Curr. Psychiat. Ther.*, 6:172-176.

10073 **ROBINSON, L. D.** (1973), A program for deaf mental patients. *Hosp. & Community Psychiat.*, 24:40-42.

10074 **ROBINSON, L. D.** (1965), Psychiatric services for deaf patients: ii. group psychotherapy using manual communication. *Ment. Hosp.*, 16:172-174.

10075 **ROBINSON, L. H.** (1974), Group work with parents of retarded adolescents. *Amer. J. Psychother.*, 18:397-408.

10076 **ROBINSON, M.**, and **JACOBS, A.** (1970), Focused video-tape feedback and behavior change in group psychotherapy. *Psychother.: Theory, Res. & Pract.*, 7:169-172.

10077 **ROBINSON, M. B.** (1968), Effects of video tape feedback versus discussion session feedback on group interaction, self awareness and behavioral change among group psychotherapy participants. *Dissert. Abstr. Internat.*, 29:1178-1179.

10078 **ROBINSON, M. B.** (1970), A study of the effects of focused video-tape feedback in group counseling. *Compar. Group Studies*, 1:47-75.

10079 **ROBINSON, P. A.** (1978), Parents of "beyond control" adolescents. *Adolescence*, 13:109.

10080 **ROBINSON, R. M.** (1979), The relationship of dimensions of interpersonal trust with group cohesiveness, group status, and immediate outcome in short-term group counseling. *Dissert. Abstr. Internat.*, 40:5016B.

10081 **ROBINSON, V. P.** (1972), Review of *Carl Rogers on Encounter Groups*. *J. Otto Rank Assn.*, 7:50-64.

10082 **ROBITAILLE, N. D.** (1965), The organization of a patient council. *Perspect. Psychiat. Care*, 3:23-25.

10083 **ROCHE, M. P.** (1974), Elementary group Co-counseling by disenchanted junior high school students and its effect on their self–concept, interpersonal relationships, attitude toward school and school performance. *Dissert. Abstr. Internat.*, 34:6984A.

10084 **ROCHEBLAUE-SPENLE, A. M.** (1969/1970), (Role and psychodrama.) *Bull. de Psychol.*, (Paris) 23:816-819.

10085 **ROCHESTER, S. R.**, **VACHON, M. L.**, and **LYALL, W. A.** (1974), Immediacy in language: a channel to care of the dying patient. *J. Community Psychol.*, 2:75-76.

10086 **ROCHKIND, M.**, and **CONN, J. H.** (1973), Guided fantasy encounter. *Amer. J. Psychother.*, 27:516-528.

10087 **ROCK, S. A.** (1975), Differential effects of three models of undergraduate growth groups. *Dissert. Abstr. Internat.*, 36:3418A.

10088 **ROCK, S. A.** (1980), *This Time Together*. Grand Rapids: Zondervan Publishing House.

10089 **ROCK, W.** (1979), Psychology of development and group dynamics in the psychoanalytical theory of education. *Dynam. Psychiat.*, (Berlin) 12:305.
10090 **ROCKWELL, D.** (1971), Some observations on "living in." *Psychiatry*, 34:214-223.
10091 **ROCKWELL, W. J., MOORMAN, J. C., HAWKINS, D.,** and **MUSANTE, G.** (1976), Individual vs. group: brief treatment outcome in a university mental health service. *J. Amer. Coll. Health Assn.*, 24:186-190.
10092 **RODRIGUEZ, I. D.** (1971), Group work with hospitalized Puerto Rican patients. *Hosp. & Community Psychiat.*, 22:219-220.
10093 **RODRIGUEZ PORRAS, J. M.** (1972), T-group and their application to instruction. *Rev. Psicol. Apl.*, (Paris) 27:707-717.
10094 **ROE, J. E.** (1977), The relationship of two process measurement systems in encounter groups. *Dissert. Abstr. Internat.*, 38:1901B.
10095 **ROE, J. E.,** and **EDWARDS, K. J.** (1978), Relationship of two process measurement systems for group therapy. *J. Consult. & Clin. Psychol.*, 46:1545-1546.
10096 **ROEMELE, V.,** and **GRUNEBAUM, H.** (1967), Helping the helpers. *Internat. J. Group Psychother.*, 17:343-355.
10097 **ROESSLER, R., COOK, D.,** and **LILLARD, D.** (1977), Effects of systematic group counseling on work adjustment clients. *J. Couns. Psychol.*, 24:313-317.
10098 **ROETHER, H. A.** (1972), Definitive outcome study of a group psychotherapy program with probational sex offenders. *Dissert. Abstr. Internat.*, 33:1865A.
10099 **ROETHER, H. A.,** and **PETERS, J. J.** (1972), Cohesiveness and hostility in group psychotherapy. *Amer. J. Psychiat.*, 128:1014-1017.
10100 **ROGAL, R. A.** (1970), Group counseling for counselors: Its effect upon the growth of behavior cognition and its relationship to counselor effectiveness. *Dissert. Abstr. Internat.*, 31:1022A.
10101 **ROGENESS, G. A.,** and **STEWART, J. T.** (1978), The positive group: a therapeutic technique in the hospital treatment of adolescents. *Hosp. & Community Psychiat.*, 29:520-526.
10102 **ROGERS, A. H.** (1968), Videotape feedback in group psychotherapy. *Psychother.: Theory, Res. & Pract.*, 5:37-39.
10103 **ROGERS, C.** (1971), Carl Rogers describes his way of facilitating encounter groups. *Amer. J. Nursing*, 71:528-531.
10104 **ROGERS, C.** (1973), *Carl Rogers on Encounter Groups*. New York: Harper and Row.
10105 **ROGERS, C.** (1971), Facilitating encounter groups. *Amer. J. Nursing*, 11:275-279.
10106 **ROGERS, C.** (1969), The group comes of age. *Psychol. Today*, 3:27-31, 58-61.
10107 **ROGERS, C., ROBACK, H., McKEE, E.,** and **CALHOUN, D.** (1976), Group psychotherapy with homosexuals: review. *Internat. J. Group Psychother.*, 26:3-27.
10108 **ROGERS, C. R.** (1970), *Carl Rogers on Encounter Groups*. New York: Harper and Row.
10109 **ROGERS, C. R.** (1971), *Encounter groups*. New York: Penguin Press.
10110 **ROGERS, C. R.** (1979), Groups in two cultures. *Personnel & Guid. J.*, 58:11-15.
10111 **ROGERS, J., MacBRIDE, A., WHYLIE, B.,** and **FREEMAN, S. J. J.** (1978), The use of groups in the rehabilitation of amputees. *Internat. J. Psychiat. Med.*, 8:243-255.
10112 **ROGERS, K.** (1973), Group dynamics for marketing managers. *J. Advert. Res.*, 13:7-14.

10113 **ROGERS, K.** (1972), Group processes in police-community relations. *Bull. Menninger Clinic*, 36:515-534.
10114 **ROGERS, R. E.** (1972), Sensitivity training: caveat emptor. *J. Nursing Admin.*, 2:48-54.
10115 **ROGOW, A. A.** (1970), *The Psychiatrists*. New York: G. P. Putnam's Sons.
10116 **ROHAN, W. P.** (1970), A follow-up study of hospitalized problem drinkers. *Diseases Nerv. System*, 31:259-265.
10117 **ROHLF, D.** (1977), A Review of R. Chessick's *Intensive Psychotherapy of the Borderline Patient. Group*, 1:265-266.
10118 **RÖHLING, G.** (1977), Ego-structural approaches in the psychodynamics of addictions. *Dynam. Psychiat.*, (Berlin) 10:17-22.
10119 **RÖHR, D.** (1974), Group dynamics: an approach to the rehabilitation of patients with myocardial infarction. *Der Rehab.*, (Stuttgart) 13:141-144.
10120 **ROHRBACHER, R.** (1973), Influence of a special camp program for obese boys on weight loss, self-concept, and body image. *Res. Quart. Amer. Assn. Health Phys. Ed. Res.*, 44:150-157.
10121 **ROHRBAUGH, M.** (1975), Patterns and correlates of emotional arousal in laboratory training. *J. Appl. Behav. Science*, 11:220-240.
10122 **ROHRBAUGH, M.**, and **BARTELS, B. D.** (1975), Participants' perceptions of "curative factors" in therapy and growth groups. *Small Group Behav.*, 6:430-456.
10123 **ROI, G.** (1952), Group psychotherapy of schizophrenics at the Padua Psychiatric Hospital. *Riv. Sper. Freniatria*, (Florence) 26:279-288.
10124 **ROI, G.** (1951), La struttura dello psicodramma nella psicoterapia di gruppo degli schizofrenici. (The use of psychodrama in group psychotherapy with schizophrenics.) *Rev. Sper. Freniatria*, (Florence) 5:279-282.
10125 **ROJAS-BERMUDEZ, J. G.** (1969), The "intermediary object." *Group Psychother., Psychodrama & Sociometry*, 22:149-154.
10126 **ROJAS-BERMUDEZ, J. G.** (1969/1970), The intermediate object: the contribution of the use of marionettes in psychodrama. *Bull. de Psychol.*, (Paris) 23:940-943.
10127 **ROLAND, P. E.** (1948), An exploratory training technique for the reeducation of catatonics. *Amer. J. Psychiat.*, 105:353-356.
10128 **ROLL, E. J.**, and **ROLL, S.** (1979), Claimed and disclaimed action in psychodrama. *Group Psychother., Psychodrama & Sociometry*, 32:89-93.
10129 **ROLL, W. V.** (1976), Feed-back training for encounter group facilitators. *Dissert. Abstr. Internat.*, 36:4177.
10130 **ROLLA, B. H.** (1962), Codificatión en los analisis de larga duración. (Codification in analysis of long duration.) *Acta Psiquiát. Psicol. Argentina*, (Buenos Aires) 8:115-118.
10131 **ROLLA, E.**, and **NOEMI, M.** (1967), Group psychotherapy with industrial, publicity and commercial executives. *Psychother. & Psychosomat.*, (Basel) 15:57.
10132 **ROMAN, M.** (1967), Current conceptual and methodological issues in group psychotherapy research: introduction to panel—part ii. *Internat. J. Group Psychother.*, 17:192-195.
10133 **ROMAN, M.** (1957), *Reaching Delinquents through Reading*. Springfield, IL: C. C. Thomas.
10134 **ROMAN, M.** (1976), Symposium: family therapy and group therapy —similarities and differences. introduction. *Internat. J. Group Psychother.*, 26:281-287.
10135 **ROMAN, M.** (1965), The treatment of the homosexual in the group. *Topical Probl. Psychol. & Psychother.*, 5:170-175.
10136 **ROMAN, M.** (1955), Tutorial group therapy: a study of the integration of remedial reading and group therapy in the treatment of delinquents. *Dissert. Abstr. Internat.*, 15:1761.

10137 **ROMAN, M.,** and **MELTZER, B.** (1977), Cotherapy: a review of current literature (with special references to therapeutic outcome). *J. Sex & Marital Ther.*, 3:63-77.

10138 **ROMAN, M.,** and **PORTER, K.** (1978), Combining experiential and didactic aspects in a new group therapy training approach. *Internat. J. Group Psychother.*, 28:371-387.

10139 **ROMANELLA, P. A.** (1974), Values and facilitativeness as determinants of significant others in a group experience. *Dissert. Abstr. Internat.*, 35:1990-1991.

10140 **ROMANO, J. L.,** and **QUAY, A. T.** (1974), Follow-up of community college group participants. *J. Coll. Student Personnel*, 15:278-283.

10141 **ROMANO, M. D.** (1973), Sexual counseling in groups. *J. Sex. Res.*, 9:69-78.

10142 **ROME, H. P.** (1945), Audio-visual aids in psychiatry. *Hosp. Corps Quart.*, 18:37-38.

10143 **ROME, H. P.** (1945), Group psychotherapy. *Diseases Nerv. System*, 6:237-241.

10144 **ROME, H. P.** (1962), Group psychotherapy: a twenty-year retrospectus. *Internat. J. Group Psychother.*, 12:295-300.

10145 **ROME, H. P.** (1945), Military group psychotherapy. *Amer. J. Psychiat.*, 101:494-497.

10146 **ROME, H. P.** (1946), Psychopathology and group psychotherapy. *Res. Publicat. Assn. Nerv. & Ment. Diseases*, 25:162-170.

10147 **ROME, H. P.** (1945), Therapeutic films and group psychotherapy. *Sociometry*, 8:485-492.

10148 **ROMOFF, V.,** and **SLAVINSKY, S.** (1973), Nurse therapy for lower socioeconomic psychiatric outpatients. *Perspect. Psychiat. Care*, 11:10-15.

10149 **RON, H., LURIE, A.,** and **WEISSMAN, J.** (1969), Methods of altering role relationships of young schizophrenics. *Amer. J. Orthopsychiat.*, 39:329-330.

10150 **RONCAL, R. B.** (1970), Chronically ill, self-sustaining patients in a state mental hospital. *N.Y. State J. Med.*, 70:2328-2331.

10151 **RONNING, H. G.** (1963), *Can You Talk It Out? A Panel Discussion Manual.* Los Angeles: Central Guidance Clinic.

10152 **ROOS, P.** (1968), Initiating socialization programs for socially inept adolescents. *Ment. Retard.*, 6:13-17.

10153 **ROOS, P.** (1963), Psychological counseling with parents of retarded children. *Ment. Retard.*, 1:345-350.

10154 **ROOSENBURG, A.** (1962), (Difficulties and possibilities in social therapy and psychotherapy of mentally disturbed delinquents.) *Nederl. Tijschr. Geneeskunde*, (Amsterdam) 106:1746-1747.

10155 **ROOTES, L.** (1974), The effect of achievement motivation training on women prisoners. *Crim. Justice & Behav.*, 1:131-138.

10156 **ROPER, P.** (1967), The effects of hypno-therapy on homosexuality. *Can. Med. Assn. J.*, (Ottawa) 96:319-327.

10157 **ROSÉ, A. E., BRAWN, C. E.,** and **METCALFF, E. V.** (1959), Music therapy at Westminister Hospital. *Ment. Hosp.*, 43:93-104.

10158 **ROSE, A. L., THOMMES, M. J., Van ORSHOVEN, T.,** and **LONGFELLOW, L. A.** (1972), The evolution of the wheel. *Psychol. Today*, 5:45-53.

10159 **ROSE, A. M.** (1956), *Sociology: The Study of Human Relationships.* New York: Knopf.

10160 **ROSE, D., BUTLER, C. M.,** and **EATON, F. L.** (1954), Play group therapy with psychotic adolescent girls. *Internat. J. Group Psychother.*, 4:303-311.

10161 **ROSE, J.,** and **GARFINKEL, P. E.** (1980), A parents' group in the management of anorexia nervosa. *Can. J. Psychiat.*, (Ottawa) 25:228-233.

10162 **ROSE, M.** (1972), Peper Harow: a therapeutic community for boys who have found difficulties in their lives. *Health*, 9:24-29.

10163 **ROSE, S.** (1953), Application of Karen Horney's theories to group analysis. *Internat. J. Group Psychother.*, 3:270-279.

10164 **ROSE, S.** (1958), Group psychoanalysis: the group striving for unity and union. *Amer. J. Psychoanal.*, 18:69-79.

10165 **ROSE, S.** (1957), Group psychotherapy from the points of view of various schools of psychology: ii. Horney concepts in group psychotherapy. *Internat. J. Group Psychother.*, 7:376-384.

10166 **ROSE, S.** (1952), Some advantages of group analysis. *Amer. J. Psychoanal.*, 12:79-80.

10167 **ROSE, S.** (1951), Tentative formulations in group analysis. *Amer. J. Psychoanal.*, 11:85-88.

10168 **ROSE, S. D.** (1969), A behavioral approach to the group treatment of parents. *Soc. Work*, 14:21-29.

10169 **ROSE, S. D. (Ed.)** (1979), *Casebook in Group Therapy: A Behavioral-Cognitive Approach*. Englewood Cliffs, NJ: Prentice-Hall.

10170 **ROSE, S. D.** (1977), *Group Therapy: A Behavioral Approach*. Englewood Cliffs, NJ: Prentice-Hall.

10171 **ROSE, S. D.** (1976), *Group Therapy: A Behavioral Approach*. New York: Prentice-Hall.

10172 **ROSE, S. D.** (1974), Group training of parents as behavior modifiers. *Soc. Work*, 19:156-162.

10173 **ROSE, S. D.** (1980), Review of D. Upper's and S. M. Ross's *Behavioral Group Therapy, 1979: An Annual Review*. *Contemp. Psychol.*, 25:833.

10174 **ROSE, S. D.** (1972), *Treating Children in Groups*. San Francisco: Jossey-Bass.

10175 **ROSE, S. D., CAYNER, J. J.,** and **EDELSON, J. L.** (1977), Measuring interpersonal competence. *Soc. Work*, 22:125-129.

10176 **ROSE, S. D., SIEMON, J. B.,** and **O'BRYANT, K.** (1979), Use of the group in therapy by members of AABT. *Behav. Ther.*, 2:21.

10177 **ROSEN, A. C.** (1970), Changes in the perception of mental illness and mental health. *Percept. & Motor Skills*, 31:203-208.

10178 **ROSEN, A. C.,** and **GOLDEN, J. S.** (1975), The encounter-sensitivity training group as an adjunct to medical education. *Internat. Rev. Appl. Psychol.*, (Liverpool) 24:61-70.

10179 **ROSEN, B., KATZOFF, A., CARRILLO, C.,** and **KLEIN, D. F.** (1976), Clinical effectiveness of "short" vs. "long" psychiatric hospitalization: i. inpatient results. *Arch. Gen. Psychiat.*, 33:1316-1322.

10180 **ROSEN, C. E.** (1972), The effects of sociodramatic play on problem solving behavior among culturally disadvantaged pre-school children. *Dissert. Abstr. Internat.*, 32:4111A.

10181 **ROSEN, H. G.,** and **ROSEN, S.** (1969), Program profiles. Group therapy as an instrument to develop a concept of self-worth in the adolescent and young adult mentally retarded. *Ment. Retard.*, 7:52-55.

10182 **ROSEN, I.** (1959), Developing and sustaining group therapy problems. *Ment. Hosp.*, 10:28-29.

10183 **ROSEN, I. M.,** and **CHASEN, M.** (1949), Study of resistance and its manifestations in therapeutic groups of chronic psychotic patients. *Psychiatry*, 12:279-283.

10184 **ROSEN, S.,** and **KASSAN, M.** (1972), Recent experiences with gestalt, encounter and hypnotic techniques. *Amer. J. Psychoanal.*, 32:90-105.

10185 **ROSENBAUM, A., O'LEARY, D.,** and **JACOB, R. G.** (1975), Behavioral intervention with hyperactive children: group consequences as a supplement to individual contingencies. *Behav. Ther.*, 6:315-323.

10186 **ROSENBAUM, M.** (1968), The academic and the clinical. *J. Group Psychoanal. & Process*, (London) 1:5-10.
10187 **ROSENBAUM, M.** (1975), The challenge of group psychoanalysis. In: *Group Psychotherapy and Group Function*, eds. M. Rosenbaum and M. M. Berger. New York: Basic Books.
10188 **ROSENBAUM, M.** (1952), The challenge of group psychoanalysis. *Psychoanal.*, 1:42-58.
10189 **ROSENBAUM, M.** (1969), College students as a source of attendant help. *Perspect. Psychiat. Care*, 7:228-234.
10190 **ROSENBAUM, M.** (1973), *Drug Abuse and Drug Addiction*. London, New York: Gordon and Breach.
10191 **ROSENBAUM, M.** (1974), *Group Psychotherapy from the Southwest*. London: Gordon and Breach.
10192 **ROSENBAUM, M.** (1974), *Group Psychotherapy from the Southwest*. New York: Gordon and Breach.
10193 **ROSENBAUM, M.** (1960), Obstacles to research in psychotherapy. *Psychoanal. Rev.*, 47:97-105.
10194 **ROSENBAUM, M.** (1963), Resistance to group psychotherapy in a community mental health clinic. *Internat. J. Soc. Psychiat.*, (London) 9:180-183.
10195 **ROSENBAUM, M.** (1970), The responsibility of the group psychotherapy practitioner for a therapeutic rationale. *J. Group Psychoanal. & Process*, (London) 2:5-17.
10196 **ROSENBAUM, M.** (1971), The responsibility of the psychotherapist for a theoretic rationale. *Group Process*, (London) 3:41-47.
10197 **ROSENBAUM, M.** (1980), Review of S. R. Slavson's and M. Schiffer's *Dynamics of Group Psychotherapy*. *Contemp. Psychol.*, 25:631.
10198 **ROSENBAUM, M.** (1966), Some comments on the use of untrained therapists. *J. Clin. Psychol.*, 30:292-294.
10199 **ROSENBAUM, M.** (1960), What is the place of combined psychotherapy? a comment and critique. *Topical Probl. Psychol. & Psychother.*, 2:86-96.
10200 **ROSENBAUM, M.**, and **BERGER, M.** (1963), *Group Psychotherapy and Group Function*. New York: Basic Books.
10201 **ROSENBAUM, M.**, and **BERGER, M. M.** (1975), *Group Psychotherapy and Group Function*, 2d ed. New York: Basic Books.
10202 **ROSENBAUM, M.**, and **HARTLEY, E.** (1962), A summary review of current practices of ninety-two group psychotherapists. *Internat. J. Group Psychother.*, 12:194-198.
10203 **ROSENBAUM, M.**, and **KRAFT, I. A.** (1975), Group psychotherapy for children. In: *Group Psychotherapy and Group Function*, 2d ed., eds. M. Rosenbaum and M. M. Berger. New York: Basic Books.
10204 **ROSENBAUM, M.**, and **SNADOWSKY, A.** (1976), *The Intensive Group Experience*. New York: Free Press.
10205 **ROSENBAUM, M., SNADOWSKY, A.**, and **HARTLEY, E.** (1966), Group psychotherapy and the integration of the Negro. *Internat. J. Group Psychother.*, 16:86-90.
10206 **ROSENBERG, G.**, and **COLTOFF, P.** (1967), A community participation program for the hospitalized mental patient. *J. Jewish Communal Serv.*, 43:253-259.
10207 **ROSENBERG, H.**, and **BONOMA, T. V.** (1974), A social influence rating method for group interaction and some pilot results on group therapy process. *Perspect. Soc. Psychiat.*, 1:259-262.
10208 **ROSENBERG, I. H.** (1961), An experimental investigation of some effects on stutterers of pacatal-aided group psychotherapy: a comparison of the effects on male adult stutterers of group psychotherapy with and without

the tranquilizer pacatal as an adjuvant. *Dissert. Abstr. Internat.*, 21:3168. (University Microfilms No. 61-00347.)

10209 **ROSENBERG, J.** (1979), Inpatient group therapy for older children and pre-adolescents. *Internat. J. Group Psychother.*, 29:393-406.

10210 **ROSENBERG, J. B.**, and **LINDBLAD, M. B.** (1978), Behavior therapy in a family context: treating elective mutism. *Fam. Process*, 17:77-82.

10211 **ROSENBERG, J. M.** (1962), Ethnodrama as a research method in anthropology. *Group Psychother., Psychodrama & Sociometry*, 15:236-243.

10212 **ROSENBERG, J. M.** (1960), Perceptual differences in sociometric patterning. *Group Psychother., Psychodrama & Sociometry*, 13:47-55.

10213 **ROSENBERG, J. M.** (1961), Role playing: a useful tool in understanding the impact of industrial automation on the displaced worker. *Group Psychother., Psychodrama & Sociometry*, 14:44-47.

10214 **ROSENBERG, L.**, and **MOOSBRUKER, J.** (1967), The participation of working class mental patients in a mixed-class therapeutic group. *Soc. Science & Med.*, 1:85-96.

10215 **ROSENBERG, P.** (1952), An experimental analysis of psychodrama. Unpublished doctoral dissertation, Radcliffe College.

10216 **ROSENBERG, P.**, and **CHILGREN, R.** (1973), Sex education discussion groups in a medical setting. *Internat. J. Group Psychother.*, 23:23-41.

10217 **ROSENBERG, P. P.** (1972), The medical student discussion group as an effective data-gathering technique. *Internat. J. Group Psychother.*, 22:243-249.

10218 **ROSENBERG, P. P.** (1962), Methodology for an objective analysis of the content of a group protocol. *Internat. J. Group Psychother.*, 12:467-475.

10219 **ROSENBERG, P. P.**, and **FULLER, M.** (1957), Dynamic analysis of the student nurse. *Group Psychother., Psychodrama & Sociometry*, 10:22-39.

10220 **ROSENBERG, P. P.**, and **FULLER, M. L.** (1955), Human relations seminar: a group work experience in nursing education. *Ment. Hygiene*, 39:406-432.

10221 **ROSENBLATT, A.**, and **WIGGINS, L. M.** (1967), Characteristics of the parents served. *Soc. Casework*, 48:639-647.

10222 **ROSENBLATT, D.** (1975), *Opening Doors: What Happens in Gestalt Therapy*. New York: Harper and Row.

10223 **ROSENFELD, D.** (1970), Nuevos enfoques en psicoterapia grupal: introducción a las teorías de Jean P. Sartre. (A new focus in group therapy: an introduction to the theories of Jean P. Sartre.) *Rev. Argentina Psicol.*, (Buenos Aires) 2:41-62.

10224 **ROSENFELD, E. M.** (1969), Intervening in hostile behavior through dyadic and/or group intervention. *J. Psychiat. Nursing*, 7:251

10225 **ROSENFELD, J. M.**, and **ORLINSKY, N.** (1961), The effect of research on practice: research and decrease in noncontinuance. *Arch. Gen. Psychiat.*, 5:176-182.

10226 **ROSENGREN, T. M.** (1972), A leaderless group model designed to increase self-referent verbal behavior. *Dissert. Abstr. Internat.*, 33:976A.

10227 **ROSENGREN, W. R.** (1959), Symptom manifestations as a function of situational press: a demonstration in socialization. *Sociometry*, 22:113-123.

10228 **ROSENHEIM, E.**, and **ELIZUR, A.** (1977), Group therapy for trauma. *Curr. Psychiat. Ther.*, 17:143-148.

10229 **ROSENSTEIN, S. H.**, and **HERSEN, M.** (1969), Resistances encountered in outpatient group psychotherapy with male juvenile probationers. *Correct. Psychiat. & J. Soc. Ther.*, 15:45-49.

10230 **ROSENSTOCK, H. A.** (1978), Early a.m. group therapy. *J. Nat. Assn. Priv. Psychiat. Hosp.*, 9:37.

10231 **ROSENSTOCK, H. A.**, and **HANSEN, D. B.** (1974), Toward better school

adaptability: an early adolescent group therapy experiment. *Amer. J. Psychiat.*, 131:1397-1399.
10232 **ROSENSTOCK, H. A.,** and **VINCENT, K. R.** (1979), Parental involvement as a requisite for successful adolescent therapy. *J. Clin. Psychiat.*, 40:132.
10233 **ROSENTHAL, B. G.,** and **de LONG, A. J.** (1972), Complementary leadership and spatial arrangement of group members. *Group Psychother., Psychodrama & Sociometry*, 25:34-52.
10234 **ROSENTHAL, D., FRANK, J. D.,** and **NASH, E. H.** (1954), The self-righteous moralist in early meetings of therapeutic groups. *Psychiatry*, 17:215-223.
10235 **ROSENTHAL, L.** (1961), Aspects of similarity and difference in levels of group treatment of adults in social agency settings. *J. Jewish Communal Serv.*, 37:4.
10236 **ROSENTHAL, L.** (1964), Basic dynamics of activity group therapy. *Pathways Child Guid.*, 6:7.
10237 **ROSENTHAL, L.** (1956), Child guidance. In: *The Fields of Group Psychotherapy*, ed. S. R. Slavson. New York: International Universities Press.
10238 **ROSENTHAL, L.** (1953), Countertransference in activity group therapy. *Internat. J. Group Psychother.*, 3:431-440.
10239 **ROSENTHAL, L.** (1951), Group psychotherapy in a child guidance clinic. *Soc. Casework*, 8:337-342.
10240 **ROSENTHAL, L.** (1953), Group therapy with problem children and their parents. *Fed. Probat.*, 17:4-27.
10241 **ROSENTHAL, L.** (1978), An investigation of the relationship between therapists' orientations and their preferences for interventions in group psychotherapy. *Dissert. Abstr. Internat.*, 39:3757B.
10242 **ROSENTHAL, L.** (1976), The resolution of group-destructive resistance in modern group analysis. *Mod. Psychoanal.*, 1:2.
10243 **ROSENTHAL, L.** (1977), Review of S. deSchill's *Challenge for Group Psychotherapy: Present and Future. Psychoanal. Rev.*, 63:642-644.
10244 **ROSENTHAL, L.** (1977), Qualifications and tasks of therapist in group therapy with children. *Clin. Soc. Work*, 5:191-199.
10245 **ROSENTHAL, L.** (1958), Some aspects of a triple relation: group-group-therapist-supervisor. In: *New Frontiers in Child Guidance*, ed. A. Esman. New York: International Universities Press.
10246 **ROSENTHAL, L.** (1968), Some aspects of interpretation in group therapy. In: *Use of Interpretation in Treatment*, ed. E. F. Hammer. New York: Grune and Stratton.
10247 **ROSENTHAL, L.** (1971), Some dynamics of resistances and therapeutic management in adolescent group therapy. *Psychoanal. Rev.*, 58:353-366.
10248 **ROSENTHAL, L.** (1963), A study of resistances in a member of a therapy group. *Internat. J. Group Psychother.*, 13:315-327.
10249 **ROSENTHAL, L.** (1966), Training for group therapy: the contributions of individual supervisory and group training modalities. *Pathways Child Guid.*, 9:3-4.
10250 **ROSENTHAL, L.,** and **APAKA, W.** (1959), The group psychotherapy literature, 1958. *Internat. J. Group Psychother.*, 9:239-256.
10251 **ROSENTHAL, L.,** and **APAKA, W.** (1960), The group psychotherapy literature, 1959. *Internat. J. Group Psychother.*, 10:227-245.
10252 **ROSENTHAL, L.,** and **BLACK, M.** (1970), Modification in therapeutic technique in the group treatment of delinquent boys. In: *New Approaches in Child Guidance*, ed. E. H. Stream. New York: Scarecrow Press.
10253 **ROSENTHAL, L.,** and **GARFINKEL, A.** (1957), The group psychotherapy literature, 1956. *Internat. J. Group Psychother.*, 7:196-211.

10254 **ROSENTHAL, L.**, and **GARFINKEL, A.** (1958), The group psychotherapy literature, 1957. *Internat. J. Group Psychother.*, 8:193-213.

10255 **ROSENTHAL, L.**, and **HOLLOWITZ, E.** (1955), The group therapy literature, 1954. *Internat. J. Group Psychother.*, 5:213-217.

10256 **ROSENTHAL, L.**, and **HOLLOWITZ, E.** (1954), The group therapy literature, 1953. *Internat. J. Group Psychother.*, 4:218-222.

10257 **ROSENTHAL, L.**, and **NAGELBERG, L.** (1956), Limitations of activity group therapy: a case presentation. *Internat. J. Group Psychother.*, 6:166-179.

10258 **ROSENTHAL, L.**, and **SCHAMESS, G.** (1961), The group psychotherapy literature, 1960. *Internat. J. Group Psychother.*, 11:219-235.

10259 **ROSENTHAL, L.**, and **SCHAMESS, G.** (1962), The group psychotherapy literature, 1961. *Internat. J. Group Psychother.*, 12:240-259.

10260 **ROSENTHAL, L.**, and **SCHAMESS, G.** (1963), The group psychotherapy literature, 1962. *Internat. J. Group Psychother.*, 13:219-238.

10261 **ROSENTHAL, L., SCHAMESS, G.**, and **LEIBOWITZ, M.** (1964), The group psychotherapy literature, 1963. *Internat. J. Group Psychother.*, 14:227-241.

10262 **ROSENTHAL, L., GABRIEL, B., KOLODNEY, E., LIEBERMAN, F., NAGELBERG, L.**, and **PFEFFER, D.** (1960), Family relations as a consideration in selection for activity group therapy. *Internat. J. Group Psychother.*, 10:78-89.

10263 **ROSENTHAL, L. V.**, and **NAGELBERG, L.** (1955), Validation of selection of patients for activity group therapy. *Internat. J. Group Psychother.*, 5:38-45.

10264 **ROSENTHAL, M. S.**, and **BIASE, D. V.** (1969), Phoenix houses: therapeutic communities for drug addicts. *Hosp. & Community Psychiat.*, 20:26-30.

10265 **ROSENTHAL, P.** (1947), The death of the leader in group psychotherapy. *Amer. J. Orthopsychiat.*, 17:266-277.

10266 **ROSENTHAL, P. A.** (1979), Sudden disappearance of one parent with separation and divorce: the grief and treatment of pre-school children. *J. Divorce*, 3:43.

10267 **ROSENTHAL, T. L., LINEHAN, K. S., KELLER, J. E., ROSENTHAL, R. H., THEOBALC, D. E.**, and **DAVIS, A. F.** (1978), Group aversion by imaginal, vicarious and shared recipient-observer shocks. *Behav. Res. & Ther.*, 16:421-427.

10268 **ROSENTHAL, V.**, and **SHIMBERG, E.** (1958), A program of group therapy with incarcerated narcotic addicts. *J. Crim. Law & Criminol.*, 49:140-144.

10269 **ROSENTHAL, W. A.** (1970), A theory of beginnings in social group work process. *Dissert. Abstr. Internat.*, 31:3050.

10270 **ROSENZWEIG, N.** (1967), Planning a psychiatric program for the general hospital. *Hospitals*, 41:58-65.

10271 **ROSENZWEIG, S.**, and **SHAKOW, D.** (1937), Play technique in schizophrenia and other psychoses: i. rationale. *Amer. J. Orthopsychiat.*, 7:32-35.

10272 **ROSENZWEIG, S.**, and **SHAKOW, D.** (1937), Play techniques in schizophrenia and other psychoses: ii. schizophrenic construction. *Amer. J. Orthopsychiat.*, 7:36-47.

10273 **ROSENZWEIG, S. P.**, and **FOLMAN, R.** (1974), Patient and therapist variables affecting premature termination in group psychotherapy. *Psychother.: Theory, Res. & Pract.*, 11:76-79.

10274 **ROSIN, A. J.** (1975), Group discussions: a therapeutic tool in a chronic diseases hospital. *Geriatrics*, 30:45-48.

10275 **ROSKIN, G., KASSNOVE, R.**, and **ADAMS, J.** (1978), Group vocational rehabilitation counselling for drug abusers as an outreach technique in the schools. *Drug Forum*, 7:35-40.

10276 **ROSOW, H. M.,** and **KAPLAN, L.** (1954), Integrated individual and group therapy. *Internat. J. Group Psychother.*, 4:381-393.

10277 **ROSS, A. L.** (1974), Combining behavior modification and group work techniques in a day treatment center. *Child Welfare*, 53:435-444.

10278 **ROSS, D.** (1975), Toward a theory of process psychotherapy. *Fam. Ther.*, 2:237-258.

10279 **ROSS, D. L.** (1977), Poetry therapy versus traditional supportive therapy: a comparison of group process. *Dissert. Abstr. Internat.*, 38:1417B.

10280 **ROSS, D. M., UECKER, S. L. P., POWELL, S. R., MILLER, S. P.,** and **BEAN, J. A.** (1980), The impact of group and individual therapy on socialization of residents in an institutional setting. *Issues Ment. Health Nursing*, 2:33-42.

10281 **ROSS, E. K.,** and **ANDERSON, R.** (1968), Psychotherapy with least expected: modified group therapy with blind clients. *Rehab. Lit.*, 29:73-76.

10282 **ROSS, F. T.** (1971), Touch and go. *Group Process*, (London) 3:89-94.

10283 **ROSS, G.,** and **WEINSTEIN, P.** (1967), Groupwork in hospital and the community. *Soc. Serv. Quart.*, (London) 41:15-19.

10284 **ROSS, H.** (1944), Group psychotherapy related to group trauma. *Amer. J. Orthopsychiat.*, 14:609-615.

10285 **ROSS, J. L.** (1965), Alcoholics Anonymous: a neglected adjunct to hospital treatment. *J. Kansas Med. Soc.*, 66:23-27.

10286 **ROSS, L. E.** (1962), Note: persisting inhibitory effect found in both classical and instrumental learning situations. *Psychol. Reports*, 11:691-692.

10287 **ROSS, L. H.,** and **ALLEN, R. M.** (1975), Two statistical approaches to two types of group confrontation. *Small Group Behav.*, 6:220-228.

10288 **ROSS, M.** (1975), Community geriatric group therapies: a comprehensive review. In: *Group Psychotherapy and Group Function*, 2d ed., eds. M. Rosenbaum and M. M. Berger. New York: Basic Books.

10289 **ROSS, M.** (1959), Recent contributions to gerontologic group psychotherapy. *Internat. J. Group Psychother.*, 9:442-450.

10290 **ROSS, S. M.** (1974), Behavioral group therapy with alcohol abusers. In: *Modification of Behavior of the Mentally Ill: Rehabilitation Approaches*, eds. R. E. Hardy and G. Cull. Springfield, IL: C. C. Thomas.

10291 **ROSS, S. N.** (1978), Evaluation of a model to train paraprofessionals to conduct assertive training groups. *Dissert. Abstr. Internat.*, 39:4595B.

10292 **ROSS, W. D.** (1948), Group psychotherapy with patients' relatives. *Amer. J. Psychiat.*, 104:623-626.

10293 **ROSS, W. D.** (1948), Group psychotherapy with psychotic patients and their relatives. *Amer. J. Psychiat.*, 105:383-386.

10294 **ROSS, W. D.** (1971), Some psychiatric aspects of sensitivity groups. *Can. Psychiat. Assn. J.*, (Ottawa) 16:83-86.

10295 **ROSS, W. D.,** and **BRISSENDEN, A.** (1961), Some observations on the emotional position of the group psychotherapist. *Psychiat. Quart.*, 35:516-522.

10296 **ROSS, W. D., BLOCK, S. L.,** and **SILVER, H.** (1958), Integrating training in group psychotherapy with psychiatric residency training. *Internat. J. Group Psychother.*, 8:323-328.

10297 **ROSS, W. D., KLIGFELD, M.,** and **WHITMAN, R. W.** (1971), Psychiatrists, patients, and sensitivity groups. *Arch. Gen. Psychiat.*, 25:178-180.

10298 **ROSS, W. F., McREYNOLDS, W. T.,** and **BERZINS, J. L.** (1974), Effectiveness of marathon group psychotherapy with hospitalized female narcotic addicts. *Psychol. Reports*, 34:611-616.

10299 **ROSSBERG, R.,** and **JAQUES, M.** (1961), The role of the group in patient evaluation, counseling, and management. *Personnel & Guid. J.*, 40:135-142.

10300 **ROSSBERG, R. H.** (1956), The use of group therapy in a counseling program with paraplegics: a comparative study of the effects of the incorporation of group therapy in a counseling program on the behavior and certain attitudes of paraplegics. Unpublished doctoral dissertation, New York University.

10301 **ROSSEL, R. D.** (1979), Humor and hard play in group therapy. *Internat. J. Group Psychother.*, 29:407-418.

10302 **ROSSI, J. J.** (1957), A process analysis of three types of group psychotherapy with hospitalized alcoholics. Unpublished doctoral dissertation, University of Ottawa.

10303 **ROSSMAN, M.** (1979), *New Age Blues*. New York: Dutton.

10304 **ROSTOV, B. W.** (1965), Group work in the psychiatric hospital: a critical review of the literature. *Soc. Work*, 10:23-31.

10305 **ROSZELL, B. L.** (1971), Pretraining, awareness, and behavioral group therapy approaches to assertive behavior training. *Dissert. Abstr. Internat.*, 32:3649B.

10306 **ROT, N.** (1975), (The individual in the group.) *Anali Zavoda Ment. Zdravlje*, 7:25-33.

10307 **ROTAR, F.** (1980), A group counseling approach using the "human development program" in grades kindergarten through six. *Dissert. Abstr. Internat.*, 40:5326A. (University Microfilms No. 8007312.)

10308 **ROTH, B. E.** (1980), Review of L. Ormont's and H. Strean's *The Practice of Conjoint Therapy*. *Group*, 4:63.

10309 **ROTH, B. E.** (1980), Understanding the development of a homogeneous identity impaired group through a countertransference phenomenon. *Internat. J. Group Psychother.*, 30:405.

10310 **ROTH, R.** (1964), The effect of time limited group psychotherapy on underachieving male college freshmen: ii. achievement, self concept, and attitudes. Unpublished doctoral dissertation, Adelphi University.

10311 **ROTH, R.** (1977), A transactional analysis group in residential treatment of adolescents. *Child Welfare*, 56:776-786.

10312 **ROTH, R. M., MAUKSCH, H. O.,** and **PEISER, K.** (1967), The non-achievement syndrome, and group therapy and achievement change. *Personnel & Guid. J.*, 46:393-398.

10313 **ROTH, S.,** and **STIGLITZ, M.** (1971), The shared patient: separate therapists for group and individual psychotherapy. *Internat. J. Group Psychother.*, 21:44-52.

10314 **ROTH, S. A.** (1974), Group reinforcement contingency systems under varying conditions of monetary payment and individual feedback. *Dissert. Abstr. Internat.*, 41:699B.

10315 **ROTHAUS, P.** (1964), Instrumented role-playing in psychiatric training laboratory. *Arch. Gen. Psychiat.*, 11:400-410.

10316 **ROTHAUS, P.** (1966), Participation and sociometry in autonomous and trainer–led patient groups. *J. Couns. Psychol.*, 13:68-76.

10317 **ROTHAUS, P.** (1967), Sentence completion test prediction of autonomous and therapist–led group behavior. *J. Couns. Psychol.*, 14:28-34.

10318 **ROTHAUS, P., HANSON, P. G.,** and **CLEVELAND, S. E.** (1966), Art and group dynamics. *Amer. J. Occupat. Ther.*, 20:182-187.

10319 **ROTHAUS, P., JOHNSON, D. L.,** and **LYLE, F. A.** (1964), Group participation training for psychiatric patients. *J. Couns. Psychol.*, 11:230-238.

10320 **ROTHAUS, P., HANSON, P. G., JOHNSON, D. L., LYLE, F. A.,** and **MOYER, R.** (1966), The anticipation and management of crisis on an open psychiatric ward. *J. Appl. Behav. Science*, 2:431-447.

10321 **ROTHAUS, P., MORTON, R. B., JOHNSON, D. L., CLEVELAND, S. E.,** and **LYLE, F. A.** (1963), Human relations training for psychiatric patients. *Arch. Gen. Psychiat.*, 8:572-581.

10322 **ROTHENBERG, A.**, and **VOGEL, E. F.** (1964), Patient cliques and the therapeutic community. *Brit. J. Med. Psychol.*, (London) 37:143-151.

10323 **ROTHMAN, G.** (1961), Psychodrama and autogenic relaxation. *Group Psychother., Psychodrama & Sociometry*, 14:26-29.

10324 **ROTHMAN, R.** (1956), Group counseling with parents of visually handicapped children. *Internat. J. Group Psychother.*, 6:317-323.

10325 **ROTHSCHILD, B.** (1967), Experiences in a drawing group in the Burghölzlii University Clinic, Zurich: contributions to the subject of the meeting. *Schweiz. Arch. Neurol., Neurochir. & Psychiat.*, (Zurich) 99:165-168.

10326 **ROTHSCHILD, J.** (1960), Play therapy with blind children. *New Outlook Blind*, 54:329-333.

10327 **ROTHSLEIN, A.** (1979), Mental health program at the Lexington School for the Deaf. In: *Hearing and Hearing Impairment*, eds. L. J. Bradford and W. G. Hardy. New York: Grune and Stratton.

10328 **ROTHSTEIN, E., NORTON, B. A., LAHAGE, E. H.**, and **MUELLER, S. R.** (1966), An experimental alcoholism unit in a psychiatric hospital. *Quart. J. Studies Alcohol*, 27:513-516.

10329 **ROTMAN, C. B.**, and **CLAYMAN, C. S.** (1971), Human relations training for camp staff members. *Camping Mag.*, 43:10.

10330 **ROTMAN, C. B.**, and **GOLBURGH, S. J.** (1967), Group counseling mentally retarded adolescents. *Mental Retard.*, 5:13-16.

10331 **ROTTER, H.** (1958), Über die funktion der beratungsstellen bei der ambulanten behandlung alkoholkranker. (On the function of consultation clinics in the ambulant treatment of alcoholics.) *Wiener Med. Wochenschr.*, (Vienna) 108:487-489.

10332 **ROTTER, J. B.** (1960), Psychotherapy. In: *Annual Review of Psychology, Vol. II*, eds. P. R. Farnsworth and Q. Nemar. Palo Alto: Annual Reviews, pp. 381-414.

10333 **ROUNSAVILLE, B., LIFTON, N.**, and **BIEBER, M.** (1979), The natural history of a psychotherapy group for battered women. *Psychiatry*, 42:63-78.

10334 **ROURKE, P. G.** (1974), Consultant role and member learning in the small experiential group. *Dissert. Abstr. Internat.*, 34:5691B.

10335 **ROUSLIN, S.** (1973), Relatedness in group psychotherapy. *Perspect. Psychiat. Care*, 11:165-171.

10336 **ROUSOS, I. C.** (1960), Planning occupational therapy for schizophrenic children. *Amer. J. Occupat. Ther.*, 14:137-139.

10337 **ROUTH, T. A.** (1958), Psychodrama and the blind. *Group Psychother., Psychodrama & Sociometry*, 11:213-215.

10338 **ROUTH, T. A.** (1962), Psychotherapy as used in a rehabilitation centre for the blind. *Indian J. Soc. Work*, (Bombay) 23:173-178.

10339 **ROUTH, T. A.** (1957), A study of the use of group psychotherapy in rehabilitation centers for the blind. *Group Psychother., Psychodrama & Sociometry*, 10:38-50.

10340 **ROWAN, J.** (1975), Encounter group research: no joy? *J. Human. Psychol.*, 15:19-28.

10341 **ROWE, W.** (1972), The effect of short–term group counseling and cognitive learning on a measure of self–actualization of counselors in training. *Dissert. Abstr. Internat.*, 32:4965A.

10342 **ROWE, W.**, and **WINBORN, B. B.** (1973), What people fear about group work: an analysis of 36 selected critical articles. *Educat. Technol.*, 13:53-57.

10343 **ROWE, W. S.** (1967), The treatment of homosexuality and associated perversions by psychotherapy and aversion therapy. *Med. J. Austral.*, (Glebe) 2:637-639.

10344 **ROWITCH, J.** (1968), Group consultation with school personnel. *Hosp. & Community Psychiat.*, 19:261-266.

01345 **ROWLAND, K. F.** (1978), Evaluation of a sexual enhancement program for elderly couples. *Dissert. Abstr. Internat.*, 38:6171B. (University Microfilms No. 7807922.)

10346 **ROWLAND, K. F.**, and **HAYNES, S. N.** (1978), A sexual enhancement program for elderly couples. *J. Sex & Marital Ther.*, 4:91-113.

10347 **ROY, J. J.** (1972), A study of the processes and outcomes of a group achievement counselling program for "underachieving" students. *Dissert. Abstr. Internat.*, 32:3702A.

10348 **ROYER de GARCIA REINOSO, G.** (1970), (Violence and aggression or, better, violence and repression?) *Rev. de Psicoanal.*, (Buenos Aires) 27:271-305.

10349 **RÓZYCKI, A.** (1972), (Psychotherapy and therapeutic community.) *Ceskoslov. Psychiat.*, (Prague) 68:257-263.

10350 **RUBENSTEIN, A.** (1973), The effect of social modeling and humanistic group procedures upon teacher classroom behavior and student perceptions. *Dissert. Abstr. Internat.*, 33:4100A.

10351 **RUBENSTEIN, B.** (1945), Therapeutic use of groups in an orthopedic hospital school. *Amer. J. Orthopsychiat.*, 15:662-674.

10352 **RUBENSTEIN, B. O.**, and **LEVITT, M.** (1957), Some observations regarding the role of fathers in child psychotherapy. *Bull. Menninger Clinic*, 21:16-27.

10353 **RUBENSTEIN, M. A., NEMIROFF, R. A.**, and **CHIPMAN, A.** (1967), Simultaneous hospitalization of a mother and daughter. *Amer. J. Orthopsychiat.*, 37:350-351.

10354 **RUBES, H.** (1975), New opening technique in group psychotherapy. In: *Psychotherapie in Sozialistichen Landern*, (*Psychotherapy in Socialist Countries*), ed. M. Hausner. Leipzig: Thieme.

10355 **RUBES, J.** (1970), Public psychodrama in Prague. *Group Psychother., Psychodrama & Sociometry*, 23:57-59.

10356 **RUBIN, B.**, and **EISEN, S. B.** (1958), The old-timers' club: an autonomous patient group in a state mental hospital. *Arch. Neurol. Psychiat.*, 79:113-121.

10357 **RUBIN, H. E.**, and **KATZ, E.** (1946), Auroratone films for the treatment of psychotic depressions in an army general hospital. *J. Clin. Psychol.*, 2:333-340.

10358 **RUBIN, H. E.**, and **KATZ, E.** (1946), Motion picture psychotherapy of psychotic depressions in an army general hospital. *Sociometry*, 9:86-89.

10359 **RUBIN, H. S.**, and **COHEN, H. A.** (1974), Group counseling and remediation: a two-faceted intervention approach to the problem of attrition in nursing education. *J. Educat. Res.*, 67:195-198.

10360 **RUBIN, J. A.**, and **LEVY, P.** (1975), Art-awareness: a method for working with groups. *Group Psychother., Psychodrama & Sociometry*, 28:108-117.

10361 **RUBIN, S.** (1978), Parent's group in a psychiatric hospital for children. *Soc. Work*, 23:416-417.

10362 **RUDHYAR, E. F.** (1951), Methods of sound and movement as an adjunct to psychodrama. *Group Psychother., Psychodrama & Sociometry*, 4:94-99.

10363 **RUDHYAR, E. F.**, and **BRANHAM, B.** (1953), The development of a psychodrama department in a mental hospital. *Group Psychother., Psychodrama & Sociometry*, 6:110-114.

10364 **RUDMAN, S.** (1970), Positive changes in self–concept as a function of participation in encounter groups and encounter tape groups. *Dissert. Abstr. Internat.*, 31:5674B.

10365 **RUDOLF, G.** (1955), An experiment in group therapy. *Internat. J. Soc. Psychiat.*, (London) 1:49-53.

10366 **RUDOLF, G.** (1955), An experiment in group therapy with mental defectives. *Internat. J. Soc. Psychiat.*, (London) 1:24-27.

10367 **RUEL, M.** (1980), Process without structure: some anthropological observations on the large group. *Group Anal.*, (London) 13:99-109.

10368 **RUEVENI, U.** (1970), The application and use of sensitivity training in the development of human relation skills with medical students. *J. Psychiat. Nursing*, 3:28-29.

10369 **RUEVENI, U.** (1971), Using sensitivity training with junior high school students. *Children*, 18:69-72.

10370 **RUEVENI, U.**, and **SPECK, R. V.** (1969), Using encounter group techniques in the treatment of the social network of the schizophrenic. *Internat. J. Group Psychother.*, 19:495-500.

10371 **RUFFIN, J. E.** (1973), Racism as counter-transference in psychotherapy groups. *Perspect. Psychiat. Care*, 11:172-178.

10372 **RUGER, U.** (1976), (Catamnestic outcomes of a sample of 21 outpatients 5 years after group therapy.) *Gruppenpsychother. & Gruppendynam.*, (Goettingen) 10:313-330.

10373 **RUGER, U.** (1977), (Later emotional attitudes of patients towards group-dynamic processes five years after termination of an analytic group psychotherapy.) *Gruppenpsychother. & Gruppendynam.*, (Goettingen) 11:122-129.

10374 **RUGER, U.** (1980), Various regressive processes and their prognostic value in inpatient group psychotherapy. *Internat. J. Group Psychother.*, 30:95-106.

10375 **RUHE, J.**, and **EATMAN, J.** (1977), Effects of racial composition on small work groups. *Small Group Behav.*, 8:479-486.

10376 **RUINON, K. B.** (1976), The effects of activity group guidance on children's self-concept and social power. *Dissert. Abstr. Internat.*, 36:5057A.

10377 **RUITENBEEK, H. M.** (1973), *The Analytic Situation: How Patient and Therapist Communicate*. Chicago: Aldine.

10378 **RUITENBEEK, H. M.** (1969), *Group Therapy Today: Styles, Methods, and Techniques*. New York: Atherton Press.

10379 **RUITENBEEK, H. M.** (1970), *The New Group Therapies*. New York: Discus Books.

10380 **RUIZ, A. S.** (1975), Chicano group catalysts. *Personnel & Guid. J.*, 53:462-466.

10381 **RUIZ, C.** (1969), (Group therapy: supervised musicotherapy and ergotherapy in a psychiatric setting.) *Laval Med.*, (Quebec) 40:189-197.

10382 **RUIZ, E. J.** (1975), Influence of bilingualism on communication in groups. *Internat. J. Group Psychother.*, 25:391-395.

10383 **RUIZ, P.** (1972), On the perception of the "mother-group" in t-groups. *Internat. J. Group Psychother.*, 22:488-491.

10384 **RUIZ, P.** (1975), Symposium: group therapy with minority group patients—introduction. *Internat. J. Group Psychother.*, 25:389-390.

10385 **RUIZ, R. A.**, and **BURGESS, M. M.** (1968), Group psychotherapy: a preliminary teaching model. *J. Med. Educat.*, 43:455-463.

10386 **RUIZ–OGARA, C.** (1961), ("Group analysis" with schizophrenic patients.) *Medicina*, (Barcelona) 29:77-80.

10387 **RUIZ–OGARA, C.** (1967), (On the psychotherapy of schizophrenia in the psychiatric hospital.) *Actas Luso Españolas Neurol. Psiquiat.*, (Madrid) 26:277-286.

10388 **RUIZ–OGARA, D. C.** (1953), Operación al estudio de la psicoterapia en grupo. (Operating a group psychotherapy office.) *Med. & Cir. Guerra*, (Madrid) 15:235-240.

10389 **RULE, B. G., KRIEGER, M. H.,** and **SCHER, M.** (1966), Patient group membership and outcome of psychiatric hospitalization. *Internat. J. Group Psychother.*, 16:304-312.

10390 **RUMKE, H. C.** (1951), Group psychotherapy in Utrecht, Holland. *Internat. J. Group Psychother.*, 1:374-376.

10391 **RÜMMELE, W.** (1974), Report and considerations on group psychotherapy in a prison. *Schweiz. Arch. Neurol., Neurochir. & Psychiat.*, (Zurich) 115:359-368.

10392 **RUNDLE, F. L.,** and **BRIGGS, D. L.** (1957), Beginning of a therapeutic community: establishing group meetings on a closed ward. *U.S. Armed Forces Med. J.*, 8:811-819.

10393 **RUNDLE, F. L.,** and **BRIGGS, D. L.** (1957), Development of a therapeutic community: problems encountered in daily community meetings. *U.S. Armed Forces Med. J.*, 8:1339-1349.

10394 **RUPKEY, J. T.** (1973), The effects of teacher directed group counseling on self-esteem, congruence of student and teacher perception of group climate and achievement of teacher's goals for group climate. *Dissert. Abstr. Internat.*, 34:4889A.

10395 **RUSCONI, S.** (1969), (Psychologic training and the Balint group.) *Rev. Med. Psychosom.*, (Paris) 11:165-168.

10396 **RUSH, A. J., SHAW, B.,** and **KHATANI, M.** (1980), Cognitive therapy of depression: utilizing the couples system. *Cognitive Ther. Rev.*, 4:103.

10397 **RUSKIN, I. W.** (1953), Analytic group psychotherapy for husbands and wives. First Annual Report, Group Psychotherapy Association of Southern California, pp. 25-31.

10398 **RUSKIN, I. W.** (1952), Analytic group psychotherapy for wives and husbands. *California Med.*, 77:140-145.

10399 **RUSSAW, E. H.** (1970), Nursing in a narcotic–detoxification unit. *Amer. J. Nursing*, 70:1720.

10400 **RUSSELL, A.,** and **WINKLER, R.** (1977), Evaluation of assertive training and homosexual guidance service groups designed to improve homosexual functioning. *J. Consult. & Clin. Psychol.*, 45:1-13.

10401 **RUSSELL, B. M.** (1980), Didactic group counseling as it affects the trainable mentally retarded's self concept, communication skills, peer acceptance, and perceived social standing. *Dissert. Abstr. Internat.*, 41:2523A. (University Microfilms No. 8027136.)

10402 **RUSSELL, E. W.** (1978), The facts about encounter groups: first facts. *J. Clin. Psychol.*, 34:130-137.

10403 **RUSSELL, J.** (1975), Personal growth through structured group exercises. In: *The Innovative Psychological Therapies: Critical and Creative Contributions*, eds. R. M. Suinn and R. G. Weigel. New York: Harper and Row.

10404 **RUSSELL, J.** (1971), Personal growth through structured group exercises. *Voices*, 7:28-36.

10405 **RUSSELL, J. M.,** and **EASTON, J.** (1979), Teaching the design, leadership and evaluation of structured groups. *Personnel Guid. J.*, 57:426-428.

10406 **RUSSELL, R. K., MILLER, D. E.,** and **JUNE, L. N.** (1975), A comparison between group systematic desensitization and cue controlled relaxation in the treatment of test anxiety. *Behav. Ther.*, 6:172-177.

10407 **RUSSELL, R. K., MILLER, D. E.,** and **JUNE, L. N.** (1974), Group cue-controlled relaxation in the treatment of text anxiety. *Behav. Ther.*, 5:572-573.

10408 **RUSTIN, L.** (1978), An intensive group programme for adolescent stammerers. *Brit. J. Disorders Communication*, (London) 13:85-92.

10409 **RUSTIN, S. L.** (1970), Therapist authenticity in group and individual psychotherapy with college students. *J. Contemp. Psychol.*, 3:45-50.

10410 **RUSTIN, S. L.**, and **WOLK, R. L.** (1963), The use of specialized group psychotherapy techniques in a home for the aged. *Group Psychother., Psychodrama & Sociometry*, 16:25-29.

10411 **RUTAN, J. S.**, and **ALONSO, A.** (1980), Sequential cotherapy of groups for training and clinical care. *Group*, 4:40-50.

10412 **RUTAN, J. S.**, and **ALONSO, A.** (1978), Some guidelines for group therapists. *Group*, 2:4-13.

10413 **RUTENBERG, H.** (1974), Group processes. *Hosp. Prog.*, 55:60-75.

10414 **RUTSCHMAN, D. F.** (1970), Affective versus cognitive groups with precollege blind youth. *Dissert. Abstr. Internat.*, 32:1283A.

10415 **RUTTER, D. R.**, and **STEPHENSON, G. M.** (1972), Visual interaction in a group of schizophrenic and depressive patients: a follow-up study. *Brit. J. Sociol. & Clin. Psychol.*, (London) 11:410-411.

10416 **RUZICKA, M. F.**, **PALISI, A. T.**, **KELLY, M. D.**, and **CORRADO, N. R.** (1979), Relation of perceptions by leaders and members to creative group behavior. *J. Psychology*, 103:95-102.

10417 **RYAN, T.** (1973), Goal-setting in group counseling. *Educat. Technol.*, 13:19-25.

10418 **RYAN, W.** (1958), Capacity for mutual dependence and involvement in group psychotherapy. Unpublished doctoral dissertation, Boston University.

10419 **RYAN, W.** (1960), Predicting continuation in group therapy with the Rorschach. *Amer. Psychologist*, 15:416.

10420 **RYBACK, R. S.** (1971), Schizophrenics anonymous: a treatment adjunct. *Psychiat. in Med.*, 2:247.

10421 **RYBAK, W. S.** (1963), Disguised group therapy: an approach to the treatment of hospitalized teen-aged patients. *Psychiat. Quart. Suppl.*, 37:44-55.

10422 **RYEN, A. H.** (1974), Determining the causes of inequity: the effects of group outcome, individual inputs, and reward expectation on intra- and intergroup reward allocation. *Dissert. Abstr. Internat.*, 35:2470B.

10423 **RYKER, M.** (1970), Group work with students in a university mental health service. *J. Amer. Coll. Health Assn.*, 18:296-300.

10424 **RYLE, A.** (1976), Group psychotherapy. *Brit. J. Hosp. Med.*, (London) 15:239.

10425 **RYLE, A.**, and **LIPSHITZ, S.** (1976), An intensive case study of a therapeutic group. *Brit. J. Psychiat.*, (Ashford) 128:581-587.

10426 **RZADKOWOLSKA, E.** (1964), (Group psychotherapy of neuroses.) *Neurol. & Neurochir. Polska*, (Warsaw) 14:929-933.

S

10427 **SABATH, G.** (1962), Intertransference: transference relationships between members of the psychotherapy team. *Internat. J. Group Psychother.*, 12:492-495.
10428 **SABATH, G.** (1965), Parental negative suggestion as a stimulant for antisocial behavior. *Correct. Psychiat. & J. Soc. Ther.*, 11:323-326.
10429 **SABATH, G.** (1964), The treatment of hard-core voluntary drug addict patients. *Internat. J. Group Psychother.*, 14:307-317.
10430 **SABOTINI, S. G.** (1976), An investigation of play group counseling. *Dissert. Abstr. Internat.*, 36:7875A.
10431 **SACHS, A. H.** (1972), Group leadership as a factor in attitude change: a field Q study. *Dissert. Abstr. Internat.*, 33:1574A.
10432 **SACHS, D. L.** (1975), The impact of group counseling on self-esteem and other personality characteristics. *Dissert. Abstr. Internat.*, 35:7068.
10433 **SACKMAN, H.** (1973), Community prototype experience in re-educating drinking drivers. *Proceed., 81st Annual Convention*, American Psychological Association, Montreal, Canada, 8:946.
10434 **SACKS, H. R.** (1959), The use of psychodrama and role playing in improving the interpersonal skills of attorneys. *Group Psychother., Psychodrama & Sociometry*, 12:240-249.
10435 **SACKS, J. M.** (1970), *Introduction to Psychodrama*. Philadelphia: AAP Tape Library, Vol. 43.
10436 **SACKS, J. M.** (1965), The judgement technique in psychodrama. *Group Psychother., Psychodrama & Sociometry*, 18:69-72.
10437 **SACKS, J. M.** (1973), Psychodrama: an underdeveloped group resource. *Educat. Technol.*, 13:37-39.
10438 **SACKS, J. M.** (1960), Psychodrama and psychoanalysis. *Group Psychother., Psychodrama & Sociometry*, 13:199.
10439 **SACKS, J. M.** (1977), Reminiscences of J. L. Moreno. *Group*, 1:194-200.
10440 **SACKS, J. M.**, and **BERGER, S.** (1954), Group therapy techniques with hospitalized chronic schizophrenic patients. *J. Couns. Psychol.*, 18:297-302.
10441 **SACKS, J. M.**, **HOFFMAN, J. M.**, **CUTTER, H. S. G.**, and **HAEFNER, D. P.** (1960), Changes in perception and interaction in group therapy. *Group Psychother., Psychodrama & Sociometry*, 13:101-109.
10442 **SACKS, L. A.** (1974), Group interaction as a variable effecting the individual's perception of the meaning of his existence. *Dissert. Abstr. Internat.*, 35:2061A.
10443 **SACHS, R. H.**, **EIGENBRODE, C. R.**, and **KRUPER, D. C.** (1979), Psychology and dentistry. *Prof. Psychol.*, 10:521-528.
10444 **SADDLER, D. L.** (1973), Effects of activity interview group counseling on performance of adolescent educable mentally retarded students. *Dissert. Abstr. Internat.*, 33:3305A.
10445 **SADLER, H.**, and **RUBIN, S.** (1950), Observations in treatment of patients with psychosomatic disorders using subshock insulin in a group setting. *Amer. J. Psychiat.*, 107:350-356.
10446 **SADOCK, B.**, and **GOULD, R. E.** (1964), A preliminary report on short-term group psychotherapy on an acute adolescent male service. *Internat. J. Group Psychother.*, 14:465-473.
10447 **SADOCK, B. J.** (1976), Review of I. D. Yalom's *Theory and Practice of Group Psychotherapy*. *Amer. J. Psychiat.*, 133:594.
10448 **SADOCK, B. J.**, and **KAPLAN, H. I.** (1969), Group psychotherapy with psychiatric residents. *Internat. J. Group Psychother.*, 19:130-142.

10449 **SADOCK, B. J.**, and **KAPLAN, H. I.** (1970), Long-term intensive group psychotherapy with psychiatric residents as part of residency training. *Amer. J. Psychiat.*, 126:1138-1143.

10450 **SADOCK, B. J., KAPLAN, H. I.**, and **FREEDMAN, A. M.** (1968), Integrated group psychotherapy training and psychiatric residency. *Arch. Gen. Psychiat.*, 18:276-279.

10451 **SADOCK, B. J., NEWMAN, L.**, and **NORMAND, W. C.** (1968), Short-term group psychotherapy in a psychiatric walk-in clinic. *Amer. J. Orthopsychiat.*, 38:724-732.

10452 **SADOFF, R. L.** (1973), The group that failed. *Psychiat. Quart.*, 47:110-116.

10453 **SADOFF, R. L.**, and **COLLINS, D. J.** (1968), Passive dependency in stutterers. *Amer. J. Psychiat.*, 124:1126-1127.

10454 **SADOFF, R. L.**, and **SIEGEL, J. R.** (1965), Group psychotherapy for stutterers. *Internat. J. Group Psychother.*, 15:72-80.

10455 **SADOFF, R. L., RESNIK, H. L.**, and **PETERS, J. J.** (1968), On changing group therapists. *Psychiat. Quart. Suppl.*, 42:156-166.

10456 **SADOFF, R. L., ROETHER, H. A.**, and **PETERS, J. J.** (1971), Clinical measure of enforced group psychotherapy. *Amer. J. Psychiat.*, 128:224-227.

10457 **SADOVNIKOFF, V., BENSON, R. M.**, and **PACKARD, G. M.** (1963), Problems encountered in establishing an "institution-to-community" group therapy program for delinquents. *Internat. J. Group Psychother.*, 13:156-166.

10458 **SAFAN, D.** (1969), A short introduction to gestalt group therapy. *Rev. Interamer. Psicol.*, 3:177-191.

10459 **SAFER, D. J.** (1965), Conjoint play therapy for the young child and his parent. *Arch. Gen. Psychiat.*, 13:320-326.

10460 **SAFIAN, M. Z.** (1978), Review of M. Seligman's *Group-Counseling and Group-Psychotherapy with Rehabilitation Clients. Internat. J. Group Psychother.*, 28:419-421.

10461 **SAFIRSTEIN, S. L.** (1970), Aftercare in a general hospital. *Sandoz Psychiat. Spectator*, 6:2-3.

10462 **SAGER, C. J.** (1953), Aspects of clinical training in psychotherapy. *Amer. J. Psychiat.*, 7:633-640.

10463 **SAGER, C. J.** (1960), Combined individual and group psychoanalysis: Symposium—2. concurrent individual and group analytic psychotherapy. *Amer. J. Orthopsychiat.*, 30:225-241.

10464 **SAGER, C. J.** (1970), Discussion of symposium: the relationship of group psychotherapy to other group modalities in mental health. *Internat. J. Group Psychother.*, 20:540-544.

10465 **SAGER, C. J.** (1959), The effects of group psychotherapy on individual psychoanalysis. *Internat. J. Group Psychother.*, 9:403-419.

10466 **SAGER, C. J.** (1968), The group psychotherapist: bulwark against alienation. *Internat. J. Group Psychother.*, 18:419-431.

10467 **SAGER, C. J.** (1964), Insight and interaction in combined therapy. *Internat. J. Group Psychother.*, 14:403-412.

10468 **SAGER, C. J.** (1965), Insight and interaction in concurrent individual and group therapy. *Curr. Psychiat. Ther.*, 5:140-144.

10469 **SAGER, C. J.** (1964), A symposium on combined individual and group psychotherapy: insight and interaction in combined therapy. *Internat. J. Group Psychother.*, 14:403-412.

10470 **SAGER, C. J.**, and **KAPLAN, H. S.** (1971), *Progress in Group and Family Therapy*. New York: Brunner/Mazel.

10471 **SAGER, C. J.**, and **KAPLAN, H. S.** (1972), *Progress in Group and Family Therapy*. New York: Brunner/Mazel.

10472 **SAGER, C. J.**, and **KAPLAN, H. S.** (1973), *Progress in Group and Family Therapy*. New York: Brunner/Mazel.
10473 **SAHAKIAN, W. S.** (1969), *Psychotherapy and Counseling: Studies in Technique*. Chicago: Rand McNally.
10474 **SAINSBURY, M. J.** (1968), Therapeutic communities and admission centres. *Med. J. Austral.*, (Glebe) 1:871.
10475 **SAINT-LAURENT-SIMAND, L.** (1974), (Practical views on group psychotherapy.) *Vie Med. Can. Française*, (Quebec) 3:772-781.
10476 **SAKLES, C. J.** (1978), Review of L. Yablonsky's *Psychodrama: Resolving Emotional Problems through Role-Playing. J. Nerv. & Ment. Diseases*, 166:145-146.
10477 **SAKURAI, M. M.** (1975), Small group cohesiveness and detrimental conformity. *Sociometry*, 38:340-357.
10478 **SALAS, E., FORTI, L., SAMOVICI, E.**, and **DIROTA, A.** (1969), Group therapy for children and mothers in emergency situations arising from dental treatment of children. *Rev. Psiq. & Psicol. Med.*, 9:16-38.
10479 **SALES, A. P.** (1972), Rehabilitation counselor candidate change resulting from sensitivity group experiences. *Dissert. Abstr. Internat.*, 5554A.
10480 **SALIH, H. A.** (1969), Phobics in group psychotherapy. *Internat. J. Group Psychother.*, 19:28-34.
10481 **SALOMON, E.** (1972), The encounter experience examined in the light of the functional helping process. *Otto Rank Assn. J.*, 7:30-40.
10482 **SALOSHIN, H. E.** (1954), Development of an instrument for the analysis of the social group work method in therapeutic settings. *Dissert. Abstr. Internat.*, 14:1473-1474.
10483 **SALTMARSH, R. E.**, and **HUBELE, G. E.** (1974), Basic interaction behaviors: a microcounseling approach for introductory courses. *Counselor Educat. & Supervision*, 13:246-249.
10484 **SALTS, C. J.** (1980), Effects of postseparation/postdivorce counseling groups on adjustment and self-concept. *Dissert. Abstr. Internat.*, 40:4262A. (University Microfilms No. 8001114.)
10485 **SALUM, I.**, and **BORJESON, O.** (1957), On bibliotherapy and its significance in the mental patient's ward. *Soc. Med. & Ther.*, 34:7-12.
10486 **SALVENDY, J. T.** (1977), Education in psychotherapy: challenges and pitfalls. *Can. Psychiat. Assn. J.*, (Ottawa) 22:435.
10487 **SALVENDY, J. T.** (1980), Group psychotherapy: a quest for standards. *Can. Psychiat. Assn. J.*, (Ottawa) 25:394-402.
10488 **SALVENDY, J. T.** (1980), Review of M. Grotjahn's *The Art and Technique of Analytic Group Therapy. Can. Psychiat. Assn. J.*, (Ottawa) 25:523-524.
10489 **SALZBERG, H. C.** (1962), Effects of silence and redirection on verbal responses in group psychotherapy. *Psychol. Reports*, 11:455-461.
10490 **SALZBERG, H. C.** (1969), Group psychotherapy screening scale: a validation study. *Internat. J. Group Psychother.*, 19:226-228.
10491 **SALZBERG, H. C.** (1978), Review of G. G. Harris' *The Group Treatment of Human Problems: A Social Learning Approach. Contemp. Psychol.*, 23:526.
10492 **SALZBERG, H. C.** (1967), Verbal behavior in group psychotherapy with and without a therapist. *J. Couns. Psychol.*, 14:24-27.
10493 **SALZBERG, H. C.**, and **BIDUS, D. R.** (1966), Development of a group therapy screening scale: an attempt to select suitable candidates and predict successful outcome. *J. Clin. Psychol.*, 22:478-481.
10494 **SALZBERG, H. C.**, and **HECKEL, R. V.** (1963), Psychological screening utilizing the group approach. *Internat. J. Group Psychother.*, 13:214-215.
10495 **SALZBERG, H. C., BROKAW, J. R.**, and **STRAHLEY, D. F.** (1964), Effects of group stability on spontaneity and problem-relevant verbal behavior in group psychotherapy. *Psychol. Reports*, 14:687-694.

10496 **SALZBERG, H. C., CLARK, J. B., DRENNEN, W. T., HAMILTON, J. W., HECKEL, R. V., LONG, T. E.,** and **MARR, M. J.** (1962), The effects of multiple therapists in relinquishing a delusional system. *J. Clin. Psychol.*, 18:218-220.

10497 **SALZMAN, C.** (1977), The effects of marijuana on small group process. *Amer. J. Drug & Alcohol Abuse*, 4:251-256.

10498 **SAMELSON, C. F.,** and **FISCHER, W. G.** (1972), Group psychotherapy with selected lower extremity amputees in a physical medicine rehabilitation setting. *Proceed. Annual Convention*, American Psychological Association, 7:703-704.

10499 **SAMENOW, S. E.** (1968), The college dropout: a study in self-definition. *Dissert. Abstr. Internat.*, 29:1179B.

10500 **SAMPSON, E. E.** (1972), Leader orientation and t-group effectiveness. *J. Appl. Behav. Science*, 8:564-575.

10501 **SAMPSON, E.,** and **MARTHAS, M. S.** (1977), *Group Process for the Health Professions.* New York: J. Wiley and Sons.

10502 **SAMUEL-LAJEUNESSE, B.** (1977), Indications for group psychotherapy. *Sem. Hop.-The.*, 53:336-338.

10503 **SAMUELS, A. S.** (1964), Use of group balance as a therapeutic technique. *Arch. Gen. Psychiat.*, 11:411-420.

10504 **SAMUELS, S. D.** (1971), Games therapists play. *Transactional Anal. J.*, 1:95-99.

10505 **SAMUELS, S. D.** (1971), Stroke strategy: i. the basis of therapy. *Transactional Anal. J.*, 1:23-24.

10506 **SAMUELSON, W. G.** (1968), A comparative study of the changes in self-understanding of counselor–trainees as a result of small group discussion and the use of existential literature. *Dissert. Abstr. Internat.*, 28:3977-3978.

10507 **SAMULEWICZ, E.** (1975), The effects of critical thinking and group counseling upon behavior problem students. *Dissert. Abstr. Internat.*, 36:2645A.

10508 **SANBURG, D. L.** (1974), Assertive training in groups. *Personnel & Guid. J.*, 53:117.

10509 **SANCHEZ, M. A.** (1970), The effect of client-centered group counseling on self-concept and certain attitudes of seventh and eighth grade students. *Dissert. Abstr. Internat.*, 30:3283A-3284A.

10510 **SANCHEZ, M. G.** (1968), (Introduction to group psychotherapy and mental judgment.) *Actas Luso Espanoles Neurol. Psiquiat.*, (Madrid) 27:115-164.

10511 **SANCHEZ, V. C., LEWINSOHN, P. M.,** and **LARSON, D. W.** (1980), Assertion training: effectiveness in the treatment of depression. *J. Clin. Psychol.*, 36:526.

10512 **SANDEL, S. L.** (1978), Movement therapy with geriatric patients in a convalescent home. *Hosp. & Community Psychiat.*, 29:738.

10513 **SANDER, K.** (1974), (Outcome and conditions of change in client-centered therapy groups (KSE-groups).) *Gruppenpsychother. & Gruppendynam.*, (Goettingen) 8:41-53.

10514 **SANDERS, R. W.,** and **SAVINO, A. B.** (1973), Working with abusive parents: group therapy and home visits. part 2. *Amer. J. Nursing*, 73:482-484.

10515 **SANDERS, S.** (1976), Mutual group hypnosis as a catalyst in fostering creative problem solving. *Amer. J. Clin. Hypnosis*, 19:62-66.

10516 **SANDERS, S.** (1977), Mutual group hypnosis and smoking. *Amer. J. Clin. Hypnosis*, 20:131-135.

10517 **SANDERS, S.** (1978), Review of A. Starr's *Psychodrama: Rehearsal for Living—Illustrated Therapeutic Techniques. Contemp. Psychol.*, 23:687.

10518 **SANDERSON, M. R.** (1979), Problems displayed "in vivo": a particular advantage of group therapy. *Perspect. Psychiat. Care*, 17:176-186.

10519 **SANDHU, H.** (1966), Group sessions in a reformatory school in the Punjab (India). *Correc. Psychiat. & J. Soc. Ther.*, 12:393-403.

10520 **SANDHU, H. S.** (1970), Therapy with violent psychopaths in an Indian prison community. *Internat. J. Offender Ther.*, (London) 14:138-144.

10521 **SANDISON, R. A.** (1975), Group therapy and drug therapy. In: *Group Psychotherapy and Group Function*, 2d ed., eds. M. Rosenbaum and M. M. Berger. New York: Basic Books.

10522 **SANDISON, R. A.** (1955), Group therapy in a provincial out-patient department. *Internat. J. Soc. Psychiat.*, (London) 1:28-32.

10523 **SANDISON, R. A.** (1959), The role of psychotropic drugs in group therapy. *Proceed. World Health Organizat.*, 21:505-515.

10524 **SANDISON, R. A.**, and **CHANCE, E.** (1948), The measurement of the structure and behaviour of therapeutic groups. *J. Ment. Science*, (London) 94:749-763.

10525 **SANDLER, G. B.** (1973), Improving participant observation: the t-group as an answer. *J. Appl. Behav. Science*, 9:51-61.

10526 **SANDNER, D.** (1975), (Bion's analytic theory of groups and its relation to group psychotherapy and group dynamics.) *Gruppenpsychother. & Gruppendynam.*, (Goettingen) 9:1-17.

10527 **SANDNER, D.** (1980), (Psychodynamics of schizophrenics in analytic group psychotherapy with neurotic and psychotic patients.) *Gruppenpsychother. & Gruppendynam.*, (Goettingen) 15:32-50.

10528 **SANDNER, D.** (1980), Thoughts on Walter Schindler's contribution to group analysis theory and technique. *Group*, 13:161-164.

10529 **SANDNER, D.**, and **DIETER OHLMEIER, G.** (1978), *Psychodynamik in Kleingruppen: Theorie der Affektiven Geschehens in Slebsterfahrungs. und Therapiegruppen (Salbstanalyt. Gruppen)*. Munich: E. Reinhardt.

10530 **SANDRON, L.** (1973), Psychodrama: a dramatic impact. *J. Rehab.*, 39:31-33.

10531 **SANDS, P. M.**, and **HANSON, P. G.** (1971), Psychotherapeutic groups for alcoholics and relatives in an outpatient setting. *Internat. J. Group Psychother.*, 21:23-33.

10532 **SANDS, P. M., HANSON, P. G.**, and **SHELDON, R. B.** (1967), Recurring themes in group psychotherapy with alcoholics. *Psychiat. Quart.*, 41:474-482.

10533 **SANDS, R. M.** (1956), Methods of group therapy for parents. *Soc. Work*, 1:48-56.

10534 **SANDS, R. M.** (1965), Changes in the individual effected through group therapy: studies of two men in two father's groups. *Topical Probl. Psychol. & Psychother.*, 5:102-125.

10535 **SANDS, R. M.**, and **FISCHMAN, H. S.** (1963), Experimentation with group techniques with ego-disturbed mothers. *Internat. J. Group Psychother.*, 13:187-195.

10536 **SANDS, R. M.**, and **GOLUB, S.** (1974), Breaking the bonds of tradition: a reassessment of group treatment of latency-age children. *Amer. J. Psychiat.*, 131:662-665.

10537 **SANFORD, N.** (1953), Group therapy. In: *Annual Review of Psychology*, ed. C. P. Stone. Stanford: Annual Reviews, pp. 317-325.

10538 **SANSBURY, D. L.** (1974), Assertive training in groups. *Personnel & Guid. J.*, 53:117-122.

10539 **SANTA MARIA, C. H.** (1951), A new workshop: the VA hospital. *Educat. Theatre J.*, 3:207-211.

10540 **SANTIAGO De COLON, L.** (1964), A group work experience for mothers of adolescents with epilepsy. *Bull. Assn. Med. Puerto Rico*, 56:51-57.

10541 **dos SANTOS, O.** (1964), (Dramatization in psychiatry.) *J. Brasil. Psiquiat.*, (Rio de Janeiro) 13:219-237.

10542 **dos SANTOS, O.** (1964), (Group occupational therapy.) *J. Brasil. Psiquiat.*, (Rio de Janeiro) 13:205-217.

10543 **SANTUCCI, A. A.** (1972), The effects on t-group process and study skill training on self–confidence levels of economic opportunity and college freshmen. *Dissert. Abstr. Internat.*, 32:6138A.

10544 **SAPER, B.** (1974), Patients as partners in a team approach: Forst Hospital, Des Plaines, Illinois. *Amer. J. Nursing*, 74:1844-1847.

10545 **SAPER, M. B.** (1968), Bibliotherapy as an adjunct to group psychotherapy. *Dissert. Abstr. Internat.*, 28:4302B.

10546 **SAPIR, E.** (1968), Group. *J. Group Psychoanal. & Process*, (London) 1:37-46.

10547 **SAPORITO, T. J.** (1977), The effects of group size and leader style on level of empathic understanding and self-concept of members of an experiential course in group counseling. *Dissert. Abstr. Internat.*, 38:1234A.

10548 **SARASON, I. G.**, and **GANZER, V. J.** (1973), Modeling and group discussion in the rehabilitation of juvenile delinquents. *J. Couns. Psychol.*, 20:442-449.

10549 **SARAVAY, S. M.** (1975), Group psychology and the structural theory: a revised psychoanalytic model of group psychology. *J. Amer. Psychoanal. Assn.*, 23:69-89.

10550 **SARAVAY, S. M.** (1978), A psychoanalytic theory of group development. *Internat. J. Group Psychother.*, 28:481-507.

10551 **SARBIN, J. R.**, and **FARBEROW, N. L.** (1952), Contributions to role taking theory: a clinical study of self and role. *J. Abnorm. Psychol.*, 47:117-125.

10552 **SARBIN, T. M.** (1945), Spontaneity training of the feebleminded. *Sociometry*, 8:389-393.

10553 **SARBIN, T. R.** (1943), The concept of role-taking. *Sociometry*, 6:273-285.

10554 **SARBIN, T. R.**, and **ALLEN, V. L.** (1968), Increasing participation in a natural group setting: a preliminary report. *Psychol. Record*, 18:1-7.

10555 **SARETSKY, T.** (1978), *Active Techniques and Group Psychotherapy*. New York: J. Aronson.

10556 **SARETSKY, T.** (1971), The application of t-group techniques to ongoing psychotherapy. *Group Process*, (London) 3:57-60.

10557 **SARETSKY, T.** (1972), Resistance in a group as a function of the therapist's countertransference expectations. *Psychother.: Theory, Res. & Pract.*, 9:265-266.

10558 **SARETT, M., CHEEK, F.**, and **OSMOND, H.** (1966), Reports of wives of alcoholics on effects of LSD-25 treatment of their husbands. *Arch. Gen. Psychiat.*, 14:171-178.

10559 **SARGENT, A. G.** (1974), Laboratory education: what is it? *Supervisor Nurse*, 5:29-30.

10560 **SARGENT, L.** (1979), Poetry in therapy. *Soc. Work*, 24:156.

10561 **SARLIN, C. N.**, and **BEREZIN, M. A.** (1946), Group psychotherapy on a modified analytic basis. *J. Nerv. & Ment. Diseases*, 104:611-667.

10562 **SARLIN, M. B.**, and **ALTSHULER, K. Z.** (1968), Group psychotherapy with deaf adolescents in a school setting. *Internat. J. Group Psychother.*, 18:337-344.

10563 **SARREL, P. M.** (1967), The university hospital and the teenage unwed mother. *Amer. J. Pub. Health*, 57:1308-1313.

10564 **SARRI, R. C.** (1974), Behavioral theory and group work. In: *Individual Change through Small Groups*, eds. P. Glasser, R. Sarri, and R. Vinter. New York: Free Press.

10565 **SARRO, R.** (1966), The essence of psychodrama: essay of psychodramatic trilogy. *Group Psychother., Psychodrama & Sociometry*, 19:126-139.
10566 **SASLOW, J. A.** (1972), Four therapeutic programs compared through training mothers to increase children's verbal behavior. *Dissert. Abstr. Internat.*, 32:5458-5459B.
10567 **SATA, L. S.** (1975), Laboratory training for police officers. *J. Soc. Issues*, 31:107-114.
10568 **SATA, L. S.** (1974), Group methods: the volunteers and the paraprofessional. *Internat. J. Group Psychother.*, 24:400.
10569 **SATA, L. S.** (1974), Training new mental health personnel in group methods: iii. group methods, the volunteer and the paraprofessional. *Internat. J. Group Psychother.*, 24:400-407.
10570 **SATA, L. S.**, and **DERBYSHIRE, R. L.** (1969), Breaking the role barrier: a psychotherapeutic necessity. *Ment. Hygiene*, 53:110-117.
10571 **SATCHELL, B. M.**, **FINCH, J.**, and **BREGG, E.** (1970), Are five weeks enough? *Nursing Outlook*, 18:38-40.
10572 **SATIR, V. M.** (1971), A humanistic approach. *Internat. J. Psychiat.*, 9:245-246.
10573 **SATORE, R.** (1974), The mirror image approach to classroom counseling. *Elem. School Guid. & Couns.*, 9:235-236.
10574 **SATTERFIELD, W. C.** (1977), Short-term group therapy for people in crisis. *Hosp. & Community Psychiat.*, 28:539-541.
10575 **SATTERLEE, R. L.**, and **SORENSON, A. G.** (1958), A sociometric procedure for use in selecting teacher candidates. *Group Psychother., Psychodrama & Sociometry*, 11:114-120.
10576 **SATTIN, S. M.** (1975), The psychodynamics of the "holiday syndrome." *Perspect. Psychiat. Care*, 13:156-162.
10577 **SATZ, P.**, and **BARAFF, A.** (1962), Changes in the relation between self-concepts and ideal-concepts of psychotics consequent upon therapy. *J. Gen. Psychol.*, 67:291-298.
10578 **SAUL, L. J.** (1975), A note on tension, creativity and therapy. *J. Amer. Acad. Psychoanal.*, 3:277.
10579 **SAUL, S. R.**, and **SAUL, S.** (1974), Group psychotherapy in a proprietary nursing home. *Gerontologist*, 14:446-450.
10580 **SAUL, S. R.**, and **SAUL, S.** (1973), Old people talk about death. *Omega: J. Death & Dying*, 4:27-35.
10581 **SAUL, S. R.**, and **SAUL, S.** (1970), Social group work in community mental health. *Hosp. & Community Psychiat.*, 21:234-235.
10582 **SAULNIER, L.**, and **SIMMARD, T.** (1973), *Personal Growth and Interpersonal Relations*. Englewood Cliffs, NJ: Prentice Hall.
10583 **SAUNDERS, A. M.**, and **LAMB, W.** (1977), Group experience with parents of hemophiliacs: viable alternative to group therapy. *J. Clin. Child Psychol.*, 6:79-82.
10584 **SAUTER, A.** (1971), Die selbsterfahrungsgruppe in der erziehungsberatung. (The self-experience group in parental counseling.) *Praxis Kinderpsychol. & Kinderpsychiat.*, (Goettingen) 20:214-219.
10585 **SAVIN, H.** (1976), Multi-media group treatment with socially inept adolescents. *Clin. Psychologist*, 29:14-17.
10586 **SAVINO, A. B.**, and **SANDERS, R. W.** (1973), Working with abusive parents: group therapy and home visits. *Amer. J. Nursing*, 73:482-484.
10587 **SCANDRETT, S. L.** (1980), Positive critical incidents in group psychotherapy: a communication analysis (volumes i and ii). *Dissert. Abstr. Internat.*, 40:6056A. (University Microfilms No. 8012418.)
10588 **SCANLAN, B. K.** (1971), Sensitivity training clarifications, issues, insights. *Personnel J.*, 50:546-552.

10589 **SCARBOROUGH, L. F.** (1956), Management of convulsive patients by group therapy. *Diseases Nerv. System*, 17:223.

10590 **SCARINCI, A.** (1961), (Comparative study of the psychodrama play of children according to age.) *Rev. Neuropsychiat. Infantile*, (Paris) 9:230-233.

10591 **SCHAAP, C. P.** (1977), (Treating relationships.) *Gedrag*, (Tilburg) 5:400-416.

10592 **SCHACHERI, B.** (1970), Theater as social psychotherapy. *Riv. Sper. Freniatria*, (Emilia) 94:801-804.

10593 **SCHACHTER, R. S.** (1974), Kinetic psychotherapy in the treatment of children. *Amer. J. Psychother.*, 18:430-437.

10594 **SCHAEFER, A.** (1965), Participants: not patients. *Amer. J. Nursing*, 65:94-95.

10595 **SCHAEFER, J. W., PALKES, H. S.,** and **STEWART, M. A.** (1974), Group counseling for parents of hyperactive children. *Child Psychiat. & Human Develop.*, 5:89-94.

10596 **SCHAEFER, L. C.** (1965), View of a former group analysand. *Topical Probl. Psychol. & Psychother.*, 5:11-16.

10597 **SCHAEFFER, D. S.** (1969), Effects of frequent hospitalization on behavior of psychotic patients in multiple group therapy program. *J. Clin. Psychol.*, 25:104-105.

10598 **SCHAEFFER, D. T.,** and **von NESSEN, R.** (1968), Intervention for disadvantaged girls: insight for school faculties. *Amer. J. Orthopsychiat.*, 38:666-671.

10599 **SCHAEFFER, D. T.,** and **von NESSEN, R. W.** (1967), An intervention technique for acting out adolescent girls: implications for bringing insight to school faculties regarding the disadvantaged. *Amer. J. Orthopsychiat.*, 37:376.

10600 **SCHAFFNER, B.** (1957), *Group Processes: Transactions of the Third Conference.* New York: Josiah Macy, Jr. Foundation.

10601 **SCHAG, D., LOO, C.,** and **LEVIN, M. M.** (1978), The group assessment of interpersonal traits (GAIT): differentiation of measures and their relationship to behavioral response modes. *Amer. J. Community Psychol.*, 6:47-62.

10602 **SCHAIBLE, T. D.,** and **JACOBS, A.** (1975), Feedback iii: sequence effects—enhancement of feedback acceptance and group attractiveness by manipulation of the sequence and valence of feedback. *Small Group Behav.*, 6:151-173.

10603 **SCHAIN, J.** (1980), The application of Kleinian theory to group psychotherapy. *Internat. J. Group Psychother.*, 30:319-332.

10604 **SCHAMESS, G.** (1976), Group treatment modalities for latency-age children. *Internat. J. Group Psychother.*, 26:455-473.

10605 **SCHAPIRA, H. J.** (1970), Psychotherapy termination as a group experience with hospitalized psychiatric patients. *Psychother.: Theory, Res. & Pract.*, 7:155-160.

10606 **SCHAUER, G.** (1951), The function of an audience analyst in psychodrama. *Group Psychother., Psychodrama & Sociometry*, 4:197-205.

10607 **SCHAUER, G.** (1945), Patients as therapeutic agents in a mental hospital. *Sociometry*, 8:394-395.

10608 **SCHAUER, G.** (1951), Repetition-compulsion and spontaneity. *Group Psychother., Psychodrama & Sociometry*, 3:339-343.

10609 **SCHAUER, J. R.** (1970), Personal change groups and counseling. *Dissert. Abstr. Internat.*, 31:5779A.

10610 **SCHAUL, B. H.** (1972), A comparison of cognitive-experiential pre-training and the effects of verbal behavior in a group psychotherapy technique. *Dissert. Abstr. Internat.*, 6662B.

10611 **SCHAUSS, A. G.** (1979), Differential outcomes among probationers comparing orthomolecular approaches to conventional casework counseling. *J. Ortho-Psychiat.*, 8:158-168.
10612 **SCHAYE, Z.**, and **GARMIZA, C.** (1976), On "medication patients" and their treatment: the advantages of groups. *J. Group Dynam. Psychother.*, 7:31-34.
10613 **SCHECTER, D. E.** (1961), The integration of group therapy with individual psychoanalysis. *Curr. Psychiat. Ther.*, 1:145-151.
10614 **SCHECTER, D. E.** (1969), The integration of group therapy with individual psychoanalysis. *Psychiatry*, 22:267-276.
10615 **SCHEDLER, D. E.** (1980), The impact of the Ohlsen triad model of group counseling in treatment: training workshops for clergy and spouses. *Dissert. Abstr. Internat.*, 41:2459A. (University Microfilms No. 8029174.)
10616 **SCHEER, R. M.**, and **SHARP, W. M.** (1965), Group work as a treatment. *Ment. Retard.*, 3:23-25.
10617 **SCHEFF, T. J.** (1962), Perceptual orientation and role performance of staff members in a mental hospital ward. *Internat. J. Soc. Psychiat.*, (London) 8:113-121.
10618 **SCHEFF, T. J.** (1972), Reevaluation counseling: social implications. *J. Human. Psychol.*, 12:58-71.
10619 **SCHEIDEL, T.**, and **CROWELL, L.** (1966), Feedback in small group communication. *Quart. J. Speech*, 52:273-278.
10620 **SCHEIDEMAN, J.** (1976), Remotivation: involvement without labels. *J. Psychiat. Nursing*, 14:41-42.
10621 **SCHEIDLINGER, S.** (1947), Activity group therapy with primary behavior disorders in children. In: *The Practice of Group Therapy*, ed. S. R. Slavson. New York: International Universities Press.
10622 **SCHEIDLINGER, S.** (1966), The concept of empathy in group psychotherapy. *Internat. J. Group Psychother.*, 16:413-424.
10623 **SCHEIDLINGER, S.** (1955), Concepts of identification in group psychotherapy. *Amer. J. Psychother.*, 6:661-672.
10624 **SCHEIDLINGER, S.** (1966), The concept of latency: implications for group treatment. *Soc. Casework*, 47:363-367.
10625 **SCHEIDLINGER, S.** (1968), The concept of regression in group psychotherapy. *Internat. J. Group Psychother.*, 18:3-20.
10626 **SCHEIDLINGER, S.** (1953), The concepts of social group work and of group psychotherapy. *Soc. Casework*, 34:292-297.
10627 **SCHEIDLINGER, S.** (1967), Current conceptual and methodological issues in group psychotherapy research: introduction to panel—part i. *Internat. J. Group Psychother.*, 17:53-56.
10628 **SCHEIDLINGER, S.** (1968), Current trends in group therapy with children and adolescents: introductory remarks. *Internat. J. Group Psychother.*, 18:445-446.
10629 **SCHEIDLINGER, S.** (1960), Experiential group treatment of severely deprived latency-age children. *Amer. J. Orthopsychiat.*, 30:356-368.
10630 **SCHEIDLINGER, S.** (1952), Freudian group psychology and group psychotherapy. *Amer. J. Orthopsychiat.*, 22:710-717.
10631 **SCHEIDLINGER, S.** (1960), Group process in group psychotherapy: i. current trends in the integration of individual and group psychology. *Amer. J. Psychother.*, 14:104-120.
10632 **SCHEIDLINGER, S.** (1960), Group process in group psychotherapy: ii. current trends in the integration of individual and group psychology. *Amer. J. Psychother.*, 14:346-363.
10633 **SCHEIDLINGER, S.** (1952), Group psychotherapy. In: *Progress in Clinical Psychology, Vol. 1*, eds. D. Brower and L. Abt. New York: Grune and Stratton.

10634 **SCHEIDLINGER, S.** (1954), Group psychotherapy. *Amer. J. Orthopsychiat.*, 24:140-145.
10635 **SCHEIDLINGER, S.** (1968), Group psychotherapy in the sixties. *Amer. J. Psychother.*, 22:170-184.
10636 **SCHEIDLINGER, S.** (1977), Group psychotherapy research: open forum. *Internat. J. Group Psychother.*, 27:135-137.
10637 **SCHEIDLINGER, S.** (1948), Group therapy: its place in psychotherapy. *Soc. Casework*, 29:299-304.
10638 **SCHEIDLINGER, S.** (1977), Group therapy for latency-age children: a bird's eye view. *J. Clin. Child Psychol.*, 6:40-43.
10639 **SCHEIDLINGER, S.** (1964), Identification, the sense of belonging and of identity in small groups. *Internat. J. Group Psychother.*, 14:291-306.
10640 **SCHEIDLINGER, S.** (1974), On the concept of the "mother-group." *Internat. J. Group Psychother.*, 24:417-428.
10641 **SCHEIDLINGER, S.** (1952), *Psychoanalysis and Group Behavior: A Study in Freudian Group Psychology.* New York: Norton.
10642 **SCHEIDLINGER, S.** (1980), *Psychoanalytic Group Dynamics: Basic Readings.* New York: International Universities Press.
10643 **SCHEIDLINGER, S.** (1980), The psychology of leadership revisited: an overview. *Group*, 4:5-17.
10644 **SCHEIDLINGER, S.** (1969), Reply to Hersch. *Amer. Psychologist*, 24:170.
10645 **SCHEIDLINGER, S.** (1956), Social group work and group psychotherapy. *Soc. Work*, 1:36-42.
10646 **SCHEIDLINGER, S.** (1970), Symposium on the relationship of group psychotherapy to other group modalities in mental health. *Internat. J. Group Psychother.*, 20:470-472.
10647 **SCHEIDLINGER, S.** (1978), Symposium: inpatient group therapy—some current perspectives. *Internat. J. Group Psychother.*, 28:319-320.
10648 **SCHEIDLINGER, S.** (1955), The relationship of group therapy to other group influence attempts. *Ment. Hygiene*, 39:376-390.
10649 **SCHEIDLINGER, S.** (1968), Therapeutic group approaches in community mental health. *Soc. Work*, 13:87-95.
10650 **SCHEIDLINGER, S.** (1970), Therapeutic group approaches with ghetto youth: summary of workshops. *Newsl. Amer. Orthopsychiat. Assn.*, 14:16-17.
10651 **SCHEIDLINGER, S.** (1965), Three group approaches with socially deprived latency-age children. *Internat. J. Group Psychother.*, 15:434-445.
10652 **SCHEIDLINGER, S.**, and **HOLDEN, M. A.** (1966), Group therapy of women with severe character disorders: the middle and final phases. *Internat. J. Group Psychother.*, 16:174-189.
10653 **SCHEIDLINGER, S.**, and **PORTER, K.** (1980), Group therapy combined with individual psychotherapy. In: *Specialized Techniques in Individual Psychotherapy*, eds. T. B. Karasu and L. Bellak. New York: Brunner/Mazel.
10654 **SCHEIDLINGER, S.**, and **PYRKE, M.** (1961), Group therapy of women with severe dependency problems. *Amer. J. Orthopsychiat.*, 31:776-785.
10655 **SCHEIDLINGER, S.**, and **SAREKA, A.** (1969), Mental health consultation-education program with group service agencies in a disadvantaged community. *Community Ment. Health J.*, 5:164-171.
10656 **SCHEIDLINGER, S.**, **EISENBERG, M. S.**, **KING, C. H.**, and **OSTROWER, R.** (1962), Activity group therapy of a dull boy with severe body ego problems. *Internat. J. Group Psychother.*, 12:41-55.
10657 **SCHEIDLINGER, S.**, **PECK, H. B.**, **FRANK, J. D.**, and **KELMAN, H. C.** (1963), A symposium on the relationship of group psychotherapy to group dynamics: discussion. *Internat. J. Group Psychother.*, 13:433-451.
10658 **SCHEIN, E. H.**, and **BENNIS, W. G.** (1965), *Personal and Organizational*

Change through Group Methods: The Laboratory Approach. New York: J. Wiley and Sons.
10659 **SCHER, J.** (1973), Professionally directed existential group therapy in methadone maintenance rehabilitation. *Proceed. Nat. Conf. Methadone Treatment*, 2:1191-1202.
10660 **SCHER, M. J.** (1976), Changes in self-acceptance of homosexual males who participated in heterogeneous and homogeneous group experiences with heterosexual and homosexual facilitators. *Dissert. Abstr. Internat.*, 36:6453B.
10661 **SCHER, J. M.** (1960), The concept of self in schizophrenia. *Existent. Psychiat.*, 1:64-88.
10662 **SCHER, J. M.** (1959), Two disruptions of the communication zone: a discussion of action and role playing techniques. *Group Psychother., Psychodrama & Sociometry*, 12:127-133.
10663 **SCHER, M.** (1973), Observations in an aftercare group. *Internat. J. Group Psychother.*, 23:322-337.
10664 **SCHER, M.**, and **JOHNSON, M. H.** (1964), Attendance fluctuations in an after-care group. *Internat. J. Group Psychother.*, 14:223-224.
10665 **SCHER, S. C.**, and **DAVIS, H. R.** (1960), *The Out-Patient Treatment of Schizophrenia.* New York: Grune and Stratton.
10666 **SCHERER, S. E.**, and **FREEDBERG, E. J.** (1976), Effects of group videotape feedback on development of assertiveness skills in alcoholics: a follow-up study. *Psychol. Reports*, 39:983-992.
10667 **SCHIBALSKI, W.** (1978), Modes of therapist acting out and its structural significance. *Dynam. Psychiat.*, (Berlin) 11:252-265.
10668 **SCHIBALSKI, W.** (1980), The problem of ego–structurally directed therapy with psychosomatic patients in a dynamic psychiatric clinic. *Dynam. Psychiat.*, (Berlin) 13:347-361.
10669 **SCHIFF, S. B.**, and **GLASSMAN, S. M.** (1969), Large and small group therapy in a state mental health center. *Internat. J. Group Psychother.*, 19:150-157.
10670 **SCHIFF, S. K.**, and **KELLAM, S. G.** (1969), Parent participation in a communitywide mental health program for first graders. *Amer. J. Orthopsychiat.*, 39:282-283.
10671 **SCHIFFER, A. L.** (1967), The effectiveness of group play therapy as assessed by specific changes in a child's peer relations. *Amer. J. Orthopsychiat.*, 37:219-220.
10672 **SCHIFFER, A. L.** (1966), The effectiveness of group play therapy as assessed by specific changes in a child's peer relations. *Dissert. Abstr. Internat.*, 27:972. (University Microfilms No. 66-06167.)
10673 **SCHIFFER, M.** (1977), Activity group therapy: implications in community agency practice. *Group*, 1:211-221.
10674 **SCHIFFER, M.** (1947), Activity group therapy with exceptional children. In: *The Practice of Group Therapy*, ed. S. R. Slavson. New York: International Universities Press.
10675 **SCHIFFER, M.** (1977), Activity interview group psychotherapy: theory, principles, and practice. *Internat. J. Group Psychother.*, 27:377-388.
10676 **SCHIFFER, M.** (1946), Group therapy for the exceptional child. *J. Exceptional Child*, 12:97-105.
10677 **SCHIFFER, M.** (1952), Permissivism versus sanction in activity group therapy. *Internat. J. Group Psychother.*, 2:255-261.
10678 **SCHIFFER, M.** (1969), *The Therapeutic Play Group.* New York: Grune and Stratton.
10679 **SCHIFFER, M.** (1952), Trips as a treatment tool in activity group therapy. *Internat. J. Group Psychother.*, 2:139-149.
10680 **SCHIFFER, M.** (1960), The use of the seminar in training teachers and

counselors as leaders of therapeutic play groups for maladjusted children. *Amer. J. Orthopsychiat.*, 30:154-165.

10681 **SCHILDER, P.** (1936), The analysis of ideologies as a psychotherapeutic method, especially in group treatment. *Amer. J. Psychiat.*, 93:601-617.

10682 **SCHILDER, P.** (1940), The cure of criminals and prevention of crime. *J. Crim. Psychopathol.*, 2:149-161.

10683 **SCHILDER, P.** (1940), Introductory remarks on groups. *J. Soc. Psychol.*, 12:83-100.

10684 **SCHILDER, P.** (1939), Results and problems of group psychotherapy in severe neuroses. *Ment. Hygiene*, 23:87-99.

10685 **SCHILDER, P.** (1975), Results and problems of group psychotherapy in severe neuroses. In: *Group Psychotherapy and Group Function*, 2d ed., eds. M. Rosenbaum and M. M. Berger. New York: Basic Books.

10686 **SCHILLER, P.** (1974), A sex attitude modification process for adolescents. *J. Clin. Child. Psychol.*, 3:50-51.

10687 **SCHINDLE, W.** (1976), (Development of group psychotherapy.) *Praxis der Psychother.*, 21:59-67.

10688 **SCHINDLER, E. M.** (1958), The roles of social group workers and educators in adult education. *Group Psychother., Psychodrama & Sociometry*, 11:121-127.

10689 **SCHINDLER, R.** (1957), (Basic principles of group psychodynamics.) *Psyche*, (Stuttgart) 11:308-314.

10690 **SCHINDLER, R.** (1963), (Bifocal group psychotherapy.) *Annales Medico-Psychol.*, (Paris) 2:19-30.

10691 **SCHINDLER, R.** (1961), Der gruppentherapeut und seine position in der gruppe. (The group therapist and his position in the group.) *Praxis der Psychother.*, 6:1-8.

10692 **SCHINDLER, R.** (1959), Der soziodynamische aspekt in der "bifokalen gruppentherapie." (The sociodynamic aspect in "bifocal group therapy.") *Acta Psychother., Psychosomat. Orthopaedagog.*, 7:207-220.

10693 **SCHINDLER, R.** (1960), Group psychotherapy in Austria. *Internat. J. Sociometry & Sociatry*, 2:88-90.

10694 **SCHINDLER, R.** (1977), (Interferences with self-discovery in the group: impediment and resistance.) *Praxis der Psychother.*, 22:159-164.

10695 **SCHINDLER, R.** (1959), Meaning, purpose and structure of the "oesterreichische arbeitskreis fuer gruppentherapie und gruppendynamik. (OeAGG)." *Wiener. Med. Wochenschr.*, (Vienna) 109:1004-1005.

10696 **SCHINDLER, R.** (1960), (On the mutual influence of conversation components, group position and ego figure in psychoanalytic group therapy.) *Psyche*, (Stuttgart) 14:382-392.

10697 **SCHINDLER, W.** (1980), *Die Analytische Gruppentherapie nach dem Familienmodell: Ausgew: Beitr.* Munich: E. Reinhardt.

10698 **SCHINDLER, W.** (1973), Das selbst und die gruppen analyse. (Self and group analysis.) *Dynam. Psychiat.*, (Berlin) 6:165-176.

10699 **SCHINDLER, W.** (1951), Family pattern in group formation and therapy. *Internat. J. Group Psychother.*, 1:100-105.

10700 **SCHINDLER, W.** (1951), "Family-pattern": group therapy of sex disorders. *Internat. J. Sexol.*, (Bombay) 4:142-149.

10701 **SCHINDLER, W.** (1952), The "group personality" concept in group psychotherapy. *Internat. J. Group Psychother.*, 2:311-315.

10702 **SCHINDLER, W.** (1971), (Observations concerning techniques of analytic group psychotherapy.) *Psychother. & Med. Psychol.*, (Stuttgart) 21:27-35.

10703 **SCHINDLER, W.** (1960), (On the range of application of analytic group psychotherapy.) *Zeit. Psychother. Med. Psychol.*, (Stuttgart) 10:183-191.

10705 **SCHINDLER, W.** (1966), The role of the mother in group psychotherapy. *Internat. J. Group Psychother.*, 16:198-202.

10706 **SCHINDLER-RAINMAN, E.** (1969), Communicating with today's teenagers: an exercise between generations. *Children*, 16:218-223.

10707 **SCHINKE, S. P.** (1976), Behavioral assertion training in groups: a comparative clinical study. *Dissert. Abstr. Internat.*, 36:5554A.

10708 **SCHINKE, S. P.**, and **ROSE, S. D.** (1976), Interpersonal skill training in groups. *J. Couns. Psychol.*, 23:442-448.

10709 **SCHLACHET, P. J.** (1977), Review of Edward T. Hall's *Beyond Culture. Group*, 1:70-72.

10710 **SCHLACHET, P. J.** (1980), Review of M. Grotjahn's *The Art and Technique of Analytic Group Therapy. Group*, 4:78-80.

10711 **SCHLACHET, P. J.** (1978), Review of M. Rosenbaum's and A. Snadowsky's *The Intensive Group Experience: A Guide. Group*, 2:247-250.

10712 **SCHLACHET, P. J.** (1977), Tea and theory with Helen Durkin. *Group*, 1:132-139.

10713 **SCHLAFER, R. J.** (1974), A comparison of selected test variables between structured versus unstructured marathon encounter group counseling. *Dissert. Abstr. Internat.*, 34:6391A.

10714 **SCHLEGEL, L.** (1975), (Components of analytic group-therapy.) *Gruppenpsychother. & Gruppendynam.*, (Goettingen) 9:18-25.

10715 **SCHLESINGER, H. J.**, and **HOLZMAN, P. S.** (1970), The therapeutic aspects of the hospital milieu. *Bull. Menninger Clinic*, 34:1-11.

10716 **SCHLOSS, J. J.** (1970), The effect of video and audio playback in group counseling on personality change. *Dissert. Abstr. Internat.*, 30:3284A.

10717 **SCHMALBACH, K.** (1961), (A psychiatric day clinic as part of the psychiatric polyclinic.) *Nervenarzt*, 32:222-224.

10718 **SCHMID, W. L.** (1974), The team approach to rehabilitation after mastectomy. *Aorn. J.*, 19:821-836.

10719 **SCHMIDBAUER, W.** (1969), (Schamanism and psychotherapy.) *Psychol. Rundchau*, (Goettingen) 20:29-47.

10720 **SCHMIDHOFER, E.** (1952), Mechanical group therapy. *Science*, 115:120-123.

10721 **SCHMIDT, F. L.**, and **JOHNSON, R. H.** (1973), Effect of race on peer ratings in an industrial situation. *J. Appl. Psychol.*, 57:237-241.

10722 **SCHMIDT, H. G.**, and **BOUHUIJS, P. A. J.** (1980), *Onderwijs in Taakgerichte Groepen*. DeMeern: Spectrum.

10723 **SCHMIDT, R. A.** (1969), Effects of group counseling on reading achievement and sociometric status. *Dissert. Abstr. Internat.*, 30:1406A.

10724 **SCHMIDT, S. A.**, and **LIEBOWITZ, B.** (1969), Adolescent girls and their parents: sexual problems and parallels. *Amer. J. Orthopsychiat.*, 39:328-329.

10725 **SCHMITT, G. M.** (1980), (Client-centered group psychotherapy in the treatment of anorexia nervosa.) *Praxis Kinderpsychol. & Kinderpsychiat.*, (Goettingen) 29:247-251.

10726 **SCHMITT, V. G. M.** (1980), Client-centered group psychotherapy in the treatment of analytic group therapy. *Group*, 4:78-80.

10727 **SCHMUCK, R.**, and **SCHMUCK, P.** (1971), *Group Processes in the Classroom*. Dubuque: Wm. C. Brown.

10728 **SCHMUCK, R. A.**, and **SCHMUCK, P. A.** (1975), *Group Processes in the Classroom*, 2d ed. Dubuque: Wm. C. Brown.

10729 **SCHMULOWITZ, J. S.** (1976), Effectiveness of group counseling as a function of state/trait anxiety in reducing problematic speech in children. *Dissert. Abstr. Internat.*, 37:1928B.

10730 **SCHNADT, F.** (1955), Techniques and goals in group psychotherapy with schizophrenics. *Internat. J. Group Psychother.*, 5:185-193.

10731 **SCHNEEMAN, R. T.** (1964), Een experiment met de q-sortmethode bij een zevental gestoorde pubers in groepstherapie. (An experiment with the q-sort method in 7 mentally disturbed adolescents undergoing group psychotherapy.) *Nederl. Tijdschr. Psychol.*, (Amsterdam) 19:136-164.

10732 **SCHNEEMANN, R.** (1978), (Group talk psychotherapy with adolescents.) *Aerzh. Jugendkunde*, (Leipzig) 69:341-347.

10733 **SCHNEER, H. I., GOTTSFELD, H.**, and **SALES, A.** (1957), Group therapy as an aid with delinquent pubescents in a special public school. *Psychiat. Quart. Suppl.*, 31:246-260.

10734 **SCHNEIDER, B.** (1970), Relationships between various criteria of leadership in small groups. *J. Soc. Psychol.*, 82:253-261.

10735 **SCHNEIDER, E. H.** (1959), *Music Therapy, 1958 Vol. VIII.* Eighth book of proceedings of the National Association for Music Therapy. Lawrence, KS.: National Association for Music Therapy.

10736 **SCHNEIDER, G.** (1967), (Formation of an analytic group therapy sector in a psychiatric hospital.) *J. Brasil. Psiquiat.*, (Rio de Janeiro) 16:347-354.

10737 **SCHNEIDER, L. I.** (1955), A proposed conceptual integration of group dynamics and group therapy. *J. Soc. Psychol.*, 42:173-191.

10738 **SCHNEIDER, P.** (1975), Contribution to combined technique in psychotherapy: terminal phase of therapy in a small group. *Dynam. Psychiat.*, (Berlin) 8:7-40.

10739 **SCHNEIDER, P. B.** (1965), (Analytic group psychotherapy: technical problems, indications.) *Inform. Psychiat.*, 14:657-671.

10740 **SCHNEIDER, P. B.** (1954), Experiment in progress: group psychotherapy of psychopaths according to Maxwell Jones. *Schweizer. Arch. Neurol., Neurochir. & Psychiat.*, (Zurich) 73:463-469.

10741 **SCHNEIDER, P. B.** (1965), *Pratique de la Psychothérapie de Groupe: Compte Rendu du Seminaire Internationale de Psychothérapie de Groupe. (Practice of Group Therapy: Proceedings of the International Seminar on Group Psychotherapy,* Lausanne, 1963.) Paris: Presses Universitaires de France.

10742 **SCHNEIDER, P. B., BARRELET, M., JORDI, P.**, and **DELALOYE, R.** (1959), Cases of failure and refusal of individual psychotherapy treated by group psychotherapy. *Acta Psychother., Psychosomat. Orthopaedagog. Suppl.*, (Basel) 7:338-349.

10743 **SCHNEIDERMAN, G.**, and **SEGAL, B.** (1969), A volunteer program for psychiatric inpatients in a general hospital: a pilot project. *J. Jewish Communal Serv.*, 45:274-278.

10744 **SCHNEIDM, B.**, and **McGUIRE, L.** (1976), Group therapy for non-orgasmic women: two age levels. *Arch. Sexual Behav.*, 5:239-247.

10745 **SCHNEIDMUHL, A. M.** (1951), Group psychotherapy program at the Spring Grove State Hospital. *Group Psychother., Psychodrama & Sociometry*, 4:41-55.

10746 **SCHNIDMAN, R. E.** (1979), A multi-modal assessment of didactic vs. rehearsal group assertiveness training. *Dissert. Abstr. Internat.*, 40:1384B.

10747 **SCHOENAKER, T.** (1978), Individualpsychologische gruppentherapie bei erwachsenen stotternden. (An Adlerian approach in group therapy with adult stutterers.) *Sprache-Stimme-Gehor*, (Stuttgart) 4:136-144.

10748 **SCHOENBERG, B.** (1966), Consultation in multidisciplinary group teaching program: the counterpart method. *Nursing Forum*, 5:65-81.

10749 **SCHOENBERG, B.**, and **SENESCU, R.** (1966), Group psychotherapy for patients with chronic multiple somatic complaints. *J. Chronic Diseases*, 19:649-657.

10750 **SCHOENBERGER, L.**, and **BRASWELL, C.** (1971), Music therapy in rehabilitation. *J. Rehab.*, 37:30-31.

10751 **SCHOFIELD, J. W.** (1979), The impact of positively structured contact

on intergroup behavior: does it last under adverse conditions. *Soc. Psychol.*, 42:280-284.
10752 **SCHOFIELD, L. J.**, and **WONG, S.** (1975), Operant approaches to group therapy in a school for handicapped children. *Develop. Med. & Child Neurol.*, (London) 17:425-433.
10753 **SCHOFIELD, L. J., Jr., HEDLUND, C.**, and **WORLAND, J.** (1974), Operant approaches to group therapy and effects on sociometric status. *Psychol. Reports*, 35:83-90.
10754 **SCHOMBURG, E.**, and **WIPPERMAN, E.** (1953), Wie unser märchenteppich entstad. (How our magic carpet originated.) *Schweizer. Zeit. Psychol. Anwendungen*, (Berne) 12:39-51.
10755 **SCHONBAR, R. A.** (1973), Group co-therapist and sex role identification. *Amer. J. Psychother.*, 27:539-547.
10756 **SCHONFELD, W. A.** (1969), Trends in adolescent psychiatry. In: *Current Psychiatric Therapies*, ed. J. H. Masserman. New York: Grune and Stratton.
10757 **SCHÖNHALS-ABRAHAMSOHN, M.** (1978), *Modellseminare "Eltern mit Kinderu": Eine Issenschaftliche Analyse zu Problemen und Möglichkeiten der Seminararbeit/Durchgefuhrt von der Psychologischen Forschungsgruppe Schönhals.* Stuttgart: W. Kohlhammer.
10758 **SCHÖNKE, M.** (1975), Psychodrama in school and college. *Group Psychother., Psychodrama & Sociometry*, 28:168-179.
10759 **SCHÖNKE, M.** (1975), (Psychodrama in school and college: an empirical study.) *Gruppendynam.*, (Stuttgart) 2:109-116.
10760 **SCHÖNKE, M.** (1979), (The use of a double in psychodrama.) *Praxis Kinderpsychol. & Kinderpsychiat.*, (Goettingen) 28:303-308.
10761 **SCHOONMAKER, J.**, and **THOMAS, C. S.** (1970), Mental health center attempts interracial public education. *Hosp. & Community Psychiat.*, 21:123-126.
10762 **SCHOTT, J. F.** (1973), Breaking down barriers with alcoholics: marathons. *Proceed., 81st Annual Convention*, American Psychological Association, Montreal, Canada, 8:391-392.
10763 **SCHRADER, W. K., ALTMAN, S.**, and **LEVENTHAL, T.** (1969), A didactic approach to structure in short-term group therapy. *Amer. J. Orthopsychiat.*, 39:493-497.
10764 **SCHRAMM, L.** (1968), Arbeitstragung—Der landesgemeinschaft fur erziehungsberatung BadenWurttemberg vom 26-28, 10, 1967 in Wiesneck. (Meeting of the Baden-Wurttemberg State Assoc. for education guidance from October 26-28, 1967 in Wiesneck.) *Praxis Kinderpsychol. & Kinderpsychiat.*, (Goettingen) 17:107-108.
10765 **SCHRAMSKI, T. G.** (1979), A systematic model of psychodrama. *Group Psychother., Psychodrama & Sociometry*, 32:20-30.
10766 **SCHREIBER, M.** (1965), Some basic concepts in social group work and recreation with the mentally retarded. *Rehab. Lit.*, 26:194-203.
10767 **SCHREIBER, M.**, and **BROMFIELD, S. H.** (1966), Adolescents who want to help: some experiences with teen volunteers in a group work setting. *Ment. Retard.*, 4:13-19.
10768 **SCHREIBER, S. C.** (1969), Some special forms of aggressiveness in activity group therapy and their impact on the therapists. *Smith Coll. Studies Soc. Work*, 39:138-146.
10769 **SCHREINER, P. J.** (1967), An exploratory study of the nature of advocacy and inquiry in problem–solving. *Dissert. Abstr. Internat.*, 27:3532.
10770 **SCHRELER, K.** (1966), (Experiences of a nurse in sociotherapy of mental patients.) *Deutsche Zentralblatt Krankenpflege*, (Stuttgart) 10:453-455.
10771 **SCHRETER, R. K.** (1980), Treating the untreatable: a group experience

with somaticizing borderline patients. *Internat. J. Psychiat. & Med.*, 10:205.

10772 **SCHRETER, R. K.** (1978/1979), Treating the untreatables: identifying the somaticizing borderline patient. *Internat. J. Psychiat. & Med.*, 9:207.

10773 **SCHRÖDER, R. G.** (1968), Stationary group therapy of stuttering children on a juvenile psychiatric ward. *Agnes Karll Schwest*, 22:509-510.

10774 **SCHROEDER, C. C.** (1976), Adventure training for resident assistants. *J. Coll. Student Personnel*, 17:11-15.

10775 **SCHROEDER, K.** (1973), Systematic human relations training for resident assistants. *J. Coll. Student Personnel*, 14:313-316.

10776 **SCHROEDER, M. G.** (1936), Group psychotherapy in a state hospital. *Elgin State Hosp. Papers*, 2:174-178.

10777 **SCHRUM, J. D.** (1972), The effects of empathy, self-disclosure, and the social desirability response set on interpersonal relationships within encounter groups. *Dissert. Abstr. Internat.*, 922B.

10778 **SCHUAL, F., SALTER, H.,** and **PALEY, M. G.** (1968), Hospitalized alcoholic patients: ii. the rationale of a residential program. *Hosp. & Community Psychiat.*, 19:204-206.

10779 **SCHUAL, F., SLATER, H.,** and **PALEY, M. G.** (1971), "Thematic" group therapy in the treatment of hospitalized alcoholic patients. *Internat. J. Group Psychother.*, 21:226-233.

10780 **SCHUBERT, M.** (1978), The impact of consciousness raising groups on women and their committed relationships. *Dissert. Abstr. Internat.*, 38:5042B.

10781 **SCHUBERT, P.** (1972), Personality type and self-perceived change resulting from sensitivity group experience. *Dissert. Abstr. Internat.*, 32:4360A.

10782 **SCHUERGER, J. L., LONG, T. J., BOSSHART, D. A.,** and **MENGES, R. J.** (1971), Fluctuation in psychological state during two encounter-group weekends. *Psychol. Reports*, 29:267-274.

10783 **SCHUKER, E.** (1979), Psychodynamics and treatment of sexual assault victims. *J. Amer. Acad. Psychoanal.*, 7:553.

10784 **SCIRE, H. G.** (1958), Changes in behavior and personality following use of chlorpromazine and reserpine: adjunct, group therapy—comparison of the immediate administration of a chemotherapeutic program with group therapy and administration of a chemotherapeutic program after a delay, i.e., after a period of exposure to group therapy. Unpublished doctoral dissertation, New York University.

10785 **SHOSENBERG, N.** (1980), Self-help groups for parents of premature infants. *Can. Nurse*, (Ottawa) 76:30-34.

10786 **SHULMAN, B. H.** (1962), The use of dramatic confrontation in group psychotherapy. *Psychiat. Quart. Suppl.*, 36:93-99.

10787 **SCHULMAN, B. M.** (1975), Group process: an adjunct in liaison consultation psychiatry. *Internat. J. Psychiat. & Med.*, 6:489-499.

10788 **SCHULMAN, G. I.** (1967), Asch conformity studies: conformity to the experimenter and/or to the groups? *Sociometry*, 30:26-40.

10789 **SCHULMAN, G. L.** (1973), Treatment of intergenerational pathology. *Soc. Casework*, 54:462-472.

10790 **SCHULMAN, I.** (1956), Delinquents. In: *The Fields of Group Psychotherapy*, ed. S. R. Slavson. New York: International Universities Press.

10791 **SCHULMAN, I.** (1955), Dynamics and treatment of anti-social psychopathology in adolescents. *Nerv. Child*, 11:35-41.

10792 **SCHULMAN, I.** (1952), The dynamics of certain reactions of delinquents to group psychotherapy. *Internat. J. Group Psychother.*, 2:334-343.

10793 **SCHULMAN, I.** (1957), Modifications in group psychotherapy with antisocial adolescents. *Internat. J. Group Psychother.*, 7:310-317.

10794 **SCHULMAN, I.** (1959), Transference, resistance and communication problems in adolescent psychotherapy groups. *Internat. J. Group Psychother.*, 9:496-503.

10795 **SCHULTZ, I. M.**, and **ROSS, D.** (1955), Group psychotherapy with psychotics in partial remission. *Psychiat. Quart.*, 29:273-279.

10796 **SCHULTZ, J. H.** (1957), Über einige gruppenpsychotherapeutische erfahrungen in autogenen training. (Concerning some group therapy experiences in autogenic training.) *Zeit. Diagnost. Psychol.*, 5:236-243.

10797 **SCHULTZ, K. A.** (1978), The use of groups in the rehabilitation of offenders on probation: an experimental study. *Dissert. Abstr. Internat.*, 38:5044.

10798 **SCHULTZE-GÖRLITZ, F.**, and **KRACK, E.** (1972), (The role of contemplation in a music therapy group.) *Zeit. Psychother. Med. Psychol.*, (Stuttgart) 22:66-69.

10799 **SCHULZ, E.** (1979), Group discussions in psychiatric long-term treatment. *Psychotherapy*, 29:226.

10800 **SCHULZ, J.** (1965), (Experiences in an analytic psychotherapy ward.) *Zeit. Psychosomat. Med. & Psychoanal.*, (Goettingen) 11:104-119.

10801 **SCHULZE, H.** (1971), Erfahrungen mit gruppentherapie in geschlossenen ferienkursen. (Experiences with group therapy in closed vacation courses.) *Praxis der Psychother.*, 16:137-142.

10802 **SCHUMACHER, R.** (1980), Parenting groups: a process for change. *J. Special. Group Work*, 5:135-139.

10803 **SCHUMACHER, R. R.** (1974), The influence of differential group composition on the effectiveness of group counseling with second, third, fourth, and fifth grade male children. *Dissert. Abstr. Internat.*, 35:1992-1993.

10804 **SCHUMACHER, W.** (1973), (Group psychotherapy: concept models, forms and indications.) *Med. Welt*, (Stuttgart) 24:1053-1057.

10805 **SCHUMAN, S. H.**, **MARCUS, D.**, and **NESSE, D.** (1973), Puppetry and the mentally ill. *Amer. J. Occupat. Ther.*, 28:484-486.

10806 **SCHUMANN, H. J. von.** (1970), Combined single and group psychotherapy in functional sexual disorders. *Med. Monatsschr.*, 24:538-542.

10807 **SCHURMANS, D.** (1969), (Dynamic and methodologic analysis of group psychotherapy.) *Evolut. Psychiat.*, (Toulouse) 34:179-214.

10808 **SCHURRMANS, M. J.** (1964), Five functions of the group therapist. *Amer. J. Nursing*, 64:108-110.

10809 **SCHUSTER, F. P., Jr.** (1959), Summary description of multiple impact psychotherapy. *Texas Report Biol. Med.*, 17:426-430.

10810 **SCHUTAENBERGER, A. A.** (1966), *Précis de Psychodrame.* (*Review of Psychodrama.*) Paris: Editions Universitaires.

10811 **SCHUTTMANN, H.** (1966), Supervision sozialpadagogischer gruppenarbeit in kinder- und jugendheimen. (Supervision of social-pedagogical group work in children and youth homes.) *Praxis Kinderpsychol. & Kinderpsychiat.*, (Goettingen) 15:298-301.

10812 **SCHUTZ, W.** (1975), Not encounter and certainly not facts. *J. Human. Psychol.*, 15:7-18.

10813 **SCHUTZ, W. C.** (1973), *Elements of Encounter.* Big Sur: Joy Press.

10814 **SCHUTZ, W. C.** (1971), *Here Comes Everybody: Bodymind and Encounter Culture.* New York: Harper and Row.

10815 **SCHUTZ, W. C.** (1967), *Joy.* New York: Grove Press.

10816 **SCHUTZ, W. C.** (1967), *Joy: Expanding Human Awareness.* New York: Grove Press.

10817 **SCHUTZ, W. C.** (1968), *Joy: Expanding Human Awareness.* New York: Grove Press, Section 3.

10818 **SCHUTZ, W. C.**, and **ALLEN, V. L.** (1966), The effects of a t-group laboratory on interpersonal behavior. *J. Appl. Behav. Science*, 2:265-286.

10819 **SCHUTZENBERGER, A. A.** (1960), Groupe Français d'études de sociométrie dynamique des groupes et psychodrame en France. (The French Group studies of sociometry, group dynamics, and psychodrama in France.) *Internat. J. Sociometry & Sociatry*, 2:103.

10820 **SCHUTZENBERGER, A. A.** (1966), Marquis de Sade: a French precursor of psychodrama. *Group Psychother., Psychodrama & Sociometry*, 19:46-48.

10821 **SCHUTZENBERGER, A. A.** (1964), Premier Congrès International de Psychodrame. (First International Congress on Psychodrama.) *Internat. J. Sociometry & Sociatry*, 4:52-55.

10822 **SCHUTZENBERGER, A. A.** (1976), (The triadic group: group analysis, group dynamics, and psychodrama.) *Connexions*, (Paris) 17:119-129.

10823 **SCHUURMAN, C. J.** (1964), (Group discussions as a contribution to mental hygiene.) *Nederl. Tijdschr. Geneeskunde,* (Amsterdam) 108:500-503.

10824 **SCHWAB, D. S.** (1976), Review of L. R. Wolberg's and M. L. Aronson's *Group Therapy 1974: An Overview. Internat. J. Group Psychother.*, 26:249-250.

10825 **SCHWAB, S. I.** (1907), The use of social intercourse as a therapeutic agent in the psychoneuroses: a contribution to the art of psychotherapy. *J. Nerv. & Ment. Diseases*, 34:497-503.

10826 **SCHWABE, C.** (1966), Methodische probleme der gruppensingtherapie bei der behandlung von neurosen in sociodynamischer sicht. (Methodical problems of group singing therapy in the treatment of neuroses from the socio-dynamic viewpoint.) *Zeit. Psychother. Med. Psychol.*, (Stuttgart) 16:183-189.

10827 **SCHWAITZ, E. K.** (1972), Why group therapy now? *Psychiat. Annals*, 2:26.

10828 **SCHWARTZ, A. H.**, and **FARMER, R. G.** (1968), Providing milieu treatment in a military setting. *Hosp. & Community Psychiat.*, 19:271-276.

10829 **SCHWARTZ, A. H., HARROW, M., ANDERSON, C., FEINSTEIN, A. E.**, and **SCHWARTZ, C. C.** (1970), Influence of therapeutic task orientation on patient and therapist satisfaction in group psychotherapy. *Internat. J. Group Psychother.*, 20:460-469.

10830 **SCHWARTZ, A. J.** (1974), Comparative effectiveness of three group oriented interventions with college undergraduates. *J. Amer. Coll. Health Assn.*, 23:114-123.

10831 **SCHWARTZ, A. L.** (1969), Developing community group work services: the learnings from an NIMH project. *Ment. Retard. Abstr.*, 6:722.

10832 **SCHWARTZ, A. N.** (1970), Volunteers help build patients' self-esteem. *Hosp. & Community Psychiat.*, 21:87-89.

10833 **SCHWARTZ, A. N.**, and **HAWKINS, H. L.** (1965), Patient models and affect statements in group therapy. *Proceed., 73d Annual Convention*, American Psychological Association, 265-266.

10834 **SCHWARTZ, E. D.**, and **GOODMAN, J. I.** (1952), Group therapy of obesity in elderly diabetics. *Geriatrics*, 7:280-283.

10835 **SCHWARTZ, E. K.** (1972), Group process laboratories as a teaching method. *Internat. J. Group Psychother.*, 22:16-21.

10836 **SCHWARTZ, E. K.** (1965), Group psychotherapy: the individual and the group. *Psychother. & Psychosomat.*, (Basel) 13:142-149.

10837 **SCHWARTZ, E. K.** (1972), Is there place for the traditional in group therapy? In: *Innovations in Psychotherapy*, eds. G. D. Goldman and D. S. Milman. Springfield, IL: C C Thomas.

10838 **SCHWARTZ, E. K.** (1965), Leadership and the psycho–therapist. *Topical Probl. Psychol. & Psychother.*, 5:72-79.

10839 **SCHWARTZ, E. K.** (1972), The treatment of obsessive patient in the group therapy setting. *Amer. J. Psychother.*, 26:352-361.
10840 **SCHWARTZ, E. K.** (1971), The trend to grouping. *Internat. J. Psychiat.*, 9:205-211.
10841 **SCHWARTZ, E. K.** (1972), Why group therapy, now? *Psychiatric Annals*, 2:26-37.
10842 **SCHWARTZ, E. K.**, and **WOLF, A.** (1968), The interpreter in group therapy: conflict resolution through negotiation. *Arch. Gen. Psychiat.*, 18:186-193.
10843 **SCHWARTZ, E. K.**, and **WOLF, A.** (1964), On countertransference in group psychotherapy. *J. Psychology*, 57:131-142.
10844 **SCHWARTZ, E. K.**, and **WOLF, A.** (1963), Psychoanalysis in groups: resistance to its use. *Amer. J. Psychother.*, 17:457-464.
10845 **SCHWARTZ, E. K.**, and **WOLF, A.** (1961), Psychoanalysis in groups: some comparisons with individual analysis. *J. Gen. Psychol.*, 64:153-191.
10846 **SCHWARTZ, E. K.**, and **WOLF, A.** (1960), Psychoanalysis in groups: the mystique of group dynamics. *Topical Probl. Psychol. & Psychother.*, 2:119-154.
10847 **SCHWARTZ, E. K.**, and **WOLF, A.** (1957), Psychoanalysis in groups: three primary parameters. *Amer. Imago*, 14:281-297.
10848 **SCHWARTZ, H. P.** (1972), Group roles as an indicator of potential counselor effectiveness. *Dissert. Abstr. Internat.*, 33:977A.
10849 **SCHWARTZ, L.** (1971), The therapeutic community for fatherless adolescent boys: a family approach. Paper presented at the Annual Meetings of the American Orthopsychiatric Assn., Washington, D.C.
10850 **SCHWARTZ, L. A.** (1945), Group psychotherapy in the war neuroses. *Amer. J. Psychiat.*, 101:498-500.
10851 **SCHWARTZ, L. H., MARCUS, R.**, and **CONDON, R.** (1978), Multidisciplinary group therapy for rheumatoid arthritis. *Psychosomatics*, 19:289-293.
10852 **SCHWARTZ, L. J.**, and **SCHWARTZ, R.** (1971), Therapeutic acting out. *Psychotherapy*, 8:205-207.
10853 **SCHWARTZ, M.** (1960), Recent observations on group psychotherapy with adolescent delinquent boys in residential treatment: analytic group psychotherapy. *Internat. J. Group Psychother.*, 10:195-212.
10854 **SCHWARTZ, M. D.** (1977), An information and discussion program for women after a mastectomy: the Transition Center and the Department of Psychiatry, Yale University School of Medicine. *Arch. Surgery*, 112:276-281.
10855 **SCHWARTZ, M. D.** (1975), Situation/transition groups: a conceptualization and review. *Amer. J. Orthopsychiat.*, 45:744-755.
10856 **SCHWARTZ, M. L.**, and **CAHILL, R.** (1971), Psychopathology associated with myasthenia gravis and its treatment by psychotherapeutically oriented group counseling. *J. Chronic Diseases*, 24:543-552.
10857 **SCHWARTZ, M. S.**, and **NASH, K. B.** (1970), Use of the group as a method of intervention in urban schools: summary of workshops. *Newsl. Amer. Orthopsychiat. Assn.*, 14:21-22.
10858 **SCHWARTZ, R.**, and **SCHWARTZ, L. J.** (1969), Growth encounters. *Voices*, 5:7-16.
10859 **SCHWARTZ, R.**, and **SCHWARTZ, L. J.** (1972), Psychotherapy with patients with acting–out disorders. In: *The Theory and Practice of Psychotherapy with Specific Disorders*, ed. M. Hammer. Springfield, IL: C. C. Thomas.
10860 **SCHWARTZ, S.** (1968), Group therapy, social competence, and hospital stay. *Arch. Gen. Psychiat.*, 18:559-561.

10861 **SCHWARTZ, W.** (1979), Review of N. McCaughan's *Group Work, Learning and Practice. Contemp. Psychol.*, 24:858.
10862 **SCHWARTZ, W.**, and **PAPAS, A. T.** (1968), Verbal communication in therapy. *Psychosomatics*, 9:71-74.
10863 **SCHWARTZBERG, A. Z., MULLEN, B. N.**, and **GROCER, M. N.** (1971), Diagnostic groups in an adolescent treatment program. *Hosp. & Community Psychiat.*, 22:217-219.
10864 **SCHWARZ, B.** (1971), (Significance of social therapy for mental disorders associated with aging.) *Zeit. Aerztl. Fortbildung*, (Jena) 65:854-858.
10865 **SCHWARZ, O.** (1952), Therapeutic drama club. *Diseases Nerv. System*, 13:41-43.
10866 **SCHWARZEL, W.** (1974), (Nonverbal interaction training: a new market for utilization of training?) *Gruppendynamik*, (Stuttgart) 5:25-38.
10867 **SCHWEBEL, M.** (1973), Groups for the educationally distraught. *Educat. Technol.*, 13:39-44.
10868 **SCHWENK, E.** (1976), (Problems concerning out-patient group therapy of alcoholics) *Gruppenpsychother. & Gruppendynam.* (Goettingen). 11:89-99.
10869 **SCHWOBEL, G.** (1969), (Analytical group psychotherapy in obesity.) *Praxis*, (Berne) 58:1033-1039.
10870 **SCHWOBEL, G.** (1966), Zur frage der bedeutung von sterilitat, periodenstorungen, frigiditat und vaginismus: bearbeitet in einer gruppentherapie. (On the problem of the meaning of sterility, menstrual disorders, frigidity and vaginism: material developed on the basis of group therapy.) *Zeit. Psychosomat. Med. & Psychoanal.*, (Goettingen) 12:39-50.
10871 **SCHWÖT, G.** (1969), (Analytical group psychotherapy in obesity.) *Praxis*, (Berne) 58:1033-1039.
10872 **SCILLITANI, B.** (1966), La psicoterapia di gruppo "allargata." ("Extended" group psychotherapy.) *Minerva Med.*, (Turin) 57:2805-2806.
10873 **SCISSONS, E. H.**, and **NJAA, L. J.** (1973), Systematic desensitization of test anxiety: a comparison of group and individual treatment. *J. Consult. & Clin. Psychol.*, 4:470.
10874 **SCLARE, A. B.** (1979), Review of S. Zimberg's, J. Wallace's, and S. B. Blume's *Practical Approaches to Alcoholism Psychotherapy. Brit. J. Psychiat.*, (Ashford) 135:372.
10875 **SCODEL, A.** (1964), Inspirational group therapy: a study of Gamblers Anonymous. *Amer. J. Psychother.*, 18:115-125.
10876 **SCOFIELD, R. E.** (1970), The comparative effects of short-term group, individual, and regular counseling on self-concept. *Dissert. Abstr. Internat.*, 30:3286A.
10877 **SCORESBY, A. L.** (1970), An experimental comparison of confirmed and disconfirmed anticipations for verbal reinforcement in group counseling. *Dissert. Abstr. Internat.*, 31:1023A.
10878 **SCOTT, C. L.** (1980), Interpersonal trust: a comparison of attitudinal and situational factors. *Human Relat.*, 33:805-812.
10879 **SCOTT, D.**, and **CROWHURST, J.** (1975), Reawakening senses in the elderly: Alberta Hospital, Ponoka. *Can. Nurse*, (Ottawa) 71:21-22.
10880 **SCOTT, E. M.** (1966), Group therapy for schizophrenic alcoholics in a state-operated outpatient clinic: with hypnosis as an integrated adjunct. *Internat. J. Clin. & Exper. Hypnosis*, 14:232-242.
10881 **SCOTT, E. M.** (1976), Group therapy with convicts on work release in Oregon. *Internat. J. Offender Ther.*, (London) 20:225-235.
10882 **SCOTT, E. M.** (1959), Joint and group treatment for married alcoholics and their spouses. *Psychol. Reports*, 5:725-728.

10883 **SCOTT, E. M.** (1956), A special type of group therapy and its application to alcoholics. *Quart. J. Studies Alcohol*, 17:288-290.
10884 **SCOTT, E. M.** (1963), A suggested treatment plan for the hostile alcoholic. *Internat. J. Group Psychother.*, 13:93-100.
10885 **SCOTT, G.** (1980), (A nurse's experiences in an ambulatory aftercare group for alcoholics.) *Krankenpflege*, (Frankfurt) 34:19-21.
10886 **SCOTT, H.** (1976), The effects of leadership training and style on individuals involved in group therapy. *Dissert. Abstr. Internat.*, 38:1420.
10887 **SCOTT, J. D.** (1972), Comparative effectiveness of existential and behavioral group counseling in reducing pain apperception in individuals experiencing chronic low back pain. *Dissert. Abstr. Internat.*, 32:6620A.
10888 **SCOTT, J. M.**, and **ANCHOR, K. N.** (1977), Male homosexual behavior and ego function strategies in the group encounter. *J. Clin. Psychol.*, 33:1079-1084.
10889 **SCOTT, M. C.** (1970), Small groups: an effective treatment approach in residential programs for adolescents. *Child Welfare*, 49:161-164.
10890 **SCOTT, R. H.** (1961), The therapeutic community in prison. *J. Soc. Ther.*, 7:197-203.
10891 **SCOTT, W. A.**, and **ROHRBAUGH, J.** (1975), Conceptions of harmful groups: some correlates of group descriptions in three cultures. *J. Personality & Soc. Psychol.*, 31:992-1003.
10892 **SCULTHROPE, W.**, and **BLUMENTHAL, I. J.** (1965), Combined patient-relative group therapy in schizophrenia. *Ment. Hygiene*, 49:569-573.
10893 **SEABOURNE, B.** (1963), The action sociogram. *Group Psychother., Psychodrama & Sociometry*, 16:145-155.
10894 **SEAGULL, E. A.**, and **SEAGULL, A. A.** (1979), Talk to a lay group as a method of primary prevention. *J. Clin. Child Psychol.*, 8:130-132.
10895 **SEALS, J. M.**, and **MEANS, R. S.** (1972), Academic outcome for group and individually counseled reinstated students. *Cat. Selected Docum. Psychol.*, 2:78-79.
10896 **SEARLE, P. R.** (1969), The effect of videotape feedback on the behavior of counseling groups. *Dissert. Abstr. Internat.*, 29:2970A.
10897 **SEARS, R.** (1953), Leadership among patients in group therapy. *Internat. J. Group Psychother.*, 3:191-197.
10898 **SEARS, R.** (1956), Leadership among patients in group therapy: ii. a study of patients' and therapists' ratings. *Internat. J. Group Psychother.*, 5:374-382.
10899 **SECHREST, L.**, and **BOOTZIN, R.** (1975), Preliminary evaluation of psychologists in encounter groups. *Prof. Psychol.*, 6:69-79.
10900 **SECHREST, L.**, and **KESSLER, M.** (1977), Special considerations in conducting evaluations of encounter groups. *Prof. Psychol.*, 8:516-525.
10901 **SECHREST, L. B.**, and **BARGER, B.** (1961), Verbal participation and perceived benefit from group psychotherapy. *Internat. J. Group Psychother.*, 11:49-59.
10902 **SEDLMAIER, M.**, and **SISLEY, E. L.** (1972), Mural group: integration of projective drawings with standard group therapy techniques. *Psychol. Reports*, 31:475-481.
10903 **SEDMAK, T.** (1975), (Group psychotherapy of depressive patients.) *Anali Zavoda Ment. Zdravlje*, 7:131-143.
10904 **SEEBANDT, G.** (1964), Compulsive vomiting in a school child: a case report on the phenomenology and therapy of compulsive neurosis. *Acta Paedopsychiat.*, (Basel) 31:203-208.
10905 **SEELIG, J. C.** (1974), A comparison of change in counselor candidates as a result of differing group experiences. *Dissert. Abstr. Internat.*, 10:6392A.

10906 **SEEMAN, A. Z.** (1948), Group guidance: an exploratory study in methods of analysis. Unpublished doctoral dissertation, Ohio State University.

10907 **SEEMAN, K.** (1968), Multimodality outpatient group psychotherapy. *Amer. J. Psychother.*, 22:443-459; *Curr. Psychiat. Ther.*, 11:146-155.

10908 **SEEN, G. H.** (1973), An examination of observer evaluations of experimentally induced changes in perceived leadership in a task oriented leaderless discussion group. *Dissert. Abstr. Internat.*, 34:1265B.

10909 **SEGAL, R. L.** (1972), Work with patient chairman in task groups in a psychiatric hospital. *Compar. Group Studies*, 3:105-115.

10910 **SEGAL, S. P.** (1972), Research on the outcome of social work therapeutic interventions: a review of the literature. *J. Health & Soc. Behav.*, 13:3-17.

10911 **SEGEV, A.** (1975), (Treatment of stress and anxiety states after myocardial infarction by group rehabilitation.) *Harefuah*, (Tel Aviv) 88:205-208.

10912 **SEGLOW, I. M.** (1967), An experiment in group training of social workers for leadership of therapeutically orientated groups. *Psychother. & Psychosomat.*, (Basel) 15:61.

10913 **SEGLOW, I. M.** (1965), Psychodrama groups in a day-school for maladjusted children. *Assn. Psychother. Bull.*, 6:23-34.

10914 **SEGUIN, C. A.** (1947), Un experimento con psicoterapía colectiva. (An experiment with group psychotherapy.) *Rev. Neuro-Psiquiat.*, (Lima) 10:378-379.

10915 **SEGUIN, G. A.** (1959), Group psychotherapy and communication. *Group Psychother., Psychodrama & Sociometry*, 12:86-91.

10916 **SEIDERMAN, S.** (1974), Ethnotherapy: a new hope for society. *Internat. J. Group Psychother.*, 24:174-189.

10917 **SEIDLER, R.** (1966), Individual psychology in activity group therapy. *Individ. Psychologist*, 4:1-3.

10918 **SEIDLER, R.** (1936), School guidance clinics in Vienna. *Individ. Psychol. Bull.*, 2:75-78.

10919 **SEIDMAN, J. M.** (1969), *The Child: A Book of Readings*, 2d ed. New York: Holt, Rinehart and Winston.

10920 **SEIDMON, B. L.** (1980), Effects of group therapy on the deaf. *Dissert. Abstr. Internat.*, 40:5874B. (University Microfilms No. 8012696.)

10921 **SEIFERT, W.** (1975), *Gruppendynamik: Veranderung Durch Selbsterfahrung.* (*Group Dynamics: Learning Through Self-Discovery.*) Cologne: Kiepenheuer and Witsch.

10922 **SEIVER, L. M.** (1961), A layman leads a great books group in a mental hospital. *Ment. Hygiene*, 45:537-542.

10923 **SELDMAN, M.** (1971), An investigation of aspects of marathon-encounter group phenomena: types of participants and differential perception of leaders. *Dissert. Abstr. Internat.*, 32:3652B.

10924 **SELDMAN, M. L.**, and **McBREARTY, J. F.** (1975), Characteristics of marathon volunteers. *Psychol. Reports*, 36:555-560.

10925 **SELDMAN, M. L., McBREARTY, J. F.**, and **SELDMAN, S. L.** (1974), Deification of marathon encounter group leaders. *Small Group Behav.*, 5:80-91.

10926 **SELFRIDGE, F. F., WEITZ, L. J., ABRAMOWITZ, S. I., CALABRIA, F. M., ABRAMOWITZ, C. Z.**, and **STEGER, J. A.** (1975), Sensitivity-oriented versus didactically-oriented in-service counselor training. *J. Couns. Psychol.*, 22:156-159.

10927 **SELIGMAN, M.** (1977), *Group Counseling and Group Psychotherapy with Rehabilitation Clients.* Springfield, IL: C C Thomas.

10928 **SELIGMAN, M.** (1968), An investigation of verbal behavior between alternating, self-directed, and therapist-led group psychotherapy sessions. *Dissert. Abstr. Internat.*, 29:1180.

10929 **SELIGMAN, M.**, and **DESMOND, R. E.** (1973), Leaderless groups: a review. *Couns. Psychologist*, 4:70-87.

10930 **SELIGMAN, M.**, and **DESMOND, R.** (1975), The leaderless group phenomenon: a historical perspective. *Internat. J. Group Psychother.*, 25:277-290.

10931 **SELIGMAN, M.**, and **STERNE, D. M.** (1969), Verbal behavior in therapist-led, leaderless, and alternating group psychotherapy sessions. *J. Couns. Psychol.*, 16:325-328.

10932 **SELKIN, J.**, and **MEYER, G.** (1960), Group therapy enters the sheltered workshop. *J. Rehab.*, 26:8-9.

10933 **SELLER, S.**, and **TAYLOR, J.** (1965), The malevolent transformation: implications for group work practice. *Soc. Work*, 10:82-91.

10934 **SELLERS, D. J.** (1974), Teaching a self-initiated control technique to individuals and a group in college. *Internat. J. Clin. & Exper. Hypnosis*, 22:39-45.

10935 **SELLSCHOPP-RUPPELL, A.** (1977), Behavioral characteristics in in-patient group psychotherapy with psychosomatic patients. *Psychother. & Psychosomat.*, (Basel) 28:316-322.

10936 **SELTZER, J.**, and **KILMANN, R. H.** (1977), Effect of group composition on group process: homogeneity vs. heterogeneity on task and people dimensions. *Psychol. Reports*, 41:1195-1200.

10937 **SELVEY, H. A.** (1978), Review of I. A. Greenberg's *Group Hypnotherapy and Hypnotherapy*. *Amer. J. Clin. Hypnosis*, 21:58.

10938 **SELVINI, A.** (1973), An internist's experience in a doctor-patient relationship training group (Balint group). *Psychother. & Psychosomat.*, (Basel) 22:1-18.

10939 **SEMERIVA, J. P.**, and **THIBERGE, B.** (1978), (Interpretation: a matter of interpretation.) *Etudes Psychother.*, 31:51-56.

10940 **SEMINARA, B.**, and **AGOSTINI, E.** (1974), (Acting-out during group psychotherapy.) *Riv. Speri. Freniatria*, (Emilia) 98:993-1003.

10941 **SEMKE, C. W.** (1968), A comparison of the outcomes of case study structured group counseling with high ability, underachieving freshmen. *Dissert. Abstr. Internat.*, 29:128.

10942 **SEMON, R. G.**, and **GOLDSTEIN, N.** (1957), The effectiveness of group psychotherapy with chronic schizophrenic patients and an evaluation of different therapeutic methods. *J. Consult. & Clin. Psychol.*, 21:317-322.

10943 **SEMONSKY, C.**, and **ZICHT, G.** (1974), Activity group parameters. *J. Amer. Acad. Child Psychiat.*, 13:166-179.

10944 **SEMRAD, E. V.** (1948), Psychotherapy of the psychoses in a state hospital. *Diseases Nerv. System*, 9:105-111.

10945 **SEMRAD, E. V.**, and **ARSENIAN, J.** (1951), The use of group processes in teaching group dynamics. *Amer. J. Psychiat.*, 108:358-363.

10946 **SEMRAD, E. V., ARSENIAN, J.**, and **STANDISH, C. T.** (1957), Experiences with small groups in teaching group psychology. *Group Psychother., Psychodrama & Sociometry*, 10:191-197.

10947 **SEMRAD, E. V., KANTER, S., SHAPIRO, D.**, and **ARSENIAN, J.** (1963), The field of group psychotherapy. *Internat. J. Group Psychother.*, 13:452-475.

10948 **SEMRAD, E. V.** (1951), Group methods, Section 11. *Proceed. of the 3d Ment. Hosp. Inst.* Mental Hospital Service of the American Psychiatric Association, Washington, D.C., APA, pp. 133-145.

10949 **SENAY, E. C.** (1968), Innovations in administering a day treatment program: ii. the process group. *Hosp. & Community Psychiat.*, 19:183-184.

10950 **SENAY, E. C.**, and **RENAULT, P. R.** (1971), Treatment methods for heroin addicts: a review. *J. Psychedelic Drugs*, 3:47-54.

10951 **SENFT, P.** (1959), The concept of group catharsis. *Acta Psychother., Psychosomat. Orthopaedagog. Suppl.*, (Basel) 7:350-354.

10952 **SENFT, P.** (1955), Transference in group psychotherapy. *Acta Psychother., Psychosomat. Orthopaedagog.*, (Basel) 3:373-378.

10953 **SEPLOWIN, V. M.** (1972), A study of perceptions before and after a managerial development course. *Compar. Group Studies*, 3:135-158.

10954 **SERBER, M.** (1972), Teaching the nonverbal components of assertive training. *J. Behav. Ther. & Exper. Psychiat.*, 3:179-183.

10955 **SERLIN, F. R.** (1970), Techniques for the use of hypnosis in group therapy. *Amer. J. Clin. Hypnosis*, 12:177-202.

10956 **SERWER, B.**, and **LEVY, E. I.** (1966), Group therapy as part of a college-level study skills program. *Internat. J. Group Psychother.*, 16:65-77.

10957 **SETHNA, E. D.**, and **HARRINGTON, J. A.** (1971), Evaluation of group psychotherapy. *Brit. J. Psychiat.*, (Ashford) 118:641-658.

10958 **SETHNA, E. R.**, and **HARRINGTON, J. A.** (1971), A study of patients who lapsed from group psychotherapy. *Brit. J. Psychiat.*, (Ashford) 119:59-70.

10959 Setting held critical to lack of success in group therapy (1968), *Roche Report: Front. Hosp. Psychiat.*, 5:1, 2, 8.

10960 **SEVERINGHAUS, E. C.**, and **IGERSHEIMER, W. W.** (1964), An analysis of behavior in the first meeting of a therapy group. *Internat. J. Group Psychother.*, 14:49-59.

10961 **SEWELL, H. H.**, and **ABRAMOWITZ, S. I.** (1979), Flexibility, persistence, and success in sex therapy. *Arch. Sexual Behav.*, 8:497-506.

10962 **SEXTER, I. S.** (1957), A manual for the utilization of social films and television programs by counselors and teachers of group guidance in junior high schools. Unpublished doctoral dissertation, New York University.

10963 **SEYMOUR, G. E.** (1971), The concurrent validity of unobtrusive measures of conflict in small isolated groups. *J. Clin. Psychol.*, 27:431-435.

10964 **SEYMOUR, G. E.**, and **GUNDERSON, E. K. E.** (1971), Attitudes as predictors of adjustment in extremely isolated groups. *J. Clin. Psychol.*, 27:333-338.

10965 **SEYMOUR, R. M.** (1974), An experimental group for mothers of young children. *Midwife*, (London) 10:154-158.

10966 **SHAALAN, M.** (1978), Experiences with group psychotherapy in the Egyptian culture: the public hospital setting. *J. Egyptian Med. Assn. Suppl.*, 61:69-78.

10967 **SHADER, R. I.**, and **MELTZER, H. Y.** (1968), The breast metaphor and the group. *Internat. J. Group Psychother.*, 18:110-113.

10968 **SHADISH, W. R.** (1978), The development, reliability, and validity of the Interpersonal Relations Scale: the measurement of intimate behavior with special application to encounter group outcome. *Dissert. Abstr. Internat.*, 39:2520B. (University Microfilms No. 7821502.)

10969 **SHADISH, W. R.** (1980), Nonverbal interventions in clinical groups. *J. Consult. & Clin. Psychol.*, 48:164-168.

10970 **SHAFAR, S.** (1975), Group and individual analytic psychotherapy: reflections on four patients. *Group Anal.*, (London) 9:76-80.

10971 **SHAFFER, J. B. P.** (1979), Review of L. R. Wolberg's, M. L. Aronson's, and A. R. Wolberg's *Group Therapy 1978: An Overview. Contemporary Psychology*, 24:827.

10972 **SHAFFER, J. B. P.**, and **GALINSKY, M. D.** (1974), *Models of Group Therapy and Sensitivity Training*. Englewood Cliffs, NJ: Prentice-Hall.

10973 **SHAFTEL, G.**, and **SHAFTEL, F. R.** (1948), Report on the use of a "practice action level" in the Stanford University project for American ideals. *Sociatry*, 2:245-253.

10974 **SHALINSKY, W.** (1969), Group composition as an element of social group work practice. *Soc. Serv. Rev.*, 43:42-49.

10975 **SHAMBAUGH, P. W.**, and **KANTER, S. S.** (1969), Spouses under stress: group meeting with spouses of patients on hemodialysis. *Amer. J. Psychiat.*, 125:928-936.

10976 **SHANKEN, P.** (1977), Is there a "how to" of psychological growth? *J. Psychiat. Nursing*, 15:19-20.

10977 **SHANNON, D. A.** (1971), A study of the effectiveness of two procedures of counseling with small groups of underachievers with average intelligence in the eighth and ninth grades. *Dissert. Abstr. Internat.*, 32:4361A.

10978 **SHANNON, P. D.**, and **SNORTUM, J. R.** (1966), An activity group's role in intensive psychotherapy. *Amer. J. Occupat. Ther.*, 19:344-347.

10979 **SHAPIRO, D.** (1950), A study of the influence of the social field on individual behavior: as revealed in the expression of hostility and warmth by neurotics and paranoid schizophrenics in discussion group situations. *Genetic Psychol., Monogr.*, 42:161-230.

10980 **SHAPIRO, D.**, and **BIRK, L.** (1967), Group therapy in experimental perspective. *Internat. J. Group Psychother.*, 17:211-224.

10981 **SHAPIRO, D. A.**, **CAPLAN, H. L.**, **RHODE, P. D.**, and **WATSON, J. P.** (1975), Personal questionnaire changes and their correlates in a psychotherapeutic group. *Brit. J. Med. Psychol.*, (London) 48:207-215.

10982 **SHAPIRO, I. S.**, and **CREEDON, C. F.** (1958), An evaluation of parent discussion and group leadership training for public health and hospital nurses. *Nursing Res.*, 7:27-29.

10983 **SHAPIRO, J. L.** (1978), *Methods of Group Psychotherapy and Encounter: A Tradition of Innovation.* Itasca, IL: Peacock.

10984 **SHAPIRO, J. L.**, and **DIAMOND, M. J.** (1972), Increases in hypnotizability as a function of encounter group training: some confirming evidence. *J. Abnorm. & Soc. Psychol.*, 79:112-116.

10985 **SHAPIRO, J. L.**, and **GUST, T.** (1974), Counselor training for facilitative human relationships. *Counselor Educat. & Supervision*, 13:198-206.

10986 **SHAPIRO, J. N.** (1964), A comparison of certain Rorschach score patterns with psychodrama action patterns. *Dissert. Abstr. Internat.*, 25:2615-2616.

10987 **SHAPIRO, R. B.** (1977), Review of C. A. Loew's, H. Grayson's, and G. Heiman Loew's *Three Psychotherapies. Group*, 1:66-67.

10988 **SHAPIRO, R. B.** (1977), Review of Charles Brenner's *Psychoanalytic Technique and Psychic Conflict. Group*, 1:68-69.

10989 **SHAPIRO, R. B.** (1978), Working through the war with Vietnam vets. *Group*, 2:156-183.

10990 **SHAPIRO, R. J.** (1971), A comparative investigation of emotionality and multiple outcome criteria in marathon and traditional growth groups. *Dissert. Abstr. Internat.*, 32:3652B.

10991 **SHAPIRO, R. J.** (1980), Review of F. M. Sander's *Individual and Family Therapy: Toward an Integration. Fam. Process*, 19:420-422.

10992 **SHAPIRO, R. J.**, and **KLEIN, R. H.** (1975), Perceptions of the leaders in an encounter group. *Small Group Behav.*, 6:238-248.

10993 **SHAPIRO, S.** (1975), The group leadership training program at F.C.I. Lompoc. In: *The Crumbling Walls: Treatment and Counseling of Prisoners*, eds. R. H. Hosford and C. S. Moss. Urbana, IL: University of Illinois Press.

10994 **SHAPIRO, S. B.** (1950), An attempt to modify certain attitudes and personality characteristics of prejudiced individuals by group psychotherapeutic methods. *Amer. Psychologist*, 5:463.

10995 **SHAPIRO, S. B.** (1965), Orienting patients to ego therapy. *J. Psychology*, 59:315-318.

10996 **SHAPIRO, S. B.**, and **BACH, G. R.** (1948), Hostility patterns in group therapy. *Amer. Psychologist*, 3:346.

10997 **SHARMA, K. L.** (1975), Rational group counseling with anxious underachievers. *Can. Counselor*, (Ottawa) 9:132-138.

10998 **SHARMI, S.** (1979), From alienation to admiration: developmental stages of group leaders in encounters with the culturally deprived mothers. *Human Relat.*, 32:737-750.

10999 **SHARNI, S.** (1980), Groups of culturally deprived parents: a multidimensional intervention model. *Small Group Behav.*, 11:345-358.

11000 **SHARP, V.** (1977), The research act in sociology and the limits of meaning: the understanding of crisis, care and control in a therapeutic community. *Austral. & New Zeal. J. Sociol.*, (Christ Church) 13:236-241.

11001 **SHARPE, P.** (1980), Some thoughts on group processes in industrialized society. *Group Anal.*, (London) 13:25-29.

11002 **SHARPE, R.** (1975), Counseling services for school-age pregnant girls. *J. School Health*, 45:284-285.

11003 **SHASKAN, D.** (1965), The future role of a national professional organization for group psychotherapy. *Topical Probl. Psychol. & Psychother.*, 5:219-224.

11004 **SHASKAN, D. A.** (1960), Combined individual and group psychoanalysis: symposium—1. combined therapy. *Amer. J. Orthopsychiat.*, 30:223-224.

11005 **SHASKAN, D. A.** (1952), Demonstration of a common fantasy in a group. *Internat. J. Group Psychother.*, 2:250-254.

11006 **SHASKAN, D. A.** (1946), Development of group psychotherapy in a military setting. *Proceed. Assn. Res. Nerv. Diseases*, 25:311-315.

11007 **SHASKAN, D. A.** (1958), Group psychotherapy as an index of growth in a VA mental hygiene clinic. *Internat. J. Group Psychother.*, 8:285-292.

11008 **SHASKAN, D. A.** (1972), Group psychotherapy: present trends in management of the more severe emotional problems. *Psychiat. Annals*, 2:10-15.

11009 **SHASKAN, D. A.** (1947), Must individual and group psychotherapy be opposed? *Amer. J. Orthopsychiat.*, 17:290-292.

11010 **SHASKAN, D. A.** (1974/1975), Successful signs in borderlines. *Groups*, 6:15-19.

11011 **SHASKAN, D. A.** (1948), Trends in orthopsychiatric therapy: ix. evolution and trends in group psychotherapy. *Amer. J. Orthopsychiat.*, 18:447-454.

11012 **SHASKAN, D. A.** (1970), Sisyphus oder die ruckkehr zur gruppe. (Sisyphus or returning to the group.) *Dynam. Psychiat.*, (Berlin) 3:33-38.

11013 **SHASKAN, D. A.**, and **BLANK, L.** (1958), New directions in group psychotherapy. *Internat. J. Soc. Psychiat.*, (London) 4:134-139.

11014 **SHASKAN, D. A.**, and **JOLESCH, M.** (1944), War and group psychotherapy. *Amer. J. Orthopsychiat.*, 14:571-577.

11015 **SHASKAN, D. A.**, and **LINDT, H.** (1948), The theme of the aggressive mother during group therapy: analysis of a group interview. *Psychoanal. Rev.*, 35:295-300.

11016 **SHASKAN, D. A., CONRAD, D. C.**, and **GRANT, J. D.** (1950), Prediction of behavior in group psychotherapy from Rorschach protocols. *Group Psychother., Psychodrama & Sociometry*, 3:218-230.

11017 **SHASKAN, D. A., PLANK, R.**, and **BLUM, H. H.** (1949), The function of the group. *Psychoanal. Rev.*, 36:385-388.

11018 **SHASKAN, D. A., SAGER, C. J., DURKIN, H. E.**, and **GLATZER, H. T.** (1960), Combined individual and group psychoanalysis: symposium. *Amer. J. Orthopsychiat.*, 30:223-246.

11019 **SHASKAN, D. M.** (1953), Group therapy and the prevention of panic. *Internat. J. Group Psychother.*, 3:285-292.

11020 **SHATAN, C. F., BRODY, B.,** and **GHENT, E. R.** (1962), Countertransference: its reflection in the process of peer-group supervision. *Internat. J. Group Psychother.*, 12:335-346.

11021 **SHATIN, L.,** and **KYMISSIS, P.** (1975), A study of transactional group image therapy. *Amer. J. Art Ther.*, 15:13-18.

11022 **SHATIN, L.,** and **ZIMET, C. N.** (1958), Influence of music upon verbal participation in group psychotherapy. *Diseases Nerv. System*, 19:66-72.

11023 **SHATOFF, D. K.** (1980), The effects of a "developing satisfying relationships" group on college students' interpersonal behavior. *Dissert. Abstr. Internat.*, 40:5875B. (University Microfilms No. 8013341.)

11024 **SHATTAN, S. P., DeCAMP, L., FUJII, E., FROSS, G. G.,** and **WOLFF, R. J.** (1966), Group treatment of conditionally discharged patients in a mental health clinic. *Amer. J. Psychiat.*, 122:798-805.

11025 **SHATTER, F.** (1957), An investigation of the effectiveness of a group therapy program, including the child and his mother, for the remediation of reading disabilities. *Dissert. Abstr. Internat.*, 17:1032.

11026 **SHAULIK, F. H.** (1976), The relationship of interpersonal and intra-group conditions to individual change in marathon encounter groups. *Dissert. Abstr. Internat.*, 37:817A.

11027 **SHAW, D., FORE, K., RITCHIE, A., McNULTY, M.,** and **NIXON, G.** (1977), Multiple impact therapy: University of Texas Medical Branch in Galveston. *Amer. J. Nursing*, 77:246-248.

11028 **SHAW, M. E.** (1971), *Group Dynamics: The Psychology of Small Group Behavior.* New York: McGraw-Hill.

11029 **SHAW, M. E.** (1959), Organizational considerations in role playing application. *Group Psychother., Psychodrama & Sociometry*, 12:156-160.

11030 **SHAW, M. E.** (1959), Spontaneity training and role playing in industry. *Group Psychother., Psychodrama & Sociometry*, 12:293-299.

11031 **SHAW, M. E.** (1956), Training executives in action. *Group Psychother., Psychodrama & Sociometry*, 9:63-68.

11032 **SHAW, M. E.,** and **BLUM, J. M.** (1966), Effects of leadership style upon group performance as a function of task structure. *J. Personality & Soc. Psychol.*, 3:238-242.

11033 **SHAW, M. E.,** and **BLUM, J. M.** (1965), Group performance as a function of task difficulty and the group's awareness of members satisfaction. *J. Appl. Psychol.*, 49:151-154.

11034 **SHAW, M. E.,** and **HARKEY, B.** (1976), Some effects of congruency of member characteristics and group structure upon group behavior. *J. Personality & Soc. Psychol.*, 34:412-418.

11035 **SHAW, M. W.** (1976), The effects of automated group desensitization and symbolic modeling plus role rehearsal on beginning counselor-trainees' state anxiety. *Dissert. Abstr. Internat.*, 36:5060A.

11036 **SHAW, R., BLUMENFELD, H.,** and **SENF, R.** (1968), A short–term treatment program in a child guidance clinic. *Soc. Work*, 13:81-90.

11037 **SHAWVER, L.** (1974), The expression of values in group psychotherapy. *Dissert. Abstr. Internat.*, 34:5663B.

11038 **SHAWVER, L.,** and **LUBACK, J.** (1977), Value attribution in group psychotherapy. *J. Consult. & Clin. Psychol.*, 45:228-236.

11039 **SHAY, E. R.** (1964), Self-concept changes among alcoholics in group discussion. *Dissert. Abstr. Internat.*, 24:3190.

11040 **SHEA, G. F., Jr.** (1974), The effects of reality therapy oriented group counseling with delinquent, behavior-disordered students. *Dissert. Abstr. Internat.*, 34:4889A.

11041 **SHEA, J. E.** (1954), Differentials in resistance reactions in individual and group psychotherapy. *Internat. J. Group Psychother.*, 4:253-261.

11042 **SHEAR, H. J.** (1960), Group therapy with chronic psychiatric outpatients. *Delaware Med. J.*, 32:113-117.

11043 **SHEARE, J. B.**, and **LARSON, C. C.** (1978), Odd couple—effective public schools—mental health joint programming to provide educational–therapeutic services to emotionally disturbed students and their families. *Psychol. in Schools*, 15:541-544.

11044 **SHEARER, R. M.** (1969), The structure and philosophy of Georgia's halfway houses. *Hosp. & Community Psychiat.*, 20:115-118.

11045 **SHEARON, E. M.** (1978), Aspects of persuasion in psychodrama. *Group Psychother., Psychodrama & Sociometry*, 31:96.

11046 **SHEARON, E. M.** (1976), The effects of psychodrama treatment on professed and inferred self concepts of selected fourth graders in one elementary school. *Dissert. Abstr. Internat.*, 36:5161-5162.

11047 **SHEARSON, E. M.** (1980), Psychodrama with children. *Group Psychother., Psychodrama & Sociometry*, 33:142-155.

11048 **SHEATS, P. H.** (1948), Sociodrama as an aid to large group communication. *Sociatry*, 4:431-435.

11049 **SHECTMAN, F.** (1977), Conventional and contemporary approaches to psychotherapy: Freud meets Skinner, Janov, and others. *Amer. Psychologist*, 32:197-204.

11050 **SHEEHAN, V. H.** (1973), *Unmasking*. Chicago: Swallow Press.

11051 **SHEFRIN, A. P.** (1978), The use of role-playing for teaching professionalism and ethics. *J. Dental Educat.*, 42:150-152.

11052 **SHELDON, W. D.**, and **LANDSMAN, T.** (1950), An investigation of nondirective group therapy with students in academic difficulty. *J. Cons. Psychol.*, 14:210-215.

11053 **SHELDRAKE, P.**, and **TURNER, B.** (1973), Perceptions and factions in a therapeutic community. *Human Relat.*, 26:371-385.

11054 **SHELLHASE, L. J.** (1960), Acceptance of role and resultant interaction in the group psychotherapy of schizophrenia. *Group Psychother., Psychodrama & Sociometry*, 13:208-229.

11055 **SHELLHASE, L. J.** (1963), The development of a social group by schizophrenic patients within a therapeutic milieu. *Ment. Hygiene*, 47:418-420.

11056 **SHELLHASE, L. J.** (1962), A study of the self-governing activities of a schizophrenic group. *Internat. J. Soc. Psychiat.*, (London) 8:211-219.

11057 **SHELLOW, R. S.** (1958), Psychodramatic and group therapy. *Group Psychother., Psychodrama & Sociometry*, 11:227-228.

11058 **SHELLOW, R. S., WARD, J. L.**, and **RUBENFELD, S.** (1958), Group therapy and the institutionalized delinquent. *Internat. J. Group Psychother.*, 8:265-275.

11059 **SHELLY, J. A.** (1966), Daytop Lodge: halfway house for addicts on probation. *Rehab. Record*, 7:19-21.

11060 **SHELLY, M. W.**, and **STEDRY, A. C.** (1968), Toward the design of a group: a preliminary model. *Psychol. Reports*, 22:1177-1189.

11061 **SHELTON, J. T.** (1970), Habilitation of disturbed adolescent male retardates. *Ment. Retard.*, 7:132-133.

11062 **SHELTON, S. C.**, and **NIX, C.** (1979), Development of a divorce adjustment group program in a social service agency. *Soc. Casework*, 60:309-312.

11063 **SHEPHARD, C. S.** (1975), The effect of group counseling on death anxiety in children with cancer. *Dissert. Abstr. Internat.*, 36:2723A.

11064 **SHEPARD, H. A.** (1956), Test flight: a group dream. *Group Psychother., Psychodrama & Sociometry*, 9:44-62.

11065 **SHEPARD, H. A.**, and **BENNIS, W. G.** (1956), A theory of training by group methods. *Human Relat.*, 9:403-414.

11066 **SHEPARD, M.**, and **LEE, M.** (1970), *Marathon 16*. New York: G. P. Putnam's Sons.

11067 **SHEPHERD, J. C.** (1973), An evaluation of group and individual models of career counseling. *Dissert. Abstr. Internat.*, 34:3071A.

11068 **SHEPS, J.** (1964), Group therapy in schizophrenia. *Internat. Psychiat. Clinics*, 1:911-928.

11069 **SHEPSTONE, A.** (1967), Practical nursing with groups. *Nursing Times*, (London) 63:1413-1414.

11070 **SHERE, E.**, and **TEICHMAN, Y.** (1971), Evaluation of group therapy with pre-adolescent girls: assessment of therapeutic effects based on Rorschach records. *Internat. J. Group Psychother.*, 21:99-104.

11071 **SHERIDAN, E. P.**, **SHACK, J.**, **WALKER, R. E.**, **SHERIDAN, K.**, **EGAN, G.**, and **LAVIGNE, J.** (1973), A training program for small group leaders: ii. evaluation. *J. Community Psychol.*, 1:8-12.

11072 **SHERIDAN, K.**, **SHERIDAN, E. P.**, **SHACK, J.**, **WALKER, R. E.**, **EGAN, G.**, and **LAVIGNE, J.** (1973), A training program for small-group leaders: i. overview. *J. Community Psychol.*, 1:3-7.

11073 **SHERMAN, R. W.**, and **HILDRETH, A. M.** (1970), A resident group process training seminar. *Amer. J. Psychiat.*, 127:372-375.

11074 **SHERMAN, S.** (1943), A system of combined individual and group therapy as used in the medical program for merchant seamen. *Amer. J. Psychiat.*, 100:127-130.

11075 **SHERMAN, S. H.** (1967), Alcoholism and group therapy. *Rational Living*, 2:20-23.

11076 **SHERRARD, P. A. D.** (1974), Predicting group leader/member interaction: the efficacy of the Ivey taxonomy. *Dissert. Abstr. Internat.*, 34:6392-6393.

11077 **SHERRY, P.**, and **HURLEY, J. R.** (1976), Curative factors in psychotherapeutic and growth groups. *J. Clin. Psychol.*, 30:835-837.

11078 **SHERTZER, B.** (1971), *Teachers' Guide to Group Vocational Guidance*. Cambridge, MA: Bellman Publishing.

11079 **SHERWOOD, C. C.** (1956), Some recommendations for research in the field of group psychotherapy. *Group Psychother., Psychodrama & Sociometry*, 9:126-132.

11080 **SHERWOOD, M.** (1964), Bion's experiences in groups: a critical evaluation. *Human Relat.*, 17:113-130.

11081 **SHEWCHUK, L. A.** (1977), Preliminary observations on an intervention program for heavy smokers. *Internat. J. Addict.*, 12:323-336.

11082 **SHICHOR, D.** (1970), Nonconformity patterns of different types of leaders in small groups. *Compar. Group Studies*, 1:269-274.

11083 **SHIELDS, E. E.** (1970), The effect of varied group and individual counseling methods upon culturally different freshmen. *Dissert. Abstr. Internat.*, 31:2692-2693.

11084 **SHIGLEY, R. H.** (1973), A comparison of group administered punishment and individually administered punishment to suppress inappropriate classroom behavior. *Dissert. Abstr. Internat.*, 34:4028B.

11085 **SHIHADEH, E. S.** (1979), Peer counseling and parolees perceptions of rehabilitative values. *J. Psychology*, 10:135.

11086 **SHILLING, C. S.** (1979), Relationship between the assertive behavior of parents and the behavior of their children. *Amer. J. Fam. Ther.*, 7:59-64.

11087 **SHIMAHARA, N. K.** (1979), *Adaptation and Education in Japan*. New York: Holt, Rinehart and Winston.

11088 **SHINEDLING, M. M.**, **JERRY, D. W.**, and **RAVSTEN, L. A.** (1975), Short-term hedonism: therapy for patients who cannot delay gratification. *Hosp. & Community Psychiat.*, 26:133-136.

11089 **SHINFUKO, N.** (1975), (Experience of group psychotherapy at Hizen National Sanitarium.) *Kyushu Neuro-Psychiat.*, (Fukuoka) 21:200-208.

11090 **SHIPLEY, R. H.** (1977), Effect of a pregroup collective project on the cohesiveness of inpatient therapy groups. *Psychol. Reports*, 41:79-85.

11091 **SHIPTON, B.**, and **SPAIN, A.** (1980), The influence of client fees on evaluations by clients of counseling outcome. *Psychology*, 17:1-4.

11092 **SHLENSKY, R.** (1972), Issues raised in group process with blind precollege students. *Adolescence*, 7:427-434.

11093 **SHLIEN, J. M.** (1956), A criterion of psychological health. *Group Psychother., Psychodrama & Sociometry*, 9:149-152.

11094 **SHOEMAKER, R., GUY, W.**, and **McLAUGHLIN, J.** (1955), The usefulness of group therapy at atopic eczema. *Penn. Med. J.*, 58:603-609.

11095 **SHOEMAKER, R. J., GUY, W. B.**, and **McLAUGHLIN, J. T.** (1954), The usefulness of group therapy in the management of atopic eczema. *Penn. Med. J.*, 58:603-609.

11096 **SHOEMAKER, W. F.** (1972), Changes in measured self-actualization as influenced by a group counseling procedure. *Dissert. Abstr. Internat.*, 32:4361A.

11097 **SHOMER, R. W.**, and **CENTERS, R.** (1970), Differences in attitudinal responses under conditions of implicitly manipulated group salience. *J. Personality & Soc. Psychol.*, 15:125-132.

11098 **SHOOBS, N. E.** (1946), The application of individual psychology through psychodramatics. *Individ. Psychol. Bull.*, 5:3-21.

11099 **SHOOBS, N. E.** (1956), Individual psychology and psychodrama. *Amer. J. Individ. Psychol.*, 12:46-52.

11100 **SHOOBS, N. E.** (1944), Psychodrama in the schools. *Sociometry*, 7:152-168.

11101 **SHOOBS, N. E.** (1943), The psychodramatic approach to classroom problems. *Sociometry*, 6:264-265.

11102 **SHOR, J. A.** (1948), A modified psychodrama technique for rehabilitation of military psychoneurotics. *Sociatry*, 1:414-420.

11103 **SHORE, H.** (1966), The institution for the aged of the future. *J. Jewish Communal Serv.*, 42:355-363.

11104 **SHORE, M. F., MASSIMO, J. L.**, and **RICKS, D. F.** (1965), A factor analytic study of psychotherapeutic change in delinquent boys. *J. Clin. Psychol.*, 21:208-212.

11105 **SHORT, J. F.**, and **STRODTBECK, F. L.** (1956), *Group Process and Gang Delinquency.* Chicago: University of Chicago Press.

11106 **SHORT, M. C.**, and **SINGER, M. J.** (1972), Group work with youths on parole. *Soc. Work*, 17:78-85.

11107 **SHORT, R.** (1948), Role-playing in adult Spanish classes. *Sociatry*, 2:333-335.

11108 Short-term group psychotherapy aids coronary patients' wives. (1969), *Roche Report: Front. Hosp. Psychiat.*, 6:1-2, 8-11.

11109 **SHOSTROM, E. L.** (1969), Group therapy: let the buyer beware. *Psychol. Today*, 2:36-40.

11110 **SHOSTROM, E. L.** (1968), Replies to Danet, Lubin, and Hurvitz. *Amer. Psychologist*, 23:760-761.

11111 **SHOSTROM, E. L.** (1968), Witnessed group therapy on commercial television. *Amer. Psychologist*, 23:207-209.

11112 **SHRADER, W. K., ALTMAN, S.**, and **LEVENTHAL, T.** (1969), A didactic approach to structure in short-term group therapy. *Amer. J. Orthopsychiat.*, 39:493-497.

11113 **SHRADER, W. K.**, and **BECKENSTEIN, L.** (1966), Reality-oriented group therapy. *Hosp. & Community Psychiat.*, 17:239-240.

11114 **SHRAUGER, J. S.** (1972), Self-esteem and reactions to being observed by others. *J. Personality & Soc. Psychol.*, 23:192-200.

11115 **SHUBIN, S.** (1979), Rx for stress: your stress. *Nursing 79*, 9:52-55.

11116 **SHUFER, S.** (1977), Communicating with young children: teaching via the play–discussion group. part 1. *Amer. J. Nursing*, 78:1960-1962.

11117 **SHUGART, G.**, and **LOOMIS, E. A.** (1954), Psychodrama with parents of hospitalized schizophrenic children. *Group Psychother., Psychodrama & Sociometry*, 7:118-124.

11118 **SHULMAN, B.** (1957), Group psychotherapy in an army post stockade. *J. Soc. Ther.*, 3:14-18.

11119 **SHULMAN, B. H.** (1951), Group therapy with adolescent: an experiment. *Individ. Psychol. Bull.*, 9:86-91.

11120 **SHULMAN, B. H.** (1960), A psychodramatically oriented action technique in group psychotherapy. *Group Psychother., Psychodrama & Sociometry*, 13:34-39.

11121 **SHULMAN, B. H.** (1962), The use of dramatic confrontation in group psychotherapy. *Psychiat. Quart. Suppl.*, 36:93-99.

11122 **SHULMAN, M. H.** (1945), Delinquency treatment in the controlled activity group. *Amer. Sociol. Rev.*, 10:405-414.

11123 **SHULMAN, L.** (1967), Scapegoats, group workers, and preemptive intervention. *Soc. Work*, 12:37-43.

11124 **SHUNTICH, R. J.**, and **REISING, P. E.** (1977), Assumed personality characteristics of counseling center growth group participants. *J. Psychology*, 97:221-226.

11125 **SHUR, M. S.** (1976), A group counseling program for low self-esteem adolescent females in the fifth grade. *Dissert. Abstr. Internat.*, 36:5839A.

11126 **SHUTER, R. M.** (1974), The free school: a case study in environmental influence on small group behavior. *Dissert. Abstr. Internat.*, 34:6159.

11127 **SHUTTS, E. L.** (1970), The effects of group games counseling and group centered counseling with a population of hospitalized children and adolescents. *Dissert. Abstr. Internat.*, 30:5247A.

11128 **SILBERGELD, S., THUNE, E. S.**, and **MANDERSCHEID, W.** (1980), Marital role dynamics during brief group psychotherapy: assessment of verbal interactions. *J. Clin. Psychol.*, 36:480-491.

11129 **SIDMAN, J.**, and **OLSON, W. M.** (1967), Helping behavior as a function of staff and patient roles in psychotherapy groups: a pilot study. *J. Fort Logan Ment. Health Ctr.*, 4:97-113.

11130 **SIEBENTHALL, C. A.** (1973), The effect of group and individual counseling on achievement and self concept with coordinated vocational academic education students. *Dissert. Abstr. Internat.*, 33:4101A.

11131 **SIEBERT, E.** (1978), (Review of L. Kreeger's *Psychotherapy and Large Group.*) *Dynam. Psychiat.*, (Berlin) 11:82-84.

11132 **SIEBOLD, P.**, and **RABINOWITZ, O.** (1977), Problems of identity in group treatment of mothers. *Group*, 1:90-99.

11133 **SIEGEL, A.** (1970), A hospital program for young adults. *Arch. Gen. Psychiat.*, 22:166-178.

11134 **SIEGEL, B.** (1971), Group psychotherapy: its effects on mothers who rate social performance of retardates. *Amer. J. Psychiat.*, 127:9-3.

11135 **SIEGEL, E. M.** (1972), The effects of lecture–discussion and group-centered counseling on parents of moderately mentally retarded children. *Dissert. Abstr. Internat.*, 33:978A.

11136 **SIEGEL, L. J.** (1955), Homosexuality-psychotherapeutic approach and its criminogenic challenge. *Group Psychother., Psychodrama & Sociometry*, 8:321-325.

11137 **SIEGEL, M.** (1965), Group psychotherapy with gifted underachieving college students. *Community Ment. Health J.*, 1:188-194.

11138 **SIEGEL, M.** (1973), Individual and group psychotherapy: fads and foolishness. *Psychother.: Theory, Res. & Pract.*, 10:261-264.

11139 **SIEGEL, M.** (1965), Recent experience of a therapist as a patient in group psychotherapy. *Topical Probl. Psychol. & Psychiat.*, 5:5-10.

11140 **SIEGEL, M.** (1972), Special problems in group psychotherapy practice. In: *Practical Problems of a Private Psychotherapy Practice*, eds. G. D. Goldman and G. Stricker. Springfield, IL: C C Thomas.

11141 **SIEGEL, M.** (1971), Use and misuse of group techniques in education, industry, and consulting practice. *Group Process*, (London) 3:5-6.

11142 **SIEGEL, M. G.** (1944), The Rorschach test as an aid in selecting clients for group therapy and evaluating progress. *Ment. Hygiene*, 28:444-449.

11143 **SIEGEL, N. H.** (1964), What is a therapeutic community? *Nursing Outlook*, 12:49-51.

11144 **SIEGEL, S.,** and **ZAJONC, R. B.** (1967), Group risk taking in professional decisions. *Sociometry*, 30:339-349.

11145 **SIEGERT, F. A.** (1978), The cost-effectiveness of individual and group behavior therapy for parents of problem children. *Dissert. Abstr. Internat.*, 39:5088B.

11146 **SIEGLER, S.** (1971), Play production as a technique of group counseling with disadvantaged Negro adolescents. *Dissert. Abstr. Internat.*, 32:3105A.

11147 **SIEVEKING, N. A.** (1970), Systematic desensitization in groups with institutionalized adolescents. *Dissert. Abstr. Internat.*, 30:4383.

11148 **SIEVER, L. M.** (1961), A layman leads a great books group in a mental hospital. *Ment. Hygiene*, 45:537-542.

11149 **SIFNEOS, P. E.** (1969), The interdisciplinary team: an educational experience for mental health professionals. *Psychiat. Quart.*, 43:123-130.

11150 **SIGAL, J., BRAVERMAN, S.,** and **PILON, R.** (1976), Effects of teacher-led, curriculum–integrated sensitivity training in a large high school. *J. Educat. Res.*, 70:3-9.

11151 **SIGRELL, B.** (1965), (Group therapy research problems.) *Nordisk Psykol.*, (Copenhagen) 17:449-454.

11152 **SIGRELL, B.** (1971), Nagra gruppsykoterapeutiska fragestallningar. (Some group therapeutic problems.) *Nordisk Psykol.*, (Copenhagen) 23:188-199.

11153 **SIGRELL, B.** (1970), Group psychotherapy: studies of processes in therapeutic groups. *Dissert. Abstr. Internat.*, 31:3008.

11154 **SIGRELL, B.** (1968), *Group Psychotherapy: Studies of Processes in Therapeutic Groups*. Stockholm: Almqvist and Wiksell.

11155 **SIGURDSON, H. R.** (1969), Expanding the role of the non–professional. *Crime & Delinquency*, 15:420-429.

11156 **SIKES, M. P.** (1971), Police-community relations laboratory: the Houston model. *Prof. Psychol.*, 2:39-45.

11157 **SIKES, W. W.** (1971), An organizational development workshop for a college. *Soc. Change*, 4:4-6.

11158 **SILBERFORB, P. M.** (1980), Psychosocial aspects of neoplastic disease: iii. group support for the oncology nurse. *Gen. Hosp. Psychiat.*, 2:192.

11159 **SILBERGELD, S., KOENIG, G. R., MANDERSCHEID, R. W., MEEKER, B. F.,** and **HORNUNG, C. A.** (1975), Assessment of environment–therapy systems: the group atmosphere scale. *J. Consult. & Clin. Psychol.*, 43:460-469.

11160 **SILBERGELD, S., MANDERSCHEID, R. W.,** and **KOENIG, J. R.** (1977), Psychosocial environment in group therapy evaluation. *Internat. J. Group Psychother.*, 27:153-163.

11161 **SILBERGELD, S., MANDERSCHEID, R. W.,** and **SOEKEN, D. R.** (1976),

Issues at the clinical–research interface: placebo effect control groups. *J. Nerv. & Ment. Diseases*, 163:147-153.

11162 **SILBERGELD, S., MANDERSCHEID, R. W., O'NEILL, P. H., LAMPRECHT, F., and LORENZ, K. Y.** (1975), Changes in serum dopamine-beta-hydroxylase activity during group psychotherapy. *Psychosomat. Med.*, 37:352-367.

11163 **SILBERGELD, S., THUNE, E. S., and MANDERSCHEID, R. W.** (1979), The group therapist leadership role. *Small Group Behav.*, 10:176-199.

11164 Silent observers may aid group therapy (1968), *Roche Report: Front. Hosp. Psychiat.*, 5:2.

11165 **SILKWORTH, W. D.** (1939), A new approach to psychotherapy in chronic alcoholism. *Lancet*, 57:312-315.

11167 **SILVA, A.** (1979), Group dynamics and intervention with the psychiatric nursing personnel. *Minerva Psichiat.*, (Turin) 20:257-266.

11168 **SILVA, M. C.** (1979), Effects of orientation information on spouses anxiety and attitudes toward hospitalization and surgery. *Res. Nursing & Health*, 2:127-136.

11169 **SILVA, M. M.** (1971), Experiencia institucional: Reemplazo de la pareja terapéutica en un grupo de funcionamiento. (Institutional experience: replacement of a therapeutic couple in a functioning group.) *Acta Psiquiat. Psicol. Amer. Latina*, (Buenos Aires) 17:116-120.

11170 **SILVER, A.** (1950), Group psychotherapy with senile psychotic patients. *Geriatrics*, 5:147-150.

11171 **SILVER, A. W.** (1963), Delinquents in group therapy. *Amer. J. Orthopsychiat.*, 33:754-756.

11172 **SILVER, A. W.** (1967), Inter-relating group-dynamic, therapeutic, and psychodynamic concepts. *Internat. J. Group Psychiat.*, 17:139-150.

11173 **SILVER, A. W.** (1964), A therapeutic discussion group in a detention home for adolescents awaiting hospital commitment. *Internat. J. Group Psychother.*, 14:502-503.

11174 **SILVER, G. M.** (1978), Systematic presentation of pre-therapy information in group psychotherapy: its relationship to attitude and behavioral change. *Dissert. Abstr. Internat.*, 38:4481-4482B. (University Microfilms No. 7732501.)

11175 **SILVER, R. J., and CONYNE, R. K.** (1977), Effects of direct experience and vicarious experience on group therapeutic attraction. *Small Group Behav.*, 8:83-93.

11176 **SILVER, R. J., LUBIN, B., SILVER, D. S., and DOBSON, N. H.** (1980), The group psychotherapy literature, 1979. *Internat. J. Group Psychother.*, 30:491-538.

11177 **SILVERMAN, H.** (1969), Sensitivity training and the establishment. *J. Group Psychoanal. & Process*, (London) 2:89-94.

11178 **SILVERSTEIN, S.** (1969), A new venture in group work with the aged. *Soc. Casework*, 50:573-580.

11179 **SIMKINS, L., and WEST, J.** (1965), Modification of verbal interactions in triad groups: preliminary report. *Psychol. Reports*, 16:684.

11180 **SIMKINS, L., and WEST, J.** (1966), Reinforcement of duration of talking in triad groups. *Psychol. Reports*, 18:231-236.

11181 **SIMM, U.** (1961), (Group therapy with alcoholics in an institution.) *Socialmed. Tidskr.*, (Stockholm) 38:183-190.

11182 **SIMMEL, E.** (1944), War neuroses. In: *Psychoanalysis Today*, ed. S. Lorand. New York: International Universities Press, pp. 227-248.

11183 **SIMMONS, R.** (1971), Sociodrama of Black students at a White preparatory school. *Group Psychother., Psychodrama & Sociometry*, 24:121-124.

11184 **SIMMONS, R. C.** (1971), Intensity as a variable in programmed group interaction: the marathon. *Dissert. Abstr. Internat.*, 32:2494A.

11185 **SIMMONS, W. D.** (1954), The group approach to weight reduction: i. a review of the project. *J. Amer. Dietetic Assn.*, 30:437-441.

11186 **SIMNEGAR, R.** (1978), The effects of group therapy on values and behavioral adjustment of chronic hospitalized patients. *Dissert. Abstr. Internat.*, 38:6174B-6175B. (University Microfilms No. 7808138.)

11187 **SIMON, B.** (1946), The treatment of the neuropsychiatric patient in an army hospital. *Med. Clinics North Amer.*, 31:459-472.

11188 **SIMON, B., HOLZBERG, J. D., AARON, S.,** and **SAXE, C. H.** (1947), Group therapy from the viewpoint of the patient. *J. Nerv. & Ment. Diseases*, 105:156-170.

11189 **SIMON, E.** (1956), Tentative impressions about the efficacy of group therapy in psychosomatic disorders. *Acta Med. Orient.*, 15:195-200.

11190 **SIMON, F. B.** (1977), (Dangers of paradoxical communication in a "therapeutic community.") *Psychiat. Praxis*, (Stuttgart) 4:38-43.

11191 **de SIMON, G.,** and **de PERROT, E.** (1963), (First observations on a trial with 2–focus group psychotherapy.) *Annales Medico–Psychol.*, (Paris) 121:205-214.

11192 **SIMON, J.** (1977), Evaluation of EST as an adjunct to group psychotherapy in treatment of severe alcoholism. *Biosci. Communicat.*, (Basel) 3:141-148.

11193 **SIMON, J.** (1979), Review of H. Mullan's and M. Rosenbaum's *Group Psychotherapy: Theory and Practice. Amer. J. Psychiat.*, 136:1359.

11194 **SIMON, N. M.,** and **WHITELEY, S.** (1977), Psychiatric consultation with MICU nurses: the consultation conference as a working group. *Heart & Lung*, 6:497-504.

11195 **SIMON, P.,** and **ALBERT, L.** (1975), *Les Relations Interpersonnelles: Une Approache Expérientielle dans un Milieu Laboratoire.* (*Interpersonal Relations: An Experimental Approach in a Laboratory Setting.*) Montreal: Agence d'Arc.

11196 **SIMON, R. J.** (1964), Psychotherapy techniques and problems with severe schizophrenics: psychodrama versus direct analysis. *Internat. J. Sociometry & Sociatry*, 4:83-87.

11197 **SIMONS, R. A.** (1970), Diagnostic intake: variation on a theme. *Ment. Hygiene*, 54:101-104.

11198 **SIMONS, R. C.,** and **STOCKTON, W. J.** (1965), The use of an ongoing training group in a military mental hygiene clinic. *Internat. J. Group Psychother.*, 15:228-241.

11199 **SIMS, G. K.,** and **SIMS, J. M.** (1973), Does face-to-face contact reduce counselee responsiveness with emotionally insecure youth? *Psychother.: Theory, Res. & Pract.*, 10:348-351.

11200 **SINGER, D. L., ASTRACHAN, B. M., GOULD, L. J.,** and **KLEIN, E. B.** (1975), Boundary management in psychological work with groups. *J. Appl. Behav. Science*, 11:137-176.

11201 **SINGER, H. A.** (1972), Training a city in sensitivity. *Training & Develop. J.*, 26:20-30.

11202 **SINGER, J. L.,** and **GOLDMAN, G. D.** (1954), Experimentally contrasted social atmospheres in group psychotherapy with chronic schizophrenics. *J. Soc. Psychol.*, 40:23-37.

11203 **SINGER, M.** (1974), Comments and caveats regarding adolescent groups in a combined approach. *Internat. J. Group Psychother.*, 24:429-438.

11204 **SINGER, M.,** and **FISCHER, R.** (1967), Group psychotherapy of male homosexuals by a male and female co-therapy team. *Internat. J. Group Psychother.*, 17:44-52.

11205 **SINGER, R. D.** (1961), A note on the use of the semantic differential as a predictive device in milieu therapy. *J. Clin. Psychol.*, 17:376-378.

11206 **SINGER, W. B.** (1952), Post-hypnotic suggestion in group therapy: a note. *J. Clin. Psychol.*, 8:205.

11207 **SINGLER, J. R.** (1975), Group work with hospitalized stroke patients. *Soc. Casework*, 56:348-354.

11208 **SINGLETON, R. A., Jr.** (1974), Group discussion, others' decisions, others' arguments, and the choice shift phenomenon. *Dissert. Abstr. Internat.*, 34:3543.

11209 **SINICK, D.** (1979), Professional development in counseling older persons. *Counselor Educat. & Supervision*, 19:4-12.

11210 **SINROD, H.** (1964), Communication through paintings in a therapy group. *Bull. Art Ther.*, 3:133-147.

11211 **SIRBU, W. I.** (1978), Behavioral parent training in groups: an evaluation. *Dissert. Abstr. Internat.*, 38:6175B. (University Microfilms No. 7808578.)

11212 **SIROKA, E.** (1968), Spontaneity theatre as an aid to emotional education. *J. Emot. Educat.*, 8:212-219.

11213 **SIROKA, E. K.** (1974), The nonresidential therapeutic community as a treatment modality. *Dissert. Abstr. Internat.*, 35:3036-3037.

11214 **SIROKA, R.** (1964), Sociodrama and the Negro family. *Internat. J. Sociometry & Sociatry*, 4:91-93.

11215 **SIROKA, R. W.** (1978), From drama to psychodrama. *Art Psychother.*, 5:15-18.

11216 **SIROKA, R. W., SIROKA, E. K.,** and **SCHLOSS, G. A.** (1971), *Sensitivity Training and Group Encounter: An Introduction.* New York: Grosset and Dunlap.

11217 **SIROKY, H.** (1962), Diagnosticke aspekty psychodramatu. (Diagnostic aspects of psychodrama.) *Ceskoslav. Psychol.*, (Prague) 6:154-165.

11218 **SIROKY, H.** (1963), Psychodrama as a modern instrument for moral education. *Internat. J. Sociometry & Sociatry*, 3:3-4.

11219 **SISEK, I.,** and **ROBIC-KUDLEK, K.** (1976), (Group psychotherapy of schizophrenics and their parallel inclusion in the hospital ward therapeutic community.) *Soc. Psihijat.*, (Belgrade) 4:315-319.

11220 **SISNEY, V. V.,** and **SHEWMAKER, K. L.** (1964), Group psychotherapy in a church setting. *Pastoral Psychol.*, 15:36-40.

11221 **SISSON, P. J.** (1970), An interaction process analysis of extended group counseling with psychiatry residents. *Dissert. Abstr. Internat.*, 31:3887A.

11222 **SISSON, P. J.** (1973), Extended group counseling with psychiatry residents: an interaction process analysis. *Small Group Behav.*, 4:466-475.

11223 **SIVADON, P., ALIZON, J.,** and **MASSE, J.** (1952), (Group psychotherapy as a cure of a state of generalized intolerance.) *Annales Médico-Psychol.*, (Paris) 110:521-525.

11224 **SIVADON, P.,** and **BAUME, S.** (1952), Le club de post cure dépelan. (The post cure wind-down group.) *Annales Médico-Psychol.*, (Paris) 110:489-492.

11225 **SIVADON, P., FOLLIN, S.,** and **TOURNAUD, S.** (1952), Les clubs sociothérapiques a l'hôpital psychiatrique. (Sociotherapy groups in a psychiatric hospital.) *Annales Médico-Psychol.*, (Paris) 110:489-492.

11226 **SJOBERG, C.** (1967), (Sociotherapy in Lillhagen Hospital.) *Svenska Lakartidningen*, (Stockholm) 64:3488-3491.

11227 **SJOHAGEN, A.** (1958), Gruppsykoterapi i alkoholistvarden. (Group psychotherapy in hospitals for alcoholics.) *Socialmed. Tidskr.*, (Stockholm) 35:243-245.

11228 **SJOSTROM, K.** (1961), (Group activity with alcoholics in an open ward.) *Socialmed. Tidskr.*, (Stockholm) 38:329-333.

11229 **SKALIČANOVÁ, M.** (1977), Suggestive and group psychotherapy in some children's somatic diseases. *Ceskoslav. Psychiat.*, (Prague) 23:174-177.
11230 **SKINNER, K.** (1980), Support group for nurses. *Nursing Outlook*, 28:296-299.
11231 **SKJOITEN, M.**, and **BARTLETT, R. M.** (1968), Student volunteers as group leaders in elementary schools. *Children*, 15:225-228.
11232 **SKLAR, A. D.** (1970), Time-extended group therapy: a controlled study. *Compar. Group Studies*, 1:373-386.
11233 **SKLAR, N. E.**, and **BELLIS, J. M., Jr.** (1969), The challenge: adjustment of retarded adolescents in a workshop. *J. Rehab.*, 35:19-21.
11234 **SKOLNICK, N. J.** (1979), Personality change in drug abusers: a comparison of therapeutic community and prison groups. *J. Consult. & Clin. Psychol.*, 47:768-770.
11235 **SKORPEN, E.** (1971), Great tasks. *J. Religion & Health*, 10:226-245.
11236 **SKOVHOLT, T., RESNICK, J. L.**, and **DEWEY, C. R.** (1979), Weight treatment: a group approach to weight control. *Psychother.: Theory, Res. & Pract.*, 16:118.
11237 **SKYNNER, A.** (1975), An experiment in group consultation with the staff of a comprehensive school. In: *Group Psychotherapy from the Southwest*, ed. M. Rosenbaum. New York: Gordon/Breach.
11238 **SKYNNER, A. C. R.** (1968), A family of family casework agencies. *Internat. J. Group Psychother.*, 18:352-360.
11239 **SKYNNER, A. C. R.** (1977), Family therapy and group therapy: similarities and differences. *Internat. J. Group Psychother.*, 27:113-115.
11240 **SKYNNER, A. C. R.** (1977), Marital problems and their treatment. *Group*, 1:245-252.
11241 **SKYNNER, A. L.** (1969), A group-analytic approach to conjoint family therapy. *J. Child Psychol. & Psychiat.*, 10:81-106.
11242 **SKYNNER, R.** (1975), The large group in training. In: *The Large Group: Dynamics and Therapy*, ed. L. Kreeger. London: Constable.
11243 **SLAGER, J. B.** (1972), Leader personality type as a factor of change in t-groups. *Dissert. Abstr. Internat.*, 33:2724A.
11244 **SLAIKEU, K. A.** (1973), Evaluation studies on group treatment of juvenile and adult offenders in correctional institutions: a review of the literature. *J. Res. Crime & Delinquency*, 10:87-100.
11245 **SLANEY, R. B.** (1978), Review of M. Seligman's *Group Counseling and Group Psychotherapy with Rehabilitation Clients. Rehab. Couns. Bull.*, 21:266-268.
11246 **SLATER, M. R.** (1964), *Sex Offenders in Group Therapy.* Nashville: Sherbourne.
11248 **SLATER, M. R.** (1964), *Sex Offenders in Group Therapy: The Personal Experiences of a Clinical Psychologist in Criminal Group Therapy.* Los Angeles: Sherbourne Press.
11249 **SLATER, P.** (1966), *Microcosm, Structural, Psychological, and Religious Evolution in Groups.* New York: J. Wiley and Sons.
11250 **SLAVINSKA-HOLY, N.** (1975), Spatio-temporal considerations in psychoanalytic group psychotherapy of severely disturbed patients. In: *Group Therapy 1975: An Overview*, eds. L. R. Wolberg and M. L. Aronson. New York: Stratton Intercontinental Medical Books.
11251 **SLAVSON, S.** (1959), A bioquantum theory of the ego and its application to analytic group psychotherapy. *Internat. J. Group Psychother.*, 9:3-30.
11252 **SLAVSON, S. R.** (1947), Activity group therapy with character deviations in children. In: *The Practice of Group Therapy*, ed. S. R. Slavson. New York: International Universities Press.
11253 **SLAVSON, S. R.** (1950), *Analytic Group Psychotherapy with Children, Adolescents and Adults.* New York: Columbia University Press.

11254 **SLAVSON, S. R.** (1969), The anatomy and clinical applications of group interaction. *Internat. J. Group Psychother.*, 19:3-15.
11255 **SLAVSON, S. R.** (1970), Are sensitivity groups valid supplements in an emotionally dehumanized society? *Sandoz Psychiat. Spectator*, 6:6, 8-9.
11256 **SLAVSON, S. R.** (1957), Are there "group dynamics" in therapy groups? *Internat. J. Group Psychother.*, 7:131-154.
11257 **SLAVSON, S. R.** (1951), Authority, restraint and discipline in group therapy with children. *Nerv. Children*, 9:187-195.
11258 **SLAVSON, S. R.** (1971), *"Because I Live Here": The Theory and Practice of Vita-Erg Ward Therapy with Deteriorated Psychotic Women.* New York: International Universities Press.
11259 **SLAVSON, S. R.** (1959), A bioquantum theory of the ego and its application to analytic group psychotherapy. *Internat. J. Group Psychother.*, 9:3-30.
11260 **SLAVSON, S. R.** (1951), Catharsis in group psychotherapy. *Psychoanal. Rev.*, 38:39-52.
11261 **SLAVSON, S. R.** (1974), *Child Centered Group Guidance of Parents.* New York: International Universities Press.
11262 **SLAVSON, S. R.** (1953), Common sources of error and confusion in group psychotherapy. *Internat. J. Group Psychother.*, 3:3-28.
11263 **SLAVSON, S. R.** (1956), Community mental health. In: *The Fields of Group Psychotherapy*, ed. S. R. Slavson. New York: International Universities Press.
11264 **SLAVSON, S. R.** (1947), Contra-indications of group therapy for patients with psychopathic personalities. In: *The Practice of Group Therapy*, ed. S. R. Slavson. New York: International Universities Press.
11265 **SLAVSON, S. R.** (1954), A contribution to a systematic theory of group psychotherapy. *Internat. J. Group Psychother.*, 4:3-30.
11266 **SLAVSON, S. R.** (1955), Criteria for selection and rejection of patients for various types of group psychotherapy. *Internat. J. Group Psychother.*, 5:3-30.
11267 **SLAVSON, S. R.** (1962), A critique of the group therapy literature. *Acta Psychother. Psychosomat. Orthopaedagog.*, (Basel) 10:62-73.
11268 **SLAVSON, S. R.** (1951), Current trends in group psychotherapy. *Internat. J. Group Psychother.*, 1:7-15.
11269 **SLAVSON, S. R.** (1975), Current trends in group psychotherapy. *Internat. J. Group Psychother.*, 25:131-140.
11270 **SLAVSON, S. R.** (1945), Differential methods of group therapy in relation to age level. *Nerv. Children*, 4:196-210.
11271 **SLAVSON, S. R.** (1947), Differential dynamics of activity and interview group therapy. *Amer. J. Orthopsychiat.*, 17:293-302.
11272 **SLAVSON, S. R.** (1948), Discussion on group therapy. *Annual N.Y. Acad. Science*, 69:904-906.
11273 **SLAVSON, S. R.** (1951), The dynamics of analytic group psychotherapy. *Internat. J. Group Psychother.*, 1:208-217.
11274 **SLAVSON, S. R.** (1979), *Dynamics of Group Psychotherapy.* New York: J. Aronson and Sons.
11275 **SLAVSON, S. R.** (1970), Eclecticism versus sectarianism in group psychotherapy. *Internat. J. Group Psychother.*, 20:3-13.
11276 **SLAVSON, S. R.** (1957), Einige merkmale der analytischen gruppenpsychotherapie. (Some features of analytical group psychotherapy.) *Zeit. Diagnost. Psychol.*, 5:150-161.
11277 **SLAVSON, S. R.** (1947), An elementaristic approach to the understanding and treatment of delinquency. *Nerv. Children*, 6:413-423.
11278 **SLAVSON, S. R.** (1958), (Emergence of dynamic psychoanalytic factors

in group psychotherapy with adults.) *Rev. Française Psychoanal.*, (Paris) 22:693-704.

11279 **SLAVSON, S. R.** (1959), The era of group psychotherapy. *Acta Psychother., Psychosomat. Orthopaedagog.*, (Basel) 7:167-196.

11280 **SLAVSON, S. R.** (1946), Fields and objectives of group therapy. In: *Current Therapies of Personality Disorders*, ed. B. Glueck. New York: Grune and Stratton.

11281 **SLAVSON, S. R.** (1956), *The Fields of Group Psychotherapy*. New York: International Universities Press.

11282 **SLAVSON, S. R.** (1971), *The Fields of Group Psychotherapy*. New York: Schocken Books.

11283 **SLAVSON, S. R.** (1966), *The Fields of Group Psychotherapy*. New York: J. Wiley and Sons.

11284 **SLAVSON, S. R.** (1956), Freud's contributions to group psychotherapy. *Internat. J. Group Psychother.*, 6:349-357.

11285 **SLAVSON, S. R.** (1962), Further observations on group psychotherapy with adolescent delinquent boys in residential treatment: ii. patterns of acting-out of a transference neuroses by an adolescent boy. *Internat. J. Group Psychother.*, 12:211-224.

11286 **SLAVSON, S. R.** (1947), General principles and dynamics. In: *The Practice of Group Therapy*, ed. S. R. Slavson. New York: International Universities Press.

11287 **SLAVSON, S. R.** (1949), Group basis for mental health. *Ment. Hygiene*, 33:280-292.

11288 **SLAVSON, S. R.** (1947), The group in child guidance. In: *Handbook of Child Guidance*, ed. E. Harms. New York: Child Care Publications, pp. 402-412.

11289 **SLAVSON, S. R.** (1940), Group psychotherapy. *Ment. Hygiene*, 24:36-49.

11290 **SLAVSON, S. R.** (1950), Group psychotherapy. *Scient. Amer.*, 183:42-45.

11291 **SLAVSON, S. R.** (1946), Group psychotherapy. In: *Progress in Neurology and Psychology, Vol. 1*, ed. E. A. Spiegel. New York: Grune and Stratton, pp. 662-680.

11292 **SLAVSON, S. R.** (1955), Group psychotherapies. In: *Six Approaches to Group Psychotherapy*, eds. J. L. McCary and D. E. Sheer. New York: Dryden Press, pp. 127-178.

11293 **SLAVSON, S. R.** (1961), Group psychotherapy and the nature of schizophrenia. *Internat. J. Group Psychother.*, 11:3-32.

11294 **SLAVSON, S. R.** (1972), Group psychotherapy and the transference neurosis. *Internat. J. Group Psychother.*, 22:433-443.

11295 **SLAVSON, S. R.** (1970), Group psychotherapy: beginnings. *Voices*, 6:17-23.

11296 **SLAVSON, S. R.** (1950), Group psychotherapy in delinquency prevention. *J. Educat. Sociol.*, 24:45-51.

11297 **SLAVSON, S. R.** (1944), Group therapy at the Jewish Board of Guardians. *Ment. Hygiene*, 28:414-422.

11298 **SLAVSON, S. R.** (1948), Group therapy in child care and child guidance. *Jewish Soc. Serv. Quart.*, 25:203-213.

11299 **SLAVSON, S. R.** (1943), Group therapy: special section meeting, 1943, summary. *Amer. J. Orthopsychiat.*, 13:687-690.

11300 **SLAVSON, S. R.** (1945), Group therapy with children. In: *Modern Trends in Child Psychiatry*, eds. N. D. C. Lewis and B. L. Pacella. New York: International Universities Press, pp. 291-305.

11301 **SLAVSON, S. R.** (1975), In the beginning: *International Journal of Group Psychotherapy*. *Internat. J. Group Psychother.*, 25:147-151.

11302 **SLAVSON, S. R.** (1966), Interaction and reconstruction in group psychotherapy. *Internat. J. Group Psychother.*, 16:3-12.

11303 **SLAVSON, S. R.** (1951), *International Journal of Group Psychotherapy. Vol. 1, No. 1.* New York: International Universities Press.
11304 **SLAVSON, S. R.** (1943), *An Introduction to Group Therapy.* New York: Commonwealth.
11309 **SLAVSON, S. R.** (1949), Milieu and group treatment for delinquents. In: *National Conference of Social Work, Proceedings: Selected Papers, Seventy-Fifth Anniversary Meeting,* Atlantic City, New Jersey, April 17-23, 1948. New York: Columbia University Press.
11310 **SLAVSON, S. R.** (1956), The nature and treatment of acting out in group psychotherapy. *Internat. J. Group Psychother.,* 6:3-27.
11311 **SLAVSON, S. R.** (1965), Para-analytic group psychotherapy: a treatment of choice for adolescents. *Psychother. & Psychosomat.,* (Basel) 13:321-331.
11312 **SLAVSON, S. R.** (1959), Parallelisms in the development of group psychotherapy. *Internat. J. Group Psychother.,* 9:451-462.
11305 **SLAVSON, S. R.** (1953), *An Introduction to Group Therapy.* New York: International Universities Press.
11306 **SLAVSON, S. R.** (1952), *An Introduction to Group Therapy.* New York: International Universities Press.
11307 **SLAVSON, S. R. (Ed.)** (1970), *Introduction to Group Therapy.* New York: International Universities Press.
11308 **SLAVSON, S. R.** (1948), Milieu and group treatment for delinquents. In: *Bulwarks Against Crime,* Yearbook of the National Probation and Parole Assn., New York.
11314 **SLAVSON, S. R.** (1937), Personality qualifications for workers in group therapy. *Proceed. Nat. Conf. Jewish Soc. Serv.,* 14:154-159.
11315 **SLAVSON, S. R.** (1962), Personality qualifications of a group psychotherapist. *Internat. J. Group Psychother.,* 12:411-420.
11316 **SLAVSON, S. R.** (1966), The phenomenology and dynamics of silence in psychotherapy groups. *Internat. J. Group Psychother.,* 16:395-404.
11317 **SLAVSON, S. R.** (1951), Pioneers in group psychotherapy: Joseph H. Pratt. *Internat. J. Group Psychother.,* 1:95-99.
11318 **SLAVSON, S. R.** (1948), Play group therapy for young children. *Nerv. Children,* 7:318-327.
11320 **SLAVSON, S. R.** (1955), A preliminary note on the relationship of psychodrama and group psychotherapy. *Internat. J. Group Psychother.,* 5:361-366.
11321 **SLAVSON, S. R.** (1943), Principles and dynamics of group therapy. *Amer. J. Orthopsychiat.,* 13:650-659.
11322 **SLAVSON, S. R.** (1947), Qualifications and training of group therapists. *Ment. Hygiene,* 31:386-396.
11323 **SLAVSON, S. R.** (1956), Racial and cultural factors in group psychotherapy. *Internat. J. Group Psychother.,* 6:152-165.
11324 **SLAVSON, S. R.** (1960), Recent observations on group psychotherapy with adolescent delinquent boys in residential treatment: the scope and aims of the evaluation study. *Internat. J. Group Psychother.,* 10:176-179.
11325 **SLAVSON, S. R.** (1965), *Reclaiming the Delinquent by Para-Analytic Group Psychotherapy and the Inversion Technique.* New York: Free Press.
11326 **SLAVSON, S. R.** (1954), Remarks on group psychotherapy and community mental health. *Internat. J. Group Psychother.,* 4:210-217.
11327 **SLAVSON, S. R.** (1944), Some elements in activity group therapy. *Amer. J. Orthopsychiat.,* 14:578-588.
11328 **SLAVSON, S. R.** (1952), Some problems in group psychotherapy as seen by private practitioners. *Internat. J. Group Psychother.,* 2:54-66.
11329 **SLAVSON, S. R.** (1953), Sources of countertransference and group induced anxiety. *Internat. J. Group Psychother.,* 3:373-388.

11330 **SLAVSON, S. R.** (1956), Symptom versus syndrome in group psychotherapy. In: *The Fields of Group Psychotherapy*, ed. S. R. Slavson. New York: International Universities Press.
11331 **SLAVSON, S. R.** (1964), *A Textbook in Analytic Group Psychotherapy*. New York: International Universities Press.
11332 **SLAVSON, S. R.** (1943), The treatment of aggression: round table, 1943: vii. through group therapy. *Amer. J. Orthopsychiat.*, 13:419-427.
11333 **SLAVSON, S. R.** (1945), Treatment of withdrawal through group therapy. *Amer. J. Orthopsychiat.*, 15:681-689.
11334 **SLAVSON, S. R.** (1950), Transference phenomena in group psychotherapy. *Psychoanal. Rev.*, 37:39-55.
11335 **SLAVSON, S. R.** (1974), Types of group psychotherapy and their clinical applications. In: *The Challenge for Group Psychotherapy: Present and Future*, ed. S. deSchill. New York: International Universities Press.
11336 **SLAVSON, S. R.** (1945), Types of relationship and their application to psychotherapy. *Amer. J. Orthopsychiat.*, 15:267-277.
11337 **SLAVSON, S. R.** (1943), Value of the group in therapy. *Newsl. Amer. Assn. Psychiat. Soc. Work*, 13:57-59.
11339 **SLAVSON, S. R.** (1960), When is a "therapy group" not a therapy group? *Internat. J. Group Psychother.*, 10:3-21.
11340 **SLAVSON, S. R.**, and **HALLOWITZ, E.** (1949), Group psychotherapy. In: *Progress in Neurology and Psychiatry, Vol. IV*, ed. E. A. Spiegel. New York: Grune and Stratton.
11341 **SLAVSON, S. R.**, and **HALLOWITZ, E.** (1950), Group psychotherapy. In: *Progress in Neurology and Psychiatry, Vol. V*, ed. E. A. Spiegel. New York: Grune and Stratton, pp. 579-590.
11342 **SLAVSON, S. R.**, and **HALLOWITZ, E.** (1951), Group psychotherapy. In: *Progress in Neurology and Psychiatry, Vol. VI*, ed. E. A. Spiegel. New York: Grune and Stratton, pp. 518-532.
11343 **SLAVSON, S. R.**, **HALLOWITZ, E.**, and **KINSTLER, M.** (1950), *Bibliography on Group Psychotherapy*. New York: American Group Therapy Association.
11344 **SLAVSON, S. R.**, **HALLOWITZ, E.**, and **ROSENTHAL, L.** (1953), Group psychotherapy. In: *Progress in Neurology and Psychiatry, Vol. VIII*, ed. E. A. Spiegel. New York: Grune and Stratton.
11345 **SLAVSON, S. R.**, **HALLOWITZ, E.**, and **ROSENTHAL, L.** (1952), Group psychotherapy. In: *Progress in Neurology and Psychiatry, Vol. VII*, ed. E. A. Spiegel. New York: Grune and Stratton, pp. 527-540.
11346 **SLAVSON, S. R.**, **HALLOWITZ, E.**, and **ROSENTHAL, L.** (1954), Group psychotherapy. In: *Progress in Neurology and Psychiatry, Vol. IX*, ed. E. A. Spiegel. New York: Grune and Stratton.
11347 **SLAVSON, S. R.**, and **MacLENNAN, B.** (1956), Unmarried mothers. In: *The Fields of Group Psychotherapy*, ed. S. R. Slavson. New York: International Universities Press.
11348 **SLAVSON, S. R.**, and **MEYERS, G.** (1946), *Bibliography on Group Therapy*. New York: American Group Therapy Association, p. 12.
11349 **SLAVSON, S. R.**, and **SCHEIDLINGER, S.** (1947), Group psychotherapy. In: *Progress in Neurology and Psychiatry, Vol. II*, ed. E. A. Spiegel. New York: Grune and Stratton, pp. 473-490.
11350 **SLAVSON, S. R.**, and **SCHEIDLINGER, S.** (1948), Group psychotherapy. In: *Progress in Neurology and Psychiatry, Vol. III*, ed. E. A. Spiegel. New York: Grune and Stratton.
11351 **SLAVSON, S. R.**, and **SCHIFFER, M.** (1975), *Group Psychotherapies for Children: A Textbook*. New York: International Universities Press.
11352 **SLAVSON, S. R.**, **THAUN, G.**, **TENDLER, D.**, and **GABRIEL, B.** (1949), Children's activity in casework therapy. *J. Soc. Case Work*, 30:136-142.

11353 **SLAVSON, S. R., WIENER, H.,** and **SCHEIDLINGER, S.** (1945), Activity group therapy with a delinquent dull boy of eleven. *Nerv. Children*, 4:274-290.

11354 **SLAWSON, P. F.** (1965), Group psychotherapy with obese women. *Psychosomatics*, 6:206-209.

11355 **SLAWSON, P. F.** (1965), Psychodrama as a treatment for hospitalized patients: a controlled study. *Amer. J. Psychiat.*, 122:530-533.

11356 **SLIMMER, L. W.** (1978), Use of the nursing process to facilitate group therapy. *J. Psychiat. Nursing*, 16:42-44.

11357 **SLIVADON, P.** (1972), (Human environment and institutional therapy.) *Annales Medico-Psychol.*, (Paris) 2:123-127.

11358 **SLIVKIN, S. E.** (1970), One-to-one psychotherapy in a group setting with hospitalized psychotic patients. *Internat. J. Group Psychother.*, 20:63-76.

11359 **SLIVKIN, S. E.** (1976/1977), Psychiatric day hospital treatment of terminally ill patients. *Internat. J. Psychiat. Med.*, 7:123-131.

11360 **SLIVKIN, S. E.,** and **BERNSTEIN, N. R.** (1968), Goal–directed group psychotherapy for retarded adolescents. *Amer. J. Psychiat.*, 22:35-45.

11361 **SLOAN, M. B.** (1953), The special contribution of therapeutic group work in a psychiatric setting. *Group*, 15:11-18.

11362 **SLOVENKO, R.** (1977), Group-psychotherapy: privileged communication and confidentiality. *J. Psychiat. Law*, 5:405-466.

11363 **SLUGA, W.** (1970), Die psychotherapeutische situation im strafvollzug. (The psychotherapeutic situation in penal institutions.) *Zeit. Psychother. Med. Psychol.*, (Stuttgart) 20:75-83.

11364 **SLVADON, P.** (1972), (Human environment and institutional therapy.) *Annales Medico-Psychol.*, (Paris) 2:123-127.

11365 **SMAIL, D. J.** (1972), A grid measure of empathy in a therapeutic group. *Brit. J. Med. Psychol.*, (London) 45:165-170.

11366 **SMALL, I. F., MATARAZZO, R. G.,** and **SMALL, J. G.** (1963), Total ward therapy groups in psychiatric treatment. *Amer. J. Psychother.*, 14:254-265.

11367 **SMALL, I. F.,** and **SMALL, J. G.** (1963), The significance of the introduction in large group psychotherapy. *Internat. J. Soc. Psychiat.*, (London) 9:127-134.

11368 **SMALL, I. F., SMALL, G.,** and **POINER, V.** (1966), Anticipating the effects of program change. *J. Psychiat. Nursing*, 4:232-241.

11369 **SMART, R. G.** (1976), Outcome studies of therapeutic community and halfway house treatment for addicts. *Internat. J. Addict.*, 11:143-159.

11370 **SMIGEL, E. O.** (1961), A note on audience involvement and role playing in sociodrama. *Group Psychother., Psychodrama & Sociometry*, 14:66-67.

11371 **SMITH, A., SMITH, R., SANDERS, R., WEINMAN, B., KENNY, J.,** and **FITZGERALD, B.** (1963), Predicting the outcome of social therapy with chronic psychotics. *J. Abnorm. & Soc. Psychol.*, 66:351-357.

11372 **SMITH, A. B.,** and **BASSIN, A.** (1961), Application of small group therapy to crime and delinquency. *J. Soc. Ther.*, 7:76-85.

11373 **SMITH, A. B., BASSIN, A.,** and **FROEHLICH, A.** (1960), Change in attitudes and degree of verbal participation in group therapy with adult offenders. *J. Couns. Psychol.*, 24:247-249.

11374 **SMITH, A. B., BASSIN, A.,** and **FROEHLICH, A.** (1962), Interaction process and equilibrium in a therapy group of adult offenders. *J. Soc. Psychol.*, 56:141-147.

11375 **SMITH, A. B., BERLIN, L.,** and **BASSIN, A.** (1965), Hostility and silence in client-centered group therapy with adult offenders. *Group Psychother., Psychodrama & Sociometry*, 18:191-198.

11376 **SMITH, A. B., BERLIN, L.,** and **BASSIN, A.** (1963), Problems in client–centered group therapy with adult offenders. *Amer. J. Orthopsychiat.*, 33:550-553.

11377 **SMITH, A. B. W.** (1931), The impromptu theatre in New York. *Impromptu*, 1:5-7.

11378 **SMITH, A. D.** (1971), Using group methods in consultation with preschool teachers. *Hosp. & Community Psychiat.*, 22:27-29.

11379 **SMITH, A. J.** (1968), Accuracy of group members' perception of the therapist: a function of patient or therapist? *Proceed., 76th Annual Convention*, American Psychological Association, 3:515-516.

11380 **SMITH, A. J.** (1970), A manual for the training of psychiatric nursing personnel in group psychotherapy. *Perspect. Psychiat. Care*, 8:106-126.

11381 **SMITH, A. J.**, and **McGRATH, F.** (1948), Parent education and group therapy: an episode. *J. Clin. Psychol.*, 4:214-217.

11382 **SMITH, C. E.** (1964), The effect of anxiety on the performance and attitude of authoritarians in a small group situation. *J. Psychology*, 58:191-203.

11383 **SMITH, C. G.** (1969), Alcoholics: their treatment and their wives. *Brit. J. Psychiat.*, (Ashford) 115:1039-1042.

11384 **SMITH, C. S.** (1978), Enhancing the self concept of teaching disabled children through group counseling. *Dissert. Abstr. Internat.*, 10:688A.

11385 **SMITH, D.** (1980), Review of R. C. Berg's and G. L. Landreth's "Group counseling: fundamental concepts and procedures." *Internat. J. Group Psychother.*, 30:542.

11386 **SMITH, D.**, and **KINGSTON, P.** (1980), Live supervision without a one-way screen. *J. Fam. Ther.*, 2:379-387.

11387 **SMITH, D.**, and **MILLER, R.** (1979), Personal growth groups. *Small Group Behav.*, 10:263-270.

11388 **SMITH, D. A.** (1978), Review of R. E. Merritt, Jr.'s and D. D. Walley's *The Group Leader's Handbook: Resources, Techniques, and Survival Skills*. *Amer. J. Occupat. Ther.*, 32:598.

11389 **SMITH, D. J.** (1971), A comparison of the effects of short-term individual counseling, group counseling, and sensitivity training on the self-concept of male college students. *Dissert. Abstr. Internat.*, 32:1867A.

11390 **SMITH, D. S.**, and **DUANE, M. J.** (1980), Couples group treatment of chronic marital dysfunction. *J. Psychiat. Nursing*, 18:30-36.

11391 **SMITH, D. S.**, and **HAWTHORNE, M. E.** (1949), Psychiatric rehabilitation: a follow-up study of 200 cases. *Navy Med. Bull.*, 49:655-669.

11392 **SMITH, E.** (1971), Group conference for post-partum patients. *Amer. J. Nursing*, 71:112-113.

11393 **SMITH, E. E.**, and **GOODCHILDS, J. D.** (1963), The wit in large and small established groups. *Psychol. Reports*, 13:273-274.

11394 **SMITH, E. F. B.** (1973), Teaching group therapy in an undergraduate curriculum. *Perspect. Psychiat. Care*, 11:70-74.

11395 **SMITH, G. W.**, and **PHILLIPS, A. I.** (1971), *Me and You and Us*. New York: P. H. Wyden.

11396 **SMITH, H. C.** (1973), *Sensitivity Training*. Hightstown, NJ: McGraw-Hill Books.

11397 **SMITH, H. W.** (1977), Small group interaction at various ages. *Small Group Behav.*, 8:65-78.

11398 **SMITH, J. E.** (1973), The effects of group counseling on the behavior of juvenile probationers. *Dissert. Abstr. Internat.*, 33:4102A.

11399 **SMITH, J. E.** (1970), The relationship of encounter group interaction, certain process variables, and cohesiveness. *Dissert. Abstr. Internat.*, 31:1025A.

11400 **SMITH, J. L.** (1978), Determining the results of psychodrama training for the counseling professions. *Dissert. Abstr. Internat.*, 40:770A.

11401 **SMITH, J. L.** (1980), Finding your leadership style in groups. *Amer. J. Nursing*, 80:1301-1303.
11402 **SMITH, J. M.** (1973), *Leading Groups in Personal Growth*. Atlanta: John Knox Press.
11403 **SMITH, L. W.**, and **GLAD, D. D.** (1956), Client reactions to therapist operating in controlled group situations. *Group Psychother., Psychodrama & Sociometry*, 9:18-34.
11404 **SMITH, M. K.**, and **CARR, M. W.** (1967), Public health nurses form first chapter t-groups. *Can. Nurse*, (Ottawa) 63:46.
11405 **SMITH, M. R.** (1950), The "silent" auxiliary-ego technique in rehabilitating deteriorated mental patients. *Group Psychother., Psychodrama & Sociometry*, 3:92-100.
11406 **SMITH, M. R., BRYANT, J. E.**, and **TWITCHELL-ALLEN, D.** (1951), Sociometric changes in a group of adult female psychotics following an intensive socializing program. *Group Psychother., Psychodrama & Sociometry*, 4:145-155.
11407 **SMITH, M. W.** (1980), Gifted-student role and verbal interaction in counseling groups. *Dissert. Abstr. Internat.*, 40:4973A. (University Microfilms No. 8003331.)
11408 **SMITH, N. P.** (1972), An analysis of the relationship of counselor characteristics and behavior exhibited in group experience with counselor effectiveness in a selected group of counselor trainees. *Dissert. Abstr. Internat.*, 32:4229-4230B.
11409 **SMITH, O. S.**, and **GUNDLACH, R. H.** (1974), Group therapy for Blacks in a therapeutic community. *Amer. J. Orthopsychiat.*, 44:26-36.
11410 **SMITH, P. B.** (1975), Are there adverse effects of sensitivity training? *J. Human. Psychol.*, 15:29-47.
11411 **SMITH, P. B.** (1979), Changes in relationships after sensitivity training. *Small Group Behav.*, 10:414-430.
11412 **SMITH, P. B.** (1975), Controlled studies of the outcome of sensitivity training. *Psychol. Bull.*, 82:597-622.
11413 **SMITH, P. B.** (1971), Correlations among some tests of t-group learning. *J. Appl. Behav. Science*, 7:508-511.
11414 **SMITH, P. B.** (1974), Group composition as a determinant of Kelman's social influence modes. *European J. Soc. Psychol.*, (The Hague) 4:261-278.
11415 **SMITH, P. B.** (1980), *Group Processes and Personal Change*. New York: Harper and Row.
11416 **SMITH, P. B.** (1971), *Group Processes: Selected Readings*. Baltimore: Penguin.
11417 **SMITH, P. B.** (1974), *Groups within Organizations: Application of Social Psychology to Organizational Behavior*. New York: Harper and Row.
11418 **SMITH, P. B.** (1980), Personal causality and sensitivity training. *Small Group Behav.*, 11:235-250.
11419 **SMITH, P. B.** (1976), Sources of influence in the sensitivity training laboratory. *Small Group Behav.*, 7:33-348.
11420 **SMITH, P. B.** (1967), The use of t-groups in effecting individual and organizational change. *Psychol. Scene*, 1:16-18.
11421 **SMITH, P. B.**, and **LINTON, M. J.** (1975), Group composition and changes in self–actualization in t-groups. *Human Relat.*, 28:811-824.
11422 **SMITH, R. D.**, and **EVANS, J. R.** (1973), Comparison of experimental group guidance and individual counseling as facilitators of vocational development. *J. Couns. Psychol.*, 20:202-208.
11423 **SMITH, R. G.** (1974), The effects of leadership style, leader position power, and problem solving method on group performance. *Dissert. Abstr. Internat.*, 35:773A.

11424 **SMITH, R. J.** (1970), A closer look at encounter therapies. *Internat. J. Group Psychother.*, 20:192-209.
11425 **SMITH, R. L.**, and **ALEXANDER, A. M.** (1974), *Counseling Couples in Groups: A Manual for Improving Troubled Relationships.* Springfield, IL: C C Thomas Publisher.
11426 **SMITH, R. M.** (1971), The administration of human relations and sensitivity training. *Adult Leadership*, 20:170-172.
11427 **SMITH, R. R., JENKINS, W. O., PETKO, C. M.**, and **WARNER, R. W., Jr.** (1979), An experimental application and evaluation of rational behavior therapy in a work release setting. *J. Couns. Psychol.*, 26:519-525.
11428 **SMITH, R. W., SANDERS, R., SMITH, A.**, and **WEINMAN, B.** (1965), Effect of socioenvironmental therapy on awareness of others in chronic psychosis. *J. Personality & Soc. Psychol.*, 2:282-287.
11429 **SMITH, R. W.**, and **YOUNG, H. H.** (1968), Re-enforcement and changes in loquacity in group psychotherapy. *Psychol. Reports*, 23:230.
11430 **SMITH, S.**, and **HAYTHORN, W. W.** (1972), Effects of compatability, crowding, group size, and leadership seniority on stress, anxiety, hostility, and annoyance in isolated groups. *J. Personality & Soc. Psychol.*, 22:67-79.
11431 **SMITH, V. L.** (1980), Effects of group therapy on adolescents experiencing parental absence due to divorce or marital separation. *Dissert. Abstr. Internat.*, 41:947A. (University Microfilms No. 8019150.)
11432 **SMITH, W. L.** (1955), Format and acting out in psychotherapy. *Group Psychother., Psychodrama & Sociometry*, 8:170-173.
11433 **SMITH, W. L.** (1955), Moreno's "Interpersonal therapy, group psychotherapy and the function of the unconscious." *Group Psychother., Psychodrama & Sociometry*, 8:69-71.
11434 **SMITH, W. L.** (1954), Moreno's transference, countertransference and tele: a discussion. *Group Psychother., Psychodrama & Sociometry*, 7:315-317.
11435 **SMITSON, W. S.** (1967), The group process in treating culturally deprived psychotics from Appalachia. *Ment. Hygiene*, 51:108-114.
11436 **SMOLEN, E. M.**, and **LIFTON, N.** (1965), A special treatment program for schizophrenic children in a child guidance clinic. *Amer. J. Orthopsychiat.*, 35:397-398.
11437 **SMOLEN, E. M.**, and **LIFTON, N.** (1966), A special treatment program for schizophrenic children in a child guidance clinic. *Amer. J. Orthopsychiat.*, 36:736-742.
11438 **SMOYAK, S. A.** (1977), Use of gaming simulation by health care professionals. *Health Educat. Monogr.*, 5:11-17.
11439 **SMYTH, J. P.**, and **WALBERG, H. J.** (1974), Group counseling effects on several adjustment problems. *Small Group Behav.*, 5:331-340.
11440 **SNADOWSKY, A. M.**, and **BELKIN, G.** (1974), Affecting change in the phenomenal field: a cognitive technique used during an intensive group experience. *Small Group Behav.*, 5:506-512.
11441 **SNELL, J. E.** (1966), Psychiatric evaluation in open biracial groups. *Amer. J. Psychiat.*, 122:880-885.
11442 **SNIDER, R. T.** (1970), An exploratory factorial study of behavior interactions in autonomous patient groups. *Dissert. Abstr. Internat.*, 30:5701B-5702B.
11443 **SNORTUM, J. R.**, and **ELLENHORN, L. J.** (1974), Predicting and measuring of the psychological impact of nonverbal encounter. *Internat. J. Group Psychother.*, 24:217-229.
11444 **SNORTNUM, J. R.**, and **MYERS, H. F.** (1971), Intensity of t-group relationships as a function of interaction. *Internat. J. Group Psychother.*, 21:190-201.

11445 **SNOW, D. L.**, and **HELD, M. L.** (1973), Group psychotherapy with obese adolescent females. *Adolescence*, 8:407-414.

11446 **SNOWDEN, E. N.** (1940), Mass psychotherapy. *Lancet*, 11:769-770.

11447 **SNOWDON, J.** (1980), Self-help groups and schizophrenia. *Austral. & New Zeal. J. Psychiat.*, (Carlton) 14:265-268.

11448 **SNYDER, B. R.**, and **BERMAN, L.** (1960), The use of a psychoanalytic group approach with teachers at a junior high school. *Amer. J. Orthopsychiat.*, 30:767-779.

11449 **SNYDER, P. A. S.** (1974), Small group facilitators: analyses of attitudes, interests, and values among three types of successful group leaders. *Dissert. Abstr. Internat.*, 34:4008A.

11450 **SNYDER, R.**, and **SECHREST, L.** (1959), An experimental study of directive group therapy with defective delinquents. *Amer. J. Ment. Deficiency*, 64:117-123.

11451 **SNYDER, W. U.** (1958), Psychotherapy. In: *Annual Review of Psychology, 9*, eds. P. R. Farnsworth and Q. McNemar. Palo Alto: Annual Reviews.

11452 **SOBCHUK, P. A.** (1978), The relative effects of the vocational exploration group and instructional career group counseling: a multidimensional approach to assessment of career development. *Dissert. Abstr. Internat.*, 39:1446A.

11453 **SOBLE, D.**, and **GELLER, J. J.** (1964), A type of group psychotherapy in the children's unit of a mental hospital. *Psychiat. Quart.*, 38:262-270.

11454 **SODEN, E. W.** (1968), The "team" approach in the treatment of alcoholics. *Fed. Probat.*, 32:47-49.

11455 **SOHN, L.** (1952), Group therapy for young delinquents. *Brit. J. Delinquency*, 3:20-33.

11456 **SOKOLIK, Z.** (1967), (Experiences with the psychotherapeutic training team.) *Psychiat. Polska*, (Warsaw) 1:285-288.

11457 **SOLBY, B.** (1945), Group psychotherapy and the psychodramatic method. *Sociometry*, 8:288-291.

11458 **SOLBY, B.** (1939), Note on psychodrama reformatory. *Sociometry*, 2.

11459 **SOLBY, B.** (1944), The role concept in job adjustment. *Sociometry*, 7:222-229.

11460 **SOLEM, A. R.** (1956), An experimental test of two theories of involvement in role playing. *Internat. J. Sociometry & Sociatry*, 1:163-175.

11461 **SOLIMAN, P.** (1968), (Two systematized deliriums in schizophrenics.) *Annales Medico-Psychol.*, (Paris) 2:351-364.

11462 **SOLLINGER, I.** (1974), On being a faculty member in a group counseling institute. *Counselor Educat. & Supervision*, 13:226-227.

11463 **SOLMS, H.**, and **de MEURON, M.** (1969), (Group therapy for alcoholics in the psychiatric hospital environment: preliminary results of a practical experience under difficult conditions.) *Toxicomanies*, (Quebec) 2:201-216.

11464 **SOLOMON, A., LOEFFLER, F. J.**, and **FRANK, G. H.** (1953), An analysis of co-therapist interaction in group psychotherapy. *Internat. J. Group Psychother.*, 3:171-180.

11465 **SOLOMON, A. P.** (1950), Drama therapy. In: *Occupational Therapy: Principles and Practices*, eds. W. R. Dunton and S. Licht. Springfield, IL: C C Thomas, pp. 246-313.

11466 **SOLOMON, A. P.**, and **FENTRESS, T. L.** (1947), A critical study of analytically oriented group psychotherapy utilizing the technique of dramatization of the psychodynamics. *Occupat. Ther. & Rehab.*, 26:23-46.

11467 **SOLOMON, B. B.** (1968), Social group work in the adult out–patient clinic. *Soc. Work*, 13:56-61.

11468 **SOLOMON, J. C.**, and **AXELROD, P. L.** (1944), Group psychotherapy for withdrawn adolescent children. *Amer. J. Diseases Children*, 68:86-101.

11469 **SOLOMON, J. C.**, and **SOLOMON, G. F.** (1963), Group psychotherapy with father and son as cotherapists: some dynamic considerations. *Internat. J. Group Psychother.*, 13:133-140.

11470 **SOLOMON, L. N.** (1969), A group program for high-potential underachieving college freshmen. *Amer. J. Orthopsychiat.*, 39:304-305.

11471 **SOLOMON, L. N., and BERZON, B.** (1972), *New Perspectives on Encounter Groups*. San Francisco: Jossey-Bass.

11472 **SOLOMON, L. N., and BERZON, B.** (1970), *The Encounter Group: Issues and Applications*. Belmont, CA: Brooks/Cole.

11473 **SOLOMON, L. N., BERZON, B., and DAVIS, D. P.** (1970), A personal growth program for self-directed groups. *J. Appl. Behav. Science*, 6:427-452.

11474 **SOLOMON, L. N., BERZON, B., and WEEDMAN, C.** (1968), The programmed group: a new rehabilitation resource. *Internat. J. Group Psychother.*, 18:199-219.

11475 **SOLOMON, M. L., and SOLOMON, C. K.** (1970), Psychodrama as an ancillary therapy on a psychiatric ward. *Can. Psychiat. Assn. J.*, (Ottawa) 15:365-373.

11476 **SOLTZ, Z.** (1975), The application of structured scoring techniques in a comparison of the performance on the thematic apperception test with performance in psychodramatic roleplaying situation. *Dissert. Abstr. Internat.*, 36:459B.

11477 **SOLYOM, L., SHUGAR, R., BRYNTWICK, S., and SOLYOM, C.** (1973), Treatment of fear of flying. *Amer. J. Psychiat.*, 130:423-427.

11478 Somatic symptoms may mask patient's marital discord. (1967), *Roche Report: Front. Hosp. Psychiat.*, 4:1.

11479 **SOMERFELD-ZISKIND, E.** (1948), Group therapy. *Annals Western Med. & Surg.*, 2:341-346.

11480 **SOMERFELD-ZISKIND, E.** (1947), Group therapy. *Med. Women J.*, 56:24-29.

11482 **SOMERFELD-ZISKIND, E.** (1957), Report of Second International Congress of Group Psychotherapy, Zurich. *Group Psychother., Psychodrama & Sociometry*, 10:353-355.

11483 **SOMERS, B. J.** (1968), Give me what is really mine! *Voices*, 4:39-41.

11484 **SOMERS, B. J.** (1972), Reevaluation therapy: theoretical framework. *J. Human. Psychol.*, 12:42-57.

11485 **SOMERS, M. L., and GITLIN, P.** (1966), Innovations in field instruction in social group work. *J. Educat. Sociol.*, 2:52-58.

11486 **SOMERS, M. R., and POUPPIRT, P. S.** (1940), Discussion groups as an adjunct to psychotherapy. *Calif. & Western Med.*, 53:79-82.

11487 **SOMMER, M., and OVERBECK, G.** (1977), (On the psychodynamics of headaches: observations of a therapy group.) *Praxis der Psychother.*, 22:117-127.

11488 **SOMMER, R.** (1967), Small group ecology. *Psychol. Bull.*, 67:145-152.

11489 **SOMMER, R.** (1959), Studies in personal space. *Sociometry*, 22:247-260.

11490 **SOMMERS, R. A.** (1980), An assessment of the psychotherapeutic effectiveness of synectics group problem-solving procedures. *Dissert. Abstr. Internat.*, 40:5833B. (University Microfilms No. 8013087.)

11492 **SOMMERS, V. S.** (1953), An experiment in group psychotherapy with members of mixed minority groups. *Internat. J. Group Psychother.*, 3:254-269.

11493 **SOMMER-WEHRLI, A.** (1978), *Patienten im Kreis: Skizzen über eine Gruppentherapie.* (*Patients' Roundtable: Impressions of a Group Therapy.*) Berne: H. Huber.

11494 **SONE, W. R.** (1971), Individual and group implosive therapy, fear and behavior change. *Dissert. Abstr. Internat.*, 31:3081B.

11495 **SONNE, I.** (1960), (Group therapy of pubertal children.) *Ugeskr. for Laeger*, (Copenhagen) 122:1743-1751.

11496 **SONSTEGARD, M.,** and **DREIKURS, R.** (1975), The teleoanalytic group counseling approach. In: *Basic Approaches to Group Psychotherapy and Group Counseling*, ed. G. Gazda. Springfield, IL: C C Thomas.

11497 **SOO, E.** (1974), The impact of activity group therapy upon a highly constricted child. *Internat. J. Group Psychother.*, 24:207-216.

11498 **SOO, E. S.** (1977), The impact of collaborative treatment on premature termination in activity group therapy. *Group*, 1:222-234.

11499 **SOO, E. S.** (1980), The impact of transference and countertransference in activity group therapy. *Group*, 4:27-41.

11500 **SOÓKY, A.** (1967), Hypnopedic group therapy in the treatment of alcoholics. *Orvosi Hetilap*, (Budapest) 108:562-564.

11501 **SORCHER, M.,** and **GOLDSTEIN, A.** (1972), A behavior modeling approach in training. *Personnel Administrator*, 35:35-41.

11502 **SORENSEN, A.** (1973), Treating drug addicts with humanistic and behavioristic techniques: complementary modalities in therapeutic communities. *Cornell J. Soc. Relat.*, 8:139-149.

11503 **SORENSEN, E. T.** (1972), Group therapy in a community hospital dialysis unit. *J. Amer. Med. Assn.*, 221:899-901.

11504 **SORENSEN, J.,** and **CUDLIPP, E.** (1973), *The New Way to Become the Person You'd Like to Be: The Complete Guide to Consciousness Raising.* New York: D. McKay.

11505 **SORENSEN, J. A.** (1969), The effect of reinforcement counseling on dominant behavior in a group setting. *Dissert. Abstr. Internat.*, 29:4338A.

11506 **SORENSON, W. R.** (1978), From Sigmund Freud to O. Hobart Morurer: the emergence of integrity group therapy—an evaluation from the perspective of pastoral counseling. *Dissert. Abstr. Internat.*, 39:325A.

11507 **SORESI, S.** (1973), *La Psicologia dei Rapporti Umani.* (*The Psychology of Human Relations.*) San Daniele del Friuli: Grillo.

11508 **SOROKIN, P. A.** (1955), Spontaneous remarks on "The discovery of the spontaneous man." *Group Psychother., Psychodrama & Sociometry*, 8:327-328.

11509 **SORRENTINO, L. V.** (1978), Group psychotherapy in Rhode Island. *Rhode Island Med. J.*, 61:79-85.

11510 **SOSKIN, R. A.** (1970), Personality and attitude change after two alcoholism treatment programs. *Quart. J. Studies Alcohol*, 31:920-931.

11511 **SOTILE, W. M.,** and **KILMANN, P. R.** (1978), Effects of group systematic desensitization on female orgasmic dysfunction. *Arch. Sexual Behav.*, 7:477-491.

11512 **SOUTHHARD, S.** (1974), *Your Guide to Group Experience.* Nashville: Abingdon.

11513 **SOUTHWELL, M.** (1979), The catatonic: ghost of psychiatric nursing. *Free Assn.*, 6:3-4.

11514 **SOUTHWORTH, R. S.** (1966), A study of the effects of short-term group counseling on underachieving sixth grade students. *Dissert. Abstr. Internat.*, 27:1272A.

11515 **SPADONI, A. J.,** and **SMITH, J. A.** (1969), Milieu therapy in schizophrenia: a negative result. *Arch. Gen. Psychiat.*, 20:547-551.

11516 **SPALTRO, E.** (1961), The group and group therapy. *Arch. Psicol. Neurol., & Psichiat.*, (Milan) 22:331-362.

11517 **SPANJAARD, J.** (1974), Group therapy in a psychoanalytic institute: a study of the development of the transference neurosis in psychoanalytic group therapy. In: *The Challenge for Group Psychotherapy: Present and Future*, ed. S. de Schill. New York: International Universities Press.

11518 **SPANJAARD, J.** (1959), Transference neurosis and psychoanalytic group psychotherapy. *Internat. J. Group Psychother.*, 9:31-42.

11519 **SPARKS, D.**, and **INGRAM-GOODMAN, M.** (1980), The challenge process: a group problem-solving technique. *J. Special. Group Work*, 5:73-76.

11520 **SPAULDING, D. L., Jr.** (1980), Empathy, degree of client's verbal participation and client self-disclosure in group therapy. *Dissert. Abstr. Internat.*, 40:3425B. (University Microfilms No. 8001351.)

11521 **SPAZIER, D.** (1966), Gedanken zur nachgehenden Fürsorge und Rehabilitation bei psychisch Kranken. (Thoughts on aftercare and rehabilitation in psychiatric patients.) *Nervenarzt*, 37:381-387.

11522 **SPEAR, F. G.** (1960), Deterioration in schizophrenic control groups. *Brit. J. Med. Psychol.*, (London) 33:143-148.

11523 **SPECHT, F.** (1965), (Experiences with the symbol drama in children and adolescents.) *Monatsschr. Kinderheilkunde*, 113:237-238.

11524 **SPECK, R. V.** (1964), Mental health problems involving the family, the pet, and the veterinarian. *J. Amer. Vet. Med. Assn.*, 145:150-154.

11525 **SPECK, R. V.**, and **RUEVENI, U.** (1975), Network therapy: a developing concept. In: *Group Psychotherapy and Group Function*, 2d ed., eds. M. Rosenbaum and M. M. Berger. New York: Basic Books.

11526 **SPEEGLE, P. T.** (1963), The effectiveness of two techniques of counseling with students on academic probation. *Dissert. Abstr. Internat.*, 23:3469-3470.

11527 **SPEER, D. C.** (1970), Effects of marathon group therapy: short-term MMPI changes. *Compar. Group Studies*, 1:397-404.

11528 **SPEERS, R. W.**, and **LANSING, C.** (1964), Group psychotherapy with preschool psychotic children and collateral group therapy of their parents: a preliminary report of the first two years. *Amer. J. Orthopsychiat.*, 34:659-666.

11529 **SPEERS, R. W.**, and **LANSING, C.** (1965), *Group Therapy in Childhood Psychosis*. Chapel Hill, NC: University of North Carolina Press.

11530 **SPEIER, A.** (1968), *Psicoterapía del Grupo en la Infancía: Un Enfoque Centrado en la Expresión Simbólica.* (*Group Psychotherapy in Infancy: A Study in Symbolic Expression.*) Buenos Aires: Proteo.

11531 **SPEIERER, G.** (1975), (The relations and the development of closeness or distance of the group leader and group cohesion in the initial phase of analytic and client-centered therapist self-experiencing groups.) *Gruppenpsychother. & Gruppendynam.*, (Goettingen) 9:32-42.

11532 **SPEIERER, G. W.** (1978), (Theory and technique of client centered self-experiencing group: empirical results.) *Psychother. & Med. Psychol.*, (Stuttgart) 28:194-204.

11533 **SPEIERER, G. W.** (1974), (Theory, technique, and process hypotheses of the client self–experiencing group.) *Psychother. & Med. Psychol.*, (Stuttgart) 24:61-66.

11534 **SPEIERER, G. W.**, and **WEIDELT, J.** (1979), (Development and place of anxiety and stress experience in client-centered self-experiencing groups.) *Zeit. Klin. Psychol. & Psychother.*, (Freiburg) 27:135-145.

11535 **SPELTZ, M. L.** (1979), The use of group contingencies for applied behavior influence: an evaluative review. *Cat. Selected Docum. Psychol.*, 9:41.

11536 **SPENCE, R. B.** (1947), Psychodrama and education. *Sociatry*, 1:31-34.

11537 **SPENCER, A. M.** (1963), Permissive group therapy with lysergic acid diethylamide. *Brit. J. Psychiat.*, (Ashford) 109:37-45.

11538 **SPERBER, M.** (1962), Micki's world: a continuing experiment in psychodrama. *Group Psychother., Psychodrama & Sociometry*, 15:326-333.

11539 **SPERBER, Z.**, and **REISER, M.** (1971), Utilizing non-professional aides in the treatment of psychotic children at an outpatient clinic. *Psychiatry*, 8:224-230.

11540 **SPERGEL, I.** (1965), Selecting groups for street work service. *Soc. Work*, 10:47-55.

11541 **SPERLING, E.** (1969), (Group formations at the university and its relation to treatment problems in students.) *Zeit. Psychosomat. Med. & Psychoanal.*, (Goettingen) 15:251-260.

11542 **SPERLING, E.** (1971), (Psychotherapeutic experiences with groups of married couples.) *Zeit. Psychosomat. Med. & Psychoanal.*, (Goettingen) 17:335-346.

11543 **SPEROFF, B. J.** (1960), Group psychotherapy and role playing in labor relations: a case study. *Group Psychother., Psychodrama & Sociometry*, 13:87-93.

11544 **SPEROFF, B. J.** (1959), Group psychotherapy as adjunct training in handling grievances. *Group Psychother., Psychodrama & Sociometry*, 12:169-174.

11545 **SPEROFF, B. J.** (1957), Group psychotherapy in industry: a case of intragroup conflict. *Group Psychother., Psychodrama & Sociometry*, 10:3-9.

11546 **SPEROFF, B. J.** (1960), Group psychotherapy in labor relations: a case study. *Personnel J.*, 39:14-17.

11547 **SPEROFF, B. J.** (1953), The group's role in role playing. *J. Industr. Training*, 7:17-20.

11548 **SPEROFF, B. J.** (1962), Group therapy and role playing in industry. *Internat. J. Sociometry & Sociatry*, 2:116-122.

11549 **SPEROFF, B. J.** (1964), The identification of hidden sociometric leaders. *Group Psychother., Psychodrama & Sociometry*, 17:96-103.

11550 **SPEROFF, B. J.** (1966), Psychodrama with alcoholics: two brief paradigms. *Group Psychother., Psychodrama & Sociometry*, 19:214-219.

11551 **SPEROFF, B. J.** (1955), Role playing vs. acting with script. *Nursing Outlook*, 3:377-379.

11552 **SPEROFF, B. J.** (1954), Rotational role–playing used to develop executives. *Personnel J.*, 33:49-50.

11553 **SPEROFF, B. J.** (1954), Scripts vs. role–playing. *Personnel J.*, 32:304-306.

11554 **SPEROFF, B. J.**, and **SIMON, D.** (1963), Problems and approaches in child group psychotherapy in a public school milieu. *Group Psychother., Psychodrama & Sociometry*, 16:39-45.

11555 **SPEROS, T.** (1972), The final empty chair. *Group Psychother., Psychodrama & Sociometry*, 25:32-33.

11556 **SPIEGEL, D.**, and **YALOM, I. D.** (1978), A support group for dying patients. *Internat. J. Group Psychother.*, 28:233-245.

11557 **SPIEGEL, E. A.** (1963), *Progress in Neurology and Psychiatry: Vol. XVIII.* New York: Grune and Stratton.

11558 **SPIEGELBERG, N.** (1980), Support group improves quality of life: a multiple sclerosis support group. *Arn. J.*, 5:9-11.

11559 **SPIEL, W.** (1950), Über gruppen–psychotherapie. (Group therapy.) *Zeit. Individ.-Psychol.*, (Munich) 19:161-174.

11560 **SPIELBERGER, C. D.**, and **WEITZ, H.** (1964), Improving the academic performance of anxious college freshmen: a group–counseling approach to the prevention of underachievement. *Psychol. Monogr.*, 78:1-20.

11561 **SPIELMAN, R.** (1975), A new application of closed group psychotherapy in a public psychiatric hospital. *Austral. & New Zeal. J. Psychiat.*, (Carlton) 9:193-199.

11562 **SPIKER, D.** (1943), Protected groups in the treatment of young children. *Amer. J. Orthopsychiat.*, 13:659-664.

11563 **SPINKS, M.** (1968), People who need people. *Nursing Mirror*, (London) 126:33-34.

11564 **SPINKS, N. J.** (1970), The effects of male and female models in vicarious therapy pretraining on the change in self-concept of institutionalized female juvenile delinquents in group counseling. *Dissert. Abstr. Internat.*, 30:5702B-5703B.

11565 **SPITZ, H. H.**, and **KOPP, S. B.** (1957), Multiple psychotherapy. *Psychiat. Quart. Suppl.*, 31:295-311.

11566 **SPITZ, H.**, and **SADOCK, B. J.** (1973), Small interactional groups in the psychiatric training of graduate nursing students. *J. Nursing Educat.*, 12:6-13.

11567 **SPITZ, H. I.** (1979), Group approaches to treating marital problems. *Psychiat. Annals*, 9:50-72.

11568 **SPITZ, H. I.** (1980), Review of H. Kellerman's "Group psychotherapy and personality: intersecting structures." *Amer. J. Fam. Ther.*, 8:85.

11569 **SPITZ, H. I.** (1980), Review of H. Roback's, S. Abramowitz's, and D. Strassberg's "Group psychotherapy research: commentaries and selected readings." *Amer. J. Fam. Ther.*, 8:85.

11570 **SPITZ, H. I.** (1978), Structured interactional group psychotherapy with couples. *Internat. J. Group Psychother.*, 28:401-414.

11571 **SPITZ, H. I.**, **KASS, F.**, and **CHARLES, E.** (1980), Common mistakes made in group psychotherapy by beginning therapists. *Amer. J. Psychiatry*, 137:1619-1621.

11572 **SPITZ, J.** (1974), (Preparatory discussion with parents prior to children's admission to a psychiatric hospital.) *Ceskoslav. Psychiat.*, (Prague) 70:109-113.

11573 **SPITZER, R. L.**, and **KLEIN, D. F.** (1976), *Evaluation of Psychological Therapies: Psychotherapies, Behavior Therapies, Drug Therapies and Their Interactions*. Baltimore: Johns Hopkins University Press.

11574 **SPIVAK, M.**, **STEWART, T. W.**, and **MOORE, K. B.** (1962), An experimental social interaction approach to milieu treatment of schizophrenia. *Psychiat. Quart.*, 36:484-502.

11575 **SPOTNITZ, H.** (1957), The borderline schizophrenic in group psychotherapy: the importance of individualization. *Internat. J. Group Psychother.*, 7:155-174.

11576 **SPOTNITZ, H.** (1960), The concept of goals in group psychotherapy. *Internat. J. Group Psychother.*, 10:383-393.

11577 **SPOTNITZ, H.** (1972), *The Couch and the Circle*. New York: Lancer.

11578 **SPOTNITZ, H.** (1961), *The Couch and the Circle: A Story of Group Psychotherapy*. New York: Alfred A. Knopf.

11579 **SPOTNITZ, H.** (1968), Discussion of F. H. Stoller's "Accelerated interaction." *Internat. J. Group Psychother.*, 18:220-239.

11580 **SPOTNITZ, H.** (1975), Experiences in conducting demonstration groups. In: *Group Therapy 1975: An Overview*, eds. L. R. Wolberg and M. L. Aronson. New York: Stratton Intercontinental Medical Books.

11581 **SPOTNITZ, H.** (1965), Failures in group psychotherapy. *Topical Probl. Psychol. & Psychiat.*, 5:150-156.

11582 **SPOTNITZ, H.** (1972), Group psychotherapy in perspective. *Amer. J. Psychiat.*, 129:606-607.

11583 **SPOTNITZ, H.** (1971), In tribute to S. R. Slavson. *Internat. J. Group Psychother.*, 21:402-405.

11584 **SPOTNITZ, H.** (1968), The management and mastery of resistance in group psychotherapy. *J. Group Psychoanal. & Process*, (London) 1:5-22.

11585 **SPOTNITZ, H.** (1947), Observations of emotional currents in interview group therapy with adolescent girls. *J. Nerv. & Ment. Diseases*, 106:565-582.

11586 **SPOTNITZ, H.** (1968), Psychoanalytic therapy of aggression in groups.

In: *Current Psychiatric Therapies*, ed. J. H. Masserman. New York: Grune and Stratton.
11587 **SPOTNITZ, H.** (1952), A psychoanalytic view of resistance in groups. *Internat. J. Group Psychother.*, 2:3-9.
11588 **SPOTNITZ, H.** (1958), Resistance reinforcement in affect training of analytic group psychotherapy. *Internat. J. Group Psychother.*, 8:395-402.
11589 **SPOTNITZ, H.** (1972), Touch countertransference in group psychotherapy. *Internat. J. Group Psychother.*, 22:455-463.
11590 **SPOTNITZ, H.**, and **GABRIEL, B.** (1950), Resistance in analytic group therapy: a study of the group therapeutic process in children and mothers. *Quart. J. Child Behav.*, 2:71-85.
11591 **SPRATLEN, L. P.** (1976), A Black client group in day treatment. *Perspect. Psychiat. Care*, 12:176-182.
11592 **SPREI-OTT, J. E.** (1980), The use of assertiveness training and consciousness-raising groups in the treatment of depression in women. *Dissert. Abstr. Internat.*, 40:5024B. (University Microfilms No. 8008248.)
11593 **SPRINGER, L. K.** (1974), The group effect on personality. *Dissert. Abstr. Internat.*, 34:5211B.
11594 **SPRINGER, T. A.** (1970), An experimental study of the effects of group counseling upon the creative thinking of selected senior high school students. *Dissert. Abstr. Internat.*, 31:165-166A.
11595 **SPRINGMANN, R. R.** (1974), The application of interpretations in large groups. *Internat. J. Group Psychother.*, 24:333-341.
11596 **SPRINGMANN, R. R.** (1970), A large group. *Internat. J. Group Psychother.*, 20:210-218.
11597 **SPROUSE, C. L.**, and **BRUSH, D. H.** (1980), Assessment of interpersonal perception: assessing a quasi-therapy group by individual differences multi–dimensional scaling. *Small Group Behav.*, 11:35-49.
11598 **SPRUELL, M. N.** (1970), The development of facilitative training for a group of alcoholics. *Dissert. Abstr. Internat.*, 30:5679B.
11599 **SPRUIELL, V.** (1967), Countertransference and an adolescent group crisis. *Internat. J. Group Psychother.*, 17:298-308.
11600 **SQUATRIGLIA, R. W.** (1970), The impact of short-term group counseling on student values. *Dissert. Abstr. Internat.*, 31:3280-3281.
11601 **SREĆKOVIĆ, M.** (1978), (Ajuriaguerra psychotherapy based on autogenic training.) *Psihijat. Danas*, (Belgrade) 10:73-76.
11602 **von STAABS, G.** (1959), (Mode of action of the sceno-test in group therapy.) *Acta Psychother., Psychosomat. Orthopaedagog. Suppl.*, (Basel) 7:355-364.
11603 **STACEY, C. L.**, and **DeMARTINO, M. F.** (1957), *Counseling and Psychotherapy with the Mentally Retarded.* Glencoe, IL: Free Press.
11604 **STACY, D., DOLEYS, D. M.**, and **MALCOLM, R.** (1979), Effects of social-skills training in a community-based program. *Amer. J. Ment. Deficiency*, 84:152-158.
11605 **STADELI, H.** (1962), (Play therapy and development of personality.) *Praxis Kinderpsychol. & Kinderpsychiat.*, (Goettingen) 11:251-255.
11606 **STAFFORD, L. F.** (1973), The clinical specialist in the geographic unit system. *J. Psychiat. Nursing*, 11:22-25.
11607 **STAFFORD, R. R.** (1978), Attitude and behavior change in couples as a function of communication training. *Dissert. Abstr. Internat.*, 39:2526B. (University Microfilms No. 7819902.)
11608 **STAGER, P.** (1967), Conceptual level as a composition variable in small-group decision making. *J. Personality & Soc. Psychol.*, 5:152-161.
11609 **STAGGS, A. M.** (1980), Group counseling of learning disabled children in the intermediate grades enrolled in the public school special education

program: training in cognitive behavior modification. *Dissert. Abstr. Internat.*, 40:6157A. (University Microfilms No. 8012141.)

11610 **STAHL, G. R.** (1954), A statistical report of industry's experience with role playing. *Group Psychother., Psychodrama & Sociometry*, 6:202-215.

11611 **STAINBROOK, E.** (1963), A psychiatric crisis ward. *Curr. Psychiat. Ther.*, 3:257-263.

11612 **STAMBAUGH, H. M.** (1972), The training of day leaders for adlerian parent study groups. *Dissert. Abstr. Internat.*, 32:4968A.

11613 **STAMOS, T. J.** (1963), An experimental preplacement therapy group. *Ment. Hosp.*, 14:286-288.

11614 **STAMPS, L. W.** (1973), The effects of intervention techniques on children's fear of failure. *J. Genetic Psychol.*, 123:85-97.

11615 **STANDAL, S. W.** (1955), Comments on Moreno's "Transference, countertransference and tele." *Group Psychother., Psychodrama & Sociometry*, 8:71-73.

11616 **STANDISH, C. T.**, and **SEMRAD, E. V.** (1975), Group psychotherapy with psychotics. In: *Group Psychotherapy and Group Function*, 2d ed., eds. M. Rosenbaum and M. M. Berger. New York: Basic Books.

11617 **STANDISH, C. T.**, and **SEMRAD, E. V.** (1951), Group psychotherapy with psychotics. *J. Psychiat. Soc. Work*, 20:143-150.

11618 **STANDISH, C. T., GURRI, J., SEMRAD, E. V.**, and **DAY, M.** (1952), Some difficulties in group psychotherapy with psychotics. *Amer. J. Psychother.*, 109:283-286.

11619 **STANFORD, G.**, and **ROARK, A. E.** (1974), *Human Interaction in Education*. Boston: Allyn and Bacon.

11620 **STANG, J.** (1968), (Thoughts about group therapy.) *Nordisk Psychiat. Tidsskr.*, (Kungsbacha) 22:374-378.

11621 **STANKOVIC, S.** (1967), Prevention and therapy of neuroses by music and rhythmical breathing. *Psychother. & Psychosomat.*, (Basel) 15:65.

11622 **STANLEY, C. S.** (1972), The relative effects of encounter groups on interpersonal and communication skills. *Dissert. Abstr. Internat.*, 33:3408.

11623 **STANLEY, E. J., GLASER, H. H., LEVIN, D. G., ADAMS, P. A.**, and **COLEY, I. L.** (1968), The treatment of adolescent obesity: is it worthwhile? *Amer. J. Orthopsychiat.*, 38:207.

11624 **STANLEY-TUCKER, L. A.** (1975), The influence of leader intervention conditions upon cohesiveness in encounter groups. *Dissert. Abstr. Internat.*, 36:2648A.

11625 **STANNAREL, D. L.** (1973), Ideological conflict on a psychiatric ward. *Psychiatry*, 36:143-156.

11626 **STANTON, H. E.** (1975), Change in self-insight during an intensive group experience. *Small Group Behav.*, 6:487-493.

11627 **STANTON, H. E.** (1976), Hypnosis and encounter group volunteers: a validation study of the sensation-seeking scale. *J. Consult. & Clin. Psychol.*, 44:692-695.

11628 **STANTON, H. E.** (1976), Microteaching and the experiential groups. *J. Human. Psychol.*, 16:67-76.

11629 **STANTON, H. E.** (1976), Teacher education and the experiential group. *Contemp. Educat. Psychol.*, 1:89-96.

11630 **STAPLES, E. J.** (1959), The influence of the sex of the therapist and of the co-therapist technique in group psychotherapy with girls: an investigation of the effectiveness of group psychotherapy with eighth grade, behavior problem girls, comparing results achieved by a male therapist, by a female therapist, and by the two therapists in combination. *Dissert. Abstr. Internat.*, 19:2154.

11631 **STARK, J. A.** (1974), An evaluation of a semi–programmed self-modification technique designed to improve self-control with groups of emotionally disturbed adolescents. *Dissert. Abstr. Internat.*, 34:6225B.

11632 **STARK, M.** (1966), Human relations as a student personnel service. *J. Coll. Student Personnel*, 7:275-278.

11633 **STARKE, H.** (1967), (Experiences with group discussion in the psychiatric station.) *Zeit. Aerztl. Fortbildung*, (Jena) 61:420-423.

11634 **STARKEY, C. T.** (1974), An analysis of the components of a group contingency to control disruptive classroom behavior. *Dissert. Abstr. Internat.*, 34:6489A.

11635 **STARKMAN, S. S.** (1966), Psychotherapy in schools: a rationale for more useful application. *Psychol. in Schools*, 3:236-241.

11636 **STARKS, F. B.** (1977), Group work with the aged: a successful student project—Culver West Convalescent Hospital. *J. Gerontol. Nursing*, 3:30-34.

11637 **STARR, A.** (1977), *Rehearsal for Living: Psychodrama Illustrated Therapeutic Techniques*. Chicago: Nelson Hall.

11638 **STARR, A.** (1953), Psychodrama with a child's social atom. *Group Psychother., Psychodrama & Sociometry*, 5:222-225.

11639 **STARR, A.** (1951), The role of psychodrama in a child guidance clinic. *Individ. Psychol. Bull.*, 9:18-24.

11640 **STARR, A.** (1959), Role playing: an efficient technique at a business conference. *Group Psychother., Psychodrama & Sociometry*, 12:166-168.

11641 **STARR, A.**, and **CHELNEK, I.** (1955), Psychodrama at V.A. Hospital, Downey, Illinois. *Group Psychother., Psychodrama & Sociometry*, 8:20-24.

11642 **STARR, A.**, and **FOGEL, E.** (1961), Training state hospital personnel through psychodrama and sociometry. *Group Psychother., Psychodrama & Sociometry*, 14:55-61.

11643 **STATON, W. O.** (1978), A clinical evaluation of two affectively different forms of group assertion training: negative versus varied versus milieu controls. *Dissert. Abstr. Internat.*, 90:466B.

11644 **STATTON, W. O.** (1968), Lay mental health action in a community. *J. Individ. Psychol.*, 24:94-96.

11645 **STAUBLE, W. J.** (1971), Milieu therapy and the therapeutic community. *Can. Psychiat. Assn. J.*, (Ottawa) 16:197-202.

11646 **STAUBLE, W. J.** (1965), Training group psychotherapists. *Can. Psychiat. Assn. J.*, (Ottawa) 10:216-222.

11647 **STAVA, L. J.**, and **BEDNAR, R. L.** (1979), Process and outcome in encounter groups. *Small Group Behav.*, 10:200-213.

11648 **STEBBIN, D.** (1975), "Playing it by ear" in answering the needs of a group of Black teenagers. In: *Adolescents Grow in Groups*, ed. I. Berkovitz. New York: Brunner/Mazel.

11649 **STEDMAN, J. M.**, **PETERSON, T. L.**, and **CARDARELLE, J.** (1971), Application of a token system in a preadolescent boy's group. *J. Behav. Ther. & Exper. Psychiat.*, 2:23-29.

11650 **STEELE, D. D.** (1974), Self-disclosure and peak experience in intensive small groups. *Dissert. Abstr. Internat.*, 34:3476B.

11651 **STEELE, F. I.** (1970), Can t-group training change the power structure? *Personnel Administrator*, 33:48-53.

11652 **STEELE, F. I.** (1971), The socket-wrench saga. *Internat. J. Psychiat.*, 9:212-218.

11653 **STEELE, M. H.** (1949), Group meetings for relatives of mental hospital patients. *Smith Coll. Studies Soc. Work*, 19:141-170.

11654 **STEELE, R. E.**, and **NASH, K. B.** (1972), Sensitivity training and the Black community. *Amer. J. Orthopsychiat.*, 42:424-430.

11655 **STEELE, R. E.**, and **NASH, K. B.** (1971), Sensitivity training in the Black community. Paper presented at Annual Meeting of the American Orthopsychiatric Assn., Washington, D.C.

11656 **STEFFENS, E.** (1970), Using literature in group therapy. *Hosp. & Community Psychiat.*, 21:227.

11657 **STEFFEN, J. D.** (1969), The effects of two behavioral models of group counseling on the academic performance of selected college women. *Dissert. Abstr. Internat.*, 29:3427-3428.

11658 **STEGER, J. C.**, and **BROCKWAY, J. A.** (1980), Sexual enhancement in spinal cord injured patients: behavioral group treatment. *Sexual Disabil.*, 3:84-96.

11659 **STEIDEMANN, E. G.** (1964), Group treatment with resistive clients. *Soc. Casework*, 45:26-31.

11660 **STEIGER, R.** (1953), Von praktischen arbeiten in der spielgruppe. (On the general work of the group.) *Heilpaedagog. Werkbl.*, (Lucerne) 22:54-55.

11661 **STEIN, A.** (1971), Group interaction and group psychotherapy in a general hospital. *Mt. Sinai J. Med. N.Y.*, 38:89-100.

11662 **STEIN, A.** (1955), Group psychotherapy in patients with peptic ulcer. *Arch. Neurol. Psychiat.*, 73:580.

11663 **STEIN, A.** (1963), Hillside hospital and group psychotherapy. *J. Hillside Hosp.*, 12:131-133.

11664 **STEIN, A.** (1963), Indications for group psychotherapy and the selection of patients. *J. Hillside Hosp.*, 12:156-166.

11665 **STEIN, A.** (1970), The nature and significance of interaction in group psychotherapy. *Internat. J. Group Psychother.*, 20:153-162.

11666 **STEIN, A.** (1970), The nature and significance of interaction in group psychotherapy. *Sandoz Psychiat. Spectator*, 6:21-22.

11667 **STEIN, A.** (1964), The nature of transference in combined therapy. *Internat. J. Group Psychother.*, 14:413-423.

11668 **STEIN, A.** (1956), Psychosomatic disorders. In: *The Fields of Group Psychotherapy*, ed. S. R. Slavson. New York: International Universities Press.

11669 **STEIN, A.** (1952), Resistance to group psychotherapy. *J. Hillside Hosp.*, 1:79-88.

11670 **STEIN, A.** (1956), The superego and group interaction in group psychotherapy. *J. Hillside Hosp.*, 5:495-504.

11671 **STEIN, A.** (1964), A symposium on combined individual and group psychotherapy: the nature of transference in combined therapy. *Internat. J. Group Psychother.*, 14:413-424.

11672 **STEIN, A.** (1975), The training of the group psychotherapists. In: *Group Psychotherapy and Group Function*, 2d ed., eds. M. Rosenbaum and M. M. Berger. New York: Basic Books.

11673 **STEIN, A.**, and **PETERS, A.** (1968), Toward an international federation of group psychotherapists. *Internat. J. Group Psychother.*, 18:402-404.

11674 **STEIN, A.**, and **SOLOMON, I.** (1953), Group psychotherapy as an aid to patients upon discharge from the hospital. *J. Hillside Hosp.*, 2:72-79.

11675 **STEIN, A.**, and **WIENER, S.** (1978), Group therapy with medically ill patients. In: *Psychotherapeutics in Medicine*, eds. T. B. Karasn and R. I. Steinmuller. New York: Grune and Stratton.

11676 **STEIN, A., STEINHARDT, R. W.**, and **CUTLER, S. I.** (1955), Group psychotherapy in patients with peptic ulcer. *Bull. N.Y. Acad. Med.*, 31:583-591.

11677 **STEIN, A., LIPSHUTZ, D. M., ROSEN, S. R., MISCHEL, E.**, and **SHEPS, J.** (1952), Experimental and specific types of group psychotherapy in a general hospital. *Internat. J. Group Psychother.*, 2:10-23.

11678 **STEIN, A.** (1955), Group psychotherapy on the psychiatric ward of a general hospital. *J. Mt. Sinai Hosp. N.Y.*, 22:104.

11679 **STEIN, C.** (1959), A challenging group of three. *Group Psychother., Psychodrama & Sociometry*, 12:236-239.

11680 **STEIN, C.** (1960), And now there are four: minimal group psychotherapy in a family setting. *Group Psychother., Psychodrama & Sociometry*, 13:14-21.

11681 **STEIN, C.** (1962), Emotional needs of professional personnel in the training of psychodramatists and group psychotherapists. *Group Psychother., Psychodrama & Sociometry*, 15:118-122.

11682 **STEIN, C.** (1946), New experiences in group psychotherapy. *New Engl. J. Med.*, 235:112-117.

11683 **STEIN, C.** (1965), New horizons in the expanding art of psychotherapy. *Group Psychother., Psychodrama & Sociometry*, 18:11-16.

11684 **STEIN, C.** (1961), Psychodrama for nurses in a general hospital. *Group Psychother., Psychodrama & Sociometry*, 14:90-94.

11685 **STEIN, C.** (1966), Psychotherapy and psychodrama. *J. Amer. Soc. Psychosomat. Dent. & Med.*, 13:2-4.

11686 **STEIN, C.** (1976), Review of I. A. Greenberg's *Psychodrama: Theory and Therapy*. *Amer. J. Clin. Hypnosis*, 19:67-69.

11687 **STEIN, C. I.** (1973), Group-grope: the latest development bromide. *Personnel J.*, 52:19-26.

11688 **STEIN, D. D., GOLDSCHMID, M. L., WEISSMAN, H. N.,** and **SORRELLS, J.** (1969), The relationship of clinical training and practice to clinician's sex, age, and work setting. *Clin. Psychol.*, 22:137-139.

11689 **STEIN, D. K.** (1971), Expectation and modeling in sensitivity groups. Unpublished doctoral dissertation, University of Connecticut.

11690 **STEIN, D. K.** (1973), A social learning theory approach to sensitivity groups. *Amer. J. Community Psychol.*, 1:351-361.

11691 **STEIN, F.** (1972), Occupational therapists engaged in group treatment. *Amer. J. Occupat. Ther.*, 26:324.

11692 **STEIN, K., KORCHIN, S. J.,** and **SOSKIN, W. F.** (1978), Leadership style determinants of cohesiveness in adolescent groups. *Internat. J. Group Psychother.*, 28:263.

11693 **STEIN, L. L.** (1965), The psychiatric conference as a social system. *Dissert. Abstr. Internat.*, 26:2375.

11694 **STEIN, M.** (1947), Neuroses and group motivation. *U.S. Army Med. Serv. Bull.*, 7:317-321.

11695 **STEIN, M. I.** (1948), Visual aids in group psychotherapy for veterans with psychosomatic complaints. *J. Clin. Psychol.*, 4:206-211.

11696 **STEIN, R. T.** (1977), Accuracy of process consultants and untrained observers in perceiving emergent leadership. *J. Appl. Psychol.*, 62:755-759.

11697 **STEIN, R. T.** (1975), Identifying emergent leaders from verbal and non–verbal communications. *J. Personality & Soc. Psychol.*, 32:125-135.

11698 **STEIN, T. J.,** and **GAMBRILL, E. D.** (1976), Behavioral techniques in foster care. *Soc. Work*, 21:34-39.

11699 **STEIN, R. T., GEIS, F. L.,** and **DAMARIN, F.** (1973), Perception of emergent leadership hierarchies in task groups. *J. Personality & Soc. Psychol.*, 28:77-87.

11700 **STEINBACH, I.,** and **RING, C.** (1976), (Working with small groups in second grade.) *Psychol. Erziehung & Unterricht*, (Munich) 23:351-355.

11701 **STEINBERG, R. O.** (1976), The encounter group movement and the tradition of Christian enthusiasm, and mysticism. *Dissert. Abstr. Internat.*, 36:5286B.

11702 **STEINER, C.** (1972), 1971 Eric Berne memorial scientific award lecture. *Transactional Anal. J.*, 2:34-37.

11703 **STEINER, C.** (1971), The stroke economy. *Transactional Anal. J.*, 1:9-15.
11704 **STEINER, I. D.** (1966), Models for inferring relationships between group size and potential group productivity. *Behav. Science*, 11:273-283.
11705 **STEINER, J.** (1976), The group therapy of schizophrenia. *Groups*, 7:25-29.
11706 **STEINER, J.** (1979), Holistic group therapy with schizophrenic patients. *Internat. J. Group Psychother.*, 29:195-210.
11707 **STEINER, J.** (1972), Reflections on the encounter group and the therapist. *Amer. J. Occupat. Ther.*, 26:130-131.
11708 **STEINER, J.** (1973), The use of activity as an adjunct to group psychotherapy: i. *Groups*, 5:15-28.
11709 **STEINER, J.,** and **KAPLAN, S. R.** (1969), Outpatient group "work for pay" activity for chronic schizophrenic patients. *Amer. J. Psychother.*, 23:452-462.
11710 **STEINER, J.,** and **RUSK, G. H.** (1973), Partial milieu therapy: a villa in Portugal, ii. *Groups*, 5:29-43.
11711 **STEINER, L. R.** (1954), The use of radio as a medium for mental health education. *Internat. J. Group Psychother.*, 4:204-209.
11712 **STEINFELD, G. J.,** and **MABLI, J.** (1974), Perceived curative factors in group therapy by residents of a therapeutic community. *Crim. Justice & Behav.*, 1:278.
11713 **STEINHAUER, J. C.** (1972), Evaluation of a marathon encounter group by instrumental case studies, and repeated measures. *Dissert. Abstr. Internat.*, 33:478-979A.
11714 **STEINHAUER, J. C.** (1973-1974), Tacit knowing as methodology for evaluating an encounter group. *Interpersonal Develop.*, 4:1-20.
11715 **STEINIG, K. H.** (1962), (Multidimensional diagnosis and therapy in speech neuroses.) *Arch. Ohron-Nasen-, & Kehlkopfheilkunde*, 80:816-822.
11716 **STEININGER, E. H.,** and **LEPPEL, L.** (1970), Group therapy for reluctant juvenile probationers and their parents. *Adolescence*, 5:67-77.
11717 **STEINMAN, B.** (1976), (Group therapy [editorial].) *Akt. Gerontol.*, (Stuttgart) 6:505-506.
11718 **STEINMEYER, E.** (1973), (Evaluation of the rehabilitation outcome in a therapeutic community with the help of sociometry and variables of the personality structure. *Die Rehabilitation*, (Stuttgart) 12:218-220.
11719 **STEMMLER, W.** (1960), A contribution to group psychotherapy: psychological principles and description of a course of therapy.) *Psyche*, (Stuttgart) 14:427-441.
11720 **STEPHAN, V.** (1975), (Group-dynamic treatment methods in juvenile delinquency institutions: results of a research project.) *Praxis Kinderpsychol. & Kinderpsychiat.*, (Goettingen) 24:64-70.
11721 **STEPHENSON, N. L., BOUDEWXNS, P. A.,** and **LESSING, R. A.** (1977), Long-term effects of peer group confrontation therapy used with polydrug users. *J. Drug Issues*, 7:135-149.
11722 **STEPHENSON, R. M.,** and **SCARPITTI, F. R.** (1974), *Group Interaction as Therapy: The Use of the Small Group in Corrections.* Westport, CT: Greenwood Press.
11723 **STEPNER, A. L.,** and **TUMARKIN, B.** (1961), The role of group therapy in psychiatry. *J. Florida Med. Assn.*, 47:793-797.
11724 **STERK, S.** (1973), Psychomat: an experiential group for university students. *Adolescence*, 8:219-224.
11725 **STERN, D. J.** (1965), Comments on the use of psychodrama as a teaching technique. *Group Psychother., Psychodrama & Sociometry*, 18:142-161.
11726 **STERN, E.** (1949), Uber gruppenpsychotherapie. (Group psychotherapy.) *Nervenarzt*, 20:371-379.

11727 **STERN, E. M.** (1959), Group psychoanalysis with individuals manifesting sexually deviate patterns. *Acta Psychother., Psychosomat. Orthopaedagog. Suppl.*, (Basel) 7:365-376.

11728 **STERN, H.**, and **GROSZ, H. J.** (1966), Personality correlates of patient interactions in group psychotherapy. *Psychol. Reports*, 18:411-414.

11729 **STERN, H.**, and **GROSZ, H. J.** (1966), Verbal interactions in group psychotherapy between patients with similar and with dissimilar personalities. *Psychol. Reports*, 19:1111-1114.

11730 **STERNBACH, J. C.** (1969), Interaction process and social structure of social work treatment groups in a maximum security prison. *Dissert. Abstr. Internat.*, 30:2160A.

11731 **STERN, K., SMITH, J. M.**, and **FRANK, M.** (1953), Mechanisms of transference and countertransference in psychotherapeutic and social work with the aged. *J. Gerontol.*, 8:328-332.

11732 **STERNBACH, O.** (1947), The dynamics of psychotherapy in the group. *J. Child Psychiat.*, 1:91-112.

11733 **STERNBACH, O.** (1948), Techniques in group therapy. *Jewish Soc. Serv. Quart.*, 25:221-224.

11734 **STERNBERG, D.** (1965), Legal frontiers in prison group psychotherapy. *J. Crim. Law & Criminol.*, 56:446-449.

11735 **STERNE, D. M.**, and **SELIGMAN, M.** (1971), Further comparisons of verbal behavior in therapist-led, leaderless, and alternating group psychotherapy sessions. *J. Couns. Psychol.*, 18:472-477.

11736 **STERNER, G. A.** (1972), Facilitating short-term group psychotherapy using modeling and didactic methods. *Dissert. Abstr. Internat.*, 2824B.

11737 **STERNLICHT, M.** (1964), Establishing an initial relationship in group psychotherapy with delinquent retarded male adolescents. *Amer. J. Ment. Deficiency*, 69:39-41.

11738 **STERNLICHT, M.** (1969), Parent counseling in an experimental rehabilitation center. *J. Rehab.*, 35:15-16.

11739 **STERNLICHT, M.** (1966), Treatment approaches to delinquent retardates. *Internat. J. Group Psychother.*, 16:91-93.

11740 **STERNLICHT, M.**, and **SULLIVAN, I.** (1974), Group counseling with parents of the MR: leadership selection and functioning. *Ment. Retard.*, 12:11-13.

11741 **STERNLIEB, S. F.** (1963), The development of group psychotherapy for psychosomatic manifestations in various existing settings. *S. Dakota J. Med. Pharmacol.*, 16:32-35.

11742 **STETTNER, J. W.** (1970), Pastoral counseling in the age of Aquarius. *Pastoral Psychol.*, 21:7-14.

11743 **STEVENIN, L.** (1965), (Directed theatrical expression.) *Hygiene Ment. Can.*, (Ottawa) 54:217-222.

11744 **STEVENIN, L., DARS, E.**, and **BENOIT, J. C.** (1961), (Directed dramatic expression: its application in psychotherapy.) *Annales Medico-Psychol.*, (Paris) 119:936-944.

11745 **STEVENS, E.** (1957), Psychodrama in a speech clinic. *Sociatry*, 1:56-58.

11746 **STEVENS, E.** (1946), The use of psychodrama in the treatment of children with articulatory defects. *Sociometry*, 9:283-289.

11747 **STEVENS, J. H.** (1974), The home learning project: a group consultation model of parent education. *Child Care Quart.*, 4:246-254.

11748 **STEVENS, L. F.** (1963), Nurse-patient discussion groups. *Amer. J. Nursing*, 63:67-69.

11749 **STEVENS, S. E.** (1961), Talking it over on a disturbed ward. *Ment. Hosp.*, 12:11-12.

11750 **STEVENS, S. E.** (1965), Techniques for treatment team meetings. *Ment. Hosp.*, 16:258-259.

11751 **STEVENSON, G. S.** (1956), *Mental Health Planning for Social Action.* New York: Blakiston Division, McGraw-Hill Books.

11752 **STEWART, D. A.** (1955), Dynamics of fellowship as illustrated in Alcoholics Anonymous. *Quart. J. Studies Alcohol*, 16:251-262.

11753 **STEWART, D. A.** (1954), Empathy in the group therapy of alcoholics. *Quart. J. Studies Alcohol.*, 15:74-110.

11754 **STEWART, D. A.** (1954), Ethical aspects of the group therapy of alcoholics. *Quart. J. Studies Alcohol*, 15:288-303.

11755 **STEWART, K. K.**, and **AXELROD, P. L.** (1947), Group therapy in a children's psychiatric ward: experiment combining group therapy with individual therapy and resident treatment. *Amer. J. Orthopsychiat.*, 17:312-325.

11756 **STEWART, L., DAWSON, D.**, and **BYLES, J. A.** (1976), Using peer-group intervention with problem students in a secondary school. *Hosp. & Community Psychiat.*, 27:572-574.

11757 **STEWART, L. G.** (1970), Perceptions of selected variables of the counseling relationship in group counseling with deaf college students. *Dissert. Abstr. Internat.*, 31:1026A.

11758 **STEWART, R. V.** (1970), The effects of group counseling on acceptance of self, acceptance of others, grade point averages, and teacher rated behavior of failing tenth grade students. *Dissert. Abstr. Internat.*, 30:4236A-4237A.

11759 **STEWART, W.** (1975), Nursing and counseling: a conflict of roles? *Nursing Mirror*, (London) 140:71-73.

11760 **STIEPER, D. R.** (1963), Three concepts related to group therapy and group therapy training. *Ment. Hygiene*, 47:490-496.

11761 **STIERLIN, H.** (1973), Group fantasies and family myths: some theoretical and practical aspects. *Fam. Process*, 12:111-125.

11762 **STIERLIN, H.** (1975), *Von der Psychoanalyse zur Familientherapie: Theori, Klinik.* (*Psychoanalysis and Family Therapy: Theory and Clinical Practice.*) Stuttgart: J. Klett.

11763 **STILLMAN, S.** (1971), Mental illness and peer group popularity. *J. Clin. Psychol.*, 27:202-203.

11764 **STILLMAN, S.** (1972), The relationship of selected individual characteristics to group behavior in two risk taking situations. *Dissert. Abstr. Internat.*, 32:4195-4196B.

11765 **STIMAC, M. F.** (1973), The effects of long-term group counseling on academic performance and certain noncognitive personality variables of students in a general education program. *Dissert. Abstr. Internat.*, 34:1631A.

11766 **STIMPSON, D. V.** (1975), T-group training to improve counseling skills. *J. Psychology*, 89:89-94.

11767 **STINSON, J. E.**, and **HELLEBRANDT, E. T.** (1972), Group cohesiveness, productivity, and strength of formal leadership. *J. Soc. Psychol.*, 87:99-105.

11768 **STINSON, M.** (1972), Group communication for the deaf. *Volta Rev.*, 74:52-54.

11769 **STINSON, M.** (1971), Group communication for the deaf. *J. Rehab.*, 37:42-44.

11770 **STIRT, S. S.** (1940), Overt mass masturbation in a classroom. *Amer. J. Orthopsychiat.*, 10:801-809.

11771 **ST. JEAN, R.** (1970), Reformulation of the value hypothesis in group risk taking. *Proceed., 78th Annual Convention*, American Psychological Association, 339-340.

11772 **STOCK, D.** (1962), Interpersonal concerns during the early sessions in therapy groups. *Internat. J. Group Psychother.*, 12:14-26.

11773 **STOCK, D.**, and **LIEBERMAN, M. A.** (1962), Methodological issues in the assessment of total-group phenomena in group therapy. *Internat. J. Group Psychother.*, 12:312-325.
11774 **STOCK, D.**, and **WHITMAN, R. M.** (1957), Patients' and therapists' apperceptions of an episode in group therapy. *Human Relat.*, 10:367-384.
11775 **STOCK, D., WHITMAN, R. M.**, and **LIEBMAN, M. H.** (1958), The deviant member in therapy group. *Human Relat.*, 11:341-372.
11776 **STOCK, H. V.** (1978), The effects of a humanistic–relational parent education group on neurologically impaired children and their parents. *Dissert. Abstr. Internat.*, 38:6127B. (University Microfilms No. 7809414.)
11777 **STOCKBRIDGE, M. E.** (1966), The third fountain. *Brit. J. Psychiat. Soc. Work*, (Birmingham) 8:43-45.
11778 **STOCKEY, M. R.** (1961), A comparison of the effectiveness of group counseling, individual counseling, and employment among adolescent boys with adjustment problems. Ph.D. thesis, University of Michigan.
11779 **STOCKTON, N.** (1980), Behavioral group counseling. *J. Special. Group Work*, 5:189-195.
11780 **STOCKTON, R.** (1980), The education of group leaders: a review of the literature with suggestions for the future. *J. Special. Group Work*, 5:55-62.
11781 **STOCKTON, R.** (1978), Reviews and bibliographies of experiential small group research: survey and perspective. *Small Group Behav.*, 9:435.
11782 **STOCKTON, R.**, and **MORRAN, D. K.** (1980), The use of verbal feedback in counseling groups: toward an effective system. *J. Special. Group Work*, 5:10-14.
11783 **STOFFLER, F.** (1972), (Group therapy with schizophrenic women.) *Med. Welt*, (Stuttgart) 24:781-783.
11784 **STOFFLER, F.** (1975), (Treatment of the addict by Alcoholics Anonymous.) *Med. Welt*, (Stuttgart) 23:1154-1156.
11785 **STOKES, J. P.**, and **TAIT, R. C.** (1979), The group incidents questionnaire: a measure of skill in group facilitation. *J. Couns. Psychol.*, 26:250-254.
11786 **STOKOLS, D.** (1974), Some determinants of alienation in the small group. *Dissert. Abstr. Internat.*, 34:4721B.
11787 **STOKVIS, B.** (1955), Das uber tragungsphanomen in der gruppenpsychotherapeutischen behandlung psychosomatischer patienten mittels der psycho und soziodramas. (On transference aspects of group psychotherapy in treating psychosomatic patients with psychotherapy and sociotherapy.) *Acta Psychother. Psychosomat. Orthopaedagog.*, (Basel) 3:58-67.
11788 **STOKVIS, B.** (1955), Das uber tragungsphanomen in der gruppenpsychotherapeutischen behandlung psychosomatischer patienten mittels der psycho und soziodramas. (Transference phenomenon in a group-psychotherapy of psychosomatic patients utilizing psychodrama and sociodrama.) *Acta Psychother. Psychosomat. Orthopaedagog.*, (Basel) 3:250-259.
11789 **STOKVIS, B.** (1954), Group psychodrama of eneuretic children by psychodrama and sociodrama. *Amer. J. Psychother.*, 8:265-275.
11790 **STOKVIS, B.** (1954), Gruppenpsychologie unlerschung der veltbilder van pahenten mit psychosomatischen storungen. (Utilizing a group psychology perspective with those presenting psychosomatic complaints.) *Schweiz. Arch. Neurol., Neurochir. & Psychiat.*, (Zurich) 74:404-414.
11791 **STOKVIS, B.** (1959), Gruppenpsychotherapeutische erfahrungen bei asthmatikern. (Experience in group psychotherapy with asthmatics.) *Acta Psychother., Psychosomat. Orthopaedagog.*, (Basel) 7:220-232.
11792 **STOKVIS, B.** (1953), Leidner erfahrungen mit dem psycho- und soziodrama. (Experiences with psycho- and sociodrama in Leyden.) In: *Die*

Vortrage der 4. Lindauer Psychotherapiewoche, ed. E. Speer. Stuttgart: George Thieme.

11793 **STOKVIS, B.** (1960), (The principles and current status of group psychotherapy.) *Zeit. Psychother. Med. Psychol.*, (Stuttgart) 10:129-140.

11794 **STOKVIS, B.** (1961), *Psychotherapie fuer den Praktischen Arzt.* (*Psychotherapy for the General Practitioner.*) Basel: S. Karger.

11795 **STOKVIS, B.** (1959), *Second International Congress of Group Psychotherapy.* New York: S. Karger.

11796 **STOKVIS, B.** (1960), Wie man zur gruppenpsychotherapie gekommen ist. (How one comes to group therapy.) *Praxis der Psychother.*, 5:205-207.

11797 **STOKVIS, B.**, and **WELMAN, A. J.** (1955), Groeps-en sociotherapie als adjurans ter behandeling vans lijders aan asthma bronchiale. *Nederl. Tijdschr. Geneeskunde*, (Amsterdam) 99:690-693.

11798 **STOKVIS, B.**, and **WELMAN, A. J.** (1955), La thérapeutique de groupe et la sociothérapie comme adjuvant dans le traitment d'asthmatique. (Group therapy and sociotherapy as adjuncts in the treatment of asthmatics.) *Evolut. Psychiat.*, (Toulouse) 4:695-710.

11799 **STOKVIS, B.**, and **WELMAN, A. J.** (1955), (Psychodrama and sociodrama as psychotherapy in psychosomatic disorders.) *Nederl. Tijdschr. Geneeskunde*, (Amsterdam) 99:1482-1488.

11800 **STOKVIS-WARNAAR, J.**, and **STOKVIS, B.** (1962), Psychodrama of enuresis nocturna in boys. *Group Psychother., Psychodrama & Sociometry*, 15:179-196.

11801 **STOLLAK, G. E.** (1968), The experimental effects of training college students as play therapists. *Psychother.: Theory, Res. & Pract.*, 5:77-80.

11802 **STOLLBERG, D.** (1972), Some specifics about the psychoanalytic group work with theologians. *Dynam. Psychiat.*, (Berlin) 5:35.

11803 **STOLLER, F. H.** (1968), Accelerated interaction: a time–limited approach based on the brief, intensive group. *Internat. J. Group Psychother.*, 18:220-258.

11804 **STOLLER, F. H.** (1970), Encountertapes. *Psychol. Today*, 4:18, 22.

11805 **STOLLER, F. H.** (1978), Group psychotherapy on television: innovation with hospitalized patients. In: *Videotape Techniques in Psychiatric Training and Treatment*, ed. M. M. Berger. New York: Brunner/Mazel.

11806 **STOLLER, F. H.** (1967), Group psychotherapy on television: an innovation with hospitalized patients. *Amer. Psychologist*, 22:158-162.

11807 **STOLLER, F. H.** (1967), The long weekend. *Psychol. Today*, 1:28-33.

11808 **STOLLER, F. H.** (1970), The marathon group as a model for growth and change. In: *The Encounter Group: Issues and Applications*, eds. L. N. Solomon and B. Berzon. Belmont, CA: Brooks/Cole.

11809 **STOLLER, F. H.** (1970), Psychotherapy and the time grain: pace in progress. *Compar. Group Studies*, 1:410-418.

11810 **STOLLER, F. H.** (1970), A synergic model of human growth. *Compar. Group Studies*, 1:405-409.

11811 **STOLLER, F. H.** (1970), Therapeutic concepts reconsidered in light of video tape experience. *Compar. Group Studies*, 1:5-17.

11812 **STOLLER, F. H.** (1968), Use of videotape (focused feedback) in group counseling and group therapy. *J. Res. & Develop. Educat.*, 1:30-44.

11813 **STOLLER, F. H.** (1969), Videotape feedback in group setting. *Psychiat. Digest*, 30:72.

11814 **STOLLER, F. H.** (1969), Videotape feedback in the group setting. *J. Nerv. Ment. Diseases*, 148:457-466.

11815 **STOLLER, F. H.** (1978), Videotape feedback in marathon and encounter group. In: *Videotape Techniques in Psychiatric Training and Treatment*, ed. M. M. Berger. New York: Brunner/Mazel.

11816 **STOLLER, F. H.,** and **BERGER, M. M.** (1970), Discussants: video-tape papers. *Compar. Group Studies*, 1:177-190.

11817 **STOLZOFF, G. H.** (1980), Parent training approaches: a follow-up evaluation of parent effectiveness training, Adlerian study groups, and behavior modification. *Dissert. Abstr. Internat.*, 41:701B. (University Microfilms No. 8017819.)

11818 **STOMPS, L. W.** (1970), The effects of intervention techniques on fear of failure behavior. *Dissert. Abstr. Internat.*, 31:2267-2268.

11819 **STONE, A.,** and **LEVINE, L.** (1950), Group therapy in sexual maladjustment. *Amer. J. Psychiat.*, 107:195-202.

11820 **STONE, A. A.** (1971), The quest of the counter-culture. *Internat. J. Psychiat.*, 9:219-226.

11821 **STONE, A. R.** (1950), The caseworker's contribution to the social rehabilitation of an intellectually limited hospitalized psychotic patient; group psychotherapy research project. *J. Psychiat. Soc. Work*, 19:115-122.

11822 **STONE, A. R., PARLOFF, M. B.,** and **FRANK, J. D.** (1954), The use of "diagnostic" groups in a group therapy program. *Internat. J. Group Psychother.*, 4:274-284.

11823 **STONE, G. C.** (1979), A specialized doctoral program in health psychology: considerations in its evolution. *Prof. Psychol.*, 10:596-604.

11824 **STONE, J.** (1963), Patient participation in group therapy rehash. *J. Fort Logan Ment. Health Ctr.*, 1:45-46.

11825 **STONE, L. A.,** and **KRISTJANSON, R. W.** (1975), Computer-assisted group encounter. *Small Group Behav.*, 6:457-468.

11826 **STONE, P. A.** (1972), Comparative effects of group encounter, group counseling and study skills instructions on academic performance of underachieving college students. *Dissert. Abstr. Internat.*, 33:2724A.

11827 **STONE, W. N.** (1975), Dynamics of the recorder-observer in group psychotherapy. *Comprehens. Psychiat.*, 16:49-54.

11828 **STONE, W. N.,** and **GREEN, B. L.** (1978), Learning during group therapy leadership training. *Small Group Behav.*, 9:373-386.

11829 **STONE, W. N.,** and **WHITMAN, R. M.** (1977), Contribution of psychology of self to group process and group therapy. *Internat. J. Group Psychother.*, 27:343-359.

11830 **STONE, W. N., BLAZE, M.,** and **BOZZUTO, J.** (1980), Late dropouts from group psychotherapy. *Amer. J. Psychother.*, 34:401-413.

11831 **STONE, W. N., SCHENGBER, J.,** and **SEIFRIED, S. F.** (1966), The treatment of a homosexual woman in a mixed group. *Internat. J. Group Psychother.*, 16:425-433.

11832 **STONE, W.** (1971), Screening for t-groups: the myth of healthy candidates. *Amer. J. Psychiat.*, 127:1485-1490.

11833 **STONE, W. O.** (1972), A study of pre-recorded relaxation training, rational-emotive and personal-growth group counseling intervention techniques in the reduction of state anxiety in Black multi-occupational trainees. *Dissert. Abstr. Internat.*, 32:6772A.

11834 **STONE, W. R.** (1971), Individual and group implosive therapy: fear and behavior change. *Dissert. Abstr. Internat.*, 32:3018B.

11835 **STOOZLOF, G. H.** (1979), Parent training approaches. A follow-up evaluation of parent effectiveness training, Adlerian study groups, and behavior modification. *Dissert. Abstr. Internat.*, 41:701B.

11836 **STOTSKY, B. D.,** and **ZOLIK, E. S.** (1965), Group psychotherapy with psychotics: 1921-1963—a review. *Internat. J. Group Psychother.*, 15:321-344.

11837 **STOUDENMIRE, J.** (1975), A comparison of muscle relaxation training and music in the reduction of state and trait anxiety. *J. Clin. Psychol.*, 31:490-492.

11838 **STOUDENMIRE, J.** (1973), Group counseling in hospital trainees coming from "culturally deprived" backgrounds. *Community Psychol.*, 1:235-238.

11839 **STOUTE, A.** (1950), Implementation of group interpersonal relationships through psychotherapy. *J. Psychology*, 30:145-156.

11840 **STOVER, L.** (1966), Efficacy of training procedures for mothers in therapy. *Dissert. Abstr. Internat.*, 27:2147B.

11841 **STRACHSTEIN, H.** (1978), Review of M. Sugar's *The Adolescent in Group and Family Therapy*. *Group*, 2:62-64.

11842 **STRACHSTEIN, H. W.** (1960), A comparison of individual and group psychotherapy on the basis of the recognition of the transference object, the interpretation of, and the working through of, the transference. *Dissert. Abstr. Internat.*, 20:4710. (University Microfilms No. 60-01930.)

11843 **STRACHWITZ, E. V.** (1975), (Combined therapy with the child and connecting persons.) *Praxis Kinderpsychol. & Kinderpsychiat.*, (Goettingen) 24:241-245.

11844 **STRAIGHT, B.**, and **WERKMAN, S. L.** (1958), Control problems in group therapy with aggressive adolescent boys in a mental hospital. *Amer. J. Psychiat.*, 114:998-1001.

11845 **STRAIGHT, E. M.** (1960), Evaluation of group psychotherapy by follow-up study of formerly hospitalized patients. *Group Psychother., Psychodrama & Sociometry*, 13:110-118.

11846 **STRAIN, P.** (1975), Increasing social play of severely retarded preschoolers with sociodramatic activities. *Ment. Retard.*, 13:7-9.

11847 **STRANAHAN, M.**, and **SCHWARTZMANN, C.** (1959), An experiment in reaching asocial adolescents through group therapy. *Annals Amer. Acad. Polit. & Soc. Science*, 322:117-125.

11848 **STRANAHAN, M., SCHWARTZMANN, C.**, and **ATKIN, E.** (1957), Group treatment for emotionally disturbed and potentially delinquent boys and girls. *Amer. J. Orthopsychiat.*, 27:518-527.

11849 **STRANDBERG, W. L.** (1969), An investigation of the effects of time as a process variable in group counseling. *Dissert. Abstr. Internat.*, 30:2345A.

11850 **STRANG, R.** (1940), Techniques and instruments of mental hygiene: diagnosis and therapy. *Rev. Educat. Res.*, 10:450-459.

11851 **STRANSKY, E.** (1949), Zur gruppenpsychotherapie. (On group psychotherapy.) *Wiener Klin. Wochenschr.*, (Vienna) 61:733-734.

11852 **STRASSBERG, D. S., GABEL, H.**, and **ANCHOR, K. N.** (1976), Patterns of self-disclosure in parent discussion groups. *Small Group Behav.*, 7:369-378.

11853 **STRASSBERG, D. S., ROBACK, H. B., ANCHOR, K. N.**, and **ABRAMOWITZ, S. L.** (1975), Self-disclosure in group therapy with schizophrenics. *Arch. Gen. Psychiat.*, 32:1259-1261.

11854 **STRAUB, H. H.** (1975), (Developmental processes dependent upon leader behavior in psychodramatic groups.) *Gruppendynamik*, (Stuttart) 2:104-108.

11855 **STRAUB, H.** (1969), (Experiences with psychodrama in treatment of compulsive neuroses.) *Zeit. Psychother. Med. Psychol.*, (Stuttgart) 19:192-202.

11856 **STRAUB, H.** (1963), (Psychodrama according to Moreno and its applicability in a psychiatric clinic.) *Zeit. Psychother. Med. Psychol.*, (Stuttgart) 13:117-124.

11857 **STRAUSS, E. B.** (1944), Comments on J. Bierer's paper. *Royal Soc. Med. Proceed.*, (London) 37:209.

11858 **STRAUSS, E. B.** (1948), Entwicklung der psychologischen richtung in der psychiatrie. (Evolution of the psychological tendency in psychiatry.) *Deutsche Med. Wochenschr.*, (Stuttgart) 73:145-147.

11859 **STRAUSS, E. B., STROMOLSEN, R.,** and **BIERER, J.** (1944), A memorandum on therapeutic social clubs in psychiatry. *Brit. Med. J.*, (London) 2:861.

11860 **STRAUSS, E. G.** (1948), Advances in group and individual therapy: opening the discussion. In: *International Congress on Mental Health, Vol. 3*, ed. J. C. Flugel. Proceedings of the International Conference on Medical Psychotherapy. New York: Columbia University Press.

11861 **STRAUSS, F. H.** (1955), Transference phenomena in a therapeutic community. *Acta Psychother. Psychosomat. Orthopaedagog.*, (Basel) 3:403-409.

11862 **STRAUSS, L.** (1980), The effect of an ongoing treatment group program in support of independent living. *Military Med.*, 145:849.

11863 **STRAYER, R.** (1961), Social integration of alcoholics through prolonged group therapy. *Quart. J. Studies Alcohol*, 22:471-480.

11864 **STRAZZULLA, M.** (1956), Nursery school training for retarded children. *Amer. J. Ment. Deficiency*, 61:141-151.

11865 **STREAN, H. S.** (1962), A means of involving fathers in family treatment: guidance groups for fathers. *Amer. J. Orthopsychiat.*, 32:719-727.

11866 **STREAN, H. S.** (1962), On introducing a new member. *Internat. J. Group Psychother.*, 12:362-368.

11867 **STREAN, H. S.** (1965), The personal impact of group training. *Topical Probl. Psychol. & Psychother.*, 5:33-38.

11868 **STREAN, H. S.** (1972), Social change and the proliferation of regressive therapies. *Psychoanal. Rev.*, 58:581-594.

11869 **STREAN, H. S.** (1960), Treating parents of emotionally disturbed children through role playing. *Psychoanal. Rev.*, 47:67-75.

11870 **STREAR, S.** (1969), A comparison of two methods of group counseling with obese adolescents. *Dissert. Abstr. Internat.*, 30:2389A.

11871 **STREET, P. A.** (1978), Towards an aesthetic and affective analysis of extra linguistic processes in the encounter group using a musical analogue. *Dissert. Abstr. Internat.*, 38:3374B.

11872 **STREETER, N. M.,** and **OWENS, W. E.** (1970), Partners in ministering: a psychiatrist and a pastor. *Community Ment. Health J.*, 6:292-299.

11873 **STRELNICK, A.** (1980), Multifamily group therapy for outpatients. *Amer. J. Fam. Ther.*, 8:72-74.

11874 **STRELTZER, N. E.,** and **KOCH, G. V.** (1968), Influence of emotional role-playing on smoking habits and attitudes. *Psychol. Reports*, 22:317-330.

11875 **STREUFERT, S.** (1966), Conceptual structure, communicator importance, and interpersonal attitudes toward conforming and deviant group members. *J. Personality & Soc. Psychol.*, 4:100-103.

11876 **STREUFERT, S., STREUFERT, S. C.,** and **CASTORE, C. H.** (1968), Leadership in negotiations and the complexity of conceptual structure. *J. Appl. Psychol.*, 52:218-223.

11877 **STRICKLAND, T.** (1980), Modifying delinquent adolescent affective responses related to self-perception and the use of drugs through a temporary group experience. *Dissert. Abstr. Internat.*, 41:605A. (University Microfilms No. 8018266.)

11878 **STRICKLER, E.** (1965), Educational group counseling with a remedial reading program. *Dissert. Abstr. Internat.*, 25:5129.

11879 **STRICKLER, M.,** and **ALLGEYER, J.** (1967), The crisis group: a new application of crisis theory. *Soc. Work*, 12:28-32.

11880 **STRIEGL, Q. B.** (1976), Self reported behavioral and attitudinal changes influenced by participation in women's consciousness-raising groups. *Dissert. Abstr. Internat.*, 36:4112A.

11881 **STRNAD, M.** (1975), (Conditions and limits of group psychotherapy in old people particularly in the homes for the aged.) *Ceskoslav. Psychiat.*, (Prague) 71:315-318.

11882 **STROENSTEIN, H. W.** (1960), A comparison of individual and group psychotherapy. *Dissert. Abstr. Internat.*, 20:4710.

11883 **STROH, G.** (1958), A therapist's reactions as reflected in his reporting on a psychotherapeutic group. *Internat. J. Group Psychother.*, 8:403-409.

11885 **STROMSTA, C.** (1965), A procedure using group consensus in adult stuttering therapy. *J. Speech & Hearing Disorders*, 30:277-279.

11886 **STROPKS, A. J.** (1976), Logoanalysis and guided imagery as group-treatments for existential vacuum. *Dissert. Abstr. Internat.*, 37:992B.

11887 **STROTZKA, H.** (1961), (Nature and significance of social psychiatry.) *Wiener Klin. Wochenschr.*, (Vienna) 73:389-392.

11888 **STROTZKA, H.,** and **BUCHINGER, K.** (1975), (Group dynamic aspects of a casework-supervisor-training group.) *Gruppenpsychother. & Gruppendynam.*, (Goettingen) 9:55-76.

11889 **STRUM, I. E.** (1969), Note on psychodrama in a "helping relationship." *Group Psychother., Psychodrama & Sociometry*, 22:191-193.

11890 **STRUNK, C.,** and **WITKIN, L. J.** (1974), The transformation of a latency-age girls' group from unstructured play to problem-focused discussion. *Internat. J. Group Psychother.*, 24:460-470.

11891 **STRUNK, P.** (1976), Review of Uchtenhagen's *Group Therapy and Social Environment*, 4:295-296.

11892 **STRUPP, H. H.** (1973), The experiential group and the psychotherapeutic enterprise. *Internat. J. Group Psychother.*, 23:115-124.

11893 **STRUPP, H. H.** (1962), Psychotherapy. *Annual Rev. Psychol.*, 13:445-478.

11894 **STRUPP, H. H.,** and **BERGIN, A. E.** (1969), Some empirical and conceptual bases for coordinated research in psychotherapy: a critical review of issues, trends, and evidence. *Internat. J. Psychiat.*, 7:18-90.

11895 **STRUPP, H. H.,** and **BLOXOM, A. L.** (1975), Preparing lower-class patients for group psychotherapy: development and evaluation of a role-induction film. In: *Group Psychotherapy and Group Function*, 2d ed., eds. M. Rosenbaum and M. M. Berger. New York: Basic Books.

11896 **STRUPP, H. H.,** and **BLOXUM, A. L.** (1973), Preparing lower-class patients for group psychotherapy: development and evaluation of a role-induction film. *J. Consult. & Clin. Psychol.*, 41:373-384.

11897 **STRUPP, H. H.** (1974), *Psychotherapy and Behavior Change, 1973*. Chicago: Aldine.

11898 **STUART, B. R.** (1968), Selecting a behavioral alternative through practice. *Group Psychother., Psychodrama & Sociometry*, 21:219-221.

11899 **STUBBE, H.** (1976), Psychotherapeutic function of the South American medicine man. *Confinia Psychiat.*, (Basel) 19:68-79.

11900 **STUBBLEBINE, J. M.** (1957), Group psychotherapy with some epileptic mentally deficient adults. *Amer. J. Ment. Deficiency*, 61:725-730.

11901 **STUBBLEBINE, J. M.** (1960), The therapeutic community: a further formulation. *Ment. Hosp.*, 11:16-18.

11902 **STUBBLEBINE, J. M.,** and **ROADRUCK, R. D.** (1956), Treatment program for mentally deficient adolescents. *Amer. J. Ment. Deficiency*, 60:552-556.

11903 **STUCHLIK, J.** (1960), The development and present state of psychotherapy in Czechoslovakia. *Group Psychother., Psychodrama & Sociometry*, 13:195-198.

11904 **STUCKER, P. L.** (1976), Group therapy in crisis intervention. *J. Psychiat. Nursing*, 14:28-30.

11905 **STUCKEY, B., GARRETT, M. W.,** and **SUGAR, M.** (1971), Group supervision of student companions to psychotic children. *Internat. J. Group Psychother.*, 21:301-309.

11906 **STUDT, H. H.** (1972), Problems of combined approaches to inpatient and outpatient psychotherapy. *Praxis der Psychother.*, 17:145-152.
11907 **STUNTZ, E. C.** (1972), The boxers' hug. *Transactional Anal. J.*, 2:190.
11908 **STUNTZ, E. C.** (1971), Classification of games by positions. *Transitional Anal. J.*, 1:255-258.
11909 **STUNTZ, E. C.** (1972), Second order structure of the parent. *Transactional Anal. J.*, 2:59-61.
11910 **STURM, I. E.** (1970), A behavioral outline of psychodrama. *Psychother.: Theory, Res. & Pract.*, 7:245-247.
11911 **STURM, I. E.** (1965), The behavioristic aspect of psychodrama. *Group Psychother., Psychodrama & Sociometry*, 18:50-64.
11912 **STURM, I. E.** (1970), Neuropsychiatric hospitalization on a follow-up date as a function of ward treatment programs. *J. Clin. Psychol.*, 26:230-233.
11913 **STURM, I. E.** (1963), Psychodrama in a clinical pastoral training program. *Group Psychother., Psychodrama & Sociometry*, 16:30-35.
11914 **STURTON, S.** (1972), Developing groupwork in a casework agency. *Brit. J. Soc. Work*, (Birmingham) 2:143-153.
11915 **STURUP, G.** (1959), Group therapy with chronic criminals. *Acta Psychother., Psychosomat. Orthopaedagog. Suppl.*, (Basel) 7:377-385.
11916 **SUAREZ, R.** (1970), The silent patient in group therapy. *J. Psychiat. Nursing*, 8:10-12.
11917 **SUBOTNIK, L. S.** (1975), Client-centered group therapy compared with behavior modification in changing inappropriate behavior of elementary school children. *Psychother.: Theory, Res. & Pract.*, 25:138-141.
11918 **SUCHANEK-FROEHLICH, H.** (1959), (Group psychotherapy in psychosomatic medicine.) *Acta Psychother., Psychosomat. Orthopaedagog. Suppl.*, (Basel) 7:385-397.
11919 **SUCHANEK-FRÖHLICH, H.** (1960), Über die Bedeutung der Gruppentherapie für die Behandlung funktioneller und psychosomatischen Störungen. (The significance of group therapy in the treatment of functional and psychosomatic disorders.) *Praxis der Psychother.*, 5:208-216.
11920 **SUCZEK, R. F.** (1954), The group approach to weight control. ii. psychologic aspects of obesity and group weight reduction. *J. Amer. Dietetic Assn.*, 30:442-446.
11921 **SUESS, J. F.** (1970), Self-confrontation of videotaped psychotherapy as a teaching device for psychiatric students. *J. Med. Educat.*, 45:271-282.
11922 **SUGAR, M.** (1975), *The Adolescent in Group and Family Therapy*. New York: Brunner/Mazel.
11924 **SUGAR, M.** (1967), Group therapy for pubescent boys with absent fathers. *J. Amer. Acad. Child Psychiat.*, 6:478-498.
11925 **SUGAR, M.** (1974), Interpretive group psychotherapy with latency children. *J. Amer. Acad. Child Psychiat.*, 13:648-666.
11926 **SUGAR, M.** (1971), Multitransferences and divarications in group therapy. *Internat. J. Group Psychother.*, 21:444-455.
11927 **SUGAR, M.** (1971), Premature withdrawal from group therapy: parents of intellectually retarded girls. *Group Process*, (London) 4:60-72.
11928 **SUINN, R. M.** (1968), The desensitization of test-anxiety by group and individual treatment. *Behav. Res. & Ther.*, 6:385-387.
11929 **SUINN, R. M.**, and **HALL, R.** (1970), Marathon desensitization groups: an innovative technique. *Behav. Res. & Ther.*, 8:97-98.
11930 **SUINN, R. M.**, and **WEIGEL, R. G.** (1975), *The Innovative Psychological Therapies: Critical and Creative Contributions*. New York: Harper and Row.
11931 **SULE, F.** (1971), (Paradoxical therapeutic techniques and their applicability in group psychotherapy.) *Magyar Pszichol. Szemle*, (Budapest) 28:520.

11932 **SULE, F.** (1964), (Writing a diary in psychotherapy of alcoholism.) *Ideggyogyazati Szemle*, (Budapest) 17:251-254.

11933 **SULLIVAN, L. A.** (1945), Psychodrama in a child guidance clinic. *Sociometry*, 8:296-305.

11934 **SULLIVAN, P. C.** (1977), The effects of short term vocational group counseling on career change skills. *Dissert. Abstr. Internat.*, 37:5082A.

11935 **SUMMERLIN, M. L.**, and **WARD, G. R.** (1978), Effect of parental participation in a parent group on a child's self-concept. *J. Psychology*, 100:227-234.

11936 **SUNDEL, M.** (1974), Diagnosis in group work. In: *Individual Change through Small Groups*, eds. P. Glasser, R. Sarri, and R. Vinter. New York: Free Press.

11937 **SUNLEY, R. M.** (1969), "Thinking skills": new programming for after-school groups of cognitively deprived children. *Amer. J. Orthopsychiat.*, 39:292-294.

11938 **SUPER, D. E.** (1980), The year 2000 and all that. *Couns. Psychol.*, 8:22.

11939 **SUPPLE, L. K.** (1962), Hypnodrama, a synthesis of hypnosis and psychodrama: a progress report. *Group Psychother., Psychodrama & Sociometry*, 15:58-62.

11940 **SUPPLE, L. K.** (1951), On some American innovations in psychiatry. *Group Psychother., Psychodrama & Sociometry*, 4:70-73.

11941 **SURKIS, A. A.** (1971), (Therapeutic psychodrama: a synthesis of principles of theatre and treatment.) *Laval Med.*, (Quebec) 42:29-32.

11942 **SUSSMAN, A.** (1965), Psychodrama and method acting. *Group Psychother., Psychodrama & Sociometry*, 18:260-261.

11943 **SUSSMAN, A. E.** (1974), Group therapy with severely handicapped deaf clients. *J. Rehab. Deaf*, 8:122-126.

11944 **SUTHERLAND, J. D.** (1952), Notes on psychoanalytic group therapy: i. therapy and training. *Psychiatry*, 15:111-117.

11945 **SUTHERLAND, J. D.**, and **FITZPATRICK, G. A.** (1945), Some approaches to group problems in the British army. *Sociometry*, 8:443-455.

11946 **SUTHERLAND, J. D.**, and **GILL, H. S.** (1964), The significance of the one–way vision screen in analytic group psychotherapy. *Brit. J. Med. Psychol.*, (London) 37:185-202.

11947 **SUTHERLAND, J. D., GILL, H. S.**, and **PHILLIPSON, H.** (1967), Psychodiagnostic appraisal in the light of recent theoretical developments. *Brit. J. Med. Psychol.*, (London) 40:299-315.

11948 **SUZUKI, I.** (1962), Theory and practice of psychodramatic group supervision in social casework. *Ment. Hygiene Res.* (Jap.) 1:32-41.

11949 **SUZUKI, R.** (1974), (A trial group therapy in the day care of young children with psychiatric diseases.) *Japanese J. Nursing Art*, (Tokyo) 20:52-60.

11950 **SVENSSON, A.** (1972), (The marathon method according to Bach and Steller.) *Gruppendynamik*, (Stuttgart) 4:407-422.

11951 **SWAILS, R. G.** (1973), The effects of three group approaches on the aptitude and attitude dimensions of vocational development of ninth grade high school students. *Dissert. Abstr. Internat.*, 34:4763A.

11952 **SWAN, A. C.** (1970), Personality integration and perceived behavior in a sensitivity training group. *Dissert. Abstr. Internat.*, 31:3717-3718.

11953 **SWAN, M.**, and **WILSON, L. J.** (1979), Sexual and marital problems in a psychiatric out–patient population. *Brit. J. Psychiat.*, (Ashford) 135:310-314.

11954 **SWAN, W. S.** (1973), Effects of leadership style and videotape mediated expectancies on affect and dependency in marathon encounter groups. *Dissert. Abstr. Internat.*, 34:885B.

11955 **SWANSON, D. D.** (1972), The effects of behavioral group counseling on the self-concept of pregnant Negro teenagers using male and female co-counselors. *Dissert. Abstr. Internat.*, 33:3312A.

11956 **SWANSON, G. E.** (1974), The primary process of groups, its systematics and representation. *J. Theory Soc. Behav.*, 4:53-69.

11957 **SWANSON, M. G.** (1969), A check list for group leaders. *Perspect. Psychiat. Care*, 7:120-126.

11958 **SWARR, R. R.**, and **EWING, T. N.** (1977), Outcome effects of eclectic interpersonal-learning-based group psychotherapy with college student neurotics. *J. Consult. & Clin. Psychol.*, 45:1029-1035.

11959 **SWARTZ, M. J.** (1959), The kibbutz and its children. *Group Psychother., Psychodrama & Sociometry*, 12:92-96.

11960 **SWEENEY, A.**, and **DRAGE, E.** (1968), Group therapy: an analysis of the orientation phase. *J. Psychiat. Nursing*, 6:20-26.

11961 **SWEENEY, A., BARNES, P., SHAFFER, M.**, and **CASSIDY, R.** (1969), Courage to change. *J. Psychiat. Nursing*, 7:73-76.

11962 **SWENDSEN, L. A.** (1978), Role supplementation for new parents: a role mastery plan. *MCN: Amer. J. Maternal Child Nursing*, 3:84-91.

11963 **SWENSON, W. M.** (1951), "Round table" group psychotherapy at the St. Peter State Hospital. *Group Psychother., Psychodrama & Sociometry*, 4:63-65.

11964 **SWENSON, W. M.**, and **MARTIN, H. R.** (1976), A description and evaluation of an outpatient intensive psychotherapy center: Mayo Clinic. *Amer. J. Psychiat.*, 133:1043-1046.

11965 **SWILDENS, H.** (1979), (Is there a Rogerian group therapy?) *Tijdschr. voor Psychother.*, 5:1-7.

11966 **SWINDLEHURST, B.** (1980), Review of M. M. Ohlsen's "Group counseling." *Internat. J. Adv. Couns.*, 3:295.

11967 **SWISHER, J. D., WARNER, R. W.**, and **HERR, E. L.** (1972), Experimental comparison of four approaches to drug abuse prevention among ninth and eleventh graders. *J. Couns. Psychol.*, 19:328-332.

11968 **SWISHER, J. D., WARNER, R. W., SPENCE, C. C.**, and **UPCRAFT, M. L.** (1973), Four approaches to drug abuse prevention among college students. *J. Coll. Student Personnel*, 14:231-235.

11969 **SYMONDS, C.** (1971), A nude touchy–feely group. *J. Sex Res.*, 7:126-133.

11970 **SYMONDS, M.**, and **DAWSON, E. S.** (1974/1975), The co-therapist approach to group treatment with institutionalized early adolescent girls. *Groups*, 6:27-36.

11971 **SYMONDS, P. M.** (1947), Role playing as a diagnostic procedure in the selection of leaders. *Sociatry*, 1:43-50.

11972 **SYVÄNNE, S.** (1964), (Experiences in group therapy with parents for patients in a psychiatric department for young people.) *Nordisk Psykiat. Tidsskr.*, (Kungsbacha) 18:529-537.

11973 **SYZ, H.** (1963), (Reflections on group- or phylo-analysis.) *Acta Psychother., Psychosomat. Orthopaedagog. Suppl.*, (Basel) 11:37-88.

11974 **SYZ, H. C.** (1928), Remarks on group analysis. *Amer. J. Psychiat.*, 85:141-148.

11975 **SYZ, H. C.** (1930), Socio-individual principles in psychopathology. *Brit. J. Med. Psychol.*, (London) 10:329-343.

11976 **SYZ, H. C.** (1944), Treatment within the group as a biological entity. *Amer. J. Orthopsychiat.*, 14:603-608.

11977 **SZELENBERGER, W.** (1971), (Music therapy in the psychiatric ward.) *Psychiat. Polska*, (Warsaw) 5:69-72.

11978 **SZONDI, L.** (1963), *Schicksalsanalytische Therapie*. (*Fate Analytic Therapy*.) Berne: H. Huber.

11979 **SZÖNYI, G.** (1975), (Interpersonal exposure to danger and risk-taking in the group therapy process.) *Psychiat. Neurol. Med. Psychol.*, (Leipzig) 27:524-528.

T

11980 **TABACHNICK, N.** (1965), Isolation, transference–splitting and combined therapy. *Comprehens. Psychiat.*, 6:336-346.

11981 **TABER, R. H.** (1969), Providing mental health services to a low socio-economic Black community without requiring that people perceive themselves as patients: an ecological systems approach to a community group. *Amer. J. Orthopsychiat.*, 39:339-340.

11982 **TABER, R. H.** (1970), A systems approach to the delivery of mental health services in Black ghettos. *Amer. J. Orthopsychiat.*, 40:703-709.

11983 **TABOROFF, L. H., BROWN, W. H., KORNER, I. N., REISER, D. E., TALMADGE, M., GOATES, B. L.,** and **STEIN, E.** (1956), A note on intake diagnosis in groups. *Internat. J. Group Psychother.*, 6:193-196.

11984 **TAILEY, P.** (1968), The relation of group counseling to changes in the self-concept of Negro eighth grade students. *Dissert. Abstr. Internat.*, 28:2524A.

11985 **TAINTOR, Z.,** and **WEYMOUTH, P.** (1967), A group cycle in a developing therapeutic community. *Sandoz Psychiat. Spectator*, 4:15-16.

11986 **TAJFEL, H.** (1979), Individuals and groups in social psychology. *Brit. J. Sociol. & Clin. Psychol.*, (London) 18:183-190.

11987 **TALAVAGE, J. J.** (1974), A theory of dynamic group behavior. *Internat. J. Gen. Systems*, 1:119-130.

11988 **TALBOT, E., MILLER, S. C.,** and **WHITE, R. B.** (1961), Some aspects of self-conceptions and role demands in a therapeutic community. *J. Abnorm. & Soc. Psychol.*, 63:338-345.

11989 **TALLAND, G. A.** (1957), Do therapists and patients share norms on the content of group discussion? *Group Psychother., Psychodrama & Sociometry*, 10:10-21.

11990 **TALLAND, G. A.** (1957), Role and status structure in therapy groups. *J. Clin. Psychol.*, 13:27-33.

11991 **TALLAND, G. A.** (1955), Task and interaction process: some characteristics of therapeutic group discussion. *J. Abnorm. & Soc. Psychol.*, 50:105-109.

11992 **TALLAND, G. A.** (1954), The working system of psychotherapy groups. *Group Psychother., Psychodrama & Sociometry*, 7:67-80.

11993 **TALLAND, G. A.,** and **CLARK, D. H.** (1954), Evaluation of topics in therapy group discussions. *J. Clin. Psychol.*, 10:131-137.

11994 **TALLEY, W. M.** (1971), Some concerns about group experiences. *J. Counc. Assn. Univ. Student Personnel Serv.*, 5:22-26.

11995 **TALMADGE, M.** (1959), Values of group interaction for discharged mental patients. *Internat. J. Group Psychother.*, 9:338-344.

11996 **TALMADGE, M., HAYDEN, B. S.,** and **KULLA, M.** (1969), The alienated junior high school student: a research evaluation of a program. *Amer. J. Orthopsychiat.*, 39:299-300.

11997 **TAMERIN, J. S.** (1972), The psychodynamics of quitting smoking in a group. *Amer. J. Psychiat.*, 129:589-595.

11998 **TAMKIN, A. S.** (1968), The use of an interval timer in group therapy. *Internat. J. Group Psychother.*, 18:366-368.

11999 **TAMMINEN, A. W.,** and **SMABY, M. H.** (1978), You can be a skilled group helper. *Personnel & Guid. J.*, 56:501-507.

12000 **TANAKA, K.** (1961), The effects of sociometric regrouping on psychological structure in the school classes. *Group Psychother., Psychodrama & Sociometry*, 14:203-208.

12001 **TANG, K. S.** (1971), Inducing achievement behavior through a planned group counseling program. *Dissert. Abstr. Internat.*, 31:3888A.

12002 **TANSEY, F. M.** (1979), Videotape focused feedback techniques in marathon group therapy: effects on self-actualization and psychopathology. *Dissert. Abstr. Internat.*, 39:5592B.

12003 **TAPPAN, C. B.** (1968), A program of resocialization for a long-term regressed schizophrenic patient. *J. Psychiat. Nursing*, 6:334-335.

12004 **TARRAB, G.** (1969/1970), Happenings and psychodrama. *Bull. de Psychol.*, (Paris) 23:915-922.

12005 **TARRIER, R. B.** (1973), New trends in technology management for training group counselors. *Educat. Technol.*, 13:52-56.

12006 **TARRIER, R. B.**, and **SHAPPELL, D. L.** (1973), Groups: guidance, counseling, or therapy. *Small Group Behav.*, 4:47-54.

12007 **TASS, G.** (1976), Psychotherapeutic methods for the management of persons after attempted suicide. *Orvosi Hetilap*, (Budapest) 117:659-660.

12008 **TATARA, M.** (1963), (An analysis of success and failure in the cases of psychotherapy with children: i.) *Japanese J. Clin. Psychol.*, (Tokyo) 2:63-73.

12009 **TATE, F. E.** (1973), Counseling groups for counselor trainees: a process model. *Counselor Educat. & Supervision*, 13:68-71.

12010 **TATE, F. U.** (1958), Training in group psychotherapy: a symposium. (IV) the satisfactions for the trainee in learning group psychotherapy. *Amer. J. Psychother.*, 12:503-505.

12011 **TATE, G. T.** (1967), *Strategy of Therapy: Toward the Engineering of Social Growth*. New York: Springer.

12012 **TATER, S. M.** (1980), Psychodynamics of child abuse as seen through the conjoint psychotherapy of a mother and her abused child. *Fam. Ther.*, 7:197.

12013 **TAUBER, L. E.** (1978), Choice point analysis: formulation, strategy, intervention, and result in group process therapy and supervision. *Internat. J. Group Psychother.*, 28:163-184.

12014 **TAUBER, L. E.** (1964), Participation of the patient in the planning and evaluation of group psychotherapy. *Internat. J. Group Psychother.*, 14:224-226.

12015 **TAUBER, L. E.**, and **ISAACSON, L. E.** (1961), Group-need therapy: an approach to group planning. *J. Couns. Psychol.*, 8:260-262.

12016 **TAUSCH, A. M.** (1975), (Psychic changes and conversational behavior in person-centered encounter groups with prison inmates, judges, psychotherapy clients and psychologists.) *Psychol. Erziehung Unterricht*, (Munich) 22:161-171.

12017 **TAVANTZIS, T. N.** (1978), An investigation into the relationship between a specific theory of group counseling and its practice. *Dissert. Abstr. Internat.*, 39:4067A.

12018 **TAVDIOGLU, M.** (1973), Group therapy of the outcasts of psychiatry. *Voices*, 9:33-36.

12018 **TAVORMINA, J. B.** (1974), Basic models of parent counseling: a critical review. *Psychol. Bull.*, 81:827-835.

12019 **TAVLARIDOU, A.** (1960), Report on the committee on group psychotherapy and psychodrama in Greece. *Internat. J. Sociometry & Sociatry*, 2:103.

12020 **TAVORMINA, J. B.** (1974), Relative effectiveness of behavioral and reflective group counseling with parents of mentally retarded children. *Dissert. Abstr. Internat.*, 35:527B.

12021 **TAVORMINA, J. B.** (1975), Relative effectiveness of behavioral and reflective group counseling with parents of mentally retarded children. *J. Consult. Clin. Psychol.*, 43:22-31.

12022 **TAVRIS, E.** (1962), Some notes on group psychotherapy for severe mental defectives. *Delaware Med. J.*, 33:301-307.

12023 **TAWADROS, S. M.** (1957), An experiment in the group psychotherapy of stutterers. *Internat. J. Sociometry and Sociatry*, 1:181-189.

12024 **TAWADROS, S. M.** (1956), Factors in group therapy. *Internat. J. Psychiat.*, 2:44-50.

12025 **TAWADROS, S. M.** (1956), Spontaneity training at the Dorra Institute, Alexandria, Egypt. *Group Psychother., Psychodrama & Sociometry*, 9:164-167.

12026 **TAYLAR, E. D., STRICKLAND, C. A.,** and **LINDSAY, C. S.** (1948), The social club in a treatment of defectives. In: *Therapeutic Social Clubs*, (ed. J. Bierer. London: Lewis.

12027 **TAYLOR, A. J.** (1966), An evaluation of group psychotherapy: research report. *New Zeal. Med. J.*, (Dunedin) 65:120-122.

12028 **TAYLOR, A. J.** (1967), An evaluation of group psychotherapy in a girl's borstal. *Internat. J. Group Psychother.*, 17:168-177.

12029 **TAYLOR, A. J.** (1962), Group therapy and the prison theatre. *New Zeal. Med. J.*, (Dunedin) 61:352-355.

12030 **TAYLOR, A. J. W.** (1964), An approach to the diagnosis and group treatment of criminal psychopathy. *Human Relat.*, 17:243-250.

12031 **TAYLOR, A. J. W.** (1961), A therapeutic group in prison. *Internat. J. Group Psychother.*, 11:180-187.

12032 **TAYLOR, A. J. W.** (1963), Therapeutic groups outside a prison. *Internat. J. Group Psychother.*, 13:308-314.

12033 **TAYLOR, C. T.** (1978), A group experience for parents of children with malignancy. *J. So. Carolina Med. Assn.*, 74:290-292.

12034 **TAYLOR, D. W.** (1971), Group systematic desensitization with test-anxious college students. *Dissert. Abstr. Internat.*, 31:4347.

12035 **TAYLOR, F. K.** (1961), *The Analysis of Therapeutic Groups*. Fair Lawn, NJ: Oxford University Press.

12036 **TAYLOR, F. K.** (1961), *The Analysis of Therapeutic Groups*. London: Oxford University Press.

12037 **TAYLOR, F. K.** (1958), A history of group and administrative therapy in Great Britain. *Brit. J. Med. Psychol.*, (London) 31:153-173.

12038 **TAYLOR, F. K.** (1949), Experimental investigation of collective social and libidinal motivations in therapeutic groups. *Brit. J. Med. Psychol.*, (London) 22:169-182.

12039 **TAYLOR, F. K.** (1957), Group therapy with in- and out-patients. *Internat. J. Soc. Psychiat.*, (London) 3:36-43.

12040 **TAYLOR, F. K.** (1952), On some principles of group therapy. *Brit. J. Med. Psychol.*, (London) 25:128-134.

12041 **TAYLOR, F. K.** (1950), The pattern of friendliness and dominance in a therapeutic group. *J. Ment. Science*, (London) 96:407-425.

12042 **TAYLOR, F. K.** (1951), Quantitative evaluation of psychosocial phenomena in small groups. *J. Ment. Science*, (London) 97:690-717.

12043 **TAYLOR, F. K.** (1967), Some doubts about sensitivity training. *Austral. Psychologist*, (Brisbane) 1:171-179.

12044 **TAYLOR, F. K.** (1950), The therapeutic factors of group-analytical treatment. *J. Ment. Science*, (London) 96:976-997.

12045 **TAYLOR, F. K.** (1954), The three-dimensional basis of emotional interactions in small groups. i. *Human Relat.*, 7:441-471.

12046 **TAYLOR, F. K.,** and **REY, J. H.** (1953), The scapegoat motif in society and its manifestations in a therapeutic group. *Internat. J. Psycho-Anal.*, (London) 34:253-264.

12047 **TAYLOR, H. F.** (1968), Balance, tension, and tension release in the two-person group. *Human Relat.*, 21:59-74.

12048 **TAYLOR, J.** (1978), Review of K. D. Mackenzie's *A Theory of Group Structures, Vol. 1: Basic Theory; Vol. 2: Empirical Tests. J. Communicat.*, 28:227-229.

12049 **TAYLOR, J. L.** (1975), A group counseling program for adopting parents. *Amer. J. Orthopsychiat.*, 45:266-267.

12050 **TAYLOR, M. G. K.** (1972), Some effects of an intensive group experience on social influence, internal-external control and individual attraction to the group. *Dissert. Abstr. Internat.*, 2359B

12051 **TAYLOR, M. H.** (1975), Effects of a pre-programmed, leaderless personal growth group. *J. Coll. Student Personnel*, 16:201-204.

12052 **TAYLOR, M. H.** (1974), Encountertapes for personal growth groups. *Western Carolina Univ. J. Educat.*, 6:16-19.

12053 **TAYLOR, M. H.** (1976), Encountertapes for personal growth groups: how useful? *Small Group Behav.*, 7:397-406.

12054 **TAYLOR, M. H.** (1975), A rational-emotive workshop on overcoming study blocks. *Personnel & Guid. J.*, 53:458-462.

12055 **TAYLOR, T. D.** (1970), Effects of group counseling on self-concept and academic achievement of selected high school sophomore health classes. *Dissert. Abstr. Internat.*, 3:1582A.

12056 **TAYLOR, W. F.** (1971), Direct vs. indirect intervention in elementary group counseling. *Dissert. Abstr. Internat.*, 32:1069A.

12057 **TAYLOR, W. F.,** and **HOEDT, K. C.** (1974), Classroom-related behavior problems: counsel parents, teachers, or children? *J. Couns. Psychol.*, 21:3-8.

12058 **TAYONA, S.** (1975), Remotivation at the National Mental Hospital Mandaluyong, Rizal. *Philippine J. Nursing*, (Manila) 44:32-34.

12059 **TCHACK, E.** (1972), Self-actualization and clarity of perception of self and others during sensitivity training. *Dissert. Abstr. Internat.*, 33:2183-2184A.

12060 **TEAHAN, J. E.** (1966), Effect of group psychotherapy on academic low achievers. *Internat. J. Group Psychother.*, 16:78-85.

12061 **TEAHAN, J. E.** (1975), Role-playing and group experience to facilitate attitude and value changes among Black and White police officers. *J. Soc. Issues*, 31:35-45.

12062 **TEBOUL, R.** (1967), Traitement de psychotiques en groupe restreint. (Treatment of psychotics in a restricted group.) *Annales Medico-Psychol.*, (Paris) 1:776.

12063 **TEC, L.** (1956), A psychiatrist as a participant observer in a group of "delinquent" boys. *Internat. J. Group Psychother.*, 6:418-429.

12064 **TECHUMI, S. A.** (1974), Changes in self concept resulting from a crisis intervention marathon group process treatment for non-achieving two-year college freshmen. *Dissert. Abstr. Internat.*, 34:5647A.

12065 **TEFFT, B. M.,** and **SIMEONSSON, R. J.** (1979), Psychology and the creation of health care settings. *Prof. Psychol.*, 10:558-570.

12066 **TEICHER, A.** (1962), The use of conflicting loyalties in combined individual and group psychotherapy with separate therapists. *Internat. J. Group Psychother.*, 12:75-81.

12067 **TEICHER, A., DeFRIENTAS, L.,** and **OSHERSON, A.** (1974), Group psychotherapy and the intense group experience: a preliminary rationale for encounter as a therapeutic agent in the mental health field. *Internat. J. Group Psychother.*, 24:159-173.

12068 **TEICHER, J. D.** (1945), Experiences with group psychotherapy. *Nav. Med. Bull.*, 44:753-755.

12069 **TEICHER, J. D.** (1966), Group psychotherapy with adolescents. *Calif. Med.*, 105:18-21.

12070 **TEICHMAN, Y., SPIEGEL, Y.,** and **TEICHMAN, M.** (1978), Crisis intervention with families of servicemen missing in action. *Amer. J. Community Psychol.*, 6:315-326.

12071 **TEIRICH, H.** (1960), (Group psychotherapy in American prisons.) *Med. Klinik*, (Munich) 55:1168-1170.

12074 **TEIRICH, H. R.** (1955), Gruppenpsychotherapie im spiegel einer patienzeichnung. *Med.*, 12:432-435.

12075 **TEIRICH, H. R.** (1957), Gruppentherapie mit studenten. (Group therapy with students.) *Zeit. Diagnost. Psychol.*, 5:260-270.

12072 **TEIRICH, H. R.** (1951), Group psychotherapy in Austria. *Group Psychother., Psychodrama & Sociometry*, 4:107-111.

12073 **TEIRICH, H. R.** (1952), Group psychotherapy with women patients in a mental hospital. *Internat. J. Group Psychother.*, 2:369-376.

12076 **TEIRICH, H. R.** (1958), *Musik in der Medizin.* (*Music in Medicine.*) Stuttgart: G. Fischer.

12077 **TEIRICH, H. R.** (1959), Patientenklubs in der privatpraxis. (Patients' clubs in private practice: a report on experience.) *Acta Psychother., Psychosomat. Orthopaedagog.*, (Basel) 7:232-239.

12078 **TEIRICH, H. R.** (1953), Psychiatrisches turnen im rahmen gruppentherapeutischer Bestrebungen. (Psychiatric exercises in a group therapy setting at Bestrebungen.) *Hippokrates*, (Stuttgart) 24:461-464.

12079 **TEIRICH, H. R.** (1954), Rangordnungsprobleme in der gruppe bei mensch und tier. (Group hierarchy problems among men and animals.) *Zeit. Psychother. Med. Psychol.*, (Stuttgart) 4:193-201.

12080 **TEIRICH, H. R.** (1953), Ruhebilder in der gruppentherapie. *Der Psychologie*, (Berne) 9:347-352.

12081 **TEIRICH, H. R.** (1951), Schools rather than hospitals: about group psychotherapy in Austria. *Group Psychother., Psychodrama & Sociometry*, 4:77-79.

12082 **TEIRICH, H. R.** (1957), Soziometrie und gruppenpsychotherapie. (Sociometry and group psychotherapy.) *Zeit. Psychother. Med. Psychol.*, (Stuttgart) 7:41-47.

12083 **TEIRICH, H. R.** (1949), Theorie und praxis der gruppenpsychotherapie. (Group psychotherapy: theory and practice; preliminary report.) *Wiener Med. Wochenschr.*, (Vienna) 99:617-618.

12084 **TEIRICH, H. R.** (1954), Ubertragungs-und rang-ordnungsprobleme in der gruppentherapie. (Transference and hierarchy problems in group therapy.) *Acta Psychother., Psychosomat. Orthopaedagog.*, (Basel) 3:409-413.

12085 **TEIRICH, H. R.** (1955), The use of video methods in group psychotherapy. *Group Psychother., Psychodrama & Sociometry*, 8:47-48.

12086 **TEIRICH, H. R.** (1951), Was ist gruppenpsychotherapie? (What is group psychotherapy?) *Zeit. Psychother. Med. Psychol.*, (Stuttgart) 1:26-30.

12087 **TEITELBAUM, H. A., HOEKSTRA, C. S., GOLDSTEIN, D. N., HARRIS, I. D.,** and **WOODS, R. M.** (1946), The treatment of psychiatric disorders due to combat by means of a group therapy program and insulin subshock doses. *J. Nerv. & Ment. Diseases*, 104:123-143.

12088 **TEITELBAUM, S. H.,** and **SUINN, R. M.** (1964), A group therapy program with orthopedic patients. *Group Psychother., Psychodrama & Sociometry*, 17:49-55.

12089 **TEITELMAN, E., GLASS, J. B., BLYN, C.,** and **JENNINGS, D.** (1979), The treatment of female borderlines. *Schiz. Bull.*, 5:111-117.

12090 **TEIXEIRA, I. J.** (1973), Critical considerations about therapy in group in Guanabara. *Neurobiologia*, (Pernambuco) 36:41-44.

12091 **TELSCHOW, E. F.** (1950), The role of the leader in nondirective group psychotherapy. Unpublished doctoral dissertation, Columbia University.

12092 **TENBRUNSEL, T. W., LOTTMAN, T. J., COBY, W. F.,** and **OZIEL, L. J.**

(1971), A group token program for the education of the mentally ill. *Psychol. Reports*, 28:743-746.
12093 **TENENBAUM, B.** (1961), Group therapy with LSD-25: a preliminary report. *Diseases Nerv. System*, 22:459-462.
12094 **TENENBAUM, S.** (1970), A discussion of the therapy that resides in a group. *Psychother.: Theory, Res. & Pract.*, 7:253-255.
12095 **TENENBAUM, S.** (1968), *A Psychologist Looks at Marriage*. New York: A. S. Barnes.
12096 **TENENBAUM, S.** (1970), School grades and group therapy. *Ment. Hygiene*, 54:525-529.
12097 **TENFLOTH, I.**, and **RACKENSPERGER, W.** (1975), Study of efficacy of training emotional behavior in groups. *Arch. Psychiat. & Nervenkrankheiten*, 220:237-243.
12098 **TENG, S. M.** (1980), Practicing group psychotherapy in a psychiatric ward. *Hu Li Tsa Chih*, (Hong Kong) 27:9-17.
12099 **TEPPERMAN, J. H.** (1977), The effectiveness of short term group therapy upon the pathological gambler and wife. *Dissert. Abstr. Internat.*, 37:5383B.
12100 **TERHUNE, W. B.**, and **DICKENSON, J. R.** (1948), Progress in group psychotherapy: a summary of the literature. *New Engl. J. Med.*, 239:854-859.
12101 **TERLESKI, D. R.** (1970), The relationship between unstructured and structured sensitivity group experiences and self-perceived changes of group members. *Dissert. Abstr. Internat.*, 31:5139-5140A.
12102 **TERNER, J. R.**, and **PEW, W. L.** (1978), *The Courage to Be Imperfect: The Life and Work of Rudolf Dreikurs*. New York: Hawthorne Books.
12103 **TERRELL, D. L.** (1973), A comparison of individual, group and individual plus group interventions by non-professional child aides. *Dissert. Abstr. Internat.*, 34:2320B.
12104 **TERWILLIGER, K. D.** (1972), The effect of group counseling on the vocal recital performance of undergraduate education vocal music majors. *Dissert. Abstr. Internat.*, 33:577A.
12105 **TEUWSEN, E.** (1975), (Client-centered groups with emphasis on self-experience at student counseling centers.) *Gruppendynamik*, (Stuttgart) 6:250-255.
12106 **THAKAR, B.** (1974), An evaluation of the effectiveness of rehabilitated schizophrenics as co-leaders in a selected group counseling situation. *Dissert. Abstr. Internat.*, 35:4200B.
12107 **THAMM, R.** (1972), Self-acceptance and acceptance-of-others: an exploration into personality syndromes. *Transactional Anal. J.*, 2:139-147.
12108 **THAYER, J. A.** (1968), The effects of group counseling on achievement and behavior of junior high school students. *Dissert. Abstr. Internat.*, 29:1111-1112.
12109 **THEINER, E. C.** (1969), An approach to the manpower problem: psychodrama as conducted in a military setting. *Amer. Psychologist*, 24:686-687.
12110 **THELAN, A. M.** (1969), The effectiveness of required individual and group guidance procedures in promoting change in selected characteristics of high risk junior college freshmen. *Dissert. Abstr. Internat.*, 30:178A.
12111 **THELAN, H. A.** (1951), Social process versus community deterioration. *Group Psychother., Psychodrama & Sociometry*, 4:206-212.
12112 **THELEN, M. H.**, and **HARRIS, C. S.** (1968), Personality of college underachievers who improve with group psychotherapy. *Personnel & Guid. J.*, 46:561-566.
12113 **THELEN, M. H.**, and **LASOSKI, M.** (1980), The separate and combined

effects of focusing information and videotape self-confrontation feedback. *J. Behav. Ther. & Exper. Psychiat.*, 11:173-178.

12114 Therapist's own conflicts may be resolved during group leadership. (1969), *Roche Report: Front. Hosp. Psychiat.*, 6:3.

12115 **THIEL, G., STEINBACH, I.,** and **TAUSCH, A. M.** (1978), (Pupils have helpful talks with pupils.) *Psychol. Erziehung & Unterricht*, (Munich) 25:75-81.

12116 **THIEMANN, J.** (1944), Part-time protective environment as an adjuvant in therapy for alcohol addiction. *New Engl. J. Med.*, 231:9-11.

12117 **THIESSEN, J. D.** (1980), Facilitating postdivorce adjustment through communication skills training. *Dissert. Abstr. Internat.*, 40:3974B.

12118 **THIS, C.** (1964), (Therapeutic clay modeling and psychotics in a hospital environment.) *Confinia Psychiat.*, (Basel) 7:38-46.

12119 **THISTLE, L.** (1976), The effects of consciousness-raising vs. encounter and same vs. mixed sex groups on sex role attitudes and self-perceptions of graduate students in a counselor/psychotherapist training program. *Dissert. Abstr. Internat.*, 36:7222-7223.

12120 **THOMA, E.** (1964), Group psychotherapy with underachieving girls in a public high school. *J. Individ. Psychol.*, 20:96-100.

12121 **THOMAS, C. A.** (1974), Human relations training in the Army Medical Department. *Military Med.*, 139:731-733.

12122 **THOMAS, C. A., JR.** (1967), Return-to-duty oriented group psychotherapy in an army psychiatric treatment center. *Military Med.*, 132:716-721.

12123 **THOMAS, G. W.** (1943), Group psychotherapy: a review of the recent literature. *Psychosomat. Med.*, 5:166-180.

12124 **THOMAS, J. D.** (1974), Effectiveness of a group counseling procedure in changing work values of college students. *Dissert. Abstr. Internat.*, 34:3893A.

12125 **THOMAS, J. E.** (1972), Group work and adult education. *Austral. J. Adult Educat.*, (Sydney) 12:15-19.

12126 **THOMAS, N. L.** (1974), The effects of a sensitivity encounter group experience upon self-concept and school achievement in adolescent underachieving girls. *Dissert. Abstr. Internat.*, 35:1066B.

12127 **THOMAS, P. H.** (1974), An evaluation of a fight training treatment program: the elements and effects of constructive fighting. *Dissert. Abstr. Internat.*, 35:527.

12128 **THOMAS, S. D.** (1973), Effectiveness of a group counseling procedure in changing work values of college students. *Dissert. Abstr. Internat.*, 34:3893A.

12129 **THOMBS, M. R.** (1973), Group counseling and the sociometric status of second grade children. *Elem. School Guid. Couns.*, 7:194-197.

12130 **THOMPSON, A.,** and **GROSS, A. E.** (1965), Problems in evaluating industrial therapy programs. *Psychiat. Quart. Suppl.*, 39:136-141.

12131 **THOMPSON, C. E.,** and **KOLB, W. P.** (1953), Group psychotherapy in association with Alcoholics Anonymous. *Amer. J. Psychiat.*, 110:29-33.

12132 **THOMPSON, D. D.** (1971), A review and analysis of the reported experimental research on group counseling in higher education between 1955 and 1967. *Dissert. Abstr. Internat.*, 31:5612B.

12133 **THOMPSON, D. G.** (1978), Effectiveness of values clarification and social-spectrum behavioral group counseling with ninth-grade boys in a residential school. *Dissert. Abstr. Internat.*, 39:4742A.

12134 **THOMPSON, D. S.** (1967), Remotivation to motivation. *Can. Nurse*, (Ottawa) 63:32-35.

12135 **THOMPSON, E. F.,** and **GLAD, D. D.** (1972), Relationships between emotional projection test responses and the process of improvement in a therapy group of paranoid schizophrenics. *J. Colorado-Wyoming Acad. Science*, 4:82-83.

12137 **THOMPSON, H. S.** (1952), An experience of a nonalcoholic in Alcoholics Anonymous leadership. *Quart. J. Studies Alcohol*, 13:271-295.

12136 **THOMPSON, G.** (1970), Having a thought. *Internat. J. Group Psychother.*, 20:170-184.

12138 **THOMPSON, J. A.**, and **NEUBAUER, P. B.** (1951), A discussion of the case of Jean Case. *Internat. J. Group Psychother.*, 1:169-171.

12139 **THOMPSON, J. K.** (1969), "I'm the most geriatric of them all": community placement of geriatric patients. *Ment. Hygiene*, 53:375-380.

12140 **THOMPSON, K.** (1948), The in-patient club. In: *Therapeutic Social Clubs*, ed. J. Bierer. London: Lewis.

12141 **THOMPSON, R.** (1980), Psychotherapy: a refined form of hell on earth. *Nursing Mirror*, (London) 150:33-35.

12142 **THOMPSON, S.**, and **KAHN, J. H.** (1970), *The Group Process as a Helping Technique: A Textbook for Social Workers, Psychologists, Doctors, Teachers, and Other Workers in Community Service.* New York: Pergamon Press.

12143 **THOMPSON, W. R.** (1973), A comparison of the relative effectiveness of two different group approaches with sixth grade pupils. *Dissert. Abstr. Internat.*, 34:3893A.

12144 **THOMPSON, W. R.**, and **RANDOLPH, D. L.** (1973), A comparison of the relative effectiveness of two different group approaches to counseling with sixth grade pupils. *Southern J. Educat. Res.*, 7:66-79.

12145 **THOMSON, C. P.** (1968), Developing a day program at the Royal Edinburgh Hospital. *Hosp. & Community Psychiat.*, 19:14-17.

12146 **THOMSON, G.** (1972), The identification of ego states. *Transactional Anal. J.*, 2:196-211.

12147 **THOMSTAD, H.** (1964), Group supervision of student nurses training groups. *Acta Psychiat. Scand., Suppl.*, (Copenhagen) 40:119.

12148 **THORDAL, B. K.** (1976), The differential effects of group emotional climate in four types of counseling groups. *Dissert. Abstr. Internat.*, 36:4741-4742.

12149 **THORESEN, C. E.**, and **POTTER, B.** (1975), Behavioral group counseling. In: *Basic Approaches to Group Psychotherapy and Group Counseling*, ed. G. Gazda. Springfield, IL: C. C. Thomas.

12150 **THORESON, R. W.** (1963), An analysis of mental patient role perceptions: own and attributed norms. *Dissert. Abstr. Internat.*, 24:1276-1277.

12151 **THORLEY, A. S.**, and **CRASKE, N.** (1950), Comparison and estimate of group and individual methods of treatment. *Brit. Med. J.*, (London) 1:97-100.

12152 **THORN, J. P.** (1974), The prediction of the individual's in-group verbal behavior. *Dissert. Abstr. Internat.*, 35:3438A.

12153 **THORPE, G. L.** (1975), (Desensitization, behavioral rehearsal, self-instructional training and placebo effects on assertive-refusal behavior.) *European J. Behav. Anal. & Modificat.*, (Munich) 1:30-44.

12154 **THORPE, J. J.** (1956), Addicts. In: *The Fields of Group Psychotherapy*, ed. S. R. Slavson. New York: International Universities Press.

12155 **THORPE, J. J.**, and **SMITH, B.** (1952), Operational sequence in group therapy with young offenders. *Internat. J. Group Psychother.*, 2:24-33.

12156 **THORPE, J. J.**, and **SMITH, B.** (1953), Phases in group development in the treatment of drug addicts. *Internat. J. Group Psychother.*, 3:66-78.

12157 **THORTON, C. E.** (1979), Sexuality counseling of women with spinal cord injuries. *Sexual Disabil.*, 2:267-277.

12158 **THUNE, E. S., MANDERSCHIELD, R. W.**, and **SILBERGELD, S.** (1980),

Personal vs. relationship orientation as a dimension of sex role differentiation. *Psychol. Reports*, 46:455.

12159 **THUNE, E. S., MANDERSCHEID, R. W.,** and **SILBERGELD, S.** (1980), Status or sex roles as determinants of interaction patterns in small, mixed-sex groups. *J. Soc. Psychol.*, 112:51-65.

12160 **THURSTON, A. S.** (1959), An experimental study of the relative effectiveness of group counseling and the orientation course in assisting college freshmen. Unpublished doctoral dissertation, George Washington University.

12161 **THURSZ, D.** (1960), *Volunteer Group Advisors in a National Social Group Work Agency*. Washington, D.C.: Catholic University of America Press.

12162 **TIBBETTS, P.** (1974), Sensitivity training: a possible application for librarianship. *Spec. Libraries*, 65:493-498.

12163 **TIBBITTS, G. E.** (1974), Group psychotherapy reporting. *Australasian Nurses J.*, (Port Adelaide) 2:11.

12164 **TICHENER, J. L., SHELDON, M. B.,** and **ROSS, W. D.** (1959), Changes in blood pressure of hypertensive patients with and without group psychotherapy. *J. Psychosomat. Res.*, 4:10-12.

12165 **TIEBOUT, H. M.** (1943), Therapeutic Mechanisms of Alcoholics Anonymous. *Amer. J. Psychiat.*, 100:468-473.

12166 **TIEDEMANN, J. G.** (1961), An investigation of the influence of group standards and deviate member behavior on the exhibited racial prejudice of an individual. Ph.D. thesis, American University.

12167 **TIEGERMAN, S.,** and **KASSINOVE, H.** (1977), Effects of assertive training and cognitive components of rational therapy on assertive behaviors and interpersonal anxiety. *Psychol. Reports*, 40:535-542.

12168 **TIERNEY, M.** (1945), Psychodramatic therapy for the alcoholics. *Sociometry*, 8:76-78.

12169 **TIETZ, W.** (1970), Establishing a small group treatment home in the Mexican ghetto. *Amer. J. Orthopsychiat.*, 40:242.

12170 **TILEY, E.** (1966), Ingrebourne Centre: a therapeutic community. *Nursing Times*, (London) 62:1399-1401.

12171 **TILLICH, M.** (1948), My experience on the psychodrama stage. *Sociatry*, 2:65-66.

12173 **TIMMONS, E. O., RICKARD, H. C.,** and **TAYLOR, R. E.** (1960), Reliability of content-free group verbal behavior. *Psychol. Record*, 10:297-305.

12172 **TILLMANN, W. A., HARRIS, L. H., PHIPPS, M. A.,** and **HOWE, J. L.** (1968), Group therapy amongst persons involved in frequent automobile accidents. Defense documentation center for scientific and technical information, 1964, 82 pp. As reported in *Occupat. Ment. Health Notes*, (Feb.) pp. 45-46.

12174 **TINDALL, J.** (1979), Time-limited and time–extended encounter group. *Small Group Behav.*, 10:402-413.

12175 **TINDALL, J. H.** (1971), A comparative procedural descriptive analysis of the time limited and time extended encounter groups. *Dissert. Abstr. Internat.*, 32:5051A.

12176 **TIRONA, M.** (1966), A study of some of the effects of group experience on mothers' understanding of the problems of sibling rivalry: abstract of thesis. *Smith Coll. Studies Soc. Work.*, 37:85.

12177 **TOBIASON, R. V. C.** (1972), The relative effectiveness of individual and group desensitization in reducing student nurses' anxiety. *Dissert. Abstr. Internat.*, 3707A.

12178 **TOBIESSEN, J.,** and **SHAI, A.** (1971), A comparison of individual and group mental health consultation with teachers. *Community Ment. Health J.*, 7:218-226.

12179 **TOBIN, M. W.** (1973), Effects of axiotherapy in groups. *Dissert. Abstr. Internat.*, 33:3295B.

12180 **TODD, D. M. P.** (1971), An assessment of group counseling effectiveness with educable mentally retarded junior high school students. *Dissert. Abstr. Internat.*, 32:2426A.

12181 **TODD, K. M.** (1944), The therapy of play. *Ment. Health Digest*, 5:3-7.

12182 **TODD, R.** (1971), Notes on corporate man. *Atlantic*, 228:83-88.

12183 **TODD, W. E.**, and **PINE, I.** (1968), Peer supervision of individual psychotherapy. *Amer. J. Psychiat.*, 125:780-784.

12184 **TOELLE, R.** (1960), (The psychiatric station as a group: on group psychotherapy of schizophrenics.) *Nervenarzt*, 31:264-267.

12185 **TOEMAN, Z.** (1945), Audience reactions to therapeutic films. *Sociometry*, 8:493-497.

12186 **TOEMAN, Z.** (1946), Clinical psychodrama: auxiliary ego double and mirror techniques. *Sociometry*, 9:178-183.

12187 **TOEMAN, Z.** (1948), The "double situation" in psychodrama. *Sociatry*, 1:436-446.

12188 **TOEMAN, Z.** (1947), Psychodrama: its relation to stage, radio and motion pictures. *Sociatry*, 1:119-126.

12189 **TOEMAN, Z.** (1944), Role analysis and audience structure. *Sociometry*, 7:205-221.

12190 **TOEMAN, Z.** (1945), A sociodramatic audience test. *Sociometry*, 8:399-409.

12191 **TOEMAN, Z.** (1948), Synthesis between a group psychotherapy, a psychodrama and a sociodrama session. *Sociatry*, 2:417-418.

12192 **TÖGEL, I.** (1964), (On experiences with certain auxiliary psychotherapeutic methods.) *Psychiat., Neurol. & Med. Psychol.*, (Leipzig) 16:412-419.

12193 **TOKER, E.** (1972), The scapegoat as an essential group phenomenon. *Internat. J. Group Psychother.*, 22:320-332.

12194 **TOLAND, J. J., Jr.** (1970), Inmate behavior: interaction sentiment and activity in a therapeutic community for abnormal offenders. *Dissert. Abstr. Internat.*, 31:1392A.

12195 **TOLDSON, I. L.**, and **PASTEUR, A. B.** (1975), Developmental stages of Black self-discovery: implications for using Black art forms in group interaction. *J. Negro Educat.*, 44:130-138.

12196 **TOLL, N.** (1968), Non-conformist group therapies. *Voices*, 4:44-45.

12197 **TOLL, N.** (1965), Patients' reactions to group psychotherapy in private practice. *Group Psychother., Psychodrama & Sociometry*, 18:271-273.

12198 **TOLLINTON, H. J.** (1969), The organization of a psychotherapeutic community. *Brit. J. Med. Psychol.*, (London) 42:271-275.

12199 **TOLOR, A.** (1970), The effectiveness of various therapeutic approaches: a study of subprofessional therapists. *Internat. J. Group Psychother.*, 20:48-62.

12200 **TOLOR, A.**, and **GRIFFIN, A.** (1969), Group therapy in a school setting. *Psychol. in Schools*, 6:59-62.

12201 **TOMIM, B.**, and **GLENN, A. G.** (1968), Psychotherapy with drug abusers in a male admitting service. *Psychiat. Quart. Suppl.*, 42:144-155.

12202 **TOMPKINS, R. P.**, and **GALLO, F. T.** (1978), Social groupwork: a model for goal formulation. *Small Group Behav.*, 9:307-318.

12203 **TOMSOVIC, M.** (1976), Group therapy and changes in self-concept of alcoholics. *J. Studies Alcohol*, 37:53-57.

12204 **TOMSOVIC, M.** (1968), Hospitalized alcoholic patients: i. a two-year study of medical, social, and psychological characteristics. *Hosp. & Community Psychiat.*, 19:197-203.

12205 **TONDLOVÁ, H.** (1976), (Psychotherapy of chronic schizophrenic patients with personality defect in ambulant conditions.) *Ceskoslav. Psychiat.*, (Prague) 72:51-54.

12206 **TONGAS, P. N.** (1979), The Kaiser permanent smoking control program: its purpose and implications for an HMO. *Prof. Psychol.*, 10:409-418.

12207 **TOPEL, S. I.** (1967), Of crisis, family, and therapist: a preliminary guide to a therapeutic process in a disadvantaged Los Angeles Community. *Amer. J. Orthopsychiat.*, 37:280.

12208 **TORDA, C.** (1970), An effective therapeutic method for the LSD user. *Percept. & Motor Skills*, 30:79-88.

12209 **TORGERSEN, S.** (1980), Personality and experience in an encounter-group. *Scand. J. Psychol.*, (Stockholm) 21:139-141.

12210 **TORRANCE, E. P.** (1957), What happens to the sociometric structure of small groups in emergencies and extreme conditions. *Group Psychother., Psychodrama & Sociometry*, 10:212-220.

12211 **TORRANCE, E. P.**, and **MASON, R.** (1956), The indigenous leader in changing attitudes and behavior. *Internat. J. Sociometry & Sociatry*, 1:23-28.

12212 **TORRANCE, P.** (1948), The student personnel program. *Sociatry*, 2:368-375.

12213 **TORRE, M.**, and **TORRE, E.** (1973), Adaptations of the group psychotherapy approach for use in poverty area elementary schools. *Group Process*, (London) 5:75-84.

12214 **TORRE, M. P.** (1947), Group psychotherapy for college students. *Proceed., American Student Health Association*, 29:35-38.

12215 **TOSELAND, R.** (1977), A problem-solving group workshop for older persons. *Soc. Work*, 22:325-326.

12216 **TOSHNEY, J.** (1978), Alcoholism: an alcoholism and detoxification centre—University Hospital of South Manchester. part 2. *Nursing Times*, (London) 74:573-574.

12217 **TOSI, D. J., UPSHAW, K., LANDE, A.**, and **WALDRON, M. A.** (1971), Group counseling with nonverbalizing elementary students: differential effects of premack and social reinforcement techniques. *J. Couns. Psychol.*, 18:437-440.

12218 **TOSQUELLES, F., GENTIS, R., ENKIN, M.**, and **BONNET, F.** (1959), On group therapy within the general framework of institutional therapeutics. *Acta Psychother., Psychosomat. Orthopaedagog.*, (Basel) 7:239-242.

12219 **TOUGH, A.** (1972), Two movements interacting: human potential and adult education. *Adult Leadership*, 20:335-338.

12220 **TOUGH, H.** (1980), A cognitive-augmented approach to the definition of group therapist style. *Group Anal.*, (London) 13:118-121.

12221 **TOUKMANIAN, S. G.**, and **RENNIE, D. L.** (1975), Microcounseling versus human relations training: relative effectiveness with undergraduate trainees. *J. Couns. Psychol.*, 22:345-352.

12222 **TOURAINE, G.** (1975), (The psychodrama of Moreno.) *Encephale*, (Paris) 1:249-253.

12223 **TOWEY, M. R., SEARS, S. W., WILLIAMS, J. A., KAUFMAN, N.**, and **CUNNINGHAM, M. K.** (1966), Group activities with psychiatric inpatients. *Soc. Work*, 11:50-56.

12224 **TOWLE, M.** (1980), Organizing parent groups. *J. Learning Disabil.*, 13:165-167.

12225 **TOWNE, R. D.** (1954), Group therapy in a military hospital. *U.S. Forces Med. J.*, 5:853-859.

12226 **TOWNSEND, R. E., HOUSE, J. F.**, and **ADDARIO, D.** (1975), A comparison of biofeedback–mediated relaxation and group therapy in the treatment of chronic anxiety. *Amer. J. Psychiat.*, 132:598-601.

12227 **TRABAUD, P., EXBRAYAT, C., COUDRAY, J. P.**, and **TOURAME, G.**

(1978), (Group–psychotherapy–psychodrama.) *Annales Medico-Psychol.*, (Paris) 136:642.

12228 **TRACEY, D. A., BRIDDELL, D. W.,** and **WILSON, G. T.** (1974), Generalization of verbal conditioning to verbal and nonverbal behavior: group therapy with chronic psychiatric patients. *J. Appl. Behav. Anal.*, 7:391-402.

12229 **TRACEY, J.** (1970), Parent guidance groups: is this therapy? *J. Psychiat. Nurs.*, 8:11-12.

12230 **TRACY, J. F.** (1971), Analysis of patient guidance groups. *J. Psychiat. Nurs.*, 9:18-19.

12231 **TRAKAS, D. A.,** and **LLOYD, G.** (1971), Emergency management in a short-term open group. *Comprehens. Psychiat.*, 12:170-175.

12232 **TRAPPE, M.** (1971), A therapeutic vacation community. *Praxis der Psychother.*, 16:129-137.

12233 **TRAUER, T.** (1980), Correlates of patient participation in the large group meetings of a therapeutic community. *Brit. J. Med. Psychol.*, (London) 53:109-118.

12234 **TRAUTMAN, E. C.** (1962), Suicide as a psychodramatic act. *Group Psychother., Psychodrama & Sociometry*, 15:159-161.

12235 **TRAVER, T.** (1979), Relationship between large group meetings and patients estimates of ward tension. *Brit. J. Med. Psychol.*, (London) 52:205-214.

12236 **TRAVIS, K. I.** (1972), The effects of modifying interruptions of organized behavioral and cognitive sequences. *Dissert. Abstr. Internat.*, 32:7326-7327.

12237 **TRAXLER, S.** (1980), (Psychotherapeutic group work with psychiatric patients: a clinical study.) *Psychiat. Praxis*, (Stuttgart) 7:113-122.

12238 **TREADWELL, T.,** and **TREADWELL, J.** (1972), The pioneer of the group encounter movement. *Group Psychother., Psychodrama & Sociometry*, 25:16-26.

12239 **TREADWELL, V.** (1977), Group and individual counseling: effects on college grades. *J. Non-White Concerns Personnel & Guid.*, 5:73-80.

12240 **TREAT, R. J.** (1977), An additional note on the stroking profile. *Transactional Anal. J.*, 7:248.

12241 Treatment failures in children tied to clinic setting. (1969), *Roche Report: Front. Hosp. Psychiat.*, 6:5-6.

12242 **TRECKER, H. B.** (1956), *Group Work in the Psychiatric Setting*. Proceedings of an institute conducted by the American Association of Group Workers. New York: Whiteside and Morrow.

12243 **TRECKER, H. B.** (1948), *Social Group Work: Principles and Practices.* New York: Women's Press.

12244 **TREDGOLD, R. F.** (1972), Michael Balint and medical students. *Psychiat. Med.*, 3:385-388.

12245 **TREESH, E. O.** (1966), Multiple impact therapy: the creative process in psychiatry in a private clinic—assumptions and rationale in retrospect. *J. Kansas Med. Soc.*, 67:26-29.

12246 **TREFFERT, D. A.** (1968), Children and adolescents: hospital treatment programs. *Hosp. & Community*, 19:237-240.

12247 **TREGER, H.,** and **TREGER, S.** (1968), Use of the small group in vocational rehabilitation of the disabled poor. *J. Rehab.*, 34:22-25.

12248 **TRENT, R. D.,** and **NOTTAGE, W.** (1957), Changing the concept of a physically inadequate self through group work in a physical education setting. *Psychiat. Quart. Suppl.*, 31:56-65.

12249 **TRENZ, R. C.** (1971), Cognitive dissonance and the t-group: the effects of social context on the selective avoidance phenomenon. *Dissert. Abstr. Internat.*, 32:573B.

12250 **TREPPA, J. A.**, and **FRICKE, L.** (1972), Effects of a marathon group experience. *J. Couns. Psychol.*, 19:466-467.
12251 **TRESEMER, D.** (1976), Observing social interaction: methodological models. *Small Group Behav.*, 7:47-58.
12252 **TRETAKOFF, M.** (1969), Counseling parents of handicapped children: a review. *Ment. Retard.*, 7:31-34.
12253 **TREUDLEY, M. B.** (1944), Psychodrama and social casework. *Sociometry*, 7:169-178.
12254 **TREXLER, L. D.**, and **KARST, T. O.** (1972), Rational emotive therapy, placebo, and nontreatment effects on public-speaking anxiety. *J. Abnorm. & Soc. Psychol.*, 79:60-67.
12255 **TRICE, H. M.** (1956), Alcoholism: group factors in etiology and therapy. *Human Organizat.*, 152:33-40.
12256 **TRIDENTI, A.** (1978), Thérapie du couple à travers la psychothérapie d'un seul de ses members. *Psychother. & Psychosomat.*, (Basel) 29:198-202.
12257 **TRIMBLE, R. W.** (1979), Review of E. Kramer's *Beginning Manual for Psychotherapists*. *Contemp. Psychol.*, 24:865.
12258 **TRIMBLE, R. W.** (1979), Review of J. H. Paul's *Farm and Technique of Psychotherapy*. *Contemp. Psychol.*, 24:865.
12259 **TROESTER, J. D.**, and **DARBY, J. A.** (1976), The role of the mini-meal in therapeutic play groups. *Soc. Casework*, 57:97-103.
12260 **TROJE, E.** (1977), *Porträt einer Gruppe: Aus d. Praxis e. Selbsthifegruppe von Studenten.* (*Portrait of a Group: On the Practice of a Student Self-Help Group.*) Munich: Juventa-Verlag.
12261 **TROJE, E.** (1978), (Self-help groups for students.) *Gruppenpsychother. & Gruppendynam.*, (Goettingen) 13:228-239.
12262 **TROPP, E.** (1973), Group counseling, disability, and social service goals. *Pub. Welfare*, 31:25-32.
12263 **TROPP, E.** (1968), The group: in life and in social work. *Soc. Casework*, 49:267-274.
12264 **TROPP, N. D.** (1976), Behavior change through self-control compared with group therapy and a control group. *Dissert. Abstr. Internat.*, 37:2532B.
12265 **TROTTER, H. D.** (1970), The effectiveness of group psychotherapy in the treatment of academic underachievement in college freshmen. *Dissert. Abstr. Internat.*, 32:573-574B.
12266 **TROTZER, J. P.** (1977), *The Counselor and the Group: Integrating Theory, Training, and Practice.* Monterey, CA: Brooks/Cole Publishing.
12267 **TROTZER, J. P.** (1970), The effect of group-centered and topic-centered methods on group process and outcomes. *Dissert. Abstr. Internat.*, 30:4237A.
12268 **TROTZER, J. P.** (1971), Process comparison of encounter groups and discussion groups using videotaped excerpts. *J. Couns. Psychol.*, 18:358-361.
12269 **TROTZER, J. P.** (1973), Using communication exercises in groups. *Personnel & Guid. J.*, 51:373-377.
12270 **TROTZER, J. P.**, and **KASSERA, W. J.** (1973), Guidelines for selecting communication techniques in group counseling. *School Counselor*, 20:299-301.
12271 **TROTZER, J. P.**, and **SEASE, W. A.** (1971), The effect of group-centered and topic-centered methods on volunteer college students' self-concepts. *J. Coll. Student Personnel*, 12:292-296.
12272 **TRUAS, C. B.**, and **CARKHUFF, R. R.** (1965), Personality change in hospitalized mental patients during group psychotherapy as a function of the use of alternate sessions and vicarious therapy pretraining. *J. Clin. Psychol.*, pp. 225-228.

12273 **TRUAS, C. B., CARKHUFF, R. R.,** and **KODMAN, F.** (1965), Relationships between therapist–offered conditions and patient change in group psychotherapy. *J. Clin. Psychol.*, 21:327-329.

12274 **TRUAX, C. B.** (1971), Degree of negative transference occurring in group psychotherapy and client outcome in juvenile delinquents. *J. Clin. Psychol.*, 27:132-136.

12275 **TRUAX, C. B.** (1971), The initial status of the client and the predictability of psychotherapeutic change. *Compar. Group Studies*, 2:3-16.

12276 **TRUAX, C. B.** (1971), Perceived therapeutic conditions and client outcome. *Compar. Group Studies*, 2:301-310.

12277 **TRUAX, C. B.** (1961), *The Process of Group Psychotherapy.* Washington, D.C.: American Psychological Association.

12278 **TRUAX, C. B.** (1960), The process of group psychotherapy: relationships between hypothesized therapeutic conditions and intrapersonal exploration. *Dissert. Abstr. Internat.*, 21:676.

12279 **TRUAX, C. B.** (1961), The process of group psychotherapy: relationship between hypothesized therapeutic conditions and intrapersonal exploration. *Psychol. Monogr.*, 75.

12280 **TRUAX, C. B.** (1966), Therapist empathy, warmth, and genuineness and patient personality change in group psychotherapy: a comparison between interaction unit measures, time sample measures, patient perception measures. *J. Clin. Psychol.*, 22:225-229.

12281 **TRUAX, C. B.** (1968), Therapist interpersonal reinforcement of client self-exploration and therapeutic outcome in group psychotherapy. *J. Couns. Psychol.*, 15:225-231.

12282 **TRUAX, C. B.** (1971), Effects of alternate sessions, vicarious therapy pre–training, and patient self-exploration with hospitalized mental patients during group therapy. *Can. Counselor*, (Ottawa) 5:31-40.

12283 **TRUAX, C. B.,** and **LISTER, J. L.** (1970), Effects of therapist persuasive potency in group psychotherapy. *J. Clin. Psychol.*, 26:396-397.

12284 **TRUAX, C. B.,** and **WARGO, D. G.** (1969), Effects of vicarious therapy pretraining and alternate sessions on outcome in group psychotherapy with outpatients. *J. Consult. & Clin. Psychol.*, 33:440-447.

12285 **TRUAX, C. B., SCHULDT, W. J.,** and **WARGO, D. G.** (1968), Self-ideal concept congruence and improvement in group psychotherapy. *J. Consult. & Clin. Psychol.*, 32:47-53.

12286 **TRUAX, C. B., SHAPIRO, J. G.,** and **WARGO, D. G.** (1968), The effects of alternate sessions and vicarious therapy pre-training on group psychotherapy. *Internat. J. Group Psychother.*, 18:186-198.

12287 **TRUAX, C. B., WARGO, D. G.,** and **SILBER, L. D.** (1966), Effects of group psychotherapy with high accurate empathy and nonpossessive warmth upon female institutionalized delinquents. *J. Abnorm. & Soc. Psychol.*, 71:267-274.

12288 **TRUAX, C. B., WARGO, D. G.,** and **VOLKSDORF, N. R.** (1970), Antecedents to outcome in group counseling with institutionalized juvenile delinquents: effects of therapeutic conditions, patient self-exploration, alternate sessions, and vicarious therapy pretraining. *J. Abnorm. & Soc. Psychol.*, 76:235-242.

12289 **TRUAX, C. B., WITTMER, J.,** and **WARGO, D. G.** (1971), Effects of therapeutic conditions of accurate empathy, non-possessive warmth, and genuineness on hospitalized mental patients during group therapy. *J. Clin. Psychol.*, 27:137-142.

12290 **TRUAX, C. B., CARKHUFF, R. R., WARGO, D. G., KODMAN, F.,** and **MOLES, E. A.** (1966), Changes in self-concepts during group psychotherapy as a function of alternate sessions and vicarious therapy pretraining in institutionalized mental patients and juvenile delinquents. *J. Couns. Psychol.*, 30:309-314.

12291 **TRUAX, C. B., WARGO, D. G., FRANK, J. D., IMBER, S. D., BATTLE, C. C., HOEHN-SARIC, R., NASH, E. H.,** and **STONE, A. R.** (1966), The therapist's contribution to accurate empathy, non–possessive warmth, and genuineness in psychotherapy. *J. Clin. Psychol.*, 22:331-334.

12292 **TRUAX, R.,** and **TOURBEY, G.** (1971), Male homosexuals in group psychotherapy: a controlled study. *Diseases Nerv. System*, 32:707-711.

12293 **TRUDEL, R. M.** (1978), Group therapy with women alcoholics: a perspective for rehabilitation. *Dissert. Abstr. Internat.*, 38:6182-6183B.

12294 **TRUE, J. E.** (1974), Training new mental health personnel in group methods: i. education and work performance of associate degree mental health workers as related to group therapy. *Internat. J. Group Psychother.*, 24:383-392.

12295 **TRUPIN, E. W., GILCHRIST, L., MAIVRO, R. D.,** and **FAY, G.** (1979), Social skills training for learning: disabled children. In: *Behavioral Systems for the Developmentally Disabled, Vol. II*, ed. L. A. Hamerlynck. New York: Brunner/Mazel.

12296 **TRUSS, T. T.** (1971), The effects of focused videotape feedback on changes in self–concept and ideal self–concept in a group therapy setting. *Dissert. Abstr. Internat.*, 32:6063B.

12297 **TRUSSELL, W. E.** (1973), Groups for young people from the drug using community. In: *Drug Abuse and Drug Addiction*, ed. M. Rosenbaum. London: Gordon and Breach.

12298 **TSAI, M.,** and **WAGNER, N. N.** (1978), Therapy groups for women sexually molested as children. *Arch. Sexual Behav.*, 7:417-427.

12299 **TSCHUMI, S. A.** (1974), Changes in self-concept resulting from a crisis intervention marathon group process treatment for non-achieving two-year college freshmen. *Dissert. Abstr. Internat.*, 34:5647A.

12300 **TSCHUSCHKE, V., VOLK, W.,** and **EHLERS, W.** (1980), The applicability of the Gottschalk-Gleser content analysis of verbal behavior for examining the progress of a psycho-analytically structured group psychotherapy (exemplified by a quantitative description of the course of anxiety and aggressiveness within an analytical group.) *Gruppenpsychother. & Gruppendynam.*, (Goettingen) 16:240-256.

12301 **TUBBS, A.** (1970), Nursing intervention to shorten anxiety-ridden transition periods. *Nurs. Outlook*, 18:27.

12302 **TUCKER, J.,** and **FRIEDMAN, S. T.** (1972), Population density and group size. *Amer. J. Sociol. Res.*, 77:742-749.

12303 **TUCKER, J. E.** (1956), Group psychotherapy with chronic psychotic soiling patients. *J. Couns. Psychol.*, 20:430.

12304 **TUCKMAN, B. W.** (1965), Developmental sequence in small groups. *Psychol. Bull.*, 63:384-399.

12305 **TUCKMAN, B. W.** (1976), Feedback and the change process. *Phi Delta Kappa*, 57:341-344.

12306 **TUCKMAN, B. W.,** and **JENSEN, M. C.** (1977), Stages of small-group development revisited. *Group & Organizat. Studies*, 2:419-427.

12307 **TUFF, R. J.** (1977), A comparison of the effects of a counseling skills training group and a treatment group with peer-counselor trainees. *Dissert. Abstr. Internat.*, 38:1910B.

12308 **TUMILTY, E. M.** (1966), Hypomania-mania: a nursing care study. *Nursing Times*, (London) 62:430-432.

12309 **TUOIT, P. L.** (1978), Videotape feedback vs. verbal feedback in time-limited group therapy with acute schizophrenics. *Dissert. Abstr. Internat.*, 39:5093B.

12310 **TURBOW, S. R.** (1975), Geriatric group day care and its effect on independent living: a thirty-six-month assessment. *Gerontologist*, 15:508-510.

12311 **TURCOT, G. H.** (1961), (The psychiatric service of a general hospital and the milieu therapy.) *Union Med. Can.*, (Montreal) 90:713-717.
12312 **TURK, J. L.** (1974), Power as the achievement of ends: a problematic approach in family and small group research. *Fam. Process*, 13:39-52.
12313 **TURNBLOM, M.**, and **MYERS, J. S.** (1952), A group discussion program with families of aphasic patients. *J. Speech & Hearing Disorders*, 17:393-396.
12314 **TURNER, C. H.** (1968), Psychoanalytically–oriented psychiatric guidance. *Psychiat. Quart.*, 42:62-80.
12315 **TURNER, H. B.** (1976), A therapeutic community for chronic mental patients. *Health & Soc. Work*, 1:96-112.
12316 **TURNER, J. W.** (1955), Tele and transference from the point of view of Jungian psychology. *Amer. Psychologist*, 8:76-78.
12317 **TURQUET, P.** (1975), Threats to identity in the large group. In: *The Large Group: Dynamics and Therapy*, ed. L. Kreeger. London: Constable.
12318 **TURQUET, P. M.**, and **WOODHOUSE, D.** (1967), *The Use of Small Groups in Training*. Hertfordshire: Codicote Press.
12319 **TUTAJ, G. A.** (1975), The effectiveness of group counseling in alleviating depression among the aged. *Dissert. Abstr. Internat.*, 36:2653A.
12320 **TUTTLE, J. F.**, and **PETERS, J. J.** (1965), Group techniques and ward administration in a military hospital. *Internat. J. Group Psychother.*, 15:97-103.
12321 **TUTTMAN, S.** (1980), The question of group therapy: from a psychoanalytic viewpoint. *J. Amer. Acad. Psychoanal.*, 8:217.
12322 **TWAROG, J. E.** (1976), The effect of group and individual client-centered case consultation on teacher behavior toward and teacher perception of behavior problem students. *Dissert. Abstr. Internat.*, 36:4184B.
12323 **TWITCHELL-ALLEN, D.** (1950), Round table on psychodrama of the American Psychological Association Meeting. *Group Psychother., Psychodrama & Sociometry*, 3:246-249.
12324 **TWITCHELL-ALLEN, D.**, and **STEPHENS, F. M.** (1951), Some theoretical and practical aspects of group psychotherapy. *Group Psychother., Psychodrama & Sociometry*, 4:9-16.
12325 **TYLER, E. A., TRUUMAA, A.**, and **HENSHAW, P.** (1962), Family group intake by a child guidance clinic team. *Arch. Gen. Psychiat.*, 6:214-218.
12326 **TYLER, F. B.** (1979), Psychosocial competence differences among adolescents on entering group counseling. *Psychol. Reports*, 44:811-822.
12327 **TYSON, H. A.** (1966), The acts according to Moreno. *Group Psychother., Psychodrama & Sociometry*, 19:220-230.

U

12328 **UDELMAN, H. D.**, and **UDELMAN, D. L.** (1978), Group therapy with rheumatoid arthritic patients. *Amer. J. Psychother.*, 32:288-299.
12329 **UGELSTAD, E.** (1964), Some experiences in group psychotherapy with psychotic patients. *Acta Psychiat. Scand. Suppl.*, (Copenhagen) 40:259.
12330 **UHES, M. J.** (1971), Expression of hostility as a function of an encounter group experience. *Psychol. Reports*, 28:733-734.
12331 **UHLEMANN, M. R.**, and **WEIGEL, R. G.** (1977), Behavior change outcomes of marathon group treatment. *Small Group Behav.*, 8:269-280.
12332 **UKERITIS, M. D.** (1977), A study of value convergence in a group psychotherapy setting. *Dissert. Abstr. Internat.*, 38:4488.
12333 **ULMAN, E.** (1959), Implications of art for psychotherapy and psychodrama. *Group Psychother., Psychodrama & Sociometry*, 12:327-328.
12334 **ULLMANN, L. P.** (1957), Selection of neuropsychiatric patients for group psychotherapy. *J. Couns. Psychol.*, 21:277-280.
12335 **ULLMANN, L. P., KRASNER, L.**, and **COLLINS, B. J.** (1961), Modification of behavior through verbal conditioning: effects in group therapy. *J. Abnorm. & Soc. Psychol.*, 62:128-132.
12336 **ULRICH, I.**, and **TANELI, S.** (1976), (Psychotherapy with children suffering from bronchial asthma.) *Praxis Kinderpsychol. & Kinderpsychiat.*, (Goettingen) 25:4-8.
12337 **UMANSKY, A. L.** (1944), Psychodrama and the audience. *Sociometry*, 7:179-189.
12338 **UMEZU, K.** (1970), The study of autistic children with behavior therapy. 3. group therapy. *Bull. Seishin Igaku Inst.*, 17:61-70.
12339 **UNDERWOOD, P. R.** (1971), Communication through role playing. *Amer. J. Nursing*, 71:1184-1186.
12340 **UNGER, J. A.** (1972), The differential effects of marathon and weekly groups' self–perceptions and interpersonal feelings. *Dissert. Abstr. Internat.*, 33:168A.
12341 **UNIVERSITY OF MASSACHUSETTS COUNSELING CENTER STAFF** (1972), Effects of three types of sensitivity groups on changes in measures of self-actualization. *J. Couns. Psychol.*, 19:253-254.
12342 **UPPER, D.**, and **ROSS, S. M.** (1980), *Behavioral Group Therapy 1980: An Annual Review*. Champaign, IL: Research Press.
12343 **UPPER, D.**, and **ROSS, S. M.** (1977), Behavior group therapy: emotional avoidance and social skills problems of adults. In: *Progress in Behavior Modification*, ed. M. Hersen. New York: Academic Press.
12344 **URBIN, M. A.** (1971), A commitment to care. *Nursing Clinics North Amer.*, 6:757-767.
12345 **URCUYO, L.** (1972), A particular "group" experience. *Amer. J. Psychoanal.*, 32:215-216.
12346 **URDAL, B.** (1971), The differential indication for individual versus family therapy in adolescent psychiatry. *Tiddskr. Norske Laegeforen*, (Stockholm) 91:358-361.
12347 **URIOSTE, M. M.** (1978), Multicultural experiential group counseling versus multicultural didactic instruction on the attitudes of high school females. *Dissert. Abstr. Internat.*, 39:4743A.
12348 **USANDIVARAS, R. J.** (1975), The argonauts' expedition and groups. In: *Group Therapy 1975: An Overview*, eds. L. R. Wolberg and M. L. Aronson. New York: Stratton Intercontinental Medical Books.
12349 **USANDIVARAS, R. J.** (1979), (Frequent errors in group psychotherapy.) *Acta Psiquiat. Psicol. Amer. Latina*, (Buenos Aires) 25:15-23.

12350 **USANDIVARAS, R. J.** (1974), (Group and myth.) *Acta Psiquiat. Psicol. Amer. Latina*, (Buenos Aires) 20:161-167.

12351 **USANDIVARAS, R. J.** (1973), Psicoterapia breve en grupos: reflexiones sobre una experiencia. (Brief psychotherapy in groups: reflections after an experience.) *Acta Psiquiat. Psicol. Amer. Latina*, (Buenos Aires) 19:169-177.

12352 **USANDIVARAS, R. J., GRIMSON, W. R., HAMMOND, H., ISSAHAROFF, E.**, and **ROMANOS, D.** (1967), The marbles test: a test for small groups. *Arch. Gen. Psychiat.*, 17:111-118.

12353 **USDIN, G. L., ROND, P. C., HINCHCLIFFE, J. A.**, and **ROSS, W. D.** (1952), The meaning of disulfiram to alcoholics in group psychotherapy. *J. Studies Alcohol*, 13:590-595.

12354 **USHER, S.**, and **POLLACK, H.** (1972), The marketing of the movement: a critical look at the selling of encounter groups. *Ontario Psychologist*, (Toronto) 4:232-241.

12355 **USORHORST-SMEENK, F.** (1977), How do children feel about having asthma? *J. Asthma Res.*, 14:169-188.

12356 **UTENA, T.** (1970), (Attendance patterns of the mentally disturbed in psychodramatic group therapy.) *Japanese J. Psychol.*, (Tokyo) 41:78-83.

V

12357 **VACHON, M. L.** (1980), A controlled study of self-help intervention for widows. *Amer. J. Psychiat.*, 137:1380-1384.
12358 **VACHON, M. L. S.**, and **LYALL, W. A. L.** (1976), Applying psychiatric techniques to patients with cancer. *Hosp. & Community Psychiat.*, 27:582-584.
12359 **VAESSEN, M. L.** (1964), (Criteria for the indication for psychotherapy.) *Zeit. Psychosomat. Med. Psychol.*, (Stuttgart) 10:198-209.
12360 **VAIL, D.** (1955), An unsuccessful experiment in group therapy. *Amer. J. Ment. Deficiency*, 60:144-151.
12361 **VAIL, D. J.** (1966), *Dehumanization and the Institutional Career.* Springfield, IL: C. C. Thomas.
12362 **VAIL, D. J.** (1972), Milieu therapy and psychoanalytic psychotherapy processes compared. In: *Innovations in Psychotherapy*, eds. G. D. Goldman and D. S. Milman. Springfield, IL: C. C. Thomas.
12363 **VAIL, J. P.** (1970), The effects of encounter tapes for personal growth on certain specific aspects of the intellectual, behavioral, and self-concept development of culturally disadvantaged Negro girls. *Dissert. Abstr. Internat.*, 31:5141A.
12364 **VALENTICH, M.**, and **GRIPTON, J.** (1975), Teaching human sexuality to social work students. *Fam. Coordinator*, 24:273-280.
12365 **VALENTINE, L. R.** (1970), Self-care through group learning. *Amer. J. Nursing*, 70:2140-2142.
12366 **VALINE, W. J.** (1971), Focused feedback with videotape: an aid in group counseling of underachieving college freshmen. *Dissert. Abstr. Internat.*, 31:5784A.
12367 **VALINE, W. J.** (1974), Focused feedback with videotape as an aid in counseling underachieving college freshmen. *Small Group Behav.*, 5:131-143.
12368 **VALINE, W. J.**, and **AMOS, L. C.** (1973), High school transfer students: a group approach. *Personnel & Guid. J.*, 52:40-42.
12369 **VALKO, R. J.** (1976), Group therapy for patients with hysteria (Briquets disorder). *Diseases Nerv. System*, 37:484.
12370 **VALLES, J.**, and **SIKES, M. P.** (1964), A program for the treatment and study of alcoholism in a Veterans Administration Hospital. *Quart. J. Studies Alcohol*, 25:101-107.
12371 Value conflicts create psychiatric problems. (1969), *Roche Report: Front. Hosp. Psychiat.*, 6:3.
12372 Value of encounter groups questioned by group therapist (1970). *Roche Report: Front. Hosp. Psychiat.*, 7:3.
12373 **van AUKEN, K. G.** (1971), Further view on laboratory education. *Monthly Labor Rev.*, 94:63-65.
12374 **van BROK, W.** (1953), Development of group psychotherapy. *Geneeskundige Gids*, (Amusfoort) 31:27-32.
12375 **VANCE, H., FINKLE, L.**, and **McGEE, H. J.** (1977), Group counseling with mentally retarded persons. *Personnel & Guid. J.*, 56:148-153.
12376 **van COPPE, H.** (1976), Evaluation of therapeutic evolution and procedures by patients in clinical group psychotherapy settings. *Tijdschr. voor Psychother.*, 18:100-109.
12377 **van de POL, J.** (1980), (Effects of disorder severity on the structuring of psychodrama and group psychotherapy.) *Tijdschr. voor Psychother.*, 6:210-218.

12378 **van der DOES, M.**, and **Van der POOL, M.** (1978), (Women learn to love themselves.) *Tijdschr. voor Psychother.*, 4:265-272.

12379 **van der HOOF, T. J.** (1970), The effects of group counseling on low achieving students' perception of their college environment. *Dissert. Abstr. Internat.*, 30:4237A-4238A.

12380 **van der KOLK, C.** (1976), Popular music in group counseling. *School Counselor*, 23:206-211.

12381 **van der MAY, J.**, and **PEAKE, T.** (1980), Psychodrama as a psychotherapy supervision technique. *Group Psychother., Psychodrama & Sociometry*, 33:25-32.

12382 **van der VOORT, F. J.** (1975), (Psychotherapy, individual or group therapy: why, when, where?) *Nederl. Tijdschr. Geneeskunde*, (Amsterdam) 119:1141-1147.

12383 **van der VOORT, H. E.**, and **BLANK, J. E.** (1975), A sex counseling program in a university medical center. *Couns. Psychologist*, 5:64-67.

12384 **van der ZYL, S.**, **ERNSET, C.**, and **SALINGER, H. J.** (1979), Role expectations: a significant concern for the nurse-therapist. *J. Psychiat. Nursing*, 17:23-27.

12385 **van DYCK, B. J.** (1980), An analysis of selection criteria for short-term group counseling clients. *Personnel & Guid. J.*, 59:226-230.

12386 **van EMDE BOAS, C.** (1967), (Emotional consequences of situational differences in analytically oriented collective therapy and in individual analysis.) *Rev. Psiquiat. Psicol. Med.*, (Rome) 8:167-173.

12387 **van EMDE BOAS, C.** (1950), Group therapy of anorgastic women. *Internat. J. Sexol.*, (Bombay) 4:1-6.

12388 **van GEE, S. J.** (1979), Alcoholism and the family: a psychodrama approach. *J. Psychiat. Nursing*, 17:9-12.

12389 **van HOOSE, W. H.**, and **KOTTLER, J. A.** (1977), *Ethical and Legal Issues in Counseling and Psychotherapy*. San Francisco: Jossey-Bass.

12390 **van INEVE, P.** (1977), Review of J. Huinck's *Getting Acquainted with Group Therapy*. *Tijdschr. voor Psychother.*, 19:816.

12391 **van KREVELEN, D. A.** (1962), On the problem of therapeutic pairing in neurotic youngsters. *Acta Psychother. Psychosomat. Orthopaedagog*, (Basel) 10:233-245.

12392 **van OSTENBERG, D. L.** (1973), Therapy groups for staff and interns. *Hosp. & Community Psychiat.*, 24:474-475.

12393 **van PUTTEN, T.**, and **MAY, P. R. A.** (1976), Milieu therapy of the schizophrenias. In: *Treatment of Schizophrenia: Progress and Prospects*, eds. L. J. West and D. E. Flinn. New York: Grune and Stratton.

12394 **van QUEKELBERGHE, R.**, and **DROSTE, G.** (1975/1976), Bibliography of marathon group research: 1966-1975. *Interpersonal Develop.*, 6:42-47.

12395 **van REE, F.** (1974), (Couples group therapy in relation to continued education of nurses with diploma B. 2. application as educational internship.) *Tijdschr. Ziekenverplaging*, (Lochem) 27:1062-1067.

12396 **van ROOIJEN-SMOOR, T. G.** (1974), An experiment in group counseling of young non-married mothers. *Impact*, 6:24-30.

12397 **van SCOY, H.** (1972), Activity group therapy: a bridge between play and work. *Child Welfare*, 51:528-534.

12398 **van STONE, W. W.**, and **GILBERT, R.** (1972), Peer confrontation groups: what, why, and whether. *Amer. J. Psychiat.*, 129:583-588.

12399 **van THIEL, S.** (1974), Applying group dynamics to a seminar. *J. Thought*, 9:168-171.

12400 **van VLACK, L. L.** (1975), The utility of non-verbal procedures in the first group meeting. *Dissert. Abstr. Internat.*, 36:1421B.

12401 **van VLEET, P.** (1949), Rhythmic activity: a project in group therapy with children. *Amer. J. Orthopsychiat.*, 19:79-86.

12402 **van WEEL, C.** (1980), Group based care: does it change problem behavior. *J. Royal Coll. Gen. Pract.*, 30:665.
12403 **VARGAS, M. J.** (1960), A group therapeutic project involving a total admission ward. *Group Psychother., Psychodrama & Sociometry*, 13:173-181.
12404 **VARGAS, M. J.** (1961), Uses of humor in group psychotherapy. *Group Psychother., Psychodrama & Sociometry*, 14:198-202.
12405 **VARENHORST, B. B.** (1973), Game theory, simulations and group counseling. *Educat. Technol.*, 13:40-43.
12406 **VARENHORST, B. B.** (1975), Training adolescents as peer counselors. *Personnel & Guid. J.*, 53:271-275.
12407 **VARNER, E. B.** (1970), Impact of basic group encounter on self-actualization of junior college students. *Dissert. Abstr. Internat.*, 31:2120A.
12408 **VARON, E.** (1953), Recurrent phenomena in group psychotherapy. *Internat. J. Group Psychother.*, 3:49-58.
12409 **VARON, E.** (1960), Transition into the therapeutic phase of group therapy. *Internat. J. Group Psychother.*, 10:321-332.
12410 **VASCO, J. B.** (1964), (The emergence of the leader in the therapeutic group.) *J. Brasil. Psiquiat.*, (Rio de Janeiro) 13:355-363.
12411 **VASEY, I. T.** (1968), Experiences in the use of group therapy as a specific treatment modality for adolescents in the child guidance center. *Acta Paedopsychiat.*, (Basel) 35:267-273.
12412 **VASILE, R. G.**, and **O'LOUGHLIN, M.** (1977), Initiation of fees in a non-paying group. *Psychiat. Annals*, 7:77-84.
12413 **VASS, I.** (1965), The acting-out patient in group therapy. *Amer. J. Psychother.*, 19:302-308.
12414 **VASSILOU, G.** (1969), Discussion: as part of panel on interaction and insight in group psychotherapy. AGPA Conf., 1968. *Internat. J. Group Psychother.*, 19:281-287.
12415 **VASSILOU, G.** (1973), What general systems theory offers to the group therapist. *Internat. Ment. Health Res. Newsl.*, 15:8.
12416 **VASSILIOU, G.**, and **VASSILIOU, V. G.** (1977), On the alternation of group transaction patterns and its therapeutic actualization. *Internat. J. Group Psychother.*, 27:75-85.
12417 **VASSILIOU, G.**, and **VASSILIOU, V. G.** (1974), On the synallactic aspects of the grouping process. In: *Group Therapy 1974: An Overview*, eds. L. R. Wolberg and M. L. Aronson. New York: Stratton Intercontinental Medical Books.
12418 **VASSILIOU, G.**, and **VASSILIOU, V.** (1974), A source of discordance: across milieu variations of affective expressions during group transaction. In: *Social Psychiatry, Vol. 1*, eds. J. Masserman and V. Schwab. New York: Grune and Stratton.
12419 **VASSILIOU, V. G.**, and **VASSILIOU, G.** (1974), Variations of the group process across cultures. *Internat. J. Group Psychother.*, 24:55-65.
12420 **VATTANO, A. J.** (1972), Power to the people: self help groups. *Soc. Work*, 17:7-15.
12421 **VAZQUEZ, AGUILOR, A. C.**, and **PEREZ IBORES, O.** (1975), (The psychotherapeutic experience of a group evaluated by means of the Rorschach test.) *Neurol.-Neurocir.-Psiquiat.*, (Mexico City) 16:263.
12422 **VELASCO de ONGAY, M. E.** (1977), Group psychotherapy: experience with a changing process at a clinic of ISSSTE. *Neurol.-Neurocir.-Psiquiat.*, (Mexico City) 18:135-139.
12423 **VELASCO, LAFARGA, M. G.** (1978), (Measurement of change in encounter groups.) *Enseñanza & Investig. Psicol.*, (Mexico City) 4:126-131.
12424 **VELAZQUEZ AGUILAR, A., et al.** (1977), Group psychotherapy with an

analytical orientation in the Matelolco Neuro-Psychiatric Clinic. *Neurol.-Neurocir.-Psiquiat.*, (Mexico City) 18:141-155.
12425 **VELTIN, A.** (1968), (The group conversation in the therapeutic community.) *Zeit. Psychother. Med. Psychol.*, (Stuttgart) 18:50-57.
12426 **VELTKAMP, L. J.** (1975), School phobia. *J. Fam. Couns.*, 3:47-51.
12427 **VELTKAMP, L. J.**, and **NEWMAN, K.** (1976), Parent groups: how effective? *J. Fam. Couns.*, 4:46-51.
12428 **VENINGA, R.**, and **FREDLUND, D. J.** (1974), Teaching the group approach: School of Public Health at the University of Minnesota. *Nursing Outlook*, 22:373-376.
12429 **VENINO, W. K.** (1974), A comparison of two encounter group approaches in promoting personal growth and self-actualization. *Dissert. Abstr. Internat.*, 34:6989.
12430 **VEREECKEN, J. L.** (1963), (Aspects of a suggestive-psychagogic therapy: an anthropological consideration.) *Acta Psychother., Psychosomat. Orthopaedagog.*, (Basel) 11:403-411.
12431 **VERETT, G. D.** (1970), The effect of a summer group counseling institute on selected attitudes and personality characteristics of junior college counselors. *Dissert. Abstr. Internat.*, 31:3283A.
12432 **VERHAEST, S.**, and **PIERLOOT, R.** (1980), Different models of analytic group psychotherapy: a comparative survey. *Psychother. & Psychosomat.*, (Basel) 34:1-10.
12433 **VERHOELST-VERSTRAETEN, D.** (1978), (Investigation of the theory of value in the framework of therapy of partner relationships.) *Nederl. Tijdschr. Psychol.*, (Amsterdam) 33:441-452.
12434 **VERHULST, J.**, and **HEIMAN, J. R.** (1979), An interactional approach to sexual dysfunctions. *Amer. J. Fam. Ther.*, 7:19-36.
12435 **VERINIS, J. S.** (1970), The ex-patient as a lay therapist: attitudes of group members toward him. *Psychother.: Theory, Res. & Pract.*, 7:161-163.
12436 **VERINIS, J. S.** (1970), Therapeutic effectiveness of untrained volunteers with chronic patients. *J. Consult. & Clin. Psychol.*, 34:152-155.
12437 **VERNALLIS, F. F.** (1975), Saturation group psychotherapy in a weekend clinic: an outcome study. In: *The Innovative Psychological Therapies: Critical and Creative Contributions*, eds. R. M. Suinn and R. G. Weigel. New York: Harper and Row.
12438 **VERNALLIS, F. F.**, and **REINERT, R. E.** (1961), An analysis of a goal-directed group psychotherapy with hospitalized patients. *Group Psychother., Psychodrama & Sociometry*, 14:5-12.
12439 **VERNALLIS, F. F.**, and **REINERT, R. E.** (1966), Group treatment methods in a weekend hospital. *Psychother.: Theory, Res. & Pract.*, 3:91-93.
12440 **VERNALLIS, F. F.**, and **REINERT, R. E.** (1963), The weekend hospital. *Ment. Hosp.*, 14:254-258.
12441 **VERNALLIS, F. F., HOLSON, D. G., SHIPPER, J. C.**, and **BUTLER, D. C.** (1972), The treatment process in saturation group therapy. *Psychother.: Theory, Res. & Pract.*, 9:135-138.
12442 **VERNALLIS, F. F., SHIPPER, J. C., BUTLER, J. C.**, and **TOMLINSON, T. M.** (1970), Saturation group psychotherapy in a weekend clinic: an outcome study. *Psychother.: Theory, Res. & Pract.*, 7:144-152.
12443 **VERNALLIS, F. F., STRAIGHT, E. M., COOK, A. D.**, and **STIMPERT, W. E.** (1965), The group therapist in the treatment of chronic schizophrenics. *Group Psychother., Psychodrama & Sociometry*, 18:241-246.
12444 **VERNER, M.** (1957), *Psychologia v Zdravotnictve.* (*Psychology in Health Service.*) Bratislava: Solvenska Akademiz Vied.
12445 **VERNOT, G. G.** (1975), A study of the effectiveness of group counseling

using a human relations treatment program with disruptive tenth grade boys. *Dissert. Abstr. Internat.*, 36:3420A.

12446 **VERNY, T. R.** (1974), *Inside Groups: A Practical Guide to Encounter Groups and Group Therapy*. New York: McGraw-Hill.

12447 **VERVEN, N., WALDFOGEL, S.**, and **YOUNG, R. A.** (1956), Modified psychodrama and group therapy in a treatment camp. *Internat. J. Group Psychother.*, 6:291-299.

12448 **VERWOERDT, A.**, and **EISDORFER, C.** (1967), Geropsychiatry: the psychiatry of senescence. *Geriatrics*, 22:139-149.

12449 **VESTRE, N. D., GREENE, R. L.**, and **MARKS, M. W.** (1978), Psychological adjustment of persons seeking sensitivity group experiences. *Psychol. Reports*, 42:1295-1298.

12450 **VESZY-WAGNER, L.** (1973), (Destructiveness against individuals and groups.) *Dynam. Psychiat.*, (Berlin) 6:414.

12451 **VICARS, W. M.** (1978), Review of J. W. Pfeiffer's and J. E. Jones' *The 1978 Annual Handbook for Group Facilitators. Personnel Psychol.*, 31:930-933.

12452 **VICINO, F. L., KRUSELL, J., BASS, B. M., DECI, E. L.**, and **LANDY, D. A.** (1973), The impact of PROCESS: self-administered exercises for personal and interpersonal development. *J. Appl. Behav. Science*, 9:737-756.

12453 **VIDART, L.** (1968), (Applications of the method of directed scenic expression in adult epileptics.) *Annales Medico-Psychol.*, (Paris) 2:376-381.

12454 **VIDMAR, N. J.** (1968), Leadership and role structure in negotiation and other decision-making groups. *Dissert. Abstr. Internat.*, 28:3267-3268.

12455 **VIDOJKOVIĆ, P.** (1978), (Problems of the group therapist.) *Psihijat. Danas*, (Belgrade) 10:111-112.

12456 **VIDOJKOVIĆ, S.**, and **DUKIĆ, T.** (1979), (Therapist and observer in group psychotherapy.) *Psihijat. Danas*, (Belgrade) 11:31-37.

12457 **VIEFHUES, H.** (1961), (Group therapeutic institutions outside of the hospital. The protected working place for mental patients and the patient club.) *Nervenarzt*, 32:211-217.

12458 **VIEHWEG, W.** (1974), (Psycho- and social therapy of aging.) *Zeit. Alternsforschung*, (Dresden) 29:43-50.

12459 **VILHAR, V.** (1975), (Autogenic training in the group.) *Anali Zavoda Ment. Zdravlje*, 7:123-130.

12460 **VINOKUR, A.** (1969), Distribution of initial risk levels and group decisions involving risk. *J. Personality & Soc. Psychol.*, 13:207-214.

12461 **VINOKUR, A.** (1971), Review and theoretical analyses of the effects of group process upon individual and group decisions involving risk. *Psychol. Bull.*, 76:231-250.

12462 **VINSON, A.** (1968), Television and group-centered learning. *Soc. Work Educat. Reporter*, 16:32-33.

12463 **VINTER, R. D.**, and **SARRI, R. C.** (1965), Malperformance in the public school: a group work approach. *Soc. Work*, 10:3-13.

12464 **VIOLA, H.**, and **RIVERE, B.** (1976), Assertive therapy in outpatient clinic and psychiatric hospital. *Perspect. Psychiat. Care*, 58:313.

12465 **VISHER, J. S.**, and **BROWN, D. T.** (1961), Procedures in integrating group psychotherapy in a mental hygiene clinic. *Internat. J. Group Psychother.*, 11:175-179.

12466 **VITALE, J. H., PRESTON, L., MARKFELD, J.**, and **MULLIN, S.** (1973), Small group method on a general hospital nursing unit. *J. Psychiat. Nursing*, 11:9-12.

12467 **VITALO, R. L.** (1969), Implications of training in interpersonal dimensions for the treatment of psychiatric patients. *Dissert. Abstr. Internat.*, 30:2428B.

12468 **VITALO, R. L.** (1971), Teaching improved interpersonal functioning as a preferred mode of treatment. *J. Clin. Psychol.*, 27:166-177.

12469 **VOGEL, S.** (1957), Some aspects of group psychotherapy with alcoholics. *Internat. J. Group Psychother.*, 7:302-309.

12470 **VOGELER, E. J., Jr.**, and **GREENBERG, I. A.** (1968), Psychodrama and audience with emphasis on closed-circuit television. *Group Psychother., Psychodrama & Sociometry*, 21:4-11.

12471 **VOGL, G.** (1965), (Group therapy in a child guidance center.) *Praxis Kinderpsychol. & Kinderpsychiat.*, (Goettingen) 14:54-58.

12472 **VOGT, H.** (1971), An invitation to group counseling. *Fed. Probat.*, 35:30-32.

12473 **VOKATY, D. A.** (1978), The development of an instrument for the measurement of group therapy process. *Dissert. Abstr. Internat.*, 40:680B.

12474 **VOLD, G.** (1958), *Theoretical Criminology*. New York: Oxford University Press.

12475 **VOLK, W.** (1978), (Origin of group therapy.) *Praxis der Psychother.*, 23:293-296.

12476 **VOLK, W.**, and **HERMES, M.** (1980), Aspects of satisfaction with group psychotherapy. *Gruppenpsychother. & Gruppendynam.*, (Goettingen) 16:257-267.

12477 **VOLKAN, V. D.** (1980), Narcissistic personality organization and reparative leadership. *Internat. J. Group Psychother.*, 30:131-152.

12478 **VOLKAN, V. D.**, and **HAWKINS, D. R.** (1972), The learning group. *Amer. J. Psychiat.*, 128:1121-1126.

12479 **VOLKMAR, F. R., BACON, S., SHAKIR, S. A.**, and **PFEFFERBAUM, A.** (1981), Group therapy in the management of manic-depressive illness. *Amer. J. Psychother.*, 35:226-234.

12480 **VOL'PERT, I. E.** (1968), Vosproizvedenie obraza kak metod psikhoterapii. (Reproduction of the image as a method of psychotherapy.) *Zh. Nevropat. & Psikhiat. Korsakov*, (Moscow) 68:902-906.

12481 **VOLTERRA, V.**, and **MOLINARI, S.** (1968), (The patient with character disorder in mixed group open to discussion.) *Riv. Psichiat.*, (Rome) 3:377-381.

12482 **VOLTERRA, V.**, and **SOVERINI, S.** (1969), Borderline subjects and situations in a mixed group open to discussion. *Riv. Psichiat.*, (Rome) 4:391-394.

12483 **VOLTOLINA, E. J., MOSKOWITZ, M. M.**, and **KAMMERER, W. G.** (1971), Adaptation of crisis intervention group to navy out–patient psychiatric clinic population. *Military Med.*, 136:546-548.

12484 **von KLOCK, K. B.** (1966), An investigation of group and individual counseling as remedial methods for working with junior high school underachieving boys. *Dissert. Abstr. Internat.*, 27:1276A.

12485 **von RAD, M.** (1979), Comments on theory and therapy of psychosomatic patients with a follow–up study. *Psychother. & Psychosomat.*, (Basel) 32:118.

12486 **von RAD, M.**, and **RUPPELL, A.** (1975), Combined inpatient and outpatient group psychotherapy: a therapeutic model for psychosomatics. *Psychother. & Psychosomat.*, (Basel) 26:237-243.

12487 **von SCOY, H.** (1971), An activity group approach to seriously disturbed latency boys. *Child Welfare*, 50:413.

12488 **von UEXBULL, T.** (1972), System and crisis: a psychosomatic of human development. *Psychiat. in Med.*, 3:417.

12489 **von WALLENBERG PACHALY, A.** (1978), (The ego development of a psychosomatical patient as a result of psychotherapy in a dynamic psychiatric hospital.) *Dynam. Psychiat.*, (Berlin) 11:241-251.

12490 **von WIESE, L.** (1952), Role playing as a method of academic education. *Group Psychother., Psychodrama & Sociometry*, 5:73-77.

12491 **von XYLANDER, E.** (1958), (Discussion of wishes.) *Psychol. Rundschau*, (Goettingen) 9:192-201.

12492 **VORDENBERG, W.** (1970), A technique for goal-setting in group work. *Personnel & Guid. J.*, 48:479-480.

12493 **VORSTER, C.** (1980), An investigation into the effect of relationship oriented therapy on the drinking behavior of alcoholics. *Dissert. Abstr. Internat.*, 40:3975B.

12494 **VOSKRESENSKAIA, A. M.** (1965), (Experience with group psychotherapy [culture therapy] in a day clinic.) *Zh. Nevropat. & Psikhiat. Korsakov*, (Moscow) 65:766-769.

12495 **VOTH, A. C.** (1963), Group therapy with hospitalized alcoholics: a twelve-year study. *Quart. J. Studies Alcohol*, 24:289-303.

12496 **VOTOS, A. S.** (1953), Group techniques in overcoming medical students' resistance to learning psychiatry. *Internat. J. Group Psychother.*, 3:293-301.

12497 **VRAA, C.** (1971), Influence of need for inclusion on group participation. *Psychol. Reports*, 28:271-274.

12498 **VRAA, C. W.** (1974), Emotional climate as a function of group composition. *Small Group Behav.*, 5:105-120.

12499 **VRAA, C. W.**, and **GERSZEWSKI, M. C.** (1972), Personality characteristics and level of genuineness in group interaction. *Psychol. Reports*, 31:383-386.

12500 **VRIEND, J.** (1979), Brief answers to 20 questions about group counseling. *J. Employment Couns.*, 16:133-142.

12501 **VRIEND, J.** (1973), A fully equipped computer-assisted group counseling research and training lab. *Educat. Technol.*, 13:57-60.

12502 **VRIEND, J.**, and **DYER, W. W.** (1973), Applied technology in group counseling. *Educat. Technol.*, 13:9.

12503 **VRIEND, J.**, and **DYER, W. W.** (1973), A case for a technology of group counseling and delineation of major group categories. *Educat. Technol.*, 13:12-18.

12504 **VRIEND, J.**, and **DYER, W. W.** (1973), *Counseling Effectively in Groups*. Englewood Cliffs, NJ: Educational Technology Publications.

12505 **VRIEND, J.**, and **DYER, W. W.** (1975), Effectively handling silence in counseling groups. *Can. Counsellor*, (Ottawa) 9:2-8.

12506 **VRIEND, T. J.** (1969), High -performing inner-city adolescents assist low-performing peers in counseling groups. *Personnel & Guid. J.*, 47:897-903.

12507 **VRIEND, T. J.** (1969), Utilizing peer leaders in counseling and study groups to modify academic achievement: a demonstration study in an inner-city high school. *Dissert. Abstr. Internat*, 30:178A-179A.

12508 **VURSLEYS, H. P.** (1980), The remediation of role disorders through focused group work. *Amer. J. Occupat. Ther.*, 34:609.

W

12509 **WACHSPRESS, M.** (1965), Use of groups in various modalities of hospital treatment. *Internat. J. Group Psychother.*, 15:17-22.
12510 **WACHTEL, A. B., STEIN, A.,** and **BALDINGER, M.** (1979), Dynamic implications of videotape recording and playback in analytic group psychotherapy: paradoxical effect on transference resistance. *Internat. J. Group Psychother.*, 29:67-85.
12511 **WACKER, A. S.** (1972), A comparison of two methods of selecting applicants for a group experience. *Dissert. Abstr. Internat.*, 32:5557A.
12512 **WACKS, J.** (1970), Some effects on the group psychotherapist in the group situation. *J. Group Psychoanal. Process*, 2:37-44.
12513 **WADE, R., JORDAN, G.,** and **MYERS, G.** (1969), Sociopsychiatric rehabilitation in a black urban ghetto. 3. the view of the paraprofessional. *Amer. J. Orthopsychiat.*, 39:677-683.
12514 **WADSWORTH, S. D.** (1972), A critical evaluation of Camp Tokhir: an environmental therapy laboratory for communicative disordered children. *Dissert. Abstr. Internat.*, 33:2205A.
12515 **WAGNER, F. F.** (1965), (The significance of a patient's club in psychiatric follow-up treatment: a 5-year retrospect.) *Ugeskr. for Laeger*, (Copenhagen) 127:1667-1668.
12516 **WAGNER, F. F.** (1965), Suicide prevention and social clubs. *Internat. J. Soc. Psychiat.*, (London) 11:116-117.
12517 **WAGNER, M.** (1972), The blaming game. *Transactional Anal. J.*, 2:181-185.
12518 **WAGNER, M. K.** (1968), Reinforcement of the expression of anger through role-playing. *Behav. Res. & Ther.*, 6:91-95.
12519 **WAGNER, M. N.** (1966), Reinforcement of verbal productivity in group therapy. *Psychol. Reports*, 19:1217-1218.
12520 **WAGNER, P. S.** (1969), Prospects for psychiatry and psychoanalysis. *Internat. Psychiat. Clinics*, 6:5-28.
12521 **WAGONER, J. H.** (1980), The Emotional Projection Test as an instrument to differentiate affective qualities of personality profiles and as a measure of affective change in four different therapy groups. *Dissert. Abstr. Internat.*, 40:5835B. (University Microfilms No. 8013149.)
12522 **WAGONFELD, S.,** and **WOLOWITZ, H. M.** (1968), Obesity and the self-help group: a look at TOPS. *Amer. J. Psychother.*, 125:249-252.
12523 **WAHLER, R. G.** (1980), The insular mother: her problems in parent-child treatment. *J. Appl. Behav. Anal.*, 13:207-219.
12524 **WAHLER, R. G.,** and **AFTON, A. D.** (1980), Attentional processes in insular and non–insular mothers: some differences in their summary reports about child problem behaviors. *Child Behav. Ther.*, 2:25-41.
12525 **WAHRMAN, R.** (1974), Some observations on sensitivity training research. *Small Group Behav.*, 5:321-329.
12526 **WAISMAN, M. M.** (1964), Sociometric perception and self-other attitudes. *Internat. J. Sociometry & Sociatry*, 4:43-50.
12527 **WALDMAN, K. R.** (1976), Leader expectations and predictability of encounter group outcome. *Dissert. Abstr. Internat.*, 36:6571A.
12528 **WALDMAN, M.** (1961), The effects of group counseling in a controlled workshop setting on attitude, manual dexterity and ability to perceive correct spatial relations. *Dissert. Abstr. Internat.*, 22:328-329.
12529 **WALDMAN, M.,** and **REISER, M.** (1961), Group psychotherapy and personality factors in a work adjustment process. *J. Jewish Communal Serv.*, 38:167-170.

12530 **WALDORF, D.** (1971), Social control in therapeutic communities for the treatment of drug addicts. *Internat. J. Addict.*, 6:29-44.

12531 **WALEN, S. R.** (1980), Cognitive factors in sexual behavior. *J. Sex & Marital Ther.*, 6:87-101.

12532 **WALKER, B. A.** (1972), Effects of short-term group counseling on changes in attitudes of flexibility, tolerance, and non–authoritarianism. *Dissert. Abstr. Internat.*, 32:3708A.

12533 **WALKER, C.** (1978), Effect of group psycho–therapy on bereavement with spouses of dying cancer patients. *Dissert. Abstr. Internat.*, 38:5049B.

12534 **WALKER, C.** (1978), Time-limited group psychotherapy in a mental hospital: Alberta Hospital, Ponoka. *Can. J. Psychiat. Nursing*, (Winnipeg) 19:9-12.

12535 **WALKER, D. N.** (1975), A dyadic interaction model for nonverbal touching behavior in encounter groups. *Small Group Behav.*, 6:308-324.

12536 **WALKER, J. R.**, and **HAMILTON, L. S.** (1973), A Chicano/Black/White encounter. *Personnel & Guid. J.*, 51:471-477.

12537 **WALKER, K. D.** (1979), Covert sensitization vs. reappraisal therapy in the modification of drinking tendencies. *Dissert. Abstr. Internat.*, 40:5876B.

12538 **WALKER, L.** (1975), Nutritional concerns of addicts in treatment: Methadone Maintenance Treatment Program, Los Angeles, California. *J. Psychiat. Nursing*, 13:21-26.

12539 **WALKER, R. E., SHACK, J. R., EGAN, G., SHERIDAN, K.**, and **SHERIDAN, E. P.** (1972), Changes in self-judgments of self–disclosure after group experience. *J. Appl. Behav. Science*, 8:248-251.

12540 **WALKER, T. G.** (1973), Behavior of temporary members in small groups. *J. Appl. Psychol.*, 58:144-146.

12541 **WALKER, T. G.** (1976), Leader selection and behavior in small political groups. *Small Group Behav.*, 7:363-368.

12542 **WALKER, W. L.**, and **MITCHELL, L. E.** (1965), Group decision-making in an apprenticeship program for youth. *Amer. J. Orthopsychiat.*, 35:378-379.

12543 **WALKER, W. L.**, and **MITCHELL, L. E.** (1967), Group decision–making in an apprenticeship program for youth. *Amer. J. Orthopsychiat.*, 37:101-106.

12544 **WALKER, W. S.** (1958), A participant-observer analysis of group process and individual and group behavior at Highfield's project. Unpublished doctoral dissertation, New York University.

12545 **WALL, K. E.** (1978), Effects of all female and mixed sex assertion training groups on the assertive behavior of females. *Dissert. Abstr. Internat.*, 38:6184B-6185B.

12546 **WALL, S. M.**, and **BRYANT, N. D.** (1979), Behavioral self-management of academic test performance in elementary classrooms. *Psychol. in Schools*, 16:558-567.

12547 **WALLACE, D. H.**, and **BARBACH, L. G.** (1974), Preorgasmic group treatment. *J. Sex & Marital Ther.*, 1:146-154.

12548 **WALLACE, S. B.** (1980), Efficacy of the use of group psychotherapy with adolescents who have a seizure disorder. *Dissert. Abstr. Internat.*, 40:3976B. (University Microfilms No. 8004844.)

12549 **WALLACH, M. A.**, and **KOGAN, N.** (1967), Group risk taking and field dependence-independence of group members. *Sociometry*, 30:323-338.

12550 **WALLACH, M. A., KOGAN, N.**, and **BURT, R. B.** (1968), Are risk takers more persuasive than conservatives in group discussion? *J. Exper. Soc. Psychol.*, 4:76-88.

12551 **WALLACH, M. A., KOGAN, N.**, and **BURT, R. B.** (1965), Can group members recognize the effects of group discussion upon risk taking? *J. Exper. Soc. Psychol.*, 1:379-395.

12552 **WALLEN, V.** (1970), Motivation therapy with the aging geriatric veteran patient. *Military Med.*, 135:1007-1010.

12553 **WALLER, C. A.** (1976), Therapy preparation and its effect on group member behavior. *Dissert. Abstr. Internat.*, 37:995B.

12554 **WALLERSTEIN, R. S.** (1958), Psychologic factors in chronic alcoholism. *Annals Internal Med.*, 48:114-122.

12555 **WALLIA, C. S.** (1966), Effect of differential perception of access to information in a four member decision-making group on their participation. *Dissert. Abstr. Internat.*, 26:4068.

12556 **WALLINGA, J. V.** (1964), A study of adolescent auto theft. *J. Child Psychiat.*, 3:126-139.

12557 **WALSH, H. E.** (1954), The group approach to weight reduction. iii. as the nutritionist sees it. *J. Amer. Dietetic Assn.*, 30:447-449.

12558 **WALSH, J. A.**, and **PHELAN, T. W.** (1974), People in crisis: an experimental group. *Community Ment. Health J.*, 10:3-8.

12559 **WALSH, R. T.** (1978), Nonspecific influences in group counter-conditioning: a methodological and conceptual critique. *Can. Psychol. Rev.*, 19:224.

12560 **WALTER, G. A.** (1975), Effects of video tape feedback and modeling on the behaviors of task group members. *Human Relat.*, 28:121-138.

12561 **WALTER, G. A.**, and **MILES, R. E.** (1974), Changing self-acceptance: task groups and videotape feedback or sensitivity training? *Small Group Behav.*, 5:356-364.

12562 **WALTER, R.** (1977), *Der Alkoholkranke und die Nachbehandlung in Gruppen: e. Unters, uber Interaktionen u. Erwartungen d. Gruppenmitglieder in Kreuzbundgruppen*. Hamm: Hoheneck-Verlag.

12563 **WALTON, D. R.** (1973), Effects of personal growth groups on self-actualization and creative personality. *J. Coll. Student Personnel*, 14:490-494.

12564 **WALTON, H.** (1961), Group methods in hospital organization and patient treatment as applied in the psychiatric treatment of alcoholism. *Amer. J. Psychiat.*, 118:410-418.

12565 **WALTON, H. (Ed.)** (1971), *Small Group Psychotherapy*. Harmondsworth, England: Penguin.

12566 **WALTON, H. J.**, and **McPHERSON, F. M.** (1968), Phenomena in a closed psychotherapeutic group. *Brit. J. Med. Psychol.*, (London) 41:61-72.

12567 **WALTON, R. E.** (1970), A problem-solving workshop on border conflicts in eastern Africa. *J. Appl. Behav. Science*, 6:453-496.

12568 **WALUM, L. R.** (1968), Group perception of threat of non–members. *Sociometry*, 31:278-284.

12569 **WANGER, J. C.** (1957), Factors contributing to positive social interaction in groups of schizophrenics. Unpublished doctoral dissertation, Columbia University.

12570 **WARD, C. A.** (1980), An evaluation of short-term personality changes as a result of a marathon, large group encounter training. *Dissert. Abstr. Internat.*, 41:1129B. (University Microfilms No. 8020627.)

12571 **WARD, C. D.** (1968), Seating arrangement and leadership emergence in small discussion groups. *J. Soc. Psychol.*, 74:83-90.

12572 **WARD, D. J.** (1974), Group therapy innovation at psychiatric out-patient clinics. *Irish Med. J.*, (Dublin) 67:391-396.

12573 **WARD, E., JACKSON, C.**, and **CAMP, T.** (1973), Remotivation: a growing family of therapeutic techniques. *Hosp. & Community Psychiat.*, 24:629-630.

12574 **WARD, J. L.** (1961), The psychodrama of the LSD experience: some comments on the biological man. *Group Psychother., Psychodrama & Sociometry*, 14:121-128.

12575 **WARD, J. L., RUBENFELD, S.**, and **SHELLOW, R. S.** (1958), Counter-

transference as a factor in the delinquent's resistance to psychotherapy. *Group Psychother., Psychodrama & Sociometry*, 11:229-243.
12576 **WARD, J. S.** (1972), An evaluation of group therapy in process. *Dissert. Abstr. Internat.*, 33:1809B.
12577 **WARD, J. T.** (1974), The sounds of silence: group psychotherapy with non–verbal patients. *Perspect. Psychiat. Care*, 12:13-19.
12578 **WARD, L. C., Jr.** (1960), An examination of processes occurring in two methods of group psychotherapy with schizophrenics. *Dissert. Abstr. Internat.*, 20:3848-3849.
12579 **WARD, M.** (1955), Group therapy for 11 preschool cerebral palsied children. *Except. Children*, 21:207-214.
12580 **WARD, M. H.** (1945), Note on psychomusic and musical group psychotherapy. *Sociometry*, 8:476-479.
12581 **WARD, N. G.** (1980), Analysis of the self: a cognitive relabeling technique. *Psychother.: Theory, Res. & Pract.*, 17:30-36.
12582 **WARDROP, K. R. H.** (1976), Group therapy with adult offenders in Scotland. *Internat. J. Offender Ther.*, (London) 20:236-241.
12583 **WARE, J. R.**, and **BARR, J. E.** (1977), Effects of a nine-week structured and unstructured group experience on measures of self-concept and self–actualization. *Small Group Behav.*, 8:95-100.
12584 **WARE, L. M.**, and **LEVY, E. Z.** (1969), "The meeting": a step toward a therapeutic community in an adolescent unit. *Bull. Menninger Clinic*, 33:352-363.
12585 **WARKENTIN, J.** (1975), An experience in teaching psychotherapy by means of group therapy. In: *Group Psychotherapy and Group Function*, 2d ed., eds. M. Rosenbaum and M. M. Berger. New York: Basic Books.
12586 **WARKENTIN, J.** (1955), An experience in teaching psychotherapy by means of group therapy. *Prog. Educat.*, 32:79-82.
12587 **WARKENTIN, J., JOHNSON, N. L.**, and **WHITAKER, C. A.** (1951), A comparison of individual and multiple psychotherapy. *Psychiatry*, 14:415-418.
12588 **WARNER, G. D.** (1970), The didactic auxiliary chair. *Group Psychother., Psychodrama, & Sociometry*, 23:31-34.
12589 **WARNER, G. D.** (1971), Psychodrama: a special group approach in the psychiatric hospital. *Group Psychother., Psychodrama & Sociometry*, 24:131-134.
12590 **WARNER, G. D.** (1970), Psychodrama: a special group approach in the psychiatric hospital. *Sandoz Psychiat. Spectator*, 6:9-12.
12591 **WARNER, R. W.** (1971), Alienated students: six months after receiving behavior group counseling. *J. Couns. Psychol.*, 18:426-430.
12592 **WARNER, R. W.**, and **HANSEN, J. C.** (1970), Verbal-reinforcement and model–reinforcement group counseling with alienated students. *J. Couns. Psychol.*, 17:168-172.
12593 **WARNER, S. G.** (1980), The effects of Human Potential Laboratory groups on self-actualization, self-esteem and anxiety. *Dissert. Abstr. Internat.*, 40:3794A. (University Microfilms No. 7928623.)
12594 **WARNER, S. G.**, and **JEPSEN, D. A.** (1979), Differential effects of conceptual level and group counseling format on adolescent career decision-making processes. *J. Couns. Psychol.*, 26:497-503.
12595 **WARNER, W. J.** (1955), Some common denominators in theory for psychotherapy. *Group Psychother., Psychodrama & Sociometry*, 8:82-86.
12596 **WARREN, L. W.** (1976), The therapeutic status of consciousness-raising groups. *Prof. Psychol.*, 7:132-140.
12597 **WARSCHAWSKI, P.** (1979), (Therapy groups with patients and nursing staff in a geriatric hospital.) *Akt. Gerontol.*, (Stuttgart) 9:329-335.
12598 **WARWICK, C. E.** (1964), Relationship of scholastic aspiration and group

cohesiveness to the academic achievement of male freshmen at Cornell University. *Human Relat.*, 17:155-168.
12599 **WASHINGTON, E. L.** (1974), Effects of group counseling and role playing upon selected behaviors of institutionalized male delinquents. *Dissert. Abstr. Internat.*, 35:2703A.
12600 **WASHINGTON, K. S.** (1970), A comparison of the effectiveness of two group counseling formats. *Dissert. Abstr. Internat.*, 31:4479A.
12601 **WASSELL, B.** (1966), *Group Analysis*. New York: Citadel Press.
12602 **WASSELL, B.** (1952), Group composition and patient selection. *Amer. J. Psychoanal.*, 12:80.
12603 **WASSELL, B. B.** (1959), *Group Psychoanalysis*. New York: Philosophical Library.
12604 **WASSERMAN, T. H.**, and **VOGRIN, D. J.** (1979), Long-term effects of a token economy on target and off-task behaviors. *Psychol. in Schools*, 16:551-557.
12605 **WATERHOUSE, J.** (1978), Group work in intermediate treatment. *Brit. J. Soc. Work*, (Birmingham) 8:127-144.
12606 **WATKINS, J. T.**, **NOLL, G. A.**, and **BREED, G. R.** (1975), Changes toward self-actualization. *Small Group Behav.*, 6:272-281.
12607 **WATSON, J. P.** (1972), Possible measures of change during group psychotherapy. *Brit. J. Med. Psychol.*, (London) 45:71-77.
12608 **WATSON, J. P.** (1970), A repertory grid method of studying groups. *Brit. J. Psychiat.*, (Ashford) 117:309-318.
12609 **WATSON, J. P.**, and **LACEY, J. H.** (1974), Therapeutic groups for psychiatric inpatients. *Brit. J. Med. Psychol.*, (London) 47:307-312.
12610 **WATSON, J. P.**, **MULLETT, G. E.**, and **PILLAY, H.** (1973), The effects of prolonged exposure to phobic situations upon agoraphobic patients treated in groups. *Behav. Res. & Ther.*, 11:531-545.
12611 **WATSON, K. W.**, and **BOVERMAN, H.** (1968), Preadolescent foster children in group discussions. *Children*, 15:65-70.
12612 **WATZLAWICK, P.**, and **WEAKLAND, J. H.** (1977), *Interactional View: Studies at the Mental Research Institute*. New York: W. W. Norton.
12613 **WAX, J.** (1965), Analyzing a therapeutic community meeting. *Internat. J. Group Psychother.*, 15:29-36.
12614 **WAXENBERG, S. E.** (1965), Leadership style: interaction and group climate. *Psychother.: Theory, Res. & Pract.*, 2:164-168.
12615 **WAXENBERG, S. E.**, and **FLEISCHL, M. F.** (1965), Referring therapists' impressions of a therapeutic social club. *Internat. J. Soc. Psychiat.*, (London) 11:173-179.
12616 **WAXER, P. H.** (1977), Short-term group psychotherapy: some principles and techniques. *Internat. J. Group Psychother.*, 27:33-42.
12617 **WAYBRIGHT, E. W.** (1978), The manner in which that which is intersubjectively possible comes to be actualized within the dialectical relationship of kaiserian small group therapy. *Dissert. Abstr. Internat.*, 38:5601B.
12618 **WAYMIRE, T. R.** (1971), An exploratory study of the normative dimensions emphasized by t-group trainers. *Dissert. Abstr. Internat.*, 32:2831A.
12619 **WAYNE, J. L.**, and **FEINSTEIN, B. B.** (1978), Group work outreach to parents by school social workers. *Soc. Casework*, 59:345-351.
12620 **WAYSON, W. W.** (1974), Head start parents in participant groups: i. statistics and stereotypes. *J. Appl. Behav. Science*, 10:250-256.
12621 **WEARNE, T. D.** (1973), Outcomes in individual and group counseling with ninth grade girls. *Dissert. Abstr. Internat.*, 33:6678A.
12622 **WEARNE, T. D.**, and **POWELL, J. C.** (1976), A comparison of outcomes in individual and group counseling with ninth grade girls. *Alberta J. Educat. Res.*, (Edmonton) 22:254-261.

12623 **WEATHERS, O. D.**, and **BULLOCK, S. C.** (1978), Therapeutic group home care for adolescent girls: an interagency development. *J. Nat. Med. Assn.*, 70:331-334.

12624 **WEAVER, S.** (1979), Review of H. Tajfel's *Differentiation between Social Groups: Studies in the Social Psychology of Intergroup Relations. Brit. J. Psychol.*, (London) 70:581.

12625 **WEAVER, S.** (1979), Review of L. Berkowitz's *Group Processes. Brit. J. Psychol.*, (London) 70:582.

12626 **WEBER, A.** (1977), (Special schooling, education counseling, psychotherapy and pharmacotherapy in children with minimal brain damage.) *Ther. Umschau*, (Berne) 34:24-28.

12627 **WEBER, L.**, and **HILL, T.** (1973), A therapy group of juvenile delinquent boys. *Psychiat. Forum*, 3:25-33.

12628 **WEBER, L. A.** (1980), The effect of videotape and playback on an inpatient adolescent group. *Internat. J. Group Psychother.*, 30:213-227.

12629 **WEBER, W. J.** (1980), Representatives and generalizability of interpersonal behavior in a psychotherapy group. *Dissert. Abstr. Internat.*, 41:704B. (University Microfilms No. 8016597.)

12630 **WEBSTER, C. T.** (1979), Group therapy for behavior–problem children in a rural junior high school. *Child Welfare*, 53:53-57.

12631 **WEBSTER, E. J.** (1968), Procedures for group parent counseling in speech pathology and audiology. *J. Speech & Hearing Disorders*, 33:127-131.

12632 **WEBSTER, J.** (1966), Nursing families in a therapeutic community. *Internat. J. Nursing Studies*, 3:1-7.

12633 **WEBSTER, T. G.**, and **HARRIS, H. I.** (1958), Modified group psychotherapy, an experiment in group psychodynamics for college freshmen. *Group Psychother., Psychodrama & Sociometry*, 11:283-298.

12634 **WECHSLER, I. R.** (1962), The "sociometric field": a new training and research tool. *Group Psychother., Psychodrama & Sociometry*, 15:123-125.

12635 **WECHSLER, J. D.** (1971), Improving the self–concepts of academic underachievers through maternal group counseling. *Calif. J. Educat. Res.*, 22:96-103.

12636 **WEDDIG, T. M.** (1974), Focusing and crisis fantasy in experiential group psychotherapy. *Psychother.: Theory, Res. & Pract.*, 11:289.

12637 **WEDLER, H. L.** (1975), (Proceedings: therapeutic group work in the hospital.) *Munchen Med. Wochenschr.*, (Munich) 117:842.

12638 **WEDLER, H. L.** (1975), Therapeutic group work in a medical clinic. *Verh. Deutsche Gesamte Inn. Med.*, 81:1738-1740.

12639 **WEEKS, H. A.** (1953), Preliminary evaluation of the Highfields Project. *Amer. Sociologist*, 18:280-287.

12640 **WEEKS, H. M.** (1965), An evaluation of self-awareness group therapy with chronic schizophrenic patients. *Dissert. Abstr. Internat.*, 26:1177-1178.

12641 **WEEKS, M. J.** (1974), A study of the relationship between group facilitative involvement and relative effectiveness of group counseling professionals. *Dissert. Abstr. Internat.*, 34:310B.

12642 **WEIANT, P. A.** (1980), An experiment in voluntary group centered counseling: Dedham house of correction. *Dissert. Abstr. Internat.*, 31:2120A.

12643 **WEICH, H. J.**, and **ROLLINS, E.** (1966), Short-term group psychotherapy with acutely psychotic patients. *Psychiat. Quart.*, 40:80-87.

12644 **WEIDEMANN, J.** (1961), Soziale verhaltensweisen des kranken kindes. (Patterns of social behavior in the ill child.) *Acta Paedopsychiat.*, (Basel) 28:241-248.

12645 **WEIGEL, R. D.**, and **WARNATH, C. F.** (1968), The effects of group therapy on reported self-disclosure. *Internat. J. Group Psychother.*, 18:31-41.

12646 **WEIGEL, R. G.** (1968), Outcomes of marathon group therapy and marathon group topical discussion. *Dissert. Abstr. Internat.*, 29:1182.
12647 **WEIGEL, R. G.** (1977), The marathon encounter: requiem for a social movement. *Small Group Behav.*, 8:201-222.
12648 **WEIGEL, R. G.**, and **CORAZZINI, J. G.** (1978), Small group research: suggestions for solving common methodological and design problems. *Small Group Behav.*, 9:193-220.
12649 **WEIGEL, R. G.**, and **DINGES, N.** (1972), Perceived self-disclosure, mental health, and who is liked in group treatment. *J. Couns. Psychol.*, 19:47-52.
12650 **WEIGEL, R. G.**, and **STRAUMFJORD, A. A.** (1970), The dog as a therapeutic adjunct in group treatment. *Voices*, 6:108-110.
12671 **WEIL, P. G.** (1965-1970), Psychodrama and psychoanalysis. *Bull. de Psychol.*, (Paris) 23:726-735.
12652 **WEINAPPLE, M.** (1977), Review of A. W. Rachman's *Identity Group Psychotherapy with Adolescents. Contemp. Psychol.*, 22:215-216.
12653 **WEINBERG, J.** (1946), Group psychotherapy as developed in a military setting. *Psychiat. Quart.*, 20:470-484.
12654 **WEINBERGER, A.**, and **ENGELHART, R. S.** (1976), Three group treatments for reduction of speech anxiety among students. *Percept. & Motor Skills*, 43:1317-1318.
12656 **WEINER, H. B.** (1975), Living experiences with death: a journeyman's view through psychodrama. *Omega: J. Death & Dying*, 6:251-274.
12655 **WEINBERGER, P. M.** (1975), Frequency of group counseling as a variable affecting student self-esteem and classroom behavior with male students at the seventh grade level. *Dissert. Abstr. Internat.*, 36:1517B.
12657 **WEINER, H. B.** (1968), J. L. Moreno: Mr. group psychotherapy. *Group Psychother., Psychodrama & Sociometry*, 21:144-150.
12658 **WEINER, H. B.** (1966), An overview of the use of psychodrama and group psychotherapy in the treatment of alcoholism in the United States and abroad. *Group Psychother., Psychodrama & Sociometry*, 19:159-165.
12659 **WEINER, H. B.** (1966), A report on the use of psychodrama on a television show: "Alcoholism, our great failure." *Internat. J. Sociometry & Sociatry*, 5:11-32.
12660 **WEINER, H. B.** (1965), Treating the alcoholic with psychodrama. *Group Psychother., Psychodrama & Sociometry*, 18:27-49.
12661 **WEINER, M. B.**, and **WEINSTOCK, C. S.** (1979), Group progress of community elderly as measured by tape recordings, group tempo and group evaluation. *Aging*, 10:177.
12662 **WEINER, M. F.** (1969), In defense of the therapist. *Psychosomatics*, 10:156-158.
12663 **WEINER, M. F.** (1974), Genetic versus interpersonal insight. *Internat. J. Group Psychother.*, 24:230-237.
12664 **WEINER, M. F.** (1975), Group therapy. *J. Amer. Med. Assn.*, 234:1181-1182.
12665 **WEINER, M. F.** (1975), "Individual" versus conjoint therapy. *Diseases Nerv. System*, 36:546-549.
12666 **WEINER, M. F.** (1971), Levels of intervention in group psychotherapy. *Group Process*, (London) 3:67-81.
12667 **WEINER, M. F.** (1980), Review of H. B. Roback's and S. I. Abramowitz's, *Group Psychotherapy Research: Commentaries and Selected Readings. Internat. J. Group Psychother.*, 30:374.
12668 **WEINER, M. F.** (1972), Self-exposure by the therapist as a therapeutic technique. *Amer. J. Psychother.*, 26:42-51.
12669 **WEINER, M. F.** (1973), Termination of group psychotherapy. *Group Process*, (London) 5:85-96.

12670 **WEINGOLD, J. T.,** and **HORMUTH, R. P.** (1953), Group guidance of parents of mentally retarded children. *J. Clin. Psychol.*, 9:118-124.

12671 **WEINHOLD, B.** (1977), Restoring natural power through group counseling. *Personnel & Guid. J.*, 56:235-239.

12672 **WEINMAN, B., SANDERS, R., KLEINER, R.,** and **WILSON, S.** (1970), Community based treatment of the chronic psychotic. *Community Ment. Health J.*, 6:13-21.

12673 **WEINSCHENK, C.** (1973), When is a procedure a form of therapy? comments on the paper of A. Heigl-Evers and F. Heigel, "Group psychotherapy: methods and technics." *Nervenarzt*, 44:274.

12674 **WEINSTEIN, H. G.** (1971), Special classes and group therapy: an evaluation of their effects on achievement and behavior in a public school setting. *Dissert. Abstr. Internat.*, 32:1930A.

12675 **WEINSTEIN, M. S.,** and **HANSON, R.** (1975), Leader experience level and patterns of participation in sensitivity training groups. *Small Group Behav.*, 6:123-140.

12676 **WEINSTEIN, M. S.,** and **POLLACK, H. B.** (1972), The use of exercises in sensitivity training: a survey. *Compar. Group Studies*, 3:497-512.

12677 **WEINSTEIN, R. S.** (1974), Reading groups and teacher-child interaction in the first grade classroom. *Dissert. Abstr. Internat.*, 34:5696B.

12678 **WEINSTOCK, A.** (1979), Group treatment of characterologically damaged, developmentally disabled adolescents in a residential treatment center. *Internat. J. Group Psychother.*, 29:369-382.

12679 **WEINSTOCK, M.** (1974), Toward a treatment of alienation: a comparison of group counseling approaches. *Dissert. Abstr. Internat.*, 35:2785A.

12680 **WEIR, J. M., DUBITZKY, M.,** and **SCHWARTZ, J. L.** (1969), Counselor style and group effectiveness in a smoking withdrawal study. *Amer. J. Psychother.*, 23:106-118.

12681 **WEISBERG, P. S.** (1979), Group therapy with adolescents. In: *Short Course in Adolescent Psychiatry*, ed. J. R. Novello. New York: Brunner/Mazel.

12682 **WEISBERG, P. S.** (1973), Intensive group therapy with college-age students as suicide prevention. *Groups*, 5:45-48.

12683 **WEISE, K.** (1965), (Pantomime as part of sociotherapy in the psychiatric clinic.) *Nervenarzt*, 36:463-468.

12684 **WEISE, K.** (1967), (Pantomime in the framework of group psychotherapy.) *Zeit. Psychother. Med. Psychol.*, (Stuttgart) 17:17-22.

12685 **WEISE, K.** (1968), (Possibilities of psychiatric treatment near the community with special reference to day and night treatment.) *Zeit. Aerztl. Fortbildung*, (Jena) 62:42-49.

12686 **WEISER, C.,** and **WEISER, C.** (1973), *Not So Loud, I Can't Hear You!* Philadelphia: Fortress Press.

12687 **WEISKOTT, G. N.** (1975), Assertiveness, territoriality, and personal space behavior as a function of group assertion training with a college population. *Dissert. Abstr. Internat.*, 36:2726A.

12688 **WEISKOTT, G. N.,** and **CLELAND, C. C.** (1977), Assertiveness, territoriality, and personal space behavior as a function of group assertion training. *J. Couns. Psychol.*, 24:111-117.

12689 **WEISS, B. J.** (1972), The development of cohesiveness in marathon growth groups. *Dissert. Abstr. Internat.*, 32:6065B.

12690 **WEISS, F. A.** (1955), Group psychoanalysis: a panel discussion. *Amer. J. Psychoanal.*, 15:31-44.

12691 **WEISS, M. H.,** and **McKENZIE, D. H.** (1972), The effects of videotape focused feedback on facilitative genuineness in interracial encounters. *Compar. Group Studies*, 3:247-259.

12692 **WEISS, R.** (1949), Haripuy hak'vutsati. (Group therapy.) *L'maan Hayeled V'hanoar*, No. 38.

12693 **WEISSELBERGER, D.** (1973), Acting-out behavior in group psychotherapy: a reappraisal. *Groups*, 5:57-61.

12694 **WEISSELBERGER, D.** (1977), Developmental phases in activity interview group psychotherapy with children. *Groups*, 8:20-26.

12695 **WEISSELBERGER, D.** (1976), Sexual acting out in group therapy: a reassessment. *Groups*, 7:35-37.

12696 **WEISSMAN, H. N.** (1969), The psychiatric team as a differential decision-maker with child patients. *Psychol. Reports*, 25:11-17.

12697 **WEISSMAN, H. N., GOLDSCHMID, M. L., GORDON, R.,** and **FEINBERG, H.** (1977), Changes in self-regard, creativity, and inter–personal behavior as a function of audio-tape encounter-group experiences. *Psychol. Reports*, 31:975-981.

12698 **WEISSMAN, H. N., SELDMAN, M.,** and **RITTER, K.** (1971), Changes in awareness of impact upon others as a function of encounter and marathon group experiences. *Psychol. Reports*, 28:651-661.

12699 **WEITZ, P.,** and **BAGANZ, C. N.** (1952), Application of group therapy principles to hospital administration. *Internat. J. Group Psychother.*, 2:245-249.

12700 **WELCH, V. O.,** and **SIGMAN, M.** (1980), Group psychotherapy with mildly retarded, emotionally disturbed adolescents. *J. Clin. Child Psychol.*, 9:209-212.

12701 **WELKOWITZ, J.** (1960), Behavior patterns in group psychotherapy sessions in two Veterans Administration hospitals. *Dissert. Abstr. Internat.*, 20:4202-4203. (University Microfilms No. 60-01165.)

12702 **WELLINGTON, J.** (1965), Group therapy with pre-adolescent girls. *Psychother.: Theory, Res. & Pract.*, 2:171-173.

12703 **WELLMAN, M.** (1963), Basic principles of Moreno's contributions to psychology. *Group Psychother., Psychodrama & Sociometry*, 16:260-284.

12704 **WELLS, C. G.** (1962), Psychodrama and creative counseling in the elementary schools. *Group Psychother., Psychodrama & Sociometry*, 15:244-252.

12705 **WELLS, C. G.** (1961), Psychodrama with children in a sociometrically structured setting. *Group Psychother., Psychodrama & Sociometry*, 14:160-163.

12706 **WELLS, G. D., MAZER, J.,** and **CLINE, B.** (1958), Fostering the involvement of the psychiatric patient in group activities. *Psychiatry*, 21:259-268.

12707 **WELLS, R. A.** (1975), Training in facilitative skills. *Soc. Work*, 20:242-243.

12708 **WELLS, R. A.,** and **DEZEN, A. C.** (1978), Ideologies, idols, (and graven images?): rejoinder to Gruman and Kniskern. *Fam. Process*, 17:283-286.

12709 **WELSH, R. L.** (1978), The use of group strategies with the visually impaired: a review. *J. Visual Impair. Blindness*, 72:131-138.

12710 **WELTER, P. R.** (1968), Group counseling and the assessment of affective learning. *Dissert. Abstr. Internat.*, 29:1114A.

12711 **WEMHOFF, R. T.** (1978), The effects of two different counseling orientations and procedures on self-actualization of group counseling participants. *Dissert. Abstr. Internat.*, 37:3386B.

12712 **WENAR, C.,** and **RUTTENBERG, B. A.** (1969), Therapies for autistic children. In: *Current Psychiatric Therapies*, ed. J. H. Masserman. New York: Grune and Stratton.

12713 **WEND, H.** (1970), Principal problems in the psychotherapy of alcoholics. *Psychiat., Neurol. & Med. Psychol.*, (Leipzig) 22:365-369.

12714 **WENDER, H. B.** (1950), Experiences in group psychotherapy with insulin treated patients. *Psychiat. Quart.*, 24:314-323.
12715 **WENDER, L.** (1951), Current trends in group psychotherapy. *Amer. J. Psychother.*, 5:381-404.
12716 **WENDER, L.** (1936), The dynamics of group psychotherapy and its application. *J. Nerv. & Ment. Diseases*, 84:54-60.
12717 **WENDER, L.** (1975), The dynamics of group psychotherapy and its application. In: *Group Psychotherapy and Group Function*, 2d ed., eds. M. Rosenbaum and M. M. Berger. New York: Basic Books.
12718 **WENDER, L.** (1945), Group psychotherapy. *Sociometry*, 8:346-349.
12719 **WENDER, L.** (1940), Group psychotherapy: a study of its application. *Psychiat. Quart.*, 14:708-718.
12720 **WENDER, L.** (1946), Group psychotherapy within the psychiatric hospital. In: *Current Therapies of Personality Disorders*, ed. B. Glueck. New York: Grune and Stratton, pp. 46-58.
12721 **WENDER, L.** (1963), The psychodynamics of group psychotherapy. *J. Hillside Hosp.*, 12:134-139.
12722 **WENDER, L.** (1951), Reflections on group psychotherapy. *Quart. Rev. Psychiat.*, 6:246-248.
12723 **WENDER, L.** (1951), Selection of patients for group psychotherapy. *Internat. J. Group Psychother.*, 1:55-58.
12724 **WENDER, L.**, and **STEIN, A.** (1949), Group psychotherapy as an aid to out-patient treatments. *Psychiat. Quart.*, 23:415-424.
12725 **WENDER, L.**, and **STEIN, A.** (1953), The utilization of group psychotherapy in the social integration of patients: ii. *Internat. J. Group Psychother.*, 3:320-329.
12726 **WENDER, L.**, and **STEIN, A.** (1953), The utilization of group psychotherapy in the social integration of patients: an extension of the method to self-governing patient groups. *Internat. J. Group Psychother.*, 3:210-218.
12727 **WENDLAND, L. V.** (1955), A therapeutic group with husbands and wives of poliomyetic patients. *Group Psychother., Psychodrama & Sociometry*, 8:25-32.
12728 **WENDT, H.** (1975), Group round. *Psychiat. Neurol. & Med. Psychol.*, (Leipzig) 27:134-139.
12729 **WENDT, H.** (1960), (On the practice of group therapy.) *Deutsche Gesundh.*, (Berlin) 15:1604-1608.
12730 **WENKART, A.** (1965), Comments on existential changes in a woman. *Topical Probl. Psychol. & Psychiat.*, 5:146-149.
12731 **WENTWORTH-ROHR, I.** (1969), Origin of the primary group: a contribution to theory of groups. *J. Group Psychoanal. & Process*, (London) 2:19-28.
12732 **WEPPNER, R. S.** (1973), Some characteristics of an ex-addict self-help therapeutic community and its members. *Brit. J. Addict.*, 68:243-250.
12733 **WERBIN, J.**, and **HYNES, K.** (1975), Transference and culture in a Latino therapy group. *Internat. J. Group Psychother.*, 25:396-401.
12734 **WERMERS, D. F.**, and **WISE, M.** (1969), A technique to integrate the social isolate in a group activity. *Internat. J. Group Psychother.*, 19:229-233.
12735 **WERNER, J. A.** (1972), Group systematic desensitization of test anxiety in relation to measured changes in scholastic probation students. *Dissert. Abstr. Internat.*, 33:1031A.
12736 **WERNER, J. A.** (1970), Relating group theory to nursing practice. *Perspect. Psychiat. Care*, 8:248-261.
12737 **WERNER, R. S.** (1972), Group counseling with underachievers in a community college. *Dissert. Abstr. Internat.*, 32:3708A.

12738 **WERNER, V., MADDIGMAN, R. F.,** and **WATSON, C. G.** (1969), A study of two treatment programs for chronic mentally ill patients in occupational therapy. *Amer. J. Occupat. Ther.*, 23:132-136.

12739 **WERT, P. M.** (1978), The use of selected psychological tests in determining treatment outcome and group therapy behavior with sex offenders. *Dissert. Abstr. Internat.*, 39:685A.

12740 **WERTH, E. M.** (1979), A comparison of pretraining methods for encounter group therapy. *Dissert. Abstr. Internat.*, 40:1390B.

12741 **WERTHEIM, J.,** and **BIRCHER, L. M.** (1976), (Geriatric group psychotherapy.) *Akt. Gerontol.*, (Stuttgart) 6:519-529.

12742 **WERTLIEB, D.** (1979), A preventive health paradigm for health care psychologists. *Prof. Psychol.*, 10:548-557.

12744 **WEST, J. H.** (1965), England's Caldecott community: environmental therapy and its treatment orientation. *Ment. Hygiene*, 49:351-355.

12743 **WERTLIEB, D.,** and **BUDMAN, S. H.** (1979), Concluding remarks: dimensions of role conflict for health care psychologists. *Prof. Psychol.*, 10:640.

12745 **WEST, M., McILVAINE, R.,** and **SELLS, C. J.** (1979), Interdisciplinary health care settings experience with groups for parents of children having specific disabilities. *Soc. Work & Health Care*, 4:287-298.

12746 **WEST, W.** (1978), Combined approaches in the treatment of the orally regressed masochistic character disorder. *J. Contemp. Psychother.*, 9:155-161.

12747 **WEST, W. G.** (1972), The effects of two types of group counseling procedures with junior college students. *Dissert. Abstr. Internat.*, 32:3709A.

12748 **WESTBROOK, F. D.** (1974), A comparison of three methods of group vocational counseling. *J. Consult. & Clin. Psychol.*, 21:502-506.

12749 **WESTENDORP, F., ABRAMSON, B.,** and **WIRT, R. D.** (1962), Group psychotherapy in a public school setting. *Group Psychother., Psychodrama & Sociometry*, 15:30-35.

12750 **WESTFALL, M. P., SCHATZBERG, A. F., BLUMETTI, A. B.,** and **BIRK, C. L** (1975), Effeminacy: ii. variation with social context. *Arch. Sexual Behav.*, 4:43-51.

12751 **WESTFIELD, D. R.** (1972), Two years' experience of group methods in the treatment of male alcoholics in a Scottish mental hospital. *Brit. J. Addict.*, 67:267-276.

12752 **WESTMAN, J. C.** (1961), Group psychotherapy with hospitalized delinquent adolescents. *Internat. J. Group Psychother.*, 11:410-418.

12753 **WESTMAN, J. C.** (1960), An overview of group psychotherapy. *Arch. Gen. Psychiat.*, 2:271-277.

12754 **WESTMAN, J. C.** (1967), Setting the treatment focus in a child psychiatry clinic. *Amer. J. Orthopsychiat.*, 37:271-272.

12755 **WESTMAN, J. C., KANSKY, E. W., ERIKSON, M. E., ARTHUR, B.,** and **VROOM, A. L.** (1963), Parallel group psychotherapy with the parents of emotionally disturbed children. *Internat. J. Group Psychother.*, 13:52-60.

12756 **WESTNEY, O. E.** (1972), The comparative effects of a group discussion program and a lecture program on the self concept, attitudes toward pregnancy and manifest anxiety of unwed, primigravid Negro adolescent girls. *Dissert. Abstr. Internat.*, 33:91A.

12757 **WESTRATE, R. M.** (1973), T-group composition using a personality criterion and related considerations to validate the outcome of human relations training. *Dissert. Abstr. Internat.*, 34:4765A.

12758 **WETHERHORN, M. H.** (1958), Chlorpromazine: alone and an adjunct to group psychotherapy in the treatment of chronic paranoid and catatonic schizophrenias. Unpublished doctoral dissertation, Florida State University.

12759 **WETZEL, M. C., KINNEY, J. M., BEAVERS, M. E., HARVEY, R. T.,** and **URBANCIK, G. W.** (1976), Action laboratory: behavioral group therapy in a traditional context. *Internat. J. Group Psychother.*, 26:59-70.

12760 **WEWETZER, K. H.,** and **FREUDENFREG, D.** (1956), Über verlauf und erfolg einer speilgruppentherapie. (Progress and success in group plan therapy.) *Zeit. Diagnost. Psychol.*, 4:59-82.

12761 **WEXLER, J. M.,** and **STEELE, T. E.** (1978), Termination of one therapist in co-led group psychotherapy. *Clin. Soc. Work J.*, 6:211-220.

12762 **WEYMOUTH, P.,** and **TAINTOR, Z.** (1968), A group cycle in a developing therapeutic community. *Internat. J. Group Psychother.*, 18:75-85.

12763 **WHALEN, C.** (1969), Effects of a model and instructions on group verbal behaviors. *J. Consult. & Clin. Psychol.*, 33:509-521.

12764 **WHALEN, C. K.,** and **HENKER, B. A.** (1971), Pyramid therapy in a hospital for the retarded: methods, program evaluation, and long-term effects. *Amer. J. Ment. Deficiency*, 75:414-434.

12765 **WHALEN, E. F.,** and **BARRELL, R. P.** (1970), Utilizing group techniques: a training program for psychiatric nurses. *J. Psychiat. Nursing*, 8:27.

12766 **WHEELER, W.** (1972), Effects of encounter group methods upon selected measures of the body image. *Dissert. Abstr. Internat.*, 32:4436A.

12767 **WHEELWRIGHT, J. B.** (1955), Comments on Moreno's "transference and tele." *Group Psychother., Psychodrama & Sociometry*, 8:80-81.

12768 **WHIPPLE, D. W.** (1979), Group analysis as an adjunct to the termination process. *Psychoanal. Rev.*, 66:215-226.

12769 **WHIPPLE, S. B.,** and **MAANING, D. E.** (1978), Anorexia nervosa: commitment of a multifaceted treatment program. *Psychother. & Psychosomat.*, (Basel) 3:161.

12770 **WHITAKER, C. A.** (1951), Discussion of the symposium on group psychotherapy, theory and practice. *Group Psychother., Psychodrama & Sociometry*, 4:38-40.

12771 **WHITAKER, C. A., WARKENTIN, J.,** and **JOHNSON, N.** (1949), A philosophical basis for brief psychotherapy. *Psychiat. Quart.*, 23:439-443.

12772 **WHITAKER, D. S.** (1965), The processes by which change occurs and the role of insight. *Psychother. & Psychosomat.*, (Basel) 13:126-141.

12773 **WHITAKER, D. S.,** and **LIEBERMAN, M. A.** (1964), Assessing interpersonal behavior in group therapy. *Percept. & Motor Skills*, 18:763-764.

12774 **WHITAKER, D. S.,** and **LIEBERMAN, M. A.** (1968), *Psychotherapy Through the Group Process*. Englewood Cliffs, NJ: Prentice-Hall.

12775 **WHITAKER, D. S.,** and **LIEBERMAN, M. A.** (1964), *Psychotherapy Through the Group Process*. Hawthorne, NY: Aldine Publishing.

12776 **WHITAKER, D. S.,** and **LIEBERMAN, M. A.** (1964), *Psychotherapy Through the Group Process*. London: Prentice-Hall.

12777 **WHITAKER, D. S.,** and **LIEBERMAN, M. A.** (1964), *Psychotherapy Through the Group Process*. New York: Atherton Press.

12778 **WHITAKER, D. S.,** and **THELEN, H. A.** (1975), Emotional dynamics and group culture. In: *Group Psychotherapy and Group Function*, 2d ed., eds. M. Rosenbaum and M. M. Berger. New York: Basic Books.

12779 **WHITAKER, L.,** and **DEIKMAN, A.** (1980), Psychotherapy of severe depression. *Psychother.: Theory, Res. & Pract.*, 17:85.

12780 **WHITAKER, L. H.** (1954), Group therapy: review and report on its use in therapeutic community. *Med. J. Austral.*, (Glebe) 1:899-904.

12781 **WHITE, A., FICHTENBAUM, L.,** and **DOLLARD, J.** (1964), Measures for predicting dropping out of psychotherapy. *J. Consult. & Clin. Psychol.*, 28:326-332.

12782 **WHITE, E. M.** (1970), Race relations: a call for action. *Nurs. Outlook*, 18:31-33.

12783 **WHITE, J.** (1974), The human potential laboratory in the community college. *J. Coll. Student Personnel*, 15:96-100.
12784 **WHITE, K. R.** (1972), A study of self-concept change as a result of "normal" and "fish-bowl" methods of t-group interaction. *Dissert. Abstr. Internat.*, 33:1452A.
12785 **WHITE, K. R.** (1974), T-groups revisited: self-concept change and the "fish-bowling" technique. *Small Group Behav.*, 5:473-485.
12786 **WHITE, L. A.** (1972), The effects of leader personality on group outcomes in interracial encounter groups. *Dissert. Abstr. Internat.*, 33:4107A.
12787 **WHITE, N. F.** (1972), The descent of milieu therapy. *Can. Psychiat. Assn. J.*, (Ottawa) 17:41-50.
12788 **WHITE, R. E.**, and **BUTTS, W. M.** (1963), Near sociometric investigations of group membership survival. *Group Psychother., Psychodrama & Sociometry*, 16:182-188.
12789 **WHITE, T. D.** (1972), Training parents in a group situation to use behavior modification techniques to reduce frequency of maladaptive behavior in their learning disabled child. *Dissert. Abstr. Internat.*, 32:1776B.
12790 **WHITE, W. A.** (1950), Comments on Moreno's "Psychological organization of groups in the community." *Group Psychother., Psychodrama & Sociometry*, 3:189-195.
12791 **WHITE, W. A.**, and **HALL, R. W.** (1945), Group psychotherapy: a symposium. *Sociometry*, 8:243-561.
12792 **WHITE, W. F.**, and **ALLEN, W. R.** (1966), Psychodramatic effects of music as a psychotherapeutic agent. *J. Music Ther.*, 3:69-71.
12793 **WHITEHEAD, C. E.** (1973), St. Columba, Emmanuel Centre. *Queen's Nursing J.*, (London) 16:185-186.
12794 **WHITEHORN, J. C.** (1963), The situational part of diagnosis. *Internat. J. Group Psychother.*, 13:290-299.
12795 **WHITEHOUSE, F. A.** (1967), The concept of therapy: a review of some essentials. *Rehab. Lit.*, 28:238-247.
12796 **WHITELAW, B.**, **WALWYN, M.**, **FLEISCHAKER, K.**, and **EDSALL, B.** (1980), Different drummers. *J. Special. Group Work*, 5:212-215.
12797 **WHITELEY, J. S.**, and **GORDON, J.** (1979), Review of *Group Approaches in Psychiatry*. *Psychol. Med.*, (London) 9:599.
12798 **WHITELEY, R. M.** (1973), Women in groups. *Couns. Psychologist*, 4:27-43.
12799 **WHITMAN, E. B.** (1954), Personality of fourth grade children as measured by modified t.a.t. and improvisation techniques. *Group Psychother., Psychodrama & Sociometry*, 7:255-261.
12800 **WHITMAN, H.**, **GUSTAFSON, J. P.**, and **COLEMAN, F.** (1979), Supportive group therapy for cancer patients. *Amer. J. Nursing*, 19:910-913.
12801 **WHITMAN, H. H.**, **GUSTAFSON, J.**, and **COLEMAN, F. W.** (1979), Group approaches for cancer patients, leaders and members. *Amer. J. Nursing*, 79:910-913.
12802 **WHITMAN, R. M.** (1973), Dreams also of the group: an approach to the problem of group psychology. *Internat. J. Group Psychother.*, 23:408-420.
12803 **WHITMAN, R. M.** (1956), The rating and group dynamics of the psychiatric staff conference. *Psychiatry*, 19:333-340.
12804 **WHITMAN, R. M.**, and **STOCK, D.** (1958), The group focal conflict. *Psychiatry*, 21:269-276.
12805 **WHITMAN, R. M.**, **LIEBERMAN, M. A.**, and **STOCK, D.** (1960), The relation between individual and group conflicts in psychotherapy. *Internat. J. Group Psychother.*, 10:259-286.
12806 **WHITMAN, T. L.** (1972), Aversive control of smoking behavior in a group context. *Behav. Res. & Ther.*, 10:97-104.
12807 **WHITMORE, H. L.** (1970), Group satisfaction: a function of the client

selection procedures using interpersonal needs. *Dissert. Abstr. Internat.*, 31:3891A.
12808 **WHITNEY, D. M.** (1970), An experimental study of three methods of implementing confrontation and their effects on the facilitative dimensions of interpersonal and small group processes. *Dissert. Abstr. Internat.*, 30:3744A-3745A.
12809 **WHITTAKER, J. K.** (1976), Differential use of program activities in child treatment groups. *Child Welfare*, 55:459-467.
12810 **WHITTAKER, J. K.** (1970), Models of group development: implications for social group work practice. *Social Serv. Rev.*, 44:308-322.
12811 **WHITTAKER, L.** (1967), The effects of group counseling on academic achievement and certain personality factors of college students with academic deficiencies. *Dissert. Abstr. Internat.*, 27:2834A.
12812 **WHYCHERLEY, J.** (1974), A symposium on the rehabilitation of the stroke patient. *Nursing Mirror*, (London) 139:73-76.
12813 **WIBERLEY, J. A.** (1961), Changes in school administrators' attitudes toward others as an outcome of a group-centered discussion. Ph.D. thesis, Syracuse University.
12814 **WICKS, L. K.** (1977), Transsexualism: a social work approach. *Health & Soc. Work*, 2:179-193.
12815 **WIDLÖCHER, D.** (1961), (The observation of psychodrama with children and adolescents.) *Rev. Neuropsychiat. Infantile*, (Paris) 9:413-418.
12816 **WIDLÖCHER, D.** (1962), (Psychodrama.) *Med. Infantile*, (Paris) 69:475-478.
12817 **WIEDER, D.**, and **HICKS, J.** (1973), A study of motivational techniques in the long-term sheltered workshop. *Training School Bull.*, 70:43-50.
12818 **WIEDORN, W. S., Jr.** (1957), Modified group therapy in training psychiatric aides. *Psychiat. Quart. Suppl.*, 31:42-49.
12819 **WIEINAS, M. J.** (1972), Quarter-way-house for the hospitalized mentally ill. *Soc. Work*, 17:72.
12820 **WIEMER, M. J.** (1975), Cognitive restructuring therapy. *Scand. J. Behav. Ther.*, 4:3-10.
12821 **WIERINGA, C. F.** (1973), (Feedback.) *Gruppendynamik*, (Stuttgart) 1:42-56.
12822 **WIESENHUTTER, E.** (1970), Entwicklung, keifung, retardation, regression. (Development, maturity, retardation, regression.) *Praxis der Psychother.*, 15:122-132.
12823 **WIESENHUTTER, E.** (1961), Gestaltungs und gruppentherapie bei jugendlichen. (Gestalt and group therapy in young subjects.) *Praxis der Psychother.*, 6:155-160.
12824 **WIGELL, W. W.** (1960), A content analysis of tape recordings of group counseling sessions with gifted underachieving ninth grade students. Ed.D. thesis, University of Illinois.
12825 **WIGELL, W. W.**, and **OHLSEN, M. M.** (1962), To what extent is affect a function of topic and referent in group counseling? *Amer. J. Orthopsychiat.*, 32:728-735.
12826 **WIGGINS, S. L.** (1965), Conditioning against silences and direct comments to the therapist in group psychotherapy by the use of auditory stimulation. *Dissert. Abstr. Internat.*, 25:6088-6089.
12827 **WIGGINS, S. L.**, and **SALZBERG, H. C.** (1966), Conditioning against silences and therapist-directed comments in group psychotherapy using auditory stimulation. *Psychol. Reports*, 18:591-599.
12828 **WIJESINGHE, O. B.**, and **WOOD, R. R.** (1976), A repertory grid study of interpersonal perception within a married couples psychotherapy group. *Brit. J. Med. Psychol.*, (London) 49:287-293.
12829 **WIJSENBEEK, H.**, and **MUNITZ, H.** (1970), (Group treatment in a he-

modialysis center.) *Psychiat., Neurol., Neurochir.*, (Amsterdam) 73:213-220.

12830 **WIKLUND, D.** (1958), Terapigrupp och totalgrepp ger framgang i amerikanskt nykterhetsframjande. (Progress in group therapy and "total push" in treatment of alcoholics in America.) *Soc. Meddelanden*, (Stockholm) 10:570-579.

12831 **WILBUR, B. M., SALKIN, D.,** and **BIRNBAUM, H.** (1966), The response of tuberculous alcoholics to a therapeutic community. *Quart. J. Studies Alcohol*, 27:620-635.

12832 **WILCOX, E. J.,** and **HILL, W. F.** (1957), Group process problems in a team research program. *Provo Papers*, 1:37-53.

12833 **WILCOX, G. T.** (1957), Changes in adjustment of institutionalized female defectives following group psychotherapy. Unpublished doctoral dissertation, Pennsylvania State University.

12834 **WILCOX, G. T.** (1957), *Changes in Adjustment of Institutionalized Female Defectives Following Group Psychotherapy*. Ann Arbor: University Microfilms.

12835 **WILCOX, G. T.,** and **GUTHRIE, G. M.** (1957), Changes in adjustment of institutionalized female defectives following group psychotherapy. *J. Clin. Psychol.*, 13:9-13.

12836 **WILD, H. J.** (1973), (Conflict-centered group discussion in the industrial outpatient clinic.) *Zeit. Aerztl. Fortbildung*, (Jena) 67:390-393.

12837 **WILD, H. J.** (1977), (Group-therapy system of treatment in a psychiatric ambulatory.) *Psychiat. Neurol. & Med. Psychol.*, (Leipzig) 29:221-230.

12838 **WILDE, R. K.** (1973), The effects of structured motivation program approach and a non-structured group approach on self-actualizing attitudes, scholastic motivation among high school juniors. *Dissert. Abstr. Internat.*, 33:4862A.

12839 **WILDER, J.** (1974), Group analysis and the insights of the analyst. In: *The Challenge for Group Psychotherapy: Present and Future*, ed. S. de Schill. New York: International Universities Press.

12840 **WILDER, J.** (1952), Group analysis as an adjunct to long lasting psychoanalysis. *Group Psychother., Psychodrama & Sociometry*, 5:64-67.

12841 **WILDER, J.** (1959), Group analysis in the course of long-term individual psychoanalysis as a method of self-supervision. *Acta Psychother., Psychosomat. Orthopaedagog. Suppl.*, (Basel) 7:398-403.

12842 **WILDER, J.** (1942), The psychodrama as compared with other methods of psychotherapy. *Sociometry*, 5:185-190.

12843 **WILE, D.** (1973), What do trainees learn from a group therapy workshop? *Internat. J. Group Psychother.*, 23:185-203.

12844 **WILE, D. B.,** and **BRON, G. D.** (1970), Preliminary validational evidence for the group therapy questionnaire. *J. Consult. & Clin. Psychol.*, 34:367-374.

12845 **WILE, D. B., BRON, G. D.,** and **POLLACK, H. B.** (1970), The group therapy questionnaire: an instrument for study of leadership in small groups. *Psychol. Reports*, 27:263-273.

12846 **WILENSKY, H.,** and **HERZ, M. I.** (1966), Problem areas in the development of a therapeutic community. *Internat. J. Soc. Psychiat.*, (London) 12:299-308.

12847 **WILETT, J. R.** (1974), The effect of instructions, modeling and reinforcement on training communication skills in small groups. *Dissert. Abstr. Internat.*, 35:2454B.

12848 **WILKE, R. B.** (1974), *The Pastor and Marriage Group Counseling*. Nashville: Abingdon Press.

12849 **WILKINS, F. H.** (1978), An investigation to determine the effectiveness of video tape feedback in increasing self awareness of pupils in group counseling. *Dissert. Abstr. Internat.*, 39:8339A.

12850 **WILKINSON, A. E., PRADO, W. M., WILLIAMS, W. O.,** and **SCHNADT, F. W.** (1971), Psychological test characteristics and length of stay in alcoholism treatment. *Quart. J. Studies Alcohol*, 32:60-65A.

12851 **WILKINSON, C. B.** (1973), Problems in Black/White encounter groups. *Internat. J. Group Psychother.*, 23:155-165.

12852 **WILKINSON, G. S.** (1977), Small group counseling with elementary school children of divorce. *Dissert. Abstr. Internat.*, 37:6287A.

12853 **WILLAGE, D. E.,** and **MEYER, R. G.** (1978), The effects of varying levels of confidentiality on self-disclosure. *Group*, 2:88-97.

12854 **WILLCOX, A. F.** (1970), The new professionals: practical aspects of the use of new careerists in public service agencies. *Ment. Hygiene*, 54:347-356.

12855 **WILLEFORD, W.** (1967), Group psychotherapy and symbol formation. *J. Anal. Psychol.*, (London) 12:137-160.

12856 **WILLEFORD, W.** (1966), Gruppenpsychotherapie und symbolbildung. (Group psychotherapy and symbol formation.) *Psychother. & Psychosomat.*, (Basel) 14:282-297.

12857 **WILLEKE, C.,** and **GÜNTHER, H.** (1975), *Kritische Beiträge zur Gruppendynamik.* (*Critical Contributions on Group Dynamics.*) Stuttgart: Seewald.

12858 **WILLETT, E. A.** (1973), Group therapy in a methadone treatment program: an evaluation of changes in interpersonal behavior. *Internat. J. Addict.*, 8:33-39.

12859 **WILLEY, R. deV.,** and **ANDREW, D. C.** (1955), *Modern Methods and Techniques in Guidance.* New York: Harper and Row.

12860 **WILLIAMS, C. C.** (1977), The intensive care unit: social work intervention with the families of critically ill patients. *Social Work & Health Care*, 2:391-398.

12861 **WILLIAMS, C. L.** (1979), Empathic communication and its effect on client outcome. *Issues Ment. Health Nursing*, 2:15-26.

12862 **WILLIAMS, C. L.** (1980), Nurse therapist high empathy and nurse therapist low empathy during therapeutic-group work as factors in changing the self–concept of the institutionalized aged. *Dissert. Abstr. Internat.*, 40:3095B. (University Microfilms No. 8001353.)

12863 **WILLIAMS, H.** (1976), Smokers' advice centres and smoking cessation methods: Drayton Park Centre, London. group therapy in a smokers' advice centre—methods and aims. *Health*, 12:14-18.

12864 **WILLIAMS, H. B.,** and **FOLGER, J. K.** (1948), Role-playing in the education work conference. *Sociatry*, 2:338-347.

12865 **WILLIAMS, I.** (1975), Remotivation therapy keeps patients alert. *Dimens. Health Serv.*, (Toronto) 52:39.

12866 **WILLIAMS, I.** (1975), Remotivation therapy: the search for a spark of interest. *Can. J. Psychiat. Nursing*, (Winnipeg) 16:11.

12867 **WILLIAMS, J., LEWIS, C., COPELAND, F., TUCKER, L.,** and **FEAGAN, L.** (1978), A model for short-term group therapy on a children's inpatient unit. *Clin. Soc. Work J.*, 6:21-32.

12868 **WILLIAMS, J. A.** (1978), Cohesiveness in growth groups: the effects of similarity of values and self–esteem upon interpersonal attraction and attraction-to-the-group. *Dissert. Abstr. Internat.*, 39:5962A.

12869 **WILLIAMS, J. C.** (1977), The evolution of a psychotherapy group on a children's inpatient unit. *Smith Coll. Studies Soc. Work*, 48:3-8.

12870 **WILLIAMS, J. R., CSALANY, L.,** and **MISEUIC, G.** (1967), Drug therapy with or without group discussion: effects of various regimens on the behavior of geriatric patients in a mental hospital. *J. Amer. Geriat. Soc.*, 15:34-40.

12871 **WILLIAMS, J. R., KRIAUCIUNAS, R.**, and **RODRIQUIZ, A.** (1970), Physical, mental, and social rehabilitation for elderly and infirm patients. *Hosp. & Community Psychiat.*, 21:130-132.

12872 **WILLIAMS, L.** (1958), An experiment in group therapy. *Brit. J. Addict.*, 54:109-125.

12873 **WILLIAMS, M.** (1966), Limitations, fantasies, and security operations of beginning group psychotherapists. *Internat. J. Group Psychother.*, 16:150-162.

12874 **WILLIAMS, M.** (1962), *An Evaluation of an Intensive Group Living Program with Schizophrenic Patients.* Washington, D.C.: American Psychological Association.

12875 **WILLIAMS, M.**, and **JACKSON, R. D.** (1972), A small group living program for Vietnam–era veterans. *Hosp. & Community Psychiat.*, 23:141-144.

12876 **WILLIAMS, M., KITTLESON, S. K.**, and **HALPERIN, L.** (1957), An investigation of the effects of a group living program with withdrawn schizophrenic patients. *Group Psychother., Psychodrama & Sociometry*, 10:161-168.

12877 **WILLIAMS, M., ROBACK, H.**, and **PRO, J.** (1980), A geriatric "growth group." *Group*, 4:43-48.

12878 **WILLIAMS, M. J.** (1972), The effect of group counseling upon selected personality and behavioral variables in delinquent adolescents. *Dissert. Abstr. Internat.*, 32:3710A.

12879 **WILLIAMS, M. J. S.** (1964), Reference group relationships and dogmatism as determinants of influence and interpersonal conflict. *Dissert. Abstr. Internat.*, 24:3006.

12880 **WILLIAMS, R. A.** (1976), Contract for co-therapists in group psychotherapy. *J. Psychiat. Nursing*, 14:11-14.

12881 **WILLIAMS, R. I.**, and **BLANTON, R. L.** (1968), Verbal conditioning in a psychotherapeutic situation. *Behav. Res. & Ther.*, 6:97-103.

12882 **WILLIAMS, R. L.** (1970), A social systems model applied to a rehabilitation program for institutionalized patients. *J. Rehab.*, 36:20-23.

12883 **WILLIAMS, R. L.**, and **GASDICK, J. M.** (1970), Practical applications of psychodrama: an action therapy for chronic patients. *Hosp. & Community Psychiat.*, 21:187-189.

12884 **WILLIAMS, W. C., Jr.** (1972), The efficacy of group counseling on the academic performance of Black college freshmen with low-predicted grade point averages. *Dissert. Abstr. Internat.*, 32:4974A.

12885 **WILLIAMS, Y. D.** (1979), Multiple groups needs assessment in preventive community mental health. *Dissert. Abstr. Internat.*, 40:5469B.

12886 **WILLINGER, B. H.** (1980), Modified group psychotherapy with chronic renal dialysis patients. *Group*, 4:46-55.

12887 **WILLIS, R. H.**, and **HALE, J. F.** (1963), Dyadic interaction as a function of amount of feedback and instructional orientation. *Human Relat.*, 16:149-160.

12888 **WILLIS, R. J.** (1972), A search for predictors of growth through interpersonal interaction. *Dissert. Abstr. Internat.*, 32:1300B.

12889 **WILLIS, S. L.** (1974), Individual induced affect as a preventative pre–training technique for encounter group stress. *Dissert. Abstr. Internat.*, 35:3049B.

12890 **WILLMS, H.** (1973), (Music therapy: basis, mode of action and indications.) *Deutsche Krankenpflege-Zeit.*, (Stuttgart) 26:4-10.

12891 **WILLNER, G.** (1953), The problem of anxiety in group psychotherapy on a chronic mental hospital service. *Psychiat. Quart. Suppl.*, 27:92-104.

12892 **WILLNER, G.** (1954), Report on further developments in group psychotherapy on a chronic service of a mental hospital. *Psychiat. Quart. Suppl.*, 28:54-67.

12893 **WILLNER, G.** (1954), The use of dream interpretation in group psychotherapy in a state hospital. *Psychiat. Quart. Suppl.*, 28:228-241.

12894 **WILLNER, G. P.** (1952), Preliminary report of the introduction of group psychotherapy on a chronic ward in a mental hospital. *Psychiat. Quart. Suppl.*, 26:86-92.

12895 **WILLS, B. S.** (1974), Personality variables which discriminate between groups differing in level of self-actualization. *J. Couns. Psychol.*, 21:222-227.

12896 **WILMER, H.** (1956), A psychiatric service as a therapeutic community. *U.S. Armed Forces Med. J.*, 7:640-654.

12897 **WILMER, H. A.** (1966), Free association of people: observations on the changing constellations in large group meetings. *Internat. J. Soc. Psychiat.*, (London) 12:44-51.

12898 **WILMER, H. A.** (1968), Innovative uses of videotape on a psychiatric ward. *Hosp. & Community*, 19:129-133.

12900 **WILMER, H. A.** (1958), *Social Psychiatry in Action: A Therapeutic Community.* Springfield, IL: C. C. Thomas.

12901 **WILMER, H. A.** (1952), *This is Your World: A Book for the Orientation of Professional Workers to the Emotional Problems of the Chronically Ill Patient—Tuberculosis and the Individual.* Springfield, IL: C. C. Thomas.

12902 **WILMER, H. A.** (1957), The use of sound recordings in group psychotherapy. *Internat. J. Soc. Psychiat.*, (London) 3:102-109.

12903 **WILMER, H. A.** (1967), The use of stereophonic audiotape recording in supervision of psychotherapy. *Amer. J. Psychiat.*, 123:1162-1165.

12904 **WILMER, H. A.** (1967), "You know": observations on interjectory, seemingly meaningless phrases in group psychotherapy. *Psychiat. Quart.*, 41:296-323.

12905 **WILMER, H. A., MARKS, I.,** and **POGUE, E.** (1966), Group treatment of prisoners and their families. *Ment. Hygiene*, 50:380-389.

12906 **WILSON, A. L.** (1971), Group therapy for parents of handicapped children. *Rehab. Lit.*, 32:332-335.

12907 **WILSON, A. R.** (1968), An investigation into the psychological aspects of pregnancy and the puerperium using the technique of group analysis. *J. Psychosomat. Res.*, 12:73-82.

12908 **WILSON, A. T. M., DOYLE, M.,** and **KELNAR, J.** (1947), Group techniques in a transitional community. *Lancet*, 252:735-738.

12909 **WILSON, C. G.** (1973), The effects of time limited group counseling on the level of functioning of chronic home hemodialysis patients. *Dissert. Abstr. Internat.*, 34:1633A.

12910 **WILSON, C. J.** (1973), The effects of time-limited group counseling on the level of functioning of chronic home hemodialysis patients. *Dissert. Abstr. Internat.*, 34:1633A.

12911 **WILSON, C. J., MUZEKARI, L. H., SCHNEPS, S. A.,** and **WILSON, D. M.** (1974), Time-limited group counseling for chronic home hemodialysis patients. *J. Couns. Psychol.*, 21:376-379.

12912 **WILSON, D. C.** (1954), Group psychotherapy and manic-depressive psychosis. *Amer. J. Psychiat.*, 110:911-915.

12913 **WILSON, D. L., WILSON, M. E., Jr., SAKATA, R.,** and **FRUMKIN, R. M.** (1967), Effects of short–term group interaction on social adjustment in a group of mentally retarded clients. *Psychol. Reports*, 21:716.

12914 **WILSON, E. L.** (1962), Group therapy experience with eight physically disabled homebound students in a prevocational project. *Except. Children*, 29:164-169.

12915 **WILSON, E. L.** (1970), Group therapy in a rehabilitation program. *New Outlook for Blind*, 64:237-239.

12916 **WILSON, E. L.** (1972), Programming individual and adjunctive therapeutic services for visually impaired clients in a rehabilitation center. *New Outlook for Blind*, 66:215-220.

12917 **WILSON, E. S.**, and **CANADA, R. M.** (1980), Preschool groups: a vehicle for teaching life coping skills. *J. Special. Group Work*, 5:131-134.

12918 **WILSON, G.**, and **RYLAND, G.** (1949), *Social Group Work Practice*. Boston: Houghton Mifflin.

12919 **WILSON, G. S.**, and **KONOPKA, G.** (1944), Social group work in a psychiatric setting. *Newsl. Amer. Assn. Psychiat. Soc. Work*, 14:35-43.

12920 **WILSON, J.**, and **HASTEROK, J.** (1975), We are important too: report on a growth group experiment for student wives. *J. Amer. Coll. Health Assn.*, 23:350-352.

12921 **WILSON, J. E.** (1972), The trend in laboratory education for managers organization training or sensitivity? *Training & Develop. J.*, 26:18-25.

12922 **WILSON, J. M.**, and **SNODGRASS, J. D.** (1969), The prison code in a therapeutic community. *J. Crim. Law & Criminol.*, 60:472-478.

12923 **WILSON, J. P.** (1974), The effects of congruent and incongruent social structures on group performance. *Dissert. Abstr. Internat.*, 34:6749A.

12924 **WILSON, S. R.** (1969), The effect of the laboratory situation on experimental discussion groups. *Sociometry*, 32:220-236.

12925 **WILSON, S. R.** (1968), A study of the effects of the observer on small experimental groups under conditions of high and low task saliency. *Dissert. Abstr. Internat.*, 28:4293-4294.

12926 **WILSON, W.**, and **KAYATANI, M.** (1968), Intergroup attitudes and strategies in games between opponents of the same or of a different race. *J. Personality & Soc. Psychol.*, 9:24-30.

12927 **WILTZ, N. A.** (1973), Behavioral therapy techniques in treatment of emotionally disturbed children and their families. *Child Welfare*, 52:483-492.

12928 **WILTZ, N. A., Jr.** (1970), Modification of behaviors of deviant boys through parent participation in a group technique. *Dissert. Abstr. Internat.*, 30:4786A-4787A.

12929 **WINBORN, B. B.** (1960), The effectiveness of short-term group counseling upon the academic achievement of potentially superior but underachieving college freshmen. Ph.D. thesis, Indiana University.

12930 **WINDELL, J. O.**, and **WINDELL, E. A.** (1977), Parent group training programs in juvenile courts: a national survey. *Fam. Coordinator*, 26:459-463.

12931 **WINDER, A.**, and **STIEPER, D. R. A.** (1956), A prepracticum seminar in group psychotherapy. *Internat. J. Group Psychother.*, 6:410-417.

12932 **WINDER, A. E.**, and **HERSKO, M.** (1958), A thematic analysis of an outpatient psychotherapy group. *Internat. J. Group Psychother.*, 8:293-300.

12933 **WINDER, A. E.**, and **SAVENKO, N.** (1970), Group counseling with neighborhood youth corps trainees. *Personnel & Guid. J.*, 48:561-567.

12934 **WINDER, A. E.**, and **TIERNEY, S.** (1968), A conjoint use of casework and group psychotherapy with the parents of emotionally disturbed children. *Child Welfare*, 47:7-16.

12935 **WINDER, A. E., FERRINI, L.**, and **GABY, G. E.** (1965), Group therapy with parents of children in a residential treatment center. *Child Welfare*, 44:266-271.

12936 **WINDISCHMANN, H.** (1970), (Group therapy with alcoholics.) *Zeit. Aerztl. Fortbildung*, (Jena) 64:285-288.

12937 **WINE, D. B.**, and **CRUMPTON, E.** (1968), Group psychotherapy with twenty-seven starving men. *Psychiat. Digest*, 29:17-20.

12938 **WINEMAN, D.** (1949), Group therapy and casework with ego disturbed children. *J. Soc. Casework*, 30:110-113.

12939 **WINETT, R. A.**, and **VACHON, E. M.** (1974), Group feedback and group contingencies in modifying behavior of fifth graders. *Psychol. Reports*, 34:1283-1292.

12940 **WING, G.**, and **POLLACK, K.** (1973), The use of groups in a city psychiatric hospital. *Psychiat. Quart.*, 43:71-81.

12941 **WINGETT, W. R.** (1976), A comparison of two models of group counseling in teaching communication skills to nursing students. *Dissert. Abstr. Internat.*, 36:4278A.

12942 **WINICK, C.**, and **HOLT, H.** (1961), Seating position as nonverbal communication in group analysis. *Psychiatry*, 24:171-182.

12943 **WINICK, C.** (1965), Process and interaction in group psychotherapy. *Topical Probl. Psychol. & Psychiat.*, 5:67-71.

12944 **WINICK, C.**, and **HOLT, H.** (1962), Eye and face movements as nonverbal communication in group psychotherapy. *J. Hillside Hosp.*, 11:67-79.

12945 **WINICK, C.**, and **HOLT, H.** (1961), Some external modalities of group psychotherapy and their dynamic significance. *Amer. J. Psychother.*, 15:56-62.

12946 **WINICK, C.**, and **HOLT, H.** (1960), Uses of music in group psychotherapy. *Group Psychother., Psychodrama & Sociometry*, 13:76-86.

12947 **WINICK, C.**, **KADIS, A. L.**, and **KRAMER, J. D.** (1961), The training and practice of American group psychotherapists. *Internat. J. Group Psychother.*, 11:419-430.

12948 **WINKELMANN, F.** (1975), Sudden changing of therapist within analytic individual and group psychotherapy. *Dynam. Psychiat.*, (Berlin) 8:41-51.

12949 **WINKLER, H. A.** (1978), Review of M. Seligman's "Group counseling and group psychotherapy with rehabilitation clients." *Amer. J. Psychiat.*, 135:263.

12950 **WINKLER, W. T.** (1966), Indikation und prognose zur psychotherapie der psychosen. (Indication and prognosis for psychotherapy of the psychoses.) *Zeit. Psychother. Med. Psychol.*, (Stuttgart) 16:42-51.

12951 **WINN, A.** (1970), Forbidden games. *Internat. J. Group Psychother.*, 20:356-365.

12952 **WINN, A.** (1972), (Reflections on the strategy of the t-group and the role of the change agent in organizational development.) *Bull. de Psychol.*, (Paris) 25:250-256.

12953 **WINN, A.** (1972), (T-groups on camera.) *Bull. de Psychol.*, (Paris) 25:700-704.

12954 **WINN, A.** (1969), The use of group processes in organization development. *J. Group Psychoanal. & Process*, (London) 2:5-17.

12955 **WINSHIP, B. J.**, and **KELLEY, J. D.** (1976), A verbal response model of assertiveness. *J. Couns. Psychol.*, 23:215-220.

12956 **WINSTON, A.**, and **PAPERNIK, D. S.** (1970), Establishing a therapeutic community in a municipal hospital. *Hosp. & Community Psychiat.*, 21:397-400.

12957 **WINTER, D. A.**, and **TRIPPETT, C. J.** (1977), Serial change in group psychotherapy. *Brit. J. Med. Psychiat.*, (London) 50:341-348.

12958 **WINTER, S. K.** (1976), Developmental stages in the roles and concerns of group co-leaders. *Small Group Behav.*, 7:349-362.

12959 **WINTHROP H.** (1971), Abuses of sensitivity training on the American campus. *Bull. Menninger Clinic*, 35:28-41.

12960 **WINZELER, H.** (1969), Twelve years of group therapy in a gynecological practice demonstrated on an example of psychogenic amenorrhea and sterility. *Gynaecologia*, (Basel) 167:137-139.

12961 **WIRT, R. D.**, and **WIRT, A. L.** (1963), Psychotherapeutic processes. *Ann. R. Psychol.*, 14:365-390.
12962 **WIRTH, M. G.** (1973), Counselor positive mental health as a factor in group participants' growth. *Dissert. Abstr. Internat.*, 34:1634A.
12963 **WISE, L. J.** (1970), Alienation of present-day adolescents. *J. Amer. Acad. Child Psychiat.*, 9:264-277.
12964 **WISE, P. S.** (1980), Methods of teaching revisited: character play and role play. *J. Continuing Educat. Nursing*, 11:37-38.
12965 **WISE, T. N.** (1977), Utilization of group process in training oncology fellows. *Internat. J. Group Psychother.*, 27:105-112.
12966 **WITEK, J.** (1980), (The effectiveness of group-dynamic sensitivity training.) *Zeit. Exper. & Angewondte Psychol.*, (Goettingen) 27:335-345.
12967 **WITENBERG, M. J.**, and **BRUSILOFF, P.** (1972), A therapeutic group in a day care center. *Internat. J. Child Psychiat.*, 1:17-33.
12968 Witnessed group therapy on television: therapeutic or not? *Amer. Psychologist*, 23:759-761.
12969 **WITTE, P. G.** (1977), Group therapy with multiple sclerosis couples. *Health & Soc. Work*, 2:188-195.
12970 **WITTENBERG, R.** (1944), Psychiatric concepts in group work. *Amer. J. Orthopsychiat.*, 14:76-83.
12971 **WITTENBERG, R. M.**, and **BERG, J.** (1952), The stranger in the group. *Amer. J. Orthopsychiat.*, 22:89-97.
12972 **WITTGENTSTEIN, O. G.** (1966), Gruppenbildung und (oder) isolierung. (Group formation and/or isolation.) *Psychother. & Psychosomat.*, (Basel) 14:264-281.
12973 **WITTICH, G. H.** (1966), Der altere mensch in der psychotherapeutischen gruppe. (The older person in the psychotherapeutic group.) *Psychiat. Neurol. & Med. Psychol.*, (Leipzig) 18:141-145.
12974 **WITTICH, G. H.**, and **ENKEFERC, E.** (1968), Multidimensional integrated group therapy in psychosomatic rehabilitation. *Psychother. & Psychosomat.*, (Basel) 16:261-270.
12975 **WITTICH, G. H.**, and **FERCHLAND, E.** (1967), Mehrdimensionale integrierte gruppentherapie in der psychosomatischen rehabilitation. (Multidimensional integrated group therapy in psychosomatic rehabilitation.) *Psychother. & Psychosomat.*, (Basel) 15:70.
12976 **WITTKOWER, E. D.** (1964), Treatment of psychosomatic disorders. *Can. Med. Assn. J.*, (Ottawa) 90:1055-1060.
12977 **WITTMER, J.** (1976), Race relations training with correctional officers. *Personnel & Guid. J.*, 54:302-306.
12978 **WITTMER, J.**, and **LOESCH, L.** (1974), A workshop for facilitating teacher-student communication. *School Counselor*, 22:100-106.
12979 **WITTMER, J., TRUAX, C. B.**, and **WARGO, D. G.** (1971), Effects of therapeutic conditions of accurate empathy, non-possessive warmth, and genuineness on hospitalized mental patients during group therapy. *J. Clin. Psychol.*, 27:137-142.
12980 **WITTSON, C. L., AFFLECK, D. C.**, and **JOHNSON, V.** (1961), Two-way television in group therapy. *Ment. Hosp.*, 12:22-23.
12981 **WITZIG, J. S.** (1968), The group treatment of male exhibitionists. *Amer. J. Psychiat.*, 125:179-185.
12982 **WODARSKI, J. S.** (1973), Group counseling and anti-social children: a social learning perspective. *Correct. & Soc. Psychiat*, 19:6-14.
12983 **WODARSKI, J. S.**, and **PEDI, S. J.** (1978), The empirical evaluation of the effects of different group treatment strategies against a controlled treatment strategy on behavior exhibited by antisocial children, behaviors of the therapist, and two self-rating scales that measure antisocial behavior. *J. Clin. Psychol.*, 34:471-489.

12984 **WODARSKI, J. S., FELDMAN, R. A.,** and **FLAX, N.** (1974), Group therapy and antisocial children: a social learning theory perspective. *Small Group Behav.*, 5:182-210.

12985 **WOGAN, M.** (1970), Effect of therapist–patient personality variables on therapeutic outcome. *J. Consult. & Clin. Psychol.*, 35:356-361.

12986 **WOGAN, M.** (1965), A study of the relationship between personality similarity in psychotherapeutic dyads and the quality of the therapeutic experience. *Dissert. Abstr. Internat.*, 26:1787.

12987 **WOGAN, M., GETTER, H., AMOUR, M. J., NICHOLS, M. F.,** and **OKMAN, G.** (1977), Influencing interaction and outcomes in group psychotherapy. *Small Group Behav.*, 8:25-46.

12988 **WOHL, T. H.** (1967), The group approach to the asthmatic child and family. *J. Asthma Res.*, 4:237-239.

12989 **WOHL, T. H.** (1963), The role of group psychotherapy for mothers in a rehabilitative approach to juvenile intractable asthma. *Ment. Hygiene*, 47:150-155.

12990 **WOHLFORD, P.** (1974), Head Start parents in participant groups. *J. Appl. Behav. Science*, 10:222-249.

12991 **WOHLKING, W.,** and **WIENER, H.** (1971), Structured and spontaneous role playing contrast and comparison. *Training & Develop. J.*, 25:8-15.

12992 **WOLBERG, A.** (1972), Intensifying the group process in psychoanalytic group psychotherapy. *Psychiat. Annals*, 2:70-73.

12993 **WOLBERG, A.** (1960), The psychoanalytic treatment of the borderline patient in the individual and group setting. *Topical Probl. Psychol. & Psychiat.*, 2:174-197.

12994 **WOLBERG, L.** (1965), Methodology in short term therapy. *Amer. J. Psychiat.*, 122:135-140.

12995 **WOLBERG, L. R.** (1972), Intensifying the group process: ii. experiential groups—can they enhance adaptation? *Psychiat. Annals*, 2:51-70.

12996 **WOLBERG, L. R.** (1967), *The Technique of Psychotherapy*, 2d ed. New York: Grune and Stratton.

12997 **WOLBERG, L. R.,** and **ARONSON, M. L.** (1980), *Group and Family Therapy 1980: An Overview*. New York: Brunner/Mazel.

12998 **WOLBERG, L. R.,** and **ARONSON, M. L.** (1978), *Group Psychotherapy 1978: An Overview*. New York: Stratton Intercontinental Medical Books.

12999 **WOLBERG, L. R.,** and **ARONSON, M. L.** (1976), *Group Therapy 1976: An Overview*. New York: Stratton Intercontinental Medical Books.

13000 **WOLBERG, L. R.,** and **ARONSON, M. L.** (1974), *Group Therapy 1974: An Overview*. New York: Stratton Intercontinental Medical Books.

13001 **WOLBERG, L. R.,** and **ARONSON, M. L.** (1975), *Group Therapy 1975: An Overview*. New York: Stratton Intercontinental Medical Books.

13002 **WOLBERG, L. R.,** and **ARONSON, M. L.** (1979), *Group Therapy 1979: An Overview*. New York: Stratton Intercontinental Books.

13003 **WOLBERG, L. R.,** and **ARONSON, M. L.** (1977), *Group Therapy 1977: An Overview*. New York: Stratton Intercontinental Medical Books.

13004 **WOLBERG, L. R.,** and **SCHWARTZ, E. R.** (1973), *Group Therapy 1973: An Overview*. New York: Stratton Intercontinental Medical Books.

13005 **WOLD, P.,** and **STEGER, J.** (1976), Social class and group therapy in a working class population. *Community Ment. Health J.*, 12:335-341.

13006 **WOLF, A.** (1969), *Beyond the Couch: Dialogues in Teaching and Learning Psychoanalysis in Groups*. New York: Science House.

13007 **WOLF, A.** (1952), On the irrelevance of group psychotherapy in mass conflict. *Group Psychother., Psychodrama & Sociometry*, 5:78-79.

13008 **WOLF, A.** (1949), The psychoanalysis of groups. i. *Amer. J. Psychother.*, 3:525-558.

13009 **WOLF, A.** (1950), The psychoanalysis of groups. ii. *Amer. J. Psychother.*, 4:16-50.

13010 **WOLF, A.** (1964), Psychoanalytic group therapy. *Curr. Psychiat. Ther.*, 4:166-174.

13011 **WOLF, A.** (1974), Psychoanalysis in groups. In: *The Challenge for Group Psychotherapy: Present and Future*, ed. S. de Schill. New York: International Universities Press.

13012 **WOLF, A.** (1969), Training in psychoanalysis in groups without face-to-face contact. *Ment. Health Digest*, 1:33-35.

13013 **WOLF, A., and SCHWARTZ, E. K.** (1962), *Psychoanalysis in Groups.* New York: Grune and Stratton.

13014 **WOLF, A., and SCHWARTZ, E. K.** (1964), Psychoanalysis in groups as creative process. *Amer. J. Psychoanal.*, 24:46-59.

13015 **WOLF, A., and SCHWARTZ, E. K.** (1959), Psychoanalysis in groups: clinical and theoretic implications of the alternate meeting. *Acta Psychother., Psychosomat. Orthopaedagog. Suppl.*, (Basel) 7:404-437.

13016 **WOLF, A., and SCHWARTZ, E. K.** (1960), Psychoanalysis in groups: the alternate session. *Amer. Imago*, 17:101-108.

13017 **WOLF, A., and SCHWARTZ, E. K.** (1959), Psychoanalysis in groups: the role of values. *Amer. J. Psychoanal.*, 19:37-52.

13018 **WOLF, A., and SCHWARTZ, E. K.** (1955), The psychoanalysis of group: implications for education. *Internat. J. Soc. Psychiat.*, (London) 1:9-17.

13019 **WOLF, A., SCHWARTZ, E. K., McCARTY, G. J., and GOLDBERG, I. A.** (1970), *Beyond the Couch: Dialogues in Teaching and Learning Psychoanalysis in Groups.* New York: Science House.

13020 **WOLF, A., SCHWARTZ, E. K., McCARTY, G. J., and GOLDBERG, J. A.** (1969), Training in psychoanalysis in groups without face-to-face contact. *Amer. J. Psychother.*, 23:488-494.

13021 **WOLF, A., LOCKE, N., ROSENBAUM, M., HILLPERN, E. P., GOLDFARB, W., KADIS, A. L., OBERS, S. J., MILBERG, I. L., and ABELL, R. G.** (1952), The psychoanalysis of groups: the analyst's objections. *Internat. J. Group Psychother.*, 2:221-231.

13022 **WOLF, A., BROSS, R., FLOWERMAN, S., GREENE, J. S., KADIS, A. L., LEOPOLD, H., LOCKE, N., MILBERG, I., MULLAN, H., OBERS, S. J., and ROSENBAUM, M.** (1954), Sexual acting out in the psychoanalysis of groups. *Internat. J. Group Psychother.*, 4:369-380.

13023 **WOLF, A. S.** (1967), Participation of the aged in the group process. *Ment. Hygiene*, 51:381-386.

13024 **WOLF, S. R., and HALL, R. C. W.** (1971), The use of psychodrama to diminish transcultural distance in psychotherapy. *Group Psychother., Psychodrama & Sociometry*, 24:17-23.

13025 **WOLFE, D. A.** (1980), Group and individual parent training with child abusers. *Dissert. Abstr. Internat.*, 41:2353B. (University Microfilms No. 8028942.)

13026 **WOLFE, E. L.** (1952), Group psychotherapy in naval neuropsychiatric center. *U.S. Forces Med. J.*, 3:1195-1203.

13027 **WOLFE, H. H., and SOLOMON, E. B.** (1973), Individual and group psychotherapy: complementary growth experiences. *Internat. J. Group Psychother.*, 23:177-184.

13028 **WOLFE, J. L.** (1972), How integrative is integrative therapy? *Couns. Psychologist*, 3:42-49.

13029 **WOLFE, L. A.** (1965), Moreno and Mowrer on "The new group therapy." *Group Psychother., Psychodrama & Sociometry*, 18:171-176.

13030 **WOLFF, H. H.** (1964), (Group dynamics in self-experimenting group of students learning psychotherapy.) *Zeit. Psychother. Med. Psychol.*, (Stuttgart) 14:111-117.

13031 **WOLFF, K.** (1967), Comparison of group and individual psychotherapy with geriatric patients. *Diseases Nerv. System*, 28:384-386.

13032 **WOLFF, K.** (1964), The confused geriatric patient. *J. Amer. Geriat. Soc.*, 12:266-270.

13033 **WOLFF, K.** (1966), Emotional rehabilitation. *J. Amer. Geriat. Soc.*, 14:75-79.

13034 **WOLFF, K.** (1963), Goals and limitations of group psychotherapy with geriatric patients in a psychiatric hospital. *Internat. J. Sociometry & Sociatry*, 3:17-21.

13035 **WOLFF, K.** (1966), Group psychotherapy of geriatric patients. *Curr. Psychiat. Ther.*, 6:202-203.

13036 **WOLFF, K.** (1967), Group psychotherapy with geriatric patients in a psychiatric hospital: goals, limitations and results. *Internat. J. Soc. Psychiat.*, (London) 13:275-277.

13037 **WOLFF, K.** (1962), Group psychotherapy with geriatric patients in a psychiatric hospital: six-year study. *J. Amer. Geriat. Soc.*, 10:1077-1080.

13038 **WOLFF, K.** (1959), Group psychotherapy with geriatric patients in a state hospital setting: results of a three-year study. *Group Psychother., Psychodrama & Sociometry*, 12:218-222.

13039 **WOLFF, K.** (1961), Group psychotherapy with geriatric patients in a Veterans Administration Hospital. *Group Psychother., Psychodrama & Sociometry*, 14:85-89.

13040 **WOLFF, K.** (1967), Group therapy for alcoholics. *Ment. Hygiene*, 51:549-551.

13041 **WOLFF, K.** (1968), Hospitalized alcoholic patients: iii. motivating alcoholics through group psychotherapy. *Hosp. & Community Psychiat.*, 19:206-209.

13042 **WOLFF, K.** (1971), Rehabilitating geriatric patients. *Hosp. & Community Psychiat.*, 22:8-11.

13043 **WOLFF, K.** (1976), (Review of Vohtenhagen's *Group Therapy and Social Milieu.*) *Der Psychologie*, (Berne) 35:165-166.

13044 **WOLFF, R. A.** (1975), Therapeutic experiences through group art expression. *Amer. J. Art Ther.*, 14:91-98.

13045 **WOLFF, S.** (1964), Group discussions with nurses in a hospital for alcoholism. *Internat. J. Soc. Psychiat.*, (London) 10:301-312.

13046 **WOLFF, T. J.** (1969), Community mental health on campus: evaluating group discussion led by dormitory advisors and graduate students. *Dissert. Abstr. Internat.*, 30:1910B-1911B.

13047 **WOLFF, W.** (1956), *Contemporary Psychotherapists Examine Themselves*. Springfield, IL: C. C. Thomas.

13048 **WOLFGANG, A.**, and **PIERSON, D.** (1977), The relationship of group research and current practices in group counseling and therapy in metro Toronto. *Can. Counselor*, (Ottawa) 11:185-191.

13049 **WOLK, D. J.** (1979), From Tavistock to human relations. *Small Group Behav.*, 10:295-298.

13050 **WOLK, D. J.** (1967), Sensitization seminars for students. *Perspect. Psychiat. Care*, 5:136-140.

13051 **WOLK, R. L.** (1963), The relationship of group psychotherapy to institutional adjustment. *Group Psychother., Psychodrama & Sociometry*, 16:141-144.

13052 **WOLK, R. L.**, and **GOLDFARB, A. I.** (1967), The response to group psychotherapy of aged recent admissions compared with long-term mental hospital patients. *Amer. J. Psychiat.*, 123:1251-1257.

13053 **WOLK, R. L.**, and **REID, R.** (1964), A study of group psychotherapy results with youthful offenders in detention. *Group Psychother., Psychodrama & Sociometry*, 17:56-60.

13054 **WOLKENSTEIN, A. S.** (1977), The fear of committing child abuse: a discussion of eight families. *Child Welfare*, 56:249-257.

13055 **WOLLAN, K. I.** (1951), Application of group therapy principles to institutional treatment of adolescents. *Internat. J. Group Psychother.*, 1:356-364.

13056 **WOLLAN, K. I.** (1941), A new treatment program for juvenile delinquents. *J. Crim. Law & Criminol.*, 31:712-719.

13057 **WOLLERSHEIM, J. P.** (1970), Effectiveness of group therapy based upon learning principles in the treatment of overweight women. *J. Abnorm. & Psychol.*, 76:462-474.

13058 **WOLLERSHEIM, J. P.** (1969), The effectiveness of learning theory based group therapy in the treatment of overweight women. *Dissert. Abstr. Internat.*, 30:396B.

13059 **WOLLERSHEIM, J. P.** (1977), Follow-up of behavioral group therapy for obesity. *Behav. Ther.*, 8:996-998.

13060 **WOLLERT, R. W., KNIGHT, B.,** and **LEVY, L. H.** (1980), Make today count: a collaborative model for professionals and self-help groups. *Prof. Psychol.*, 11:130-138.

13061 **WOLMAN, B.** (1960), Group psychotherapy with latent schizophrenics. *Internat. J. Group Psychother.*, 10:301-312.

13062 **WOLMAN, B. B.** (1964), Hostility experiences in group psychotherapy. *Internat. J. Soc. Psychiat.*, (London) 10:57-63.

13063 **WOLMAN, B. B.** (1969), Interactional group psychotherapy with schizophrenics. *Psychother.: Theory, Res. & Pract.*, 6:194-198.

13064 **WOLMAN, B. B.** (1976), Success and failure in group psychotherapy. *Small Group Behav.*, 7:99-113.

13065 **WOLMAN, C.** (1970), Group therapy in two languages, English and Navajo. *Amer. J. Psychother.*, 24:677-685.

13066 **WOLMAN, C. S.** (1976), Therapy groups for women. *Amer. J. Psychiat.*, 133:274-278.

13067 **WOLMAN, R. N.** (1970), "Through the one-way mirror": an analysis of the dynamics in the observation of psychotherapy. *Psychother.: Theory, Res. & Pract.*, 7:108-110.

13068 **WOLOSHIN, A. A., TARDI, G.,** and **TOBIN, A.** (1966), De-institutionalization of mentally retarded men through use of a half-way house. *Ment. Retard.*, 4:21-25.

13069 **WOLOSIN, R. J.** (1975), Cognitive similarity and group laughter. *J. Personality & Soc. Psychol.*, 32:503-509.

13070 **WOLOWIK, W. M.** (1977), (Group therapy of schizophrenia in the initial phase of the disease.) *Psychiat. Neurol. & Med. Psychol.*, (Leipzig) 29:587-592.

13071 **WOLSTEIN, B.** (1961), Existential analysis in search of a therapy. *Amer. J. Psychother.*, 15:382-394.

13072 **WOLTMAN, A. G.** (1943), Puppetry as a means of psychotherapy. In: *Encyclopedia of Child Guidance*, ed. R. B. Winn. New York: Philosophical Library.

13073 **WONDOLOWSKI, M.** (1978), Interpersonal problem–solving training groups for hospitalized aged psychiatric patients. *Dissert. Abstr. Internat.*, 39:1975B.

13074 **WONG, M. R.** (1978), Males in transition and the self-help group. *J. Couns. Psychol.*, 7:46-49.

13075 **WONG, N.** (1979), Clinical considerations in group treatment of narcissistic disorders. *Internat. J. Group Psychother.*, 29:325-346.

13076 **WONG, N.** (1980), Combined group and individual treatment of borderline and narcissistic patients: heterogeneous vs. homogeneous groups. *Internat. J. Group Psychother.*, 30:389-404.

13077 **WONG, N.** (1964), Out-patient group psychotherapy with paranoid schizophrenic patients. *Psychiat. Quart.*, 38:665-677.
13078 **WONG, N.** (1980), Review of H. Mullan's and M. Rosenbaum's *Group Psychotherapy*, 2d ed. *Bull. Menninger Clinic*, 44:397.
13079 **WOOD, C.** (1978), Community resources for sexual counseling. In: *Gynaecology, Sex and Psyche*, eds. L. Dennerstein, G. Burrows, L. Cox, and C. Wood. Carlton: Melbourne University Press.
13080 **WOOD, J. C.** (1975), An experience in poetry therapy: Wright-Patterson Air Force Base Medical Center Psychiatry Service. *J. Psychiat. Nursing*, 13:27-31.
13081 **WOOD, J. E.**, and **SIMON, W. B.** (1971), Psychotherapy in a public mental hospital. *Ment. Hygiene*, 55:221-224.
13082 **WOOD, P. E., MILLIGAN, M., CHRIST, D.**, and **LIFF, D.** (1978), Group counseling for cancer patients in a community hospital. *Psychosomatics*, 19:555-564.
13083 **WOODALL, T. E.** (1971), From crisis to collaboration: thoughts on the use of laboratory method in resolving Black-White issues. *Soc. Change*, 1:1-3.
13084 **WOODBURY, M. A., LEVIN, I.**, and **WOODBURY, M.** (1967), Report on the first year of operation of an emergency and home hospitalization programme. *Psychother. & Psychosomat.*, (Basel) 15:71.
13085 **WOODGER, J. H.** (1966), The Gio social club. *Nursing Times*, (London) 62:679.
13086 **WOODHOUSE, D. J.** (1974), An examination of the immediate and long-range effects of participation in a self-exploration group upon participants' self–acceptance and acceptance of others. *Dissert. Abstr. Internat.*, 35:3536A.
13087 **WOODS, L. W.** (1970), Group psychotherapy in a general hospital. *Can. Psychiat. Assn. J.*, (Ottawa) 15:357-359.
13088 **WOODS, M.**, and **MELNICK, J.** (1979), Review of group therapy selection criteria. *Small Group Behav.*, 10:155-175.
13089 **WOODS, M. M.** (1980), Relevance, activity, and intermember familiarity as parameters of group structure: effects on early group development. *Dissert. Abstr. Internat.*, 41:705B. (University Microfilms No. 8018273.)
13090 **WOODS, S. M.** (1969), A course for medical students in the psychology of sex: training in sociocultural sensitivity. *Amer. J. Psychiat.*, 125:1508-1519.
13091 **WOODS, T. L.** (1974), A group method of engaging parents at a child psychiatry clinic. *Child Welfare*, 53:394-401.
13092 **WOODS, T. L.** (1972), Parents preparation group. *Compar. Group Studies*, 3:201-211.
13093 **WOODWARD, W.** (1951), Spontaneous personality synthesis in group therapy. *Internat. J. Group Psychother.*, 1:123-125.
13094 **WOODY, R. H.** (1972), Conceptualizing the "shared patient": treatment orientations of multiple therapists. *Internat. J. Group Psychother.*, 22:228-233.
13095 **WOODY, R. H.** (1971), Self-understanding seminars: the effects of group psychotherapy in counselor training. *Counselor Educat. & Supervision*, 10:112-119.
13096 **WOODY, R. H.**, and **BILLY, J. T.** (1966), Counseling and psychotherapy for the mentally retarded: a survey of opinions and practices. *Ment. Retard.*, 4:20-23.
13097 **WOODY, R. H.**, and **WOODY, J. D.** (1975), Behavioral group counseling for adolescent females with behavioral problems. *Psychol. Reports*, 36:421-422.
13098 **WOOL, M. L., KANTER, S. S.**, and **GRAY, W.** (1955), Group psychotherapy

in preventive psychiatry: a preliminary report. *Internat. J. Group Psychiat.*, 5:404-414.
13099 **WOOLF, V. V.** (1973), The relationship between peer involvement in a drug rehabilitation group and judgments of moral maturity on kohlberg moral maturity stages. *Dissert. Abstr. Internat.*, 34:1388A.
13100 **WOOLLAMS, S. J.** (1967), Using a tape recorder in group therapy. *Hosp. & Community Psychiat.*, 18:315.
13101 **WOOLMER, T.** (1980), Psychoanalysis, language and groups. *Group Anal.*, (London) 13:191-201.
13102 **WORCHEL, P.** (1957), The control of hostility in group training. *Group Psychother., Psychodrama & Sociometry*, 10:319-327.
13103 **WORMSER, R.** (1976), *Sensitiv-Spiele: Wie Man Neuartigekontakte Knüpft und Überraschende Erfahrungen Macht.* Munich: Mosaik Verlag.
13104 **WORST, R. W., VANSICKLE, R.,** and **McDANIEL, E.** (1969), Coalitions: a measure of the differential extension of parental perceptions by delinquent girls. *Internat. J. Group Psychother.*, 19:346-360.
13105 **WORTHEN, V. K.,** and **MALONY, H. N.** (1973/1974), Potential strengths: a comparative study of positive and negative oriented marathon group experiences for couples. *Interpersonal Develop.*, 4:243-253.
13106 **WORTIS, J.,** and **FREUNDLICH, D.** (1964), Psychiatric work therapy in the Soviet Union. *Amer. J. Psychiat.*, 121:123-128.
13107 **WOTRING, N. N. R.** (1980), The effects of small guidance groups on children's self-concepts. *Dissert. Abstr. Internat.*, 40:6158A. (University Microfilms No. 8013051.)
13108 **WRETMARK, G.** (1969), (Organization plan of the psychiatric clinic in Linköping, Sweden: the psychiatric hospital as group therapeutic situation.) *Zeit. Psychother. Med. Psychol.*, (Stuttgart) 19:229-240.
13109 **WRETMARK, G., PAUSER, H.,** and **WANNERDAHL, U.** (1958), Gruppsykoterapi vid alkoholism: preliminara erfarenheter. (Group psychotherapy in alcoholism: preliminary observations.) *Svenska Lakartidningen*, (Stockholm) 55:1071-1079.
13110 **WRIGHT, B. H.** (1948), *Practical Handbook for Group Guidance.* Chicago: Science Research Associates.
13111 **WRIGHT, E. R.** (1968), Comparative study of units in a small state hospital. *Diseases Nerv. System*, 29:189-192.
13112 **WRIGHT, F.** (1977), Review of Z. A. Liff's "The leader in the group." *Group*, 1:65-66.
13113 **WRIGHT, F., BUIRSKI, P.,** and **SMITH, N.** (1978), The implications of leader transparency for the dynamics of short-term process groups. *Group*, 2:210-219.
13114 **WRIGHT, G. L.** (1980), The effects of co-leader similarity/dissimilarity on group cohesion and outcome. *Dissert. Abstr. Internat.*, 40:4906A. (University Microfilms No. 8005964.)
13115 **WRIGHT, K. W.** (1952), Goals of group psychotherapy. *Group Psychother., Psychodrama & Sociometry*, 5:51-53.
13116 **WRIGHT, K. W.** (1946), Group therapy in extramural clinics. *Psychiat. Quart.*, 20:322-331.
13117 **WRIGHT, L.** (1979), A comprehensive program for mental health and behavioral medicine in a large children's hospital. *Prof. Psychol.*, 10:458-466.
13118 **WRIGHT, L.** (1976), Indirect treatment of children through principle–oriented parent consultation. *J. Consult. & Clin. Psychol.*, 44:148.
13119 **WRIGHT, L. S.,** and **McKENZIE, C. D.** (1973), A talking group therapy for hyperactive 11 year old boys. *Devereux Sch. Forum*, 8:1-24.

13120 **WRIGHT, M. E.** (1971), Self-help groups in the rehabilitation enterprise. *Psychol. Aspects Diseases*, 18:43-45.

13121 **WRIGHT, R. G.** (1973), A multidisciplinary seminar for training in group work. *Hosp. & Community Psychiat.*, 24:240-241.

13122 **WRIGHT, W. T., Jr.** (1959), An investigation of an adjunctive two-therapist group therapy procedure designed to improve the process of consensual validation in the mother-child relationship: the mother. Unpublished doctoral dissertation, Denver University.

13123 **WUBBOLDING, R.**, and **OSBORNE, L. B.** (1974), An awareness game for elementary school children. *School Counselor*, 21:223-227.

13124 **WULBERT, R.** (1965), Inmate pride in total institutions. *Amer. J. Sociol.*, 71:1-9.

13125 **WYATT, W.** (1949), Present trends in psychotherapy. *Med. J. Austral.*, (Glebe) 1:417-419.

13126 **WYATT, W. C.** (1970), Responsible use of sensitivity training. *Nursing Outlook*, 18:39-40.

13127 **WYBORNY, D. G.** (1979), The community mental health ideologies, career plans, and therapeutic orientations of advanced graduate students: a comparative, evaluative study. *Dissert. Abstr. Internat.*, 41:705B.

13128 **WYCKOFF, H.** (1970), Radical psychiatry and transactional analysis in women's groups. *Transactional Anal. Bull.*, 9:128-133.

13129 **WYER, R. S., Jr.** (1966), Effects of incentive to perform well, group attention, and group acceptance on conformity in a judgmental task. *J. Personality & Soc. Psychol.*, 4:21-26.

13130 **WYERS, N. L.** (1969), Adaptations of the social group work method. *Soc. Casework*, 50:513-518.

13131 **WYLIE, H. W., Jr., LAZAROFF, P.** and **LOWY, F.** (1964), A dying patient in a psychotherapy group. *Internat. J. Group Psychother.*, 14:482-490.

13132 **WYNNE, A. R.** (1978), Movable group therapy for institutionalized patients. *Hosp. & Community Psychiat.*, 29:516-519.

13133 **WYSE, H.** (1980), What does group analysis mean to me? *Group Anal.*, (London) 13:48-49.

13134 **WYSOCKI, S. R.** (1976), Differential effects of three group treatments on self-actualization and attitudes toward the sex roles of women. *Dissert. Abstr. Internat.*, 36:7316A.

13135 **WYSOR, B.** (1971), Encounter games: a dangerous new trend. *Harper's Bazaar*, 104:60-61.

X

13136 **von XYLANDER, E.** (1959), (The discussion of wishes.) *Acta Psychother., Psychosomat. Orthopaedagog. Suppl.*, (Basel) 7:438-439.

Y

13137 **YABLONSKY, L.** (1954), Future-projection-technique. *Group Psychother., Psychodrama & Sociometry*, 7:303-305.
13138 **YABLONSKY, L.** (1972), Humanizing groups through psychodrama. *Group Psychother., Psychodrama & Sociometry*, 25:7-15.
13139 **YABLONSKY, L.** (1955), Preparing parolees for essential social roles. *Group Psychother., Psychodrama & Sociometry*, 8:38-39.
13140 **YABLONSKY, L.**, and **ENNEIS, J. M.** (1969/1970), Theory and practice of psychodrama. *Bull. de Psychol.*, (Paris) 23:765-770.
13141 **YAHALOM, I.** (1964), Complementary therapy of severely disturbed children and their parents in a day care center. *J. Jewish Communal Serv.*, 40:269-350.
13142 **YAILLEN, E.** (1968), The crisis in group work and Jewish center practice. *J. Jewish Communal Serv.*, 45:86-96.
13143 **YALOM, I. D.** (1971), Encounter group casualties. *Sandoz Psychiat. Spectator*, 7:11-12.
13144 **YALOM, I. D.** (1974), Group therapy and alcoholism. *Annals N.Y. Acad. Science*, 233:85-103.
13145 **YALOM, I. D.** (1961), Group therapy of incarcerated sexual deviants. *J. Nerv. & Ment. Diseases*, 132:158-170.
13146 **YALOM, I. D.** (1966), Problems of neophyte group therapists. *Internat. J. Soc. Psychiat.*, (London) 12:52-59.
13147 **YALOM, I. D.** (1977), Research in est. *Amer. J. Psychiat.*, 134:213.
13148 **YALOM, I. D.** (1966), A study of group therapy: dropouts. *Arch. Gen. Psychiat.*, 14:393-414.
13149 **YALOM, I. D.** (1970), *The Theory and Practice of Group Psychotherapy.* New York: Basic Books.
13150 **YALOM, I. D.** (1975), *The Theory and Practice of Group Psychotherapy*, 2d ed. New York: Basic Books.
13151 **YALOM, I. D.**, and **GREAVES, C.** (1977), Group therapy with the terminally ill. *Amer. J. Psychiat.*, 134:396-400.
13152 **YALOM, I. D.**, and **LIEBERMAN, M. A.** (1971), A study of encounter group casualties. *Arch. Gen. Psychiat.*, 25:16-30.
13153 **YALOM, I. D.**, and **MOOS, R.** (1965), The use of small interactional groups in the teaching of psychiatry. *Internat. J. Group Psychother.*, 15:242-246.
13154 **YALOM, I. D.**, and **RAND, K.** (1966), Compatibility and cohesiveness in therapy groups. *Arch. Gen. Psychiat.*, 15:267-275.
13155 **YALOM, I. D.**, and **TERRAZAS, F.** (1968), Group therapy for psychotic elderly patients. *Amer. J. Nursing*, 68:1690-1694.
13156 **YALOM, I. D., BROWN, S.**, and **BLOCH, S.** (1975), The written summary as a group psychotherapy technique. *Arch. Gen. Psychiat.*, 32:605-613.
13157 **YALOM, I. D., BLOCH, S., ZIMMERMAN, E.**, and **FRIEDMAN, L.** (1977), The impact of a weekend group experience on individual therapy. *Arch. Gen. Psychiat.*, 34:399-415.
13158 **YALOM, I. D., HOUTS, P. S., NEWELL, G.**, and **RAND, K. H.** (1967), Preparation of patients for group therapy: a controlled study. *Arch. Gen. Psychiat.*, 17:416-427.
13159 **YALOM, I. D., HOUTS, P. S., ZIMERBERG, S. M.**, and **RAND, K. H.** (1967), Prediction of improvement in group therapy: an exploratory study. *Arch. Gen. Psychiat.*, 17:159-168.
13160 **YALOM, I. D., BLOCH, S., BOND, G., ZIMMERMAN, E.**, and **QUALLS, B.** (1978), Alcoholics in interactional group therapy: an outcome study. *Arch. Gen. Psychiat.*, 35:419-425.

13161 **YAMAZAKI, M.**, and **IMOTO, M.** (1971), A trial of integrating with brief individual intervention and group treatment for school phobic children. *J. Ment. Health*, 19:93-116.

13162 **YANNETT, W. M.** (1965), The effectiveness of individual and group counseling among high school boys with school behavior problems. Unpublished doctoral dissertation, St. John's University.

13163 **YANO, B. S.** (1977), What about us? Group therapy for oncology nurses. *J. Pract. Nursing*, 27:28-29.

13164 **YAROSZ, E. J.** (1966), Group counseling with engineering freshmen: academic achievement and student reactions. *Dissert. Abstr. Internat.*, 27:403A.

13165 **YAROSZ, E. J.**, and **BRADLEY, H.** (1963), The relationship between physical distance and sociometric choices in two residence halls. *Internat. J. Sociometry & Sociatry*, 3:42-55.

13166 **YARYAN, R. B.**, and **FESTINGER, L.** (1961), Preparatory action and belief in the probable occurrence of future events. *J. Abnorm. & Soc. Psychol.*, 63:603-606.

13167 **YAZQUEZ, AGUÍLAR, A. C.**, and **PÉREZ IBARES, O.** (1975), (The psychotherapeutic experience of a group evaluated by means of the Rorschach test.) *Neurol.-Neurocir.-Psiquiat.*, (Mexico City) 16:263-272.

13168 **YEARWOOD, A. C.**, and **HESS, S. K.** (1979), How can an alcoholic change in 28 days? *Amer. J. Nursing*, 79:1436-1438.

13169 **YEAWORTH, R.** (1970), Learning through group experience. *Nursing Outlook*, 18:29-32.

13170 **YEH, M. F.** (1978), Clinical therapeutic group activities. *Hu Li Tsa Chih*, (Hong Kong) 25:50-53.

13171 **YEOMANS, N. T.** (1961), Notes on a therapeutic community: ii. *Med. J. Austral.*, (Glebe) 48:829-830.

13172 **YITZCHAK, B.** (1971), An Israeli experimental group with primary school dropouts outside the school setting. *Child Welfare*, 50:336-340.

13173 **YOGMAN, H. T.** (1959), Group guidance practices in selected New Jersey senior high schools. Unpublished doctoral dissertation, Rutgers University.

13174 **YONG, J.** (1971), Advantages of group therapy in relation to individual therapy for juvenile delinquents. *Correct. Psychiat. & J. Soc. Ther.*, 2:34-40.

13175 **YONG, J. N.** (1969), Effects of group therapy on severely sociopathic offenders. *Corr. Psychiat. & J. Soc. Ther.*, 15:48-54.

13176 **YONGE, K. A.**, and **O'CONNOR, N.** (1954), Measurable effects of group psychotherapy with defective delinquents. *J. Ment. Science*, (London) 100:944-952.

13177 **YOSHIMURA, T.** (1965), (Experience of the cycling–therapy of psychotics.) *Iryo*, (Tokyo) 19:1058-1065.

13178 **YOSHIMURA, T.** (1963), (Psychotherapy and patient meetings.) *Iryo*, (Tokyo) 17:285-286.

13179 **YOST, O. R.** (1953), *A Key to Emotional Health: An Aid to Group Psychotherapy Among Patients*. Orangeburg, SC: Edgewood Sanitarium Foundation.

13180 **YOUMANS, R. D.** (1974), Differences in behavior related to participation and non–participation in jail group counseling. *Dissert. Abstr. Internat.*, 35:596A.

13181 **YOUNG, E. R.**, and **JACOBSON, L. I.** (1970), Effects of time-extended marathon group experiences on personality characteristics. *J. Couns. Psychol.*, 17:247-251.

13182 **YOUNG, J. G.**, and **ANDREWS, D. A.** (1974), Short-term structured group counseling and prison adjustment. *Can. J. Criminol. & Correct.*, (Ottawa) 16:5-13.

13183 **YOUNG, K. R.** (1974), The comparative effectiveness of individual versus group token reinforcement contingencies. *Dissert. Abstr. Internat.*, 34:6472A.

13184 **YOUNG, L. H.** (1972), Comparison of the effects of encounter groups and sociodrama on the attitudes of various ethnic groups in a junior high school. *Dissert. Abstr. Internat.*, 32:6773A.

13185 **YOUNG, R. A., MILLER, L.,** and **VERVEN, N.** (1951), Treatment techniques in a therapeutic camp. *Amer. J. Orthopsychiat.*, 21:819-826.

13186 **YOUNG, R. G.** (1974), Perceptions of a group experience by counseling students as related to self-concept and therapeutic functioning. *Dissert. Abstr. Internat.*, 35:1454A.

Z

13187 **ZABARENKO, L.**, and **ZABARENKO, R. N.** (1966), A suggested method for studying small group seminars in psychiatry. *J. Nerv. & Ment. Diseases*, 143:239-247.

13188 **ZACHARIAS, J.** (1965), Psychodrama with teenagers. *Group Psychother.*, 18:262-266.

13189 **ZACHARIAS, J. L.** (1966), Psychodrama of an unwed mother. *Group Psychother., Psychodrama & Sociometry*, 19:198-200.

13190 **ZACHEPITSKII, R. A.** (1980), Review of S. Kratochvil's *Group Psychotherapy. Vop. Psikhol.*, 3:168.

13191 **ZACHER, A. N.** (1961), The use of psychodrama in pastoral therapy. *Group Psychother., Psychodrama & Sociometry*, 14:164-168.

13192 **ZACKER, J.** (1972), Understanding one's clients: an attempt to improve sensitivity and morale in police recruits. *Psychol. Reports*, 31:999-1008.

13193 **ZACKER, J.**, and **BARD, M.** (1973), Effects of conflict management training on police performance. *J. Appl. Psychol.*, 58:202-208.

13194 **ZAGONA, S. V., WILLIS, J. E.**, and **MacKINNON, W. J.** (1967), Group effectiveness in creative problem-solving tasks: an examination of relevant variables. *J. Psychology*, 62:111-137.

13195 **ZAHND, W. F.**, and **BERECOCHEA, J. E.** (1973), Group process training in a correctional institution. *Internat. J. Addict.*, 8:443-450.

13196 **ZAIDENS, S. H.** (1963), Psychiatric treatment of the neurodermatoses. *Industr. Med. Surg.*, 32:261-265.

13197 **ZAKS, M. S.**, and **WALTERS, R. H.** (1959), A group comparison of Negro narcotic addicts with non-addicted Negro and White controls. *Group Psychother., Psychodrama & Sociometry*, 12:300-307.

13198 **ZAKUS, G., CHIN, M. L., KEOWN, M., HEBERT, F.**, and **HELD, M.** (1979), Group behavior modification approach to adolescent obesity. *Adolescence*, 14:481-490.

13199 **ZALBA, S. R.**, and **ABELS, P.** (1970), Training the nurse in psychiatric group work. *J. Psychiat. Nursing*, 8:7-12.

13200 **ZANDER, A.** (1972), Attributed pride or shame in group and self. *J. Personality & Soc. Psychol.*, 23:346-352.

13201 **ZANDER, A.** (1979), Study of group behavior during four decades. *J. Appl. Behav. Science*, 15:272-282.

13202 **ZANDER, A.**, and **FORWARD, J.** (1968), Position in group, achievement motivation, and group aspirations. *J. Personality & Soc. Psychol.*, 8:282-288.

13203 **ZANDER, A.**, and **LIPPITT, R.** (1944), Reality–practice as educational method. *Sociometry*, 7:129-151.

13204 **ZANDER, A. F.** (1947), Role playing: a technique for training the necessarily dominating leader. *Sociatry*, 1:225-235.

13205 **ZANDER, W.** (1977), Possibilities and limitations of group therapy. *Praxis der Psychother.*, 22:209-216.

13206 **ZANDER, W.** (1974), (Special conclusions concerning conjoint individual and group therapy based on experience with a demonstration group.) *Gruppenpsychother. & Gruppendynam.*, (Goettingen) 8:122-130.

13207 **ZANI, L. P.** (1969), Intensive vs. protracted counselor directed group counseling with underachieving secondary school students. *Dissert. Abstr. Internat.*, 30:1834A.

13208 **ZANKER, A.**, and **MITCHELL, S. D.** (1948), The use of music in group therapy. *J. Ment. Science*, (London) 94:737-748.

13209 **ZARA, E.** (1968), (Experiences with motion pictures and therapeutic panel discussions in the hospital environment.) *Ospedale Psychiat.*, (Naples) 36:88-138.

13210 **ZARLE, T. H.**, and **BOYD, R. C.** (1977), An evaluation of modeling and experiential procedures for self-disclosure training. *J. Couns. Psychol.*, 24:118-124.

13211 **ZARLE, T. H.**, and **WILLIS, S.** (1975), A pregroup training technique for encounter group stress. *J. Couns. Psychol.*, 22:49-53.

13212 **ZARNARI, O.** (1969), Group work with parents of mentally retarded children. *Ment. Retard.*, 6:726.

13213 **ZAX, M.**, and **STRICKER, G.** (1969), *The Study of Abnormal Behavior: Selected Readings*, 2d ed. New York: Macmillan.

13214 **ZDRAVKOVIC, J.** (1973), A large group of chronic psychotic patients in a therapeutic community. *Anali Zavoda Ment. Zdravdge*, 5:113-119.

13215 **ZEFF, L. H.**, and **IVERSON, M. A.** (1966), Opinion conformity in groups under status threat. *J. Personality & Soc. Psychol.*, 3:383-389.

13216 **ZEGANS, L. S.** (1969), A mental health center's response to racial crisis in an urban high school. *Psychiatry*, 32:252-264.

13217 **ZEICHNER, A. M.** (1957), Observations on individual and group counseling of the individual with cerebral palsy. *Except. Children*, 23:305-352.

13218 **ZEIGER, J. A. H.** (1974), The effects of videotaped modeling and behavior rehearsal through group training on assertive behavior. *Dissert. Abstr. Internat.*, 34:7543.

13219 **ZIEGLER, P.** (1977), Social stresses of medical students: a couples group approach. *Group*, 1:235-244.

13220 **ZILBERGELD, B.**, and **ELLISON, C. R.** (1979), Social skills training as an adjunct to sex therapy. *J. Sex & Marital Ther.*, 5:340-350.

13221 **ZEILBERGER, J.**, **SAMPEN, S. E.**, and **SLOANE, H. N., Jr.** (1968), Modification of a child's problem behaviors in the home with the mother as therapist. *J. Appl. Behav. Anal.*, 1:47-53.

13222 **ZEILLER, B.**, **TOMKIEWICZ, S.**, and **FINDER, J.** (1973), (Evolution of juvenile delinquents: report on 108 very difficult adolescents cared for and educated in a semi-free setting.) *Encephale Suppl.*, (Paris) 62:16-30.

13223 **ZEISE, W. J.**, and **ELSAESSER, E.** (1965), Individual observations during psychoanalytic group therapy with adolescents. *Psychother. & Psychosomat.*, (Basel) 13:314-320.

13224 **ZEITLYN, B. B.** (1975), Group greed and group need: an occupational hazard for psychiatric personnel? *Brit. J. Psychiat.*, (Ashford) 126:193-195.

13225 **ZEITLYN, B. B.** (1968), (Therapeutic community: reality or fantasy?) *Rev. Med. Psychosomat.*, (Toulouse) 10:359-365.

13226 **ZEITZ, P.** (1974), Establishing trust in the informal classroom. *Reading Teacher*, 27:451-453.

13227 **ZELDOW, P. B.** (1977), Outline for a seminar in milieu therapy: a blind spot in clinical training. *Prof. Psychol.*, 8:109-115.

13228 **ZELDOW, P. B.**, and **ANSELL, P.** (1976), Bibliography: milieu therapy and administrative psychiatry. *Cat. Selected Docum. Psychol.*, 7:71.

13229 **ZELENSKI, J. F.** (1973), Factors influencing changes in affective sensitivity and self–actualization as the result of a t-group experience. *Dissert. Abstr. Internat.*, 33:4863A.

13230 **ZELENY, L. D.** (1956), The sociodrama as an aid in teaching international relations and world history. *Internat. J. Sociometry & Sociatry*, 1:29-33.

13231 **ZELLERMAYER, J.** (1964), (Objectives and therapeutic methods in an open psychiatric department.) *Harefuah*, (Tel Aviv) 66:288-292.

13232 **ZEMORE, R.** (1975), Systematic desensitization as a method of teaching

a general anxiety-reducing skill. *J. Consult. & Clin. Psychol.*, 43:157-161.
13233 **ZERFAS, P. G.** (1965), Effects of induced expectancies and therapist activity upon patient behavior in group psychotherapy. *Dissert. Abstr. Internat.*, 26:2874.
13234 **ZERITSKY, S. A.** (1951), Experiences in group therapy among veterans. *Arch. Neurol. Psychiat.*, 65:125.
13235 **von ZERSSEN, D.** (1964), (Hospital group psychotherapy of relatively young schizophrenics.) *Psyche*, (Stuttgart) 18:532-545.
13236 **ZEUSCHNER, R. F., Jr.** (1974), The measurement of communication variables in the small group: models, instruments and theory. *Dissert. Abstr. Internat.*, 34:4467A.
13237 **ZGLICZYNSKI, S. M.** (1978), Multimodal behavior therapy with groups of aged. *Dissert. Abstr. Internat.*, 39:4159A.
13238 **ZIDE, M. M.** (1973), Group dynamics techniques. *Personnel & Guid. J.*, 51:620-622.
13239 **ZIEGLER, J. S.** (1973), A comparison of the effect of two forms of group psychotherapy on the treatment of marital discord. *Dissert. Abstr. Internat.*, 34:143A.
13240 **ZIERL, W.** (1959), Therapeutisches rollenspiel im Sceno-Test ("Scenodrama"). (Therapeutic role playing with the Sceno test: Sceno drama.) *Praxis Kinderpsychol. & Kinderpsychiat.*, (Goettingen) 8:113-124.
13241 **ZIFERSTEIN, I.** (1961), Dynamic psychotherapy in the Soviet Union. *Group Psychother., Psychodrama & Sociometry*, 14:221-233.
13242 **ZIFERSTEIN, I.** (1972), Group psychotherapy in the Soviet Union. *Amer. J. Psychiat.*, 129:595-600.
13243 **ZIFERSTEIN, I.** (1959), The role of identification in group psychotherapy. *Acta Psychother., Psychosomat. Orthopaedagog. Suppl.*, (Basel) 7:440-445.
13244 **ZIFERSTEIN, I.**, and **GROTJAHN, M.** (1957), Group dynamics of acting out in analytic group psychotherapy. *Internat. J. Group Psychother.*, 7:77-85.
13245 **ZIFERSTEIN, I.**, and **GROTJAHN, M.** (1954), Working through acting out, and psychodrama. *Group Psychother., Psychodrama & Sociometry*, 7:321-322.
13246 **ZILBACH, J. J.**, and **GRUNEBAUM, M. G.** (1964), Pregenital components in incest as manifested in two girls in activity group therapy. *Internat. J. Group Psychother.*, 14:166-177.
13247 **ZILBERGELD, B.** (1980), Alternatives to couples counseling for sex problems: group and individual therapy. *J. Sex & Marital Ther.*, 6:3-18.
13248 **ZILLER, R. C.** (1977), Group dialectics: the dynamics of groups over time. *Human Develop.*, 20:293-308.
13249 **ZIMBERG, S.**, **LIPSCOMD, H.**, and **DAVIS, E. B.** (1971), Sociopsychiatric treatment of alcoholism in an urban ghetto. *Amer. J. Psychiat.*, 127:1670-1674.
13250 **ZIMET, C.** (1979), Developmental task and crisis groups: the application of group psychotherapy to maturational processes. *Psychother.: Theory, Res. & Pract.*, 16:2-8.
13251 **ZIMET, C. N.** (1960), Character defense preference and group therapy interaction. *Arch. Gen. Psychiat.*, 3:168-175.
13252 **ZIMET, C. N.** (1964), Ego identity and group interaction: a preliminary report. *Internat. J. Group Psychother.*, 14:500-502.
13253 **ZIMET, C. N.** (1969), Group psychotherapy: current practices and future trends. *Internat. Psychiat. Clin.*, 6:213-234.
13254 **ZIMET, C. N.**, and **FINE, H. J.** (1958), Methodology and evaluation in

group psychotherapy. *Group Psychother., Psychodrama & Sociometry,* 11:189-196.

13255 **ZIMET, C. N.,** and **FINE, H. J.** (1955), Personality changes with a group therapeutic experience in a human relations seminar. *J. Abnorm. & Soc. Psychol.,* 51:68-73.

13256 **ZIMET, C. N.,** and **SCHNEIDER, C. J.** (1966), Character structure and group interaction. *Proceed., 74th Annual Convention,* American Psychological Association, pp. 189-190.

13257 **ZIMET, C. N.,** and **SCHNEIDER, C.** (1969), Effects of group size on interaction in small groups. *J. Soc. Psychol.,* 77:177-187.

13258 **ZIMKOWSKI, A. M.** (1978), Traditional psychodrama and "scene fixing" effects on growth experience outcome. *Dissert. Abstr. Internat.,* 39:1003B.

13259 **ZIMMER, D.,** and **UCHTENHAGEN, A.** (1979), (Social therapeutic group with schizophrenic out-patients.) *Gruppenpsychother. & Gruppendynam.,* (Goettingen) 14:155-165.

13260 **ZIMMERMA, R.** (1976), Review of I. D. Yalom's *Group Psychotherapy: Principles and Methods. Praxis der Psychother.,* 21:92.

13261 **ZIMMERMAN, D.** (1968), Notes on the reaction of a therapeutic group to termination of treatment by one of its members. *Internat. J. Group Psychother.,* 18:86-94.

13262 **ZIMMERMAN, D.** (1967), Some characteristics of dreams in group-analytic psychotherapy. *Internat. J. Group Psychother.,* 17:524-535.

13263 **ZIMMERMAN, D.** (1961), (Various characteristic features of dreams in psychoanalytic group psychotherapy.) *Zeit. Psychosomat. Med. & Psychoanal.,* (Goettingen) 7:279-288.

13264 **ZIMMERMAN, W. M.** (1980), Effects of short-term group counseling on gifted elementary students. *Dissert. Abstr. Internat.,* 40:6214A. (University Microfilms No. 8013891.)

13265 **ZIMMERMANN, D.** (1960), Application of group psychotherapy to the teaching of dynamic psychiatry and understanding student resistances. *Internat. J. Group Psychother.,* 10:90-97.

13266 **ZIMMERMANN, D.** (1969), *Estudios Sobre Psicoterapia Analítica de Grupo. (Studies on Analytic Group Psychotherapy.)* Buenos Aires: Ediciones Hormé.

13267 **ZIMMERMAN-TANSELLA, C.** (1979), Preparation courses for childbirth in primapar: a comparison. *J. Psychosomat. Res.,* (London) 23:277.

13268 **ZIMMERT, R.** (1962), (On the beginning of a polyclinical group.) *Zeit. Psychosomat. Med. & Psychoanal.,* (Goettingen) 8:49-54.

13269 **ZIMPFER, D.** (1971), Needed: professional ethics for working with groups. *Personnel & Guid. J.,* 50:280-287.

13270 **ZIMPFER, D. G.** (1967), Expression of feelings in group counseling. *Personnel & Guid. J.,* 45:703-708.

13271 **ZIMPFER, D. G.** (1976), *Group Work in the Helping Professions: A Bibliography.* Washington: Association for Specialists in Groupwork.

13272 **ZINBERG, N. E.** (1967), A group approach with the school teacher in the integration crisis. *Ment. Hygiene,* 51:289-298.

13273 **ZINBERG, N. E.,** and **FRIEDMAN, L. J.** (1967), Problems in working dynamic groups. *Internat. J. Group Psychother.,* 17:447-456.

13274 **ZINBERG, N. E.,** and **GLOTFELTY, J. A.** (1968), The power of the peer group. *Internat. J. Group Psychother.,* 18:155-164.

13275 **ZINBERG, N. E.,** and **SHAPIRO, D.** (1963), A group approach in the contexts of therapy and education. *Ment. Hygiene,* 47:108-116.

13276 **ZINGER, N. G.** (1975), A working paper for group auxiliary egos. *Psychother. & Psychosomat.,* (Basel) 28:152-156.

13277 **ZINKER, J. C.** (1970), Beginning the therapy. *Voices,* 6:29-31.

13278 **ZINKER, J. C.** (1971), Dreamwork as theatre. *Voices,* 7:18-21.

13279 **ZISFEIN, L.**, and **ROSEN, M.** (1974), Effects of a personal adjustment training group counseling program. *Ment. Retard.*, 12:50-53.
13280 **ZISFEIN, L.**, and **ROSEN, M.** (1973), Personal adjustment training: a group counseling program for institutionalized mentally retarded persons. *Ment. Retard.*, 11:16-20.
13281 **ZOHN, J.**, and **CARMODY, T.** (1978), Training opportunities in group treatment methods in APA-approved clinical psychology programs. *Prof. Psychol.*, 9:50-62.
13282 **ZONGKER, C. E.** (1973), The effect of selected group counseling approaches on the self–concept of student teachers. *Dissert. Abstr. Internat.*, 34:1763A.
13283 **ZOURAS, N. L.**, and **RESNICK, M.** (1968), Summer camp therapy for underachieving adolescents. *Sandoz Psychiat. Spectator*, 5:14-16.
13284 **ZUCKER, A.** (1961), Group psychotherapy and the nature of drug addiction. *Internat. J. Group Psychother.*, 11:209-218.
13285 **ZUCKER, A. H.**, and **WAKSMAN, S.** (1973), Results of group therapy with young drug addicts. *Internat. J. Soc. Psychiat.*, (London) 18:267-279.
13286 **ZUCKER, R. A.**, and **van HORN, H.** (1972), Sibling social structure and oral behavior drinking and smoking in adolescence. *Quart. J. Studies Alcohol*, 33:193-197.
13287 **ZUEHLKE, T. E.**, and **WATKINS, J. T.** (1975), The use of psychotherapy with dying patients: an exploratory study. *J. Clin. Psychol.*, 31:729-732.
13288 **ZUK, G. H.** (1965), On the pathology of silencing strategies. *Fam. Process*, 4:32-49.
13289 **ZUK, G. H.** (1971), Triadic-based therapy. *Internat. J. Psychiat.*, 9:247-248.
13290 **ZUK, G. H.** (1979), Value systems and psychopathology in family therapy. *Internat. J. Fam. Ther.*, 1:133.
13291 **ZULLO, J. R.** (1972), T-group laboratory learning and adolescent ego development. *Dissert. Abstr. Internat.*, 32:2799B.
13292 **ZUMPE, V.** (1970), (Verbal communications in the therapeutic group.) *Zeit. Psychother. Med. Psychol.*, (Stuttgart) 20:139-146.
13293 **ZUPNICK, S. M.** (1971), The effects of varying degrees of a peer model's performance on the extinction of a phobic response in an individual or group setting. *Proceed., Annual Convention*, American Psychological Association, 6:433-434.
13294 **ZUSMAN, J.** (1969), "No-therapy", a method of helping persons with problems. *Community Ment. Health J.*, 5:482-486.
13295 **ZUSMAN, W.** (1967), (Countertransferential insight and projective identification.) *J. Brasil. Psiquiat.*, (Rio de Janeiro) 16:311-317.
13296 **ZUSMAN, Z.** (1966), Our expectations influence our patients. *Hosp. & Community Psychiat.*, 17:110.
13297 **ZWEBACK, S.** (1976), Use of concrete reinforcement to control content of verbal initiations in group therapy with adolescents. *Psychol. Reports*, 38:1051-1057.
13298 **ZWEBACK, S.** (1972), Use of token reinforcement to control the content of verbal initiations in adolescent group therapy. *Dissert. Abstr. Internat.*, 33:2364B.
13299 **ZWEBEN, J. E.**, and **HAMMANN, K.** (1970), Prescribed games: a theoretical perspective on the use of group techniques. *Psychother.: Theory, Res. & Pract.*, 7:22-27.
13300 **ZWEIBEL, A.** (1947), A technique in group psychotherapy. *Individ. Psychol. Bull.*, 6:69-70.
13301 **ZWEIBELSON, I.**, and **LODATO, F. J.** (1967), Counseling parents and problem children. *Correct. Psychiat. & J. Soc. Ther.*, 13:204-208.
13302 **ZWIER, M.** (1973), Efficacy of small group practice with intractable neu-

ropsychiatric patients. *Proceed., 81st Annual Convention*, American Psychological Association, Montreal, Canada, 8:1059-1060.

13303 **ZYTOWSKI, D. G.** (1964), Diagnostic psychodrama with a college freshman. *Group Psychother., Psychodrama & Sociometry*, 17:123-128.

13304 **ZYTOWSKI, D. G.** (1963), Obligatory counseling with college underachievers. *Group Psychother., Psychodrama & Sociometry*, 16:8-15.

Subject Index

A

Abortion
00092, 01103, 01759, 04417, 04418
Accreditation
00346, 01272, 02906, 03072, 05988, 05998, 06343, 06773, 06811, 07076, 07684, 08340, 08341, 08689, 08924, 08936, 09078, 09113, 09925, 09926, 09928, 10195, 10196, 11003, 11362, 11673, 11754, 11775, 13269
Acting Out, Character Disorder, Sociopath
00176, 00211, 00411, 00663, 00878, 01437, 01448, 01449, 01451, 01500, 01553, 01628, 01695, 01727, 01754, 01909, 02346, 03001, 03024, 03058, 03206, 03368, 03382, 03387, 03714, 04005, 04131, 04265, 05417, 05562, 06098, 06272, 06492, 06867, 06957, 06959, 07080, 07112, 07247, 07487, 08129, 08193, 08442, 08500, 08556, 08638, 08657, 08775, 09332, 09346, 09563, 09838, 09934, 09959, 09960, 10079, 10520, 10599, 10652, 10667, 10740, 10852, 10859, 10940, 11088, 11264, 11285, 11310, 11313, 11432, 12030, 12413, 12481, 12678, 12693, 12695, 12746, 13022, 13062, 13175, 13244, 3245
Activity Group Therapy
00057, 00406, 00920, 00921, 00975, 01283, 01406, 01626, 01679, 01710, 01985, 02033, 02543, 02563, 02610, 02640, 02806, 03097, 03105, 03229, 03231, 03314, 03316, 03572, 03743, 03792, 03857, 03966, 04126, 04141, 04142, 04210, 04827, 04869, 04871, 04872, 04990, 05292, 05503, 05707, 05715, 06300, 06301, 06506, 06788, 06968, 07140, 07508, 07520, 07533, 07551, 07673, 07977, 07998, 08059, 08266, 08293, 08503, 08632, 08681, 08695, 08698, 09024, 09168, 09176, 09300, 09384, 09413, 09501, 09522, 09872, 10012, 10023, 10236, 10238, 10257, 10262, 10263, 10376, 10444, 10621, 10656, 10673, 10674, 10675, 10676, 10677, 10679, 10768, 10917, 10943, 10978, 11122, 11228, 11252, 11271, 11327, 11353, 11497, 11498, 11499, 11708, 11709, 12397, 12401, 12487, 12694, 12734, 13120, 13246
Adlerian
00110, 00111, 00112, 00120, 00510, 01190, 01215, 02914, 02921, 02922, 02927, 02931, 02933, 03451, 03770, 03791, 03847, 04026, 04133, 04677, 05307, 05704, 06765, 07851, 07950, 08744, 08809, 08868, 08869, 08874, 09080, 10747, 11612, 11817, 11835
Adolescents
00004, 00021, 00073, 00090, 00108, 00119, 00155, 00206, 00223, 00251, 00310, 00402, 00455, 00485, 00488, 00499, 00519, 00561, 00609, 00612, 00640, 00644, 00660, 00661, 00674, 00866, 00876, 00909, 00915, 00916, 00920, 00921, 00932, 01056, 01057, 01058, 01111, 01188, 01257, 01259, 01284, 01386, 01387, 01393, 01404, 01420, 01437, 01469, 01516, 01518, 01519, 01520, 01531, 01532, 01533, 01534, 01536, 01537, 01538, 01539, 01540, 01544, 01545, 01553, 01557, 01560, 01561, 01570, 01580, 01586, 01618, 01634, 01659, 01666, 01674, 01691, 01694, 01702, 01708, 01726, 01732, 01785, 01793, 01803, 01804, 01806, 01831, 01859, 01867, 01901, 01914, 01923, 01942, 01950, 02033, 02045, 02062, 02094, 02128, 02141, 02154, 02174, 02195, 02221, 02235, 02266, 02267, 02269, 02270, 02313, 02314, 02317, 02318, 02335, 02434, 02446, 02447, 02458, 02474, 02504, 02529, 02530, 02534, 02535, 02570, 02583, 02591, 02604, 02626, 02636, 02669, 02745, 02777, 02779, 02846, 02879, 02899, 02973, 02977, 02984, 02986, 02997, 03035, 03054, 03094, 03146, 03148, 03157, 03180, 03193,

03194, 03206, 03210, 03228, 03229, 03232, 03242, 03247, 03254, 03274, 03282, 03326, 03373, 03376, 03419, 03455, 03464, 03486, 03487, 03488, 03492, 03503, 03530, 03531, 03547, 03553, 03599, 03707, 03777, 03813, 03831, 03847, 03851, 03857, 03865, 03868, 03889, 03940, 03944, 03945, 03946, 03950, 03986, 04002, 04005, 04021, 04029, 04035, 04051, 04052, 04078, 04135, 04205, 04209, 04212, 04227, 04294, 04295, 04304, 04324, 04330, 04331, 04374, 04387, 04397, 04475, 04493, 04535, 04587, 04594, 04659, 04748, 04751, 04753, 04852, 04876, 04878, 04892, 04938, 04980, 04988, 04992, 04993, 05000, 05048, 05066, 05087, 05099, 05100, 05104, 05112, 05146, 05171, 05190, 05225, 05237, 05245, 05246, 05271, 05273, 05277, 05296, 05315, 05317, 05325, 05336, 05351, 05352, 05383, 05422, 05466, 05480, 05513, 05552, 05564, 05567, 05568, 05577, 05602, 05603, 05615, 05625, 05661, 05692, 05724, 05737, 05738, 05739, 05760, 05787, 05831, 05840, 05951, 05956, 05963, 05971, 05972, 05997, 06019, 06045, 06077, 06098, 06100, 06133, 06147, 06158, 06325, 06331, 06434, 06435, 06448, 06449, 06458, 06461, 06471, 06556, 06574, 06587, 06593, 06594, 06595, 06642, 06671, 06711, 06769, 06822, 06831, 06838, 06839, 06853, 06907, 06921, 06927, 06947, 06948, 06968, 06984, 06991, 07013, 07079, 07080, 07086, 07090, 07178, 07231, 07246, 07371, 07390, 07421, 07502, 07517, 07518, 07519, 07526, 07527, 07698, 07728, 07732, 07745, 07759, 07760, 07782, 07783, 07825, 07837, 07867, 07901, 07950, 08010, 08050, 08092, 08103, 08104, 08116, 08119, 08144, 08147, 08151, 08160, 08203, 08237, 08241, 08252, 08253, 08265, 08266, 08280, 08286, 08288, 08289, 08290, 08319, 08422, 08631, 08653, 08712, 08724, 08773, 08780, 08786, 08813, 08866, 08891, 08942, 08980, 08981, 08987, 09000, 09004, 09007, 09072, 09089, 09154, 09197, 09255, 09275, 09294, 09327, 09339, 09342, 09406, 09407, 09413, 09489, 09517, 09522, 09561, 09584, 09615, 09660, 09685, 09686, 09709, 09730, 09731, 09732, 09736, 09739, 09744, 09771, 09811, 09812, 09813, 09814, 09857, 09891, 09894, 09968, 09973, 09976, 09977, 09983, 09986, 10011, 10054, 10061, 10064, 10071, 10075, 10079, 10083, 10101, 10152, 10160, 10161, 10181, 10209, 10231, 10232, 10247, 10330, 10369, 10408, 10421, 10444, 10446, 10509, 10540, 10562, 10585, 10598, 10599, 10628, 10686, 10724, 10725, 10731, 10732, 10756, 10767, 10791, 10793, 10794, 10849, 10853, 10863, 10889, 10962, 10977, 11002, 11061, 11119, 11127, 11146, 11147, 11150, 11173, 11203, 11233, 11285, 11311, 11313, 11324, 11360, 11431, 11445, 11468, 11523, 11585, 11594, 11599, 11623, 11630, 11648, 11649, 11692, 11756, 11758, 11778, 11841, 11844, 11847, 11870, 11877, 11902, 11922, 11923, 11951, 11967, 11970, 11996, 12055, 12069, 12108, 12120, 12133, 12246, 12326, 12346, 12347, 12368, 12391, 12406, 12411, 12445, 12484, 12506, 12507, 12542, 12543, 12548, 12556, 12584, 12594, 12623, 12628, 12652, 12655, 12678, 12681, 12700, 12702, 12752, 12756, 12815, 12838, 12878, 12963, 13053, 13055, 13097, 13162, 13173, 13184, 13188, 13198, 13207, 13216, 13222, 13223, 13283, 13286, 13291, 13297, 13298

Aftercare
09534

Alcoholics
09294, 09481

Alcoholics Anonymous
00153, 00253, 00313, 00579, 00598, 01439, 03088, 03604, 03690, 03691, 04199, 05063, 05409, 05443, 08065, 08857, 09491, 10285, 11752, 11784, 12131, 12137, 12165

Alcoholism
00109, 00126, 00130, 00187, 00203, 00320, 00337, 00474, 00592, 00597, 00599, 00601, 00787, 00831, 00848, 00879, 00892, 00917, 01210, 01216, 01291, 01359, 01360, 01417, 01431, 01439, 01501, 01504, 01560, 01564,

01663, 01681, 01682, 01684, 01685, 01686, 01758, 01772, 01779, 01810, 01823, 01872, 01876, 01877, 01878, 01930, 01932, 01971, 01972, 02108, 02316, 02321, 02327, 02452, 02469, 02490, 02571, 02574, 02584, 02768, 02774, 02736, 02738, 02852, 02952, 02967, 03089, 03167, 03200, 03264, 03265, 03266, 03267, 03268, 03269, 03293, 03316, 03377, 03378, 03391, 03394, 03401, 03420, 03431, 03464, 03503, 03518, 03545, 03556, 03564, 03600, 03616, 03688, 03689, 03692, 03696, 03776, 03810, 03975, 03976, 03977, 04018, 04065, 04076, 04154, 04256, 04257, 04259, 04282, 04283, 04284, 04285, 04286, 04350, 04351, 04515, 04658, 04729, 04768, 04771, 04772, 04935, 04944, 04984, 05018, 05030, 05031, 05084, 05108, 05111, 05199, 05355, 05419, 05507, 05516, 05572, 05632, 05702, 05703, 05793, 05801, 05836, 05839, 05885, 05945, 05962, 06035, 06075, 06215, 06345, 06469, 06500, 06561, 06672, 06695, 07018, 07019, 07020, 07021, 07022, 07024, 07057, 07078, 07095, 07126, 07235, 07369, 07494, 07495, 07501, 07541, 07544, 07545, 07599, 07726, 07727, 07835, 07847, 07858, 07870, 07871, 07872, 07873, 07874, 07875, 07876, 07877, 07878, 07903, 07939, 07958, 07971, 08002, 08003, 08005, 08085, 08102, 08145, 08155, 08182, 08183, 08185, 08191, 08205, 08209, 08210, 08211, 08306, 08307, 08308, 08592, 08605, 08618, 08637, 08647, 08658, 08688, 08766, 08770, 08792, 08804, 08811, 08880, 08894, 08927, 08940, 09008, 09015, 09056, 09098, 09132, 09133, 09207, 09208, 09294, 09394, 09395, 09485, 09533, 09534, 09539, 09562, 09652, 09655, 09672, 09711, 09716, 09759, 09803, 09880, 09988, 10116, 10209, 10302, 10328, 10331, 10433, 10531, 10532, 10558, 10666, 10762, 10778, 10779, 10868, 10874, 10880, 10882, 10883, 10884, 10885, 11039, 11075, 11165, 11181, 11192, 11227, 11228, 11383, 11454, 11463, 11500, 11510, 11550, 11598, 11753, 11754

Allergies
00706, 01839, 08163, 08164

Analytic Group Therapy
06119, 06348

Aphasia
00129, 00642, 01261, 01344, 02044, 02312, 02492, 03190, 09859

Armed Forces
00027, 00028, 00565, 01160, 01376, 01575, 01978, 06149, 07743, 07795, 08109, 08185, 08941, 10357, 10358, 11695.
(*See also* Military Applications and Veterans)

Art
00304, 00503, 00707, 00708, 01731, 01949, 02549, 02698, 02699, 02890, 02933, 03078, 04122, 04126, 04841, 04978, 05098, 05110, 05712, 05717, 05816, 05869, 06737, 06795, 07553, 07626, 08098, 08164, 08675, 08699, 08721, 08722, 08836, 09496, 09598, 09599, 09965, 10318, 10325, 10360, 10488, 11210, 12195, 12333, 13044

Art Therapy
00763, 00964

Assertiveness Training
00109, 01797, 01814, 02857, 02862, 03168, 03455, 03456, 03936, 03957, 03958, 04088, 04373, 04853, 05035, 05036, 05361, 05388, 05463, 05585, 05747, 05796, 05851, 05895, 06296, 06325, 06402, 06439, 07124, 07242, 07341, 07357, 07622, 07656, 07681, 07682, 08195, 08516, 08806, 08984, 09223, 09318, 09319, 09804, 09945, 10003, 10006, 10291, 10305, 10400, 10508, 10511, 10538, 10666, 10707, 10746, 10954, 11592, 11643, 12167, 12464, 12545, 12687, 12688, 12955, 13218

Asthma
00038, 00041, 06032

Audio-visual Aids
00577, 00578, 00658, 00919, 00940, 01070, 01117, 01119, 01120, 03094,

03320, 03349, 06246, 10716, 07812, 08148, 09023, 09308, 09625, 09836, 09972, 10040, 10063, 10142, 10147, 10716, 10962, 11111, 11711, 11805, 11806, 12185, 12462, 12697, 12902, 12903, 12968, 12980, 13100
Autism
02161, 05266, 07784
Autogenic Training
00365, 01206, 01207, 01208, 01394, 02436, 03890, 04592, 06646, 06689, 07298, 09482, 10323, 11601, 12459

B

Behavioral Group Therapy
00626, 00906, 01133, 01270, 02332, 02632, 02868, 03119, 03192, 03770, 03801, 03878, 05425, 05464, 05523, 06713, 06876, 06909, 06931, 06960, 07048, 08128, 08301, 08714, 08754, 08890, 08939, 09306, 09532, 09574, 09698, 09829, 09858, 10176, 10290, 10314, 10746, 10873, 11505, 11649, 12092, 12228, 12236, 12338, 12537, 13097
Behavior Modification
01108, 02080, 03607
Behavior Therapy
00030, 00063, 00138, 00177, 00253, 00301, 00335, 00350, 00351, 00359, 00361, 00413, 00447, 00479, 00495, 00510, 00593, 00620, 00624, 00643, 00644, 00813, 01101, 01238, 01363, 01620, 01669, 01935, 01936, 01938, 02033, 02074, 02135, 02137, 02175, 02208, 02441, 02562, 02598, 02599, 02600, 02601, 02622, 02630, 02633, 02634, 02636, 02693, 02746, 02755, 02756, 02811, 02812, 02830, 02831, 02843, 02867, 02869, 02957, 02973, 03026, 03051, 03126, 03172, 03325, 03539, 03543, 03546, 03564, 03586, 03697, 03749, 03780, 03899, 03912, 03959, 04017, 04029, 04050, 04059, 04090, 04091, 04118, 04138, 04174, 04310, 04346, 04349, 04431, 04436, 04465, 04489, 04518, 04548, 04566, 04594, 04690, 04701, 04702, 04714, 04722, 04808, 04866, 04904, 04910, 04912, 04985, 05056, 05127, 05132, 05219, 05265, 05270, 05297, 05303, 05304, 05410, 05411, 05442, 05511, 05515, 05759, 05851, 05858, 05859, 05880, 05894, 05895, 05897, 06094, 06095, 06099, 06146, 06162, 06239, 06278, 06319, 06390, 06509, 06539, 06558, 06559, 06601, 06641, 06683, 06688, 06890, 06899, 06900, 06931, 06954, 07000, 07014, 07068, 07074, 07099, 07100, 07128, 07129, 07130, 07131, 07163, 07204, 07245, 07292, 07342, 07363, 07497, 07558, 07668, 07681, 07682, 07698, 07699, 07712, 07846, 07899, 07902, 07937, 07938, 07946, 07962, 07968, 07985, 07987, 08018, 08040, 08077, 08092, 08155, 08182, 08183, 08195, 08242, 08246, 08249, 08250, 08297, 08334, 08513, 08537, 08661, 08726, 08727, 08764, 08789, 08859, 08888, 08904, 08925, 08932, 08946, 08972, 09045, 09104, 09169, 09187, 09214, 09215, 09308, 09417, 09498, 09642, 09759, 09760, 09795, 09837, 09839, 09882, 09927, 09932, 09947, 09964, 10002, 10026, 10066, 10168, 10169, 10170, 10171, 10172, 10173, 10185, 10210, 10267, 10277, 10305, 10343, 10406, 10407, 10707, 10752, 10753, 10887, 11035, 11084, 11145, 11147, 11179, 11180, 11211, 11429, 11494, 11502, 11511, 11535, 11573, 11657, 11658, 11698, 11779, 11834, 11835, 11898, 11910, 11911, 11917, 11928, 11929, 11955, 12020, 12021, 12034, 12149, 12153, 12177, 12335, 12342, 12343, 12519, 12546, 12559, 12591, 12592, 12604, 12735, 12759, 12763, 12789, 12826, 12827, 12881, 12927, 12928, 12939, 13059, 13117, 13183, 13198, 13232, 13237, 13297, 13298
Bibliographies
02278, 02352, 02353, 04824, 04825, 04830, 04875, 04947, 05290, 05811, 05852, 06191, 06306, 06563, 06564, 07307, 07314, 07407, 07408, 07522,

07528, 07529, 07530, 07531, 07532, 07534, 07535, 08071, 08335, 09378, 09704, 09848, 09850, 09851, 09852, 10137, 10202, 10250, 10251, 10253, 10254, 10255, 10256, 10258, 10259, 10260, 10261, 11176, 11343, 11348, 11781, 12394, 13228, 13271
Bibliotherapy
00139, 00718, 01263, 01661, 02485, 04111, 08191, 08301, 10485, 10545
Bi-focal Group Therapy
00401, 01465, 01509, 01986, 02732, 02733, 04035, 06269, 06763, 10690, 10692
Bioenergetics
01346
Blindness
00485, 01667, 01844, 02065, 03858, 05218, 06646, 07614, 07616, 08089, 08396, 08893, 10281, 10337, 10338, 10339, 10414, 11092, 12709, 12916
Books: Group Counseling
01011, 01055, 01104, 01341, 02322, 02323, 02470, 02826, 02950, 02951, 03044, 03353, 03414, 03921, 03922, 04061, 04062, 04064, 04069, 04209, 04249, 04414, 04929, 04930, 04932, 05435, 05742, 06194, 06196, 06462, 06463, 06680, 06859, 07526, 07563, 07566, 07608, 07797, 08650, 08913, 08914, 08915, 08919, 08944, 10473, 11225, 12266, 12389, 12504, 12848, 12859, 13110
Books: Group Therapy
00061, 00256, 00331, 00344, 00395, 00497, 00532, 00562, 00651, 00691, 00700, 00739, 00740, 00741, 00742, 00743, 00744, 00745, 00746, 00747, 00748, 00749, 00750, 00751, 00752, 00769, 00804, 00945, 00974, 01026, 01054, 01089, 01091, 01092, 01099, 01207, 01218, 01219, 01220, 01229, 01230, 01275, 01320, 01454, 01537, 01540, 01699, 01784, 01818, 01829, 01919, 01973, 02161, 02186, 02290, 02341, 02394, 02470, 02510, 02511, 02677, 02726, 02728, 02745, 02782, 02944, 03008, 03009, 03010, 03011, 03041, 03077, 03102, 03163, 03199, 03355, 03374, 03400, 03410, 03436, 03466, 03493, 03549, 03612, 03670, 03673, 03679, 03680, 03681, 03682, 03683, 03684, 03689, 03719, 03725, 03726, 03746, 03803, 03806, 03846, 03864, 03903, 03934, 03990, 04008, 04061, 04062, 04063, 04066, 04069, 04168, 04169, 04171, 04194, 04213, 04230, 04241, 04242, 04251, 04252, 04354, 04378, 04430, 04440, 04458, 04500, 04501, 00571, 04636, 04640, 04712, 04713, 04716, 04894, 04937, 04946, 04973, 04986, 05112, 05151, 05177, 05197, 05216, 05267, 05346, 05372, 05433, 05434, 05492, 05751, 05752, 05779, 05791, 05824, 05875, 05864, 05877, 05878, 05889, 05917, 05918, 05921, 05923, 05972, 05985, 05986, 06053, 06054, 06056, 06057, 06163, 06332, 06339, 06340, 06360, 06362, 06363, 06387, 06459, 06474, 06526, 06530, 06555, 06649, 06751, 06995, 07033, 07058, 07065, 07098, 07181, 07183, 07184, 07187, 07202, 07204, 07240, 07276, 07290, 07307, 07309, 07314, 07315, 07385, 07387, 07388, 07398, 07408, 07427, 07428, 07435, 07473, 07506, 07526, 07527, 07571, 07749, 07776, 07984, 08047, 08077, 08106, 08162, 08215, 08369, 08370, 08379, 08380, 08381, 08476, 08477, 08481, 08518, 08519, 08538, 08575, 08615, 08616, 08617, 08618, 08700, 08831, 08864, 08865, 08971, 09011, 09047, 09066, 09217, 09221, 09222, 09230, 09275, 09353, 09398, 09408, 09409, 09410, 09444, 09451, 09468, 09492, 09600, 09603, 09640, 09692, 09723, 09732, 09820, 09914, 10036, 10054, 10088, 10151, 10169, 10170, 10171, 10174 10191, 10192, 10200, 10201, 10246, 10303, 10377, 10378, 10379, 10470, 10471, 10472, 10473, 10529, 10546, 10555, 10600, 10641, 10658, 10678, 10697, 10727, 10728, 10735, 11087, 11154, 11247, 11253, 11274, 11280, 11281, 11282, 11283, 11303, 11304, 11305, 11306, 11307, 11308, 11319, 11325, 11331, 11348, 11351, 11416, 11493, 11512, 11529, 11530, 11573, 11578, 11603, 11722, 11762, 11794, 11795, 11897, 11930, 12011, 12035, 12036, 12260,

12389, 12446, 12562, 12565, 12601, 12603, 12770, 12776, 12777, 12857, 12996, 12997, 12998, 12999, 13000, 13001, 13003, 13004, 13006, 13013, 13019, 13149, 13150, 13179, 13266

Books: HRT
00227, 00354, 00487, 00545, 00546, 00548, 00611, 00986, 01293, 01295, 01354, 01378, 01776, 01777, 01803, 01953, 02144, 02145, 02166, 02217, 02280, 02380, 03099, 03100, 03101, 03103, 03160, 03895, 04366, 04367, 04368, 04550, 04565, 04742, 04755, 04856, 05073, 05203, 05492, 05496, 06059, 06340, 06740, 06772, 06999, 07091, 07161, 07443, 07444, 07445, 07482, 07591, 07600, 07634, 07642, 07773, 07805, 08033, 08139, 08225, 08517, 08562, 08785, 08854, 08856, 08884, 09005, 09006, 09010, 09047, 09397, 09399, 09400, 09827, 09909, 09911, 09929, 10104, 10108, 10109, 10204, 10501, 10582, 10658, 10813, 10814, 10816, 10921, 10983, 11050, 11066, 11194, 11395, 11396, 11402, 11415, 11471, 11472, 11491, 11507, 12142, 12686, 12774, 12775, 13103

Books: Psychodrama
00342, 00691, 01300, 01917, 03204 04027, 04763, 05056, 06009, 06930, 07630, 08337, 08341, 08353, 08369, 08384, 08386, 08388, 08411, 08412, 08418, 08429, 08430, 08450, 08458, 08463, 08464, 08472, 08476, 08795, 09692, 10435, 10810

Books: Other
00200, 00341, 00357, 00368, 00430, 00470, 00492, 00552, 00596, 00718, 00726, 00893, 00983, 01060, 01061, 01095, 01096, 01141, 01183, 01228, 01279, 01513, 01542, 01633, 01645, 01883, 01913, 01951, 01964, 02019, 02079, 02093, 02206, 02227, 02254, 02285, 02289, 02357, 02379, 02511, 02577, 02664, 02825, 02851, 02859, 02860, 02891, 02908, 02920, 02931, 02959, 02965, 02994, 03042, 03076, 03104, 03248, 03285, 03319, 03372, 03556, 03603, 03708, 03709, 03738, 03871, 03972, 04020, 04068, 04087, 04131, 04175, 04233, 04313, 04415, 04430, 04490, 04521, 04538, 04573, 04591, 04613, 04851, 04889, 04948, 04989, 04995, 05016, 05112, 05164, 05210, 05211, 05215, 05294, 05340, 05345, 05412, 05491, 05579, 05931, 06097, 06177, 06192, 06197, 06221, 06249, 06250, 06251, 06326, 06330, 06341, 06599, 06694, 06779, 06787, 06869, 06913, 06951, 06992, 07071, 07081, 07132, 07135, 07164, 07346, 07397, 07398, 07471, 07525, 07540, 07577, 07581, 07593, 07627, 07636, 07656, 07662, 07708, 07769, 07777, 07898, 07952, 08027, 08133, 08173, 08187, 08200, 08268, 08721, 08781, 08783, 08838, 08898, 09101, 09110, 09111, 09112, 09114, 09230, 09309, 09396, 09401, 09402, 09444, 09468, 09545, 09553, 09554, 09555, 09556, 09888, 09920, 10004, 10011, 10115, 10133, 10159, 10190, 10222, 10642, 10665, 10722, 10757, 10815, 10817, 10919, 11028, 11078, 11105, 11247, 11249, 11258, 11261, 11417, 11504, 11577, 11619, 11637, 11751, 12076, 12095, 12102, 12161, 12243, 12277, 12319, 12342, 12361, 12474, 12612, 12874, 12900, 12901, 12918, 12997, 13047, 13213

Book Review
00067, 00113, 00358, 00410, 00421, 00441, 00471, 00521, 00560, 00656, 00941, 00963, 01644, 01796, 02129, 03154, 03276, 03443, 03789, 03930, 04843, 05819, 05880, 06639, 06640, 06821, 06536, 06955, 07204, 07243, 07331, 07380, 07511, 07573, 07792, 07963, 08047, 08052, 08088, 08261, 08280, 08309, 08627, 08719, 08974, 09118, 09119, 09120, 09121, 09122, 09123, 09124, 09125, 09126, 09290, 09446, 09447, 09483, 09576, 09811, 09930, 09931, 09946, 09974, 09975, 10117, 10197, 10308, 10447, 10460, 10476, 10488, 10491, 10517, 10709, 10711, 10824, 10861, 10874, 10937, 10971, 10987, 10988, 10991, 11131, 11193, 11245

Borderline
00246, 00336, 00963, 01420, 02682, 03390, 03942, 03948, 04580, 05032, 05472, 05835, 06259, 06957, 07490, 08945, 09449, 10771, 10772, 11010, 12089, 12482, 13076

C

Cancer
09288, 12358, 13164
Case Histories
00091, 00146, 00166, 00218, 00223, 00418, 00457, 00466, 00509, 00583, 00704, 00705, 00834, 01080, 01090, 01167, 01476, 01493, 01502, 01517, 01538, 01643, 01693, 01740, 01949, 02092, 02102, 02103, 02597, 02617, 02620, 02666, 02699, 02738, 02903, 02942, 03077, 03280, 03522, 03617, 03877, 03878, 03919, 03978, 03979, 04140, 04370, 04466, 04524, 04580, 04679, 04680, 04729, 04965, 05048, 05064, 05131, 05425, 05704, 06032, 06214, 06400, 06779, 07139, 07299, 07546, 07746, 07753, 07783, 07848, 07912, 08146, 08157, 08177, 08272, 08293, 08321, 08322, 08327, 08336, 08337, 08374, 08420, 08421, 08423, 08424, 08428, 08446, 08465, 08501, 08527, 08620, 08668, 08699, 08735, 08888, 08927, 09085, 09094, 09244, 09311, 09349, 09437, 09548, 09821, 09831, 09881, 10162, 10169, 10257, 10333, 10353, 10363, 10425, 10904, 11126, 11237, 11285, 11353, 11391, 11543, 11545, 11546, 11710, 11713, 11821, 11888, 12008, 12058, 12138, 12171, 12260, 12656
Character Disorder
02453
Child Abuse
00885, 01357, 02483, 02694, 04863, 05974, 07963, 10514, 12012
Children: Disturbed
00219, 00220, 00274, 00283, 00284, 00638, 00856, 00927, 00971, 00984, 00998, 01061, 01066, 01171, 01187, 01188, 01254, 01255, 01327, 01350, 01413, 01426, 01465, 01467, 01468, 01492, 01522, 01617, 01675, 01746, 01834, 01896, 01898, 01970, 01981, 01985, 01988, 01990, 01998, 02014, 02082, 02138, 02142, 02161, 02196, 02205, 02233, 02234, 02272, 02363, 02424, 02444, 02612, 02766, 02841, 03010, 03011, 03153, 03457, 03820, 03931, 03990, 04020, 04034, 04039, 04053, 04276, 04371, 04486, 04487, 04502, 04682, 04752, 04959, 05266, 05279, 05504, 05523, 05837, 05838, 05948, 05953, 06335, 06349, 06439 06479, 06494, 06717, 06982, 06995, 07142, 07182, 07191, 07192, 07657, 07667, 07713, 07784, 08267, 08523, 08642, 08645, 08744, 08779, 09001, 09185, 09195, 09279, 09501, 09684, 09808, 09864, 10013, 10336, 10595, 10773, 11117, 11848, 11869, 11905, 11950, 12338, 12487, 12630, 12712, 12927, 12934, 12935, 12938, 12982, 12983, 13091, 13119, 13141, 13161, 13221
Children: Handicapped
00001, 00056, 01000, 01107, 01364, 01410, 01630, 01968, 01985, 02058, 02164, 02211, 02228, 02374, 02387, 02451, 02465, 02558, 02593, 03055, 03152, 03337, 03576, 04301, 04552, 00562, 04866, 05180, 05815, 05967, 06024, 06169, 06503, 06543, 06860, 06982, 07121, 07213, 07232, 07616, 08199, 08263, 08746, 10033, 10324, 10326, 10752, 11776, 12033, 12252, 12295, 12579, 12745, 12906
Children: Somatic
00051, 00052, 00053, 00659, 01969, 02084, 02153, 02164, 05137, 06543, 06544, 07752, 07811, 07942, 12626, 12988, 12989
Children: Other
00043, 00054, 00058, 00252, 00279, 00408, 00464, 00500, 00517, 00639, 00643, 00653, 00662, 00692, 00717, 00788, 00866, 00967, 00968, 01008, 01052, 01056, 01108, 01134, 01154, 01170, 01283, 01301, 01321, 01340, 01466, 01469, 01579, 01607, 01638, 01679, 01747, 01757, 01806, 01835, 01851, 01937, 01940, 01945, 01966, 01977, 02038, 02119, 02126, 02135,

02137, 02157, 02158, 02207, 02210, 02328, 02442, 02466, 02483, 02485, 02514, 02531, 02543, 02549, 02592, 02602, 02622, 02625, 02629, 02635, 02638, 02639, 02694, 02735, 02736, 02744, 02749, 02756, 02819, 02870, 02903, 02905, 02953, 02964, 02987, 03026, 03031, 03081, 03118, 03181, 03219, 03227, 03230, 03289, 03305, 03306, 03309, 03348, 03358, 03360, 03447, 03739, 03743, 03744, 03758, 03808, 03850, 03858, 03908, 03947, 03952, 03961, 03979, 03992, 04009, 04035, 04097, 04125, 04140, 04142, 04145, 04192, 04213, 04214, 04215, 04216, 04217, 04220, 04221, 04228, 04281, 04290, 04329, 04337, 04374, 04395, 04446, 04449, 04460, 04461, 04484, 04485, 04507, 04508, 04584, 04595, 04753, 04777, 04821, 04823, 04827, 04840, 04861, 04928, 04994, 05079, 05135, 05140, 05173, 05195, 05214, 05246, 05254, 05264, 05273, 05280, 05303, 05304, 05307, 05490, 05500, 05511, 05515, 05517, 05526, 05574, 05578, 05707, 05709, 05713, 05717, 05769, 05811, 05819, 05858, 05894, 05920, 06002, 06046, 06087, 06090, 06173, 06220, 06224, 06225, 06306, 06328, 06470, 06483, 06506, 06510, 06521, 06542, 06547, 06573, 06589, 06629, 06630, 06643, 06690, 06709, 06739, 06802, 06803, 06879, 06921, 06931, 06963, 06979, 06984, 07001, 07038, 07054, 07062, 07084, 07107, 07111, 07141, 07190, 07234, 07262, 07300, 07320, 07340, 07346, 07348, 07359, 07372, 07381, 07390, 07393, 07419, 07436, 07437, 07438, 07450, 07520, 07533, 07551, 07574, 07618, 07619, 07648, 07666, 07673, 07677, 07731, 07739, 07763, 07764, 07766, 07780, 07809, 07834, 07836, 07849, 07853, 07868, 07890, 07905, 07963, 07967, 08016, 08034, 08077, 08083, 08259, 08272, 08286, 08298, 08329, 08485, 08486, 08487, 08513, 08559, 08560, 08621, 08635, 08646, 08651, 08681, 08687, 08691, 08698, 08699, 08732, 08773, 08794, 08795, 08801, 08805, 08841, 08844, 08847, 08852, 08913, 08914, 08920, 08960, 08980, 08981, 08988, 08993, 08994, 09004, 09028, 09062, 09066, 09094, 09161, 09175, 09237, 09291, 09297, 09310, 09349, 09350, 09351, 09416, 09432, 09478, 09488, 09496, 09502, 09542, 09609, 09642, 09650, 09753, 09777, 09779, 09822, 09871, 09896, 09900, 09901, 09937, 09957, 09971, 09972, 09985, 09989, 10021, 10026, 10046, 10057, 10069, 10120, 10174, 10180, 10203, 10209, 10237, 10239, 10240, 10244, 10252, 10266, 10307, 10352, 10353, 10361, 10376, 10459, 10478, 10536, 10566, 10583, 10590, 10593, 10604, 10621, 10628, 10629, 10638, 10651, 10670, 10671, 10672, 10674, 10676, 10680, 10803, 10904, 10914, 11025, 11036, 11046, 11047, 11063, 11086, 11104, 11127, 11135, 11145, 11229, 11252, 11257, 11270, 11288, 11298, 11300, 11318, 11352, 11384, 11436, 11437, 11453, 11495, 11497, 11523, 11528, 11530, 11554, 11562, 11572, 11590, 11609, 11614, 11638, 11639, 11700, 11746, 11755, 11843, 11864, 11924, 11925, 11927, 11933, 11935, 11937, 11959, 11978, 12008, 12020, 12021, 12057, 12176, 12246, 12298, 12325, 12338, 12471, 12523, 12524, 12546, 12611, 12627, 12644, 12670, 12677, 12694 12696, 12705, 12755, 12789, 12799, 12809, 12815, 12857, 12867, 12869, 12917, 12939, 13054, 13107, 13117, 13118, 13122, 13123, 13212, 13264, 13301

Class Method
01552, 01712, 04393, 04805, 07485, 09298, 09314, 09627, 09628, 09635, 09636, 09653

Client-centered Group Therapy
00035, 00491, 01012, 02122, 02446, 02812, 03210, 03747, 04035, 04406, 05188, 05209, 05332, 05333, 05470, 05997, 06682, 07177, 08064, 08559, 08673, 09211, 09227, 09490, 09770, 10509, 10513, 10725, 10726, 11375, 11376, 11531, 11532, 11534, 11917, 11965, 12105, 12322, 12642, 12979

Clinics
01380, 01492, 01746, 02663, 02736, 02764, 02752, 02866, 02924, 03155, 03227, 03741, 03808, 03826, 03913, 03969, 03976, 04010, 04035, 04081, 04098, 04099, 04217, 04219, 04390, 04446, 04532, 04556, 04840, 04928,

04987, 05005, 05017, 05106, 05145, 05485, 05571, 05574, 05612, 05638, 05706, 05800, 05809, 05848, 05849, 06017, 06133, 06262, 06336, 06338, 06542, 06590, 06709, 06814, 06945, 07215, 07478, 07717, 07718, 07870, 07871, 07872, 07873, 07874, 07875, 07876, 07877, 07878, 08130, 08485, 08540, 08707, 08804, 08988, 09050, 09218, 09225, 09310, 09313, 09371, 09506, 09507, 09536, 09562, 09609, 09917, 09976, 10194, 10239, 10325, 10451, 10668, 10717,
10880, 10918, 11007, 11024, 11036, 11198, 11436, 11437, 11467, 11539, 11639, 11745, 11856, 11933, 12241, 12245, 12325, 12422, 12424, 12437, 12464, 12465, 12494, 12572, 12683, 12754, 13091, 13116

Cognitive Factors
10396

Cognitive Methods
00030, 00517, 00608, 00858, 01135, 01190, 01244, 02546, 02978, 03163, 03164, 05214, 05410, 06089, 06514, 06539, 06843, 06960, 07902, 08516, 09476, 09693, 09964, 10169, 11609, 12220, 12531, 12581

College Students
00089, 00271, 00276, 00287, 00289, 00489, 00571, 01010, 01067, 01069, 01133, 01341, 01352, 01365, 01493, 01507, 01588, 01620, 01660, 01752, 01770, 01771, 01805, 01824, 01846, 01946, 02052, 02070, 02089, 02140, 02197, 02256, 02333, 02356, 02441, 02588, 02699, 02700, 02761, 02775, 02833, 02843, 02885, 03038, 03171, 03196, 03202, 03308, 03406, 03412, 03471, 03516, 03894, 03982, 04026, 04079, 04087, 04161, 04189, 04190, 04309, 04327, 04514, 04568, 04870, 04917, 04920, 04962, 05023, 05132, 05133, 05188, 05272, 05298, 05331, 05363, 05498, 05860, 05912, 05961, 06099, 06154, 06174, 06263, 06304, 06535, 06539, 06540, 06558, 06609, 06696, 06698, 06738, 06799, 06892, 06954, 07055, 07241, 07275, 07285, 07295, 07306, 07382, 07484, 07537, 07797, 07824, 07970, 08011, 08089, 08168, 08186, 08213, 08245, 08247, 08251, 08316, 08546, 08555, 08565, 08664, 08665, 08677, 08714, 08799, 08947, 08959, 09105, 09169, 09211, 09239, 09251, 09316, 09369, 09375, 09427, 09760, 09768, 09787, 09788, 09980, 09987, 10091, 10140, 10189, 10310, 10409, 10423, 10499, 10543, 10758, 10759, 10830, 10956, 11023, 11137, 11157, 11389, 11470, 11541, 11560, 11657, 11724, 11757, 11801, 11826, 11958, 11968, 12034, 12064, 12075, 12110, 12112, 12124, 12128, 12160, 12214, 12221, 12239, 12265, 12671, 12299, 12366, 12367, 12379, 12407, 12431, 12598, 12633, 12654, 12682, 12737, 12747, 12783, 12811, 12884, 12920, 12929, 13127, 13164, 13165, 13303, 13304

Combined Somatic and Group Therapy
01205, 05627

Comments, Critiques, Observations, Reflections
00069, 00071, 00169, 00175, 00207, 00258, 00314, 00360, 00431, 00439, 00462, 00475, 00524, 00555, 00605, 00633, 00668, 00673, 00677, 00734, 00738, 00756, 00758, 00766, 00779, 00781, 00782, 00785, 00795, 00796, 00797, 00801, 00807, 00820, 00825, 00837, 00838, 00839, 00842, 00894, 00895, 00896, 00901, 00902, 00908, 00918, 00960, 00965, 00988, 00989, 01017, 01019, 01020, 01026, 01029, 01036, 01064, 01065, 01083, 01149, 01150, 01158, 01172, 01217, 01221, 01222, 01223, 01224, 01225, 01226, 01227, 01242, 01252, 01274, 01281, 01294, 01299, 01317, 01318, 01338, 01342, 01381, 01382, 01391, 01403, 01456, 01474, 01479, 01487, 01520, 01532, 01546, 01558, 01559, 01591, 01593, 01595, 01598, 01623, 01625, 01653, 01662, 01781, 01791, 01796, 01811, 01821, 01822, 01828, 01881, 01893, 01895, 01910, 01918, 01922, 01963, 01967, 02013, 02066, 02206, 02333, 02338, 02369, 02371, 02471, 02479, 02480, 02482, 02515, 02516, 02557, 02563, 02564, 02605, 02616, 02667, 02683, 02695, 02717, 02771, 02792, 02809, 02816, 02856, 02865, 02898, 02915, 02919, 02923, 02930,

02941, 02976, 03018, 03139, 03145, 03147, 03205, 03212, 03213, 03215, 03229, 03317, 03322, 03336, 03337, 03402, 03444, 03445, 03446, 03448, 03449, 03474, 03495, 03515, 03522, 03524, 03561, 03572, 03598, 03654, 03655, 03793, 03850, 03885, 03950, 03995, 04184, 04269, 04335, 04338, 04348, 04360, 04376, 04381, 04468, 04520, 04522, 04553, 04572, 04618, 04619, 04620, 04628, 04630, 04632, 04633, 04642, 04652, 04691, 04706, 04731, 04736, 04759, 04761, 04762, 04773, 04822, 04838, 04877, 04890, 04924, 04927, 04999, 05009, 05031, 05052, 05068, 05082, 05114, 05147, 05163, 05218, 05224, 05229, 05232, 05247, 05257, 05283, 05366, 05379, 05382, 05414, 05429, 05438, 05456, 05471, 05475, 05489, 05495, 05535, 05537, 05542, 05543, 05545, 05546, 05554, 05555, 05558, 05613, 05637, 05638, 05640, 05647, 05649, 05652, 05655, 05658, 05664, 05665, 05688, 05718, 05721, 05729, 05750, 05774, 05775, 05792, 05827, 05901, 05942, 05965, 05994, 06013, 06063, 06064, 06077, 06129, 06189, 06201, 06202, 06210, 06217, 06228, 06347, 06365, 06366, 06372, 06385, 06386, 06395, 06409, 06416, 06429, 06432, 06497, 06498, 06696, 06700, 06703, 06716, 06730, 06761, 06785, 06788, 06809, 06810, 06811, 06815, 06818, 06864, 06878, 06880, 06887, 06920, 06935, 06941, 06987, 07006, 07034, 07049, 07050, 07051, 07063, 07092, 07112, 07137, 07146, 07198, 07222, 07225, 07237, 07252, 07274, 07281, 07321, 07323, 07360, 07361, 07366, 07404, 07504, 07514, 07541, 07543, 07549

Comments

07552, 07560, 07590, 07637, 07643, 07672, 07689, 07700, 07710, 07729, 07734, 07748, 07755, 07758, 07774, 07775, 07965, 08000, 08001, 08023, 08024, 08025, 08053, 08062, 08066, 08069, 08075, 08086, 08157, 08174, 08332, 08339, 08342, 08343, 08350, 08354, 08356, 08357, 08358, 08359, 08361, 08363, 08364, 08368, 08375, 08377, 08383, 08387, 08392, 08393, 08394, 08395, 08400, 08401, 08402, 08406, 08409, 08410, 08415, 08419, 08432, 08440, 08441, 08443, 08448, 08455, 08456, 08479, 08483, 08497, 08510, 08570, 08603, 08622, 08625, 08670, 08694, 08704, 08707, 08731, 08734, 08736, 08756, 08803, 08830, 08839, 08870, 08908, 08909, 08978, 09001, 09002, 09017, 09054, 09055, 09077, 09087, 09138, 09139, 09259, 09261, 09270, 09283, 09295, 09296, 09341, 09343, 09406, 09422, 09439, 09557, 09559, 09587, 09591, 09593, 09617, 09646, 09688, 09726, 09737, 09743, 09775, 09785, 09791, 09793, 09805, 09845, 09849, 09890, 09916, 09923, 09940, 09963, 09976, 09992, 10031, 10043, 10090, 10106, 10158, 10177, 10182, 10186, 10199, 10227, 10230, 10295, 10304, 10312, 10342, 10352, 10437, 10439, 10445, 10464, 10475, 10530, 10565, 10570, 10576, 10594, 10618, 10644, 10663, 10702, 10712, 10719, 10827, 10840, 10891, 10939, 10948, 11001, 11045, 11048, 11109, 11110, 11169, 11191, 11203, 11235, 11272, 11279, 11299, 11357, 11508, 11536, 11538, 11563, 11579, 11583, 11585, 11602, 11615, 11620, 11660, 11679, 11682, 11683, 11687, 11717, 11723, 11749, 11793, 11796, 11809, 11857, 11887, 11931, 11940, 11961, 11973, 11974, 11976, 11992, 11994, 12000, 12018, 12024, 12040, 12046, 12068, 12074, 12078, 12080, 12083, 12084, 12090, 12100, 12111, 12136, 12138, 12141, 12163, 12212, 12222, 12256, 12315, 12317, 12323, 12327, 12337, 12345, 12348, 12398, 12399, 12408, 12409, 12417, 12418, 12430, 12525, 12559, 12566, 12606, 12664, 12703, 12708, 12715, 12716, 12717, 12721, 12722, 12730, 12753, 12767, 12770, 12790, 12791, 12815, 12816, 12842, 12897, 12952, 12957, 13007, 13051, 13109, 13125, 13138, 13205, 13253

Communications/Interactions

00227, 00428, 00505, 01021, 01022, 01033, 01034, 01035, 01118, 02096, 02170, 02259, 02542, 02607, 02628, 02649, 02684, 02781, 02872, 02914, 02969, 02991, 03057, 03091, 03121, 03124, 03125, 03140, 03206, 03224, 03236, 03245, 03286, 03482, 03505, 03528, 03585, 03908, 03980, 03984,

04112, 04164, 04177, 04216, 04232, 04263, 04313, 04334, 04367, 04368, 04414, 04415, 04440, 04448, 04494, 04523, 04565, 04607, 04608, 04609, 04624, 04711, 04856, 04886, 04888, 04890, 04951, 05018, 05041, 05202, 05252, 05254, 05258, 05266, 05267, 05124, 05309, 05310, 05324, 05441, 05518, 05621, 05693, 05854, 05996, 06048, 06060, 06061, 06068, 06136, 06142, 06172, 06181, 06238, 06491, 06591, 06710, 06722, 06760, 06770, 06780, 06801, 06820, 06834, 06852, 06858, 06911, 06992, 06993, 07080, 07106, 07233, 07257, 07277, 07374, 07445, 07588, 07669, 07687, 07766, 07781, 07859, 07943, 07969, 07975, 07983, 07991, 08051, 08054, 08084, 08180, 08508, 08509, 08577, 08606, 08638, 08644, 08720, 08730, 08760, 08773, 08778, 08815, 08816, 08817, 08837, 08876, 08882, 08911, 08918, 08938, 08942, 09052, 09165, 09187, 09199, 09326, 09605, 09649, 09697, 09853, 10025, 10037, 10042, 10061, 10074, 10382, 10441, 10442, 10467, 10468, 10483, 10483, 10489, 10492, 10495, 10566, 10587, 10619, 10662, 10706, 10862, 10866, 10901, 10915, 10928, 10931, 10954, 11022, 11054, 11076, 11128, 11184, 11190, 11199, 11221, 11254, 11302, 11373, 11374, 11397, 11407, 11443, 11520, 11566, 11570, 11574, 11607, 11622, 11665, 11666, 11670, 11697, 11730, 11768, 11769, 11782, 11803, 11991, 11995, 12045, 12113, 12117, 12152, 12159, 12173, 12251, 12269, 12270, 12400, 12414, 12519, 12535, 12569, 12577, 12614, 12677, 12847, 12861, 12887, 12888, 12904, 12913, 12942, 12943, 12944, 12978, 12987, 13063, 13236, 13252, 13256, 13257, 13292

Community, Therapeutic Community

00060, 00130, 00188, 00300, 00306, 00587, 00723, 00900, 01029, 01260, 01348, 01516, 01599, 01656, 01748, 01793, 02005, 02046, 02047, 02072, 02075, 02077, 02132, 02248, 02500, 02533, 02544, 02572, 02655, 02687, 02747, 02847, 02848, 02849, 02960, 02996, 03076, 03098, 03123, 03182, 03185, 03261, 03262, 03263, 03272, 03312, 03343, 03541, 03559, 03602, 03795, 03810, 03839, 03966, 04011, 04031, 04042, 04099, 04109, 04164, 04219, 04224, 04250, 04411, 04439, 04457, 04472, 04528, 04529, 04760, 04854, 04925, 04989, 05071, 05083, 05172, 05321, 05422, 05487, 05493, 05519, 05635, 05692, 05731, 05773, 05814, 05837, 05849, 05873, 05883, 05905, 05929, 05935, 05940, 06168, 06218, 06271, 06272, 06451, 06452, 06492, 06499, 06505, 06535, 06542, 06625, 06627, 06628, 06743, 06744, 06847, 06946, 06955, 07007, 07039, 07082, 07190, 07251, 07270, 07319, 07371, 07542, 07586, 07652, 07653, 07674, 07678, 07703, 07704, 07743, 07751, 07778, 07801, 07850, 07982, 08030, 08031, 08128, 08129, 08176, 08205, 08253, 08315, 08399, 08405, 08544, 08552, 08582, 08586, 08686, 08786, 08828, 08833, 08900, 09183, 09184, 09266, 09273, 09276, 09331, 09343, 09385, 09389, 09417, 09419, 09463, 09498, 09592, 09675, 09702, 09707, 09781, 09812, 09813, 09907, 09967, 09976, 09993, 10194, 10296, 10264, 10283, 10288, 10302, 10392, 10393, 10457, 10474, 10581, 10649, 10655, 10670, 10673, 10831, 10849, 10890, 11000, 11053, 11143, 11190, 11213, 11219, 11234, 11263, 11326, 11369, 11409, 11604, 11644, 11645, 11712, 11861, 11901, 11981, 11985, 11988, 12170, 12194, 12198, 12232, 12233, 12403, 12425, 12530, 12584, 12613, 12632, 12732, 12744, 12762, 12780, 12831, 12846, 12896, 12908, 12922, 12956, 13079, 13171, 13214, 13225 (*See also:* Milieu Therapy)

Conditioning

02309, 03776, 03894, 04702, 05129, 07099, 09307, 10286

Consciousness-raising Groups

00575, 00588, 00615, 01199, 02050, 02670, 03056, 03550, 04140, 05421, 06647, 07153, 07159, 07271, 07627, 08198, 10780, 11592, 11880, 12119, 12596

Co-therapy and Co-therapists

00268, 00647, 00985, 01240, 01568, 02100, 02535, 02573, 02678, 02707,

02769, 02799, 02993, 03180, 03344, 03924, 03988, 03989, 04146, 04155, 04156, 04239, 04294, 04295, 04297, 04380, 04444, 04497, 04609, 04900, 05090, 05116, 05121, 05234, 05235, 05371, 05502, 05561, 05639, 06140, 06157, 06379, 06764, 06861, 07026, 07318, 07322, 07339, 07465, 07516, 07925, 07936, 08223, 08231, 08234, 08581, 08793, 08826, 09219, 09353, 09441, 09442, 09477, 09718, 09720, 09941, 10083, 10137, 10313, 10411, 10496, 10755, 11204, 11464, 11469, 11630, 11872, 11955, 11970, 12106, 12761, 12880, 12958, 13094, 13114, 13122

Counseling: Guidance

00095, 01189, 01201, 01979, 02256, 02258

Couples

01805, 02316, 06684, 07547, 11390

Creavity, 04016, 10578

Crime and Delinquency

00021, 00028, 00048, 00063, 00064, 00087, 00088, 00117, 00119, 00127, 00136, 00139, 00178, 00292, 00293, 00317, 00319, 00370, 00403, 00442, 00483, 00484, 00565, 00693, 00720, 00844, 00871, 00944, 00947, 01100, 01160, 01216, 01248, 01249, 01250, 01382, 01424, 01427, 01500, 01516, 01527, 01556, 01565, 01659, 01721, 01744, 01816, 01817, 01862, 01909, 01910, 01911, 01923, 01942, 02086, 02109, 02121, 02343, 02374, 02438, 02472, 02501, 02524, 02534, 02560, 02631, 02648, 02675, 02780, 02807, 03098, 03140, 03141, 03156, 03161, 03220, 03229, 03232, 03251, 03257, 03281, 03282, 03326, 03364, 03373, 03376, 03387, 03413, 03414, 03441, 03512, 03577, 03687, 03695, 03711, 03757, 03759, 03848, 03889, 03918, 03950, 03977, 04003, 04021, 04077, 04143, 04144, 04147, 04148, 04159, 04160, 04209, 04293, 04332, 04378, 04450, 04575, 04586, 04653, 04797, 04801, 04814, 04815, 04816, 04852, 04900, 04905, 04938, 04976, 04977, 05163, 05213, 05237, 05239, 05078, 05089, 05095, 05096, 05099, 05100, 05042, 05044, 05046, 05047, 05048, 05327, 05375, 05391, 05423, 05502, 05524, 05570, 05660, 05671, 05672, 05673, 05675, 05705, 05737, 05738, 05739, 05760, 05767, 05768, 05793, 05847, 05896, 05903, 05963, 05972, 05997, 06012, 06082, 06097, 06103, 06213, 06294, 06295, 06358, 06460, 06464, 06663, 06683, 06793, 06794, 06822, 06862, 06863, 07018, 07019, 07020, 07021, 07023, 07024, 07058, 07077, 07178, 07278, 07353, 07476, 07539, 07580, 07650, 07662, 07664, 07679, 07759, 07760, 07788, 07789, 07813, 07835, 07881, 07893, 07894, 07895, 07896, 07910, 08115, 08141, 08172, 08178, 08195, 08203, 08310, 08424, 08478, 08529, 08541, 08594, 08674, 08729, 08742, 08829, 08863, 08879, 08885, 08889, 08934, 08991, 08998, 09039, 09042, 09044, 09060, 09064, 09092, 09115, 09167, 09197, 09252, 09275, 09293, 09332, 09333, 09334, 09345, 09348, 09406, 09411, 09417, 09438, 09518, 09553, 09626, 09736, 09738, 09789, 09854, 09855, 09856, 09857, 09867, 09875, 09891, 09922, 09944, 10133, 10136, 10154, 10155, 10229, 10252, 10268, 10391, 10457, 10519, 10520, 10548, 10682, 10733, 10790, 10792, 10797, 10853, 10881, 10890, 11040, 11058, 11059, 11085, 11104, 11105, 11106, 11122, 11136, 11171, 11234, 11244, 11247, 11248, 11277, 11285, 11296, 11308, 11309, 11324, 11325, 11353, 11363, 11372, 11373, 11374, 11375, 11376, 11398, 11450, 11455, 11458, 11564, 11716, 11720, 11730, 11734, 11737, 11739, 11848, 11877, 11915, 12016, 12029, 12031, 12032, 12063, 12071, 12155, 12194, 12274, 12287, 12288, 12290, 12474, 12556, 12575, 12582, 12599, 12627, 12752, 12878, 12905, 12922, 12928, 13053, 13056, 13104, 13124, 13139, 13145, 13174, 13176, 13180, 13182, 13195, 13222 (*See also:* Acting Out, Character Disorder, Sociopath, Adolescents, Psychodrama, Correctional)

Crisis Intervention

00160, 00182, 00184, 00185, 00979, 01258, 01278, 01292, 01326, 01420, 01672, 02339, 02631, 02850, 02873, 02876, 02968, 03128, 03523, 03537,

03731, 03808, 04404, 04417, 04907, 05053, 05694, 06208, 06222, 06426, 06543, 06544, 06962, 07816, 07885, 08097, 08161, 08205, 08557, 08903, 09276, 09592, 09662, 09966, 10320, 10574, 10842, 11493, 11611, 11879, 11904, 12064, 12070, 12207, 12299, 12483, 12558, 12567, 13142, 13250, 13272

Cultural Factors
03238, 03321

D

Dance Therapy
00140, 00141, 00142, 00584, 01297, 01741, 01887, 01991, 01992, 02018, 02029, 03485, 05969, 09057, 10362, 10512

Day Hospital
00034, 01175, 01254, 02586, 02819, 02861, 02971, 03436, 03696, 03793, 03801, 03901, 04373, 04475, 05098, 05101, 05236, 05408, 05584, 05612, 06314, 06553, 06677, 06782, 06783, 07227, 07273, 07802, 08903, 09145, 09271, 09280, 09425, 09426, 09480, 09970, 10060, 10277, 10717, 10949, 11359, 11591, 12145, 12439, 12440, 12494, 0112685, 12967

Death and Death Anxiety
00016, 00245, 00418, 00571, 01008, 01643, 01723, 02168, 02319, 02985, 03340, 03929, 04776, 06256, 06334, 06532, 06533, 07013, 07329, 07547, 08135, 09858, 09954, 10085, 10580, 11063, 11556, 13131, 13287

Depression
00070, 00215, 00436, 00671, 00672, 00798, 00969, 01145, 01197, 01780, 02110, 02589, 03136, 03190, 03191, 03341, 03885, 03912, 03973, 04291, 04343, 04893, 05405, 05749, 05909, 06044, 06278, 06433, 06843, 07017, 07066, 07100, 07253, 07418, 07558, 08107, 08184, 08520, 08715, 09053, 09059, 09247, 09483, 10052, 10357, 10358, 10396, 10415, 10511, 10903, 11592, 12319, 12479, 12779

Diagnosis
00100, 00467, 00561, 00591, 00767, 00870, 01030, 01146, 01406, 01434, 01436, 01460, 01631, 01641, 02083, 02435, 03566, 03842, 04401, 04403, 04487, 04703, 04850, 05011, 05146, 05227, 05455, 05948, 06259, 06569, 06657, 06742, 06854, 06862, 06913, 06928, 06939, 07302, 07671, 07757, 08060, 08194, 08444, 08453, 08507, 08578, 08579, 08580, 08667, 08979, 09183, 09391, 09436, 09453, 09725, 09861, 10299, 10502, 10576, 10863, 11197, 11217, 11330, 11715, 11729, 11822, 11850, 11936, 11947, 11971, 11983, 12030, 12190, 12346, 12352, 12794, 12850, 13303

Discussion Group Therapy
01988

Disturbed Children
01522, 01532, 01533, 01539, 01544

Dramatics
00001, 00526, 00592, 00692, 00862, 00972, 01052, 01882, 01972, 02560, 02660, 02912, 04476, 05446, 06081, 06667, 06675, 06676, 06715, 06862, 06901, 06961, 06990, 07047, 07085, 07568, 07663, 08193, 08403, 08626, 08655, 09392, 09499, 09674, 09831, 09887, 10211, 10541, 10786, 10865, 11121, 11215, 11377, 11465, 11466, 11523, 11743, 11744, 11941, 11942, 12029, 12683, 12684, 13278

Dreams
00367, 00409, 00753, 00775, 01127, 01441, 01442, 01444, 01997, 03090, 03091, 03458, 03459, 04311, 04543, 05582, 05639, 06051, 06070, 06383, 06407, 06675, 06686, 07313, 07550, 08374, 08607, 08825, 08843, 11064, 12802, 12893, 13262, 13263, 13277

Dropouts, Failures and Complications
00156, 00166, 00316, 00405, 00537, 00539, 00603, 00670, 00693, 00737, 00864, 00877, 00883, 01001, 01042, 01043, 01087, 01637, 01841, 01849, 01899, 02007, 02008, 02115, 02287, 02350, 02371, 02653, 02999, 03122, 03880, 04546, 04547, 04627, 04728, 04732, 04854, 05013, 05113, 05178, 05308, 05340, 05455, 05558, 05639, 05666, 05983, 06120, 06245, 06344, 06403, 06422, 06537, 06739, 07039, 07180, 07365, 07376, 07500, 07542, 07605, 07771, 07844, 08943, 09304, 09481, 09532, 09586, 09967, 10154, 10265, 10273, 10452, 10499, 10742, 10958, 10959, 11012, 11140, 11152, 11262, 11581, 11818, 11830, 12008, 12241, 12349, 12360, 12781, 12850, 13064, 13148, 13261, 13273

Drugs
00953, 01682, 01868, 01946, 02488, 03155, 03517, 03782, 03809, 04040, 04160, 05015, 05045, 05078, 05098, 05162, 05513, 06993, 07935, 08017, 08652, 08792, 08941, 08943, 09007, 09327, 09771, 10950, 12201, 12208, 12538, 13285 (*See also:* Narcotics)

Drug Abuse
00030, 00050, 00145, 00229, 00288, 00405, 00474, 00574, 00674, 00757, 00759, 00787, 00806, 00831, 00846, 00847, 00848, 00954, 01003, 01217, 01253, 01289, 01502, 01553, 01557, 01561, 01562, 01584, 01634, 01641, 01647, 01709, 01727, 01732, 01760, 01831, 01854, 01867, 01914, 02214, 02240, 02309, 02631, 02655, 02665, 02973, 03082, 03146, 03148, 03318, 03364, 03555, 03623, 03810, 03811, 03887, 04068, 04258, 04689, 05078, 05317, 05345, 05419, 05513, 05524, 05692, 05797, 05873, 05898, 05950, 05991, 06055, 06123, 06124, 06125, 06126, 06166, 06236, 06254, 06270, 06302, 06669, 06677, 06716, 06722, 06747, 06759, 06831, 06851, 07079, 07082, 07112, 07334, 07389, 07442, 07683, 07916, 08900, 08983, 09008, 09040, 09042, 09043, 09044, 09073, 09100, 09183, 09184, 09325, 09374, 09455, 09495, 09522, 09535, 09613, 09614, 09739, 09757, 10118, 10190, 10264, 10268, 10275, 10298, 10399, 10429, 10497, 11059, 11234, 11333, 11369, 11502, 11721, 11877, 11967, 11968, 12154, 12156, 12297, 12530, 12574, 12732, 12858, 13099, 13197, 13284

Drug Therapy
00494

Dying
09299

E

Encounter Group
00601, 00679, 00982, 01348, 01349, 03310, 03412, 03551, 03628, 03629, 03630, 03815, 08046, 12126, 12570, 12593

Epilepsy
01051, 01206, 01678, 02638, 02639, 02743, 06031, 06273, 07040, 09769, 10540, 11900, 12453

Ethics, Values, Cultural Factors
00191, 01152, 01399, 01416, 01890, 01898, 01974, 02101, 02432, 02906, 02916, 03321, 03529, 03863, 03864, 04303, 04305, 04600, 04839, 05306, 05407, 05439, 05453, 05586, 05626, 05648, 05857, 06038, 06938, 07486, 07594, 08227, 08378, 08499, 08950, 08981, 09525, 10487, 10998, 11037, 11038, 11051, 11083, 11186, 11218, 11337, 12332, 12371, 12389, 12733, 13071

Evaluation of Group Therapy
01860, 02618, 02644, 02756, 02817, 02977, 02995, 03059, 03167, 03256, 03296, 03323, 03438, 03462, 03471, 03481, 03518, 03549, 03601, 03674,

04147, 04193, 04598, 04709, 04715, 04746, 05489, 05567, 05573, 05634, 05771, 05772, 05847, 05858, 05865, 05913, 05914, 05916, 05946, 06088, 06246, 06378, 06541, 06753, 06783, 06942, 06949, 07002, 07104, 07249, 07328, 07423, 07606, 07609, 07697, 07838, 07901, 07909, 07929, 07933, 07992, 08038, 08207, 08209, 08224, 08457, 08471, 08526, 08536, 08879, 08895, 08900, 09143, 09201, 09202, 09208, 09209, 09249, 09322, 09346, 09364, 09386, 09411, 09421, 09517, 09696, 09762, 09818, 09933, 09982, 09999, 10013, 10345, 10405, 10807, 10957, 11070, 11080, 11142, 11159, 11160, 11189, 11192, 11211, 11244, 11427, 11573, 11631, 11714, 11845, 11996, 12014, 12027, 12028, 12042, 12376, 12576, 12639, 12640, 12661, 12794, 12874, 13254

Existentialism
01456, 01723, 03307, 04312, 04320, 04902, 05409, 05436, 05437, 07211, 07917, 08167, 08360, 08433, 08598, 08599, 08600, 08733, 08972, 09339, 09344, 09956, 10506, 10659, 10887, 11886, 12730, 13071

F

Family and Group Therapy (Couples Therapy, Marital Therapy)
00067, 00105, 00147, 00149, 00272, 00281, 00302, 00362, 00544, 00618, 00762, 01137, 01379, 01398, 01410, 01461, 01462, 01465, 01475, 01495, 01497, 01522, 01643, 01671, 01716, 01735, 01738, 01779, 01827, 01932, 02058, 02082, 02084, 02123, 02134, 02152, 02172, 02215, 02226, 02327, 02375, 02435, 02518, 02536, 02571, 02602, 02659, 02725, 02802, 02842, 02866, 02981, 02997, 03055, 03068, 03069, 03114, 03128, 03134, 03183, 03287, 03312, 03327, 03346, 03367, 03529, 03533, 03556, 03558, 03597, 03605, 03633, 03702, 03703, 03752, 03873, 03916, 03954, 04137, 04156, 04173, 04195, 04282, 04284, 04285, 04286, 04471, 04551, 04593, 04636, 04671, 04714, 04935, 04939, 04940, 04961, 05027, 05038, 05217, 05242, 05263, 05291, 05293, 05306, 05348, 05371, 05375, 05494, 05505, 05525, 05744, 05745, 05805, 05872, 05875, 05933, 05964, 05966, 05968, 06006, 06101, 06215, 06350, 06388, 06408, 06684, 06740, 06741, 06847, 06973, 06975, 06976, 07029, 07130, 07131, 07164, 07210, 07283, 07346, 07505, 07585, 07665, 07746, 07814, 07888, 08050, 08141, 08181, 08190, 08262, 08429, 08445, 08544, 08569, 08579, 08591, 08706, 08767, 09083, 09084, 09134, 09187, 09268, 09417, 09777, 09833, 09942, 09954, 09966, 10134, 10210, 10308, 10396, 10397, 10398, 10470, 10471, 10472, 10699, 10700, 10849, 10882, 10991, 11043, 11128, 11214, 11238, 11239, 11240, 11241, 11390, 11425, 11478, 11542, 11567, 11607, 11680, 11761, 11841, 11865, 11873, 11922, 12070, 12095, 12207, 12313, 12325, 12395, 12828, 12848, 12860, 12905, 12927, 12969, 12988, 13054, 13105, 13219, 13239, 13247, 13290

Frequency of Sessions
00946, 01306, 03034, 03787, 05978, 05979, 07239, 08755, 12282, 12284, 12286, 12288, 12290, 12655, 13016

G

General Considerations
00023, 00024, 00076, 00081, 00264, 00440, 00504, 01177, 01178, 01906

Geriatrics, Gerontology
00180, 00325, 00441, 00845, 00922, 00970, 01023, 01024, 01045, 01063, 01478, 01661, 01676, 01764, 01765, 01766, 01767, 01768, 01769, 01780, 01813, 01888, 01904, 01995, 02095, 02248, 02439, 02641, 02697, 02864, 02975, 03064, 03065, 03136, 03253, 03277, 03380, 03501, 03751, 03860,

03973, 04223, 04225, 04362, 04384, 04443, 04494, 04624, 04688, 04708, 04709, 04769, 04809, 04847, 04990, 05497, 05620, 05668, 05696, 05716, 05846, 05891, 05899, 06110, 06212, 06226, 06262, 06268, 06275, 06549, 06598, 06612, 06613, 06760, 06768, 06780, 06902, 06932, 06965, 07067, 07083, 07101, 07113, 07156, 07162, 07172, 07173, 07174, 07175, 07176, 07200, 07205, 07206, 07208, 07209, 07493, 07584, 07596, 07599, 07607, 07615, 07832, 07972, 07979, 07980, 08059, 08107, 08166, 08175, 08176, 08318, 08752, 08768, 08769, 08892, 09381, 09387, 09611, 09683, 09801, 09883, 09910, 10060, 10288, 10289, 10345, 10346, 10356, 10410, 10512, 10579, 10834, 10864, 11103, 11170, 11178, 11209, 11636, 11881, 12139, 12215, 12310, 12319, 12448, 12458, 12552, 12597, 12661, 12741, 12862, 12870, 12871, 12877, 12973, 13023, 13031, 13032, 13034, 13035, 13036, 13037, 13038, 13039, 13042, 13052, 13073, 13155, 13277

Gestalt
00256, 00684, 01013, 02023, 02547, 02690, 02956, 02961, 02993, 03070, 03374, 03408, 03615, 03638, 03639, 03645, 03647, 03648, 03986, 04400, 04669, 04921, 04961, 04963, 05103, 05360, 06065, 06066, 06171, 06538, 06557, 08121, 08505, 08675, 08891, 08907, 08954, 09178, 10184, 10222, 10458, 11706, 12823

Group Casework
07772

Group Composition
01336, 01569, 01722, 02764, 02765, 02766, 02834, 03048, 03170, 03259, 03478, 03567, 03568, 03785, 03872, 03932, 03933, 03934, 04569, 04596, 04671, 04674, 04969, 05091, 05179, 05285, 05311, 05329, 05378, 05457, 05630, 05865, 06037, 06121, 06461, 06625, 06839, 06937, 07009, 07167, 07230, 07456, 07673, 07686, 08045, 08196, 08325, 08695, 08740, 08765, 09096, 09196, 09281, 09473, 09844, 10263, 10273, 10490, 10493, 10494, 10936, 10974, 11142, 11266, 11414, 11421, 11608, 11613, 11664, 11866, 12302, 12334, 12359, 12385, 12498, 12511, 12545, 12549, 12602, 12723, 12807, 12972, 13088

Group Counseling
00093, 00097, 00132, 00145, 00248, 00271, 00287, 00288, 00289, 00292, 00352, 00353, 00356, 00407, 00410, 00465, 00493, 00565, 00571, 00625, 00658, 00660, 00662, 00670, 00696, 00715, 00716, 00725, 00864, 00873, 00903, 00939, 00950, 00967, 00997, 01006, 01008, 01010, 01069, 01109, 01133, 01136, 01159, 01160, 01164, 01215, 01285, 01290, 01321, 01336, 01340, 01578, 01580, 01647, 01648, 01713, 01756, 01798, 01799, 01830, 01846, 01892, 01903, 01908, 01937, 01943, 01959, 01966, 01975, 02027, 02036, 02063, 02069, 02070, 02112, 02140, 02197, 02221, 02247, 02269, 02322, 02323, 02504, 02505, 02540, 02569, 02570, 02580, 02581, 02582, 02583, 02588, 02595, 02596, 02629, 02635, 02651, 02669, 02700, 02749, 02761, 02775, 02777, 02821, 02833, 02843, 02857, 02899, 02900, 02913, 02953, 02972, 02974, 02986, 03031, 03033, 03038, 03039, 03040, 03043, 03061, 03071, 03085, 03094, 03190, 03270, 03271, 03275, 03305, 03320, 03347, 03407, 03413, 03422, 03426, 03484, 03507, 03579, 03607, 03742, 03800, 03802, 03818, 03848, 03893, 03905, 04009, 04016, 04035, 04041, 04049, 04051, 04052, 04061, 04062, 04064, 04069, 04070, 04073, 04079, 04121, 04130, 04134, 04170, 04176, 04179, 04180, 04186, 04188, 04189, 04190, 04204, 04209, 04215, 04217, 04249, 04288, 04299, 04304, 04326, 04334, 04375, 04386, 04387, 04390, 04418, 04464, 04537, 04552, 04554, 04562, 04563, 04564, 04568, 04584, 04600, 04653, 04661, 04678, 04724, 04748, 04757, 04758, 04861, 04865, 04885, 04886, 04914, 04918, 04919, 04920, 04930, 04931, 04932, 04941, 04996, 05000, 05010, 05062, 05088, 05093, 05104, 05159, 05163, 05171, 05188, 05214, 05216, 05233, 05253, 05271, 05278, 05303, 05304, 05325, 05330, 05349, 05365, 05383, 05430,

05435, 05451, 05452, 05462, 05466, 05482, 05500, 05510, 05511, 05526, 05552, 05563, 05567, 05577, 05601, 05607, 05615, 05624, 05678, 05706, 05735, 05742, 05765, 05777, 05783, 05797, 05807, 05810, 05811, 05831, 05840, 05845, 05846, 05850, 05886, 05892, 05893, 05902, 05912, 05961, 05977, 05997, 06012, 06038, 06069, 06080, 06096, 06099, 06121, 06149, 06157, 06158, 06161, 06172, 06174, 06181, 06191, 06193, 06219, 06220, 06241, 06263, 06274, 06282, 06320, 06331, 06380, 06388, 06521, 06540, 06561, 06671, 06678, 06679, 06698, 06723, 06736, 06738, 06769, 06781, 06784, 06796, 06797, 06802, 06803, 06850, 06853, 06859, 06879, 06892, 06909, 06933, 06942, 07001, 07004, 07018, 07019, 07020, 07021, 07024, 07041, 07044, 07055, 07073, 07121, 07185, 07232, 07241, 07306, 07318, 07333, 07338, 07358, 07421, 07463, 07502, 07509, 07544, 07545, 07556, 07564, 07565, 07578, 07611, 07616, 07617, 07628, 07648, 07651, 07675, 07698, 07705, 07720, 07722, 07728, 07739, 07740, 07745, 07796, 07797, 07834, 07840, 07846, 07851, 07866, 07881, 07882, 07889, 07890, 07903, 07905, 07951, 07953, 07961, 07970, 07973, 07975, 08008, 08017, 08037, 08038, 08041, 08048, 08095, 08103, 08104, 08147, 08148, 08213, 08237, 08241, 08245, 08250, 08255, 08259, 08294, 08296, 08304, 08312, 08504, 08509, 08515, 08550, 08649, 08653, 08691, 08712, 08723, 08728, 08746, 08748, 08749, 08753, 08762, 08799, 08807, 08816, 08821, 08845, 08846, 08851, 08901, 08902, 08905, 08916, 08917, 08918, 08920, 08934, 08947, 08960, 09000, 09027, 09028, 09039, 09041, 09062, 09063, 09071, 09073, 09094, 09103, 09105, 09161, 09169, 09175, 09179, 09189, 09191, 09237, 09247, 09251, 09294, 09310, 09312, 09315, 09317, 09328, 09329, 09342, 09368, 09369, 09375, 09393, 09549, 09561, 09584, 09596, 09609, 09613, 09614, 09648, 09661, 09685, 09701, 09711, 09744, 09760, 09773, 09774, 09854, 09855, 09856, 09857, 09895, 09900, 09908, 09931, 09956, 09962, 09972, 09981, 09987, 09997, 09998, 10019, 10046, 10078, 10080, 10097, 10100, 10237, 10239, 10275, 10299, 10300, 10307, 10330, 10341, 10359, 10394, 10401, 10417, 10432, 10484, 10507, 10509, 10547, 10573, 10584, 10595, 10609, 10615, 10713, 10716, 10723, 10803, 10856, 10876, 10877, 10896, 10906, 10941, 10962, 10977, 10997, 11036, 11040, 11063, 11085, 11096, 11125, 11127, 11146, 11209, 11221, 11222, 11288, 11384, 11385, 11398, 11407, 11408, 11422, 11439, 11452, 11462, 11496, 11514, 11560, 11564, 11594, 11600, 11609, 11657, 11740, 11757, 11758, 11765, 11778, 11779, 11782, 11785, 11812, 11826, 11833, 11838, 11849, 11865, 11934, 11938, 11955, 11966, 11984, 12006, 12009, 12017, 12020, 12021, 12049, 12055, 12056, 12057, 12104, 12106, 12108, 12119, 12128, 12129, 12132, 12133, 12148, 12149, 12160, 12180, 12217, 12230, 12262, 12270, 12288, 12307, 12319, 12325, 12326, 12347, 12366, 12367, 12375, 12379, 12380, 12385, 12396, 12405, 12411, 12431, 12445, 12471, 12472, 12500, 12501, 12502, 12503, 12505, 12506, 12507, 12528, 12532, 12591, 12592, 12594, 12599, 12600, 12621, 12626, 12635, 12655, 12670, 12671, 12679, 12710, 12711, 12737, 12747, 12811, 12824, 12825, 12849, 12852, 12878, 12884, 12909, 12910, 12911, 12929, 12933, 12941, 12949, 12982, 13048, 13096, 13162, 13164, 13173, 13182, 13217, 13264, 13270, 13279, 13280, 13282

Group Culture, Group Climate, Group Structure
00031, 00077, 00106, 00167, 00170, 00193, 00205, 00244, 00366, 00427, 00433, 00437, 00452, 00454, 00507, 00538, 00540, 00553, 00596, 00599, 00606, 00645, 00688, 00712, 00713, 00730, 00731, 00735, 00754, 00755, 00789, 00828, 00851, 00863, 00884, 00936, 00987, 00992, 01050, 01059, 01067, 01129, 01193, 01232, 01381, 01384, 01388, 01419, 01421, 01422, 01438, 01445, 01447, 01455, 01471, 01472, 01482, 01506, 01552, 01555, 01585, 01630, 01636, 01646, 01654, 01692, 01722, 01728, 01734, 01755, 01789, 01794, 01806, 01824, 01833, 01840, 01853, 01865, 01869, 01924, 01952, 01956, 01962, 01973, 01980, 01983, 02003, 02004, 02028, 02032,

02041, 02056, 02078, 02081, 02099, 02116, 02124, 02125, 02129, 02155, 02160, 02168, 02193, 02220, 02231, 02268, 02360, 02365, 02372, 02494, 02542, 02579, 02686, 02835, 02928, 03226, 03284, 03397, 03430, 03519, 03571, 03582, 03621, 03627, 03631, 03701, 03717, 03728, 03734, 03737, 03838, 03897, 03974, 04082, 04127, 04129, 04298, 04308, 04334, 04351, 04407, 04422, 04527, 04536, 04579, 04585, 04664, 04735, 04738, 04744, 04779, 04899, 04908, 04955, 04968, 04972, 04975, 04997, 05006, 05395, 05726, 05808, 05975, 06028, 06039, 06292, 06293, 06297, 06333, 06334, 06489, 06508, 06720, 06943, 06944, 06979, 07059, 07060, 07088, 07094, 07097, 07150, 07256, 07352, 07510, 07623, 07761, 07841, 07887, 07914, 08079, 08216, 08317, 08398, 08500, 08534, 08535, 08587, 08665, 08747, 08768, 08769, 08862, 08954, 09164, 09224, 09256, 09390, 09412, 09715, 09816, 10003, 10080, 10284, 10394, 10422, 10477, 11033, 11034, 11144, 11393, 11430, 11706, 11763, 11771, 11786, 11875, 12047, 12148, 12304, 12306, 12460, 12497, 12498, 12508, 12583, 12614, 12778, 12803, 12838, 13069, 13089, 13129, 13154, 13166, 13194, 13200, 13202, 13215, 13224, 13248

Group Development
01421, 01422, 01472

Group Discussion
00135, 00136, 00230, 00280, 00282, 00284, 00293, 00464, 00470, 00482, 00512, 00518, 0522, 00617, 00694, 00727, 00792, 00882, 00956, 00962, 01048, 01094, 01115, 01171, 01204, 1303, 01368, 01457, 01463, 01464, 01550, 01861, 02048, 02253, 02319, 02367, 02460, 02491, 02498, 02501, 02502, 02512, 02744, 02855, 02949, 02951, 03096, 03105, 03175, 03340, 03345, 03366, 03393, 03498, 03527, 03554, 03566, 03789, 03909, 03910, 03940, 04181, 04228, 04255, 04264, 04278, 04355, 04436, 04455, 04601, 04663, 04684, 04901, 04960, 04993, 05099, 05100, 05114, 05137, 05295, 05362, 05416, 05454, 05468, 05782, 05803, 05937, 05976, 06001, 06026, 06076, 06276, 06436, 06457, 06583, 06697, 06786, 06865, 06869, 06878, 06966, 06967, 07005, 07030, 07105, 07125, 07189, 07337, 07345, 07508, 07612, 07838, 07854, 07936, 08094, 08135, 08295, 08303, 08639, 08682, 08684, 08790, 08855, 09169, 09228, 09287, 09301, 09388, 09389, 09414, 09429, 09489, 09578, 09659, 09663, 09664, 09699, 09710, 09713, 09717, 09782, 09798, 09800, 09871, 09926, 09928, 09978, 10077, 10216, 10217, 10274, 10344, 10433, 10506, 10548, 10799, 10823, 10854, 10979, 10982, 11039, 11173, 11208, 11486, 11633, 11748, 11852, 11890, 11989, 11991, 11993, 12001, 12094, 12268, 12313, 12491, 12550, 12551, 12571, 12611, 12646, 12756, 12813, 12836, 12870, 12924, 13046, 13054, 13136, 13169, 13209

Group Dynamics
02706, 03516, 06338, 06994, 09446, 09447, 11166

Group Evaluation
01413, 02585, 04799, 04966, 05020, 05102, 07680

Group Guidance
00717, 03320

Group Play
03570

Group Psychoanalysis
01640, 01689, 01773, 01774, 01775, 01794, 02078, 02135, 02370

Group Psychotherapy
01392, 01508, 01528, 01536, 01541, 01608, 01609, 01625, 01680, 01872, 01978, 01998, 02003, 02005, 02006, 02008, 02009, 02010, 02011, 02015, 02017, 02020, 02022, 02038, 02039, 02040, 02041, 02044, 02046, 02047, 02051, 02052, 02054, 02056, 02081, 02082, 02097, 02099, 02105, 02107, 02108, 02109, 02111, 02141, 02156, 02158, 02159, 02160, 02162, 02163,

02164, 02178, 02181, 02185, 02188, 02195, 02196, 02202, 02203, 02205, 02216, 02436, 02437, 02444, 02448, 02450, 02451, 02495, 02499, 03165, 03308, 03309, 03508, 03970, 03988, 04009, 04018, 05352, 05372, 05678, 05745, 05762, 06886, 06897, 06919, 11320

Group Selection

01915

Group Therapist/Group Leader

00116, 00119, 00270, 00422, 00423, 00463, 00513, 00530, 00604, 00711, 00718, 00726, 00818, 00897, 00924, 00925, 00949, 01031, 01098, 01106, 01162, 01193, 01245, 01291, 01319, 01320, 01331, 01337, 01368, 01384, 01415, 01526, 01528, 01530, 01531, 01541, 01574, 01583, 01597, 01735, 01762, 01782, 01845, 01849, 01891, 01897, 01900, 02045, 02091, 02133, 02200, 02202, 02219, 02255, 02257, 02259, 02261, 02311, 02317, 02320, 02370, 02462, 02459, 02525, 02545, 02595, 02658, 02728, 02752, 02787, 02789, 02790, 02791, 02793, 02794, 02795, 02801, 02804, 02807, 02824, 02827, 02829, 02864, 02877, 02896, 02932, 02956, 02963, 02985, 03043, 03047, 03048, 03051, 03052, 03063, 03067, 03129, 03179, 03222, 03241, 03244, 03314, 03339, 03347, 03385, 03392, 03428, 03467, 03474, 03488, 03585, 03593, 03595, 03597, 03653, 03698, 03745, 03802, 03840, 03856, 03904, 03974, 04013, 04061, 04135, 04162, 04166, 04247, 04275, 04288, 04289, 04361, 04448, 04452, 04453, 04539, 04577, 04597, 04607, 04631, 04639, 04657, 04662, 04669, 04720, 04827, 04843, 04853, 04873, 04874, 04933, 04945, 04956, 04991, 05006, 05022, 05092, 05105, 05115, 05119, 05161, 05249, 05252, 05286, 05287, 05402, 05403, 05404, 05406, 05489, 05521, 05588, 05592, 05593, 05595, 05598, 05602, 05603, 05618, 05641, 05677, 05695, 05714, 05765, 05776, 05818, 05832, 05834, 05939, 05975, 06040, 06042, 06079, 06098, 06111, 06112, 06115, 06242, 06286, 06346, 06348, 06424, 06429, 06430, 06431, 06457, 06473, 06496, 06507, 06508, 06519, 06528, 06529, 06557, 06614, 06629, 06685, 06731, 06745, 06798, 06834, 06958, 06980, 07075, 07087, 07108, 07110, 07125, 07170, 07177, 07181, 07197, 07249, 07264, 07277, 07308, 07310, 07326, 07354, 07355, 07401, 07458, 07459, 07492, 07521, 07533, 07554, 07556, 07562, 07610, 07686, 07756, 07771, 07787, 07826, 07827, 07924, 07955, 07956, 07959, 07960, 08188, 08243, 08258, 08524, 08548, 08601, 08702, 08711, 08739, 08750, 08785, 08791, 08796, 08797, 08798, 08817, 08853, 08862, 08886, 08933, 08935, 08968, 09059, 09127, 09165, 09171, 09246, 09303, 09355, 09462, 09609, 09710, 09728, 09756, 09782, 09826, 09863, 09884, 09940, 09952, 10039, 10096, 10232, 10241, 10245, 10265, 10273, 10409, 10412, 10416, 10431, 10455, 10466, 10492, 10500, 10504, 10547, 10596, 10643, 10660, 10667, 10691, 10734, 10768, 10788, 10808, 10829, 10838, 10848, 10923, 10925, 10928, 10931, 10982, 10992, 10993, 10998, 11032, 11072, 11076, 11082, 11139, 11163, 11231, 11243, 11315, 11322, 11379, 11401, 11403, 11423, 11449, 11531, 11571, 11612, 11624, 11630, 11691, 11692, 11699, 11707, 11735, 11740, 11750, 11767, 11774, 11780, 11854, 11876, 11883, 11954, 11957, 11971, 12066, 12091, 12114, 12137, 12207, 12211, 12220, 12266, 12273, 12280, 12283, 12289, 12291, 12372, 12384, 12410, 12443, 12454, 12507, 12512, 12527, 12541, 12571, 12614, 12662, 12668, 12729, 12782, 12801, 12826, 12827, 12845, 12873, 12948, 12983, 12985, 13045, 13112, 13113, 13146, 13204, 13296

Group Therapy and Group Process

00051, 00052, 00053, 00054, 00086, 00098, 00131, 00158, 00266, 00294, 00324, 00424, 00468, 00495, 00562, 00589, 00590, 00614, 00615, 00679, 00756, 00758, 00760, 00764, 00765, 00768, 00769, 00770, 00772, 00774, 00776, 00777, 00778, 00790, 00791, 00793, 00800, 00803, 00809, 00812, 00814, 00816, 00827, 00835, 00845, 00934, 00951, 00960, 01003, 01012, 01031, 01037, 01108, 01161, 01211, 01256, 01316, 01324, 01328, 01329,

01303, 01331, 01334, 01385, 01386, 01387, 01389, 01401, 01409, 01412, 01416, 01426, 01432, 01433, 01434, 01435, 01436, 01438, 01439, 01440, 01444, 01446, 01454, 01468, 01469, 01471, 01472, 01473, 01479, 01482, 01484, 01487, 01489, 01496, 01499, 01500, 01503, 01505, 01519, 01521, 01528, 01529, 01531, 01535, 01538, 01541, 01543, 01544, 01546, 01547, 01551, 01555, 01556, 01560, 01563, 01564, 01565, 01567, 01570, 01571, 01572, 01573, 01574, 01575, 01579, 01582, 01586, 01588, 01589, 01590, 01592, 01597, 01600, 01601, 01602, 01605, 01606, 01612, 01613, 01614, 01615, 01616, 01618, 01619, 01621, 01622, 01623, 01626, 01628, 01632, 01637, 01638, 01639, 01640, 01644, 01649, 01650, 01651, 01653, 01654, 01660, 01663, 01664, 01665, 01666, 01668, 01669, 01670, 01671, 01673, 01674, 01676, 01677, 01678, 01682, 01683, 01684, 01685, 01686, 01687, 01691, 01694, 01695, 01696, 01697, 01699, 01700, 01701, 01705, 01706, 01707, 01710, 01715, 01717, 01718, 01720, 01721, 01723, 01724, 01725, 01726, 01728, 01730, 01731, 01732, 01742, 01744, 01745, 01747, 01748, 01749, 01750, 01753, 01754, 01755, 01759, 01764, 01765, 01766, 01767, 01769, 01770, 01779, 01783, 01784, 01785, 01786, 01795, 01801, 01804, 01807, 01811, 01812, 01813, 01816, 01817, 01821, 01822, 01824, 01839, 01840, 01841, 01842, 01843, 01844, 01846, 01847, 01849, 01850, 01851, 01853, 01854, 01855, 01856, 01857, 01858, 01859, 01867, 01868, 01873, 01874, 01884, 01891, 01894, 01898, 01900, 01901, 01910, 01916, 01920, 01922, 01924, 01925, 01927, 01928, 01930, 01931, 01941, 01942, 01945, 01947, 01950, 01954, 01955, 01960, 01971, 01974, 01980, 01999, 02007, 02013, 02014, 02015, 02019, 02032, 02034, 02037, 02042, 02050, 02055, 02057, 02059, 02061, 02065, 02075, 02076, 02077, 02084, 02090, 02101, 02102, 02103, 02106, 02110, 02115, 02119, 02120, 02121, 02126, 02128, 02138, 02142, 02143, 02146, 02147, 02151, 02152, 02153, 02154, 02167, 02168, 02180, 02182, 02183, 02184, 02186, 02187, 02191, 02194, 02199, 02200, 02201, 02207, 02211, 02212, 02213, 02218, 02224, 02225, 02226, 02228, 02230, 02231, 02233, 02234, 02235, 02236, 02237, 02238, 02241, 02242, 02244, 02245, 02248, 02249, 02252, 02256, 02257, 02258, 02261, 02262, 02264, 02268, 02270, 02271, 02274, 02275, 02276, 02281, 02282, 02289, 02293, 02294, 02295, 02296, 02297, 02298, 02299, 02300, 02303, 02304, 02305, 02306, 02307, 02308, 02310, 02311, 02312, 02313, 02314, 02315, 02317, 02318, 02321, 02324, 02327, 02328, 02332, 02333, 02335, 02336, 02337, 02341, 02342, 02345, 02349, 02350, 02351, 02352, 02353, 02354, 02355, 02356, 02358, 02361, 02362, 02363, 02365, 02368, 02369, 02371, 02372, 02373, 02374, 02375, 02376, 02377, 02433, 02434, 02438, 02439, 02441, 02442, 02443, 02446, 02447, 02453, 02454, 02455, 02456, 02459, 02461, 02463, 02465, 02466, 02468, 02469, 02471, 02472, 02473, 02475, 02476, 02478, 02479, 02480, 02482, 02486, 02487, 02492, 02493, 02494, 02517, 02518, 02523, 02527, 02537, 02540, 02565, 02575, 02590, 02613, 02622, 02640, 02653, 02674, 02677, 02691, 02710, 02740, 02741, 02745, 02762, 02792, 02810, 02820, 02832, 02879, 02888, 02891, 02910, 02913, 02930, 02980, 02983, 02991, 03007, 03009, 03012, 03017, 03020, 03026, 03060, 03082, 03108, 03120, 03140, 03165, 03191, 03198, 03199, 03214, 03243, 03258, 03276, 03283, 03352, 03369, 03370, 03374, 03377, 03386, 03389, 03395, 03399, 03411, 03415, 03440, 03442, 03443, 03450, 03453, 03469, 03470, 03477, 03500, 03514, 03540, 03542, 03557, 03578, 03580, 03584, 03587, 03591, 03593, 03609, 03621, 03627, 03632, 03651, 03652, 03655, 03664, 03672, 03681, 03683, 03694, 03706, 03712, 03715, 03716, 03718, 03724, 03732, 03733, 03735, 03756, 03763, 03764, 03769, 03789, 03812, 03814, 03832, 03833, 03841, 03843, 03852, 03853, 03854, 03859, 03873, 03874, 03876, 03877, 03878, 03891, 03900, 03928, 03939, 03962, 03963, 03965, 03967, 03981, 03990, 03991, 03993, 04007, 04019, 04024, 04025, 04032, 04037, 04045, 04054, 04066, 04067, 04073, 04075,

04083, 04084, 04101, 04102, 04103, 04117, 04124, 04126, 04128, 04153, 04167, 04185, 04186, 04191, 04198, 04229, 05107, 04236, 04243, 04251, 04253, 04254, 04260, 04274, 04292, 04318, 04319, 04327, 04378, 04379, 04399, 04412, 04419, 04423, 04425, 04426, 04430, 04442, 04451, 04454, 04459, 04492, 04512, 04517, 04533, 04534, 04559, 04566, 04580, 04614, 04622, 04625, 04626, 04647, 04650, 04654, 04655, 04668, 04676, 04683, 04705, 04737, 04749, 04753, 04769, 04770, 04774, 04782, 04783, 04784, 04786, 04787, 04788, 04793, 04812, 04813, 04833, 04834, 04867, 04895, 04897, 04904, 04914, 04922, 04942, 04958, 04976, 04985, 05021, 05036, 05053, 05075, 05085, 05090, 05125, 05114, 05155, 05157, 05158, 05187, 05212, 05222, 05242, 05258, 05278, 05183, 05208, 05299, 05337, 05339, 05343, 05344, 05353, 05358, 05364, 05374, 05376, 05399, 05430, 05440, 05469, 05471, 05472, 05527, 05534, 05539, 05540, 05541, 05578, 05611, 05615, 05619, 05670, 05722, 05734, 05748, 05762, 05777, 05784, 05788, 05794, 05844, 05862, 05872, 05908, 05926, 05943, 05980, 05981, 05987, 06004, 06071, 06072, 06073, 06115, 06119, 06163, 06164, 06165, 06171, 06180, 06183, 06184, 06185, 06186, 06235, 06252, 06339, 06355, 06376, 06377, 06401, 06404, 06405, 06410, 06524, 06525, 06538, 06575, 06587, 06592, 06625, 06626, 06627, 06641, 06646, 06653, 06655, 06664, 06668, 06674, 06693, 06719, 06725, 06726, 06728, 06735, 06741, 06751, 06777, 06792, 06804, 06806, 06820, 06823, 06824, 06825, 06843, 06904, 06915, 06923, 06972, 06978, 07010, 07012, 07017, 07026, 07028, 07052, 07070, 07089, 07098, 07118, 07145, 07157, 07158, 07207, 07220, 07246, 07287, 07288, 07296, 07304, 07314, 07325, 07327, 07364, 07370, 07373, 07378, 07384, 07395, 07400, 07402, 07416, 07422, 07433, 07443, 07444, 07490, 07511, 07582, 07597, 07604, 07618, 07619, 07629, 07635, 07638, 07658, 07660, 07707, 07709, 07711, 07737, 07756, 07780, 07784, 07900, 07908, 07918, 07919, 07922, 07932, 07971, 07988, 07994, 07995, 07996, 08015, 08032, 08074, 08090, 08091, 08170, 08188, 08197, 08204, 08243, 08270, 08290, 08292, 08331, 08352, 08371, 08408, 08508, 08516, 08521, 08530, 08557, 08558, 08585, 08590, 08595, 08596, 08654, 08659, 08701, 08710, 08738, 08789, 08808, 08811, 08814, 08815, 08842, 08893, 08906, 08999, 09067, 09068, 09075, 09081, 09082, 09102, 09108, 09109, 09135, 09141, 09150, 09165, 09182, 09210, 09221, 09253, 09264, 09269, 09271, 09272, 09274, 09286, 09321, 09336, 09352, 09354, 09356, 09431, 09434, 09437, 09443, 09476, 09477, 09504, 09520, 09539, 09546, 09566, 09567, 09576, 09597, 09607, 09645, 09707, 09727, 09741, 09752, 09754, 09756, 09765, 09783, 09784, 09789, 09833, 09853, 09862, 09865, 09913, 09930, 09931, 09950, 09964, 09965, 09975, 09977, 10003, 10031, 10095, 10099, 10113, 10119, 10134, 10143, 10146, 10169, 10173, 10197, 10244, 10278, 10301, 10302, 10388, 10390, 10413, 10418, 10424, 10443, 10510, 10518, 10529, 10537, 10587, 10603, 10631, 10632, 10633, 10634, 10635, 10637, 10648, 10657, 10693, 10694, 10737, 10787, 10801, 10822, 10835, 10841, 10894, 10897, 10898, 10914, 10920, 10936, 10945, 10960, 10966, 10996, 10999, 11001, 11008, 11023, 11092, 11105, 11128, 11129, 11153, 11167, 11175, 11176, 11246, 11248, 11256, 11268, 11269, 11286, 11289, 11290, 11291, 11292, 11316, 11325, 11339, 11340, 11341, 11342, 11344, 11345, 11346, 11349, 11350, 11401, 11431, 11435, 11451, 11479, 11480, 11481, 11483, 11490, 11509, 11516, 11519, 11520, 11559, 11568, 11571, 11582, 11625, 11658, 11680, 11706, 11726, 11732, 11761, 11829, 11830, 11851, 11862, 11877, 11893, 11903, 11956, 12006, 12013, 12015, 12041, 12065, 12072, 12086, 12098, 12191, 12193, 12224, 12226, 12227, 12237, 12242, 12258, 12265, 12266, 12282, 12377, 12402, 12404, 12419, 12422, 12441, 12447, 12450, 12455, 12456, 12461, 12473, 12476, 12479, 12508, 12521, 12548, 12628, 12629, 12692, 12700, 12718, 12742, 12743, 12795, 12832, 12855, 12856, 12857, 12862, 12872, 12886, 12904, 12917, 12954, 12961, 12965,

12995, 13048, 13078, 13096, 13098, 13133, 13190, 13201, 13242, 13274, 13275
Group Training
02190
Guidance and Counseling
02083

H

High School
04205
History of Group Therapy
00329, 00332, 00543, 00779, 01026, 01247, 01368, 01594, 01596, 01627, 02227, 02239, 02338, 02507, 02681, 02751, 02918, 03004, 03465, 04785, 04798, 05576, 05683, 05730, 06058, 06804, 06812, 06921, 07193, 07387, 08022, 08026, 08345, 08346, 08349, 08365, 08366, 08382, 08738, 09074, 09193, 09452, 09457, 09472, 09509, 09510, 09511, 09729, 09735, 09915, 09990, 09991, 10144, 10687, 10754, 10930, 11295, 11301, 11312, 11317, 11858, 12037, 12374, 12475, 12657
History of Psychodrama
02567, 02904, 08397, 08438, 08459, 08496, 08563, 10820
HRT: Encounter
00062, 00161, 00172, 00277, 00525, 00545, 00546, 00548, 00569, 00573, 00610, 00616, 00682, 00683, 00874, 00878, 00898, 00899, 00961, 00969, 00982, 00990, 00999, 01071, 01116, 01120, 01161, 01191, 01246, 01288, 01294, 01296, 01348, 01349, 01452, 01524, 01619, 01677, 01778, 01799, 02035, 02089, 02094, 02246, 02277, 02283, 02287, 02325, 02366, 02368, 02428, 02432, 02503, 02553, 02621, 02642, 02647, 02654, 02757, 02758, 02759, 02760, 02788, 02793, 02800, 02802, 02808, 02845, 02871, 02895, 02901, 02962, 03074, 03106, 03129, 03166, 03177, 03195, 03222, 03310, 03412, 03433, 03479, 03551, 03575, 03628, 03629, 03630, 03754, 03817, 03862, 03870, 03938, 04314, 04341, 04347, 04364, 04398, 04416, 04480, 04498, 04503, 04583, 04685, 04859, 04891, 04915, 04969, 05019, 05081, 05139, 05248, 05321, 05354, 05362, 05512, 05514, 05579, 05580, 05586, 05604, 05618, 05701, 05766, 05891, 06052, 06135, 06153, 06195, 06287, 06289, 06291, 06304, 06382, 06406, 06475, 06476, 06673, 06718, 06748, 06771, 06807, 06856, 07144, 07148, 07160, 07295, 07343, 07344, 07451, 07454, 07479, 07557, 07562, 07591, 07601, 07602, 07603, 07642, 07692, 07693, 07706, 07721, 07742, 07808, 07826, 07865, 07917, 07995, 07996, 08046, 08054, 08189, 08218, 08219, 08232, 08298, 08324, 08508, 08555, 08690, 08823, 08872, 08933, 09025, 09038, 09052, 09142, 09262, 09325, 09365, 09383, 09552, 09587, 09589, 09692, 09694, 09703, 09730, 09733, 09809, 09830, 09874, 09954, 10007, 10048, 10056, 10086, 10094, 10103, 10104, 10105, 10108, 10109, 10129, 10178, 10184, 10340, 10364, 10370, 10402, 10481, 10555, 10713, 10777, 10782, 10812, 10858, 10899, 10900, 10923, 10925, 10984, 10992, 11206, 11216, 11399, 11224, 11622, 11624, 11647, 11701, 11707, 11713, 11714, 11804, 11815, 11820, 11825, 11826, 11871, 11969, 12016, 12053, 12067, 12119, 12174, 12175, 12209, 12238, 12268, 12330, 12372, 12407, 12423, 12429, 12446, 12527, 12535, 12536, 12593, 12636, 12697, 12698, 12740, 12766, 12786, 12851, 12877, 12889, 13135, 13143, 13152, 13184, 13211
HRT: Group Dynamics
00227, 01282, 01958, 02149, 03140, 04152, 04287, 04309, 05054, 05061, 05205, 05226, 05390, 05527, 05699, 05949, 06994, 08033, 08542, 08614, 09983, 10139, 10334, 11194, 11368, 12478, 13086, 13238

HRT: Marathon
00066, 00290, 00529, 00530, 00533, 00534, 00535, 00536, 00576, 01213, 01256, 01620, 01635, 01871, 01965, 02001, 02023, 02284, 02449, 02488, 02611, 02685, 02768, 02796, 02797, 02798, 02817, 02818, 03087, 03129, 03195, 03311, 03328, 03432, 03641, 03642, 03643, 03644, 03645, 03647, 03648, 03649, 03650, 03781, 03811, 04076, 04112, 04113, 04346, 04400, 04421, 04696, 04697, 04858, 04900, 04921, 05103, 05272, 05284, 05659, 05812, 05906, 05910, 05911, 06279, 06280, 06281, 06283, 06284, 06285, 06287, 06289, 06291, 06305, 06323, 06582, 06866, 06893, 07012, 07038, 07043, 07244, 07693, 07694, 07730, 07823, 07883, 07916, 07941, 08082, 08186, 08220, 08224, 08225, 08226, 08233, 08273, 08555, 08680, 08890, 09025, 09040, 09042, 09043, 09044, 09132, 09133, 09543, 09589, 09692, 09694, 09704, 09733, 09734, 09735, 10298, 10713, 10762, 10872, 10923, 10924, 10925, 10990, 11026, 11184, 11232, 11527, 11713, 11807, 11808, 11815, 11884, 11929, 11950, 12064, 12250, 12299, 12331, 12340, 12646, 12647, 12689, 13105, 13181
HRT: Sensitivity
00095, 00419, 00550, 00556, 00602, 00649, 00905, 01355, 01751, 01895, 01963, 01989, 02028, 02133, 02166, 02204, 02278, 02279, 02291, 02326, 02378, 02380, 02409, 02411, 02477, 02509, 02525, 02548, 02556, 02618, 02649, 02689, 02816, 02880, 03080, 03121, 03135, 03209, 03450, 03676, 03996, 04038, 04149, 04150, 04182, 04201, 04202, 04203, 04314, 04315, 04316, 04317, 04542, 05296, 05381, 05393, 05401, 05514, 05521, 05530, 05531, 05586, 05590, 05591, 05841, 05946, 05958, 06148, 06152, 06154, 06211, 06305, 06413, 06425, 06584, 06699, 06771, 06773, 06775, 06872, 06882, 07115, 07171, 07275, 07343, 07344, 07447, 07448, 07462, 07491, 07676, 07762, 07787, 07969, 07986, 08172, 08256, 08300, 08531, 08532, 08533, 08745, 08820, 08827, 08874, 08922, 09014, 09090, 09190, 09405, 09430, 09473, 09524, 09542, 09543, 09544, 09571, 09788, 09842, 09843, 09844, 09846, 09847, 09885, 09890, 09924, 10114, 10178, 10294, 10297, 10368, 10369, 10479, 10588, 10781, 10926, 11150, 11177, 11201, 11216, 11255, 11389, 11410, 11411, 11412, 11418, 11419, 11622, 11655, 11689, 11690, 11952, 12043, 12059, 12101, 12126, 12162, 12341, 12449, 12525, 12561, 12675, 12676, 12921, 12959, 12966, 13050, 13090, 13126
HRT: T-Groups
00103, 00122, 00269, 00278, 00513, 00514, 00724, 00875, 00952, 00993, 01105, 01162, 01163, 01186, 01274, 01322, 01356, 01358, 01365, 01512, 01863, 01962, 01979, 02064, 02091, 02116, 02193, 02276, 02277, 02278, 02283, 02286, 02288, 02292, 02320, 02525, 02552, 02566, 02794, 02814, 03158, 03159, 03328, 03528, 03753, 03784, 03896, 03911, 03917, 03983, 04246, 04445, 04447, 04540, 04561, 04695, 04898, 04902, 04933, 04998, 05007, 05192, 05367, 05588, 05592, 05593, 05595, 05596, 05598, 05736, 05780, 05781, 05871, 05957, 06076, 06093, 06114, 06131, 06136, 06209, 06230, 06238, 06309, 06324, 06399, 06443, 06496, 06507, 06605, 06636, 06705, 06714, 06857, 07003, 07072, 07116, 07151, 07169, 07244, 07303, 07410, 07449, 07453, 07460, 07461, 07624, 07661, 07808, 07904, 07947, 08029, 08046, 08137, 08156, 08158, 08314, 08532, 08536, 08633, 08743, 08959, 09099, 09262, 09357, 09461, 09612, 09643, 09708, 09756, 09767, 09828, 10001, 10005, 10067, 10093, 10121, 10140, 10316, 10317, 10321, 10383, 10500, 10525, 10543, 10556, 10559, 10818, 11243, 11404, 11413, 11420, 11421, 11651, 11766, 11832, 12249, 12373, 12618, 12757, 12784, 12785, 12952, 12953, 13229, 13291
HRT: Other
00089, 00094, 00106, 00107, 00160, 00173, 00182, 00196, 00202, 00265, 00298, 00299, 00327, 00333, 00334, 00346, 00355, 00363, 00382, 00387, 00421, 00428, 00466, 00476, 00487, 00547, 00594, 00619, 00678, 00680,

00681, 00695, 00868, 00937, 01112, 01250, 01327, 01376, 01377, 01388, 01408, 01414, 01457, 01485, 01494, 01506, 01515, 01583, 01587, 01612, 01646, 01652, 01662, 01740, 01753, 01838, 01894, 01961, 01984, 02025, 02104, 02117, 02118, 02146, 02148, 02171, 02173, 02227, 02302, 02415, 02423, 02425, 02457, 02706, 03036, 03037, 03225, 03329, 03350, 03375, 03480, 03516, 03605, 03608, 03619, 03635, 03636, 03637, 03638, 03639, 03640, 03788, 04085, 04456, 04481, 04819, 04908, 04909, 04936, 04982, 05001, 05037, 05311, 05312, 05313, 05369, 05457, 05481, 05565, 05733, 05756, 05763, 05868, 05934, 06005, 06071, 06290, 06438, 06533, 06650, 06704, 06980, 06998, 07046, 07060, 07155, 07285, 07405, 07412, 07455 07741, 07891, 07921, 07966, 07978, 08045, 08121, 08206, 08316, 08547, 08548, 08554, 08565, 08608, 08777, 08784, 08875, 08878, 08883, 08955, 08956, 09106, 09330, 09358, 09531, 09537, 09552, 09564, 09583, 09610, 09658, 09690, 09714, 09958, 10022, 10028, 10029, 10061, 10068, 10087, 10122, 10220, 10329, 10403, 10404, 10775, 10985 11077, 11124, 11387, 11440, 11473, 11626, 11632, 11892, 12056, 12052, 12121, 12219, 12271, 12365, 12445, 12563, 12868, 12920, 13255

Hypno Drama
01633

Hypnosis
00137, 00140, 00141, 00142, 00362, 00879, 01315, 01316, 01655, 02746, 03686, 03793, 03915, 04410, 04521, 04544, 04922, 05023, 05689, 06420, 06600, 06617, 06675, 07348, 07442, 07999, 08177, 08385, 08467, 08708, 08709, 09030, 09056, 09257, 10156, 10184, 10515, 10516, 10880, 10937, 10955, 11206, 11500, 11627, 11939

I

Individual and Group Counseling
07852, 08718

Individual and Group Therapy
00022, 00102, 00275, 00328, 00411, 00415, 00416, 00417, 00425, 00465, 00566, 00623, 00706, 00762, 00786, 00794, 00805, 00808, 00810, 00811, 00824, 01005, 01016, 01124, 01126, 01130, 01155, 01165, 01168, 01169, 01266, 01428, 01611, 01688, 01761, 0200, 02053, 02080, 02165, 02272, 02329, 02340, 02359, 02458, 02578, 02698, 02714, 02854, 02882, 02893, 02894, 02989, 03022, 03054, 03086, 03097, 03133, 03150, 03180, 03181, 03246, 03303, 03363, 03468, 03509, 03510, 03538, 03607, 03738, 03808, 03827, 03828, 038330, 03894, 03907, 03936, 04060, 04290, 04293, 04462, 04504, 04516, 04518, 04692, 04727, 04803, 04814, 04815, 04823, 04934, 04957, 05058, 05060, 05072, 05156, 05220, 05241, 05245, 05250, 05259, 05181, 05331, 05371, 05377, 05391, 05394, 05538, 05544, 05585, 05636, 05744, 05746, 05869, 05876, 06064, 06077, 06118, 06204, 06364, 06366, 06407, 06550, 06566, 06656, 06692, 06701, 06707, 06734, 06756, 06763, 06910, 07025, 07063, 07113, 07142, 07242, 07265, 07266, 07351, 07419, 07640, 07880, 08019, 08028, 08030, 08076, 08146, 08163, 08191, 08230, 08319, 08527, 08544, 08692, 08701, 08727, 08847, 08861, 08894, 08904, 08948, 08949, 09079, 09080, 09085, 09194, 09275, 09282, 09338, 09450, 09490, 09550, 09575, 09655, 09712, 09761, 09780, 09792, 09870, 09925, 09935, 09984, 10008, 10091, 10185, 10249, 10276, 10280, 10306, 10313, 10409, 10463, 10467, 10468, 10469, 10613, 10614, 10631, 10632, 10653, 10738, 10742, 10806, 10836, 10845, 10876, 10895, 10934, 10970, 10991, 11004, 11009, 11018, 11041, 11067, 11074, 11083, 11084, 11130, 11138, 11145, 11203, 11389, 11422, 11494, 11671, 11755, 11778, 11834, 11842, 11860, 11882, 11928, 11975, 11980, 11986, 12066, 12103, 12110, 12151,

12177, 12178, 12239, 12322, 12382, 12386, 12484, 12544, 12587, 12621, 12622, 12665, 12805, 12841, 12916, 12948, 12993, 13025, 13027, 13031, 13076, 13157, 13161, 13162, 13174, 13183, 13206, 13217, 13247, 13293
Industrial Applications
01280, 01353, 01355, 01373, 01388, 01399, 01430, 01458, 01486, 01514, 01545, 01697, 01863, 01974, 02048, 02280, 02282, 02348, 03335, 03762, 03804, 03938, 03964, 04089, 04181, 04413, 05069, 06411, 06412, 06472, 06872, 06873, 06874, 06875, 06910, 07446, 07570, 07805, 08061, 08588, 08788, 08957, 09284, 09359, 09363, 09359, 09405, 10131, 10213, 10721, 11001, 11030, 11141, 11156, 11459, 11545, 11546, 11548, 11652, 12130, 12182, 12354, 12836, 12921
Infants
01643
Infertility
00006
Inpatient
00020, 00058, 00096, 00150, 00152, 00187, 00194, 00213, 00310, 00361, 00420, 00456, 00570, 00581, 00601, 00613, 00653, 00666, 00702, 00780, 00784, 00887, 00942, 00964, 00972, 00984, 01004, 01102, 01105, 01182, 01185, 01217, 01253, 01265, 01314, 01323, 01345, 01390, 01392, 01402, 01437, 01478, 01501, 01548, 01584, 01590, 01604, 01650, 01651, 01683, 01684, 01698, 01702, 01727, 01743, 01783, 01807, 01823, 01856, 01859, 01873, 01874, 01875, 01877, 01878, 01881, 01884, 01900, 01904, 01944, 01947, 01991, 02003, 02004, 02039, 02041, 02057, 02062, 02095, 02128, 02149, 02154, 02158, 02167, 02178, 02237, 02244, 02250, 02273, 02466, 02468, 02551, 02640, 02806, 02844, 02902, 02971, 03013, 03066, 03067, 03075, 03079, 03095, 03108, 03200, 03282, 03331, 03332, 03455, 03500, 03523, 03617, 03948, 04123, 04154, 04279, 04322, 04357, 04377, 04443, 04749, 04940, 05017, 05063, 05131, 05310, 05357, 05448, 05522, 05762, 05797, 06033, 06034, 06233, 06255, 06276, 06315, 06403, 06556, 06621, 06768, 06813, 06814, 06829, 06837, 06848, 06902, 06936, 07011, 07037, 07069, 07075, 07202, 07203, 07234, 07236, 07250, 07254, 07350, 07357, 07425, 07536, 07821, 07822, 07888, 08072, 08502, 08583, 08592, 08678, 08888, 08983, 08994, 08997, 09071, 09130, 09206, 09210, 09226, 09247, 09327, 09377, 09428, 09432, 09508, 09515, 09551, 09565, 09569, 09570, 09610, 09724, 09746, 09834, 09944, 09969, 10018, 10092, 10116, 10150, 10206, 10209, 10220, 10283, 10298, 10320, 10353, 10374, 10387, 10399, 10421, 10440, 10448, 10461, 10485, 10527, 10605, 10647, 10743, 10773, 10860, 10935, 11058, 11090, 11127, 11133, 11147, 11148, 11173, 11181, 11186, 11207, 11227, 11355, 11358, 11364, 11463, 11475, 11661, 11678, 11766, 11805, 11806, 11906
Interpersonal Relationships
00143, 00841, 00954, 01045, 01076, 01425, 01642, 01838, 01870, 01944, 01957, 02037, 02090, 02173, 02175, 02183, 02275, 02296, 02450, 02476, 02554, 02555, 02589, 02671, 02812, 02878, 02927, 03026, 03093, 03135, 03138, 03187, 03503, 03587, 03588, 04273, 04359, 04364, 04440, 04494, 04565, 04856, 04893, 05027, 05207, 05236, 05310, 05459, 05599, 05921, 06067, 06142, 06144, 06176, 06190, 06216, 06227, 06230, 06256, 06310, 06313, 06338, 06393, 06440, 06473, 06487, 06588, 06634, 06762, 06772, 06820, 06855, 06910, 06912, 07056, 07059, 07115, 07170, 07188, 07199, 07201, 07270, 07356, 07357, 07432, 07437, 07457, 07458, 07459, 07502, 07579, 07595, 07631, 07769, 07779, 07803, 07844, 07957, 07960, 07976, 08129, 08168, 08312, 08390, 08391, 08416, 08513, 08632, 08702, 09016, 09050, 09059, 09136, 09140, 09146, 09182, 09245, 09255, 09267, 09367, 09428, 09516, 09698, 09832, 09843, 09895, 09544, 10010, 10016, 10083, 10175, 10207, 10335, 10434, 10591, 10671, 10672, 10708, 10777, 10818,

10878, 10968, 11023, 11195, 11336, 11425, 11597, 11622, 11728, 11729, 11772, 11839, 11875, 11979, 12158, 12340, 12433, 12452, 12467, 12468, 12493, 12629, 12697, 12773, 12828, 12858, 12879, 13049, 13251

L

Large Groups
00033, 00336, 01547, 01711, 02480, 04534, 06908, 07120, 07340, 07581, 08260, 10367, 10669, 11242, 11595, 12233, 12317, 12570, 12897
Leaderless Group
03247, 09009, 10908
Leaderless Method
00096, 00312, 00451, 00621, 00676, 00859, 01117, 01119, 01122, 01123, 01231, 01463, 01478, 01486, 01541, 01581, 01588, 01752, 01825, 01871, 02039, 02192, 02255, 02259, 02260, 02261, 02270, 02487, 02553, 02614, 02615, 02679, 02737, 02868, 02958, 03290, 03350, 03371, 03409, 03748, 03823, 03909, 03961, 04138, 04244, 04385, 04558, 05024, 05191, 05217, 05406, 05418, 05443, 05465, 05576, 05604, 05608, 05609, 05721, 05804, 05843, 06104, 06105, 06106, 06117, 06312, 06394, 06418, 06419, 06665, 06724, 06980, 07026, 07089, 07154, 07189, 07317, 07383, 07387, 07388, 07420, 07617, 08217, 08703, 08803, 08876, 09020, 09367, 09388, 09389, 09432, 09500, 09663, 09664, 10020, 10049, 10063, 10226, 10492, 10928, 10929, 10930, 10931, 11442, 11735, 12051, 12261, 12420, 12522, 12726, 12732, 13074, 13120
Leadership Method
00033
Letter Writing
06607, 06608
Literature Review
00495, 01074, 01765, 01943, 02277, 02480, 02737, 02818, 03699, 04184, 04770, 05963, 06287, 07008, 07070, 07114, 07263, 07312, 07409, 07413, 07414, 07415, 10288, 10304, 10342, 10929, 10947, 11176, 11267, 12123, 12709, 13088

M

Medication
00060, 00771, 00824, 00826, 00829, 00917, 01185, 01351, 01407, 01448, 01832, 02574, 02708, 02854, 02883, 03089, 03130, 03315, 03359, 03786, 03855, 04424, 04515, 04818, 05072, 05427, 05790, 06078, 06308, 06677, 06840, 06847, 06851, 07253, 07334, 07362, 07598, 08473, 08525, 09225, 09232, 09233, 09234, 09236, 09326, 09585, 09740, 10208, 10521, 10523, 10558, 10612, 10659, 10784, 11162, 11537, 11573, 12087, 12093, 12714, 12758, 12870
Mental Deficiency
00010, 00057, 00212, 00248, 00353, 00455, 00476, 01007, 01429, 01698, 02055, 02165, 02211, 02705, 02736, 02777, 03348, 03363, 03486, 03534, 04106, 04108, 04390, 04429, 04551, 04702, 05450, 05566, 05567, 05568, 05638, 05783, 06019, 06045, 06130, 06402, 06629, 06791, 06942, 06947, 06982, 06983, 07038, 07107, 07111, 07254, 07305, 07320, 07618, 07619, 07780, 07806, 07907, 08016, 08111, 08119, 08504, 08514, 08523, 08651, 08681, 08687, 08724, 08813, 08841, 08852, 09070, 09240, 09241, 09435, 09561, 09753, 09763, 09779, 09951, 09962, 10009, 10071, 10075, 10181, 10330, 10552, 10766, 10932, 11061, 11134, 11135, 11233, 11360, 11737,

11739, 11740, 11846, 11864, 11900, 11902, 11927, 12020, 12021, 12022, 12375, 12670, 12764, 12822, 12912, 13068, 13096, 13212, 13280
Mental Hospitals
00026, 00104, 00309, 00310, 00780, 00782, 00783, 01392, 01402, 01423, 01473, 01476, 01477, 01491, 01522, 01548, 01551, 01572, 01590, 01651, 01657, 01667, 01725, 01763, 01825, 01856, 01900, 01906, 01944, 01991, 01994, 02015, 02030, 02041, 02082, 02156, 02173, 02178, 02196, 02226, 02237, 02295, 02297, 02360, 02439, 02445, 02454, 02487, 02568, 02646, 02647, 02661, 02662, 02734, 02884, 03046, 03120, 03177, 03261, 03385, 03502, 03531, 03559, 03560, 03563, 03614, 03725, 03796, 03820, 03884, 03951, 04002, 04012, 04096, 04105, 04107, 04154, 04183, 04224, 04245, 04255, 04257, 04383, 04433, 04441, 04472, 04496, 04504, 04587, 04602, 04704, 04750, 04756, 04791, 04792, 04811, 04839, 04845, 04880, 04881, 04960, 04983, 05005, 05085, 05172, 05221, 05318, 05322, 05487, 05520, 05755, 05798, 05820, 05836, 05928, 05932, 06151, 06170, 06200, 06223, 06271, 06308, 06337, 06353, 06356, 06368, 06374, 06398, 06421, 06650, 06681, 06832, 06846, 06881, 06884, 06965, 07136, 07197, 07464, 07472, 07499, 07621, 07696, 07697, 07716, 07732, 07888, 07979, 07980, 08174, 08399, 08645, 08800, 08835, 08937, 08996, 09036, 09061, 09069, 09152, 09156, 09157, 09172, 09174, 09212, 09250, 09305, 09538, 09563, 09606, 09610, 09641, 09654, 09787, 09877, 09878, 09887, 09992, 10044, 10123, 10304, 10328 10356, 10361, 10363, 10389, 10607, 10617, 10736, 10745, 10776, 10909, 10922, 10944, 11225, 11226, 11453, 11561, 11572, 11653, 11663, 11844, 11912, 12073, 12098, 12489, 12588, 12589, 12590, 12720, 12751, 12764, 12870, 12891, 12892, 12894, 13034, 13036, 13037, 13038, 13052, 13081, 13111, (*See also:* Psychoses)
Mental Hygiene
01404, 01550, 01578, 01589, 01656, 01897, 02005, 02067, 02087, 02304, 02561, 02572, 02603, 02730, 02766, 02917, 02929, 03272, 03291, 03292, 03323, 03429, 03714, 03783, 03800, 03825, 03888, 04014, 04015, 04511, 04651, 05298, 05334, 05439, 05536, 05660, 06107, 06391, 06527, 06542, 06624, 06898, 06945, 06946, 07045, 07228, 07269, 07291, 07397, 07948, 08130, 09265, 09273, 09274, 09385, 10464, 10646, 10649, 10655, 10669, 10670, 10761, 10823, 10976, 11007, 11024, 11043, 11093, 11149, 11198, 11263, 11287, 11326, 11524, 11644, 11711, 11850, 12178, 12465, 12649, 12962, 13046, 13216
Mental Retardation
00356, 00627, 01170, 01200, 01259, 01301, 01340, 03274, 03484, 03511, 04293, 04333, 04992, 05625, 07648, 10153, 10401, 10444, 10731, 12180, 12700
Milieu Therapy
00032, 00033, 00065, 00190, 00191, 00192, 00224, 00242, 00430, 00479, 00511, 00613, 00714, 00728, 00760, 00774, 00854, 01001, 01002, 01284, 01423, 01711, 02021, 02095, 02114, 02232, 02240, 02308, 02464, 02508, 02696, 02747, 03173, 03523, 03552, 03614, 04047, 04245, 04378, 04443, 04483, 04588, 04598, 04741, 04860, 04989, 05085, 05302, 05316, 05328, 05486, 05838, 05931, 06258, 06349, 06350, 06368, 06435, 06602, 06627, 06727, 07069, 07104, 07702, 07845, 08512, 08528, 08812, 08993, 08995, 09144, 09547, 09808, 09860, 09886, 10014, 10082, 10715, 10828, 11055, 11205, 11309, 11515, 11574, 11645, 11710, 12311, 12362, 12393, 12787, 13227, 13278
Military Applications
00151, 00698, 01002, 01053, 01156, 01233, 01262, 01264, 01376, 01575, 01978, 02185, 02187, 02212, 02264, 02564, 02942, 02990, 03045, 03089, 03107, 03330, 03331, 03332, 03333, 03594, 03656, 03720, 03755, 03811, 03882, 03883, 03884, 04477, 04513, 04621, 04800, 04882, 04883, 05032,

05548, 05674, 05813, 05965, 06033, 06423, 06850, 07228, 07269, 07670, 08549, 08666, 08822, 09181, 09216, 09254, 09283, 09335, 09532, 09619, 09658, 09893, 10041, 10070, 10145, 10539, 10850, 10989, 11006, 11007, 11014, 11102, 11118, 11182, 11187, 11945, 12070, 12087, 12109, 12121, 12122, 12225, 12320, 12370, 12483, 12552, 12653, 12701, 12875, 13026, 13039, 13234

Minority Issues: Low Income
00404, 00465, 00661, 00984, 01470, 01977, 02128, 02986, 05222, 09596, 09894, 10148, 11982, 13005

Minority Issues: Sex
01773, 01905, 02535, 02658, 02670, 02678, 03061, 03129, 03179, 03441, 03577, 03595, 03829, 04022, 04533, 04848, 05036, 05314, 06843, 06944, 07124, 07271, 07816, 09513, 09906, 11630, 11833, 12545

Minority Issues: Other
00082, 00233, 00956, 01078, 01195, 01198, 01326, 01495, 01659, 01744, 02088, 02808, 03761, 03885, 08447, 09278, 10384, 11492

Minority Issues: Race and Ethnic
00102, 00285, 00322, 00717, 01120, 01567, 01568, 01943, 01946, 01947, 02063, 02091, 02293, 02482, 02587, 02588, 02610, 02988, 03403, 03405, 03622, 03910, 03982, 04119, 04204, 04205, 04226, 04533, 04888, 04891, 04898, 05014, 05115, 05119, 05320, 05330, 05350, 05498, 05802, 05813, 06158, 06260, 06393, 06444, 06480, 06572, 06596, 06609, 06610, 06747, 06779, 06802, 07001, 07004, 07075, 07285, 07295, 07336, 07550, 07579, 07595, 07747, 07970, 08073, 08122, 08266, 08324, 08660, 08723, 08834, 08987, 08990, 09042, 09192, 09238, 09248, 09424, 09469, 09573, 09685, 09854, 09855, 09949, 09953, 10030, 10110, 10205, 10371, 10375, 10380, 10520, 10721, 10761, 10916, 11107, 11146, 11183, 11214, 11323, 11409, 11441, 11648, 11654, 11654, 11899, 11955, 11981, 11982, 11984, 12166, 12169, 12195, 12363, 12513, 12536, 12691, 12733, 12756, 12782, 12851, 12884, 12926, 12977, 13065, 13083, 13184, 13197, 13216

Multiple Therapy
02932, 03046, 03556, 03936, 04070, 04832, 05874, 07381, 08141, 08619, 08851, 10024, 10851, 11565, 12245, 12588, 12885

Music, Music Therapy
07949, 08656, 08741, 08782

Music
00208, 00212, 00865, 01269, 01389, 01795, 01943, 02773, 03707, 03966, 03968, 03969, 04048, 04206, 04754, 05130, 05302, 05651, 05661, 05953, 06478, 06484, 06485, 06486, 06964, 07172, 07418, 08244, 08257, 08428, 08676, 09426, 09904, 10157, 10381, 10735, 10750, 10798, 11022, 11621, 11837, 11871, 11977, 12076, 12104, 12380, 12580, 12792, 12890, 12946, 13208

N

Narcotics
01003, 05078 (*See also:* Drugs)

Neuroses
00002, 00003, 00009, 00176, 00336, 00635, 01267, 01406, 01475, 01484, 01535, 01639, 01847, 01856, 01858, 01864, 01947, 01990, 02034, 02358, 02434, 02623, 02966, 02990, 03032, 03282, 03390, 03423, 03656, 03879, 03882, 03883, 03935, 03946, 03955, 03968, 04116, 04267, 04362, 04406, 04635, 04636, 04683, 04749, 04750, 04789, 04800, 04805, 04841, 05065, 05256, 05281, 05145, 05320, 05352, 05550, 05629, 05789, 05924, 05925, 05941, 05969, 06094, 06167, 06452, 06453, 06454, 06572, 06631, 06661,

06662, 06754, 06755, 06758, 06787, 06819, 06840, 06841, 06842, 06948, 07224, 07253, 07345, 07386, 07468, 07580, 07733, 07845, 08012, 08076, 08093, 08101, 08246, 08428, 08571, 08584, 08782, 08926, 09031, 09032, 09085, 09180, 09244, 09527, 09601, 09633, 09638, 09639, 09651, 09838, 09839, 10055, 1022, 10426, 10496, 10527, 10608, 10684, 10685, 10825, 10826, 10839, 10850, 10904, 10979, 11102, 11182, 11187, 11294, 11313, 11517, 11518, 11621, 11694, 11715, 11855, 11958, 12369, 12391, 13075

Night Hospital
07507

Non-directive Group Therapy
00030, 00187, 01374, 01466, 03451, 03570, 04389, 04428, 04430, 05337, 05490, 06589, 06799, 06899, 06918, 07202, 07203, 08522, 09048, 09049, 09322, 09323, 09324, 09806, 11052, 12091 (*See also:* Client-centered Group Therapy)

Nursing
00049, 00222, 00272, 00276, 00300, 00481, 00570, 00792, 00887, 00888, 01081, 01610, 01649, 01658, 01719, 01720, 01735, 01888, 01908, 01912, 01939, 02042, 02110, 02156, 02197, 02213, 02319, 02481, 02498, 02502, 02526, 02529, 02627, 02641, 02697, 02776, 02785, 02803, 02838, 02840, 02853, 02945, 02976, 02993, 03036, 03053, 03073, 03280, 03304, 03313, 03383, 03545, 03631, 03751, 03985, 04000, 04001, 04031, 04087, 04137, 04156, 04240, 04289, 04292, 04437, 04456, 04553, 04847, 04858, 04863, 04954, 05110, 05116, 05128, 05204, 05228, 05242, 05302, 05382, 05408, 05464, 05497, 05512, 05635, 05900, 05936, 05946, 06018, 06299, 06329, 06598, 06697, 06753, 06766, 06808, 06880, 06956, 06957, 06959, 07022, 07061, 07083, 07199, 07201, 07335, 07475, 07536, 07708, 07954, 07961, 08039, 08095, 08135, 08291, 08304, 08306, 08326, 08511, 08558, 08567, 08745, 08793, 08828, 08836, 08905, 08959, 09003, 09065, 09130, 09144, 09170, 09243, 09379, 09425, 09592, 09684, 09858, 09876, 09917, 09948, 09979, 10148, 10219, 10220, 10359, 10399, 10770, 10885, 10982, 11069, 11115, 11158, 11166, 11167, 11230, 11356, 11380, 11404, 11513, 11563, 11566, 11606, 11684, 11748, 11759, 12147, 12177, 12301, 12308, 12344, 12384, 12395, 12428, 12466, 12597, 12632, 12736, 12765, 12793, 12862, 12941, 13045, 13163, 13199

O

Obesity
00031, 00138, 00359, 00434, 00580, 00593, 00911, 01270, 01315, 01316, 01446, 01520, 01669, 01704, 01935, 01936, 02017, 02224, 02329, 02331, 02883, 03454, 03550, 03590, 04388, 04478, 04479, 04590, 04594, 04702, 04824, 04825, 04892, 04922, 05039, 05040, 05246, 054113, 05442, 05462, 06001, 06064, 06232, 06534, 06545, 06552, 06560, 06567, 06568, 06681, 06861, 07212, 07345, 07572, 07856, 07857, 08013, 08672, 08722, 09058, 09239, 09242, 09797, 10120, 10725, 10834, 10869, 10871, 11185, 11236, 11354, 11445, 11623, 11870, 11920, 12522, 12557, 13057, 13058, 13059, 13198

Observers and Observation
00216, 00994, 01347, 01926, 02538, 02992, 03461, 03634, 04300, 04723, 05376, 06011, 06236, 06611, 06670, 07738, 08466, 08711, 08923, 09443, 09467, 09487, 09663, 11114, 11164, 11696, 11827, 12063, 12456, 12554, 12815, 12904, 12925, 13067, 13223

Occupational Therapy
00247, 00519, 00653, 00930, 01367, 02251, 02619, 02671, 03849, 04136, 04347, 04355, 04483, 05400, 05424, 05503, 05508, 05835, 06845, 07216,

07466, 07551, 07559, 07843, 08072, 09286, 09588, 09774, 09889, 09971, 10330, 10542, 12738

Orientation and Structure

00815, 01201, 01606, 02246, 02250, 02318, 02511, 02513, 02702, 03057, 03286, 03483, 04033, 04057, 04379, 04394, 04495, 04526, 04597, 04606, 04718, 04723, 04778, 04860, 04913, 04971, 05144, 05174, 05184, 05185, 05358, 05384, 05454, 05762, 05788, 05795, 06303, 06477, 06517, 06638, 06713, 06797, 06868, 07229, 07426, 08010, 08090, 08105, 08159, 08254, 09476, 09721, 09961, 10500, 10524, 10751, 10829, 10830, 10995, 11044, 11112, 11174, 11367, 11960, 12101, 12454, 12553, 12711, 12740, 12901, 12923, 13158, 13267

Outpatient

00168, 00184, 00337, 00440, 00561, 00582, 00817, 00943, 00949, 00959, 01004, 01302, 01361, 01362, 01380, 01491, 01533, 01675, 01746, 01748, 01749, 01750, 01760, 01801, 01909, 02068, 02241, 02469, 02576, 02626, 02688, 02716, 02770, 02832, 02852, 02866, 02975, 03089, 03178, 03246, 03326, 03610, 03706, 03721, 03727, 04044, 04145, 04556, 04831, 04840, 04944, 04987, 05095, 05096, 05326, 05662, 05686, 05900, 05967, 06021, 06294, 06295, 06336, 06338, 06444, 06445, 06505, 06621, 06689, 06958, 07162, 07174, 07175, 07176, 07247, 07248, 07253, 07345, 07481, 07620, 07784, 07870, 07871, 07872, 07873, 07874, 07875, 07876, 07877, 07878, 08107, 08136, 08154,08201, 08243, 08520, 08540, 08685, 08707, 08804, 08943, 09019, 09024, 09073, 09095, 09128, 09225, 09247, 09340, 09458, 09481, 09508, 09536, 09666, 09750, 09810, 09838, 09919, 10148, 10229, 10372, 10522, 10531, 10664, 10665, 10868, 10880, 10907, 11042, 11213, 11467, 11521, 11539, 11674, 11709, 11873, 11906, 11953, 11964, 12039, 12205, 12284, 12486, 12572, 12724, 12837, 12932, 13077, 13259

Overview

09057, 09204, 09336, 09106, 09137, 11535, 12132

P

Pain

03304, 04292, 04436, 08753

Paraprofessionals

00116, 00889, 01105, 01209, 01358, 01740, 02555, 02561, 03062, 03063, 03247, 03860, 04278, 04452, 04493, 04567, 04675, 04699, 05033, 05168, 05277, 05080, 05305, 05502, 05708, 05719, 05991, 06018, 06123, 06124, 06219, 06220, 06558, 06579, 06906, 06940, 07451, 07478, 07483, 07503, 07612, 07675, 07881, 07950, 07964, 08067, 08188, 08245, 08264, 08291, 08593, 08602, 08764, 08822, 09172, 09173, 09204, 09787, 09995, 10198, 10291, 10568, 10569, 10832, 11085, 11148, 11155, 11231, 11539, 11756, 11801, 11999, 12103, 12106, 12115, 12199, 12307, 12406, 12435, 12436, 12507, 12513, 12641, 12854, 13046

Parents

00029, 00038, 00039, 00041, 00051, 00052, 00053, 00055, 00056, 00101, 00125, 00229, 00250, 00295, 00296, 00301, 00356, 00359, 00407, 00464, 00469, 00470, 00472, 00482, 00490, 00510, 00520, 00558, 00617, 00641, 00659, 00677, 00850, 00856, 00860, 00882, 00885, 00967, 00968, 01000, 01006, 01048, 01066, 01134, 01154, 01164, 01171, 01187, 01188, 01190, 01195, 01204, 01254, 01301, 01303, 01357, 01361, 01579, 01605, 01617, 01638, 01706, 01707, 01831, 01834, 01835, 01885, 01896, 01937, 01970, 01998, 02026, 02085, 02119, 02126, 02136, 02139, 02205, 02208, 02211, 02233, 02266, 02295, 02443, 02460, 02465, 02493, 02506, 02550, 02558, 02593, 02612, 02626, 02629, 02638, 02639, 02694, 02718, 02744, 02755,

02756, 02823, 02824, 02870, 02905, 02972, 03009, 03010, 03011, 03014, 03023, 03050, 03081, 03132, 03152, 03184, 03230, 03233, 03270, 03271, 03306, 03348, 03381, 03387, 03416, 03492, 03511, 03521, 03539, 03576, 03633, 03790, 03866, 03940, 03941, 03947, 03954, 04035, 04039, 04125, 04130, 04145, 04192, 04215, 04217, 04271, 04276, 04281, 04294, 04295, 04301, 04355, 04356, 04446, 04449, 04508, 04511, 04552, 04562, 04670, 04683, 04904, 04906, 04959, 05067, 05097, 05104, 05137, 05173, 05180, 05190, 05195, 05223, 05307, 05317, 05364, 05375, 05389, 05398, 05451, 05506, 05513, 05574, 05607, 05642, 05711, 05713, 05778, 05815, 05830, 05894, 05920, 05948, 05967, 05973, 05990, 06002, 06010, 06046, 06090, 06169, 06173, 06241, 06321, 06488, 06494, 06501, 06536, 06543, 06544, 06679, 06709, 06739, 06765, 06795, 06803, 06838, 06860, 06931, 06963, 06977, 06991, 07054, 07107, 07111, 07213, 07234, 07300, 07320, 07340, 07346, 07391, 07394, 07618, 07619, 07685, 07752, 07766, 07800, 07811, 07836, 07867, 07868, 07903, 07945, 07981, 07985, 07991, 08083, 08094, 08125, 08153, 08199, 08202, 08262, 08267, 08281, 08288, 08488, 08568, 08630, 08642, 08651, 08666, 08687, 08725, 08732, 08744, 08746, 08763, 08776, 08802, 08805, 08841, 08844, 08852, 08913, 09062, 09072, 09175, 09213, 09220, 09222, 09275, 09279, 09328, 09329, 09349, 09350, 09351, 09415, 09416, 09419, 09478, 09597, 09609, 09659, 09686, 09753, 09763, 09779, 09782, 09807, 09815, 09901, 09943, 10013, 10033, 10057, 10061, 10075, 10079, 10153, 10161, 10168, 10173, 10221, 10232, 1024o, 10266, 10324, 10352, 10353, 10361, 10428, 10459, 10478, 10533, 10534, 10535, 10540, 10566, 10583, 10584, 10586, 10595, 10640, 10670, 10705, 10724, 10785, 10965, 10982, 10998, 10999, 11015, 11025, 11086, 11117, 11132, 11134, 11135, 11145, 11211, 11381, 11528, 11572, 11590, 11612, 11716, 11738, 11740, 11747, 11776, 11817, 11840, 11852, 11865, 11869, 11924, 11927, 11935, 11962, 11972, 12012, 12018, 12020, 12021, 12033, 12049, 12057, 12176, 12224, 12229, 12252, 12427, 12523, 12524, 12619, 12620, 12631, 12670, 12745, 12755, 12789, 12906, 12928, 12930, 12934, 12935, 12989, 12990, 13025, 13091, 13092, 13104, 13118, 13122, 13141, 13212, 13221, 13301

Peer Group

02214

Perception

01121, 01159, 01205, 01319, 01332, 01334, 01801, 02209, 02541, 02778, 02871, 02974, 03294, 03788, 04526, 04717, 05181, 05599, 05818, 06775, 07039, 07059, 07119, 07257, 07431, 07489, 07863, 08034, 08040, 08524, 08986, 09469, 09516, 09520, 09928, 09956, 10212, 10350, 10383, 10416, 10441, 10442, 10617, 10898, 10953, 10992, 11053, 11085, 11188, 11379, 11774, 12059, 12322, 12340, 12526, 12555, 12568, 13104, 13186

Personality Factors, Traits

00036, 00145, 00292, 00486, 00551, 00585, 00906, 01578, 01631, 01648, 01875, 01877, 01903, 02016, 02024, 02064, 02120, 02275, 02596, 02880, 02953, 03002, 03047, 03383, 03443, 03574, 04321, 04401, 05081, 05761, 05866, 05936, 05947, 06074, 06163, 06166, 06172, 06211, 06282, 06285, 06365, 06405, 06414, 06425, 06464, 06467, 06493, 06718, 06914, 06953, 07389, 07511, 07521, 07548, 07650, 07728, 07742, 07787, 07807, 07808, 07831, 07958, 07959, 07966, 08004, 08017, 08172, 08255, 08256, 08270, 08298, 08299, 08304, 08314, 08509, 08553, 08657, 08767, 08849, 08902, 08922, 08989

Personality Factors

09089, 09102, 09239, 09362, 09584, 09783, 09794, 09819, 09895, 10006, 10432, 10601, 10661, 10716, 10981, 10994, 11124, 11243, 11314, 11315, 11382, 11568, 11593, 11614, 11718, 11728, 11764, 12107, 12112, 12209, 12280, 12431, 12477, 12499, 12521, 12529, 12757, 12878, 12895, 12985, 12986, 13181, 13255

Phobias
00138 00201, 00413, 00620, 00624, 00664, 01752, 01782, 01843, 01902, 01931, 02183, 02184, 02271, 02306, 02441, 02475, 02476, 02477, 02633, 03192, 04090, 04091, 04818, 04910, 04911, 04912, 06632, 06717, 07002, 09306, 10480, 12426, 12610, 13161, 13293
Physically Handicapped
00622, 00876, 01373, 01464, 01545, 01697, 01968, 02772, 02925, 03092, 03111, 03193, 04196, 04488, 04537, 04566, 04682, 05638, 06150, 06226, 06543, 06646, 06769, 06791, 06859, 07034, 07279, 07311, 07411, 07617, 07670, 07840, 08568, 09522, 10111, 10300, 10327, 10498, 10562, 11658, 11943, 12157, 12247, 12262, 12914
Play Therapy
00013, 00058, 00161, 00211, 00492, 00978, 01200, 01466, 01481, 01757, 01898, 02137, 02531, 03005, 03221, 03941, 04053, 04172, 04214, 04218, 04220, 04221, 04296, 04389, 04457, 04476, 04538, 04676, 05209, 05265, 05266, 05458, 05490, 05616, 05617, 05710, 06225, 06433, 06643, 06712, 06907, 06918, 06982, 06983, 07666, 07915, 08016, 08055, 08501, 08560, 09177, 09281, 09297, 10160, 10271, 10272, 10326, 10430, 10459, 10590, 10671, 10672, 10680, 11116, 11318, 11605, 11801, 11846, 12181, 12259, 12964
Poetry
01710, 03237, 06951, 07022, 07400, 09117, 09433, 09766, 10560, 13080
Pregnancy
01885
Prevention
00007, 00164, 00978, 01458, 01550, 01672, 01760, 01793, 01885, 02082, 02187, 02189, 02443, 05471
Private Practice
01032, 01889, 02071, 02709, 02937, 02938, 02946, 05532, 05551, 06096, 06957, 07324, 07328, 07726, 07880, 08039, 08604, 08634, 09079, 09162, 09163, 09976, 11328, 12077, 12197
Probation and Parole
01216
Projective Techniques
01479, 01861, 01888, 01928, 02150, 02668, 03855, 05927, 05970, 05995, 06428, 06580, 06637, 07390, 07768, 08006, 08112, 08113, 08273, 08425, 08695, 09086, 09116, 09131, 09745, 10419, 10902, 10986, 11016, 11070, 11142, 12421, 12799, 13137, 13167, 13295
Psychoanalysis
00022, 00338, 00339, 04346
Psychoanalysts
02200, 02770, 02813, 03110, 07665, 07667
Psychoanalytic Group Therapy
00008, 00012, 00013, 00036, 00044, 00061, 00079, 00080, 00084, 00114, 00128, 00165, 00167, 00168, 00195, 00196, 00234, 00235, 00237, 00238, 00241, 00242, 00243, 00245, 00263, 00340, 00343, 00367, 00409, 00497, 00503, 00508, 00563, 00564, 00572, 00616, 00655, 00657, 00669, 00714, 00729, 00814, 00822, 00836, 00843, 00878, 00911, 00912, 00913, 00914, 00996, 01036, 01074, 01093, 01140, 01144, 01145, 01147, 01238, 01271, 01309, 01384, 01391 01425, 01443, 01507, 01525, 01576, 01577, 01704, 01729, 01818, 01848, 01920, 01932, 01958, 01997, 02012, 02090, 02102, 02132, 02192, 02198, 02229, 02243, 02440, 02484, 02565, 02656, 02673, 02681, 02701, 02708, 02709, 02710, 02712, 02713, 02714, 02716, 02717, 02719, 02720, 02721, 02723, 02727, 02728, 02729, 02889, 02947, 02992, 03022, 03025, 03090, 03091, 03115, 03133, 03179, 03180, 03181, 03186, 03203, 03211, 03246, 03281, 03282, 03297, 03298, 03299, 03300, 03301,

03302, 03303, 03324, 03367, 03384, 03423, 03451, 03457, 03493, 03548, 03657, 03658, 03659, 03660, 03661, 03662, 03663, 03665, 03666, 03667, 03668, 03669, 03670, 03671, 03673, 03675, 03676, 03677, 03678, 03681, 03683, 03684, 03700, 03704, 03740, 03757, 03768, 03797, 03831, 03834, 03907, 03942, 03952, 03953, 03963, 04023, 04025, 04092, 04095, 04115, 04146, 04165, 04268, 04328, 04382, 04391, 04463, 04466, 04468, 04484, 04485, 04498, 04545, 04570, 04610, 04611, 04612, 04617, 04629, 04634, 04635, 04637, 04638, 04642, 04643, 04645, 04729, 04745, 04903, 04978, 05049, 05060, 05109, 05140, 05141, 05142, 05143, 05149, 05151, 05152, 05153, 05154, 05173, 05175, 05195, 05261, 05316, 05397, 05485, 05553, 05560, 05630, 05631, 05633, 05634, 05643, 05663, 05679, 05800, 05828, 05925, 05938, 05992, 06042, 06043, 06058, 06159, 06204, 06205, 06234, 06235, 06370, 06515, 06516, 06518, 06520, 06562, 06576, 06591, 06612, 06613, 06632, 06640, 06706, 06729, 06731, 06732, 06733, 06734, 06735, 06737, 06767, 06794, 06822, 06873, 06875, 06907, 06922, 06926, 06929, 07027, 07063, 07165, 07179, 07238, 07268, 07283, 07297, 07308, 07309, 07313, 07315, 07470, 07480, 07490, 07568, 07569, 07602, 07649, 07749, 07901, 08027, 08055, 08056, 08106, 08108, 08110, 08192, 08260, 08318, 08498, 08538, 08551, 08610, 08640, 08641, 08702, 08705, 08714, 08761, 08765, 08912, 08928, 08929, 08930, 08931, 08961, 08962, 08963, 08965, 08966, 08967, 08969, 09285, 09446, 09447, 09448, 09452, 09526, 09528, 09541, 09602, 09618, 09658, 09683, 09719, 09722, 09730, 09742, 10130, 10164, 10166, 10167, 10187, 10188, 10242, 10348, 10373, 10386, 10397, 10398, 10463, 10488, 10527, 10528, 10546, 10561, 10596, 10641, 10696, 10698, 10702, 10703, 10704, 10710, 10714, 10726, 10736, 10739, 10800, 10822, 10844, 10845, 10846, 10847, 10853, 10869, 10871, 10967, 10970, 11017, 11018, 11241, 11250, 11251, 11253, 11259, 11260, 11273, 11276, 11278, 11311, 11448, 11465, 11517, 11518, 11531, 11584, 11586, 11587, 11588, 11590, 11595, 11727, 11802, 11944, 11946, 11973, 11974, 12038, 12044, 12300, 12314, 12321, 12350, 12383, 12386, 12432, 12447, 12510, 12651, 12690, 12768, 12839, 12840, 12841, 12907, 12942, 12948, 12992, 12993, 13008, 13009, 13010, 13011, 13012, 13014, 13015, 13016, 13017, 13018, 13019, 13020, 13021, 13022, 13029, 13101, 13223, 13244, 13262, 13263

Psychodrama

00002, 00003, 00016, 00037, 00068, 00069, 00070, 00071, 00078, 00127, 00162, 00174, 00175, 00183, 00189, 00217, 00255, 00257, 00258, 00338, 00339, 00340, 00369, 00431, 00467, 00475, 00555, 00583, 00633, 00636, 00637, 00654, 00673, 00690, 00872, 00955, 00981, 01075, 01076, 01110, 01192, 01194, 01252, 01273, 01299, 01369, 01370, 01380, 01396, 01403, 01417, 01427, 01440, 01467, 01473, 01474, 01476, 01477, 01493, 01502, 01514, 01523, 01593, 01594, 01595, 01596, 01603, 01604, 01624, 01629, 01631, 01675, 01680, 01690, 01703, 01709, 01780, 01781, 01788, 01789, 01790, 01791, 01792, 01805, 01808, 01809, 01820, 01823, 01837, 01864, 01888, 01917, 01923, 01934, 01948, 01967, 02024, 02030, 02031, 02066, 02130, 02131, 02174, 02210, 02223, 02334, 02339, 02343, 02346, 02347, 02440, 02474, 02490, 02496, 02497, 02508, 02515, 02567, 02617, 02620, 02631, 02666, 02667, 02668, 02691, 02692, 02736, 02762, 02767, 02887, 02889, 02902, 02903, 02904, 02937, 02938, 02942, 03068, 03069, 03110, 03137, 03146, 03148, 03149, 03203, 03204, 03215, 03216, 03217, 03308, 03309, 03322, 03331, 03332, 03333, 03334, 03335, 03336, 03337, 03366, 03382, 03383, 03483, 03494, 03495, 03496, 03581, 03599, 03611, 03711, 03761, 03762, 03765, 03766, 03767, 03804, 03844, 03868, 03869, 04034, 04089, 04145, 04161, 04227, 04294, 04295, 04325, 04339, 04358, 04377, 04397, 04410, 04413, 04427, 04457, 04460, 04473, 04505, 04514, 04520, 04521, 04522, 04524, 04538, 04700, 04756, 04757, 04758, 04759, 04760,

04761, 04762, 04764, 04765, 04766, 04767, 04819, 04820, 04850, 04858, 04887, 04893, 04924, 04925, 04926, 04927, 04965, 04967, 04970, 05003, 05004, 05005, 05009, 05042, 05042, 05045, 05046, 05047, 05048, 05099, 05100, 05166, 05169, 05189, 05227, 05228, 05229, 05230, 05231, 05282, 05286, 05357, 05366, 05386, 05392, 05407, 05415, 05417, 05423, 05426, 05444, 05445, 05447, 05448, 05449, 05509, 05510, 05695, 05709, 05712, 05740, 05798, 05799, 05817, 05826, 05870, 05884, 05915, 05924, 06025, 06137, 06175, 06176, 06228, 06233, 06316, 06317, 06318, 06319, 06421, 06440, 06495, 06626, 06651, 06652, 06653, 06654, 06655, 06656, 06657, 06658, 06686, 06808, 06821, 06826, 06840, 06863, 06878, 06886, 06887, 06889, 06896, 06897, 06919, 06921, 06925, 06927, 06928, 06929, 06953, 06984, 06986, 06988, 06989, 06996, 07015, 07016, 07031, 07049, 07050, 07051, 07092, 07224, 07260, 07261, 07262, 07264, 07281, 07299, 07302, 07321, 07336, 07488, 07536, 07625, 07633, 07671, 07749, 07754, 07757, 07781, 07790, 07804, 07848, 07849, 07912, 07934, 07965, 08023, 08026, 08068, 08086, 08124, 08149, 08171, 08178, 08189, 08212, 08238, 08276, 08286, 08287, 08313, 08327, 08328, 08329, 08330, 08338, 08350, 08351, 08360, 08362, 08372, 08374, 08385, 08387, 08392, 08393, 08394, 08396, 08397, 08404, 08409, 08410, 08413, 08414, 08415, 08417, 08419, 08420, 08421, 08422, 08423, 08424, 08425, 08426, 08427, 08428, 08431, 08432, 08438, 08444, 08445, 08446, 08447, 08448, 08452, 08453, 08455, 08456, 08459, 08461, 08465, 08466, 08467, 08469, 08473, 08474, 08484, 08485, 08486, 08487, 08488, 08489, 08490, 08491, 08492, 08493, 08495, 08496, 08507, 08556, 08563, 08594, 08622, 08662, 08663, 08664, 08665, 08667, 08670, 08708, 08709, 08734, 08735, 08742, 08775, 08793, 08810, 08819, 08825, 08832, 08843, 08869, 08873, 08941, 08954, 08957, 08975, 08978, 08979, 08989, 08996, 08997, 09021, 09064, 09070, 09152, 09153, 09155, 09156, 09157, 09185, 09289, 09290, 09391, 09418, 09435, 09439, 09480, 09487, 09503, 09505, 09509, 09510, 09511, 09538, 09548, 09594, 09595, 09619, 09620, 09622, 09671, 09674, 09724, 09740, 09775, 09824, 10043, 10044, 10064, 10084, 10124, 10125, 10126, 10128, 10180, 10215, 10323, 10337, 10355, 10362, 10363, 10434, 10436, 10437, 10438, 10476, 10517, 10530, 10565, 10590, 10592, 10606, 10758, 10759, 10760, 10765, 10819, 10820, 10821, 10822, 10913, 10986, 11045, 11046, 11047, 11048, 11098, 11099, 11100, 11101, 11102, 11117, 11120, 11121, 11183, 11196, 11212, 11214, 11215, 11217, 11218, 11320, 11355, 11370, 11400, 11458, 11475, 11476, 11508, 11536, 11538, 11550, 11637, 11638, 11639, 11641, 11642, 11681, 11684, 11686, 11725, 11745, 11746, 11787, 11788, 11789, 11792, 11799, 11800, 11846, 11854, 11855, 11856, 11889, 11910, 11911, 11913, 11933, 11939, 11941, 11942, 11948, 12004, 12019, 12025, 12109, 12168, 12171, 12186, 12187, 12188, 12190, 12191, 12222, 12227, 12234, 12253, 12323, 12327, 12333, 12337, 12356, 12377, 12381, 12388, 12470, 12574, 12588, 12589, 12590, 12651, 12656, 12657, 12658, 12659, 12660, 12703, 12704, 12705, 12792, 12815, 12816, 12842, 12883, 13024, 13138, 13140, 13184, 13188, 13189, 13191, 13203, 13230, 13245, 13258, 13276, 13303

Psychodrama and Group Psychotherapy
08668, 08669, 08676, 08692, 11057, 11457, 11685

Psychokinetics
01114, 03646, 10741

Psychoses
00025, 00029, 00112, 00123, 00127, 00144, 00147, 00149, 00150, 00152, 00154, 00155, 00168, 00169, 00194, 00209, 00221, 00261, 00308, 00401, 00426, 00430, 00450, 00456, 00458, 00459, 00469, 00494, 00516, 00557, 00652, 00686, 00699, 00711, 00799, 00830, 00843, 00850, 00852, 00853, 00855, 00880, 00881, 00886, 00923, 00926, 00946, 00959, 01245, 01263, 01297, 01313, 01362, 01428, 01491, 01509, 01522, 01547, 01571, 01572,

01589, 01617, 01639, 01651, 01754, 01807, 01820, 01834, 01836, 01857, 01875, 01960, 01982, 01986, 01994, 02046, 02047, 02051, 02060, 02068, 02105, 02175, 02177, 02178, 02205, 02226, 02230, 02297, 02486, 02526, 02550, 02576, 02594, 02608, 02619, 02637, 02640, 02645, 02657, 02687, 02688, 02707, 02734, 02738, 02739, 02753, 02806, 02830, 02863, 02912, 02935, 02936, 02961, 02982, 02985, 02991, 02995, 03053, 03116, 03117, 03127, 03191, 03218, 03228, 03362, 03379, 03385, 03390, 03417, 03418, 03424, 03435, 03439, 03448, 03510, 03513, 03537, 03610, 03614, 03617, 03768, 03786, 03793, 03822, 03904, 03906, 03914, 03923, 03942, 03960, 04022, 04043, 04046, 04058, 04080, 04100, 04184, 04223, 04234, 04235, 04255, 04302, 04325, 04336, 04337, 04361, 04372, 04396, 04402, 04405, 04406, 04409, 04424, 04530, 04555, 04660, 04721, 04741, 04780, 04817, 04844, 05003, 05004, 05022, 05032, 05070, 05086, 05097, 05134, 05189, 05227, 05281, 05424, 05427, 05441, 05460, 05461, 05473, 05480, 05553, 05644, 05684, 05685, 05689, 05691, 05780, 05781, 05814, 05832, 05834, 05856, 05904, 06010, 06049, 06078, 06102, 06110, 06116, 06143, 06233, 06247, 06258, 06301, 06308, 06231, 06322, 06352, 06374, 06378, 06390, 06414, 06415, 06447, 06498, 06516, 06523, 06546, 06554, 06603, 06606, 06631, 06633, 06634, 06635, 06709, 06761, 06789, 06844, 06894, 06903, 06905, 06964, 06969, 07011, 07037, 07075, 07138, 07142, 07165, 07182, 07196, 07202, 07203, 07221, 07223, 07298, 07332, 07386, 07434, 07439, 07440, 07441, 07452, 07467, 07469, 07498, 07512, 07554, 07559, 07583, 07594, 07595, 07597, 07639, 07641, 07719, 07733, 07734, 07767, 07772, 07815, 07818, 07819, 07820, 07828, 07829, 07830, 07931, 07933, 07934, 08015, 08032, 08036, 08070, 08096, 08100, 08125, 08136, 08149, 08152, 08201, 08202, 08236, 08337, 08338, 08421, 08430, 08431, 08473, 08502, 08503, 08545, 08582, 08585, 08660, 08671, 08679, 08703, 08860, 08861, 08869, 08877, 08887, 08899, 08939, 08953, 08993, 09009, 09019, 09153, 09218, 09231, 09232, 09233, 09234, 09236, 09335, 09403, 09458, 09527, 09536, 09540, 09568, 09572, 09595, 09604, 09652, 09653, 09724, 09751, 09799, 09808, 09904, 09921, 10052, 10123, 10124, 10127, 10149, 10150, 10160, 10183, 10271, 10272, 10293, 10336, 10357, 10358, 10370, 10386, 10387, 10415, 10420, 10440, 10527, 10577, 10597, 10661, 10665, 10730, 10795, 10880, 10892, 10942, 10944, 10979, 11054, 11055, 11056, 11068, 11117, 11170, 11196, 11202, 11219, 11258, 11293, 11338, 11358, 11371, 11406, 11428, 11435, 11436, 11437, 11447, 11461, 11513, 11515, 11522, 11528, 11529, 11539, 11574, 11575, 11616, 11617, 11618, 11705, 11706, 11709, 11783, 11821, 11836, 11853, 11905, 12003, 12062, 12106, 12118, 12135, 12184, 12205, 12228, 12303, 12309, 12315, 12329, 12356, 12393, 12443, 12479, 12569, 12578, 12640, 12643, 12672, 12758, 12822, 12874, 12876, 12883, 12912, 12940, 12950, 13061, 13063, 13070, 13077, 13155, 13177, 13214, 13235, 13259, 13302

Psychosomatics
00038, 00039, 00041, 00054, 00055, 00056, 00068, 00235, 00473, 00477, 00568, 00649, 00650, 00722, 00761, 00801, 00807, 00819, 00829, 00854, 00951, 01114, 01127, 02456, 02484, 02742, 02902, 02998, 03624, 03823, 03783, 04023, 04380, 04581, 04582, 04747, 05341, 05342, 05343, 05344, 05348, 05529, 05630, 05631, 05633, 05634, 06023, 06396, 06397, 06641, 06644, 06827, 07195, 07763, 07764, 07812, 07836, 08123, 08127, 08274, 08275, 09349, 09350, 09351, 09482, 09630, 09657, 09700, 09834, 09837, 09783, 10058, 10445, 10668, 10771, 10772, 10935, 11094, 11095, 11162, 11189, 11487, 11662, 11668, 11676, 11695, 11741, 11787, 11788, 11790, 11791, 11797, 11798, 11799, 11918, 11919, 12164, 12355, 12485, 12486, 12488, 12489, 12769, 12797, 12975, 12976, 12988, 12989, 13196

Psychotherapy, technique
00096, 00099, 00110, 00157, 01533

Puppets
00976, 00977, 04601, 05076, 05079, 06547, 07474, 08681, 09403, 10126, 10805, 13072

R

Reality Therapy
01976, 02095, 02446
Recreational Therapy
03491, 05336, 05385, 05522, 08549, 09292, 09983, 12248
Reflections
04184
Rehabilitation/Aftercare
00027, 00060, 00309, 003190, 00333, 00334, 00978, 01064, 01673, 02055, 02121, 02472, 02561, 02676, 02754, 03108, 03111, 03790, 03960, 03971, 04126, 04175, 04347, 04356, 04467, 04780, 04801, 05029, 05120, 05255, 05310, 05328, 05440, 05497, 05508, 05620, 05930, 06161, 06226, 06447, 06478, 06703, 06712, 06727, 06859, 06864, 06991, 07037, 07079, 07333, 07469, 07614, 07764, 07842, 07907, 07908, 08002, 08003, 08130, 08199, 08937, 09518, 09529, 09748, 09949, 09950, 10111, 10338, 10339, 10479, 10498, 10548, 10750, 10885, 10911, 11391, 11405, 11474, 11738, 12247, 12293, 12513, 12871, 12975, 13120
Religion
00872, 01013, 01053, 01369, 01370, 01401, 01402, 01487, 01488, 01542, 10743, 01762, 01961, 02031, 02130, 02470, 02909, 03472, 03629, 04505, 04754, 05056, 050557, 05223, 05268, 05269, 05286, 05399, 05622, 05743, 05881, 05888, 05959, 05960, 06091, 06244, 06248, 06249, 06265, 06267, 06425, 07032, 07033, 07035, 07036, 07073, 07096, 07246, 07289, 07359, 07986, 08033, 08573, 08824, 08944, 09173, 09376, 09548, 09558, 09658, 09810, 10615, 11220, 11297, 11506, 11701, 11742, 11913, 13191
Remedial Reading
00491, 01062, 03525, 03526, 03579, 05220, 07272, 07421, 09251, 09276, 10136, 11025
Remotivation Therapy
00273, 01241, 01893, 02676, 02697, 03515, 03794, 04494, 04828, 05520, 06660, 07083, 07897, 08043, 08175, 09465, 09497, 09883, 10155, 10620, 10879, 12058, 12134, 12552, 12573, 12865, 12866, 13033
Reports, National and International
00203, 00210, 00232, 00315, 00317, 00318, 00438, 00443, 00461, 00619, 00733, 00823, 00892, 00981, 01075, 01077, 01088, 01194, 01325, 01592, 01788, 01790, 01808, 01929, 02233, 02234, 02235, 02236, 02237, 02238, 02239, 02559, 02565, 02754, 02784, 03003, 03425, 03596, 03868, 04469, 04829, 05069, 05169, 05274, 05275, 05533, 05547, 05549, 05853, 06025, 06456, 06652, 06655, 06816, 06924, 06963, 06996, 07102, 07392, 07700, 07754, 07804, 08021, 08081, 08287, 08320, 08323, 08482, 08539, 08613, 08708, 08709, 08832, 09074, 09619, 09620, 09621, 09671, 09917, 09939, 10192, 10741, 10764, 10819, 10821, 10966, 10973, 11089, 11482, 11557, 12019, 12025, 12216, 12444, 12892, 12894, 12920, 13084, 13106, 13108
Research: Comparative
00035, 00277, 00601, 00620, 00639, 00675, 00906, 01244, 01935, 02023, 02317, 02401, 02589, 02812, 02815, 02843, 02857, 02953, 03026, 03069, 03475, 03770, 03774, 03973, 04010, 04051, 04234, 04689, 04719, 04904, 04941, 04943, 05104, 05363, 05452, 05691, 05698, 06035, 06089, 06220, 06406, 06445, 06669, 06790, 06876, 06899, 07012, 07292, 07539, 07698, 07915, 08009, 08121, 08134, 08232, 08506, 08522, 08536, 08891, 08920,

09037, 09137, 09375, 09485, 09880, 10020, 10035, 10179, 10279, 10610, 10611, 10745, 10873, 10876, 10887, 11234, 11510, 11643, 11951, 12143, 12144, 12254, 12264, 12600, 12622, 12679, 12748, 12941, 12983, 12984, 13031, 13134, 13207
Research: Outcome
00048, 00191, 00196, 00335, 00374, 00420, 00463, 00563, 00564, 00566, 00676, 00682, 00683, 00721, 00886, 00944, 01315, 01418, 01483, 01704, 02873, 02479, 03584, 03586, 03723, 03736, 03787, 04672, 04706, 04855, 04920, 04953, 05001, 05030, 05278, 05701, 05921, 05972, 05973, 06034, 06047, 06115, 06128, 06155, 06187, 06274, 06281, 06285, 06288, 06289, 06297, 06298, 06438, 06469, 06774, 07154, 07347, 07429, 07592, 07770, 07803, 07858, 07884, 08058, 08236, 09091, 09146, 09147, 09148, 09149, 09245, 09314, 09404, 09454, 09474, 09475, 09477, 09580, 09581, 09648, 09788, 09905, 10034, 10035, 10098, 10347, 10389, 10611, 10666, 10941, 10990, 11369, 11647, 11718, 12276, 12281, 12284, 12437, 12442, 12527, 12607, 12622, 12739, 12756, 12757, 12786, 12987, 13159, 13160, 13233
Research: Process
00018, 00132, 00209, 00324, 00446, 00460, 00932, 00980, 00995, 01328, 01395, 02261, 03562, 03722, 03729, 03730, 03760, 03888, 03899, 03943, 03999, 04028, 04494, 04599, 05077, 05289, 05347, 05467, 05614, 05701, 06849, 07316, 07347, 08165, 08797, 09147, 09516, 09678, 09679, 09680, 09681, 09783, 09806, 10279, 10302, 10347, 11607, 12278, 12279
Research: Other
00020, 00122, 00231, 00260, 00381, 00392, 00396, 00445, 00458, 00459, 00600, 00649, 00933, 00937, 00939, 00991, 01196, 01235, 01385, 01408, 01415, 01432, 01433, 01434, 01435, 01436, 01459, 01485, 01490, 01523, 01527, 01544, 01574, 01587, 01600, 01611, 01638, 01664, 01692, 01722, 01730, 01736, 01737, 01841, 01886, 01888, 01891, 01978, 01987, 02012, 02052, 02124, 02131, 02255, 02276, 02278, 02286, 02292, 02315, 02393, 02552, 02724, 02791, 02792, 03143, 03249, 03437, 04072, 04073, 04163, 04667, 04707, 04832, 04949, 04964, 05118, 05123, 05126, 05193, 05238, 05335, 05359, 05589, 05594, 05600, 06050, 06134, 06145, 06206, 06311, 06384, 06446, 06468, 06658, 06985, 07117, 07380, 07410, 07920, 07940, 07956, 08982, 08985, 09199, 09493, 09494, 09600, 09677, 09796, 09841, 09907, 10027, 10036, 10059, 10121, 10132, 10193, 10207, 10218, 10225, 10287, 10365, 10366, 10456, 10602, 10627, 10636, 10833, 10878, 10963, 10964, 10980, 11000, 11079, 11151, 11161, 11175, 11364, 11720, 11773, 11894, 12275, 12285, 12312, 12394, 12416, 12525, 12608, 12634, 12648, 12667, 13147, 13158
Research: Evaluation
02106, 02507, 03084, 03284, 04070, 04826, 05001, 06404, 06970, 07138, 11091, 11597
Residential Settings
00320, 00483, 00643, 00644, 00646, 00697, 01056, 01427, 02142, 02524, 03136, 03229, 03278, 03547, 03599, 03620, 03856, 04151, 04158, 04225, 04293, 04324, 04332, 04333, 04525, 04557, 04576, 04604, 04698, 05029, 05099, 05100, 05140, 05239, 05282, 05329, 05417, 05419, 05474, 05476, 05916, 05917, 05918, 06027, 06029, 06030, 06216, 06236, 06268, 06275, 06357, 06429, 06430, 06435, 06458, 06744, 06800, 06863, 06865, 06995, 07112, 07200, 07683, 07765, 07837, 07935, 08063, 08119, 08265, 08315, 08697, 08742, 09000, 09029, 09089, 09252, 09347, 09406, 09456, 09553, 09554, 09555, 09611, 09682, 09864, 09897, 10011, 10280, 10311, 10410, 10512, 10519, 10778, 10853, 10889, 11285, 11324, 11458, 11755, 11881, 11970, 12133, 12623, 12819, 12935
Resistance
00969, 01015, 01018, 01149, 02711, 03497, 03750, 03950, 04266, 04392,

05170, 06565, 06582, 06656, 07217, 08527, 08638, 08848, 08964, 08967, 08969, 08970, 09020, 09117, 09120, 09129, 09442, 09691, 09868, 10183, 10194, 10229, 10242, 10247, 10248, 10557, 10794, 10844, 11041, 11584, 11587, 11588, 11590, 11659, 11669, 12496, 12510, 12575, 13265

Review of the Literature
01411, 01429, 02447, 02448, 02591, 04523, 04640, 04672, 04714, 04715, 10910, 11780, 11781, 11836

Role-playing
00015, 00689, 00869, 00947, 00955, 01360, 01375, 01411, 01545, 01698, 01736, 01921, 02545, 02715, 02805, 02837, 02840, 02941, 03040, 03146, 03275, 03804, 03868, 03869, 04161, 04413, 04514, 04700, 04756, 05191, 05509, 05799, 05915, 06138, 06139, 06147, 06178, 06389, 06442, 06888, 07030, 07188, 07263, 07293, 07317, 07348, 07351, 07576, 07631, 07644, 07645, 07646, 07647, 08118, 08120, 08142, 08150, 08330, 08566, 08794, 08795, 09361, 09363, 09722, 09817, 09994, 10053, 10071, 10213, 10315, 10434, 10551, 10553, 10662, 11029, 11030, 11051, 11107, 11370, 11460, 11543, 11547, 11548, 11551, 11552, 11553, 11610, 11640, 11869, 11874, 11895, 11896, 11971, 12061, 12189, 12339, 12490, 12518, 12599, 12864, 12991, 13204, 13240, 13243

Roundtable Method
01828, 01829, 02723, 06687, 06896, 07861, 07862, 08070, 11332, 11963, 12728

S

Schools
00284, 00626, 00694, 00703, 00882, 00927, 00958, 01055, 01061, 01244, 01414, 01500, 01586, 01603, 01607, 01648, 01679, 01691, 01694, 01793, 01851, 01892, 01901, 01940, 01948, 01959, 02038, 02054, 02080, 02115, 02126, 02207, 02210, 02221, 02269, 02284, 02367, 02586, 02651, 02718, 02748, 02846, 02997, 03026, 03031, 03153, 03157, 03184, 03309, 03372, 03407, 03507, 03553, 03569, 03581, 03640, 03759, 03771, 03772, 03798, 03813, 03820, 04051, 04069, 04119, 04200, 04227, 04290, 04326, 04503, 04548, 04584, 04677, 04764, 04765, 04766, 04767, 04926, 04930, 04931, 04945, 04992, 04996, 05012, 05165, 05214, 05240, 05511, 05563, 05566, 05568, 05569, 05579, 05724, 05769, 05841, 05876, 05922, 06002, 06011, 06014, 06146, 06169, 06209, 06229, 06309, 06459, 06479, 06483, 06754, 06765, 06853, 06934, 07178, 07186, 07262, 07284, 07513, 07563, 07565, 07566, 07654, 07698, 07809, 07817, 07915, 07951, 07962, 08103, 08203, 08240, 08255, 08280, 08328, 08561, 08648, 08653, 08664, 08712, 08723, 08779, 08905, 08920, 08925, 09028, 09176, 09342, 09596, 09661, 09701, 09773, 09900, 09957, 09997, 09998, 10231, 10275, 10307, 10351, 10562, 10573, 10599, 10733, 10752, 10758, 10759, 10803, 10857, 10918, 10962, 11043, 11084, 11100, 11101, 11107, 11141, 11231, 11514, 11554, 11609, 11634, 11635, 11756, 11770, 11937, 12000, 12081, 12096, 12180, 12200, 12426, 12463, 12484, 12507, 12546, 12621, 12630, 12673, 12704, 12749, 12813, 12852, 13172, 13207, 13226

Seating
00505, 01343, 03070, 04523, 04951, 05207, 05380, 06490, 08760, 09370, 12571, 12942

Selection of Patients (Group Composition)
00222, 00269, 01113, 01393, 01566, 01817, 02554, 02556, 02700, 03186, 03500, 03706, 04093, 04094, 04129, 04178, 04270, 04365, 05117, 07791, 07956, 09368, 09535, 10803

Self-Disclosure

00179, 00259, 00260, 00261, 00312, 00588, 00636, 00861, 01006, 01046, 01047, 01116, 01549, 01597, 01850, 01871, 01900, 01974, 02020, 02064, 02094, 02116, 02147, 02151, 02213, 02370, 02731, 02789, 02790, 02795, 02797, 02801, 02802, 02901, 03018, 03129, 04359, 04398, 04408, 04453, 04661, 04997, 05081, 05087, 05560, 05601, 05867, 06040, 06297, 06511, 07093, 07241, 07294, 07406, 07449, 07491, 07826, 07827, 07911, 08243, 08547, 08548, 08934, 09182, 09369, 09462, 09705, 09706, 09708, 09938, 10777, 11520, 11650, 11852, 11853, 12539, 12649, 12853, 13210, 00206, 00407, 00464, 00470, 00482, 00506, 00617, 00973, 01049, 01119, 01739, 01744, 01878, 01907, 01935, 01936, 02049, 02084, 02222, 02483, 02615, 03050, 03088, 03521, 03823, 03867, 04050, 04175, 04530, 05036, 05078, 05217, 05294, 05418, 05597, 05711, 05843, 06104, 06126, 06208, 06330, 06766, 07055, 07271, 07340, 07496, 07499, 07770, 07963, 08188, 08261, 08268, 08269, 09159, 09277, 09288, 09299, 09687, 09782, 10113, 10785, 11230, 11447, 11558, 12261, 12353, 12420, 12522, 12645, 12732, 13060

Sensitivity Training
02133, 04087

Sex: Deviation
01629, 01789, 02347, 05323, 05327, 07496, 07799, 08282, 11727, 12814, 13145

Sex: Dysfunction
00226, 00585, 00629, 00630, 00631, 00891, 01128, 01655, 02209, 02839, 03361, 04196, 04197, 04537, 04790, 04864, 05027, 05459, 05785, 06062, 06970, 06971, 07122, 07123, 07168, 07301, 07377, 08042, 08181, 08506, 08658, 08858, 08859, 09320, 09669, 09755, 09795, 09833, 10744, 10806, 10870, 11953, 12387, 12960, 13079

Sex: Exhibitionists
04267, 06214, 07793, 07794, 07798, 09380, 12981

Sex: Homosexuality
00658, 01007, 01125, 01165, 01236, 01240, 01733, 02382, 03142, 03509, 03810, 04139, 04794, 04795, 04796, 04801, 04803, 04804, 05417, 05860, 05874, 06141, 06207, 07282, 08230, 08305, 08643, 08818, 09486, 09902, 10107, 10135, 10156, 10343, 10400, 10660, 10888, 11136, 11204, 11831, 12292

Sex: Offenders
01816, 01817, 02364, 07855, 11246, 11248

Sex: Voyeur
04267

Sex: Other
00105, 00385, 00386, 02335, 02455, 02473, 02477, 02764, 02974, 03815, 04507, 04615, 04623, 04694, 04703, 04751, 04862, 05026, 05028, 05484, 05850, 06080, 06127, 06133, 06180, 06448, 06504, 06578, 06621, 06769, 07053, 07367, 07375, 07664, 08115, 08116, 08131, 08190, 08543, 09018, 09340, 09366, 09560, 09615, 09918, 09919, 10098, 10141, 10216, 10345, 10346, 10680, 10700, 10724, 10783, 10961, 11223, 11819, 11969, 12298, 12383, 12531, 12739, 12750, 13090, 13220, 13247

Short-Term, Brief Psychotherapy
00133, 00134, 00137, 00177, 00608, 00671, 00672, 00860, 00978, 01079, 01080, 01234, 01498, 01715, 01716, 01717, 01747, 01782, 01860, 01945, 01996, 02058, 02062, 02114, 02152, 02209, 02265, 02518, 02624, 02703, 02797, 02847, 02866, 02874, 02954, 02974, 03176, 03177, 03227, 03230, 03270, 03271, 03347, 03373, 03376, 03511, 03593, 03616, 03894, 04064, 04071, 04076, 04207, 04482, 04562, 04917, 04974, 05098, 05253, 05276, 05571, 05667, 05691, 05697, 05892, 05945, 06044, 06090, 06095, 06150, 06151, 06213, 06255, 06261, 06277, 06427, 06506, 06570, 06577, 06669, 06684, 06711, 06796, 07062, 07098, 07108, 07110, 07202, 07203, 07211,

07219, 07292, 07459, 07558, 07585, 07617, 07712, 08013, 08080, 08245, 08278, 08279, 08284, 08285, 08631, 08666, 08732, 08834, 08847, 08883, 08912, 09000, 09094, 09095, 09153, 09223, 09226, 09311, 09411, 09440, 09464, 09561, 09594, 09702, 09748, 09771, 09937, 09980, 10310, 10341, 10446, 10451, 10571, 10574, 10763, 10876, 11036, 11108, 11112, 11128, 11389, 11514, 11527, 11600, 11736, 11803, 12099, 12174, 12231, 12309, 12351, 12385, 12532, 12616, 12643, 12771, 12867, 12910, 12911, 12912, 12929, 12994, 13113, 13182, 13264

Silence
00099, 01366, 04358, 05129, 07103, 11097, 11316, 11916

Sleep Therapy
03356, 03357, 03358, 03360, 03559, 04138, 04474, 05582

Sociodrama
00019, 00958, 01157, 01259

Social Case Work
00515, 00520, 00640, 04277, 04279, 04281, 07810, 07832, 09310, 10789, 11352, 11948, 12253

Social Group Work
00291, 00408, 00574, 00661, 00667, 00802, 00847, 00848, 00965, 01009, 01014, 01345, 01429, 01430, 01438, 01563, 01803, 01870, 01879, 01918, 02006, 02032, 02083, 02179, 02186, 02327, 02704, 02891, 03081, 03388, 03398, 03408, 03563, 03700, 03708, 03777, 03821, 03885, 03929, 04020, 04021, 04183, 04248, 04280, 04384, 04432, 04506, 05251, 05425, 05488, 06015, 06016, 06109, 06360, 06460, 06470, 06502, 06513, 06527, 06529, 06531, 06805, 06838, 06891, 07013, 07192, 07227, 07471, 07587, 07607, 07944, 08087, 08117, 08589, 08715, 08774, 08791, 08801, 08829, 09022, 09060, 09090, 09160, 09293, 09382, 09466, 09764, 09802, 09886, 10092, 10235, 10269, 10482, 10581, 10611, 10616, 10626, 10645, 10688, 10766, 10767, 10802, 10910, 10933, 10974, 11123, 11361, 11371, 11467, 11485, 11730, 11731, 11777, 11914, 12125, 12161, 12202, 12243, 12263, 12605, 12619, 12637, 12796, 12810, 12814, 12860, 12918, 12919, 12970, 13130, 13259

Sociometry
00195, 00251, 00468, 00552, 01251, 01362, 01499, 01785, 01851, 01957, 01962, 02267, 02462, 02499, 02652, 02941, 03196, 03611, 03622, 03845, 03937, 04305, 04306, 04307, 04509, 04726, 05043, 05059, 05165, 05244, 05490, 05515, 05650, 05669, 05670, 05822, 05823, 05829, 05993, 06144, 06156, 06160, 06551, 06691, 06826, 06845, 06846, 06851, 07538, 08179, 08277, 08319, 08347, 08348, 08373, 08376, 08407, 08439, 08449, 08468, 08475, 08494, 08561, 08566, 08736, 08771, 08772, 08840, 09097, 09512, 09514, 09515, 09563, 09619, 09799, 09979, 10212, 10316, 10575, 10753, 10893, 11406, 11489, 11549, 11642, 11718, 12082, 12129, 12210, 12526, 12634, 12705, 12788, 13165

Somatic Diseases, Organic Diseases
00039, 00124, 00180, 00349, 00432, 00498, 00565, 00659, 00665, 01202, 01203, 01208, 01246, 01286, 01503, 01582, 01700, 01701, 01712, 01783, 01835, 01839, 01842, 01860, 01995, 01996, 02022, 02084, 02092, 02111, 02122, 02153, 02164, 02190, 02216, 02249, 02303, 02308, 02468, 02502, 02609, 02740, 02911, 02970, 03108, 03109, 03321, 03340, 03345, 03396, 03520, 03539, 03580, 03606, 03625, 03783, 03790, 03827, 03892, 03946, 03979, 04050, 04107, 04192, 04375, 04467, 04659, 04724, 04734, 04740, 04775, 04776, 04831, 05135, 05136, 05167, 05242, 05338, 05396, 05872, 05954, 06023, 06090, 06132, 06179, 06548, 06648, 06876, 06883, 06952, 07013, 07140, 07214, 07255, 07349, 07350, 07399, 07463, 07606, 07651, 07746, 07750, 07811, 07869, 07913, 08126, 08214, 08262, 08284, 08285, 08893, 08912, 08951, 08952, 09026, 09041, 09166, 09220, 09228, 09229,

09299, 09301, 09471, 09484, 09635, 09686, 09695, 09711, 09748, 09749, 09750, 09776, 09954, 10065, 10072, 10074, 10119, 10274, 10478, 10583, 10589, 10718, 10749, 10834, 10851, 10854, 10856, 10887, 10911, 10975, 11063, 11108, 11158, 11168, 11207, 11229, 11359, 11478, 11503, 11556, 11558, 11675, 11757, 11768, 11769, 11919, 12088, 12328, 12336, 12533, 12548, 12626, 12638, 12644, 12727, 12800, 12801, 12812, 12829, 12860, 12886, 12909, 12910, 12911, 12969, 13082, 13131, 13151, 13217, 13287 (*See also:* Allergies, Cancer, Epilepsy, Tuberculosis)

Special Populations: Doctors
01076, 06137

Special Populations: Low Income
01959, 02076, 02077, 02128, 02190, 04290, 04380, 05184, 05185, 06008, 06586, 07079, 07346, 07524, 08208, 08252, 09263, 09628, 09948, 09994, 09996, 10180, 10214, 10650, 11895, 11896, 12213, 12247

Special Populations: Smokers
01101, 01485, 01505, 01586, 03279, 04896, 05008, 05761, 06239, 06420, 06895, 07014, 07074, 07712, 08850, 09030, 09825, 10516, 11083, 11997, 12206, 12670, 12806, 12863, 13286

Special Populations: Women
00474, 00585, 00615, 00629, 01049, 01084, 01543, 016212, 01759, 01784, 01814, 02152, 02501, 02754, 02807, 02833, 02885, 03009, 03056, 03168, 13069, 03256, 03257, 03364, 04187, 05747, 05972, 06008, 06103, 06161, 06207, 06263, 06277, 06381, 06647, 06843, 06952, 07109, 07124, 07153, 07271, 07340, 07487, 07488, 07552, 07553, 07613, 07622, 07627, 07659, 07835, 07856, 07913, 08020, 08080, 08184, 08235, 08598, 08658, 08901, 08984, 09042, 09239, 09247, 09293, 09820, 09838, 09854, 09964, 10003, 10047, 10155, 10298, 10333, 10652, 10654, 10780, 10854, 11524, 11592, 11880, 12089, 12293, 0112357, 12378, 12730, 12798, 12833, 12834, 12835, 13057, 13058, 13066, 13128, 13134

Special Populations: Other
00005, 00323, 01376, 01409, 02498, 02504, 02512, 02528, 02548, 02694, 02943, 02964, 03593, 03895, 04340, 04488, 05002, 05037, 05167, 05295, 05416, 05428, 05458, 05587, 05642, 05711, 06020, 06041, 06086, 06532, 06708, 07418, 08114, 08132, 08248, 08271, 08624, 08926, 08973, 09013, 09235, 09372, 09445, 09470, 09479, 09665, 10073, 10112, 10234, 10292, 10293, 10329, 10368, 10563, 10567, 10867, 10875, 11347, 11392, 11448, 11477, 11955, 12016, 12060, 12061, 12172, 12392, 12396, 12699, 12937, 13189, 13192, 13193

Special Populations: Pregnancy
00090, 01214, 01257, 01518, 01519, 01570, 01574, 01580, 01784, 01885, 02293, 02504, 02526, 02604, 03176, 03867, 04304, 02907, 13267

Speech Defects
00297, 00554, 00632, 00634, 00866, 00890, 01613, 01614, 01615, 01699, 02019, 02020, 02119, 02492, 02593, 02858, 03234, 03365, 03583, 04180, 04369, 04404, 04531, 04532, 04765, 04887, 05200, 05426, 05698, 06752, 06981, 06986, 06990, 08635, 09051, 10208, 10408, 10453, 10454, 10729, 10747, 10773, 11715, 11745, 11746, 11885, 12023, 12313, 12631 (*See also:* Aphasia)

Speech Therapy
00517, 12514

Spouses
02502, 02740, 02779, 03190, 03293, 03316, 03693, 04409, 04637, 04638, 05250, 05632, 05842, 05909, 06170, 06500, 06561, 06883, 06950, 07495, 08498, 08579, 08986, 09207, 09491, 09834, 10558, 10615, 10882, 10975, 11108, 11168, 11383, 12533, 12727, 12920

Suicide

00164, 00436, 01197, 01489, 02018, 02110, 02242, 03083, 03342, 03343, 03774, 03775, 04774, 05471, 05694, 06257, 07879, 08157, 08557, 09004, 09618, 12007, 12234, 12516, 12682

Supervision

00011, 00014, 00181, 00345, 00478, 01073, 01140, 01159, 01333, 02176, 02650, 03112, 03287, 03354, 04157, 04211, 04238, 04239, 04261, 04480, 04603, 04644, 04645, 04646, 04686, 04952, 05465, 05984, 06535, 06974, 07064, 07701, 07923, 07926, 07993, 08221, 08222, 08311, 09088, 09188, 09360, 09361, 09523, 09585, 09891, 09899, 09953, 10381, 10811, 11020, 11386, 11888, 11905, 11948, 12013, 12147, 12183, 12381, 12841, 12903

Support Groups

02323, 04605, 07752, 10544

Surveys

01069, 01162, 02258, 04846, 05198, 06108, 06328, 07226, 07392, 07403, 08307, 09582, 09676, 11781, 12844, 12845, 12930

T

Teaching and Teacher Training

00017, 00576, 00624, 00701, 00898, 01072, 01186, 01345, 01355, 01396, 01371, 01405, 01414, 01552, 01581, 01852, 01940, 02580, 02783, 02897, 03085, 03403, 03506, 03861, 03989, 04074, 04086, 04097, 04307, 04414, 04473, 04561, 04646, 04700, 04761, 04806, 04837, 04919, 05088, 05362, 05435, 05556, 056ll, 05741, 05764, 05833, 05884, 05915, 06138, 06237, 06243, 06495, 06651, 06654, 06865, 06898, 07015, 07016, 07027, 07046, 07358, 07424, 07569, 07633, 07654, 07785, 07817, 07839, 08009, 08011, 08049, 08208, 08312, 08628, 08629, 08716, 08717, 08795, 09058, 09374, 09418, 09454, 09549, 09643, 09907, 10068, 10385, 10748, 10835, 10934, 10945, 10946, 11078, 11378, 11628, 11629, 11725, 11921, 12322, 12364, 12468, 12585, 12586, 12917, 12964, 13153, 13203, 13230, 13265, 13272, 13282

Techniques of Group Therapy

00586, 00595, 00685, 01307, 01308, 01312, 01333, 01375, 01382, 01383, 02672, 02722, 02750, 02780, 02787, 02815, 02875, 02878, 02881, 02934, 02940, 03049, 03055, 03195, 03200, 03201, 03245, 03255, 03295, 03368, 03452, 03463, 03494, 03499, 03504, 03565, 03587, 03588, 03589, 03591, 03602, 03618, 03756, 03815, 03816, 03819, 03836, 03837, 03850, 03904, 03919, 03920, 03925, 03926, 03927, 04222, 04231, 04510, 04660, 05479, 05557, 05623, 05654, 05700, 05724, 05740, 05760, 05770, 05825, 05832, 05855, 05863, 05870, 05879, 05882, 05896, 05930, 05944, 05974, 06577, 06597, 07555, 07639, 07659, 07711, 07714, 07736, 07737, 07817, 07860, 07906, 07943, 07974, 07997, 08007, 08111, 08138, 08169, 08867, 08871, 08910, 09003, 10436, 10503, 10593, 10681, 10695, 10730, 10796, 10809, 10883, 10916, 11011, 11013, 11021, 11049, 11062, 11113, 11146, 11196, 11335, 11338, 11427, 11428, 11450, 11525, 11526, 11567, 11570, 11580, 11585, 11656, 11677, 11721, 11733, 11833, 11868, 11998, 12170, 12179, 12186, 12187, 12192, 12196, 12244, 12305, 12480, 12492, 12581, 12616, 12617, 12650, 12666, 12668, 12669, 12673, 12706, 12719, 12725, 12734, 12760, 12769, 12808, 12809, 12817, 12820, 12821, 12908, 12915, 12945, 12951, 12971, 13024, 13028, 13102, 13147, 13156, 13178, 13185, 13231, 13241, 13258, 13268, 13276, 13277, 13288, 13289, 13294, 13299, 13300

Techniques and Programs

00002, 00003, 00134, 00159, 00178, 00179, 00204, 00214, 00225, 00249, 00254, 00286, 00303, 00305, 00320, 00348, 00364, 00414, 00417, 00444, 00451, 00473, 00480, 00481, 00496, 00502, 00531, 00549, 00612, 00625,

00646, 00655, 00657, 00663, 00669, 00687, 00690, 00707, 00708, 00767, 00775, 00857, 00867, 00868, 00880, 00881, 00891, 00929, 00935, 00938, 00942, 00950, 00957, 01003, 01028, 01041, 01057, 01065, 01084, 01131, 01132, 01135, 01192, 01212, 01213, 01234, 01285, 01290, 01305, 01335, 01397, 01445, 01450, 01453, 01480, 01481, 01491, 01501, 01510, 01526, 01545, 01548, 01553, 01554, 01557, 01560, 01589, 01636, 01650, 01651, 01657, 01659, 01668, 01683, 01686, 01690, 01694, 01703, 01710, 01714, 01738, 10743, 01761, 01791, 01797, 01799, 01809, 01819, 01857, 01865, 01884, 01913, 01920, 01933, 01942, 01944, 01954, 01955, 01964, 01972, 01987, 01993, 02009, 02010, 02046, 02047, 02050, 02060, 02061, 02068, 02073, 02086, 02143, 02153, 02157, 02163, 02164, 02180, 02182, 02194, 02202, 02203, 00218, 02241, 02250, 02257, 02262, 02266, 02299, 02300, 02307, 02310, 02314, 02328, 02330, 02336, 02337, 02342, 02348, 02354, 02361, 02367, 02452, 02467, 02478, 02532, 02624, 02625, 02640, 02656, 02692, 02710, 02713, 02715, 02828, 02886, 02907, 02926, 02936, 02978, 03015, 03019, 03065, 03071, 03149, 03162, 03174, 03217, 03223, 03237, 03242, 03288, 03331, 03421, 03434, 03705, 03767, 03871, 03954, 03972, 04110, 04141, 04208, 04265, 04266, 04319, 04320, 04323, 04324, 04352, 04357, 04358, 04363, 04364, 04372, 04395, 04415, 04438, 04470, 04541, 04670, 04687, 04739, 04770, 04774, 04819, 04820, 04842, 04844, 04846, 04847, 04849, 04889, 04916, 04923, 04979, 04981, 04986, 05013, 05094, 05112, 05138, 05150, 05050, 05174, 05212, 05230, 05231, 05300, 05301, 05356, 05445, 05447, 05448, 05449, 05469, 05483, 05510, 05532, 05747, 05807, 05875, 05887, 05962, 05982, 06000, 06020, 06060, 06061, 06086, 06119, 06231, 06268, 06307, 06316, 06317, 06327, 06335, 06342, 06351, 06354, 06359, 06367, 06373, 06375, 06415, 06441, 06446, 06446, 06482, 06512, 06554, 06615, 06627, 06666, 06885, 07017, 07350, 07421, 07512, 07589, 07786, 07927, 07928, 07972, 08149, 08171, 08188, 08229, 08232, 08238, 08239, 08276, 08283, 08299, 08372, 08386, 08409, 08426, 08427, 08474, 08490, 08491, 08492, 08493, 08495, 08576, 08589, 08600, 08652, 08662, 08663, 08787, 08868, 08873, 08980, 08988, 09021, 09152, 09154, 09157, 09158, 09590, 09667, 09673, 09840, 10395, 10528, 10554, 01606, 10720, 10760, 10826, 10855, 10969, 11005, 11019, 11027, 11120, 11237, 11270, 11446, 11474, 11519, 11533, 11555, 11596, 11641, 11725, 11750, 11792, 11824, 11862, 12412, 12514, 12804

Techniques of Group Psychotherapy
03955, 03971, 04693, 05074, 05249, 05255, 06092, 06188, 06481, 06739, 06741, 06749, 06750, 06753, 06757, 06785, 06870, 06871, 06889, 06916, 06917, 06937, 07033, 07042, 07078, 07113, 07147, 07149, 07166, 07194, 07196, 07218, 07231, 07258, 07368, 07396, 07431, 09064, 09093, 09128, 09155, 09186, 09195, 09203, 09258, 09289, 09316, 09373, 09416, 09420, 09423, 09455, 09459, 09460, 09503, 09521, 09529, 09547, 09579, 09608, 09622, 09644, 09647, 09668, 09689, 09693, 09751, 09758, 09766, 09824, 09835, 09879, 09898, 09936, 09955, 10000, 10001, 10051, 10101, 10118, 10224, 10252, 10282, 10319, 10350, 10354, 10378, 10410

Tele
00078, 00162, 00189, 00321, 01277, 01624, 01796, 02927, 03144, 03902, 05890, 06113, 07361, 07775, 08355, 08367, 08434, 08435, 08451, 08460, 08839, 09593, 11434, 11615, 12316, 12767

Theory: Adhesion
00066, 00321, 02920, 09076, 10917, 11098, 11099

Theory: Behavioral
06746, 07834, 09244, 09956, 10564

Theory: Group Therapy
00910, 01922, 02182, 02203, 02300, 02345, 02354, 02413

Theory: Psychoanalytic

00234, 00528, 00736, 00821, 00832, 01148, 01166, 01237, 01239, 01729, 01848, 02203, 02720, 03260, 03817, 03996, 04344, 04345, 04445, 01616, 06007, 06751, 06758, 07127, 07267, 07283, 07561, 07567, 07632, 07637, 08228, 08333, 08958, 09691, 09866, 09991, 10044, 10089, 10163, 10165, 10438, 10465, 10526, 10549, 10550, 10603, 10613, 10614, 10623, 10624, 10625, 10630, 10639, 10951, 10988, 11172, 11251, 11284, 11405, 11670, 12520

Theory: Psychodrama
00002, 00003, 02344, 04435

Theory: Other
00023, 00024, 00045, 00059, 00072, 00083, 00085, 00115, 00127, 00148, 00197, 00198, 00199, 00238, 00239, 00240, 00297, 00330, 00383, 00435, 00447, 00448, 00449, 00501, 00523, 00527, 00541, 00542, 00609, 00700, 00710, 00719, 00905, 00931, 01097, 01153, 01174, 01179, 01180, 01181, 01184, 01276, 01422, 01515, 01609, 01742, 01773, 01800, 1879, 01931, 01939, 01983, 01987, 02125, 02134, 02169, 02203, 02289, 02298, 02299, 02301, 02322, 02323, 02405, 02448, 02822, 03001, 03006, 03016, 03017, 03560, 00559, 04676, 04730, 04739, 05051, 05206, 05243, 05262, 05288, 05528, 05645, 05646, 05656, 05657, 05676, 05727, 05728, 05786, 06253, 06255, 06342, 06455, 06604, 06776, 06828, 06885, 06997, 07143, 07152, 07430, 07489, 07735, 07847, 08344, 08384, 08389, 08436, 08437, 08454, 08462, 08470, 08480, 08572, 08574, 08609, 08693, 08696, 08737, 09035, 09046, 09107, 09186, 09198, 10015, 10017, 10062, 10196, 10223, 10572, 10622, 10683, 10689, 10701, 10804, 11049, 11060, 11200, 11266, 11275, 11321, 11414, 11433, 11460, 11484, 11488, 11506, 11576, 11704, 11810, 11987, 12054, 12317, 12324, 12415, 12595, 12663, 12731, 12772, 12804, 13093, 13115

Therapeutic Community
00429, 00773, 01423, 01517, 01554, 01559, 01561, 01591, 01634, 01981, 02113, 02132, 02803, 02945, 03185, 03927, 05931, 07724, 07733, 10349, 11224, 11366

Therapeutic Social Clubs (Support Groups)
00155, 00163, 00188, 00506, 00621, 00849, 00922, 01173, 01176, 01183, 01268, 01511, 01981, 04030, 04175, 04578, 04605, 05373, 06299, 06369, 06830, 07705, 07706, 07842, 09790, 10349, 11158, 11859, 11862, 12026, 12457, 12515, 12516, 12615, 13085

Theses and Dissertations
00019, 00048, 00062, 00088, 00103, 00107, 00132, 00145, 00177, 00205, 00230, 00248, 00267, 00282, 00287, 00290, 00301, 00324, 00350, 00407, 00419, 00422, 00423, 00429, 00434, 00437, 00465, 00476, 00478, 00486, 00493, 00510, 00516, 00517, 00518, 00553, 00558, 00565, 00569, 00571, 00575, 00576, 00580, 00588, 00610, 00612, 00623, 00635, 00662, 00670, 00672, 00674, 00675, 00701, 00711, 00717, 00719, 00724, 00858, 00859, 00861, 00863, 00875, 00884, 00900, 00903, 00906, 00919, 00928, 00932, 00944, 00946, 00950, 00961, 00962, 00997, 00999, 01010, 01013, 01059, 01109, 01116, 01133, 01155, 01162, 01189, 01190, 01199, 01201, 01204, 01215, 01216, 01243, 01244, 01246, 01256, 01283, 01290, 01298, 01315, 01316, 01321, 01400, 01419, 01447, 01498, 01499, 01500, 01528, 01529, 01553, 01562, 01570, 01578, 01580, 01583, 01586, 01597, 01618, 01620, 01642, 01646, 01648, 01651, 01652, 01653, 01654, 01659, 01673, 01694, 01713, 01734, 01751, 01763, 01771, 01782, 01786, 01797, 01802, 01814, 01819, 01830, 01831, 01838, 01845, 01846, 01849, 01850, 01851, 01852, 01871, 01879, 01884, 01892, 01900, 01902, 01903, 01904, 01933, 01935, 01936, 01939, 01940, 01942, 01943, 01945, 01955, 01959, 01975, 01977, 01979, 01983, 01989, 02000, 02016, 02027, 02028, 02036, 02038, 02044, 02059, 02064, 02069, 02070, 02074, 02080, 02088, 02089, 02094, 02107,

02120, 02122, 02126, 02133, 02140, 02175, 02190, 02197, 02218, 02221, 02224, 02231, 02266, 02267, 02269, 02271, 02306, 02313, 02320, 02332, 02356, 02360, 02377, 02433, 02434, 02439, 02441, 02445, 02446, 02458, 02461, 02485, 02489, 02503, 02504, 02505, 02508, 02513, 02523, 02524, 02525, 02527, 02535, 02569, 02570, 02580, 02582, 02583, 02588, 02589, 02594, 02595, 02596, 02598, 02610, 02621, 02628, 02629, 02642, 02650, 02669, 02679, 02700, 02731, 02735, 02741, 02749, 02755, 02761, 02777, 02802, 02804, 02806, 02807, 02808, 02811, 02812, 02833, 02845, 02846, 02855, 02857, 02868, 02871, 02872, 20878, 02880, 02885, 02899, 02900, 02901, 02953, 02986, 02989, 02995, 03031, 03033, 03036, 03038, 03043, 03051, 03054, 03057, 03061, 03066, 03067, 03084, 03085, 03094, 03106, 03121, 03129, 03135, 03136, 03138, 03158, 03168, 03171, 03187, 03189, 03190, 03197, 03202, 03218, 03222, 03224, 03239, 03247, 03256, 03283, 03286, 03347, 03348, 03366, 03396, 03432, 03433, 03475, 03480, 03483, 03511, 03516, 03532, 03535, 03544, 03546, 03553, 03592, 03628, 03630, 03685, 03758, 03770, 03777, 03781, 03787, 03800, 03802, 03847, 03848, 03881, 03894, 03905, 03914, 03936, 03941, 03962, 03973, 03982, 03983, 03984, 03986, 04005, 04006, 04014, 04026, 04049, 04050, 04051, 04059, 04064, 04079, 04106, 04120, 04121, 04149, 04174, 04176, 04198, 04199, 04202, 04204, 04227, 04290, 04293, 04297, 04298, 04299, 04304, 04309, 04310, 04326, 04334, 04341, 04358, 04361, 04365, 04373, 04375, 04379, 04400, 04401, 04405, 04406, 04407, 04408, 04416, 04421, 04448, 04462, 04480, 04488, 04503, 04519, 04522, 04526, 04530, 04554, 04558, 04559, 04560, 04561, 04566, 04568, 04574, 04577, 04583, 04596, 04597, 04681, 04684, 04688, 04689, 04722, 04748, 04750, 04808, 04813, 04823, 04824, 04825, 04853, 04857, 04858, 04861, 04864, 04865, 04884, 04888, 04900, 04905, 04913, 04914, 04917, 04920, 04921, 04933, 04941, 04943, 04969, 04974, 04977, 04982, 04994, 05000, 05024, 05030, 05036, 05062, 05079, 05081, 05086, 05088, 05103, 05104, 05133, 05171, 05182, 05188, 05189, 05191, 05205, 05209, 05213, 05214, 05220, 05233, 05245, 05249, 05252, 05253, 05254, 05271, 05272, 05278, 05284, 05297, 05303, 05319, 05323, 05325, 05330, 05331, 05337, 05349, 05350, 05361, 05363, 05364, 05366, 05383, 05391, 05401, 05403, 05411, 05421, 05430, 05452, 05458, 05462, 05463, 05466, 05481, 05490, 05498, 05510, 05511, 05514, 05515, 05518, 05521, 05526, 05563, 05567, 05577, 05582, 05583, 05585, 05601, 05603, 05606, 05614, 05618, 05691, 05692, 05693, 05697, 05702, 05714, 05739, 05747, 05765, 05767, 05783, 05788, 05802, 05807, 05812, 05830, 05831, 05832, 05846, 05850, 05851, 05858, 05876, 05881, 05891, 05894, 05905, 05906, 05907, 05909, 05910, 05912, 05913, 05922, 05937, 05946, 05947, 05955, 05957, 05997, 05998, 06014, 06067, 06080, 06095, 06096, 06111, 06117, 06121, 06128, 06135, 06136, 06157, 06158, 06162, 06174, 06181, 06211, 06213, 06220, 06230, 06252, 06263, 06274, 06275, 06278, 06281, 06292, 06297, 06303, 06306, 06309, 06324, 06406, 06425, 06441, 06443, 06444, 06445, 06464, 06467, 06493, 06507, 06539, 06540, 06550, 06558, 06584, 06630, 06636, 06669, 06683, 06705, 06710, 06711, 06713, 06718, 06719, 06736, 06738, 06747, 06765, 06781, 06784, 06782, 06790, 06792, 06796, 06802, 06803, 06805, 06853, 06852, 06860, 06866, 06876, 06879, 06909, 06910, 06949, 06955, 06960, 06966, 06979, 06980, 07001, 07002, 07003, 07004, 07012, 0730, 07039, 07044, 07055, 07059, 07073, 07087, 07093, 07099, 07110, 07118, 07119, 07121, 07124, 07138, 07139, 07170, 07203, 07211, 07214, 07241, 07244, 07245, 07256, 07280, 07285, 07295, 07306, 07316, 07330, 07343, 07358, 07369, 07382, 07389, 07421, 07437, 07447, 07451, 07476, 07479, 07488, 07489, 07492, 07502, 07503, 07539, 07555, 07556, 07558, 07562, 07578, 07611, 07617, 07622, 07631, 07650, 07654, 07657, 07661, 07675, 07681, 07682, 07692, 07698, 07720, 07739, 07740, 07745, 07787, 07796, 07807, 07808, 07809, 07812, 07823, 07826,

07851, 07852, 07864, 07869, 07882, 07883, 07889, 07899, 07903, 07904, 07915, 07916, 07917, 07921, 07935, 07946, 07951, 07953, 07955, 07961, 07964, 07969, 07970, 07975, 07978, 07986, 07990, 07995, 08009, 08014, 08017, 08037, 08038, 08040, 08041, 08054, 08057, 08073, 08078, 08082, 08095, 08103, 08107, 08121, 08135, 08147, 08148, 08159, 08172, 08181, 08186, 08189, 08190, 08195, 08203, 08210, 08213, 08237, 08241, 08242, 08243, 08245, 08255, 08258, 08259, 08266, 08273, 08296, 08298, 08302, 08304, 08312, 08318, 08324, 08325, 08500, 08508, 08513, 08516, 08520, 08547, 08550, 08555, 08559, 08633, 08637, 08640, 08653, 08675, 08683, 08714, 08723, 08724, 08728,08730, 08744, 08746, 08749, 08751, 08752, 08753, 08754, 08762, 08764, 08767, 08768, 08790, 08791, 08799, 08808, 08817, 08820, 08821, 08836, 08851, 08890, 08891, 08895, 08896, 08901, 08902, 08920, 08932, 08934, 08935, 08938, 08947, 08956, 08960, 08972, 08990, 09000, 09024, 09025, 09028, 09030, 09037, 09052, 09059, 09062, 09067, 09071, 09089, 09092, 09094, 09095, 09099, 09100, 09102, 09132, 09136, 09151, 09165, 09168, 09169, 09182, 09184, 09187, 09189, 09211, 09237, 09242, 09245, 09247, 09249, 09251, 09294, 09297, 09318, 09320, 09322, 09328, 09339, 09342, 09352, 09367, 09368, 09369, 09375, 09388, 09404, 09418, 09424, 09431, 09450, 09469, 09473, 09517, 09520, 09524, 09549, 09552, 09561, 09574, 09584, 09596, 09611, 09612, 09613, 09643, 09649, 09658, 09661, 09670, 09676, 09685, 09687, 09694, 09698, 09701, 09705, 09708, 09711, 09717, 09744, 09747, 09756, 09760, 09768, 09787, 09788, 09797, 09798, 09806, 09809, 09818, 09823, 09857, 09858, 09874, 09875, 09880, 09882, 09892, 09895, 09903, 09905, 09908, 09954, 09957, 09961, 09964, 09972, 09980, 09981, 09985, 09987, 10002, 10005, 10007, 10010, 10020, 10033, 10040, 10046, 10059, 10077, 10080, 10083, 10087, 10094, 10098, 10100, 10129, 10136, 10139, 10180, 10208, 10215, 10226, 10241, 10269, 10279, 10291, 10300, 10302, 10305, 10307, 10310, 10314, 10334, 10341, 10345, 10347, 10350, 10364, 10376, 10394, 10401, 10414, 10418, 10422, 10430, 10431, 10432, 10442, 10444, 10479, 10482, 10484, 10499, 10506, 10507, 10509, 10543, 10545, 10547, 10566, 10587, 10609, 10610, 10615, 10660, 10672, 10707, 10713, 10729, 10746, 10769, 10777, 10780, 10781, 10784, 10803, 10848, 10876, 10877, 10886, 10887, 10896, 10905, 10906, 10908, 10920, 10923, 10928, 10941, 10962, 10968, 10977, 10986, 10990, 11025, 11026, 11035, 11037, 11039, 11040, 11046, 11063, 11067, 11076, 11083, 11084, 11096, 11125, 11126, 11127, 11130, 11135, 11145, 11146, 11147, 11153, 11174, 11184, 11186, 11208, 11211, 11213, 11221, 11243, 11384, 11389, 11398, 11399, 11400, 11407, 11408, 11423, 11431, 11449, 11452, 11476, 11490, 11491, 11494, 11505, 11506, 11514, 11520, 11526, 11564, 11592, 11593, 11594, 11600, 11607, 11609, 11612, 11622, 11624, 11630, 11631, 11634, 11643, 11650, 11657, 11689, 11693, 11701, 11713, 11730, 11757, 11758, 11764, 11765, 11776, 11778, 11786, 11817, 11818, 11826, 11833, 11834, 11835, 11840, 11842, 11849, 11870, 11871, 11877, 11878, 11880, 11882, 11886, 11934, 11951, 11952, 11954, 11955, 11984, 12001, 12002, 12017, 12020, 12034, 12050, 12055, 12056, 12059, 12064, 12091, 12099, 12101, 12103, 12104, 12106, 12108, 12110, 12117, 12119, 12124, 12126, 12127, 12128, 12132, 12133, 12143, 12148, 12150, 12152, 12160, 12166, 12175, 12176, 12177, 12179, 12180, 12194, 12236, 12249, 12264, 12265, 12267, 12278, 12293, 12296, 12299, 12307, 12309, 12319, 12322, 12340, 12347, 12363, 12366, 12379, 12400, 12407, 12431, 12445, 12454, 12467, 12473, 12484, 12493, 12507, 12511, 12514, 12521, 12527, 12528, 12532, 12533, 12537, 12544, 12545, 12548, 12553, 12554, 12569, 12570, 12576, 12578, 12593, 12599, 12600, 12617, 12618, 12621, 12629, 12640, 12641, 12642, 12646, 12655, 12673, 12677, 12679, 12687, 12689, 12701, 12710, 12711, 12735, 12737, 12739, 12740, 12747, 12756, 12757, 12758, 12766, 12784, 12786, 12789, 12807, 12808, 12811,

12826, 12833, 12838, 12847, 12849, 12852, 12862, 12868, 12878, 12879, 12884, 12885, 12888, 12889, 12909, 12910, 12923, 12925, 12941, 12962, 12986, 13025, 13046, 13058, 13073, 13086, 13089, 13099, 13107, 13114, 13122, 13127, 13134, 13162, 13164, 13173, 13180, 13183, 13184, 13186, 13207, 13218, 13229, 13233, 13236, 13237, 13239, 13258, 13264, 13282, 13291, 13298

Time Orientation
01367, 01400, 01989

Training
00047, 00088, 00093, 00097, 00132, 00193, 00202, 00214, 00244, 00268, 00300, 00307, 00340, 00343, 00347, 00352, 00412, 00452, 00453, 00602, 00606, 00607, 00610, 00696, 00709, 00724, 00732, 00822, 00833, 00840, 00889, 00903, 00945, 01015, 01027, 01038, 01040, 01057, 01068, 01073, 01082, 01136, 01151, 01152, 01209, 01277, 01291, 01296, 01322, 01337, 01360, 01379, 01384, 01405, 01415, 01430, 01454, 01514, 01563, 01572, 01599, 01652, 01656, 01713, 01751, 01753, 01756, 01763, 01798, 01863, 01869, 01870, 01894, 01933, 01950, 01958, 01979, 01993, 02002, 02012, 02021, 02045, 02067, 02075, 02136, 02156, 02194, 02200, 02252, 02257, 02263, 02270, 02282, 02295, 02311, 02320, 02330, 02435, 02475, 02529, 02545, 02566, 02595, 02606, 02650, 02695, 02786, 02787, 02872, 02909, 03043, 03062, 03113, 03121, 03158, 03159, 03187, 03188, 03239, 03383, 03404, 03426, 03473, 03485, 03508, 03532, 03710, 03753, 03772, 03804, 03860, 03868, 03898, 03985, 03997, 03998, 04008, 04034, 04056, 04057, 04087, 04118, 04119, 04340, 04379, 04421, 04434, 04436, 04491, 04493, 04523, 04545, 04549, 04574, 04610, 04656, 04686, 04733, 04743, 04802, 04807, 04810, 04820, 04832, 04836, 04898, 04936, 04970, 04971, 04974, 05001, 05012, 05182, 05183, 05204, 05264, 05309, 05314, 05420, 05431, 05476, 05477, 05478, 05501, 05559, 05575, 05581, 05605, 05622, 05678, 05720, 05723, 05754, 05796, 05802, 05806, 05821, 05826, 05893, 05921, 05952, 05985, 05986, 06139, 06149, 06175, 06182, 06203, 06224, 06371, 06389, 06392, 06417, 06474, 06571, 06585, 06622, 06623, 06650, 06659, 06702, 06762, 06778, 06817, 07891, 06940, 06956, 06974, 07004, 07005, 07031, 07087, 07259, 07260, 07291, 07335, 07373, 07379, 07403, 07477, 07478, 07515, 07521, 07523, 07575, 07655, 07661, 07663, 07688, 07691, 07720, 07723, 07831, 07899, 07952, 07982, 07989, 07990, 07993, 08035, 08068, 08078, 08137, 08140, 08174, 08191, 08196, 08281, 08453, 08469, 08564, 08611, 08674, 08713, 08761, 08785, 08822, 08881, 08894, 08921, 08968, 09012, 09013, 09088, 09205, 09260, 09302, 09330, 09388, 09389, 09431, 09437, 09456, 09469, 09476, 09482, 09580, 09581, 09687, 09697, 09723, 09772, 09778, 09827, 09869, 09912, 09995, 10002, 10029, 10038, 10138, 10249, 10296, 10315, 10341, 10405, 10411, 10449, 10450, 10462, 10486, 10569, 10680, 10774, 10866, 10886, 10905, 10912, 10926, 10938, 10982, 10993, 11031, 11035, 11065, 11071, 11072, 11073, 11198, 11242, 11322, 11380, 11394, 11408, 11438, 11456, 11501, 11540, 11544, 11566, 11571, 11612, 11642, 11646, 11672, 11681, 11688, 11719, 11760, 11780, 11801, 11817, 11823, 11828, 11838, 11867, 11888, 11913, 11944, 12005, 12009, 12010, 12097, 12117, 12119, 12147, 12294, 12318, 12406, 12428, 12634, 12707, 12765, 12789, 12818, 12843, 12847, 12930, 12931, 12933, 12947, 12965, 12977, 13012, 13020, 13025, 13030, 13090, 13095, 13121, 13187, 13193, 13195, 13199, 13220, 13281 (*See also:* Group Therapists and Supervision)

Transactional Analysis
00121, 00252, 00402, 00559, 00864, 00867, 00891, 01021, 01022, 01085, 01097, 01099, 01665, 01865, 02043, 02127, 02362, 02956, 03027, 03028, 03029, 03030, 03207, 03208, 03235, 03249, 03250, 03251, 03254, 03255, 03705, 03771, 03772, 03778, 03779, 04132, 04400, 04457, 04835, 04836,

04868, 04919, 04981, 05011, 05315, 05398, 05415, 05785, 05999, 06000, 06083, 06084, 06085, 06122, 06198, 06199, 06426, 06450, 06630, 06721, 06833, 07714, 08005, 08143, 08636, 08692, 08891, 08907, 08976, 08977, 08992, 09089, 09211, 09269, 09519, 09530, 09577, 09924, 10032, 10311, 10504, 10505, 11702, 11703, 11907, 11908, 11909, 12107, 12146, 12240, 12517, 13128

Transference and Countertransference
00021, 00042, 00046, 00078, 00162, 00189, 00225, 00246, 00321, 00530, 00538, 00628, 00647, 00948, 01016, 01138, 01139, 01142, 01143, 01277, 01304, 01310, 01311, 01339, 01568, 01576, 01624, 01796, 01806, 01834, 01865, 02011, 02096, 02098, 02201, 02243, 02482, 02678, 02763, 02829, 02948, 02983, 03021, 03144, 03273, 03301, 03303, 03351, 03423, 03427, 03460, 03573, 03593, 03713, 03835, 03902, 04081, 04262, 04266, 04272, 04392, 04402, 04533, 04643, 04649, 04729, 04781, 05175, 05478, 05538, 05550, 05561, 05679, 05680, 05681, 05682, 05856, 05890, 06113, 06242, 06312, 06348, 06392, 06735, 06897, 07209, 07326, 07361, 07375, 07775, 08015, 08031, 08056, 08234, 08355, 08367, 08434, 08435, 08451, 08460, 08597, 08612, 08757, 08758, 08759, 08839, 08968, 08970, 09441, 09593, 09719, 09733, 09238, 09309, 10371, 10427, 10557, 10794, 10843, 10952, 11020, 11294, 11313, 11329, 11334, 11434, 11499, 11517, 11518, 11589, 11599, 11615, 11667, 11671, 11731, 11787, 11788, 11842, 11861, 11926, 11980, 12274, 12316, 12510, 12575, 12733, 12767, 13295

Tuberculosis
00118, 05572, 06266, 06427, 06437, 07690, 09627, 09628, 09631, 09632, 09634, 09636, 09637, 12831, 12898, 12901

V

Veterans
00074, 00075, 03333, 03334, 06469, 09610

Video Tape
00265, 00312, 00863, 00994, 01032, 01039, 01040, 01044, 01379, 01636, 01654, 01872, 01977, 02014, 02305, 02495, 02520, 02521, 02628, 02872, 03135, 03218, 03310, 03433, 03931, 03957, 04055, 04238, 04239, 04377, 04710, 04865, 04977, 05034, 05079, 05370, 05386, 05563, 05564, 05610, 06624, 06784, 06893, 07316, 07317, 07494, 07695, 07720, 07731, 07741, 07744, 07760, 07823, 07833, 08044, 08054, 08148, 08489, 08637, 09034, 09167, 09182, 09622, 09624, 09670, 09957, 09962, 09972, 10040, 10076, 10077, 10078, 10102, 10357, 10358, 10666, 10896, 11811, 11812, 11813, 11814, 11815, 11816, 11895, 11896, 11921, 12002, 12085, 12268, 12296, 12309, 12366, 12367, 12510, 12560, 12561, 12691, 12849, 12899, 13209, 13218

Visual Aids
00171, 00595, 01100, 02188, 02189, 02519, 02522, 02693, 03366, 04299, 04339, 05392, 06107, 06108, 06238, 06264, 07434, 07905, 08212, 08417, 08623, 09352, 10716, 11111, 11695, 12188, 12470, 12628

Vocational Counseling
00135, 00701, 00715, 00716, 00950, 01189, 01974, 02777, 02833, 02843, 03038, 08048, 08080, 08294, 12594

Warm Up
01252, 02131, 02334, 03496, 09070

Cited Periodicals

Acad. Manag. J.
Acad. Ther.
Acta Allergologica, (Copenhagen), (in Engl.)
Acta Med. Scand. Supply. (Stockholm), (in Engl.)
Acta Neurol. & Psychiat. Belgica, (Brussels), (in Engl.)
Acta Neurol. & Psychiat. Hellenica, (Salonica), (in Engl.)
Acta Obstet. Ginecol. Hispano-Lusitania, (Barcelona)
Acta Paedopsychiat., (Basel), (in Engl.)
Acta Psiquiat. Psicol. Amer. Latina, (Buenos Aires)
Acta Psychiat. Scand. Supply., (Copenhagen), (in Engl.)
Acta Psychol., (Amsterdam)
Acta Psychother., Psychosomat. Orthopaedagog., (Basel)
Actas Luso Espanoles Neurol. Psiquiat., (Madrid)
Activ. Nerv. Superior, (Prague), (in Engl.)
Addict. Behav.,
Addict. Diseases
Adolescence
Adult Educat.
Adult Leadership
Aerzh. Jugendkunde, (Leipzig)
Aggiornam. Psicother. Psicol. Clin.
Akt. Gerontol., (Stuttgart)
Alcohol Health & Res. World
Alkoholikysymys, (Helsinki)
Amer. Acad. Polit. & Soc. Sciences
Amer. Annals Deaf
Amer. Anthropol.
Amer. Arch. Rehab. Ther.
Amer. Behav. Scientist
Amer. Coll. Health Assn. J.
Amer. Coll. Nurse-Midwives Bull.
Amer. Corrective Ther. J.
Amer. Educat. Res. J.
Amer. Fam. Physician
Amer. Health Care Assn. J.
Amer. Heart J.
Amer. Imago
Amer. J. Art Ther.
Amer. J. Clin. Hypnosis
Amer. J. Clin. Med.
Amer. J. Community Psychol.
Amer. J. Correct.
Amer. J. Digestive Diseases
Amer. J. Fam. Ther.
Amer. J. Maternal Child Nursing
Amer. J. Ment. Deficiency
Amer. J. Nursing
Amer. J. Occupat. Ther.
Amer. J. Orthopsychiat.
Amer. J. Psychiat.
Amer. J. Psychother.

Amer. J. Pub. Health
Amer. J. Sociol. Res.
Amer. Psychol. Assn. Monitor
Amer. Psychologist
Amer. Rev. Respirat. Disease
Amer. Scientist
Amer. Scholar
Amer. Sociol Rev.
Amer. Surgeon
Amer. Vocat. J.
ANA Clin. Sessions
ANA in Action
Analyt. Psychol., (Basel)
Annales Espanoles Pediat., (Madrid)
Annales Med. Internae Fenniae, (Helsinki)
Annales Med. Legale, (Paris)
Annales Medico-Psychol., (Paris)
Annals Allergy Psychiat.
Annals Internal Med.
Annals of Allergy
Annals N.Y. Acad. Science
Annals Prog. Child Psychiat.
Appl. Anthropol.
Arch. de Psychol., (Geneva), (in Engl. & Fr.)
Arch. Dermatol. & Syph.
Arch. Environ. Health
Arch. Gen. Psychiat.
Arch. Hosp. Univ., (Havana)
Arch. Neurobiol., (Madrid)
Arch. Neurol. Psychiat.
Arch. Pediat. Ureguay, (Montevideo)
Arch. Physical Med. & Rehab.
Arch. Psicol., Neurol. & Psichiat., (Milan), (in Engl.)
Arch. Psychiat. & Nervenkrankheiten, (in Engl. or Ger.)
Arch. Sexual Behav.
Arch. Surgery
Arq. Brasil. Psicol. Apl., (Rio de Janeiro)
Arq. Neurol-Psychiat., (São Paulo), (in Engl.)
Art Psychother.
Austral. & New Zeal. J. Psychiat., (Carlton)
Austral. & New Zeal. J. Sociol., (Christ Church)
Austral. J. Adult Educat., (Sydney)
Austral. J. Psychol., (Parkville)
Austral. Psychologist, (Brisbane)
Australasian Nurses J., (Port Adelaide)

Baseler Nationalzeit.
Behav. Biology
Behav. Engineering
Behav. Res. & Ther.
Behav. Science Res.
Behav. Ther.
Bibl. Psychiat. & Neurol., (Basel)
Boston Med. Surgery J.
Brit. J. Addict., (Edinburgh)
Brit. J. Criminol., (London)

Brit. J. Disorders Communicat., (London)
Brit. J. Educat. Technol., (London)
Brit. J. Guid. & Couns., (Cambridge)
Brit. J. Hosp. Med., (London)
Brit. J. Med. Educat., (Oxford)
Brit. J. Med. Psychol., (London)
Brit. J. Ment. Subnorm., (Birmingham)
Brit. J. Psychiat., (Ashford)
Brit. J. Psychiat. Soc. Work
Brit. J. Psychother.
Brit. J. Psychiat. Soc. Work, (Birmingham)
Brit. J. Sociol. & Clin. Psychol., (London)
Brit. J. Venereal Diseases, (London)
Brit. Med. J., (London)
Brit. Psychol. Soc. Bull., (London)
Bronches, (Paris)
Bull. Amer. Coll. Neuropsychiat.
Bull. Art Ther.
Bull. de Psychol., (Paris)
Bull. Grad. Estudies Psychol. Univ. Paris
Bull. Johns Hopkins Hosp.
Bull. Menninger Clinic

Cahiers Psychol. & Reeducat., (Montreal)
Calif. Med.
Calif. Ment. Health Res. Digest
Can. Counselor, (Ottawa)
Can. J. Behav. Science, (Montreal), (in Engl.)
Can. J. Criminol. & Correct., (Ottawa), (in Engl.)
Can. J. Occupat. Ther., (Toronto), (in Engl.)
Can. J. Psychiat. Nursing, (Winnipeg), (in Engl.)
Can. J. Psychol., (Toronto), (in Engl.)
Can. J. Pub. Health, (Ottawa), (in Engl.)
Can. Med. Assn. J., (Ottawa), (in Engl.)
Can. Ment. Health Suppl.,
Can. Nurse, (Ottawa), (in Engl.)
Can. Psychiat. Assn. J., (Ottawa), (in Engl.)
Can. Psychologist
Cardiology, (Basel), (in Engl.)
Cat. Selected Docum. Psychol.
Cerebral Palsy Rev.
Ceskoslav. Psychiat., (Prague)
Ceskoslav. Psychol., (Prague)
Child Develop.
Child Psychiat. & Human Develop.
Child Study J.
Child Welfare
Children
Children Today
Christian Cent.
Cleft Palate J.
Clin. Pediat.
Clin. Psychologist
Clin. Soc. Work J.
Coll. Student J.
Colorado-Wyoming Acad. Science J.

Community Ment. Health J.
Compar. Group Studies
Comprehens. Psychiat.
Confinia Psychiat., (Basel), (in Engl.)
Connexions, (Paris)
Contemp. Drug Probl.
Contemp. Psychol.
Correct. Psychiat. & J. Soc. Ther.
Correct. & Soc. Psychol.
Couns. & Values
Couns. Psychologist
Counselor Educat. & Supervision
Crime & Delinquency
Crim. Justice & Behav.
Curr. Psychiat. Ther.

Death Educat.
Der Psychologie, (Berne)
Der Rehab., (Stuttgart)
Delaware State Med. J.
Deutsche Gesundh., (Berlin)
Deutsche Krankenpflege-Zeit., (Stuttgart)
Deutsche Schwesternzeit., (Stuttgart)
Deutsche Zentralblatte Krankenpflege, (Stuttgart)
Develop. Med. & Child Neurol., (London)
Develop. Psychobiol.
Diabetes
Dialysis & Transplantation
Digestive Neurol. & Psychiat.
Dimens. Health Services, (Toronto), (in Engl.)
Diseases Nerv. System
Dissert. Abstr. Internat.
Duodecim, (Helsinki)
Drug Forum
Dynam. Psychiat., (Berlin), (in Engl.)

Educat. & Training, (London)
Educat. & Training Ment. Retard.
Educat. & Urban Soc.
Educat. Digest, (Toronto), (in Engl.)
Educat. Leadership
Educat. Rev., (Birmingham)
Educat. Technol.
Elem. School Guid. & Couns.
Elem. School J.
Elgin State Hosp. Papers
Encephale Suppl., (Paris)
Ensenanza & Investig. Psichol., (Mexico City)
Epilepsia
European J. Soc. Psychol., (The Hague), (in Engl.)
European J. Toxicol., (Paris), (in Engl.)
Evolut. Psychiat., (Toulouse)
Except. Children
Existent. Psychiat.
Exper. Med. & Surgery

Fam. Coordinator
Fam. Process
Fam. Ther.
Fed. Probat.
Federator
Focus Except. Children
Folia Clin. Internac., (Barcelona)
Formosa Med. Assn. J., (Taipei), (in Engl.)
Fortschr. Neurol., Psychiat. & Grenzgebiete, (Stuttgart)

Gedrag, (Tilburg)
Geriatrics
Gerontol. Clin., (Basel)
Gerontologie, (Paris)
Gerontologist
Gerontology, (Basel), (in Engl.)
Gerontology, (Tel Aviv), (in Engl.)
Gifted Children Quart.
Ginecol. & Obstet., (Buenos Aires)
Group
Group Anal., (London)
Group Process, (London)
Group & Organizat. Studies
Group Psychother., Psychodrama & Sociometry
Groups
Gruppendynamik, (Stuttgart)
Gruppenpsychother. & Gruppendynam., (Goettingen)
Gynaecologia, (Basel), (in Engl.)

Harefuah, (Tel Aviv)
Harvard J. Legislat.
Harvest Years
Health & Soc. Serv. J., (London)
Health & Soc. Work
Health Visitor, (London)
Hearing Rehab. Quart.
Heart & Lung
Heilpaedagog. Werkbl., (Lucerne)
Hexagon Roche, (Basel), (in Engl.)
Helvetica Med. Acta Suppl., (Basel), (in Engl.)
Hippokrates, (Stuttgart)
Homosexual Couns. J.
Hospital, (Rio de Janeiro)
Hosp. & Community Psychiat.
Hosp. Prog.
Hospitals
Howard J. Penol. & Crime Prevention, (London)
Hu Li Tsa Chih, (Hong Kong), (in Engl.)
Human Organizat.
Human Relat.
Humanist
Hydrocarb. Processing
Hygeia
Hygiene Ment. Can., (Ottawa)

Ideggyogyaszati Szemle, (Budapest)

Illinois Med. J.
Indian J. Soc. Work, (Bombay)
Individ. Psychologist
Infirmiere Can., (Ottawa)
Infirmiere Française, (Paris)
Insights
Internat. Arch. Allergy
Internat. Assn. Pupil Personnel Workers J.
Internat. J. Addict.
Internat. J. Aging & Human Develop.
Internat. J. Clin. & Exper. Hypnosis
Internat. J. Clin. Pharmacol. & Biopharmacy, (Munich), (in Engl.)
Internat. J. Fam. Couns.
Internat. J. Fertility
Internat. J. Group Psychother.
Internat. J. Group Tensions
Internat. J. Health Educat., (Geneva), (in Engl.)
Internat. J. Nursing Studies
Internat. J. Obesity
Internat. J. Offender Ther., (London)
Internat. J. Psychiat. Med.
Internat. J. Psycho-Anal., (London)
Internat. J. Psychoanal. Psychother.
Internat. J. Sexol., (Bombay)
Internat. J. Soc. Psychiat., (London)
Internat. Ment. Health Res. Newsl.
Internat. Nursing Rev., (Geneva), (in Engl.)
Internat. Pharmopsychiat., (Basel), (in Engl.)
Internat. Rev. Appl. Psychol., (Liverpool)
Internat. Psychiat. Clinics
Internist. Praxis, (Munich)
Interpersonal Develop.
Isr. Annals Psychiat., (Jerusalem), (in Engl.)
Isr. J. Psychol. Couns. Educat.
Issues Ment. Health Nursing

Japanese J. Child Psychiat., (Tokyo)
Japanese J. Nursing Res., (Tokyo)
Japanese J. Psychol., (Tokyo)
J. Abnorm. & Soc. Psychol.
J. Advert. Res.
J. All-India Inst. Ment. Health, (New Delhi), (in Engl.)
J. Amer. Acad. Child Psychiat.
J. Amer. Coll. Health Assn.
J. Amer. Coll. Neuropsychiat.
J. Amer. Dietetic Assn.
J. Amer. Geriat. Soc.
J. Amer. Med. Assn.
J. Amer. Soc. Psychosomat. Dent. & Med.
J. Anal. Psychol., (London)
J. Appl. Behav. Anal.
J. Appl. Behav. Science
J. Appl. Psychol.
J. Appl. Rehab. Couns.
J. Asthma Res.
J. Arkansas Med. Soc.

J. Behav. Ther. & Exper. Psychiat.
J. Brasil. Med., (Rio de Janeiro)
J. Brasil. Psiquiat., (Rio de Janeiro)
J. Bronx State Hosp.
J. Child Asthma Res.
J. Child Psychol. & Psychiat.
J. Chronic Diseases
J. Clin. & Pastoral Soc. Work
J. Clin. Child Psychol.
J. Clin. Psychol.
J. Coll. Student Personnel
J. Coll. Placement
J. Communicat.
J. Communicat. Disorders
J. Community Psychol.
J. Confl. Resolut.
J. Consult. & Clin. Psychol.
J. Contemp. Psychother.
J. Couns. Psychol.
J. Creative Behav.
J. Correct. Educat.
J. Correct. Psychol.
J. Crim. Law & Criminol.
J. Crim. Psychopathol.
J. Curriculum Studies, (London)
J. Dent. Educat.
J. Divorce
J. Drug Educat.
J. Drug Issues
J. Educat.
J. Educat. Psychol.
J. Educat. Res.
J. Educat. Soc. Work
J. Educat. Sociol.
J. Emerg. Nursing
J. Employment Couns.
J. Except. Child
J. Exper. Child Psychol.
J. Exper. Educat.
J. Exper. Psychol.
J. Exper. Soc. Psychol.
J. Fam. Couns.
J. Fam. Practice
J. Fort Logan Ment. Health Ctr.
J. Gen. Psychol.
J. Genetic Psychol.
J. Geriat. Psychiat.
J. Gerontol. Nursing
J. Group Psychoanal. & Process, (London)
J. Health & Soc. Behav.
J. Health, Physical Educat. & Recreat., (Tokyo)
J. Higher Educat.
J. Hillside Hosp.
J. Homosexuality
J. Human. Psychol.
J. Human Relat.

J. Human Stress
J. Individ. Psychol.
J. Jewish Commmunal Serv.
J. Kansas Med. Soc.
J. Learning Disabil.
J. Maine Med. Assn.
J. Marital & Fam. Ther.
J. Marriage & Fam.
J. Marriage & Fam. Couns.
J. Med. Assn. Georgia
J. Med. Bordeaux
J. Med. Educat.
J. Medico, (Porto)
J. Med. Soc. N.J.
J. Ment. Health
J. Ment. Health Technol.
J. Ment. Science
J. Missouri Med. Assn.
J. Music Ther.
J. Nat. Assn. Deans Women
J. Nat. Assn. Priv. Psychiat. Hosp.
J. Neurol., Neurosurg. & Psychiat., (London)
J. Nerv. & Ment. Diseases
J. Nursing Admin.
J. Nursing Educat.
J. Occupat. Med.
J. Operat. Psychiat.
J. Pastoral Care & Couns.
J. Pediat.
J. Personality
J. Personality & Soc. Psychol.
J. Personality Assessment
J. Polit. Science Admin.
J. Postgrad. Med.
J. Pract. Nursing
J. Project. Tech. & Personality Assessment
J. Psychedelic Drugs
J. Psychiat. Nursing
J. Psychiat. Res., (London)
J. Psychiat. Soc. Work
J. Psychology
J. Psychol. & Theology
J. Psychosomat. Res.
J. Rehab.
J. Religion & Health
J. School Health
J. Sex & Marital Ther.
J. Soc. Casework
J. Soc. Issues
J. Soc. Policy, (London)
J. Soc. Psychol.
J. Spec. Educat. & Ment. Retard.
J. Special. Group Work
J. Speech & Hearing Disorders
J. Studies Alcohol
J. Transpersonal Psychol.

J. Visual Impair. & Blindness
J. Vocat. Behav.
J. Youth & Adolescence

Koelner Zeit. Soziol. & Sozialpsychol., (Wiesbaden)
Kinderaerztliche Praxis, (Leipzig)
Krankenpflege, (Frankfurt)
Kyusho Neuro-Psychiat., (Fukuoka)
Lancet
Landarzt, (Stuttgart)
Laval Med., (Quebec)
Lavoro Neuropsichiat., (Rome)
Life-Threatening Behav.
Lijecnicki Vjesnik, (Zagreb)

Magyar Pszichol. Szemle, (Budapest)
Manag. Internat. Rev., (Wiesbaden), (in Engl.)
Marriage & Fam. Living
Mass. Health J.
MCN: Amer. J. Maternal Child Nursing
Med. Annals D.C.
Medicina, (Buenos Aires)
Med. Glasnik, (Belgrade)
Med. & Cir. Guerra, (Madrid)
Med. Insight
Med. Health
Med. Hosp.
Med. Hygiene
Med. Klinik, (Munich)
Med. J. Austral., (Glebe)
Med. Times
Med. Trial Tech. Quart.
Med. Welt, (Stuttgart)
Med. World, (London)
Med. World News
Megamot, (Jerusalem)
Mens & Onderneming, (Meppel)
Mensch & Arbeit, (Munich)
Ment. Health Digest
Ment. Health & Soc., (Basel), (in Engl.)
Ment. Hosp.
Ment. Hygiene
Ment. Retard.
Ment. Retard. Abstr.
Michigan J. Secondary Educat.
Michigan Nurse
Midwest Educat. Rev.
Midwife, (London)
Military Med.
Minerva Med., (Turin)
Minerva Psichiat., (Turin)
Mod. Psychoanal.
Monatsschr. Psychiat. & Neurol., (Basel), (in Engl.)
Multivar. Behav. Res.
Munchen Med. Wochenschr., (Munich)

Nat. Cath. Guid. Conf. J.
Nat. Med. Assn. J.
Nederl. Tijdschr. Geneeskunde, (Amsterdam)
Nederl. Tijdshcr. Gerontol., (Dwenter)
Nederl. Tijdschr. Psychiat., (Meppel)
Nederl. Tijdschr. Psychol., (Amsterdam)
Negro Educat. Rev.
Neurobiologia, (Pernambuco), (in Engl.)
Neurochirurgia, (Genoa)
Neuropsychiatry
Neuropsihijatrija, (Zagreb)
Nervennartz
Neurologia, (Bucharest)
Neurol. & Neurochir. Polska, (Warsaw)
Neurol.-Neurocir.-Psiquiat., (Mexico City)
New Dir. Teaching
New Engl. J. Med.
New Era, (London)
New Outlook for Blind
New Zeal. Psychologist, (Wellington)
New Zeal. Med. J., (Dunedin)
Newsl. Amer. Assn. Psychiat. Soc. Workers
Newsl. Amer. Orthopsychiat. Assn.
Newsl. Res. Ment. Health & Behav. Sciences
Newsl. Res. Psychol.
Nordisk Med., (Copenhagen)
Nordisk Psykiat. Tidsskr., (Kungsbacha)
Nordisk Psykol., (Copenhagen)
Norsk Pedagog. Tidskr., (Troundheim)
North Carolina Med. J.
Northwestern Med.
Nursing Clinics North Amer.
Nursing Digest
Nursing Forum
Nursing Forum, (Aukland)
Nursing Homes
Nursing Mirror, (London)
Nursing Outlook
Nursing Papers, (Montreal), (in Engl.)
Nursing Res.
Nursing '76
Nursing Times, (London)
N.Y. State Med. J.
N.Y. State Assn. Occupat. Ther.

Occupat. Ther. & Rehab.
Oesterreich. Aerztezeit., (Vienna)
Ofakim, (Tel Aviv)
Offender Rehab.
Ohio Med. J.
Omega: J. Death & Dying
Ontario Psychologist, (Toronto)
Organizat. Behav. & Human Perf.
Orvosi Hetilap, (Budapest)
Ospedale Psychiat., (Naples)
Otto Rank Assn. J.

Pacific Sociol. Rev.
Paedagog. Rundschau, (Kastellaun)
Paediat. & Grenzebiete, (Berlin)
Pastoral Psychol.
Patient Care
Peabody J. Educat.
Pediatrics
Percept. & Motor Skills
Personality & Soc. Psychol. Bull.
Personnel Administrator
Personnel & Guid. J.
Personnel J.
Personnel Psychol.
Perspect. Psychiat., (Paris)
Perspect. Psychiat. Care
Philippine Fed. Priv. Med. Pract. J., (Manila), (in Engl.)
Police, (Surrey)
Policlinico, (Rome)
Polish Psychol. Bull., (Warsaw), (Eng. or Fr.)
Polski Tygodnik Lekarski, (Warsaw)
Postgrad. Med.
Postgrad. Med. J., (Oxford)
Praxis der Psychother.
Praxis Kinderpsychol. & Kinderpsychiat., (Goettingen)
Probation, (Surrey)
Proceed. Amer. Prison Assn.
Proceed. Assn. Res. Nerv. Diseases
Prof. Psychol.
Prog. Educat.
Prog. Psychiat. Res.
Przeglad Lekarski, (Warsaw)
Przeglad Psychol., (Warsaw)
Psihijat. Danas, (Belgrade)
Psihoterapija, (Zagreb)
Psyche, (Heidelburg)
Psyche, (Stuttgart)
Psychiat. Annals
Psychiat. Clin., (Basel)
Psychiat. Communicat.
Psychiat. Digest
Psychiat. Forum
Psychiat. in Med.
Psychiat. & Neurol. Japonica, (Tokyo)
Psychiat., Neurol., Neurochir., (Amsterdam)
Psychiat. Opinion
Psychiat. Polska, (Warsaw)
Psychiat. Praxis, (Stuttgart)
Psychiat. Quart. Suppl.
Psychiatry
Psychoanal. Rev.
Psychol. Aspects Diseases
Psychol. Bull.
Psychol. Française, (Paris)
Psycho. in Schools
Psychol. Med., (London)

Psychol. Reports
Psychol. Rundschau, (Goettingen)
Psychol. Studies, (Mysore)
Psychol. Today
Psychol. Women Quart.
Psychol. Wychowawcza, (Warsaw)
Psychologie, (Paris)
Psychometrika
Psychopathol. Africaine, (Dakar-Fann), (in Engl.)
Psychosomatics
Psychosomatic Med.
Psychother. & Med. Psychol., (Stuttgart)
Psychother. & Psychosomat., (Basel), (in Engl.)
Psychotherapy
Pub. Health, (London)
Pub. Welfare
Pediat. Process
Penn. Pract.
Physiol.

Quad. Criminol. Clin., (Rome)
Quart. J. Geriat.
Quart. J. Speech
Quart. J. Studies Alcohol
Quart. Rev. Biol.

RN
Rass. Studi Psichiat., (Siena)
Rational Living
Reformatio, (Berne)
Rehab. Couns. Bull.
Rehab. Lit.
Rehab. Psychol.
Rehab. Record
Rehab. Res. & Pract. Rev.
Relig. Educat.
Res. Pub. Assess. Nerv. & Ment. Diseases
Rev. Argentina Psicol., (Buenos Aires)
Rev. Brasil. Psiquiat., (São Paulo)
Rev. Chilena Psychol., (Santiago)
Rev. Columbia. Psiquiat., (Bogota)
Rev. Cubana Med., (Havana)
Rev. de Enfermagen, (Lisbon)
Rev. de l'Infirmiere, (Paris)
Rev. de Medicina, (Bucharest)
Rev. de Psicoanal., (Buenos Aires)
Rev. de Psiquiat., (Santiago)
Rev. Educat. Res.
Rev. Exist. Psychol. & Psychiat.
Rev. Française Psychoanal., (Paris)
Rev. Interamer. Psicol., (in Engl.)
Rev. Internat. Serv. Sante Armees, (Paris), (in Engl.)
Rev. Hosp. Clin. Fac. Med. São Paulo, (in Engl.)
Rev. Med. Chile, (Santiago)
Rev. Med. Costa Rica, (San José)
Rev. Med. Interna, Neurol., Psihiat., (Bucharest)

Rev. Med. Psychosomat., (Toulouse)
Rev. Mexicana Anal. Conducta, (Mexico City), (in Engl.)
Rev. Mexicana Psicol., (Jalisco)
Rev. Neuro-Psiquiat., (Lima)
Rev. Neuropsychiat. Infantile, (Paris)
Rev. Paulista Med., (São Paulo)
Rev. Psicol. Normal. & Patol., (São Paulo)
Rev. Psicol. Soc. & Arch. Ital. Psicol. Gen.
Rev. Psychol. & Sci. Educat., (Liege)
Rev. Psychol. Appl., (Paris)
Rev. Psychol. Peuples, (Le Havre)
Riv. Patol. Nerv. & Ment., (Florence), (in Engl.)
Riv. Psichiat., (Rome)
Riv. Sper. Freniatria, (Emilia)
Roche Report: Front. Hosp. Psychiat.
Rocky Mtn. Med. J.
Rocky Mtn. Soc. Science J.
Royal Army Med. Corps J., (Liverpool)
Royal Soc. Med. Proceed., (London)

Sairaanhoitaja Sjukskoterskan, (Helsinki)
Scand. J. Rehab. Med. Suppl., (Stockholm), (in Engl.)
Schiz. Bull.
School & Soc.
School Guid. Worker, (Toronto)
School Health Rev.
School Counselor
Schweiz. Aertezeit., (Berne)
Schweiz. Akad. Med. Wissenschaftern Bull., (Basel), (in Engl.)
Schwiez. Arch Neurol., Neurochir. & Psychiat., (Zurich), (in Engl.)
Schweiz. Med. Wochenschr., (Basel)
Schweiz. Spital-Veska, (Aarau)
Schweiz. Zeit. Psychol. Anwendungen, (Berne)
Schwestern Rev., (Wuerzburg)
Science & Vie, (Paris)
Science Digest
Scient. Amer.
Secondary Educat.
Sistema Nerv., (Milan)
Slow Learning Child, (Brisbane)
Small Group Behav.
Smith Coll. Studies Soc. Work
Soc. Advance. Manag. J.
Soc. Casework
Soc. Change
Soc. Forces
Soc. Probl.
Soc. Psihijat., (Belgrade)
Soc. Psychiat.
So. African Nurses J., (Pretoria)
So. Calif. Psychoanal. Inst. Bull.
Soc. Science & Med.
Soc. Serv. Quart., (London)
Soc. Serv. Rev.
Soc. Work
Soc. Worker, (Ottawa)

Soc. Work & Health Care
Soc. Work Educat. Reporter
Socialmed. Tidskr., (Stockholm)
Sociol. Inquiry
Sociol. Rev., (Keele)
Sociol. Ruralis, (Assen), (in Engl.)
Socil. Quart.
Southern Med. J.
Sociometry
Sprache-Stimme-Gehour, (Stuttgart)
St. John's Hosp. Dermatol. Soc. Trans.
Strausbourg Med.
Studies Personnel Psychol., (Ottawa)
Suicide & Life-Threatening Behav.
Supervisor Nurse
Svenska Lakartidningen, (Stockholm)
Sygeplejersken, (Copenhagen)
Sykepleien, (Oslo)

Teachers Coll. Record
Teaching Psychol.
Texas Med.
Texas Personnel & Guid. Assn. J.
Ther. Gegenwart, (Munich)
Therapiewoche, (Karlsruhe)
Therapeut. Umschau, (Berne)
Tidskr. Sveriges Sjukskoeterskor, (Stockholm)
Tijdschr. Ziekenverplaging, (Lochem)
Today's Educat.
Today's Health
Together: J. Special. Group Work
Topical Probl. Psychol. & Psychiat.
Toulouse Med.
Toxicomanies, (Quebec)
Training & Develop. J.
Training School Bull.
Trans. Amer. Neurol. Assn. J.
Trans. Ment. Health Res. Newsl.
Transactional Anal. J.
Transcult. Psychiat. Res. Rev., (Montreal), (in Engl.)
Transnat. Ment. Health Res. Newsl.
Travail & Methodes, (Paris)
Treatment Serv. Bull.

Ugeskr. for Laeger, (Copenhagen)
Uni Nova, (Basel)
Union Med. Can., (Montreal)
Univ. Ottawa Psychiat. J.
U.N.A. Nursing J., (Melbourne)
Urban Educat.
U.S. Navy Med. Bull.
U.S. Vet. Admin. Tech. Bull.
Utah Nurse

Veterinary Med.
Vie Med. Can. Française, (Quebec)

Virginia Med. Monthly
Vocat. Guid. Quart.
Voices
Volta Rev.
Vop. Psikhiat. & Nevropatol., (Leningrad)
Vop. Psikhol., (Moscow)

W. Virginia Med. J.
Welfare
Wiad. Lekarski, (Warsaw)
Wiener Klin. Wochenschr., (Vienna)
Wiener Med. Wochenschr., (Vienna)
Wiener Zeit. Nervenheilk., (Vienna)
Wirklichkeit & Weischeit, (Dusseldorf)

Yahrb. Psychol.

Zeit. Aertztl. Fortbildung, (Jena)
Zeit. Allegemeinmed., (Stuttgart)
Zeit. Exper. & Angewandte Psychol., (Goettingen)
Zeit. Gerontol., (Darmstadt)
Zeit. Gesamte Hygiene, (Berlin)
Zeit. Individ. Psychol., (Munich)
Zeit. Klin. Psychol. & Psychother., (Freiburg)
Zeit. Klin. Psychol.—Forschung & Praxis, (Goettingen)
Zeit. Kinder- & Jugendpsychiat., (Berne)
Zeit. Psychosomat. Med. & Psychoanal., (Goettingen)
Zeit. Psychother. Med. Psychol., (Stuttgart)
Zh. Nevropat. & Psikiat. Korsakov, (Moscow)
Zh. Vysshei Nerv. Deyatl'nosti Pavlova, (Moscow)
Ziekenhuis, (Lochem)